American Foreign Policy

Pattern and Process

SEVENTH EDITION

EUGENE R. WITTKOPF
Late, Louisiana State University

CHRISTOPHER M. JONES
Northern Illinois University

WITH CHARLES W. KEGLEY, JR.
University of South Carolina

THOMSON
™
WADSWORTH

Australia • Brazil • Canada • Mexico • Singapore
Spain • United Kingdom • United States

THOMSON

WADSWORTH

American Foreign Policy:
Pattern and Process, **Seventh Edition**
Eugene R. Wittkopf and Christopher M. Jones
with Charles W. Kegley, Jr.

Publisher: Michael Rosenberg
Managing Development Editor: Karen Judd
Assistant Editor: Christine Halsey
Editorial Assistant: Megan Garvey
Technology Project Manager: Stephanie Gregoire
Marketing Manager: Karin Sandberg
Marketing Assistant: Kathleen Tosiello
Marketing Communications Manager: Heather Baxley
Project Manager, Editorial Production: Paul Wells
Creative Director: Rob Hugel

Art Director: Maria Epes
Print Buyer: Karen Hunt
Permissions Editor: Roberta Broyer
Production Service: International Typesetting
   and Composition
Copy Editor: Lunaea Weatherstone
Cover Designer: Ellen Pettengell
Cover Image: © CORBIS
Compositor: International Typesetting and Composition
Printer: Thomson/West

1 2 3 4 5 6 7 11 10 09 08 07

Library of Congress Control Number: 2006934481

ISBN 13: 978-0-534-60337-3
ISBN 10: 0-534-60337-8

Thomson Higher Education
10 Davis Drive
Belmont, CA 94002–3098
USA

For more information about our products, contact us at:
Thomson Learning Academic Resource Center
1-800-423-0563

For permission to use material from this text or product, submit a request online at
http://www.thomsonrights.com.
Any additional questions about permissions can be submitted by e-mail to
thomsonrights@thomson.com.

This book is dedicated to the memory of Eugene R. Wittkopf (1943–2006), who passed away unexpectedly as this edition neared completion. For more than three decades, Gene was a prolific scholar within the fields of international relations and foreign policy analysis. He consistently generated work that was theoretically sensitive, analytically sound, meticulously researched, and adeptly written. These commendable qualities extended to the many successful textbooks that Gene produced over the course of his impressive career. Titles bearing the Wittkopf name stood the test of time and introduced thousands of individuals to the study of world politics and American foreign policy. Gene's skill as a scholar, teacher, and editor, coupled with his unwavering commitment to excellence, led each edition to encompass the most recent scholarship and up-to-date analysis, while remaining accessible to the average student. Nowhere was this more apparent than in American Foreign Policy: Pattern and Process, a book that he envisioned, took great pride in, and shepherded through seven editions. We miss him, and we hope that he would be proud of the final product.

For Barbara, Debra and Jason, Jonathan and Randee,
my mother and the memory of my father,
and Katie, the newest member of the family
E.R.W.

Kristen, Trevor, Leanna, and Ian
C.M.J.

Debra
C.W.K.

Brief Contents

Contents

Preface

The months and years since terrorists attacked the World Trade Center and the Pentagon in September 2001 have been tumultuous ones for the United States and its foreign policy. The presidency of George W. Bush will forever be linked with those fateful events. The global war on terrorism launched by the president, the war in Afghanistan and the controversial war in Iraq, and the unprecedented disaffection of many policy makers and peoples around the world toward the United States and its policies have profoundly shaped the character of world politics in the first decade of the new millennium.

The United States remains the world's preeminent power. Yet an array of challenges confront its leaders. These formidable tasks include thwarting new terrorist attacks; halting the further proliferation of nuclear and other weapons of mass destruction; meeting threats to national security while simultaneously protecting Americans' civil liberties; stanching the roiling conflicts across the Middle East and Southwest Asia; addressing the controversy over the costs and benefits of the globalization of the world political economy; and protecting the fragile ecosphere generally, and coping with global warming in particular. Perhaps most vexing is the reality that these difficult issues and many others must be confronted without the predictability that marked the global contest with the Soviet Union that dominated much of the last half of the twentieth century. Despite declarations by policy makers that the United States is once again in the midst of a "long war" that could span decades, building a domestic consensus around a set of guiding principles and strategies that offer the same clarity and unity of purpose as during the Cold War has proven elusive.

As policy makers today seek to define a new and enduring policy posture, we are reminded of the choices the immediate post–World War II generation faced, and how those choices shaped nearly half a century of American foreign policy. In the wake of the Japanese surprise attack on Pearl Harbor and the dawning of the nuclear age over Hiroshima, America's rise to globalism and the onset of the Cold War triggered sweeping changes in the nation's world role. The results were a new activism toward others (internationalism), a unity of purpose (anticommunism), an expansive grand strategy (containment), and recurrent patterns of foreign policy behavior (global activism, military might for offense and defense, and interventionism). The contest between capitalism and communism also provided the rationale for a substantially expanded, multipronged foreign policy bureaucracy designed to pursue America's new global role with strength and determination. Relations between the White House and Congress often evolved in a consensual fashion, encouraging congressional deference to presidential preeminence in the making and execution of foreign policy.

That harmonious view changed with the Watergate scandal, the Vietnam War, and the war in Central America reinforced by the Iran-Contra affair during the Reagan administration. Both George H. W. Bush and Bill Clinton complained of the sour, often deadlocked relations between Congress and the White House. Even the fall of the Berlin Wall and the end of the Cold War failed to repair the partisanship and ideological differences that increasingly caused dissensus where consensus was sought. Absent elite consensus, there was little that other Americans could embrace as a widely accepted view of a foreign policy grand strategy around which a new foreign policy consensus could be built.

President George H. W. Bush sought grounds for that consensus by drawing on Wilsonian idealism. In the wake of the Cold War, he envisioned a new world order based on the rule of law and an effective and legitimate United Nations. President Bill Clinton, a liberal internationalist like his predecessor, also embraced Wilsonianism. His vision of the post–Cold War world included a world political economy built on the principles and promises of globalization, and an international political system in which peace could be achieved by promoting democracy and democratic capitalism. George W. Bush went to Washington with, at best, a vague foreign policy program. To him, a paramount goal was avoiding the domestic policy mistakes his father had made. Another goal was avoiding what he viewed as Clinton's foreign policy mistakes, including humanitarian intervention and nation-building.

Then came 9/11, a watershed event much like Pearl Harbor sixty years earlier. Suddenly, everything seemed to have changed. Bush announced a policy to prevent further attacks on the United States, pursuing transnational terrorists wherever they may be, and punishing states that harbored them. He warned other states they were either with the United States or against it. And he later added democracy promotion and putting an end to tyranny throughout the world as embellishments to what became known as the *Bush Doctrine*—a new foreign policy grand strategy for the post-9/11 era.

The last edition of this book was published only a few months after the terrorist attacks of 9/11. It assessed how new, post–Cold War opportunities, challenges, aspirations, and old constraints intermixed to shape President Bill Clinton's efforts to devise a new American foreign policy. That book also set the stage for this new, seventh edition of *American Foreign Policy: Pattern and Process,* in which we make a critical assessment of the Bush administration in the context of the patterns and processes that have long shaped American foreign policy. The post-9/11 world has certainly posed new challenges and opportunities, but we will also find that the president and his administration have been constrained by past practices and new imperatives. Thus the Bush administration perpetuates in fundamental ways the consistency and continuity of American foreign policy evident throughout past decades. The seventh edition of *American Foreign Policy: Pattern and Process* draws on recent events and scholarship to provide comprehensive coverage and analysis of the significant impact the September 11, 2001, terrorist attacks and the first six years of the George W. Bush administration have had on early twenty-first century American foreign policy. Our fifteen chapters have been thoroughly revised and substantially updated and, in some cases, completely rewritten to capture the many sweeping changes that have transpired since the twin towers of the World Trade Center fell. Thus the book is very much an in-depth examination of how the Bush administration sought to reshape national strategy, policies, and structures, the domestic and international actions that have been initiated in the name of national security, and the immediate implications and possible long-term consequences of these developments. Retaining the accessibility that has marked previous editions of the book has been our goal throughout.

As in previous editions, we rely on a proven and resilient conceptual framework that frames the examination of the different sources of American foreign policy. This new edition continues to place the contemporary issues, debates, challenges, and opportunities in their historical context in order to assess the changes of today's post-9/11 world in the broader sweep of the nation's enduring principles, values, and interests: peace and prosperity, stability and security, democracy and defense. Our conceptual framework allows us to utilize relevant theories effectively, and our placement of the contemporary debates in their historical context allows students both to see and to assess the forces underlying continuity and change in American foreign policy. Readers familiar with the book will note that we have retained the overall structure and thematic thrust of previous editions, which effectively harness the conceptual, theoretical, and historical components appropriate for the analysis of American foreign policy. Our analytical framework stresses five foreign policy sources that collectively influence decisions about foreign policy goals and the means chosen to realize them: the *external* (global) environment, the *societal* environment of the nation, the *governmental* setting in which policy making occurs, the *roles* occupied by policy makers, and the *individual* characteristics of foreign policy-making elites.

After establishing the analytical approach of the text (Part I) and considering the broad patterns of goals and policy instruments (Part II), we elaborate on these five sources in the nine chapters comprising Parts III through VII. Our final section and chapter (Part VIII) returns to the challenges of the post-9/11 era and considers the choices Americans will face as President Bush prepares the final chapters of his legacy.

As we tackled the task of bringing our text fully into the post-9/11 era, we made countless changes and revisions in each part. Among them, our readers will find the following:

Part I, Chapter 1 introduces grand strategy as a key concept used to frame national security policy. We discuss how the Bush Doctrine and its elements comprise an American foreign policy grand strategy, and we return to it repeatedly later in the book. The discussion sets the stage for continuing assessments in later chapters of the Bush administration's emphasis on a strategy of primacy (hegemony) and alternative approaches toward twenty-first century national security strategies. The war on terrorism is evident throughout. Chapter 1 also draws attention to globalization. It briefly outlines the positive and negative aspects of globalization, a phenomenon that commands less immediate attention than in the 1990s, when it dominated the pace of world politics, but which has proceeded nonetheless. It further recognizes that both the ends and means of American foreign policy remain broadly disputed.

The presentation of the analytical framework around which we organize the book (Chapter 2) remains sharp and concise, and we have added new examples to demonstrate its continued utility for understanding twenty-first century American foreign policy.

Part II has been substantially revised and updated. In Chapter 3, we examine the goals of American foreign policy in historical perspective, with an emphasis on the concepts of internationalism and isolationism, realism and idealism, and power, principle, and pragmatism. Our discussion of American foreign relations from the birth of the Republic through the decade preceding the September 11, 2001, attacks is presented more concisely. The reprioritization of the American foreign policy agenda since the Clinton administration is reflected in our new and considerable attention to the war on terrorism, the Bush Doctrine (with its historic elements of preemptive war, unilateralism, hegemony), homeland security, countering the proliferation of weapons of mass destruction, and democracy promotion.

Chapter 4 focuses entirely on military power and intervention, taking special care to consider developments in the Bush administration including the global campaign against terrorism and the conflicts in Iraq and Afghanistan. The examination of military force and political purposes has been sharpened with an up-to-date emphasis on coercive diplomacy and force-short-of-war. In addition, the discussion of ballistic missile threats and the national missile defense program has been updated and expanded.

Chapter 5 retains its focus on four forms of nonmilitary interventionism: covert action, foreign aid, sanctions, and public diplomacy. We have enlarged the discussion of counterterrorism and today's challenges for covert action to reflect recent developments in the war on terrorism. Our examination of foreign assistance has been thoroughly restructured to include a discussion of the full range of contemporary U.S. bilateral foreign economic assistance programs, including new Bush administration initiatives—the Global HIV/AIDS Initiative, the Millennium Challenge Account, and debt relief. Our updated discussion of foreign military aid and sales highlights the link between such assistance and the war on terrorism. We give attention to the growing importance of public diplomacy in the post-9/11 era with special emphasis on the Department of State's efforts under the leadership of Colin Powell and Condoleezza Rice to counter powerful anti-American sentiment worldwide.

In Part III, we survey the international political and economic environments in their historical and contemporary variants as a source of American foreign policy. In Chapter 6, we consider how the characteristics of the international political system shape American foreign policy choices. Our discussion reflects explicitly on the current global context, in which the United States enjoys primacy but must contend with emergent powers and the rise of "soft balancing," and the continuing challenges of transnational terrorism and globalization. Key global challenges that extend beyond traditional great power politics are also examined, including the threat of global climate change, expanded coverage of failed states, and an updated and more streamlined discussion of non-state actors.

In Chapter 7, we stress America's continuing centrality in the world political economy and the profound challenges and changes that globalization poses to its economic hegemony. Recent efforts to preserve and extend U.S. preponderance and the responses of others to them are examined. Our discussion concentrates on monetary and trade policy, including a section on the Bush administration's preference for negotiated free trade agreements (FTAs) and its emphasis on Latin America.

In Part IV, we assess the dynamics of the societal sources of American foreign policy. In Chapter 8, we address the nation's political culture and public opinion as it relates to foreign policy. In an environment undergoing rapid political and demographic change pointing toward increased multiculturalism, we have added to our coverage of liberalism a new section on *civil religion,* which shows how the nation's predominantly Christian values and beliefs have become intertwined with the dominant political culture. The chapter now includes greater attention to whether and how the recent influx of (largely Hispanic) immigrants poses a challenge to the dominant political culture. The public opinion section examines in some detail how the war on terrorism and especially the war in Iraq have affected attitudes toward President Bush, adding to a remarkable drop in his popularity with Americans since 9/11.

In Chapter 9, we examine evidence supporting (or refuting) two popular views of the policy-making process in the United States: elitism and pluralism. We find the evidence as it relates to foreign policy leans toward the elitist model. We note the corporate connections of the Bush administration, widely criticized for its "Big Business" orientation, and briefly discuss the Project for the New American Century (PNAC) as a source of both the neoconservative ideas and personnel that achieved dominance in the Bush administration. Our examination of the role of the media in the policy process has been sharpened with greater attention on the media's "framing" role. And our attention to presidential elections continues to raise questions about their decisiveness as it relates to foreign policy, even in the 2004 presidential campaign when the war in Iraq was a key issue.

In Part V, we focus on the governmental sources of American foreign policy. We examine the president's role and a cluster of factors that affect presidential leadership in Chapter 10, including the setting (for example, the Constitution and the courts) and the structures that presidents use to exercise policy leadership. Given the Bush administration's determined effort to considerably expand presidential power, our discussion has been refocused around the themes of presidential preeminence and the post-9/11 return of the "imperial presidency." New sections on the Homeland Security Council and the enhanced foreign policy role of Vice President Richard B. Cheney have been added. Our discussion of the National Security Council system has been updated to include the tenures of Condoleezza Rice and Stephen Hadley as national security advisers.

Our substantial revision to Chapter 11 includes recent developments in the foreign policy bureaucracy. The Department of State section includes a thorough discussion of Colin Powell's four-year revitalization effort at Foggy Bottom as well as Condoleezza Rice's subsequent emphasis on transformational diplomacy. The discussion of the Department of Defense examines the significant impact of Donald Rumsfeld's assertive leadership and his efforts to "transform" the Pentagon. Our coverage of the U.S. intelligence community includes the many structural and procedural changes associated with post-9/11 intelligence reforms (including the establishment of a director of national intelligence), an updated and more streamlined analysis of the Central Intelligence Agency, a discussion of the militarization of U.S. intelligence, and new sections on the Federal Bureau of Investigation, the Drug Enforcement Agency, and the Department of Homeland Security.

Chapter 12 focuses on Congress and its foreign policy roles and instruments of influence. Numerous insights and evidence from the post-9/11 era have been added. We also give renewed emphasis to the War Powers Resolution that includes issues and developments related to the Bush administration's military campaigns in Afghanistan and Iraq. In addition, our discussion of treaty politics now encompasses new material on the ratification of arms control treaties.

In Part VI, we consider roles as sources of American foreign policy. Chapter 13 examines decision making with an emphasis on the impact of position on policy preferences and policy making. In this context, we assess rational actor and bureaucratic politics models. Our revised discussion of the nature, sources, characteristics, and consequences of bureaucratic behavior and politics includes post-9/11 examples related to counterterrorism policy, a new section on risk aversion, and an expanded discussion of policy makers' reliance on historical analogies, including an analysis of the similarities and dissimilarities between the Iraq and Vietnam conflicts.

In Part VII, we focus on individual sources, stressing the characteristics of leaders. Chapter 14 includes consideration of the character, style, and personality of foreign policy makers, as well as the conditions in which their individual idiosyncrasies matter most. Our revision updates and expands our discussion of President Bush's character and leadership style. New sketches of other recent officials explore the influence of personality, style, and personal background on foreign policy making.

In Part VIII (Chapter 15), we reflect on the future of American foreign policy and the prospects for a second American Century. Our concluding thoughts reflect on the legacy of George W. Bush and how those who follow in his leadership path may assess his foreign policies and postures. We reexamine elements of the Bush Doctrine and the grand strategy it comprises. We also consider the interplay of the five sources of American foreign policy discussed in previous chapters as they have shaped or constrained Bush's effort to engineer a new policy paradigm for a new American Century.

Although Bush's foreign policy as been described as "revolutionary," we conclude that that description is wanting. Certainly his legacy will shape the future, just as the two great wars and the decades-long Cold War of the twentieth century have shaped the world in which we live today. But revolutions are rare in a democratic society where the forces of change face substantial countervailing pressures. Our own conclusion about the impact of 9/11 and the future of American foreign policy is captured in the following comment by the managing editor of the prominent magazine *Foreign Policy:*

> If you look closely at the trend lines since 9/11, what is remarkable is how little the world has changed. The forces of globalization continue unabated; indeed, if anything, they have accelerated. The issues of the day that we were debating on that morning in September are largely the same. Across broad measures of political, economic, and social data, the constants outweigh the variations. And, five years later, the United States' foreign policy is marked by no greater strategic clarity than it had on September 10, 2001.
>
> *(William J. Dobson, Foreign Policy, September/October 2006, 23)*

Readers of our book may not agree with this conclusion. But we hope it invites them to engage in spirited discussions as they make their own judgment about the future of American foreign policy after Bush.

In addition to these conclusions and the many revisions we have made in our analyses, we have continued our determination to make the new edition accessible and conducive to effective teaching and learning. Our readers will find more organizational breaks and sections in each chapter designed to assist the student and help to structure readings and discussions. The book retains the textual highlights of the previous edition. To further its pedagogical value, we have provided new, shorter list of key terms at the end of each chapter, new suggested readings, and a thoroughly updated glossary. Tables, figures, and focus boxes have also been updated throughout to reflect recent developments. Finally, we remain committed to connecting our historical and contemporary discussions to broader themes, concepts, and theories. Doing so promotes greater critical and analytical thinking, better explanation and evaluation, and a more coherent consideration of the pattern and process of American foreign policy.

This overview captures just a few of the many changes, large and small, in this edition of *American Foreign Policy: Pattern and Process.* Our text now reflects a vision of the unfolding new century. But just as change and continuity describe the reality of contemporary American foreign policy, our book continues to be shaped by the many people who have contributed to it from its inception to the present. The contributions have come from our professional colleagues and critics, from "comment cards" sent to our publisher, ideas shared with our sales representatives, student evaluations, and other means. All have shaped our efforts to provide superior scholarship and an effective teaching and learning tool.

We are pleased to acknowledge the special contributions to this edition made by others. Cameron Thies made major contributions to the revisions of Chapters

6 and 7. Mark A. Boyer participated in updating some of the early chapters. And James M. Scott, coauthor of the previous edition, will recognize the continuing influence of his work. We also are pleased to recognize the contributions of Rachel Bzostek, Scott Crichlow, Lui Hebron, Shaun Levine, Kathryn McCall, John Mueller, and Sam Robison, who contributed in large and small ways to the project. We also recognize the professionals at Wadsworth Publishing for their contributions in bringing this edition to fruition, among them Michael Rosenberg, David Tatom, Karen Judd, Paul Wells, Marti Paul, Patrick Rooney, Karin Sandberg, Christine Halsey, Ben Kolstad, Mona Tiwary, Divya Kapoor, Lunaea Weatherstone, and Marlene Veach.

Finally, we are pleased and proud to recognize our wives and children. Without their unwavering love and support, this book would not have been possible.

Eugene R. Wittkopf
Christopher M. Jones
Charles W. Kegley, Jr.

About the Authors

Eugene R. Wittkopf was the R. Downs Poindexter Professor Emeritus at Louisiana State University (LSU). He also held appointments at the University of Florida and the University of North Carolina. He received his doctorate from the Maxwell School of Citizenship and Public Affairs at Syracuse University. He published more than thirty books on international politics and foreign policy and several dozen refereed articles in professional journals and chapters in books. He held offices in professional associations and served on the editorial boards of numerous profession journals. In 2002, he received the Distinguished Scholar Award of the Foreign Policy Section of the International Studies Association. Earlier, Professor Wittkopf was named the 1996 Distinguished Research Master of Arts, Humanities, and Social Studies at Louisiana State University. This is the highest award given by LSU in recognition of faculty contributions to research and scholarship.

Christopher M. Jones is associate professor and chair within the Department of Political Science at Northern Illinois University (NIU). He has also served as assistant chair and director of undergraduate studies. He received his doctorate from the Maxwell School of Citizenship and Public Affairs at Syracuse University, where he received university-wide awards in research and teaching. He has published more than twenty journal articles and book chapters related to American foreign and defense policy, and co-edited *The Future of American Foreign Policy* (1999) with Eugene R. Wittkopf. Professor Jones has been recognized for teaching excellence by student organizations, the American Political Science Association, the National Political Science Honor Society, *Who's Who among America's Teachers,* and three universities. In 2002, he became the youngest recipient of Northern Illinois University's Excellence in Undergraduate Teaching Award, the institution's longest-standing faculty honor.

Charles W. Kegley, Jr., is corporate secretary on the board of trustees of the Carnegie Council for Ethics in International Affairs and a Moynihan Faculty Research Associate in the Moynihan Institute of Global Affairs at Syracuse

University. He has held appointments at Georgetown University, the University of Texas, Rutgers University, the People's University of China, and the Graduate Institute of International Studies, Geneva. He received his doctorate from the Maxwell School of Citizenship and Public Affairs at Syracuse University. He has written and edited more than forty-five books and more than one hundred journal articles and book chapters. He is past president of the International Studies Association (ISA) and a recipient of the Distinguished Scholar Award of ISA's Foreign Policy Section. Professor Kegley is also Distinguished Pearce Professor of International Relations Emeritus at the University of South Carolina.

Analytical and Thematic Perspectives on American Foreign Policy

1

In Search of American Foreign Policy:

A Thematic Introduction

> There are times when only America can make the difference between war and peace, between freedom and repression, between hope and fear.
> PRESIDENT WILLIAM JEFFERSON CLINTON, 1996

> America has no empire to extend or utopia to establish. We wish for others only what we wish for ourselves—safety from violence, the rewards of liberty, and the hope for a better life.
> PRESIDENT GEORGE W. BUSH, 2002

America the invincible. Long a part of the nation's political heritage, that description is no longer accurate—if it ever was. On September 11, 2001, nineteen hijackers armed with only a few box cutters commandeered four commercial jetliners packed with jet fuel and smashed them into the World Trade Center (WTC), the Pentagon, and the hills of Pennsylvania. Nearly three thousand people were killed on that day, more than were killed at Pearl Harbor on December 7, 1941. Like December 7, 9/11 will long remain etched on the nation's psyche.

Almost immediately after the attack, President George W. Bush declared the United States at war with terrorism and the states and non-state actors who would perpetrate it—most notably the transnational terrorist organization *Al Qaeda.*

As the president prepared the country for a long, dogged search for and destruction of terrorist havens in southwest Asia and elsewhere, he also employed conventional military force to bring about regime change in Afghanistan and Iraq. Parallels were evident between the war on terrorism and the three global wars that animated the great powers in the twentieth century—World Wars I and II and the Cold War. Just as their outcomes profoundly shaped the world in which we live today, the war on terrorism has also reshaped the lives of millions of Americans and others around the world and will continue to do so. The war against terrorism—which some commentators call *World War IV*—is in many ways a replay of those prior conflicts, as the struggle over power and principle remains central to the conflicts between the antagonists and protagonists. As in the twentieth century, the war on terrorism initially animated the patriotic sentiments of the American people, tilted the constitutional balance of power away from Congress toward the president, placed restraints on Americans' civil liberties, rationalized sharp increases in defense spending, and then became a divisive national political issue.

Differences between the war on terrorism and the twentieth century global wars are also evident, of course. The perpetrators of terrorism may have connections to states, but they are transnational actors unconstrained by the boundaries of sovereign states, long the central focus of international politics. Religious fanaticism animates most terrorists with global reach, and they have demonstrated a willingness to sacrifice their own lives to achieve their goals: causing the death and destruction of their enemies and instilling fear. Thus the Cold War strategy of *deterrence* relied upon by the United States to prevent an attack by the Soviet Union on the United States or its allies is ineffective in the war on terror. How do you deter someone who does not fear death?

The war on terrorism is also an asymmetrical war. As defined by the U.S. military, **asymmetrical warfare** comprises "attempts to circumvent or undermine an opponent's strengths while exploiting his weaknesses using methods that differ significantly from the opponent's usual mode of operations" (cited in Barnett 2004). U.S. strengths in wartime are its technologically sophisticated conventional military capabilities and its nuclear deterrent. Its weaknesses derive from its attraction as an open and free society. The nineteen hijackers who sacrificed their own lives in the 9/11 attacks entered the United States quite freely. And their weapons of choice differed significantly from the United States' preferred instruments of war: they used civilian passenger planes as weapons of mass destruction. The Vietnam War, the Persian Gulf War, and the war in Iraq all also revealed techniques used by weaker states against a dominant U.S. military force, including roadside bombings, the taking of hostages, using human shields, commingling insurgents and guerilla antagonists with civilian populations, hiding enemy forces in religious centers, and engaging in environmental devastation.

Terrorism is not new to the twenty-first century; indeed, its practice is centuries old. In pursuit of their objectives, today's terrorists have taken advantage of the open borders and advanced technologies fostered by globalization processes unleashed during the 1990s, such as disposable cell phones, rapid-fire financial transactions, and the Internet. In the end, however, **terrorism** remains what it has always been: politically motivated violence waged by the weak against the strong. And no one is stronger today than the United States.

THE AMERICAN CENTURIES

In 1941, Henry Luce, the noted editor and publisher of *Time, Life,* and *Fortune* magazines, envisioned his era as the dawn of the "American Century." He based his prediction on the conviction that "only America can effectively state the aims of this war" (World War II). The aims included "a vital international economy" and "an international moral order."

In many ways Luce's prediction proved prophetic, not just as it applied to World War II but also to the decades-long Cold War contest with the Soviet Union that quickly followed. But even Luce might be surprised that the twenty-first century looks to be an even more thoroughly American century than his. Today, in the early years of the new century, the facts are simple and irrefutable: compared with other countries, the United States is in a class by itself. No other country can match the productivity of its economy, the extent of its scientific and technological prowess, its ability to sustain massive levels of defense spending, or the power, sophistication, and global reach of its armed forces. The terrorist attacks on the American homeland on September 11, 2001, did considerable harm to the economy and jolted the ethos of invincibility, but they did nothing to challenge the preeminent power of the United States in the world. Indeed, the attacks helped to settle priorities along lines preferred by the Republican party: an assertive America.

Today, America's power extends even beyond the traditional measures Luce considered, encompassing a wealth of less tangible assets broadly conceived as *soft power* (Nye 2004). In contrast to the *hard power* of military might, soft power includes the attraction of America's culture, values, and political beliefs and the ability of the United States to establish rules and institutions it favors. Thus the United States continues to set much of the agenda in the international organizations it helped to establish in the 1940s, and democracy and market economies have spread throughout the world. American culture—ranging from hip-hop music, blue jeans, and McDonald's to PCs, Windows operating systems, and Internet communications in English—exhibits nearly universal appeal in our globalizing world. Impressed with the global reach of America's soft power, one analyst observed that "One has to go back to the Roman Empire for a similar instance of cultural hegemony. . . . We live in an 'American age,' meaning that American values and arrangements are most closely in tune with the new Zeitgeist" (Joffe 1997).

Powerful as the United States may be, America's "second" century will still be profoundly shaped by the three global wars of the twentieth century. Three times in eighty years—in World War I, World War II, and the Cold War—the world experienced international contests for power and position of global proportions and with global consequences, forcing the United States to confront its role as its political, economic, and military importance grew. All of these conflicts will continue to cast their shadows across the contours of world politics as the twenty-first century unfolds.

The presidents who occupied the White House during these contests shared a common vision of the nation's future, grounded in *liberalism* and *idealism.* Woodrow Wilson, under whose leadership the United States entered the war against Germany in 1917 and fought to create "a world safe for democracy," called for an association of states that he promised would guarantee the "political independence and territorial integrity [of] great and small states alike." Franklin D. Roosevelt, president during World War II until his death in April 1945, portrayed the moral basis for American involvement in World War II as an effort to secure *four freedoms*—freedom of speech and expression, freedom of worship, freedom from want, and freedom from fear. He, too, supported creation of a new association of the United Nations, as the allies were called, to secure and maintain the structure of peace once the war against Germany and Japan was ended. Like Wilson, Roosevelt's vision of the postwar world championed the principles of self-determination and an open international marketplace. Harry S. Truman, Roosevelt's successor, carried much of Roosevelt's vision forward, eventually adapting its principles to his own definition of the post–World War II world order.

George H. W. Bush perpetuated the liberal tradition following the third twentieth century contest for power and position—the Cold War. It ended in November 1989 when the Berlin Wall came tumbling down. For nearly thirty years the wall had stood as perhaps the most emotional symbol of the "iron curtain" that separated the East from the West, and of the Cold War that had raged between the United States and the Soviet Union since World War II. Less than a year later, Iraq invaded the tiny desert kingdom of Kuwait. The United States, now with the unprecedented support of the Soviet Union in the United Nations Security Council, took the lead in organizing a military response to Iraq's aggression, based on the same principle of collective security that Wilson, Roosevelt, and Truman had embraced. President Bush evoked images of the "next American century" and a "new world order" in which the "rule of law" would reign supreme. He extolled America's leadership role, urging that "only the United States of America has the moral leadership and the means to back it up."

Once before, however, the United States had rejected the world's call for leadership and responsibility. Wilson failed in his bid to have the United States join the League of Nations, of which he had been the principal architect. In this and other ways the United States turned away from the challenge of international involvement that World War I had posed. Instead, it opted to return to its historic pattern of isolation from the machinations it associated with Europe's power politics, which Wilson had characterized as an "old and evil order," one marked by "an arrangement of power and suspicion and dread." The strategy contributed to the breakdown of order and stability in the decades following World War I, thus setting the stage for the twentieth century's second global contest for international power and position.

World War II was geographically more widespread and militarily more destructive than World War I—and it transformed world politics irrevocably. The place of the United States in the structure of world politics also was altered dramatically as it emerged from the war with unparalleled capabilities.

World War II not only propelled the United States to the status of an emergent superpower, it also transformed the way the country responded to the challenges of the postwar world. *Isolationism* fell to the wayside, as American leaders and eventually the American people embraced *internationalism*—a new vision predicated on political assumptions derived from their experience in World War II and the turmoil that preceded it. Wilsonian idealism now became intertwined with the doctrine of *political realism,* which focused on power, not ideals. Containment became the preferred strategy for dealing with the Soviet Union in the latest contest for power and position, demanding resources and commitment beyond anything the United States had previously experienced. Some forty years later, the United States would emerge "victorious" in this contest, as first the Soviet external empire and then the Soviet Union itself disintegrated. The ideology of communism also fell into widespread disrepute.

Ironically, the end of the Cold War removed the very things that had given structure and purpose to post–World War II American foreign policy: fear of communism, fear of the Soviet Union, and a determination to contain both. These convictions also stimulated the internationalist ethos accepted by the American people and especially their leaders following World War II. Absent them, the decade between the end of the Cold War and 9/11 was marked by a search for a new ***grand strategy*** that would guide the nation into the new century. The concept refers to "the full range of goals that a state should seek, but it concentrates primarily on how the military instrument should be employed to achieve them. It prescribes how a nation should wield its military instrument to realize its foreign policy goals" (Art 2003). The first step in defining a grand strategy, then, is the determination of a state's national interests and hence its goals. Political Scientist Robert J. Art suggests six such national interests for the United States (see Focus 1.1), arranged roughly from "vital" (preventing an attack) to "important" (spreading democracy and stopping global warming). He also suggests eight grand strategies to secure those interests and goals. We will touch on them briefly later in this chapter.

Even as the United States debated—and continues to debate—a strategy for the future, forces unleashed in the decade leading to 9/11 markedly reshaped the global environment. The spread of democracy to nearly every corner of the world gave millions of people freedom to control their own destinies in ways only recently deemed imaginable. Because democracies rarely engage in violent conflict with one another, *global democratization* gave rise to the hope that this century will be less marked by violence, warfare, and bloodshed than the last. Furthermore, democracy is often accompanied by the spread of *economic liberalism*. As market forces are unleashed, greater economic opportunity and rising affluence hold forth the promise of improved living standards and enhanced quality of life.

The globalization of the world political economy accompanied the spread of political democracy and market economies, contributing to a homogenization of social and cultural forces worldwide. ***Globalization***

F O C U S   1.1   The National Interests of the United States

1. Prevent an attack on the American homeland
2. Prevent great-power Eurasian wars and, if possible, the intense security competition that makes them more likely
3. Preserve access to a reasonably priced and secure supply of oil
4. Preserve an open international economic order
5. Foster the spread of democracy and respect for human rights abroad
6. Protect the global environment, especially from the adverse affects of global warming and severe climate damage

SOURCE: Quoted and adapted from Robert J. Art, *A Grand Strategy for America*. Ithaca, NY: Cornell University Press, 2003, p. 7. Reprinted by permission.

---

refers to the rapid intensification and integration of states' economies, not only in terms of markets but also ideas, information, and technology, which is having a profound impact on political, social, and cultural relations across borders. The economic side of globalization often dominates the headlines of financial pages and computer trade journals. But the causes and consequences of globalization extend beyond economics (see Focus 1.2).

Globalization seemed to stall following the U.S. invasion of Iraq in 2003 and the antipathy toward the United States that followed—"a disaster for globalization" is how one noted international economist, Joseph Siglitz, described that year. But systematic data collected by the A. T. Kearney Corporation and the Carnegie Endowment for International Peace reveals that globalization "is a phenomenon that runs deeper than the political crises of the day" (A. T. Kearney, Inc. and Carnegie Endowment 2005). Instead, it is an ongoing process that stems from "the onrush of economic and ecological forces that demand integration and uniformity and that mesmerize the world with fast music, fast computers, and fast food—with MTV, Macintosh, and McDonald's, pressing nations into one commercially homogenous global network: one McWorld tied together by technology, ecology, communications, and commerce" (Barber 1992). This is the environment that led an admiring German journalist to ask us to "Think of the United States as a gambler who can play simultaneously at each and every table that matters—and with more chips than anybody else. Whichever heap you choose, America sits on top of it" (Joffe 1997). Despite global discontent with the direction of American foreign policy, this assessment remains true a decade later. The United States continues to dominate each table that matters.

Because the political boundaries separating states are transparent to the cross-border trends unleashed by globalization, the trends pose challenges to the United States at home and abroad. Domestically, globalization "is exposing a deep fault line between groups who have the skills and mobility to flourish in global markets and those who either don't have these advantages or perceive the expansion of unregulated markets as inimical to social stability and deeply held norms." Understandably, this results in "severe tension between the market and social groups such as workers, pensioners, and environmentalists, with governments stuck in the middle" (Rodrik 1997).

Internationally, the forces unleashed by globalization are also "producing a powerful backlash from those brutalized or left behind in the new system," which is defined by an "inexorable integration of markets, nation-states, and technologies to a degree never witnessed before" (Friedman 1999). Thus globalization may be a force beyond states' control.

Collectively, the "dark side" of globalization has given rise to antiglobalists in the United States and abroad who have joined forces to slow—even stop—"the onrush of economic and ecological forces that demand integration and uniformity."

FOCUS 1.2 The Shrinking World

Contacts between the world's people are widening and deepening as natural and artificial barriers fall. Huge declines in transport and communication costs have reduced natural barriers. Shipping is much cheaper: between 1920 and 1990 maritime transport costs fell by more than two-thirds. Between 1960 and 1990 operating costs per mile for the world's airlines fell by 60 percent.

Communication is also much easier and cheaper. Between 1940 and 1970 the cost of an international telephone call fell by more than 80 percent, and between 1970 and 1990 by 90 percent. In the 1980s telecommunication traffic was expanding by 20 percent a year. The Internet, the take-off point for the information superhighway, is now used by 50 million people, with the number of subscribers tapping into it doubling every year.

Toppling Trade Barriers

Artificial barriers have been eased with the reduction in trade barriers (tariffs, quotas, and so on) and exchange controls. In 1947 the average tariff on manufactured imports was 47 percent; by 1980 it was only 6 percent, and with full implementation of the Uruguay Round, it should fall to 3 percent.

Other artificial barriers were removed with the resolution of political conflicts that have divided the world for decades, such as the Cold War and the apartheid system in South Africa.

Spurred by the fall of barriers, global trade grew twelve-fold in the postwar period. Now more than $4 trillion a year, it is expected to grow 6 percent annually for the next ten years.

The Rising Tide of Finance

The expansion of capital flows has been even more dramatic. Flows of foreign direct investment in 1995 reached $315 billion, nearly a six-fold increase over the level for 1981–1985. Over the same period world trade increased by little more than half.

Less visible, but infinitely more powerful, are the world's financial markets. Between the mid-1970s and 1996 the daily turnover in the world's foreign exchange markets increased from around $1 billion to $1.2 trillion. Most private capital flows went to industrial countries, but a growing share is going to developing countries. Between 1987 and 1994 the flows to developing countries rose from $25 billion to $172 billion, and in 1995 they received a third of the global foreign direct investment flows.

These changes are significant, but need to be placed in historical context. Much of this has happened before. For 17 industrial countries for which there are data, exports as a share of GDP in 1913 were 12.9 percent, not much below the 1993 level of 14.5 percent. And capital transfers as a share of industrial country GDP are still smaller than in the 1890s. Earlier eras of globalization also saw far greater movement of people around the world. Today immigration is more restricted.

The modern era of globalization is distinguished less by the scale of the flows than by their character. In

---

Antiglobalists endeavor to preserve cultural identities, to protect the environment from degradation by profit-driven multinational corporations, and to stem the "rush to the bottom" in labor markets caused in part by *outsourcing* jobs to countries with the cheapest labor. Ironically, post-9/11 efforts to cope with terrorism have also tightened restrictions on foreign travel and other transborder activities in ways that have conformed to the antiglobalists' vision.

Widespread *intranational conflict* fed by ethnic and religious feuds, often centuries old, is another troublesome development that bloomed in the last decade of the twentieth century. The United States responded, increasingly involving itself in *humanitarian interventions,* such as peacekeeping, peacemaking, and nation-building activities in places like Somalia and the former Yugoslavia. After the 78-day air war in the Yugoslav province of Kosovo in 1998, President Clinton, in what became known as the *Clinton Doctrine,* pledged that the United States would intervene in ethnopolitical conflicts when it was within its power to stop them. In contrast, President George W. Bush campaigned in 2000 on the promise that he would not engage in nation-building abroad. But he quickly became involved in that process in Afghanistan and Iraq after forcing regime change in both countries following 9/11.

trade, for example, a much smaller share by value consists of commodities (partly a reflection of lower prices relative to manufactures) and a larger share is services and intracompany trade. Finance too is different: net flows may be similar, but gross flows are larger— and the flows come from a wider variety of sources. And multinational corporations are leaders in mobilizing capital and generating technology.

Global Technology . . .

Some of the changes in international trade and finance reflect advances in technology. The lightning speed of transactions means that countries and companies now must respond rapidly if they are not to be left behind.

Technological change is also affecting the nature of investment. Previously, high-technology production had been limited to rich countries with high wages. Today technology is more easily transferred to developing countries, where sophisticated production can be combined with relatively low wages.

The increasing ease with which technology can accompany capital across borders threatens to break the links between high productivity, high technology, and high wages. For example, Mexico's worker productivity rose from a fifth to a third of the U.S. level between 1989 and 1993, in part as a consequence of increased foreign investment and sophisticated technology geared toward production for the U.S. market. But the average wage gap has narrowed far more slowly, with the Mexican wage still only a sixth of the U.S. wage. The availability of higher levels of technology all over the world is putting pressure on the wages and employment of low-skilled workers.

. . . And a Global Culture

Normally, globalization refers to the international flow of trade and capital. But the international spread of cultures has been at least as important as the spread of economic processes. Today a global culture is emerging. Through many media— from music to movies to books— international ideas and values are being mixed with, and superimposed on, national identities. The spread of ideas through television and video has seen revolutionary developments. There now are more than 1.2 billion TV sets around the world. The United States exports more than 120,000 hours of television programming a year to Europe alone, and the global trade in programming is growing by more than 15 percent a year.

Popular culture exerts more powerful pressure than ever before. From Manila to Managua, Beirut to Beijing, in the East, West, North and South, styles in dress (jeans, hairdos, t-shirts), sports, music, eating habits, and social and cultural attitudes have become global trends. Even crimes— whether relating to drugs, abuse of women, embezzlement, or corruption— transcend frontiers and have become similar everywhere. In so many ways, the world has shrunk.

SOURCE: From *Human Development Report 1997*, by United Nations Development Programme, copyright © 1997 by the United Nations Development Programme. Used by permission of Oxford University Press, Inc.

TOWARD A GRAND STRATEGY FOR THE SECOND AMERICAN CENTURY

For forty years, *containment* of the Soviet Union defined America's foreign and national security policy. The strategy was based on the premises of *political realism* and *liberal internationalism,* "logics" of American foreign policy that emphasize power and international cooperation, respectively (Callahan 2004). Presidents Bush and Clinton continued to embrace these logics in the 1990s, but neither successfully designed an overarching grand strategy for the post–Cold War world around which a domestic and global consensus could be built.

Political scientist Robert Art has analyzed eight proposed grand strategies, assessing their fit for realizing America's six interests and goals described in Focus 1.1. He identifies and briefly compares them this way:

> *Dominion* aims to transform the world into what America thinks it should look like. This strategy would use American military power in an imperial fashion to effect the transformation. *Isolationism* aims to maintain a free hand for the United States, and

its prime aim is to keep the United States out of most wars. *Offshore balancing* generally seeks the same goals as isolationism, but would go one step further and cut down an emerging hegemon in Eurasia so as to maintain a favorable balance of power there. *Containment* aims to hold the line against a specific aggressor that either threatens American interests in a given region or that strives for world hegemony, through both deterrent and defensive uses of military power. *Collective security* aims to keep the peace by preventing war by any aggressor. *Global collective security* and *cooperative security* aim to keep the peace everywhere; *regional collective security* to keep peace within specified areas. All three variants of collective security do so by tying the United States to multilateral arrangements that guarantee military defeat for any aggressor that breaches the peace. Finally, *selective engagement* aims to do a defined number of things well.

(Art 2003, 83)

Selective Engagement

Art concludes from his assessment of these eight strategies that most are either undesirable or politically infeasible. He argues that *selective engagement* is the preferred strategy for realizing America's six national interests and goals as he defines them.

Selective engagement is a strategy that aims to preserve America's key alliances and its forward-based forces. It keeps the United States militarily strong. With some important changes, it continues the internationalist path that the United States chose in 1945. It establishes priorities. . . . It steers a middle course between not doing enough and attempting too much: it takes neither an isolationist, unilateralist path at one extreme nor a world-policeman role at the other. Selective engagement requires that the United States remain militarily

involved abroad for its own interests. . . . Central to selective engagement are certain tasks that the United States must do well if its security, prosperity, and values are to be protected. Small in number, these tasks are large in scope and importance, and neither easy nor cheap to attain. If properly conceived and executed, however, selective engagement is politically feasible and affordable.

(Art 2003, 10)

Art's preference for a strategy of selective engagement is shared by others, but they are not without their critics. Advocates generally focus attention on great power relations in Eurasia, believing that it "sinks into warfare when the United States is absent, not when it is present; and once it does, we ultimately regret it" (Posen and Ross 1997). Left out of this scenario is a formula for prioritizing among the multiple challenges now facing the United States, including, for example, the compelling needs of millions of people in the **Global South** who live in poverty and without hope. In the absence of prioritizing guidelines, critics argue, the United States must be selective, guided by a pragmatic determination of where its true national interests lie.

Furthermore, a wide range of alternative preferences is cogently argued by others in the burgeoning literature on grand strategies. A neo-isolationist strategy, for example, is not easily dismissed.

Neo-isolationism

Neo-isolationists share with other grand strategists an overriding concern with the role of power in the global arena. However, they place a decidedly different spin on its meaning for today's foreign and national security policy. Who, they ask, poses a realistic challenge to America's overwhelming military power? North Korea? Iran? They concede that "nuclear weapons have increased the sheer capacity of others to threaten the safety of the United States," but they also argue that the U.S. nuclear arsenal makes it "nearly inconceivable" that any other state could seriously challenge the United States militarily (Posen and Ross 1997). As one group of analysts put it, "isolationism in the 1920s was inappropriate, because conquest on a continental scale was then possible. Now, nuclear weapons assure great power sovereignty—and certainly America's defense" (Gholz, Press, and Sapolsky 1997). Even after 9/11, neo-isolationists argue that "the U.S. should do less in the world. If the U.S. is less involved, it will be less of a target" (Posen 2001/2002).

To be sure, if the United States is drawn into conflicts around the world, it will become the hated object of machinations by others, including those who practice terrorism or seek to develop biological and chemical as well as nuclear weapons of mass destruction. Arguably the insurgency in Iraq is illustrative of this hatred.

The prescription for neo-isolationists that follows is the same as the nation's first president recommended two centuries ago: avoid foreign entanglements. Today this includes distancing the United States from the United Nations and other international organizations when they seek to make or enforce peace in roiling conflicts. This means less *multilateralism*—working in concert with others, usually on the basis of some principle such as collective security—to promote its policy ends.

Most advocates of neo-isolationism do not propose total withdrawal from the world. Even journalist and one-time Republican party presidential hopeful Pat Buchanan's (1990) popular call that America should be "first—and second, and third" does not prescribe that (see also Buchanan 2004). Nor does military retrenchment necessarily imply a resort to economic nationalism, as "a vigorous trade with other nations and the thriving commerce of ideas" are not incompatible with military restraint (Gholz, Press, and Sapolsky 1997). Thus American national interests remain unchanged: "The United States still seeks peace and prosperity. But now this preferred state is best obtained by restraining America's great power, a power unmatched by any rival and unchallenged in any important dimension. Rather than lead a new

crusade, America should absorb itself in the . . . task of addressing imperfections in its own society" (Gholz, Press, and Sapolsky 1997).

Neoconservatism

Retreat from international organizations has long been popular among isolationists and neo-isolationists, many of whom are also politically conservative. Even among them, however, some—who are often called *neoconservatives* (see Boot 2004)—bitterly oppose conflict avoidance through withdrawal from the world. Charles Krauthammer, for example, a neoconservative syndicated columnist, bitterly attacks the current version of neo-isolationism. "Isolationism is an important school of thought historically, but not today," he writes, "because it is so obviously inappropriate to the world of today—a world of export-driven economies, of massive population flows, and of 9/11, the definitive demonstration that the combination of modern technology and transnational primitivism has erased the barrier between 'over there' and over here."

For Krauthammer, *democratic globalism* is the appropriate U.S. strategy in a *unipolar world,* one in which the United States alone is unchallenged by others. He defines democratic globalism as "a foreign policy that defines the national interest not as power but as values, and that identifies one supreme value, what John Kennedy called 'the success of liberty'."

> Democratic globalism sees as the engine of history not the will to power but the will to freedom. As President Bush put it in his speech at Whitehall [in November 2003], "The United States and Great Britain share a mission in the world beyond the balance of power or the simple pursuit of interest. We seek the advance of freedom and the peace that freedom brings."
>
> Beyond power. Beyond interest. Beyond interest defined as power. That is the credo of democratic globalism.
>
> *(Krauthammer 2004, at www.aei.org)*

Krauthammer's provocative vision of the future has been criticized (see Buchanan 2004; Dorrien 2003; Fukuyama 2004b), but it enjoys wide sympathy among neoconservatives in the Bush White House, Bush's "war cabinet" and others in the Bush administration, and influential journalists, writers, and think-tank analysts. Liberty and freedom figure prominently in their vision, but getting there requires power. The United States is in a unique position to wield it, and the Bush administration is determined to maintain it.

Power, liberty, and freedom became defining features of the Bush administration's foreign policy following the vicious 9/11 terrorist attacks and is spelled out in the president's *National Security Strategy* statement, a report to Congress that followed a year later.

The Bush Doctrine

The night of the terrorist attacks, the president declared in a speech before Congress: "We will pursue nations that provide aid or safe haven to terrorism. Every nation, in every region, now has a decision to make. Either you are with us, or you are with the terrorists." Thus the United States will "make no distinction between the terrorists who committed these acts and those who harbor them."

These statements seemed to lay the basis for the later military interventions in Afghanistan and Iraq and became the cornerstone of the *Bush Doctrine* (for critiques see Jervis 2003 and Hoffmann 2003). Bush would also pledge to stem the proliferation of nuclear and other weapons of mass destruction, and to promote liberty and democracy throughout the world. The Middle East would be the starting place, with Iraq standing as a symbol of stability that other states in the strife-ridden region could emulate. The administration issued a "Roadmap to Peace" designed to push the inflammatory Israeli-Palestinian conflict toward some kind of resolution, a step believed to be critical in moving toward peace and stability throughout the Middle East.

As a grand strategy, the Bush Doctrine encompasses three critical concepts. One is the defense strategy of *preemptive war*—striking militarily an adversary who poses an imminent threat before the adversary can strike first (see Taylor 2004 for an assessment of the concept "imminent"). The United States has always reserved the right of preemption as a means of self-defense, but never before has this right been displayed so prominently or codified so explicitly. Although applicable anywhere, the "doctrine of preemption" is closely tied to the war on terrorism. "The war on terror will not be won on the defensive," according to Bush. Instead, "we must take the battle to the enemy, disrupt his plans, and confront the worst threats before they emerge. . . . Our security will require all Americans to be . . . ready for preemptive action when necessary." (See Frum and Pearle 2003 for an aggressive strategy to defeat terrorism and promote liberty.)

Preemption is one of the elements of a Bush grand strategy (Gaddis 2004). *Unilateralism*—conducting foreign affairs individually rather than acting in concert with others—is the second. *Hegemony* (*primacy*) is the third. It calls for a preponderance of power in the hands of the United States beyond challenge by any other state or combination of states.

Political scientist Robert Jervis argues that "the perceived need for preventive wars is linked to the fundamental unilateralism of the Bush Doctrine, since it is hard to get a consensus for such strong actions and other states have every reason to let the dominant power carry the full burden." Many of the most important U.S. allies in Europe, particularly France and Germany, opposed the U.S. invasion of Iraq. Though this was disadvantageous in some ways, Jervis reasons that "the strong opposition of allies to overthrowing Saddam gave the United States the opportunity to demonstrate that it would override strenuous objections from allies if this was necessary to reach its goals. While this horrified multilateralists, it showed that Bush was serious about his doctrine" (Jervis 2003).

The wisdom and appropriateness of a grand strategy built around hegemony or primacy have been extensively scrutinized with the post–Cold War rise of the United States to the status of the world's sole superpower.[1] During the nineteenth century, as the United States spread "from sea to shining sea," continental hegemony was necessary to make certain that "no other great power gained sovereignty within geographic proximity of the United States" (Gaddis 2004). Today, with the forces of globalization having the effect of making the United States "geographically proximate" to the entire world, advocates of hegemony or primacy argue that global power projection is essential to secure national security.

Hegemony requires leadership, and leaders require followers. However, when combined with preemption and unilateralism, it is not clear whether the addition of hegemonic leadership is a recipe for peace and stability or a witch's brew leading to *unilateral imperialism*. Consider the following.

While on the campaign trail in the 2000 presidential election against rival Al Gore, George W. Bush declared: "If we're an arrogant nation, [foreigners] will resent us. If we're a humble nation but strong, they'll welcome us. . . . We've got to be humble." Today, much of the world sees the United States not as humble but as arrogant. An outpouring of global sympathy for the United States followed 9/11. The French newspaper *Le Monde*, a frequent platform for criticism of the United States, declared on September 12, "we are all Americans." The United States and its allies quickly intervened militarily against the ruling Taliban government in Afghanistan in retaliation for its harboring of Al Qaeda and its leader, Osama bin Laden. The multilateral intervention reflected the widespread support of key U.S. allies and others around the world.

The sympathy showered on the United States in the aftermath of 9/11 quickly evaporated following the invasion of Iraq in March 2003, an unpopular war in most other countries around the world. Echoing such sentiment, political economist Clyde Prestowitz described the United States as a *rogue nation* (2003), one whose actions abroad exceed widely accepted norms of international behavior. Similarly, Harvard political scientist Stanley Hoffmann (2003) concluded that "the Bush Doctrine proclaims the emancipation of a colossus from international constraints (including from the restraints that the United States itself enshrined in networks of international and regional

organizations after World War II). In context, it amounts to a doctrine of global domination." Survey research in other countries on political attitudes toward the United States (Holsti 2004) confirmed the erosion of support not only for its policies but also for the attractiveness of its traditions, values, and democratic institutions—its soft power.

Hegemony smacks of what Art calls a grand strategy of dominion. "Dominion," as we have seen, "aims to transform the world into what America thinks it should look like." The strategy would transform the United States from today's preponderant power into tomorrow's unilateral imperialist. Imperialism would require that the United States expend vast treasure to control an increasingly large number of countries militarily and politically. This might lead to *imperial overstretch* (Kennedy 1987), which caused the decline of previous hegemonic powers by extending them abroad beyond what their resources at home could sustain. In addition, dominion—imperialism—also challenges fundamental American traditions and values, which imposes additional constraints. For example, American journalists and citizens will demand that their leaders outline an "exit strategy" soon after troops hit the ground. The hegemonic powers and empires of past centuries were largely spared such pressure.

Wilsonian Liberalism

Former Democratic senator Gary Hart (2004) takes a decidedly different approach than the neoconservatives toward devising a grand strategy for the future. He is uniquely positioned to do so. As co-chair with former Republican senator Warren Rudman of *The United States Commission on National Security/21st century* (United States Commission on National Security 1999), the former lawmakers issued an incisive and stinging report on the state of U.S. national security in the waning days of the Clinton administration. Its conclusions and recommendations proved startlingly prophetic. The commission warned that terrorist attacks on the United States itself were imminent, that a federal department of homeland security should be created to shield the country from them, and that fear would come to dominate the American psyche.

Against this background, Hart (2004) is mindful that the post-9/11 environment offers a propitious time for designing a new grand strategy. But he worries that the terrorist threat is a thin thread with which to weave a tapestry for the future: "Few would argue that this war *by itself* represents an American grand strategy—the application of its powers to large national purposes—worthy of a great nation. Rather, terrorism and the responses it requires might best be seen as a metaphor for an emerging new revolutionary age to which a national grand strategy must respond." He proposes instead a strategy in the tradition of **Wilsonian liberalism,** the soft power of the nation's ideals and values rather than the hard power of its military strength. It is based on the "premise that America is the world's leader, that its leadership must be exercised in a revolutionary world, that its principles are one of its most important resources and powers, and that it will and must remain a democratic republic within the context of those principles."

Hart has little sympathy for the language of imperialism and triumphalism that has emerged since 9/11, particularly among neoconservative circles. "There is always the possibility that the American people, out of fear of terrorism, desire for cheap oil, or just sheer arrogance of power, are now prepared to become imperialists and colonists," he writes.

> However, strategists of empire should not bank on this character transformation, particularly when the costs of empire come due. Larger armies and navies, more invasions, systematic loss of troops to hostile guerilla factions, higher taxes, larger deficits—all have distinctly sobering effects. Even more sobering will be the fundamental changes wrought within our own society: loss of a sense of idealism; erosion of national self-respect; anger at systematic deception by our government; alienation from the global community; loss of popular sovereignty, and dedication to

> the common good; and sacrifice of any notion of nobility.
> *(Hart 2004, 132)*

Despite Hart's view that terrorism is not a firm foundation on which to build a grand strategy, it is clear that the foreign and national security policies of the George W. Bush administration rest heavily on its threat. The 2004 presidential election, in which the war on terrorism and the war in Iraq were divisive issues—and, for some, decisive issues—also made clear that the American people and their friends and allies abroad have yet to rally around a single grand strategy for the future. During the Cold War, policy makers and the American people often disagreed about the means of containing the threat of Soviet communism, but the ends of the strategy of containment were widely shared. Today, both the ends and means of American foreign and national security policy remain broadly disputed.

TOWARD EXPLANATION

The struggle against terrorism is likely to be prolonged, extending well beyond the Bush administration and its successors, much as the Cold War encompassed the administrations of eight presidents stretching over decades. Whether the Bush grand strategy will realize its ambitious goals is therefore problematic. That holds for the other grand strategies we have touched on. Regardless, all of them share a concern for the definition of U.S. interests in the changing global environment, of the challenges the United States faces now or may face in the future, and of the prospects for linking American traditions and values to its foreign policy objectives.

Just as we can safely predict the war against terrorism is unlikely to be won quickly or soon, so too we can predict that none of the competing strategies we have discussed will guide American foreign policy in quite the way its proponents would like. The reason is simple: American foreign policy is not the product of a mechanical calculus of the nation's goals and interests. Instead, its determination is the product of a complex political process anchored in tradition and colored by contemporary developments at home and abroad. As former Secretary of State Dean Rusk remarked some years ago, "the central themes of American foreign policy are more or less constant. They derive from the kind of people we are . . . and from the shape of the world situation."

Our purpose in this book is to anticipate the shape of American foreign policy in the "second American century." To do so, we must understand much about the world, about the United States and its system of government, about the behavior of political leaders and others responsible for its foreign policy, and about the competing world views that animate the American people and their leaders. We must also understand how these forces have interacted in the past to create today's American foreign policy, as the United States finds itself bound by history even as many of the fears and strategies that once shaped it have dissipated and others have emerged.

KEY TERMS

Al Qaeda
asymmetrical warfare
Bush Doctrine
globalization

Global South
grand strategy
hegemony
multilateralism

neo-isolationism
preemptive war
selective engagement
soft power

terrorism
unilateralism
Wilsonian liberalism

SUGGESTED READINGS

Art, Robert J. *A Grand Strategy for America.* Ithaca, NY: Cornell University Press, 2003.

Barnett, Thomas M. P. *The Pentagon's New Map: War and Peace in the Twenty-First Century.* New York: Putnam, 2004.

Daalder, Ivo H., and James M. Lindsay. *America Unbound: The Bush Revolution in Foreign Policy.* Washington, DC: Brookings Institution Press, 2003.

Gaddis, John Lewis. *Surprise, Security, and the American Experience.* Cambridge, MA: Harvard University Press, 2004.

Halper, Stefan, and Jonathan Clarke. *America Alone: The Neo-Conservatives and the Global Order.* Cambridge, MA: Cambridge University Press, 2004.

Hart, Gary. *The Fourth Power: A Grand Strategy for the United States in the Twenty First Century.* New York: Oxford University Press, 2004.

Johnson, Chalmers. *Blowback: The Costs and Consequences of American Empire.* New York, NY: Metropolitan Books, 2000.

Korb, Larry. *Strategies for U.S. National Security: Winning the Peace in the 21ˢᵗ Century.* Muscatine, IA: Stanley Foundation, 2003.

Laqueur, Walter. *The New Terrorism: Fanaticism and the Arms of Mass Destruction.* New York: Oxford University Press, 2000.

Mead, Walter Russell. *Power, Terror, Peace, and War: America's Grand Strategy in a World at Risk.* New York: Knopf, 2004.

Ninkovich, Frank A. *The Wilsonian Century: U.S. Foreign Policy Since 1900.* Chicago: University of Chicago Press, 1999.

Nye, Joseph S. Jr. *The Paradox of American Power: Why the World's Only Superpower Can't Go It Alone.* New York: Oxford University Press, 2002.

Posen, Barry. "Command of the Commons: The Military Foundation of U.S. Hegemony," *International Security* 28 (Summer 2003): 5–45.

Prestowitz, Clyde. (2003) *Rogue Nation: American Unilateralism and the Failure of Good Intentions.* New York: Basic Books.

NOTES

1. In addition to the references in the text and the suggested readings, see, e.g., Bacevich 2002; Brzezinski 1998; Calleo 2003; Ferguson 2003a, 2004; Gingrich 2003; Huntington 1993, 1999; Ikenberry 2002; Kagan 1998, 2003; Krauthammer 2003/2004; Kagan and Kristol 2000; Layne 1998; Nye 2002a; Simes 2003, 2003/2004; and Snyder 1991, 2003.

2

Pattern and Process
in American Foreign Policy
An Analytical Perspective

A long-term consistency of behavior is bound to burden American
democracy when the country rises to the stature of a great power.
FRENCH POLITICAL SOCIOLOGIST ALEXIS DE TOCQUEVILLE, 1835

Decisions and actions in the international arena can be understood,
predicted, and manipulated only in so far as the factors influencing the
decisions can be identified.
AMERICAN POLITICAL SCIENTIST ARNOLD WOLFERS, 1962

Foreign policy embraces the goals that the nation's
officials seek to attain abroad, the values that
give rise to those objectives, and the means or instruments used to pursue them. We try in this book
to understand how and why the interaction of values, ends, and means shapes American foreign policy—sometimes stimulating change and promoting
innovation, sometimes constraining the nation's
ability to respond innovatively to new challenges,
even when circumstances demand it. We direct
particular attention to the more than six decades
since World War II, when the United States emerged

as the dominant power in world politics and the
American people rejected isolationism in favor of
global activism. We argue that the adaptations in
American foreign policy that occurred during the
Cold War (roughly 1947 to 1989) were confined
largely to the means used to achieve persistent ends
sustained by immutable values. We also argue that
the same confluence of values and political forces
persists today, even as a transformed United States
struggles to find a new grand strategy for dealing
with a world also transformed by the shocking events
of September 11, 2001.

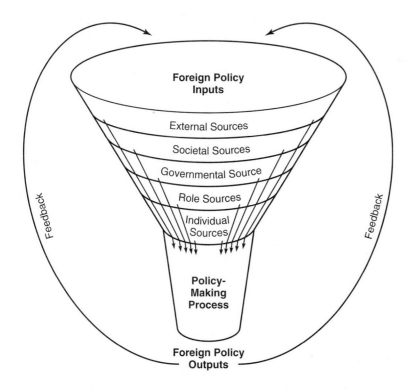

FIGURE 2.1 The Sources of American Foreign Policy as a Funnel of Causality

Our hypothesis that the values and goals underlying American foreign policy are resistant to change prompts consideration of the reasons why. To answer this seemingly simple question we adapt a framework for analysis first proposed by political scientist James N. Rosenau (1966, 1980). The framework postulates that all of the factors that explain why states behave as they do in international politics can be grouped into five broad **source categories:** the *external* (global) environment, the *societal* environment of the nation, the *governmental* setting in which policy making occurs, the *roles* occupied by policy makers, and the *individual* characteristics of foreign policy-making elites. Clearly each of these categories encompasses a much larger group of more discrete variables, but together they help us to think systematically about the forces that shape America's foreign policy. Thus they suggest guidelines for assessing the performance of the United States in world politics and the conditions that will shape its course as it responds to the challenges of the twenty-first century.

THE SOURCES OF AMERICAN FOREIGN POLICY

Our analytical framework says that each of the broadly defined sources of American foreign policy is a *causal agent* that helps to explain why the United States behaves in world politics as it does. The five causal agents together paint this portrait, as illustrated in Figure 2.1. It describes a theoretical *funnel of causality*[1] that shows how the five sources collectively shape what the United States does abroad.

The figure depicts the *inputs* to the foreign policy-making process as the external, societal, governmental, role, and individual categories that make up the analytical framework. The inputs give shape and direction to the actions the United States pursues abroad, which can be thought of as the *outputs* of the foreign policy-making process. In the language of scientific inquiry, the foreign policy behavior of the United States is the ***dependent variable***—*what* we hope to explain—and the source categories and the variables they comprise are the ***independent variables***—*how* we hope to explain it.

Note, however, that whether we are attempting to explain a single foreign policy event or a sequence of related behaviors, no source category by itself fully determines foreign policy behavior. Instead, the categories are interrelated and *collectively* determine foreign policy decisions, and hence foreign policy outputs. They do so in two ways:

- Generating the necessity for foreign policy decisions that result in foreign policy action

- Influencing the decision-making process that converts inputs into outputs

The policy-making process is what converts inputs into outputs. Here is where those responsible for the nation's foreign policy make the actual choices that affect its destiny. The process is complex because of its many participants and because policy-making procedures cannot be divorced from all of the multiple sources that shape decision makers' responses to situations demanding action. Still, we can think of the foreign policy-making process as the *intervening variable* that links foreign policy inputs (independent variables) into outputs (dependent variables). Although it is sometimes difficult to separate the process from the resulting product, once that conversion has been made we can begin to examine the recurring behaviors that describe and explain how the United States responds to the world around it.

Figure 2.1 also tells us something about the constraints under which policy makers must operate, as each of the interrelated sources of American foreign policy is "nested" within an ever-larger set of variables. The framework views individual decision makers as constrained by their policy-making roles, which typically are defined by their positions within the policy-making institutions comprising the governmental source category. Those governmental variables in turn are cast within their more encompassing societal setting, which is nested within an even larger international environment consisting of other states, non-state actors, and global trends and issues to which the United States, as a global actor, believes it must respond.

EXPLAINING POLICY PATTERNS

Our framework's attention to the multiple sources of American foreign policy implicitly rejects the widespread impulse to search for its single cause, whose simplicity most of us intuitively find satisfying. Political pundits who seek to shape policy opinion often use the rhetoric of particular explanations to promote their political causes. For some, the seemingly dictatorial powers of private interest groups, which are often thought to put their personal gain ahead of the national interest, explain what the United States does abroad, and why. For others, the predatory characteristics of its capitalist economic system explain the nation's global impulses. Both "explanations" of American foreign policy may contain kernels of truth, and under some circumstances they may account for certain aspects of policy more accurately than competing explanations. However, because foreign policy actions almost invariably result from multiple sources, we are well advised to think in *multicausal* terms if our goal is to move beyond rhetoric toward an understanding of the complex reality underlying the nation's foreign policy.

Our dissatisfaction with single-factor explanations of American foreign policy is based in part on empirical observation and in part on the logic underlying the analytical framework we employ. Let us turn, therefore, to a fuller explication of the source categories that organize and inform our later analyses.

External Sources

The ***external source category*** refers to the attributes of the international system and to the characteristics and behaviors of the state and non-state actors comprising it. It includes all "aspects of America's external environment or any actions occurring abroad that condition or otherwise influence the choices made by its officials" (Rosenau 1966). Geopolitical changes stemming from the demise of the Soviet Union, the rise of religious zealotry, and global environment challenges are examples that stimulate and shape decisions made by foreign policy officials. Others include more structural elements, such as changing distributions of power, deepening interdependence, expansive globalization, and the like. Thus the external source category draws attention to the characteristics of other states, how they act toward the United States, and how their attributes and actions influence American foreign policy behavior.

The idea that a state's foreign policy is conditioned by the world around it enjoys a long tradition and wide following. ***Political realists*** in particular argue that the distribution of power in the international system, more than anything else, influences how its member states act. States in turn are motivated to acquire power to their own advantage. Because all states are assumed to be motivated by the same drives, the principal way to understand international politics and foreign policy, according to this perspective, is to monitor the interactions of states in the international arena or, in other words, to focus on the external source category.

Political realists' perspective is compelling and will inform much of our analyses in the chapters that follow, especially in Chapters 6 and 7. Still, we must be cautious before accepting the proposition that the external environment alone dictates foreign policy. Instead, it is more reasonable to assume that "factors external to the actor can become determinants only as they affect the mind, the heart, and the will of the decision maker. A human decision to act in a specific way . . . necessarily represents the last link in the chain of antecedents of any act of policy. A geographical set of conditions, for instance, can affect the behavior of a nation only as specific persons perceive and interpret these conditions" (Wolfers 1962). Thus external factors alone cannot determine how the United States behaves in world politics, but they do exert a powerful influence.

Societal Sources

The ***societal source category*** comprises those characteristics of the domestic social and political system that shape its orientation toward the world. Robert Dallek's *The American Style of Foreign Policy: Cultural Politics and Foreign Affairs* (1983) and Richard Payne's *The Clash with Distant Cultures: Values, Interests, and Force in American Foreign Policy* (1995) are illustrative interpretations of American foreign policy that rest on societal explanations. Neo-Marxist critics of American foreign policy, for example, identified its driving forces as the nation's capitalist economic system and its need to safeguard foreign markets for American economic exploitation. Even today the popular principle of "free trade" is viewed by some as an "ideology" (Callahan 2004). The United States uses the ideology to promote open markets for American goods abroad, but is quick to abandon the "magic of the marketplace" and may use protectionist measures when its own producers are threatened by foreign competition.

The development of the United States into a hegemon power also rests on an understanding of American society. U.S. territorial expansion and imperialism in the nineteenth century were often rationalized by references to ***manifest destiny*** and the belief that Americans were a "chosen people" with a divine right to expand. In turn, many accounts argue that American ideological preferences influenced American policies toward peoples outside the state's territorial jurisdiction.

Because American foreign policy is deeply rooted in its history and culture, the impact of societal forces is potentially strong. As one analyst pointedly argued, "To change [America's] foreign policy, its internal structure must change" (Isaak 1977). In Chapters 8 and 9 we will give special attention to the impact of societal variables on American foreign policy.

Governmental Sources

Richard M. Nixon once noted, "If we were to establish a new foreign policy for the era to come, we had to begin with a basic restructuring of the process by which policy is made." Jimmy Carter echoed this theme repeatedly in his 1976 presidential campaign by maintaining that to change policy one must first change the machinery that produces it. Three decades later, the same theme dominated the conclusions and recommendations of *The 9/11 Commission Report: Final Report of the National Commission on Terrorist Attacks Upon the United States.* The commission bluntly stated that coping effectively with the continuing threat of terrorism "will require a government better organized than the one that exists today, with its national security institutions designed half a century ago to win the Cold War. Americans should not settle for incremental, ad hoc adjustments to a system created a generation ago for a world that no longer exists."

The assumption underlying the 9/11 Commission's conclusions (and recommendations for change) is that the way the U.S. government is *organized* for foreign policy-making affects the *substance* of American foreign policy itself. This is the core notion of a governmental influence on foreign policy. These institutions lie at the core of the ***governmental source category.*** It embraces "those aspects of a government's structure that limit or enhance the foreign policy choices made by decision makers" (Rosenau 1966).

The politics realizing the 9/11 Commission's vision of a revitalized national security structure will be played out principally between Congress and the president, the primary foreign policy-making institutions in the U.S. presidential system of government.

The Constitution purposefully seeks to constrain any one branch of government from exercising the kind of dictatorial powers wielded by Britain's King George III, against whom the American colonists revolted. Thus, it is not surprising that governmental variables typically constrain what the United States can do abroad and the speed with which it can do it, rather than enhancing its ability to act with innovation and dispatch. As the French political sociologist Alexis de Tocqueville ([1835] 1969) observed, "Foreign politics demand scarcely any of those qualities which a democracy possesses; and they require, on the contrary, the perfect use of almost all those faculties in which it is deficient." We will examine governmental source variables in Chapters 10, 11, and 12.

Role Sources

The structure of government and the roles that people occupy within it are closely intertwined. The ***role source category*** refers to the impact of the office on the behavior of its occupant. Roles are important because decision makers indisputably are influenced by the socially prescribed behaviors and legally sanctioned norms attached to the positions they occupy. Because the positions they occupy shape their behavior, policy outcomes are inevitably influenced by the roles extant in the policy-making arena.

Role theory goes far in explaining why, for example, American presidents act, once in office, so much like their predecessors and why each has come to view American interests and goals in terms so similar to those held by previous occupants of the Oval Office. Roles, it seems, determine behavior more than do the qualities of individuals.[2] Consider the evolutions of U.S. policies toward terrorists in general and Iraq in particular briefly summarized in Focus 2.1. Although the second Bush administration is credited with articulating a policy of preemption and of carrying it out through regime change in Iraq—presumed to have weapons of mass destruction and to have maintained ties to Al Qaeda—in fact its policies built on a policy history that was laid out by Ronald Reagan and elaborated by Bill Clinton.

More broadly, historian John Lewis Gaddis (2004) has argued that the Bush administration's emphasis on preemption, unilateralism, and hegemony is a reincarnation of nineteenth century American foreign policy, as the country spread from the east coast to the west.

The role concept is especially useful in explaining the kinds of policy recommendations habitually made by and within the large bureaucratic organizations. Role pressures typically lead to attitudinal conformity within bureaucracies and in

---

FOCUS 2.1   The Evolution of U.S. Policies toward Iraq and Terrorists

"There should be no place on earth where terrorists can rest and train and practice their skills. . . . [Self-defense] is not only our right, it is our duty."
Ronald Reagan, 1986

"Saddam Hussein must not be allowed to develop nuclear arms, poison gas, biological weapons, or the means to deliver them. . . . So long as Saddam remains in power, he will remain a threat to his people, his region, and the world. . . . [T]he best

way to end the threat that Saddam poses . . . is for Iraq to have a different government."
Bill Clinton, 1998

"The war on terror will not be won on the defensive. We must take the battle to the enemy, disrupt his plans, and confront the worst threats before they emerge. . . . [O]ur security will require all Americans to be forward-looking and resolute, to be ready for preemptive action when necessary."
George W. Bush, 2002

---

deference to their orthodox views. "To get along, go along" is a timeworn aphorism from which few in bureaucratic settings are immune. Because the system places a premium on behavioral consistency and constrains the capacity of individuals to make a policy impact, people at every level of government find it difficult to escape their roles by rocking the boat and challenging conventional thinking. For example, the bitingly critical, bipartisan Senate Intelligence Committee's *Report of the U.S. Intelligence Community's Prewar Intelligence Assessment on Iraq* (July 7, 2004) used the concept "groupthink" to describe how attitudinal conformity in the intelligence community contributed to its failures in Iraq. Thus role restraints on policy innovation go a long way in explaining the resistance of American foreign policy to change even as the world changes. We examine their impact more completely in Chapter 13.

Individual Sources

Finally, our explanatory framework identifies as a fifth policy source the individual characteristics of decision makers—the skills, personalities, beliefs, and psychological predispositions that define the kind of people they are and the types of behavior they exhibit. The ***individual source category*** embraces the values, talents, and prior experiences that distinguish one policy maker from another and that

distinguishes his or her foreign policy choices from others.

Clearly every individual is unique, so it is not difficult to accept the argument that what they might do in foreign policy settings will differ. Consider the following questions:

- Why did Secretary of State John Foster Dulles publicly insult Chou En-Lai of the People's Republic of China by refusing at the 1954 Geneva Conference to shake Chou's extended hand? Could it be that Dulles, a devout Christian, viewed the Chinese leader as a symbol of an atheistic doctrine so abhorrent to his own values that he chose to scorn the symbol?

- Why did the United States persist in bombing North Vietnam for so long in the face of clear evidence that the policy of bombing the North Vietnamese into submission was failing and, if anything, was hardening their resolve to continue fighting? Could it be that President Johnson could not admit failure, and that he had a psychological need to preserve his positive self-image by "being right"?

- Why did the first President Bush personalize the 1991 war against Iraq following its invasion of Kuwait, demonizing Saddam Hussein as "another Hitler"? Did his belief that "history is biography" and his penchant for personal diplomacy cause him to view the war as a contest between individual leaders rather than a conflict between competing national interests?

- Why, after campaigning vigorously in 1992 for a forceful U.S. response to ethnic cleansing in Bosnia, did Bill Clinton act so cautiously once he became president? Was his reluctance a product of the Vietnam War, not only his lack of personal military experience at that time but also of the belief embraced by many of the Vietnam generation that negotiation and compromise are sometimes preferable to the use of force, even when dealing with aggressors?

- Why, despite reports from several reputable sources that the reasons used to justify war against Iraq were based on faulty evidence, did George W. Bush continue to defend them throughout his first term in office rather that concede he had been mistaken? Could his seeming denial have been a product of a Manichean, black or white, good or evil worldview, characteristic of much official thinking during the Cold War?

Theories emphasizing the personal characteristics and experiences of political leaders enjoy considerable popularity. This is partly because democratic theory leads us to expect that individuals elected to high public office will be able either to sustain or to change public policy to accord with popular preferences, and because the electoral system compels aspirants for office to emphasize how their administration will be different from that of their opponents. However, in the same way that other single-factor explanations of American foreign policy are suspect, we must be wary of ascribing too much importance to the impact of individuals. Individuals may matter, and in some instances they clearly do, but the mechanisms through which individuals influence foreign policy outcomes are likely to be much more subtle than popular impressions would have us believe. This is the subject of Chapter 14.

THE MULTIPLE SOURCES OF AMERICAN FOREIGN POLICY

The explicitly multicausal perspective of our analytical framework begins with the premise that we must look in different places if we want to find the origins of American foreign policy; and it tells us where to look, thus providing a helpful guide to understand policy and how it is made. We can illustrate its utility using a strategy common among historians known as *counterfactual reasoning*. The strategy poses a series of questions that effectively drop a key variable from the equation and then asks us to speculate about what might have been. Regardless of how we respond to the counterfactual questions, the simple act of posing them facilitates appreciation of the numerous forces shaping foreign policy. We can use counterfactual reasoning to highlight how we might assess the dominant theme of American foreign policy since World War II: the containment of the Soviet Union. Why was it so durable? Why did change come so gradually even as changes in world politics seemed to demand innovation?

To answer these questions, we must look in a variety of places. At the level of the international system, for instance, the advent of nuclear weapons and the subsequent fear of destruction from a Soviet nuclear attack promoted a status quo American policy designed primarily to deal with this paramount fear. Would the United States have acted differently over the course of Cold War history had international circumstances been different? What if plans proposed by the United States immediately following World War II to establish an international authority to control nuclear know-how had succeeded? Might the Cold War never have started? What if Soviet leaders had decided against putting offensive nuclear weapons in Cuba in 1962, which precipitated the most dangerous crisis of the Cold War era? Would the absence of this challenge to American preeminence in the Western Hemisphere have reduced the superpowers' later reliance on nuclear deterrence and a strategy of *mutual assured destruction* to preserve peace?

Might the Cold War have ended earlier by exposing nonmilitary weaknesses in the Soviet system, which were masked by the military-centric Cold War competition (Gaddis 1997)? Consider also what might have occurred in the Cold War contest had developments in the United States unfolded differently. Would the preoccupation with Soviet communism have endured so long had nationalistic sentiments ("my country, right or wrong!") dissipated as the nation rapidly urbanized and its foreign-born population came increasingly from non-European countries? Or if a mobilized American public freed of fear of external enemies had revolted against the burdens of monstrously high levels of peacetime military expenditures? Or if the anticommunist, witch-hunting tactics Senator Joseph McCarthy initiated after communist forces came to power in China in 1949 had been discredited from the start rather than later?

Or turn instead to the governmental sector. Would American foreign policy have changed more rapidly had foreign policy making not become dominated by the president and the presidency—if instead the balance between the executive and legislative branches anticipated in the Constitution had been preserved throughout the 1960s? Indeed, would American foreign policy have been different and more flexible if "Cold Warriors" had not populated the innermost circle of presidential advisers in the 1950s and 1960s, and if career professionals within the foreign affairs bureaucracy had successfully challenged their singular outlook?

Then consider whether officials responsible for the seemingly ideological orthodoxy of America's anticommunist foreign policy had experienced fewer pressures for conformity. Would the decisions reached during the Cold War decades have been different had decision-making roles been less institutionalized, encouraging advocacy of more diverse opinions? Might American policy makers have sought more energetically to move, in George H. W. Bush's words, "beyond containment," prior to his presidency had policy-making roles encouraged more long-range planning and less timidity in responding to new opportunities?

Finally, consider the hypothetical prospects for change in American policy had other individuals risen to positions of power during this period. Would the cornerstone of American postwar policy have been so virulently anticommunist if Franklin D. Roosevelt had lived out his fourth term in office? If Adlai Stevenson and not Dwight D. Eisenhower had been responsible for American policy throughout the 1950s? If John F. Kennedy's attempt to improve relations with the Soviets had not ended with his assassination? If Hubert Humphrey had managed to obtain the 400,000 extra votes in 1968 that would have made him, and not Nixon, president? If George McGovern's call for America to "come home" had enabled him to keep Nixon from a second term? If Ronald Reagan's bid to turn Jimmy Carter out of office in 1980 had failed? If the 1988 election—a time of dramatic developments in Eastern Europe and the Soviet Union—had put Michael Dukakis in the Oval Office instead of George H. W. Bush?

Moving beyond the Cold War, would the United States' response to Iraq's invasion of Kuwait have been the same if Bill Clinton—the first American president born after World War II and whose formative years included the war in Vietnam—had been in the White House instead of George H. W. Bush, a World War II Navy combat pilot? Or would Clinton, too, have found that the responsibilities of his office moved him inexorably in the direction of a military response to Iraq's aggressive challenge? Would leadership strategies in the war on terrorism have turned out differently if Al Gore had picked up the few errant Florida votes necessary to elect him, not George W. Bush, the nation's 43rd president? Would Gore have regarded the 9/11 terrorist attacks on the World Trade Center as criminal acts, continuing the policy of his predecessor? Or would he, too, have regarded them as acts of war? Similarly, if John Kerry had won Ohio in 2004 and replaced Bush to become the 44th president, would he have been able to reverse the tide of world opinion toward the war in Iraq, convincing traditional U.S. allies to join in the war effort? Or would the role constraints on his presidency imposed by the commitments and policies of his predecessor have forced him to stay the course rather than striking out in new directions? In short, would different policy makers with different personalities, psychological needs, and political dispositions have made a difference in American foreign policy during the many decades since World War II?

Counterfactual historiography based on "what if " questions rarely reveals clear-cut answers about what might have been. Asking the questions, however, makes us more aware of the problem of tracing causation by forcing us to consider different possibilities and influences. Thus, to answer even partially the question "Why does the United States act the way it does in its foreign policy relations?" we need to examine each of its major sources. Collectively, these identify the many constraints and stimuli facing the nation's decision makers, thus providing insight into the factors that promote continuity and change in America's relations with others.[3]

LOOKING AHEAD

We begin our inquiry into the pattern and process of American foreign policy in Part II, where we examine the goals and instruments of policy. We will show there that the central themes of American foreign policy and the enduring patterns of behavior that both reveal and sustain them are marked by persistence and continuity, even in the face of dramatic changes and challenges at home and abroad. The values of freedom, democracy, peace, and prosperity that animate American foreign policy have not always resulted in similar goals and tactics in the face of changing circumstances. But they have endured, thus contributing to a long-term consistency in American foreign policy.

Then, recognizing that the multiple sources of American foreign policy constrain decision makers' latitude, we will conduct our exploration of the causes of America's foreign policy persistence and continuity in descending order of the "spatial magnitude" of each of the explanatory categories. We turn first to the external environment (Part III), the most comprehensive of the categories influencing decision makers. Next we will examine societal sources (Part IV) and then proceed to the way in which the American political system is organized for foreign policy making (Part V). From there we will shift focus again to role sources (Part VI), which partly flow from and are closely associated with the governmental setting. Finally, we will consider the importance of individual personalities, preferences, and predispositions in explaining foreign policy outcomes (Part VII).

By looking at external, societal, governmental, role, and individual sources of American policy independently, we can examine the causal impact that each exerts on America's behavior toward the rest of the world. Our survey will show that certain factors are more important in some instances than in others. In Chapter 15, where we probe the future of American foreign policy, we will speculate about how interrelationships among the sources of American foreign policy might affect its course in the new century.

KEY TERMS

counterfactual reasoning
dependent variable
external source category

foreign policy
governmental source category
independent variables

individual source category
intervening variable
manifest destiny
political realists

role source category
societal source category
source categories

SUGGESTED READINGS

Bolton, M. Kent. *U.S. Foreign Policy and International Politics: George W. Bush, 9/11, and the Global-Terrorist Hydra.* Upper Saddle River, NJ: Pearson/Prentice Hall, 2005.

Brown, Seyom. *The Faces of Power: Constancy and Change in United States Foreign Policy from Truman to Clinton.* New York: Columbia University Press, 1994.

Bucklin, Steven J. *Realism and American Foreign Policy: Wilsonians and the Kennan-Morgenthau Thesis.* Westport, CT: Praeger Publishers, 2000.

Gaddis, John Lewis. *Surprise, Security, and the American Experience.* Cambridge, MA: Harvard University Press, 2004.

Greenstein, Fred I., and John P. Burke. *How Presidents Test Reality: Decisions on Vietnam, 1954 and 1965.* New York: Russell Sage Foundation, 1989.

Hermann, Charles F. "Changing Course: When Governments Choose to Redirect Foreign Policy," *International Studies Quarterly* 34 (March 1990): 3–21.

Hogan, Michael J., and Thomas G. Paterson, eds., *Explaining the History of American Foreign Relations.* New York: Cambridge, 1991.

Ikenberry, G. John, ed., *American Foreign Policy: Theoretical Essays*, 5th ed. New York: Pearson/Longman, 2005.

Neack, Laura, Jeanne A. K. Hey, and Patrick J. Haney, eds., *Foreign Policy Analysis: Continuity and Change in Its Second Generation.* Englewood Cliffs, NJ: Prentice Hall, 1995.

Trubowitz, Peter. *Defining the National Interest: Conflict and Change in American Foreign Policy.* Chicago: University of Chicago Press, 1998.

Zelikow, Philip. "Foreign Policy Engineering: From Theory to Practice and Back Again," *International Security* 18 (Spring 1994): 143–71.

NOTES

1. The funnel metaphor draws on the classic study of the American voter by Angus Campbell, Philip E. Converse, Warren E. Miller, and Donald E. Stokes (1960).

2. The view that the office makes the person has been expressed thus: *If we accept the proposition . . . that certain fundamentals stand at the core of American foreign policy, we could argue that any president is bound, even dictated to, by those basic beliefs and needs. In other words, he has little freedom to make choices wherein his distinctive style, personality, experience, and intellect shape America's role and position in international relations in a way that is uniquely his. It might be suggested that a person's behavior is a function not of his individual traits but rather of the office that he holds and that the office is circumscribed by the larger demands of the national interest, rendering individuality inconsequential.* (Paterson 1979, 93)

3. See Bolton (2005) for a critique of the argument that continuity rather than change marks American foreign policy even in the post-9/11 world. Bolton uses the framework outlined in this book and the events surrounding 9/11 to assess its impact on policy. He concludes that 9/11 represents "a fundamental, substantive, and enduring juncture in U.S. foreign policy."

PART II

Patterns of American Foreign Policy

3

Principle, Power, and Pragmatism

The Goals of American Foreign Policy in Historical Perspective

> The ultimate test of our foreign policy is how well our actions measure up to our ideals.... Freedom is America's purpose.
> SECRETARY OF STATE MADELEINE K. ALBRIGHT, 1998

> We have a place, all of us, in a long story... of a new world that became a friend and liberator of the old, a story of a slave-holding society that became a servant of freedom, the story of a power that went into the world to protect but not possess, to defend but not to conquer.
> PRESIDENT GEORGE W. BUSH, 2001

Peace and prosperity, stability and security, democracy and defense—these are the enduring values and interests of American foreign policy. Freedom from the dictates of others, commercial advantage, and promotion of American ideas and ideals are among the persistent foreign policy goals tied to these values and interests. Isolationism and internationalism are competing strategies the United States has tried during its two-century history as means to its policy ends. Historically these strategies have also been closely intertwined with idealism and realism, competing visions of the nature of humankind, of international politics and states' foreign policy motivations, and of the problems and prospects for achieving a peaceful and just world order.

During World War I, Woodrow Wilson articulated the premises of *idealism*, summarizing them in a famous speech before Congress in January 1918, which contained fourteen points. They included a call for open diplomacy, freedom of the seas, removal of barriers to trade, self-determination, general disarmament, and, most importantly, abandonment of the balance-of-power system of international politics—an "arrangement of power and of suspicion and of dread"—in favor of a new, **collective security** system grounded in an international organization, the League of Nations. Under the system envisioned by Wilson, states would pledge themselves to join together to oppose aggression by any state whenever and wherever it occurred. Together, Wilson's revolutionary ideas called for a new world order completely alien to the experiences of the European powers, which lay exhausted from four years of bitter war.

Europe's bloody history led its leaders to embrace **political realism,** not idealism, as an approach to the problem of war. For them, *realpolitik,* as realism is sometimes called, translated into a foreign policy based on rational calculations of power and the national interest. The approach built on the political philosophy of the sixteenth century Italian theorist Niccolò Machiavelli, who emphasized in *The Prince* a political calculus based on interest, prudence, and expediency above all else, notably morality. Moral crusades—such as "making the world safe for democracy," as Wilson had sought with U.S. entry into World War I—are anathema to realist thinking. Similarly, "realists view conflict as a natural state of affairs rather than a consequence that can be attributed to historical circumstances, evil leaders, flawed sociopolitical systems, or inadequate international understanding and education" (Holsti 1995).[1] In contrast, "Wilson's idea of world order derived from Americans' faith in the essentially peaceful nature of man and an underlying harmony of the world. It followed that democratic states were, by definition, peaceful; people granted self-determination would no longer have reason to go to war or to oppress others. Once all the peoples of the world had tasted of the blessings of peace and democracy, they would surely rise as one to defend their gains" (Kissinger 1994a). American history and American foreign policy have never been free of the debate between idealists and realists or from contentions about the role of ideals and self-interest. As one former policy maker observed in the aftermath of the Persian Gulf War, "we and the British ... are still divided about

whether the foreign policy of a democracy should be concerned primarily with the structure and dynamics of world politics, the balance of power, and the causes of war, or whether we should leave such cold and dangerous issues to less virtuous and more cynical peoples, and concentrate only on the vindication of liberty and democracy" (Rostow 1993).

In Part II of *American Foreign Policy: Pattern and Process,* we examine the goals and instruments of American foreign policy over the course of the nation's history and the strategies and tactics used to realize them. We begin in this chapter with a brief look at the nation's philosophy and behavior as it first sought to ensure its independence and then expanded to become a continental nation and eventually an imperial power. Isolationism dominated thinking (if not always action) during this period, and it reasserted itself between World Wars I and II, interludes when the United States, contrary to isolationist warnings, participated actively in European balance-of-power politics. We then turn to the decades-long Cold War contest between the United States and the Soviet Union. This was a time of internationalism, indeed, *global activism,* as the United States actively sought to shape the structure of world peace and security. We conclude with a discussion of contemporary issues that illustrate the continuing contention among power, principle, and pragmatism as the United States faces a new century.

We continue our inquiry in Chapters 4 and 5, where we direct primary attention to America's rise to globalism in the decades following World War II. We will examine how military might and interventionism were brought into the service of America's foreign policy goals during the Cold War and ask about their continued relevance.

PRINCIPLE AND PRAGMATISM, 1776–1941: ISOLATIONISM, EXPANSIONISM, AND IMPERIALISM

Two motivations stimulated the colonists who came to America two centuries ago: "material advantages and utopian hopes" (Gilbert 1961). Freedom from England and, more broadly, from the machinations of Europe's great powers became necessary for their realization.

John Adams, a revolutionary patriot and the new nation's second president, urged that "we should separate ourselves, as far as possible and as long as possible, from all European politics and wars." George Washington had enshrined that reasoning in the nation's enduring convictions when he warned the nation in his farewell address to "steer clear of permanent alliances with any portion of the foreign world." "Why," he asked, "by interweaving our destiny with that of any part of Europe, entangle our peace and prosperity in the toils of European ambition, rivalship, interest, humor, or caprice?" He worried that participation in balance-of-power politics with untrustworthy and despotic European governments would lead to danger abroad and the loss of democratic freedoms at home. If the country interacted with corrupt governments, it would become like them: Lie down with dogs, get up with fleas. Ironically, however, an alliance with France was the critical ingredient in ensuring the success of the American revolution.

Hamilton, Jefferson, and American Continentalism

With freedom won, the new Americans now had to preserve it. Thomas Jefferson and Alexander Hamilton posed alternative postures to meet the challenge and to move the nation beyond it—toward greatness.[2] Jefferson, Washington's secretary of state and the nation's third president, saw the preservation of liberty as the new nation's quintessential goal. For him, a policy of aloofness or political detachment from international affairs—*isolationism*—was the best way to preserve and develop the nation as a free people. He did recognize, though, that foreign trade was necessary to secure markets for American agricultural exports and essential imports. Thus he was prepared to negotiate commercial treaties with others and to protect the nation's ability to trade. "For that, however, the country needed no more than a few diplomats and a small navy. 'To aim at such a navy as the greater nations of Europe possess, would be a foolish and wicked waste of the energies of our countrymen'" (Hunt 1987).

Hamilton, the first secretary of the Treasury, offered quite different prescriptions. Beginning with assumptions about human nature central to the perspective of classical realism—that, in his words, "men are ambitious, vindictive, and rapacious"— Hamilton concluded pessimistically that "conflict was the law of life. States no less than men were bound to collide over those ancient objects of ambition: wealth and glory" (Hunt 1987). Thus the goals of American foreign policy were clear: develop the capabilities necessary to enable the United States to be (again in Hamilton's own words) "ascendant in the system of American affairs . . . and able to dictate the terms of the connection between the old and the new world." Hamilton's immediate impact on American political life ended when he was fatally wounded in a duel with Aaron Burr in 1804, but the influence of his ideas on foreign and domestic policy and the perceived need for strong executive leadership continued. As president, for example, Jefferson himself acted in Hamiltonian ways: he threatened an alliance with Britain to counter France's reacquisition of the Louisiana territory ceded to Spain in the 1763 Treaty of Paris and, having acquired the territory, threatened to take the Floridas from Spain. The power of the presidency grew accordingly.

Jefferson was more interested in the port of New Orleans as a vehicle to promote commercialism abroad than in all of the vast Louisiana territory, but the territorial expansion of the United States continued in the half-century following the Louisiana Purchase. The Floridas and portions of Canada were annexed next, followed by Texas, the Pacific Northwest, California, and portions of the present-day southwestern United States. The war with Mexico, precipitated by President James K. Polk, led to Mexico's cession of the vast California territory. Polk's threatened military action over the Oregon Country also helped to add the Northwest to the new nation. The expansionist spirit that animated these episodes is reflected in the policy rhetoric of their proponents. In 1846, for example, William H. Seward, who later became secretary of state, pledged, "I will engage to give you the possession of the American continent and the control of the world."

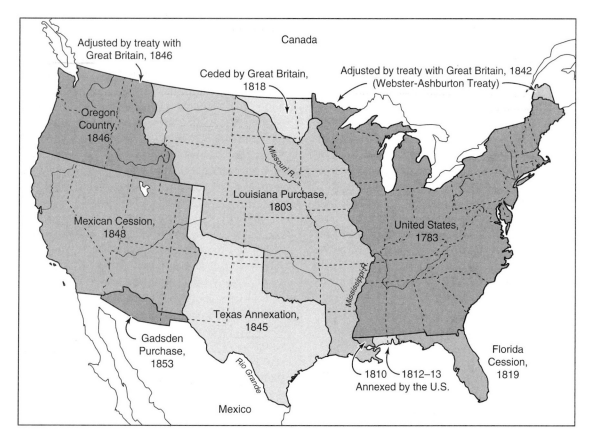

M A P 3.1 Birth of a Continental Nation: U.S. Territorial Expansion by the Mid-Nineteenth Century
SOURCE: Walter LaFeber, *The American Age: United States Foreign Policy at Home and Abroad,* 2nd ed. New York: Norton, 1994, 132.

By midcentury the United States had expanded from sea to shining sea (see Map 3.1). ***Manifest destiny,*** the widespread belief that the United States was destined to spread across the North American continent and eventually embody it, captured the nation's mood. In the process, however, conflict over how to treat the issue of slavery in the newly acquired territories rended American society and politics. Four years of civil war suspended the progress of America's manifest destiny. It also resulted in more American casualties than any other conflict in the nation's history.

A Nation Apart

Beginning in 1796, the Napoleonic Wars raged in Europe intermittently for nearly two decades.

Although the War of 1812, the North American theater of this conflict, briefly involved the United States in the Europeans' competition for "wealth and glory," the years following it saw isolationism take on the trappings of "a divine privilege, the perceived outcome of American national wisdom and superior virtue" (Serfaty 1972). Manifest destiny embodied the conviction that Americans had a higher purpose to serve in the world than others. Theirs was not only a special privilege but also a special charge: to protect liberty and to promote freedom. That purpose was served best by isolating the American republic from the rest of the world, not becoming involved in it.

In 1823, President James Monroe sought to remove the United States from Europe's intrigues by distancing himself from its ongoing quarrels. In a message to Congress he declared the Western Hemisphere "hands off" from European encroachment: "We owe it . . . to candor and to the amicable relations existing between the United States and [European] powers to declare that we should consider any attempt on their part to extend their system to any portion of this hemisphere as dangerous to our peace and safety." What would later be known as the ***Monroe Doctrine*** in effect said that the New World would not be subject to the same forces of colonization perpetrated by the Europeans on others. Little noticed at the time, Monroe's declaration shaped thinking about interventionism and the role and responsibilities of the United States toward its hemispheric neighbors well into the twentieth century.

Intrigue with foreign powers punctuated the contest between North and South during the Civil War, but in its aftermath the state turned inward—a pattern repeated in the twentieth century. Even as it focused on reconstruction, however, the nation's expansionist drive continued. Alaska was purchased from Russia in the 1860s, and Native Americans in the West were systematically subdued as the United States consolidated its continental domain. Here manifest destiny was little more than a crude euphemism for a policy of expulsion and extermination of Native Americans who were, in contemporary terminology, "non-state nations." Thereafter, the advocates of expansionism increasingly coveted Cuba, Latin America, Hawaii, and various Asian lands. Not until the end of the nineteenth century, however, would the United States assert its manifest destiny beyond the North American continent—this time in pursuit of empire. By then, moralism had become closely intertwined with the Americans' perception that they were a nation apart, one with a special mission in world politics.

Democratic promotion—to make the world safe for democracy—would dominate much of American foreign policy in the twentieth century, but in the nineteenth it sought liberty. Equality and democracy were not typically within its purview. Democracy refers to political processes. Today we describe a country as democratic if "nearly everyone can vote, elections are freely contested, and the chief executive is chosen by popular vote or by an elected parliament, and civil rights and civil liberties are substantially guaranteed" (Russett 1998). Liberty (individual freedom) and ***liberalism*** (the advocacy of liberty) instead focus on individual freedom. Not until the 1830s, with the election of Andrew Jackson, could the United States begin to be properly called a democracy. At that time Alexis de Tocqueville, a French political sociologist, published his famous treatise *Democracy in America,* which focused on the role that ordinary people played in its political processes as he described America's uniqueness.

Although the American republic was the champion of liberty in its first century, its approach was passive, not active. It chose to act as an example, "a beacon of light on liberty," demonstrating to the world how a free society could run its affairs and holding itself as a model for others to emulate. But the United States would not assume responsibility for the world, even in the name of freedom; it would not be an agent of international reform, seeking to impose on others its way of life. Secretary of State John Quincy Adams prescribed the nation's appropriate world role in an often-quoted speech, delivered on July 4, 1821: "Wherever the standard of freedom and independence has been or shall be unfurled, there will [America's] heart, her benedictions, and her prayers be. But she goes not abroad in search of monsters to destroy" (see also Kennan 1995; Gaddis 2004).

The United States was not unengaged, however. Even as its ideals colored its self-perceptions, pragmatism dictated the exercise of power. Crises and military engagements with European powers and Native Americans were recurrent as the United States expanded across the continent. Elsewhere the rule was ***unilateralism,*** not acting in concert with others. Thus the United States alone fostered the creation of Liberia in the 1820s, opened Japan to commercial relations in the 1850s, and scrambled to control Samoa in the 1880s. Then, in 1895, it asserted its self-proclaimed Monroe Doctrine prerogatives against the British in a dispute involving Venezuela. The United States now effectively claimed that it alone enjoyed supremacy in the Western Hemisphere, and it was evident that the United States had the capability to back its claim.

In the decades following the Civil War, the United States emerged as the world's major industrial power. By 1900 it had surpassed Great Britain as the world's leading producer of coal, iron, steel, and textiles. The stage was being set for the United States to assume Britain's mantle as the world's leading economic power and rule maker—a global hegemon.

Isolationism under Siege: Imperialism and Interventionism

Diplomatic historians credit jingoistic "yellow journalism" (press sensationalism) with a role in provoking the United States to declare war against Spain in 1898. In fact, multiple motives—all centered on Cuba, which for several years had engaged in insurrection against Spain—caused President William McKinley to seek congressional authorization for the use of force to end the Cuban war. They ranged from humanitarian concerns to commercial interests and growing expansionist sentiments. Senator Albert Beveridge, for example, speaking in 1898, referred to Americans as "a conquering race." "We must obey our blood," he urged, "and occupy new markets and if necessary new lands."

With victory in the "splendid little war" with Spain, the United States gained a primary goal: suzerainty over Cuba. The Philippines now also became a U.S. territory in the Pacific, joining Hawaii, which had been annexed in 1898. Puerto Rico and Guam also joined the new imperium. The United States was suddenly transformed into an imperial power rivaling the great powers of Europe. Thus the Spanish-American War is properly regarded as a watershed in American foreign policy, as it opened a new era in America's relations with the rest of the world.

McKinley eschewed outright annexation of Cuba, but the Philippines posed a more vexing choice. McKinley was interested principally in the port at Manila, and he worried about the problem of governing the Filipinos. The popular story of how McKinley decided to colonize the Philippines came from his revelation before church leaders in 1899:

I walked the floor of the White House night after night until midnight; and I am not ashamed to tell you . . . that I went down on my knees and prayed Almighty God for light and guidance more than one night. And one night it came to me. . . . [T]here was nothing left to do but take them all, and educate the Filipinos, and uplift and civilize them as our fellow men. . . . And then I went to bed, and . . . slept soundly.
(LaFeber 1994, 213)

Although historians are skeptical of this story, they do not deny that the United States then embarked on a project that persists until the present—to sponsor democracy elsewhere. First, however, it was necessary to put down a Filipino rebellion, which proved to be a bloody, four-year battle, "the first of many antirevolutionary wars fought by the United States in the twentieth century" (LaFeber 1994). Only then could the United States concern itself with the Philippines' internal political processes. Attention to Philippine political development meant that democratic promotion—not just the abstraction of liberty—was now America's concern (Smith 1994a).

The McKinley administration is also credited with advancing American interests in China. In 1899, John Hay, McKinley's secretary of state, sought to enlist European support for the traditional nineteenth-century (unilateral) American policy of free competition for trade with China—that is, an ***Open Door policy*** toward China. In 1900, he advised European powers in the second of his "open-door notes" that the United States would not tolerate the division of China into "spheres of influence." He insisted instead that China's territorial integrity be respected. Regarded by some as an expression of the United States' growing foreign commercial interests and by others as an expression of American moralism and naiveté about balance-of-power politics, the Open Door was also based on a pragmatic appraisal of American power. Hay himself advised McKinley in terms Alexander Hamilton would surely have approved: "The inherent weakness of our position is this: we do not want to rob China ourselves, and our public opinion will not permit us to interfere, with an army, to prevent others from robbing her. Besides, we have no army. The talk of the papers about 'our preeminent moral position giving the authority to dictate to the world' is mere flap-doodle" (LaFeber 1994).

Foreign policy issues figured prominently in the election of 1900. William Jennings Bryan, the Democratic Party candidate and later Woodrow Wilson's secretary of state, carried the anti-imperialist banner. Theodore (Teddy) Roosevelt, McKinley's vice presidential running mate, was the champion of imperialism. Roosevelt had served in the Navy Department early in the McKinley administration and, with Captain Alfred Mahan, an early geopolitical strategic thinker, had promoted the development of sea power as a route to American greatness.

Roosevelt succeeded to the presidency when an assassin's bullet felled McKinley. The shooting occurred only one day after McKinley claimed, in a speech on America's new world role, that "isolation is no longer possible or desirable." Roosevelt is remembered for speaking softly while carrying a big stick. A leader of the "Rough Riders" cavalry regiment during the Spanish-American War as well as an advocate of strong naval power, Roosevelt marked his presidency (1901–1909) by a series of power assertions and interventions, primarily in Latin America. The United States forced Haiti to clear its debts with European powers, fomented insurrection in Panama to win its independence from Colombia and secure American rights for a trans-isthmian canal, established a financial protectorate over the Dominican Republic, and occupied Cuba. Roosevelt also mediated the end of the Russo-Japanese War (1904–1905), from which Japan emerged as an increasingly aggressive Far Eastern power.

Many of Roosevelt's specific actions were rationalized in his corollary to the Monroe Doctrine. In 1904, in response to economic chaos in the Dominican Republic, which threatened foreign involvement, Roosevelt announced to Congress that "the adherence of the United States to the Monroe Doctrine may force the United States, however

reluctantly, . . . to the exercise of international police power." In fact, however, the *Roosevelt Corollary* went well beyond Monroe's initial intentions (LaFeber 1994). The United States would now oppose Latin American revolutions, not support them. It would not only oppose European intervention into hemispheric affairs but support its own. It would use American power to bring hemispheric economic affairs under its tutelage. And it would now use military force to set hemispheric affairs straight, unlike Monroe, who saw no need to flex military muscle. Thus the Roosevelt Corollary to the Monroe Doctrine set the stage for a new era in U.S. relations with its southern neighbors—most of whom came to resent the colossus to the North.

Although intervention was indeed characteristic of this era, the term *dollar diplomacy* best describes the period from 1900 to 1913. As American business interests in the Caribbean and Central America mushroomed, the United States flexed its Roosevelt Corollary principles and corresponding muscles to protect them. Roosevelt's interventionist tactics were continued by his successor, William Howard Taft, who at one point described his administration's policies as "substituting dollars for bullets" (hence the term "dollar diplomacy").

Little changed with Woodrow Wilson's election in 1912, as the data in Focus 3.1. make clear. Until the outbreak of war in Europe, Wilson was consumed by foreign policy challenges in China, Mexico, and the Caribbean, often resorting to military intervention to achieve his ends. "Determined to help other peoples become democratic and orderly, Wilson himself became the greatest military interventionist in U.S. history. By the time he left office in 1921, he had ordered troops into Russia and half a dozen Latin American upheavals" (LaFeber 1994). Intervention arguably was not inconsistent with Wilsonian idealism, but in some sense it reflected its failure. "Wilson wanted elections, real change, order, and no foreign interventions—all at once," observes historian Walter LaFeber (1994). "He never discovered how to pull off such a miracle."

In May 1915, a German submarine torpedoed the *Lusitania,* pride of the British merchant marine.

F O C U S 3.1   **Dawn of a New Millennium: The Use of American Armed Forces Abroad Initiated during the Roosevelt, Taft, and Wilson Administrations, 1901–1921**

Theodore Roosevelt

1901 Columbia (State of Panama).

U.S. troops protect American property and keep transit lines open on the isthmus during revolutionary disturbances.

1902 Colombia. U.S. forces protect American lives and property at Bocas del Toro during civil war.

1902 Colombia (State of Panama).

U.S. troops are used to keep railroads running and to prevent the landing of Colombian troops in Panama.

1903 Honduras. U.S. forces protect the American consulate at Puerto Cortez.

1903 Dominican Republic. Marines land at Santo Domingo to protect American interests.

1903 Syria. U.S. forces protect the consulate in Beirut.

1903–1904 Abyssinia. Marines protect the U.S. Consul General during treaty negotiations.

1903–1914 Panama. U.S. forces protect American interests and lives following the revolution for independence for construction of the Panama canal.

1904 Dominican Republic. American and British forces establish a no-fighting zone and protect American lives and interests during revolutionary fighting.

1904 Tangier, Morocco. A marine guard lands to protect the consul general.

1904 Panama. U.S. troops protect American interests and lives at Ancon during a threatened insurrection.

1904–1905 Korea. A marine guard is sent to protect the American legation at Seoul during the Russo-Japanese War.

1906–1909 Cuba. U.S. forces seek to restore order, protect foreigners, and establish a stable government.

1907 Honduras. U.S. troops protect American interests in Trujillo, Ceiba, Puerto Cortez, San Pedro, Laguna, and Choloma during war between Honduras and Nicaragua.

William Howard Taft

1910 Nicaragua. U.S. forces protect American interests at Bluefields.

1911 Honduras. American troops protect American lives and interests during civil war.

1911 China. U.S. troops dispatched at various sites as the nationalist revolution approaches.

1912 Honduras. A small U.S. force temporarily lands at Puerto Cortez.

1912 Panama. U.S. troops supervise Panamanian elections outside the canal zone.

1912 Cuba. U.S. forces protect American interests in the province of Oriente and Havana.

1912 China. U.S. troops protect American lives and interests during revolutionary activities.

Nearly 1,200 lives were lost, including 128 Americans. The attack precipitated a crisis with the United States on the issue of neutrals' rights on the high seas. Wilson's attention now shifted from Asia and the Western Hemisphere to Europe, leading to U.S. intervention in World War I. Wilson also began to call for a new collective security system to replace the war-prone balance of power and for other fundamental reforms in international relations. Wilson's efforts to implement his vision failed during his lifetime, however. The refusal of the United States Senate to approve the Versailles peace settlement and U.S. membership in the League of Nations was a particularly devastating personal defeat for Wilson. Without American participation, the League was doomed to failure. Still, the principles of Wilsonian idealism have never been extinguished. Indeed, La-Feber writes that Wilson was the first American president "to face the full blast of twentieth-century revolutions," and that his "responses made his policies the most influential in twentieth-century American foreign policy. 'Wilsonianism' became a

1912 Turkey. U.S. forces guard the American legation at Constantinople during the Balkan War.

1912–1925 Nicaragua. U.S. forces dispatched to protect American interests remain to promote peace and stability.

1912–1941 China. U.S. troops engage in continuing protective action following disorders that began with the Kuomintang rebellion.

Woodrow Wilson

1913 Mexico. U.S. Marines evacuate American citizens and others.

1914 Haiti. U.S. forces protect American nationals.

1914 Dominican Republic. U.S. forces protect Puerto Plata and Santo Domingo City.

1914–1917 Mexico. Undeclared Mexican-American hostilities.

1915–1934 Haiti. U.S. forces maintain order during chronic threatened insurrection.

1916 China. U.S. forces land to quell rioting on American property in Nanking.

1916–1924 Dominican Republic. U.S. forces maintain order during chronic threatened insurrection.

1917 China. U.S. troops land to protect American lives at Chungking.

1917–1918 Germany and Austria-Hungary. World War I.

1917–1922 Cuba. U.S. forces protect American interests during and following insurrection.

1918–1919 Mexico. U.S. troops enter Mexico pursuing bandits and fight Mexican troops at Nogales.

1918–1920 Panama. U.S. troops act as police during election disturbances and later.

1918–1920 Soviet Russia. U.S. troops protect the American consulate at Vladivostok and remain as part of an allied occupation force; later American troops intervene at Archangel in response to the Bolshevik revolution.

1919 Dalmatia. U.S. forces act as police in feud between Italians and Serbs.

1919 Turkey. U.S. Marines protect the American consulate during the Greek occupation of Constantinople.

1919 Honduras. U.S. troops maintain order during attempted revolution.

1920 China. U.S. troops protect lives during a disturbance at Kiukiang.

1920 Guatemala. U.S. troops protect the American legation and interests.

1920–1922 Russia (Siberia). U.S. Marines sent to protect U.S. radio station and property on Russian Island, Bay of Vladivostok.

SOURCE: Adapted from Ellen C. Collier, "Instances of Use of United States Armed Forces Abroad, 1778–1993," *CRS Report for Congress,* October 7, 1993.

term to describe later policies that emphasized internationalism and moralism and that were dedicated to extending democracy." We will return to that insight later in this chapter.

Isolationism Resurgent: Interwar Idealism and Withdrawal

The League of Nations as an American foreign policy program died in the presidential election of 1920. Warren G. Harding defeated James M. Cox, who had received the Democratic Party's nomination after Wilson was stricken with a debilitating stroke while campaigning nationwide for the League. Harding's foreign policy program called for a *return to normalcy,* effectively one that sought "relief from the burdens that international engagement brings" (Mandelbaum 1994).

Disillusionment with American involvement in World War I would eventually set in, undermining Americans' "confidence in the old symbols of internationalism and altruistic diplomacy" and their "assurance that America's mission should be one of magnanimous service to the rest of the world" (Osgood 1953). Disillusionment became especially prevalent in the 1930s, as isolationism again emerged as the dominant American foreign policy strategy. Initially, however, idealism was still accepted, perhaps out of popular indifference. Military intervention in Latin America and China also perpetuated the unilateralist thrust of American foreign policy evident even before the turn of the century.

Although the United States practiced interventionism during the 1920s, thus perpetuating a now firmly established policy pattern, American policy makers also enthusiastically pursued key elements of the idealist paradigm. With the Washington Naval Conference of 1921, the United States sought, through arms limitations, to curb a triangular naval arms race involving the United States, Japan, and Britain. A series of treaties designed to maintain the status quo in the Far East followed. The program conformed to idealist precepts, but no enforcement provisions were included. Thus realists argue that "the transient thrill afforded by the Washington Conference was miserable preparation for the test of political leadership provided by the ominous events that undermined the Far Eastern settlement a decade later" (Osgood 1953).

Realists also criticize the 1928 Pact of Paris, popularly known as the **Kellogg-Briand Pact** (after the U.S. Secretary of State, Frank B. Kellogg, and the French Foreign Minister, Aristide Briand, who negotiated it). The agreement sought to deal with the problem of war by making it illegal. Realists thus regard it as "the perfect expression of the utopian idealism which dominated America's attempts to compose international conflicts and banish the threat of war in the interwar period. . . . The Pact of Paris simply declared that its signatories renounced war as an instrument of national policy . . . It contained absolutely no obligation for any nation to do anything under any circumstances" (Osgood 1953).[3]

As fascism rose during the 1930s and the world political economy fell into deep depression, neither the outlawry of war nor the principle of collective security stemmed the onslaught of renewed militarism. Germany, Italy, and Japan repeatedly challenged the post–World War I order, Britain and France seemed powerless to stop them, and the United States retreated into an isolationist shell. In the U.S. Senate a special committee chaired by the extreme isolationist Gerald P. Nye held hearings that attributed American entry into World War I to war profiteers—"merchants of death," as they were called. Congress passed a series of neutrality acts between 1935 and 1937 whose purpose was to steer America clear of the emerging European conflict. The immediate application came in Spain, where, with the help of Hitler, General Francisco Franco sought to overthrow the Spanish republic and replace it with a fascist regime. The neutrality acts effectively barred the United States from assisting the antifascist forces.

The Great Depression reinforced isolationist sentiments in the United States. As noted earlier, Britain was the world's preeminent economic power in the nineteenth century. As the preponderant power in politics as well as economics—a global hegemon—it promoted an open international economic system based on free trade. Its power began to wane in the late nineteenth century, however. Following World War I, Britain's ability to exercise the leadership role necessary to maintain the open world political economy was severely strained. The United States was the logical candidate to assume this role, but it refused.[4]

Britain's inability to exercise leadership and the United States' unwillingness to do so were primary causes of the Great Depression. Economic nationalism now became the norm. Tariffs erected by one state to protect its economy from foreign inroads led to retaliation by others. The volume of international trade contracted dramatically, causing reduced living standards and rising economic hardship. Policy makers who sought to create a new world order following World War II would conclude that economic nationalism was a major cause of the breakdown of international peace. Indeed, the perceived connectedness of peace and prosperity is one of the major lessons of the 1930s that continues to inform American foreign policy even today.

Another lesson was learned when Britain's policy of trying to appease Hitler failed. In September

1938—meeting in Munich, Germany—Britain and France made an agreement with Hitler that permitted Nazi Germany to annex a large part of Czechoslovakia in return for what British Prime Minister Neville Chamberlain called "peace in our time." Instead, on September 1, 1939, Hitler attacked Poland. Britain and France, honoring their pledge to defend the Poles, declared war on Germany two days later. World War II had begun. The lesson drawn from the 1938 *Munich Conference*—that aggressors cannot be appeased—would also inform policy makers' thinking for decades to come.

In the two years that followed Hitler's initial onslaught against Poland—years that saw German attacks on France, Britain, and the Soviet Union—President Franklin D. Roosevelt deftly nudged the United States away from its isolationist policies in support of the Western democracies. Germany's blatant exercise of *machtpolitik* (power politics) challenged the precepts of idealism that had buttressed the isolationism of the 1930s. Still, Roosevelt was careful not to jettison idealism as he prepared the nation for the coming conflict. He understood "that only a threat to their security could motivate [the American people] to support military preparedness. But to take them into a war, he knew he needed to appeal to their idealism in much the same way that Wilson had.... What he sought was to bring about a world community compatible with America's democratic and social ideals as the best guarantee of peace" (Kissinger 1994a).

In the spring of 1941, Congress passed and Roosevelt signed the *Lend-Lease Act*. The act permitted the United States to assist others deemed vital to U.S. security, thus committing the United States to the Allied cause against the Axis powers, Germany and Italy. The proposal provoked a bitter controversy in the United States. Senator Arthur Vandenberg, then a staunch isolationist (converted to internationalism after the war), remarked that Lend-Lease was the death-knell of isolationism: "We have tossed Washington's Farewell Address into the discard," he wrote in his diary. "We have thrown ourselves squarely into the power politics and the power wars of Europe, Asia, and Africa. We have taken a first step upon a course from which we can

never hereafter retreat" (Serfaty 1972). The next step occurred when Japan attacked Pearl Harbor on December 7, 1941. No longer could America's geographic isolation from the world support its political isolation.

With the onset of World War II the United States began to reject its isolationist past. The ethos of *liberal internationalism*—"the intellectual and political tradition that believes in the necessity of leadership by liberal democracies in the construction of a peaceful world order through multilateral cooperation and effective international organizations" (Gardner 1990)—now animated the American people and their leaders as they embarked on a new era of unprecedented global activism.

POWER AND PRINCIPLE, 1946–1989: GLOBAL ACTIVISM, ANTICOMMUNISM, AND CONTAINMENT

"Every war in American history," writes historian Arthur Schlesinger (1986), "has been followed in due course by skeptical reassessments of supposedly sacred assumptions." World War II, more than any other, served such a purpose. It crystallized a mood and acted as a catalyst for it, resolved contradictions and helped clarify values, and produced a consensus about the nation's world role. Most American leaders were now convinced that the United States should not, and could not, retreat from world affairs as it had after World War I. The isolationist heritage was pushed aside as policy makers enthusiastically plunged into the task of shaping the world to American preferences. Thus a new epoch in American diplomacy unfolded as—with missionary zeal—the United States once more sought to build a new world order on the ashes of Dresden and Berlin, Hiroshima and Nagasaki.

In 1947 President Harry S. Truman set the tone of postwar American policy in the doctrine that bears his name: "The free peoples of the world look to us for support in maintaining their freedoms....

If we falter in our leadership, we may endanger the peace of the world—and we shall surely endanger the welfare of our own nation." Later policy pronouncements prescribed America's missionary role. "Our nation," John F. Kennedy asserted in 1962, was "commissioned by history to be either an observer of freedom's failure or the cause of its success." Ronald Reagan echoed that sentiment nearly two decades later: "We in this country, in this generation, are, by destiny rather than choice, the watchmen on the walls of world freedom."

Internationalism Resurgent

Secretary of State Dean Rusk declared in 1967 that "Other nations have interests. The United States has responsibilities." Consistent with its new sense of global responsibility—and drawing on a sometimes uncertain blend of its idealist and realist heritage—the United States actively sought to orchestrate nearly every significant global initiative in the emergent Cold War era.

It was a primary sponsor and supporter of the United Nations. It engineered creation of regional institutions, such as the Organization of American States, and promoted American hegemony in areas regarded as American spheres of influence. It campaigned vigorously for the expansion of foreign trade and the development of new markets for American business abroad.[5] It launched an ambitious foreign aid program. And it built a complex network of military alliances, both formal and informal. Its pursuit of these ambitious foreign policy objectives created a vast American "empire" circling the globe. Focus 3.2. summarizes the scope of America's commitments and involvements abroad in 1991, when the United States emerged as the world's sole remaining superpower—and exactly half a century after the Japanese attack on Pearl Harbor. Against this background, a phrase used by President Carter's national security adviser, Zbigniew Brzezinski, accurately described the United States: "the first global society." Indeed, for half a century few aspirants to the White House would risk challenging the nation's active leadership role. Had they done so, they would have attacked a widely accepted and deeply ingrained national self-image that both led to and was sustained by extensive global interests and involvements.

Global activism is the first of three tenets uppermost in the minds of American policy makers following World War II. The others focused on the post–World War II challenge of Soviet communism. Together the three tenets defined a new orthodoxy that not only replaced the isolationist mood of the 1930s but also shaped a half-century of American foreign policy. The trilogy summarized below describes the new orthodoxy:

- The United States must reject isolationism and embrace an active responsibility for the direction of international affairs.
- Communism represents a dangerous ideological force in the world, and the United States should combat its spread.
- Because the Soviet Union is the spearhead of the communist challenge, American foreign policy must contain Soviet expansionism and influence.

The Communist Challenge to American Ideas and Ideals

Fear of communism—and an unequivocal rejection of it—played a major part in shaping the way the United States perceived the world throughout the Cold War. Communism was widely seen as a doctrinaire belief system diametrically opposed to "the American way of life," one intent on converting the entire world to its own vision. Because communism was perceived as inherently totalitarian, antidemocratic, and anticapitalist, it also was perceived as a potent threat to freedom, liberty, and prosperity throughout the world.

Combating this threatening, adversarial ideology became an obsession—to the point, some argued, that American foreign policy itself became ideological (Commager 1983; Parenti 1969). The United States now often defined its mission as much in terms of the beliefs it opposed as those it supported. In words and deeds, America seemingly stood less *for* something, as in the nineteenth

---

F O C U S 3.2   **America's Half Century: Nonmilitary and Military Dimensions of Global Activism at the End of the Cold War**

Nonmilitary Involvements

- The United States maintained diplomatic offices in 160 nations and participated in over fifty major international organizations and eight hundred international conferences.

- U.S. broadcasting services promoted America's message and world view in forty-eight languages beamed throughout the world.

- The value of U.S. exports reached $421.7 billion, while its imports from abroad stood at $487.1 billion. In 1941 total U.S. trade with the rest of the world—exports plus imports—totaled $8.8 billion.

- U.S. economic aid to ninety countries exceeded $11.0 billion, bringing to $246.1 billion the total amount of foreign economic assistance granted to other countries since World War II. From June 1941 through June 1945 the United States spent $49 billion on foreign aid, all for military objectives.

- U.S. direct investment abroad stood at $361.5 billion.

Military Involvements

- Bilateral and multilateral treaties, executive agreements, and policy declarations committed the United States to the defense of over forty nations.

- In 1990, prior to the Persian Gulf buildup, 435,000 troops were stationed at 395 major military bases and hundreds of minor bases in thirty-five foreign countries. In 1940, one year before the Lend-Lease Act was passed, the entire U.S. Army consisted of 269,000 officers and enlisted personnel.

- 47,000 Navy and Marine Corps personnel were aboard ships outside U.S. territorial waters. Another 10,000 were stationed at military bases on American territories in the Pacific. In 1940, one year before Pearl Harbor was attacked, the entire U.S. Navy consisted of 54,000 officers and enlisted personnel.

- 12,000 strategic nuclear warheads were deployed on 1,600 intercontinental and seabased missiles and 260 intercontinental bombers.

- Nonstrategic forces levels included more than 8,000 tactical nuclear weapons, 16,000 battle tanks, 7,000 combat aircraft, 2,000 attack helicopters, and 300 aircraft carriers and major ships.

- The United States agreed to sell $20.9 billion of military equipment to other nations, bringing the total value of sales since the Korean War to $210 billion. Another $81.6 billion was spent in other forms of military aid and training.

- The nation's budget for military preparedness stood at $320.9 billion—a figure that exceeded the gross national product (GNP) of all but a handful of the world's other nations. In 1940—the same year that Nazi Germany attacked and occupied Belgium, the Netherlands, and France—the combined budgets of the Army and Navy departments was nearly $1.8 billion—1.8 percent of the nation's GNP.

---

century, than *against* something: the communist ideology of Marxism-Leninism.

Official pronouncements about America's global objectives as they developed in the formative decade following World War II routinely stressed the menace posed by Marxist-Leninist (communist) doctrine. "The actions resulting from the communist philosophy," charged Harry Truman in 1949, "are a threat." President Dwight D. Eisenhower later warned that "We face a hostile ideology—global in scope, atheistic in character, ruthless in purpose, and insidious in method." "Unhappily," he continued, "the danger it poses promises to be of indefinite duration."

One popular view of "the beast" that helped sustain the anticommunist impulse was the belief that communism was a cohesive monolith to which all adherents were bound in united solidarity. The passage of time steadily reduced the cogency of that viewpoint, as communism revealed itself to be more polycentric than monolithic. Communist Party leaders became increasingly vocal about their own divisions and disagreements concerning communism's fundamental beliefs. The greatest fear that some felt was regarding the motives of other communist states. Moreover, even if communism was in spirit an expansionist movement, it proved to be more flexible than initially assumed, with no timetable for the conversion of nonbelievers. Regardless, the perception of communism as a global monolith was a driving force behind America's Soviet-centric foreign policy.

A related conviction saw communism as endowed with powers and appeals that would encourage its continued spread. The view of communism as an expansionist, crusading force intent on converting the entire world to its beliefs, whose doctrines, however evil, might command widespread appeal was a potent argument. The **domino theory**, a popular metaphor in the 1960s, asserted that one country's fall to communism would stimulate the fall of those adjacent to it. Like a row of falling dominoes, an unstoppable chain reaction would unfold, bringing increasing portions of the world's population under the domination of totalitarian, communist governments. "Communism is on the move. It is out to win. It is playing an offensive game," warned Richard Nixon in 1963. Earlier in his political career Nixon had chastised Truman's secretary of state, calling him the "dean of the cowardly college of Communist containment" and recommended "dealing with this great Communist offensive" by pushing back the Iron Curtain with force. The lesson implied by the domino metaphor is that only American resistance could abate the seemingly inevitable communist onslaught. Reinforced by the image of communism as a monolithic force, the domino theory was especially potent in explaining America's resolve to fight in Vietnam.

The anticommunist goal became a bedrock of the foreign policy consensus that emerged after World War II. From the late 1940s until the United States became mired in the Vietnam War, few in the American foreign policy establishment challenged this consensus. Policy debates centered largely on how to implement the anticommunist drive, not on whether communism posed a threat. Some of the

ideological fervor of American rhetoric receded during the 1970s with the Nixon-Kissinger effort to limit communist influence through a strategy of *détente*. References in policy statements to communism itself as a force in world politics also declined. President Carter went so far as to declare in the aftermath of the Vietnam War that "we are now free of that inordinate fear of communism which once led us to embrace any dictator who joined us in our fear."

But the anticommunist underpinnings of American foreign policy did not vanish. Instead, the belief that "communism is the principal danger" gained renewed emphasis under President Ronald Reagan, whose Manichean world view depicted the world as a place where the noncommunist "free world," led by the United States, engaged in continuous battle with the communist world led by the Soviet Union, which he described as an "evil empire." Later he would confront the Soviet empire on its very doorstep. On a trip to Berlin—divided since 1961 by a wall built by communist East Germany that stood as perhaps the most emotional symbol of the division between East and West—Reagan challenged Soviet President Mikhail Gorbachev, saying, "Mr. Gorbachev, tear down this wall."

The more virulent forms of anticommunism waned as domestic change in Eastern Europe and the Soviet Union itself accelerated during Reagan's second term in office. Richard Schifter, an assistant secretary of state in the administration of George H. W. Bush, declared that "communism has proven itself to be a false god." Rejected gods do not need to be condemned. The first Bush administration nonetheless chose to emphasize a worldwide transition to democracy inspired by the desire to extirpate the curse of communist ideology from the world. Secretary of State James A. Baker, III: "Our idea is to replace the dangerous period of the Cold War with a democratic peace—a peace built on the twin pillars of political and economic freedom."

The historical import of anticommunism should be neither minimized nor forgotten, as the impact of the beliefs about communism in the

American policy-making community was enormous. Successful opposition to communism became one of America's most important interests, coloring not only what happened abroad but also much of what took place at home, requiring the expenditure of enormous psychological and material treasure—and sometimes threatening cherished domestic values.

The Containment of Soviet Influence

As the physically strongest and the most vocal Marxist-Leninist state, the Soviet Union stood at the vanguard of the communist challenge. Hence the third tenet of the new orthodoxy emergent after World War II: The United States must contain Soviet expansionism and influence.

Four corollary beliefs buttressed the determination to contain Soviet communism:

- The Soviet Union is an expansionist power, intent on maximizing communist power through military conquest and "exported" revolutions.

- The Soviet goal of world domination is permanent and will succeed unless blocked by vigorous counteraction.

- The United States, leader of the "free world," is the only state able to repel Soviet aggression.

- Appeasement will not work: Force must be met with force if Soviet expansionism is to be stopped.

A Soviet-centric foreign policy flowed from this interrelated set of beliefs, whose durability persisted for decades. Furthermore, the precepts of political realism, which focus on power, not principle, now came to dominate American foreign policy, as the purpose of the **containment** strategy was the preservation of the security of the United States "through the maintenance of a balance of power in the world" (Gaddis 1992; see also Gaddis 1982 and Kissinger 1994b). As one scholar put it, "[political] realists sought to reorient United States policy so that American policy makers could cope with

Soviet attempts at domination without either lapsing into passive unwillingness to use force or engaging in destructive and quixotic crusades to 'make the world safe for democracy.' Their ideas were greeted warmly by policy makers, who sought . . . to 'exorcise isolationism, justify a permanent and global involvement in world affairs, [and] rationalize the accumulation of power'" (Keohane 1986a).[6] To understand what brought about these durable assumptions, the containment strategy derived from them, and the doctrine of political realism that sustained them, it is useful to trace briefly alternative interpretations of the origins of the Cold War and, following that, the strategies of containment that America's Cold War presidents pursued.

The Origins of the Cold War: Competing Hypotheses   Three hypotheses compete for attention as we seek to explain the origins of the Cold War: a conflict of interests, ideological incompatibilities, and misperceptions.

A Conflict of Interests   Rivalry between the emergent superpowers following World War II was inescapable. Indeed, a century earlier Alexis de Tocqueville foresaw that the United States and Russia were destined by fate and historical circumstance to become rivals. "Each," he said, "will one day hold in its hands the destinies of half of mankind." Tocqueville could not have foreseen the ideological differences between the United States and the Soviet Union. Instead, the logic of *realpolitik* explains his prediction. From this perspective, the status of the United States and the Soviet Union at the top of the international hierarchy and the interests they held most dear made each suspicious of the other. And each had reasons to counter the other's potential global hegemony. Thus, in the observations of one political realist:

> The principal cause of the Cold War was the essential duopoly of power left by World War II, a duopoly that quite naturally resulted in the filling of a vacuum (Europe) that had once been the center of the

international system and the control of which would have conferred great, and perhaps decisive, power advantage to its possessor. . . . The root cause of the conflict was to be found in the structural circumstances that characterized the international system at the close of World War II.
(Tucker 1990, 94)

But was the competition necessary? During World War II, the United States and the Soviet Union had both demonstrated an ability to subordinate their ideological differences and competition for power to larger purposes—the destruction of Hitler's Germany. Neither relentlessly sought unilateral advantage. Instead, both practiced accommodation to protect their mutual interest. Their success in remaining alliance partners suggests that Cold War rivalry was not predetermined, that continued collaboration was possible.

After the war, American and Soviet leaders both expressed their hope that wartime collaboration would continue (Gaddis 1972). Harry Hopkins, for example, a close adviser to President Roosevelt, reported that "The Russians had proved that they could be reasonable and farseeing and there wasn't any doubt in the minds of the President or any of us that we could live with them and get along with them peacefully for as far into the future as any of us could imagine."

Roosevelt argued that it would be possible to preserve the accommodative atmosphere the great powers achieved during the war if the United States and the Soviet Union each respected the other's national interests. He predicated his belief on an informal agreement that suggested each great power would enjoy dominant influence in its own sphere of influence and not oppose the others in their areas of influence (Morgenthau 1969; Schlesinger 1967). As presidential policy adviser John Foster Dulles noted in January 1945, "The three great powers which at Moscow agreed upon the 'closest cooperation' about European questions have shifted to a practice of separate, regional responsibility." Agreements about the role of the Security Council in the new United Nations (in which each great power would enjoy a veto) obligated the United States and the Soviet Union to share responsibility for preserving world peace, further symbolizing the expectation of continued cooperation.

If these were the superpowers' hopes and aspirations when World War II ended, why did they fail? To answer that question, we must go beyond the logic of *realpolitik* and probe other explanations of the origins of the Cold War.

Ideological Incompatibilities Another interpretation holds that the Cold War was simply an extension of the superpowers' mutual disdain for each other's political system and way of life—in short, ideological incompatibilities. Secretary of State James F. Byrnes embraced this thesis following World War II. He argued that "there is too much difference in the ideologies of the United States and Russia to work out a long term program of cooperation." Thus the Cold War was a conflict "not only between two powerful states, but also between two different social systems" (Jervis 1991).

The interpretation of the Cold War as a battle between diametrically opposed systems of belief contrasts sharply with the view that the emergent superpowers' differences stemmed from discordant interests. Although the adversaries may have viewed "ideology more as a justification for action than as a guide to action," once the interests they shared disappeared, "ideology did become the chief means which differentiated friend from foe" (Gaddis 1983). From this perspective, the Cold War centered less on a conflict of interests between rivals for global power and prestige than on a contest between opposing belief systems about alternative ways of life. Such contests allow no room for compromise, as they pit right against wrong, good against evil; diametrically opposed belief systems require victory. Adherents, animated by the righteousness of their cause, view the world as an arena for religious war—a battle for the allegiance of people's minds. Thus American policy rhetoric—like that employed to justify past religious wars and religious persecutions—advocated "sleepless hostility to Communism—even preventive war"

(Commager 1965). Such an outlook virtually guarantees pure conflict: Intolerance of competing belief systems is rife, and cooperation or conciliation with the ideological foe entails no virtue. Instead, adversaries view the world in *zero-sum* terms: When one side wins converts, the other side necessarily loses them.

Lenin thus described the predicament—prophetically, it happened: "As long as capitalism and socialism exist, we cannot live in peace; in the end, either one or the other will triumph—a funeral dirge will be sung either over the Soviet Republic or over world capitalism."

Misperceptions A third explanation sees the Cold War rooted in psychological factors, particularly the superpowers' misperceptions of each other's motives, which their conflicting interests and ideologies reinforced. Mistrustful parties see in their own actions only virtue and in those of their adversaries only malice. Hostility is inevitable in the face of such "we-they," "we're OK, you're not" mirror images. Moreover, as a state's perceptions of its adversary's evil intentions become accepted as dogma, its prophecies also become self-fulfilling (White 1984).

A month before Roosevelt died, he expressed to Stalin his desire, above all, to prevent "mutual distrust." Yet, as noted, mistrust soon developed. Indeed, its genesis could be traced to prewar years, particularly in the minds of Soviet leaders, who recalled American participation in the 1918–19 Allied military intervention in Russia, which turned from its initial mission of keeping weapons out of German hands into an anti-Bolshevik undertaking. They also were sensitive to the United States' failure to recognize the Soviet Union diplomatically until 1933 in the midst of a depression (perceived as a sign of capitalism's weakness and its ultimate collapse).

The wartime experience did little to assuage Soviet leaders; rather, their anxieties were fueled by disquieting memories:

- U.S. procrastination before entering the war against the fascists
- America's refusal to inform the Soviets of the Manhattan Project or to apprise them of

wartime strategy to the same extent as the British

- The delay in sending promised Lend-Lease supplies
- The failure to open up the second front (leading Stalin to suspect that American policy was to let the Russians and Germans destroy each other)
- The use of the atomic bomb against Japan, perhaps perceived as a maneuver to prevent Soviet involvement in the Pacific peace settlement

Those suspicions were later reinforced by the willingness of the United States to support previous Nazi collaborators in American-occupied countries, notably Italy, and by its pressure on the Soviet Union to abide by its promise to allow free elections in areas vital to Soviet national security, notably Poland. Soviet leaders also were resentful of America's abrupt cancellation of promised Lend-Lease assistance, which Stalin had counted on to facilitate the postwar recovery. Thus Soviet distrust of American intentions stemmed in part from fears of American encirclement that were exacerbated by America's past hostility.

To the United States, on the other hand, numerous indications of growing Soviet belligerence warranted distrust. They included:

- Stalin's announcement in February 1946 that the Soviet Union was not going to demilitarize its armed forces, at the very time that the United States was engaged in the largest demobilization by a victorious power in world history
- The Soviet Union's unwillingness to permit democratic elections in the territories it had liberated from the Nazis
- Its refusal to assist in postwar reconstruction in regions outside of Soviet control
- Its removal of supplies and infrastructure from Soviet-occupied areas
- Its selfish and often obstructive behavior in the fledgling new international organizations

---

F O C U S 3.3   Mirror Images: The Onset of the Cold War

The Soviet Image of the United States
- **They (the rulers) are bad.** The Wall Street bankers, politicians, and militaries want a war because they fear loss of wealth and power in a communist revolution.

  They are surrounding us with military bases. They send spies (in U-2 planes and otherwise) to destroy the workers' fatherland.

  They are like the Nazis—rearming the Germans against us.
- **They are imperialistic.** The capitalist nations dominate colonial areas, keep them
- in submission.

  The Latin-American regimes (except Cuba) are puppets of the USA.
- **They exploit their own people.** All capitalists live in luxury by exploiting workers, who suffer insecurity, unemployment, and so on.
- **They are against democracy.** Democratic forms are mere pretense; people can vote only for capitalist candidates.

  Rulers control organs of propaganda, education, and communication. They persecute anyone favoring communist ideas.
- **They distort the truth.** They falsely accuse the USSR of desiring to impose ideology by force.
- They are immoral, materialist, selfishly individualistic. They are only out for money.
- They (the people) are good. The American people want peace.

The American Image of the Soviet Union
- **They (the rulers) are bad.** The men in the Kremlin are aggressive, power-seeking, brutal in suppressing Hungary, ruthless in dealing with their people.

  They are infiltrating the western hemisphere to attack us.

  They engage in espionage and sabotage to wreck our country.

  They are like the Nazis—an aggressive expansionist dictatorship.
- **They are imperialistic.** The communists want to dominate the world.

  They rigidly control the satellite puppet governments.
- **They exploit their own people.** They hold down consumer goods, keep standards of living low except for communist bureaucrats.
- **They are against democracy.** Democratic forms are mere pretense; people can vote only for communist candidates.

  Rulers control organs of propaganda, education, and communication. They persecute anyone favoring western democracy.
- **They distort the truth.** They pose as a friend of colonial people in order to enslave them.
- **They are immortal, materialistic.** They are preventing freedom of religion.
- **They (the people) are good.** The Soviet people want peace.

SOURCE: Ralph K. White, *New York Times*, 5 September 1961, 5.

- Its occasional opportunistic disregard for international law and violation of agreements and treaties
- Its infiltration of Western labor movements

Harry Truman typified the environment of distrust. Upon assuming the presidency after Roosevelt's death he declared: "If the Russians did not wish to join us they could go to hell" (Tugwell 1971). In this climate of suspicion and distrust, the

Cold War grew (see Focus 3.3). "Each side thought that it was compelled by the very existence of the other to engage in zero-sum competition, and each saw the unfolding history of the Cold War as confirming its view" (Garthoff 1994).

Historians have long been intrigued about the origins of the Cold War and the weights that should be attached to competing explanations. Their task was made more difficult because nearly all sources of information came from the United States and the other western countries. Now, however, Russian authorities have begun to open Soviet archives from the early Cold War years, permitting new insights. Interestingly, the new evidence tends to confirm that the United States responded defensively to recurrent patterns of Soviet belligerence. Reinforcing this interpretation are historians' findings that Joseph Stalin's perceptions of and antipathy toward the west may have precluded the possibility of avoiding an East-West confrontation. Although the United States may have believed that the atomic bomb gave it the "the ultimate weapon" for dealing with Soviet intransigence on the issues unresolved in 1945, archival research now challenges that conclusion. Indeed, it shows that Stalin regarded the United States and its allies as wimps. Illustrative is Stalin's remark in December 1949 that "America, though it screams of war, is actually afraid of war more than anything else" (Haslam 1997). It is notable that his remark came shortly after the United States signed a mutual defense pact that formed the North Atlantic Treaty Organization (NATO) and less than a year before North Korea—with Soviet support—attacked South Korea, precipitating the Korean War.

Historians may eventually alter their first impressions about the origins of the Cold War as now revealed in newly acquired information from Russian archives.[7] Unlikely to change is the conclusion that a combination of power, principle, and pragmatism colored the way political leaders on both sides of the Iron Curtain played out this global contest for power and position. From the perspective of American foreign policy, the key issue was how best to apply the strategy of containment to curtail expansion of Soviet power and influence.

America's Containment Strategies: Evolutionary Phases   The history of American foreign policy since World War II is largely the story of how the containment doctrine was interpreted and applied. Figure 3.1 illustrates the pattern of conflict and cooperation the United States directed toward the Soviet Union during the Cold War and the Soviets' responses. The information charted summarizes hundreds of verbal and physical actions the two powers directed toward one another as revealed in systematic analyses of media

accounts of their behavior. The evidence reveals three patterns of Soviet-American interactions during the Cold War:

1. Conflict was the characteristic mode of Soviet-American interactions.

2. The acts of conflict and cooperation directed by one power toward the other were typically responded to in kind. Periods when the United States directed friendly initiatives toward the Soviets were also periods when the Soviets acted with friendliness toward the United States; periods of U.S. belligerence were periods of Soviet belligerence. Thus *reciprocity* describes the powers' patterns of behavior toward one another.

3. Although different presidents are identified with periodic shifts in the pattern of conflict and cooperation toward the Soviet Union during the Cold War, the historical record reveals "no detectable systematic differences in the way administrations regularly [built] on their own past behavior or in the way they [responded] to the Soviet Union" (Dixon and Gaarder 1992). Instead, regardless of the party affiliation or political ideology of those in the Oval Office, continuity rather than change is the hallmark of America's Cold War behavior toward the Soviet Union.

Cold War Confrontation, 1947–1962   A brief period of wary friendship preceded the onset of Cold War confrontation, but by 1947 all pretense of collaboration ceased, as the antagonists' vital security interests collided over the issues surrounding the structure of post–World War II European politics.

In February 1946, Stalin gave a speech in which he spoke of the inevitability of conflict with the capitalist powers. Urging the Soviet people not to be deluded that the end of the war with Germany meant the state could relax, he called for intensified efforts by the Soviet people to strengthen and defend their homeland. Many Western leaders saw Stalin's first major postwar address as a declaration of World War III. Shortly after this, George F.

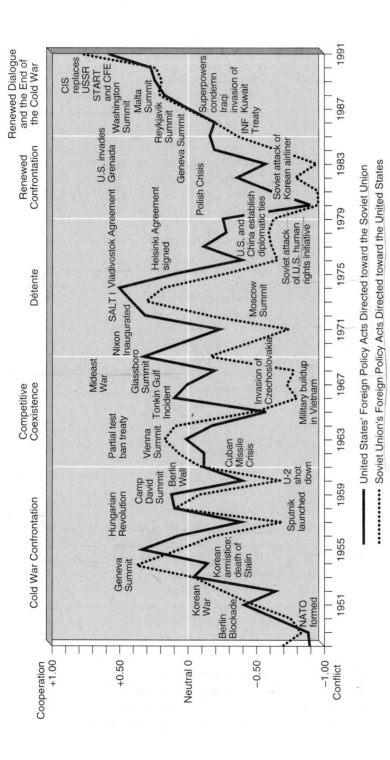

FIGURE 3.1 Soviet-American Relations, 1948–1991

NOTE: The index is the net proportion of cooperative acts and conflictual acts.

SOURCE: Adapted from Edward E. Azar and Thomas J. Sloan, *Dimensions of Interaction* (Pittsburgh: Center for International Studies, 1973), and supplemented with data from the Conflict and Peace Data Bank. Data for 1966–1991 are from the World Event Interaction Survey, as compiled by Rodney G. Tomlinson.

Kennan, then a U.S. diplomat in Moscow, sent to Washington his famous "long telegram" assessing the sources of Soviet conduct. Kennan's conclusions were ominous: "We have here a political force committed fanatically to the belief that with [the] United States there can be no permanent modus vivendi, that it is desirable and necessary that the internal harmony of our society be disrupted, our traditional way of life be destroyed, the international authority of our state be broken, if Soviet power is to be secure."

Kennan's ideas were circulated widely when, in 1947, the influential journal *Foreign Affairs* published them in an anonymous article Kennan signed "X." In it, he argued that Soviet leaders would forever feel insecure about their political ability to maintain power against forces both within Soviet society and the outside world. Their insecurity would lead to an activist—and perhaps aggressive—Soviet foreign policy. Yet it was within the power of the United States to increase the strain on the Soviet leadership, which eventually could lead to a gradual mellowing or final end of Soviet power. "In these circumstances" Kennan concluded, "it is clear that the main element of any United States policy toward the Soviet Union must be that of a long-term, patient but firm and vigilant *containment* of Russian expansive tendencies" (Kennan 1947, emphasis added).

Not long after that, Harry Truman made this prescription the cornerstone of American postwar policy. Provoked in part by domestic turmoil in Turkey and Greece—which he and others believed to be communist inspired—Truman responded: "I believe that it must be the policy of the United States to support free peoples who are resisting attempted subjugation by armed minorities or by outside pressures."

Few declarations in American history were as powerful and important as this one, which eventually became known as the ***Truman Doctrine.*** "In a single sentence Truman had defined American policy for the next generation and beyond. Whenever and wherever an anti-Communist government was threatened, by indigenous insurgents, foreign invasion, or even diplomatic pressure . . . , the United States would supply political, economic, and, most of all, military aid" (Ambrose 1993).

Whether the policy of containment was appropriate, even at the time of its origination, remains controversial. Journalist Walter Lippmann wrote a series of articles in the *New York Herald Tribune,* later collected in a short book called *The Cold War* (Lippmann 1947), in which he argued that global containment would be costly for the United States, that it would militarize American foreign policy, and that eventually the United States would have to support any regime that professed anticommunism, regardless how distasteful it might be. Henry Wallace, a third-party candidate who opposed Harry Truman for the presidency, joined in Lippmann's concern when he warned of the dilemma the United States would eventually face: "Once America stands for opposition to change, we are lost. America will become the most hated nation in the world."

Lippmann's critique proved prophetic in all its details. Before the Cold War had run its course, the United States had spent trillions of dollars on national defense, had developed permanent peacetime military alliances circling the globe, and had found itself supporting some of the most ruthless dictatorships in the world—in Argentina, Brazil, Cuba, the Dominican Republic, Guatemala, Greece, Haiti, Iran, Nicaragua, Paraguay, the Philippines, Portugal, South Korea, South Vietnam, Spain, and Taiwan—whose only shared characteristic was their opposition to communism. In the process, America's revolutionary heritage as a beacon of liberty often was set aside as the country found itself opposing social and political change elsewhere, choosing instead to preserve the status quo in the face of potentially disruptive revolutions.

As the Cold War persisted, the inability of the superpowers to maintain the sphere-of-influence posture tacitly agreed to earlier contributed to their propensity to interpret crises as the product of the other's program for global domination. When the Soviets moved into portions of Eastern Europe, American leaders interpreted this as confirmation that they sought world conquest.

The Soviet Union, however, had reason to think that the Americans would readily accede to Soviet domination in the east. In 1945, for example, Secretary of State James Byrnes stated that the "Soviet Union has a right to friendly governments along its borders." Undersecretary of State Dean Acheson spoke of "a Monroe Doctrine for eastern Europe." These viewpoints and others were implied in the Yalta agreements, concluded by the Allies late in the war against Nazi Germany and designed to shape Europe's postwar political and security character. They reinforced the Soviet belief that the Western powers would accept the Soviets' need for a buffer zone in Eastern Europe, which had been the common invasion route into Russia for more than three centuries. Hence, when the U.S. government began to challenge Soviet supremacy in eastern Germany and elsewhere in Eastern Europe, the Soviet Union felt that previous understandings had been violated and that the West harbored "imperialist designs" (see also Focus 3.3).

A seemingly unending eruption of Cold War crises followed. They included the Soviet refusal to withdraw troops from Iran in 1946, the communist coup d'état in Czechoslovakia in 1948, the Soviet blockade of West Berlin in June of that year, the communist acquisition of power on the Chinese mainland in 1949, the outbreak of the Korean War in 1950, the Chinese invasion of Tibet in 1950, and the on-again, off-again Taiwan Straits crises that followed. Hence the "war" was not simply "cold"; it became an embittered worldwide quarrel that threatened to escalate into open warfare, as the two powers positioned themselves to prevent the other from achieving preponderant power.

The United States enjoyed clear military superiority at the strategic level until 1949. It alone possessed the ultimate "winning weapon" and the means to deliver it. The Soviets broke the American atomic monopoly that year, much sooner than American scientists and policy makers had anticipated. Thereafter, the Soviet quest for military equality and the superpowers' eventual relative strategic strengths influenced the entire range of their relations. As the distribution of world power became **bipolar**—with the United States and its allies comprising one pole, the Soviet Union and its allies the other—the character of superpower relations took on a different cast, sometimes more collaborative, sometimes more conflictual.

Europe, where the Cold War first erupted, was the focal point of the jockeying for influence. The principal European allies of the superpowers divided into NATO and the Warsaw Treaty Organization. These military alliances became the cornerstones of the superpowers' external policies, as the European members of the Eastern and Western alliances willingly acceded to the leadership of their respective patrons.

To a lesser extent, alliance formation also enveloped states outside of Europe. The United States in particular sought to contain Soviet (and Chinese) influence on the Eurasian landmass by building a ring of pro-American allies on the very borders of the communist world. In return, the United States promised to protect its growing number of clients from external attack. Thus the Cold War extended across the entire globe.

In the rigid two-bloc system of the 1950s the superpowers talked as if war were imminent, but in deeds (especially after the Korean War) both acted cautiously. President Eisenhower and his secretary of state, John Foster Dulles, promised a "rollback" of the Iron Curtain and the "liberation" of the "captive nations" of Eastern Europe. They pledged to respond to aggression with "massive [nuclear] retaliation." And they criticized the allegedly "soft" and "reactive" Truman Doctrine, claiming to reject containment in favor of an ambitious "winning" strategy that would finally end the confrontation with "godless communism." But communism was not rolled back in Eastern Europe, and containment was not replaced by a more assertive strategy. In 1956, for example, the United States failed to respond to Hungary's call for assistance in its revolt against Soviet control. American policy makers, despite their threatening language, promised more than they delivered. "'We can never rest,' Eisenhower swore in the 1952 presidential campaign, 'until the enslaved nations of the world have in the fullness of freedom the right to choose their own path.' But rest they did, except in their speeches" (Ambrose 1993).

Nikita Khrushchev assumed the top Soviet leadership position after Stalin's death in 1953. He claimed to accept *peaceful coexistence* with capitalism, and in 1955 the two superpowers met at the Geneva summit in a first, tentative step toward a mutual discussion of world problems. But the Soviet Union also continued, however cautiously, to exploit opportunities for advancing Soviet power wherever it perceived them to exist, as in Cuba in the early 1960s. Thus the period following Stalin's death was punctuated by continuing crises and confrontations. Now—in addition to Hungary—Cuba, Egypt, and Berlin became the flash points. Moreover, a crisis resulted from the downing of an American U-2 spy plane deep over Soviet territory in 1960. Nuclear brinkmanship and massive retaliation were symptomatic of the strategies of containment through which the United States at this time hoped to balance Soviet power and perhaps force the Soviets into submission.

Competitive Coexistence, 1962–1969 The Soviets' surreptitious placement of missiles in Cuba in 1962, the onset of the Vietnam War at about the same time, and the beginning of a seemingly unrestrained arms race cast a shadow over the possibility of superpower coexistence. The most serious test of the ability of the United States and the Soviet Union to avert catastrophe and to manage confrontation peacefully was the 1962 **Cuban missile crisis**—a catalytic event that transformed thinking about how the Cold War could be waged and expanded awareness of the suicidal consequences of a nuclear war. The superpowers stood eyeball to eyeball, in the words of then Secretary of State Dean Rusk. Fortunately, one blinked. Building from the recognition that common interests between the superpowers did indeed exist, President Kennedy, at American University's commencement exercises in 1963, explained why tension reduction had become imperative and war could not be risked:

> Among the many traits the people of [the United States and the Soviet Union] have in common, none is stronger than our mutual abhorrence of war. Almost unique among the major world powers, we have never been at war with each other. . . . Today, should total war ever break out again—no matter how—our two countries would become the primary targets. It is an ironical but accurate fact that the two strongest powers are the two in the most danger of devastation. . . . So let us not be blind to our differences, but let us also direct attention to our common interests and to the means by which those differences can be resolved. And if we cannot end now our differences, at least we can help make the world safe for diversity.

Kennedy is also remembered for his clarion inaugural address two years earlier. "Let every nation know, whether it wishes us well or ill, that we shall pay any price, bear any burden, meet any hardship, support any friend, oppose any foe to assure the survival and the success of liberty." For some, the challenge was a renewal of America's Cold War challenge to the Soviet Union. For others, it was an expression of America's idealist heritage.[8]

Kennedy's inaugural address defined an approach as resolutely anti-Soviet as that of his predecessors, but—especially following the missile crisis—his administration began in both style and tone to depart from the confrontational tactics of the past. Thus competition for advantage and influence continued, but the preservation of the status quo was also tacitly accepted, as neither superpower proved willing to launch a new war to secure new geostrategic gains. As the growing parity of American and Soviet military capabilities made coexistence or nonexistence the alternatives, finding ways to adjust their differences became compelling. This alleviated the danger posed by some issues and opened the door for new initiatives in other areas. For example, the Geneva (1955) and Camp David (1959) experiments in summit diplomacy set precedents for other tension-reduction activities. Installation of the "hot line," a direct communication link between the White House and the Kremlin, followed in 1963. So did the 1967 Glassboro summit and several negotiated agreements, including the 1963 Partial Test Ban Treaty, the 1967 Outer Space Treaty, and the 1968 Nuclear Non-Proliferation Treaty. In addition, the United States tacitly accepted a divided Germany and Soviet hegemony in Eastern Europe, as illustrated by its unwillingness to respond forcefully to the Warsaw Pact invasion of Czechoslovakia in 1968.

Détente, 1969–1979 With the inauguration of Richard Nixon as president and the appointment of Henry Kissinger as his national security adviser, the United States tried a new approach toward containment, officially labeled *__détente.__* In Kissinger's words, détente sought to create "a vested interest in cooperation and restraint," "an environment in which competitors can regulate and restrain their differences and ultimately move from competition to cooperation." Several considerations prompted the new approach. They included recognition that a nuclear attack would prove mutually suicidal, a growing sensitivity to the security requirements of both superpowers, and their shared concern for an increasingly powerful and assertive China.

To engineer the relaxation of superpower tensions, Nixon and Kissinger fashioned the *linkage theory.* Predicated on the expectation that the development of economic, political, and strategic ties between the United States and the Soviet Union would bind the two in a common fate, linkage would foster mutually rewarding exchanges. In this way, it would lessen the superpowers' incentives for war. Linkage also made the entire range of Soviet-American relations interdependent, which made cooperation in one policy area (such as arms control) contingent on acceptable conduct in others (intervention outside traditional spheres of influence).

As both a goal of and a strategy for expanding the superpowers' mutual interest in restraint, détente symbolized an important shift in their global relationship. In diplomatic jargon, relations between the Soviets and Americans were "normalized," as the expectation of war receded. In terms of containment, on the other hand, the strategy now shifted more toward self-containment on the Soviets' part than American militant containment. As one observer put it, "Détente did not mean global reconciliation with the Soviet Union. . . . Instead, détente implied the selective continuation of containment by economic and political inducement and at the price of accommodation through concessions that were more or less balanced" (Serfaty 1978). When militarily superior, the United States had practiced containment by coercion and force. From a new position of parity, containment was now practiced by seduction. Thus détente was "part of the Cold War, not an alternative to it" (Goodman 1975).

Paralleling its conviction to normalize relations with the Soviet Union, the Nixon administration sought to terminate the long, costly, and unpopular war in Vietnam. U.S. involvement escalated in the mid-1960s, but the war became increasingly unpopular at home as casualties mounted and the purposes of U.S. engagement remained vague and unconvincing. Thus the Vietnam War coincided with—indeed, caused—popular pleas for a U.S. retreat from world affairs. President Nixon's declaration in 1970 (later known as the *Nixon Doctrine*) that the United States would provide military and economic assistance to its friends and allies but would hold these states responsible for protecting their own security took cognizance of a resurgent isolationist mood at home.

Securing Soviet support in extricating itself from Vietnam was a salient American goal sought through the détente process, but arms control stood at the center of the new dialogue. The *Strategic Arms Limitation Talks (SALT)* became the test of détente's viability. Initiated in 1969, the SALT negotiations sought to restrain the threatening, expensive, and spiraling arms race. They produced two sets of agreements. The SALT I agreement limiting offensive strategic weapons and the Antiballistic Missile (ABM) Treaty were signed in 1972. The second pact, SALT II, was concluded in 1979. With their signing, each of the superpowers gained the principal objective it had sought in détente. The Soviet Union gained recognition of its status as the United States' equal; the United States gained a commitment from the Soviet Union to moderate its quest for preeminent power in the world.

The SALT II agreement was not brought to fruition, however. It was signed but never ratified by the United States. The failure underscored the real differences that still separated the superpowers. By the end of the 1970s, détente lost nearly all of its momentum and much of the hope it had symbolized only a few years earlier. During the SALT II treaty ratification hearings, the U.S. Senate expressed concern about an agreement with a rival that continued high levels of military spending, that sent arms to states outside its traditional sphere of influence (Algeria, Angola, Egypt, Ethiopia, Somalia, Syria, Vietnam, and elsewhere), and that stationed military forces in Cuba. These complaints all spoke to the persistence of Americans' deep-seated distrust of the Soviet Union and their understandable concern about Soviet intentions.

Renewed Confrontation, 1979–1985   The Soviet invasion of Afghanistan in 1979 ended the Senate's consideration of SALT II—and détente. "Soviet aggression in Afghanistan—unless checked—confronts all the world with the most serious strategic challenge since the Cold War began," declared President Jimmy Carter. In response the United States initiated a series of countermoves, including enunciation of the **Carter Doctrine** declaring the willingness of the United States to use military force to protect its security interests in the Persian Gulf region. Thus antagonism and hostility once more dominated Soviet-American relations. And once more the pursuit of power dictated the appropriate strategy of containment as Eisenhower's tough talk, Kennedy's competitiveness, and even Truman's belligerence were rekindled. Before Afghanistan, Carter had embarked on a worldwide campaign for human rights, an initiative steeped in Wilsonian idealism directed as much toward the Soviet Union as others. This, too, now fell victim to the primacy of power over principle.

Following his election in 1980, President Ronald Reagan and his Soviet counterparts delivered a barrage of confrontational rhetoric reminiscent of the 1950s. In one interview, Reagan went so far as to say, "Let's not delude ourselves, the Soviet Union underlies all the unrest that is going on. If they weren't engaged in this game of dominoes, there wouldn't be any hot spots in the world." In another speech before the British parliament, he implored the nations of the free world to join one another to promote worldwide democracy. That ambitious call reflected Wilsonian idealism and long-standing moralistic strains in American foreign policy. It also implied renewal of the challenge to Soviet communism that British Prime Minister Winston Churchill launched in Fulton, Missouri, in 1946, where he declared "an Iron Curtain has descended" across Europe and called for the English-speaking nations to join together for the coming "trial of strength" with the communist world. Reagan policy adviser Richard Pipes' bold charge in 1981 that the Soviets would have to choose between "peacefully changing their Communist system . . . or going to war" punctuated the tense atmosphere.

In many respects, the early 1980s were like the 1950s, as tough talk was not matched by aggressive action. But the first Reagan term did witness some assertive action, notably resumption of the arms race. The United States now placed a massive rearmament program above all other priorities, including domestic economic problems. American policy makers also spoke loosely about the "winability" of a nuclear war through a "prevailing" military strategy, which included the threat of a "first use" of nuclear weapons should a conventional war break out.

The superpowers also extended their confrontation to new territory, such as Central America, and renewed their public diplomacy (propaganda) efforts to extol the ascribed virtues of their respective systems throughout the world. A series of events punctuated the renewal of conflict:

- The Soviets destroyed Korean Airlines flight 007 in 1983.
- Shortly thereafter the United States invaded Grenada.
- Arms control talks then ruptured.
- The Soviets boycotted the 1984 Olympic Games in Los Angeles (in retaliation for the U.S. boycott of the 1980 Moscow Olympics).

The Reagan administration also embarked on a new program, the ***Reagan Doctrine,*** which pledged U.S. support of anticommunist insurgents (euphemistically described as "freedom fighters") who sought to overthrow Soviet-supported governments in Afghanistan, Angola, and Nicaragua. The strategy "expressed the conviction that communism could be defeated, not merely contained." Thus "Reagan took Wilsonianism to its ultimate conclusion. America would not wait passively for free institutions to evolve, nor would it confine itself to resisting direct threats to its security. Instead, it would actively promote democracy" (Kissinger 1994a).

Understandably, relations between the United States and the Soviet Union were increasingly strained by the compound impact of these moves, countermoves, and rhetorical flourishes. The new Soviet leader, Mikhail Gorbachev, summarized the alarming state of superpower relations in the fall of 1985 by fretting that "The situation is very complex, very tense. I would even go so far as to say it is explosive." The situation did not explode, however. Instead, the superpowers resumed their dialogue and laid the basis for a new phase in their relations.

Renewed Dialogue and the End of the Cold War, 1985– 1991 Prospects for a more constructive phase improved measurably under Gorbachev. At first his goals were hard to discern, but it soon became clear that he felt it imperative for the Soviet Union to reconcile its differences with the capitalist West if it wanted any chance of reversing the deterioration of its economy and international position. In Gorbachev's words, these goals dictated "the need for a fundamental break with many customary approaches to foreign policy." Shortly thereafter, he chose the path of domestic reform, one marked by political democratization and a transition to a market economy. And he proclaimed the need for "new thinking" in foreign and defense policy to relax superpower tensions.

To carry out "new thinking," in 1986 Gorbachev abrogated the long-standing Soviet ideological commitment to aid national liberation movements struggling to overthrow capitalism. "It is inadmissible and futile to encourage revolution from abroad," he declared. He also for the first time embraced ***mutual security,*** proclaiming that a diminution of the national security of one's adversary reduces one's own security. Soviet spokesperson Georgy Arbatov went as far as to tell the United States that "we are going to do a terrible thing to you—we are going to deprive you of an enemy."

Gorbachev acknowledged that the Soviet Union could no longer afford both guns and butter. To reduce the financial burdens of defense and the dangers of an arms race, he offered unprecedented unilateral arms reductions. "We understand," Gorbachev lamented, "that the arms race . . . serves objectives whose essence is to exhaust the Soviet Union economically." He then went even further, proclaiming his desire to end the Cold War altogether. "We realize that we are divided by profound historical, ideological, socioeconomic, and cultural differences," Gorbachev noted during his first visit to the United States in 1987. "But the wisdom of politics today lies in not using those differences as a pretext for confrontation, enmity, and the arms race."

Meanwhile, the Reagan administration began to moderate its hard-line posture toward the new Soviet regime. Reagan himself would eventually call Gorbachev "my friend." Arms control was a centerpiece of the new partnership. In 1987 the United States and the Soviet Union agreed to eliminate an entire class of weapons (intermediate-range nuclear missiles) from Europe. Building on this momentum and fueled by high-level summitry, Reagan and Gorbachev agreed to a new START treaty (Strategic Arms Reduction Treaty) that called for deep cuts in the strategic nuclear arms arsenals of the two sides. That treaty has since gone through two additional iterations that call for even more cuts in the world's most lethal weapons, although final approval has been stalled in the Russian parliament.

The premises underlying containment appeared increasingly irrelevant in the context of these promising pronouncements and opportunities. As

Strobe Talbott (1990), later deputy secretary of state in the Clinton administration, put it, "Gorbachev's initiatives...made containment sound like such an anachronism that the need to move beyond it is self-evident." Still, the premises of the past continued to exert a powerful grip. Fears that Gorbachev's reforms might fail, that Gorbachev himself was an evil genius conning the West, or that his promises could not be trusted were uppermost in the minds of Ronald Reagan and, later, George H. W. Bush. "The Soviet Union," Bush warned in May 1989, had "promised a more cooperative relationship before—only to reverse course and return to militarism." Thus, although claiming in May 1989 its desire to move "beyond containment," the Bush administration did not abandon containment. Instead, it resurrected the linkage strategy.

Surprisingly, demands of linkage were soon met. Soviet troops were withdrawn from Afghanistan in 1989. A year later the United States sought and received Soviet support for Operation Desert Shield. Gorbachev then announced that the Soviet Union would terminate its aid to and presence in Cuba, and he promised that it would liberalize its emigration policies and allow greater political and religious freedom.

The normalization of Soviet-American relations now moved apace.[9] The Cold War, which had begun in Europe and centered there for forty-five years, ended there. All the communist governments in the Soviet "bloc" in Eastern Europe permitted democratic elections, in which Communist party candidates routinely lost. Capitalist free market principles also replaced socialism. To the surprise of nearly everyone, the Soviet Union acquiesced in these revolutionary changes. Without resistance, the Berlin Wall came tumbling down. Before long the Germanys would be united and the Warsaw Pact dismantled. As these seismic changes shook the world, the Soviet Union itself sped its reforms to promote democracy and a market economy, and eagerly sought cooperation with and economic assistance from the West.

The failed conservative coup against Gorbachev in August 1991 put the final nail in the coffin of Communist Party control in Moscow, the very heartland of the international communist movement. By that Christmas, the Soviet Union had ceased to exist, replaced instead by Russia and fourteen newly independent states (including Ukraine, Belarus, Kazakhstan, Georgia, and others). With communism now in retreat everywhere, the face of world politics was transformed irrevocably, setting the stage for a postcontainment American foreign policy.

The End of the Cold War: Competing Hypotheses   With the end of the Cold War, the proposition that George Kennan advanced in his famous 1947 "X" article appeared prophetic. "The United States has it in its power," he wrote, "to increase enormously the strains under which Soviet policy must operate, to force upon the Kremlin a far greater degree of moderation and circumspection than it has had to observe in recent years, and in this way to promote tendencies which must eventually find their outlet in either the break-up of or the gradual mellowing of Soviet power." That was precisely what *did* happen—over forty years later.

Left unsettled, however, were the causes of this "victory" over communism. Did militant containment force the Soviet Union into submission? If so, nuclear weapons played a critical role in producing what historian John Lewis Gaddis (1986) has called "the long peace." The drive to produce them also may have helped to bankrupt the Soviet planned economy. In particular, the Reagan administration's anti-ballistic-missile "Star Wars" program—officially known as the Strategic Defense Initiative (SDI)—arguably convinced Gorbachev and his advisers that they could not compete with the United States (Fitzgerald 2000). From this perspective, power played a key role in causing the end of the Cold War. People on the conservative side of the political spectrum in the United States were quick to embrace this view, thus crediting Ronald Reagan and his policies with having "won" the Cold War.

Others, particularly on the liberal side of the spectrum, placed greater emphasis elsewhere. They saw Soviet leaders succumbing to the inherent political and economic weaknesses of their own system, which left them unable to conduct an imperial policy abroad or retain communist control at home. This is much like the demise of Soviet power Kennan envisioned decades earlier. Recall that Soviet leaders were convinced they were the vanguard of a socialist-communist movement that would ultimately prevail over the West. This provided the ideological framework within which the geostrategic conflict with the United States took place. Only when Soviet leaders themselves repudiated this framework—as Gorbachev did—was it possible to end the Cold War. From this perspective,

> the West did not . . . win the Cold War through geopolitical containment and military deterrence. Still less was the Cold War won by the Reagan military buildup and the Reagan doctrine. . . . Instead, "victory" came when a new generation of Soviet leaders realized how badly their system at home and their policies abroad had failed. What containment did do was to preclude any temptations on the part of Moscow to advance Soviet hegemony by military means. . . . Because the Cold War rested on Marxist-Leninist assumptions of inevitable world conflict, only a Soviet leader could have ended it. And Gorbachev set out deliberately to do just that.
>
> *(Garthoff 1994, 11–12; see also Mueller 2004–2005; compare Pipes 1995.)*

Just as historians have debated the causes of the Cold War for decades, explaining its demise quickly became a growth industry.[10] The reasons are clear and compelling: if we can learn the causes of the Cold War's rise and demise, we will learn much about the roles of power and principle, about ideals and self-interest, as the United States devises new foreign policy strategies for a new century. Clearly, however, a historical watershed is now behind us— and another has been crossed, now symbolized not by a wall dividing a city, but by aggressive, transboundary terrorists.

IN SEARCH OF A RATIONALE: FROM THE BERLIN WALL TO 9/11 AND BEYOND

The decade preceding 9/11 proved to be a transitional one for American foreign policy. It began with hope and ended in tragedy. A reprioritized American foreign policy agenda followed. At the conclusion of the Persian Gulf War in 1991, President George H. W. Bush proclaimed that "we can see a new world coming into view. . . . In the words of Winston Churchill, a world order in which 'the principles of justice and fair play protect the weak against the strong. . . .' A world where the United Nations—freed from Cold War stalemate—is poised to fulfill the historic vision of its founders. A world in which freedom and respect for human rights find a home among all nations." He also highlighted the necessity of American leadership: "In a world where we are the only remaining superpower, it is the role of the United States to marshal its moral and material resources to promote a democratic peace. It is our responsibility . . . to lead." Thus "Bush anticipated American dominance that would be both legitimate and, to some extent, welcomed by the global community" (Brilmayer 1994). In short, this would be a *new world order.*

Bush's vision punctuated the continuing appeal of Wilsonian idealism. To be sure, power rather than principle was often the overriding element in the Cold War strategy of containment—to the point that principles themselves were sometimes bastardized. Nonetheless, Henry Kissinger, himself an ardent realist, recounts in his book *Diplomacy* how elements of the idealist paradigm shaped the policies of presidents from Franklin Roosevelt to Bill Clinton. He concludes that at the twilight of the twentieth century "Wilsonianism seemed triumphant. . . . For the third time in [the twentieth] century, America . . . proclaimed its intention to build a new world order by applying its domestic values to the world at large" (Kissinger 1994a).

William Jefferson Clinton went to Washington on the strength of his domestic policy program, but his foreign policy agenda was also ambitious. It included "preventing aggression, stopping nuclear proliferation, vigorously promoting human rights and democracy, redressing the humanitarian disasters that normally attend civil wars," virtually the entire "wish-list of contemporary American internationalism" (Hendrickson 1994). Wilsonian idealism was at the core of the agenda.

Clinton's priorities also reflected the view that the end of the Cold War had opened a Pandora's box of new challenges to America's enduring values and interests. Clinton described them in a 1994 address to the United Nations:

> The dangers we face are less stark and more diffuse than those of the Cold War, but they are still formidable—the ethnic conflicts that drive millions from their homes; the despots ready to repress their own people or conquer their neighbors; the proliferation of weapons of mass destruction; the terrorists wielding their deadly arms; the criminal syndicates selling those arms or drugs or infiltrating the very institutions of a fragile democracy; a global economy that offers great promise but also deep insecurity and, in many places, declining opportunity; diseases like AIDS that threaten to decimate nations; the combined dangers of population explosion and economic decline . . . ; [and] global and local environmental threats.

As globalization gained momentum, Clinton told the American Society of Newspaper Editors near the end of his administration that the challenges ahead involved "a great battle between the forces of integration and the forces of disintegration; the forces of globalism versus tribalism; of oppression against empowerment."

Clinton left to George W. Bush, his more conservative successor, a liberal legacy regarding democracy promotion, trade liberalization, stemming the proliferation of weapons of mass destruction, and the promotion of human rights and international values that would help shape the policies of the forty-third president. By the end of his

administration Clinton had also elevated international terrorism to the forefront of his concerns (Clarke 2004). Although he launched a cruise missile attack on Osama bin Laden's terrorist training camps in Afghanistan, his administration apparently missed other opportunities to "eliminate" (i.e., kill) the terrorist threat posed by the Islamic fundamentalist. Following September 11, 2001, transnational terrorism became the defining element of the new administration's foreign policy.

We will discuss below how the Bush and Clinton administrations' foreign policy agendas regarding weapons proliferation, democracy promotion, market economies and free trade, human rights and values, and related issues intersected to promote continuity as well as change in American foreign policy. First, however, we direct our attention to the war on terrorism.

The Bush Doctrine and the War on Terrorism: Uniquely Unilateralist?

As we saw in Chapter 1, three principles define the Bush administration's national security agenda, its grand strategy: preemptive war—striking militarily an adversary who poses an imminent threat before the adversary can strike first; unilateralism—acting by itself rather than in concert with others; and hegemony—a preponderance of power in U.S. hands. All are encapsulated in the ***Bush Doctrine*** of 2002 and profoundly colored the administration's approach to the threat of transnational terrorism.

Before Bush's controversial victory in the 2000 election, Condoleezza Rice, Bush's first-term national security adviser and second-term secretary of state, hinted at a foreign policy approach based squarely on the tenets of realism. According to Rice (2000), the Bush administration would "refocus the United States on the national interest and the pursuit of key priorities." Bush began to flesh out these interests and priories in his first inaugural address, where he also made clear he would protect and promote the enduring values of the United States. "The enemies of liberty and our country should make no mistake," he proclaimed. "America remains engaged in the world by history and by choice, shaping a balance of power that favors freedom. We will defend our allies and our interests. We will show purpose without arrogance. We will meet aggression and bad faith with resolve and strength. And to all nations, we will speak for the values that gave our nation birth." These words and their broad appeal to historical values were echoed after 9/11 in the president's 2002 State of the Union address when he stated that "we have a greater objective than eliminating threats and containing resentment. We must seek a just and peaceful world beyond the war on terror." These statements implied a proactive engagement in world affairs of a different sort than witnessed in previous administrations.

Although Bush promised collaboration with others and "purpose without arrogance," the unilateralist thrust of decisions early in his first term affronted U.S. allies. They included his rejection of U.S. membership in the International Criminal Court; ceasing negotiations on the Kyoto Protocol to the global climate treaty designed to reduce emissions of global warming gases; and abrogation of the 1972 Anti-Ballistic Missile treaty with Russia, paving the way for deployment of a national ballistic missile defense system and massive increases in U.S. defense spending. In each case Bush touted his vision of a "distinctly American internationalism that reflects the union of our values and our national interests." That, in short, meant putting U.S. interests first.

The 9/11 terrorist attacks initially pushed Bush toward the Clinton legacy of multilateralism. "Allies are essential for success in the war on terrorism," observed one policy analyst (Posen 2001/2002). That, he said, explained the determination of the Bush administration "to build a broad coalition [of supporters]." One result is that Russia, China, and Pakistan soon enjoyed warmer relations with the United States than they had in years, as the administration concentrated its policy efforts on the anti-terror campaign. Before long, however, aggressive unilateralism became the characteristic *modus operandi*. It was particularly evident when the United States intervened militarily in Iraq in March 2003, despite the opposition of Germany and France, longtime NATO allies, and Russia and China, newfound post–Cold War friends.

The policies that led from 9/11 to the invasion of Iraq were spelled out in a series of presidential speeches and statements. On September 20, 2001, the president promulgated what initially became known as the Bush Doctrine when he declared before a joint session of Congress that the United States "will pursue nations that provide aid or a safe haven for terrorism." He continued, saying "Every nation, in every region, now has a decision to make. Either you are with us, or you are with the terrorists. . . . [A]ny nation that continues to harbor or support terrorism will be regarded . . . as a hostile regime."

A year later, in his 2002 State of the Union address, Bush introduced Americans to the "axis of evil"—Iraq, Iran and North Korea—and began to lay the groundwork for military action against Iraq. The threat of preemptive action against threats to U.S. security—arguably the basis for the invasion of Iraq—is, as we have seen, a centerpiece of the more widely known and fully formed Bush Doctrine. Bush defended the policy at the West Point commencement exercises in June 2002. A few months later he affirmed the new strategy in his *National Security Strategy of the United States of America*, a quadrennial national security report required by Congress. He declared that threats facing the United States "will require all Americans to be forward-looking and resolute, to be ready for preemptive action when necessary to defend our liberty and to defend our lives." To do this, the president argued, "America has and intends to keep, military strengths beyond challenge"—in short, it would maintain its global hegemony. The *National Security Strategy* defended the preemptive policy this way:

> The United States has long maintained the option of preemptive actions to counter a sufficient threat to our national security. The greater the threat, the greater is the risk of inaction—and the more compelling the case for taking anticipatory action to defend ourselves, even if uncertainty

remains as to the time and place of the enemy's attack. To forestall or prevent such hostile acts by our adversaries, the United States will, if necessary, act preemptively.

The document also emphasized that the United States would act alone, if necessary, when its vital interests were at stake.

Bush's approach to Iraq differed from Afghanistan. There the United States sought to topple the Taliban government, an Islamic fundamentalist regime that had harbored Osama bin Laden, where he trained terrorist followers like those who destroyed the World Trade Center's Twin Towers. The Afghan intervention enjoyed widespread international support. This was not the case in Iraq. Regime change was an often repeated rationale for the war—getting rid of Saddam Hussein, a tyrant of the worst order who also allegedly had ties with Al Qaeda and hence was a key to the war on terrorism. Ridding Iraq of its presumed programs to produce and stockpile of biological, chemical, and nuclear weapons of mass destruction was also a centerpiece of the rationale for war. Neither argument—nor many others used by the administration, as illustrated in Figure 3.2)—carried the day abroad.

In the end, a "coalition of the willing" joined the United States in Iraq. It included several countries from the newly expanded NATO alliance, which now counted most former members of the Warsaw Pact (with the notable exception of Russia) among its ranks. Excluding Britain, however, few members of the coalition made significant contributions to what would become a vicious, urban campaign against Iraqi insurgents. Weapons of mass destruction were never found. Ties to Al Qaeda were never substantiated. Both proved significant when the United States sought, but failed, to win multilateral support for Iraqi reconstruction efforts. With the legitimacy of its actions in Iraq and elsewhere in tatters (Nye 2004; Tucker and Hendrickson 2004), the United States may find it even more difficult to gain international support for a future preemptive project.

The Bush agenda does draw on the themes of defending liberty and the promotion of democracy,

as we elaborate below. Still, many analysts have pointed to the Bush Doctrine as a dramatic departure from the historical patterns of American involvement in world affairs (Dombrowski and Payne 2003; Gaddis 2002; Jervis 2003; compare Gaddis 2004, 2005). Interestingly, although the doctrine does emphasize an assertive promotion and defense of American interests, political realists uncomfortable with its neoconservative thrust are among its strongest detractors (see Jervis 2003; Mearsheimer and Walt 2003).

Homeland Security

In addition to preemptive war and other key elements of the Bush foreign policy, the war on terror embraces a distinctive domestic component. President Bush often said it is preferable to fight the terrorists in Afghanistan, Iraq, and elsewhere than to fight them in the United States. He and others in his administration also repeatedly reminded the country that "America's enemies need to be right only once. Our intelligence and law enforcement professionals . . . must be right every single time." Achieving that measure of security requires a significant antiterrorist campaign at home as well as abroad.

Winning congressional approval of the Uniting and Strengthening America by Providing Appropriate Tools Required to Intercept and Obstruct Terrorism Act of 2001, known as the USA PATRIOT Act, or simply as the Patriot Act, was one of Bush's first post-9/11 moves. Much discussed during the 2004 presidential campaign, the now controversial law greatly expands the ability of the government to monitor the private activities of Americans, including, for example, what books they check out at public libraries or buy at bookstores. Government review of private medical records and e-mail messages is fair game in the name of stopping terrorism, as are "sneak and peek" searches of one's home and property without prior notice. Americans' civil liberties, critics argue, are at risk. Shortly after the 2004 election, Congress passed another law with a provision that further expanded the government's right to engage in domestic surveillance

W ant a reason for war with Iraq? Here are 21. A study by Devon Largio, a recent graduate of the University of Illinois, Urbana-Champaign, reveals that between September 2001 and October 2002, 10 key players in the debate over Iraq presented at least 21 rationales for going to war. Largio examines the public statements of President George W. Bush, Vice President Dick Cheney, Senate Democratic leader Tom Daschle, Sens. Joseph Lieberman and John McCain, Richard Perle (then chairman of the Defense Policy Review Board), Secretary of State Colin Powell, National Security Advisor Condoleezza Rice, Secretary of Defense Donald Rumsfeld, and Deputy Secretary of Defense Paul Wolfowitz.

The table below illustrates who deployed each rationale.

To prevent the proliferation of weapons of mass destruction: Bush, Cheney

For regime change: Bush, Cheney, Daschle, Lieberman, McCain

To further the war on terror: Bush, Cheney, Daschle, Lieberman, McCain, Perle, Powell, Rice

Because of Iraq's violations or U.N. resolutions: Bush, Cheney, Lieberman, McCain, Perle, Powell, Rice, Rumsfeld, Wolfowitz

Because of Saddam Hussein's evil dictatorship and actions: Bush, Cheney, Lieberman, McCain, Perle, Powell, Rice, Rumsfeld, Wolfowitz

Because of a lack of weapons inspections in Iraq: Bush, Lieberman, Perle, Powell, Rice, Rumsfeld, Wolfowitz

To liberate Iraq: Bush, McCain, Powell, Rice, Wolfowitz

Because of Iraq's links to al Qaeda: Bush, Cheney, Lieberman, Perle, Rice, Rumsfeld, Wolfowitz

Because Iraq was an imminent threat: Bush, Perle, Perle, Rice, Rumsfeld

To disarm Iraq: Bush, Perle, Powell, Rumsfeld, Wolfowitz

To conclude the Gulf War of 1991: Lieberman, McCain, Perle, Rice, Rumsfeld

Because Hussein was a threat to the region: Bush, Cheney, Powell, Powell

For the safety of the world: Bush, Daschle, Powell, Rumsfeld

To support the United Nations: Bush, Powell, Rice

Because the United States could (easy victory): Perle, Rumsfeld

To preserve peace around the world: Bush

Because Iraq was a unique threat: Rumsfeld

To transform the region: Perle

As a warning to other terrorist nations: Perle

Because Hussein hates the United States and will act against it: Lieberman

Because history calls the United States to action: Bush

CHART BY JARED SCHNEIDMAN FOR *FP*

F I G U R E 3.2 21 Rationales for War

NOTE: This list does not cover all statements made by this group of officials during this period or after October 2002.

SOURCE: "Rationales for War," *Foreign Policy* 144 (September/October, 2004), p. 18.

of Americans' activities. The provision was part of a sweeping reorganization of the foreign intelligence community consisting of the Central Intelligence Agency (CIA) and more than a dozen other civilian and military organizations, such as the Defense Department's National Reconnaissance Office (NRO), responsible for intelligence collection using space-based satellites.

The intelligence reorganization law with its domestic "spying" provisions grew directly from 9/11. Several inquiries were launched soon after the terrorist attacks that asked what caused the evident breakdown of security leading to the events of that fateful day. Most visible among them was the 9/11 Commission appointed by Congress and the president. Its findings shaped the national debate about what went wrong and what to do in the future. Almost unanimously the inquiries concluded that a breakdown in intelligence efforts abroad and counterintelligence efforts at home were at fault. The conclusions and recommendations were not unlike studies of Pearl Harbor following World War II. They, too, revealed that information about the impending Japanese attack was available but scattered throughout the government and hence, for all practical purposes, useless. Creation of the CIA in 1947—whose purpose was centralization of foreign intelligence in one place—was the response. The Intelligence Reform and Terrorism Prevention Act of 2004 continues the trend toward centralization. The law creates a director of national intelligence who is given broad authority over intelligence budgets, personnel, and missions, and who reports directly to the president.

The Department of Homeland Security (DHS) is another government reorganization project flowing directly from 9/11. Like the CIA, centralization was the theme, but this time it focused on bringing together domestic counterintelligence and law enforcement information about potential terrorists and otherwise protecting the security of the territorial United States. A product of congressional initiatives, the department groups under a single bureaucratic roof a broad range of agencies responsible for policies related to emergency management, immigration, travel and transportation security, and threat protection, among others. Its charge includes continuation of priorities the Clinton administration attached to new challenges to U.S. security, such as cyberterrorism. Worms, viruses, and other evidence of the work of computer hackers are familiar to any computer user. The havoc they could wreak on the country's security, energy, transportation, and other sophisticated computer-driven systems is unimaginable. Assuring homeland security is thus a daunting task. If the United States must be certain all of the time, but terrorists must be right only once in ten tries, total security from a terrorist attack is an impossible goal. Indeed, serious terrorist experts do not expect it. The question is not whether terrorists will again strike the homeland. It is where, when, and how.

Homeland security figured prominently in the 2004 presidential contest. Bush's challenger, Democrat Senator John Kerry of Massachusetts, directed particular attention to the dangers posed by the thousands of unchecked, unmonitored cargo containers that daily enter U.S. ports of entry carrying foreign-produced goods to the U.S. market. Protecting the United States from the potential threat posed to U.S. ports and commercial traffic generally, and the possible surreptitious entry of weapons of mass destruction, is a daunting task, but, as Kerry charged, it is also a matter of priorities. Analyst Stephen Flynn (2004b, 22–23) described during the campaign season what he sees as "the neglected home front": "Although the CIA has concluded that the most likely way weapons of mass destruction (WMD) would enter the United States is by sea, the federal government is spending more every three days to finance the war in Iraq than it has provided over the past three years to prop up the security of all 361 U.S. commercial seaports." Flynn, like others, worries that terrorists could use cargo containers as Trojan horses to smuggle weapons of mass destruction into the country or in other ways to interrupt the import supply chain for lethal purposes. And containerized cargo is only one of many vulnerabilities the United States faces (see Flynn 2004a). The question remains, then: When, where, and how will terrorists strike again?

Countering the Proliferation
of Weapons of Mass Destruction

Combating the spread of weapons of mass destruction (WMD) was a central theme in the prelude to the war against Iraq, as we have noted. Likewise it was a central feature of the Bush administration's national security posture and its doctrine of anticipatory military action.

Counterproliferation, a concept that implies the United States itself will act as the sole global arbiter and destroyer of weapons of mass destruction, is a long-standing goal of American foreign policy. In fact, how to stop the global spread of WMD, particularly nuclear weapons, is an issue as old as "the bomb" itself. In 1946, the Truman administration devised a plan that would have placed the development of raw materials and facilities for production of atomic energy under the control of an international body. The plan fell victim to the emerging Cold War conflict with the Soviet Union.

Two decades later, in 1968, the United States and more than a hundred other countries signed the *Nuclear Non-Proliferation Treaty (NPT).* It remains in force today. Policed by the International Atomic Energy Agency (IAEA), the NPT declares that nuclear states will transfer to non-nuclear states nuclear know-how for peaceful purposes in return for the promise that that knowledge will not be used to make nuclear weapons. The new wrinkle in this long-standing global issue is the threat posed by nuclear weapons in the hands of terrorists or rogue states. As stated in the Bush administration's *National Security Strategy,* "Rogue states and terrorists do not seek to attack us using conventional means. They know such attacks would fail. Instead, they rely on acts of terror and, potentially, the use of weapons of mass destruction—weapons that can be easily concealed, delivered covertly, and used without warning."

Currently eight countries—China, France, India, Israel, Pakistan, Russia, the United Kingdom, and the United States—are widely regarded as nuclear powers (see Focus 3.4). But the list could quickly expand. Harvard University security expert Graham Allison cogently frames the issue: "In addition [to the eight now known to have nuclear weapons], the CIA estimates that North Korea has enough plutonium for one or two nuclear weapons. And two dozen additional states possess research reactors with enough highly enriched uranium (HEU) to build at least one nuclear bomb on their own. According to best estimates, the global nuclear inventory includes more than 30,000 nuclear weapons, and enough HEU for 240,000 more" (Allison 2004a, 65–66). The vast majority of weapons are in the control of the United States and Russia.

Pakistani nuclear scientist A. Q. Khan, who began his career in the Netherlands, recently highlighted the immediacy of the nuclear threat all too clearly. Architect of Pakistan's nuclear weapons capability, which is designed to counter India's, Khan is now regarded as a Pakistani national hero. For decades he ran a rogue nuclear network apparently used to pass atomic secrets to more than a dozen countries. He visited still others with perhaps ulterior motives. The list is formidable. According to the *New York Times* (December 26, 2004, A1, 12), it included Turkey, Syria, Spain, Saudi Arabia, Egypt, Malaysia, South Africa, Iran, North Korea, Libya, Malaysia, and Dubai (a major transportation node in the nuclear network), among others. Many are Islamic countries where anti-Americanism runs high.

Khan reportedly obtained the blueprint for a bomb from China and shared it with Libya. Others—particularly Iran—may also have received what a Bush administration official characterized as "a nuclear starter kit—everything from centrifuge designs to raw uranium fuel to the blueprints for the bomb." Whether Pakistan's military was a party to the rogue black market remains uncertain.

For years Pakistan's military sought to build a nuclear weapon and a missile delivery system to counter India's nuclear program. This soured U.S.-Pakistani relations. The United States imposed sanctions on Pakistan and in other ways tried to derail Pakistan's aspirations and efforts. In the end its policies failed.

While other states that once pursued the nuclear option, such as Argentina, Brazil, South Africa,

F O C U S 3.4   Nuclear Weapons: Who has What?

Nuclear-Weapon States
The following states are parties to the Nuclear Non-Proliferation Treaty and are recognized as nuclear-weapon states by that international agreement.

China	More than 100 warheads
France	Approximately 350 strategic warheads
Russia	4,978 strategic warheads, approximately 3,500 operational tactical warheads, and more than 11,000 stockpiled strategic and tactical warheads
United Kingdom	Less than 200 strategic warheads
United States	5,968 strategic warheads, more than approximately 1,000 operational tactical weapons, and approximately 3,000 reserve strategic and tactical nuclear weapons

De facto Nuclear-Weapon States
The following states have never signed the Nuclear Non-Proliferation Treaty, but possess nuclear weapons. They are not recognized as nuclear weapon states under the treaty.

India:	45 to 95 nuclear warheads
Israel:	Between 75 and 200 nuclear warheads
Pakistan	30 to 50 nuclear warheads

The following state withdrew from the Nuclear Non-Proliferation Treaty in 2003.

North Korea	One to two nuclear weapons, according to CIA estimates and possesses enough spent

nuclear fuel that could be reprocessed into fissile material for as many as six nuclear weapons.

States of Immediate Proliferation Concern:

Iran	No known nuclear weapons or sufficient fissile material stockpiled to build weapons. However, it has undertaken covert nuclear activities to establish the capacity to indigenously produce fissile material. Iran is a signatory of the Nuclear Non-Proliferation Treaty.

States Who Returned Nuclear Weapons to Russia after the Soviet Union's Collapse

Belarus

Kazakhstan

Ukraine

States Who Have Abandoned Nuclear Weapon Programs

Argentina

Brazil

Iraq

Libya

South Korea

Taiwan

SOURCE: Adapted from Arms Control Association, *Fact Sheet: Nuclear Weapons: Who Has What at a Glance*, April 2005, www.armscontrol.org/factsheets/Nuclearweaponswhohaswhat.asp, Accessed December 22, 2006.

and Libya, abandoned their ambitions, India and Pakistan pushed forward. Both refused to sign the NPT, and their own rivalry combined with India's fear of China propelled their nuclear programs forward. India first tested a nuclear device in 1974. By the mid-1980s it was clear that Pakistan also enjoyed a nuclear capability built through largely clandestine means. Then, in May 1998, both carried out a series of underground nuclear tests, shocking the world with their "in-your-face" defiance of prevailing global sentiments and the long-standing global testing moratorium. The United States continued to seek to punish Pakistan for its "misbehavior." But 9/11 ended all pretense that the United States would distance itself from Pakistan. Instead the Bush administration embraced Pakistan's military government, headed by General Pervez Musharraf, as a strategic partner in the war against terrorism. (As shown in Map 3.2, Pakistan borders Afghanistan and Iran.) In turn, as intelligence on the expansiveness of A. Q. Khan's nuclear black market network developed, the Bush administration did nothing. Meanwhile, the Musharraf government exonerated Khan of any wrongdoing and refused to let American intelligence officials speak with him directly. Jack Pritchard, a former Clinton administration official who later worked as a State Department envoy to North Korea under Bush, reacted to the dramatic developments this way: "It is an unbelievable story, how this [Bush] administration has given Pakistan a pass on the single worst case of proliferation in the past half century.... We've given them a pass because of Musharraf's agreement to fight terrorism" (quoted in the *New York Times*, December 26, 2004, p. A12).

North Korea and Iran are particularly troublesome proliferation threats. Although among the original "axis of evil" states identified by George W. Bush in early 2002, by the end of his first term the president had backed off the notion that "regime change" or other measures used against Iraq could deal with the nuclear rogues. But for how long?

Iran has an acknowledged nuclear program that has long been suspected of receiving equipment and other assistance from Russia, China, North Korea—and now Pakistan's Dr. Khan. It insists its nuclear program is designed for peaceful purposes only but has refused to cease production of weapons-grade materials. Furthermore, in late 2004 reports surfaced that Iran was seeking to adapt its existing missile system to carry a nuclear weapon. Iranian missiles have ranges capable of reaching anywhere in the Middle East, including Israel. The missile threat added new fuel to the international debate on proliferation issues. Intense pressure by the IAEA and several European states nonetheless failed to convince Iran to abandon its nuclear efforts. The United States, meanwhile, often found itself at loggerheads with both the international watchdog agency and its European allies. The threat of punitive sanctions or aggressive military action against the Persian state loomed large as the Bush administration entered its second term, causing concern among analysts that Iran could be the next U.S. Iraq.

Like Iran, North Korea is a signatory of the NPT. But monitoring the development of this closed society's nuclear program has been difficult because it is a ground-up operation, much like that leading to the atomic bomb the United States used against Japan in August 1945. South Korean defense officials estimated in October 2006 that North Korea possessed enough plutonium to manufacture seven nuclear bombs (*Boston Globe*, 26 October 2006, www.boston.com). North Korea also has a vigorous missile development program and is believed to have missiles capable of hitting Japan and perhaps the Aleutian Islands in Alaska.

North Korea's drive to obtain the bomb boldly challenged Clinton's priorities. The administration first adopted a bellicose posture toward the communist regime but eventually struck a bargain with North Korea that would provide it with proliferation-resistant nuclear reactors for energy production (and copious amounts of oil) in return for its promise to dismantle its nuclear weapons program. North Korea broke the agreement, posing continuing problems for the Bush administration. Although recurrent crises over the past decade have ended short of war, North Korea's nuclear ambitions came to a head in January 2003 when it withdrew from the NPT and again in October 2006 when it became the eighth country in history to test

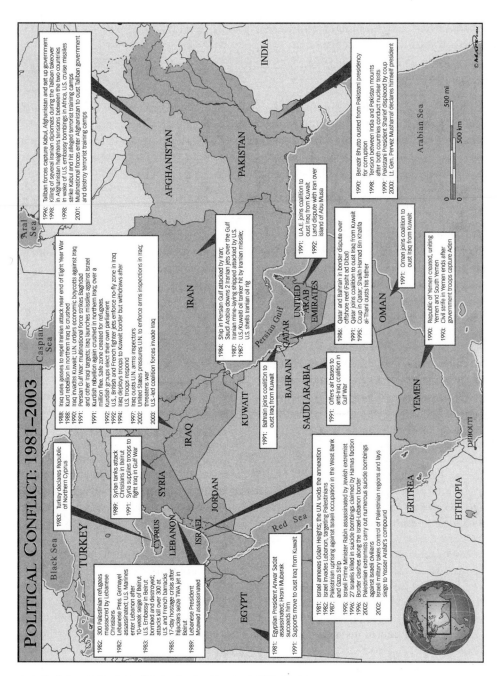

MAP 3.2 Political Conflict in the Middle East 1981–2003.

SOURCE: Used by permission of Maps.com.

a nuclear device. Bush administration efforts to deter the North Korean program centered on six-party talks among the United States, North Korea, South Korea, China, Russia, and Japan. Those talks began August 2003, but stalled in 2005. Although North Korea expressed interested in continuing the talks in 2006, its nuclear test placed their future in doubt. Even if the meetings were reestablished, it is questionable whether they would produce meaningful results. Earlier sessions illustrated that little consensus exists among the parties as to the tactics that might induce North Korea to disarm.

Although unsuccessful with North Korea, the Clinton administration did notch some victories on the nonproliferation front. In 1995, 175 countries agreed to extend the NPT indefinitely. Additionally, in 1997, the administration gained ratification of the _**Chemical Weapons Convention (CWC)**_ in the Senate, which ensured that the United States would join over 160 countries in banning the development, production, acquisition, transfer, stockpiling, and use of chemical weapons. "The United States is now destroying the 30,000 tons of chemical weapons and agents it accumulated during the Cold War and Russia is destroying its 40,000 tons of chemical weapons. Seven or eight other countries are suspected of having some chemical weapons, but none is know to have a large stockpile" (Cirincione 2005, 1). Furthermore, the United States helped to persuade China to join both of these agreements and the Biological Weapons Convention while curtailing some of its support for nuclear programs in Iran and Pakistan (Berger 2000). "Both the United States and Russia have ended their offensive biological weapons programs; only three other states may now have biological agents in actual weapons" (Cirincione 2005, 1). Clinton was not successful in winning Senate approval for the _**Comprehensive Test Ban Treaty (CTBT)**_, which if approved by the forty-four countries that possess nuclear power and research reactors, would ban all explosive testing of nuclear weapons. At the time of the Senate rejection in October 1999, the treaty had already been approved by a large number of other states.

A major breakthrough in counterproliferation efforts occurred during the first Bush term. In 2003

Libya agreed to turn over to the United States its nuclear gear and plans based on Khan's technology. They revealed a sophisticated nuclear program that went far beyond a mere "starter kit." The result of British intelligence initiatives, Libya agreed to renounce nuclear, chemical, and biological weapons in exchange for the lifting of UN and U.S. economic sanctions leveled against the country due to its complicity in a terrorist attack on Pan Am flight 103 over Lockerbie, Scotland, in 1988, which claimed 259 lives. President Bush signed the order lifting U.S. sanctions against Libya a year later. Shortly thereafter Libyan president Muammar Gaddafi declared that "if we are not recompensed [further for our decision], other countries will not follow our example and dismantle their programs." Whether such a "pay for disarmament" approach will become a model for others has yet to be determined. But it seems unlikely.

The ballistic missiles Pakistan, India, Iran, and North Korea are developing could move their small cache of atomic weapons into launch-ready nuclear arsenals. This, too, is troubling to nonproliferation advocates. In 1987, seven of the world's most advanced suppliers of missile-related technology established the _**Missile Technology Control Regime (MTCR)**_ in an effort to slow the development of missiles capable of delivering weapons of mass destruction. As of late 2004, thirty-four countries formally subscribed to its principles. The MTCR remains an informal, voluntary arrangement, however, and thus is best described as an irritant against further missile development. Still, it has been credited with some success in slowing or stopping several missile programs around the world (_Arms Control Association,_ "Fact Sheet: The Missile Technology Control Regime at a Glance," September 2004).

The Bush administration added another informal group outside the IAEA framework—the Proliferation Security Initiative—whose purpose is to interdict illicit nuclear, biological, and chemical trade through sea or air transportation routes. And in May 2004 it announced the Global Threat Reduction Initiative. It is modeled after the bilateral U.S.-Russian agreement designed to secure the Russian nuclear arsenal. The Global Threat

Reduction Initiative, like the U.S.-Russian program, seeks to collect and secure weapons-grade plutonium and enriched plutonium that might be used in weapons production.

Promoting Democracy

During President Clinton's first term in office, no goal seemed more important than promoting democracy abroad. "In a new era of peril and opportunity," Clinton declared in 1993, "our overriding purpose must be to expand and strengthen the world's community of market-based democracies." The centrality of democracy promotion rested squarely on the belief that democracies are more peaceful than other political systems. That conviction, a bedrock of Wilsonian idealism, enjoys a long heritage going back at least to Immanuel Kant's eighteenth-century treatise *Perpetual Peace*. Democracies are as willing and capable of waging war as others, but scholarly inquiry demonstrates conclusively what Kant argued two centuries ago: democracies do not engage in war with one another. Furthermore, democracies are more likely to use nonviolent forms of conflict resolution than others.[11] Thus Clinton and others in his administration "converted that proposition into a security policy manifesto. Given that democracies do not make war with each other, ... the United States should seek to guarantee its security by promoting democracy abroad" (Carothers 1994a).[12]

The combination of the end of the Cold War, the support of the United States and other democratic states, and the broad appeal of liberal democracy led to a wave of democratic experiments during Clinton's presidency. At one point during the 1990s, more than half of the world's governments would embrace some variety of democratic political procedures. Sustaining the momentum proved difficult, however. Political turmoil and economic setbacks in Russia stalled efforts to build a new democratic state there.[13] Strained relations over issues involving Iran, the Middle East, and the Balkans also dampened U.S. enthusiasm for aiding its former adversary. Russian President Vladimir Putin would make a surprising intervention into the

2004 presidential campaign, saying at an October Central Asian summit that a defeat of President Bush "could lead to the spread of terrorism to other parts of the world." Bush would continue to express friendship toward Putin and applaud their close working relationship. Nonetheless, Putin's continued drift toward authoritarianism was a matter of growing concern to the United States.

Elsewhere during the Clinton era, interventions in Haiti and Bosnia designed to promote democracy quickly confronted the realities of grinding poverty and ethnic animosities that had prevented democracy and civil society in the first place. In the Middle East, the United States faced the uncomfortable fact that its security and economic interests were closely linked to authoritarian states, where democracy promotion might produce instability, not peace. In Africa, a region where democracy promotion activities were often emphasized, the otherwise low priority assigned to the region worked against substantial efforts or expenditures toward realizing the goal of liberal democracy.

Despite earlier setbacks and disappointments, democracy promotion remained a foreign policy priority when George W. Bush first took over the Oval Office. The highest profile applications of the theme came in Afghanistan immediately following 9/11 and later in Iraq. In both cases, however, it was difficult to separate the goals of promoting democracy with those of the war on terror.

In a November 2003 speech, President Bush argued:

> Our commitment to democracy is ...
> [being] tested in the Middle East ... Some
> skeptics of democracy assert that the
> traditions of Islam are inhospitable to the
> representative government. This "cultural
> condescension," as Ronald Reagan termed
> it, has a long history ... [but] more than
> half of all the Muslims in the world live in
> freedom under democratically constituted
> governments. They succeed in democratic
> societies, not in spite of their faith, but
> because of it. A religion that demands
> individual moral accountability, and

encourages the encounter of the individual with God, is fully compatible with the rights and responsibilities of self-government.

(For a powerful critique of this viewpoint, see Ottaway and Carothers 2004; also Hobsbawm 2004.)

Although these words provided a foundation for the pursuit of democracy throughout the world, they also produced tension with American allies and helped to polarize American politics. It is one thing to espouse democracy, but quite another to intervene actively in the affairs of sovereign states. For this and other reasons, the United States had few supporters when it moved into Iraq in 2003 (although it did enjoy multilateral support for its earlier efforts in Afghanistan).

To the Bush administration's credit, some commentators believed that it had chosen its approach to democracy promotion wisely. If one begins from the premise that the chief threats to world order and security come from weak, collapsed, or failed states, then pursuing a policy that promotes nation-building and democracy is a logical policy course to follow (Fukuyama 2004a). Thus, intervening in, and ultimately rebuilding, Afghanistan and Iraq in a democratic image fit closely with the pursuit of American interests in the world. As we know from earlier in the chapter and have been reminded recently (see Kinzer 2003), intervention to promote democracy enjoys a long history, at least at the level of official rhetoric. But as with so many American interventions historically, the primary problem with implementing this approach to democracy promotion is an inability to plan adequately for the post-intervention rebuilding phase (Fukuyama 2004a). In both Afghanistan and Iraq many unexpected developments, including brutal insurgency and rising costs, hampered Bush's plans. Moreover, the moves toward democratic elections in both countries were fraught with charges of fraud and an overarching American presence that at least implied continued American dominance in the post-conflict political era.

Protecting Human Rights and Promoting International Values

The boundaries of the Bush approach to nation-building are illustrated by its lack of attention to the failed state of Sudan. Like its predecessor's (non)-response to the Rwandan genocide in the 1990s, the Bush administration refrained from getting involved in the decades-long Sudanese civil war, even though some estimates put the number of casualties of the fighting at more than two million (Lowry 2004; Naimark 2004). Most recently, the United States refused to intervene in the Darfur region of Sudan, where widespread human rights abuses and genocidal fighting provoked by the Sudanese government and government-backed armed militia broke out in February 2003. Nearly four years later, an estimated 450,000 people had died from disease and violence in Darfur and another 2.5 million people were displaced (*Washington Post*, 11 November 2006, p. A21). Secretary of State Colin Powell and his successor, Condoleezza Rice, helped focus international attention on the violence and abuses in Darfur and urged United Nations involvement in addressing the issue. But without a direct perceived threat to American security, Sudan remained off the Bush administration's intervention priority list.

In the previous administration, protecting human rights and promoting international values was a major policy goal, although it evolved slowly and, as Rwanda illustrates, unevenly. During the 1992 campaign, Bill Clinton criticized President George H. W. Bush for doing too little to stop ethnic conflict in Bosnia, where a systematic pattern of genocide widely described as ethnic cleansing was unfolding. In 1993, however, President Bill Clinton chose not to become involved in the Balkans' roiling ethnic conflict. Not until 1995 did the United States actively seek a settlement of the bloody dispute.

Haunted by the images of Rwanda and Bosnia, Clinton moved more forcefully in support of a military response to civil conflict in the Serbian province of Kosovo in 1999. Together with its NATO partners, the United States launched a sustained military attack on Serbia designed to ensure the autonomy of Kosovo and to stem the tide the bloodletting perpetrated there on ethnic Albanians by Serbian military, paramilitary, and police forces.

Some analysts, drawing on statements President Clinton sounded following NATO's intervention, characterized the rationale underlying the campaign as the **_Clinton Doctrine._**[14] Speaking during the Group of 8 (G-8) summit in Germany in 1999, Clinton remarked that "We may never have a world that is without hatred or tyranny or conflict, but at least instead of ending this century with helpless indignation in the face of it, we instead begin a new century and a new millennium with a hopeful affirmation of human rights and human dignity." Then, speaking before soldiers stationed in Macedonia, Clinton defined in dramatically more assertive terms America's role in enforcing international values:

> People should not be killed, uprooted or destroyed because of their race, their ethnic background or the way they worship God. . . . Never forget if we can do this here [the Balkans], and if we can then say to the people of the world, whether you live in Africa, or Central Europe, or any other place, if somebody comes after innocent civilians and tries to kill them en masse because of their race, their ethnic background or their religion, and it's within our power to stop it, we will stop it.

According to Clinton's National Security Adviser Sandy Berger (2000), such engagement is critical not only in promoting liberal values but also in preserving the ability of the United States to exercise leadership and global hegemony in the twenty-first century (Callahan 2004). We will examine the Clinton Doctrine and other ideas regarding the proper use of force in greater detail in Chapter 4.

As in the case of promoting democracy, promoting international values, especially through military force, may fade with time. Whatever its end purpose, the Kosovo campaign was a "war by committee." Keeping the NATO allies united proved difficult, as a combination of domestic and international concerns within its member countries colored their commitment. In part to maintain cohesion,

military operations were conducted in ways designed to minimize NATO casualties. Still, the war strained NATO to the point that it seemed unlikely to soon engage in another "out of area" exercise to promote international values. In the words of one Italian policy maker, "Obviously, nobody in his right mind would look with relish at the prospect of repeating this experience" (Gellman 1999).

In contrast to Clinton's emphasis on the promotion of international values, particularly as they focused on humanitarian reasons for intervention, the Bush administration took a much more narrow view of international values that focused on the development of democratic institutions and respect for individual freedom in countries around the world. One conservative commentator called this approach a "liberty doctrine," centering on the promotion of individual freedoms abroad. Such an approach emphasizes "first the containment and then the elimination of those forces opposed to liberty, be they individuals, movements, or regimes" (McFaul 2002, 4). This thinking about the potential for a proactive American role in democracy promotion and nation-building was one of the underlying themes of what has since been called the Bush Doctrine.

But even though the rationale for military intervention took on a different tone from that of Clinton's approach in Bosnia and Kosovo, it is interesting to note that the military difficulties confronted by each administration in implementing its policies were similar. In short, the Bush administration had as many difficulties in executing its value promotion policies in both Afghanistan and Iraq as the Clinton team did in its two major interventions. Oddly, the similarities between these two sets of experiences may provide more commentary about the efficacy of military solutions to contemporary foreign policy problems than they provide about the policy guidelines themselves.

Promoting Open Markets

Clinton's 1992 drive for the White House emphasized economics. One of Clinton's most quoted sound bites from that campaign was "It's the economy, stupid," as he tried to paint President George H. W. Bush as out of touch with the economic realities of the average American. Clinton's agenda included domestic economic rejuvenation, enhanced competitiveness in foreign markets, and the promotion of sustainable development in the Global South. Then Undersecretary of the Treasury Lawrence H. Summers highlighted the intersection of Clinton's security and economic priorities when he observed that "the two key pillars of any viable foreign policy are the maintenance of security and the maintenance of prosperity." Meanwhile, the Commerce Department, normally a backwater in the foreign affairs government, brimmed with activity as it sought to return the United States to an era when "the business of America is business." Clinton's foreign economic agenda focused on four general categories of issues.

First, he worked to build an overall "architecture" of rules and institutions through renewal of the General Agreement on Tariffs and Trade (GATT), which included provisions for a new World Trade Organization (WTO), as well as additional efforts toward financial coordination. He also worked toward regional trade arrangements to expand U.S. markets, reduce barriers to trade, and integrate economies through such efforts as the North American Free Trade Agreement (NAFTA) linking the United States, Canada, and Mexico in a free trade zone and initiatives toward free trade zones in the Western Hemisphere and the Pacific Basin. The Clinton administration also focused on bilateral approaches toward specific trade partners, including Japan, Europe, China, and aggressively pursued a Big Emerging Markets (BEM) strategy around the world. In addition to tough negotiating postures toward Japan, and the European Union on salient trade issues, Clinton negotiated an agreement for Permanent Normal Trade Relations (PNTR) with China and that country's accession to the World Trade Organization. In fact, by the time the Clinton administration ended, it could claim some three hundred market-opening agreements with other countries. Finally, the Clinton administration also took steps to improve the infrastructure and policies for U.S. exports and export promotion,

streamlining export assistance and licensing procedures and expanding government efforts to advocate for U.S. exporters overseas.

Clinton's emphasis on shoring up the U.S. position in the world economy arguably produced some of his administration's most notable achievements (Walt 2000). The initiatives also fit well into the tapestry of economic liberalism (the existence or development of market economies) central to Wilsonian ideals. Indeed, the promotion of democratic capitalism almost invariably came coupled with the goal of democratic enlargement (Brinkley 1997). Hence creating market economies was not only good for business, it was also good for peace.

Not surprisingly, the Bush administration also remained committed to open markets and the further expansion of global trade. It continued to support Clinton's decision on China's accession to the WTO. Nonetheless, characteristic of the more aggressive and unilateralist tone of the administration's first-term foreign policy, China was viewed less as a "strategic partner," as during the Clinton administration, and more as a "strategic competitor" to the United States in world markets (Hook 2004). Even so, the United States continued to engage Chinese officials in dialogue about monetary exchange rate issues and opening markets and free trade at such forums as the Asia-Pacific Economic Cooperation (APEC) summit in Chile in 2004 as a way of leading up to the WTO meetings planned for Hong Kong in 2005. As elsewhere, however, China's cooperation in the war on terrorism tended to mute other differences between the United States and the rising Asian power.

In Europe, the Bush administration worked to balance the growing influence of an enlarged European Union by solidifying its relationships with countries in the Western Hemisphere and the Pacific Rim. Along these lines, the Bush administration imposed steel sanctions on the European Union in 2001 for almost two years and was at odds with many countries who saw this as a violation of the spirit, if not the letter, of WTO regulations. To some, the sanctions were a thinly veiled attempt to appeal to swing voting states prior to the 2004 election. In the end, the administration lifted the tariffs in December 2003 and avoided a trade war with the European Union over the issue (Blecker 2004).

On a more positive policy approach, the administration sought to expand its trading relationships with Canada and Mexico under NAFTA, while trying to avoid adopting initiatives such as a common external tariff for NAFTA that might be perceived as threatening American economic sovereignty. What remains unanswered is whether the three countries can continue to move forward economically without becoming more highly integrated politically (Pastor 2004). In addition, the North American trio, led by the United States, has also sought the expansion of NAFTA to include others in the Western Hemisphere and many around the Pacific Rim. Economic ministers from thirty-four countries met in Miami in November 2003 to work out an agreement that would create a Free Trade Area of the Americas by 2005, though few officials viewed that deadline as feasible—and it was not met. Similar discussions aimed at expanding free trade and countering EU expansion were held at the November 2004 APEC summit mentioned above. These included proposed bilateral trading agreements between the United States and Australia, Japan, and Chile and also the possible creation of a Free Trade Area of the Asia-Pacific. This last proposed agreement was wholeheartedly endorsed by the APEC Business Council, a group of business leaders lobbying for expanded free trade access in the region.

In sum, the Bush approach to opening markets aggressively worked to counter perceived economic threats from China and the European Union, while seeking to maintain American economic dominance throughout the Americas and even around the Pacific Rim. Moreover, its distinctly pro-business tone unabashedly focused on promoting exports and investment, even if critics argued that continued free trade expansion would allow further outsourcing of American jobs and the migration of more American businesses to lower cost production sites. Others, however, supported the Bush approach and argued that "outsourcing is less [a problem] of economics than of psychology—people

feel that their jobs are threatened" (Drezner 2004). This more optimistic view sees free trade as "lifting all boats" economically and merely requiring workers to migrate to other productive sources of employment.

PRINCIPLE, POWER, OR PRAGMATISM: SHOULD POWER NOW BE FIRST?

The Clinton administration's last (1999) *National Security Strategy* statement sought to elevate welfare issues to the status of strategic issues. The report states, for example, that "Environmental threats such as climate change...directly threaten the health and well-being of U.S. citizens." It added that "Diseases and health risks can no longer be viewed solely as a domestic concern. With the movement of millions of people per day across international borders and the expansion of international trade, health issues as diverse as importation of dangerous infectious diseases and bioterrorism preparedness profoundly affect our national security." Instead, the reprioritization of the American foreign policy agenda following 9/11 clearly shifted the attention away from the *low politics* of global well-being to the *high politics* of peace and security. Hence none of the issues Clinton championed figured prominently on the Bush administration's first foreign policy agenda.

The United States did initiate a modestly funded program to fight AIDS in Africa, but global climate change, emphasized during the Clinton years, was shunted aside. Instead the Bush administration refused to recognize the widespread international agreement of the scientific community pointing to the impact of human activity on global warming. On this and other issues American national interests and a unilateral pursuit of them now replaced the preferences and multilateralist thrust of the Clinton years.

In a foreign policy speech during a visit to Canada in December 2004, his first since winning reelection, Bush seemed to move away from his first-term unilateralist foreign policy posture to one more sensitive to the concerns of America's traditional allies and friends abroad. He pledged to "foster a wide international consensus" behind three basic goals. Fighting terrorism and promoting democracy were among them. But the first, declared the president, would be "building effective multinational and multilateral institutions supporting effective multilateral actions." The speech was laced with allusions to prior events and issues that continued to reflect the hegemonic, almost defiant posture of Bush's first term. The speech nonetheless seemed to set a more modest course for the second term, a course that became far more certain with Democratic control of both the House and Senate following the midterm elections of November 2006 and the resignation of Secretary of Defense Donald Rumsfeld that same month.

KEY TERMS

bipolar
Bush Doctrine
Carter Doctrine
Chemical Weapons
    Convention (CWC)
Clinton Doctrine
collective security
Comprehensive Test
    Ban Treaty (CTBT)
containment
Counterproliferation
Cuban missile crisis

détente
dollar diplomacy
domino theory
economic liberalism
idealism
isolationism
Kellogg-Briand Pact
Lend-Lease Act
liberal internationalism
liberalism
linkage theory
manifest destiny

Missile Technology
    Control Regime
    (MTCR)
Monroe Doctrine
Munich Conference
mutual security
new world order
Nixon Doctrine
Nuclear Non-
    Proliferation Treaty
    (NPT)
Open Door policy

political realism
Reagan Doctrine
Roosevelt Corollary
Strategic Arms Limitation Talks (SALT)
Truman Doctrine
unilateralism
zero-sum

SUGGESTED READINGS

Brokaw, Tom. *The Greatest Generation.* New York: Random House, 2004.

Bush, George, and Brent Scowcroft. *A World Transformed.* New York: Knopf, 1998.

Fromkin, David. *In the Time of the Americans: FDR, Truman, Eisenhower, Marshall, MacArthur—The Generation that Changed America's Role in the World.* New York: Knopf, 1995.

Gaddis, John Lewis. *Strategies of Containment: A Critical Appraisal of American National Security Policy During the Cold War.* Revised and Expanded Edition. New York: Oxford University Press, 2005.

Garthoff, Raymond L. *The Great Transition: American-Soviet Relations and the End of the Cold War.* Washington, DC: Brookings Institution Press, 1994.

Halberstam, David. *War in a Time of Peace: Bush, Clinton, and the Generals.* New York: Scribners, 2001.

Hendrickson, David C. "In Our Own Image: The Sources of American Conduct in World Affairs," *The National Interest* 50 (Winter 1997–1998): 9–21.

Melanson, Richard A. *American Foreign Policy Since the Vietnam War: The Search for Consensus from Nixon to Clinton.* Armonk, NY: M. E. Sharpe, 2000.

Moens, Alexander. *The Foreign Policy of George W. Bush: Values, Strategy and Loyalty.* Burlington, VT: Ashgate Publishing, 2004.

Mueller, John, "What Was the Cold War About? Evidence from Its Ending," *Political Science Quarterly* 119 (Winter 2004–2005): 609–631.

Smith, Tony. *America's Mission: The United States and the Worldwide Struggle for Democracy in the Twentieth Century.* Princeton: Princeton University Press, 1994.

The United States Commission on National Security 21st Century. *Seeking National Strategy: A Concert for Preserving Security and Promoting Freedom.* Phase II Report on a U.S. National Security Strategy for the 21st Century. Washington, DC: United States Commission on National Security/21st Century, 2000.

Woodward, Bob. *Plan of Attack.* New York: Simon and Schuster, 2004.

NOTES

1. The classic statements of realism as an explicit theory can be found in Carr (1939), Kennan (1954), Morgenthau (1985), Niebuhr (1947), and Thompson (1960). Classical realism today is challenged by "neorealism," or "structural realism." This variant of realism focuses not on humankind's innate lust for power—a central construct in classical realism—but instead on states' drive for security in an anarchical world which causes them to behave in similar ways, resulting in efforts to secure power for survival. In this chapter we build primarily on classical realism as we focus on the contest of ideas about international politics as it has informed American foreign policy. In Chapter 6 we will draw on structural (neo)realism to explain how the external environment now and in the past informs our understanding of American foreign policy. For critical discussions of both classical and structural (neo)realism, see Kegley (1995), Keohane (1986b), Mansbach and Vasquez (1981), Smith (1987), Vasquez (1983), and Waltz (1979).

2. The discussion of the Jefferson and Hamilton models for coping with the challenges the new Americans faced draws on Hunt (1987), especially pages 22–28.

3. "Legalism" is often treated with moral idealism as characteristic of the American worldview (Kennan 1951). Its manifestations are the tendencies of American leaders to justify foreign policy actions by citing legal precedents, to assume that disputes necessarily involve legal principles, to rely on legal reasoning to define the limits of permissible behavior for states, and to seek legal remedies for conflicts. Thus, when confronted with a policy predicament, American policy makers are prone to ask not, "What alternative best serves the national interest?" but instead, "What is the legal thing to do?"

4. Herman M. Schwartz (1994) argues that U.S. international economic policy in the 1920s and 1930s was deadlocked by two domestic economic groups, "nationalists," who were oriented toward the domestic market, and "internationalists," who, while also oriented toward the domestic market, were competitive in the global marketplace. The inability of either group to achieve dominance made U.S. efforts to realize a larger international role "only hesitant and erratic." After World War II the United States shifted its policy toward leadership, in part because the nationalists shifted their own calculation. Policy also shifted, Schwartz argues, because of the emergence of a third small but influential group, "security internationalists." Fervently anticommunist and supporters of expanded military spending, the security internationalists joined other internationalists in favoring an expanded overseas presence, but like the nationalists, they feared strong labor unions at home. "This emerging third group resolved the old prewar deadlock, for now two groups could line up along a common axis of interests against the remaining group."

5. The popular aphorism (coined by Calvin Coolidge) that "the business of America is business" captures the belief that American foreign policy is often dominated by business interests and capitalistic impulses. While that view, typically ascribed to "revisionists" (see, for example, Kolko [1969], Magdoff [1969], and Williams [1972, 1980]), was once popular, others dispute its veracity. Political scientist Ronald Steel (1994), for example, categorically asserts that "It is simply not possible to explain U.S. foreign policy in essentially economic terms. The oscillation between isolation and intervention, the persistent emphasis on morality, the obsession with freedom and democracy, the relentless proselytization cannot be stuffed into an economic straitjacket. American foreign policy may often be naive or hypocritical, but it cannot be confined to a balance sheet." See also Garthoff

(1994). Economic revisionism, which is referred to here, is not to be confused with other revisionist accounts that address the expansionist tendencies of the United States. Economic revisionists see the United States expanding in search of world markets for the surpluses of capitalism, whereas the diplomatic revisionist school sees the creation of an American imperium as the product of the American pursuit of national power or of its quest to impose its political system on others. For discussions of empire as a component of America's efforts to achieve political, not economic, preeminence, see Blachman and Puchala (1991), Hoffmann (1978), Liska (1978), and Lundestad (1990).

6. Realist critics warn of the dangers of a foreign policy rooted in messianic idealism, as moral absolutes rationalize the harshest punishment of international sinners, without limit or restraint, to the detriment of American interests (Kennan 1951). Arthur Schlesinger (1977), an adviser in the Kennedy administration, observes worriedly that "All nations succumb to fantasies of innate superiority. When they act on those fantasies ... they become international menaces."

7. Research on the origins and evolution of the Cold War, always extensive, has grown dramatically in recent years. In addition to Gaddis (1997), examples include Holloway's (1994) *Stalin and the Bomb* and the essays on *The Origins of the Cold War in Europe* in Reynolds (1994). The Spring 1997 issue of *Diplomatic History* is a useful summary of new insights based on recent historiography. Melvyn P. Leffler (1996) reviews several studies and reaches conclusions from them somewhat at variance with those of other scholars. Earlier works include Gaddis (1972), Kolko (1968), Melanson (1983), Schlesinger (1986), Spanier (1988), Ulam (1985), and Yergin (1978).

8. See Bostdorff and Goldzwig (1994) for an analysis of Kennedy's often simultaneous use of idealist and pragmatic rhetoric, with special emphasis on Vietnam.

9. For a lively account of the end of the Cold War that focuses on Bush, Gorbachev, and their advisers, see Beschloss and Talbott (1993).

10. Kegley (1994) provides a useful overview of competing arguments.

11. For useful overviews and a sampling of the extensive scholarly literature on the democratic peace, see Caprioli (1999), Caprioli and Boyer (2001), Chan (1997), Doyle (1986, 1995), Gowa (1999), Owen (1994), Ray (1995), Russett and Oneal (2000), and Spiro (1994).

12. See Hendrickson (1994–1995) for a trenchant critique of democratic promotion and related elements of the Clinton strategy of enlargement.

13. In 1999, British writer John Lloyd, who spent five years in Moscow as bureau chief for *The Financial Times*, wrote an article asking "Who lost Russia?" The phrase is emotionally charged in American politics, as it refers to the "loss of China" in 1949 when communist forces took over the mainland. Not long after that, Senator Joseph McCarthy of Wisconsin launched an anticommunist purge directed at the State Department and others in the foreign affairs government alleged to have been responsible for the "loss." Ironically, the United States today finds itself divided by the same contentious judicial and constitutional challenges it once pursued as it sought to protect itself domestically from communism's challenges to the American way of life. Racial profiling—the identification of people not by what they may have done but by how they look—has become a popular yet controversial approach law enforcement agencies now use to deal with potentially criminal elements in American society. The line separating domestic liberal and conservative values seems to have changed little in the process.

14. *Newsweek* reported in its July 26, 1999, issue that the president had planned to make a speech outlining a "Clinton Doctrine" for humanitarian intervention. The administration delayed the event after analyses of the effectiveness of the air campaign against Kosovo began to be questioned and other elements of the intervention, including in particular the conduct of "war by committee" (referring to the nineteen-member NATO alliance), raised doubts about applicability of the Kosovo experience elsewhere.

4

Instruments of Global Influence:

Military Might and Interventionism

> Military power is an essential part of diplomacy.
> LAWRENCE S. EAGLEBURGER, UNDER SECRETARY OF STATE, 1984

> This will be a campaign unlike any other in history. A campaign
> characterized by shock, by surprise, by flexibility, by the employment of
> precise munitions on a scale never before seen, and by the application of
> overwhelming force.
> U.S. ARMY GENERAL TOMMY FRANKS, 2003

1950

NSC

NSC-68

In April 1950, about a year after the Soviet Union successfully tested an atomic bomb, the **National Security Council (NSC),** a top-level interagency body that advises the president on foreign policy matters, completed a policy review and issued its now-famous, top-secret memorandum known as **NSC-68.** This document set in motion the militarization of American foreign policy and the containment strategy that would persist for decades. A decisive sentence in NSC-68 asserted that "Without superior aggregate military strength, in being and readily mobilizable, a policy of 'containment' . . . is no more than a policy of bluff." NSC-68 also called for a nonmilitary counteroffensive against the Soviet Union, which included covert economic, political, and psychological warfare designed to foment unrest and revolt in Soviet bloc countries. Soon American foreign policy would become highly dependent on a range of powerful—but often controversial—military, paramilitary, and related instruments to pursue fundamental goals. America's domestic priorities also would be shaped by its preference for military might and interventionism, as defense spending would for decades comprise the largest share of discretionary (nonentitlement) federal expenditures.

As the Cold War ended, some analysts, recalling NSC-68 as an example of successful strategic planning that made U.S. "victory" in the Cold War possible, called for a similar planning effort to guide the nation into the twenty-first century. One particularly significant aspect of the needed planning, many argued, was the place military instruments of policy would occupy in the dramatically changing global environment. Despite the Bush administration's grand strategy of preemption, unilateralism, and hegemony, as of yet no such strategic *plan* has emerged in response to the military threats posed by Iran, North Korea, and, more broadly, radical Islam and the global war on terrorism (O'Halloran 2005). Our purpose in this chapter and the next is to examine the instruments of American foreign policy captured in the themes of military might and interventionism. These comprise the means used to achieve the political objectives of foreign policy. They include the threatened use of force, war and other forms of military intervention, propaganda, clandestine operations, military aid, the sale of arms, economic sanctions, and economic assistance. Here, in Chapter 4, our primary concern is the role that the actual and threatened use of military force, conventional and nuclear, have played during the past six decades as instruments of both compellence and deterrence designed to defend homeland security and the survival of the United States and its allies. We will also assess their continuing relevance in a changed and changing world. Since foreign policy refers to the sum of objectives and programs the government uses to cope with its external environment, our attention is on that subset of foreign policy known as ***national security policy***—the weapons and strategies the United States relies on to ensure security and survival in an uncertain, dangerous, and often hostile global environment.

THE COMMON DEFENSE: MILITARY GLOBALISM AND CONVENTIONAL FORCES

The logic of *realpolitik* encourages the practice of coercive behavior abroad. The potential dominance of military thinking on foreign policy planning is one symptom of that instinct. The militarization of American foreign policy following World War II occurred in part because the nation's policy makers routinely defined international political problems in terms of military. Not until they digested the painful Vietnam experience did many Americans begin to understand that military firepower and political influence are not synonymous.

American leaders' rhetoric consistently emphasizes the martial outlook derived from the assumptions of political realism. Indeed, the premises underlying the martial spirit have been reiterated so often that they have become dogma. The unexpectedly rapid diminution of clearly defined threats to the United States and its allies in the Cold War's wake called into question this martial spirit. Adjusting the nation's military capabilities to new challenges, including transnational terrorism, demanded new introspection. Inevitably that means we must understand past patterns of military preparedness and interventionist practices, which both inform and constrain future possibilities. We begin by considering the role of conventional military power in promoting and protecting the nation's interests.

Conventional Military Power during the Cold War

When the United States determined in 1990 to counter Iraq's invasion of Kuwait, it maintained a network of more than four hundred overseas military bases with nearly half a million soldiers and sailors assigned to posts and ships outside the United States itself. They reflected a national commitment to perceived global responsibilities shaped by a nearly half-century commitment to the containment of communism.

The importance of U.S. overseas troop deployments to American security has nowhere been greater than in Western Europe, where the United States maintained thousands of troops since the 1950s as a bulwark against a hostile encroachment by the Soviet Union and its Warsaw Pact allies. Even today thousands remain in Europe as a backstop to the post–Cold War expansion of the NATO alliance. With it, the number of countries the United States is now committed to defend has actually expanded, not contracted.

Early in the Cold War the Eisenhower administration's European conventional military strategy rested on the concept of a ***trip wire:*** in the event of an attack by Warsaw Pact forces against Western Europe, the presence of American troops virtually ensured that some would be killed. In this way the "wire" leading to an American retaliation would be "tripped" because policy makers would find themselves in a situation where they were militarily obligated to respond.

Later, the Kennedy administration's strategy of ***flexible response,*** adopted as the official NATO defense posture in 1967, became the means for credibly coping with conventional war threats. The strategy implied that the United States and its allies possessed the capabilities (and will) to respond to an attack by hostile forces at whatever level might be appropriate, ranging from conventional to nuclear weapons. Indeed, the NATO alliance reserved the right of first use of nuclear weapons if that proved necessary to repel a Soviet attack against the West. ***Theater nuclear forces*** provided the link between U.S. conventional and strategic nuclear forces, thus tying American nuclear capabilities to a regional threat and the defense of its allies. The term itself suggested the possibility of region-wide conflict (as in Europe during World War II) involving ***tactical nuclear weapons*** (weapons designed for the direct support of combat operations) without an escalation to global conflagration involving ***strategic weapons*** (nuclear and other weapons of mass destruction capable of annihilating an adversary).

The strategy of flexible response envisioned increased conventional war capabilities as a substitute for reliance on strategic nuclear weapons to deter Soviet aggression. In 1962 the ability to wage "two and one-half wars" became official policy. The United States would prepare to fight simultaneously a conventional war in Europe with the Soviet Union, an Asian war, and a lesser engagement elsewhere.

Nixon changed the two-and-a-half war strategy to one-and-a-half wars. Conventional and tactical nuclear forces would now meet a major communist attack in *either* Europe or Asia and contend with a lesser contingency elsewhere. The reorientation of military doctrine was part of the reordering of the country's world role envisioned in the ***Nixon Doctrine.*** It called for a lower American profile in the post-Vietnam era and for greater participation by U.S. allies in their own defense. Simultaneously, the United States adopted a ***twin pillars strategy*** toward the Middle East. Designed to protect American interests by building up the political and military stature of both Iran and Saudi Arabia, the plan included the sale of billions of dollars of highly sophisticated U.S. military equipment to both Iran and Saudi Arabia.

Events in Afghanistan (the Soviet invasion) and the Persian Gulf (the Islamic revolution in Iran) during the Carter administration quickly undermined the twin pillars strategy. They also spurred plans already in the works to develop a Rapid Deployment Force (RDF) capable of intervening quickly in world trouble spots. (Now called the U.S. Central Command and a permanent element of the Pentagon command structure, it was responsible for directing Operations Desert Shield [1990], Desert Storm in the Persian Gulf War [1991], and Operation Iraqi Freedom in the Iraq war [2003]. The ***Carter Doctrine,*** enunciated in the president's 1980 State of the Union address, affirmed the determination of the United States to intervene in the Middle East militarily, if necessary, to safeguard American security interests. That, of course, has since happened. ***Extended deterrence***, a strategy that seeks to dissuade an adversary from attacking one's allies, which once focused largely on Europe and Asia, now also brought the Middle East under America's protective umbrella.

The Reagan administration initially adopted a markedly more combative posture toward the Soviet Union than did Carter. It jettisoned the belief that any conventional war with the Soviet Union would be short and settled either by negotiation or escalation to a nuclear confrontation. Instead, military planners now assumed that such a war would be protracted and global in scope, with fighting in numerous locations around the world but without necessarily precipitating a nuclear catastrophe. The aggressive posture fostered the development of new defensive concepts in Europe, such as the *Air-Land Battle,* which anticipated close air force support of army combat maneuvers on the ground—a style of warfare vividly illustrated in the Persian Gulf War and again in the Iraq war. The administration also adopted a more aggressive posture toward conflict situations outside the European core area, notably in Africa, Central America, and Southwest Asia.

On the Soviet side, change also was in the wind. In a speech before the United Nations in 1988, Soviet President Mikhail Gorbachev announced large-scale unilateral reductions in Soviet military forces that went far beyond what Western military planners only a short time earlier had dreamed possible. Before long, renewed negotiations between NATO and the Warsaw Pact on European conventional forces resulted in a treaty that called for eliminating thousands of tanks, artillery pieces, armored personnel carriers, infantry fighting vehicles, and heavy armament combat vehicles. Shortly before that, the superpowers took an unprecedented move when they agreed to dismantle and remove from Europe all of their intermediate-range missiles, their first experiment in disarmament.

On another front, in 1990 the United States and the Soviet Union agreed to stop production and significantly reduce their stockpiles of chemical weapons. Each also pledged further reductions once a multilateral agreement banning chemical weapons was reached. That promise was realized in 1992 with the Chemical Weapons Convention. The agreement (discussed in Chapter 3) came into force in 1997, thus bringing the world's major chemical arsenals under a modicum of international control.

Conventional Military Power for a New Era

In early 1990, the first Bush administration issued a new defense planning document designed to shape the military strategy necessary to cope with threats the United States might face in the next few years. The Bush plan recognized that the security environment in Europe was less threatening due to the revolutionary changes that had occurred in Eastern Europe. Thus it sought to reduce significantly each superpower's armed forces in the "central zone" of Europe. It also laid the groundwork for the 1991 decision to remove tactical nuclear weapons from Europe and Korea and from U.S. warships and submarines. Gorbachev followed Bush's lead, thus further reducing the once awesome levels of conventional military and tactical nuclear power deployed in Europe. However, despite the dramatic changes unfolding in the force postures of the NATO and Warsaw Pact alliances, the planning document anticipated continued Soviet-American rivalry. This led critics to charge that the administration was blind to new, rapidly unfolding opportunities.

As arms reductions in Europe continued, the Persian Gulf War provided the United States with a unique opportunity to test the weapons and strategies that for decades had been designed for, but untested in, Europe. Iraq had been armed with Soviet weapons and schooled in its military thinking. The result for Iraq was disastrous—and humiliating for Soviet military strategy. "Arguably, the Iraqis were inept in exercising Soviet plans with Soviet equipment," observed one analyst, "but many Russians privately [expressed] their dismay at the mismatch and [wondered] how much better they might have fared" (Snow 1998).

The Bush administration moved cautiously in assimilating the lessons of the forty-two-day Persian Gulf War (viewed by many as a precursor to the renewal of the U.S. global policeman role in disrepute since Vietnam) and in adjusting to the collapse of the Soviet Union, which came less than a year after the Gulf victory. In early 1992, news media reported that a working version of the Pentagon's periodic planning document known as the *Defense Policy Guidance* was being developed, whose purpose was to "set the nation's direction for the next century." It laid out the rationale for a *Base Force* of 1.6 million active-duty troops (compared with 2.1 million at the time and 1.4 million in recent years). The *Defense Policy Guidance* document also asserted that the United States should prevent the emergence of a rival superpower by maintaining military dominance capable of "deterring potential competitors from even aspiring to a larger regional or global role" (Gellman 1992b); see also Gellman (1992a). Written by then Secretary of Defense Dick Cheney and Under Secretary for Policy Paul Wolfowitz, the controversial document defined the basic architecture of the neoconservative defense posture of the second Bush presidency, including its grand strategy based on preemption, unilateralism, and hegemonism.

The Base Force proposal became the first Bush administration's military blueprint for the post–Cold War era. The United States would now prepare for more military contingencies, not fewer. Colin Powell, chairman of the Joint Chiefs of Staff, defended the new plan. "The central idea in the [new national military] strategy is the change from a focus on global war-fighting to a focus on regional contingencies," he wrote in *Foreign Affairs*. "When we were confronted by an all-defining, single, overwhelming threat—the Soviet Union—we could focus on that threat as the yardstick in our strategy, tactics, weapons, and budget . . . . [Now] we must concentrate on the capabilities of our armed forces to meet a host of threats and not a single threat" (Powell 1992–1993).

The Clinton administration's defense plans were based for the most part on Bush's Base Force plan. In particular, the focus on regional conflicts remained. U.S. forces would be called upon to carry out a *two-war strategy* in which they would be able to fight two major regional conflicts (MRCs) on the scale of the Persian Gulf War nearly simultaneously. Thus the administration emphasized that highly trained and well-equipped forces should be retained to meet regional contingencies rapidly and without prior warning. It also anticipated that American forces would have to be prepared to fight in these conflicts without major support from U.S. allies.

In 1997, the Pentagon released its *Quadrennial Defense Review*, a major report mandated by Congress to assess periodically the nation's future military strategy, force structure, and the resources necessary to support them. The review anticipated five future dangers to the United States: (1) regional challenges, including attacks on friendly nations, ethnic conflict, religious wars, and state sponsored terrorism; (2) weapons of mass destruction, including Russian nuclear arms and the global proliferation of biological, chemical, and nuclear weapons; (3) transnational dangers, such as terrorism, drug trafficking, organized crime, and uncontrolled migration; (4) asymmetric attacks, including terrorism, information warfare, the use of unconventional weapons, and environmental sabotage; and (5) "wild card" scenarios, such as a new technological threat or the takeover of a friendly nation by anti-American factions (Cohen 1997). The two-MRCs concept remained a central element in the defense review, even as it called for a further streamlining of U.S. military forces to levels fully one-third less than during the Cold War. Before long critics would argue that the decisions made during the 1990s constrained the ability of the United States to prosecute vigorously the war in Iraq while simultaneously maintaining U.S. commitments elsewhere throughout the world. "Citizen soldiers"—members of the reserve and National Guard—were now called on to play a much larger combat role than in previous conflicts.

In late 2001, George W. Bush's Defense Department completed its first *Quadrennial Defense Review*. Led by Secretary of Defense Donald Rumsfeld, the review sought a more fundamental transformation of American military forces in the face of an environment characterized by a greater degree of uncertainty about the origins of security threats. It thus sought to shift U.S. national security planning from a "threat-based" to a "capabilities-based" model. Such planning would focus on how potential adversaries might act, rather than on the potential adversary or regional threat scenario. Capabilities-based planning would therefore stress the resources and capabilities necessary to counter or preempt such actions. High among the list of such potential threats, even before 9/11, were "asymmetric threats" such as terrorism, biological, chemical, and nuclear attacks, and cyberattacks. Long term, as President Bush outlined at a speech at Annapolis in May 2005, the goal the military transformation sought was to make U.S. forces "faster, lighter, more agile, and more lethal," and thus better positioned to counter new and emerging threats. Rumsfeld jettisoned the two-MRC planning concept that sought to ready the military to fight two major wars simultaneously. Instead, the armed forces embraced a **win–hold–win strategy.** That is, the United States would be prepared to fight and "win decisively" a single major conflict in one theater while it conducted a defensive holding operation against another opponent in a second theater. Once it defeated the first opponent, it would shift its attention and resources to win decisively in the second theater.

Building U.S. transformational capabilities also requires repositioning bases from overseas and placing a greater emphasis on those in the United States. Simultaneously, new bases were built abroad. Many were in former communist countries, including republics of the former Soviet Union. The goal was to redeploy U.S. forces nearer to the conflict-prone Middle East, but it opened the United States to criticism for promoting democratic values abroad at the same time it maintained troops in nondemocratic states. Those who defend the practice argue that "the strategic benefits of having U.S. bases close to important theaters such as Afghanistan outweigh the political costs of supporting unsavory host regimes." Some also argue that "a U.S. military presence in repressive countries gives Washington additional leverage to press them to liberalize" (Cooley 2005).

Rumsfeld's reform efforts were guided in part by earlier reports from the Joint Chiefs of Staff (*Joint Vision 2010*, and *Joint Vision 2020*) designed to improve the integration of the country's armed forces and to realize a fundamental transformation in warfare referred to among military planners as a revolution in military affairs. Pentagon planners have been receptive to the emerging vision in part because they see it as a way to cope with limited resources and to reduce the number of combatant and noncombatant lives lost in future wars, a matter of considerable political sensitivity.

A **revolution in military affairs (RMA)** can be defined as "a rapid and radical increase in the effectiveness of military units that alters the nature of warfare and changes the strategic environment."

The RMA currently sweeping the U.S. military draws heavily on information technologies developed in the private sector, leading to continued advances in weapons, computer, and intelligence technology that will afford it "increased stealth, mobility, and dispersion, and a higher tempo of operations, all under the shield of information superiority" (Metz 1997); see also Cohen (1996) and Nye and Owens (1996). All have been widely evident in the Iraq war even as media attention to the insurgency and grueling urban fighting eclipsed much of the high-tech warfare.

The world first caught a glimpse of the changing nature of warfare stimulated by technological advances in the 1991 Persian Gulf War, when, following a massive bombing campaign, Iraq's army, believed to have been the fourth largest in the world, was routed in only 100 hours of combat. Particularly impressive was the far greater accuracy of precision-guided munitions, or "smart" bombs, fired by stealthy F-117A fighters compared with older-design aircraft using unguided bombs.

The effectiveness of NATO's air campaign against Serbia involving its province of Kosovo eight years later was even more striking. According the U.S. Air Force, NATO aircraft flew more than 38,000 sorties and dropped some 27,000 bombs, many guided to their targets by lasers and satellites after being launched from aircraft and ships hundreds of miles away. Remarkably, NATO did not suffer a single casualty in the seventy-eight-day bombardment. Some civilian casualties were sustained due to "collateral damage" or by errant bombs (including China's embassy), but in the annals of modern warfare, their numbers were small indeed.

Operations against Afghanistan in October 2001 further revealed the potential for RMA-driven warfare. RMA expert Eliot Cohen asserted that "this war is going to give you the revolution in military affairs" (Ricks 2001b)—and, indeed, it revealed remarkable advances beyond what was first revealed in the Persian Gulf War. Not only did U.S. forces rely almost exclusively on precision-guided munitions deployed by most of its attack aircraft and by strategic bombers based in the United States, but other new technologies were also used. Unmanned drones, for example, provided battlefield video to both air and ground forces. Some were outfitted with antitank missiles enabling them to not only survey targets for others, but also to fire at the emerging targets. Information used to guide ground operations was gathered on the ground, in the air, and from space. The mobility, range, and firepower of U.S. forces represented a qualitative shift from past military operations, including the Persian Gulf War only ten years earlier. At the same time, some low-tech options were also exploited. In one early battle, American and anti-Taliban Afghan forces mounted horseback to launch a cavalry attack replete with sophisticated shoulder-fired, precision guided weapons.

Despite Pentagon enthusiasm for the RMA and the battlefield successes to which it has contributed, the defense community continues to debate its value. Some analysts worry about its relationship to traditional modes of warfare, such as the use of ground forces (Betts 1996; O'Hanlon 1998–1999; Orme 1997–1998; and the discussion and essays on the RMA in Zelikow 2001). Others wonder whether the new directions implied in the RMA will lead once more to preparing for the last war, not for unforeseen future challenges. Lieutenant General William Wallace framed the problems the United States faced in Iraq this way: "The enemy we're fighting is a bit different than the one we war-gamed against" (quoted in Dwyer 2003). So while it is clear that a military transformation is underway, its exact character and potential effectiveness in the coming years remains a point of dispute and will certainly continue as a Pentagon work in progress.

As the United States pursues the RMA, some analysts also worry that other states may respond with varying defensive strategies. The more wealthy of the industrial states may pursue RMAs of their own. Others who cannot afford to develop sophisticated information-based weapons may instead choose weapons of mass destruction (WMD)—particularly the so-called NBC weapons (nuclear, biological, and chemical). (Following the Persian Gulf War, an Indian general was asked what he learned about how to deal with the United States militarily. He reputably remarked: "If you have nuclear weapons, use them early and often.") Alternatively, information warfare of the sort now practiced by computer hackers may help level the playing field for others. Furthermore, multiple forms of terrorist attacks on the United States itself, including the possible use of weapons of mass destruction, for which it is ill-prepared, would constitute a third option, one made more pressing by the 9/11 terrorist strikes in New York and Washington, D.C. (Allison 2004b; Betts 1998; Carter, Deutch, and Zelikow 1998). Ironically, then, the pursuit of a high-tech conventional weapons posture may stimulate a new arms race or open an already open society to new forms of unconventional threats.

Simultaneously, the ability to reduce casualties may have important foreign policy consequences for the United States by lowering the bar for choosing the military option to deal with challenges from abroad. As Boston University foreign policy expert Andrew Bacevich observes, "The advent of precision weapons—and the ability to deliver those weapons with minimal risk to U.S. forces—has chipped away at old inhibitions regarding the use of force. The policy elite has become comfortable not simply with the notion of possessing great military power, but of using it" (cited in Ricks 2001c).

Military Force and Political Purposes

The discussions of conventional war planning here and of strategic doctrine later in this chapter show that *deterrence*—a strategy intended to prevent an adversary from using force by convincing it that the costs of such action outweigh potential gains—is a primary purpose of American military might. In addition to deterrence, American forces are also used to change the behavior of others. For instance, "coercive diplomacy employs threats or limited force to persuade an opponent to call off or undo an encroachment—for example, to halt an invasion or give up territory that has been occupied. Coercive diplomacy therefore differs from the strategy of deterrence,... which employs threats to dissuade an opponent from undertaking an action that he has not yet initiated" (Craig and George 1990).

TABLE 4.1 U.S. Coercive Diplomacy Cases, 1990–2001

Case	Specific U.S. Goals
Somalia 1992–94	End starvation and reconstruct the government
Haiti 1994	Install a new government
North Korea 1994	Freeze the nuclear weapons program
Bosnia 1995	Reduce Serbian conquest and end the Bosnian war
China 1996	Demonstrate U.S. resolve and stop China from coercing Taiwan
Iraq 1990–98	Free Kuwait and destroy Iraq's weapons of mass destruction
Kosovo 1999	End Serb repression of Albanian Kosovars
Terrorism 1993, 1998, and 2001	Retaliate against terrorists and force state actors to yield them up

SOURCE: Robert J. Art, "Introduction," *The United States and Coercive Diplomacy.* Washington, DC: United States Institute of Peace Press, 2003, p. 12. Reprinted by permission of United States Institute of Peace.

Coercive diplomacy also differs from the application of brute force against an adversary. Instead it seeks to persuade the opponent to cease his aggression rather than to bludgeon him into stopping. In contrast to the crude use of force to repel the opponent, coercive diplomacy emphasizes the use of threats to demonstrate resolution to protect one's interests and to emphasize the credibility of one's determination to use more force if necessary (Craig and George 1990, 197). In short, coercive diplomacy, in the words of analyst Alexander George, is synonymous with forceful persuasion: "the attempt to get a target—a state, a group (or groups) within a state, or a nonstate actor—to change its objectionable behavior through either the threat to use force or the actual use of limited force" (Art 2003c; citing George 1992).

The long conflict between the United States and Iraq is replete with instances of forceful persuasion intermixed with strategies of containment and deterrence. The massive buildup of U.S. and allied forces following Iraq's invasion of Kuwait in 1990 was initially intended to force Iraq to withdraw from the small state. When coercive diplomacy failed, the coalition, led by the United States, marched in.

Over the next decade the United States engaged in a series of diplomatic and military maneuvers designed to forestall further aggressive behavior by Iraq and force its compliance with United Nations resolutions. In late 1998 the United States and Britain launched Operation Desert Fox, a seventy-hour aerial bombardment designed to punish Saddam Hussein for his refusal to let UN observer teams continue their efforts to root out Iraq's ability to develop weapons of mass destruction. Five years later, with WMD still at issue, the United States abandoned coercive diplomacy in favor of the full application of force.

The practice of coercive diplomacy was widespread during and before the Cold War. Was it successful? The record is not clear. The outcome of the Cuban missile crisis says yes, but the failure of the United States to prevent the Japanese attack on Pearl Harbor counsels otherwise.

Evidence from the immediate post–Cold War decade is also ambiguous. Of eight instances between 1990 and 2001 when the United States used coercive diplomacy in pursuit of its goals (see Table 4.1), it failed more often than not. Based on extensive research by Robert J. Art and his colleagues, Art concludes that forceful persuasion succeeded in only two of the eight cases described in Table 4.1: Haiti and Bosnia. The China case, when the United States sought to influence the outcome of a conflict between mainland China and the island of Taiwan, is

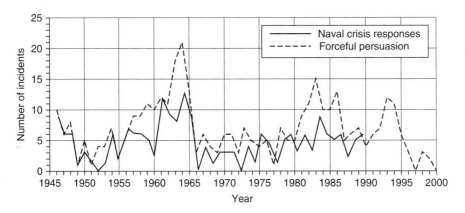

FIGURE 4.1 Force-Short-of-War: The Use of Military Force for Political Purposes, 1946–2000

SOURCE: Data for 1946–1995 from Benjamin O. Fordham, "U.S. Uses of Force, 1870–1995," at http://bingweb.binghamton. edu/~bfordham/data.html; data for 1996–2000 from William Howell (Harvard University) and Jon Pevehouse (University of Wisconsin), provided with compliments of the researchers. The authors thank Professor Fordham for permission to use his data collection.

ambiguous. In the remaining five cases (described in detail in Art and Cronin 2003) the evidence points to failure.[1]

Force-short-of-war is another commonly used application of conventional military force to achieve political objectives. Like deterrence and coercive diplomacy, force-short-of-war is designed to persuade, not to coerce. Compellence, deterrence, or a combination of both may characterize particular instances of the use of force-short-of-war. The objective, however, is the same: to persuade an adversary to change his own political calculations in the face of U.S. military might.

Examples of America's reliance on force-short-of-war as an instrument of influence abound. Following the Soviet invasion of Afghanistan in 1979, the United States augmented its Indian Ocean naval patrols as a signal to the Soviet Union not to extend its invasion westward. In 1983, the United States stationed a carrier task force in the Mediterranean to dissuade Libyan dictator Muammar Qaddafi from launching an attack on Sudan. In the same year, it staged naval maneuvers on both sides of the Honduran isthmus in hopes of intimidating leftist guerrillas active in Central America and deterring Cuba, Nicaragua, and the Soviet Union from supporting them. In 1989, additional U.S. troops were sent to

Panama following General Manuel Noriega's disregard of the results of the Panamanian election, a signal to Noriega that the United States might take further action (it did). In 1994, the United States sent 35,000 troops to the Persian Gulf to deter Saddam Hussein from hostile maneuvers that might have been a prelude to the resumption of warfare over Kuwait. In the years that followed it engaged in numerous shows of force designed to alter Saddam's political calculations. In 1996, a U.S. aircraft carrier battle group steamed into the Taiwan Strait in response to Chinese military exercises near the island state it considers a rogue province, but which the United States is legally bound to support. On these and many other occasions, the use of force-short-of-war was designed for purposes other than protecting the immediate physical security of the nation or its allies. Instead, the purpose was to influence the political calculations and behavior of others.

Figure 4.1 charts the frequency of these displays of force-short-of-war from 1946 to 2000. The data shows that the United States subtly but surely threatened to unleash its military might to influence the decisions of other states roughly 400 times, or about seven times a year since the onset of the Cold War. There has been a marked decline in their frequency beginning in 1996, but this is likely due to changes in reporting rules, not "objective" reality. The 1996–2000 data do not include force-short-of war activities by forces already deployed; those from 1946–1995 do. So the downturn in activity may simply be an artifact of data collection rules, a conclusion supported by the vigorous military activity undertaken during the first four years of the Clinton administration compared with the last. The record of the Bush administration has not yet been researched.

Military Intervention

The maintenance of a high military profile abroad, the practice of military deterrence, coercive diplomacy, and displays of force-short-of-war are four elements of the interventionist thrust of America's globalist foreign policy posture. Outright military intervention is a fifth. Here, too, there has been a striking consistency in the willingness of American commanders-in-chief to intervene in the affairs of others. On twelve conspicuous occasions—in Korea (1950), Lebanon (1958), Vietnam (1962), the Dominican Republic (1965), Grenada (1983), Panama (1989), Iraq (1991), Haiti (1994), Bosnia (1995), Serbia/Kosovo (1999), Afghanistan (2001), and Iraq (2003)—the United States intervened overtly with military power in another country to accomplish its foreign policy objectives. The first five account more than anything for the label "interventionist" widely used to describe America's Cold War foreign policy. Anticommunism is the thread that ties all five together.

Intervention is not unusual in American history, even before the Cold War, as we saw in Chapter 3. But with the onset of that global conflict, interventionism became a part of the ideological struggle between Soviet communism and the "free world." Previously, commerce and economic profits were primary motivations of U.S. behavior. Now interventionism became a key element in the conflict between competing ways of life.

Panama and especially Iraq in 1991 are widely viewed abroad if not always at home as post–Cold War expressions of America's pursuit of global hegemony. They and others that followed arguably represent the U.S. response to the emerging asymmetric threats of the twenty-first century. Bosnia and Serbia/Kosovo (to which we might add the 1992 intervention in Somalia) are cases of humanitarian intervention. U.S. troops (and those of its allies) intervened militarily to protect a people from abuses by its own government or, in the case of Somalia, from the violent anarchy that characterized a failed state. These were the kinds of situations the new administration of George W. Bush promised to avoid.

The wars in Afghanistan and Iraq quickly changed that. Motivated by the threat of transnational terrorism, the United States now found itself involved not only in bloody wars but also in massive state-building efforts involving virtually all elements of the society, economy, and government in the two Islamic countries.

The Afghanistan intervention enjoyed considerable support among other countries, as it dealt with an immediate terrorist threat—Osama bin Laden—and the Taliban regime that protected his operations. President Bush launched Operation Enduring Freedom in October 2001. As he articulated in speeches before Congress and the American people, its purposes included the destruction of terrorist training camps and infrastructure within Afghanistan, the capture of Al Qaeda leaders, and the cessation of terrorist activities in Afghanistan. By mid-2005, U.S. forces in Afghanistan had grown to 20,000. NATO in its first-ever engagement outside of Europe joined the fight almost immediately, contributing another 8,000 troops in mid-2005 (O'Hanlon and Kamp 2005, 5).

The war in Iraq, however, despite efforts by the United States to link it to WMD, bin Laden, and terrorism,[2] was distinctly unpopular throughout the world, if not in the United States itself. Approved neither by the United Nations nor by NATO, the U.S.-led intervention was widely perceived in the Arab and Muslim worlds as an occupying foreign power—the *infidel*—in an Islamic state. The United States nonetheless made a major commitment when it launched Operation Iraqi Freedom in March 2003. It was supported by a "coalition of the willing," once comprising thirty or more states. Britain, led by Prime

Minister Tony Blair, was the major partner of the United States. In mid-2005, it had 8,000–10,000 military personnel in Iraq, while the remaining non-U.S. coalition partners (roughly two dozen) had 15,000 troops. The United States contributed 138,500 to the combined international troop strength in Iraq (O'Hanlon and Kamp 2006), where the war turned into a vicious urban conflict between the multinational forces and newly trained Iraqi forces, on one hand, and Iraqi and foreign insurgents on the other.

The intervention in the Middle East in 1990–1991, which culminated in the Persian Gulf War, stands apart from the others in important ways. More American troops were sent there than to Vietnam (750,000 troops from the United States and elsewhere comprised the coalition marshaled against Iraq), yet remarkably few casualties were sustained in a high-tech war that lasted only forty-two days. (In contrast, the Vietnam Veterans Memorial on the Mall in the nation's capital commemorates the nearly 60,000 Americans who lost their lives in a war that spanned two Republican and two Democratic administrations.) Moreover, it was the first overt intervention since World War II that enjoyed the acquiescence of the Soviet Union. Thus it was a clear instance of collective security, with enforcement measures approved by the UN Security Council against an aggressor on behalf of the world community. Also, the intervention was not rationalized in anticommunist terms.

The Kosovo air war also is remarkable for the absence of casualties, as we noted earlier. Like the Persian Gulf War, it, too, was a multilateral effort, but in this case the action was not sanctioned by the United Nations, a contentious point which impeded efforts to negotiate an end to the prolonged bombardment.[3] Instead, NATO, in its first-ever combat activity, was the enforcer. Still, the United States supplied most of the firepower. At the height of the bombing campaign some 800 U.S. aircraft and 37,500 troops were committed to the fight.

Absent the alleged communist threats to Korea, Lebanon, Vietnam, the Dominican Republic, and Grenada, what explains U.S. interventionist behavior beyond Iraq's clear-cut violation of Kuwait's inviolate international border in August 1990? The term new interventionism was used in the early 1990s to describe responses to a changed and changing environment in which humanitarian concerns and international values often trumped other explanations of state behavior. The interventions in Somalia (1992), Haiti (1994), Bosnia (1995), and Serbia/Kosovo (1999) fit the pattern. All involved coercive diplomacy (see Table 4.1), but the motivations clearly diverged from the anticommunist impulse evident before the disintegration of the Soviet empire.[4]

The New Interventionism

Arguably, the last decade of the twentieth century witnessed greater sensitivity to humanitarian values as a reason to join military power to diplomacy. Britain's Prime Minister Tony Blair made that case in Kosovo, describing NATO's intervention there as "a moral cause." The most proactive supporter of the Atlantic alliance's military actions asserted that "We are fighting for a world where dictators are no longer able to visit horrific punishments on their own peoples in order to stay in power." In fact, in addition to vital and important interests that might require the application of U.S. force, the 1999 U.S. *National Security Strategy for a New Century* also posited a third category of "humanitarian and other interests," which included human rights concerns and support for democratization. In these cases, the strategy suggested, U.S. military intervention *may* be appropriate to respond to, relieve, and/or restrict the consequences of the humanitarian catastrophe.[5] A willingness to intervene in such conflicts, especially those *within* states, is the defining characteristic of the **new interventionism.** As defined during the Clinton years, the emphasis on humanitarian and international values distinguishes the new interventionism from the interventionist thrust of the Bush Doctrine, discussed in Chapter 3.

The underpinnings of the new interventionism rest in the Clinton administration's efforts in several crises dating from its first term, including Somalia, Rwanda, Haiti, and Bosnia. Presidential Decision Directive 56 (May 1997) on "Complex Contingency Operations" also shaped policy by establishing some general guidelines and processes for designing such an intervention. As we discussed in Chapter 3, Clinton later articulated the basis for U.S. involvement in internal conflicts in other states. The Clinton Doctrine called for using U.S. military power to halt ethnic cleansing of peoples based on their race, ethnicity, or religion.

The use of troops for purposes of *peacekeeping* (keeping contending parties apart) and *peace enforcement* (imposing a settlement on disputants) are key policy instruments underlying the new interventionism. The Persian Gulf experience in collective security first ignited enthusiasm for using the United Nations as an instrument of both peacekeeping and peace enforcement. Within a short time thousands of troops were carrying out more UN operations than at any other time. The United States eagerly supported many of these operations, whose interests they served. Eventually, however, its enthusiastic embrace of multilateralism waned, blunted by its experience in Somalia where eighteen American lives were claimed in combat.[6]

President George H. W. Bush launched the Somalia intervention (called Operation Restore Hope), hoping to bring relief from famine to thousands of starving Somalis. Earlier it had initiated Operation Provide Comfort, another multilateral initiative designed to protect the Kurdish people in Iraq from death and destruction at the hands of Saddam Hussein following the Persian Gulf War. Both were distinguished from other interventions by serving humanitarian purposes, not overtly political ones. Under Clinton, the Somalia intervention gradually escalated until American troops were involved in military activities against one of the factions. In October 1993, when American forces took casualties on one such operation, public and congressional outcries persuaded the administration to end the U.S. deployment.

In 1994, the Clinton administration participated in another—albeit much more limited—humanitarian intervention in Rwanda, where hundreds of thousands of refugees faced intolerable conditions following months of genocidal, ethnic bloodletting. Shortly after that, former President Jimmy Carter negotiated the safe passage of Haiti's

military leaders to Panama, paving the way for a U.S.-led multinational force to return Haiti's elected president to power. By ridding Haiti of its military regime, Operation Restore Democracy also sought to eliminate the human rights abuses the military regime had perpetrated on its own people.

Just as enthusiasm for multilateralism followed in the wake of the successful collective security effort in the Persian Gulf, support for humanitarian intervention grew as civil and ethnic conflict erupted elsewhere. It also flowed naturally from the apparent "triumph" of Wilsonian liberalism at the conclusion of the Cold War. As one analyst put it, "The new interventionism has its roots in longstanding tendencies of American foreign policy—missionary zeal, bewilderment when the world refuses to conform to American expectations, and a belief that for every problem there is a quick and easy solution" (Stedman 1992–1993). Thus the new interventionism combined "an awareness that civil war is a legitimate issue of international security with a sentiment for crusading liberal internationalism." A more skeptical characterization referred to it as "foreign policy as social work" (Mandelbaum 1996).

Laudable as they may be, humanitarian interventions raise troublesome moral, political, and legal questions. What level of human suffering is necessary before intervention is warranted? If intervention is required to relieve human suffering in Somalia and Rwanda, then why not in countless other places—the Sudan, for example, where by the end of 2006 an estimated 450,000 people had died in the Darfur region without the lifting of a single international hand—or countless other failed states around the world, where poverty, starvation, ethnic violence, and the inhumanity of governments toward their own people have been daily occurrences? Is the restoration of law and order a legitimate reason to intervene? To protect—or promote—democracy? What obligation, and for how long, does the intervener have to ensure that its stated goals are achieved? Particularly troublesome is a World Bank finding that "within five years, half of all countries emerging from civil unrest fall back into conflict in a cycle of collapse" ("Failed State Index," *Foreign Policy,* July/August 2005, 58).

Peace enforcement operations are plagued by many of the same questions as humanitarian interventions designed to keep peace by separating the antagonists. The interventions in Bosnia and Kosovo stand out. In Bosnia in particular many United Nations peacekeepers were killed by Serbian fighters as they sought to carry out their international mission.

Conflict erupted in Bosnia-Herzegovina between ethnic Muslims and Serbs following the breakup in 1992 of Yugoslavia, of which it had been a part. The United Nations sent a peacekeeping force to the country believing it could contain the violence, but it proved ineffectual. Ethnic cleansing, the practice by one side (notably Bosnian Serbs backed by the Yugoslav military from the republic of Serbia) to kill or drive from their homes people of the other side (Bosnian Muslims), became rampant. In April 1994, NATO launched air strikes against Bosnian Serbs, hoping to protect UN forces. Later the following year it launched a sustained bombing campaign designed to force negotiations between the antagonists. Finally, in late 1995, Assistant Secretary of State Richard Holbrooke brokered a cease-fire and an agreement designed to stop the ethnic conflict. The agreement called for intervention by an Implementation Force (IFOR), whose purpose was to enforce the peace settlement in which keeping Bosnia as a separate state was a central element. Negotiators rejected the alternative of partitioning it along ethnic lines reflecting the power positions of the antagonists.

President Clinton promised that U.S. forces would be in Bosnia for no more than a year. Three years later, 6,000 American troops remained as part of the NATO-led peace enforcers and their stay was extended indefinitely. By then some success in promoting democracy and reconstruction could be claimed, but the bitter antagonisms between rival ethnic groups remained rampant, dimming prospects for building a multiethnic Bosnian state. And Radovan Karadžić, the Bosnian Serb president indicted for genocide by the International War Crimes Tribunal in the Hague for his role in perpetrating ethnic cleansing during the long years of violence, remained at large.

The war crimes tribunal later indicted Slobodan Milošević for his role in the ethnic cleansing of the Serbian province of Kosovo, the home of thousands of ethnic Albanians which had long enjoyed autonomy from the central government in Belgrade. Serbian military, paramilitary, and police forces carried out the genocide of Kosovar Albanians. Ironically, ending that conflict required negotiating with the alleged criminal, Milošević. And when the hundreds of thousands of ethnic Albanians who had been driven from their homeland by Serbs returned, widespread violent revenge took place. Now, it seemed, was the time for the Serbs to leave Kosovo—and thousands did. Although a NATO-led force of 50,000 troops (7,000 from the United States) came committed to maintaining the province's multiethnic composition, the prospects for achieving that goal seemed remote. Indeed, some critics of U.S. and NATO actions predicted an "occupation" of Kosovo that could last decades.

Although the nature and causes of the ethnic violence in Bosnia and Kosovo and the peace efforts to resolve them were similar, there was one important difference. Bosnia had been recognized by the United States and the members of the European Union as a sovereign state. Kosovo never was. No one doubted its status as a province of the Republic of Serbia, even though it was overwhelmingly populated by ethnic Albanians whose embrace of Islam, not the Eastern Orthodox Christianity of the Serbs, fueled separatist sentiments. Milošević rose to power in part on his pledge to strip Kosovo of its autonomy. An agreement negotiated in Rambouillet, France, sought to restore that autonomy. Regardless, the United States and its NATO partners never challenged Serbia's sovereignty over the province.

Sovereignty is a cardinal principle in international law and politics that affirms that no authority is above the state. It protects the territorial inviolability of the state, its freedom from interference by others, and its authority to rule its own population. The United Nations is predicated on the sovereign equality of its members. Article 2, Section 7 of the UN charter specifically states that nothing in the charter should be construed to permit interference in matters essentially within the domestic jurisdiction of member states.

In this context, the campaign against terrorism that began in October 2001 raises difficult questions. Al Qaeda, the terrorist organization responsible for the attacks on the U.S., is a non-state actor. U.S. efforts to destroy its sprawling network are fundamentally interventionist and an intrusion on the principle of sovereignty. Moreover, they also constitute, as a putative general rule, an effort to hold governments responsible for the actions of individuals or groups within their borders. Does the United States have the right to intervene in states that harbor terrorists, as it claims in the Bush Doctrine? As one senior foreign policy adviser explained: "We must eliminate the scourge of international terrorism. In order to do that, we need not only to eliminate the terrorists and their networks, but also those who harbor them."

Terrorism aside, some legal scholars believe that "humanitarian intervention is legally permissible in instances when a government abuses its people so egregiously that the conscience of humankind is shocked." From this perspective, the humanitarian interventions in Iraq (Kurdistan) and Somalia in the early 1990s "represented the triumph over national sovereignty of international law designed to protect the fundamental human rights of citizens in every state" (Joyner 1993); see also Joyner (1992) and Fixdal and Smith (1998), but compare Stedman (1995) and Lund (1995).

Still, as international legal scholar Christopher Joyner observes,

> . . . little evidence suggests that states in the early 21st century have accepted a lawful right of humanitarian intervention. The bottom line today is that states continue to value their sovereignty and political free will above the value they place on the protection of foreign peoples' human rights. Put bluntly, few governments are willing to risk their national blood or treasure to safeguard or rescue the lives of strangers in strange lands.
>
> (Joyner 2005, 178)

Finally, just as there are differences of opinion about when and where to intervene, there are differences about what is at stake. Journalist Michael Elliott put the issue succinctly: "'Values' are a slippery concept on which to base the expenditure of blood and treasure. Reasonable, civilized men and women can disagree about which values are worth dying for" (*Newsweek,* 26 April 1999, 37).

Arguably, George W. Bush laid out a significantly more demanding criteria for the use of force than did his immediate predecessor. In an October 2000 presidential debate, for example, Bush explained when he would commit U.S. troops:

> Well, if it's in our vital national interests. And that means whether or not our territory—our territory is threatened, our people could be harmed, whether or not our alliances—our defense alliances are threatened, whether or not our friends in the Middle East are threatened. That would be a time to seriously consider the use of force. Secondly, whether or not the mission was clear, whether or not it was a clear understanding as to what the mission would be. Thirdly, whether or not we were prepared and trained to win, whether or not our forces were of high morale and high standing and well equipped. And finally, whether or not there was an exit strategy. . . . I would be guarded in my approach. . . . I believe the role of the military is to fight and win war and, therefore, prevent war from happening in the first place.

While the U.S. response in Afghanistan to the September 2001 terrorist strikes seemed to meet this more exacting standard, the criteria would appear to limit the use of force to a relatively few situations. One could also argue, however, that once the decision for involvement is made under such restrictions, the commitment is larger and more significant than under the interventionist approach advocated by the Clinton team. Certainly that became the case in Iraq where, some two years into the war, debate about the apparent absence of an exit strategy erupted domestically. Debates about the torture of prisoners, the maintenance of secret CIA prisons in others countries where torture, correctly or not, was believed rampant, the civil rights of "enemy combatants," and the applicability of the Geneva Accords on the rules of war and the treatment of prisoners also churned the country.

As support for the war began to unravel at home (in late 2005 over half of those surveyed by Gallup indicated a preference for withdrawing U.S. troops from Iraq within a year), Bush laid out in his second inaugural address a broad agenda for the future. "America, in this young century, proclaims liberty throughout all the world, and to all the inhabitants thereof," he said. And he reiterated his belief that people everywhere yearn for democracy, concluding "There is no justice without freedom." To many observers his speech was a clarion call for greater U.S. military intervention abroad to promote values embraced by the United States. It also provoked recollections of the warnings of a former legal counsel to the Senate Foreign Relations committee made at the time of the Kosovo air war: "No one, as yet, has devised safeguards sufficient to guarantee that power will not be misdirected to undermine the values it was established to protect" (Glennon 1999; see also Rieff 1999 and Franck 1999).

To Intervene or Not to Intervene?

In the aftermath of the divisive Vietnam War, American policy makers worried about intervening in world trouble spots. Constrained by the Vietnam syndrome, they feared that prolonged involvement requiring substantial economic costs and many casualties would undermine support in Congress and among the American public. The death of 241 Marines in Beirut in 1983, who had been sent to Lebanon as part of a multinational peacekeeping force during the Lebanese civil war, and the death of another 18 American soldiers in Somalia in 1993, reinforced the reluctance to intervene abroad militarily—especially with combat troops. Bill Clinton

reflected that thinking when he stated emphatically at the outset of NATO's campaign against Serbia that "I do not intend to put our troops in Kosovo to fight a war."[7]

Eliminating the invasion option from the beginning may actually have intensified Milošević's resolve to stand up to NATO, thus prolonging the destructive conflict. As a study of the threat and actual use of force during the Bush and Clinton administrations (prior to Kosovo) concluded,

> There is a generation of political leaders throughout the world whose basic perception of U.S. military power and political will is one of weakness, who enter any situation with a fundamental belief that the United States can be defeated or driven away. This point of view was expressed explicitly and concisely by Mohamed Farah Aideed, leader of a key Somali faction, to Ambassador Robert Oakely, U.S. special envoy to Somalia, during the disastrous U.S. involvement there in 1993–1995: "We have studied Vietnam and Lebanon and know how to get rid of Americans, by killing them so that public opinion will put an end to things."
> *(Blechman and Wittes 1999, 5)*[8]

Ironically, then, an unwillingness to incur casualties may actually diminish the effectiveness of U.S. military threats, thus requiring the actual use of force, as during the Persian Gulf War. A study of eight post–Cold War cases in which "the United States utilized its armed forces demonstratively in support of political objectives" found that George H. W. Bush and Bill Clinton both had acted timidly, "taking some action but not the most effective possible action to challenge the foreign leaders threatening the United States" (Blechman and Wittes 1999).

Efforts by the George W. Bush administration to build support for U.S. operations against terrorism in general and military action in Afghanistan and elsewhere sought "to prepare the public to accept the loss of American lives in combat"

(DeYoung and Milbank 2001). As the Iraq conflict in particular lingered, Bush repeatedly said that the United States would not "cut and run" in the face of a growing casualty list; instead, it would "stay the course," remaining engaged as long as necessary to achieve its military and foreign policy goals.

Although support for U.S. efforts to exercise military dominance on a global scale was widely popular in the United States following 9/11, it waned thereafter, as we noted. Studies by John Mueller (1971, 1973, 2005) and others show there is a kind of inevitability in the decline among democratic societies in their support for war. Rising casualties are often linked to a decline of support (Larson 1996; Larson and Savych 2005).

Following the disaster in Lebanon early in the Reagan administration, Secretary of Defense Caspar Weinberger articulated a set of six principles, known as the ***Weinberger Doctrine,*** to govern the use of force abroad. He stated that force should be used only when vital national interests are at stake, sufficient resources are committed, and objectives are clearly defined. Additionally, there must be a willingness to adjust military force as events on the ground dictate along with a reasonable expectation that lawmakers and the public will support the operation. Last, force should be used only after all other options have been exhausted, suggesting that force and diplomacy operate on separate tracks. A decade later, Colin Powell, in what is widely referred to as the ***Powell Doctrine,*** synthesized these ideas. "Powell stressed the importance of going into a conflict with all the forces at hand and winning quickly and decisively. Like Weinberger's six tests, the Powell Doctrine aimed at keeping U.S. troops out of wars to which the nation was not fully committed" (Jordan, Taylor, and Mazarr 1999). The Persian Gulf War fit the parameters of the Powell Doctrine; the Bosnia conflict, which erupted shortly thereafter, apparently did not. As the first Bush's Secretary of State James Baker reportedly said, "We don't have a dog in that fight."

Whether it is Bosnia, Afghanistan, or Iraq, does the United States still have interests that can be advanced best through intervention? If the United States does intervene, can it stay the course, as great powers historically have done (Luttwak 1994)? Or do the domestic political costs of prolonged engagement outweigh the foreign policy benefits?

As the Bush administration proceeded through its second term in office, it increasingly faced these questions, not only from Democrats but also some Republicans. As noted, multiple issues ranging from exit strategies to torture of prisoners provoked doubts. Interestingly, public support for the war in Iraq fell markedly as casualties mounted, surpassing 2,800 as Veterans Day was celebrated on November 11, 2006. In the annals of warfare, this is a relatively low number for combat that has stretched beyond three and a half years. But, as we have seen, the threshold of public tolerance of combat casualties has dropped markedly since the denouement of the Cold War, seemingly in lockstep with the premises and promises of information-based warfare embraced in the revolution of military affairs.

The war in Iraq is the longest and bloodiest conflict in which the United States has engaged since Vietnam. As it progresses, the parallels with Vietnam also grow (Laird 2005). In particular, as the domestic mood about the war changes, does this portend a "Iraq syndrome" not unlike that that followed the evident failure in Vietnam (Laird 2005)?

Political scientist John Mueller, an expert on domestic influences on foreign policy, warns that many of the sharpest elements of the Bush grand strategy marked out in his first term have already begun to lose their cutting edge. He writes:

> Among the casualties of the Iraq syndrome could be the Bush doctrine, universalism, preemption, preventive war, and indispensable-nationhood. Indeed, these once-fashionable . . . concepts are already picking up growing skepticism about various key notions: that the United States should take unilateral military action to correct situations or overthrow regimes it considers reprehensible but that present no immediate threat to it, that it can and should forcibly bring democracy to other nations not now so blessed, that it has the duty to

rid the world of evil, that having by far the largest defense budget in the world is necessary and broadly beneficial, that international cooperation is of only very limited value, and that Europeans and other well-meaning foreigners are naive and decadent wimps.

(Mueller 2005, 53–54; see also Jervis 2005b)

Does this forecast a new phase of introversion and isolationism similar to that which typically followed U.S. military involvement in past wars? Or, instead, does it portend a return to the liberal internationalism and bipartisanship of the early post–World War II years?

STRATEGIC DOCTRINE THEN AND NOW: NUCLEAR WEAPONS AS INSTRUMENTS OF COMPELLENCE AND DETERRENCE

The clocks of Hiroshima stopped at 8:15 on the morning of August 6, 1945, when, in the blinding flash of a single weapon and the shadow of its mushroom cloud, the international arena was transformed from a balance-of-power to a balance-of-terror system. No other event marked more dramatically the change in world politics that would shape the next half century. The United States has not used atomic weapons in anger since August 1945, but it sought throughout the Cold War to gain bargaining leverage by relying heavily on nuclear force as an instrument of strategic defense (the defense of its homeland) and as a means "to defend its interests wherever they existed" (Gaddis 1987–1988). The latter implied its willingness not only to threaten but actually to use nuclear weapons. Even today nuclear weapons figure prominently in the design of American national security policy. As the Pentagon stated in its 1993 report on the roles and missions of American military forces after the Cold War, nuclear forces "truly do safeguard our way of life."

Strategic Doctrine during America's Atomic Monopoly, 1945–1949

The seeds of the atomic age were planted in 1939 when the United States launched the Manhattan Project, a program at the cutting edge of science and technology designed to construct a superweapon that could be used successfully in war. J. Robert Oppenheimer, the atomic physicist who directed the Los Alamos, New Mexico, laboratory during the development of the A-bomb, observed that "We always assumed if [atomic bombs] were needed they would be used." Thus the rationale was established for a military strategy based on, and backed by, extraordinary means of destruction with which to deal with enemies. President Truman's decision to drop the A-bomb on Hiroshima and, three days later, on Nagasaki was the culmination of that thinking. "When you have to deal with a beast you have to treat him as a beast," Truman reasoned.

Why did the United States use the bomb, which demolished two Japanese cities and took over one hundred thousand lives?[9] The official explanation is simple: The bomb was dropped "in order to end the war in the shortest possible time and to avoid the enormous losses of human life which otherwise confronted us" (Stimson and Bundy 1947). Whether the bomb was necessary to end the war remains in dispute, however. Hiroshima and Nagasaki were largely civilian, not military, targets, and there is now credible evidence that the Japanese wanted to surrender to the United States on acceptable terms.

Many historians now contend that the real motivation behind the bomb's use was preventing the expansion of the Soviet Union's postwar influence in the Far East, not a desire to save lives, whether American or Japanese.[10] A parallel interpretation contends that the United States wanted to impress Soviet leaders with the awesome power of its new weapon and America's willingness to exploit the advantages it now gave them. Regardless of its true motivations, the use of weapons of mass destruction against Japan marked the beginning of an era in which the instruments of war would be used not as means to military ends, but instead for the psychological purpose of molding others' behavior.

During the period of America's atomic monopoly, the concept of ***compellence*** (Schelling 1966) described the new American view of nuclear weapons: they would not be used to fight but rather to get others to do what they might not otherwise do. Thus nuclear weapons became instruments of coercive diplomacy, the ultimate means of forceful persuasion (George 1992).

President Truman and Secretary of War Henry L. Stimson counted on the new weapon to elicit Soviet acceptance of American terms for settling outstanding war issues, particularly in Eastern and Central Europe. Truman could confidently advocate "winning through intimidation" and facing "Russia with an iron fist and strong language," because the United States alone possessed the greatest intimidator of them all—the bomb. Stimson was persuaded that the United States should "use the bomb to pry the Soviets out of Eastern Europe" (LaFeber 1976). Although Stimson soon would reverse his position,[11] his first instincts anticipated the direction American strategic thinking would take during this formative period, which NSC-68 finally crystallized. The memorandum rationalized "increasing American military and allied military capabilities across the board both in nuclear and conventional weapons [and] making it clear that whenever threats to the international balance of power manifested themselves, the United States could respond" (Gaddis 1987–1988). Should it prove necessary, the bomb was a tool that could be used.[12]

Strategic Doctrine under Conditions of Nuclear Superiority, 1949–1960

The monopoly on atomic weapons the United States once enjoyed gave way to superiority in 1949, when, as we have noted, the Soviet Union also acquired the bomb. The assumption that America's adversaries could be made to bend to American wishes through atomic blackmail nonetheless became a cornerstone of the Eisenhower containment strategy, particularly as conceived by its chief architect, Secretary of State

John Foster Dulles. Dulles sought to reshape the strategy of containment around three concepts: rollback, brinkmanship, and massive retaliation, all of which revealed the perceived utility of nuclear weapons as instruments of coercive diplomacy

Rollback *Rollback* identified the goal: reject passive containment of the spread of communist influence and, instead, "roll back" the Iron Curtain by liberating communist-dominated areas. Dulles pledged that the United States would practice rollback—and not merely promise it—by employing "all means necessary to secure the liberation of Eastern Europe."

Brinkmanship *Brinkmanship* sought to harness American strategic superiority to its foreign policy goals. In defining this concept, Dulles explained how atomic power could be used for bargaining purposes:

> You have to take chances for peace, just as you must take chances in war. Some say that we were brought to the verge of war. Of course we were brought to the verge of war. The ability to get to the verge without getting into the war is the necessary art. . . . If you try to run away from it, if you are scared to go to the brink, you are lost. . . . We walked to the brink and we looked it in the face. We took strong action.
>
> *(Dulles 1952, 146)*

Massive Retaliation *Massive retaliation* became the strategic doctrine determined to convince America's adversaries it was both willing and able to carry out its threats. Labeled the "New Look" to distinguish it from Truman's strategy, massive retaliation was a countervalue nuclear weapons strategy designed to provide "the maximum deterrent at bearable cost" by threatening mass destruction of the things the Soviet leaders were perceived to value most—their population and military/industrial centers. The doctrine grew out of the Eisenhower administration's simultaneous impulses to save money and to challenge the perception that American foreign policy had become largely a reflexive reaction to communist initiatives. No longer would containment be restricted to retaliation against localized communist initiatives. Instead, it would target the very center of communist power to accomplish foreign policy goals.

Despite its bold posturing, the Eisenhower administration, for the most part, proceeded cautiously. If it did sometimes threaten to use nuclear weapons, it never carried out the threats; nor did it roll back the iron curtain, most notably when it failed to assist Hungarian revolutionaries who rose up against Soviet power in 1956. Nevertheless, faith in the utility of nuclear weapons as instruments of coercive diplomacy defined the 1950s, as the United States artfully pursued a compellent strategy.

Strategic Doctrine in Transition, 1961–1992

A shift from compellence toward a strategy of deterrence began in the late 1950s and became readily discernible during the Kennedy and Johnson years. The Soviet Union's growing strategic capability helped stimulate the change. The development of intercontinental ballistic missiles (ICBMs) in particular caused alarm, as the United States now saw itself as being as vulnerable to Soviet attack as the Soviet Union was to an American strike. "On the day the Soviets acquired [the bomb as] an instrument and the means to deliver it," Kennedy adviser George Ball (1984) observed, "the bomb lost its military utility and became merely a means of mutual suicide . . . [for] there are no political objectives commensurate with the costs of an all-out nuclear exchange."

Kennedy himself felt it necessary to educate the world to the new strategic reality, warning of its dangers in a 1961 speech to the United Nations General Assembly:

> Today, every inhabitant of this planet must contemplate the day when this planet may no longer be habitable. Every man, woman, and child lives under a nuclear sword of Damocles, hanging by the slenderest of threads, capable of being cut

at any moment by accident or miscalculation or by madness. The weapons of war must be abolished before they abolish us.

> Men no longer debate whether armaments are a symptom or cause of tension. The mere existence of modern weapons—ten million times more powerful than any that the world has ever seen, and only minutes away from any target on earth—is a source of horror, and discord and distrust.

From Compellence to Deterrence   As we have seen, deterrence means discouraging an adversary from using force by convincing the adversary that the costs of such action outweigh the potential gains. As a practical matter, strategic deterrence denotes the threatened use of weapons of mass destruction to impose unacceptably high costs directly on the homeland of a potential aggressor. To ensure that such costs can be imposed, a ***second-strike capability*** is necessary. This means that offensive strategic forces must be able to withstand an adversary's initial strike and retain the capacity to respond with a devastating second blow. In this way the aggressor will be assured of destruction, thus deterring the initial preemptive attack. Hence strategic deterrence implies sensitivity to the survivability of American strategic forces. In practice, the United States has sought survivability through a ***triad of strategic weapons*** consisting of manned bombers and land- and sea-based intercontinental ballistic missiles. It continues to do so today.

The Kennedy administration's doctrine of strategic deterrence rested on the principle of ***assured destruction***—a condition realized if the country can survive an aggressor's worst possible attack with sufficient firepower to inflict unacceptable damage on the attacker in retaliation. It differed from massive retaliation in that the latter presupposed U.S. strategic superiority, which enabled the United States to choose the time and place where nuclear weapons might be used in response to an act of Soviet aggression (as defined by the United States). In contrast, the principle of assured destruction pledged that a direct attack against the United States (or perhaps its allies) would automatically result in a devastating American retaliatory nuclear strike. Hence this strategy of survival through nuclear attack avoidance depended critically on the rational behavior of Soviet leaders who, it was assumed, would not attack first if convinced that a first strike against the United States (or perhaps its NATO allies) would lead to its own destruction.

As the Soviet arsenal grew, American strategic doctrine increasingly stressed that what held for American deterrence of Soviet aggression also held for Soviet deterrence of American assertiveness. Hence mutual deterrence, based on the principle of ***mutual assured destruction (MAD)***, soon described the superpowers' strategic relationship. A "balance of terror" based on the military potential for, and psychological expectation of, widespread death and destruction for *both* combatants in the event of a nuclear exchange now governed the superpowers' strategic relationship. In this sense mutual deterrence "is like a gun with two barrels, of which one points ahead and the other points back at the gun's holder," writes Jonathan Schell (1984). "If a burglar should enter your house, it might make sense to threaten him with this gun, but it could never make sense to fire it." Yet preservation of a MAD world was eagerly sought: Because the price of an attack by one state on its adversary would be its own destruction, ironically the very weapons of war encouraged stability and war avoidance.

From Countervalue to Counterforce The principle of assured destruction emerged in an environment characterized by American strategic superiority. By the end of the 1960s, however, it became clear that the Soviets had an arsenal roughly equivalent to that of the United States. American policy makers now confronted gnawing questions about the utility of continually attempting to enhance the destructive capabilities of the United States. As Henry Kissinger, Nixon's national security adviser and later secretary of state, observed: "The paradox of contemporary military strength is that a gargantuan increase in power has eroded its

relationship to policy.... [Military] power no longer translates automatically into influence."

By the time the first Strategic Arms Limitation Talks (SALT) agreements were signed in 1972, a new nuclear weapons orthodoxy began to emerge: Their purpose was to prevent war, not to wage it. Robert McNamara (1983), secretary of defense under Kennedy and Johnson, put it simply: "Nuclear weapons serve no military purpose whatsoever. They are totally useless except only to deter one's opponent from using them." Such reasoning stimulated growing support in the 1980s for a "no first use" declaratory policy, even though such a policy would run counter to NATO doctrine, which maintained that nuclear weapons would be used if NATO conventional forces faced defeat on the battlefield. Since 1978 the United States has pledged not to use nuclear weapons against non-nuclear states that are signatories of the Nuclear Non-Proliferation Treaty (NPT). However, successive administrations "have also maintained a policy of 'strategic ambiguity,' refusing to rule out a nuclear response to a biological or chemical attack." Arguably, strategic ambiguity applies to nuclear weapons as well, aiding deterrence "by keeping potential adversaries uncertain about a U.S. response" (Deutch 2005).

Although the SALT arms control negotiations sought to restrain the superpowers' strategic competition (see Chapter 3), qualitative improvements in their weapons systems continued unabated. Inevitably this provoked new challenges to the emerging orthodoxy about nuclear weapons as instruments of policy. The continuing strategic debate now centered on the issues of targeting policy and war-fighting strategies.

Like massive retaliation, the principle of assured destruction rested on the belief that deterrence could be realized by directing nuclear weapons at targets believed to be of greatest value to an adversary, namely, its population and industrial centers. The ***countervalue*** targeting doctrine joined the civilian and industrial centers of both Cold War adversaries in a mutual hostage relationship.

As early as 1962, Secretary of Defense McNamara suggested that the United States ought instead to adopt a *counterforce* strategy, one that targeted American destructive power on the enemy's military forces and weapons. A decade later the United States would take significant strides in this direction as it began to develop a "limited nuclear options" policy and the corresponding weapons capability to destroy heavily protected Soviet military targets. Recently declassified documents from the time show that President Nixon stimulated the new direction. Worried about the carnage a nuclear exchange (the "horror strategy") would cause and also about the credibility of a MAD strategy, Nixon finalized the search for alternative, "smaller packages" shortly before he left office (Burr 2005). The search invited the addition of another lurid acronym to the arcane language of strategic planning: **NUTS** or **NUT**—variously defined as *"nuclear utilization target selection"* or *"nuclear utilization theory."* Target selection strategy remains as controversial today as it was decades ago. The Bush administration in particular faced much criticism as it debated whether to build a new, low-yield nuclear weapon—a Robust Nuclear Earth Penetrator—capable of burrowing underground to destroy specific enemy weapons sites. Congress refused to fund research on the new weapon, leading to reports that the administration would opt instead for a conventional capability designed for the same "bunker busting" purpose (Deutch 2005; "Congress Steps Back from Nukes," *The Defense Monitor*, November/December 2005).

President Carter extended the counterforce option in the 1980s, when he signed Presidential Directive (PD) 59. Known in official circles as the *countervailing (war-fighting) strategy*, the new posture sought to enhance deterrence by targeting Soviet military forces and weapons as well as population and industrial centers. It was incorporated into the top-secret master plan for waging nuclear war known as the *Single Integrated Operational Plan (SIOP)*, which operationalizes strategic doctrine by selecting the targets to be attacked in the event of war (see Ball and Toth 1990; Hall 1998; Burr 2005).

Even as the United States modified its plans for coping with the Soviet threat, the Soviet Union continued a massive program initiated in the 1960s to enlarge and modernize Soviet strategic forces. Advantages in numbers of missiles, missile warheads, and missile throw-weight accrued to the Soviets, stimulating a growing chorus of alarm that moved the United States away from the accommodationist policies of the 1970s toward a decidedly more militant posture (see also Chapter 3). "Our ability to deter war and protect our security declined dangerously during the 1970s," scolded Ronald Reagan, setting the stage for the largest peacetime military buildup in the nation's history. The Reagan administration feared in particular that Soviet technological developments had rendered the land-based leg of the strategic triad vulnerable to a devastating first strike (which would undermine the U.S. second strike capability but not eliminate it due to its submarine-based forces). Further, it became convinced that the Soviet Union could no longer be deterred simply with the threat of assured destruction. It therefore pledged to develop capabilities sufficient not only to ensure the survival of U.S. strategic forces in the event of a first strike (so that a devastating second strike could be launched), but also to deter a second strike by threatening a third. Reagan officials claimed that making nuclear weapons more usable would enhance deterrence by making the nuclear threat more credible.

Critics disagreed, charging that making nuclear war less unthinkable made it more likely. They often pointed to the vulnerability of the nation's command, control, communications, and intelligence (C^3I) capabilities. A Soviet attack by comparatively few weapons could effectively "decapitate" the United States by killing its political leaders and destroying the communication links necessary to ensure a coordinated and coherent U.S. retaliation (Ball 1989; Schneider 1989).[13] Such dangers undermined the feasibility of conducting a limited (protracted) nuclear war, they warned. Hence, critics of Reagan's policies concluded that a strategy premised on the usability of nuclear weapons in war would actually increase the probability of nuclear conflict, not reduce it.

The first Bush administration was not explicit about its strategic assumptions. However, while it stressed publicly that America's nuclear weapons were primarily for deterrence, it quietly continued to pursue a nuclear war-fighting capability. President George H. W. Bush approved changes in the SIOP that would enhance U.S. capabilities to paralyze Soviet war-making abilities in the opening hours of conflict by "decapitating" the Soviet leadership. Critics, who averred that Bush's revised SIOP took "war fighting to dangerous extremes" (Ball and Toth 1990; see also Glaser 1992; Mazarr 1990; Toth 1989), again worried that plans to blitz Soviet leaders at the beginning of hostilities would increase rather than decrease the risk of nuclear holocaust. Because these changes were made at the very time that the Soviet threat was diminishing, they gave testimony to the persistence of old ways of thinking about national security and strategy. Indeed, Secretary of State James Baker asserted shortly before the Berlin Wall crumbled that "We are not on the verge of a perpetual peace in which war is no longer possible. We cannot disinvent nuclear weapons nor the need for continued deterrence."

From Offense to Defense Ronald Reagan launched perhaps the greatest challenge to the orthodox view of the utility of nuclear weapons with a dramatic call for a high-tech, "Star Wars" *ballistic missile defense (BMD)* system, designed to render intercontinental nuclear missiles "impotent and obsolete." The *Strategic Defense Initiative (SDI)*, as it was officially known, sought to create a "defense dominant" strategy. Believing the principle of mutual assured destruction "morally unacceptable," Reagan's program foreshadowed a distant future in which the United States would interdict offensive weapons launched toward the United States in fear or anger. The knowledge that the United States was invulnerable would also reduce the probability of war.

SDI became an object of criticism from the start, stimulating a debate that continues even today, although more muted. Many experts felt that the program created expectations that technology could not fulfill until well into the twenty-first century, if ever. Still, advocates of a defense-dominant strategy maintained that "defending through active defense is preferable to defending through terrorism—the ultimate mechanism by which deterrence through threat of retaliation operates" (Congressional Research Service 1989). Thus research on various conceptualizations of missile defense systems continued for more than a decade at the cost of many billions of dollars.

Eventually the notion of establishing an impenetrable shield that would render incoming missiles "impotent and obsolete" was abandoned in favor of a less ambitious system. As the Soviet Union imploded and the Cold War fizzled, "scenarios of a Third World strike, a renegade Russian submarine missile attack, or an accidental or unauthorized launch became the primary justifications for the system" (Han 1992–1993). The intelligence community in 1995 released a National Intelligence Estimate (NIE) that concluded the threat that one or more rogue states might build an ICBM capable of striking the United States was ten or more years into the future.

That time frame has since been shortened substantially. Today, following a 1998 congressionally mandated study headed by former Secretary of Defense Donald Rumsfeld, there seems to be widespread agreement in Washington that the threat from abroad is more imminent.[14] In particular, the Rumsfeld Commission concluded that a rogue state could build an intercontinental missile in perhaps as few as five years. In turn, that state could "inflict major damage" on the United States. North Korea and Iran were specifically cited. Both now have medium- and potentially long-range ballistic missiles.

Congressional Republicans were particularly vigorous proponents of a *national missile defense (NMD)* system. Previously the emphasis had been on *theater missile defenses (TMD)* being developed by the army and navy.[15] The former seek to protect U.S. allies in their local settings; the latter to protect the United States itself (and perhaps some allies). Thus a national missile system can threaten other states with a nuclear deterrent capability, while theater systems cannot. Accordingly, national defense systems are inherently more dangerous and threatening to the mutual deterrence system on which the long Cold War peace rested. Since Bush's election the Pentagon has dropped the distinction between national and theater systems and is adding longer range capabilities to theater defenses.

During the 1990s, when the Democrats controlled the White House, President Clinton generally stalled the Republicans' efforts. In 1996, Clinton agreed to develop a program capable of being deployed by 2003 *if* a ballistic missile threat seemed imminent. At the time such a development seemed unlikely. Then North Korea tested missiles whose anticipated capabilities would permit attacks on the United States. At about the same time, China was shown to have engaged in espionage at U.S. nuclear facilities for many years, which may have significantly advanced its nuclear capabilities.[16]

By the end of his administration, Clinton finally agreed that the United States would field a national missile defense system against a "limited missile attack" as soon as it was "technologically feasible," initially indicating his support for ground-based interceptors based in Alaska. Later he added that, while "the NMD program is sufficiently promising and affordable to justify continued development," he would defer the decision to move forward with early deployment to his successor.

The man who assumed the White House in January 2001 was less hesitant. Throughout the 2000 campaign, George W. Bush promised to create a "new strategic framework" with Russia and to "defend U.S. citizens, not outdated treaties." The reference was to the 1972 Antiballistic Missile (ABM) treaty with the then–Soviet Union. The treaty prohibited either superpower from deploying a defensive missile system. Bush committed his administration to an early deployment of a comprehensive NMD system with land, sea, and space components (which would violate the ABM). Later in campaign 2000, Bush coupled his plan for NMD with a proposal to reduce—possibly unilaterally— U.S. nuclear arsenals to the "lowest possible number consistent with our national security," and less than the thresholds established in arms control agreements. After his election, Bush reiterated his commitment to NMD and began to lay the groundwork with American allies as well as China and Russia, which included renegotiation with Russia of

elements of the ABM treaty (as Clinton had done before him). Bush made it clear, however, that the U.S. decision would not be driven by opposition from those quarters.

Then, in December 2001, shortly after the 9/11 terrorist attacks, Bush informed Russia that the United States was withdrawing from the 1972 ABM Treaty. Citing the need to defend against potential long-range terrorist threats to the American homeland, Bush stated that, "as the events of September 11th made all too clear, the greatest threats to both our countries come not from each other, or from other big powers in the world, but from terrorists who strike without warning or rogue states who seek weapons of mass destruction."

Surprisingly, perhaps, 9/11 actually muted the controversy over abrogating the ABM treaty. Russia decided to align itself with the United States in the war on terrorism, which in turn limited criticism from China and others. Domestically, the terrorists attacks were viewed by many as a reason to go forward with a planned NMD system.

> Some observers initially speculated that support for missile defense would plummet because people would want to concentrate on stopping low-tech methods of attacking the United States. Yet, most of the U.S. public drew a different lesson from September 11, namely, that some of the country's adversaries are prepared to do the unthinkable against the United States, actually using missiles if they get their hands on them. That heightened perception of the threat now helps drive the missile defense debate.
>
> *(Lindsay and O'Hanlon 2002a, 169–170)*

With the restrictions of the ABM treaty now behind the United States, Bush announced that the first phase of a deployed NMD would be put into place in the fall of 2004. Despite missile tests that often failed even within tightly constrained test parameters, the target date was met: six antimissile missiles were lowed into their hardened silos in Fort Greely, Alaska and another two were deployed at Vandenberg Air Force Base in California. Two more

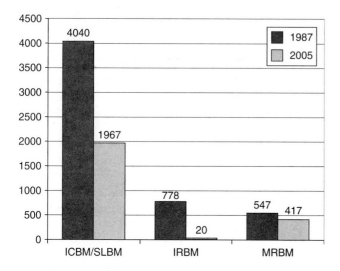

FIGURE 4.2 Long- and Medium-Range Ballistic Missiles, 1987–2005

SOURCE: Joseph Cirincione. "The Declining Ballistic Missile Threat," in *Policy Outlook*, February 2005. Washington, DC: Carnegie Endowment for International Peace, p. 11.

missiles were installed in Alaska in 2005. The first phrase of the deployed NMD tracked the Clinton plan of a land-based defensive system that would use kinetic weapons to smash into enemy payloads. The ultimate vision of the Bush administration (and potentially its successors) has yet to be articulated. As the president promised, it could involve a mix of land-, sea-, and space-based weapons systems, but what that mix will be is far from certain. Judging by the Bush administration's budget plans, a fully deployed and operational NMD system could comprise as many 2,000 interceptors (Lindsay and O'Hanlon 2002a, 165). Their successful development will likely depend critically on ideas and technologies that will only come to fruition in the decades ahead, as billions more are invested in the enterprise.

Curiously, at the same time that the United States has emphasized the ballistic missile threat, between 1987 and 2005 the number of states pursuing long-range ballistic missiles has fallen from eight to five. A study of proliferation issues by the Carnegie Endowment for International Peace reveals other unexpected trends:

- Analysis of global ballistic missile arsenals shows that there are far fewer ICBMs and long-range submarine-launched ballistic missiles (SLBMs) in the world

today than there were during the Cold War. (See Figure 4.2.)

- The number of intermediate-range ballistic missiles (IRBMs), i.e., missiles with a range of 3,000–5,000 km, has decreased in the past fifteen years by an order of magnitude.

- The overall number of medium-range ballistic missiles (MRBMs), i.e., missiles with a range of 1,000–3,000 km, has also decreased. Five new countries, however, have developed or acquired MRBMs since the late 1980s.

- The number of countries trying to develop ballistic missiles has also decreased and the nations still attempting to do so are poorer and less technologically advanced than were the nations fifteen years ago.

- The number of countries with short-range ballistic missiles (SRBMs), i.e., missiles with ranges up to 1,000 km, has remained fairly static over the past twenty years and is now beginning to decrease as aging inventories are retired.

- Today, fewer nations potentially hostile to the United State and Europe are trying to develop MRBMs compared with twenty-five years ago (. . . 2004: China, Iran, and North Korea).

- The damage from a ballistic missile attack on U.S. territory, U.S. forces, and European allies today with one or two warheads is also lower by orders of magnitude than fifteen years ago when thousand of warheads would have destroyed the country and possibly all human life on the planet.

(Cirincione 2005, 4–5)

None of this mitigates the threat that may be posed by rogue states or by terrorist groups that seek weapons of mass destruction. As we saw in Chapter 3, transnational cooperation in spreading nuclear technology from China, North Korea, and Pakistan to others, often states with actively developing missile programs, poses a serious threat. At the same time, however, the data also show that cooperation with other states may achieve tacit or more formal agreements that dampen the possibility of a global holocaust so widely anticipated during the Cold War. Indeed, the arms control agreements reached between the United States and the former Soviet Union and Russia account for much of the reduction of WMD threats since the 1960s. We will give more attention to these agreements later in this chapter.

Strategic Doctrine for a New Era

Late in 1997, and with little ceremony, Bill Clinton signed a new Presidential Decision Directive redefining existing nuclear weapons policy and strategy. The product of a Nuclear Posture Review begun years earlier, it replaced the last presidential guidance on the use of nuclear weapons in war, which Ronald Reagan had approved in 1981. That document anticipated that nuclear war would be protracted, that the president should have a menu of nuclear options from which to pick, and that limited nuclear exchanges might permit pauses during which negotiations could occur. The Soviet Union and its Eastern European allies were, of course, the prime targets, with some reports suggesting that at

the Cold War's peak 40,000 targets in the communist world had been marked for destruction (Ottaway and Coll 1995).[17]

The Clinton guidelines dramatically reduced (but did not eliminate) potential nuclear targets in the former Soviet Union. Apparently, it did not abandon the notion that a protracted nuclear war might be fought (Hall 1998), but it did shift the emphasis to a more diffuse set of threats—not just a nuclear threat from a single, powerful antagonist but to general threats caused by "instability." Included are anticipated challenges by those who might possess not only nuclear but also biological and chemical weapons of mass destruction, in particular rogue states and rising powers such as China. The common thread with previous policy is clear: nuclear weapons are designed to dissuade an adversary from attacking the United States (or its allies) by putting at risk whatever that adversary holds dear.

Although the Clinton administration's revised nuclear guidelines shifted to what some analysts regarded as a more realistic assessment of the challenges the United States now faces, critics were quick to seize on a number of unresolved issues. How many nuclear warheads are required for deterrence? Can prevention of their accidental use be assured? And can they guarantee against non-nuclear threats? The prestigious Henry L. Stimson Center addressed these issues in a series of reports on the evolving U.S. nuclear posture, which included the views of many of the nation's most knowledgeable defense experts (Goodpaster 1995, 1997). Interestingly, the center's conclusions raised doubts about the ability of nuclear weapons to deter biological or chemical weapons and recommended that the ultimate goal of U.S. policy should be a nuclear-free world.

But while the world now presents new threats to American security, the basic Cold War style American nuclear arsenal remains little changed. And although analysts urge reconsideration of the structure of American nuclear forces and policies about their use, most agree that the effectiveness of deterrence continues to be based on the credibility of a retaliatory threat (Deutch 2005; Gabel

2004–2005). The primary difference from earlier strategic policies rests in the firm commitment to missile defense and more offensively minded approach to nuclear use. But as Robert Jervis (2002) puts it, mutual assured destruction "may be in the dustbin of history, but states that employ nuclear weapons or force their adversaries to do so may find themselves there as well."

As this discussion suggests, the scholarly and policy debates about the wisdom of building nuclear weapons and their utility as instruments of foreign policy, first simulated by the use of the atomic bombs against Japan in the waning days of World War II, continues today. The debate has been reinvigorated with discussions of terrorism, chemical and biological weapons of mass destruction, the seeming ease with which some states can now develop nuclear arms, and controlling their spread. Arms control thus continues its relevance for American national security.

ARMS CONTROL AND NATIONAL SECURITY

The end of the Cold War witnessed a flurry of dramatic arms control and disarmament initiatives considered unimaginable less than two decades earlier. By then negotiated arms control agreements had become not only a generally accepted dimension of U.S. national security policy, but also an integral element of strategic deterrence. Interestingly, the initial focus was on the control and reduction of delivery systems, not on nuclear and other weapons of mass destruction. Limiting delivery systems continues to be a primary concern, as reflected in the national missile defense debate, but since the mid-1980s warheads have increasingly been the subject of scrutiny.

From SALT to START

The *Strategic Arms Limitation Talks (SALT)* negotiations were a joint effort by the Cold War adversaries to prevent the collapse of the fragile balance of terror that mutual assured destruction supported. The SALT agreements reached in 1972 (SALT I) attempted to guarantee each superpower's second-strike capability and thereby preserve the fear of retaliation on which stable deterrence presumably rested.

The first SALT agreement consisted of (1) a treaty that restricted the deployment of antiballistic missile (ABM) defense systems by the United States and the Soviet Union to equal and very low levels, and (2) a five-year interim accord on strategic offensive arms, which restricted the number of intercontinental ballistic missile (ICBM) and submarine ballistic missile (SLBM) launchers that each side was permitted to have. The interim agreement on offensive weapons was essentially a confidence-building, stopgap measure that anticipated a comprehensive, long-term treaty limiting strategic weapons. The ABM accord, although a treaty, was eventually repudiated by both of its signatories.

The SALT II treaty, signed in 1979 (but never ratified), sought to make arms limitations permanent by substantially revising the quantitative restrictions of SALT I and by placing certain qualitative constraints on the superpowers' strategic arsenals. When SALT II was signed, these limits were expected to dampen dramatically the momentum of the superpowers' arms race. Although they may have kept the total number of strategic weapons below what otherwise would have been produced, the spiral of weapons production—notably, deliverable warheads—continued.

The Reagan administration followed the "dual track" of its predecessors by pursuing simultaneously arms control talks and a military buildup. Early in its first term the Reagan team showed little willingness to discuss arms limitations, but a combination of domestic and international pressure gave impetus to two sets of negotiations—the *Strategic Arms Reduction Talks (START)*, aimed at reducing, not just capping, the superpowers' strategic forces, and the intermediate-range nuclear force (INF) talks, designed to limit theater nuclear weapons in Europe. As noted earlier, the superpowers reached a historic agreement in 1987 when they signed the INF treaty banning intermediate-range nuclear forces from Europe. Although the accord required dismantling less than five percent of the world's nuclear arsenals, it set the stage for what British Foreign Secretary Sir Geoffrey Howe called "the beginning of the beginning of the whole arms control process."

On the strategic front, negotiations first stalled and then proceeded cautiously. In 1985, the superpowers differed substantially in how those cuts should be accomplished, however, as their force compositions influenced their negotiating positions. As a traditional land power, the Soviet Union placed heavy reliance on land-based missiles. The United States sought to reduce their number, viewing them as the gravest threat to U.S. land-based forces. Conversely, the Soviets, facing an American strategic force more widely dispersed among the three legs of its strategic triad, sought cutbacks that would directly offset U.S. areas of superiority.

Eventually the principle of "deep cuts" became the mutually accepted goal. In 1991, after nine years of bargaining, the negotiators overcame their differences and concluded the START I treaty, committing each side to reduce its strategic forces by one third. The treaty also provided a baseline for future reductions in the two sides' strategic capabilities.

Almost as soon as the ink on START I was dry, President Bush responded to widespread complaints that the agreement barely began the kinds of arms reductions possible now that the threat of a Soviet attack had vanished. The United States must seize "the historic opportunity now before us," he declared. He then called long-range bombers off twenty-four-hour alert, canceled plans to deploy the long-range MX missile on rail cars, and offered to negotiate sharp reductions in the most dangerous kinds of globe-spanning missiles. Not long after that, the new Russian President Boris Yeltsin declared that Russia "no longer considers the United States our potential adversary" and announced it would stop targeting American cities with nuclear missiles. Bush responded with a series of unilateral arms cuts to which Yeltsin quickly replied. He recommended that the two powers reduce their nuclear arsenals to only 2,000 to 2,500 warheads each—far below the cuts called for in START I and almost 50 percent greater than the reductions Bush had proposed.

At the June 1992 Washington summit, Bush and Yeltsin made the surprise announcement that Russia and the United States would make additional deep cuts in their strategic arsenals. The addendum to the START accord, which was to become START II, called for a 60 percent reduction of the two powers' combined total nuclear arsenals—from about 15,000 warheads to 6,500 by the year 2003. Even more dramatically, the START II agreement, signed in early 1993, not only cut the number of warheads beyond earlier projections but also altered drastically the kinds of weapons each country could stockpile. Russia and the United States agreed to give up all multiple warheads on their land-based ICBM missiles—a particularly dangerous, "silo-busting" capability. They also pledged to reduce the number of submarine-launched ballistic missile warheads to no more than 1,750. President Bush described the hopeful future that START II portended: "With this agreement the nuclear nightmare recedes more and more for ourselves, for our children, and for our grandchildren."

Strategic Defense and Arms Control in the New Era

START II faced several nettlesome problems from the beginning. They included the presence of nuclear weapons on the territories of three other of the former Soviet republics (Belarus, Kazakhstan, and Ukraine) and stiff opposition from ardent Russian nationalists and communists in the Duma, the Russian parliament whose approval was required. Under the terms of the agreement, Russia would have to undertake expensive efforts to build new single warhead missiles to maintain strategic parity with the United States—an issue important to Russians committed to retaining its superpower status. And in the United States, congressional conservatives concerned about denuding America's nuclear capabilities were implacably opposed to the agreement. Thus START II remained unratified nearly ten years after it was signed.

Bill Clinton promised a thorough reevaluation of the nation's strategic posture paralleling the Bottom Up Review of conventional weapons. When

TABLE 4.2 Strategic Nuclear Warheads of the United States and the Soviet Union/Russia, 1990–2007

| | United States | | | Russia | | |
	1990	2005	2007[a]	1990[b]	2005	2007[a]
ICBMs	2,450	1,700	300	6,612	2,436	385
SLBMs	5,760	3,168	1,008	2,804	1,672	1,016
Bombers	2,353	1,098	700	855	624	568
Total	10,563	5,966	2,008	10,271	4,732	1,969

[a] Assumes START II is in place and START III has been successfully negotiated.
[b] Includes Belarus, Kazakhstan, Russia, and Ukraine.
SOURCE: Adapted from Arms Control Association, *ACA Fact Sheet*, 2001, 2006. WWW.armscontrol.org.

the review was completed in 1994, however, it reaffirmed previous policies but did little else. A disappointment to those who sought further reductions in strategic arms, no new initiatives were announced that would cut U.S. and Russian weapons below the 3,500/3,000 balance projected in the START II accord. Furthermore, the United States would continue to deploy nearly 500 nuclear weapons in Europe to deter an attack on American allies. And the long-standing doctrine of a "first use" of nuclear weapons was retained rather than adopting a no-first-use declaratory policy. As during the Cold War, this meant that the United States might draw the nuclear sword to fend off non-nuclear challenges, including those posed by biological and chemical weapons. Finally, Clinton approved a military plan to install more accurate missiles equipped with nuclear warheads on U.S. submarines. It was in this environment that an anonymous advocate of further reductions in offensive nuclear weapons worried that "the clay of history is beginning to harden again" (quoted in Smith 1994b; for a contrasting viewpoint, see Bailey 1995).

START II never entered into force because of persistent delays in the Russian ratification process. With U.S. strategic doctrine also seemingly stuck in the clay of history, Clinton and Russian President Yeltsin met in Helsinki, Finland, in 1997, in an effort to keep the strategic arms control process alive. There they laid the groundwork for START III, which envisioned reductions of their nuclear arms to between 2,000 and 2,500 strategic nuclear warheads by 2007. In the end, the treaty achieved

reductions roughly equivalent to 20 percent of each superpower's nuclear arsenal in 1990 (see Table 4.2). It also kept parts of the START process alive by employing START's on-site verification system that provided the foundation for confidence, transparency, and predictability in future strategic interactions.

In 2001, George W. Bush and Russian President Vladimir Putin concluded a handshake deal to further reduce nuclear arms, disagreeing only over whether to do so in a formal treaty or a simple executive agreement. Later, in May 2002, an agreement popularly called the *Moscow Treaty* was ratified that made even deeper cuts than projected by their predecessors. The **Strategic Offensive Reductions Treaty (SORT)** limited each country's total number of operationally deployed strategic nuclear weapons to 1700–2200. The projected targets are to be met by 2012, when the treaty will either expire or be extended by a follow-on agreement.

The SORT treaty does not specify how each state will determine what types of warheads will be cut nor does it require that the warheads be destroyed, only that they be removed from their delivery vehicles. This fact led Secretary of State Colin Powell in testimony before that Senate to explain that "the treaty will allow you to have as many warheads as you want." Furthermore, because the treaty refers only to *deployed* weapons (various SALT and START agreements also refer to deployed nuclear weapons), not their total number, it excludes hundreds, perhaps thousands more in storage that can be activated rather quickly and easily.

How many strategic nuclear weapons are necessary for effective deterrence? No one is sure, but some analysts believe that cutting force levels to 200 warheads for all of the major nuclear powers is sufficient. Indeed, for the United States, whose conventional power outstrips all other states, nuclear weapons are comparatively unimportant. The revolution in military affairs promises that American security interests would be better served *without* nuclear weapons than *with* them. Les Aspin, long-time chair of the House Armed Services Committee and Bill Clinton's first secretary of defense, anticipated that future when he wondered about the wisdom of having developed nuclear weapons in the first place. His words:

> Nuclear weapons were the big equalizer—the means by which the United States equalized the military advantage of its adversaries. But now the Soviet Union has collapsed. The United States is the biggest conventional power in the world. There is no longer any need for the United States to have nuclear weapons as an equalizer against other powers. If we were to get another crack at the magic wand, we'd wave it in a nanosecond. A world without nuclear weapons would not be disadvantageous to the United States. In fact, a world without nuclear weapons would actually be better. Nuclear weapons are still the big equalizer but now the United States is not the equalizer but the equalizee.

Meanwhile, the strategic arms control agenda remains unfulfilled. Stopping nuclear testing as a way to deal with proliferation remains an enduring objective. In 1996, President Clinton signed the **Comprehensive Test Ban Treaty (CTBT),** calling it "the longest-sought, hardest-fought prize in arms control history." As the name implies, the treaty sought to stall further nuclear proliferation by banning completely all explosive nuclear tests, including the underground tests permitted under the 1963 Partial Test Ban Treaty signed in the immediate aftermath of the Cuban missile crisis. By 2006, 177 states had joined the United States in signing the new treaty, including all of the then-declared nuclear powers (Britain, China, France, Russian, and the United States). Notably absent were India and Pakistan, two of the three (Israel is the other) "nondeclared" nuclear states. Because of the way it was drafted, the CTBT cannot come into force until India, which refuses even to sign the treaty, ratifies it along with the forty-three other countries that possess nuclear power and research reactors. Furthermore, although the United States is a signatory of the treaty, Congress voted in October 1999 against its ratification. The failure of the CTBT to come into force a decade after it was signed is especially troubling to counterproliferation advocates as North Korea expands its missile and weapons programs and Iran develops its capacity to build nuclear weapons programs, even in the face of strong international pressure.

At the level of conventional weapons, more than one hundred countries gathered in Ottawa, Canada, in 1997, where they signed a treaty to ban the production and use of antipersonnel weapons, commonly referred to as land mines. Diana, Princess of Wales, campaigned against these widely used weapons, which often kill or maim not just military personnel but also noncombatants long after the overt violence that precipitated their use has ended. At the time of the Ottawa gathering, analysts estimated that "anywhere from 80 million to 110 million land mines are buried in 68 nations, from Angola to Bosnia, Nicaragua to Cambodia" (Myers 1997). The United States agreed to participate in the negotiations but in the end refused to sign the *Ottawa Landmine Treaty* (formally the Convention on the Prohibition of the Use, Stockpiling, Production and Transfer of Anti-Personnel Mines and on Their Destruction). The Pentagon vigorously opposed the treaty, reasoning that antipersonnel weapons are among the most effective in protecting South Korea from a North Korean invasion. Ironically, countless land mines left behind by retreating Serbian forces posed one of the gravest dangers to NATO peacekeepers following the Kosovo air bombardment. Later, during the Iraq war, improvised explosive devices (IEDs), often planted on roadsides, proved to be a great threat to U.S. troops and the cause of many casualties. Arguably, IEDs are analogous to land mine antipersonnel weapons.

The land mine debate reveals how difficult reconciling arms control with larger national security concerns often is. Still, the United States remains committed to the principle of integrating the control of weapons of war into its overall military posture. Coping with weapons of mass destruction will command primary attention, but, as illustrated with the land mines case, other weapons may also be scrutinized. Instructively, the United States joined African and European states in Oslo, Norway, in 1998, where they endorsed measures to control the spread of light weapons, the major cause of death in today's wars.

POWER AND PRINCIPLE: IN PURSUIT OF THE NATIONAL INTEREST

The world has changed dramatically in the past two decades, but the means of American foreign policy—captured in the themes of military might and interventionism—remain durable patterns. Adjustments have been made, to be sure, but they have been confined largely to tactics, not fundamental reassessments of basic purposes or strategies. Thus we find that the nation's conventional military forces remain poised for global engagement and that nuclear weapons are still believed to provide security from attack through the threat of attack. Without a new framework for policy, old ways of thinking persist.

The outlines of a new framework remain unclear, though the reelection of George W. Bush in November 2004 may solidify a direction for some time to come. Beyond the overarching commitment to the war on terror, to many people the United States is still the dominant power in a unipolar world at the dawn of a new American century. This conviction calls out for a policy of primacy.

Will primacy carry the day beyond Bush? Liberty may remain the quintessential goal of American foreign policy, but whether the United States will go abroad in search of monsters to destroy is problematic. The spillover of dissatisfaction with the war in Iraq may spark renewed contention over the appropriate role of the United States in world affairs. Nonetheless the nation's long history of intervention in the affairs of others to remake the world in its own image is likely to survive in some form or another.

KEY TERMS

assured destruction
ballistic missile defense (BMD)
brinkmanship
Carter Doctrine
compellence
Comprehensive Test Ban Treaty (CTBT)
counterforce
countervailing (war-fighting) strategy
countervalue
deterrence
extended deterrence
flexible response
force-short-of-war

massive retaliation
mutual assured destruction (MAD)
national missile defense (NMD)
National Security Council (NSC)
national security policy
new interventionism
Nixon Doctrine
NSC-68
NUTS/NUT
peace enforcement
peacekeeping
Powell Doctrine
revolution in military affairs (RMA)

rollback
second-strike capability
Single Integrated Operational Plan (SIOP)
sovereignty
Strategic Arms Limitation Talks (SALT)
Strategic Arms Reduction Talks (START)
Strategic Defense Initiative (SDI)
Strategic Offensive Reductions Treaty (SORT)

strategic weapons
tactical nuclear weapons
theater missile defenses (TMD)
theater nuclear forces
triad of strategic weapons
trip wire
twin pillars strategy
two-war strategy
Weinberger Doctrine
win-hold-win strategy

SUGGESTED READINGS

Allison, Graham. *Nuclear Terrorism: The Ultimate Preventable Catastrophe.* New York: Henry Holt, 2004b.

Alperovitz, Gar. *The Decision to Use the Atomic Bomb and the Architecture of an American Myth.* New York: Knopf, 1995.

Art, Robert J., and Patrick M. Cronin, eds. *The United States and Coercive Diplomacy.* Washington, DC: United States Institute of Peace Press, 2003, pp. 359–420.

Brands, H. W., ed. *The Use of Force After the Cold War.* College Station, TX: Texas A&M University Press, 2000.

Daalder, Ivo H., and Michael O'Hanlon. *Winning Ugly: NATO's War to Save Kosovo.* Washington, DC: Brookings Institution, 2000.

Deutch, John. "Rethinking Nuclear Strategy," *Foreign Affairs* 84 (January/February 2005): 49–60.

Flynn, Stephen. *America the Vulnerable: How Our Government Is Failing to Protect Us from Terrorism.* New York: HarperCollins, 2004.

George, Alexander L. *The Limits of Coercive Diplomacy.* Boulder, CO: Westview, 1994.

Haass, Richard N. *The Opportunity: America's Moment to Alter History's Course.* New York: PublicAffairs Books, 2005.

Hoffman, Peter J., and Thomas G. Weiss. *Sword and Salve: Confronting New Wars and Humanitarian Crises.* Landham, MD: Rowman and Littlefield, 2006.

MacKinnon, Michael G. *The Evolution of US Peacekeeping Policy Under Clinton.* London: Frank Cass Publishers, 1999.

Rumsfeld, Donald H. "Transforming the Military," *Foreign Affairs* 81 (May/June): 20–32.

Snow, Donald M. *When America Fights: The Uses of U.S. Military Force.* Washington, DC: Congressional Quarterly Press, 2000.

Woodward, Bob. *Bush at War.* New York: Simon and Schuster, 2002.

NOTES

1. George (1992) studied seven other cases beginning in the 1930s and spanning the Cold War period. Much like Art, he concludes that coercive diplomacy succeeded in 2 percent of the cases, failed in 43 percent, and ended with ambiguous outcomes 29 percent of the time.

2. The Washington think-tank Global Security, which specializes in military issues, described the objectives of the Iraq war thus:

   The military objectives of Operation Iraqi Freedom consist of, first, ending the regime of Saddam Hussein. Second, to identify, isolate, and eliminate Iraq's weapons of mass destruction. Third, to search for, to capture, and to drive out terrorists from the country. Fourth, to collect intelligence related to terrorist networks. Fifth, to collect such intelligence as is related to the global network of illicit weapons of mass destruction. Sixth, to end sanctions and to immediately deliver humanitarian support to the displaced and to many needy citizens. Seventh, to secure Iraq's oil fields and resources, which belong to the Iraqi people. Finally, to help the Iraqi people create conditions for a transition to a representative self-government. (www.globalsecurity.org/military/ops/iraqi_ freedom.htm, accessed 10/23/06)

3. Some NATO countries, notably France and to a lesser extent Germany, believe that only the United Nations can authorize the resort to force for purposes other than self-defense. The United States, on the other hand, objects to holding NATO "hostage" to the UN Security Council, where Russia and China could veto the use of force (Daalder 1999).

4. On the use of force in the 1990s, see Betts (1994), Brands (2000), and MacKinnon (1999).

5. See Nye (1996) for an attempt to distinguish among different levels of U.S. interests and requirements associated with them.

6. On the Somalia intervention, see Schraeder (1998), Stevenson (1995), Brune (1999), and Clarke and Herbst (1997).

7. Writing before the Kosovo campaign, John A. Gentry (1998), a retired U.S. Army Reserve officer who spent time in Bosnia and at NATO headquarters working on Bosnia-related issues, wrote a scathing article entitled "Military Force in an Age of National Cowardice." He argues that "the United States presents a schizophrenic posture to the world: we crow about being the world's only superpower and claim the perquisites of that status, including the world's obeisance under the threat of sanctions, but radiate fear about using power if our people are likely to be hurt."

8. Research on public attitudes toward casualties suffered in Lebanon and in the humanitarian intervention in Somalia lends only limited support to the hypothesis that suffering casualties will cause public support of peacekeeping operations to dissipate (Burk 1999).

9. For a vivid description of the human and physical damage, see Schell (1982).

10. See Alperovitz (1985, 1989), Bernstein (1995), and Miles (1985). For rebuttals, see Alsop and Joravsky (1980), Bundy (1988), and Weinberg (1994).

11. Stimson actually became an early advocate of efforts to negotiate an agreement with the Soviet Union that might have limited the nuclear arms spiral that soon followed (Chace 1996).

12. Alperovitz and Bird (1994) discuss the role of the atomic bomb in the militarization of post–World War II American foreign policy.

13. During the Reagan era, when the expectation of nuclear war was high, Dick Cheney, then a Republican congressman, and Donald Rumsfeld, head of the Searle pharmaceutical company in Chicago, led a highly secret team who purpose was to develop a plan to ensure the survivability of the government, particularly the presidency, in the event of nuclear war, even if this required circumventing constitutional rules governing presidential succession. Fifty to sixty federal employees, including at least one member of the cabinet, participated in detailed monthly exercises designed to keep "the federal government running during and after a nuclear war with the Soviet Union" (Mann 2004a). The plan and exercises developed at the time became a blueprint, led by Cheney, to protect President Bush following the 9/11 terrorist attacks (Mann 2004a).

14. The literature on missile defense systems is substantial. For brief discussions of the pros and cons, see Glaser and Fetter (2001) and Lindsay and O'Hanlon (2002a, 2002b).

15. The Persian Gulf War stimulated the search for theater defenses, as the perceived success of the Patriot antimissile missile during the conflict gave impetus to the possibility of a successful defense against ballistic missiles. The actual performance of the Patriot in that war became a controversial matter (Hersh 1994; Postol 1992; but compare Ranger 1993.)

16. In May 1999, the House of Representatives released a three-volume, declassified version of the report by its Select Committee on U.S. National Security and Military/Commercial Concerns with the People's Republic of China, chaired by Representative Christopher Cox (R-CA). The report concluded that for twenty years China had carried out a successful espionage program that included information about all types of nuclear weapons currently deployed in the U.S. arsenal.

17. The fall of the Berlin Wall in 1989 caused Dick Cheney, secretary of defense in the first Bush administration and vice president in the second, to question the objectives of the SIOP and ultimately to dramatically reduce the number of its nuclear targets. Assumptions underlying the SIOP also began to be questioned. General George Lee Butler, who became commander of U.S. nuclear forces in 1991, would later become a vigorous advocate of the complete abolition of nuclear weapons (Smith 1997); see also Hall (1998).

5

Instruments of Global Influence:

Covert Activities, Foreign Aid, Sanctions, and Public Diplomacy

Intervention can be physical, spiritual, bilateral, multilateral, direct action, skills transfer, institution building; it can be so many things—a fabulous menu!
CHESTER A. CROCKER, CHAIR, BOARD OF DIRECTORS, U.S. INSTITUTE FOR PEACE, 1994

Reassurance is good. Cash is better.
AHMAD FAWZI, UNITED NATIONS SPOKESMAN COMMENTING ON LONG-TERM AMERICAN SUPPORT FOR AFGHANISTAN, 2002

In 1947, President Harry Truman enunciated the Truman Doctrine, thus committing the United States to an active, internationalist role in the post–World War II era. Congress passed a new National Security Act, which not only created the Department of Defense and the Joint Chiefs of Staff to coordinate the country's military establishment, but also the Central Intelligence Agency (CIA) to strengthen the ability of the United States to gather information and prevent recurrence of a catastrophe like Pearl Harbor. On June 5, 1947, at a Harvard University commencement address, Secretary of State George C. Marshall set forth in the Marshall Plan the commitment of the United States to assist in the reconstruction of war-torn Europe. The remarkably successful program not only helped rebuild the devastated economies of Western Europe, it kept the countries in the region from falling under communist influence. Two years later, in Point Four of his inaugural address, President Truman called for "a bold new program for making the benefits of our scientific advances and industrial progress available for the improvement and growth of underdeveloped areas," thus making foreign aid programs major instruments of American foreign policy. In 1953, the United States Information Agency (USIA) was established, creating an institutional home for World War II's Voice of America and other broadcasting and information programs meant to promote American ideas and interests around the globe. Along with the opportunity to use trade and access to the huge American market for foreign policy purposes, the innovations of these few years thereby established the outlines of the main instruments of American foreign policy drawn upon to this day.

As the last chapter suggested, military might soon quickly assumed a central role as a means to achieve post–World War II American objectives. American policy makers, however, have also relied on an array of nonmilitary means to achieve their strategic and political goals. In this chapter, we examine covert activities, foreign assistance, sanctions, and public diplomacy, and provide background on their historical uses. We will consider the challenges and dilemmas the twenty-first century poses to their continued relevance and utility

COVERT INTERVENTION: INTELLIGENCE COLLECTION AND COVERT ACTION

The intelligence community performs a range of functions, including collecting and analyzing information (discussed more thoroughly in Chapter 11) and covert action. In terms of instruments of global influence, it is the covert activities of the United States government that provide a means of affecting events around the world and the policies of others. The United States' persistent covert involvement in the affairs of other states contributed measurably to the interventionist label attached to post–World War II American foreign policy. NSC-68, the National

Security Council document so essential to the militarization of American foreign policy, helped push the United States in the direction of covert action as well. As noted in Chapter 4, it called for a non-military counteroffensive against the Soviet Union designed to foment unrest and revolt in Soviet bloc countries. At least some in Washington soon recognized that such undertakings could be accomplished only by the establishment of a worldwide structure for covert action.

To be sure, states have always gathered information about one another, which often means engaging in **espionage**—spying to obtain secret government information. The United States is no exception (see, for example, Andrew 1995). Indeed, during the American Revolution, the British hanged Nathan Hale, an American soldier, for spying. According to tradition, Hale's last words were "I only regret that I have but one life to lose for my country." Today, Hale's statue stands outside the entry to the headquarters of the CIA in Langley, Virginia.

Nevertheless, prior to World War II, covert activities by the United States were very limited, usually involving efforts to collect information. During World War I, intercepting and decoding enemy cable and radio messages—*cryptanalysis*—brought the application of modern technology to intelligence work. The "Black Chamber," a small U.S. military intelligence unit responsible for this activity, continued to function after the war, only to be terminated by President Herbert Hoover's secretary of state in 1929, who found the Black Chamber's activities abhorrent to America's idealist values. During the 1930s, President Franklin D. Roosevelt and his advisers received specialized intelligence briefings about Japan and Germany from a broad array of information sources (Kahn 1984), but the United States did not have secret agents operating abroad. Consequently, it could not practice **counterintelligence,** "operations undertaken against foreign intelligence services ... directed specifically against the espionage efforts of such services" (Holt 1995).

The immediate precursor to the CIA was the Office of Strategic Services (OSS), created by

President Roosevelt during World War II. Headed by General William J. "Wild Bill" Donovan, the OSS carried out covert intelligence operations against the Axis powers, marking the first time the United States moved beyond merely collecting information to shaping events actively in other countries. After World War II, the United States converted the OSS into a specialized intelligence agency charged with collecting and analyzing information and carrying out "special activities" as directed by the president.

The CIA was created by the National Security Act of 1947, and in the years that followed, the agency became infamous worldwide. According to a well-known congressional investigation of the CIA undertaken in the mid-1970s, "The CIA has been accused of interfering in the internal political affairs of states ranging from Iran to Chile, from Tibet to Guatemala, from Libya to Laos, from Greece to Indonesia. Assassinations, coups d'état, vote buying, economic warfare—all have been laid at the doorstep of the CIA. Few political crises take place in the world today in which CIA involvement is not alleged" (*Final Report,* I, 1976 *Final Report of the Select Committee to Study Governmental Operations with Respect to Intelligence Activities,* Vol. IV, 1976; hereafter cited as *Final Report,* I–IV, 1976). A growing volume of declassified documents and revelations flowing from the now-defunct Soviet empire show such characterizations of U.S. covert action to be largely accurate.

The Definition and Types of Covert Action

Covert action is a clandestine activity typically undertaken against foreign governments to influence political, economic, or military conditions abroad, where it is intended that the role of the U.S. government will not be apparent or acknowledged. Early in the Cold War, American policy makers embraced covert actions like those described above as instruments of influence chiefly because of their alleged utility as a so-called "middle option," less risky than direct military action, but more aggressive

than diplomatic pressure. Hence, the instrument appealed to many as "a prudent alternative to doing nothing" (Berkowitz and Goodman 1998).

Over time, the United States has relied on a number of such "special actions" in its foreign policy. A 1954 National Security Council directive identified the breadth of such acts:

> . . . propaganda; political action; economic warfare; escape and evasion and evacuation measures; subversion against hostile states or groups including assistance to underground resistance movements, guerrillas, and refugee liberation groups; support of indigenous and anticommunist elements in threatened countries of the free world; deception plans and operations; and all activities compatible with this directive necessary to accomplish the foregoing.
> *(Quoted in Gaddis 1982, 158)*

In the 1970s, it became clear that assassination was also part of this repertoire. Later, various forms of high-tech information warfare or "cyberwar" also joined the list.

Covert Intervention in the Early Cold War

In the early years of the Cold War, the use of covert action rested on a general consensus regarding the nature of the competition with the Soviet Union. Driven by the apparent urgency of the competition, American policy makers increasingly turned to covert interventions. Two of the CIA's boldest and most spectacular operations—the overthrow of Premier Mohammed Mossadegh in Iran in 1953 and the coup that ousted President Jacobo Arbenz of Guatemala in 1954[1]—resulted in the quick and virtually bloodless removal of two allegedly procommunist leaders. Consequently, both the agency and Washington policy makers acquired a sense of confidence in the CIA's capacity for operational success. Eventually, this reputation for results led to an enviable situation in which the CIA provided information, recommended policy programs, and then implemented them.

The invasion of Cuba at the Bay of Pigs in 1961 by a band of CIA-trained and financed Cuban exiles stands out as a classic case of CIA prominence in policy making. The CIA saw the Bay of Pigs operation as a way to eliminate the "problem" posed by Fidel Castro. Although engineered along the lines of the successful 1954 Guatemalan operation, the defeat suffered by the Cuban exiles tarnished the agency's reputation and cost Allen Dulles, the CIA director, his job.[2] Still, covert operations remained an accepted policy option. *Operation Mongoose* reflected that perspective. It consisted of paramilitary, sabotage, and political propaganda activities directed against Castro's Cuba in the aftermath of the Bay of Pigs, but with much the same purpose as the 1961 invasion. The Church committee's Senate hearings in the 1970s (discussed below) even revealed that the CIA once tried to humiliate Castro by dusting the Cuban leader's shoes with a substance that would make his hair fall out! Less humorously, the investigation reported that Castro had survived at least eight CIA-sponsored assassination plots.

From the 1950s to the 1970s, the agency made payments to Japan's conservative political party, the Liberal Democratic Party (LDP), which dominated Japanese politics for more than a generation, hoping to stave off a challenge by Japanese socialists. *Paramilitary operations* were also initiated in Southeast Asia. In Laos, over 30,000 tribesmen were organized into a kind of private CIA army. In Vietnam, where a CIA analyst would later admit that the agency "assassinated a lot of the wrong damn people" (Carr 1994), a CIA operation known as Phoenix killed over 20,000 suspected Vietcong in less than four years (Lewy 1978; Marchetti and Marks 1974).

Recent declassified documents reveal that from the end of World War II to well into the 1970s, the Atomic Energy Commission, the Defense Department, the military services, the CIA, and other agencies used prisoners, drug addicts, mental patients, college students, soldiers, even bar patrons, in a vast range of government-run experiments to test the effects of everything from radiation, LSD, and nerve gas to intense electric shocks and prolonged sensory deprivation. Why did the United States conduct these experiments, so eerily reminiscent of the horrific medical experiments performed during World War II on innocent victims by the likes of Germany's Dr. Josef Mengele and Japan General Shoro Ishii? "In the life and death struggle with communism, American could not afford to leave any scientific avenue unexplored" (*U.S. News and World Report*, 24 January 1994, 33).

The catalog of proven and alleged CIA involvement in the internal affairs of other states could be broadened extensively, but we cannot understand the reliance on either covert or military forms of intervention without recognizing how much the fear of communism and the drive to contain it motivated policy makers. According to the well-known book *The CIA and the Cult of Intelligence* (Victor Marchetti and John Marks 1974), "covert intervention may seem to be an easier solution to a particular problem than to allow events to follow their natural course or to seek a tortuous diplomatic settlement. . . . The temptation to interfere in another country's internal affairs can be almost irresistible, when the means are at hand." Not surprisingly, then, policy makers used the same tools as the other side, no matter how repugnant they might have been. A higher purpose—the "national security"—was being served.

Covert Actions in the 1970s and 1980s

During the 1970s, covert actions were described simply as those secret activities designed to further American policies and programs abroad. Chile became an early target.[3] Beginning in the 1950s, the United States mounted a concerted effort in Chile to prevent the leftist politician Salvador Allende from first gaining and then exercising political power. By the 1970s, American efforts included covert activities; a close working relationship between the government and giant United States–based multinational corporations doing business in Chile, whose corporate interests were threatened; and pressure on multilateral lending institutions to do America's bidding. Anti-communist thinking contributed to the eventual overthrow of the Allende government, but the story also illustrated American willingness to use a range of instruments to oppose those willing to experiment in leftist domestic political programs.

The revelation of these activities and others led to growing concern about the use (and misuse) of covert activities. Both the president and Congress imposed restraints on the foreign and domestic activities of the intelligence community. Senate hearings on intelligence activities, chaired by Frank Church (D-Idaho), revealed the CIA had tried to assassinate (murder for political purposes) foreign leaders and engaged in other questionable acts. As Church colorfully characterized it in the hearings, "Covert action is a semantic disguise for murder, coercion, blackmail, bribery, [and] the spreading of lies." This led President Gerald Ford to issue an executive order—still in force today but the subject of heated debate—outlawing assassination. As Congress became increasingly involved in the oversight of intelligence activities, this led to more refined definitions of and reporting requirements on covert actions (sometimes called "special activities") to ensure that presidents brought all proposed activities to the attention of appropriate congressional committees. For instance, the 1980 Intelligence Oversight Act established congressional intelligence oversight committees and required the submission of *presidential findings*—the president's certification to Congress that an executive-approved covert action is "important to the national interest." Presidential findings are to specify the need, purposes, and (general) means of the operation.

The Reagan administration's determination to exorcise the ghost of Vietnam, and to challenge this increased congressional assertiveness, was especially apparent in its drive to "unleash" the CIA (Woodward 1987). Its capacity for covert actions in terms of staff and budget were greatly reenergized under William Casey, Ronald Reagan's CIA director. Casey also enjoyed wide latitude in conducting secret wars against American enemies, virtually running his own State and Defense departments out of the CIA (Scott 1996). In addition to covert actions in places like Iran, Chad, Ethiopia, Liberia, and the Sudan, his missions included implementation of the **Reagan Doctrine.**

As stated in National Security Decision Direction 75 (January 17, 1983), the Reagan Doctrine directed American policy "to . . . weaken and, where possible, undermine the existing links between [Soviet Third World allies] and the Soviet Union. U.S. policy will include active efforts to encourage democratic movements and forces to bring about political change inside these countries." As President Reagan said in 1985, "We must not break faith with those who are risking their lives on every continent from Afghanistan to Nicaragua to defy Soviet supported aggression and secure rights which have been ours from birth."

Afghanistan and Nicaragua became the most celebrated applications of the newly enunciated doctrine (which also included Angola and Cambodia). Using Pakistan as a gateway, the CIA provided the anti-Marxist *mujahideen*, (the Islamic guerrillas challenging Soviet troops and the pro-Soviet regime in Afghanistan) with more than $3 billion in guns, ammunition, and other support, including a shoulder-fired antiaircraft missile known as the Stinger, which proved enormously successful and may have played a critical role in the Soviet Union's withdrawal from Afghanistan (Scott 1996).[4]

In Nicaragua the CIA supported the *contras* (so-called counterrevolutionaries who were themselves a creation of the agency) with arms, aid, and support for naval blockades, air strikes, espionage, and propaganda operations. Eventually, the U.S. role in Nicaragua figured prominently in the *Iran-contra affair*, a domestic scandal that rekindled fears of an abuse of power in the name of national security reminiscent of the Watergate affair a decade earlier. A central issue was whether funds diverted from the sale of arms to Iran in a secret arms-for-hostages deal violated a legal prohibition against continued CIA support of the contras' activities. The last two years of the Reagan administration were dominated by investigations of this scandal, not to mention renewed charges that the covert arms of the United States government were in need of more careful control.

Hence, as the Cold War came to a close, serious questions about the nature and desirability of covert interventions were being raised in many quarters. Because the Cold War's end took with it the basic rationale for most of the intelligence activities in which the United States had engaged, including covert interventions, many wondered what place such activities would play in the absence of the Soviet threat.

In Search of a Rationale: Intelligence and Covert Action beyond the Cold War

While most policy makers and policy analysts agree that intelligence must be collected and analyzed, the need for a continued covert action capability has historically been more controversial. In the post-9/11 world, however, debate over covert action, along with issues of intelligence gathering more generally, have at least for the short term turned to "How can we do it better?" rather than "Should we do it at all?" This shift in the debate about the need for proactive intelligence gathering and covert action is captured well in *The 9/11 Commission Report*, published in the fall of 2004:

> Three years after 9/11, Americans are still thinking and talking about how to protect our nation in this new era. The national debate continues. Countering terrorism has become, beyond a doubt, the top security priority for the United States. This shift has occurred with the full support of the Congress, both major political parties, the media and the American people (p. 361).

While this last sentence may be a bit of hyperbole about the level of support for all aspects of counterterrorism, few would question the notion that it has indeed become the primary goal for all governmental agencies dealing with security issues in the contemporary world environment. Similarly, the need to reform the intelligence community to make it more effective is beyond dispute. Although we will take up the issue of intelligence reform in more detail in Chapter 11, it is worth noting here that the centerpiece legislation for intelligence reform passed Congress and was signed by President George W. Bush in late 2004. Creating the position of director of national intelligence, this new law attempts to provide greater coordination among the diverse set of intelligence agencies within the federal government. Ambassador John Negroponte was appointed the first director and immediately set to work on the tasks of reforming the intelligence community. As stated above, counterterrorism is not the only focus of the twenty-first century CIA, but it seems likely to be the primary mission for both intelligence and covert action for the foreseeable future. Supplementing this focus on counterterrorism, the intelligence community continues to be active in interdicting drug trafficking and narco-terrorism, high-tech "info war," enviro-intelligence, and traditional state threats. We will discuss these briefly and then turn to the emerging focus on counterterrorism.

The War on Drugs   With congressional encouragement, the CIA has expanded its covert operations in the drugs and *narco-terrorism* arena, working with the Drug Enforcement Agency (DEA). As with counterterrorism, the CIA gathers information, conducts surveillance and infiltration, and provides personnel, training, resources, and operations support while the DEA makes the arrests. Recent examples of American anti-drug operations include anti-opium efforts in Afghanistan, a six-country sweep of Caribbean states that netted fifty arrested traffickers, and continued concerns with Colombian drug traffickers (Holmes 2005).

An overt connection to counterterrorism permeates many recent anti-drug efforts. One recent U.S. government report, the *2005 International Narcotics Control Strategy Report*, cited Afghanistan's opium production as "an enormous threat to world stability." Moreover, the report stated that "dangerous security conditions [within Afghanistan] make implementing counter-narcotics programs difficult." The current fragility of Afghan governmental authority and the need to find sources of income throughout the country make drug trafficking a viable enterprise and a challenging policy problem for the Afghan leadership as well as the international military forces stationed there.

Similarly, in an effort to side-step congressional limits on aid to Colombia because of human rights concerns, the Bush administration post-9/11 declared that antigovernment, narco-backed insurgents were terrorists, thus removing the limitations on aid monies to the South American government. Given that the Colombian insurgents are funded and interwoven with drug-trafficking organizations, the use of the terrorism card provides a new twist to the war on drugs in this conflict-torn country (Holmes 2005). We should also note that a steady stream of revelations in the past decade point to highly questionable alliances between the CIA and individuals connected to the drug trade in Laos, Vietnam, Afghanistan, Nicaragua, Guatemala, and others, reaching at least as far back at the 1960s.[5]

Information Warfare and Enviro-Intelligence

The CIA has undertaken new covert efforts in additional areas that reflect the changing nature of the world: information warfare and enviro-intelligence. Although these threats may seem obvious to some experts, John Serabian, Jr., a CIA information operations manager, explained information warfare this way in testimony to Congress in 2000:

> Why is [the] threat [of information warfare] so insidious and different? We have spent years building an information infrastructure that is interoperable, easy to access, and easy to use. Attributes like openness and ease of connectivity which promote efficiency and expeditious customer service are the same ones that now make the system vulnerable to attacks against automated information systems.

The National Intelligence Council reiterated this concern in 2004 with the publication of *Mapping the Global Future*:

> Over the next 15 years, a growing range of actors, including terrorists, may acquire and develop capabilities to conduct both physical and cyber attacks against nodes of the world's information infrastructure, including the Internet, telecommunications networks, and computer systems that control critical industrial processes such as electricity grids, refineries, and flood control mechanisms. Terrorists already have specified the U.S. information infrastructure as a target and currently are capable of physical attacks that would cause at least brief, isolated disruptions.

Information warfare, or "cyberwar" as it is sometimes called, is the use of or attacks on information systems for political and/or military advantage. It is a critical area of national security in which the intelligence community is increasingly involved (Berkowitz and Goodman 1998). Not only is the CIA recruiting individuals with the specialized computer skills that would be useful in intelligence gathering and analysis related to such warfare, it is also developing "techno-spies as field-deployed case officers" (*Time,* 10 April 2000, p. 51). Covert "cyber-actions" involving these individuals include efforts to deter and track down hackers, prevent attacks on information systems, detect and prevent "bugs" embedded in important information hardware and software, and operations to employ such tactics against others (Berkowitz and Goodman 1998). Increasingly, the CIA seeks "a few good geeks," as one account colorfully characterized the situation (*Time,* 10 April 2000, p. 51).

Interestingly, some experts do not see cyberwarfare as the primary threat to information security, but rather profit-minded cybercrime. David Perry puts it this way:

> The terror we're facing is the terror of spam, the terror of spyware, the terror of

network worms, but nothing associated with the nation-state . . . Although I am sure terrorists and secret agents use computers and computer hacking tools for purposes of espionage and sabotage, I don't think cyber-terrorism is quite the threat that we imagine it's going to be.

(Quoted in Coren 2005)

Instead, the threats posed by cybercriminals through such attacks as identity theft may pose a larger hazard that the government is less able to cope with, at least in the short term. But whatever the target, profit or politics, cyber threats will remain a point of significant policy focus in the coming years.

In another policy area related to information technologies, the CIA became increasingly involved in the 1990s in what some have called *enviro-intelligence* (Auster 1998b). These efforts chiefly involve intelligence-gathering efforts that employ the nation's satellites and other technical resources to monitor and forecast crises. However, the CIA also monitors compliance with international environmental treaties, and began, in 1998, to target other countries to learn their negotiating positions on environmental issues such as the Kyoto agreement (Auster 1998b). To do so, it has established an environmental center and has tasked its operatives to penetrate the negotiating teams of other countries. An indicator of the significance of this area for future covert efforts is the National Intelligence Council report, *Global Trends 2015,* which details a host of emerging environmental issues (and consequences) that will impact the United States. Such concerns with forecasting and early warning were brought to the policy foreground when a tsunami hit South Asia in December 2004. In its aftermath, countries around the world worked together to create a more effective early warning system for future threats. Such a network of sensors around the world could help identify potential environmental threats and also alert governmental officials more quickly about an imminent threat. A significant factor in the potential for success in this policy area was the nearly $1 billion of aid pledged

by President Bush in early 2005 to help develop more capable early warning systems around the world.

Targeting States

Although the number of covert operations is believed to have declined substantially with the end of the Cold War, the United States continues their use against states it has identified as security threats. Such uses of this instrument closely resemble the traditional applications of the Cold War, albeit on a smaller scale. One example was an operation directed against the Saddam Hussein regime in Iraq. When Iraq invaded Kuwait in August 1990, President George H. W. Bush ordered the CIA to prepare a covert action plan to destabilize Iraq by undermining the Iraqi economy, fomenting discontent within its military forces, and supporting internal and external resistance to Saddam. Bush submitted a presidential finding to Congress to that effect, which was immediately approved by the intelligence committees (Fletcher 1990). CIA efforts included propaganda in the form of broadcasts, leaflets, and video/audio cassettes, as well as attempts to support military officers planning a coup attempt (Kurkjian 1991; Oberdorfer 1993).

President Bill Clinton continued the operation, enlarging CIA support for the Kurdish rebels in the northern region of Iraq, and helping to establish the "Iraqi National Congress"—a coalition of anti-Saddam groups. In 1995, under pressure from the Republican-controlled Congress to take stronger action against Iraq, the United States accelerated its support to include substantial military assistance. Together the Bush I and Clinton administrations spent well over $100 million through 1996 on the action. Unfortunately, in September 1996 the effort collapsed as the Kurds disintegrated into rival factions and Hussein launched a military strike into the region. A similar action based in Jordan, supporting the Iraqi National Accord (mostly former Iraqi military officers), also collapsed about the same time when Hussein's security forces infiltrated the organization (Risen 2000). The CIA was routed and its Kurdish allies were annihilated in what two longtime analysts of CIA activities called "possibly the greatest covert action debacle since Vietnam. . . . Having relied on covert action because it was unwilling to confront Iraq overtly, America appeared weak as well as naive in the wake of the operation's failure" (Berkowitz 1998). Efforts to revive the activities in 1998 largely failed. But with suspicion of Iraq's support for the Al Qaeda terrorist network and the September 2001 attacks on the United States, new attempts to undermine Saddam Hussein's regime began in the fall of 2001 and continued until the military operations against Iraq commenced in the spring of 2003.

Another example of this kind of covert action overlaps with the growing counterterrorism efforts discussed below and concerns CIA activities in Afghanistan after the September 2001 strikes against the United States. Targeted both at the Taliban regime and the Al Qaeda terrorist network led by Osama bin Laden, this covert action was described by one insider as "the most sweeping and lethal covert action since the founding of the agency in 1947" (Woodward 2001). Almost immediately after the attacks on New York and Washington, D.C., George W. Bush signed an intelligence finding authorizing actions against the Taliban regime and the destruction of Osama bin Laden and his Al Qaeda network. As a senior official described it, "The gloves are off. The president has given the agency the green light to do whatever is necessary. Lethal operations that were unthinkable pre–September 11 are now underway" (Woodward 2001).

The CIA operation began with several objectives, including locating and targeting leaders of the Taliban and Al Qaeda, attacking the infrastructure and the communications and security apparatus of the Afghan regime and the terrorist network, and recruiting "defectors" from the Pashtun leaders in the southern areas of Afghanistan in order to remove the Taliban from power (Sipress and Loeb 2001). In addition to more than $1 billion in new funds for the covert action, the covert operation had additional muscle through its close collaboration with the U.S. military's special forces and other units in an unprecedented display

of coordination (Woodward 2004). The CIA also operated armed, unmanned drones that produced live video and could be dispatched to fire on emerging targets. Plans were in place to use other, longer-range drones in similar ways (Ricks 2001). With bin Laden still at large in 2006, covert operations along the Afghan–Pakistani border have continued to this writing. In many ways, the covert experiences in Afghanistan demonstrated the vital importance of having paramilitary teams on the ground in the target country and laid the groundwork for the Bush strategy in Iraq (Woodward 2004, 109).

Counterterrorism

Even before the September 11 attacks on the United States, counterterrorist covert operations involving the CIA and FBI had expanded in recent years. A new Counterterrorism Center at CIA headquarters in Langley, Virginia, staffed by both agencies, brought the CIA's ability to gather intelligence and engage in covert actions together with the FBI's investigative and law enforcement strengths. Also, the FBI has the authority to take action within American borders (the CIA does not). Prior to September 2001, the partnership had some successes, including the arrests of Mir Aimal Kansi (who assassinated two CIA employees outside CIA headquarters in 1993) and Mohammed Rashid (for bombing a Pan Am flight from Hawaii to Japan in 1982); the apprehension of Tsutomu Shirosaki (who attacked the United States embassy in Indonesia); the apprehension and prosecution of those who bombed the World Trade Center in 1993; and the investigation of the 1998 bombings of United States embassies in Kenya and Tanzania (Kitfield 2000).

Perhaps the most extensive of these operations has been the effort to break up and apprehend the Al Qaeda network, organized and financed by wealthy Saudi expatriate and zealous Islamic revolutionary Osama bin Laden. Since 1995, when bin Laden's network first became a major target, the CIA has tried to infiltrate the network, track, arrest, and detain its members ("disruption operations"), and thwart attacks on the United States (Loeb 1998). At one point in 1998, CIA operatives were also prepared to fight their way into Afghanistan from Pakistan in an attempt to snatch bin Laden from a base at which he was staying, but the operation was canceled at the last minute. The CIA and FBI also claim that their "millennium operation" preempted numerous terrorist attacks planned in 2000 (Kitfield 2000). In early 2001, the Clinton administration began a CI-21 (Counterintelligence for the 21st Century) program to extend this cooperation even further.

The September 11 strikes organized by Al Qaeda revealed the limited success of this counterterrorism effort and generated a new sense of urgency and mission for future actions. In addition to prompting calls for an investigation into the intelligence and law enforcement failure the attacks represented (Purdum and Mitchell 2001), the changed environment also produced an acceleration of the counterterrorism emphasis within the CIA and other intelligence and law enforcement agencies. The counterterrorism center at the CIA doubled in size after the attacks, and became the hub for planning operations in Afghanistan (and elsewhere) and for directing clandestine activities against terrorism (Pincus 2001).

At the same time, the inability of the CIA and FBI to prevent the 9/11 debacle led to recommendations for the establishment of a director of national intelligence and a National Counterterrorism Center (NCTC) to achieve better coordination among the various members of the U.S. intelligence community. Those recommendations became a reality in 2004 with the passage of the *Intelligence Reform and Terrorism Prevention Act.* A new NCTC responsible for coordinating and integrating all national counterintelligence, including a list of 325,000 suspected international terrorists or supporters, is now overseen by the director of national intelligence (Pincus and Eggen 2006). However, many of the CIA's most experienced counterterrorism analysts have gone to work for NCTC, raising concern among some observers about the CIA's future capacity to deliver quality counterterrorism intelligence. Yet some observers have pointed out that the CIA would not be under such strain if it and other bureaucracies, like the FBI and Pentagon, did not still attempt to perform all the analytic tasks that they did before the NCTC was created (for example, see Pincus 2005b). In other words, the CIA and other agencies have remained resistant to the development of a true national division of labor in the area of counterterrorism.

Challenges for Covert Intervention in the Twenty-First Century

During George W. Bush's administration, the United States has faced a number of critical challenges regarding the use of covert action in the new century. First, to play an effective and central role in twenty-first century foreign policy, the CIA has had to confront the long-term decline in the legitimacy of covert intervention but found a newly revitalized sense of mission stemming from the post–September 2001 campaign against terrorism. Yet even with greater acceptance of U.S. covert action in the post-9/11 era, questions abound about how far the CIA should be allowed to go. The extraordinary rendition program,[6] secret CIA prisons in other countries, partnerships with foreign intelligence services in nondemocratic states, harsh interrogation tactics, indefinite detention of terrorist suspects without standard legal protections, and the use of "dirty" individuals to collect intelligence and conduct operations have all been used to prosecute the war on terrorism. Yet it remains to be seen how long the majority of citizens in a democratic society will accept such practices in the name of national security. One scholar argued that the Bush administration's use of the "politics of fear" in the post-9/11 era impeded a national discussion about counterterrorism (see Naftali 2005).

Second, the administration had to contend with the new demands placed on the CIA by the nature of twenty-first century challenges. The agency's operations culture largely lost its edge and its technological advantages were eroding. Budget cuts in the 1990s exacerbated the problem substantially. Dramatic failures like the CIA's operation in Iraq have led to "an aversion to risky espionage operations" (Risen 2000), and its failure to predict, much less prevent, the September 2001 attacks on the United States raised new questions about its activities. New tasks and targets for CIA operators require difficult-to-attract recruits with skills and specializations relevant to the security challenges of the twenty-first century, among them the insurgencies in Iraq and Afghanistan and the threats posed by Iran and North Korea.

Third, the long-standing trend toward the militarization of U.S. intelligence continued and intensified during the Bush administration with a particular emphasis on the expansion of Defense Department human intelligence units and operations (detailed in Chapter 11). Nowhere was the Pentagon more active than in its use of special operations forces to conduct overseas covert action in the war on terrorism. This development led the CIA to become increasingly challenged and overshadowed in an area that it traditionally dominated. However, one analyst expressed concerns about the rising prominence of the Pentagon's shadow warriors. For instance, unlike the CIA, "the Defense Department (at least according to its interpretation of the law) can conduct covert operations abroad without local governments' permission and with little or no congressional oversight or recourse" (Kibbe 2004). This capacity raises serious issues related to democratic accountability as well as the potential for foreign policy debacles. The situation is further compounded by the fact that oversight of military intelligence activities falls within *and beyond* the purview of the congressional intelligence committees, because the House and Senate armed services committees control the budgets of the special forces. The Rumsfeld Pentagon also resisted any legislative attempt to add further clarity or restraint to the use of military forces in covert action. In fact, it sought to liberalize existing rules and practices. Moreover, unlike CIA covert action plans, which must pass through the National Security Council system, Defense Department covert military operations are not reviewed by outside actors and committees, removing yet another layer of oversight (Kibbe 2004).

Additionally, there was the question of whether the CIA or the Pentagon was better positioned to deliver effective covert action. The Defense Department has more personnel and budgetary resources, whereas the CIA has the benefit of more experience in covert action, more local contacts, as well as stronger knowledge of foreign languages and cultures (Kibbe 2004). Regardless of the correct answer, it was clear that bureaucratic battle lines were being drawn between the CIA and the Pentagon, which raised the prospect that such tensions could ultimately hamper the effectiveness of future U.S. covert operations in the war on terrorism.

Finally, the major challenge concerned the fundamental shift in mission inherent in the transition from Cold War to twenty-first century worlds. At first, it seemed that the CIA had lost its mandate for covert intervention with the end of the Cold War. While the rise of counterterrorism has given the agency a new intelligence polestar, it has also presented a new set of (perhaps even greater) challenges to be met. In an age of transnational terrorism and failed states, the agency faces "myriad and elusive small non-state groups or rogue regimes" difficult to pin down. Moreover, the targets "tend to shift rapidly from one hot spot to another," thereby stressing resources, logistics, and capabilities (Aizenman 1999). One experienced observer has warned that, while "the new intelligence war presents the CIA with an opportunity to excel...the campaign is also fraught with risk" (Woodward 2001). A CIA veteran notes that "the agency is being assigned a monumental task for which it is not fully equipped or trained" (cited in Woodward 2001). Among the key issues related to this challenge, discussed more fully in Chapters 11 and 13, are the personnel needs of both the intelligence and operations divisions of the agency, particularly with a renewed emphasis on the use of human intelligence. Most fundamentally, it will be interesting to see how the CIA operates as an organization under the authority of the new director for national intelligence, being a role player rather than the central force in intelligence and covert operations.

FOREIGN ASSISTANCE: INTERVENTION WITHOUT COERCION

Another instrument for exerting global influence short of military intervention is foreign assistance, both economic and military. Both power and principle have driven the use of aid over the past sixty years. However, since the end of the Cold War, the logic that sustained these programs has dissipated and their use as foreign policy tools has been heavily scrutinized.

Economic Assistance

Since World War II, the United States has provided over $375 billion in *official development assistance (ODA)*—loans and grants—to other countries (see Table 5.1). ODA, or what we commonly call *foreign economic aid,* is a combination of low interest loans and grants provided by donors to developing countries. A figure like $375 billion may seem like a large amount of money. However, it is by no means the mammoth "giveaway" ascribed to foreign aid in the popular mind, especially compared with the more than $456 billion spent for the Department of Defense's budget in FY 2004 alone and which *excluded* tens of billions of dollars in supplemental funding for the military campaigns in Iraq and Afghanistan (Department of Defense, www.dod.mil/

TABLE 5.1 **Expenditures on Foreign Economic Aid (Loans and Grants), 1946–2004 (in Billions of Dollars by Fiscal Year)**

Postwar Relief Period (1946–1948)	$ 12.5
Marshall Plan Period (1949–1952)	$ 18.6
Mutual Security Act Period (1953–1961)	$ 24.1
Foreign Assistance Act Period (1962–2004)	$377.5
Grand Total	**$445.1**

Note: Numbers do not add to total due to different reporting concepts in the pre- and post-1995 periods. Figures for the four periods are in historical dollars.

SOURCE: Adapted from *U.S. Overseas Loans and Grants: Obligations and Loan Authorizations* [Greenbook], July 1, 1945 to September 30, 2004, Washington, DC: Agency for International Development, http://qesdb.cdie.org/gbk.

comptroller/defbudget/fy2007/). Moreover, when using constant dollar figures to look over time, the approximately $27 billion spent by the United States in 2004 is not much more than was spent in 1966 (about $23 billion in constant 2004 dollars). It is also dramatically less than the amount of aid provided immediately after World War II. In 1949 alone, the United States provided (in 2004 dollars) more than $520 billion in aid, most in the form of **Marshall Plan** assistance to rebuild Western Europe (USAID Greenbook, FY 2004, http://quesdb.cdie.org/gbk). Moreover, foreign aid is often tied to the purchases of goods and services in the United States. According to the U.S. Agency for International Development, which oversees much of the foreign economic aid provided by the United States, about 80 percent of American economic aid is used to purchase American products and services (quoted in Dobbs 2001).

Purposes and Programs

For much for the post–World War II period, most policy makers accepted the need and utility of economic assistance as an instrument of national interest and of principle. During the Cold War, economic assistance rested on the premise that it contributed to American security by supporting friends, providing for markets, and containing communist influence. "The security rationale provided a general and often compelling justification for U.S. foreign aid as a whole because aid for development and other purposes, it was argued, also supported U.S. security" (Lancaster 2000a). In addition to self-interest, however, United States aid policy was also built on the belief that helping poorer countries develop and providing humanitarian relief in times of disaster and crisis were principled actions on their own merits (Bobrow and Boyer 2005). More recently, aid policy has been linked with antiterrorism policies around the world, as donors try to address the roots of terrorist causes by promoting development and increasing political stability.

In practice, therefore, during the Cold War America's foreign aid programs satisfied both realists who would focus on self-interest and security concerns, and idealists who would also stress humanitarian concerns (Tisch and Wallace 1994). Hence, as long as the security and humanitarian values ran parallel, most policy makers supported economic assistance. But when they diverged, Cold War security concerns were the primary driver for foreign aid distribution. After the Cold War, uncertainty over the contribution of aid to American security interests and economic development destroyed the consensus and raised doubts about the continued utility of the foreign economic aid tool. But even without the Cold War rationale, recent research still shows that security concerns are important drivers of foreign aid (Lai 2003).

To accomplish the purposes for which U.S. foreign economic aid is provided, the United States has relied on a number of different agencies since World War II. The most prominent has been the **U.S. Agency for International Development (USAID),** which since 1961 has been responsible for administering most American economic assistance programs. As of 2005, the bilateral foreign economic aid provided by USAID was distributed across nine major accounts:

- *Child Survival and Health Programs (CSH):* Authorized by the Foreign Assistance Act of 1961, this account provides funding for basic health services and the improvement of national health systems with an emphasis on women and children. It has supported immunization, nutrition, water, sanitation, and family planning programs. The account has also been used to assist victims of human trafficking and to make U.S. contributions to global AIDS initiatives. In fiscal year 2005, roughly $1.6 billion was allocated to CSH, with Nigeria, India, Ethiopia, Bangladesh, and Uganda as the principal recipients (State/USAID 2005).

- *Development Assistance (DA):* Authorized by the Foreign Assistance Act of 1961, the **development assistance** account provides grants and loans to specific countries for specific social and economic development projects related to agriculture, education, natural resources, energy, nutrition, and rural development. In recent years, the promotion of democracy, good governance, and human rights has become a focus of DA. Disaster relief assistance also often falls under the rubric of development assistance. In fiscal year 2005, roughly $1.4 billion was allocated to the DA account, with Afghanistan, Sudan, Indonesia, Pakistan, and South Africa as the principal beneficiaries (State/USAID 2005).

- *Economic Support Fund (ESF):* Authorized by the foreign Assistance Act of 1961, the **Economic Support Fund** encompasses grants or loans to countries of special political significance to the United States. This fund is used for "enhancing political stability, promoting economic reforms important to the long-term development, promoting economic stabilization through budget and balance of payments support, and assisting countries that allow the United States to maintain military bases on their soil" (Zimmerman 1993). Because of its political and strategic significance, ESF is provided by the State Department and managed by USAID. Egypt and Israel have been the largest recipients of this type of aid since the 1978 Camp David Accords. In FY 2005, $2.5 billion was allocated to ESF, with $895 million awarded to Egypt and Israel. Other leading recipients included Pakistan, Jordan, and Afghanistan (State/USAID 2005).

- *Transition Initiatives (TI):* Authorized by the Foreign Assistance Act of 1961, the TI account provides funding to support democratic transition and long-term political development in states in crisis, with an emphasis on establishing, strengthening, or preserving democratic institutions and processes. Among the areas supported by TI are media programs, peaceful conflict resolution, election processes, civil-military relations, and judicial and human rights processes. In FY 2005, approximately $49 million was allocated, with Sudan as the largest recipient at $16 million (State/USAID 2005).

- *FREEDOM Support Act (FSA):* Authorized by the FREEDOM Support Act of 1992 and formerly known as Assistance to the Independent States of the Former Soviet Union, this account recognizes the strategic significance of Eurasia and is designed to help complete the region's transition to democratic governance and free market economies. FSA funding has been allocated for a broad range of initiatives in these areas as well as to promote better healthcare, improve domestic infrastructure, prevent the spread of weapons of mass destruction, and curb the trafficking of people and illicit narcotics. In FY 2005, roughly $556 million was appropriated for FSA, with Georgia, Russia, Ukraine, Armenia, and Azerbaijan as the principal beneficiaries (State/USAID 2005).

- *Support for East European Democracy (SEED)*: Authorized by the SEED Act of 1989 and formerly known as the Assistance for Eastern Europe and the Baltic States, this shrinking account is designed to support political, economic, and legal reforms to help ensure that regional instability (especially in South Central Europe) does not threaten U.S. security and economic interests. Additionally, SEED funds have been used to finance healthcare and environmental initiatives, curb transnational crime, and promote U.S. business in the region. In FY 2005, about $393 million was allocated to SEED (about half the amount that was awarded in 2001), with Serbia-Montenegro, Kosovo, Bosnia-Herzegovina, Macedonia, and Albania as the leading recipients (State/USAID 2005).

- *Global HIV/AIDS Initiative (GHAI)*: Authorized by the U.S. Leadership against HIV/AIDS, Tuberculosis, and Malaria Act of 2003, this account is the central means of funding President George W. Bush's Emergency Plan for AIDS Relief in fifteen targeted countries (Haiti, Vietnam, and thirteen African states). The plan has three goals: "support the treatment of two million HIV-infected people; prevent seven million new HIV infections; and support care for ten million people infected or affected by HIVS/AIDS, including orphans and vulnerable children." In FY 2005 (the second year of funding), roughly $1.4 billion was allocated, with the largest amounts provided to Uganda, Kenya, South Africa, Zambia, and Nigeria (State/USAID 2005).

- *Millennium Challenge Account (MCA)*: Authorized by the Millennium Challenge Act of 2003, MCA, like GHAI (discussed above), is another Bush administration initiative and reflects a new Republican approach and attitude toward foreign aid. It was established in an effort to circumvent a traditional feature of U.S. foreign assistance: congressional **earmarks** (statutory requirements that a minimum amount of aid be provided to a specific country or program). Administered by the Millennium Challenge Corporation (MCC) rather than USAID, MCA provides global development assistance in areas such as agriculture, education, and private entrepreneurship. MCA funds are awarded on a competitive basis to a select group of qualified countries based on sixteen indicators that seek to reward good governance, such as just rule, economic reform, and investing people (see www.mca.gov). In FY 2005 (the second year of MCA funding), Congress appropriated only $1.5 billion of the $2.5 billion requested by President Bush. This figure fell well short of Bush's 2002 proposal: to increase U.S. foreign aid by 50 percent through $15 billion in MCA funding over a three-year period (see Radelet 2003; State/USAID 2005).

- *Nonproliferation, Anti-Terrorism, Demining and Related Programs (NADR)*: Authorized by the Foreign Assistance Act of 1961, Arms Export Control Act of 1976, and the FREEDOM Support Act of 1992, the NADR account is used to assist countries in developing the means to enhance national and international security. In recent years, funding has been provided to states to train personnel and create programs designed to deter terrorist acts, prevent the proliferation of conventional and unconventional weapons and weapons-related expertise, promote respect for human rights, and support humanitarian demining missions. In FY 2005, about $400 million was allocated to NADR for three principal activities: nonproliferation, antiterrorism, and regional stability/humanitarian efforts (State/USAID 2005).

Other Forms of Economic Assistance

Beyond the many forms of bilateral foreign economic assistance, the United States provides additional support through contributions to intergovernmental organizations to finance multilateral development projects. In FY 2005, $1.54 billion was appropriated to this account to fund initiatives administered by United Nations–related agencies, such as the United Nations Development Program (UNDP) and the United Nations Children's Fund (UNICEF), as well as multilateral development (Tarnoff and Nowels 2005). Through international organizations, such as the World Bank, the United States has relegated large-scale infrastructure projects (basic facilities and systems like roads and regional irrigation systems) since the 1970s.

Another form of economic aid is *humanitarian assistance accounts,* which as of 2005 fell into accounts reserved for disaster relief, famine assistance, migration and refugee assistance, and food for peace. The last account is the best known and is widely referred to as PL (public law) 480 in reference to the Agricultural Trade Development and Assistance Act of 1954 that created it. The objectives of the ***Food for Peace program*** are "to expand exports of U.S. agricultural commodities, to combat hunger and malnutrition, to encourage economic development in developing countries, and to promote the foreign policy interests of the United States" (Zimmerman 1993). The program, in which the Department of Agriculture plays a major role, sells agricultural commodities on credit terms and makes grants for emergency relief. The Food for Peace program totaled about $60 billion by 2000, or about a fifth of all economic aid granted since PL 480 was passed. In fiscal year 2004, slightly less than $1.2 billion in food aid was administered by USAID (State/USAID 2005).

Debt relief has also become a prominent aid component in recent years. With the advent of the Brady Initiative programs in 1989, which allowed for some debt forgiveness and government guarantees for new loans to a wide array of former Soviet bloc countries, the United States and its major allies have come to recognize that much of the debt owed by developing countries will never be repaid. The demands of debt service are also creating significant obstacles for further development. As such, in June 2005, the finance ministers of the ***Group of 8 (G8)*** countries (the world's seven largest industrialized democracies and Russia) announced a plan that would eliminate 100 percent of the debt for eighteen heavily indebted African states. The plan was widely heralded internationally, and the newly appointed World Bank president, Paul Wolfowitz, a former Bush administration Pentagon official, urged that the plan be extended to include Nigeria (Africa's largest debtor) and others. To supplement this G8 initiative, President Bush also announced an additional $674 million in emergency aid for Africa for 2005 to help African countries meet their humanitarian needs (Loven 2005).

Emergency supplemental appropriations are used to address urgent needs in a particular country or region and stand as another form of economic assistance. As Table 5.2 indicates, both Afghanistan and Iraq have received substantial amounts of this type of funding in recent years. In fact, "the U.S. assistance program to Iraq [is] the largest aid initiative since the 1948–1951 Marshall Plan" (Tarnoff and Nowels 2005). American funds have been allocated to promote democratization and rebuild the Iraq's war-ravaged infrastructure, including its oil-producing sector and basic services, such as electricity, telecommunications, and water and sewage (Tarnoff and Nowels 2005). Significantly, the funds detailed in Table 5.2 do not encompass military and security assistance, which in FY 2004 alone totaled more than $1.8 billion for Iraq and roughly $570 million for Afghanistan (State/USAID 2005). The rise of Iraq and Afghanistan as major U.S. aid recipients highlights the link between foreign assistance and the war on terror since 9/11. It also helps to explain how the antiterror orientation of the Bush administration is a primary cause for the resurgence of aid expenditures from their lows in the 1990s. In fact, USAID launched an Anti-Terrorism Certification Program, which requires all aid recipients to provide

TABLE 5.2 Expenditures on Foreign Economic Aid (Loans and Grants) to Iraq and Afghanistan, 1946–2004 (in Millions of Dollars by Fiscal Year)

Years	Iraq	Afghanistan
1946–1948	$ 6.6	$ 0.0
1949–1952	$ 3.0	$ 0.0
1953–1961	$ 120.1	$ 6.2
1962–2000	$ 152.4	$ 19.3
2001	$ 0.2	$ 0.0
2002	$ 40.3	$ 78.9
2003	$3,877.0	$366.4
2004	$6,421.1	$569.5

NOTE: Figures are in constant 2004 dollars and exclude military and security assistance.

SOURCE: Adapted from *U.S. Overseas Loans and Grants: Obligations and Loan Authorizations* [Greenbook], July 1, 1945 to September 30, 2004, Washington, DC: Agency for International Development. http://qesdb.cdie.org/gbk.

assurances that they do not support terrorism (State/USAID 2005).

Economic Aid Today: In Search of a Rationale

The end of the Cold War removed the security rationale that sustained aid for more than forty years within Congress, while the budgetary constraints of ballooning deficits and debt at the outset of the

Clinton administration tested the political will of those responsible for providing aid to other countries. Moreover, consistent with the history of public support for foreign aid, a 2001 public opinion poll found that 61 percent of Americans thought foreign aid should be reduced (Program on International Policy Attitudes 2001). However, it is important to note that public attitudes about aid spending never have been entirely based in fact. Past polls have showed that American respondents select foreign aid (along with military spending) as one of the two largest federal budgetary categories, when provided with the choices of Medicare, food stamps, Social Security, military spending, and foreign aid (see Program on International Policy Attitudes 2001). As Figure 5.1 highlights, the perennial reality of federal budget allocations is much different, with foreign aid accounting for less than 1 percent of all budget expenditures compared with 21 percent for Social Security, nearly 20 percent for Defense, and more than 11 percent for Medicare.

Additional political pressure to decrease aid spending developed from studies showing that aid had not produced much in the way of economic growth (for example, see World Bank 1998; O'Hanlon and Graham 1997). The dramatic surge of overseas private investment, coupled with the apparent triumph of the neoliberal consensus on the efficacy of market solutions, sapped the force of the argument for development assistance even further.

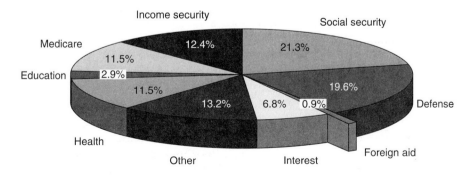

FIGURE 5.1 U.S. Budget Outlays, FY 2004

SOURCE: Curt Tarnoff and Larry Nowels. *Foreign Aid: An Introductory Overview of U.S. Programs.* Washington, DC: Congressional Research Service/The Library of Congress, 2005, p. CRS-20.

Declining support for and delivery of foreign economic assistance led to numerous efforts to restructure, reform, and refocus the economic aid instrument; as yet, none has garnered the kind of broad-gauged support that would ensure the effective use of the foreign policy tool. The controversy swirled over two interrelated issues: the structural and institutional mechanisms that administered aid and the purposes and targets of the aid. On the first issue, by 1994 USAID was under pressure from many quarters. Outside the government, policy analysts called for consolidation of USAID with the State Department, its breakup into smaller, functionally oriented agencies, and its outright elimination (see Eagleburger and Barry 1996; Ruttan 1996; Lancaster 2000a). In 1998, Congress passed, and President Clinton signed into law, the Foreign Affairs Reform and Restructuring Act, which placed USAID under the direct authority and foreign policy direction of the secretary of state, even though it left the agency structurally separate.

Though the political climate in Congress was less than sympathetic to foreign aid spending, the Clinton administration and others still sought to revitalize foreign aid as an instrument of global influence by retargeting it toward new purposes. Early efforts involved several interrelated ideas: sustainable development, chaos and crisis prevention, and democracy promotion. A major step toward new purposes occurred in September 1993, when the Task Force to Reform AID and the International Affairs Budget issued its report, *Revitalizing the AID and Foreign Assistance in the Post–Cold War Era.* The "Wharton Report" (named for Deputy Secretary of State Clifton Wharton, who chaired the commission) recommended a new global rationale to replace the conflicting demands placed on foreign aid. Recommending less military and more economic aid, the report stressed global issues such as the environment, drug trafficking, disease, population growth, and migration, among others, as the appropriate target for foreign aid policy (Nijman 1998).

Early in George W. Bush's administration, the outlines of a new approach seemed to emerge. It was not until after September 11, 2001, however, that the new policy on aid would take shape and focus on providing assistance to members of anti-terror coalitions. As already discussed above, the Bush administration has used aid to help solidify its strategic agenda around the world and especially the war on terrorism. This statement is well supported by the fact that along with long-standing beneficiaries Israel and Egypt, countries such as Iraq, Afghanistan, Pakistan, Indonesia, Colombia, Jordan, Kenya, and Sudan were among the top fifteen recipients of U.S. foreign aid in 2004. None of these eight countries were among the top U.S. foreign aid recipients in 1995 (Tarnoff and Nowels 2005). Moreover, the volume of U.S. aid has also rebounded since its lows in the mid-1990s, and the United States has once again overtaken Japan as the world's foreign aid donor. Of course, critics would be quick to point out that in terms of foreign aid as a percentage of gross national income the United States ranks below twenty other industrialized states (see Figure 5.2).

So at least for the foreseeable future, foreign aid has made a comeback relative to the financial retrenchment of the mid-1990s. Whether that will continue over the longer term will likely depend on how long the United States stays actively engaged in the war on terror and in regional conflicts. Without such overarching rationales for foreign aid outlays, it seems likely that aid will once again fall off because of the long-term lack of public and congressional support for such spending.

Military Assistance

Foreign military aid, like its economic counterpart, is now a standard instrument of American foreign policy. In this case, however, political realism, with its focus on power and the national interest, is the dominant underlying rationale. Beginning with the Korean War, grants of military aid to other countries became an essential element of Cold War defense and security planning and a tool used to pursue several national security and foreign policy goals.[7] Sales of military equipment would later join grants, and then surpass them, as the major element of American arms transfer programs.

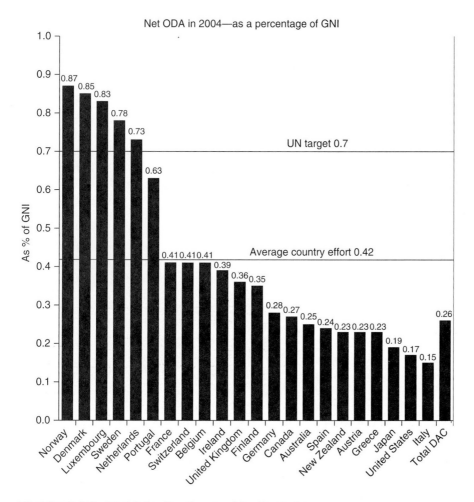

FIGURE 5.2 World's Leading Donors of Foreign Assistance

SOURCE: Cindy Williams. "Beyond Preemption and Preventive War: Increasing U.S. Budget Emphasis on Conflict Prevention," *Policy Analysis Brief*. Muscatine, IA: Stanley Foundation, 2006, p. 7.

Purposes and Programs

Foreign military grants and sales plus economic support funds comprise a broad category called *security assistance,* whose purpose is related to a multitude of United States policy objectives. The objectives of security assistance are stated clearly in the *Strategic Plan of the Defense Security Cooperation Agency* (DSCA) published in late 2002:

- Identify, develop, and advocate programs that strengthen America's alliances and partnerships

- Strengthen defense relationships that promote U.S. access and influence

- Promote interoperability with allies and friendly [states] while protecting sensitive technologies and information

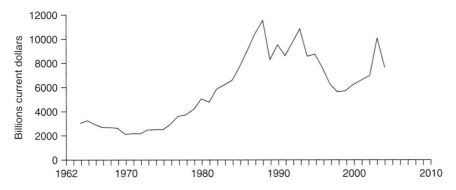

FIGURE 5.3 United States Security Assistance, 1962–2004

SOURCE: Budget of the United States Government, *Fiscal Year 2005*, Historical Tables, Federal Government Outlays by Function, p. 84 at www.whitehouse.gov/omb/budget/fy2005/pdf/hist.pdf; and Budget of the United States Government, *Fiscal Year 2006*, Historical Tables, Federal Government Outlays by Function, p. 85 at www.whitehouse.gov/omb/budget/fy2006/pdf/hist.pdf (accessed 10/29/06).

- Develop the security cooperation workforce and give it the tools to succeed
- Identify and incorporate best business practices and deploy systems that save time, energy, and money (DSCA 2002)

In addition, since 1989 it has become significantly more important to support the defense industrial base by enabling domestic arms manufacturers to export weapons in order to maintain their production lines, and this is now a key element underpinning military aid programs. In fact, one recent study found that defense contractors have actively sought out foreign sales and collaborative multinational production agreements as a means to maintain their profitability in a globalized world economy (Lavallee 2003).

Figure 5.3 provides information on the provision of security assistance over time. As Table 5.3 shows, well over $500 billion in American military aid has been extended to other states since the onset of the Korean War (including commercial sales approved by the government). Even that figure is likely to be on the conservative side, as it is based on unclassified information.

In fiscal year 2005, the United States provided its allies and friends with $5 billion in military training and equipment, which accounted for nearly a quarter of all U.S. foreign assistance that year (Tarnoff and Nowels 2005). That aid was distributed across three

TABLE 5.3 **Expenditures on Foreign Military Aid and Sales, 1950–2004 (in Billions of Dollars by Fiscal Year)**

Military Assistance Program (MAP) and Map Merger Funds	$ 60.0
International Military Education and Training (IMET) Program	$ 3.1
Foreign Military Sales (FMS) and FMS Construction Agreements	$384.8
Commercial Exports Licensed under the Arms Export Act Control	$ 89.7
Excess Defense Articles	$ 6.5
Grand Total	**$544.1**

SOURCE: Defense Security Assistance Agency. *Facts Book*. Washington, DC: Administration and Management Business Operations, DSCA, 2005 (www.dsca.mil, accessed 10/29/06).

major accounts: International Military Education and Training (IMET), Peacekeeping Operations (PKO), and Foreign Military Financing (FMF).

- *International Military Education and Training (IMET):* Authorized by the Foreign Assistance Act of 1961, IMET has governed and facilitated foreign military training since the mid-1970s. By the turn of the century, according to the State Department, IMET included 2,000 courses at 150 military schools for more than 8,000 foreign students annually (www.fas.org/asmp/campaigns/training/IMET2.html). In her 2000 report to Congress on foreign military training, Secretary of State Madeleine Albright characterized IMET as "a low-cost, highly effective component of U.S. security assistance ... to ... further the goal of regional stability ... augment the capabilities of the military forces of participant nations to support combined operations and inter-operability with U.S. forces ... and increase the ability of foreign military and civilian personnel to instill and maintain basic democratic values and protect internationally recognized human rights." In FY 2005, about $89 million was appropriated for IMET, with Turkey, Jordan, Thailand, Pakistan, and Poland as the leading beneficiaries (State/USAID 2005).

- *Peacekeeping Operations (PKO):* Authorized by the Foreign Assistance Act of 1961, this account supports voluntary multilateral peacekeeping and regional stabilization missions that advance U.S. national security interests but are not mandated by or funded through the United Nations. PKO activities have included separating adversaries, managing ceasefires, ensuring the distribution of humanitarian relief, facilitating the repatriation of refugees, demobilizing combatants, and establishing an environment in which elections and positive political, economic, and social change can occur (State/USAID 2005). In FY 2005, Congress funded PKO in the amount of approximately $103 million, with the largest allocations of aid going to Africa ($60 million),

Afghanistan ($24 million), and the Sinai Multinational Force and Observers ($16.5 million) (State/USAID 2005). The latter recipient is a byproduct of the 1978 Camp David Accords and the 1979 peace treaty between Egypt and Israel. Since 1982, an international force composed of soldiers from eleven countries, including a small contingent from the United States, has monitored the border shared by the two Middle East states in the Sinai desert.

- *Foreign Military Financing (FMF):* Authorized by the Arms Export Control Act of 1976 and the Foreign Assistance Act of 1961, FMF is the largest of the three accounts associated with foreign military assistance. It is "a grant program that enables governments to receive equipment from the U.S. government or to access equipment directly through U.S. commercial channels" (Tarnoff and Nowels 2005). During the period of 1950 to 2005, the U.S. government dispensed more than $121 billion in FMF to armed forces around the globe (Berrigan and Hartung 2005). It is important to note that FMF does not provide cash to foreign states. Rather, it finances the sale of specific military items through one of two programs. The less commonly used program, known as *Direct Commercial Sales (DCS)*, administers transactions between American companies and foreign states. The far more likely conduit for the transfer of military arms and equipment is the *Foreign Military Sales (FMS)* program, which oversees transactions between the U.S. government and the governments of foreign states. The Department of State through the Bureau of Political-Military Affairs oversees FMF, but the Pentagon's Defense Security Cooperation Agency (DSCA) manages FMF matters on a daily basis. In FY 2005, about $4.75 billion or 23.6 percent of all U.S. foreign aid was allocated to FMF (down substantially from a peak of 42 percent in FY 1984). The largest recipients were Israel ($2.2 billion), Egypt ($1.3 billion), Afghanistan ($400 million), Pakistan ($300 million), Jordan ($206 million), and Colombia ($108 million) (State/USAID 2005; Tarnoff and Nowels 2005).

Transfers in FY 2005 were representative of past years as the recipients of American arms transfers were predominantly from the Middle East. As part of the 1978 Camp David Middle East peace accords, Egypt and Israel account for roughly two-thirds of foreign military sales and credits. Other states in the region that have also made significant purchases of U.S. weapons over time include Turkey, Jordan, Saudi Arabia, Kuwait, Oman, and the United Arab Emirates. The most sought-after American weapons systems in recent years have been tanks, self-propelled guns, armored personnel carriers, supersonic combat aircraft, helicopters, surface-to-air ships, and anti-ship missiles. However, it is important to note that a substantial amount of annual U.S. arms sales to the Middle East as well as other regions involves spare parts, upgrades, and training and support (Grimmett 2004).

Another continuing pattern in 2005 was American dominance of the global arms market. Driven by the demise of the Soviet Union, once the primary arms sale competitor to the United States, and the dramatic display of new American weapons technology during the Gulf War and later the war in Iraq, the last fifteen years have been an arms bonanza for the U.S. defense industry. As overall world sales have decreased, American control of that market has increased substantially, from 24 percent in 1996–1999 to over 47 percent in 2000–2003, making the United States by far the largest supplier of weapons to the developing world. Hence, military assistance and arms sales appear to be thriving. A review of post–World War II military aid policies helps to explain why.

Military Aid during the Cold War

During the Cold War, American military aid flowed chiefly to Europe for the first decade, and then in subsequent decades to East Asia, Southeast Asia, the Middle and Near East, Africa, and Central America. Additionally, what began as grant aid shifted to military sales in the early 1960s as the Kennedy administration began to use sales as an alternative to grants due chiefly to adverse American balance of payments. Finally, by the late 1960s, United States military aid had shifted from the industrial world to the developing world. The driving purposes of military assistance were securing allies, cementing alliances, rewarding patrons, and renting overseas bases.

From Korea to Vietnam The containment policy provided a rationale for military aid to others, justified on the grounds that it augmented the capabilities of American allies to resist Soviet and Soviet-backed expansionism. The North Atlantic Treaty Organization (NATO) and the Southeast Asia Treaty Organization (SEATO) alliances thus received special attention, as did those with bilateral defensive arrangements with the United States, such as Taiwan. Military aid also was used for the rental of base rights in places such as Spain and for landing rights for ships and planes elsewhere. Economic support funds were also often used for this purpose, as in the Philippines, where sizable "side payments" were required to retain access to two large military bases, Clark Air Base and the naval facility at Subic Bay. The latter in particular increased in importance following the American withdrawal from Vietnam and the loss of the port facility at Cam Ranh Bay.

Vietnam affected other calculations as well. Between 1966 and 1975, the aid program increasingly targeted "friends," as developing states in the then-Third World commanded greater attention. During this period, South Vietnam, Cambodia, Laos, Pakistan, South Korea, and Taiwan—all bordering directly on the communist world and bound to the United States in defensive arrangements—more than doubled their military aid receipts. Similar attention characterized the economic aid program, as we noted previously.

After Vietnam The Vietnam imbroglio triggered serious concerns about U.S. military assistance policy. Some critics argued that military aid "is the 'slippery slope' that leads eventually to an over-extension of commitments and to a greater likelihood of military involvement" (Frank and Baird 1975). Others argued that American programs might have contributed to the maintenance of authoritarian regimes throughout the world, since—regardless of their intentions—the programs' consequences included a greater chance that military groups in recipient countries would intervene in or maintain their grip on the politics of those states (Rowe 1974). In the mid-1970s, for example, more than half of the recipients of American arms were dictatorships. Concern over this problem led some to try to adjust military assistance policy, but, as Figure 5.3 shows, security assistance continued to grow during this period.

The flow of arms to the Middle East achieved massive proportions during the Nixon and Ford administrations, stimulated by the Arab-Israeli conflict, the new financial resources available to Middle Eastern oil exporters from the sharp upsurge in world oil prices from 1973 to 1974, and the *Nixon Doctrine*—the pledge that the United States would provide military and economic assistance to its friends and allies but that those countries would be responsible for protecting their own security. During the 1976 presidential election, Jimmy Carter raised concern about the consistency between massive arms sales and the nation's avowed goal of seeking world peace. Once elected, he announced a new policy of "restraint" designed to curb the explosive arms trade, but Carter found it difficult to curb the use of military aid and sales to benefit American allies and friends, and rival arms exporters saw no reason to rein in their own profitable trade in arms. The Reagan administration cast aside all pretense of restraint, declaring that "the United States views the transfer of conventional arms and other defense articles as an indispensable component of its foreign policy." Reagan also decided to increase the proportion of security assistance in the overall mix of foreign aid. As before, and similar to his administration's approach to foreign economic aid, anticommunism and the perceived security threats to the United States dictated the flow of funds. One of the preferred targets was Central America. Although the Reagan administration never received support in Congress for all of the aid it sought—including military and other aid for the contras—aid levels did grow dramatically, to the point that on a per capita basis Central American states became among the most heavily funded of all aid recipients.

Hence, despite the concerns raised by Vietnam, the FMS program continued to grow during the 1970s and 1980s. Some critics worried that transfers of advanced military technology to countries and regions where conflict was frequent, as in the Middle East, would actually contribute to local aggression, not deter it (compare Kapstein 1994). As one Pentagon official described the situation in Somalia in 1992, when the Bush administration launched its humanitarian intervention there: "Between the stuff the Russians and we stuck in there during the great Cold War, there are enough arms in Somalia to fuel hostility for one hundred years" (cited in Barnet 1993). Some also pointed out how today's allies had a way of becoming tomorrow's enemies: "Much of the bitterness felt by Iranians toward the United States is traceable to twenty-five years of massive arms shipments to the Shah, much of it for use against Iranians—clubs, tear gas, and guns, and training for the dreaded secret police in how to use them" (Barnet 1993; Klare 1984).

Following the victory over Iraq in the Persian Gulf War, George H. W. Bush determined that the time was again ripe to seek restraints on the global arms trade, particularly in the Middle East. In 1992, however, as Bush faced a tough re-election bid, he broke with past practice, seeking to capitalize politically not on his arms restraint program but on the domestic benefits of arms sales abroad. In September and October 1992, he announced $20 billion in new arms sales to such countries as Taiwan and Saudi Arabia, among others, as symbols of his commitment to "do everything I can to keep Americans at work" (Hartung 1993). Bill Clinton, Bush's challenger in the 1992 presidential campaign, did not object. But the Chinese ended their participation in the P-5 arms restraint talks, marking the end of only the second serious effort in two decades to restrain the dangerous—if profitable—global trade in the weapons of war.

Military Aid during the Post–Cold War Era

Like George H. W. Bush before him, Bill Clinton was sensitive to the role of jobs in the weapons export equation. However, he took this concern to a new level. During its first year in office, the Clinton administration approved $36 billion in foreign arms sales, "a level unprecedented during the Cold War" (Honey 1997). Moreover, the administration's long-awaited conventional arms transfer policy, issued as Presidential Decision Directive (PDD) 34 in February 1995, explicitly stated among its goals a desire "to enhance the ability of the U.S. defense industrial base to meet U.S. defense requirements and maintain long-term military technological superiority at lower costs." Benefits from what some characterized as an "all come, all served" approach included export revenues, reduced unit costs for Defense Department purchases (the more units an arms maker manufactures, the lower the cost for each one), sustained assembly lines for the defense industrial base (which can produce existing weapons while gearing up for the next generation), substantial profits for the defense industry, and, of course, jobs for American workers employed in defense industries.

Given the rapidly shrinking global arms market of the 1990s, the Clinton administration was not able to sustain annual sales at the 1993 level of $36 million. However, PDD 34 coupled with liberal export restrictions and the most aggressive support for arms sales from the Departments of Commerce, Defense, and State since the Nixon era did allow the United States to emerge as the world's undisputed superpower in weapons exports during the Clinton administration (see Hartung 1995). According to the Congressional Research Service: "In 2000 the United States ranked first in the value of arms deliveries worldwide, making nearly $14.2 billion in such deliveries. [It was] the eighth year in a row that [the] United States [led] in such deliveries." The next closest competitor, the United Kingdom, sold $5.1 billion worth of weapons in 2000 (Grimmett 2001). Thus while the overall global arms market grew smaller in the 1990s, the United States carved out a far larger share of that market, controlling (on average) about a half of all sales in any given year rather than only a third during the Cold War period (Gabelnick and Rich 2000).

States in the developing world made up the preponderance of U.S. arms recipients during the 1990s. In President Clinton's first term, the United States "delivered 1,625 tanks, 2,091 armored personnel carriers, 318 combat aircraft, 203 helicopters, and 1,443 surface-to-air missiles around the world" (Broder 1997). This pattern continued in Clinton's second term. The material was increasingly sophisticated as well, as restrictions on high-tech weapons exports fell fast (for example, in 1997 the Clinton administration lifted the ban on high-tech weapons exports to Latin America) (Goozner 1997). However, according to defense policy analyst William Hartung, "these sales [were] subsidized and pushed for economic reasons with little regard to foreign policy or social concerns" (quoted in Goozner 1997). Thus, as Clinton left office, new concerns were raised about the role of the military in fueling regional conflict, instability, and civil wars, supporting repressive regimes, and diffusing advanced technology too widely, thereby assisting would-be challengers and raising the costs of American involvement in the world.

Concern over these and other issues led some lawmakers in the House and Senate in the 1990s to press for a *code of conduct on arms transfers*, which would have required foreign states to meet certain requirements before being eligible to receive U.S. weapons. In two unsuccessful bills, that criteria included: a democratic form of government; respect for citizens' rights; absence of aggression against other states; and full participation in the UN Register of Conventional Arms. After several attempts, members of Congress settled for passage of the International Arms Sales Code of Conduct of 1999 in November 1999. However, the law only required the president to start international negotiations on a global code of conduct. It did not impose a federal government-mandated set of standards to determine whether a particular foreign state could or could not receive U.S. arms.

Consequently, Bill Clinton left George W. Bush some difficult questions. One of the key issues was reconciling competing goals as they relate to the use of foreign military sales and military assistance. Can security assistance be used to achieve power and prosperity, while still supporting American principles? For example, as noted earlier, democracy promotion is on the long list of security assistance objectives. Thus we might expect foreign military sales under the Clinton administration to have been directed more toward emerging and established democracies than others. In actuality, however, there was virtually no relationship between the kind of political regime a country had and the Clinton administration's arms sales decisions. In fact, "at least 154 of the [world's] 190 independent countries [received] contracts for or deliveries of American arms in fiscal year 2000," led by many nondemocratic regimes in the Near and Middle East (Gabelnick and Rich 2000; also see Grimmett 2001). This raised anew concerns of the nature of American friends and partners.[8]

Additionally, critics of the arms-exports-for-prosperity-and-jobs argument embraced by the Clinton administration noted that the number of jobs produced for every dollar invested in the civilian sector is greater than in the military sector (Hartung 1994; *The Defense Monitor* 23(6), 1994; see also Chan and Mintz 1992). Money spent on the military is also money that cannot be spent elsewhere. Moreover, the taxpayer subsidizes arms exports through government credits and expenditures of millions for the Pentagon's arms export staff and programs (Hartung 1994). Even the exports are often balanced by "offsets," or licensing agreements that permit buyers to participate in production of the weapons system, thereby "taking business from American companies and giving it to foreign suppliers" (Hartung 1994).

The new Bush administration also had to contend with another development from the Clinton era: the globalization of the arms industry. Not only are a growing number of weapons being produced by codevelopment and coproduction schemes, in which two or more countries develop new weapons systems collaboratively, but "arms manufacturers are following the lead of their commercial counterparts and going global, pursuing transnational mergers and alliances and establishing design, production, and marketing operations abroad" (Markusen 1999). This globalization stretches the U.S. economy and impacts weapons proliferation, technology diffusion, defense procurement, and national security. It has also changed the ways weapons manufacturers do business, forcing even the once-insular U.S. industry to reach out globally for production partners (Lavallee 2003; 2005).

Military Aid Today

During the George W. Bush administration, arms sales remained a centerpiece of America's relationship with its allies and partners around the world. As in the Clinton era, the United States continued to dominate a shrinking global arms market; the Middle and Near East accounted for the bulk of annual U.S. arms transfers; and many of the same types of weapons systems along with spare parts, upgrades, and training remained the leading U.S. military exports. Also, consistent with previous patterns, the vast majority (80 percent) of weapons recipients were—as classified by the United States—either nondemocratic states or states with poor human rights records. Furthermore, many of the beneficiaries of these transactions were engaged in active conflicts. Following a decade-long trend, the United States transferred arms to eighteen of the twenty-five states engaged in active conflicts in 2003 (Berrigan and Hartung 2005).

At the same time, there were significant changes related to arms sales in the Bush II administration, which were directly tied to the realities of the post-9/11 era. From 2001 to 2005, Foreign Military Financing (FMF)—which is the largest category of U.S. military aid and includes Foreign Military Sales (FMS)—grew by more than a third (34 percent), rising from $3.5 billion in 2001 to $4.6 billion in 2005. Many of the largest recipients of this aid, such as Afghanistan, Pakistan, Jordan, Bahrain, and the Philippines, were considered critical allies in the war on terrorism. In addition, the total number of FMF recipients jumped by 48 percent, going from 48 states in 2001 to 71 states in 2006 (Berrigan and Hartung 2005). Many of new beneficiaries were previously prohibited from receiving U.S. aid due to poor human rights records, support of terrorism, or nuclear testing. However, their willingness to assist in the U.S. war on terrorism and participate in coalitions of the willing in Afghanistan and Iraq, coupled with the presence of new rules, changed their status. On the latter point, many bans and suspensions were lifted to allow the United States to reward its new partners in the war on terrorism (Berrigan and Hartung 2005). A prime example of such rewards was the 2005 decision to sell F-16 fighter jets to Pakistan. Beyond an end to a number of suspensions and bans, new post-9/11 laws and federal government policies were created to allow countries supportive of the U.S. war on terrorism to receive their American weapons and aid more quickly (Berrigan and Hartung 2005). Overall, these developments illustrate that military aid and arms sales are alive and well.

While the use of military aid and arms sales as a tool of American foreign policy in the twenty-first century shows no signs of waning, many of the perennial concerns surrounding this instrument of statecraft endure. Concerns about the stimulus of U.S. weapons sales to violent conflict, civil war, and regional instability remain. Moreover, in a world where governments and allegiances can shift significantly over time, the fear of increasingly advanced American weaponry being turned against U.S. troops and interests in some future conflict will continue to arise as the Bush administration and its successors employ the military aid instrument. Perhaps most challenging in the years ahead will be the relationship between the use of this instrument and the values and interests of the United States in the twenty-first century. On the one hand, there is the difficult balance between national security interests and fundamental democratic values. On the other hand, there is the challenge to balance the economic needs of the defense industrial sector with the military security that might come from a stronger and more comprehensive counterproliferation policy.

SANCTIONS: COERCION WITHOUT INTERVENTION?

Within a week after Iraq's tanks lumbered into Kuwait in August 1990, the world community imposed strict economic sanctions on Iraq, cutting off Iraqi oil shipments and all other forms of trade. Two years later, in May 1992, the UN Security Council again imposed mandatory sanctions, this time against Serbia and Montenegro following the outbreak of war in Bosnia-Herzegovina. And in May 1993, the Security Council imposed an embargo on oil and weapons sales to Haiti, then still under the leadership of a military regime. In all, the United Nations imposed mandatory sanctions eight times between 1991 and 1994 (Pape 1997)—six more than in all of its previous history. The United States played a principal role in each of these actions, and many other sanctions episodes over the ensuing years, making the 1990s "the sanctions decade" (Cortright and Lopez 2000).

The Nature and Purposes of Sanctions

The enthusiasm for sanctions is explained in part by the search for new instruments of foreign policy influence in domestic and global environments, characterized by limited support for military options. *Sanctions*—defined as "deliberate government actions to inflict economic deprivation on a target state or society, through the limitation or cessation of customary economic relations" (Leyton-Brown 1987)—are often seen as alternatives to military force that still permit the initiating state to express outrage at some particular action and to change the behavior of the target state. Sanctions may include boycotts (refusal to buy a state's products) and embargoes (refusal to sell to a state), among other actions. As Woodrow Wilson trumpeted in 1919, "A nation boycotted is a nation that is in sight of surrender. Apply this economic, peaceful, silent deadly remedy and there will be no need for force" (Hufbauer 1998). Thus sanctions occupy a middle ground between comparatively benign diplomatic action, on the one hand, and forceful persuasion or overt military intervention, on the other.

The use of sanctions is not new. The United States was a key player in two-thirds of the more than one hundred sanction attempts begun between the end of World War I and 1990. In four out of every five, the United States effectively acted by itself, with only minor support from other states (Elliott 1993). What is distinctive about the sanctions applied against Iraq, the former Yugoslavia, and Haiti in the 1990s is that they were multilateral. The United Nations charter has always allowed imposition of _multilateral sanctions_ against international sinners, but, as noted, this has rarely been done. Sanctions applied against the white-minority regimes in Rhodesia in 1966 and South Africa in 1977 are the only UN-sponsored initiatives taken before the action against Iraq in 1990. The difficulty in securing broad agreement for action, particularly evident during the Cold War, and the equally difficult task of maintaining discipline among the sanctioning states over a period of time, help explain the paucity of broad-based multilateral initiatives.

Iraq is a good example of the difficulty. The purpose of the sanctions against Iraq varied during the 1990s, ranging from forcing Iraq from Kuwait to the destruction of Iraq's military capabilities and creating sufficient domestic discontent to oust Saddam Hussein from power. None of these objectives was achieved, however. Sanctions remained in place after the first Gulf War to ensure Iraq's compliance with UN mandates requiring inspection of its weapons facilities and the dismantling of its nuclear, chemical, and biological weapons programs. However, those most affected (Turkey and Jordan, for example) or who wished to resume normal commercial intercourse (such as France, China, and Russia) became increasingly restive. Even the United States eventually (if only tacitly) abandoned the weapons inspection objective, preferring instead the selective application of force to cope with Iraq's defiance of the international community and its presumed potential for a continuing military threat (Gause 1999).

The evident failure of sanctions and ultimate use of force to oust Saddam Hussein from power in Iraq in 2003 raises troubling questions. Are sanctions effective? Who are their victims?

The Effectiveness of Sanctions

Determining whether sanctions are effective is difficult, as "the correlation between economic pressure and changes in political or military behavior is rarely direct" (Christiansen and Powers 1993). Even

in South Africa—where for two decades economic pressure was applied on the white-minority regime to bring an end to the segregationist apartheid system and open the way for black majority rule—the precise role that economic sanctions played in the endgame remains elusive. Analysts do generally agree, however, that sanctions were important even if not the primary determining factor ending apartheid (see, for example, Davis 1993; Minter 1986–1987; but compare Doxey 1990). The same qualified success applies to Libya. In 1999, after a decade of international pressure on Libyan dictator Muammar Qaddafi for his role in sponsoring terrorism, he finally turned over to western powers for trial two Libyans alleged to have blown up Pan Am flight 103 over Scotland in 1988, killing all 280 of its passengers. This laid the basis for Libya's renunciation of terrorism and the abandonment of its nuclear weapons program in 2003, and the restoration of full diplomatic relations between the United States and Libya in 2006.

Cuba is a case where economic coercion failed. The United States placed sanctions on the Castro regime shortly after it assumed power in 1960. It soon banned all trade with Cuba and pressured other countries to follow suit. Its goals were twofold. The United States hoped to overthrow the Castro government. Failing that, from about 1964 onward it tried to contain the Castro revolution and Cuban interventionism elsewhere in the Western Hemisphere and in Africa. The major accomplishment, however, was largely confined to "increasing the cost to Cuba of surviving and developing as a socialist country and of pursuing an international commitment" (Roca 1987).

Several factors explain Cuba's ability to withstand American pressure. The support Cuba received from the Soviet Union was especially important, but the United States' inability to persuade its allies to curtail their economic ties with Cuba counted heavily. So did Castro's charismatic leadership and popular support. Once Soviet support of Cuba ended, the United States redoubled its efforts to topple Castro through economic coercion. (This dismayed much of the rest of the world, which reproached the United States in the United Nations with a resounding repudiation of the United States embargo.) Still, Castro survived. And he made the United States "pay" for its project by permitting large numbers of disgruntled Cubans to emigrate to Florida, where the state and federal governments had to care for them.

When the Clinton administration eventually took a few halting steps to ease the decades of bitter relations with the Castro regime, conservative Republicans in Congress defended a more vigorous anti-Castro policy and passed the Helms-Burton Act in 1996, whose purpose was to punish foreign firms doing business with Cuba. By threatening secondary sanctions against others, the law set off a storm of protest in Canada, Europe, and elsewhere, arguably affecting American foreign policy interests far beyond Cuba (Haass 1997; see also Morici 1997). Meanwhile, as other countries continued to invest in and trade with Cuba, American companies pressured Clinton to lift the embargo, hoping to profit themselves. Upon taking office in 2001, George W. Bush continued to maintain American pressure to oust Castro from power through the continued support of sanctions against the island country. Some analysts and policy makers continued to view this hard-line stance as catering to Cuban émigrés living in Florida, a crucial swing voting state in both the 2000 and 2004 presidential elections.

As the Cuban case shows, sanctions often fail because other states refuse to enforce them. Systematic evidence on the use of sanctions since World War I indicates that the United States achieved its objective in only one of three cases (Elliott 1993; see also Hufbauer, Schott, and Elliott 1990).[9] During the Cold War, offsetting aid from the Soviet Union often undermined American efforts, but even today unilateral sanctions rarely prove effective.

> In most instances, other governments . . . value commercial interaction more than the United States does and are less willing to forfeit it. . . . Such thinking makes achieving multilateral support for sanctions more difficult for the United States. It usually takes something truly egregious, like Saddam Hussein's occupation of Kuwait, to overcome this anti-sanctions bias.
>
> *(Haass 1997, 78)*

If others do not go along, can *unilateral sanctions* work? Here the record is even more dismal. Between 1970 and 1990, "just five of thirty-nine unilateral U.S. sanctions [achieved] any success at all" (Elliott 1998). Furthermore, the dramatic changes in the world political economy accompanying globalization have reduced even further the number of targets vulnerable to unilateral economic coercion. Yet sanctions have continued as a preferred instrument of American foreign policy, and have been used with greater frequency since the end of the Cold War (Drury 2000). For instance, in 2003, President Bush imposed sanctions against Zimbabwe's leaders in response to the social upheaval, political intimidation, and food shortages resulting from corruption occurring in the southern African country. These sanctions prohibited American businesses from dealing with many Zimbabwean officials, including President Robert Mugabe, and froze their assets in the United States. European Union countries had previously imposed similar sanctions. To date, however, Mugabe remains in power.

Even though the prospects for success of sanctions are dubious, sanctions do sometimes succeed. Success is most likely when the goal is modest, the target is politically unstable, the initiator and target are generally friendly and carry on substantial trade with each other, the initiator is able to avoid substantial domestic costs, and the sanctions are imposed quickly and decisively (Elliott 1993). This last point highlights the idea that sanctions cannot just be threatened, but must be imposed to modify the behavior of international actors. One study of U.S. policy toward China found that simply *threatening* sanctions had little impact on Chinese behavior (Li and Drury 2004). Overall the conditions for success are difficult to realize, but they are not beyond reach. One other factor is important—and may be the determining one. The initiator must not rule out the next level: "the possibility must be clearly communicated to the target that force will be used if necessary—to enforce the sanctions, to strategically buttress their effects, or as a last resort if sanctions fail. Sanctions imposed as an alternative to force because the political will to use force is lacking are not likely to be credible and therefore not likely to be successful" (Elliott 1998). Noteworthy is the perceived failure of sanctions against Iraq in the 1990s (Cortright and Lopez 2000; 2002), which ultimately led to the decision in 2003 to use military force to oust Saddam Hussein from power.

The Victims of Sanctions

Who are sanctions' victims? Often the United States itself suffers. A study done at the Institute for International Economics in Washington estimated that economic sanctions in place in the mid-1990s "cost the United States some $20 billion in lost exports annually, depriving American workers of some 200,000 well-paid jobs." One of its principal authors added that "It would be one thing if these costs were compensated from the public purse, so that everyone shared the burden; it is quite another when the costs are concentrated episodically on individual American firms and communities" (Hufbauer 1998).

But while individual Americans and their communities may suffer economically, people in the targeted states typically suffer infinitely more. Two political scientists concluded that economic sanctions "may have contributed to more deaths during the post–Cold War era than all weapons of mass destruction throughout history" (Mueller and Mueller 1999). In Iraq alone, the United Nations estimates that some 400,000 people may have died as a result of UN-imposed sanctions in the decade preceding the second war against Iraq. This number far surpasses the fatalities suffered in the atomic bombings of Hiroshima and Nagasaki. The social costs that sanctions exacted have also been high. A former UN official responsible for the oil-for-food program in Iraq dramatized them this way:

> Iraqi families and Islamic family values have been damaged. Children have been forced to work, to become street kids, to beg, and engage in crime. Young women have been

forced into prostitution by the destitution of their families. Fathers have abandoned their families. The many problems single mothers already faced in the aftermath of the Iran-Iraq war have been compounded. Workplace progress that professional and other women had achieved in recent decades has been lost.... The education system has collapsed, with thousands of teachers leaving their posts because they are unable to work under existing conditions, and a dropout rate of some thirty percent at the primary and secondary levels. The health services are unable to handle the most basic preventable diseases—such as diarrhea, gastroenteritis, respiratory tract infections, polio—and curtail their spread to epidemic proportions. Hospitals attempt to function with collapsed water and sewage systems, without even the basic supplies for hygiene and minimal care.
> *(Halliday 1999, 66; see also Amuzegar 1997; Gause 1999)*

Thus sanctions pose a moral dilemma: "the more effective they are, the more likely that they will harm those least responsible for the wrongdoing and least able to bring about change: civilians" (Christiansen and Powers 1993). In fact, this ethical dilemma has prodded some analysts to explore the possibility that **smart sanctions** can be used to target crucial economic sectors or individuals within a target country (Cortright and Lopez 2002). By doing this, the suffering of the general population in the target country might be minimized. Others, however, question whether this idea is merely a simple solution to an extremely complex policy challenge (Drezner 2003). As UN Secretary General Kofi Annan stated, "It is not enough merely to make sanctions 'smarter.' The challenge is to achieve consensus about the precise and specific aims of the sanctions, adjust the instruments accordingly and then provide the necessary means" (quoted in Drezner 2003, 109).

Vexing as these dilemmas are, they cannot hide a central fact: ruling elites are typically immune from sanctions' effects. This is especially true in authoritarian regimes. Indeed, in spite of a war and a decade of sanctions, Saddam Hussein greeted newly elected president George W. Bush in 2001 and his new secretary of state, Colin Powell, with a cocky assertiveness stemming from his ability to survive ten years of international isolation. This attitude may have been a contributing factor in Bush's later decision to go to war in Iraq.

Political leaders in sanctioned societies may actually benefit from external economic pressure. One reason is that the typical response to economic coercion is a heightened sense of nationalism, a *laager mentality* (circle the ox wagons to face oncoming enemies), to use a phrase from the Afrikaners in South Africa. Nationalism stimulates resistance in the target state and encourages leaders to blame all hardships on outsiders. In the case of Serbia in the 1990s, for example, sanctions probably strengthened the nationalist extremists and helped to keep Serbian leader Slobodan Milošević in power for so long (Christiansen and Powers 1993; see also Woodward 1993).

Despite their checkered record of success and the troublesome ethical dilemma they pose by increasing the suffering of innocent victims, sanctions will continue to be used as foreign policy instruments, particularly in instances where the United States (and others) are unwilling to use overt military force. If nothing else, sanctions have symbolic value: they demonstrate to foreign and domestic audiences a resolve to act decisively, but short of war.

PUBLIC DIPLOMACY: USING INFORMATION AND IDEAS TO INTERVENE

United States public diplomacy is qualitatively different than interventions through clandestine intelligence operations, economic and military assistance programs, and sanctions on which the United States has relied to exercise influence over others. However, the use of information and ideas is still a part of the broad interventionist strategy generally employed by the United States to penetrate other societies. With the end of the Cold War, the anticommunist logic that once sustained the U.S. government's public diplomacy programs largely dissipated. Thus, public diplomacy's institutional independence was eliminated; programs were restructured and integrated into other agencies; and different regions of the world have become the primary targets of the U.S. government's activities in this area.

Public Diplomacy Purposes and Programs

Public diplomacy is a polite term for what many would regard as straightforward propaganda (the methodical spreading of information to influence public opinion). According to a previous executive director of the U.S. Advisory Commission on Public Diplomacy, public diplomacy "seeks to inculcate others with American values, promotes mutual understanding between the United States and other societies . . . reduces the potential for conflict . . . and dispels negative notions about the United States" (Kramer 2000). From 1953 to 1999, the United States Information Agency (USIA) was in charge of U.S. public diplomacy efforts aimed at winning greater understanding and support around the world for American society and foreign policy. Its instruments were information and cultural activities directed overseas at both mass publics and elites.

The USIA carried out its tasks through a worldwide network using a variety of media tools, including radio, television, films, libraries, and exhibitions. Among the best known are the Voice of America (VOA), which broadcasts news, political journalism, music, and cultural programs in many different languages to various parts of the globe, and Radio Free Europe and Radio Liberty (both established by the CIA), which, during the Cold War, broadcast to Eastern Europe and the Soviet Union, respectively. The Reagan administration added Radio Marti and TV Marti, which direct their messages to Cuba, and WORLDNET, a television and film service downlinked via satellite to United States embassies, television stations, and cable systems around the world. In 1994, President Clinton authorized Radio Free Asia. USIA also administered a variety of cultural exchange programs supporting travel abroad by American athletes, artists, dramatists, musicians, and scholars, as well as travel to the United States by foreign political leaders, students, and educators for study tours or other educational purposes. The Foreign Affairs Reform and Restructuring Act of 1998 abolished USIA (as of October 1, 1999) and parceled out its tasks between the State Department (for the public diplomacy and cultural programs) and a new, independent International Broadcasting Board of Governors (for VOA and the other broadcasting programs). Although less central, the White House, Central Intelligence Agency, Department of Defense, and the U.S. Agency for International Development (USAID) are also members of the U.S. public diplomacy community.

Information and cultural programs are pursued in the expectation that specialized communications can be used to make the United States' image in the world more favorable. Opinion varies widely, however, regarding the propriety and effectiveness of public diplomacy as a policy instrument. Should such efforts be designed only to provide information? Should public diplomacy aggressively promote American culture and its values? Should it be linked intimately to the political contests in which the United States becomes engaged? In practice, each role has been dominant at one time or another, dictated largely by events and contemporary challenges to U.S. foreign policy objectives.

Public Diplomacy Today

When Colin Powell assumed his duties as George W. Bush's first secretary of state in 2001, he was convinced the Department of State had to devote greater attention and resources to public diplomacy. In part, his belief was motivated by years of military and government experience where he witnessed the power of the media, especially television, in shaping the process and substance of U.S. foreign policy. Powell's initial interest in public diplomacy was also tied to the realization that USIA had been integrated within the State Department in 1999, but the department had not embraced the agency's

mission. As former secretary of defense, Frank Carlucci, who also served as U.S. Foreign Service officer, observed in 2001: "The department's professional culture remains predisposed against public outreach and engagement, thus undercutting its effectiveness at public diplomacy" (Carlucci 2001). Furthermore, Powell undoubtedly saw public diplomacy as an attractive soft power resource for the promotion of U.S. interests and values in the post–Cold War world, especially given advances in information technologies. Yet few others in the early months of the Bush administration seemed to share Powell's conviction regarding the utility of public diplomacy. As the new administration pursued a unilateralist foreign policy agenda, public diplomacy was considered a peripheral foreign policy tool.

The terrorist attacks of September 11, 2001, elevated the importance of public diplomacy exponentially. Now the Bush administration and skeptical Foreign Service officers in Powell's department had no choice but to be involved in the battle to win the hearts and minds of the world's people, particularly those living in places like the Middle East. The imperative only intensified once the United States waged an internationally unpopular war in Iraq followed by an indefinite and equally unpopular occupation. However, the need for effective public diplomacy to mollify the image of a coercive hegemon now extended beyond the anti-American attitudes of the Middle East to regions such as Latin America, Asia, and Europe. For instance, polls and studies in a number of Western European countries revealed a growing trend of public hostility toward U.S. foreign policy (see Marquis 2003; Bernstein 2003; Sachs 2004). One survey conducted nine months after the invasion of Iraq revealed that 53 percent of European Union citizens considered the United States to be a threat to world peace, tying it with Iran and North Korea. A comparative review of the State Department's polling from 2002 and 2003 illustrated that people's favorable view of the United States had dropped dramatically in Germany, France, Russia, Brazil, and Indonesia, to name just a few countries (Kohut 2003).

According to the Department of State and USAID's *Strategic Plan for Fiscal Years 2004–2009,* the U.S. government has five central goals for the conduct of public diplomacy in the post-9/11 world:

- *Communicate with younger audiences through content and means tailored to their context.* The particular focus is on the Muslim and Arab worlds.

- *Quickly counter propaganda and disinformation.* This is to be accomplished through diplomatic missions worldwide and the use of foreign citizen testimonials where appropriate.

- *Listen to foreign audiences.* International cultural and educational exchanges, public opinion polling, focus groups, and dialog with foreign press are the primary tools here.

- *Use advances in communications technology, while continuing to employ effective tools and techniques.* Gaining better access and profile in the electronic media and Internet is a crucial piece of the approach for this goal.

- *Promote international educational and professional exchanges* (pp. 31–32).

As these goals imply, this post-9/11 approach to public diplomacy centers on countering anti–United States sentiment around the world, with particular attention to the Muslim and Arab worlds. This has obvious connections to the overall anti-terror focus that has pervaded much of our discussion of the Bush administration's policies considered in this chapter.

Some specific examples show the ways in which the State Department sought to implement the new approach during the first term of the Bush administration. In 2003, *Hi* magazine, a hardcopy and Web-based publication targeting eighteen- to thirty-five-year-old Arabic-speaking individuals worldwide was launched. The magazine includes sections on music, sports, education, technology, careers, and health and is designed to engage Arabic-speaking young adults "in a constructive, interactive dialogue on the many aspects of American society." In addition, an

Arabic-language pop radio station, Radio Sawa, and a Farsi-language radio station, Radio Farda, which feature five minutes of U.S. government-produced news each hour, were established. Also, a 24-hour Arabic-language Middle East Television Network, known as Al Hurra, which features U.S. news and entertainment, began broadcasting in February 2004. Furthermore, the State Department's booklet, *Muslim Life in America,* was printed in more languages and circulated more broadly worldwide; partnerships between *Sesame Street* and Arab television stations were developed; and exchange programs involving American journalists and writers were instituted in the Arab world (see Harris 2003; Labott 2003, Wright 2004).

These steps were reinforced by organizational and personnel changes at the State Department. For example, new public diplomacy training courses were added to the curriculum at the Foreign Service Institute (see Jacobs 2003), and the Public Diplomacy Office of Policy, Planning and Resources was established in 2004 to conduct long-term strategic planning and regular studies of the effectiveness of the department's outreach programs. Moreover, high-profile officials were appointed to serve as under secretary of state for public diplomacy, a position that oversees three State Department bureaus: Education and Cultural Affairs, Public Affairs, and International Information Programs. Charlotte Beers, a leading New York advertising executive, served from 2001 to 2003. Margaret Tutwiler, a spokeswoman for former Secretary of State James Baker and a former ambassador to Morocco, served from 2003 to 2004. However, these appointments, the previously discussed initiatives, and the establishment of an Office of Global Communications within the White House to serve as the centerpiece for coordinating public diplomacy government-wide were unable to reverse the strong wave of anti-Americanism in the international community. As a result, the tenures of Beers and Tutwiler during Powell's years at the State Department were considered largely unsuccessful.

The appointment of Karen Hughes in early 2005 as the nation's chief public diplomacy officer was greeted with mixed reaction. On the one hand, she assumed a position where her predecessors had experienced considerable difficulty in altering negative global opinion toward the United States. She also enjoyed no substantive foreign policy experience. On the other hand, Hughes brought to the position a tremendous resource: her strong relationship with President Bush and his new secretary of state, Condoleezza Rice. During Bush's first eighteen months in office, Hughes worked closely with the president and his first term national security adviser, Rice, serving as a senior White House counselor. She oversaw the administration's communications, media affairs, and speechwriting during the first year of the war on terrorism and had daily contact with both Bush and Rice. Moreover, Hughes was one of Bush's most trusted aides during his two terms as governor of Texas.

Over the course of her first year of service, Hughes enjoyed unprecedented access as an under secretary of state, including regular meals with the president to share updates on the progress of her public diplomacy endeavors. This access and the accompanying clout allowed her to garner new resources and support inside and outside the State Department for a range of initiatives that won generally favorable reviews (see Kessler 2006). Examples of key changes under Hughes's leadership included an Arabic-speaking rapid response unit that monitors Arab newscasts, greater freedom for U.S. ambassadors to give overseas interviews without prior approval from Washington, and the distribution of "echo chamber" messages (prepared talking points that U.S. officials can use to address unfolding controversies). Additionally, Hughes assigned new deputy assistant secretaries for public diplomacy to each of the State Department's regional bureaus, established a regional spokesperson's office in the United Arab Emirates to respond to inquires from the Arab media, and created a new, partially classified program to determine the messages that play well in particular states along with efforts to coordinate a unified message across U.S. government agencies (Kessler 2006).

Despite these efforts, world opinion toward the United States did not improve during the same period. As Table 5.4 indicates, it worsened; and the prospect for improvement is far from encouraging. In short, U.S. practitioners of public diplomacy face a daunting task. In fact, reversing negative world opinion might be a difficult, if not impossible, mission, as long as certain U.S. policies, military actions, and global power disparities persist. Moreover, the attention, resources, and infrastructure that sustained U.S. public diplomacy efforts during the Cold War era withered in the decade between the fall of the Soviet Union and September 11. As Margaret Tutwiler observed in her confirmation hearings in 2004, "Unfortunately, our country has a problem in far too many parts of the world. [It is] a problem we have regrettably gotten into over many years through both Democrat and Republican administrations, and a problem that does not lend itself to a quick fix or a single solution or a simple plan." Thus U.S. public diplomacy was still very much in a rebuilding phase as the second term of the Bush administration unfolded. If there was a positive side

TABLE 5.4 Favorable Public Opinions of the United States

Country	1999/2000	2002	2003	2004	2005	2006
Great Britain	83%	75%	70%	58%	55%	56%
France	62%	63%	43%	37%	43%	39%
Germany	78%	61%	45%	38%	41%	37%
Spain	50%	—	38%	—	41%	23%
Russia	37%	61%	36%	47%	52%	43%
Indonesia	75%	61%	15%	—	38%	30%
Egypt	—	—	—	—	—	30%
Pakistan	23%	10%	13%	21%	23%	27%
Jordan	—	25%	1%	5%	21%	15%
Turkey	52%	30%	15%	30%	23%	12%
Nigeria	46%	—	61%	—	—	62%
Japan	77%	72%	—	—	—	63%
India	—	54%	—	—	71%	56%
China	—	—	—	—	42%	47%

SOURCE: The Pew Global Attitudes Project, June 13, 2006.

to this challenging state of affairs, it was that the post-9/11 global environment had compelled the United States to become far more sensitive to the important role of public diplomacy in contemporary international relations. Whether a more serious commitment to this foreign policy instrument over time can counter powerful anti-American sentiment in Muslim countries and worldwide remains unclear at this point.

THE INSTRUMENTS OF GLOBAL INFLUENCE TODAY

The foreign policy agenda of the twenty-first century is becoming increasingly globalized and trans-nationalized. Even the threat of terrorism—itself a transnational phenomenon—has not halted the pace of global integration.

As the United States learned in Vietnam and is now learning again in Iraq and elsewhere, power and persuasion are not synonymous. Something other than military might is necessary to shape a world conducive to the realization of American interests and objectives. The instruments of policy persuasion discussed in this chapter—covert action, economic and military aid, sanctions, and public diplomacy—have long been tried as alternatives short of overt military threats and interventions, but even they have faced challenges posed by a more complex global environment. Meanwhile force and threat of force continue to be central elements in the practice of statecraft.

Most of the policy instruments evolved during the early stages of the Cold War and were adapted to meet the challenge of Soviet communism. Whether they can be remolded to effectively meet the challenges of the post-9/11 world remains to be seen.

KEY TERMS

code of conduct on arms transfers
counterintelligence
covert action
development assistance
earmarks
Economic Support Fund (ESF)

espionage
Food for Peace program
foreign economic aid
Foreign Military Financing (FMF)
Group of 8 (G8)
laager mentality

Marshall Plan
Nixon Doctrine
presidential findings
public diplomacy
Reagan Doctrine
sanctions
security assistance
smart sanctions

U.S. Agency for International Development (USAID)

SUGGESTED READINGS

Andrew, Christopher. *For the President's Eyes Only: Secret Intelligence and the American Presidency from Washington to Bush.* New York: HarperCollins, 1995.

Arndt, Richard T. *The First Resort of Kings: American Cultural Diplomacy in the Twentieth Century.* Dulles, VA: Potomac Books, 2005.

Clarke, Duncan. *Send Guns and Money: Security Assistance and U.S. Foreign Policy.* Westport, CT: Praeger Publishers, 1997.

Cortright, David, and George A. Lopez, eds. *The Sanctions Decade: Assessing UN Strategies in the 1990s.* Boulder, CO: Lynne Rienner, 2000.

Daugherty, William J. *Executive Secrets: Covert Action and the Presidency.* Lexington, KY: University Press of Kentucky, 2004.

Godson, Roy S. *Dirty Tricks or Trump Cards: U.S. Covert Action and Counterintelligence.* New Brunswick, NJ: Transaction Publishers, 2000.

Haass, Richard N., and Meghan L. O'Sullivan, eds. *Honey and Vinegar: Incentives, Sanctions, and Foreign Policy.* Washington, DC: Brookings Institution, 2000.

Howard, Russell D., and Reid L. Sawyer. *Terrorism and Counterterrorism: Understanding the New Security Environment.* Guilford, CT: McGraw-Hill/Dushkin, 2004.

Johnson, Loch K. *Bombs, Bugs, Drugs, and Thugs: Intelligence and America's Quest for Security.* New York: New York University Press, 2002.

Kohut, Andrew, and Bruce Stokes. *America Against the World: How We Are Different and Why We Are Disliked.* New York: Times Books, 2006.

Lancaster, Carol, and Ann Van Dusen. *Organizing U.S. Foreign Aid: Confronting the Challenges of the 21st Century.* Washington, DC: Brookings Institution, 2005.

Naftali, Timothy. *Blind Spot: The Secret History of American Counterterrorism.* New York: Basic Books, 2005.

O'Sullivan, Meghan L. *Shrewd Sanctions: Statecraft and State Sponsors of Terrorism.* Washington, DC: Brookings Institution, 2003.

Rugh, William A., ed. *Engaging the Arab and Islamic Worlds through Public Diplomacy.* Washington, DC: Public Diplomacy Council.

Tarnoff, Curt, and Larry Nowels. *Foreign Aid: An Introductory Overview of U.S. Programs.* Washington, DC: Congressional Research Service/The Library of Congress, 2005.

Zimmerman, Robert F. *Dollars, Diplomacy, and Dependency: Dilemmas of U.S. Economic Aid.* Boulder, CO: Lynne Rienner, 1993.

NOTES

1. In April 2000, the CIA released a report on the action to overthrow Mossadegh. See the *New York Times Special* (www.nytimes.com/library/world/mideast/041600iran-cia-index.html) for coverage. See also "The Secret CIA History of the Iran Coup, 1953" at the National Security Archive (www.gwu.edu/~nsarchiv/NSAEBB/NSAEBB28/).

2. On the Bay of Pigs, see the CIA's own internal report, a scathing criticism of virtually all involved. Long classified and believed destroyed, the report was acquired by the National Security Archive and published in Kornbluh (1998).

3. The "facts" of the events in Chile between 1970 and 1973 are controversial. From 1998 to 2000, a series of CIA documents on the Chile operation were declassified, shedding substantial light on the extent of the American effort to first defeat and then destabilize the Allende regime. See the "Chile Documentation Project," directed by Peter Kornbluh, at the National Security Archive (www2.gwu.edu/~nsarchiv/latin_america/chile.htm), and the CIA report, "CIA Activities in Chile," released September 18, 2000 (www.lib.umich.edu/govdocs/text/ciachile.htm).

4. But see Kuperman (1999), who argues that the effect of the Stingers has been exaggerated.

Following the Soviets' withdrawal from Afghanistan, the CIA launched a covert program to buy back unused Stinger missiles. Congress reportedly provided $65 million for the program—double the cost of the roughly one thousand missiles the United States provided the mujahideen. However, only a fraction of the missiles were recovered, because the CIA does not know who controls them (Moore 1994). In 2001, Taliban forces fired Stingers in response to the U.S. air attacks on Afghanistan.

5. On the issue of the CIA-drug connection, see Johnson (2000a), Nelson (1995), and P. Scott (1998), as well as the CIA's own *The Inspector General's Report of Investigation* regarding allegations of connections between CIA and the contras in cocaine trafficking to the United States (at www.cia.gov/cia/reports/cocaine/contents.html).

6. "This program had been devised as a means of extraditing terrorism suspects from one foreign state to another for interrogation and prosecution. Critics contend that the unstated purpose of such renditions is to subject the suspects to aggressive methods of persuasion that are illegal in America—including torture" (Mayer 2005).

7. The Mutual Security Act became the umbrella legislation for economic and military aid after the

onset of Korea. Foreign military sales are now governed by the Arms Export Control Act, first passed in 1968. As of early 1995, the Foreign Assistance Act (as amended) continues to govern other military aid programs. Both statutes authorize economic assistance.

8. This is by no means limited to arms sales, either. Indeed, a criticism of the IMET program has been its problematic embrace of repressive military officers. Arguments in favor of the program stress its contribution to professionalization and the commitment to civilian government (for example, Nye 1996). In no case has this been more controversial than the School of the Americas, which has trained military officers from Latin America for several decades. Unfortunately, many of the officers have been among the most repressive in their respective countries. For example, it was IMET-funded, School of the Americas–trained soldiers in El Salvador who were guilty of the massacre of El Salvadoran civilians at El Mozote in 1981 and of the brutal murder of El Salvadoran Jesuit priests in 1989.

9. Robert A. Pape challenges even this number, arguing Hufbauer, Schott, and Elliott are too generous in their definition of "success." He argues that of 115 cases examined by Hufbauer, Schott, and Elliott, "only five cases are appropriately considered successes" (Pape 1997). For rejoinders, see Elliott (1998) and Pape (1998). See also Kaempfer and Lowenberg (1999) and essays in Haass (1998).

PART III

External Sources
of American Foreign Policy

6

Principle, Power, and Pragmatism in the Twenty-First Century:

The International Political System in Transition

Our well-being as a country depends . . . on the structural conditions
of the international system that help determine whether we are
fundamentally secure, whether the world economy is sound.
SECRETARY OF STATE GEORGE SHULTZ, 1984

The twenty-first century world is going to be
about more than great power politics.
PRESIDENT BILL CLINTON, 2000

Early in October 1994, U.S. satellite reconnaissance revealed that a division of Iraq's elite Republican Guard was moving toward the border with Kuwait. Within days, over 60,000 Iraqi troops and an armada of powerful weapons—a military force larger than the one used four years earlier to invade Kuwait and proclaim it Iraq's nineteenth province—again stood within striking distance of the tiny oil sheikdom.

President Clinton warned Saddam Hussein that "it would be a grave mistake . . . to believe that for any reason the United States would have weakened its resolve on the same issues that involved us in the conflict just a few years ago." Accordingly, he ordered additional air, naval, and ground forces to the Persian Gulf to bolster those already deployed in the oil-rich region. The United States also worked closely with its allies in Europe and the Middle East to ensure their continued support of American policies.

The U.S. response to Iraq's provocation is a classic illustration of state behavior as explained by the theory of *political realism* (discussed in Chapter 3). Perceiving its interests threatened by the aggressive behavior of an adversary seeking to upset the status quo, the United States took action to *balance* Iraq's military power. Its behavior followed the injunction of *self-help* in a system characterized by the absence of central institutions capable of conflict management and resolution. It shows how the external environment acts as a source of American foreign policy, providing both stimulants to action and constraints on its ability to realize preferred goals. We examine these external effects in this chapter and the next.

Here, in Chapter 6, we probe how the distribution of power among the world's great and lesser powers, critical global problems and developments, and the activities of non-state actors shape American foreign policy. In Chapter 7, we shift attention to the world political economy. There we examine the United States' role in managing the Liberal International Economic Order and inquire into the global and national effects of changes in the world political economy. The concepts of power and hegemony punctuate our analyses in both chapters.

THE DISTRIBUTION OF POWER AS A SOURCE OF AMERICAN FOREIGN POLICY

The theory of *political realism* holds that the distribution of power among states defines the structure of the international system. In turn, the structure determines states' behavior in world politics. Kenneth Waltz (1979), a leading proponent of *structural realism* argues that only two types of systems existed between the birth of the nation-state at the Peace of Westphalia in 1648: (1) a *multipolar* system, which existed until the end of World War II, and (2) a *bipolar* system, which characterized the distribution of power until the late twentieth century. In both, states protected their interests against external threats by balancing power with power. Coalitions—alliances—were critical in the multipolar system. States that perceived one among them as seeking hegemony (preponderance) joined together in a balancing coalition to preserve their own existence (national self-interest). Wars were recurrent and often determined who among existing and aspiring hegemons would define the world order. The United States itself was born in a contest between Britain and France over who would dominate Europe and the New World. And the historical record shows that the architects of the new American republic were acutely aware of the perquisites and perils of power that buffeted the new nation, as we saw in Chapter 3.

The situation after World War II was quite different. Now only two powers contended for preponderance. Each still sought to balance power with power, as suggested by the strategies of containment the United States pursued to parry Soviet challenges (Gaddis 1982; 2005b), but alliances were comparatively unimportant to their own survival. To be sure, the United States and the Soviet Union both tried to recruit allies to their cause. They repeatedly intervened abroad using military and other means to counter the threat each posed to the other's clients. The *North Atlantic Treaty Organization (NATO)* and the *Warsaw Pact* were pillars of their foreign policies.

Each also mirrored the behavior of the other as both developed ever more sophisticated weapons of destruction. But, structural realists argue, it was the weapons themselves—nuclear weapons in particular—that balanced the antagonists' power. As long as both enjoyed a second-strike nuclear capability, neither could dominate or destroy the other. As Waltz put it, "Nuclear weapons produced an underlying stillness at the center of international politics that made the sometimes frenzied military preparations of the United States and the Soviet Union pointless, and efforts to devise scenarios for the use of their nuclear weapons bizarre" (Waltz 1993; see also Gaddis 1986; Mearsheimer 1990a, 1990b; Waltz 1964).

The structural realist argument is not beyond dispute. Still, it usefully orients us toward an examination of historical configurations of international power and their effects on American foreign policy behavior, both in the past and in the new century.

Multipolarity and the Birth of the American Republic

From today's perspective it is difficult to believe that little more than two centuries ago the United States was a small, fledgling state whose very existence was perpetually jeopardized. With only about three million inhabitants, the thirteen colonies that proclaimed their independence from Britain were dwarfed by Europe's great powers: Britain, an island power, and France, Russia, Austria, and Prussia on the continent. Preserving the independence won at Yorktown in 1781 thus became a preoccupation. "It was the genius of America's first diplomats in this unemotional age that they realized the nature of their international opposition—which included all of the powers of the day, not excepting France—and adroitly maneuvered their country's case through the snares and traps of Europe's diplomatic coalitions until they irrevocably had secured national independence" (Ferrell 1988; see also Gilbert 1961).

The colonists' alliance with France was critical to their successful rebellion against England. France supported the United States to regain a foothold on the North American continent following an earlier defeat at the hands of the British. France and England had fought a series of wars in a century-old rivalry for preponderance in Europe and control of North America. The Seven Year's War in Europe (known as the French and Indian War in America) was the most recent. With the French defeat, the 1763 Treaty of Paris assured France's virtual elimination from North America. Canada and the Ohio Valley were ceded to the British. Louisiana was relinquished to Spain, which in turn ceded the Floridas to England. England sought to consolidate control of its empire in the years that followed. The famed Boston Tea Party was brewed by England's effort to squeeze more resources out of the colonies.

France reemerged as a principal security concern of the newly independent confederation of American states. Its policy makers were acutely aware that French support would last only as long as it served French interests. Indeed, an undeclared war erupted between the American and French navies in 1797. Ironically, however, the French Revolution and the rise of Napoleon Bonaparte, whose ambitions centered on Europe, contributed to the continental expansion of the United States. Talleyrand (Charles Maurice de Talleyrand-Périgord), the wily French foreign minister during the Reign of Terror, hoped to regain the Louisiana territory from Spain as part of a plan to recreate France's North American empire. Napoleon later became interested in the project but, facing renewed war against England, dropped it. Focused on Europe, not on recreating an empire far from the continent, he sold to the United States the vast tract of land that doubled its size. Diplomatic historian Robert Ferrell (1988) notes that "The 1803 sale of Louisiana to America was no mark of French friendship for the United States but the fortuitous result of a train of events that, but for the old world ambitions of Napoleon, would have drastically constricted American territorial expansion and might have extinguished American independence."

Napoleon's drive for European hegemony sparked more than a decade of protracted conflict and war, which finally ended in 1815 with the Congress of Vienna and the restoration of the Bourbon monarchy to the French throne. The War of 1812 was part of that system-wide conflict. The United States entered the fray against Britain, asserting its trading rights as neutral during wartime. A century later Woodrow Wilson would use similar principles to rationalize American involvement in World War I. However, unlike its position in 1917—by which time the United States had emerged as a major industrial power—in 1812 the United States was still struggling to secure its independence. History records the War of 1812 as a second American victory over the English; often forgotten is that the British successfully attacked and burned Washington, D.C., forcing President James Madison to flee the capital.

In 1823, President James Monroe enunciated what would later be called the Monroe Doctrine. Monroe's statement declared that the Americas were for Americans, as we noted in Chapter 3. At the time, the United States lacked the power to make good on its implicit threat to the European powers who were its targets. Instead, Britain's power—particularly its command of the high seas—effectively "enforced" the Monroe Doctrine for nearly seventy years. Its sea power kept other European states out of the New World and permitted the United States to develop from an agrarian society into an industrial power.

The Spanish-American War, which transformed the United States into an imperial power, had little impact on the global balance of power. In Europe, however, Germany was ascendant, challenging the French for continental hegemony in the Franco-Prussian War of 1870–1871 and posing a potential threat to England, the island power (see Kissinger 1994a). By 1914 the alliance structures of the multipolar balance-of-power system had rigidified. The guns of August that ignited World War I ended a century of great-power peace. Three years later the United States entered the war on the side of the British, French, and Russians against Germany and the Austro-Hungarian and Ottoman empires. As in the War of 1812, the legal principle of neutral rights on the high seas figured prominently in the decision for war. But political realists argue that more than principle was at stake: It was nothing less than the European balance of power, which posed potentially serious threats to American interests and security.

America entered the European war when the aggressive continental land power of Germany was about to achieve hegemony in Europe by defeating the British sea power and to acquire simultaneously the mastery of the Atlantic Ocean. The very month that war was declared by America, Britain lost 880,000 gross tons of shipping, several times more than it could possibly replace. In that same month, mutinies in the French army made France's future in the war questionable. Russia, the third member of Europe's Triple Entente, was but a few months away from its internal collapse.

(Serfaty 1972, 7–8)

The United States reverted to isolationism after World War I, choosing not to become embroiled in the machinations of European power politics. But just as its balancing behavior turned the tide against German hegemonic ambitions at the turn of the century, its power proved critical in turning back the German and Japanese challenges mounted in the 1930s and 1940s. Guided by Wilsonian idealism, the United States had hoped to replace the "ugly" balance-of-power politics of the Old World with a new collective security system, embodied in the League of Nations. When that failed, it found that it had to resort to the same strategies it once deplored: joining Britain and the Soviet Union in a balancing coalition designed to prevent the Axis powers from achieving world hegemony. Once the death and destruction ceased and the ashes began to settle, the United States found that it alone had emerged largely unscathed from the ravages of a world war that claimed 50 million lives.

Hegemonic Dominance: A Unipolar World

World War II transformed the American economy, which now stood preeminent in the world political economy. The gross national product (GNP), agricultural production, and civilian consumption of goods and services all rose dramatically. In contrast, Europe lay exhausted and destroyed. Even the Soviet Union, whose armies pushed the Nazis from Stalingrad to Berlin, had suffered grievously. Its industrial, agricultural, and transportation systems had either been destroyed or severely damaged. Nearly 7 million Soviet civilians are thought to have perished in the war. Another 11 million soldiers were killed or missing in action. Although the United States had suffered some 405,000 killed or missing in action (Ellis 1993), it had virtually no civilian casualties. Thus the ratio of Soviet to American war deaths was more than to forty to one.

The Soviet Union had, of course, secured control over much of Eastern Europe following the war, and it was over this issue that Soviet-American conflict centered. On balance, however, the United States was clearly in the superior position—a true hegemonic power. In 1947 the United States alone accounted for nearly half the world's total production of goods and services. And America's monopoly of the atomic bomb gave it military predominance. Only against this background can we begin to see how fundamental the shifts in the international distribution of power have been during the past five decades.

The post–World War II era began with the United States possessing the capability (if not the will) to exercise greater control over world affairs than perhaps any previous country. It alone possessed the military and economic might to defend unilaterally its security and sovereignty. Its unparalleled supremacy transformed the system during this interlude into a unipolar one. Perhaps his anticipation of this environment is what led Henry Luce in 1941 to predict an *American Century*—a prolonged period in which American power would shape the world to its interests.

Others worried that the United States might overextend itself. Political commentator and journalist Walter Lippmann (1943) observed that "foreign policy consists of bringing into balance . . . the nation's commitments and the nation's power." Thus "solvency" was, for Lippmann, a critical concern as the United States embarked on its rise to globalism. He later criticized the containment foreign policy strategy, arguing among other things that the regimentation required to combat Soviet communism would hurt the economy. Lippmann's concerns and criticisms anticipated the intense debate about the decline of American power that would occur four decades later. During the 1940s, however, the American century imagery was more compelling than solvency.

Still, the *unipolar moment,* a concentration of power in the hands of single country, the United States enjoyed in the immediate aftermath of World War II began to change almost as soon as it emerged. The Soviets cracked the American monopoly of the atom bomb with a successful atomic test in 1949.

Then, in 1953, they exploded a thermonuclear device, less than a year after the United States. And in 1957 they shocked the Western World as they became the first country to successfully test an intercontinental ballistic missile (ICBM) and to orbit a space satellite—feats that also signaled their ability to deliver a nuclear warhead far from mother Russia.

The Bipolar System

Bipolarity describes the concentration of power in the hands of the United States and the Soviet Union from the late 1940s until the 1962 Cuban missile crisis (see Wagner 1993). The less-powerful states looked to one or the other superpower for protection, and the two world leaders energetically competed for their allegiance. NATO, which linked the United States to the defense of Western Europe, and the Warsaw Pact, which tied the Soviet Union in a formal alliance to its Eastern European satellites, were the two major products of this early competition. The division of Europe into competing blocs also provided a solution to the German question—an implicit alliance between East and West against the center. As Lord Ismay, the first Secretary General of NATO, put it, the purpose of the Atlantic Alliance was "to keep the Russians out, the Americans in, and the Germans down."

By grouping the states of the system into two blocs, each led by a predominant power, the bipolar structure bred insecurity throughout. Believing that the power balance was constantly at stake, each side perceived a gain by one as a loss for the other—a situation known in the mathematics of game theory as a *zero-sum* outcome. Recruiting new friends and allies was thus of utmost importance, while fear that an old ally might desert the fold was ever present. The bipolar structure provided little room for compromise. Every maneuver seemed like a new initiative toward world conquest; hence, every act was perceived as hostile and required a retaliatory act. Because the antagonists believed conciliation was impossible, at best only momentary pauses in the exchange of threats, tests of resolve, and challenges to the territorial status quo could be expected (Spanier 1990). Repeated great power interventions in the Global South and recurrent crises at the brink of great power war characterized bipolarity.

Despite endemic threats and recurring crises, major war between the great powers did not occur. Instead, historian John Lewis Gaddis (1986) calls the Cold War era the *long peace*. The phrase describes the paradox that the perpetual competition and the concentration of enormous destructive power in the hands of the contestants produced caution and stability rather than recklessness and war. Gaddis as well as structural realists attribute that caution and stability to nuclear weapons.

The Bipolycentric System

A looser structure began to replace bipolarity in the wake of the Cuban missile crisis, as the superpowers stepped back from the nuclear precipice and eventually pursued a policy of détente. Both now accepted that nuclear parity preserved strategic stability, as signaled by the SALT agreements. Their intermittent pledges to avert use of nuclear weapons to settle their differences and their growing conviction that the destructiveness of modern weapons also reduced the utility of defensive alliances. Rapid technological advances in their weapons systems catalyzed further changes in the increasingly fluid international polarity structure. ICBMs in particular decreased the need for forward bases—especially important to the United States—from which to strike the adversary. As rigid bipolarity eroded, *bipolycentrism* characterized the emerging structure. The concept emphasizes the continued military superiority of the United States and the Soviet Union at this time and the continuing reliance of the weaker alliance partners on their respective superpower patrons for security. The new system also permitted measurably greater maneuverability on the part of weaker states. Hence the word "polycentrism," connoting the possibility of many centers of power and diverse relationships among those subordinate to the major powers. In the bipolycentric system, each superpower sought closer ties with the secondary powers formally aligned with its adversary (like those once nurtured between the United States and Romania and between France and the Soviet Union). The secondary powers in turn exploited those ties as they sought to enhance their bargaining position within their own alliance by establishing relationships among themselves (for example, between Poland and West Germany). While the superpowers remained militarily dominant, greater diplomatic fluidity became evident.

The Fragmentation of the Atlantic Alliance

The convergence of Soviet and American military capabilities accelerated these developments, as it reduced the credibility of the superpowers' commitment to sacrifice their own security for their allies' defense. In a system shaped by a balance of terror, European members of NATO in particular worried that the United States might not willingly sacrifice New York City for Paris or Bonn. Mounting uncertainties about the credibility of the U.S. deterrent threat led France to develop its own nuclear force and later to withdraw from the integrated NATO command. Even the *flexible response* policy adopted as official NATO strategy during the Johnson administration did not restore European confidence in American promises. The policy tried to extend to Europe the principle of assured destruction of the Soviet Union should the Warsaw Pact attack Western Europe. For many Europeans, however, it simply signaled the United States' reluctance to expose itself to destruction to ensure its allies' security.

These concerns accelerated the polycentric divisions already evident. Talk of "decoupling" Europe from American protection prompted the decision to deploy in Europe a new class of U.S. intermediate-range nuclear missiles, thus enhancing the credibility of *extended deterrence*, a strategy that seeks to deter an adversary from attacking one's allies (discussed in Chapter 4). Uneasiness persisted, however. Peace groups on both sides of the Atlantic challenged the "Atlanticist" orientation that bound the United States and Western Europe together. Increasingly, European public opinion swung toward neutralism and pacifism, even as the United States undertook a massive rearmament program designed to enhance its ability to deter Soviet aggression. The specter of Europe devastated in a limited response nuclear exchange—a nuclear attack confined to the European theater without escalating to general war between the superpowers—inspired the European quest for a new security architecture that would prevent it from becoming a nuclear battleground.

Changes in the distribution of economic strength coincided with these geostrategic developments. Already by the 1960s and 1970s many U.S. allies were vibrant economic entities, no longer weak dependents. By the end of the 1980s the combined output of Japan and the twelve members of the European Community exceeded U.S. output by nearly a trillion dollars. Thirty years earlier, in 1960, it did not even equal U.S. output. Enhanced capabilities encouraged Europe and Japan to be more assertive and accelerated the erosion of America's ability to impose its own chosen solutions on nonmilitary questions. Thus the "century" of American hegemony Henry Luce had predicted in the early 1940s gradually appeared to have been short-lived.

The Splintering of the Soviet Bloc   The fragmentation of the rigid bipolar Cold War alliances occurred in the East as well as the West. The Sino-Soviet split, dating to the 1950s, highlighted the breakup of what was thought to be a communist monolith. Reflecting ideological differences and security concerns befitting two giant neighbors, by the 1960s the dispute was elevated to rivalry for leadership of the world communist movement. This opened a new era of Washington-Moscow-Beijing triangular politics. President Nixon's historic visit to China in February 1972 is the most celebrated symbol of triangular diplomacy of the period. "Playing the China card" thereafter became a favorite U.S. maneuver in its efforts to moderate Soviet behavior around the globe.

Periodic assertions of independence also marked the behavior of the communist regimes of East Germany, Poland, and Hungary during the 1950s. In the 1960s Czechoslovakia actually pursued a democratic experiment briefly, only to have it abruptly terminated by Warsaw Pact military intervention in 1968. Fearing possible defection from the communist fold, Kremlin leaders proclaimed the **Brezhnev Doctrine** (named after the Soviet Premier Leonid Brezhnev) to justify the invasion and to put other communist states on notice about the dangers of defection from the socialist fold and the Soviet sphere of influence.

Despite that warning, East European assertions of independence from "Moscow's line" grew in the 1970s and early 1980s, presaging the far-reaching domestic and foreign policy reforms that later swept the region. In 1989, Hungary became the first socialist country in Eastern Europe to schedule free elections, Poland elected a noncommunist prime minister, East Germany's communist leadership resigned and their successors permitted destruction of the Berlin Wall, and Czechoslovakia formed a new cabinet with a noncommunist majority.

Mikhail Gorbachev's radical reforms under his policies of *glasnost* or openness required new thinking in the Soviet Union's policy toward its former Eastern European satellites, as reform at home licensed reform of communist mismanagement abroad. Hesitant to deny Soviet allies the liberalization required to save his own country, Gorbachev repudiated the Brezhnev Doctrine in favor of the "Sinatra Doctrine," which decreed that satellite states would be permitted to "do it their way." This signaled the end of the Soviet empire in Eastern Europe. In quick succession members of the Warsaw Pact renounced communist rule and endorsed free market democracies. With Europe now poised at the dawn of new era, Brent Scowcroft, President Bush's national security adviser, exclaimed that the surge of reform in Eastern Europe and the Soviet Union had brought about "a fundamental change in the whole international structure."

Toward Multipolarity: A Structural Realist Perspective on the Twenty-First Century

Changes in the structure of the international system begin with changes within states. "We know from structural theory," explains structural realist Kenneth

Waltz, "that states strive to maintain their positions in the system. Thus, in their twilight years great powers try to arrest or reverse their decline. . . . For a combination of internal and external reasons, Soviet leaders tried to reverse their country's precipitous fall in international standing but did not succeed" (see also Gilpin 1981; Kennedy 1987). Thus the end of the Cold War inevitably raised questions about future power configurations and the constraints and opportunities they might portend.

In one sense, of course, the nature of international politics remained largely unchanged with the passing of bipolarity. As political scientist Robert Jervis cautioned shortly after the implosion of the Soviet Union,

> Many of the basic generalizations of international politics remain unaltered: It is still anarchic in the sense that there is no international sovereign that can make and enforce laws and agreements. The security dilemma remains as well, with the problems it creates for states who would like to cooperate but whose security requirements do not mesh. Many specific causes of conflict also remain, including desires for greater prestige, economic rivalries, hostile nationalisms, divergent perspectives on and incompatible standards of legitimacy, religious animosities, and territorial ambitions.
> (Jervis 1991–1992, 46)

Still, the passing of Cold War bipolarity portended a very different configuration of power and possibilities, prompting scholars and policy analysts to contemplate alternative images to portray the shape of the emergent international system. A three-bloc geoeconomics model, a reinvigorated multipolar balance-of-power model, a clash-of-civilizations model, a zones-of-peace/zones-of-turmoil model, and a global village image are among them (Harkavy 1997). **Unipolarity** also competed for attention, as the United States now found itself "the sole superpower."

In the afterglow of the Persian Gulf War, syndicated columnist Charles Krauthammer (1991)

made the case not only for unipolarity as a description of system structure but also as a prescription for others' behavior. "The center of world power is the unchallenged superpower, the United States," he wrote. "There is but one first-rate power and no prospect in the immediate future of any power to rival it. . . . American preeminence is based on the fact that it is the only country with the military, diplomatic, political, and economic assets to be a decisive player in any conflict in whatever part of the world it chooses to involve itself." He predicted that other states would turn to the United States for leadership, as they did in organizing a response to Iraqi's invasion of Kuwait and, later, in the interventions in Somalia and Kosovo. "The unipolar moment means that with the close of the century's three great Northern civil wars (World War I, World War II, and the Cold War) an ideologically pacified North seeks security and order by aligning its foreign policy behind that of the United States," Krauthammer argued. "It is the shape of things to come."

The distribution of economic and military capabilities among the major powers during the 1990s supports the unipolar description, as Figure 6.1 illustrates. For comparative purposes the figure also shows the distribution in 1950. The difference between the two time periods is striking. In 1950 the United States and the Soviet Union accounted for two-thirds of the economic output of the major powers and nearly 90 percent of their military expenditures. Clearly bipolarity aptly described the distribution of power. By the 1990s and early twenty-first century, however, no other power rivaled the United States. Japan and China were its closest competitors economically, but each could claim only about a fifth of the total economic output of the major powers while the U.S. share was twice that. No one rivaled the United States militarily, whose expenditures accounted for half of all military outlays among the major powers. Against this background, along with related considerations having to do with the United States' unique geographical position, political scientist William Wohlforth (1999) concluded that "The distribution of material capabilities at the end of the twentieth

a. **Pax Britannica, 1870–1872**

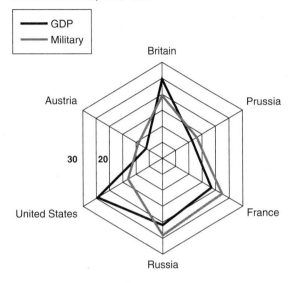

Country	GDP	Military
Britain	24	20
Prussia	11	13
France	18	22
Russia	21	24
United States	24	13
Austria	6	9

b. **Early Bipolarity, 1950**

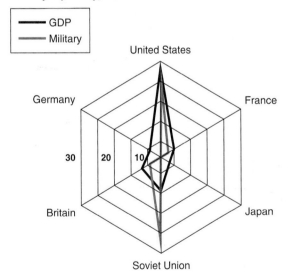

Country	GDP	Military
United States	50	43
France	8	4
Japan	5	0
Soviet Union	18	46
Britain	12	7
Germany	7	0

FIGURE 6.1 Comparing Concentrations of Power, 1870–1872, 1950, 1985, and 1996–1997

SOURCE: William C. Wohlforth, " The Stability of the Unipolar World," *International Security* 24 (Summer 1999): 14–15. Reprinted by permission.

c. **Late Bipolarity, 1985**

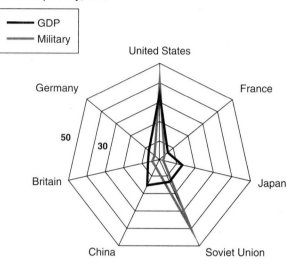

Country	GDP	Military
United States	33	40
France	6	3
Japan	13	2
Soviet Union	13	44
China	15	4
Britain	6	4
Germany	7	3

d. **Unipolarity, 1996–1997**

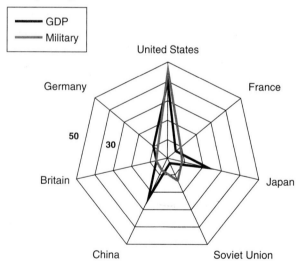

Country	GDP	Military
United States	40	50
France	6	9
Japan	22	8
Russia	3	13
China	21	7
Britain	6	6
Germany	9	7

FIGURE 6.1 *(Continued)*

century is unprecedented. . . . We are living in the modern world's first unipolar system. And unipolarity is not a 'moment.' It is a deeply embedded material condition of world politics that has the potential to last for many decades."

A recent simulation conducted by Lieber and Press (2006) found that the technological advances in

the U.S. nuclear arsenal since the end of the Cold War has left the nuclear balance decidedly tilted in its favor. Increased accuracy and yields on U.S. nuclear weapons and their delivery systems, combined with the steady degradation of Russian weapons and early warning systems, produced simulated results showing the complete destruction of all Russian nuclear weapons from a U.S. first strike. The study also found the Chinese were even more vulnerable to such a first strike. Lieber and Press conclude that the United States under President Bush is now deliberately pursuing a policy of nuclear primacy as part of a larger goal articulated in the 2002 *National Security Strategy* to achieve military primacy. Military primacy, from this point of view, is the best way to achieve global order and security.

Others challenge that view. In the words of one analyst, "To assume that international order can indefinitely rest on American hegemony is both illusory and dangerous" (Kupchan 1998). While those who embrace this competing viewpoint concede the centrality of the United States, they also argue that even now it cannot act with impunity. Sketching alternative power configurations experienced throughout history, political scientist Samuel Huntington put it this way:

> There is now only one superpower. But that does not mean the world is *unipolar.* A unipolar system would have one superpower, no significant major powers, and many minor powers. As a result, the superpower could effectively resolve important international issues alone, and no combination of other states would have the power to prevent it from doing so. For several centuries the classical world under Rome, and at times East Asia under China, approximated this model. A *bipolar* system like the Cold War has two superpowers, and the relations between them are central to international politics. Each superpower dominates a coalition of allied states and competes with the other superpower for influence among non-aligned countries. A *multipolar* system has several major powers of comparable strength that cooperate and compete with each other in shifting patterns. A coalition of major states is necessary to resolve important issues. European politics approximated this model for several centuries.
>
> *(Huntington 1999, 35–36)*

Huntington continues, saying that "contemporary international politics does not fit any of these three models. It is instead a strange hybrid, a ***uni-multipolar system*** with one superpower and several major powers." The United States has the capacity to "veto" actions initiated by other states. On the other hand, coping with "key international issues" requires its participation, "but always with some combination of other states." This configuration contrasts sharply with the unipolar moment Krauthammer anticipated in the aftermath of the Persian Gulf War, when the United States could impose its will on others.

Although Huntington's uni-multipolarity concept focuses on power, which is central to realist theory, it shares similarities with Joseph Nye's (1992) concept of ***multilevel interdependence,*** which adds attention to the integrative and disintegrative forces central to liberal theory. Nye argues that "No single hierarchy describes adequately a world politics with multiple structures. The distribution of power in world politics has become like a layer cake. The top military layer is largely unipolar, for there is no other military power comparable to the United States. The economic middle layer is tripolar and has been for two decades. The bottom layer of transnational interdependence shows a diffusion of power." Nye postulates that the "layers" of world power have an important impact on American foreign policy. Writing more than a decade ago, he argued that "the United States is better placed with a more diversified portfolio of power resources than any other country," but he concluded that the post–Cold War world would "not be an era of American hegemony." Nye (2004) has reiterated this claim by focusing on the decline of American "soft power" since President George W. Bush took office. Soft power, which refers to the attractiveness of American culture, values, and ideas, is a crucial component of hegemonic order—without it, all a state can rely on to achieve its goals is crude economic and military power. Soft power makes such goals easier to achieve because they tend to be shared by a wider global audience.

If these descriptions and prognoses are correct, we should expect that unipolarity will gradually give

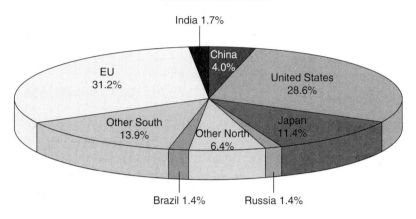

Gross National Product

FIGURE 6.2 Shares of Gross World Product, 2004

SOURCE: Adapted from the United Nations Statistics Division, National Accounts Main Aggregates Database, http://unstats.un. org/unsd/snaama/Introduction.asp, accessed 5/7/06.

way to *multipolarity,* an international system structure not unlike that which existed before World War I in which power was diffused among a comparatively small number of major powers (four or more) and a somewhat larger number of secondary powers aspiring to great power status. The United States, Japan, China, Russia, and Germany (either alone or within a united Europe) are widely regarded as the likely great powers in the system. Brazil and India are often mentioned as secondary powers that may seek great power status. Already these states account for the lion's share of gross world product, as Figure 6.2 illustrates. Hoge (2004) argues that the United States is dramatically unprepared for this inevitable shift in power to countries like China, Japan, and India. It lacks diplomats and other public officials with knowledge of Asia and Asian languages, it has failed to forge regional security agreements in Asia that could contain long-standing political–military rivalries, and it has not sought to give rising Asian powers the recognition of status that they desire in intergovernmental organizations (IGOs). The processes that will lead to the often anticipated multipolar world may take decades to unfold. Certainly a politically and militarily united Europe remains more a hope than a reality.

Several scholars, including Robert Pape (2005) and T. V. Paul (2005), have argued that the

aforementioned contenders for great power status have already begun to engage in "soft balancing" against the United States in the aftermath of the U.S. decision to invade Iraq in 2003. The assertion of President Bush through the 2002 *National Security Strategy* that the United States has the right to unilaterally attack other sovereign states without provocation is argued to have prompted states like France, Russia, China, and India to challenge the United States through international institutions, diplomatic measures to delay or undermine U.S. policy, and economic statecraft. Such soft balancing measures do not directly challenge U.S. military preponderance, but the institutional bargaining and temporary coalitions formed through soft balancing could eventually lead to hard balancing involving traditional alliances and arms buildups. On the other hand, Brooks and Wohlforth (2005) and Lieber and Alexander (2005) argue that soft balancing is much ado about nothing, and bears little relation to what is actually occurring in international politics, since U.S. grand strategy does not threaten the vital interests of any of these potential great powers.

Similarly, there is only a remote prospect that an economically dynamic power may rise to challenge the United States in the near term, as *power transition theory* predicts (Organski and Kugler 1980). Japan, the world's second largest industrial power, suffered repeated economic setbacks during the past decade. And China, often predicted to surpass the United States as the largest economic power in the world in the next decades, simply does not enjoy the technological prowess that will enable it to soon challenge the United States, whose command of information technologies is overwhelming. Finally, no conceivable coalition of major powers will arise in the near term to counter the preponderant power the United States now enjoys. Hence the prognosis that unipolarity is not a "moment" but a "material condition of world politics that has the potential to last for many decades" (Wohlforth 1999).

That said, structural realism and the long history of the rise and fall of great powers encourage us to contemplate alternative scenarios that may affect America's foreign policy future. Structural theory argues, for example, that great power status and its responsibilities are not easily shunned. This is even true for Germany and Japan, whose experience in World War II (and postwar pressures from the United States) caused both to foreswear nuclear weapons. "For a country to choose not to become a great power is a structural anomaly. For that reason, the choice is a difficult one to sustain. Sooner or later, usually sooner, the international status of countries has risen in step with their material resources . . . Japanese and German nuclear inhibitions arising from World War II will not last indefinitely; one might expect them to expire as generational memories fade" (Waltz 1993).

The United States will remain the most powerful actor for the foreseeable future, even in a multipolar system in which Germany and Japan might possess nuclear weapons. (China, India, and Pakistan already do.) The United States, then, will be the power others will seek to *balance*. As one analyst put it, "Up to a point it is a good thing for a state to be powerful. But it is not good for a state to become *too* powerful because it frightens others" (Layne 1998). Hence the structural realist proposition that "unbalanced power, whoever wields it, is a potential danger to others" (Waltz 1997). The contrast with Krauthammer's prognosis is striking: America's leadership is something that will be feared, not sought. In the emergent multipolar system others will seek to check the

dominant power, not *bandwagon* (ally) with it (Layne 1993, 1998; Walt 1990).

Ironically, the spread of democracy during the past decade, which has propelled an enthusiastic embrace of the democratic peace proposition as the road to a more peaceful world, may contribute to others' concern. Structural realist Kenneth Waltz explains:

> When democracy is ascendant, a condition that in the twentieth century attended the winning of hot wars and cold ones, the interventionist spirit flourishes. The effect is heightened when one democratic state becomes dominant, as the United States is now. Peace is the noblest cause of war. If the conditions of peace are lacking, then the country with a capability of creating them may be tempted to do so. . . . States having a surplus of power are tempted to use it, and weaker states fear their doing so.
> *(Waltz 2000a, 12)*

In a way reminiscent of the declinists' arguments advanced in the 1980s, Waltz also cautions about the strain American leadership may place on the United States itself. He writes that "The vice to which great powers easily succumb in a multipolar world is inattention; in a bipolar world, overreaction; in a unipolar world, overextension." Thus "the American effort to freeze historical development by working to keep the world unipolar is doomed. In the not very long run, the task will exceed America's economic, military, demographic, and political resources; and the very effort to maintain a hegemonic position is the surest way to undermine it. The effort to maintain dominance stimulates some countries to work to overcome it" (Waltz 2000a; see also Walt 2005).

Others' apprehension about American power is already clear, as we saw in Chapters 3 and 4. Whether the issue is military reprisals against Iraq, sanctions against Cuba and secondary sanctions against others; defending Taiwan against power incursions by China; intervening militarily in Haiti, Bosnia, and Iraq; browbeating Japan on numerical trade targets and Europe on bananas and genetically altered meat; or supporting tough standards on the distribution of international aid to economies in trouble, the United States has repeatedly found itself as "the lonely superpower at the top" in what is arguably a uni-multipolar world. From the perspective of other states, they "worry because the United States is strong enough to act pretty much as it wishes, and other states cannot be sure that Washington will not use its immense power to threaten their own interests" (Walt 2005).

Against this background, it is by no means clear how the United States should respond to the challenges of the new century in which it, not others, may be feared—and reviled. We will return to this issue in Chapter 15, where we speculate about the future of American foreign policy in a second American Century.

THE GLOBAL SOUTH IN THE TWENTY-FIRST CENTURY

The distribution of power among the world's most economically, militarily, and politically capable states is not the only feature of the international political system that affects American foreign policy. Another that promises to remain significant in the future is the relationship between the United States and the less developed countries of the world.

At the end of World War II in 1945, fewer than sixty independent states joined the new United Nations, named for the allied coalition victorious in the long and destructive war against the Axis powers. Sixty years later more than three times that number would claim seats in the world organization. Some were products of the breakup of the Soviet Union, but many others grew out of the twentieth century end of other empires: the British, French, Belgian, Dutch, Spanish, and Portuguese colonial territories in Africa and Asia amassed since the 1400s but especially during a particularly vicious wave of imperialism that swept the world in the late nineteenth century. That colonial experience helps to define what today are commonly called the developing countries. During the Cold War it also became commonplace to refer

to these states as the ***Third World,*** a concept used to distinguish them from the Western industrialized states, often called the First World.[1] Many Third World countries also embraced a foreign policy strategy of nonalignment, as they determined to strike a neutral course in the Cold War contest.

With the end of the Cold War, the term "Third World" is at once less accurate and less useful. ***Global South*** better distinguishes the states of the First World—now properly thought of as the ***Global North***—from the rest of the world. As always, placement of particular states within these categories is sometimes problematic. Russia is an obvious example, as are the emerging market economies in Eastern Europe and the ***New Independent States (NIS)*** comprising the former republics of the Soviet Union. Still, the confluence of particular characteristics along four dimensions distinguish the North from the South: politics, technology, wealth, and demography.

States comprising the Global North are democratic, technologically inventive, wealthy, and aging, as their societies tend toward zero population growth. Some in the Global South share some of these characteristics, but none share all of them. Saudi Arabia is rich but not democratic; China is technologically inventive but not wealthy. India is democratic and increasingly technologically inventive but burdened with a burgeoning population that now exceeds a billion people. Singapore is both wealthy and technologically innovative, has a comparatively modest population growth rate, but is not democratic. Beyond these are many that are not democratic, technologically innovative, or wealthy, but whose demographics project a rapidly growing population that increasingly will strain already overtaxed social and ecological systems with too few economic resources and political capabilities to match the challenge. Many are in Africa south of the Sahara.

Scholars tried to capture the differences between North and South during the new world (dis)order that emerged as the Cold War ended. Focus 6.1. encapsulates some of their ideas—and displays a remarkable degree of consensus. The vision is that of a profoundly divided world which places the United States and its closest democratic

---

F O C U S 6.1 Fault Line: The Global North versus the Global South

There is today a vast demographic-technological fault line appearing across our planet. On one side of this line are the fast-growing, adolescent, under-resourced, undercapitalized, under-educated societies; on the other side are the rich, technologically inventive yet demographically moribund, aging populations. . . . The greatest challenge global society faces today is preventing this fault line from erupting into a world-shaking crisis.

Paul Kennedy (1994, 4–5)

The key to understanding the real world order is to separate the world into two parts. One part is zones of peace, wealth, and democracy. The other part is zones of turmoil, war, and development. . . . Unfortunately, only fifteen percent of the world's population lives in the zones of peace and democracy. Most people now live in zones of turmoil and development, where poverty, war, tyranny, and anarchy will continue to devastate lives.

Max Singer and Aaron Wildavsky (1993, 3–7)

Nation-states will remain the most powerful actors in world affairs, but the principal conflicts of global politics will occur between nations and groups of different civilizations. The clash of civilizations will dominate global politics. The fault

lines between civilizations will be the battle lines of the future. . . . The world will be shaped in large measure by the interactions among seven or eight major civilizations. These include Western, Confucian, Japanese, Islamic, Hindu, Slavic-Orthodox, Latin America and possibly African civilization.

Samuel P. Huntington (1993a, 22–25)

The future of the Third World is hardly all bad news. . . . But the failures . . . will greatly outweigh the successes. . . . The global dilemmas and ills capable of coalescing into a specific body of political discontent and hostility will therefore challenge the current international system and constitute the next ideological challenge. . . . "Civilization clash" is not so much over Jesus Christ, Confucius, or the Prophet Muhammad as it is over the unequal distribution of world power, wealth, and influence, and the perceived historical lack of respect accorded to small states and peoples by larger ones.

Graham Fuller (1995, 146–154)

SOURCE: From Graham Fuller, "The Next Ideology," *Foreign Policy* 98 (Spring 1995): 145–158. Copyright © 1995 by Carnegie Endowment for International Peace. Reprinted with the permission of Foreign Policy.

---

friends, political allies, and economic partners on one side of a fault line separating them from most of the rest of the world. Although the rapid globalization of the world political economy and the spread of democracy in the past decade have blurred some of these distinctions as they apply to particular countries, the portrayal continues to show that the United States faces challenges for which many of the foreign policy instruments of balance-of-power politics are largely irrelevant.

Along the Demographic Divide:
Population and Development

The demographic divide is central to the differences between the Global North and the Global South. Nearly 80 percent of the world's wealth is concentrated in the North, while more than 80 percent of its people are in the South (see Figure 6.3). The

unequal distribution of wealth and people translates into sharply different living standards, crudely measured by differences in per capita gross national product. As illustrated in Figure 6.4, the average annual income in the Japan is nearly sixty times greater than the average income in India, home of one-sixth of the world's more than 6 billion people. And the U.S. income is nineteen times that of the other countries comprising the Global South.

These disparities—which in many other individual cases are even more stark—will widen, not narrow, in the future. At the end of the nineteenth century the ratio of average income in the richest country in the world to the poorest stood at nine to one. At the end of the twentieth century, the gap had widened to sixty to one (Birdsall 1998). Even in the unlikely event that North and South were to grow economically at the same rate, the comparatively higher population growth rates in the

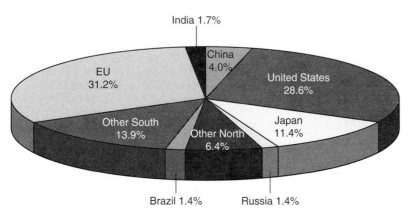

FIGURE 6.3 Shares of Gross World Product and Population, 2004

SOURCE: Adapted from the United Nations Statistics Division, National Accounts Main Aggregates Database, http://unstats.un.org/unsd/snaama/Introduction.asp, accessed 5/7/06.

South will erode income gains at a faster rate than in the North. Thus, as one analyst wryly observed, "The old saw is still correct: the rich get richer and the poor get children" (Birdsall 1998).

Although fertility rates are declining worldwide, which portends a host of problems that will have to be addressed in the second half of this century (Eberstadt 2001; Wattenberg 2004), the first half will witness a continued march toward a more crowded and stressed world. Due to population momentum as well as other factors, the world's current population of more than 6.5 billion people will grow to 8.2 billion by 2030 and more than 9 billion by the time today's college students reach retirement age.

Such dramatic growth is simply unprecedented. It took an entire century for world population to grow from 1 billion to 2 billion, but only one decade to add its last billion. By the end of the day that you read this page, the world will have added another 210,000 people to its already burgeoning number. Furthermore, as noted, nearly all of this growth will

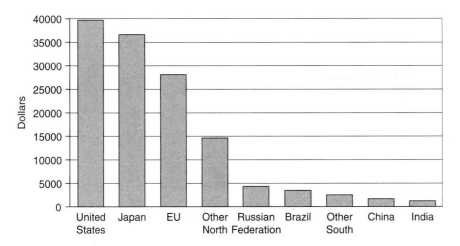

FIGURE 6.4 Global Variations in Per Capita Gross Domestic Product, 2004

SOURCE: Adapted from the United Nations Statistics Division, National Accounts Main Aggregates Database, http://unstats.un.org/unsd/snaama/Introduction.asp, accessed 5/7/06.

occur in the Global South (see Figure 6.5). Latin America's 561 million people will grow by nearly 40 percent in less than half a century. Africa's will more than double in the same time period to nearly 1.9 billion. And in Asia, which includes India and China, the population will increase by over 30 percent to 5.2 billion by midcentury (UN Population Division, *World Population Prospects: The 2004 Revision*). The result? A world a third more populated than today in only half a century.

Some countries in the Global South will escape the economic stagnation associated with a rapidly rising population. Already South Korea, Taiwan, Hong Kong, and Singapore—which, with others, belong to a group of **Newly Industrialized Economies (NIEs)**—enjoy per capita incomes comparable to many Northern countries. The reason is that their economic growth rates during much of the 1980s and 1990s far surpassed their population growth rates. Rising living standards followed.

The experience of South Korea, Taiwan, Hong Kong, and Singapore (once commonly called the "Asian tigers") has been enjoyed elsewhere in the Global South as the precepts of democratic capitalism have spread during the past decade. Liberal political economists attribute these states' success to policies that promoted a vigorous expansion of global exports and cutbacks in domestic imports. The process was spurred by the so-called **Washington Consensus,** which refers to a common outlook shared by the U.S. government, the International Monetary Fund, and the World Bank that encouraged privatization of industries and other institutions, financial deregulation, and reductions of barriers to trade as the path to economic development. Arguably the precepts of the Washington Consensus contributed importantly to the globalization process witnessed during the past decade. (See also Chapter 7).

The Global North (or many within it) has benefited handsomely from globalization, and some in the Global South have as well. As the prestigious World Watch Institute noted in its annual state-of-the-world report for 2001,

> The economic boom of the last decade has not been confined to the rich countries of the North. Much of the growth is occurring in the developing nations of Asia and Latin America, where economic reforms, lowered trade barrier, and a surge in foreign capital have fueled investment and consumption. Between 1990 and 1998, Brazil's economy grew 30 percent,

FIGURE 6.5 The Shape of the World's Population—Present and Future

SOURCE: Adapted from Population Division of the Department of Economic and Social Affairs of the United Nations Secretariat, *World Population Prospects: The 2004 Revision,* and *World Urbanization Prospects: The 2003 Revision,* http://esa.un.org/unpp, accessed 5/23/06.

India's expanded 60 percent, and China's mushroomed by a remarkable 130 percent. China now has the world's [second] largest economy if measured in purchasing power parity [PPP], and a booming middle class who work in offices, eat fast food, watch color television, and surf the Internet.[2]

(Flavin 2001, 6)

According to the *Economist's Intelligence Unit,* by 2020 China's GDP in PPP at $29.6 trillion will narrowly exceed the United States' GDP of $28.8 trillion, followed in third place by India coming in at just under $14 trillion. (*Economist,* April 1, 2006, p. 84).

But there is a dark side to globalization, as we noted in Chapter 1. Just as disparities in income between rich and poor widened during the twentieth century, the disparities between the Global North and South across a variety of measures remained stark during the economic boom of the 1990s. Worldwide over 850 million people remain malnourished; more than 1 billion do not have access to clean water; and nearly 3 billion—almost half of the world's population—survive on less than $2 a day (UN Population Fund, www.unfpa.org/pds/facts.htm). These statistics lead many observers to conclude that globalization has all too frequently produced growth without progress.

Population growth helps explain the disparate economic experiences of the world's states today and their projection into the future. Differences in history, politics, economics, and culture also play a role and are intermixed in complex and often poorly understood ways. Moreover, many Americans have the sense that world population growth is "someone else's problem, not ours." Although the population of the United States increased by more than 80 percent between 1950 and 2000, from 152 million to 276 million, much of this growth occurred through immigration, not high birth rates. To some, then, the way to halt the growth of U.S. population, which is projected to increase by nearly 25 percent in the first quarter of the twenty-first century, is to halt immigration (see also Chapter 8). President Bush's 2006 proposal to create a guest worker program and allow many illegal immigrants to pursue citizenship caused a great deal of dissent in the Republican party and among Americans in general, and also prompted a wave of popular protests by immigrants around the country.

Increasingly, however, it is clear that the momentum of global population growth poses challenges to global and national security that will affect all of the world's inhabitants, including Americans. Approximately 175 million people currently live outside their country of origin, a number expected to top 230 million by 2050 (UN Department of Economic and Social Affairs/Population Division, *International Migration Report, 2002*, pp. 9–16). Indeed, immigration itself is a result of the *push* factors that make people want to leave their own homelands, and the *pull* factors that make the United States and other countries

attractive. Thus, as John D. Steinbruner (1995), a former director of the Brookings Institution's Foreign Policy Studies program, surmised, "Both the scale and composition of this population surge will have consequences powerful enough not just to affect, but perhaps even to dominate, conceptions of international security." President Bush's 2006 proposal to use the National Guard to patrol the border reflects this securitization of the immigration issue.

Correlates and Consequences of the Demographic Divide

Conceptions of what constitutes "security" have changed dramatically since the Berlin Wall fell in 1989, as explained not only in the scholarly literature (see, for example, Klare and Thomas 1998; Nye 1999) but also in the reports of the U.S. Commission on National Security, popularly known as the Hart-Rudman Commission (http://govinfo.library.unt.edu/nssg/Reports/reports.htm). The essence of these analyses is that the twenty-first century portends dangers as well as opportunities. In a rapidly globalizing world, the Global South with its burgeoning population will figure prominently in those perils and promises.

Food Security Hunger is closely associated with poverty and population growth. Two centuries ago the Reverend Thomas Malthus predicted that the world's population would eventually outstrip its capacity to produce enough food to sustain its growing numbers. That has not happened, largely due to unprecedented increases in agricultural production since World War II. But the rate of growth in food production has slowed in recent years, and the prospects for expanding food supplies by bringing more acreage under cultivation are limited. Furthermore, degradation of soils already under cultivation caused by modern farming methods, including widespread use of agricultural chemicals and poor water management practices, has begun to take a toll on the existing production platform (Brown 2001; *World Resources 1998–99*).

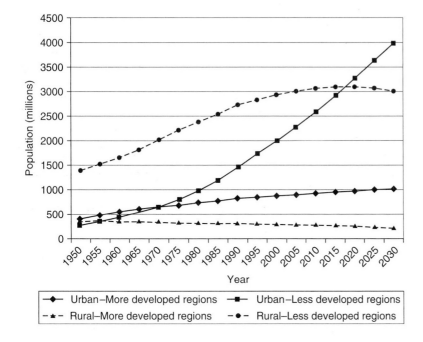

FIGURE 6.6 Estimated and Projected Urban and Rural Population of the More and Less Developed Regions, 1950–2030

NOTE: "More developed regions" conforms generally to the Global North, and "less developed regions" to the Global South.

SOURCE: Population Division of the Department of Economic and Social Affairs of the United Nations Secretariat, *World Population Prospects: The 2004 Revision,* and *World Urbanization Prospects: The 2003 Revision,* http://esa.un.org/unpp, accessed 5/23/06.

Against this background, achieving national and global food security, a long-standing goal of the international community, remains problematic. Food supplies are abundant globally, and the proportion of people who go to bed hungry has declined in the past two decades, particularly in East Asia and Latin American (Brown 2001). But where population growth remains persistently high, hunger also persists because food often does not reach those most in need. The reason is simple: many simply cannot afford to buy food because they lack the necessary income and employment opportunities. Politics and civil conflict also impede the ability of some to acquire adequate nutrition. That reality prompted the United States to launch its humanitarian intervention into Somalia in late 1992, and it continues to haunt international efforts to help those impoverished and starving in Sudan.

Poverty and inadequate food nutrition go hand in hand. The United Nations Population Fund estimates that 1.2 billion people live on less than $1 a day, with another 2.7 billion surviving on less than $2 a day (www.unfpa.org/pds/facts.htm). Not only does this limit their access to food, it also means no access to safe water, sanitation, health services, and economic opportunity. In the midst of a world of plenty, one-fifth of humanity continues to live in *absolute poverty* or without the resources to meet the basic needs for healthy living.

Poverty and Urbanization As rural poverty persists, people migrate from the countryside to cities. Urbanization is a global phenomenon, but it is especially ubiquitous in the Global South (see Figure 6.6). In 1950, New York was the only city with a population of 10 million or more. Today another eighteen cities share that distinction. Fifteen of them are in the Global South. Lagos, the capital of Nigeria, which today claims 13.4 million inhabitants, illustrates the relentless mathematics of urbanization. In 1950 Lagos had fewer than 3 million inhabitants. By 2015 it will have over 23 million. Cities like Jakarta, Indonesia, with 11 million now, will swell with more than 4 million residents each year for the next decade and a half, and Karachi, Pakistan, will grow from 11.8 million to 19.2 million by 2015 (United Nations, *World Urbanization Prospects: The 1999 Revision,* summary of findings, at www.un.org/esa/population/publications/wup1999/wup99.htm). By 2030, nearly two-thirds of the global population will be living in urban areas. Ninety percent of this urban population growth will occur in the Global South (United Nations, *World Urbanization Prospects: The 2003 Revision,* summary of findings at www.un.org/esa/population/publications/wup2003/WUP2003 Report.pdf).

The rapid urbanization of the Global South adds pressure on already stretched agricultural systems and demands for imported food. Also, already overtaxed municipalities are often unable to respond to needs for expanded social services and increased investments in social infrastructure. Environmental degradation, social unrest, and political turmoil frequently exceed governments' capacities.

Emigration and Immigration   People migrate to urban areas for many reasons, but jobs are uppermost. And jobs are few and hard to find, particularly where the ratio of dependent children to working-age adults is high—a natural consequence of rapidly growing populations, when the number of young people grows more rapidly than those who die. Today, educational and health systems in much of the Global South are burdened. These and other demands on governmental and social services encourage the immediate consumption of economic resources rather than their reinvestment to promote future economic growth.

The demand for new jobs, housing, and other human needs multiplies, but the resources to meet the demand are often scarce and typically inadequate. Before long, the Global South will also be forced to address problems like those currently facing the Global North, where increased longevity and near-zero population growth threaten to overwhelm retirement and healthcare systems, with potentially catastrophic economic, social, and political consequences (Peterson 1999; Wattenberg 2004). Modern science and medicine seem likely to continue to extend their life-saving and life-enhancing technologies worldwide, generating a similar crisis in the less developed world.

Without jobs at home, people are encouraged to emigrate. The International Labour Organization (ILO) estimates that 437 million young people will seek jobs in the Global South during this decade alone (International Labour Organization, "Overview," *World Employment Report 2001,* www.ilo.org). Two-thirds will be in Asia. Sadly, however, the ILO also expects that the number of jobseekers in Africa will be less than previously projected because of the HIV/AIDS (acquired immune deficiency syndrome caused by the human immunodeficiency virus, or HIV) pandemic. As the organization notes in its *World Employment Report 2001,* the greatest long-run cost of the HIV infection in Africa "will be the loss of human capital. . . . Losses are disproportionately high among skilled, professional, and managerial workers. The epidemic will not only reduce the stock of such workers, but also reduce the capacity to maintain future flows of trained people." As one analyst reminds us,

> The long shock waves caused by AIDS . . . are washing over many countries that are simultaneously being swamped by other diseases—malaria, tuberculosis, childhood dysentery, gonorrhea, antibiotic-resistant bacterial infections, and newly emerging infections such as severe acute respiratory syndrome (SARS) and the Marburg virus. Many of these countries also suffer from other problems that impede economic development and cause social disruption, such as military conflict and social unrest. It is therefore extremely difficult to predict how HIV/AIDS will affect these states and their societies, economies, cultures, and politics. The full impact may not be known for a generation.
>
> *(Garrett 2005, 53–54)*

Former Secretary of State Colin Powell described AIDS this way: "I was a soldier, but I know of no enemy in war more insidious or vicious than AIDS, an enemy that poses a clear and present danger to the world."

If jobs fail to materialize at home, outward pressure is inevitable. Nowhere is the connection between population pressures in the South and their social and political consequences in the North more evident. The United States has long been especially concerned about Mexico, the source of large

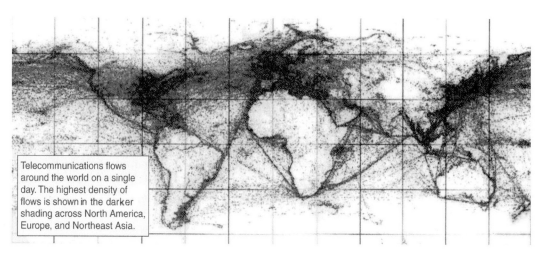

Telecommunications flows around the world on a single day. The highest density of flows is shown in the darker shading across North America, Europe, and Northeast Asia.

M A P 6.1   The Digital Divide

SOURCE: Flanagan, Frost, and Kugler (2001, 24)

numbers of illegal immigrants. There presence became an acute political issue in 2006, when President Bush proposed a "guest worker" program thought by many to be amnesty of illegal aliens. Congress also urged stronger law enforcement along the U.S.-Mexican border, which included miles of fencing along the border to staunch of flow of illegals. Still, for many of them, the urge to go North remains irresistible. As one Mexican official put it in the early 1990s, "The consequences of not creating (at least) 15 million jobs in the next 15 years are unthinkable. The youths who do not find them will have only three options: the United States, the streets, or revolution" (cited in Moffett 1994).[3]

The Digital Divide Interestingly, the digital divide may also encourage outmigration from the Global South among those equipped with today's information technology skills, as they find the pull of opportunity in the Global North more attractive than opportunities at home. Countries in the North facing a steady-state population in turn often find attractive people in the South with technical skills as they seek to fill emerging skill shortages in their own economies.

The **_digital divide_** refers broadly to the gap between people with regular access to information and communications technology (ICT) and those without such access. The demographic, economic, and social patterns that explain the digital divide are not surprising. In the United States, for example, ICT access is greatest among young urban men in higher income groups. And because educational attainment is closely correlated with income and urban residence, level of education is the single most powerful determinant of ICT access and use.

The patterns evident in the United States are matched not only elsewhere in the technologically sophisticated North but also in the Global South. But because education and income are in short supply in the South, it also is not surprising the global digital divide closely tracks the inverse of the global demographic divide. (see Map 6.1). The International Labour Organization in its *World Employment Report 2001* ("Overview," www.ilo.org) estimates that "barely six percent of the world's people have ever logged onto the Internet and eighty-five to ninety percent of them are in the industrialized countries" (see also "Measuring Globalization" 2001). These figures may also reflect that fact that the Internet itself was initially controlled directly by the U.S. government until 1998, when a quasi-private entity, the Internet Corporation for Assigned Names and Numbers

(ICANN), was created by President Clinton to administer it with continued government oversight. Attempts by other developed and developing countries to gain some control of the Internet by moving its governance to an IGO have so far fallen on deaf ears in the United States (Cukier 2005).

Lack of access and use also holds for many other ICT access devices, which include personal computers, wired and wireless telephones, and other consumer electronics, such as televisions. But the digital divide is also explained by the capacity (or incapacity) of the public and private sectors to provide financial access to ICT services and by the cognitive processes education encourages, including an ability to process and evaluate the information that information and communications technologies offer (Wilson 2002).

ICT technologies hold great promise for many of the poorer countries of the world, as they may permit them to "leapfrog" technologies in which the Global North invested heavily as they developed economically. Wireless phones, for example, enjoy both popularity and promise in many developing countries, where the cost of stringing lines from pole to pole for traditional wired phones is often prohibitive. Since the individual, social, economic, and geographic factors that have created and perpetuated the digital divide are complex, narrowing it will prove difficult and illusive.

Environmental Stress Increasingly, many migrants (internal as well as international) can be thought of as *environmental refugees,* people forced to abandon lands no longer fit for human habitation due to environmental degradation. Their number is thought to be at least 10 million, which makes them the world's largest group of displaced persons, a term that also includes victims of political instability and ethnic conflict. Some become environmental refugees as a result of catastrophic events, such as the explosion of the nuclear power plant at Chernobyl in the Ukraine in 1986. Others suffer the consequences of long-term environmental stress, such as excessive land use that results in *desertification* (a sustained decline in land productivity), often caused by population growth. But increasingly, environmental refugees are the victims of global climate change caused by global warming.

Global Warming By 2050 there may be as many as 150 million environmental refugees. The Intergovernmental Panel on Climate Change (IPCC) believes that global warming will be a primary culprit behind the movement of millions, as drought, floods, earthquakes, epidemics, and severe weather caused by global climate change, ranging from blizzards to an increased frequency of violent hurricanes, force people from their homes. The IPCC comprises a network of hundreds of scientists from around the world who, under the auspices of the United Nations, have drawn on scientific analyses to advise governments on global climate change and strategies for dealing with it. **Global warming** has been the center of its attention. The term refers to a gradual rise in the earth's temperature that occurs when gases emitted from earth are trapped by the upper atmosphere, creating the equivalent of a "greenhouse roof" by trapping heat that would otherwise escape into space. Carbon dioxide (CO_2), which is emitted by burning fossil fuels such as oil and coal, is believed to be a major cause of global warming, with methane gas, nitrous oxide, and various halocarbon gases also among the suspects. Most greenhouse gases originate in the Global North, but China and others in the Global South are increasing their emissions rapidly. The Center for Strategic and International Studies recently concluded that world energy demand will increase by 50 percent by 2020, and that at some point the Global South, led by China, will consume more than the North (Nunn and Schlesinger 2000). Already, Chinese oil consumption is increasingly blamed for the rising prices paid by Americans at the pump, as its rapid economic development has moved it from self-sufficiency in oil as late as 1993 to accounting for 30 percent of the increase in global demand for imported oil since 2000. India is not far behind as its level of economic development has increased as well (Yergin 2006).

That the earth's temperature has climbed since the industrial revolution is widely accepted (see Focus 6.2). In the twentieth century alone, the average temperature of the earth's surface rose by 0.6

FOCUS 6.2   A Warming World

Global warming can seem too remote to worry about, or too uncertain—something projected by the same computer techniques that often can't get next week's weather right. On a raw winter day you might think that a few degrees of warming wouldn't be such a bad thing anyway. And no doubt about it: Warnings about climate change can sound like an environmentalist scare tactic, meant to force us out of our cars and cramp our lifestyles.

Comforting thoughts, perhaps. But...the Earth has some unsettling news. From Alaska to the snowy peaks of the Andes the world is heating up right now, and fast. Globally, the temperature is up 1°F over the past century, but some of the coldest, most remote spots have warmed much more. The results aren't pretty. Ice is melting, rivers are running dry, and coasts are eroding, threatening communities. Flora and fauna are feeling the heat too....These aren't projections; they are facts on the ground.

The changes are happening largely out of sight. But they shouldn't be out of mind, because they are omens of what's in store for the rest of the planet. Wait a minute, some doubters say. Climate is notoriously fickle. A thousand years ago Europe was balmy and wine grapes grew in England; by 400 years ago the climate had turned chilly and the Thames froze repeatedly. Maybe the current warming is another natural vagary, just a passing thing? Don't bet on it, say climate experts. Sure, the natural rhythms of climate might explain a few of the warming signs...But something else is driving the planet-wide fever.

For centuries we've been clearing forests and burning coal, oil, and gas, pouring carbon dioxide and other heat-trapping gases into the atmosphere faster than plants and oceans can soak them up....The atmosphere's level of carbon dioxide now is higher than it has been for hundreds of thousands of years. "We're now geological agents, capable of affecting the processes that determine climate," says George Philander,

a climate expert at Princeton University. In effect, we're piling extra blankets on our planet.

Human activity almost certainly drove most of the past century's warming, a landmark report from the United Nations Intergovernmental Panel on Climate Change (IPCC) declared in 2001. Global temperatures are shooting up faster than at any other time in the past thousand years. And climate models show that natural forces, such as volcanic eruptions and the slow flickers of the sun, can't explain all that warming. As CO_2 continues to rise, so will the mercury—another 3°F to 10°F by the end of the century, the IPCC projects.

But the warming may not be gradual. The records of ancient climate...suggest that the planet has a sticky thermostat. Some experts fear today's temperature rise could accelerate into a devastating climate lurch. Continuing to fiddle with the global thermostat, says Philander, "is just not a wise thing to do." Already we've pumped out enough greenhouse gases to warm the planet for many decades to come. "We have created the environment in which our children and grandchildren are going to live," says Tim Barnett of the Scripps Institution of Oceanography. We owe it to them to prepare for higher temperatures and changed weather—and to avoid compounding the damage.

It won't be easy for a world addicted to fossil fuels to limit emissions. Three years ago the United States spurned the Kyoto Protocol, citing cost. But even Kyoto would barely slow the rise in heat-trapping gases. Controlling the increase "would take 40 successful Kyotos," says Jerry Mahlman of the National Center for Atmospheric Research. "But we've got to do it." The signs of warming...are striking enough, but they are just a taste of the havoc the next century could bring. Can we act in time to avert the worst of it? The Earth will tell.

SOURCE: Tim Appenzeller and Dennis R. Dimick, "Signs from Earth," *National Geographic*, 206 (September 2004).

---

degrees Celsius, and the 1990s was the hottest decade on record. However, even though the IPCC has concluded that the concentration of CO_2 in the atmosphere has increased by more than 30 percent since 1750, the hypothesis that human activity is the cause of the rise in temperature remains contentious. So do proposals for dealing with global

warming, even though the IPCC predicts that in this century temperatures can be expected to rise another two to three degrees Celsius.

Part of the controversy turns on the fact that over the long course of history, the earth's temperature has oscillated between eras of warmth and cold, as during the ice age. Motivated by self-interest, the global energy and petrochemical firms and countries that depend for their livelihoods on the export of fossil fuels are especially vigorous advocates of the view that temperature changes experienced in the past century and a half fit temperature patterns experienced over many millennia, rejecting the view that human activity is the cause of global warming.

Small island states in the Pacific and elsewhere are among the equally vigorous challengers of fossil fuel proponents' views. Self-interest also motivates them. Global warming threatens to cause a rise in sea levels as polar ice caps melt, which could completely inundate the island states and obliterate their peoples and cultures. Already the mean height of sea levels has risen in recent years, and evidence mounts that the ice in the polar regions is melting. In 1990 a huge chunk of Antarctica's Pine Island Glacier, measuring 100 miles wide and 30 miles long, broke off and disappeared. A decade later, scientists determined that the Arctic ice cap is thinner—and thinning more rapidly—than once thought. And Russian scientists happened onto open water in an area typically covered year round by several meters of ice.

These and other findings lead to predictions of a gradual rise in sea levels due to global warming. If that happens, coastal areas from South Carolina and Florida to Louisiana and Bangladesh would disappear—along with the small Pacific island states. The traditional weather patterns experienced in recent centuries would be disrupted dramatically (see Focus 6.3). The IPCC, first formed in 1988, has long been reluctant to attribute global warming to human activity, but in its second assessment report, completed in 1995, it stated conclusively its belief that global climate trends are "unlikely to be entirely due to natural causes." Instead, "the balance of evidence . . . suggests a discernible human influence on global climate." Six years later, it released a new report that stated even more emphatically that global warming was a manmade occurrence already well in place. "The debate is over," said Peter Gleick, president of the California-based Pacific Institute for Studies in Development, Environment, and Security. "No matter what we do to reduce

greenhouse gas emissions, we will not be able to avoid some impacts of climate change" (cited in *U.S. News and World Report,* 5 February 2001).

Deforestation and Biodiversity Deforestation often causes desertification and soil erosion. Unhappily, current trends point toward rapid deforestation worldwide. The destruction of tropical rain forests to make room for farms and ranches and to acquire exotic woods and wood products for sale in the global marketplace—as in the Amazon basin of Brazil, Indonesia, Malaysia, and Sri Lanka—is a matter of special international concern, as it contributes markedly to global warming through the greenhouse effect. Forests are "sinks" for carbon dioxide because they routinely remove CO_2 from the atmosphere during photosynthesis. When forests are cut down, these natural processes are erupted and destroyed, and, as the forests decay or are burned, they increase the amount of CO_2 discharged into the atmosphere. As a result, deforestation becomes doubly destructive.

Forests are also disappearing at a rapid rate in temperate regions as urbanization and commercial activities of various kinds lead to a loss of forests and surrounding ecosystems. With that comes degradation of watersheds, contributing to the growing shortage of fresh water around the world. Many of the remaining forests are themselves degraded by air pollution. *Acid rain* (precipitation made acidic through contact with oxides of sulfur and nitrogen), for example, has damaged forests extensively in North America and Europe. It also has degraded lakes and streams (and buildings) for many years. Although progress has been made in mitigating the causes of acid rain in the Global North, the pollutant is on the rise in the Global South, especially in Asia. Much of the region's surge in energy consumption in recent years (and projected for the future) has been fueled by burning sulfur-containing coal (especially in China) and oil, the primary sources of acid emissions. "An estimated 34 million metric tons of SO_2 [sulfur dioxide] were emitted in the Asia region in 1990, over forty percent more than in North America" (*World Resources 1998–1999*).

FOCUS 6.3 Consequences of a Warming World

Temperature rising

Temperature and CO$_2$ records

■ **Warmings trends**
The concentration of carbon dioxide in the atmosphere helps determine Earth's surface temperature. Both CO$_2$ and temperature have risen sharply since 1950.

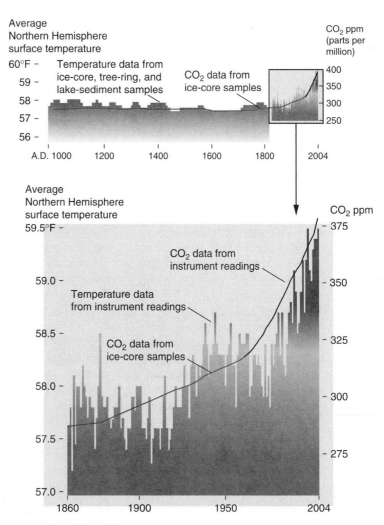

Average Northern Hemisphere surface temperature

Temperature data from ice-core, tree-ring, and lake-sediment samples

CO$_2$ data from ice-core samples

CO$_2$ ppm (parts per million)

■ Over the past 140 years, forest clearing and fossil-fuel burning have pushed up the atmosphere's CO$_2$ level by nearly 100 parts per million. The average surface temperature of the Northern Hemisphere has mirrored the rise in CO$_2$. The 1990s was the warmest decade since the mid-1800s, and 1998 the warmest year.

Average Northern Hemisphere surface temperature

CO$_2$ ppm

CO$_2$ data from instrument readings

Temperature data from instrument readings

CO$_2$ data from ice-core samples

⠿ One Degree of Change

A big difference Climate fluctuates naturally between warm and cool periods. But the 20th century has seen the greatest warming in at least a thousand years, and natural forces can't account for it all. The rise of CO$_2$ and other heat-trapping gases in the atmosphere has contributed; both greenhouse gases and temperature are expected to continue rising.

Sea level rising

Sea level change projections

■ **Coasts threatened**
As ice melts and warmer seawater expands, the oceans will rise. How much depends largely on how much CO_2 and other greenhouse gases we continue to emit. This model projects rises of between a few inches and a few feet over the

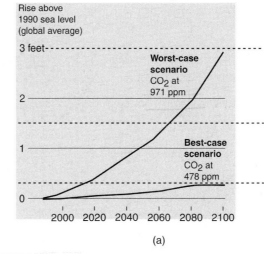

Rise above 1990 sea level (global average)

Worst-case scenario CO_2 at 971 ppm

Best-case scenario CO_2 at 478 ppm

3 feet
2
1
0

2000 2020 2040 2060 2080 2100

(a)

In Bangladesh, at just over 3 feet of rise, 70 million people could be displaced.

75 percent of coastal Louisiana wetlands would be destroyed at just over 1.5 feet.

Many low-lying South Sea islands are at further risk of flooding at about 4 inches.

Weather turning wild?

Projected weather and climate changes

■ **Storm warnings**
Higher global temperatures could fuel extreme weather. At right are computer-model projections of the chance that various weather events will be more frequent in a

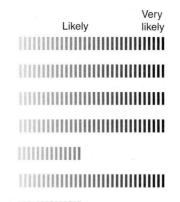

Higher maximum temperatures and more hot days

Higher minimum temperatures and fewer cold days

Higher heat index (heat plus humidity)

Higher nighttime temperatures

More drought

More intense rainfall

More intense hurricanes

Likely   Very likely

(b)

Uncertain scenarios In the next century some coastlines could migrate miles inland, displacing tens of millions of people. Siberia and northern Canada could experience a warmer, wetter climate. Other regions could suffer more frequent and severe droughts. Taking steps now to rein in greenhouse gas emissions could limit these impacts.

ART BY 5W INFOGRAPHIC. JUAN VELASCO TEMPERATURE DATA MANN AND JONES, "GEOPHYSICAL RESEARCH LETTERS." VOL 30, NO 15 (FAR LEFT, TOP), PHIL JONES, CLIMATIC RESEARCH UNIT UNIVERSITY OF EAST ANGLIA U.K. (FAR LEFT, BOTTOM) CO_2 DATA ETHERIDGE ET AL. COMMONWEALTH SCIENTIFIC AND INDUSTRIAL RESEARCH ORGANISATION AUSTRALIA, AND AUSTRALLIAN ANTARTIC DIVISON (FAR LEFT, TOP), C D KEELING SCRIPPS, INSTITUTION OF OCEANOGRAPHY (FAR LEFT, BOTTOM). ARCTIC SEA ICE DATA (MIDDLE, TOP AND BOTTOM) J COMISO, NASA PROJECTED SEA LEVEL CHANGE SCENARIOS (ABOVE,TOP) INTERGOVERNMENTAL PANEL ON CLIMATE CHANGE (IPCC). WEATHER PROJECTIONS (ABOVE, BOTTOM). IPCC, CO_2 PPM DATA (ABOVE): TOM WIGLEY, NATIONAL CENTER FOR ATMOSPHERIC RESEARCH

SOURCE: "Signs from Earth," *National Geographic,* 206 (September 2004).

FOCUS 6.4 Biological Diversity

With an estimated 13 million species on Earth (UNEP 1995, 118), few people take notice of an extinction of a variety of wheat, a breed of sheep, or an insect. Yet it is the very abundance of species on Earth that helps ecosystems work at their maximum potential. Each species makes a unique contribution to life.

- Species diversity influences ecosystem stability and undergirds essential ecological services. From water purification to the cycling of carbon, a variety of plant species is essential to achieving maximum efficiency of these processes. Diversity also bolsters resilience—an ecosystem's ability to respond to pressures—offering "insurance" against climate change, drought, and other stresses.

- The genetic diversity of plants, animals, insects, and microorganisms determines agroecosystems' productivity, resistance to pests and disease, and, ultimately, food security for humans. Extractions from the genetic library are credited with annual increases in crop productivity worth about $1 billion per year (WCMC 1992, 433); yet the trend in agroecosystems is toward the replacement of polycultures with monocultures and diverse plant seed varieties with uniform seed varieties (Thrupp 1998, 23–24). For example, more than 2,000 rice varieties were found in Sri Lanka in 1959, but just five major varieties in the 1980s (WCMC 1992, 427).

- Genetic diversity is fundamental to human health. From high cholesterol to bacteria fighters, 42 percent of the world's 25 top-selling drugs in 1997 were derived from natural sources. The global market value of pharmaceuticals derived from genetic resources is estimated at $75–150 billion. Botanical medicines such as ginseng and echinacea represent an annual market of another $20–40 billion, with about 440,000 tons of plant material in trade, much of it originating in the developing world. Not fully captured by this commercial data is the value of plant diversity to the 75 percent of the world's population that relies on traditional medicine for primary healthcare (Kate and Laird 1999:1–2, 34, 101, 334–335).

The threat to biodiversity is growing. Among birds and mammals, rates may be 100 to 1,000 times what they would be without human-induced pressures—overexploitation, invasive species, pollution, global warming, habitat loss, fragmentation, and conversion (Reid and Miller 1989). Regional extinctions, particularly the loss of populations of some species in tropical forests, may be occurring three to eight times faster than global species extinctions (Hughes et al. 1997, 691).

Destruction of forests, particularly tropical rain forests, also destroys humankind's genetic heritage, as plant and animal species become extinct even before they are identified and classified. The world's **biodiversity**—the natural abundance of plant and animal species, humankind's genetic heritage—is the inevitable victim (see Focus 6.4). Some experts worry that, due mainly to human activities, "the world is on the verge of an episode of major species extinction, rivaling five other documented periods over the past half-billion years during which a significant portion of the global fauna and flora were wiped out," each time requiring "ten million years or more for the number of species to return to the level of diversity existing prior to the event" *(World Resources 1994–1995).*

Habitat loss is the major threat to biodiversity. Ironically, perhaps, bioinvasions are now the second greatest threat to biodiversity *(World Resources 1998–1999).* The term refers to the introduction of species native to one area of the world into another. Mussels that originated from the Black Sea area are now widespread in Lake Michigan. They came in the ballast water discharged by giant ships entering the United States through the St. Lawrence Seaway. The mussels' arrival is the inevitable consequence of global trade and tourism, both elements of the rapid globalization witnessed since the 1990s. Fear of the H5N1 avian influenza virus, which originated in Asia, is a more direct threat to humans themselves (Garrett 2005b).

Origins of Top 150 Prescription Drugs in the United States of America

Origin	Total Number of Compounds	Natural Product	Semisynthetic	Synthetic	Percent
Animal	27	6	21	—	23
Plant	34	9	25	—	18
Fungus	17	4	13	—	11
Bacteria	6	5	1	—	4
Marine	2	2	0	—	1
Synthetic	64	—	—	64	43
Totals	150	26	60	64	100

Such localized extinctions may be just as significant as the extinction of an entire species worldwide. Most of the benefits and services provided by species working together in an ecosystem are local and regional. If a keystone species is lost in an area, a dramatic reorganization of the ecosystem can occur. For example, elephants disperse seeds, create water holes, and trample vegetation through their movements and foraging. The extinction of elephants in a piece of savanna can cause the habitat to become less diverse and open and cause water holes to silt up, which would have dramatic repercussions on other species in the region (Goudie 2000, 67).

Vascular Plants Threatened on a Global Scale
Of the estimated 250,000–270,000 species of plants in the world, only 751 are known or suspected to be extinct. But an enormous number—33,047, or 12.5 percent—are threatened on a global scale. Even that grim statistic may be an underestimate because much information about plants is incomplete, particularly in the tropics.

SOURCE: *World Resources 2000–2001* Washington, DC: World Resources Institute, 2000, p. 14.

Although the introduction of new species in various parts of the world has for centuries proved economically beneficial, increasingly the consequences are malign. The deliberate import of exotic species for commercial purposes or agricultural production, for example, often results in a kind of "biological pollution" that results in the destruction of both aquatic and terrestrial life. "Some ecologists predict that as the number of potential invaders increases and the supply of undisturbed natural areas declines, biological pollution by alien invaders may become the leading factor of ecological disintegration" *(World Resources 1998–1999).*

The spread of disease is caused by the same trade and travel that have increased the threat biological pollution poses to biodiversity. Millions of people travel across international borders every week. "And as people move, unwanted microbial hitchhikers tag along.... In the age of jet travel...a person incubating a disease such as Ebola can board a plane, travel twelve thousand miles, pass unnoticed through customs and immigration, take a domestic carrier to a remote destination, and still not develop symptoms for several days, infecting many other people before his condition is noticeable" (Garrett 2001).

The processes of globalization doubtless explain the rapid spread of mad cow and foot and mouth diseases throughout Europe and elsewhere in recent years. It may also explain the discovery of the West Nile virus in New York in 1999. The virus is commonly found in people, birds, and other animals in Africa, parts of Europe and Asia, and the Middle

East, but had not previously been documented in the Western Hemisphere. According to the Centers for Disease Control, there were nearly 4,200 human cases in the United States in 2006. The virus can cause encephalitis—an inflammation of the brain—which interferes with the normal functioning of the central nervous system. The spread of the avian flu virus, which originated in Asia, is another global worry.

International and Intranational Conflict

Not all threats to the global environment can be blamed on population growth. Rising consumption is also a culprit. Indeed, when it comes to finger pointing, the Global South dramatizes not its own population growth but the enormous—and disproportionate—consumption of global resources by the North (see Brown 1998; Lang 2001; Mitchell 2001; but compare Sagoff 2001). As the United Nations Development Programme notes, "on average, someone living in the developed world spends nearly $16,000 . . . on private consumption each year, compared with less than $350 spent by someone in South Asia and sub-Saharan Africa" *(World Resources 2000–2001)*. But population and consumption are intertwined in complex ways. As the demand for food increases because of population growth *and* changes in dietary habits associated with rising affluence, run-off from pesticides and fertilizers used to increase agricultural productivity pollutes waterways and contributes to the destruction of delicate coral reefs. As more energy is consumed to sustain a growing population and rising affluence, environmental degradation continues at a rapid and often accelerating pace.

As changing demographic patterns and lifestyle preferences test political wills and the ability of the earth's delicate life-support systems to support the world's six-plus billion people, the obvious question to ask is whether these developments are caldrons brewing violent international conflicts.

War inflicts human suffering that is often difficult to comprehend. But it also sometimes precipitates enormous desecration of the environment. Rome sowed salt on a defeated Carthage to prevent

its resurgence. The Dutch breached their own dikes to allow ocean saltwater to flood fertile farmlands, hoping to stop the advancing German armies during World War II. The United States used defoliants on the dense jungles in Vietnam in an effort to expose enemy guerrillas. And Iraq engaged in acts of "environmental terrorism" when it released millions of gallons of oil into the Persian Gulf during the war over Kuwait. But is the reverse true? Does desecration of the environment precipitate violent conflict?

On the surface the answer would appear to be yes, but this may be too facile a conclusion. Systematic inquiry by Thomas F. Homer-Dixon (1999) and his associates into the relationship between scarcities of critical environmental resources and violent conflict in Africa, Asia, and elsewhere leads to the conclusion that environmental scarcities "do not cause wars between countries, but they can generate severe social stresses within countries, helping to stimulate subnational insurgencies, ethnic clashes, and urban unrest." These dynamics are especially acute in the Global South, whose societies are generally "highly dependent on environmental resources and less able to buffer themselves from the social crises that environmental scarcities cause." Homer-Dixon acknowledges that many of the violent conflicts the world has witnessed in the past decade cannot be attributed to environmental scarcities, but he predicts pessimistically that "we can expect [scarcity] to become a more important influence in coming decades because of larger populations and higher per capita resource consumption rates." He adds that if a group of states he calls "pivotal" (see also Chase, Hill, and Kennedy 1996) fall on the wrong side of the "ingenuity gap"—the ability to adapt to environmental scarcity and avoid violent conflict—humanity's overall prospects will dramatically worsen. "Such a world will be neither environmentally sustainable nor politically stable. The rich will be unable to fully isolate themselves from the crises of the poor, and there will be little prospect of building the sense of global community needed to address the array of grave problems—economic, political, as well as ecological—that humanity faces."

THE NORTH–SOUTH DIVIDE: CONFLICT OR COOPERATION?

In September 2000, 147 heads of state or government leaders of 191 countries—the largest world gathering of world leaders ever—met in New York at the historic UN Millennium Summit, the brainchild of UN Secretary-General Kofi Annan (for an overview, see www.unmillenniumproject. org). The leaders gathered to set priorities for the United Nations in the new century and to assess how it might be retooled to best meet them. Quickly, however, nearly all of the policy statements and discussions boiled down to two themes common in the decades-long dispute between the Global North and South: peace and development. "Whether they were full of prose and poetry or brutally blunt, the speeches varied only in the particular aspects of the key issues that they stressed: globalization, armed conflict, human rights, HIV/AIDS, environmental degradation, nuclear weapons, education, fairer economic systems, religious and ethnic tolerance, gender equality, and corruption" (White 2000).

Bill Clinton was especially forceful in drawing the connection between peace and development. In an appearance before the UN Security Council, his last as president, he argued compellingly that "Until we confront the iron link between deprivation, disease, and war, we will never be able to create the peace that the founders of the United Nations dreamed of." That theme reflected, of course, many of the foreign policy priorities his administration had pursued during the 1990s.

The Millennium Summit was only one in a series of world conferences on peace, development, and differences between North and South that convened during the past several decades. The G-8 (the Group of Eight, comprising the world's seven largest industrialized countries plus Russia) have also from time to time discussed issues at the nexus of the North-South divide. Shortly before the Millennium Summit, for example, the G-8 concluded that closing the global digital divide was essential to bridging the gulf between the rich and poor

states. Amid controversy, an agreement was hammered out that created an information technology charter and a task force whose purpose was to investigate how Global South access to the Internet might be enhanced. Controversy arose when some leaders urged that issues such as debt relief, lack of food, housing, and basic amenities in impoverished countries deserved priority over Internet access. Proponents of the tech-thrust responded that access to technology promised an escape from the conditions of poverty that plague so many in the Global South.

In 2005, at their Summit meeting in Gleneagles, Scotland, the G-8 leaders agreed to double their aid to Africa by 2010 and committed themselves to eliminating the external debt of the world's poorest countries. Later that same year, the World Summit endorsed the Millennium Project's goals and set targets for achieving the Millennium Development Goals (MDGs) by 2015. Some progress was noted. The number of people in absolute poverty declined by 130 million, for example; child mortality rates declined from 103 deaths per 1,000 live births a year to 88; and an additional 8 percent of the developing world gained access to water. However, Kofi Annan warned, "The MDGs can be met by 2015—but only if all involved break with business as usual and dramatically accelerate and scale up action now" (United Nations, *The Millennium Development Goals Report 2005*).

Globalization also figures prominently in the most recent variant of the continuing North-South controversy, as we will note later. Globalization has once more pushed *equity* to the forefront of the North-South agenda. As argued by Theo-Ben Gurirab, Namibia's foreign minister who served as president of the UN General Assembly as the Millennium Summit took shape, "Globalization is seen by some as a force for social change, that it will help to close the gap between the rich and the poor, the industrialized North and the developing South. But it is also being seen as a destructive force because it is being driven by the very people, the colonial powers, who launched a global campaign of imperial control of peoples and resources in what we call now the third world. Can we trust them?"

Globalization and the technology themes related to it are among the most recent issues on the global agenda that relate to the millennium themes of peace and development. We will explore briefly other developments related to them during the recent past. All constitute challenges to American foreign policy provoked by the challenges and constraints of the international system.

The Earth Summit and Beyond

In 1992, the world community convened the *United Nations Conference on the Environment and Development (UNCED)* in Rio de Janeiro. Popularly known as the *Earth Summit,* it was the largest-ever world meeting of its kind, bringing together more than 150 countries, 1,400 nongovernmental organizations, and some 800 journalists. UNCED addressed how environmental and developmental issues interact with one another—something not done before, as the two issues previously had been treated on separate tracks. Statements of principles on the management of the earth's forests, conventions on climate change and biodiversity, and a program of action—*Agenda 21*—which embodied a political commitment to the realization of a broad range of environmental and development goals, were among UNCED's achievements (see Sitarz 1993).

Sustainable development, a concept encapsulating the belief that the world must work toward a model of economic development that also protects the delicate environmental systems on which humanity depends for its existence, encapsulated much of UNCED's thrust. The concept has important intergenerational implications. As first articulated in *Our Common Future,* the 1987 report of the World Commission on Environment and Development, popularly known as the Brundtland Commission (after the Norwegian prime minister who was its chair), a *sustainable society* is one that "meets the needs of the present without compromising the ability of future generations to meet their own needs." The concept of sustainable development has received a great deal of praise for promoting an interconnected approach to the issues of economic development and the environment, but others see it as only a "fashionable notion" that may have diverted policy makers' attention from specific, workable projects designed to spur development and protect the environment by focusing on a grand and somewhat obscure vision represented by the concept (Victor 2006).[4]

Population and Development   In 1994, two years after UNCED, the United Nations sponsored the World Population and Development Conference, thus carrying forward the theme of interrelationships on which sustainability depends. Family-planning programs designed to check excessive population growth were among the conference's contentious topics, but it also addressed measures to reduce poverty and improve educational opportunities with a view toward enhanced sustainability. An emphasis on the rights, opportunities, and economic roles of women—all proven critical in reducing population growth rate—was a distinctive feature of the conference. American foreign policy toward population and environmental issues has fluctuated widely during the past quarter-century. During the first United Nations population conference, held in Bucharest, Romania, in 1974, North and South quarreled about the very existence of a population problem. The United States and other rich countries embraced the view that the "population explosion" (Ehrlich and Ehrlich 1990) so impeded the economic advancement of Third World countries that nothing less than a frontal attack on the causes of population growth could cure their development illnesses. Developing states responded that the prescription was little more than another attempt by the world's rich nations to perpetuate the underdog status of the world's poor. They also pointed with anger at the consumption patterns of the North, noting that these—not population growth in the South—were the real causes of pressures on global resources.

Ten years later, at a second global population conference in Mexico City, the United States again found itself out of step with majority sentiments, but now for very different reasons. By this time the Third World had accepted the proposition that unrestrained population growth impeded progress toward economic development. They now sought more vigorous efforts by the United Nations, other multilateral agencies, and individual countries in the North to help with family planning and other programs designed to contain the "explosion." The Reagan administration, however—which at home courted the growing chorus of antiabortion sentiments—announced that population growth was not a problem. It abruptly canceled support of family planning programs, of which the United States had long been a champion. The about-face included termination of U.S. support for the United Nations Population Fund, a prohibition that continued into the senior Bush's administration.

By the time of the 1994 Population and Development Conference, which met in Cairo, the Democrats had seized control of the White House, placing domestic antiabortionist forces on the defensive. The United States now sought again to play a leading role in addressing global population issues. As we saw in Chapter 5, the Clinton administration viewed uncontrolled population growth as a cause of the chaos and crises that often engulf states in the Global South. Thus the U.S. Agency for International Development prepared for a vigorous population stabilization program, and the United States once more became a champion of the efforts by the United Nations and other governmental and nongovernmental agencies to promote family-planning programs abroad.

History seemed to repeat itself in early 2001. Just as the Clinton administration moved early to reinvigorate U.S. support of population planning programs abroad shortly after Clinton was inaugurated in 1993, the new President Bush moved early in his presidency to restrict U.S. support for global family-planning programs designed to address global population issues.

Global Climate Change   The United States has long been out of step with much of the rest of the world on climate change issues. During the 1992 Earth Summit, the United States worked hard to water down a global Framework Convention on Climate Change, but its endorsement by others set

the stage for later meetings designed to address curbs on the causes of global warming and related issues.

In 1997 states met in Japan, where they initialed the ***Kyoto Protocol to the United Nations Framework Convention on Climate.*** It was the first international accord on climate change since the Earth Summit. The protocol sought to stabilize and then reduce the concentration of greenhouse gases in the atmosphere. Vice President Al Gore played a critical role in bringing the Kyoto negotiations to a conclusion satisfactory to the United States, but the U.S. Senate refused to ratify the agreement, in part because it failed to include emissions restraints on many countries in the Global South, notably China. Powerful domestic interests in the United States also remained adamantly opposed to moving forward, citing concerns about the domestic costs perceived to result from curbs on the burning of fossil fuels, notably gasoline.

The election of George W. Bush did not bode well for advocates of a tougher U.S. position on climate change and other global environmental issues. He campaigned on a sensitive environmental issue in supporting oil exploration in protected habitats in Alaska and moved to implement that pledge shortly after his election. He quickly sought to suspend Clinton administration efforts to prevent road construction and logging in millions of acres of sensitive old-forest and other federal lands. And he renounced his campaign promise to cut carbon dioxide emissions from power plants, a central element in the Kyoto Protocol. Critics worried that this might be the death knell of Kyoto efforts to establish targets for cutting CO_2 and other greenhouse gas emissions in the coming years. In the second term of his administration Bush did seem to accept the notion that human activity may be responsible for global warming but continued to espouse a policy that left the response to the private sector and the marketplace.

Despite U.S. opposition, the Kyoto agreement came into force on February 16, 2005, after Russia ratified it the previous year. As of late 2006, 165 countries had ratified the agreement. This covered over 60 percent of the emissions from developed countries. The United States and Australia remained the notable exceptions to ratification of the agreement (United Nations Framework Convention on Climate Change, http://unfccc.int/2860.php).[5]

Biodiversity, Biotechnology, and Deforestation

When UNCED met in Rio de Janeiro, the United States found itself out of step with much of the world not only on global warming but also biodiversity. The first Bush administration refused to sign the Convention on Biodiversity. The Clinton administration reversed that decision, but the Senate refused to ratify the agreement.

Despite U.S. absence, 189 countries are now party to the convention. Served by the secretariat of the convention in Montreal, the convention seeks to promote sustainable development and a comprehensive approach to protecting the world's delicate ecosystems and their biodiversity. Signatories of the convention meet periodically to share ideas about policies and practices for the conservation and sustainable use of biodiversity with an ecosystem approach. Recent initiatives include a Biosafety Protocol, which recognizes that advances of genetically engineered plants and animals simultaneously enhance the quality of life through new plants, animals, and medicines, but also pose risks. As the biodiversity secretariat has noted, "In some countries, genetically altered agricultural products have been sold without much debate, while in others, there have been vocal protests against their use, particularly when they are sold without being identified as genetically modified."

As a leader in biotechnology, American agribusinesses have been impacted by both the promise and problems of biotechnology. Some members of the European Union, for example, have protested the use of hormone-injected cattle to produce hamburger meat for foreign export. They also have curtailed the import of genetically engineered corn originally intended for animal feedlots that inadvertently ended up in corn flake cereals and other foods consumed domestically and produced for export.

American pharmaceutical firms have also been impacted by biodiversity issues. Part of the drive to protect tropical forests where thousands of yet unnamed species thrive is because of their potential benefit in developing drugs to treat today's medical maladies. In the past many Global South countries missed out on the profits reaped from the exotic plants and animals within their borders, made possible when Northern companies "mined" their resources. The classic example comes from Madagascar. The rosy periwinkle native to tropical forests of that African island country is the source of a drug developed by Eli Lilly that was used in a revolutionary treatment of leukemia in children. Eli Lilly enjoyed profits in the tens of millions of dollars. Madagascar shared in none of them.

The Biodiversity Convention seeks to reverse this unequal exchange between North and South. Parties to the treaty recognize states' sovereignty over their natural resources and agree that access to valuable biological resources must be based on their mutual agreement and that the state of origin must share in any benefits their exploitation may yield. Cooperation might range from outright payments to sharing of biotechnical resources to profit-sharing plans.

The steps toward protecting biodiversity are halting and, as with the climate change treaty, often unenforceable. But steps are being taken—even without the formal participation of the United States in global efforts to protect the world's genetic heritage. The United States can ill afford to flaunt the will of the global community on this issue, nor has it. Despite not being a formal party to the biodiversity agreement, it continues to foster and follow policies consistent with the treaty's objectives and the goals of the world community.

Domestically, the United States has sponsored efforts to reforest areas once denuded of their natural covers. Globally, the United States shares with other industrialized countries an effort to rebuild forests lost to misuse, urban growth, and environmental degradation. The results have been encouraging. The United Nations Food and Agriculture Organization (FAO) reported in early 2001 that the rate of deforestation had declined measurably. As reported in its latest assessment, it concludes that the rate of forest loss slowed by 20 percent between 1995 and the onset of the new century. Reforestation in the Global North accounts for much of the decline. But deforestation continues unabated in the South. The FAO reports that forest destruction remains pervasive in much of Africa and Latin America. If there is a hopeful sign, it is in Asia, where deforestation has largely been compensated with reforestation programs. As a whole, however, the world community has yet to move beyond the statement of principles on the management of the earth's forests approved at the Earth Summit in 1992.

Some progress has been made in organizing to deal with a related problem, desertification. Nearly 290 countries have ratified the UN Convention to Combat Desertification (UNCCD), which came into force in 1996. The UNCCD helps to devise bottom-up approaches to sustainable development that may help prevent future desertification and roll back current and past encroachments.

The Foreign Policy Interests and Strategies of the Global South

We noted earlier that environmental stress and resource scarcities are expected to fuel social strains that may ignite violent conflict. Violence is already pervasive in much of the Global South and figures prominently in Southern states' pursuit of their foreign policy interests and strategies. The policy choices the Global South makes in responding to its problems and opportunities have important implications for American foreign policy.

During the Cold War the developing countries of the Third World embraced three identifiable strategies: (1) reform the world political economy to make it more amenable to their interests, (2) steer clear of Cold War political-military alignments, and (3) acquire modern military capabilities to protect their sovereignty and independence. This summary, of course, is an oversimplification; few in the Third World pursued all of these goals simultaneously, while many others sought goals specifically tailored to their own perceptions of their unique national interests. Still, they remain part of the legacy that informs North-South relations in the twenty-first century and that take us beyond the demographic divide in which population and development figure so prominently. A brief sketch illustrates the historic context of these strategies, the interests that motivated them, and their continuing relevance.

Reform—and Resentment   Third World efforts to reform the world political economy grew out of a perceptual lens in international politics known as **_dependency theory,_** which originated in Latin America and was quickly embraced elsewhere. Dependency theorists argued that the relationship between the rich and poor countries—the _core_ and _periphery,_ respectively—explained the persistent underdevelopment of the developing countries.

Galvanized by this logic and the evident commodity power demonstrated by the _Organization of Petroleum Exporting Countries (OPEC)_ in the 1970s, the developing countries pressed the Northern countries to replace the rules governing the _Liberal International Economic Order (LIEO)_ (discussed in detail in Chapter 7) with a new set of rules that would create a _New International Economic Order (NIEO)_ designed to reverse the dependency relationships of the past. State intervention into markets marked many of their proposals. Although pressed vigorously in a variety of international forums into the early years of the Reagan administration, the dialogue between the Global North and South over the NIEO quickly degenerated into a dialogue of the deaf.

Today little remains of Southern efforts to reform the world political economy. Instead, it continues to operate according to rules governing capital, monetary, and trade flows set by the Global North. Indeed, as political democracy spread following the Cold War, it demanded the parallel development of market economies. Thus _privatization_ became the buzzword of the 1990s. If there is a common thread joining these efforts with the NIEO drive, it is how to integrate the developing economies into the world political economy—on terms, the Global South would say, still dictated by the North, and the United States in particular.

A one-superpower world is the context in which many in the Global South now see the at the rapid advancement of globalization, which not only undermines its cultures and values but also its ability to compete in the face of rules governing commerce, labor, and the environment set in the North. In early 2000, Malaysia's then–Prime Minister Mahathir Mohamad, an outspoken leader among the Asian developing countries, pointedly reflected the concerns of many in the Global South:

What I see happening today as a result of globalization is an attempt to set up worldwide monopolies of certain businesses by a few giant corporations mainly from the West. In the future there will be at the most five banks, five automotive companies, five hypermarkets, five hotel chains, five restaurant chains and so on, all operating worldwide. All the small- and medium-sized companies in these fields and maybe others too will be absorbed by these Western owned international giants. These monopolies would, it is claimed, bring about efficiency and thus lower cost through economies of scale. The raw materials the world needs will also be produced by giant mining and plantation companies operating in poor countries, and will be carried by air and sea freighters belonging to giant transportation companies, to be processed and resold throughout the world. Some, of course, will use cheap labor in the poor countries in order to reduce costs.

It is the dream world of the super-capitalists come true. Others will merely work for the capitalists. They will earn more but they will own nothing that they can call their own. Quite obviously the great capitalists will wield immeasurable power. And they will become corrupted as they manipulate governments and international agencies so as to enable them to make more and more money for themselves.

When the Cold War ended with the defeat of communism, it was not democracy that won. It was capitalism with a big capital C. The advent of communism and socialism in the early years of the twentieth century forced capitalism to adopt a more human face. Monopolies were broken up and curbed. Today, without the challenge of communism, the true ugliness of capitalism has revealed itself. This time it will not permit any opposition or restriction.

Democracy, the rule of the majority and the concern for the poor and the small must not stand in the way of world-girdling unbridled capitalism. Through the IMF, the World Trade Organization, the international media, and the might of the most powerful and richest country on Earth, capitalism will assert its power. Before this juggernaut all must fall.

The question is, do we resist now before it is too late or do we wait until, like communism, millions have been sacrificed before we rise in rebellion?

Nonalignment—and Neglect   Diversity has always characterized the Global South. The Cold War gave it coherence, however—at least as seen through the eyes of the conflict's antagonists. Many in the Third World fed that perception through their foreign policy strategy of ***nonalignment,*** the purpose of which was to steer clear of Cold War political-military alignments. Because Third World states could not materially affect the outcome of the Cold War, they tried through nonalignment to maximize their own gains while minimizing their costs. The strategy, as preached with firebrand rhetoric at periodic summits first convened in 1961, stimulated keen efforts by each of the two superpowers to woo the uncommitted to its own side while preventing their alignment with the other. Nonalignment in effect enabled developing countries to play one side against the other in order to gain advantage for themselves. The Cold War competitors—in keeping with the sensitivity each manifested toward the other in the context of the bipolar distribution of power, perceived as a zero-sum contest—were willing players in the game.

Foreign aid was a favored foreign policy instrument the United States used to prevent defection of the nonaligned to "the other side." Between the end of the Korean War (when U.S. foreign aid efforts turned increasingly to the Third World) and 1990, the United States expended some $200 billion in foreign economic aid. Although the motivations behind these vast sums often took into account the welfare of the recipients, security concerns and an overriding emphasis on the containment of communism were the driving forces (see Chapter 5).

Soviet and Soviet bloc aid never rivaled that of the United States, and much of what was once committed apparently never actually made it to recipient countries. Nonetheless, the Soviet Union and its allies were eager competitors. Like the United States, the historic pattern of Soviet bloc aid followed the path of its strategic and geopolitical interests, with much of it concentrated in the Middle East, Southeast Asia, and the Western Hemisphere (notably Cuba and Nicaragua).

Since the 1960s, and even more markedly since the end of the Cold War, the United States and the other industrial economies of the Global North have been the principal sources of development assistance, which Southern states receive directly from individual donor countries (bilateral aid) or from international financial institutions (multilateral aid). Still, flow of aid slowed markedly during the 1990s, even as the demands for assistance to Russia and the New Independent States and to war-ravaged states like Afghanistan, Cambodia, and others grew. Although the great powers continue to rely on foreign aid as an instrument of statecraft, the United States, historically the most generous donor in dollar terms, is today the least generous as measured by the percentage of its wealth devoted to foreign assistance. A long-established goal of the United Nations is that the rich countries give 0.7 percent of their gross national product (GNP) to the poor countries. In 2004, among the twenty-two major foreign aid donors in the Global North, the United States is *dead last* at 0.16 percent. Its assistance to poor countries is but a fraction of the money Americans spend annually on alcoholic beverages, tickets to sporting events and rock concerts, and weight reduction plans.

Jeffrey Sachs (2005) wrote in *Foreign Affairs* a scathing review of U.S. developmental assistance as being long on promises, such as those contained in the Millennium Project, but short on actual delivery. Sachs suggests that most aid given by the United States is still politically motivated rather than aimed at helping countries emerge from poverty. Though his critique was aimed primarily at the United States, in fact, only a few European countries, such as Denmark (0.84), Luxembourg (0.85), Netherlands (0.74), Norway (0.87), and Sweden (0.77) actually achieve the 0.7 percent goal (OECD, www.oecd.org/dataoecd/40/3/35389786.pdf, accessed 5/23/06).

The end of the Cold War not only dissipated much of the rationale that sustained foreign aid in the past, it also removed whatever facade of strength nonalignment may once have provided the Global South. "This political device is now lost to [the states of the South]. Nonalignment died with the Cold War. More than that, the way the East-West rivalry ended, with the values and systems of the West vindicated and triumphant, undermined the very basis of the nonaligned movement, which had adopted as its foundation a moral neutrality between the two blocs" (Chubin 1993).

Still, the residue of resentment stemming from a colonial past and an underdog status in the global hierarchy persists. In a one-superpower world, the Global South is particularly sensitive to the elitist character of the United Nations Security Council, and how profoundly decisions there—where the Global South has virtually no voice but in which the United States is now dominant—can affect its future (Chubin 1993; Korany 1994). Indeed, for the Global South, the post–Gulf War world seems to reveal "the reemergence of a more open and explicit form of imperialism, in which national sovereignty is more readily overridden by a hegemonic power pursuing its own self-defined national interest" (Bienefeld 1994).

Sovereign Independence—and Intranational and International Challenges to It Global South states have always been acutely sensitive about their independence and sovereignty. Thus the increased concern in the United Nations Security Council during the 1990s with humanitarian intervention to protect human rights, promote democracy, and enhance other arguably legitimate values was often perceived as a threat to their independence and integrity.

It is important to note that the benefits Southern states may once have enjoyed as a consequence of Soviet and American efforts to win their allegiance also had their costs. More often than not, the Third World was the battleground on which the superpowers' covert activities, paramilitary operations, and proxy wars were played out. Almost all civil wars in the Cold War era occurred on Third World "killing fields," where the number of casualties ran into the tens of millions (Singer 1991). And the pattern continues: of the more than twenty active violent conflicts ongoing as of January 1, 2005, all but one were in the Global South (see Focus 6.5).

Most of these conflicts are grounded in often ravaging and bloody ethnopolitical disputes—to which traditional foreign policy instruments as well as traditional international relations theory grounded in realism and idealism are of dubious relevance. The main problem in many countries in the former Soviet Union and the Global South, explains K. J. Holsti (1998), "is not between communities within the state, but between the regime and those communities. . . . The state, rather than ethnic communities, has often been the main threat to the lives and security of its own citizens." Holsti notes, for example, that "it was the government-trained and organized militia in Rwanda in 1994 that launched the genocide of the Tutsis." A decade later, government-backed genocide in the Darfur region of Sudan in many way mirrored the atrocities perpetrated in Rwanda. Thus a basic, underlying condition of ethnopolitical conflict "is the systematic exclusion of individuals and groups from access to government positions, influence, and allocations. There is, in brief, differential treatment of specified groups by governments, which means that there are fundamental problems of justice underlying armed conflict."

Robert Kaplan (2000) likewise worries that "the coming anarchy" will be propelled by a breakdown of authority in much of the Global South. Indeed, *failed states*—states that can no longer perform basic functions such as security or governance, usually due to fractious violence or extreme poverty—are increasingly evident. Crocker (2003) argues that the Bush II administration missed the importance of failed states through its exclusive focus on rogue states that support terrorism.

State failures affect U.S. interests directly, including its advocacy of human rights, democratization, good governance and the rule of law, religious tolerance, and the promotion of U.S. export markets and investment opportunities. State failures also contribute to regional instability, the proliferation of weapons, drug trafficking, and terrorism. Although George W. Bush, as a presidential candidate in 2000, declared that he was not interested in "nation building," it has become increasingly clear to many policy makers and academics that the weak states produced by colonialism and maintained by aid and security guarantees from the Cold War adversaries are simply unable to create competent governance structures. These failing or failed states are then unable to deliver economic, social, and political opportunities to their populace, often leading to internal violence in the form of ethnic conflict, genocides, military coups, and the like. This phenomenon was first brought to the post–Cold War world's attention with the outright collapse of the Somali state in 1992, but the scope of the problem continues to widen. Scholars and methodologists have attempted to document all such failures in governance from 1955 to 2005 (see the Political Instability Task Force at http://globalpolicy.gmu.edu/pitf/). One group has identified some 293 events related to failures in governance since 1955. Another project conducted by the Fund for Peace and *Foreign Policy* magazine employs a set of twelve economic, social, military, and political indicators to evaluate individual countries' vulnerability to violent internal conflict and state failure (see www.fundforpeace.org/programs/fsi/fsindex.php and www.foreignpolicy.com/story/cms.php?story_id=3098). The resulting global ranking is depicted in Table 6.1.

F O C U S 6.5   World at War: Ongoing Significant Conflicts as of January 1, 2005

Main Warring Parties	Year Began	Contributing Causes*	Other Foreign Involvement
U.S. worldwide war on terror vs. "terrorists with global reach"	2001	Sept. 11, 2001 attacks	UN, multiple countries
Iraq government and multina-tional forces vs. Iraqi resistance and al-Qaida in Iraq.	2003	Invasion and occupation	United States, United Kingdom, Australia, Japan, S. Korea, Italy. Poland, Ukraine, Denmark, others
Israel vs. Hamas, Hezbollah, Islamic Jihad, others	1975	Religious and territorial	United States, UN, Syria, Lebanon; Iran, individuals
Afghanistan: Kabul government vs. al-Qaida and Taliban	1978	Ethnic, religious, and territorial	United States, UN, NATO, Russia, Iran, Tajikistan, Pakistan, Uzbekistan, Kyrgyzstan
India vs. Manipur insurgents, others	1986	Independence	UN, Bhutan, Myanmar, Bangladesh
Philippines vs. Abu Sayyaf	1999	Criminal, terror	United States, Malaysia, Libya, Indonesia
Nepal vs. Maoist insurgents	1996	Ideological	None
Colombia vs. National liberation Army (ELN)	1978	Drug trade, socio/economic, political	United States
Colombia vs. Revolutionary Armed Forces of Colombia (FARC)	1978	Drug trade socio/economic, political	United States
Russia vs. Chechnya	1994; 1996	Independence	Organization for Security and Cooperation in Europe (OSCE), Georgia
Democratic Republic of Congo vs. indigenous insurgents and foreign renegades	1997	Political and socio/economic using ethnic divisions	Angola, Uganda, Rwanda, Chad, Zimbabwe, France, Burundi, South Africa, Namibia, Africa Union UN
Nigeria	1970	Ethnic and religious communal violence	None
Somalia: Somaliland, Puntland, other factions	1978	Power and ethnic	UN (humanitarian aid): United States, Ethiopia, Kenya
Sudan vs. Sudan Liberation Army (splinter) and Justice and Equal-ity Movement	2003	Autonomy and ethic	UN, United States, EU, NATO

* Causes are simplifications and should not be regarded as the full explanation for what is often a very complex set of circumstances.

SOURCE: "World at War" from *The Defense Monitor,* 35 (May/June 2006), 5. Reprinted by permission of Center for Defense Information.

Elsewhere in the Global South, long-standing *security dilemmas* continue to propel apprehensions, suspicions, and violent conflict. These are vicious-circle situations in which the defensive weapons a country acquires are perceived by its adversary to be offensive, thus causing it too to build up its "defensive" arsenal. The Middle East, where bitter differences about religion and territory between

— in relation to my purpose to U.S.?

TABLE 6.1 The Failed States Index

Critical — *at most war*

1. Ivory Coast	11. Afghanistan
2. Democratic Republic of the Congo	12. Rwanda
	13. North Korea
3. Sudan	14. Colombia
4. Iraq	15. Zimbabwe
5. Somalia	16. Guinea
6. Sierra Leone	17. Bangladesh
7. Chad	18. Burundi
8. Yemen	19. Dominican Republic
9. Liberia	20. Central African Republic
10. Haiti	

In Danger

21. Bosnia and Herzegovina	31. Guatemala
22. Venezuela	32. Tanzania
23. Burma	33. Equatorial Guinea
24. Uzbekistan	34. Pakistan
25. Kenya	35. Nepal
26. Bhutan	36. Paraguay
27. Uganda	37. Lebanon
28. Laos	38. Egypt
29. Syria	39. Ukraine
30. Ethiopia	40. Peru

Borderline

41. Honduras	51. Bahrain
42. Mozambique	52. Vietnam
43. Angola	53. Cameroon
44. Belarus	54. Nigeria
45. Saudi Arabia	55. Eritrea
46. Ecuador	56. Philippines
47. Indonesia	57. Iran
48. Tajikistan	58. Cuba
49. Turkey	59. Russia
50. Azerbaijan	60. Gambia

NOTE: States are ranked in order of vulnerability to violent internal conflict. Those states listed in the critical category are most at risk. This ranking is based on twelve political, economic, military, and social indicators of instability: demographic pressures, refugees and displaced persons, group grievance, human flight, uneven development, economic decline, delegitimization of state, public services, human rights, security apparatus, fractionalized elites, and external intervention. In some instances, states receive identical instability scores.

SOURCE: Adapted from "The Failed States Index," *Foreign Policy* 149 (July/August 2005), 56–65. Reprinted by permission.

Jews and Arabs are rife, is a prominent example. So is the drive among South Asian countries to acquire nuclear weapons. China first acquired weapons of mass destruction in the 1960s. India responded with its own nuclear test in the 1970s. Pakistan followed in the 1990s. Arguably each of the triangular nuclear competitors armed for defense, not offense, but their potential adversaries perceived malevolence and responded accordingly. The result smacks of the Cold War competition between the United States and the Soviet Union: a classic arms race precipitated by competing belief systems, conflicts of interest, and potential misperceptions of the intentions of "the other side."

Traditional instruments of statecraft might be better suited to dealing with the Asian security dilemma and analogous situations elsewhere in the Global South, but, as we saw in Chapter 4, Southern states often resist the entreaties of the United States and others in the Global North, viewing them as an unwarranted interference into their sovereign independence. Iran's efforts to develop an indigenous nuclear energy program and perhaps nuclear weapons is a clear case in point. But in Iran and elsewhere in the Middle East, despite repeated initiatives by the Clinton and Bush administrations and their predecessors, the United States has routinely been perceived as favoring Jews over Muslims, angering not only Arabs but also the followers of Islam throughout the world.

Faced with seemingly endless conflict at home or abroad, it is not surprising that political elites in much of the Global South, like those in China, India, Iran, and Pakistan, would join the rest of the world in a quest to acquire modern military capabilities. Often this has meant that the *burden of military spending*—as measured by the ratio of military expenditures to GNP—is highest among those least able to bear it.

Since the end of the Cold War, military expenditures have dropped dramatically. So has their burden. In the decade ending in 1997, the military burden worldwide dropped by half, from 5.2 percent to 2.6 percent. But the decline in the Global South has been somewhat smaller, falling from 4.9 percent to 2.7 percent (U.S. Arms Control and

Disarmament Agency 2000). And some remain heavily burdened. North Korea, for example, continues to spend a tenth of its GNP on the weapons of war, even as its people face starvation requiring humanitarian assistance from others to survive. Thus the societal costs of military spending—which typically exceed expenditures on health and education—bear little relationship to the level of development.[6] Whether a state is embroiled in war with its neighbors or threatened by ethnic, religious, or tribal strife at home remains a potent explanation.

Arms imported from abroad, whether surreptitiously or openly, fuel the conflicts of a world at war. The value of arms purchased from foreign suppliers declined dramatically in the past decade, paralleling the worldwide decline in the burden of military spending. Nonetheless, demand for the weapons of war remains high in many places.

The United States figures prominently in the practice of selling arms to others. Indeed, it emerged in the wake of the implosion of the Soviet empire and the Persian Gulf War as the world's principal supplier state. During the period from 2000 to 2003, the value of all international arms transfers agreements worldwide was $127 billion. Among the top eleven suppliers, the United States accounted 46 percent of their value (Grimmett 2004, 3, 78). On the recipient side, developing states collectively accounted for a little more than 60 percent of the value of the transfer agreements. They also accounted for over half of the $148 billion in international arms deliveries from 2000 to 2003 (Grimmett 2004, 3). (The value of deliveries is often higher than the value of agreements, as they reflect the value of weapons purchase agreements often made earlier, perhaps over several years). In 2003, Saudi Arabia topped the list of recipients of arms deliveries ($5.8 billion), followed by Egypt ($2.1 billion), India ($2 billion), Israel ($1.9 billion), and China ($1 billion) (Grimmett 1999, 63). Taiwan ranked eighth ($0.5 billion), doubtless a concern to leaders on China's mainland.

The conventional weapons sold to arms buyers include the standards: submarines, tanks, self-propelled guns, armored cars, artillery pieces, combat aircraft, surface-to-air missiles, and the like. Increasingly, the export of small arms—"man-portable firearms and their ammunition primarily designed for individual use by military forces as lethal weapons," including "revolvers and self-loading pistols, rifles and carbines, assault rifles, and light machine guns" (U.S. Arms Control and Disarmament Agency 2000)—also has become a major concern (see also Klare 1994–1995). Trafficking in small arms has increased in sync with the rise of ethnopolitical conflict. Although the United Nations, in concert with the United States, has taken steps to stem the flow of small arms across borders, a "comprehensive resolution [of this problem] is unlikely in the near future" (U.S. Arms Control and Disarmament Agency 2000). The Bush administration affirmed that when it announced in June 2001 that the United States would not join a pact on small arms if it infringed on Americans' right to own guns. Meanwhile, the United Nations finds itself increasingly mired in bitter disputes in much of the Global South. While many welcomed the ability of the UN to sponsor peacekeeping missions in the aftermath of the Cold War, which they did with great regularity in the 1990s, it is clear that the pace of new peacekeeping operations has steadily increased during the early years of the twenty-first century (see Table 6.2). Some people argue that UN peacekeeping operations have the untoward effect of postponing political settlements of underlying disputes; other respond that the United Nations has played a critical role in saving lives. Regardless, unhappiness with the United Nations and other international institutions is rife in the United States.

TRANSNATIONAL INTERDEPENDENCE: AGENTS OF CHALLENGE AND CHANGE

Earlier we cited Joseph Nye's concept of a layer cake as a metaphor for the emergent global structure in which the United States now finds itself. "The

TABLE 6.2 Current UN Peacekeeping Missions, 1948–2006

Mission Name and Location	Acronym	Starting Date
UN Truce Supervision Organization—Middle East	UNTSO	May 1948
UN Military Observer Group in India and Pakistan—Kashmir	UNMOGIP	January 1949
UN Peacekeeping Force in Cyprus	UNFICYP	March 1964
UN Disengagement Observer Force—Golan Heights	UNDOF	June 1974
UN Interim Force in Lebanon	UNIFIL	March 1978
UN Mission for the Referendum in Western Sahara	MINURSO	April 1991
UN Observer Mission in Georgia	UNOMIG	August 1993
UN Interim Administration Mission in Kosovo	UNMIK	June 1999
UN Organization Mission in the Democratic Republic of the Congo	MONUC	November 1999
UN Mission in Ethiopia and Eritrea	UNMEE	July 2000
UN Mission in Liberia	UNMIL	September 2003
UN Operation in Cote d'Ivoire	UNOCI	April 2004
UN Stabilization Mission in Haiti	MINUSTAH	June 2004
UN Operation in Burundi	ONUB	June 2004
UN Mission in the Sudan	UNMIS	March 2005

SOURCE: Adapted from the United Nations Department of Peacekeeping Operations.

bottom layer of transnational interdependence," he explained, "shows a diffusion of power" (Nye 1992). Of what does that bottom layer consist? It consists of a multitude of actors who know no national boundaries but who nonetheless profoundly impact the established entities that claim sovereignty in world politics (states) and the people who live in them. These non-state actors are increasingly important in shaping contemporary global politics. International organizations and multinational corporations are the most ubiquitous among them. Transnational terrorist groups, ethnopolitical movements, and criminal entities comprise other, less-benign types. We touch on each of them briefly in this section.

International Organizations:
An Overview

The United Nations is probably the most widely known of all international organizations. It is a multipurpose organization embracing a broad array of other organizations, centers, commissions, and institutes. The distinguishing characteristic of the UN family of organizations is that governments are their members. Hence they are known as international *intergovernmental organizations (IGOs)*. There are nearly three hundred IGOs in existence, and their concerns embrace the entire range of political, economic, social, and cultural affairs that are the responsibilities of modern governments.

In addition to IGOs, the transnational layer of international politics also embraces international *nongovernmental organizations (NGOs)*. Their number grew explosively in the 1990s, from an estimated 5,000 in 1990 to perhaps five times that number by the end of the decade (*The Economist,* 11 December 1999, p. 20). The members of these international organizations (such as the International Federation of Red Cross and Red Crescent Societies) are individuals or societal groups, not governments. NGOs also deal with the entire panoply of transnational activities. It is useful to think of them as intersocietal organizations that help facilitate the achievement and maintenance of agreements among countries regarding elements of international public policy (Jacobson 1984). For example, making rules regarding security at international airports and the treatment of hijackers would not be possible without the cooperation of the International Federation of Air Line Pilots' Associations. Thus NGOs have an impact on the rules governing different policies. Their influence is arguably greatest in the Global North, where democratic institutions invite the participation of interest groups in the policy-making process. They have been particularly vigorous and visible on environmental and trade issues in recent years. Thus NGOs help to blur the distinction between domestic and foreign policy issues.

NGOs and IGOs alike mirror the same elements of conflict and cooperation that characterize international politics generally. Accordingly, not all are appropriately conceived as agents of interdependence. NATO (referenced earlier in the chapter), for example, historically has been a collective defense arrangement restricted to Canada, the United States, and states in Western Europe. Since 1999, ten Eastern European states have joined the alliance, bringing its membership to twenty-six.[7] Although an international organization, until recent years it depended for its very existence on the presence of a credible adversary, whose hostility induced cooperation among the alliance's members. Today, NATO has embraced a broader array of security tasks while retaining its commitment to the collective defense of its members (Jones 2006b). The United States was a primary mover behind the creation of NATO, the United Nations, and a multitude of other international organizations launched in the decades following World War II. It also encouraged the economic integration of Western Europe, which in 1957 culminated in the Treaty of Rome, creating the European Economic Community comprising France, Germany, Italy, Belgium, the Netherlands, and Luxembourg. The community has since been renamed the *European Union (EU)* and embraces twenty-five European countries, with further expansion promised.[8]

Although the EU counts political and security functions among its charge, its greatest successes have come in moving Europe toward a single, integrated regional economy. Today the EU has its own currency (the *euro*), is the largest market in the world, and is a major competitor as well as partner of the United States in the world political economy.

U.S. support for an integrated Europe and other international organizations flowed naturally from the international ethos that animated America's global activism following World War II. As the nature of the international system and the United States' role within it changed, however, so did American attitudes. That is nowhere more apparent than in the response of the United States to the changing United Nations.

International Organizations: The Uneasy U.S.-UN Relationship   American idealism was a motivating force behind creation of the United Nations during the waning days of World War II. American values shaped the world organization, whose political institutions were molded after its own. Almost immediately, however, the United Nations mirrored the increasingly antagonistic Cold War competition between the United States and the Soviet Union. Thus the United States sought—with considerable success—to utilize its position as the leader of the dominant Western majority in the UN to turn the organization in the direction of its own preferred foreign policy goals. That strategy became more difficult with the passage of time, however—especially as the decolonization process unfolded and the United States found itself on the defensive along with its European allies (most of which had been colonial powers) in the face of a hostile Third World coalition with which the Soviet bloc typically aligned. In 1975 that coalition succeeded in passing a General Assembly resolution (over vigorous U.S. protest) that branded Zionism "a form of racism and racial discrimination." The vote outraged Daniel P. Moynihan, then U.S. ambassador to the United Nations, who lashed out vehemently against "the tyranny of the UN's 'new majority.'" In the years that followed, U.S. attitudes toward the United Nations and many of its affiliated organizations ranged from circumspection to outright hostility. The Carter administration withdrew from the International Labour Organization (ILO) to protest what it regarded as the organization's anti-Western bias. The Reagan administration followed by withdrawing from the United Nations Educational, Scientific, and Cultural Organization (UNESCO). The administration's disenchantment with multilateralism also found expression in its indifference to an attack on the World Court and its decision to selectively withhold funds for various UN activities—a tactic the United States had long decried when the Soviet Union chose it to protest UN policies and operations it found inimical to its interests. The United States also became wary of turning to the United Nations to cope with various regional conflict situations, as it had previously done.[9]

By the end of the Reagan administration the once-prevalent retreat from multilateralism, often accompanied by a preference for a unilateral, go-it-alone posture toward global issues, began to wane. The decision of the Soviet Union under Mikhail Gorbachev's leadership to pay its own overdue UN bills and, in the wake of its misadventure in Afghanistan, to turn (or return) to the UN Security Council to deal with conflict situations in a manner recalling the original intended purpose of the UN, helped to stimulate the reassessment of U.S. policy toward the United Nations. That set the stage for Soviet-American cooperation in responding to Iraq's 1990 invasion of Kuwait.

In the years that followed, the Security Council authorized several new peacekeeping and peace enforcement operations, far outpacing any previous period in the organization's history, as we saw earlier in Table 6.2. UN Secretary-General Boutros Boutros-Ghali championed an even broader role for the UN in what President George H. W. Bush described as a new world order, proposing the creation of a volunteer force that would "enable the United Nations to deploy troops quickly to enforce a ceasefire by taking coercive action against either party, or both, if they violate it" (Boutros-Ghali 1992–1993, 1992). The rapid deployment units would go into action when authorized by the Security Council and serve under the command of the secretary-general and his designees.

This and other ideas put forward by the proactive secretary-general proved controversial, however. So, too, did the growing number of UN operations around the world. As their costs—both financial and political—mounted, disenchantment in the United States (long a critic of the UN's excessive bureaucracy and penchant toward mismanagement) also grew. The Clinton administration, as we saw in previous chapters, now elaborated rules that would sharply constrain U.S. participation in UN military operations. Secretary of State Madeleine Albright led the charge to oust Boutros-Ghali as UN Secretary-General in favor of Kofi Annan. And the new Republican majority in the House of Representatives, acting on the single foreign policy item in its "Contract with America" program put forth during the 1994 midterm elections, passed legislation that would curtail funds available for UN peacekeeping or enforcement operations and prohibit U.S. forces from serving under the command of a non-U.S. officer.

Bitter disputes between the Clinton administration and the Republican-controlled Congress would follow. U.S. arrears in its financial obligations to the United Nations mounted, topping $1 billion by the time the General Assembly opened its annual session in September 1999, putting it on the verge of losing its voting privileges. Clinton and Congress would repeatedly seek compromises permitting the debts to be paid, only to see them fall victim to partisan and ideological rancor. Senator Jesse Helms (R-North Carolina), chair of the powerful Senate Foreign Relations Committee and an outspoken conservative, effectively held the entire U.S. foreign affairs budget hostage in a continuing dispute with the administration about the role of international institutions in world politics and the challenges to U.S. sovereignty he thought they posed. An article Helms published in *The National Interest* (Helms 2000–2001) as Clinton was leaving office illustrates his views. His remarks were stimulated by an earlier speech by Secretary-General Kofi Annan in which he said the UN Security Council "is the 'sole source of legitimacy on the use of force' in the world."

Drawing on the historical legacy that warns of "entangling alliances," Helms responded that "Americans look with alarm upon the UN's claim to a monopoly on international moral legitimacy. They see this as a threat to the freedom of the American people, a claim of political authority over America and its elected leaders." He said "we want to ensure that the United States of America remains the sole judge of its own international affairs, that the United Nations is not allowed to restrict the individual rights of U.S. citizens, and the United States retains sole authority over the deployment of U.S. forces around the world." And he concluded with a warning: "If the United Nations does not respect American sovereignty, if it seeks to impose its presumed authority over the American people without their consent, then it begs for confrontation and . . . eventual U.S. withdrawal." Responding in part to the pressures of Helms and others—including many embedded in Helms-Biden legislation passed by Congress in 1999 that demanded UN reforms—U.S. Ambassador to the United Nations Richard Holbrooke brokered a deal only days before Clinton vacated the White House that would reduce U.S. contributions to the United Nations regular budget to 20 percent from 25 percent. The scale of assessments for peacekeeping operations was also revised. The U.S. share would drop from more than 30 percent to less than 28 percent beginning in 2001 and then progressively fall to about 25 percent in later years.[10]

When the new Bush administration assumed the reins of power in January 2001, it faced a world angry and disgusted with what the French rather derisively call the world's "hyperpower." The derision derives from U.S. recalcitrance about what are, after all, rather paltry sums of money by almost any standard (like the cost of fifty cruise missiles, then recently fired against Iraq). The reason, of course, is that money is not the critical issue.[11] It is a matter of who controls the destiny of states' foreign policies, including that of the United States. And on this, as Senator Helms pointedly reminds us, there is wide

and deep disagreement in a world—and a world organization—comprising nearly 200 sovereign states with widely different capabilities and divergent interests.

Robert A. Pastor, once an aide to former president Jimmy Carter, summarizes this viewpoint as seen though the eyes of American policy makers

> The United States has always been ambivalent about whether it wanted to strengthen or limit the United Nations. Its position at any given time depended, not surprisingly, on whether it viewed a specific action as serving its interests. Even in the case of the Gulf War, President George [H. W.] Bush did not consult the United Nations in making his decision to drive Saddam Hussein from Kuwait; he decided first and then sought international legitimacy and support. President Bill Clinton's request in July 1994 for a UN Security Council resolution to restore constitutional government to Haiti was similarly motivated: It was intended not to strengthen the United Nations but to support a U.S. initiative. In the case of Kosovo, NATO decided to begin the bombing of Serbia without United Nations authorization because of the opposition of Russia and China.
> *(Pastor 1999, 11)*

President George W. Bush's decision to invade Iraq occurred despite strong opposition in the UN, including the Security Council. Ultimately, plans to pursue a second resolution to explicitly authorize the invasion of Iraq were scrapped and the invasion proceeded according to U.S. plans. Thus the twenty-first century promises to be no different than the ones that have gone before, as the incentives to maximize individual gains rather than subordinate them to the collectivity persist.

Multinational Corporations   Since World War II, multinational corporations have grown enormously in size and influence, thereby dramatically changing patterns of global investment, production, and marketing. (***Multinational corporations [MNCs]*** are business enterprises organized in one society with activities abroad growing out of direct investment as opposed to portfolio investment through shareholding.) The United Nations Programme on Transnational Corporations estimates that in the early 1990s some 37,000 MNCs controlled assets in two or more countries and that they were responsible for marketing roughly 90 percent of Northern countries' trade (United Nations Programme on Transnational Corporations 1993, 99–100).

Moreover, a comparison of countries and corporations according to the size of their gross economic product shows that half of the world's top one hundred economic entities (in 1998) were multinational corporations. Among the top fifty entities, MNCs account for only fourteen, but in the next fifty they account for thirty-six (Kegley and Wittkopf 2001, 231).

Although Global South countries have spawned some multinational corporations, most remain headquartered in the developed world, where the great majority of MNC activities originate. Historically, the United States has been the home country of the largest proportion of multinational parent companies, followed by Britain and Germany. The outward stocks and flows of foreign direct investment from the United States would steadily decline in the following decades. By the 1990s the investment world appeared "tripolar," with the United States, Europe, and Japan the key actors. By mid-decade, however, American dominance in the MNC world remained unassailable. In 1996 it headquartered a third of the world's 500 largest corporations. Other liberal democracies followed in its train, as (in order) Japan, France, Germany, and Britain continued to dominate the multinational world (*Fortune,* 4 August 1997, F1.)

The dominance of MNCs located and directed from the Global North underlies much of the resentment toward globalization noted earlier in this chapter. Nonetheless, the process of extending the tentacles of these giant corporations so vividly decried by Malaysia's former prime minister Mahathir Mohamad (and others) continues relentlessly.

Although most MNCs are headquartered in the Global North, they pose little direct threat to the economies or the policy-making institutions in these large, complex societies. Not so in the case of the Global South, where the economic power and reach of multinational firms—typically American—have enabled them to become a global extension of Northern societies, serving as an engine not only for the transfer of investment, technology, and managerial skills but also of cultural values; hence Prime Minister Mahathir's concern and anger.

Today the Global South, although worried about the effects of globalization, is less fearful of the untoward effects of MNCs' involvement in their political systems than about its own ability (or inability) to attract MNC investment capital and the other perquisites that flow from it. MNCs are especially important to those who seek to emulate the economic success of the Newly Industrialized Economies (NIEs), which depends on an ability to sustain growth in exports. Foreign capital is critical in this process, even though it often comes at a high price, as suggested by the untoward effects of the Washington Consensus (see also Broad and Cavanagh 1988; Wiarda 1997). Elsewhere, however, particularly in China, which has been the target of billions in foreign direct investment, the government has effectively ignored outsiders' demands to make domestic political reforms in exchange for the economic benefits of globalization (see also Chapter 7).

Critics of multinationals—sometimes called "imperial corporations" (Barnet and Cavanagh 1994)—contend that MNCs can exact a cost on the Global North as well as the Global South. They note that while corporate executives often have a "broad vision and understanding of global issues," they have little appreciation of, or concern for, "the long-term social or political consequences of what their companies make or what they do" (Barnet and Cavanagh 1994; see also Barnet and Müller 1974 and Kefalas 1992). These allegedly include a host of maladies, including environmental degradation, a maldistribution of global resources, and social disintegration. Beyond this, critics worry that MNCs are beyond the control of national political leaders.

The formidable power and mobility of global corporations are undermining the effectiveness of national governments to carry out essential policies on behalf of their people. Leaders of nation-states are losing much of the control over their own territory they once had. More and more, they must conform to the demands of the outside world because the outsiders are already inside the gates. Business enterprises that routinely operate across borders are linking far-flung pieces of territory into a new world economy that bypasses all sorts of established political arrangements and conventions.

(Barnet and Cavanagh 1994, 19)

The United States is not immune from these processes. "Although still the largest national economy and by far the world's greatest military power, [it] is increasingly subject to the vicissitudes of a world no nation can dominate" (Barnet and Cavanagh 1994). Meanwhile, some corporate visionaries extol multinational corporations' transnational virtues. "There are no longer any national flag carriers," in the words of Kenichi Ohmae, a prominent Japanese management consultant. "Corporations must serve their customers, not governments."

International Regimes During the 1960s and 1970s, multinational corporations were the object of considerable animosity due to their size and "global reach" (Barnet and Müller 1974). Today they are widely recognized as key players in the globalization processes that engulf people everywhere. Indeed, it is inconceivable to think how the international economic system might function without them, just as it is inconceivable to think that international commerce or other forms of interaction could occur in the absence of government rules regulating their exchanges. Thus states and non-state actors coalesce to form *international regimes* that facilitate cooperative international relations. *International regimes* can be thought as "sets of implicit or explicit principles, norms, rules, and decision-making procedures around which actors' expectations converge

in a given issue area of international relations" (Krasner 1982). They are important in understanding the regularized patterns of collaboration widely evident in international politics. The international political system may appear anarchical (a central concept underlying the logic of political realism), but it is nonetheless an ordered anarchy. Regimes help explain that apparent anomaly.

The global monetary and trade systems created during and after World War II are clear examples of international regimes. Both evolved under the leadership of the United States, the hegemonic power in the postwar world political economy. Together the two regimes helped define the Liberal International Economic Order (LIEO), which embraced a set of norms, rules, and institutions that limited government intervention in the international economy and otherwise facilitated the free flow of capital and goods across national boundaries. The global system governing the extraction and distribution of oil is another example. Here governments, multinational corporations, and two international organizations, the Organization of Petroleum Exporting Countries (OPEC) and International Energy Agency (IEA), collectively play critical roles in supplying an energy-hungry world with a critical resource (see Keohane 1984).

These and other examples show that non-state actors help to build and broaden the foreign policy agendas of national decision-makers by serving as "transmission belts of policy sensitivities across national boundaries." They also help to shape attitudes among mass and elite publics, they link national interest groups in transnational structures, and they create instruments of influence enabling some governments to carry out more effectively their wishes when dealing with other governments (Keohane and Nye 1975). International regimes facilitate all of these processes. Thus, in concert with non-state actors, they play critical roles in the maintenance of international equilibrium.

Transnational Terrorism, Ethnopolitical Movements, and Transborder Criminal Operations
Transnational terrorists, ethnopolitical movements, and the activities of transborder criminal elements

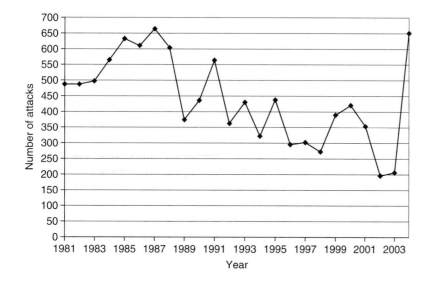

FIGURE 6.7 Total International Terrorist Attacks, 1981–2004

SOURCE: Adapted from U.S. Department of State, *Patterns of Global Terrorism* (various issues), available at www.state.gov/s/ct/rls/crt/; and Andrea Koppel, Elise LaBott and Pam Benson, "Terror Threat to U.S. Called 'Significant'," CNN, April 28, 2005, available at www.cnn.com/2005/US/04/27/terror.report/index.html, accessed 5/22/06.

are exceptions to this bold and optimistic conclusion. Their consequence and perhaps objective as non-state actors is chaos, not equilibrium. Thus they pose vexing challenges to states generally and to the United States in particular.

In its annual *Patterns of Global Terrorism* report, the State Department chronicles international terrorist attacks. As shown in Figure 6.7, international terrorist attacks steadily declined from the 1980s through the 1990s, until they reached a low point of 198 attacks in 2002. (The trends are not unrelated to the end of the Cold War, as the Soviet Union and the Communist states in Eastern Europe had provided both support and safe haven for terrorist groups.) In 2004, however, the number of attacks increased dramatically (to 651), a number not seen since the high mark of 666 attacks two decades earlier. In fact, the surge in attacks following the U.S. invasion of Iraq in 2003 was so great that Secretary of State Condoleezza Rice initially decided not to publish the numbers. The State Department received substantial criticism for this choice and eventually released them.

In August 2004, President Bush created by executive order the National Counterterrorism Center (NCTC) to serve as a focal point for government information-gathering on terrorist activities. The NCTC revised the methodological approach to counting terrorist incidents, using a much broader measure of terrorism than focusing strictly on "international terrorism," as was the practice of the State Department. As a result, the new terrorist incident numbers are not comparable to the series presented in Figure 6.7. The NCTC reported more than 11,000 terrorist attacks around the globe in 2005. The greatest number occurred in the Middle East (4,230) and South Asia (3,974). Bombings and armed attacks were the most frequently used terrorist techniques. Iraq accounted for nearly 30 percent of the attacks and over half of the deaths from them (National Counterterrorism Center, Report on Incidents of Terrorism 2005, 11 April 2006; see also www.nctc.gov). Accordingly, the United States has devoted considerable attention to terrorism and terrorist threats in recent years—all part of its global war on terrorism.

The attacks on the USS Cole in Yemen, military barracks in Saudi Arabia, and American embassies in Kenya and Tanzania, all of which resulted in considerable loss of life, are among the deadly terrorist attacks on U.S. global interests and assets leading up to September 11. The strikes against the

World Trade Center and the Pentagon, larger in scale than any previous terrorist attacks, dramatically altered the situation, however, leading to substantially greater attention and resource commitment. Although the United States has been seemingly "immune" from attacks since 9/11, Spain suffered when terrorists bombed the train system in Madrid in 2004, and London's bus and "tube" (subway) systems were bombed a year later.

Traditionally, terrorism has been a tactic of the powerless directed against the powerful. Thus political or social minorities and ethnopolitical movements often perpetrated acts of terrorism to seize the media limelight and promote their causes. Those seeking independence and sovereign statehood—like the Palestinians in the Middle East, the Basques in Spain, and the Chechen separatists in Chechnya—typified the kinds of aspirations that often animated terrorist activity.

Recently, however, as illustrated by the terrorist activities of Osama bin Laden and his followers, terrorism has become something more than "propaganda by deed" (Laqueur 1998). It has become a weapon used to inflict not just "noise," but to cause "the greatest number of casualties as possible." Bin Laden's once sprawling, transnational network of jihadists is committed to advancing a narrow view of Islam and recruiting disaffected Muslims into creating "Islamic Republics" throughout the Islamic world. The policies and presence of the United States in the Middle East has made it a principal target of these "religious fanatics" (Laqueur 1998; see also Doran 2001).

The Bush administration's global struggle against terrorism is a prime example of low-intensity conflict. Fulfilling its commitment to eradicate terrorism will not be easy, however. Terrorists have perfected their ability not only to withstand urban conflict, as in Somalia and even more vividly in Iraq, but also to stand up to the weapons of war radical Muslims believe the infidels have used against them. Often they have been actively assisted by states who find non-state actors like Al Qaeda useful outlets for pursuing their own interests.

Although radical Islamic fundamentalists are widely identified with today's international terrorist activities, a broader conception of terrorism would also incorporate government activities such as those of Serbia, which during much of the 1990s supported mass rapes and killings in Bosnia, Herzegovina, and its own province of Kosovo. "It's a war," explained one State Department official as the conflict in the Balkans raged. He added, however, that the "issue of definition is an extremely thorny and difficult one."

Thorny definitional issues aside, the spread of ethnonational movements in the past decade encouraged the weak to visit terrorism on the strong. Today it is evident that many people do not pledge their primary allegiance to the state and the government that rules them. Instead, they regard themselves as members of their nationality first and their own state second. That belief encourages the cultural, religious, ethnic, and linguistic communities within today's politico-territorial states to express their own individuality.

Even the United States—a "melting pot" of immigrants from around the world—today finds multiculturalism a growing challenge to the dominant political culture (see Chapter 8) and a large influx of illegal immigrants a challenge to its own immigration laws. Violence has sometimes accompanied expressions of multiculturalism within the United States. Often it invites expression abroad through terrorism, both within and across states.

Finally, we must acknowledge that criminal organizations also pose new dangers to the established state system and the equilibrium traditional IGOs and NGOs provide. No accounting of Russia's efforts to establish democratic capitalism during the 1990s would be complete without an understanding of how deeply ingrained criminal elements have become in its politics, economics, and society—and the consequences extend beyond Russian borders. American banks, for example, have sometimes been alleged to have unwittingly become agents of money laundering by Russian criminal elements.

On another front, illicit trading in diamonds has underlain much of the violence in Africa. Elsewhere drugs provoke conflict. Poppies used to make opium have made a comeback in Afghanistan since the United States crushed the Taliban regime in 2001.

In Columbia, where cocoa leaves are refined to make cocaine, the United States for more than a decade has been involved in a *war against drugs* first proclaimed by the senior President Bush. It has been a costly war in which the United States has invested billions in its effort to stanch the flow of drugs into the United States by targeting with military means the activities of Columbian drug lords. The second Bush administration has questioned the wisdom of dealing with the *supply side* of drug trafficking (stopping drugs at the source, which was the war-against-drugs policy launched in the first Bush presidency), and instead to focused more attention on the *demand side* of the problem, meaning drug consumption in the United States.

There is no obvious answer to coping with drugs or other criminal activities. Globalization is part of the reason. By opening states' borders to an increasingly free flow of capital and goods, all states are vulnerable to those elements in society who would take illegal advantage of others. The United States is especially vulnerable, since freedom—political and economic, the cornerstone of American society—means its open borders are easily penetrated by others. Thus it should come as no surprise that following NAFTA's launch in 1993, which sought to create a free-trade zone across the North American continent, the flow of drugs through Mexico northward also rose dramatically (Andreas 1996).[12] Meanwhile, the widespread use of computers, the Internet, and other information technologies promises that *cyberterrorism* will become an increasingly dangerous challenge.

AMERICAN FOREIGN POLICY AT THE ONSET OF A NEW CENTURY

The years immediately following World War II were filled with tremendous opportunity for the United States as it actively embraced global responsibilities and pursued an assertive foreign policy that shaped a world compatible with the American vision. Thus the character of the international political system in the decades following World War II was largely a product of the policies and programs the United States engineered and the choices it made in responding to the challenges posed by others.

The role that the United States will play in shaping the world of the twenty-first century is uncertain. As the world's sole superpower, the United States has a greater capacity than anyone to create a world order that once more is compatible with its interests and values. Paradoxically, however, the United States today also finds itself burdened with responsibilities. The institutions it promoted and once supported without reservation are sometimes the unwelcome symbols of an inhospitable and intractable international system. The emerging configuration of world power portends new challenges that already have proved more vexing than managing the Soviet menace. Many of those outside the circle of great powers remain skeptical of the impact of American power on their own interests and values, even as developments within those societies spill onto the larger global stage. And many within the circle of great powers now fear American capabilities and intentions, even as they find they must deal with an economic and military gorilla whose shadow blankets them all. Meanwhile, the relentless march of globalization and the insidious threat of terrorism pose new challenges to even a hegemonic power's ability to manage the forces that define its security and well-being.

Historically the United States has responded to external challenges either with detachment or through assertiveness. Today we live in a transitional period—one in which the old world order has passed but the shape of the new world order is not yet in full view. The events of 9/11 and the convictions of the policy makers who came to power with George W. Bush propelled a period of unilateral assertiveness. But already the Iraq war, widespread criticism from abroad and mounting concern at home have caused introspection. Whether detachment or assertiveness will characterize the U.S. response to the challenges of the second American century must still be decided.

KEY TERMS

absolute poverty
American Century
biodiversity
bipolarity
bipolycentrism
Brezhnev Doctrine
dependency theory
desertification
digital divide
environmental refugees
failed states
Global North

Global South
global warming
intergovernmental
  organizations
  (IGOs)
international regimes
Kyoto Protocol to the
  United Nations
  Framework
  Convention on
  Climate Change
long peace

multilevel interdependence
dence
multinational corporations (MNCs)
multipolarity
Newly Independent
  States (NIS)
Newly Industrialized
  Economies (NIEs)
nonalignment
nongovernmental organizations (NGOs)

security dilemmas
structural realism
sustainable
  development
Third World
uni-multipolar system
unipolarity
unipolar moment
Washington Consensus

SUGGESTED READINGS

Barnet, Richard J., and John Cavanagh. *Global Dreams: Imperial Corporations and the New World Order.* New York. Simon & Schuster, 1994.

Haass, Richard N. *The Opportunity: America's Moment to Alter History's Course.* New York: PublicAffairs Books, 2005.

Homer-Dixon, Thomas. "The Rise of Complex Terrorism," *Foreign Policy* (January/February 2002): 54–59.

Huntington, Samuel P. *The Clash of Civilizations and the Remaking of World Order.* New York: Simon & Schuster, 1996.

Keohane, Robert O., and Joseph S. Nye, Jr., *Power and Interdependence: World Politics in Transition*, 3rd ed. Glenview, IL: Longman, 2000.

Kupchan, Charles A. "After Pax Americana: Benign Power, Regional Integration, and the Sources of Stable Multipolarity," *International Security* 23 (Fall 1998): 40–96.

Neuman, Stephanie G.,ed., *International Relations Theory and the Third World.* New York: St. Martin's, 1998.

Lomborg, Bjørn. *The Skeptical Environmentalist: Measuring the Real State of the World.* New York: Cambridge University Press, 2001.

Pastor, Robert A.,ed., *A Century's Journey: How the Great Powers Shape the World.* New York: Basic Books, 1999.

Sen, Amartya. *Development as Freedom.* New York: Knopf, 1999.

"The South in the New World (Dis)Order," *Third World Quarterly*, Special Issue, 15 (March (1994): 1–176.

Walt, Stephen M. *Taming American Power: The Global Response to U.S. Primacy.* New York: Norton, 2005.

Waltz, Kenneth. "Structural Realism after the Cold War," *International Security* 25 (Summer 2000): 5–41.

Wattenberg, Ben J. *Fewer: How the New Demography of Depopulation Will Shape Our Future.* Chicago: Ivan R. Dee Publisher, 2004.

NOTES

1. The Second World in this scheme comprised the Soviet Union, its allies, and other communist societies. For them, a commitment to planned economic practices, rather than reliance on market forces to determine the supply of and demand for goods and services, was the distinguishing characteristic.

2. According to the Organisation for Economic Co-operation and Development, purchasing power parities (PPPs) "are currency conversion rates that both convert to a common currency and equalise the purchasing power of different currencies. In other words, they eliminate the differences in price levels between countries in the process of conversion" (www.oecd.org, accessed 11/27/06).

3. See Eberstadt (1991), Foster (1989), and Wattenberg (1989, 2004) for discussions of the security implications of demographic trends. Garrett (2005) addresses the security implications of the HIV/AIDS pandemic.

4. See Prugh and Assadourian (2003) for an assessment of the meaning of sustainability.

5. See the essays in the Spring 2005 issue of *Resources,* published by Resources for the Future, for commentaries on a post-Kyoto world, including the U.S. role.

6. As in the advanced industrial societies of the North, military expenditures by Global South countries are sometimes justified on grounds that they produce economic benefits. As the *World Development Report 1988* points out, "Military spending can have positive spinoff effects, such as fostering technological innovation, training personnel who later move into civilian work, providing employment opportunities, building domestic institutions, stimulating a country's tax effort, and promoting more intensive use of existing resources. Furthermore, military industries can be a focus of industrialization activities." However, the same report observes that their positive effects often are counterbalanced by long-term costs.

7. As of 2006, NATO included Belgium, Bulgaria, Canada, Czech Republic, Denmark, Estonia, France, Germany, Greece, Hungary, Iceland, Italy, Latvia, Lithuania, Luxembourg, the Netherlands, Norway, Poland, Portugal, Romania, Slovakia, Slovenia, Spain, Turkey, the United Kingdom, and the United States.

8. As of 2006, the EU included Austria, Belgium, Cyprus, the Czech Republic, Denmark, Estonia, Finland, France, Germany, Greece, Hungary, Ireland, Italy, Latvia, Lithuania, Luxembourg, Malta, the Netherlands, Poland, Portugal, Slovakia, Slovenia, Spain, Sweden, and the United Kingdom. Bulgaria and Romania are in the process of accession to the EU, possibly by 2007 or 2008. Candidate countries seeking membership include Croatia, the Former Yugoslav Republic of Macedonia, and Turkey.

9. Much of the world's antipathy toward the United States grows out of its support for Israel in the United Nations. Since 1982, for example, "the US has vetoed 32 Security Council resolutions critical of Israel, more than the total number of vetoes cast by all the other Security Council members" (Mearsheimer and Walt 2006).

10. Renegotiation of peacekeeping assessments was part of a larger effort on reforms of UN peacekeeping operations known as the Brahimi Report, named after Algerian Ambassador Lakhdar Brahimi, who chaired the panel. The panel conducted a rigorous review of all aspects of UN peacekeeping operations in an effort to make them more efficient and effective. The report was released in August 2000.

11. Funding for the UN continues to be a controversial matter, though in recent years the United States has met its current financial obligations while attempting to resolve amounts still in arrears.

12. Goods other than drugs are also often traded illicitly. Among them are ozone-depleting chemicals (chlorofluorocarbons, also known as CFCs) used in refrigerants, other products that have been banned due to their adverse effects on the atmosphere's protective ozone layer, and certain animal products, such as ivory from elephant tusks. See French and Mastny (2001).

7

The World Political Economy in Transition

Opportunities and Constraints in a Globalizing World

By transforming our hemisphere into a powerful free trade area,
we will promote democratic governance, human rights,
and economic liberty for everyone.
GEORGE W. BUSH, 2005

In the longer term, a weaker currency means that
the United States and its citizens are poorer.
MICHAEL MUSSA, FORMER CHIEF ECONOMIST,
INTERNATIONAL MONETARY FUND, 2005

"Propelled by a number of political, economic, and technological developments, the world has moved from the sharply divided international economy of the Cold War to an increasingly integrated global capitalist system. . . . Enormous increases in international trade, financial flows, and the activities of multinational corporations integrated more and more economies into the global economic system in a process now familiarly known as 'globalization.'" These concise yet prescient observations by political economist Robert Gilpin (2000) encapsulate the profound changes the world political economy has experienced in the past decade. We have moved beyond "interdependence." Today we live in a tightly integrated world political economy in which no state is immune from the economic challenges and changes other states face.

The United States sits center stage in the globalization process (compare Dunn 2001). As we discussed in Chapter 1, *globalization* refers to the rapid intensification and integration of state's economies not only in terms of markets but also ideas, information, and technology, which are having a profound impact on political, social, and cultural relations across borders. Symbolized by the Internet and fueled by the revolution in computers and telecommunications, its most visible manifestations are found in the global reach of Coca-Cola and McDonald's, of shopping centers that look the same whether they are in London or Hong Kong, Chicago or Rio de Janeiro, of rock music and designer jeans that know no political boundaries, contributing to the development of a global culture in which national identities are often submerged. As a result of these processes, the U.S. economy and American values have penetrated virtually every corner of the world. Some states and peoples accept this. Others are resentful. Regardless, the American "gorilla" is not easily dismissed.

The nation's gigantic gross national product (GNP), now in excess of $12 trillion, overshadows that of all others. American output is close to 30 percent of all of the world's production of goods and services—nearly six times its proportion of world population. The consequence of the enormous size of the U.S. economy is that little can be done in the United States without repercussions abroad. Interest rates in the United States influence interest rates abroad; domestic inflation is shared elsewhere; the general health of the U.S. economy is a worldwide concern. Once it could be said that when the United States sneezes the rest of the world catches pneumonia. That is no longer true. What remains true is that "when the United States sneezes the rest of the world catches cold" (Cooper 1988). The global importance of the American economy stems from the international position of the U.S. dollar and the United States' dominant position in the global network of trade relationships. Dollars are used by governments and private investors as reserves and for international trade and capital transactions. Today some countries (for example, Ecuador and Panama) even use the U.S. dollar as their own currency. In 2004, the United States exported nearly $1.2 trillion in merchandise to the rest of the world. And, remarkably,

American consumers bought over $1.8 trillion in goods from other countries. Little wonder that access to the U.S. market—the largest in the world—is so valued by other countries and is a common talking point in U.S. trade negotiations with other states.

The dominance of the United States in the world political economy was even greater in the years immediately following World War II than it is today. In 1947 the country accounted for 50 percent of the gross world product. It also was the world's preeminent manufacturing center and was unchallenged as its leading exporter. For at least the next twenty-five years the United States enjoyed a preponderance of power and influence so great as to warrant the label ***hegemon***.[1] Although there is no commonly accepted definition of hegemony, political scientist Joshua Goldstein (1988) suggests "hegemony essentially consists of being able to dictate, or at least dominate, the rules and arrangements by which international relations, political and economic, are conducted."

The atomic bomb symbolized the nation's awesome capabilities in the politico-military sphere, and remained largely unchallenged until the 1962 Cuban missile crisis. In the world political economy the United States derived its hegemonic status from a preponderance of material resources, of which four sets are especially important: control over markets, raw materials, and sources of capital, and a competitive advantage in the production of highly valued goods (Keohane 1984).

The enviable position the United States enjoyed in the early post–World War II years would inevitably change as Europe and Japan recovered from the ravages of war. By 1970 its proportion of gross world product had declined to about 25 percent. That would not have been especially worrisome had it not been accompanied by other developments. Although the U.S. proportion of gross world product stabilized, its share of both old manufactures ("sunset industries"), such as steel and automobiles, and new manufactures ("sunrise industries"), such as microelectronics and computers, continued to decline. Moreover, labor productivity in other countries often exceeded that in the

United States, where personal savings rates and levels of educational achievement also fell short of others' achievements. The United States' share of international financial reserves declined precipitously. And its dependence on foreign energy sources, first evident in the early 1970s, continued unabated for decades. Thus in all the areas essential to hegemony—control over raw materials, capital, and markets, and competitive advantages in production—American preponderance waned.

In this chapter, we examine the role the United States has played in building and maintaining the Liberal International Economic Order the Western industrial states created during and following World War II and have sought to maintain since. We also discuss the special responsibilities the United States exercises in the monetary and trade systems and how its changing power position has both affected and been affected by changes in the world political economy.

AMERICA'S HEGEMONIC ROLE IN THE LIBERAL INTERNATIONAL ECONOMIC ORDER: AN OVERVIEW

In 1944, the United States and its wartime allies met in the resort community of Bretton Woods, New Hampshire, to shape a new international economic structure. The lessons they drew from the Great Depression of the 1930s influenced their deliberations even as they continued their military contest with the Axis powers. The main lesson was that the United States could not safely isolate itself from world affairs as it had after World War I. Recognizing that, the United States now actively led in the creation of the rules and institutions that were to govern post–World War II economic relations. The *Liberal International Economic Order (LIEO)* was the product. The Bretton Woods system, as the LIEO is commonly called, promised to reduce barriers to the free flow of trade and capital, thus

promoting today's tightly intertwined world political economy.

The postwar Liberal International Economic Order rested on three political bases: "the concentration of power in a small number of states, the existence of a cluster of important interests shared by those states, and the presence of a dominant power willing and able to assume a leadership role" (Spero 1990). Economic power was concentrated in the developed countries of Western Europe and North America. Neither Japan nor the Third World (today's Global South) posed an effective challenge to Western dominance, and the participation of the then-communist states of Eastern Europe and the Soviet Union in the international economy was limited. The concentration of power restricted the number of states whose agreement was necessary to make the system operate effectively.

The shared interests among these states that facilitated the operation of the system included a preference for an open economic system—one based on free trade—combined with a commitment to limited government intervention, if this proved necessary. Hence the term liberal economic order (see also Gilpin 1987).

The onset of the Cold War was a powerful force cementing Western cohesion on economic issues. Faced with a common external enemy, the Western states thought economic cooperation as necessary not only for prosperity but also for security. The perception contributed to a willingness to share economic burdens. It also was an important catalyst for the assumption of leadership by only one state—the United States—and for the acceptance of that leadership role by others (see also Ikenberry 1989).

Economist Charles Kindleberger (1973) articulated the importance of leadership in maintaining a viable international economy. Kindleberger was among the first to theorize about the order and stability that preponderant powers provide as he sought to explain the Great Depression of the 1930s. He concluded that "the international economic and monetary system needs leadership, a country which is prepared, consciously or unconsciously, . . . to set standards of conduct for other countries; and to seek to get others to follow them, to take on an undue share of the burdens of the system, and in particular to take on its support in adversity." Britain played this role from the Congress of Vienna in 1815 until the outbreak of World War I in 1914; the United States assumed the British mantle in the decades immediately following World War II. In the interwar years, however, Britain was unable to play the role of leader. And the United States, although capable of leadership, was unwilling to exercise it. The vacuum, Kindleberger concluded, was a principal cause of the national and international economic traumas of the 1930s.

Hegemonic Stability Theory

Kindleberger's insights are widely regarded as a cornerstone of *hegemonic stability theory*. This theory contrasts sharply with political realism, which sees order and stability in the otherwise anarchical international political system as the product of power balances designed to thwart the aspirations of dominance-seeking states. Hegemonic stability theory focuses on the role that the preponderant power of only one state—the hegemon—plays in stabilizing the system. It also captures the special roles and responsibilities of the major economic powers in a commercial order based on market forces.

From their vantage points as preponderant powers, hegemons may range from benevolent (most interested in general benefits for all) to coercive (more exploitative and self-interested). Either type is able to promote rules for the system as a whole. In general, capitalist hegemons, like Britain in the nineteenth century and the United States in the twentieth century, prefer open (free market) systems because their comparatively greater control of technology, capital, and raw materials gives them more opportunities to profit from a system free of nonmarket restraints. But capitalist hegemons also have special responsibilities. They must make sure that countries facing balance-of-payments deficits can find the credits necessary to finance their deficits and otherwise lubricate the world political

economy. If the most powerful states cannot do this, they themselves are likely to move toward more closed (protected or regulated) domestic economies, which may undermine the open (liberal) system otherwise advantageous to them. Hence, those most able both to benefit from and influence the system also have the greatest responsibility to ensure its effective operation.

As hegemons exercise their responsibilities, they confer benefits known as public or ***collective goods.*** Collective goods are benefits everyone shares, as they cannot be excluded on a selective basis. National security is a collective good that governments provide all their citizens, regardless of the resources that individuals contribute through taxation. In international politics, "security, monetary stability, and an open international economy, with relatively free and predictable ability to move goods, services, and capital are all seen as desirable public goods.... More generally, international economic order is to be preferred to disorder" (Gill and Law 1988). States (like individuals) who enjoy the benefits of collective goods but pay little or nothing for them are *free riders.* Hegemons typically tolerate free riders, partly because the benefits they provide encourage other states to accept their dictates; thus both gain something.

All states worry about their *absolute power,* but hegemonic powers (especially benevolent ones) typically exhibit less concern about their *relative power* position than others. That is, they are less likely than others to "worry that a decrease in their power capabilities relative to those of other nation-states will compromise their political autonomy, expose them to the influence attempts of others, or lessen their ability to prevail in political disputes with allies and adversaries" (Mastanduno 1991). And they are less likely to behave defensively on international economic policy issues compared with an aspiring hegemon or with those that feel their relative power position deteriorating—hence hegemons' greater willingness to tolerate free riders. As a hegemon's preponderance erodes, however, its behavior on trade and monetary issues can be expected to change. Arguably this happened with the

United States after the Cold War, explaining its growing unwillingness to tolerate free-riding by its allies in the absence of the glue that earlier cemented them together in a common, anticommunist, anti-Soviet cause (Mastanduno 1991).

Beyond Hegemony

Why does a hegemon's power decline? Is erosion inevitable, or is it the product of lack of foresight and ill-conceived policies at home and abroad? A variety of answers have been offered. All suggest that what happens at home and abroad are tightly interconnected.

Growing concern about the United States' ability to continue its leadership role in international politics received nationwide attention with the 1987 publication of historian Paul Kennedy's treatise, *The Rise and Fall of the Great Powers,* in which he wrote:

> Although the United States is at present still in a class of its own economically and perhaps even militarily, it cannot avoid confronting the two great tests which challenge the longevity of every major power that occupies the "number one" position in international affairs: whether it can preserve a reasonable balance between the nation's perceived defense requirements and the means it possesses to maintain those commitments; and whether . . . it can preserve the technological and economic bases of its power from relative erosion in the face of ever-shifting patterns of global production.
>
> *(Kennedy 1987, 514–515)*

The danger, which Kennedy called ***imperial overstretch,*** is similar to that faced by hegemonic powers in earlier periods—notably the Spanish at the turn of the seventeenth century and the British at the turn of the twentieth. "The United States now runs the risk," he warned, "that the sum total of [its] global interests and obligations is nowadays far larger than the country's power to defend them

all simultaneously." He reiterated that theme shortly after the United States and its coalition partners attacked Iraq in January 1991: "The theory of 'imperial overstretch' . . . rests upon a truism, that a power that wants to remain number one for generation after generation requires not just military capability, not just national will, but also a flourishing and efficient economic base, strong finances, and a healthy social fabric, for it is upon such foundations that the country's military strength rests in the long term" (Kennedy 1992). As the 1990s unfolded, Kennedy would eventually disavow some of his own arguments. Still, the claim of imperial overstretch is again more common in light of the current costly conflict in Iraq and the perceived failings of the federal government to deal with the aftermath of Hurricanes Katrina and Rita in 2005, the outsourcing of American jobs abroad, record deficit spending by the federal government, record levels of public and private debt, the record current account deficit, and the steep rise in the price of oil.

Conservative critics have always argued that imperial overstretch was a ruse designed to depreciate the defense spending initiatives of the Reagan administration necessary to win the Cold War or the military interventions and expansion of intelligence gathering operations needed to support George W. Bush's war on terrorism. Others have argued that while the U.S. current account deficit and levels of debt are alarming, they are nowhere near the level of impending disaster (Levey and Brown 2005). The relationship between the health of the economy and American foreign policy is not easily dismissed, however. Indeed, a variety of commentators from both sides of the political spectrum would weigh in on the "declinist" argument, all saying that if the United States collapsed into a second-rate power, it would likely be for domestic, not foreign reasons (see Krauthammer 1991; Luttwak 1993; Nunn and Domenici 1992).

Still, the foreign dimension cannot easily be dismissed. Can the United States compete with Europe, China, and Japan? Today the answer appears self-evident, as businesses and entrepreneurs have largely reengineered the U.S. economy with sophisticated technological advances, in turn producing dramatically increased productivity among American workers. Some, in fact, have spoken so glowingly about the "new economy" that they predicted the classical business cycles of the "old economy"—characterized by periods of prosperity and low unemployment followed inevitably by inflation, resulting in rising unemployment and depressed economic activity—were now confined to the ashbin of history (see, for example, Weber 1997). That now seems dubious despite the optimistic talk of a "second American Century."

Before the extended prosperity of the 1990s, others worried that the United States might not be able to compete with Europe, China, Japan, and others not just because of what happens at home but also because of the transnational processes that erode hegemonic power (see, for example, Thurow 1992). Success in maintaining an economic order based on free trade will itself eventually undermine the power of the preponderant state. "An open international economy facilitates the diffusion of the very leading-sector cluster and managerial technologies that constitute the hegemon's advantage. As its advantage erodes, the costs of maintaining collective goods that support an open economy begin to outweigh the benefits" (Schwartz 1994).

The growing cries for protection against foreign competition heard from domestic groups disadvantaged by free trade—voiced shrilly in the 1980s and again in Seattle, Quebec, and Washington, D.C., in the 1990s as political leaders talked of further expanding the liberal economic order—reflect persistent doubts about free trade, placing pressure on the preponderant power to close the open economic order from which it otherwise benefits.

Empirical evidence that supports the central tenets of hegemonic stability theory remains inconclusive (see Isaak 1995; Schwartz 1994). The theory has its critics. Still, as our discussion of the U.S. role in the management of the international monetary and trade systems will show, hegemonic stability theory provides important insight into the dynamics of America's opportunities and constraints in a rapidly globalizing world political economy.

AMERICA'S ROLE IN THE MANAGEMENT OF THE INTERNATIONAL MONETARY SYSTEM

The agreements crafted at Bretton Woods in 1944 sought to build a postwar international monetary system characterized by stability, predictability, and orderly growth.[2] The wartime allies created the *International Monetary Fund (IMF)* to assist states in dealing with such matters as maintaining stability in their financial inflows and outflows (their balance of payments) and exchange rates (the rate used by one state to exchange its currency for another's). More generally, the IMF sought to ensure international monetary cooperation and the expansion of trade—a role, among others, that it continues to play as one of the most influential international organizations created during and after World War II. The wartime allies meeting at Bretton Woods also created the *World Bank.* Its charge was to assist in postwar reconstruction and development by facilitating the transnational flow of investment capital. Today, it is a principal means used to channel multilateral development assistance to the Global South in an effort to reduce global poverty and improve living standards.

In the immediate postwar years, however, the IMF and the World Bank proved unable to manage postwar economic recovery. They were given too little authority and too few resources to cope with the enormous economic devastation that Europe and Japan suffered during the war. The United States, now both willing and able to lead, stepped into the breach.[3]

Hegemony Unchallenged

The dollar became the key to the role that the United States assumed as manager of the international monetary system. Backed by a vigorous and healthy economy, a fixed relationship between gold and the dollar (the value of an ounce of gold was set at $35), and a government commitment to exchange

Convertible dollar
gold to dollars

gold for dollars at any time—known as ***dollar convertibility***—the dollar became "as good as gold." In fact, it was better than gold for other countries to use to manage their balance-of-payments and savings accounts. Dollars, unlike gold, earned interest, incurred no storage or insurance costs, and were in demand elsewhere, where they were needed to buy goods necessary for postwar reconstruction. Thus the postwar economic system was not simply a modified gold standard system: it was a dollar-based system. *Gold-based ⇒ Dollar-based*

Bretton Woods obligated each country to maintain the value of its own national currency in relation to the U.S. dollar (and through it to all others) within the confines of the mutually agreed exchange rate. Thus Bretton Woods was a ***fixed exchange rate system.*** In such a monetary system, governments maintain the value of their currencies at a fixed rate in relation to the currencies of other states. Governments in turn are required to intervene in the monetary market to preserve the value of their own currency by buying or selling others' currency.

Because the dollar was universally accepted, it became the vehicle for system preservation. Central banks in other countries either bought or sold U.S. dollars to raise or depress the value of their own currencies. Their purpose was to stabilize and render predictable the value of the monies needed to conduct international financial transactions.

A central problem of the immediate postwar years was how to get dollars into the hands of those who needed them most. One vehicle was the Marshall Plan, which provided Western European states with $17 billion in assistance to buy the U.S. goods necessary to rebuild their war-torn economies. The United States also encouraged deficits in its own balance of payments as a way of providing international liquidity (reserve assets used to settle international accounts) in the form of dollars.

In addition to providing liquidity, the United States assumed a disproportionate share of the burden of rejuvenating Western Europe and Japan by supporting various forms of trade competitiveness and condoning discrimination against the dollar. It willingly incurred these short-run costs because the growth that they sought to stimulate in Europe and

Japan was expected eventually to provide widening markets for U.S. exports.[4] The perceived political benefits of strengthening the Western world against the threat of communism helped to rationalize acceptance of these economic costs. In short, the United States purposely tolerated free-riding by others. Everyone benefited in this encouraging environment. Europe and Japan recovered from the war and eventually prospered. The U.S. economy also prospered, as the outflow of U.S. dollars encouraged others to buy goods and services from the United States (Spero and Hart 1997). Furthermore, the dollar's top currency role facilitated the ability of the United States to pursue a globalist foreign policy. Business interests could readily expand abroad because U.S. foreign investments were often considered desirable, and American tourists could spend their dollars with few restrictions. In effect, the United States operated as the world's banker. Other countries had to balance their financial inflows and outflows. In contrast, the United States enjoyed the advantages of operating internationally without the constraints of limited finances. Through the ubiquitous dollar, the United States came to exert considerable influence on the political and economic affairs of most other nations (Kunz 1997).

By the late 1950s, concern mounted about the long-term viability of an international monetary system based on the dollar (see Triffin 1978–1979). Analysts worried about the ability of such a system to provide the world with the monetary reserves necessary to ensure continuing economic growth. They also feared that the number of foreign-held dollars would eventually overwhelm the American promise to convert them into gold on demand, undermining the confidence others had in the soundness of the dollar and the U.S. economy. In a sense, then, the dependence of the Bretton Woods system on the United States contained the seeds of its own destruction.

Hegemony under Stress

Too few dollars (lack of liquidity) was the problem in the immediate postwar years. Too many dollars became the problem in the 1960s, which led to pressure on the value of the dollar and to trade deficits. Eventually, American leaders took action to shift some of the costs of maintaining the international monetary system onto other industrialized countries in Europe and Asia.

Beginning in the 1960s, extensive American military activities (including the war in Vietnam), foreign economic and military aid, and massive private investments produced increasing balance-of-payments deficits. Although encouraged earlier, the deficits were now out of control. Furthermore, U.S. gold holdings fell precipitously relative to the growing number of foreign-held dollars, undermining the ability of the United States to guarantee dollar convertibility. In these circumstances, others lost confidence in the dollar, becoming less willing to hold it as a reserve currency for fear that the United States might devalue it. France, under the leadership of Charles de Gaulle, went so far as to insist on exchanging dollars for gold—although arguably for reasons related as much to French nationalism as to the viability of the U.S. economy.

Along with the glut of dollars, the increasing monetary interdependence of the world's industrial economies led to massive transnational movements of capital. The internationalization of banking, the internationalization of production via multinational corporations, and the development of currency markets outside direct state control all accelerated this interconnectedness—progenitors of the process we now call "globalization" (Keohane and Nye 2000). An increasingly complex relationship between the economic policies engineered in one country and their effects on another resulted.

Changes in the world political economy also helped to undermine the Bretton Woods system. By the 1960s, the European and Japanese recoveries from World War II were complete, symbolized by their currencies' return to convertibility. Recovery meant that America's monetary dominance and the dollar's privileged position were increasingly unacceptable politically, while the return of convertibility meant that alternatives to the dollar (such as the German mark and Japanese yen) as a medium of savings and exchange were now available. The United States nonetheless continued to exercise a

disproportionate influence over these other states, even while it was unreceptive to their criticisms of its foreign economic and national security policies (such as the war in Vietnam).

From its position as the preponderant state, the United States came to see its own economic health and that of the world political economy as one and the same. In the monetary regime in particular, American leaders treasured the dollar's status as the top currency and interpreted attacks on it as attacks on international economic stability. That view clearly reflected the interests and prerogatives of a hegemon. It did not reflect the reality of a world political economy in transition: "The fundamental contradiction was that the United States had created an international monetary order that worked only when American political and economic dominance in the capitalist world was absolute. . . . With the fading of the absolute dominance, the international monetary order began to crumble" (Block 1977).

The United States sought to stave off challenges to its leadership role, but its own deteriorating economic situation made that increasingly difficult. Mounting inflation—caused in part by the unwillingness of the Johnson administration to raise taxes to pay either for the Vietnam War or the Great Society at home—was particularly troublesome. As long as the value of others' currencies relative to the dollar remained fixed, the rising cost of goods produced in the United States reduced their relative competitiveness overseas.

In 1971 for the first time in the twentieth century, the United States actually suffered a modest (extraordinarily modest by today's standards) trade deficit (of $2 billion), which worsened the next year. Predictably, demands grew from industrial, labor, and agricultural interests for protectionist trade measures designed to insulate them from foreign economic competition. Policy makers, correctly or not, laid partial blame for the trade deficit at the doorstep of major U.S. trading partners. The United States now sought aggressively to shore up its sagging position in the world political economy. In 1971, President Nixon abruptly announced that the United States would no longer exchange dollars for gold. He also imposed a surcharge on imports into the United States as part of a strategy designed to force a realignment of others' currency exchange rates. These startling and unexpected decisions—which came as a shock to the other Western industrial countries, who had not been consulted—marked the end of the Bretton Woods regime.

With the price of gold no longer fixed and dollar convertibility no longer guaranteed, the Bretton Woods system gave way to a system of *free-floating exchange rates*. Market forces rather than government intervention were now expected to determine currency values. The theory underlying the system is that a country experiencing adverse economic conditions will see the value of its currency in the marketplace decline in response to the choices of traders, bankers, and businesspeople. This will make its exports cheaper and its imports more expensive, which in turn will pull the value of its currency back toward equilibrium—all without the need for central bankers to support their currencies. In this way it was hoped that the politically humiliating devaluations of the past could be avoided. However, policy makers did not foresee that the new system would introduce an unparalleled degree of uncertainty and unpredictability into international monetary affairs.

Hegemony in Decline

Hegemonic stability theory says that international economic stability is a collective good preponderant powers provide. As a hegemon's power wanes—as arguably the relative power of the United States did in the 1970s and 1980s—economic instability should follow. It did: two *oil shocks* induced by the Organization of Petroleum Exporting Countries (OPEC) and the subsequent debt crisis faced by many Global South countries and others created a new sense of apprehension and concern about the viability of the existing international economic order. The United States—no longer able, or even willing, unilaterally to pay the costs of monetary stability—struggled to respond to the challenges.

Coping with the OPEC Decade The first oil shock came in 1973–1974, shortly after the Yom

Kippur War in the Middle East, when the price of oil increased fourfold. The second occurred in 1979–1980 in the wake of the revolution in Iran and resulted in an even more dramatic jump in the world price of oil. The impact of the two oil shocks on the United States, the world's largest energy consumer, was especially pronounced—all the more so as each coincided with a decline in domestic energy production and a rise in consumption.

A dramatic increase in U.S. dependence on foreign sources of energy to fuel its advanced industrial economy and a sharp rise in the overall cost of U.S. imports resulted. As dollars flowed abroad to purchase energy resources (a record $40 billion in 1977 and $74 billion in 1980), U.S. foreign indebtedness, also known as "dollar overhang," grew enormously and became "undoubtedly the biggest factor in triggering the worst global inflation in history" (Triffin 1978–1979). Others now worried about the dollar's value—which augmented its marked decline on foreign exchange markets in the late 1970s and early 1980s, as illustrated in Figure 7.1.

Global economic recession followed each oil shock. Ironically, however, inflation persisted. *Stagflation*—a term coined to describe a stagnant economy accompanied by rising unemployment and high inflation—entered the lexicon of policy discourse. Moreover, the changing fortunes of the dollar in the early post–Bretton Woods monetary system reflected in part the way the leading industrial powers chose to cope with the two oil-related recessions. In response to the first, they relied on fiscal and monetary adjustments to stimulate economic recovery and to avoid unemployment levels deemed politically unacceptable. In response to the second, which proved to be the longest and most severe economic downturn since the Great Depression of the 1930s, they shifted their efforts to controlling inflation through strict monetarist policies (that is, policies designed to reduce the money supply in the economy in order to control inflation). Large fiscal deficits and sharply higher interest rates resulted. Both were particularly apparent in the United States. The other industrial states also experienced higher levels of unemployment than they previously had been willing to

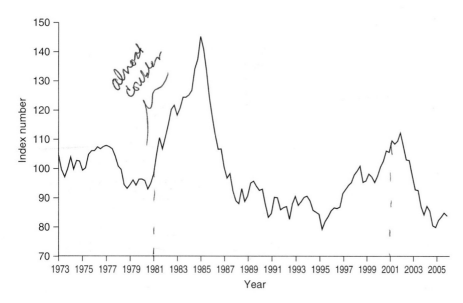

FIGURE 7.1 The Value of the Dollar, 1973–2006 (March 1973 = 100)

NOTE: The data are the *Major Currencies Index*. It is a weighted average of the foreign exchange values of the U.S. dollar against a subset of currencies in the broad index that circulate widely outside the country of issue. The weights are derived from those in the broad index. The *Broad Currencies Index* is a weighted average of the foreign exchange values of the U.S. dollar against the currencies of a large group of major U.S. trading partners. The index weights, which change over time, are derived from U.S. export shares and from U.S. and foreign import shares. For details, see Michael P. Leahy, "New Summary Measures of the Foreign Exchange Value of the Dollar," *Federal Reserve Bulletin* 84 (October 1998): 811–818.

SOURCE: www.federalreserve.gov/releases/H10/Summary/.

tolerate. World inflation already was on the rise prior to the first oil shock and may have prompted OPEC's action, but rising oil prices accentuated inflationary pressures.

The Debt Crisis   By the mid-1980s, many Global South countries and others owed enormous debts to Western banks and governments. Because these debts were often denominated in dollars and the interest rates charged on them tied to rates in the lending countries, rising interest rates in the United States and elsewhere caused their debt obligations to ratchet upward, with devastating results. A "debt crisis" soon followed, leading to what effectively became the "debt decade" (Nowzad 1990).

The specific event that triggered the debt crisis was the threat in 1982 that Mexico would default on its loans. Like Mexico, others with the largest debts, including Poland, Argentina, and Brazil, required

special treatment to keep them from going into default when they announced they did not have the cash needed to pay their creditors. Their plight was caused by heavy private and public borrowing during the 1970s, which caused private loans and investments and public loans at (nonconcessional) market rates to become more important than public foreign aid for all but the poorest of countries (Burki 1983).

The first oil shock gave impetus to the "privatization" of Global South capital flows. As dollars flowed from oil consumers in the West to oil producers in the Middle East and elsewhere, the latter—unable to invest all of their newfound wealth at home—"recycled" their petrodollars by investing in the industrial states, who were themselves the largest consumers of oil. In the process the funds available to private banks for lending increased substantially (see Spiro 1999).

Many of the developing states who were not oil exporters became the willing consumers of the private banks' investment funds. The fourfold rise in oil prices induced by the OPEC cartel hit these states particularly hard. To pay for the sharply increased cost of oil along with their other imports, many chose to borrow from abroad to sustain their economic growth and pay for needed imports. Private banks were willing lenders, as they believed *sovereign risk*—the risk that governments might default—was virtually nonexistent, while the returns on their investments in the Global South were higher than in the industrial world. For several reasons, however, the debtor states found repayment of their loans increasingly difficult. Rising interest rates were the most important factor. Sovereign risk suddenly became an ominous reality.

The IMF assumed a leadership role in securing debt relief for many debtor countries, thus keeping them from defaulting on their loans, but it did so at the cost of imposing strict conditions for domestic reform on individual debtors. Included were programs designed to curb inflation, limit imports, restrict public spending, expose protected industries, and the like. It also typically urged debtors to increase their exports, meaning it sought an export-led adjustment to the debt problem.

The IMF austerity program—vigorously pushed with strong U.S. backing until 1985—could claim considerable success from a strictly financial viewpoint (see Amuzegar 1987), but its domestic burdens and political costs simply proved overwhelming (Sachs 1989). Analysts blamed *IMF conditionality*—loans tied to the adoption of particular policies designed to resolve a country's balance of payments difficulties and promote long-term economic growth—for the overthrow of the Sudanese government of President Jaafar Nimeri in 1985, for example (see Focus 7.1). Debt and related financial issues also inflamed domestic political conflict in many other heavily indebted countries, including Argentina, Brazil, Chile, Mexico, and Nigeria. All of this encouraged political leaders in the debtor countries to adopt a more defiant posture toward the predicament they faced (see the essays in Riley 1993).

In this emotionally charged atmosphere, the United States first adopted an arm's-length policy on the debt issue, refusing to perform the hegemon's

---

FOCUS 7.1   How the IMF Works

The International Monetary Fund (IMF) and the World Bank—known as the Bretton Woods institutions—were established in 1944. The purpose of the IMF was to promote international monetary cooperation, exchange rate stability, and the expansion of international trade by acting as a lender of last resort when a member country faced an economic crisis.

In principle, the IMF has a structure akin to a financial cooperative. A member country's contributions to the IMF (called "quotas") are based on its weight in the global economy. This weight also determines its voting power and borrowing capacity (called "drawings"). Quotas amount to an exchange of assets with little direct cost to taxpayers.

For instance, in the case of the United States, its contributions entitle it to an equal amount of U.S. claims on other currencies. That is, just as other countries can draw U.S. dollars from the IMF in times of need (such as pressures on the U.S. dollar), the United States can draw on their currencies (be it the Japanese yen or the German mark) for itself. In fact, the United States has drawn on the IMF on twenty-eight different occasions. . . . By approaching the IMF, a member country facing a financial crisis has access to the fund's resources and advice. As a country's drawings become larger relative to its quotas, it must meet more exacting standards or "conditionalities," which typically mean significant changes in economic policies to ensure that the country's domestic and external deficits are drastically lowered or even eliminated. Failure to meet those conditions results in suspension, renegotiation, or even cancellation of the program.

SOURCE: Devesh Kapur, "The IMF: A Cure or a Curse?" *Foreign Policy* 111 (Summer 1998): 116.

classic stabilizer role due to its ideological antipathy toward intervention in the marketplace (Grieve 1993). Eventually, however, it would offer different plans designed to defuse a financial crisis with potentially catastrophic global proportions. Still, in the mid-1990s it would again find it necessary to arrange with the IMF a financial bailout of the Mexican economy due to a currency crisis there. Later in the decade it would seek to stimulate its own economy as a way of coping with a series of roiling Asian currency crises that plunged as much as 40 percent of the world into recession, and which again required several multibillion dollar bailouts. Even today, more than two decades after the onset of the "debt crisis" of the early 1980s, debt relief remains a primary issue on the North-South global agenda.

Toward Macroeconomic Policy Coordination

The Reagan administration's initiatives in dealing with debt crisis marked an abrupt end to what had been its passive unilateralism—commonly referred to as "benign neglect"—toward international monetary and macroeconomic policy issues. Passive unilateralism now gave way to various manifestations of pluralistic cooperation (Bergsten 1988). The latter was especially evident in the 1985 Plaza Agreement for coping with the soaring dollar. American efforts thus began to stress more multilateral coordination to shore up the international monetary system, but largely failed in the face of often competing national interests as well as powerful domestic pressures.

Passive Unilateralism, 1981–1985   The increase in U.S. interest rates, which so burdened the Global South debtor countries in the early to mid-1980s, also contributed to the changing fortunes of the dollar (see Figure 7.1). Deficit spending by the federal government contributed to rising interest rates, as the United States itself now borrowed in capital markets to cover military and other expenditures. Beyond this, three other factors helped to restore faith in the dollar: renewed economic growth in the United States; a sharp reduction in inflation (both stimulated by a decline in oil prices caused by a global oil glut); and the perception that

the United States was a safe haven for financial investments in a world otherwise marked by political instability and violence. Foreign investors therefore rushed to acquire the dollars necessary to take advantage of profitable investment opportunities in the United States. This situation contrasted sharply with the 1970s, when the huge foreign indebtedness of the United States was a principal fear.

The appreciation of the dollar was a mixed blessing for the United States. It reduced the cost of imported oil (whose price first eased and then plummeted in 1986), but it increased the cost of U.S. exports to foreign buyers, thus reducing the competitiveness of American products in overseas markets. This reality meant the loss of tens of thousands of jobs in industries that produced for export. A series of record trade deficits followed—$160 billion in 1987 alone—as imports became relatively cheaper and hence more attractive to American consumers.

The federal budget deficit also reached record portions at this time, topping $200 billion annually. Simultaneously, the United States became a debtor nation for the first time in more than a half-century, as it moved in only five years from being the world's biggest creditor to being its largest debtor. The debt legacy would eventually constrain the government's policy choices in dealing with later economic downturns, as happened with the prolonged recession of 1990 to 1992. It also raised the prospect of a long-term decline in Americans' unusually high standard of living, as money spent tomorrow to pay today's bills would not be available to meet future problems or finance future growth. By 1991, interest payments on the national debt (the accumulation of past deficits) constituted 14 percent of all federal outlays, the third largest category of expenditures (following entitlements and defense spending). Within a few years interest payments were projected to exceed defense spending (Nunn and Domenici 1992). Not until the economy turned around and the annual budget deficits reversed in the mid-to-late 1990s would Americans begin to actually pay down the long accumulating national debt.

In a normally functioning market, the combination of a strong dollar and severe trade imbalance would set in motion self-corrective processes that would return the dollar to its equilibrium value. Growing U.S. imports, for example—though beneficial to America's trade partners in generating jobs and thus stimulating their return to economic growth—should create upward pressure on the value of others' currencies. Conversely, a drop in American exports should ease the demand for dollars, thereby reducing the dollar's value in exchange markets. These mechanisms did not work, however, because of persistently high interest rates in the United States.

Pluralistic Cooperation, 1985–1988 Historically, the United States had been loath to intervene in the international marketplace to affect the value of the dollar. By 1985, however, the erosion of American trade competitiveness in overseas markets due to the overvalued dollar had become domestically unpalatable. In response, the *Group of Five (G-5)* (the United States, Britain, France, Japan, and West Germany) met secretly in the Plaza Hotel in New York and decided on a coordinated effort to bring down the dollar's value. The landmark agreement also committed the major economic powers to work with one another to manage exchange rates internationally and interest rates domestically. And it signaled the emergence of Japan as a full partner in international monetary management (Spero and Hart 1997), which led to the formation of the Group of Seven, commonly called the G-7 (the G-5 plus Canada and Italy).

When the Plaza agreement failed, the industrialized states sought other ways to manage their currencies, but the important goal of macroeconomic policy coordination remained unfulfilled (see Mead 1988–1989, 1989). The United States' inability to devise a politically acceptable budget deficit reduction strategy was a critical factor in its failure. Eventually, however, the chronic trade and budget deficits became overwhelming, helping to precipitate the dollar's long slide from the lofty heights it had achieved by mid-decade (see Figure 7.1).

The Failure of Pluralistic Cooperation, 1989–1993 After the George H. W. Bush administration assumed power in 1989, it showed little enthusiasm for multilateral venues for dealing with economic policy issues. Instead, it was content to permit the

dollar to fall to levels believed by some experts to have been below its actual purchasing power—a policy akin to the "benign neglect" of Reagan's first term.

Maintaining a weak dollar was designed to enhance the competitiveness of U.S. exports in overseas markets, but it also attracted renewed concern about economic fundamentals in the United States.[5] Simultaneously, U.S. dependence on foreign energy sources again grew to ominous proportions, contributing not only to the trade deficit but also to the nation's vulnerability to oil supply or price disruptions caused by some kind of crisis—which struck in August 1990 when Iraq invaded Kuwait. Ominously, perhaps, the value of the dollar in the international marketplace declined sharply in the early weeks of the Persian Gulf crisis. Normally a country viewed as a "safe haven" for investments during times of crisis will see the value of its currency appreciate. This had been the United States' typical role. In the Persian Gulf case, however, investors concluded that Europe and Japan were better bets. While the Bush administration practiced passive unilateralism toward the dollar, Germany's central bank—the Deutsche Bundesbank—maintained high interest rates in an aggressive effort to contain inflationary pressures generated by the cost of unifying the former East and West Germanys. Mimicking the effects on the dollar during Reagan's first term, the mark's value soared as investors now chose to hold marks rather than dollars; this further weakened a dollar already suffering from the effects of recession at home. Renewed fear about further growth in the already burgeoning domestic budget deficit caused the dollar to drop even further.

As in the monetary crises of the 1960s and 1970s, existing mechanisms of macroeconomic policy coordination proved ineffective. Even the G-7, which had begun to hold annual economic summits (and now includes Russia, making it the *Group of Eight or G-8*) proved inadequate "as a mechanism for synchronizing economic policy to exert leadership over the world economy" (Ikenberry 1993). Its failure (which continues) stemmed from "the inability of the major industrial states to make hard economic choices at home. Each government's emphasis on dealing with seemingly intractable domestic problems . . . [constrained] joint efforts to stimulate global economic growth or to manage monetary and trade relations, preventing G-7 governments from pursuing disciplined and synchronized fiscal and monetary policies" (Ikenberry 1993; see also Smyser 1993).

Hegemony Resurgent

By the end of the 1990s, world leaders would again be talking about new ways to manage the international monetary system. The currency crises of 1997 to 1998 were the principal catalysts, but, as before, macroeconomic policy coordination among the world's largest economic powers remained an elusive goal. For the United States, however, the 1990s became the longest period of sustained economic growth in its history. Still, the renewed strength of the American economy did not translate into a restoration of international economic stability, nor did it restore the American leadership of the 1950s and 1960s.

The Clinton Administration   Bill Clinton went to Washington determined to be the "economic president." Although verbally committed to a greater degree of multilateral policy making than the Bush team, the Clinton administration continued the policy of benign neglect toward the sagging dollar—this time as a mechanism of righting the trade imbalance between the United States and Japan. But there was no noticeable effect on U.S. trade with Japan—indeed, the deficit persisted despite several years in which the dollar was comparatively weak. Finally, in May 1994, the administration reversed course as it coordinated a massive, sixteen-country intervention into currency markets in an effort to prop up the sagging dollar. Additional interventions followed.

Although the Clinton administration abandoned its policy of benign neglect, its efforts to halt a further decline in the dollar fell short. The causes of the sagging dollar were baffling, as the U.S. economy was generally sound and growing, conditions that normally would cause the value of a currency to rise. Arguably, globalization was an underlying cause. The growing volume of world trade and the activities of currency speculators, who use sophisticated electronic means to carry out their transnational exchanges, became increasingly significant. By the 1990s, over $1.5 trillion in currency trading occurred each day. This exceeded the total value of foreign exchange held in countries' central banks (*New York Times,* 25 September 1992, 1; *Washington Post National Weekly Edition,* 1 March 1999, 7).

Some cited the continuing trade and government budget deficits as the causal factors. Others saw the Clinton administration's policies and performance as the primary culprit. As one senior Clinton adviser explained, "The value of the dollar on any given day is like a global referendum on all the policies of the Clinton administration combined. It is as though the world were having a huge discussion on the Internet, and the dollar's value is a snapshot of that discussion." Still others suggested that the problem lay not with the dollar but with the yen. What the Japanese called *endaka* (strong yen crisis) was, according to this reasoning, propelled by the imbalance of Japan's financial transactions with the rest of the world, leading to increased demand for the yen and hence its higher price.

Over the long term, states' economic health affects the value of their currencies. During the 1990s, the U.S. economy thrived, Japan's fell into a prolonged recession (see Gilpin 2000), and Europeans and others worried that the European Union's planned launch of a single European currency, the euro, would create uncertainty about the future—especially so since the German mark, Europe's top currency, would disappear.

Collectively, these forces contributed to a strong revival of the dollar. By the end of the decade it was priced at levels last seen in 1987 (see Figure 7.1). Now others' concern was not so much a weak dollar, but a strong dollar. Japan, for instance, would benefit from a strong dollar, because Japanese exporters could keep their prices low compared with American producers and thus compete for a greater share of the U.S. market. And, indeed, U.S. imports surged in the 1990s, as Americans consumed foreign-produced goods and services at breathtaking, record levels (over $1 trillion, in 1999, for example). Still, the Japanese worried that the soaring dollar would cause Japanese investors to invest not in Japan, which was seeking to stimulate its own economy with low interest rates, but in the United States, which promised much greater investment returns. European investors uncertain about the euro also looked once more to the United States as a safe investment haven. Again, foreign investments in the United States surged during the 1990s, especially in domestic stock markets, which experienced unparalleled capitalization growth.

Clinton's secretary of the treasury, Robert Rubin, unrelentingly supported the dollar as its value surged. "A strong dollar is in the interest of the United States," he said repeatedly. But domestically, not everyone agreed. As in the 1980s, a strong dollar hurts American firms that produce for export by making them less competitive. Thus it is not surprising that labor unions and other workers were visible in the antiglobalization protests at recent meetings of the IMF, World Bank, World Trade Organization, and the 2001 Summit of the Americas, where the second Bush administration hoped to launch a hemisphere-wide free trade zone.

American consumers, on the other hand, generally benefit from a strong dollar. Tourists get more value for their money when they travel abroad. At home, foreign-produced goods are cheaper, which in turn makes them attractive to consumers. Lower-priced imports also help to keep inflation low, as domestic producers are unable to increase prices.

So what is the "proper" value of the dollar? There is no clear-cut answer to that question. There are winners and losers domestically. And there are winners and losers in other countries.

George W. Bush Administration

Foreign economic policy received scant attention from the Bush presidency. Economist Jeffrey Garten (2005) puts it succinctly:

> For the last four years, global finance, trade, and development, and the cultiva-
tion of overseas relationships to advance U.S. interests in these areas, were not given the priority that they generally received in the preceding half-century. During the Cold War, lowering barriers to trade and investment, granting generous foreign aid, and strengthening international economic institutions—all in close cooperation with U.S. allies—were a central part of Washington's fight against communism. After the Soviet Union collapsed, the administrations of George H. W. Bush and Bill Clinton geared much of their foreign and domestic policy to enhancing U.S. competitiveness in global markets and to spreading U.S.-style capitalism abroad.
>
> *(Garten 2005, 37)*

The second Bush administration, however, initially foundered over its approach to global economic matters. But 9/11 clarified its views: global economics would definitely take a back seat to global politics, as the primacy of the war on terrorism and U.S. national security was evident in rhetoric and practice. "There has been little time, interest, or energy for anything else" (Garten 2005).

Reflecting a general pro-market orientation, the administration preferred not to take a stand on the "proper" value of the dollar. Yet, rhetorically and eventually practically speaking, it moved away from the "strong dollar" stand of the Clinton administration. Bush's first treasury secretary, Paul O'Neill, stated in February 2001 that "We are not pursuing, as often said, a policy of a strong dollar. In my opinion, a strong dollar is the result of a strong economy." When the dollar dropped as a result of his comments, the Treasury Department issued a clarification the next day: "The secretary supports a strong dollar. There is no change in policy." Federal Reserve Governor Ben Bernanke told the National Economists Club meeting in November 2002 that "the secretary of the treasury has expressed the view that the determination of the value of the U.S. dollar should be left to free market forces." O'Neill, to whom Bernanke was referring, was asked to resign by President Bush just a few weeks later. Yet

O'Neill's successor, John Snow, was able to suggest publicly in 2003 that a weaker dollar would help the United States retain manufacturing jobs—a particular worry for the Bush in the middle of a campaign. Fred Bergsten noted at the time that the "strong-dollar policy is dead and buried." Bergsten estimated that a 1 percent decline in the value of the dollar narrowed the trade gap by about $10 billion (Benjamin 2003). The Bush administration was now worried much more about the trade gap with China than Japan. Of course, a weaker dollar does not help the trade deficit with China (see Figure 7.3), since the yuan has been pegged to the dollar since 1994. Efforts to convince the Chinese to revalue the yuan have so far fallen largely on deaf ears, including those of President Hu on his 2006 visit to the United States. In 2005, the Chinese allowed the yuan to appreciate by a mere 2 percent against the dollar, when some economists have estimated that it is undervalued by 20 to 25 percent (though there is not universal agreement on this point—see Hughes 2005).

The Bush administration's policy on the dollar seemed to favor a market-driven determination of its value, which left the dollar near its weakest point in the past three decades (see Figure 7.1). Yet, a weak dollar does not seem to limit Americans' appetite for foreign products as the United States continues to run record trade deficits (see Figure 7.2). Cajoling the Chinese to appreciate the yuan to limit the size of the trade deficit with that country has not paid off substantially either.

Garten (2005) suggests that the Bush administration will likely quietly allow the dollar to depreciate 15 to 20 percent to make the current account deficit more sustainable. Factors including the uncertainty posed by the ongoing war in Iraq, record deficit spending and overall levels of federal government debt, and low to moderate economic growth are certainly unlikely to increase the value of the dollar either. In sum, the Bush administration's approach to monetary and fiscal policy looks like a return to "benign neglect," or perhaps just neglect, according to critics. Some even suggest that the United States itself will soon face a debt crisis that could lead to the collapse of the dollar, though it appears unlikely in the short run (Levey and Brown 2005).

Globalization Again

Alan Greenspan, former chair of the Federal Reserve System, remarked in testimony before Congress in the mid-1990s that the ability of the Federal Reserve System to prop up the dollar by buying it in foreign exchange markets "is extraordinarily limited and probably in a realistic sense non-existent." The internationalization of finance and the removal of barriers to transnational capital flows also have, in Greenspan's words, "[exposed] national economies to shocks from new and unexpected sources, with little if any lag." They came with a vengeance later in the 1990s, as the globalization of finance led to an era of "mad money" largely outside the control of governments (Strange 1998).

Global Financial Crises The susceptibility of states to global financial shocks became painfully obvious during exchange rate crises in Latin America, East Asia, and Russia at various times during the 1990s. These crises not only destabilized the economies of the immediately affected countries, but also sent shock waves throughout the entire world economy. Indeed, the crises that pummeled East Asia, Latin America, and Russia toward the end of the decade were often cited as posing the most serious challenge to global economic stability since the Great Depression of the 1930s. The utility of the international institutions created after World War II now also came under close scrutiny.

The Asian Financial Crisis began in Thailand, an attractive investment opportunity among the Asian Newly Industrializing Economies (NIEs). *New York Times* foreign economic correspondent Thomas L. Friedman describes what happened:

> On the morning of December 8, 1997, the government of Thailand announced that it was closing fifty-six of the country's fifty-eight top finance houses. Almost overnight, these private banks had been bankrupted by the crash of the Thai currency, the baht. The finance houses had borrowed heavily in U.S. dollars and lent those dollars out to Thai businesses for the

building of hotels, office blocks, luxury apartments, and factories. The finance houses all thought they were safe because the Thai government was committed to keeping the Thai baht at a fixed rate against the dollar. But when the government failed to do so, in the wake of massive global speculation against the baht—triggered by a daring awareness that the Thai economy was not a strong as previously believed—the Thai currency plummeted by thirty percent. This meant that businesses that had borrowed dollars had to come up with thirty percent more Thai baht to pay back each one dollar of loans. Many businesses couldn't pay the finance houses back, many finance houses couldn't repay their foreign lenders and the whole system went into gridlock, putting 20,000 white-collar employees out of work.

(Friedman 1999, ix; see also Lewis 1998)

These processes would soon be repeated elsewhere in Asia, then Latin America and Russia. In fact, the Asian Financial Crisis seems to fit a general model of the stages of development of a financial crisis: displacement, expansion, euphoria, distress, revulsion, crisis, and contagion (Kindleberger 1988; see also Gilpin 2000).

Displacement occurs when some asset becomes an object of speculation, thereby disrupting the equilibrium in the market for investments, creating a "boom." Expansion occurs when this boom is fed by increased liquidity (e.g., bank credit, margin buying), thereby forming the basis for a "bubble." As more and more investors are drawn to the expansion, euphoria takes over, leading to trading on the basis of the price of the asset alone, without regard to the underlying fundamental value of the asset. Distress sets in when investors begin to recognize the market is weak or that the limits of liquidity have been reached. Revulsion occurs when those privileged with information recognize that assets are overvalued and/or that liquidity has dried up. Insiders sell off their assets, often leading to the

crisis stage when the bubble bursts. Crisis may quickly spread through contagion to other markets through the highly interdependent financial and commodity markets. The financial crisis ends when asset prices fall to appropriate levels for their underlying value, trading is halted by some governmental authority, or a lender of last resort steps in to provide the necessary liquidity to ease the crisis into a soft landing.

With the support of the United States (which, as we noted earlier, reduced its own interest rates to stimulate economic recovery elsewhere), the IMF stepped forward to help the ailing economies in Asia and elsewhere—but with the expectation they would follow IMF advice on reforms that could prevent recurrence of the financial collapses. The IMF itself became the object of criticism for not having foreseen the impending debacle (see, for example, Kapur 1998).

Part of the controversy surrounding the IMF interventions concerns what is often described as the *moral hazard* problem (Kapstein 1999). The term refers to the willingness of private investors to make risky choices when investing in emerging markets based on their expectation that the IMF or someone else (the United States?) will bail them out if the countries in which they invest face economic instability or, worse, collapse. In short, if private investors are protected from failure by public authorities, they are likely to take higher risks (with other people's money) than would otherwise be warranted. In the end, the public (taxpayers) foots the bill for private investors' failed choices, who in effect bear none of the costs of failure.

Toward a New Financial Architecture? The Asian contagion and the criticism of the IMF that followed spurred widespread discussions among policy makers about how to create a new financial architecture. Policy makers recognized that the policy trade-offs posed by the "unholy trinity" of exchange rate policy, monetary policy, and capital mobility had serious consequences in the contemporary world (see Sobel 2005, 318–320). First posited by economists Robert Mundell and J. Marcus Fleming and, the unholy trinity recognizes the inability of states to maintain stable exchange rates, domestic autonomy in monetary policy, and capital mobility. According to the Mundell-Fleming thesis, governments can at most attain two of the three components of the trinity at any one time. For example, during the Asian Financial Crisis (and other financial crises to follow), currency speculators saw an incompatibility between government exchange rate policy and monetary policy. Capital mobility allowed these speculators to challenge government policy to either surrender exchange rate stability or monetary policy, or reassert capital controls. The IMF recommended allowing currencies to float, thereby preserving capital mobility and monetary policy autonomy, although states that adopted the IMF's advice generally faired poorly compared to those who limited capital mobility (Stiglitz 2003).

At the level of the states, many policy makers began to believe that they had little or no control over their domestic economies. In these states, policy makers and scholars began to debate the wisdom of dollarization. Dollarization proposes that other countries abandon their own currencies and officially adopt the U.S. dollar for all of their financial transactions. Some argue that by dollarizing, countries can avoid the unsettling swings in currency values that inevitably seem to plague weaker currencies (and weaker economies) (see, for example, Hausmann 1999). Others counter that this would make other states' economies subject to monetary policies in the United States dictated by the Federal Reserve Board not on the basis of their welfare, but on economic considerations in the United States. Hence "dollarization is an extreme solution to market instability, applicable in only the most extreme cases. The opposite approach—a flexible exchange rate between the national currency and the dollar—is much more prudent for most developing countries" (Sachs and Larrain 1999).

States that adopted official dollarization, such as Ecuador and El Salvador, or currency boards that pegged the national currency to the dollar, such as Argentina, have had mixed success. Argentina's currency board failed, leading the government to suspend payment on its $155 billion worth of

external debt and requiring a substantial IMF bailout. The general consensus in light of the Argentine case is that dollarization is not a substitute for deeper internal reforms generally recommended by the IMF. Dollarization for developing countries is certainly not a policy advocated by the United States or the IMF. Of course, pegging to the dollar is not the only option available to developing countries. Some states have even considered officially adopting the euro, launched by the EU in 2002, which has held its own against the U.S. dollar in currency markets.

At the international level, various proposals for reform were made, ranging from scuttling the IMF to improving private and public financial institutions in developing countries and other emerging markets, to simply generating better data on economic conditions. The last alternative is sometimes called "transparency" (see Florini 1998), which means providing open information akin to what financial analysts call "market efficiency" when they talk about access to information about publicly traded stocks and bonds.

Treasury secretary Robert Rubin became heavily involved in discussions about a new financial architecture and a leading spokesperson for transparency. Others were vocal in their antagonism toward the IMF. "Led by the unlikely team of former Secretary of State George Shultz, former treasury secretary William Simon, and former Citicorp chairman Walter Wriston, the IMF's critics called the organization 'ineffective, unnecessary, and obsolete.' They claim that 'it is the IMF's promise of massive intervention that has spurred a global meltdown of financial markets'" (Kapstein 1999).

In the end, changing the system proved too difficult.[6] Even Rubin conceded there are "no easy answers and no magic wands for overhauling financial institutions to make the world safe for capitalism." Paraphrasing a famous remark by Winston Churchill about democracy, Rubin also surmised that "the floating exchange rate system is the worst possible system, except for all others."

Although the IMF weathered the storm, it remains jostled in the rough sea that marks a world political economy in transition. Early in the George W. Bush administration, treasury secretary Paul O'Neill said the agency must do more to prevent, not simply respond to, crises. In his words, "I envision that the IMF, while sharpening its ability to respond to financial disruptions swiftly and appropriately, does so less frequently because it has succeeded in preventing crises from developing in the first place."

As its largest financial contributor, the United States is in a position to nudge the IMF toward reform. Indeed, responding to U.S. concerns, the IMF policy-setting committee declared in April 2001 that "strong and effective crisis preventions" should be a top priority of the fund. Although critical of the current practices of the organization, it is noteworthy that the Bush administration did not call for its abolition. Perhaps it is heeding the opinions of those who believe the role of the IMF cannot be minimized. In the words of one analyst, "Should the IMF fade into irrelevance, new institutions to stabilize the world economy will be needed" (Kapstein 1999).

While candidate George W. Bush campaigned against the financial bailouts of Mexico, the Asian countries, Brazil, and Russia that occurred during the Clinton administration, Bush has supported substantial bailouts in Argentina and Turkey during his tenure as president. The United States also firmly supported the Washington Consensus and the IMF's role in promoting it throughout the developing world, despite conflicting opinions on the effect of those types of policies implemented during the Asian Financial Crisis.

Similarly, many conservatives in Bush's party were strong critics of the World Bank's antipoverty mission developed under bank president James Wolfensohn's ten-year reign. Some critics even argued for the bank's abolition. Bush's selection of Paul Wolfowitz (former Deputy Secretary of Defense and one of the chief architects of the Bush Doctrine) as president of the World Bank in 2005 was thought to auger important changes in its mission, yet in office Wolfowitz largely endorsed the bank's antipoverty agenda (Einhorn 2006).

AMERICA'S ROLE IN THE MANAGEMENT OF THE INTERNATIONAL TRADE SYSTEM

The volume and value of international trade have increased exponentially during the past half century. Over this period states have vacillated between erecting barriers to trade designed to meet their domestic economic goals and opening their borders to realize the benefits that free trade promises.

Globalization is a product of the vanishing borders free trade implies, but it also has provoked increasingly vocal criticism in the United States and elsewhere among people and groups who believe the costs of globalization outweigh its benefits. Some states also worry, as during the Asian Financial Crisis, that globalization threatens their sovereign prerogatives (see Chapter 6). Thus, ironically, the very success of the LIEO and its open, multilateral trade regime has stimulated the backlash that encourages its closure

An Overview of the International Trade Regime

Management responsibilities in the postwar economic system as envisaged at Bretton Woods were to have been entrusted not only to the IMF and the World Bank but also to an International Trade Organization (ITO), whose purpose was to lower restrictions on trade and set rules of commerce. Policy planners hoped that these three organizations could assist in avoiding repetition of the international economic catastrophe that followed World War I.

In particular, the zero-sum, beggar-thy-neighbor policies associated with the intensely competitive economic nationalism of the interwar period were widely regarded as a major cause of the economic catastrophe of the 1930s, which ended in global warfare. (*Beggar-thy-neighbor policies* are efforts by one country to reduce its unemployment through currency devaluations, tariffs, quotas, export subsidies, and other strategies that enhance domestic welfare by promoting trade surpluses that can only be realized at another's expense.) Thus priority was assigned to trade liberalization, which means removing barriers to trade, particularly tariffs. Implementing this essential objective was to have been the ITO's charge, but it was stillborn, as its charter became so watered down by other countries' demands for exemptions from the generalized rules that Congress refused to approve it. In its place, the United States sponsored the **General Agreement on Tariffs and Trade (GATT).** Although initially designed as a provisional arrangement, the GATT treaty framework became the cornerstone of the liberalized trading scheme originally embodied in the international organization that was to be known as the ITO.

Trade liberalization was to occur through the mechanism of free and unfettered international trade, of which the United States has been a strong advocate for more than half a century. Free trade rests on the **normal-trade-relations (NTR)** principle, until recently known as the **most-favored-nation (MFN) principle.** Both principles say that the tariff preferences granted to one state must be granted to all others exporting the same product. The principle ensures equality in a state's treatment of its trade partners. Thus nondiscrimination is a central norm of the trade regime. Under the aegis of GATT and the most-favored-nation principle, states undertook a series of multilateral trade negotiations, called "rounds," aimed at reducing tariffs and resolving related issues. The eighth session, the Uruguay Round, completed in 1993, replaced GATT with a new **World Trade Organization (WTO),** thus resurrecting the half-century-old vision of a global trade organization "with teeth." The excruciatingly long, often contentious Uruguay negotiations reflected increasing strain on the liberal trading regime, particularly as states moved beyond the goal of tariff reduction to confront more ubiquitous and less tractable forms of new protectionism that have become widespread.[7] *Nontariff barriers* are among the most ubiquitous.

Nontariff barriers **(NTBs)** to trade cover a wide range of government regulations that have the effect of reducing or distorting international trade,

including health and safety regulations, restrictions on the quality of goods that may be imported, government procurement policies, domestic subsidies, and antidumping regulations (designed to prevent foreign producers from selling their goods for less abroad than they cost at home). NTBs comprise one of several new protectionist challenges to the principle of free trade, often called neomercantilist challenges. (**Neomercantilism** is state intervention in economic affairs to enhance national economic fortunes. More precisely, it is "a trade policy whereby a state seeks to maintain a balance-of-trade surplus and to promote domestic production and employment by reducing imports, stimulating home production, and promoting exports" [Walters and Blake 1992].) Neomercantilist practices have assumed greater prominence in American foreign economic policy in recent decades. They are also evident in other countries, as witnessed by the concern among America's trade partners about the consequences of genetically engineered agricultural products, of which the United States is the leading exporter (see Paarlberg 2000).

Hegemony Unchallenged

The United States was the principal stimulant to all of the multilateral negotiating sessions designed to reduce trade barriers. From the end of World War II until at least the 1960s, it also willingly accepted fewer immediate benefits than its trading partners in anticipation of the longer-term benefits of freer international trade. In effect, the United States was the locomotive of expanding world production and trade. By stimulating its own growth, the United States became an attractive market for others' exports, and the outflow of dollars stimulated their economic growth as well. Evidence supports the wisdom of this strategy: as the average duty levied on imports to the United States declined by more than half between the late 1940s and the early 1960s, world exports nearly tripled.

On the Periphery in the Global South   Not all shared in the prosperity of the U.S.-backed LIEO.

Many states in the emerging Global South failed to grow economically or otherwise to share in the benefits of economic liberalism. Instead, their economies remained closely tied to their former colonizers. Holdovers from the imperial period of the late 1800s, time-worn trade patterns perpetuated unequal exchanges that did little to break the newly independent states out of the yoke of their colonial past. Thus the developing countries on the periphery[8] were largely irrelevant as the new economic order emerged. They enjoyed too little power to shape effectively the rules of the game, which nonetheless seriously affected their own well-being.

The Second World The Soviet Union and its socialist allies in Eastern Europe were also outside the decision-making circle—but largely by choice. During World War II, Western planners anticipated the Soviet Union's participation in the postwar international economic system, just as they originally anticipated Soviet cooperation in maintaining the postwar political order. But enthusiasm for establishing closer economic ties between East and West began to wane once the war ended. 1947 was the critical year, as President Truman then effectively committed the United States to an anticommunist foreign policy strategy and Secretary of State George Marshall committed the United States to aid the economic recovery of Europe. Although American policy makers thought the Soviet Union might participate in the Marshall Plan, much of the congressional debate over the plan was framed in terms of the onslaught of communism—rhetoric that certainly did not endear the recovery program to Soviet policy makers.

Furthermore, Soviet leaders were determined to pursue a policy of economic autarky that would eliminate any dependence on other countries. Thus they rejected the offer of American aid. They also refused to permit Eastern European countries to accept Marshall Plan assistance. Thereafter East and West developed essentially separate economic systems, which excluded one another. Meanwhile, the United States moved to exclude the communist countries from most-favored-nation trade treatment. With its allies, it also restricted exports of goods that might bolster Soviet military capabilities or those of its allies, thus threatening Western security. Many would remain in place until they began to be dismantled in the 1990s (see Cupitt 2000).

Hegemony Under Stress

Domestically, four major statutes (as amended) have framed the U.S. approach to international trade issues and the multilateral negotiations that flowed from them: (1) the Reciprocal Trade Agreements Act of 1934, (2) the Trade Expansion Act of 1962, (3) the Trade Act of 1974, and (4) the Omnibus Trade and Competitiveness Act of 1988. Beginning in 1974 and reaffirmed until 1994, Congress (Constitutionally responsible for trade policy) also granted the president fast-track authority to negotiate trade agreements with other countries.

Fast-track authority, now referred to as **_trade promotion authority,_** does not guarantee that Congress will approve a trade agreement negotiated by the president, but it does promise that Congress will consider the agreement in a timely fashion and will either vote it up or down, without making any amendments.[9] Presidents for two decades found fast-track procedures to their liking, but in 1994 Congress permitted that authority to expire. Clinton sought to renew it in 1997 in an effort to move beyond NAFTA toward a hemispheric-wide _Free Trade Area of the Americas (FTAA)._ "At issue," Clinton argued with some justification, "is America's leadership and credibility in the eyes of our competitors." Nonetheless, Congress rebuffed him.

A year later, Republican Speaker of the House of Representatives Newt Gingrich would again seek to renew that authority, and again Congress refused. By this time labor and environmental interests had become outspoken critics of the costs of free trade stimulated by globalization (Destler 1999), as we will discuss more fully later. Interestingly, President Bush would later ask for—and get—the same authority from the Republican Congress that it denied Clinton, also with the intent of creating a Free Trade Area of the Americas.

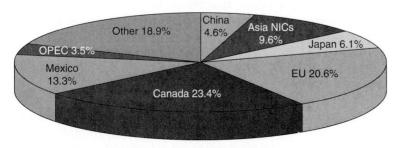

Exports

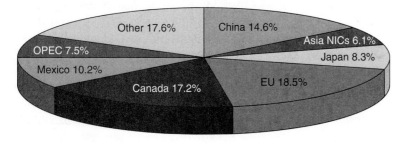

Imports

FIGURE 7.2 U.S. Trade Partners, 2005

SOURCE: Adapted from U.S. Bureau of the Census, www.census.gov/foreign-trade/balance/, accessed 11/10/06.

The European Union The Kennedy Round of negotiations in the mid-1960s marked the high point of the movement toward a liberalized trade regime. The negotiations grew out of the 1962 Trade Expansion Act. The rhetoric surrounding the act's passage cloaked trade liberalization in the mantle of national security, and the act itself was described as an essential weapon in the Cold War struggle with Soviet communism. Nonetheless, it was motivated in part by concern for maintaining U.S. export markets in the face of growing economic competition from the European Economic Community (EEC), which later became the European Community (EC). It specifically granted the president broad power to negotiate tariff rates with EEC members.

Today, as during most of the past quarter century, the European Union (EU), of which the EEC and EC are progenitors, figures prominently in U.S. trade policy. With Canada, China, Japan, and Mexico, it is among the most important U.S. trade partners (see Figure 7.2). Although the United States has officially supported European efforts to create an integrated economic union, transatlantic relations have not always been smooth, as the devil is in the details. Agricultural issues have proved especially vexing.

The Kennedy Round made progress on industrial tariffs, to the point that by 1975, when the Tokyo Round began, the United States and the European Community had reduced tariff rates on industrial products to negligible levels, but on the important question of agricultural commodities little headway was made. Although agricultural trade fell beyond the purview of GATT as originally conceived, it became a matter of growing importance to the United States. Europe's *Common Agricultural Policy (CAP)* posed the immediate challenge. Initiated in 1966—and still a centerpiece of EU policy—CAP was (is) a protectionist tariff wall designed to maintain politically acceptable but artificially high prices for farm products produced within the European Union. That curtailed American agricultural exports to the region. The lack of progress and later disagreements on this issue began to raise doubts among American policy makers about the wisdom of promoting expansionist economic policies from which others benefited. Even today, agricultural issues remain among the most troublesome in U.S.-EU trade relations.

By the time the Tokyo Round commenced in 1975, trade negotiators found themselves in a radically different environment from that of the previous GATT sessions. Trade volume had grown exponentially worldwide, economic interdependence among the world's leading industrial powers had reached unprecedented levels, tariffs were no longer the principal barriers to trade, and the United States was no longer an unfaltering economic giant. In this new environment, reducing barriers to the free flow of agricultural products and coping with nontariff barriers to trade received increased emphasis.

A measure of success was achieved on NTBs. No progress was made on agriculture, however. This shortcoming "probably more than any other single factor . . . helped to undermine the integrity and credibility of the trading system" (Low 1993). Thus, in the years between the end of the Tokyo Round and the beginning of the Uruguay Round, GATT's rules seemed increasingly irrelevant to state practices. Protectionism in violation of the principle of nondiscrimination became increasingly rife. Growing concern about the challenge of the more economically advanced developing nations was also apparent.

Challenge from the Global South   As noted earlier, the postwar international monetary and multilateral trading systems evolved primarily under the aegis of the Western industrial states, whose interests and objectives they served. Developing countries on the periphery were largely outside the privileged circle. Many came to view the existing international economic structure as a cause of their underdog status. Their challenge was especially vigorous in the immediate aftermath of the first OPEC-induced oil shock, but eventually subsided in the 1980s as more and more developing countries sought to integrate themselves into the globalizing political economy.

During the 1950s, developing states began to devise a unified posture toward others on security issues and to press for consideration of their special problems and needs in the context of the global economic structure, as we saw in Chapter 6. It would take almost another decade before their efforts bore fruit. Then, during the 1964 United Nations Conference on Trade and Development (UNCTAD), called at the behest of the developing countries, the *Group of 77 (G-77)* was formed as a coalition of the world's poor to press for concessions from the world's rich. From its original 77 founding members, the G-77 today numbers over 130 and remains a significant voice in pressing the interests of the South in its dialogue with the North. At a summit in Havana in 2000, for example, the G-77 called for a New Global Human Order designed to spread the world's wealth and power.

The G-77 scored a major victory with the Sixth Special Session of the United Nations General Assembly, held in 1974, when it used its superior numbers to secure passage of the Declaration on the Establishment of a *New International Economic Order (NIEO)*. Inspired in the wake of OPEC's price squeeze by the belief that "commodity power" endowed the Global South with the political strength necessary to challenge the industrial North, the G-77 sought a substantial alteration of the rules and institutional structures governing the transnational flow of goods, services, capital, and technology. Simply put, the New International Economic Order sought regime change—a revision of the rules, norms, and procedures of the Liberal International Economic Order to serve the interests of the South rather than the North (Krasner 1985).

The Global South's drive for regime change derived from its belief that the structure of the world political economy perpetuates developing states' underdog status. International economic institutions, such as the IMF and GATT, were (are) widely perceived as "deeply biased against developing countries in their global distribution of income and influence" (Hansen 1980). The perception was buttressed—then and now—by a legacy of colonial exploitation, the continued existence of levels of poverty and deprivation unheard of in the Global North, and a conviction that relief from many of the economic and associated political ills of the South can result only from changes in the policies of the North, in whose hands responsibility for prevailing conditions and the means to correct them were (are) thought to lie.

The Global North—then and now—rejected those views. Accepting them would have been tantamount to relinquishing control over key international institutions and a fundamental redistribution of global resources—two unlikely prospects. Instead, it located the cause of the Global South's economic woes in the domestic systems of developing countries themselves (see, for example, Bissell 1990). Thus proposals to radically alter existing international economic institutions, as well as the more modest elements of the program advanced during the 1970s and early 1980s, met with resistance and resentment. The United States was especially intransigent, as it continued to view the Global South primarily through an East–West prism, showing little interest in those aspects of Southern objectives related to transforming the Liberal International Economic Order.

As the unifying force of commodity power receded and different countries were affected in different ways by the changing economic climate of the 1980s, latent fissures within the G-77 became evident. As a result, the Global South no longer spoke with a unified voice. The differences between the Newly Industrializing Economies (NIEs) and the least-developed of the less-developed countries had the effect of dividing the G-77 into competing groups rather than uniting them behind a common cause.

Today the Global South's determination to replace the LIEO with a New International Economic Order is little more than a footnote to the history of the continuing contest between the world's rich and poor countries. Still, many of the issues raised retain their relevance. Central among them is the role of the state in managing international economic transactions. Whereas the LIEO rests on the premise of limited government intervention, ***economic nationalists*** or mercantilists assign the state a more aggressive role in fostering national economic welfare. Economic nationalism (mercantilism) undergirded the "Asian Miracle," a term widely used to describe the spectacular economic performance of Hong Kong, Singapore, South Korea, and Taiwan, often called the "Asian Tigers," that began in the 1970s and then spread elsewhere in the region as export-led growth gained popularity and momentum. In the wake of the Asian contagion of the late 1990s, however, mercantilism once more came under criticism. "Crony capitalism" symbolized the difference between liberalism and mercantilism.

Crony capitalism refers to the tightly knit relationships among corporate and other economic agents in Asian societies, including government officials, that often dictate their economic decisions, regardless of economic imperatives. Family-and-friend ties are especially prominent, as in Indonesia, where the Suharto government (and family) fell victim to the Asian Financial Crisis.

Analysts are not agreed on whether the economic development models of Western capitalism or the Asian models, which embrace strong state roles in the economy (neomercantilism) and cultural values (such as crony capitalism), have won the day (Lim 2001). A decade ago the United States and other Western countries marveled at the Japanese economic miracle and sought to understand its underlying logic. Today Japan is experiencing economic doldrums, and the Washington Consensus, although increasingly under attack (see Naim 2000), animates thinking in the most powerful states.

As a principal driving force behind the Washington Consensus, the United States figures prominently in any discussion of North-South relations. Trade is among the persistent issues. As the largest economy in the world, the Global South sees access to the U.S. market as a key to its economic success. Although the United States from time to time has sought to accommodate Southern objectives, it retains significant barriers to imports from the Global South. NTBs sometimes figure in these exclusions.

More broadly, the new drive of the United States—strongly supported by some domestic groups—to impose on Global South exporters labor and environmental standards similar to those in the United States, poses significant challenges to new entrants to U.S. markets (see Destler and Balint 1999). Not only are these standards seen as inapplicable in labor markets where labor is cheap and capital dear, environmental standards like those in the United States tax government resources in developing countries beyond their capabilities. Not surprisingly, then, the contention over the costs and benefits of globalization have taken on a global flavor, as U.S. efforts to extend its own environmental and labor standards are viewed in the Global South as thinly veiled forms of protectionism.

The Second World Again   The economic isolation of East from West that began in the early Cold War continued for more than a decade. Not until the late 1960s and early 1970s did the Soviets and the Americans begin to significantly shift their views about commercial ties with "the other side." The change was especially evident once détente became official policy on both sides of the Cold War divide. Trade now became part of a series of concrete agreements across a range of issues that would contribute to what Nixon's national security adviser Henry Kissinger described as the superpowers' "vested interest in mutual restraint." For their part, the Soviets saw expanded commercial intercourse as an opportunity to gain access to the Western credits and technology necessary to rejuvenate the sluggish Soviet economy.

The high point of détente was reached at the 1972 Moscow summit, when the two Cold War antagonists initialed the first Strategic Arms Limitation Talks (SALT) agreement. SALT was the cornerstone of détente, but expanded East-West trade was part of the mortar. A joint commercial commission was established at the summit, whose purpose was to pave the way for the granting of most-favored-nation status to the Soviet Union and the extension of U.S. government-backed credits to the Soviet regime. Neither happened as envisioned. Over the objection of President Ford and Secretary of State Kissinger, Congress made MFN status contingent on the liberalization of communist policies regarding Jewish emigration. (Congress did not limit the provisions of the law to the Soviet Union or to Jews, so they also applied to others, including China, into the 1990s.) Restrictions were also placed on Soviet (and Eastern European) access to American government-backed credits. Eventually Soviet leaders repudiated the 1972 trade agreement in response to what they regarded as an unwarranted intrusion into Soviet domestic affairs.

In part because of congressional constraints, East-West trade stagnated in the second half of the 1970s. Furthermore, the Carter administration's commitment to a worldwide human rights campaign often led to American attacks on the Soviet Union's human rights policies. Carter also tried to use trade to moderate objectionable Soviet behavior in the Global South and to sanction the Soviets for their invasion of Afghanistan in 1979. Reagan would follow a similar path, with the added twist that his administration saw trade as a stick that could be used to punish Soviet leaders for unwanted behavior (Spero and Hart 1997). Still, there was no measurable change in Soviet behavior.

A recurring feature of this period is that U.S. allies did not always share U.S. views on how to deal with the Soviet Union in the economic sphere. For example, many Europeans saw U.S. policy as hypocritical in that it attempted to pressure its allies into not selling the Soviets energy technology at the same time as the United States sold them grain. Other examples could be cited.

Against this background, today's European views of U.S. attitudes toward Russia have a distinctly familiar ring. Bush's national security adviser Condoleezza Rice took Germany's chief diplomatic aide to Germany's Chancellor Gerhard Schröder by surprise when she advised him to "be tough" with the Russians. (*New York Times*, 7 May 2001). For Europeans, smoother relations with Russia are preferred, and moving forward on addressing global environmental concerns, on which the Bush administration proved intransigent, were more salient. The gulf in the policy positions of the transatlantic allies was reminiscent of the earlier 1980s, when they tussled over the wisdom of supporting the construction of a Soviet energy pipeline into Europe. The Reagan administration worried that this would increase European dependence on Soviet energy supplies. Europeans viewed it as an opportunity to increase access to scarce energy resources.

Meanwhile, the future of Russia itself remains in doubt. *Mayfiya* groups have subverted government efforts to modernize the economy (Handelman 1994). The quality of life is deteriorating, as witnessed by decreased life-expectancy rates. And democratization is threatened, as media sources and political groups that do not toe the government line are systematically harassed. These and other conditions led the prestigious *Atlantic Monthly* to publish an article in mid-2001 titled "Russia Is Finished" (Tayler 2001). The article's topic line was especially ominous: "The unstoppable descent of a once great power into social catastrophe and strategic irrelevance."

Even as Russia struggles politically and economically, it has pursued joining the World Trade Organization, which would help to integrate it further into the capitalist world political economy. Doing so will require difficult internal Russian reforms. A major step toward Russia's entry into the WTO was taken in November 2006 when the United States and Russia concluded 12 years of difficult negotiations and reached a major trade reduction agreement. The United States was the only state within the 149-member WTO that was still withholding its consent for Russia's entry. With the U.S.-Russia accession protocol in place and legislative approval assured in both countries, Russia is expected to join the global trade body by the middle of 2007 following a successful round of multilateral trade talks with the WTO.

Meanwhile, countries in Eastern Europe have made enormous strides in converting from socialist command economies to capitalist market economies. Several have also joined the WTO and the European Union with others expected to follow. "The former communist countries sought to integrate themselves into the capitalist world economy not only to benefit from trade and investment but also as part of a larger effort to make their political and economic transitions irreversible" (Spero and Hart 1997).

From Free Trade to Fair Trade

Historically, the United States has espoused a laissez faire attitude toward trade issues, believing that market forces are best able to stimulate entrepreneurial initiatives and investment choices. During the 1980s, however, it came to believe that "the playing field is tilted." This implies that American businesspeople are unable to compete on the same basis as others—notably the continental European states, Japan, and the more advanced developing countries, where governments, playing the role of economic nationalists, routinely intervene in their economies and play entrepreneurial and developmental roles directly. Senator Lloyd M. Bentsen, a longtime advocate of free trade and later Secretary of the Treasury in the Clinton administration, captured the shifting sentiment toward free trade during the debate over the 1988 omnibus trade act: "I think in theory, it's a great theory. But it's not being practiced, and for us to practice free trade in a world where there's much government-directed trade makes as much sense as unilateral disarmament with the Russians."

Not only were sentiments toward free trade shifting rapidly in the United States—at one time during the 1980s, some three hundred bills were pending before Congress that offered protection to almost every industrial sector—but signs of closure characterized the trade system itself. By the time the Uruguay Round of trade negotiations began in 1986, the system was rife with restrictive barriers, subsidies, invisible import restraints, standards for domestic products that foreign producers could not meet, and other unfair trade practices that went beyond GATT's principles (see also Anjaria 1986). To cope with the changing environment at home and abroad, the United States mounted a series of responses. ***Multilateralism*** was one.

The Multilateral Venue   Other countries were not quick to accept the United States' analogy of an uneven playing field skewed to its disadvantage. As one observer put it caustically, "The more inefficient and backward an American industry is, the more likely the U.S. government will blame foreign countries for its problems" (Bovard 1991). Still, other states were sensitive to the need to keep protectionist sentiments in the United States at bay. Because U.S. imports stimulated the economic growth of its trade partners, they conceded that new trade talks (the Uruguay Round) should not only consider traditional tariff issues and the new protectionism but also issues traditionally outside the GATT framework of special concern to the United States due to its comparative advantages.

The new issues included barriers to trade in services (insurance, for example), intellectual property rights (such as copyrights on computer software, music, and movies), and investments (stocks and bonds). Agriculture also remained a paramount issue, as the economic well-being of American agriculture depends more heavily on exports than do other sectors of the economy.

Because world trade in agriculture evolved outside of the main GATT framework, it was not subject to the same liberalizing influences as industrial products (Low 1993; Spero and Hart 1997). Agricultural trade policy is especially controversial because it is deeply enmeshed in the domestic politics of producing states, particularly those, like the United States and some members of the European Union, for which the global market is an outlet for surplus production. The enormous subsidies that governments of some leading producers pay farmers to keep them internationally competitive are at the core of differences. The perceived need for subsidies reflects fundamental structural changes in the global system of food production. New competitors have emerged among Global South producers, and markets traditionally supplied by Northern producers have shrunk as a consequence of technological innovations enabling expanded agricultural production in countries that previously experienced food deficits.

During the Uruguay Round, the United States aggressively proposed to phase out all agricultural subsidies and farm trade protection programs within a decade. It gained some support from others but faced stiff opposition from Europeans (particularly France), which viewed it as unrealistic. Sharp differences on the issue led to an impasse in the

Uruguay Round negotiations, delaying conclusion of the talks beyond the original 1990 target date.

Three years later, when the talks finally concluded, the United States could claim a measure of success, as the European Union (then called the European Community) and others agreed to new (but limited) rules on subsidies and market access. Some domestic groups in the United States worried that increased agricultural efficiency would eventually drive small American farmers out of business. But for the industry as a whole, liberalization was perceived as more beneficial to American farmers than to producers elsewhere due to the Americans' greater efficiency. Liberalization of agricultural trade was also expected to benefit agricultural exporters in the Global South by providing them with greater access to markets in the Global North.

By the time of the Uruguay Round, many developing states had initiated trade liberalization on their own, thus coming to participate more fully in the GATT trade regime. In some areas, however, long-standing North-South differences continued to color issues of importance to the United States (see the essays in Tussie and Glover 1993). Trade-related intellectual property rights (TRIPs)—one of the new issues confronted at Uruguay—was among them. The United States (and other Northern states) wanted protection of copyrights, patents, trademarks, microprocessor designs, and trade secrets, as well as prohibitions on unfair competition. (TRIPs would figure prominently in future U.S. trade talks with China.) Developing states vigorously resisted these efforts along with the concept of "standardized intellectual property norms and regulations throughout the world" (Low 1993).[10] Thus little significant headway was made on TRIPs. U.S. efforts regarding trade-related investment measures (TRIMs) and services (such as banking and insurance) and the Clinton administration's efforts to abolish European restrictions on non-European produced movies and television programs (read, "American") also met widespread resistance.

The United States did realize a long-standing goal when the World Trade Organization was approved as GATT's replacement. Proponents of the WTO saw it as a useful element in states' efforts to keep the instrumentalities of the liberal trade regime consonant with state practices in the increasingly complex world political economy. It was not without detractors, however. Critics were especially antagonistic to WTO's dispute settlement procedures. They were concerned that the findings of its arbitration panels would be binding on the domestic laws of participating states. More broadly, the very title of the new organization suggested potential threats to American decision-making prerogatives, which sparked the ire of conservative critics in particular. Presidential hopeful Pat Buchanan's reaction is illustrative: "The glittering bribe the globalists are extending to us is this: enhanced access to global markets—in exchange for our national sovereignty" (Rabkin 1994).

Environmentalists—often on the other end of the political spectrum—also worried about the WTO. They feared it would further erode their ability to protect hard-won domestic victories against the charge that environmental protection laws restrict free trade.[11] GATT's controversial rulings that a U.S. ban on the import of tuna caught by merchants who also ensnare encircling dolphins is illegal—popularly known as the "GATTzilla versus Flipper" debate—symbolized their apprehensiveness. Environmentalists were also concerned that the World Trade Organization would perpetuate the "elitist" character of GATT (dispute panelists are appointed, not elected, and make their decisions behind closed doors), and that controls in a wide range of areas with environmental implications would be expanded and nontariff trade barriers designed purposely to protect the environment (including dolphins) disallowed. In short, they argued that the environment and sustainable development were given insufficient attention in the design of the WTO (French 1993). Their fears were reaffirmed in 1998, when the WTO, in a case similar to the dolphin-tuna controversy, overturned American policies designed to keep out of U.S. markets shrimp caught in nets without turtle-excluder devises (Destler and Balint 1999).

The Doha Round of negotiations, launched in 2001, was set to deal with a wide range of difficult issues, most of which were first broached in the Uruguay Round. Twenty-one subjects were covered by the Doha declaration, including implementation of current WTO agreements, agriculture, services, market access, TRIPs, TRIMs, trade and competition policy, transparency in government procurement, trade facilitation, WTO rules on anti-dumping and subsidies, WTO rules on regional trade agreements, dispute settlement, trade and the environment, electronic commerce, and a variety of issues pertinent to developing countries. The Doha Round was marked by an overall lack of progress. This reality led the Bush administration to pursue both regional and bilateral initiatives on trade (which probably in turn impeded the success of multilateral talks within the WTO). China and Taiwan were admitted to the WTO shortly after the launch of the talks in 2001, but most subsequent negotiations were nonetheless characterized by sharp disagreements among the industrial states and between them and developing countries.

Aggressive Unilateralism At the same time that the Clinton administration pushed the Uruguay Round to successful conclusion, it pursued policies toward Europe, Japan, and others with means best characterized as aggressive unilateralism. The approach contrasted sharply with the laissez-faire attitudes of the previous Bush administration, captured by the quip allegedly made by one of its economic advisers: "Potato chips, computer chips, what's the difference. They're all chips. A hundred dollars of one or a hundred dollars of the other is still a hundred dollars." Aggressive unilateralism, in contrast, says it matters very much what an economy produces and what kind of labor and environmental standards are followed in the production process. For example, Clinton threatened to withdraw China's most-favored-nation trade status in the aftermath of the Tiananmen Square incident unless specific criteria for respecting human rights were met. The administration's posture toward China fulfilled a campaign promise that smacked of Cold War tactics—the belief that tough economic pressure can secure explicitly political ends. Carter and Reagan had both tried this, and both failed. In the end, so did Clinton.

Faced with the reality that China had become one of the nation's most important trade partners

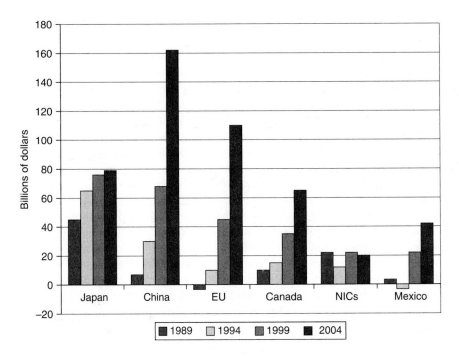

FIGURE 7.3 U.S. Trade Deficit with Principle Trading Partners

SOURCE: U.S. Census Bureau, www.census.gov/foreign-trade/balance/, accessed 11/10/06.

(see Figure 7.3), however, the Clinton administration unabashedly abandoned its human rights posture and an earlier campaign promise. Secretary of State Warren Christopher announced that a policy of "comprehensive engagement" would become the focus of U.S. policy, calling it "the best way to influence China's development." The purported change echoed the senior Bush administration's earlier emphasis on market incentives toward political liberalization—an approach Clinton vigorously attacked during the 1992 presidential campaign. Critics charged that profits had won out over principles. Later, however, Clinton could claim victory when, after threatening to impose higher tariffs on Chinese goods, he won a commitment from the Chinese to halt their piracy of compact discs and other items in violation of intellectual property rights standards.

The administration's trade policies toward Europe, Japan, and Korea bore some resemblance to its China policies in that they rested on the premise that economic security and national security would go hand in hand in the post–Cold War world. As Clinton declared early in his administration, "It is time for us to make trade a priority element of American security." "Security" and "war" would often punctuate administration rhetoric and others' interpretations of it (see Friedman 1994a; see also Chapter 3). In the fight during his second term to win congressional approval for granting China normal-trade-relations status, which paved the way for its entry into the WTO, Clinton and National Security Adviser Sandy Berger would often invoke the national security symbol as the administration pursued its goal. During its first term, however, its actions are best understood through the lens of fair trade, managed trade, and strategic trade. Together they infused American trade policies with a distinctly neomercantilist cast.

Fair Trade **Fair trade** implies that American exporters should be given the same access to foreign markets that foreign producers enjoy in the United

States (see also Prestowitz 1992). As Clinton put it, "We will continue to welcome foreign products and services into our market, but insist that our products and services be able to enter theirs on equal terms." Fair trade is often closely associated with *reciprocity,* which increasingly in recent years has meant "equal market access in terms of outcomes rather than equality of opportunities." Together the two concepts lay the basis for an interventionist trade policy (Low 1993).

Section 301 of the 1974 Trade Act embodies this interventionist thrust. It permits the United States to retaliate against others engaged in "unreasonable" or "unjustifiable" trade policies that threaten American interests. Liberalization, however—not retaliation—is the primary purpose of Section 301, and this was achieved in about one-third of the cases raised between 1975 and 1990. Retaliation occurred in about one-tenth of them (Low 1993).

Frustrated with the tedious process of resolving disputes under Section 301, but especially with what it regarded as trade practices believed responsible for the persistent U.S. trade deficits of the 1980s, Congress incorporated "Super 301" in the 1988 Omnibus Trade and Competitiveness Act. Unlike the earlier provision, **Super 301** *required* that the president identify countries engaged in unfair trade practices and either seek negotiated remedies or threaten them with U.S. retaliation. Although Super 301 was "almost unanimously viewed abroad as a clear violation of the GATT" (Walters and Blake 1992), Congress's resentment of the trade policies of Japan and the four Asian Newly Industrialized Economies (NIEs)—Hong Kong, Singapore, South Korea, and Taiwan—was glaring.

Japan was often viewed in the United States as the preeminent neomercantilist power, based on the belief that its persistent balance-of-trade and payments surpluses resulted from an intimate government-business alliance that tilted the playing field in its favor. The continuing trade imbalance between Japan and the United States—which runs into the tens of billions of dollars each year, as Figure 7.3 shows—reinforces the belief that Japan's trade policies are inherently detrimental to American business interests (see Fallows

1994; for a contrasting view, see Emmott 1994; also Bergsten and Noland 1993).

There is little doubt that Japan's protectionist trade policies inhibit penetration of its market by American firms. Japanese business practices, including cross-shareholding patterns known as *keiretsu,* which result in informal corporate bargains, also make foreign penetration difficult regardless of government policies. American consumers, however, continue to show marked preferences for Japanese products. Such preferences are not shared by their counterparts on the other side of the Pacific Basin, where cultural traditions reinforce the view that foreign products are ill-suited to the Japanese consumer.

American exports to Japan have increased considerably in recent years, in part a product of continuing negotiations between the two countries. Among them was the Structural Impediments Initiative (SII), launched in 1989 shortly after Japan was named as one of three countries engaged in unfair trade practices under Super 301 (Brazil and India were the others).

The administration of George H. W. Bush was clearly uncomfortable with the confrontational, unilateralist thrust of Super 301—not one case of retaliation was initiated (see Low 1993)—and thus was pleased to see it expire after 1990. Four years later, the Clinton administration revived the section's provisions via executive agreement following the breakdown of the latest series of Japanese-American trade negotiations, known as the "framework" talks.

Managed Trade The tactics of **managed trade**—a system in which a government intervenes to steer trade relations in a direction that the government itself has predetermined—played out during the framework talks. Once the negotiations began, the United States insisted on using certain quantitative indicators to monitor whether Japan was in fact opening its markets in various sectors, including autos, telecommunications, insurance, and medical equipment. Its intransigence on the issue led to a breakdown of negotiations in early 1994, as the Japanese retorted that numerical standards would require Japan to engage in managed trade—in effect responding to a demand for a minimum U.S. share of the Japanese market. Clinton would later deny that the United States ever demanded numerical import quota commitments from Japan. All the United States sought, according to U.S. Trade Representative Mickey Kantor, was an agreement on "objective criteria" to show progress in opening up Japan's markets to all foreign (not just American) goods. Japan did eventually agree that quantitative measures could be used to measure progress in opening Japanese markets in insurance, glass, and medical and telecommunications equipment, but it refused to guarantee the United States any specific market shares—thus sidestepping the contentious issue of "numerical targets." Furthermore, no agreement was reached on automobiles and auto parts. To keep pressure on the Japanese in these markets, the Clinton administration promptly set in motion the process that could lead to sanctions, although it chose to use Section 301 of the 1974 Trade Act rather than the more aggressive Super 301 provision. It then threatened stiff tariff increases on luxury Japanese automobiles produced for the U.S. market unless U.S. car companies and spare-parts manufacturers were guaranteed greater access to the Japanese market.

An eleventh-hour agreement was reached in mid-1995. Both sides claimed victory. The United States said the agreement set "numerical benchmarks" that would yield measurable results in opening the Japanese market; Japanese negotiators replied they had agreed to no numbers and would bear no responsibility for achieving any numerical targets. Thus, that round in the often tense U.S.-Japanese trade dispute ended without a definitive deal—as had happened so often in the past.

Managed trade between the United States and Japan as pursued by the Clinton administration was not without precedent. In 1986, the Reagan administration made an agreement with Japan to guarantee foreign companies a share of the Japanese semiconductor market. President Bush renewed it in 1991. He also led a trade mission to Japan that included a contingent of American auto executives, thus giving it an unabashedly neomercantilist

coloration. The mission seemed to confirm the view expressed by Leon Britain, competition commissioner of the European Community, that the Bush administration was "drifting toward a preference for managed trade" and that it sought "a certain share of the Japanese market on political rather than commercial grounds." Shortly thereafter the speaker of the Japanese Diet (parliament), Yoshio Sakurauchi, described the United States as "Japan's subcontractor" and American workers as lazy and illiterate. "Japan bashing" in turn became a popular American sport.

Despite the Reagan-Bush precedents, the Clinton administration was sensitive to criticisms of its tactics and objectives. Deputy Secretary of the Treasury Roger C. Altman (1994) defended them in *Foreign Affairs,* charging that "The Japanese government that berates the United States on charges of managed trade has long been in the business of targeting market outcomes itself."

Despite Altman's spirited—even hawkish—defense, other states were suspicious of U.S. motives, fearing that the United States sought a bilateral deal with Japan that would come at their expense. European governments were especially critical of the determination of the United States to threaten unilateral sanctions in the auto industry dispute rather than let the new World Trade Organization settle the issue. Similarly, Peter Sutherland, head of GATT, warned of the dangers of managed trade: "Governments should interfere in the conduct of trade as little as possible. Once bureaucrats become involved in managing trade flows, the potential for misguided decisions rises greatly."

Strategic Trade Sutherland's views arguably apply even more strongly to the application of strategic trade to "level the playing field." **Strategic trade** is a form of industrial policy that seeks to create comparative advantages by targeting government subsidies toward particular industries. The strategy challenges the premises of classical trade theory and its touchstone, the principle of comparative advantage.

Classical theory shows how international trade contributes to the welfare of trading partners. It attributes the basis for trade to underlying differences among states: some are better suited to the production of agricultural products, such as coffee, because they have vast tracts of fertile land, while others are better suited to the production of labor-intensive goods, such as consumer electronics, because they have an abundance of cheap labor. Economists now recognize, however, that comparative advantages take on a life of their own.

> Much international trade . . . reflects national advantages that are created by historical circumstance, and that then persist or grow because of other advantages to large scale either in development or production. For example, the development effort required to launch a new passenger jet aircraft is so large that the world market will support only one or two profitable firms. Once the United States had a head start in producing aircraft, its position as the world's leading exporter became self-reinforcing. So if you want to explain why the United States exports aircraft, you should not look for underlying aspects of the U.S. economy; you should study the historical circumstances that gave the United States a head start in the industry.
>
> *(Krugman 1990, 109)*

If the contemporary pattern of international trade reflects historical circumstances, states may conclude it is in their interests to try to create advantages that will redound to the long-run benefit of their economies. Curiously, then, the logic of comparative advantage can itself be used to justify government intervention in the economy. Although the returns on strategic trade policies are often marginal (Krugman 1990), the fact that some states engage in such practices encourages others to do likewise. Indeed, the United States became increasingly sensitive to the logic of strategic trade as the Soviet threat ended and its own power position compared with Japan and Germany, among others, declined, thus making it more aware of the costs of free-riding by its Cold War allies and principal economic partners (Mastanduno 1991; see also Snidal 1991).

The Clinton administration's early decision to grant tax breaks and redirect government spending to high-tech industries to enhance their competitive advantages demonstrated its willingness to follow the path of others. Clinton's attack on the EU's subsidies for the Airbus shortly after his first inauguration marked in dramatic style the approach and was likely influenced by the thinking of his newly chosen chair of the Council of Economic Advisers, Laura D'Andrea Tyson. Tyson's book, *Who's Bashing Whom? Trade Conflict in High-Technology Industries* (1992)—which includes a detailed examination of the aircraft industry, among others—articulates a "cautious activist agenda" for enhancing American competitiveness along the lines strategic trade theory prescribes.

The success of government efforts to target subsidies toward particular ("strategic") industries is, as noted, mixed. While the record of Pacific Rim countries is arguably positive, it is also marked by some conspicuous failures. Notable among them is "the Japanese government's reluctance in the 1950s to support a little start-up company named Tokyo Tsushin Kogyo. The company is now known as Sony Corporation" (Blustein 1993). The key issue, then, is the ability of governments to pick winners and losers.

In the particular case of the aircraft industry, Europeans are especially critical of the proposition that they grant subsidies while the United States does not. They correctly note that the commercial sector in the United States benefited enormously from the billions of dollars in military aerospace research and development the Pentagon spent during the Cold War, which helped to create an unequaled aerospace industry—commercial as well as military. Moreover, as the theory of strategic trade suggests, Europe's ability to compete in the industry is severely circumscribed by the advantages historical circumstances conferred on the United States.

A concern for competitiveness ties together many of the Clinton administration's initial trade policy thrusts. Clinton pledged repeatedly during and after his 1992 campaign to create more "high wage, high skill" jobs for Americans. Government intervention in the economy—neomercantilism—flows naturally from that pledge. Thus in early 1994, after Clinton personally played a role in nudging

Saudi Arabia toward a $6 billion commercial aircraft deal with Boeing and McDonnell Douglas rather than the European Airbus Industry consortium, the president would crow that this proved "that we can compete" (see also Barnes 1994).

Implicit in the concern for competitiveness was the notion that trade competition from others—particularly Japan and low-wage producers on the Pacific Rim—had diminished the living standards of American workers. The policy implications were clear: only an aggressive campaign to enhance U.S. competitiveness could reverse the trends.

Not everyone agreed with that viewpoint. Economist Paul Krugman, whose challenges to the assumptions of classical trade theory form much of the basis of current thinking about strategic trade, was especially critical of what he called the "dangerous obsession" with competitiveness (Krugman 1994a, 1994b). In particular, he criticized the view that "the nation's real income [had] lagged as a result of the inability of many U.S. firms to sell in world markets" (Krugman and Lawrence 1994). He noted that almost all of the decline in American living standards between 1973 and 1990 could be explained by a decline in domestic productivity. The same was true in Europe and Japan. "The moral is clear," Krugman continued:

> As a practical, empirical matter the major nations of the world are not to any significant degree in economic competition with each other. Of course, there is always a rivalry for status and power—countries that grow faster will see their political rank rise. So it is always interesting to compare countries. But asserting that Japanese growth diminishes U.S. status is very different from saying that it reduces the U.S. standard of living—and it is the latter that the rhetoric of competitiveness asserts.
>
> (Krugman 1994A, 35)[12]

Regionalism and Bilateralism The Bush administration's 2006 National Security Strategy asserts that "A strong world economy enhances our national security by advancing prosperity and freedom in the rest of the world. Economic growth supported by free trade and free markets creates new jobs and higher incomes. It allows people to lift their lives out of poverty, spurs economic and legal reform, and the fight against corruption, and it reinforces the habits of liberty." The promotion of political and economic freedoms were thus seen as a cornerstone of U.S. national security and the war on terror. The Clinton administration had also linked trade liberalization and national security through the "democratic peace proposition," as we saw in Chapter 3. But during the Bush administration much of international monetary and trade policy took a backseat to security concerns, as we have noted. Its activity with regard to free trade agreements (FTAs) thus stands out as notable compared to the general lack of action on many other global economic issues.

The Trade Act of 2002 gave the president trade promotion authority (TPA; previously fast track authority), which Bush used to launch an unprecedented number of FTAs. As indicated in Table 7.1, the

TABLE 7.1 U.S. Free Trade Agreements

In Force	Pending	In Negotiation
Australia	CAFTA-DR[1]	Andean[2]
Bahrain	Colombia	FTAA[3]
Chile	Oman	Malaysia[4]
Israel	Peru	Panama
Jordan		Thailand
Morocco		South African Customs Union
NAFTA[5]		United Arab Emirates
Singapore		

[1] The Central American-Dominican Republic Free Trade Agreement (CAFTA-DR) includes Costa Rica, Dominican Republic, El Salvador, Guatemala, Honduras, Nicaragua, and United States.

[2] The proposed U.S.-Andean Free Trade Agreement involves Colombia, Ecuador, Peru, and the United States.

[3] The proposed Free Trade of the Americas (FTAA) involves the thirty-four democracies of the region.

[4] In 2006, Malaysia and the United States expressed an intention to negotiate a free trade agreement.

[5] The North American Free Trade Agreement (NAFTA) includes Canada, Mexico, and the United States.

SOURCE: U.S. Government Export Portal, www.export.gov/fta, accessed 12/22/06.

United States has nearly twenty FTAs in force, pending, or under negotiation, the vast majority of which are a product of the Bush administration. The particulars of the FTA schemes may differ, but they share a common goal: trade liberalization. By reducing barriers to trade, all parties expect to benefit from liberalization, which promises greater efficiencies through specialization and hence potential benefits, not only to producers but also to consumers, that will enhance their living standards—at least that is the theory. Hegemonic theory also tells us that the United States will benefit handsomely, as its greater control of capital and technology gives it advantageous access to both opportunities and rewards.

The foundations of current efforts to build new FTAs are lodged in part in the regionally based initiatives the United States launched in the 1980s and 1990s. Ironically, those regional schemes may also threaten the perpetuation of globalization processes. This is especially the case with the bilateral agreements popular with the George W. Bush administration. In both cases (regional and bilateral) norms may be established that deviate from a global LIEO open to all and subject to the same rules and procedures, hence threatening the liberal regime itself. Nonetheless, regionalism and (increasingly) bilateralism join multilateralism and aggressive unilateralism as prominent instrumentalities in American policy makers' responses to the changes and challenges of a world political economy in transition.

Notable examples of regionalism include the Caribbean Basin Initiative, a program of tariff reductions and tax incentives launched in 1984 to promote industry and trade in Central America and the Caribbean, and the North American Free Trade Agreement (NAFTA), approved in 1993, which links the United States with Canada and Mexico in a free trade area. Post-NAFTA initiatives include the Asia-Pacific Economic Cooperation (APEC) forum, which seeks creation of a Pacific Rim free trade scheme by the year 2020, and the Free Trade Area of the Americas (FTAA), which anticipates a free trade area encompassing the Western Hemisphere much earlier than that.

Of particular note is the Central America-Dominican Republic Free Trade Agreement (CAFTA-DR), which will join the United States, Costa Rica, El Salvador, Guatemala, Honduras, Nicaragua and ultimately the Dominican Republic in an FTA. CAFTA-DR has received substantial criticism from U.S. domestic agriculture interests. The FTAA has also received substantial criticism from Latin American leaders like Hugo Chavez of Venezuela, and the leaders of the Mercosur countries who met at the 2006 Summit of the Americas in Mar del Plata, Argentina. The summit failed to produce agreement on relaunching the FTAA, despite the Bush administration's strong push to unite the hemisphere in a single FTA. Meanwhile, the Bush administration began to partner with friendly states in the Persian Gulf region as part of its effort to transform the political and economic character of the Middle East.

CAFTA-DR is in some sense an extension of North American Free Trade Agreement (NAFTA). Its purpose was to intertwine Mexico and Canada with the United States as a prelude to a wider Western Hemispheric economic partnership, embodied in the senior Bush administration's Enterprise for the Americas Initiative. NAFTA itself was an emotionally charged, high-profile issue during the 1992 presidential campaign and later as Congress faced its approval. Third-party candidate Ross Perot made a big splash with the charge that a "giant sucking sound" would be heard as American jobs rushed to Mexico should NAFTA be approved. Journalist and presidential hopeful Pat Buchanan (1993) charged that "NAFTA is not really a trade treaty at all, but the architecture of the New World Order.... NAFTA would supersede state laws and diminish U.S. sovereignty." In the end Congress approved the pact, in part because of side agreements on labor and environmental issues the Clinton administration initiated. These agreements, as we note later, have led to important if unintended consequences.

NAFTA was directed in part (as was Buchanan's invective) against the European Union. Since the 1950s, European leaders have tried methodically to build a more united Europe, beginning especially in the economic sphere with a European-wide common market. In the mid-1980s they boldly committed themselves to create a single market by 1992 and, later, a single European currency, the euro. They also promised closer cooperation on foreign political and military affairs. The latter goal has proven elusive, particularly as the conflicts in the Balkans during the 1990s tested the EU's political resolve. On the economic front, however, Europe now comprises the largest market in the world. The euro has been successfully inaugurated as a replacement for the multiple national currencies of many of its members. (Informally called "Euroland," the countries adopting the euro are Austria, Belgium, Finland, France, Germany, Greece, Ireland, Italy, Luxembourg, the Netherlands, Portugal, and Spain.) Eventually the euro may challenge the top currency role of the dollar. The EU anticipates expanding further to include the democratic states in Eastern Europe. Hence it continues its relentless push to create a continent-wide economic union with Brussels as its centerpiece (but compare Martin and George 1999).

Increasingly the EU's economic clout has caused friction with the United States. C. Fred Bergsten (2001), director of the Institute of International Economics, worries that the United States and Europe "are on the brink of a major trade and economic conflict." Their differences contributed to the foundering of the Doha Round of trade negotiations launched in 2001. However, instead of pursuing unilateral retribution, the Bush administration still chose to pursue many of its claims through the multilateral venue of the dispute resolution body of the WTO. Matters referred to it includes the dispute with the EU subsidies on large aircraft and the use of bovine growth hormone in American beef. Europe and the United States also continue to differ markedly on global warming issues, as we saw in Chapter 6. Those issues have important implications for a wider array of energy and related environmental policies.

Regional concerns extend beyond Europe. Japan has long been the dominant economic power in Asia. The United States, viewing itself as a Pacific power, took the initiative in creating the Asia-Pacific Economic Cooperation (APEC) forum, hoping to play a leading role in shaping the future of Asian economic relations in the global competition for regional economic power.

For years scholars and policy makers have speculated about the possible emergence of three large currency and trade blocs, one in Europe centered on the EU and the euro; one in the Western Hemisphere centered on the United States and the U.S. dollar; and the third in Asia centered on Japan and the Japanese yen. Japan, however, has showed little interest in playing a leadership role in creating an Asian economic area with Tokyo as the leader. Indeed, its imperial past continues to ignite passionate resentment and fear throughout much of Asia. The Asian region as a whole is moving toward preferential trading arrangements, and steps are being taken toward coordinating currency values. Asian leadership may now be contested by a rapidly developing China, despite the fact that the Chinese yuan lacks reserve currency status comparable to the Japanese yen (Calder 2006).

The status of a supposed North American regional bloc is also in question as the United States is now widely regarded as "losing Latin America" since the election of strong Leftist leaders in Venezuela, Bolivia, and Brazil, the general failure to move forward with the FTAA,[13] and the growing Chinese interest in the region. In fact, President Hu of China twice visited Latin America before making his first trip to the United States in 2006. Illegal immigration continues to be a troublesome and divisive issue as well (Hakim 2006).

The French and Dutch rejection of the proposed EU constitution in 2005, which reflected underlying unhappiness with freedom-of-movement rules in the single market, the euro and EU monetary policy, and enlargement of the union suggest that the EU may not yet be ready to function as a solid bloc either (Cohen-Tanugi 2005). The possibility and implications of regionally oriented political economies centered on Asia, Europe, and North America thus remain unclear (see, for example, Kahler 1995; Mansfield and Milner 1997; Trade

Blocs 2000). Although NAFTA and related regional initiatives in Africa, Asia, and Latin America were thought by some to be consistent with GATT's rules, other analysts worried that they violated the principle of nondiscrimination underlying the liberal trade system, thus taking it one more step toward closure. The same is true with the vast array of new, regionally based schemes now in sight (see Trade Blocs 2000). Although such cooperative arrangements might lead to trade liberalization *within* each region, they arguably would promote that liberalization by discriminating against those *outside* the region. This has long been a complaint lodged against the European Union. Already a substantial portion of trade in Asia, Europe, and North America derives from imports and exports among the countries comprising the three regions.

Others are concerned with the impact that transforming economic relationships into regional centers may have on security relationships and consequences. One line of reasoning suggests that "bitter economic rivalry" is a likely outcome of a triangular world political economy because of fear that "there can be enduring national winners and losers from trade competition" (Borrus et al. 1992)—which is the logic underlying strategic trade theory. Strategic trade practices combined with the way technology develops and the changing relationship between civilian and military research and development will tempt states to "'grab' key technologies and markets before others can. Doing so would guarantee domestic availability of the industrial resources needed to field state-of-the-art military forces and eliminate the need to make unacceptable concessions." The result? Mercantile rivalry among the world's principal trading blocs, in which "fear of one another" may be the only force binding them together (Borrus et al. 1992).

Globalization Again

The strategic trade/managed trade fracas with Japan over automobiles and auto parts—and competitiveness—would pass as the economic fortunes of Japan and the United States reversed

course during the 1990s. As we have noted, Japan stumbled into a prolonged economic slump while the U.S. economy soared. Interestingly, dramatic increases in the productivity of American workers widely attributed to the spread of information and communications technologies undergirded the prolonged period of prosperity and growth. Hegemony resurgent again became an appropriate aphorism.

It is notable that the growing trade imbalances of the United States with its principal trading partners between 1994 and 2004 (see Figure 7.3) were not accompanied by the harsh, protectionist politics of the 1980s and early 1990s. Prosperity at home explained part of this. Who was threatened? Also notable is that the product mix coming from abroad in the latter half of the 1990s was notably different than earlier. By the end of the decade, for example, China rivaled Japan as having the largest trade imbalance with the United States. Still, this did not provoke the vociferous criticism from domestic political interests that the automobile controversy with Japan ignited. Arguably one reason is that the products China exports to the United States are no longer products in which American producers choose to compete. The George W. Bush administration, despite its general pro–free trade orientation, imposed tariffs on both imported steel and Canadian softwood lumber. American producers are competing in both areas, and the political timing of the steel tariffs in 2002 (prior to Congressional midterm elections), was strongly suspected as the impetus behind these protectionist measures. The steel tariffs were later rescinded when the WTO declared them illegal.

Bush generally avoided the use of Super 301 for retaliatory purposes, instead relying on Sections 201 (anti-dumping) and 301 when needed as well as seeking redress through the dispute resolution mechanisms of NAFTA and WTO. The Bush administration also argued that the popular Byrd Amendment (2000), which funnels roughly $1 billion in anti-dumping duties back to the "injured" U.S. firms per year, should be repealed. A WTO panel ruled against the Byrd Amendment in 2002, but it took the Congress until January 2006 to repeal it. The law will officially expire on October 1, 2007.

Today many products imported from abroad are produced and distributed globally by American companies, so it is difficult to determine who benefits from trade liberalization and who pays for trade competition. Indeed, "made in America" is an increasingly rare find. Even American automobiles (such as Chrysler) are produced by foreign-owned companies, and companies that are not foreign-owned buy many of their components from foreign producers or make them in co-production schemes with foreign companies. Wal-Mart, the world's largest corporation, virtually requires its suppliers to produce goods in China and other low-cost countries, which it then distributes throughout the world at its famous low prices. Wal-Mart alone purchased $18 billion of goods from U.S. and foreign companies with production facilities in China, making the giant retailer by itself (in 2004) China's eighth largest trading partner (Hughes 2005).

The Politics of U.S. Trade Policy We have referred repeatedly in this chapter to the way in which labor and environmental groups have become energized on trade issues in recent years. At one time, labor was a champion of free trade, and environmental interests were focused largely at home. Neither is true today. Hence the politics of U.S. trade policy have changed in ways that have important consequences for a world political economy in transition, but one in which the United States remains a key player (see Hockin 2001; Das 2001; Rothgeb 2001). Indeed, environmental and labor issues arguably now comprise the "new protectionism" (Stokes 1999–2000). Simultaneously, rules governing trade are increasingly merging with domestic regulator law. And in a globalizing world, the U.S. Food and Drug Administration "effectively set health and safety rules for the Asian, European, and Latin American pharmaceutical industries by establishing norms for the world's largest market (the United States) and for some of the world's largest drug companies (American firms)" (Stokes and Choate 2004).

During the early post–World War II decades, a broad domestic consensus supported trade liberalization, but labor groups began to defect in the 1970s and 1980s, as the declining competitiveness of U.S. exports and the loss of jobs to foreign competitors affected them adversely. American workers' income also began to stagnate in the 1970s, a trend that persisted into the twenty-first century. Meanwhile, workers' rights related to workshop conditions (such as child labor and "sweatshops") and unionization in other countries where organized labor is weak gained importance (see Kapstein 1996; Newland 1999), as did related issues, such as China's human rights practices. Globalization was behind these developments. By 1993, labor (a backbone of support for the Democratic party) had become even more antagonistic to trade liberalization issues, leading it to oppose NAFTA. Clinton won that fight only with the strong support of congressional Republicans and their business allies.

Globalization also animated environmentalists' interests in trade issues. We have noted some of their concerns as they relate to the ability of the WTO (and GATT before it) to overturn hard-won domestic environmental victories in the name of free trade. Hence labor and environmentalists, otherwise odd political bedfellows, were seen marching together in globalization protests in Seattle, Quebec, and Washington, D.C. (see Cohen 2001).

I. M. Destler and Peter Balint (1999) use the phrase "trade and . . ." to encapsulate how American trade politics have moved beyond simply reconciling competing commercial interests to accommodating a wider array of issues that globalization has magnified. They describe the "trade and . . ." issues as those that "involve not the balance to be struck *among* U.S. commercial interests, but the proper balance *between* these interests and others that society values." Principal among them, as we have noted, are issues that "involve labor and environmental standards enforced (or not enforced) by U.S. trading partners and the impact that the global trade regime may have on U.S. capacity to strengthen or maintain prolabor and proenvironmental measures here at home." The side agreements the Clinton administration negotiated to win approval of NAFTA stimulated much of the debate over "trade and . . ." issues. Three agreements related to environmental enforcement and workers' rights were deemed important to winning approval of the agreement. Faced with opposition within his own party, Clinton would later seek to make these issues a centerpiece of future efforts to devise new trade liberalization rules. Other countries, however, were not pleased. Many in the Global South, for example, viewed the extension of American labor standards through multilateral trade agreements as yet another form of Northern trade protectionism. Environmentalists continued to worry about the erosion of domestic laws in the face of others' rulings. Business interests, on the other hand, worried that labor and environmentalist demands would erode their ability to compete in the world marketplace.

Dissension over "trade and . . ." issues has figured prominently in the unwillingness of Congress to grant the president renewal of trade promotion authority, as this would permit him to negotiate agreements with other countries that would either include or exclude these items as he saw fit, without the ability to Congress to make changes in those agreements. Yet trade promotion authority is viewed by pro-trade internationalists as essential to the ability of the United States to continue to exercise a leadership role in the world political economy. Without that leadership, they argue, regionalism, mercantilism, protectionism—all anathema to the LIEO—will surge.

Recognizing these realities, President George W. Bush asked Congress shortly after the Third Summit of the Americas in Quebec to grant him trade promotion authority that would enable the United States to move toward creation of a Free Trade Area of the Americas. His proposal sought to placate the competing interests evident in the trade fights Clinton faced by suggesting a "labor and environmental toolbox" that could be used by international organizations to urge countries to comply with international labor standards and environmental practices. The implication is that the agreements the Bush administration might negotiate would not include enforceable labor or environmental standards, as none would be linked directly to the new agreements. Not surprisingly, the reception was less than warm among Democrats, for whom these issues have become salient.

"The toolbox is empty," is the way one Democratic lawmaker responded. Yet, at least the rhetoric of labor and environmental standards has been incorporated into all FTAs negotiated by the Bush administration.

THE POLITICS OF MONEY AND GRADE IN A GLOBALIZING WORLD: PRIMACY AND MUDDLING THROUGH

American leadership in the world political economy and in the international political system has long been prized not only in the United States but also in other countries. Increasingly, however, others are concerned about the exercise of American leadership. Concepts and terms we have used in this and previous chapters, and those we will introduce in Chapter 8, suggest something about the apprehension of others. Primacy, aggressive unilateralism, hard-line, hyperpower, neomercantilism—these are among the phrases that other states often associate with an arrogance of power. Our theories of international politics predict that an arrogance of power will lead to balancing behavior by others, not the bandwagoning witnessed during the Cold War. Certainly many of the behaviors of other states in the world political economy during recent years are consistent with balancing behavior.

Globalization has enhanced the soft power of the United States. It has also opened states' borders to forces over which they sometimes have little control. The United States is not immune from the vanishing borders phenomenon, as we have seen. Liberal internationalists believe that further liberalization of the world political economy is necessary if the fruits of progress experienced in the 1990s are to be sustained in the new century. They also believe that American leadership is essential to that process. American policy makers, on the other hand, can no longer count on broad-based domestic support for liberalization. Instead, they must balance domestic and international interests. Often this offends one or the other, sometimes both. This has been especially evident on the issue of protecting America's border with Mexico.

Repeated calls for new institutions to cope with new realities have been heard. Certainly the rules guiding the economic institutions operating today are vastly different from the way they looked when the Bretton Woods system was launched in the 1940s. But it seems unlikely that institutions whose purposes depart radically from those already in place will be launched. Thus we find ourselves in a challenging, transitional world political economy in which only incremental adjustments can be expected. In the words of one analyst commenting at the time of the 1997–1998 global currency crises, "The best we can expect for the foreseeable future is a muddle-through strategy based on existing cooperative frameworks" (Kapstein 1999).

KEY TERMS

beggar-thy-neighbor
   policies
collective goods
dollar convertibility
economic nationalists
fair trade
fixed exchange rate
   system
free-floating exchange
   rates
free riders
General Agreement on
   Tariffs and Trade
   (GATT)

globalization
Group of 77 (G-77)
Group of Eight (G-8)
hegemon
hegemonic stability
   theory
IMF conditionality
imperial overstretch
International Mone-
   tary Fund (IMF)
Liberal International
   Economic Order
   (LIEO)
managed trade

most-favored-nation
   (MFN)
multilateralism
neomercantilism
New International
   Economic Order
   (NIEO)
nontariff barriers
   (NTBs)
normal-trade-relations
   (NTR)
strategic trade
Super 301

trade promotion
   authority
World Bank
World Trade
   Organization
   (WTO)

SUGGESTED READINGS

Bhagwati, Jagdish N. *The Wind of a Hundred Days: How Washington Mismanaged Globalization.* Cambridge, MA: MIT Press, 2001.

Destler, I. M., and Peter J. Balint. *The New Politics of American Trade: Trade, Labor, and the Environment.* Washington, DC: Institute for International Economics, 1999.

Eichengreen, Barry J. *Toward a New Financial Architecture: A Practical Post-Asia Agenda.* Washington, DC. Institute for International Economics, 1999.

Friedman, Thomas L. *The Lexus and the Olive Tree: Understanding Globalization.* New York: Farrar, Straus, Giroux, 1999.

Gilpin, Robert. *The Challenge of the Global Capitalism: The World Economy in the 21st Century.* Princeton, NJ: Princeton University Press, 2000.

Kunz, Diane B. *Butter and Guns: America's Cold War Economic Diplomacy.* New York: Free Press, 1997.

Schaeffer, Robert K. *Understanding Globalization: The Social Consequences of Political, Economic, and Environmental Change,* 3rd ed. Lanham, MD: Rowman and Littlefield, 2005.

Mansfield, Edward D., and Helen V. Milner, eds., *The Political Economy of Regionalism.* New York: Columbia University Press, 1997.

Narlikar, Amrita. *The World Trade Organization: A Very Short Introduction.* Oxford: Oxford University Press, 2005

Nye, Joseph S., and John D. Donahue, eds. *Governance in a Globalizing World.* Washington, DC: Brookings Institute Press, 2000.

Rothgeb, John M., Jr. *U.S. Trade Policy: Balancing Economic Dreams and Political Realities.* Washington, DC: CQ Press, 2001.

Stiglitz, Joseph E. *Globalization and Its Discontents.* New York: Norton, 2003.

Yergin, Daniel, and Joseph Stanislaw. *The Commanding Heights: The Battle Between Government and the Marketplace that Is Remaking the Modern World.* New York: Simon & Schuster, 1999.

NOTES

1. We confine the use of hegemon or hegemony to America's role in the world political economy, recognizing, however, that there is a close interaction between economic and political dominance.

2. For a concise overview of the international monetary system that places the Bretton Woods system in the broader context of the nineteenth and early twentieth centuries, as well as the post–Bretton Woods period after 1973, see Eichengreen (1998).

3. Our discussion of the international monetary and trade systems draws on Spero (1990) and Spero and Hart (1997). See also Schwartz (1994) and Walters and Blake (1992).

4. Declassified documents from the Truman and Eisenhower administrations clarify the role the United States played in encouraging aggressive Japanese exports to the United States. They also reveal how concern for communism in Asia stimulated choices based on political rather than economic criteria, whose consequences contributed to the ability of Japan to challenge the United States economically decades later. See Auerbach (1993) for a summary.

5. "The theology in government that a gradually declining dollar is good for U.S. competitiveness is a dangerous oversimplification," argued Jeffrey E. Garten, investment banker and author of *A Cold Peace: America, Japan, and Germany and the Struggle for Supremacy.* He added that "there is no precedent in history where a major industrial power has been competitive while its currency was depreciating" (cited in Mufson 1992).

6. The G-77 did agree in early 1999 to establish a modest forum whose purpose would be to foster consultations on exchange rate fluctuations and other problems related to the Asian contagion, including movements in international hedge funds (*New York Times,* 21 February 1999, 14).

7. As is often the case, the meaning of "new protectionism" has changed and today encompasses concerns about environmental issues and labor standards that we discuss later in this chapter. See Stokes (1999–2000).

8. The concept is from dependency theory, which classifies states into core (industrialized countries) and periphery (developing countries), according to their position in the international division of labor. For discussions, see Caporaso (1978), Shannon (1989), Sklair (1991), and Velasco (2002).

9. Trade policy expert I. M. Destler explains:

   Fast-track [now known as trade promotion authority] is Washington's solution to a bedrock constitutional dilemma. The president and the executive branch can negotiate all they like, but Congress makes U.S. trade law. Other nations know that our highly independent legislature will not necessarily deliver on executive promises. So in negotiations where broad-ranging commitments to open markets are exchanged, they refuse to bargain seriously unless U.S. officials can assure that Congress will write their concessions into U.S. statutes. Fast-track offers that assurance, with its promise that Congress will vote up or down, within a defined time period, on legislation submitted by the president or implement specific trade agreements.
   (Destler 1999, 27)

10. Developing states had earlier opposed inclusion of counterfeiting on the GATT agenda. The practice—which involves such things as Rolex watches, Apple computers, and photo-reproduced college textbooks—is widespread in much of the Global South. The United States has been especially critical of China, arguing that it engages in widespread piracy of computer software, musical compact discs, and video laser discs. At the time the Uruguay Round ended, such practices were alleged to have cost American companies as much as $1 billion a year (*New York Times,* 24 July 1994, 8).

11. The environmental consequences of free trade are subject to often vigorous dispute. For contrasting viewpoints, see Bhagwati (1993, 2001), Daly (1993), Destler and Balint (1999), Esty (1994), and French (1993).

12. For a critique of Krugman's arguments and a rejoinder, see especially the essays by Clyde V. Prestowitz, Jr., Lester C. Thurow, Stephen S. Cohen, and Krugman in the July/August 1994 issue of *Foreign Affairs.*

13. Shortly after the 2006 election of Evo Morales as president of Bolivia, and following on the heels of Venezuela's election of anti-American president Hugo Chavéz, *USA Today* correspondent David J. Lynch headlined an article saying, "Anger over free-market reforms fuels leftward swing in Latin America." "Across the region," he wrote on February 9, 2006, "leaders railing against 'savage capitalism' are now the norm, and major U.S. initiatives such as the Free Trade Area of the Americas lie dormant."

PART IV

Societal Sources of American Foreign Policy

8

Americans' Values, Beliefs, and Preferences:

Political Culture and Public Opinion in Foreign Policy

America has never been united by blood or birth or soil. We are bound by ideals that move us beyond our backgrounds, lift us above our interests, and teach us what it means to be citizens.
PRESIDENT GEORGE W. BUSH, 2001

Nobody can know what it means for a President to be sitting in that White House working late at night and to have hundreds of thousands of demonstrators charging through the streets. Not even earplugs could block the noise.
PRESIDENT RICHARD M. NIXON, 1977

Foreign policy is often believed to be "above politics." Domestic interests are subservient to national interests, according to this viewpoint. When national security is at stake, Americans lay aside their partisan differences and support their leaders as they make the tough choices necessary to promote and protect the national interest in an anarchical world. *Politics,* in short, *stops at the water's edge.*

Consider what happened in the days following the 9/11 terrorist attacks on the United States. Public approval of President Bush's job performance shot from 55 percent to 90 percent, the highest level ever recorded by the Gallup Organization (see also Murray and Spinosa 2004). As "politics as usual" were pushed aside, Congress, with strong bipartisan support, quickly passed a resolution granting the president wide latitude in framing a response to those responsible for the acts of terrorism. Shortly thereafter, again with strong bipartisan support, Congress passed the USA Patriot Act. Even at the expense of civil liberties long enjoyed by Americans, the Patriot Act gave the president more discretion in pursuing terrorist suspects intent on penetrating American society and avoiding attention until they could strike again. Before the end of the year, the president would create a White House Office of Homeland Security, precursor of the Department of Homeland Security, a product of the largest reorganization of the federal government in decades.

"Rally round the flag" effects typically occur when the nation faces crises or peril. But typically the effects are short-lived and rarely as dramatic as the 2001 rally, as "politics as usual" regains a foothold in foreign and national security debates. The war against Iraq is illustrative. Although initiated under a sweeping congressional mandate and with equally widespread public support, by the time sovereignty was transferred to a new Iraqi government in mid-2004, less than half of the American public believed that going to war against Iraq had been worthwhile. About the same time, a bipartisan Senate committee issued a stinging critique of pre-war intelligence used to justify the war. Senator John Rockefeller (D-West Virginia), ranking minority member of the Senate Committee on Intelligence that issued the report, concluded that "We in Congress would not have authorized that war—we would NOT have authorized that war—with 75 votes if we knew what we know now."

The growing divisions over Iraq helped shape the 2004 presidential campaign, as both the motives for the war and its prosecution were fiercely contested. Thirty-five years earlier, the country was similarly bitterly divided as the United States waged a fierce war in Vietnam.

War is not the only issue that transcends the political mythology that "politics stops at the water's edge." Even seemingly less contentious issues like promoting human rights abroad or raising the homeland terrorist security threat level from "guarded" to "elevated" often arouse deep-seated partisan and ideological differences.

In politically charged environments, it is not unreasonable to expect that policy makers will be concerned about the domestic repercussions of the choices they face. As one former policy maker lamented,

> [American leaders have shown a] tendency to make statements and take actions with regard not to their effect on the international scene to which they are ostensibly addressed but rather to their effect on those echelons of American opinion . . . to which the respective [leaders] are anxious to appeal. The questions, in these circumstances, [become] not: How effective is what I am doing in terms of the impact it makes on our world environment? but rather: How do I look, in the mirror of domestic American opinion, as I do it? Do I look shrewd, determined, defiantly patriotic, imbued with the necessary vigilance before the wiles of foreign governments? If so, this is what I do, even though it may prove meaningless, or even counterproductive, when applied to the realities of the external situation.
> *(Kennan 1967, 53)*

This viewpoint suggests that foreign policy decisions are likely to be guided more by concern for the reactions they might provoke at home than abroad. Preserving one's power base and the psychological desire to be admired encourage foreign policy decisions designed to elicit favorable domestic responses. At the extreme, theater substitutes for rational policy choice; spin control becomes an overriding preoccupation.

Our purpose in this chapter is to ask how America's political culture—Americans' beliefs about their political system and the way it operates—and the public's foreign policy attitudes and preferences—public opinion—shape American foreign policy. Then, in Chapter 9, we explore the roles that interest groups, the mass media, and presidential elections play in transmitting beliefs, attitudes, and preferences into the policymaking process. Throughout, we seek to understand how these societal forces constrain leaders' foreign policy behavior and when and how they encourage policy change.

POLITICAL CULTURE AND FOREIGN POLICY

The characteristics that make the United States the kind of nation it is shape Americans' self-image and their perceptions of their country's proper world role. In the waning days of the Cold War, many analysts worried that the relative decline of the United States in the world community would make it more like an "ordinary" country. Today, however, it is clear the United States remains far from typical. It is the world's fourth-largest country in geographical size and third in population. It is endowed with vast natural resources, wealth, technology, and overwhelming military might—a "hyperpower" among the democratic market economies of the Global North and throughout the world.

Americans and their leaders generally share the notion that the United States is set apart from others. Indeed, it is commonplace to observe that "the nation was explicitly founded on particular sets of values, and these made the United States view itself as different from the nations of the Old World from which it originated" (McCormick 1992). Because it is set apart, the reasoning continues, the United States has special responsibilities and obligations toward others. In short, American foreign policy may be different from the policies of other states because the United States itself is unique.

The concept of *political culture* refers to the political values, ideas, and ideals about American society and politics held by the American people. What are these core values, ideas, and ideals? Analysts' views differ (see Elazar 1994; Huntington 2004a; Huntington 2004b; Kingdon 1999; Lipset 1996; McClosky and Zaller 1984; Morgan 1988; Parenti 1981) not only because many of the latest immigrant groups want to maintain their cultural heritage, making it difficult to generalize safely about the degree to which some values are

universally embraced, but also because the nation's "loosely bounded culture" (Merelman 1984) is fluid and pluralistic. It allows the individual citizen freedom to practice his or her own philosophy while still upholding a commitment to the nation. Thus the American political tradition emphasizes majoritarianism but simultaneously tolerates disagreement, parochial loyalties, and counter allegiances.

The Liberal Tradition

Despite diversity, and respect for it, certain norms dominate. There are values and principles to which most Americans respond regardless of the particular political philosophy they espouse. Although no single definition adequately captures its essence, the complementary assumptions that comprise "mainstream" American political beliefs may be labeled *liberalism.* Basic to the liberal legacy is Thomas Jefferson's belief, enshrined in the Declaration of Independence, that the purpose of government is to secure for its citizens their inalienable rights to life, liberty, and the pursuit of happiness. The "social contract" among those who created the American experiment, which sought to safeguard these rights, is sacred. So, too, is the people's right to revolt against the government should it breach the contract. "Whenever any form of government becomes destructive of those ends," Jefferson concluded, "it is the right of the people to alter or abolish it."

In the liberal creed, as Jefferson affirmed, legitimate political power arises only from the consent of the governed, whose participation in decisions affecting public policy and the quality of life is guaranteed. Other principles and values embellish the liberal tradition, rooted in the seventeenth-century political philosophy of the English thinker John Locke. Among them are individual liberty, equality of treatment and opportunity before the law ("all men are created equal"), due process, self-determination, free enterprise, inalienable (natural) rights, majority rule and minority rights, freedom of expression, federalism, the separation of powers within government, equal opportunity to participate in public affairs, and legalism ("a government of laws, not of men"). All are consistent with Locke's belief that government should be limited to the protection of the individual's life, liberty, and property through popular consent.

Together, these tenets form the basis of *popular sovereignty,* which holds that "the only true source of political authority is the will of those who are ruled, in short the doctrine that all power arises from the people" (Thomas 1988). Abraham Lincoln's embrace of government of, by, and for the people affirms this fundamental principle. Because the American ethos subscribes enthusiastically to this principle, Americans think of themselves as a "free people."

American leaders—regardless of their partisan or philosophical labels—routinely reaffirm the convictions basic to the *Lockean liberal tradition.* So do the documents Americans celebrate on national holidays. Even those who regard themselves as political conservatives are in fact "traditional liberals who have kept faith with liberalism as it was propounded two hundred years ago" (Lipsitz and Speak 1989). Thus it is not surprising that other countries typically see few differences in the principles on which American foreign policy rests, even when political power shifts from one president to another or from one political party to the other.

Liberalism and American Foreign Policy Behavior

In a classic treatise on *The Liberal Tradition in America,* Louis Hartz (1955) argues that Lockean liberalism has become so embedded in American life that Americans may be blind to what it really is—namely, an ideology. The basis for the ideology of liberalism, so the reasoning holds, is the *exceptional American experience.* It includes the absence of pronounced class and religious strife at the time of the nation's founding, complemented by the fortuitous gift of geographic isolation from European political and military turmoil.

To mobilize public support for U.S. actions abroad and endow policy decisions with moral value, American leaders often have cloaked their actions in the rhetoric of the ideological precepts of American exceptionalism and Lockean liberalism.

Principles such as self-determination and self-preservation are continually invoked to justify policy action, as "concern with wealth, power, status, moral virtue, and the freedom of mankind were successfully transformed into a single set of mutually reinforcing values by the paradigm of Lockean liberalism" (Weisband 1973).

Remaking the world in America's image also springs from the nation's cultural traditions. As President Ronald Reagan once put it, "Our democracy encompasses many freedoms—freedom of speech, of religion, of assembly, and of so many other liberties that we often take for granted. These are rights that should be shared by all mankind." Accordingly, in 1983 Reagan launched the *National Endowment for Democracy (NED),* a controversial program whose purpose is to encourage worldwide the development of autonomous political, economic, social, and cultural institutions to serve as the foundations of democracy and the guarantors of individual rights and freedoms (see Carothers 1994b). NED continues to operate. And just as liberty and democracy infused much of its mission, so, too, the foreign policy of the current Bush administration builds heavily on those long-standing values.

The promotion of democracy abroad also rests on a set of beliefs that blend the premises of classical democratic theory and capitalism into a deeply entrenched ideology of **democratic capitalism.** While democracy and capitalism have common historical and philosophical roots, at home they have sometimes been in conflict. Capitalism in particular has led to great inequalities in income and wealth. According to the U.S. Census Bureau, for example, between 1973 and 2002 the share of U.S. income held by the wealthiest 20 percent of American households grew from 44 percent to 50 percent, while the share held by the bottom fifth fell from 4.2 percent to only 3.5 percent. Abroad, however, the premises of democratic capitalism embedded in the American culture help explain Americans' distaste for socialism and why they viewed Soviet communism as a threat to "the American way of life." The same premise motivated the Clinton administration's post–Cold War "democratic enlargement" policies, whose intent was the "enlargement of the world's free community of market economies."

The cultural ethos in the United States supports equality of opportunity, not equality of outcome. That may help explain what appears to be public indifference to the plight of so many poor people around the world. Noteworthy is that "the spread of democracy has made more visible the problem of income gaps, which can no longer be blamed on poor politics—not on communism in Eastern Europe and the former Soviet Union nor on military authoritarianism in Latin America. Regularly invoked as the handmaiden of open markets, democracy looks more and more like their accomplice in a vicious cycle of inequality and injustice" (Birdsall 1998; see also *World Development Report 2000/2001*).

Despite its seemingly negative consequences for equality of outcome, the liberal tradition influences in other ways how the United States seeks to promote democratic capitalism abroad.

> Guided by faith in the liberal tradition's nostrums and by the mechanistic notion learned in civics class that a community is built by balancing competing interests, American foreign policy experts urge societies riven by conflict to play nice: to avoid "winner takes all" politics and to guarantee that, regardless of election results, the weaker party will have a voice in national political and cultural affairs. To accomplish this, coalition governments, the guaranteed division of key offices, and a system of "mutual vetoes," are always recommended.
>
> *(Schwarz 1998, 69)*

A political system constructed this way is expected to ameliorate conflict, much as Americans believe their own balance-of-power political system does. Noteworthy is that the United States designed just such an arrangement for the interim government in Iraq as it planned for the transfer of sovereignty to the Iraqis in June 2004: each of the principal ethnic groups—the Kurds, the Sunnis, and the Shia—were to have sufficient power to balance the others so as to protect their own interests and integrity.

The American way of war also has roots in the liberal tradition. Among the industrialized countries, more Americans than anywhere else are churchgoers and profess that religion is an important part of their life. Not surprisingly, then, in every war America's side is God's side (Lipset 1996). Less flattering is the argument that the American penchant to resort to military force abroad is sustained by a culture of violence at home (Payne 1996).

Civil Religion

For more than a decade, the Gallup Poll has reported that nearly six of every ten Americans regard religion as "very important" in their lives. Religiosity and values associated in particular with evangelical Protestants figured prominently in the reelection of George W. Bush in 2004. Religion is important to the life of the country in other ways. Described as civil religion (Bellah 1980, 1992; Bellah and Hammond 1988), religiosity provides much of the glue that knits together the nation's predominantly Christian culture around a single theme or cause without violating the constitutional division of church and state. Indeed, the civil religion reinforces (and arguably is part of) the transcendent purposes at the birth of the new American republic. If nothing else, the religious pluralism evident in the tolerance of diversity among the early settlers laid the basis for civil religion. The nation could embrace a religious "creed," much as it embraced the political philosophy of liberalism.

Civil religion manifests itself in many ways. Public spaces, monuments, and political figures are treated as part of the nation's hallowed and sacred heritage. Often they are associated with war and other violent challenges to America: the Gettysburg battlefield (and Address); Arlington National Cemetery, Washington's obelisk and Lincoln's memorial on the Washington mall, where monuments to the veterans of Vietnam, Korea, and World War II have recently been added to the nation's hallowed areas. So, too, has the site of the 9/11 tragedy. Family and friends of the victims of the terrorist attacks as well as those responsible for reconstruction of the World Trade Center—to be renamed the "freedom tower"—have taken great strides to ensure that honor and preservation will mark the "footprints" and other ground where the twin towers once stood as symbols of the world's most vibrant capitalist, market economy

George W. Bush embraced the civil religion in his prosecution of the war on terrorism. Other presidents, notably Jimmy Carter and Ronald Reagan, appealed to Americans' religious faith to support their foreign policy initiatives, but no president before Bush so openly and unabashedly appealed to Americans' religiosity. In an April 2004 speech and national news conference on Iraq, for example, Bush spoke with missionary zeal about his foreign policy goals: "Freedom is the Almighty's gift to every man and woman in this world. And as the greatest power on the face of the Earth, we have an obligation to help the spread of freedom. . . . It's a conviction that's deep in my soul."

In his 2002 State of the Union address, Bush branded Iraq, Iran, and North Korea an "axis of evil." The phrase evoked memories of the Axis totalitarian powers of the 1930s—Germany, Italy, and Japan—whose aggressive behavior sparked World War II. The word "evil" carried sinister Biblical overtones. Earlier, in the days immediately following 9/11, Bush described the war on terror as a "crusade." That touched off a storm of criticism in the Muslim world, where "crusade" recalls Christian military expeditions against Muslims during the Middle Ages, whose purpose was to retake the Holy Land from the Arabs.

Rhetoric shapes policy debates, often powerfully so. So the rhetoric of civil religion in combination with constraints of the political culture arguably enhances and also limits the range of foreign policy actions the American people find acceptable. Policy makers themselves may also rule out certain options because of their anticipation of public disapproval. Assassination of foreign political leaders (murder for political purposes) has been against U.S. law since the 1970s. The war against terrorism has renewed a vigorous debate in Washington about the veracity of this prohibition. Is the

political culture (and the subtext on civil religion) limiting the range of choice on this policy issue?

The *law of anticipated reactions* captures the potential constraining effects of the political culture. It posits that decision makers screen out certain alternatives because they foresee they will be adversely received—an anticipation born of their intrinsic image of the American political culture, which helps to define in their minds the range of the permissible. As one analyst put it, political culture's influence "lies in its power to set reasonably fixed limits to political behavior and provide subliminal direction for political action . . . all the more effective because of [the] subtlety whereby those limited are unaware of the limitations placed on them" (Elazar 1970).

Robert F. Kennedy's argument against using an air strike to destroy the missiles the Soviet Union surreptitiously placed in Cuba in 1962 illustrates this subtle screening process. As he himself described it:

> Whatever validity the military and political arguments were for an attack in preference to a blockade, America's traditions and history would not permit such a course of action. Whatever military reasons [former Secretary of State Dean Acheson] and others could marshal, they were nevertheless, in the last analysis, advocating a surprise attack by a very large nation against a very small one. This, I said, could not be undertaken by the U.S. if we were to maintain our moral position at home and around the globe. Our struggle against communism throughout the world was far more than physical survival—it had as its essence our heritage and our ideals, and these we must not destroy.
> *(Kennedy 1969, 16–17; see also Evan 2000)*

This screening process has sometimes failed, of course—especially when principle clashes with power. Thus fear of communism helps to explain how a country committed to individual rights and liberties sometimes suppressed them in the name of national security. Is history repeating itself with the war on terrorism? Is the discretion accorded the president and the presidency in the USA Patriot Act (renewed as a permanent statute in 2006) the appropriate symbol?

Similarly, the ascent of the United States to the status of a global power after World War II helps explain how a country committed to "limited government" nonetheless could permit the rise of an "imperial presidency," undeterred by the constitutional system of checks and balances, and justify the creation and maintenance of a gigantic peacetime military establishment (see Deudney and Ikenberry 1994). Again, is history repeating itself? Is the Department of Homeland Security the appropriate symbol?

We also must underscore that the ideas and ideals comprising the political culture are open to competing interpretations and are often in flux. Demographic and other domestic developments as well as challenges from abroad may coalesce to generate changes in otherwise durable values and beliefs. Because the political culture is not immutable, policy makers may feel less constrained by anticipated reactions to their policy choices than would otherwise be the case.

Political Culture in a Changing Society

Consider what happened to the 1960s' generation. Raised to believe that the United States was a splendidly virtuous country, young Americans learned—from the Bay of Pigs invasion of Cuba; racial discrimination in Selma, Alabama, and elsewhere; the assassinations of President Kennedy, his brother Robert, and Martin Luther King, Jr.; and then Vietnam—that ideals were prostituted in practice. Outraged, large numbers of alienated Americans protested the abuses that undermined seemingly sacred assumptions. Simultaneously, the faith the American people placed in their political and other social institutions declined precipitously. They also began to question traditional American values.

With the political culture in flux, the climate of opinion encouraged policy change. A war ended ignominiously. Two American presidents were

toppled: one (Lyndon Johnson) in the face of intense political pressure, the other (Richard Nixon) in disgrace. Legal barriers to racial equality were dismantled. New constraints were placed on the use of military force abroad, both overt and covert, and the range of permissible action (e.g., assassination) was reduced in ways that continue to shape policy thinking today. Thus it appears that changes in the political culture—whether they stem from public disillusionment, policy failure, or other causes—can affect the kinds of policies that leaders propose and the ways they are later carried out.

Today the core values comprising American society and its political culture continue to be split along lines that mirror the 1960s and 1970s. Many of the "baby boomers" who came of age politically during these decades show greater tolerance toward homosexuals and others who have suffered discrimination and toward practices ranging from interracial marriage to premarital sex that once might have been condemned. The free expression of controversial views is also seemingly more tolerated (Broder and Morin 1999).

While greater tolerance of diversity characterizes some Americans' views, in other ways the United States has become sharply divided on values issues. The "culture war" that began in the aftermath of Vietnam now profoundly shapes political differences among Americans, as revealed in the 2004 presidential election. Moral values became the defining issue in the outcome of the election, eclipsing both the war on terrorism and the war in Iraq. Differences between evangelical Protestants and others colored voting outcomes throughout the country, with George W. Bush the clear preference among evangelicals.

The political culture faces another divisive challenge that promises to further test its tolerance and other core values: ***multiculturalism.*** "At the core of multiculturalism . . . is an insistence on the primacy of ethnicity over the individual's shared and equal status as a citizen in shaping his or her identity and, derivatively, his or her interests" (Citrin et al. 1994; see also Huntington 2004b; Gilpin 1995). Thus multiculturalism promotes *communal rights,* whereas liberalism rejects them in favor of *individual rights* and equal opportunity.

Multiculturalism challenges the conception of the United States as a pluralistic society, one embodied in the nation's original motto, *e pluribus unum*—out of many, one. The motto reflects Americans' immigrant heritage, which led President Reagan to describe the United States as an "island of freedom," a land placed here by "divine Providence" as a "refuge for all those people in the world who yearn to breathe free." It also reflects the conviction that diversity itself can be a source of national pride and unity, something no other nation has ever tried or claimed. The American effort to build a multiethnic society, argues historian Arthur Schlesinger (1992), is "a bolder experiment than we sometimes remember."

The *melting pot* became a popular metaphor to describe the process that assimilated the newly arrived into the dominant social and political ethos—that combination of ideas and ideals Swedish social scientist Gunnar Myrdal (1944) described more than half a century ago as "the American creed."[1] That metaphor aptly describes how the mostly European immigrants in the nineteenth and early twentieth century embraced the American creed. Today, however, most immigrants come from Asia and Central and South America, especially Mexico. In 2002, 32.5 million foreign-born people lived in the United States, comprising 11.5 percent of the population. More than a third of them came from Mexico or another Central American country. Already they have changed the composition of American society—and will continue to do so. Combined with other demographic trends, it is now possible to foresee a future in which Americans of European stock will no longer comprise a majority of what will then be the nation's more than 420 million residents. As President Clinton observed in commemorating Martin Luther King, Jr. Day in the waning days of his presidency, "America is undergoing one of the great demographic transformations in our history. . . . Today there is no majority racial or ethnic group in Hawaii or California or Houston or New York City. In a little more than fifty years, there will be no majority race in America."[2]

With the American creed under stress, the nation's immigration policy also is under attack. Where migrants of European origin were once given preferential access, today the emphasis is on the skills migrants will bring with them, not their national origin. Meanwhile, many Americans have jettisoned the melting pot metaphor. A 1993 *Newsweek* poll (9 August 1993) found that only 20 percent of the American people believed the United States is still a melting pot, compared with two-thirds who felt that today's immigrants "maintain their national identity more strongly." Many Americans fear that immigrants threaten their jobs or end up on states' welfare rolls. Seven years after the *Newsweek* poll, during a time of booming economic activity, the Pew Research Center for the People and the Press (2000) found that nearly 40 percent of the American people embraced the view that "immigrants today are a burden on our country because they take our jobs, housing, and health care." Reflecting that sentiment, the citizens of Arizona voted during the 2004 presidential election in favor of a state proposition designed to deny illegal immigrants access to public services. Earlier, in 1996, President Clinton signed into law the Illegal Immigration Reform and Immigrant Responsibility Act, which restricted public benefits for foreign nationals.

The impact of the growing number of Hispanic immigrants on the United States is the subject of a controversial book titled *Who Are We?* written by Harvard political scientist Samuel Huntington (2004a; see also Huntington 2004b). Hispanics, he argues, threaten American society, values, and its way of life. What is the basis of those values and way of life? Huntington replies that "mainstream Anglo-Protestant culture" is what unites the diverse subcultures that make up American society:

> One has only to ask: Would America be the America it is today if in the seventeenth and eighteenth centuries it had been settled not by British Protestants but by French, Spanish, or Portuguese Catholics? The answer is no. If would not be America; it would Quebec, Mexico, or Brazil.
>
> *(Huntington 2004a, 59)*

Protestant religion, then, is central to Huntington's conception of the "American ethos." He criticizes our earlier characterization of the United States as a "liberal" society built on the premises of John Locke's liberal political philosophy. This, he writes, gives "a secular interpretation to the religious sources of American values." Recognizing that economic and other motives led the early settlers to the New World, he retorts that "religion still was central." He further argues that "The twenty-first century . . . is dawning as a century of religion. Virtually everywhere, apart from Western Europe, people are turning to religion for comfort, guidance, solace, and identity." He notes in particular that "Evangelical Christianity has become an important force" in America. The outcome of the 2004 presidential campaign vividly illustrates that force.

Against this background, Huntington worries that the influx of Hispanics, Mexicans in particular, challenge the very foundations of America. The seeming inability or unwillingness of Hispanics to assimilate into the "mainstream Anglo-Protestant culture" lies at the heart of his concern. The alleged unwillingness of Hispanics to learn English and the de facto spread of Spanish as a second national language symbolize Hispanics' failure to assimilate culturally. Huntington reinforces his anti-Mexican immigrant argument by asking what would happen if Mexican immigration were to stop abruptly:

> The annual flow of legal immigrants would drop by about 175,000, closer to the level recommended by the 1990s Commission on Immigration Reform. . . . Illegal entries would diminish dramatically. The wages of low-income U.S. citizens would improve. Debates over the use of Spanish and whether English should be made the official language of state and national governments would subside. Bilingual education and the controversies it spawns would virtually disappear, as would controversies over welfare and other benefits for immigrants. The debate over whether immigrants pose an economic burden on state and federal governments would be decisively resolved in the negative. The average education and skills of the immigrants continuing to arrive would reach their highest levels in U.S. history. The inflow of immigrants would again become highly diverse, creating increased incentives for all immigrants to learn English and absorb U.S. culture. And most important of all, the possibility of a de facto split between a predominantly Spanish-speaking United States and an English-speaking United States would disappear, and with it, a major potential threat to the country's cultural and political integrity.
>
> *(Huntington 2004b, 32–33)*

The foreign policy implications of multiculturalism in general and immigration in particular are not entirely clear, but they are potentially profound. Already governments must cope with widespread diasporas. These are "transnational ethnic or cultural communities whose members identify with a homeland that may or may not have a state" (such as the Palestinians) (Huntington 2004a). Huntington estimates the size of the Mexican diasporas as 20–23 million people. They maintain not only a close identity with Mexico but also close ties through travel, trade, and other financial transactions. The same is true of other diasporas. All have grown in size and importance through the globalization processes widely evident in the 1990s. As one political analyst observed,

> Globalization has greatly expanded the means through which people in one country can remain actively involved in another country's cultural, economic, and political life. In fact, money transfers, travel and communications, networks and associations of nationals living abroad, and other new or improved opportunities for expatriates to "live" in one country even as they reside in another may be creating a powerful tool for development.
>
> *(Naim 2002, 96)*

Diasporas have the capacity to shape foreign policy makers' choices, much as interest groups already do. The vast increase in Mexican immigrants, both legal and illegal, has certainly shaped U.S.-Mexican relations in recent years. More broadly, Huntington writes that the nation's interests "derive from national identity."

> If American identity is defined by a set of universal principles of liberty and democracy, then presumably the promotion of those principles in other countries should be the primary goals of American foreign policy ... If the United States is primarily a collection of cultural and ethnic entities, its national interest is in the promotion of the goals of those entities and we should have a "multicultural foreign policy." If the United States is primarily defined by its European cultural heritage as a Western country, then it should direct its attention to strengthening its ties with Western Europe. If immigration is making the United States a more Hispanic nation, we should orient ourselves primarily toward Latin America.
>
> (Huntington 2004a, 10)

Huntington concluded this way: "Conflicts over what we should do abroad are rooted in conflicts over who we are at home."

One final note on the potential impact of multiculturalism on American foreign policy. The "elite" who have shaped that policy since the early twentieth century and especially since World War II have generally been European-stock leaders who embraced and promoted the logic of liberal internationalism. Multiculturalism may well diminish their influence domestically, pushing the United States away from the hegemonic posture now evident in the Bush administration's policies or the accommodationist agenda of its predecessors. Will future leaders, responding to the country's changing demographic patterns, pull back from the globalist posture—whether liberal or hegemonic—embraced for decades? Will some form of regionalism, even isolationism, emerge dominant as the character of

American foreign policy as the United States itself changes? Knowing the nature of the political culture in a changing society will help us to better anticipate how these questions will be answered.

PUBLIC OPINION AND FOREIGN POLICY: A SNAPSHOT

Like America's diplomatic history, public attitudes toward the U.S. role in the world have alternated between periods of introversion and extroversion, between isolation from the world's problems and active involvement in shaping them to fit American preferences. Public support for global activism dominated the Cold War era. The nature of internationalism has undergone fundamental changes, however, especially during and since the Vietnam War. Internationalism is now also under challenge in some quarters, as the costs in blood and treasure of hegemony take their toll.

Coming to grips with the twenty-first century challenge will be difficult, as the American people embrace sometimes competing foreign policy goals:

- They favor global activism, but prefer multilateralism over unilateralism.

- They yearn for peace through strength, but are wary of international institutions.

- They enjoy the benefits of free trade and globalization, but worry their own jobs may be outsourced.

- They oppose the use of American troops abroad, but back presidents when they choose force of arms.

- They support preemptive war at least "sometimes," but reject the view that the United States should assume the role of global policeman.

Little wonder that the role public opinion plays in shaping the country's conduct is poorly understood and often suspect, and why policy makers sometimes disparage it. John F. Kennedy's view, as described by his aide Theodore C. Sorensen (1963) is a timeless insider's view: "Public opinion is often erratic, inconsistent, arbitrary, and unreasonable—with a compulsion to make mistakes. . . . It rarely considers the needs of the next generation or the history of the last. . . . It is frequently hampered by myths and misinformation, by stereotypes and shibboleths, and by an innate resistance to innovation."

Despite this viewpoint—whether accurate or not—a vast coterie of media, political, and private groups now spend millions of dollars every year to determine what the American people think. Although modern polling ranges far beyond politics to touch virtually every aspect of Americans' private and public lives, political polling is extraordinarily pervasive (and intrusive). The seemingly axiomatic importance of political attitudes in today's world explains the compulsion to measure, manipulate, and master public opinion. As one observer put it, "Politicians court it; statesmen appeal to it; philosophers extol or condemn it; merchants cater to it; military leaders fear it; sociologists analyze it; statisticians measure it; and constitution-makers try to make it sovereign" (Childs 1965).

FOREIGN POLICY OPINION AND ITS IMPACT

Democratic theory presupposes that citizens will make informed choices about the issues of the day and ultimately about who will best represent their beliefs in the councils of government. The American people in turn expect their views to be considered when political leaders contemplate new policies or revise old ones, because leaders are chosen to represent and serve the interests of their constituents. The Constitution affirms the centrality of American citizens by beginning with the words "We the people."

The notion that ***public opinion,*** citizens' foreign policy attitudes and preferences, somehow conditions public policy is appealing, but it raises troublesome questions. Do public preferences lead American foreign policy, as democratic theory would have us believe, or is the relationship more

subtle and complicated? Do changes in foreign policy result from shifts in American public attitudes? Or is the relationship one of policy first and opinion second? Indeed, are the American people capable of exercising the responsibilities expected of them?

The Nature of American Public Opinion

The premise of democratic theory—that the American people will make informed policy choices—does not hold up well under scrutiny. That most Americans do not possess even the most elementary knowledge about their own political system, much less international affairs, is an inescapable fact. Moreover, people's "information" is often so inaccurate that it might better be labeled "misinformation." The following reveal the often startling levels of ignorance:

- In 1985, 28 percent of those surveyed thought that the Soviet Union and the United States fought each other in World War II; 44 percent did not know the two were allies at that time.

- In 1964, only 58 percent of the American public thought that the United States was a member of NATO; almost two-fifths believed the Soviet Union was a member.

- In 1997, as the Clinton administration pushed for expanding NATO, eight in ten Americans knew the United States was a member of the alliance, but less than 60 percent knew that Russia was not. After Hungary, Poland, and the Czech Republic were invited to join NATO, only one in ten Americans could recall the names of any of the invitees.

- In 1993, after more than a year of bitter conflict in the former Yugoslavia, only 25 percent of the American people could correctly identify the Serbs as the ethnic group that had conquered much of Bosnia and surrounded the capital city of Sarajevo—this despite reports that half or more of them had followed events in the region.

- In 1994, 46 percent of the electorate believed that foreign aid, which accounted for less than 1 percent of the federal budget, was one of its two biggest items.

- In 1999, just as the United States embarked on a military campaign against Serbia, only 37 percent of the American people knew the United States was supporting the Albanian Kosovars in the conflict.

- In 1985, only 63 percent of the public knew that the United States supported South Vietnam in the Vietnam War, a violent conflict that cost 58,000 American lives.

- In 2004, after numerous high profile reports refuted the claim that Iraq had weapons of mass destruction before the Iraq war, and even after the Bush administration itself had disavowed the allegation as a rationale for the war, over 70 percent of Republicans, 50 percent of independents, and 30 percent of Democrats still embraced that view (Jacobson 2007, 140).

Evidence demonstrating the extent of political misunderstanding and ignorance about basic issues could be expanded considerably, but it would only reinforce the picture of a citizenry ill-informed about major issues of public policy and ill-equipped to evaluate government policy making. Noteworthy is that the issues about which the public is persistently ignorant are not fleeting current events but typically ones that have long figured prominently on the national or global political agendas.

The absence of basic foreign affairs knowledge does not stem from deficiencies in U.S. educational institutions. It stems from disinterest. Public ignorance is a function of public inattention, because people are knowledgeable about what is important to them. More Americans are concerned about the outcome of major sporting events than with the shape of the political system or participating in it. Consider, for example, turnout rates in presidential elections: the percentage of eligible voters who voted in the fifteen presidential elections since World War II has ranged from 49 percent (1996) to

63 percent (1960). Ronald Reagan in 1980 and George H. W. Bush in 1988 were both elected president by only a third of the eligible electorate. In 1996, voter turnout dropped below 50 percent for the first time since 1925. In 2000, George W. Bush and Al Gore split almost evenly the 50 percent of the voting age population who participated in the election. Turnout "surged" to 55 percent in 2004. George W. Bush captured 50.7 percent of the vote, or just 28 percent of the voting age population, to win a second term. Strikingly, among modern presidents "only [Lyndon] Johnson ...won his first election by more than fifty-five percent of the two-party vote" (Brace and Hinckley 1993).

Turnout rates in congressional elections have been even lower, and other forms of political participation are confined to a select few. Between 1952 and 1998, for example, the proportion of Americans who profess to have worked for a political party or candidate during a congressional or presidential campaign never exceeded 7 percent (Conway 2000). In 1998, only 2 percent of the entire population indicated they had written or spoken to a public official about a foreign affairs issue in the preceding three or four years (Gallup Poll survey for the Chicago Council on Foreign Relations). In short, the United States purports to be a participatory system of democratic governance, but few are deeply involved in politics and most lack the interest and motivation to become involved. That reality applies to domestic as well as foreign affairs.[3]

Lack of interest, knowledge, and involvement led Gabriel A. Almond (1960) to conclude in his classic study, *The American People and Foreign Policy,* that public opinion toward foreign policy is appropriately thought of as "moods" that "undergo frequent alteration in response to changes in events," instead of resting on some kind of "intellectual structure." He argued that "The characteristic response to questions of foreign policy is one of indifference. A foreign policy crisis, short of the immediate threat of war, may transform indifference to vague apprehension, to fatalism, to anger; but the reaction is still a mood, a superficial and fluctuating response."

Are Interest and Information Important?

Almond's conclusion has long been regarded as conventional wisdom, but there are important reasons to question it (Caspary 1970; Holsti 1996, 2004). Most Americans may be uninformed about and seemingly indifferent to the details of policy, but they are still able to discriminate among issues and to identify those that are salient. Foreign and national security policy issues are typically among them, often jockeying with economic concerns (inflation, unemployment, deficits and debt, recession) for primacy. By the time of the 2004 presidential election—coming after both the 9/11 terrorist attacks and the onset of the war in Iraq—foreign and security policy issues again trumped domestic concerns, as was often true during the Cold War.

As the Pew Research Center summarized the results of a survey taken shortly before the election:

> Americans are often accused of being oblivious beyond their borders. In this [2004] election year, however, events overseas have eclipsed events at home as the most important issue to the voting public for the first time since Vietnam. For most of the 1990s, fewer than 10% of Americans rated foreign policy as the most important problem facing the nation. Today [August 2004], 41% cite defense, terrorism, or foreign policy as the most important national problem, compared with 26% who mention economic issues.
>
> (Pew Research Center 2004, 19. Commentary by Lee Feinstein, James M. Lindsay, and Max Boot.)

If the conclusion that the American people are indifferent to foreign policy is questionable—which it is—the relevance of their lack of knowledge is also suspect. Few people, including corporate executives, legislative aides, and political science majors and their professors would perform uniformly well on the kinds of knowledge and information questions pollsters and journalists pose to measure how well the general public is informed.

More important than interest and knowledge is whether the American people are able, in the aggregate, to hold politically relevant foreign policy beliefs. Their beliefs and the corresponding attitudes that both inform and spring from them may not satisfy political analysts when they evaluate the theory and practice of American democracy. Comparatively unsophisticated foreign policy beliefs may nonetheless be both coherent and germane to the political process.

Three examples on use-of-force issues make the point.

- *In Central America:* During the 1980s, many Americans proved unable to identify where in Central America El Salvador and Nicaragua are or who the United States supported in the long-simmering conflicts there. But they were nonetheless unwavering in their conviction that young Americans should not be sent to fight in the region. From the perspective of policy makers in Washington, the latter was the important political fact.

- *In the Middle East:* Few Americans could correctly identify Kuwait or Saudi Arabia as monarchies rather than democratic political systems, but they were still willing in 1990–1991 to send American men and women to protect them and to help them win their "freedom." To policy makers in the first Bush administration, the latter point was the politically relevant one.

- *In Europe:* Although unable to locate the ethnic conflict on a map, a significant majority of Americans in 1999 supported U.S. and NATO military intervention to stop Serbian aggression against the people of Kosovo. However, less than half of those polled favored the use of U.S. ground troops. The latter piece of data shaped President Clinton's decision to launch an air war against Serbia while pledging not to employ group troops.

To understand the frequent discrepancy between what Americans know, on the one hand, and how they respond to what they care about, on the other, it is useful to explore the differences between opinions and beliefs.

Foreign Policy Opinions

The Gallup Organization and major mainstream media routinely ask Americans what they think about many subjects. In a July 2000 survey, at a time when the Clinton administration was actively seeking to broker an agreement between Israel and the Palestinians governing the status of Jerusalem, Gallup found that 41 percent of Americans said their sympathies rested with the Israelis; only 14 percent sided with the Palestinians. In May of that year, as tensions between China and Taiwan mounted, by a 6 percent margin more Americans opposed the use of American military force to defend Taiwan than supported it. In the same month, by a 56 to 37 percent margin, they favored Congress passing a law that would grant China normal trade relations, permitting its admission to the World Trade Organization. A year earlier, in June 1999, as the United States and its NATO allies wrapped up a successful air bombardment campaign against Serbia's "ethnic cleansing" of Kosovar Albanians, four in ten Americans thought the United States had made a mistake in sending military forces to fight in the Balkans. Despite the fact there were no combat deaths suffered, only two in three also favored U.S. participation in an international peacekeeping force in Kosovo. And as the 2000 presidential election heated up, more than half of the American people supported building a national missile defense system favored by both major political parties (although they differed markedly on details). (These data may be accessed at www.galluppoll.com.) These poll data capture what we normally think of as *public opinion*. Often the opinions (attitudes) volunteered are highly volatile—and some may in fact be *nonattitudes* (individuals often do not have opinions on matters of interest to pollsters, yet, when asked, they will give an answer). The character of the issue, the pace of events, new information, or a friend's opinion may provoke change. So may "herd instincts": attitude change is stimulated by the

desire to conform to what others may be thinking—especially opinion leaders, political pundits, and policy makers themselves. Indeed, it is perhaps ironic that those who are most attuned to foreign policy issues are often the most supportive of global activism and what policy makers or other opinion influentials want (Zaller 1992). Hence Americans' opinions about specific issues appear susceptible to quick and frequent turnabouts as they respond to cues and events in the world around them.

Public attitudes change, but even in the short run they are less erratic than often presumed. Stability rather than change is demonstrably the characteristic response of the American people to foreign and national security policy issues (Shapiro and Page 1988).[4] Furthermore, changes observed in otherwise long stretches of stable attitudes are predictable and understandable—not "formless and plastic," as Almond once described them.

Consider two prominent and intertwined patterns of American foreign policy stretched across the past six decades: the wisdom of global activism and the costs of global interventionism.

Opinions about Global Activism   *Internationalism,* broadly defined as the conviction that the United States should take an active role in world affairs, enjoyed persistent public support throughout the forty-plus years of the Cold War and the nearly two decades that followed. Since the 1940s, various pollsters have asked Americans if they "think it will be best for the future of the country if we take an active part in world affairs or if we stay out." Following the end of World War II in 1945, 71 percent said active involvement would be best; in 2002, the percentage was exactly the same, dropping slightly, to 67, in 2004. Even so, measurable fluctuations are evident in this long record (see Figure 8.1).

During the 1960s and 1970s, in particular, support for global activism declined. It reached its ebb during the mid-1970s as a combination of worrisome concerns undermined the international ethos. The wrenching Vietnam experience challenged the assumption that military power by itself could achieve American foreign policy objectives; détente called

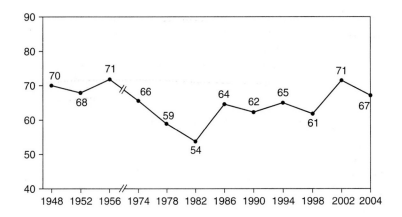

FIGURE 8.1 Support for the View that the United States Should Take an Active Role in World Affairs

SOURCE: Marshall M. Bouton. *Global Views 2004: American Public Opinion and Foreign Policy.* Chicago: Chicago Council on Foreign Relations, 2004, p. 17. Marshall M. Bouton. *Worldviews 2002: American Public Opinion and Foreign Policy.* Chicago: Chicago Council on Foreign Relations, 2002, p. 13.

into question the wisdom of the containment foreign policy strategy; and Watergate challenged the convictions that American political institutions were uniquely virtuous and that a presidency preeminent in foreign policy continued to be necessary. Despite these concerns, support for internationalism rebounded in the decade following Vietnam. That picture remained largely unchanged as the Cold War waned, despite the frequent claim that the American people turned inward following the fall of the Berlin Wall (see Figure 8.1). The perception was fueled by a mix of concern for domestic priorities and public apathy, not antagonism toward the rest of the world (Lindsay 2000a, 2000b; Bouton 2004).

Support for internationalism remained relatively stable during the 1990s, as the data in Figure 8.1 show. The figure also shows a sharp upturn in internationalism following Al Qaeda's terrorist attacks on the United States. This is perhaps a mirror image of the predictable "rally round the flag" phenomenon that typically accompanies crises. An isolationist response might also have been predictable, as survey data show that a third or more of Americans ascribe some responsibility for inviting the vicious attacks on the United States (Pew Research Center 2004, 30). (See Figure 8.2.)

Even as Al Qaeda stimulated internationalism, the Pew Research Center (2006a) recorded a sharp spike in support for *isolationism,* a policy of aloofness or political detachment from international affairs. When Americans were asked if the United States "should mind its own business internationally

and let others get along the best they can on their own," forty-two percent responded positively in 2005, an increase of twelve percentage points in just three years (Figure 8.2). The Pew Center expressed surprise at this finding: "In more than 40 years of polling, only in 1976 and 1995 did public opinion tilt this far toward isolationism" (Pew 2006a). President Bush perhaps sensed this growing sentiment when he exhorted Americans in his 2006 State of the Union address to reject "the false comfort of isolationism." Several challenges to and

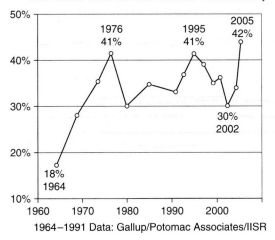

FIGURE 8.2 An Uptick in Isolationism?

SOURCE: *America's Place in the World 2005.* Washington, DC: Pew Research Center for the People and the Press, 2005, p. 1.

alleged shortfalls of the president's policies might be cited as examples what Bush saw as growing isolationist sentiment, with growing dissatisfaction with the war in Iraq as the principal cause.

Opinions about the Costs of Global Interventionism War and interventionism have commanded considerable attention in recent years. Public approval of war appears to occur just prior to and after its inception, followed—predictably perhaps—by a gradual but steady decline in bellicose attitudes and a corresponding rise in antiwar sentiments. The pattern suggests that American attitudes toward war are episodic rather than steady: in the context of actual war involvement, public attitudes range from initial acceptance to ultimate disfavor (Campbell and Cain 1965). The cost in treasure and blood appears to be the cause, as the wars in Korea (1950–1953), Vietnam (1962–1973), and Iraq (2003–present) illustrate. During each, enthusiasm closely tracked casualty rates: as casualty rates went up, support for the wars declined (Mueller 1971, 1973, 2005).[5]

Consider Iraq. With Korea and Vietnam, it is one of only three post–World War II conflicts in which the United States was "drawn into sustained ground combat and suffered more than 300 deaths in action" (Mueller 2005, 44). In each, initial enthusiasm was replaced with eventual disenchantment. Three years into the Iraq war, and more than 2,300 casualties later, a solid majority of Americans concluded that the war "was not worth it" (see Figure 8.3). John Mueller, a pioneer in the study of war and public opinion, concludes that the rapid decline in support for the Iraq intervention is one of its most striking characteristics. "By early 2005," he writes, "when combat deaths were around 1,500, the percentage of respondents who considered the Iraq war a mistake—over half—was about the same as the percentage who considered the war in Vietnam a mistake at the time of the 1968 Tet offensive, when nearly 20,000 soldiers had already died" (Mueller 2005, 45). Thus, "casualty for casualty, support [for Iraq] . . . declined far more quickly than it did during either the Korean War or the Vietnam War." He adds pessimistically, "If history is any indication, there is little the Bush administration can do to reverse this decline."

Why such a sharp decline? Mueller explains:

> This lower tolerance for casualties [was] largely due to the fact that the American public [placed] less value on the stakes in Iraq than it did on those in Korea and Vietnam [threat of communism]. The main threats Iraq was thought to present to

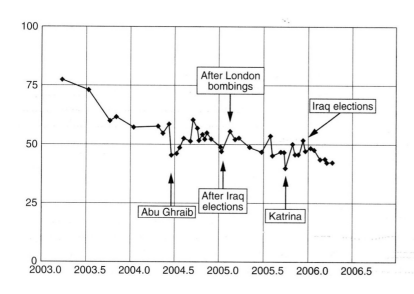

FIGURE 8.3 The Decline of Public Support for the War in Iraq, 2003–2006

NOTE: The poll question asked, "In view of the developments since we first sent our troops to Iraq, do you think we made a mistake in sending troops?"

The authors thank Professor Mueller for permission to use his data.

SOURCE: John E. Mueller, http://psweb.sbs. ohio-state.edu/faculty/jmueller/links.htm, accessed 11/11/06.

the United States when troops went in—weapons of mass destruction and support for international terrorism—[were], to say the least, discounted. With those justifications gone, the Iraq war [was] left as something of a humanitarian venture, and, as Francis Fukuyama . . . put it, a request to spend "several hundred billion dollars and several thousand American lives in order to bring democracy to . . . Iraq" would "have been laughed out of court."

(Mueller 2005, 45)

Mueller adds that "Given the evaporation of the main reasons for going to war and the unexpectedly high level of American casualties, support for the war in Iraq [was], if anything, higher than one might [have expected]—a reflection of the fact that many people still [connected] the effort there to the 'war' on terrorism, an enterprise that [continued] to enjoy huge support."

The *casualty hypothesis* for which Mueller's research provides important empirical support, is now widely recognized as the conventional wisdom. It says that Americans' tolerance for war is limited by the number of casualties suffered by its soldiers.[6] The hypothesis is supported by considerable research that extends beyond Korea, Vietnam, and Iraq (Larson 1996; Larson and Savych 2005). Distressingly, perhaps, American adversaries have also embraced those findings. As we noted in Chapter 4, Somalian warlord Aideed declared during the disastrous U.S. involvement in Somalia in the early 1990s, "We have studied Vietnam and Lebanon and know how to get rid of Americans, by killing them so that public opinion will put an end to things" (Blechman and Wittes 1999). Osama bin Laden, Slobodan Milošević, and Saddam Hussein also made similarly disquieting calculations (Feaver and Gelpi 2004).

Although the casualty hypothesis enjoys widespread acceptance, it continues to provoke inquiry. Political scientists Peter Feaver and Christopher Gelpi (2004), for example, maintain that the American people are "defeat phobic, not casualty phobic." Drawing on important surveys that seek to assess the correspondence between public and military leaders' attitudes, they note that policy makers can "tap into a large reservoir of support" for military missions and argue that Americans "appear capable of making reasoned judgments about their willingness to tolerate casualties to the extent that they view the missions as important for American foreign policy" (see also Laird 2005; but compare Mueller 2005).

Examinations of opinions about the humanitarian interventions of the 1990s add weight to their viewpoint. They show that the American people have proved to be "pretty prudent" when it comes to assessing the circumstances that might call for military intervention (Kohut and Toth 1994; Jentleson 1992, 1998). In particular, the use of military might to force change within other countries is less popular than situations that seek to impose restraint on others' foreign policies. Furthermore, Americans are not unwilling to support multilateral intervention, even if American lives are at risk, if the purposes are convincing (Burk 1999).

As with internationalism, the foregoing shows that the reasons underlying Americans' changing views of involvement in violent conflict are often compelling—suggesting once more that the public is better able to make prudent political judgments than political pundits would sometimes have us believe.

Foreign Policy Beliefs

The long-term stability and predictability in public attitudes are, as we have seen, intimately related to changes that have occurred at home and abroad, thus contributing to the rise of new foreign policy beliefs.

Although support for active involvement in world affairs rebounded in the 1980s from its nadir in the 1970s, internationalism or global engagement in the wake of the Vietnam tragedy came to wear two faces—a cooperative one and a militant one. Cooperative and *militant internationalism* grow out of differences among the American people not only on the question of *whether* the United States ought to be involved in the world (a central tenet of classical internationalism), but also on *how* it should be involved (Wittkopf 1990).

The domestic consensus favoring classical internationalism captured elements of both conflict and cooperation, of unilateralism and multilateralism. The United States was willing to cooperate with others to solve global as well as national problems; but if need be, it would also intervene in the affairs of others, unilaterally and with military force, if necessary, to defend its self-perceived vital national interests. In the years following World War II, a consensus emerged in support of these forms of involvement, but in the wake of Vietnam, concern about conflict and cooperation came to divide rather than unite Americans. Attitudes toward communism, the use of American troops abroad, and relations with the Soviet Union distinguished proponents and opponents of the alternative forms of internationalism.

Four identifiable belief systems flowed from these concerns, which inhered among elites as well as the mass of the American people (Holsti 2004; Wittkopf 1990):

- **Internationalists** supported active American involvement in international affairs, favoring a combination of conciliatory and conflictual strategies reminiscent of the pre-Vietnam internationalist foreign policy paradigm.
- **Isolationists** opposed both types of international involvement, as the term implies.
- **Hardliners** tended to view communism as a threat to the United States, to oppose détente with the Soviet Union, and to embrace an interventionist predisposition.
- **Accommodationists** emphasized cooperative ties with other states, particularly détente with the Soviet Union, and rejected the view that the United States could assume a unilateralist, go-it-alone posture in the world.

Although accommodationists and hardliners are appropriately described as "internationalists," it is clear their prescriptions for the United States' world role often diverged markedly. Hence they are best

described as *selective* internationalists. Accommodationists tend toward the "trusting" side in dealing with foes as well as friends. They prefer multilateralism over unilateralism as a means of conflict management and resolution and typically eschew the use of force. Accommodationists would choose sanctions over force, for example, and UN peacekeeping over U.S. peace enforcement.

Hardliners, on the other hand, believe in the utility of forceful persuasion and in projecting the United States to the forefront of the global agenda. For them, "indispensable nation" is a label to be embraced, not shunned. Thus, unlike internationalists, who join issues of cooperation and conflict as they relate themselves to global challenges and opportunities, accommodationists and hardliners are divided by them. To use a military analogy, *engagement* describes the preferences of both, but their interpretation of the *rules* of engagement typically differs markedly. Thus the emergence of two groups of selective internationalists undermined the broad-based domestic support for foreign policy initiatives that presidents in the Cold War era counted on, and made the task of coalition building, which more recent presidents have faced, more difficult.

Figure 8.4 shows the distribution of the mass public across the four belief systems described by the cooperative and militant internationalism dimensions in the two decades from 1974 through 1994. The differences in the proportion of Americans in each quadrant is not great.[7] Generally, however, the number of internationalists is greatest, followed by accommodationists, hardliners, and then isolationists. The political significance lies in the bifurcation of the internationalist/isolationist continuum and the different interpretations of internationalism offered by accommodationists and hardliners. Those differences were plainly evident in the 2000 presidential election, which pitted the accommodationist Al Gore against the hardliner George W. Bush.

Beliefs are important in understanding why public attitudes are often less fickle than might be expected. A **belief system** acts as "a set of lenses through which information concerning the physical and social environment is received. It orients the

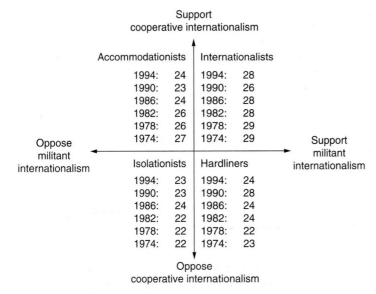

FIGURE 8.4 The Distribution of the Mass Public among the Four Types of Foreign Policy Beliefs, 1974–1994

SOURCE: Eugene R. Wittkopf. *Faces of Internationalism.* Durham, NC: Duke University Press, 1990, p. 26; Eugene R. Wittkopf, "Faces of Internationalism in a Transitional Environment," *Journal of Conflict Resolution* 38 (September 1994), 383; Eugene R. Wittkopf, "What Americans Really Think About Foreign Policy," *Washington Quarterly* 18 (Summer 1996), 94–95, author's data.

individual to his environment, defining it for him and identifying for him its salient characteristics" (Holsti 1962).

Belief systems also establish goals and order preferences. They enable people to systematically relate information about one idea to others. Importantly, this ability is not a function of information or knowledge; in fact, social cognition theory demonstrates that individuals use information shortcuts, based on their beliefs, to cope with ambiguous messages about the external environment. Paradoxically, then, ordinary citizens hold coherent attitude structures not because they *possess* detailed knowledge about foreign policy but because *they lack it.* "A paucity of information does not impede structure and consistency; on the contrary, it motivates the development and employment of structure. [Individuals attempt] to cope with an extraordinarily confusing world ... by structuring views about specific foreign policies according to their more general and abstract beliefs" (Hurwitz and Peffley 1987).

Because of their nature, beliefs are remarkably stable. Most images concerning foreign affairs are formed during adolescence and remain more or less fixed unless somehow disturbed. Peer group influences and authority figures may exert a modifying impact on images, but only the most dramatic of international events (war, for example) have the capacity to completely alter foreign policy beliefs (Deutsch and Merritt 1965). Relevant here is philosopher Charles Sanders Pierce's instructive comment on the dynamics of image change: "Surprise is your only teacher." Thus core beliefs, formed through early learning experiences, serve as *perceptual filters* through which individuals orient themselves to their environment and structure how they interpret international events they encounter later in life. If beliefs do change, they are likely to be replaced by new images that continue to simplify the world, albeit in new terms.

World War II, and the events that led to it, indelibly imprinted the world views of many Americans—including an entire generation of policy makers (Neustadt and May 1986). For the *Munich generation,* the message was clear: Aggressors cannot be appeased. To others, Vietnam was an equally traumatic event (Holsti and Rosenau 1984). For the *Vietnam generation,* the lesson was equally simple: There are limits to American power and the utility of military force in international politics.

(A dramatically different but now popular view holds that war, once begun, should not be prosecuted "with one arm tied behind our back.") The emergence of the distinctive beliefs associated with cooperative and militant internationalism in the wake of Vietnam thus conforms to our understanding of how beliefs change.

Did the end of the Cold War—dramatized by the crumbling of the Berlin Wall, long a symbol of the bitter East-West conflict—have a similar effect on Americans' foreign policy beliefs? Or did cooperative and militant internationalism, whose Cold War roots included fear of communism and dissension over how to deal with the now moribund Soviet Union, continue to describe differences among the American people about whether and how to be involved in the world in the last decade of the twentieth century? The evidence shows they did.

Individuals often ignore information that might cause them to change their beliefs or to engage in purposeful or inadvertent behavior that would otherwise reorient their perceptions to new realities.[8] Beyond belief system rigidity, the alternative internationalist orientations described above are not bound to the specific historical circumstances of the Cold War but transcend it (see Murray 1994; Russett, Hartley, and Murray 1994; Wittkopf 1996). The two faces of internationalism closely track *idealism* and *realism* (Holsti 1992)—competing visions of how best to deal with transnational problems, which predate the Cold War and persisted as new issues called for attention in the post–Cold War era, as we have seen in previous chapters. Thus in the 1990s, proponents of militant internationalism (particularly hardliners) were more likely than others to support the use of U.S. troops in places like Europe, the Middle East, and Korea, and to approve of CIA involvement abroad. Proponents of cooperative internationalism (particularly accommodationists), on the other hand, expressed greater support for extending NATO's protective umbrella eastward, normalizing relations with Cuba, Iran, Iraq, and Vietnam, supporting international institutions financially, and backing U.S. participation in UN and other multilateral peacekeeping and peace enforcement operations (Hinckley 1993;

Wittkopf 1994c, 1996, 2000; see also Kull, Destler, and Ramsay 1997; Holsti 1994, 2004; Murray 1994). The varying preferences track long-standing differences in realist and idealist prescriptions for coping with security challenges.

What about 9/11? Regrettably, data are not available that would permit an extension of the systematic analyses underlying the belief system clusters described above. Still, other information leads to the conclusion that the American people continue to be divided not only between internationalists and isolationists, but between two groups of selective internationalists: accommodationists and isolationists.

We have already seen that the terrorist attacks on that day boosted the proportion of Americans who supported an active U.S. world role. Particularly noteworthy is that the American people proved to be decidedly more multilateralist than unilateralist in orientation, a key element of both accommodationist foreign policy beliefs and traditional internationalism. Many surveys show this posture. A 2005 Pew Research Center survey (2005, 13) found that only 12 percent of the respondents thought the United States should strive to be the single world leader (25 percent preferred a "shared leadership" role). This is nearly identical to the proportion who held that view prior to 9/11 (Pew Research Center 1997). Another poll taken in 2004 found that a near majority (49 percent) believed "the nation's foreign policy should strongly take into account the interests of U.S. allies rather than be based mostly on the national interests of the United States" (Pew Research Center 2004, 2). Interestingly, there was little rancor separating Republicans and Democrats about the military action in Afghanistan, a truly multilateral effort from early in the conflict. Its purpose was to boot bin Laden from his training sanctuaries and, as in Iraq, force regime change by overthrowing the Islamic Taliban regime.

Before the 1991 Persian Gulf War, much of the domestic debate turned on the question of whether to continue to pursue sanctions against Saddam Hussein or resort to force. Colin Powell, then chairman of the Joint Chiefs of Staff, argued for sanctions, but eventually led the massive multinational coalition that defeated Iraqi forces on the ground. A decade later, now secretary of state, Powell mounted an effort in one of his first diplomatic initiatives to revise the sanctions approach to make it more selective and hence less harmful to the Iraqi people themselves and target more directly the Iraqi governing regime. That bid failed. As the threat of war mounted, the debate in Congress, the White House, and, arguably, among the American people, turned on whether to continue to rely on arms inspectors to verify the nature of Saddam Hussein's military force or resort to force of arms. Sanctions versus force; verification versus force—accommodationists versus hardliners.

Noteworthy in this respect is that partisanship and ideology are closely correlated with the two faces of internationalism. Conservatives and Republicans tend toward the hard-line belief system, liberals and Democrats toward the accommodationist. Partisan support and opposition to the Persian Gulf War, once launched, averaged about 20 percent (Holsti 2004, 173). Although comparatively large in relation to prior conflicts, the differences paled compared to the strikingly sharp divisions that accompanied the Iraq war a decade later. Republican President George H. W. Bush was himself a committed internationalist. It showed in his approach to the Gulf War. He determined with respect to the Iraqi invasion of Kuwait that "this will not stand," and he quickly moved U.S. troops to defend Saudi Arabia against an Iraqi encroachment. Then, using his extensive network of personal ties with other world leaders, he put together an overwhelming coalition of hundreds of thousands of troops to carry out mandates approved by the United Nations Security Council.

The purpose and strategy of the Iraq war was crafted by neoconservatives whose preference was to use American military power to spread American values. They advised a Republican president who had already demonstrated a unilateral thrust in his policies, as witnessed in the decisions about missile defense and the ABM treaty, and about global warming and the Kyoto agreement. Furthermore, widespread opposition to Bush's plans for Iraq was evident around the world. In the end, the United Nations Security Council refused to endorse the Bush plan, and the "coalition of the willing" that joined the United States was but a dim reflection of the coalition that routed Iraqi forces in 1991. From the very beginning, then, the Iraq war had a very distinctive "hard-line" cast that eventually opened deep partisan divisions in the American polity, the kind that persistence of the two faces of internationalism would anticipate.

Once war broke out, the president's party gave Bush more support than did the Democrats, as we would expect. But increasingly the Iraq intervention proved to be a deeply divisive, partisan issue—casting aside all notion that politics stops at the water's edge. In fact, compared with five other post–World War II interventions (Korea, Vietnam, Persian Gulf, Kosovo, and Afghanistan), the Iraq war proved to be by far the most divisive of all (Jacobson 2007). Republicans remained steady in their support of the Bush administration's policies; initial support from Democrats and independents quickly eroded (see Figure 8.5). Bush found that he had to spend much of the "political capital" earned in his 2004 reelection bid on the war. But to no avail. As we will discuss in more detail below, by the third anniversary of the invasion of Iraq, less than 40 percent of the public approved of the way Bush handled his job as president. Disaffection with the war and its rationale were primary causes of the widespread disillusionment with the president. Focus 8.1 summarizes findings of a Gallup survey taken in March 2006, three years after the war began. On virtually every dimension of the reasons related to war's onset, the American people registered pessimism and declining support. Meanwhile, on the critical issue of when the troops would come home, the president said that decision would be left to his successor and the new Iraqi government—hardly a popular response.

The Public "Temperament": Nationalistic and Permissive The responsiveness of the American people to events and the political information directed at them is—for better or worse—nowhere more apparent than in the support they accord their

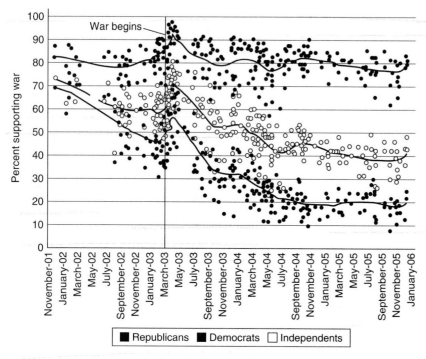

FIGURE 8.5 The Partisan Gap: Party Identification and Support for the Iraq War*

*Various question wordings.

SOURCE: Gary C. Jacobson, *A Divider, Not a Uniter: George W. Bush and the American People.* New York: Pearson/Longman, 2007, 132.

political leaders during times of crisis and peril. Like the citizens of other countries, Americans embrace **nationalism:** they value loyalty and devotion to their own country and promotion of its culture and interests as opposed to those of other countries. Nationalism sometimes includes the ethnocentric belief that the United States is (or should be recognized as) superior to others, and should therefore serve as a model for them to emulate.

No one would argue that all Americans always think nationalistically on all foreign policy issues. Generally, however, they perceive international problems in terms of "in-group loyalty and out-group competition" (Rosenberg 1965). In the extreme, nationalism results in a world view that accepts the doctrine, "my country, right or wrong." And because citizens often equate loyalty to the nation with loyalty to the current leadership, they

sometimes confuse admiration for their representatives in government with affection for country and its symbols: "my president, right or wrong." The public's nationalistic temperament stems in part from its tendency to view "things foreign" with hostility and fear. International politics often appears esoteric, secret, complicated, and unfamiliar—a cacophony of problems better left to experts who allegedly know better (and who, in turn, are quite willing to perpetuate the notion)—rendering public attitudes in the realm of foreign policy vulnerable to manipulation. People who feel threatened are prone to seek strong leadership to deal with the perceived threatening agent, a tendency policy makers have long recognized. Nazi leader Hermann Goering expressed this idea, contending, "Voice or no voice, the people can always be brought to do the bidding of the leaders. That is easy. All you have to do is to

---

F O C U S 8.1   Three Years of War in Iraq: The American People Respond

- The poll [conducted March 10–12, 2006] shows that 60% of Americans today say the war is not worth it, while in March 2003, just after the invasion of Iraq began, only 29% said it was not worth it to go to war.

- At the time, 69% of Americans said the United States would "certainly" win; today just 22% have that level of confidence. Also, at the time the war was launched, just 4% of the public thought it either unlikely the United States would win or certain it would not win; today 41% are that pessimistic.

- By 73% to 24%, Americans said the war was morally justified when it began; today the public is divided, with 47% saying it is morally justified and 50% saying it is not.

- Part of the Bush administration's justification for going to war was that such an undertaking would be part of the wider war on terrorism. Americans were divided on this issue in January 2003, with 50% agreeing and 48% disagreeing with the Bush administration. By August 2003, the public agreed by a larger margin, 57% to 41%. Today Americans reject the link between the war in Iraq and the wider war on terrorism by 53% to 44%.

- Shortly before the war began, 51% of Americans thought the war to overthrow Saddam Hussein targeted a leader who had personally been involved in the 9/11 terrorist attacks, while 41% disagreed. Today, by 54% to 39%, Americans say the Iraqi leader was not personally involved in the attacks.

- When no weapons of mass destruction were found in Iraq, a May/June 2003 CNN/*USA Today*/Gallup poll showed most Americans rejected the charge that the Bush administration deliberately misled the public about the matter, by 67% to 31%. Today, a slight majority, 51% to 46%,

believes the Bush administration did deliberately mislead the public.

- Though no weapons of mass destruction were found in Iraq after the invasion, today 57% of Americans express some degree of certainty that such weapons or programs to develop them were in Iraq just before the fighting began—29% feel definite about it, and another 28% think the weapons were there, though they have some doubt. In January 2003, two months before the war started, 86% of Americans thought such weapons might be there, including 41% who felt they definitely were there.

- Whatever change in opinion about the war that has occurred in the past three years, most Americans continue to believe that at least the Iraqi people are better off today than they were before the war. In May 2004, 72% of the public expressed that view, compared with 67% in the current poll.

- After three years of fighting by U.S. troops, Americans forecast a decidedly pessimistic future for Iraq—55% think it is more likely the situation there will degenerate into chaos and civil war, while just 40% expect the Iraqis to establish a stable government.

- This pessimism no doubt gives rise to the majority view that U.S. troops should be withdrawn from Iraq within a year—54% want either immediate withdrawal (19%) or withdrawal by March 2007 (35%). Another 39% say U.S. troops should remain as long as necessary to turn control over to the Iraqis. Four percent would send more troops to fight.

SOURCE: The Gallup Poll, Gallup Poll News Service, "Three Years of War Have Eroded Public Support," March 17, 2006 (www.galluppoll.com/content/?CI=21952, accessed 11/25/06).

---

tell them they are being attacked and denounce the pacifists for lack of patriotism."

Nationalistic sentiments find expression in the way Americans respond to the initiatives of their leaders during crises or threats from abroad, where the public's response is typically permissive. Presidents frequently realize their widest freedom of action in such circumstances, because the American people typically acquiesce in and support the decisions of their leaders.

The impact of dramatic foreign policy events and initiatives on presidential performance evaluations reveals clear evidence of the permissiveness of public attitudes. Typically such events produce the *"rally round the flag" phenomenon* that boosts a president's short-term popularity and offers strong public support for the use of executive power in the name of national security. Examples abound:

- George W. Bush's popularity with the American people spiked eight percentage points after Saddam Hussein was captured in December 2003.

- Bill Clinton's popularity jumped eleven percentage points following the June 1993 American cruise missile attack on Iraqi intelligence headquarters in Baghdad and nine points following the occupation of Haiti a year later.

- George H. W. Bush's popularity climbed by eighteen points following the initiation of military action against Iraq in January 1991.

- Ronald Reagan's approval notched upward by six points following the bombing of Libya in April 1986.

- Jimmy Carter's popularity jumped by thirteen points following the September 1978 Camp David accords between Israel and Palestinians.

- George W. Bush's popularity jumped a remarkable 35 percent after the 9/11 terrorist attacks. His popularity skyrocketed from 55 percent to 90 percent, the highest popularity rating ever recorded by Gallup, even surpassing his father's 89 percent rating following the 1991 military initiative against Iraq.

Such changes are evident across a broad range of foreign policy events, including wars, crises, peace initiatives, and summit conferences—all of which demonstrate the nationalistic and permissive responses of the American people to their leaders' policy initiatives and the challenges they face.

But the American people are also discriminating. Ronald Reagan's popularity plummeted by sixteen percentage points following the Iran-Contra revelations in late 1986, the largest drop ever recorded by the Gallup Poll (other polls recorded even steeper declines). Contrast this with John F. Kennedy, who found that his public approval actually rose to its peak (83 percent)

following the Bay of Pigs fiasco. Both involved mistakes in judgment, but the way each president handled his mistake appears to have significantly affected public perceptions of him. (In the Iran-Contra affair, not only did the American people disapprove of the sale of arms to Iran, they disbelieved the president's version of what happened and thought the administration was engaged in a cover-up similar to the Watergate affair [Ostrom and Simon 1989].) More typically, international crises are *approval-enhancing* events, whereas political scandals are *approval-diminishing* events (Ostrom and Simon 1989).

The Politics of Prestige

Presidents care about their popularity with the American people because it affects their ability to work their will with others involved in the policy process. Richard Neustadt (1980) explains the underlying logic in his classic book *Presidential Power:* "The Washingtonians who watch a president have more to think about than his professional reputation. They also have to think about his standing with the public outside of Washington. They have to gauge his popular prestige. Because they think about it, public standing is a source of [presidential] influence." In short, the more popular a president is, the more likely he is to accomplish his political agenda. This is the essence of what Dennis Simon and Charles Ostrom (1988) call the ***politics of prestige.***

Presidents also care about their popularity because it affects their political latitude. Both the absolute and relative levels of presidents' popularity, evidence suggests, are important in explaining America's political use of force short of war: the more popular presidents are, the more they are "freed" from domestic constraints to do as they wish abroad (Ostrom and Job 1986; also James and Oneal 1991; compare Lian and Oneal 1993; Meernik 1994). As one member of Congress commented on Bush's popularity following the invasion of Panama in 1989, "If the president's popularity is at eighty percent, I think [he] can do whatever he wants."

Rally-round-the-flag events, such as missile attacks on Iraq and Afghanistan or showing the flag in the Taiwan Strait, significantly affect presidents' popularity. Indeed, one presidential scholar (Lowi 1985a) argues that foreign policy comprises the only arena available to presidents that permits them to improve their popularity ratings once in office. But the state of the economy is the most potent predictor of presidential popularity. It was the principal factor that undermined the first Bush presidency and caused his 1992 reelection bid to fail.

George W. Bush, too, suffered from Americans' perception of the state of the economy and how he handled it. A Gallup poll taken at the time of the president's second inauguration revealed that only four in ten Americans (41 percent) thought the economy was "excellent" or "good"; the number was virtually the same a year earlier (Gallup Poll 2006, 3). At about the same time, a CNN/*USA Today*/Gallup poll survey found that over 60 percent of the American people disapproved of Bush's handling of the economy. Only 37 percent approved. Much like the war in Iraq, a sharp partisan gap characterized the responses on Bush's handling of the economy, with Republicans approving and Democrats and independents disapproving. ("Poll: Bush Approval Mark at All-Time Low," November 14, 2005, www.cnn.com/2005/POLITICS/11/14/bush.poll, accessed 11/26/06).

Still, the American people want peace as well as prosperity. Thus foreign policy sometimes figures prominently in the long-term erosion of support as well as the short-term boosts that most presidents experience. For Truman, the Korean War was the significant factor explaining the dramatic loss of public confidence in his leadership; for Johnson, the Vietnam War and riots in the cities were critical; for Nixon, it was the continuation of the Vietnam War and Watergate; for Carter, it was his inability to secure the release of Americans held hostage in Iran; and for George W. Bush, it is the war in Iraq.

Trends in presidential popularity are described in Figure 8.6. Presidents historically have been thought to begin their presidencies with a honeymoon—a crucial first few months after an election, in which the president is relatively free of harsh public criticism—only to find that in the long term their popularity declines. Interestingly, however,

none of the four most recent presidents experienced very enthusiastic honeymoons. The specific reasons vary, but the closeness of their electoral victories combined with increasingly bitter partisan polarization in the country doubtless undermined their early influence with Congress and the public. This is particularly evident with President George W. Bush.

As noted, specific events often cause erosion of presidential support, but it may also be stimulated by growing public dissatisfaction and lost patience with unfulfilled campaign promises, or perhaps by the adage that "familiarity breeds contempt."[9] With every presidential decision (or "nondecision"), opposition forms or becomes more vocal, Congress looks increasingly to its own parochial concerns, and the president's support seems to ooze away imperceptibly but steadily in what one scholar has described as a "cycle of decreasing influence" (Light 1991; see also Brace and Hinckley 1992). The tendency is symptomatic of the difficulties of running a government, managing a complex economy, and executing the nation's foreign policy in a manner satisfactory to a majority of Americans.

The experiences of our last three presidents—George H. W. Bush, Bill Clinton, and George W. Bush, deserve special comment—the first Bush because he failed in his reelection bid in 1992 despite having achieved the highest approval ratings ever given a president since modern polling began more than half a century earlier; Bill Clinton because he left office with the highest approval ratings since modern polling began despite being only the second president in American history to have been impeached; and the second Bush because the war on terrorism sustained him into his second term, but, like Harry Truman and Lyndon Johnson, he found himself dogged by an unpopular ground war that not only eroded his once lofty approval ratings but may also scar his historical legacy.

George H. W. Bush experienced the devastating effect of a declining economy on a president's popularity, which led to his defeat by Bill Clinton in 1992. The intriguing question is why Bush could not parlay his extraordinarily high popularity levels—89 percent according to the Gallup Poll in March 1991—into political survival

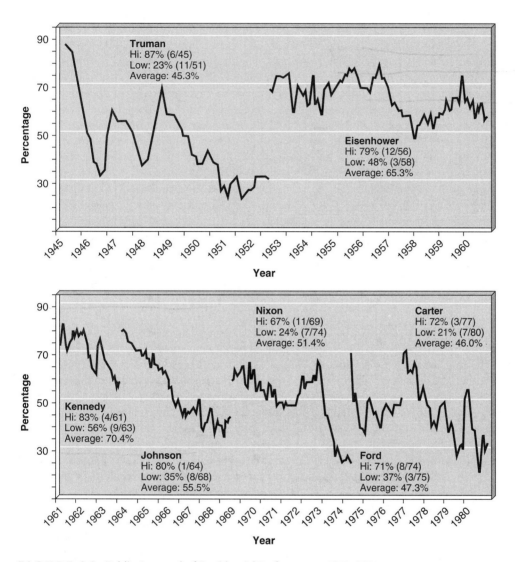

FIGURE 8.6 Public Approval of Presidential Performance, 1945–2001

NOTES: Data appear in monthly intervals beginning in June 1945 and ending in January 2002. In months with multiple polls, the last poll is used. In months where no poll was taken, the data are extrapolated using preceding and/or succeeding monthly data. The panels in the figure contain unequal numbers of monthly intervals.

SOURCE: Adapted from *The Gallup Opinion Index*, OctoberNovember 1980; various issues of *The Gallup Report* and *The Gallup Poll Monthly*, and available at www.gallup.com/poll/releas.

and longevity. The evidence suggests two answers to the question.

First, Bush's popularity manifested far wider gyrations than any of his predecessors over comparable periods in office. Ronald Reagan's popularity changed by more than five percentage points

only twice during his first three years in office, but Bush's changed by this amount nearly seven times as often, leading modern presidents in this kind of fluctuation (Brace and Hinckley 1993).

Second, Bush's sometimes unusually high but wildly fluctuating approval ratings did not sustain him

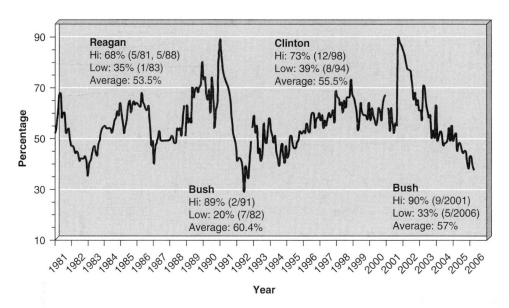

FIGURE 8.6 *continued*

because they were "tied less to George Bush the individual and more to a remarkable clustering of events" (Brace and Hinckley 1993). Most of these were international events, including the invasion of Panama, the crisis over Kuwait and the Persian Gulf War, the fall of the Berlin Wall, and the demise of communism in Eastern Europe. The White House played on each of these developments with considerable political drama, but it paid scant attention to domestic economic policy. Thus Bush's popularity appears to have been sustained almost entirely by international events of comparatively low salience to most Americans (Edwards, Mitchell, and Welch 1995). This made his popularity unstable and highly susceptible to damaging negative events. "With approval maintained at an artificial high point through a series of dramatic positive events," argue political scientists Paul Brace and Barbara Hinckley (1993), "any other events and presidential activities drove the polls down." In short, Bush's approval rating with the American people was not only higher than other presidents, it was also more vulnerable to losses.

Bill Clinton's story is less easily explained. The honeymoon during his first term was neither as long

nor his approval rating as high as some of his predecessors, a reflection perhaps not only of his comparatively weak electoral base but also his controversial decision to focus immediate attention on the issue of homosexuals in the military. Partisan disputes over his economic program and proposed tax increases and continuing concern about the state of the economy also plagued the new president. Moreover, the media cut him little slack. During his first eighteen months in office, nearly two-thirds of television news evaluations of Clinton were negative, compared with the evenly balanced coverage Bush had received previously. Press coverage was also markedly less positive than Clinton's approval ratings with the mass public ("They're No Friends of Bill: TV News Coverage of the Clinton Administration," Media Monitor, 1994, www. cmpa.com/mediaMonitor/documents/julaug94.pdf, accessed 11/12/06).

Gradually, however, Clinton's popularity gained momentum. No single foreign policy event explained this; instead, it was the increasingly vibrant state of the U.S. economy, which extended from the first through most of his second term. The enigma of that term is that the domestic scandals that dogged him throughout his presidency, leading to his impeachment in December 1998, cost him very little in the polls. Again, the bubbling U.S. economy contributed to his continued positive job approval ratings.[10] As Alan Greenspan, the powerful chairman of the Federal Reserve Board, chirped in a May 1998 meeting with the president, "This is the best economy I've ever seen in fifty years of studying it" (Woodward 2000). At the time, Clinton's approval rating stood at 64 percent, well above the 57 percent he experienced shortly after his second inauguration. Remarkably, this was after four months of investigations into Clinton's dalliance with a White House intern by Whitewater independent counsel Kenneth Starr. Starr pursued his investigation relentlessly. In August 1998, Clinton found himself before a federal grand jury, a first for a president, answering difficult questions about his affair with the intern and other matters. Four months later he was impeached by the House of Representatives on perjury and obstruction of justice charges. Clinton's approval rating was 66 percent the day after his grand jury testimony. Shortly after his impeachment, it stood at a stunning 73 percent, an all-time high. And two years later, his 67 percent approval rating ranked as the highest of any other outgoing president—even surpassing Dwight Eisenhower and Ronald Reagan.

Faced with such penetrating domestic scandal and partisan invective, how is it possible to explain Clinton's remarkably resilient popularity? "It's the economy, stupid!"—Clinton's 1992 campaign rallying cry—comes readily to mind. But is that answer sufficient? The historical record is replete with examples of presidents' undoing in the face of a potentially approval-diminishing scandal. But Clinton was immune. The reason, it appears, is because the American people were, at that time, seemingly willing to separate private morality from their assessment of a person's job performance. As two veteran Washington reporters wrote at the time of Clinton's grand jury testimony, the public "sees two very different Bill Clintons: the president whose stewardship of the nation's economy and decisiveness in foreign affairs they continue to applaud, and

the man whose scandal-plagued personal life is viewed with increased disgust, embarrassment, and even sadness" (Broder and Morin 1998; see also Kernell 1999). Interestingly, the apparent separation of private life and professional competence may have benefited George W. Bush. Just before the 2000 presidential election, news accounts reported that Bush had been arrested in 1976 for driving under the influence of alcohol, but the revelation had no discernible impact on voters' evaluations of his qualifications for the presidency.

The election of George W. Bush in 2000 was by far the closest and most contentious in a century or more. He lost the popular vote but won the electoral college vote (and the Supreme Court's). Not surprising, then, his incoming popular approval was substantially less than Clinton's outgoing approval, and it dropped even further almost immediately. For him, 9/11 was an enormously important approval-enhancing event, as his approval jumped to 90 percent. Bush quickly portrayed himself a forceful leader, a "war-time president" committed to stamping out international terrorism, however long it might take. His antiterrorist commitment sustained his entire presidency and was a critical factor contributing to his reelection in 2004.

All presidents seem to experience a low point at some time in their presidency. But can they survive? Shortly before Ronald Reagan's reelection campaign the country found itself in a seriously deep recession. Reagan's popularity fell accordingly, as can be seen easily in the low point of his approval rating in 1983. But the economy rebounded, and so did Reagan.

In contrast, George W. Bush faced an increasingly unpopular war. He retained high marks on character, leadership style, and the war on terrorism, especially among his core supporters (Republicans and conservatives). But even among Republicans, Bush's overall approval rating eroded, dropping to 74 percent in late April 2006 from an average of 91 percent across his entire presidency (www.galluppoll.com, accessed 11/12/06). Meanwhile, others began to separate the war in Iraq, including Saddam Hussein's connection to Al Qaeda, from the war on terrorism. Furthermore, an early 2006 decision to approve (reportedly without the president's personal knowledge[11]) a plan that would have put government-owned Dubai Ports World in charge of several key U.S. ports rattled the confidence even his core supporters had in Bush's commitment to protect the United States against terrorists.

Along the way the president suffered other setbacks: tales of torture and inhumane treatment of Iraqi prisoners at the U.S.-run Abu Ghraib prison in Iraq; an inability to stem the development of either North Korea's or Iran's nuclear weapons program; a burgeoning trade imbalance with China; and soaring costs for imported oil and gasoline at the pump. Domestically, concern erupted over the speed and competence of the administration in responding to Hurricane Katrina, which devastated the Gulf coast in August 2005 in what may have been the largest natural disaster ever experienced by the United States. Concern also mounted in Congress among Republicans as well as Democrats about revelations that Vice President Cheney's national security adviser had allegedly disclosed the name of an undercover CIA agent (Bush himself later acknowledged he had declassified portions of the National Intelligence Estimate in which the pertinent information could be found), and that the President had authorized—without court order—wiretaps of Americans engaged in overseas conversations with possible terrorist suspects. In most of these situations, but not all (e.g., the wiretaps), public opinion polls revealed that most Americans regarded the events as approval-diminishing.

As the president approached the 2006 midterm congressional elections, when Bush, his policies, and his party would be under review by the electorate, he unveiled a strategy reminiscent of the one that returned him to the White House in 2004: determined on the war on terrorism; committed to democracy in Iraq; strong on national defense. However, the strategy failed to achieve the same results. With growing public dissatisfaction over the situation in Iraq, Democrats secured a sweeping victory, winning control of both the House and the Senate. This result coupled with the president's lame duck status raised serious questions about his capacity to carry out his foreign policy agenda during his final years in office.

Public Opinion and Foreign Policy: An Addendum

The preceding discussion could be expanded in several ways. Here we briefly make two additional observations: the components of the concept *public opinion,* and the political and sociodemographic correlates of foreign policy opinions and beliefs.

The Public Opinion Pyramid   American society is structured like a pyramid, with a very small proportion of *policy influentials* (people who are knowledgeable about foreign affairs and who have access to decision makers) and decision makers at the top. Policy influentials and opinion leaders together are often thought of as elites. Opinion leaders overlap with both policy influentials and a more familiar group comprising the *attentive public* (those knowledgeable about foreign affairs but not necessarily with access to decision makers). By definition, the rest of the population makes up the *mass public.* The pyramid represents the three strata that make up the aggregate concept public opinion. While estimates vary about the distribution of Americans among the three groups, they suggest that policy influentials or elites commonly comprise less than 2 percent of the population, opinion leaders and the attentive public between 5 and 10 percent, and the mass public, by definition, the rest (see Figure 8.7).

One of the sharpest distinctions in public attitudes occurs between elites, on the one hand, and the mass public, on the other. Support for *liberal internationalism*—defined by U.S. Ambassador Richard Gardner (1990) as "the intellectual and political tradition that believes in the necessity of leadership by liberal democracies in the construction of a peaceful world order through multilateral cooperation and effective international organizations"—is demonstrably greater among elites than the general public. For example, a 1997 survey by Pew Research Center (Pew Research Center for the People and the Press 1997) revealed that "The

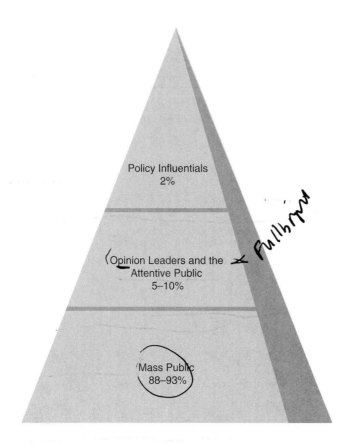

FIGURE 8.7 The Public Opinion Pyramid*
*Percentages are estimates.

public feels the United States should be no more or less active than any other country, restrained in its commitment of troops and resources to foreign adventures. In contrast, a majority of influential Americans ranging from union leaders to national security experts believes the U.S. role should be prominent and forceful." Analysts Andrew Kohut and Robert Toth (1998) concluded that "Never before has the difference on such a fundamental issue as America's place in the world been so wide." The number of leaders willing to pursue an assertive leadership role dropped significantly by 2005, to 44 percent, but it still far outstripped the mass public. Leaders were also nearly unanimous in their opinion that an active world role is best for the country.

Table 8.1 illustrates these and other differences between opinion leaders and other Americans. It also shows important similarities. Leaders and the mass public alike determined that closer cooperation with others is the most important lesson of 9/11. They also show overwhelming support for U.S. participation in several important (if sometimes controversial) international agreements and institutions. Interestingly, opinion leaders and the mass public alike would support World Trade Organization decisions even if they adversely affected the United States. Both groups would also support U.S. participation in international peacekeeping efforts in Afghanistan and would send American troops to stop genocide practiced by another government.

There are other situations where leaders and masses come close to sharing opinions. Of the ten countries where the pollsters asked if there was support for long-term military bases, there was comparatively close agreement in half the cases and much wider disagreements in the other half: Turkey, Guantanamo Bay, Iraq, Saudi Arabia, and Pakistan. Otherwise leaders and the masses differ widely on

TABLE 8.1 Differences in the Foreign Policy Preferences of American Leaders and the Mass Public, 2004–2005 (Percentages)

	Leaders	Public	Gap*
America's World Role			
Best for U.S. future if it plays an active world role	97	67	+30
The U.S. should assume a shared leadership role but also be the most active among the leading states	44	25	+19
Most important lesson of 9/11			
U.S. needs to work more closely with other countries to fight terrorism	84	73	+11
U.S. needs to act on its own more to fight terrorism	9	23	−14
Multilateralism			
The U.S. should participate in:			
Treaty prohibiting worldwide nuclear testing	85	87	−2
Treaty banning all use of land mines	80	80	0
Kyoto agreement to reduce global warming	72	71	+1
Agreement with International Criminal Court to try individuals for war crimes, genocide, crimes against humanity if their own countries will not	70	76	−6
U.S. should abide by decisions of the World Trade Organization even if against U.S.	85	69	+16
Very Important U.S. Foreign Policy Goals			
Prevent the spread of nuclear weapons	87	73	+14
Combat international terrorism	84	71	+13
Combat world hunger	67	43	+24
Improve living standards in less developed countries	64	18	+46
Improve the global environment	61	47	+14
Secure adequate supplies of energy	57	69	−12
Stop the flow of illegal drugs into the U.S.	46	63	−17
Protect the jobs of American workers	41	78	−38
Strengthen the United Nations	40	38	+2
Maintain military superiority	37	50	−13
Protect weak nations against aggression	33	18	+15
Bring democracy to other countries	29	14	+15
Control illegal immigration	21	59	−37
Use of Military Force			
Favor use of U.S. troops:			
To participate in international peacekeeping force in Afghanistan	86	75	+11
To stop a government from practicing genocide and killing its own people	86	75	+11
If North Korea invaded South Korea	82	43	+79
To participate in international peacekeeping force to enforce a peace agreement between Israel and Palestinians	81	52	+29
If Arab forces invaded Israel	64	43	+21
If China invaded Taiwan	51	33	+18
To ensure the supply of oil	36	54	−18
To fight drug lords in Colombia	27	51	−34

(Continued)

T A B L E 8.1 *Continued*

	Leaders	Public	Gap*
Military Bases Abroad			
Should have long-term military bases in:			
South Korea	71	62	+9
Turkey	63	46	+18
Japan	56	52	+4
Germany	54	57	−3
Guantanamo Bay, Cuba	47	58	−11
Afghanistan	43	47	−7
Iraq	27	42	−15
Saudi Arabia	25	50	−25
Uzbekistan	25	30	−5
Pakistan	20	39	−19
Options for Coping with Terrorists			
Work through UN to strengthen and enforce international laws against terrorism	94	87	+7
Make effort to be more even-handed in Israeli-Palestinian conflict	89	64	+25
Air strikes against training camps/facilities	83	83	0
Trial in International Criminal Court	80	82	−2
U.S. ground troops against training camps/facilities	74	76	−2
Assassination of terrorist leaders	52	68	−16
Restrict immigration	36	76	−40
Impact of NAFTA			
NAFTA is mostly good for:			
American companies	84	50	+34
Consumers like [me]	79	55	+24
Creating jobs in Mexico	79	69	+10
The U.S. economy	74	42	+32
[My] own standard of living	65	51	+14
Creating jobs in the U.S.	49	31	+18
Job security for American workers	34	25	+9
The environment	32	34	−2
Economic Issues**			
Globalization is mostly good for the U.S.	87	64	+23
Outsourcing is mostly a good thing because it lowers prices in the U.S.	56	22	−34
China practices unfair trade	—	51	—
Japan practices unfair trade	—	35	—
South Korea practices unfair trade	—	35	—
European Union practices unfair trade	—	26	—

*Leaders minus public. All percentages based on those holding an opinion except for the second entry ("The U.S. should be the most active leading nation"), which includes "don't know" responses. For the leadership sample on this item, the word "assertive" was used instead of "active."

**Dashes indicate not available.

SOURCE: Data on the most active of leading states adapted from *America's Place in the World 2005* (Pew Research Center for the People and the Press, 2005), pp. 52–53. All other data adapted from Marshall M. Bouton, *Global Views 2004: American Public Opinion and Foreign Policy* (Chicago: Chicago Council on Foreign Relations, 2004.

committing troops abroad, including such Cold War situations as a Chinese invasion of Taiwan or a North Korean invasion of South Korea.

On dealing with terrorists, seeking a more balanced U.S. policy toward the Israeli-Palestinian conflict produces distinct differences: by a 25 percent margin leaders prefer a more balanced approach to the conflict than does the mass public. The mass public, on the other hand, is more supportive of assassination of terrorist leaders than are opinion leaders. They also call for more restrictive policies toward immigrants, a posture that reflects their greater attention to domestically oriented "very important U.S. foreign policy goals" shown in the table. Similarly, the mass public sees comparatively less utility in NAFTA, especially on the critical issue of affording American workers job security. Respondents similarly place little value on outsourcing of jobs even if it means lower consumer prices.

Several factors explain differences, even sometimes yawning gaps, between leaders and masses on particular foreign policy issues and on general postures. Interest in foreign affairs, access to information about what is happening in the world, and socialization experiences are among them. Some also argue that the gap is a product of elites' failure to understand what most Americans really think (Kull and Destler 1999).

Yet American leaders and the mass public share much in common. In particular, the belief systems derived from the cooperative and militant orientations used earlier to describe mass foreign policy attitudes apply to American leaders as well. Thus elite and mass preferences diverge on specifics, but they converge on cooperative and militant internationalism as alternative orientations toward the elements comprising America's foreign policy ends and means. The similarities and differences between the general and the specifics manifest themselves this way: since Vietnam, opinion leaders have consistently subscribed to internationalist and accommodationist values in greater proportions than the mass public; the mass public has been more likely to embrace hard-line values (Holsti and Rosenau 1990, 2004; Wittkopf 1990, 1994c, 1996, 2000). During George W. Bush's first term in office neoconservatives

(hardliners) were much in evidence as they firmly held the reins of power. Since then, however, the multilateralist thrust of accommodationists and internationalists, led by Secretary of State Condoleezza Rice, has again been more prominent. Thus the structure of elite and mass attitudes is similar, even as the specific policy preferences of each diverge.

Political and Sociodemographic Correlates of Foreign Policy Attitudes Partisanship and political ideology (conservative versus liberal) are important correlates of foreign policy beliefs. As noted earlier, Republicans and conservatives are more likely to be hardliners, whereas Democrats and liberals tend to be accommodationists. In addition to these differences, public attitudes on specific foreign policy issues often vary by such factors as age, educational, gender, income, occupation, racial background, religious identification, and region of the country (see, for example, Bardes and Oldendick 2003; Holsti 2004; Trubowitz 1992; Wilcox, Ferrara, and Allsop 1993). For policy makers, knowledge about these variations is important politically, because it allows them to court some groups while ignoring others.

Income, occupation, and education are important in distinguishing the attentive public from the mass public. People in higher income groups, in professional occupations, and with more education are typically better informed about international affairs than their counterparts in other societal groups. These are the people most likely to support what foreign policy leaders want. In March 1999, for example, the Gallup Organization found Americans ambivalent about U.S. participation in NATO air strikes against Serbia (46 percent favored, 43 percent opposed). But among the 36 percent who indicated they were following the situation in Kosovo closely, 58 percent supported what by then was U.S. policy (*Poll Releases,* March 24, 1999). Similarly, in late 1994 only 42 percent of the mass public supported NATO's expansion into Eastern Europe—a central tenet of the Clinton administration's Partnership for Peace program—but the move was supported by 55 percent of those who closely followed news about U.S. foreign relations (based on a Gallup Poll survey for the Chicago Council on Foreign Relations).

Gender differences on foreign policy issues, particularly those related to the use of force, are among the correlates of foreign policy attitudes that have attracted attention in recent years. A "gender gap" first became evident in the 1980 election, when Ronald Reagan was found to enjoy markedly less support among female voters than among male voters. The differences, which were repeated four years later, appear to have been related to a greater fear among women of Reagan's bellicose foreign policy pronouncements and concerns about his ability to manage the risks of war (Frankovic 1982).[12]

Evidence from early in the 1988 presidential campaign indicated that Bush inherited women's distrust of Reagan, but by the time of the election in November 1988 gender differences had largely dissipated (Farah and Klein 1989; Taylor 1988; compare Bendyna and Lake 1995). With the onset of the crisis and war in the Persian Gulf, however, wide differences between men and women on use-of-force issues were again revealed. An August 1990 survey showed, for example, that 79 percent of the male respondents would support sending U.S. troops to defend Saudi Arabia against a possible Iraqi attack, but only 51 percent of the females would. Five months later, as the United Nations deadline for Iraq's withdrawal from Kuwait approached, another survey asked whether the United States should go to war against Iraq if it failed to comply. Of the women, 54 percent said yes, compared with 73 percent of the men. Women were also less likely than men to approve of Bush's handling of the crisis in Kuwait. Whether these differences had an effect on the 1992 presidential election is problematic, but it is clear that Bill Clinton was sensitive to gender-based issues as he mounted his campaign, and comparatively larger numbers of women did vote for him instead of for Bush or Perot. (Single women, who "often believed that they had been harmed by Reagan and Bush's policies" were especially prone to vote for Clinton [Abramson, Aldrich, and Rohde 1994].)

Democrats (Clinton and Gore) continued in the next two elections to garner more votes from

women than Republicans. Interestingly, however, after 9/11 the Council on Foreign Relations concluded from a survey of defense issues that "women's opinion on defense policies has been transformed"; on missile defense, defense spending, and related issues their views now looked like men's (Eichenberg 2003).

Political scientist Richard Eichenberg (2003) examined responses to nearly 500 survey questions to determine gender support (or opposition) for the use of U.S. military force from the Persian Gulf War through the ongoing wars in Afghanistan and Iraq. He draws four important conclusions:

> First, ... women are less supportive of the use of military force for any purpose. Second, variations in the magnitude of gender differences largely confirm past theory and research: women are relatively more sensitive to humanitarian concerns and to the loss of human life. Third, it is nonetheless also true that women are hardly pacifists, and men are not uniformly bellicose. Any difference occurs at the margins in response to specific circumstances and the particular military actions being contemplated. Fourth, given the magnitude of some gender differences on some issues involving force, such differences have the potential to be a significant factor in political decisions to employ military force and in the political response to the use of force. ... [In particular], "no politician can ignore the potential impact of her or his actions on the potential for gendered responses in the voting booth.
> *(Eichenberg 2003, 112–113 138)*

Like gender, *race* divides Americans sharply on use-of-force issues. African Americans from virtually all demographic groups—political party, ideology, gender, region of the country and age—were less likely to support the war in Iraq than other groups (Holsti 2004, 23). Ole R. Holsti (2004), drawing on others' research, offers an explanation that draws a parallel between the attitudes of women and blacks:

FOCUS 8.2 Cycles of Introversion (Isolationism) and Extroversion (Internationalism) in America's Foreign Policy

American policy makers historically have been unable to reconcile the advantages of withdrawing from the world with the benefits of reforming it. Hence the nation's global posture has alternated between periods of *introversion* and *extroversion*— that is, between periods of isolationist withdrawal and global involvement. Periods of extroversion are marked by a "willingness to use direct pressure (economic, diplomatic, or military) on other nations, while introversion stresses domestic concerns as well as normal economic, diplomatic, and humanitarian relations with other nations" (Klingberg 1996).

Debates among policy makers as to which role best serves the national interest have never been resolved conclusively. America's vacillation between introversion (isolationism) and extroversion (internationalism) appears to fluctuate in rhythmic cycles, with each taking twenty-five to thirty years (a political generation) to run its course, as summarized below.

Introversion	Extroversion
1776–1798	1798–1824
1824–1844	1844–1871
1871–1891	1891–1919
1919–1940	1940–1967
1967–1987	1987–?

"Alienation arising from structural features of American society may complement other more specific properties of these two groups." Race, then, like gender, may be emerging as an important element of cleavages in American society on foreign policy issues.

Generational changes also deserve consideration. Earlier, in commenting on the impact of Vietnam, a contrast was drawn between the Munich generation and the Vietnam generation. The electoral battle between George H. W. Bush, a World War II veteran, and Bill Clinton, a Vietnam War dissenter, epitomizes the generational changes now taking place in American policy-making circles. With it come potentially important implications for the foreign policy thinking that the next generation of policy makers may bring into positions of power (see Holsti and Rosenau 1980, 1984). The cyclical swings between global activism and withdrawal in American diplomatic history, argues Frank Klingberg (1983, 1990), are largely generational in nature, with oscillations between each mood occurring every twenty-five to thirty years quite independently of public dissatisfaction with particular experiments (such as humanitarian interventions or democracy promotion). If he is correct, we should expect that within the next decade the United States will change from its current extrovert phase toward introversion. This development would correspond with the complete political maturation of the Vietnam generation.

Although detailed evidence supporting the generational thesis remains elusive (Holsti 2004), the long history of swings between introversion and extroversion identified by Klingberg and others (summarized in Focus 8.2) suggests that generational effects may be especially potent as the United States moves forward in the new century. They may be particularly important in explaining the gulf in attitudes between the men and women with military service and a growing cadre of political leaders without that experience (Feaver and Gelpi 2004; Holsti 1998–1999; Ricks 1997).

A PUBLIC IMPACT ON AMERICAN FOREIGN POLICY?

"Polls are not only part of the news today, they are news. They not only sample public opinion, they define it." That observation by a former director of polling at CBS News (Frankovic 1998) underscores not only the ubiquity but also the importance of public opinion polls in contemporary America. Not all policy makers would openly admit to this. In

March 2006, for example, Vice President Dick Cheney appeared on CBS's commentary program *Face the Nation* after a particularly difficult week for the president in which members of his own party and others called for a shake-up of the White House senior staff. "I don't think we can pay any attention to that kind of thing," Cheney said. "The president has got a job to do. . . . He ignores the background noise that's out there in the polls that are taken on a daily basis."

Policy makers nonetheless are acutely aware of the importance of polling. Cheney's comments themselves make the point. The unceasing presidential job approval question asked by many media and other polling organizations effectively subjects the president to a *perpetual election,* and presidents are, for good reason, sensitive to where they stand in that "election," as we have seen. Does this also mean that policy makers "pander" to the public?

That policy makers are guided by public whim rather than principled conviction is a widely accepted belief. It is not warranted. Although there is a close correspondence between public preferences and public policy, the fit has widened, not narrowed, in recent years (Monroe 1998). The gulf between public preferences and government action was never more evident than during the impeachment trial of President Clinton. Survey data showed unambiguously that the majority of Americans preferred not to see Clinton removed from office, despite his transgressions, but the Republican-controlled Congress continued to press ahead anyway.

Systematic evidence compiled by political scientists Lawrence Jacobs and Robert Shapiro (2000), much of it based on interviews with Washington policy makers, shows that politicians use public opinion but are not abused by it. "The irony of contemporary politics," they write, "is that politicians both slavishly track public opinion and, contrary to the myth of 'pandering,' studiously avoid simply conforming policy to what the public wants." Instead of conforming to public preferences, politicians themselves use systematic polling to decide what they want to do; "their purpose [is] to exert the 'leadership skills to shape public opinion' and 'educate the people'" (compare Harris 2001).

That conclusion affirms the viewpoint of Kennedy adviser Theodore Sorensen, who some years ago put it this way: "No president is obliged to abide by the dictates of public opinion. . . . He has a responsibility to lead public opinion as well as respect it— to shape it, to inform it, to woo it, and win it. It can be his sword as well as his compass" (Sorensen 1963). In this vein, the Bush administration was quite effective in mobilizing support around its rationale for invading Iraq in March 2003, particularly on the issue of weapons of mass destruction for which then–Secretary of State Colin Powell made a powerful and persuasive public case before the United Nations Security Council.

The notion that policy makers see public opinion as something to be shaped, not followed, is understandable when we recall the tendency of the public to acquiesce to government decisions. The propensity to accede to leaders' choices and not to mobilize to alter them minimizes the impact on foreign policy that the public can exert. The conclusion that follows is that the American public participates (through elections, for example) without exercising power. It is involved but does not have influence.

Rather than asking if there is a direct causal connection between public opinion and the content of foreign policy, then, it may be better to inquire into the functions of public attitudes in the process itself.

Public Opinion as a Constraint on Foreign Policy Innovation

One of the reasons American foreign policy has proved so resistant to change for so long is that public images of international politics are themselves resistant to change. As we have already noted, fundamental beliefs regarding foreign relations are typically inflexible:

> Almost nothing in the world seems to be able to shift the images of forty percent of the population in most countries, even within one or two decades. Combinations of events that shift the images and attitudes even of the remaining fifty or sixty percent

of the population are extremely rare, and these rare occasions require the combination and mutual reinforcement of cumulative events with spectacular events and substantial governmental efforts as well as the absence of sizable cross-pressures.

(Deutsch and Merritt 1965, 183)

The particular numbers may have changed in the decades since these two prominent scholars made their observations, but the resistance of images to change and the tendency of party identification to define how voters choose whom and whose policies to support reinforces their observations. Public opinion thus acts as a brake on policy change, not by stopping innovations but by limiting modifications because of policy makers' perceptions of the inflexibility (and unpredictability) of public opinion. *Anticipated future opinions* is the concept John Zaller (cited in Holsti 2004) uses to describe the interplay between policy makers and public opinion.

The constraining impact of the Vietnam syndrome illustrates the tendency. If decision makers think the public voice will not permit certain initiatives and fear that the public may become mobilized against innovations, that in itself may restrict the kinds of alternatives considered. As one pollster put it, political leaders regard public opinion "as the great gorilla in the political jungle, a beast that must be kept calm" (Sussman 1988). Their task, then, is to "keep things quiet," which means they seek "to stifle public debate on matters that people care about, or should care about." It is perhaps for these political and psychological reasons that American foreign policy is perceived by so many analysts and political leaders to be constrained by public attitudes: "Mass opinion may set general limits, themselves subject to change over time, within which government may act" because the "opinion context . . . fixes the limitations within which action may be taken" (Key 1961). "Fear of electoral punishment," even if unrealistic, serves to limit what decision makers are likely to do—if for no other reason than their (often erroneous) assumption that "the public will never stand for it" (Waltz 1971).

An interesting example of limits and a perceived lack of fear of electoral punishment occurred in early 2006, when the Bush administration approved a deal that would have placed management of six key U.S. ports in the hands of Dubai Ports World. Although widely recognized for its quality management of ports throughout the world, the company was owned by the Dubai government, a member of the United Arab Emirates. Congress, which was not consulted, rose up in arms as soon as the deal was announced. Republicans joined Democrats in their criticism of the decision, and Bush threatened his first veto if Congress passed legislation halting or slowing implementation of the impending deal, which was scheduled to take place in only a few days. Congress demanded time to make its own investigation, but before that happened Dubai withdrew from the plan.

Not only was Congress miffed at the process, the American public followed the story with unusual interest and was adamantly opposed to the decision—this despite the president's determined effort to shape opinion in his favor. In an early March 2006 CNN/*USA Today*/Gallup Poll survey, three in four respondents said they had followed the story closely, and by a four-to-one margin (66 to 17 percent), they opposed the deal. In fact, 39 percent of those surveyed described the Dubai Ports World deal as a "major threat" to U.S. security. Certainly that sentiment contributed to Bush's declining popularity and bruised Republicans' reputation as strong on national security and terrorism issues.

Did public opinion drive this decision? Or Congress? In all likelihood it was both. In an election year, members of Congress probably felt they could more easily challenge the president and his "trust me" approach to national security than in other circumstances. And they were likely to have looked at the polls to determine they had little to fear from their constituents if they did.

Political constraints shape presidential behavior, not just congressional. In the run-up to the 1991 Persian Gulf War, George H. W. Bush determined that for political, not constitutional, reasons, he needed the support of Congress. On the one hand, historian Gary Hess reports (2006), it would help

Secretary of State James Baker in his negotiations with the Iraqis, then taking place in Geneva. On the other hand, domestic political considerations shaped Bush's decisions. "An opinion poll in early January [1991] showed that 60 percent of Americans believed that Bush needed congressional authority before taking the country to war.... It was clear to the White House that the greater political risk would have been to act without going to Congress."

Still, although sometimes moved by political (public opinion) considerations, the president is more likely to shape public opinion than be shaped by it. Richard Sobel examines the impact of public opinion on American foreign policy in four interventionist episodes: (1) Vietnam, beginning with the Johnson administration and extending through Nixon's; (2) Nicaragua, where during the Reagan administration the United States sought through support of counterrevolutionary forces to topple the government of the pro-Marxist Sandinista regime; (3) the Persian Gulf War, prosecuted to successful battlefield conclusion during the first Bush administration; and (4) Bosnia, where initial U.S. humanitarian intervention during the Bush administration culminated in multilateral intervention under U.S. leadership during the Clinton administration.

Based on systematic evidence as well as interviews with key policy makers during each of these conflict situations, Sobel's conclusions reinforce the long-standing argument that public opinion limits the range of policy makers' foreign policy choices. But his conclusions also extend another long-standing observation: that public opinion may constrain policy makers' latitude, but it does not shackle them. "The public's attitudes set the limits within which policy makers may operate," Sobel (2001) writes. "Within those parameters of permissive consensus, decision makers may operate with less or more political costs and relative discretion about which policies to choose." He also adds that "discretion is wider when conflicts are less salient and [public] support is higher."

In short, public permissiveness invites presidents to act first and create support later, particularly on foreign and national security policy. Often they are successful. Two examples related to the "rally round the flag" phenomenon make the point. Before

Johnson announced his Vietnam policy in 1965, which called for a dramatic escalation of U.S. direct involvement, only 42 percent of the public favored such an approach; after the announcement, 72 percent favored it. Before the first President Bush invaded Panama in December 1989 in an effort to overthrow General Manuel Noriega, 59 percent of the public opposed it; following the military action, 80 percent viewed it as justified.

The public's historical tendency to follow decision makers' leads encourages them to think that if they do not enjoy a climate of public support for their actions, they can create it. Theodore Roosevelt put it bluntly: "I did not 'divine' what the people were going to think. I simply made up my mind what they ought to think and then did my best to get them to think it." Similarly, George Elsey, an adviser to President Truman, confided that "The president's job is to lead public opinion, not to be a blind follower. You can't sit around and wait for public opinion to tell you what to do.... You must decide what you're going to do and do it, and attempt to educate the public to the reasons for your action."

Public Opinion as a Stimulus to Foreign Policy Innovation

Exceptions to the general rule of public permissiveness may be rare, as in the Dubai Ports World case, but there are instances when changes in public opinion precede rather than follow changes in policy. Consider the issue of American policy toward mainland China's admission to the United Nations. A growing proportion of the public favored admission at the same time that influential segments of the policy-making community remained in rigid opposition to it. In 1950 no more than 15 percent of the American public favored admission, but by 1969 more than half supported it (Mueller 1973), a level that may have made the eventual U.S. decision not to block admission possible. In much the same way, support for the diplomatic recognition of China by the United States rose dramatically in the decade before President Carter extended it in 1978 (Shapiro and Page 1988).[13]

Another instance where changes in public attitudes were ahead of policy shifts was the Vietnam imbroglio, where public disaffection with continued intervention was often deeper and more vocal than among government leaders. Similarly, public demonstrations of outrage in 1985 by a small group of activists toward South Africa's racial policy of apartheid appeared to rally public opinion and to be critical in bringing congressional pressure to bear on the administration to abandon its South Africa policy known as "constructive engagement." It also may have contributed to the congressional decision a year later to override a presidential veto to place sanctions on South Africa.

More recently, a plurality of the general public and an even larger number of opinion leaders supported normalization of relations with Vietnam long before the Clinton administration took this initiative (Rielly 1991, 1995). Large numbers also support entering into negotiations with Cuba and North Korea toward this end (Rielly 1995). Public support of multilateral intervention in Bosnia also was higher than unilateral action before the Clinton administration embraced NATO's active involvement in the conflict (Sobel 2001).

In these cases, it appears that public preferences laid the basis for foreign policy innovation or change. But we must be careful not to assert that public opinion *caused* policy either. It is probably more accurate to argue that the public can influence the course of policy, even when it is mobilized, only indirectly, by changing "the image of public opinion held by persons capable of affecting policy decisions" or by altering "the image of public opinion held by the public itself" (Rosenberg 1965). In this way public opinion affects how policy makers think about the international environment, the climate of domestic opinion, and the latitude available for their decisions within an otherwise constraining environment.

Public Opinion as a Resource in International Bargaining

Ironically, the constraining influence of public opinion may sometimes work to the United States' advantage in dealing with other states. American diplomats, for instance, may enhance their ability to get their way at the bargaining table by claiming that "the

American people will never tolerate this." By describing themselves as victims of popular preferences, diplomatic negotiators may indeed gain considerable bargaining leverage. "The fact that this decisional process may not in reality originate in the will of the people does not diminish the significance or usefulness of symbolically casting the threshold of national tolerance in terms of public opinion" (Fagen 1960; see also Putnam 1988).

In practice, of course, Congress is often the expression of public opinion on diplomatic matters. Knowing this, presidents sometimes seek to portray their policies at home as supported by "the American people," in effect using their opinions as bargaining leverage not only with other governments but also with Congress. Sometimes their strategies are successful, sometimes not. Clinton, for example, was able to parlay broad public support for establishing normal trade relations with China into a wider margin of victory in Congress than initially thought possible. But he was not able convince key segments of American society or Congress to support the Kyoto Protocol to the United Nations Framework Convention on Climate Change.

The Opinion-Policy Nexus: Correlation or Causation?

The foregoing observations about the functions of public opinion demonstrate the complexity of linkages between Americans' preferences and the nation's foreign policy behavior. "A democratic myth" is what Gabriel Almond (1960) called the notion "that the people are inherently wise and just, and that they are the real rulers of the republic." That conclusion is unassailable as far as it goes. It is also true, however, that the complex, still poorly understood relationship between opinion and policy is affected by a cluster of intervening factors, including the nature of the issue, the leadership, policy makers' perceptions, and the international and domestic circumstances prevailing at the time of decision.

To this we should add that over time there is a strong correspondence between public preferences and the foreign policy ends and means American leaders choose.[14] That point may seem paradoxical, since much evidence supports the existence of short-run discrepancies between preferences and policies. Yet the paradox itself speaks to an enduring question: How is it that "a policy-making system which has mastered all the modes of resistance to outside opinion nevertheless seems, from a long-run perspective, to accommodate to it"? (Cohen 1973)

We have already suggested some answers to this puzzle, particularly in the ability of presidents to mold public opinion to fit their preferred policy choices. Still, when presidents mount what Theodore Roosevelt called "the bully pulpit," they may risk later becoming prisoners of their own past efforts. Public opinion is thus typically a conservative force, a source of inertia that acts as a restraint on policy innovation. Or, as Alan Monroe (1979) concludes in a comparative study of consistency between public preferences and public policy, the policy-making system makes it "more difficult to pass publicly approved changes than to maintain the status quo."

POLITICAL CULTURE, PUBLIC OPINION, AND AMERICAN FOREIGN POLICY

The nature of American society and politics is conducive to strong domestic influences on its foreign policy behavior. Comparatively speaking, the United States is a *society-dominant system* (Friedberg 1992; Katzenstein 1977; Risse-Kappen 1991). Thus, unlike, say, France and Germany, which are state-dominated political systems, the nature of domestic structures in the United States—buttressed by a political culture that emphasizes individualism and pluralism—facilitates the expression of public opinion on foreign policy issues. It provides multiple access points to decision makers. It also demands that policy makers monitor that opinion as they maneuver to build coalitions of support for their policies. President George H. W. Bush's determined effort to build and maintain public support in Congress and elsewhere for his policies in the Persian Gulf—which were haunted by the dreaded Vietnam syndrome—illustrates how even in the area of national security (long believed to be "above politics"), societal forces often exert a profound impact on American foreign policy. Indeed, some lament that "foreign policy is essentially politics driven," with seemingly greater attention given to poll results than to policy effectiveness (Schneider 1990). Still, the limits to permissible behavior may be elastic, but they cannot be ignored completely without risking policy failure. Johnson learned that in Vietnam, as did Nixon in the Watergate affair, Reagan during the Iran-Contra scandal, George H. W. Bush in his neglect of the domestic economy despite an enviable record of foreign policy successes, and—perhaps—George W. Bush and Iraq.

In Chapter 9, we will look more closely at the access points through which public opinion and the political culture are sometimes expressed. These include interest groups and the electoral process. We will also examine the role of the media, a highly visible transmission belt through which politically relevant ideas circulate in the American polity.

KEY TERMS

accommodationists
attentive public
belief system
casualty hypothesis
civil religion
democratic capitalism
exceptional American
    experience

hardliners
internationalism
internationalists
isolationism
isolationists
law of anticipated
    reactions
liberal internationalism

liberalism
mass public
militant
    internationalism
multiculturalism
nationalism
policy influentials
political culture

politics of prestige
public opinion
"rally round the flag"
    phenomenon
society-dominant
    system

SUGGESTED READINGS

Almond, Gabriel A. *The American People and Foreign Policy.* New York: Praeger, 1960.

America's Place in the World 2005. Washington, DC: Pew Research Center for the People and the Press, 2005.

Bouton, Marshall M. *Global Views 2004: American Public Opinion and Foreign Policy.* Chicago: Chicago Council on Foreign Relations, 2004.

Dallek, Robert. *The American Style of Foreign Policy: Cultural Politics and Foreign Affairs.* New York: Knopf, 1983.

Holsti, Ole R. *Public Opinion and American Foreign Policy.* Ann Arbor, MI: University of Michigan Press, 2004.

Jacobson, Gary C. *A Divider, Not a Uniter: George W. Bush and the American People, the 2006 Election and Beyond.* New York: Pearson/Longman, 2007.

Kennedy, David M. "Can We Still Afford to Be a Nation of Immigrants?" *The Atlantic Monthly* 278 (November 1996): 52–68.

Kull, Steven, and I. M. Destler. *Misreading the Public: The Myth of a New Isolationism.* Washington, DC: Brookings Institution Press, 1999.

Larson, Eric V., and Bogdan Savych. *American Public Support for U.S. Military Operations from Mogadishu to Baghdad.* Santa Monica, CA: Rand Corporation Arroyo Center, 2005.

Page, Benjamin I., and Robert Y. Shapiro. *The Rational Public: Fifty Years of Trends in Americans' Policy Preferences.* Chicago: The University of Chicago Press, 1992.

Shapiro, Robert Y., ed. *The Meaning of American Democracy.* New York: Academy of Political Science, 2005.

Small, Melvin. *Democracy and Diplomacy: The Impact of Domestic Politics on U.S. Foreign Policy, 1789–1994.* Baltimore: Johns Hopkins University Press, 1996.

Sobel, Richard. *The Impact of Public Opinion on U.S. Foreign Policy Since Vietnam: Constraining the Colossus.* New York: Oxford University Press, 2001.

Wittkopf, Eugene R. *Faces of Internationalism: Public Opinion and American Foreign Policy.* Durham, NC: Duke University Press, 1990.

Wolfe, Alan. *One Nation, After All: What Middle Class Americans Really Think About God, Country, Family, Racism, Welfare, Immigration, Homosexuality, Work, the Right, the Left, and Each Other.* New York: Viking, 1999.

Zaller, John R. *The Nature and Origins of Mass Opinion.* New York: Cambridge University Press, 1992.

NOTES

1. Huntington (2004b) argues that advocates of multiculturalism believe that "America is not and should not be a society with a single pervasive national culture. The melting pot and tomato soup metaphors do not describe the true America. America is instead a mosaic, a salad, or even a 'tossed salad'."

2. The U.S. Census Bureau regards "Hispanic" or "Latino" as an ethnicity rather than a race. Most Hispanics classify themselves as "white." Projecting into the future, then, the United States may remain a predominantly "white" population, but the proportion of European-stock white Americans will decline.

3. Such findings invite a negative estimate of the intelligence of the American people and their importance in the political system by suggesting, as Friedrich Nietzsche concluded, that "the masses are asses." It also invites the conclusion that leaders should ignore the opinions of the masses, along the lines of Oscar Wilde's famous adage that "those who try to lead the people can only do so by following the mob." Although some may be attracted to these viewpoints, neither conclusion is warranted by the evidence, as we will demonstrate in the next section.

4. See also Graham (1986), Russett and Graham (1988), Wittkopf (1990) and, for a contrasting viewpoint, Holsti (1987).

5. Although the 1991 Persian Gulf War was short and comparatively few casualties were sustained, Mueller (1994) concludes from available data as well as

scenarios of increasing casualties posed in opinion surveys that the rate of decline in public support for the war would have followed the same pattern of decline as in Korea and Vietnam.

6. Referring to the Iraq war, John Mueller describes sardonically how the "casualty hypotheses" is sometimes interpreted:

The notion that public opinion sours as casualties increase has somehow turned into "support drops when they start seeing the body bags"—a vivid expression that some in the Bush administration . . . apparently [took] literally. As a result, the military . . . worked enterprisingly to keep Americans from seeing pictures of body bags or flag-draped coffins in the hope that this [would] somehow arrest the decline in enthusiasm for the war effort. (Mueller 2005, 46)

7. The statistical procedures used to generate the groups maximize similarities within groups and minimize similarities between them.

8. The classic study of belief system rigidity is Ole R. Holsti's (1962) examination of John Foster Dulles's image of the Soviet Union (see Chapter 14). Other studies that address the factors influencing the development of political attitudes and beliefs among mass and elite publics and why they are often resistant to change include Conover and Feldman (1984), Converse (1964), Festinger (1957), Herrmann (1986), Hirshberg (1993), Hurwitz and Peffley (1987, 1990, 1992), Larson (1985), Neuman (1986), and Zaller (1992).

9. Much of the literature that seeks to explain fluctuations in presidential popularity focuses on the impact of economic variables. The pioneering work incorporating foreign policy was done by John Mueller (1973). Ostrom and Simon (1985, 1989) extend that work to the impact of political drama on presidential popularity.

10. A *New York Times*/CBS News survey in February 1998 found that the public's approval of Clinton's handling of the economy exceeded his overall approval rating, something that had not happened for two decades except for one month of the Reagan presidency in 1983.

11. The decision was made by the Committee on Foreign Investments in the United States. Chaired by the Treasury Department, this is a long-standing interagency committee responsible for approving foreign direct investment in the United States. As in the private sector, it is not unusual that government (like corporate) decisions are made in the name of the president (CEO) without his or her direct involvement or knowledge.

12. See also Fite, Genest, and Wilcox (1990), Shapiro and Mahajan (1986), and Smith (1984).

13. Relevant case studies on the impact of public opinion in the foreign policy domain include Gilboa (1987), Kusnitz (1984), Leigh (1976), and Levering (1976). Powlick (1991) also shows that American foreign policy officials generally accord greater weight to public opinion than is sometimes thought, and that when opposition to a decision emerges, they try to change public opinion by "educating" it to their preferences.

14. See Monroe (1979, 1998), Page (1994), Page and Shapiro (1992), and Stimson, MacKuen, and Erikson (1994).

9

The Transmission of Values, Beliefs, and Preferences

Interest Groups, Mass Media, and Presidential Elections

The government of the United States . . . is a foster child
of special interests.
PRESIDENT WOODROW WILSON, 1913

We in the media do not focus on the national interest,
but on what interests the nation. It's the policy makers
who must keep the national interest clear.
TED KOPPEL, *NIGHTLINE* ANCHOR AND MANAGING EDITOR,
ABC NEWS, 1995

When you turn on your TV screen and see innocent people die day
in and day out, it affects the mentality of our country.
GEORGE W. BUSH, 2006

According to liberal democratic theory, leaders are chosen to reflect societal values by converting public preferences into policy. By extension, American foreign policy ultimately is an expression of Americans' sentiments. As James Schlesinger, a former presidential adviser and secretary of defense put it, "Foreign policy does not rest upon a definition of the national interest. It rests on public opinion." How realistic is that viewpoint? We concluded in the last chapter that, because the

United States is a society-dominant political system, public opinion is likely to play a more important role in shaping American foreign policy than in other political systems, where the power of both the state and societal groups is more centralized than in the United States. Still, it is not clear whose opinions are heard. Often the disjunction between elite and mass preferences is large. Moreover, the American political system may be premised on the value that "all men are created equal," but clearly that is not the case. Some people have more access to policy makers than others, and some have more influence.

Disparities within the American polity like these raise important questions about who really controls American foreign policy and policy making. Do elected and appointed leaders indeed devise policies that reflect public preferences? Do they instead pursue policies that cater to a privileged elite from which the leaders themselves are drawn? Or policies that appeal to specialized interests? In short, what is the correspondence between the theory and practice of democratic liberalism in America?

We seek an answer to that question in this chapter by focusing on the access points through which public opinion and the political culture may be expressed. Specifically, we examine the social background characteristics of American leaders, the nature and influence of special interest groups on American foreign policy, the role of the mass media in shaping and transmitting information and opinions, and, finally, the impact of foreign policy attitudes and issues on presidential elections.

DEMOCRATIC LIBERALISM IN THEORY AND PRACTICE

Two models compete to explain how societal preferences are translated into the political process: *elitism* and *pluralism.* As summarized in Focus 9.1, elitism emphasizes the influence of a few, and pluralism emphasizes how a broader array of preferences are translated into the policy process. Both models provide important insights into the societal sources of American foreign policy, but each also raises

troublesome questions in a political culture premised on "we the people." We begin this chapter by focusing on those questions as they relate to American foreign policy.

Does a Power Elite Control American Foreign Policy?

The United States is undeniably a democratic society. The complication with that description is that it is also a special-interest society as well as a bureaucratic, information, and mass consumption society. So if we ask whether those who make American foreign policy share the characteristics and convictions of Americans generally, perplexing findings emerge.

Who Is Chosen to Lead?   In terms of numbers, not many. Only a few thousand individuals out of nearly 300 million Americans decide issues of war and peace. In principle, everyone is eligible. In practice, few are. People are selectively recruited, and those outside the mainstream are denied access and the opportunity to serve. At the top levels—because of family connections, income, and education—foreign policy makers are not drawn proportionately from a cross-section of American society. The result is an *elite*—not only in the sense that a small minority controls policy-making power but also because America's foreign policy managers are typically drawn from an unrepresentative national coterie.

The elitist character of foreign policy making becomes apparent when policy makers' backgrounds are cataloged. Remarkably similar characteristics describe America's foreign policy establishment since its rise to globalism, or even before. Consistent with the meaning of "elite," the group is comparatively small and its composition enduring, having changed little in more than half a century. Since World War II (and even more so before), the top positions have been filled by people from the upper class who were educated at the nation's best schools. They are, as the title of a prize-winning book put it, *The Best and the Brightest* (Halberstam 1972).[1] Furthermore, they have generally come from predominantly white,

F O C U S 9.1 How Elitism and Pluralism Differ in Their Views of Power and Society

	Elite Theory	Pluralist Theory
Most Important Political Division(s) in Society	Elites who have power, and masses who do not.	Multiple competing groups (economic racial, religious, ideological, etc.) that make demands upon government.
Structure of Power	Hierarchical, with power concentrated in a relatively small set of institutional leaders who make key society decisions.	Polyarchal, with power dispersed among multiple leadership groups who bargain and compromise over key societal decisions.
Interaction among Leaders	Consensus over values and goals for society, with disagreements largely limited to means of achieving common goals.	Conflict and competition over values and goals as well as means of achieving them.
Sources of Leadership	Common backgrounds and experiences in control of institutional resources; wealth, education, upper socioeconomic status; slow continuous absorption of persons who accept prevailing values.	Diversity in backgrounds and experiences and activism in organizations; continuous formation of new groups and organizations; skills in organizational activity and gaining access to government.
Principal Institutions of Power	Corporations, banks, investment firms, media giants, foundations, "think tanks," and other private organizations, as well as government.	Interest groups, parties, and the legislative, executive, and judicial branches of government
Principal Direction of Political Influence	Downward from elites to masses through mass media, education, civic, and cultural organizations.	Upward from masses to elites through interest groups, parties, elections, opinion polls, etc.
View of Public Policy	Public policy reflects elite preferences, as modified by both altruism and desire to preserve the political system from mass unrest; policy changes occur incrementally when elites redefine their own interests.	Public policy reflects balance of competing interest groups; policy changes occur when interest groups gain or lose influence, including mass support.
Principal Protection for Democratic Values	Elite commitments to individual liberty, free enterprise, and tolerance of diversity, and their desire to preserve the existing political system.	Competition among groups; countervailing centers of power each checking the ambitions of others.

SOURCE: Thomas R. Dye and Harmon Zeigler, *The Irony of Democracy: An Uncommon Introduction to American Politics.* Copyright © The Wadsworth Group, a division of Thomson Learning.

Anglo-Saxon, Protestant (WASP) backgrounds; a disproportionate number have been trained in law; and many have had extensive experience in big business. Indeed, most policy makers' prior careers were spent as managers or owners of major corporations and financial institutions or on the faculties of the country's elite universities. More often than not, they served in appointed rather than elected positions while in government. In essence, the presence of this governing elite makes popular sovereignty fictional—a myth used "to legitimate the rule not of the people, but of a small and privileged elite" (Thomas 1988).

The evidence from the Kennedy through Reagan administrations on the career experience of executive officials in the "inner cabinet" (the secretaries of state, defense, and treasury and the attorney general) confirms this viewpoint. Eight of ten previously served in the national government, nearly half worked in private business, three-fifths were attorneys, and over a quarter had academic careers (Lowi and Ginsberg 1990). The pattern continued into the first Bush presidency. Of its cabinet-level appointees, 90 percent held previous government posts, 35 percent had corporate positions, 40 percent had careers in law, and half were educated in the Ivy League (Dye and Zeigler 1990).

Bill Clinton campaigned in 1992 on the promise that he would make his administration "look like America," but the picture that later emerged was quite different. Clinton did appoint a larger number of women and minorities to top jobs in his administration than his predecessors had. He also relied more heavily on people who had held government positions before (many in elected offices) and were trained in law, but he picked few with backgrounds in business or the military. Thus Thomas R. Dye surmised that *if* the Clinton administration looked like America, "then America has become a nation of lawyers and lobbyists" (Dye 1995).

In other ways, however, the Clinton administration looked very much like its predecessors: "Its appointees [were] drawn overwhelmingly from among the most privileged, best educated, well connected, upper- and upper-middle-class segments of America. There [was] very little 'diversity' in the educational and social backgrounds of top Clinton advisors" (Dye 1995). *Meritocracy* is how one observer characterized the unusually high levels of educational attainment of Clinton's first-term appointees: "Perhaps more than any in our history, Clinton's [was] a government of smart people." It was also "the most networked. Friendships formed at elite colleges and law schools [were] sustained through an archipelago of think tanks, foundations, councils, and associations" (Ignatius 1994).

George W. Bush continued the tradition of appointing women and minorities to high level positions. But the distinctive characteristic of his administration was the extraordinary number of appointees who had served in prior Republican administrations, including his father's, or in prominent corporate positions. Dick Cheney (vice president) and Colin Powell (secretary of state) stand out. Both had served as architects of the senior Bush's Persian Gulf standoff of Saddam Hussein, arguably his crowning foreign policy achievement. Prior to that, Cheney had served as chief of staff in the Ford administration and Powell as national security adviser to President Reagan.

Bush's first secretary of defense, Donald Rumsfeld, had served previously as defense secretary during the Ford administration. The man chosen to succeed Rumsfeld, Robert Gates, was deputy national security adviser and director of central intelligence in the Bush I administration. George W. Bush's first secretary of the treasury, Paul O'Neill, worked in the Ford administration in the Office of Management and Budget. Furthermore, the second President Bush, like his father and grandfather before him, graduated from Yale, among the nation's most prestigious private universities. He would later add Harvard to his résumé with a graduate degree in business administration before seeking his fortune in the Texas oil patch.

Interestingly, the women who have become increasingly visible in the nation's institutional elite, particularly in government, themselves share social characteristics much like their predominantly male predecessors or counterparts. Women, too, are educated in disproportionate number at the nation's most prestigious private colleges, have advanced graduate degrees, and, in the case of those in higher-level government positions, are recruited more often from within government than without (Dye 1995).

African Americans, on the other hand, have yet to penetrate the institutional elite in sufficient numbers to warrant broad characterizations (see Dye 1995). Still, it is noteworthy that the most visible minority appointees in the Clinton administration typically had law or other advanced graduate degrees. Clinton's Commerce Secretary Ron Brown, among the most prominent African Americans appointed by Clinton to a top job, had extensive political experience, which included chairing the National Democratic Party as it sought to capture the White House in 1992. Tragically, Brown was killed in an airplane accident while on a trade mission to the Balkans. Colin Powell, like Brown, grew up in Harlem, but unlike Brown, his career took a military route that led rapidly to the rank of general. Eventually, however, he too would become a political appointee, serving during the Reagan and first Bush administrations as national security adviser and, later, as chairman of the Joint Chiefs of Staff late in the first Bush and early Clinton administrations. He would become George W. Bush's first secretary of state.

Alabama native Condoleezza Rice, George W. Bush's national security adviser during his first term and secretary of state during his second term, rose through academic ranks with a Ph.D. from the University of Denver's Graduate School of International Studies as an expert on Eastern Europe and the Soviet Union. This led eventually to a prestigious Council on Foreign Relations fellowship and then a position on the first Bush president's National Security Council staff. She would later return to Stanford University, also a prestigious private university, where she became provost. She left Stanford to join the campaign trail of the man who would become the first president elected in the twenty-first century.

In addition to training and government experience, Rice shared another characteristic reminiscent of the traditional, pre- and post-Clinton foreign policy elite: close corporate connections. Rice was a member of the board of directors of three multinational companies: Charles Schwab, Chevron, and Transamerica Corporation. The Center for Responsive Politics reports that Chevron's board was "so charmed" by Rice that they named one of their tankers after her.

After serving the first Bush president as secretary of defense, Dick Cheney became chief executive of Halliburton, a military contractor and the world's largest oil field services company. Through its European subsidiaries Halliburton sold spare parts to Iraq's oil industry in violation of UN sanctions against that country. Later it enjoyed millions of dollars of no-bid contracts to assist the United States in the Iraq war. Cheney's formal ties with Halliburton ended when he became vice president, but he continued to received deferred salary payments from the company well into 2006.

Powell, too, built corporate connections in the years preceding his appointment as secretary of state. Many other Bush appointees enjoyed close ties with key American industrial and financial interests. The corporate connections of members of Bush's "inner cabinet" are summarized in Focus 9.2. To a person, each of them brought to his or her new position a rich experience with corporate America.

What do these career and socialization experiences tell us about foreign policy making? Commonality of experience—reinforced by the short line of elites in front of the revolving door between government service and the private sector and prestigious universities—fosters uniformity in foreign policy attitudes. The continuity of American foreign policy during the Cold War can be traced in part to the shared characteristics of the self-selecting, self-recruiting, and self-perpetuating "governing elite" in charge. Likeminded individuals "guarded" American foreign policy by instructing incumbent administrations on similar policy principles (Domhoff 1984).

More recently, observers skeptical of the George W. Bush administration's reemphasis of traditional national security issues—which included a national missile defense system, enhanced military spending, a propensity toward unilateral action, and a reduced interest in and concern about the kinds of

FOCUS 9.2   George W. Bush's Inner Circle: The Corporate Connection

Cabinet Position	Cabinet Official	Corporate Connections
Agriculture Secretary	Mike Johanns	ADM, Kraft, Tyson Foods, ConAgra Foods
Attorney General	Alberto Gonzalez	Vinson & Elkins
Commerce Secretary	Carlos Gutierrez	Kellog's
Defense Secretary	Robert Gates	Fidelity Investments, Brinker International
Education Secretary	Margaret Spellings	None
Energy Secretary	Samuel Bodman	Fidelity Investments, Cabot
Health and Human Services Secretary	Michael Leavitt	None
Homeland Security Secretary	Michael Chertoff	None
Housing and Urban Development Secretary	Alphonso Jackson	American Electric Power
Labor Secretary	Elaine Chao	Northwest Airlines, Clorox, Bank of America
Secretary of State	Condoleezza Rice	Chevron, Charles Schwab, Transamerica
Transportation Secretary	Mary Peters	HDR
Treasury Secretary	Henry Paulson	Goldman Sachs
Veteran Affairs Secretary	Jim Nicholson	None

NOTE: As of December 18, 2006.

SOURCE: "Bush Administration: Corporate Connections," Center for Responsive Politics, www.opensecrets.org/bush/cabinet.asp (accessed 12/22/06).

post–Cold War security issues that animated the Clinton administration—wondered if that reorientation might be explained by the recall of Cheney, Powell, Rumsfeld, and others steeped in the ethos of their administrative experiences serving Cold War presidents. Critics also worried that the administration's "tilt" on other issues, notably environmental protection, reflected its close corporate connections. Noteworthy is that the identity of the individuals Vice President Cheney assembled early in the Bush administration to craft a national energy policy was never revealed. Although the group was believed to be heavily weighted in favor of "big oil,"

its secrecy was protected under the guise of "executive privilege," a claim ultimately sustained by the Supreme Court.

Some, but not all, of George W. Bush's inner circle of advisers are part of the foreign policy elite that has shaped American foreign policy since World War II and before. Often called *the establishment* or the *wise men,* these men (for the most part) believed they possessed the training and experience necessary to make the right foreign policy decisions—and that public opinion would support their choices. The roster of names is lengthy. Excluding presidents, prominent examples include Robert

McNamara, Henry Stimson, Averell Harriman, James F. Byrnes, Allen Welsh Dulles and John Foster Dulles, George F. Kennan, Dean Acheson, Clark Clifford, Paul Nitze, Nelson Rockefeller, Colin Powell, William Bundy and McGeorge Bundy, Dean Rusk, George Ball, Henry Kissinger, Zbigniew Brzezinski, James Schlesinger, Cyrus Vance, George Shultz, Alexander Haig, William Casey, Caspar Weinberger, Donald Rumsfeld, James A. Baker, Brent Scowcroft, Lawrence Eagleburger, Warren Christopher, Leslie Gelb, Anthony Lake, Joseph Nye, and Samuel Berger. Many more could be added. Nearly every American president since World War II found himself dependent on this coterie of elites for personnel and advice. Perhaps this is what led John F. Kennedy to respond, when urged during his 1960 campaign to hit his critics harder, "That is not a very good idea. I'll need them all to run this country."

The Council on Foreign Relations   The recruitment and advisory roles of the ***Council on Foreign Relations*** illuminate the channels through which American elites and their preferences have often been funneled into the foreign policy-making process. The council is the embodiment of the establishment (the liberal Northeastern establishment, in the eyes of its critics). It has been described as "the most influential policy-planning group in foreign affairs" (Dye 1990); and its journal, *Foreign Affairs,* has been described by *Time* magazine as the most influential magazine in the country. Its limited membership (about 4,200) is drawn from among the most prestigious and best connected of the nation's financial and corporate institutions, universities, foundations, media, and government bodies. Its members (who are gate-keepers for new entrants), past and present, include most of those previously named as having moved through the revolving door of government service. "Every person of influence in foreign affairs," writes Thomas Dye (1990), including presidents, has been a member.

The council sees its role as building elite consensus on important foreign policy issues. "It initiates new policy directions by first commissioning scholars to undertake investigations of foreign policy questions. . . . Upon their completion, the [council] holds seminars and discussions among its members and between its members and top government officials." Furthermore, *Foreign Affairs* is "considered throughout the world to be the unofficial mouthpiece of U.S. foreign policy. Few important initiatives in U.S. policy have not been first outlined in articles in this publication" (Dye 1995). Although the council's influence has waned since the end of the Cold War, it remains an important voice for liberal internationalism and the corollary principle that American leadership is essential.

Other Policy Planning Groups   The Council on Foreign Relations is the most important private policy-planning entity linking the elite in American society to the government, but it is not alone. An array of privately run public policy research organizations, more commonly referred to as ***think-tanks*** seek to exercise influence across the broad spectrum of American foreign policy, including national security and foreign economic policy. Among them are the Brookings Institution, the Carnegie Endowment for International Peace, the Cato Institute, the Center for Strategic and International Studies, the Committee for Economic Development, the Business Roundtable, the American Enterprise Institute, the Institute for International Economics, the Heritage Foundation, the Overseas Development Council, the Center for Defense Information, the Population Reference Bureau, and the Worldwatch Institute.

The socialization experiences of many in the administration of George W. Bush tracked the contours of the traditional foreign policy establishment, as we have noted. But Bush himself and others outside his "inner cabinet" of foreign policy officials in another sense mirrored trends that have moved the country in a more politically conservative direction since Vietnam. Terms like "counter-establishment" (Blumenthal 1988) and "counterculture" (Atlas 1995) have been used to describe the shift toward conservative values among the country's leaders. The conservative Federalist Society is one group that lends cohesion to many in the Bush administration at the cabinet and sub-cabinet levels, in which individuals are committed to bringing their conservative ideas into mainstream legal thought.

Small chapters of the Federalist Society have been active on college campuses for many years, where they have focused on the current state of the legal order. The society was "founded on the principles that the state exists to preserve freedom, that the separation of governmental powers is central to our Constitution, and that it is emphatically the province and duty of the judiciary to say what the law is, not which it should be" (Edsall 2001). President Bush's two successful nominees to the Supreme Court—Chief Justice John Roberts and Associate Justice Samuel Alito—were both members of the Federalist Society at the time of their appointment.

The **Project for the New American Century (PNAC)** became the touchstone think-tank that provided the new Bush administration with both foreign policy ideas and personnel. A self-described educational group (www.newamericancentury.org), PNAC was formed in the 1990s to promote the principles and strategies that would inform the administration's grand strategy built on the principles of unilateralism, hegemony, and preemption. That included advocacy of the invasion of Iraq. PNAC had in fact urged the Clinton administration to pursue regime change in Iraq much earlier.

Many of PNAC's members were originally liberal internationalists who soured with the strategy and outcome of the Vietnam War. These became the neoconservatives who embraced the view that American power should be exercised not with restraint but proactively to promote American values and ideals. Military strength and moral clarity were cornerstones of their convictions (Mann 2004b). Vice President Dick Cheney was among the original, closely knit PNAC members, as was former Defense Secretary Rumsfeld and his deputy, Paul Wolfowitz. Powerful neoconservative voices outside the government, including William Kristol, editor of the influential *Weekly Standard* and head of PNAC, promoted PNAC's message. In addition to

its call for the exercise of American power to promote its ideals, it shunned or was skeptical of the role that alliances and other forms of multilateral cooperation played in protecting American security and promoting liberty abroad.[2] Instead, American interests would come first. As President Bush would later say, his administration called for a "distinctly American internationalism that reflects the union of our values and our national interests."

Elite Attitudes and Behavior Democracy encourages the participation of different people and the expression of their often divergent preferences. Therefore, the consistency between government policy and the recommendations of a cadre of statesmen-advisers-financiers outside of government does not necessarily pose a problem for liberal democratic theory. But what if we ask the related questions: Are the values and outlook of foreign policy-making elites and others with influence different from those of the American people they presumably represent? If leaders are different from those they lead, does a small minority actually control the majority?

Evidence on these questions is mixed. Elites generally have been *public regarding,* perceiving themselves as "guardians of the public good." Indeed, they are vigorous protectors of the public weal as embraced in the liberal ethos of the prevailing political culture. That includes "a willingness to take the welfare of others into account as part of one's own well-being and a willingness to use governmental power to correct perceived wrongs done to others. It is a philosophy of noblesse oblige—elite responsibility for the welfare of the poor and downtrodden, particularly blacks" (Dye and Zeigler 2000).

Although "average" Americans have generally registered approval of elites' policies (a notable exception is Vietnam), elites' views of the wisdom of "the people" are not flattering (see Bouton 2004). Moreover, the liberal ethos when applied elsewhere in the world, which means extending (imposing?) American values about liberty and democratic capitalism to others, has led to a continuing record of intervention into the affairs of others who do not share American ideas and ideals. Violent conflict and bloodshed have often resulted. Furthermore, there are limits to elites' commitment to liberal democratic values as they promote their self-interests. That is particularly evident in a globalizing world political economy.

Corporate elites sacrifice long-term economic growth for short-term, windfall, paper profits, knowing that the nation's competitive position in the world is undermined by shortsighted "bottom-line" policies. Elites move factories and jobs out of the United States in search of low-paid workers and higher profits. Global trade and unchecked immigration lower the real wages of American workers. Inequality in America increases, and elites and masses grow further apart (Dye and Zeigler 2000).

Ironically, elites' self-interest is also the glue that keeps the social/economic/political system together. "The only effective check on irresponsible elite behavior is their own realization that the system itself will become endangered if such behavior continues unrestrained. So periodically elites undertake reforms, mutually agreeing to curb the most flagrant abuses of the system" (Dye and Zeigler 2000). Reforms are typically incremental rather than revolutionary, however. Elites' willingness to change policies is tempered by their zeal to protect their interests. Existing policies may be reformed, but they are seldom replaced.

A Military-Industrial Complex?

The argument that American foreign policy is democratic because the foreign policy elite represents the public at large is challenged by those who see elite opinion diverging from that of the mass public. Indeed, a *power elite* (Mills 1956) consisting of a select few allegedly governs America without direction from the majority. Actual government authority does not reside with the people—the Lockean liberal tradition and the doctrine of popular sovereignty notwithstanding. Instead, it rests in the hands of a select minority who exercise substantial power over foreign policy making and public policy in general. In short, the American political system gives the public participation (elections, for example) without

power and involvement without influence, while a small set of elites, acting both openly and behind closed doors, makes the important decisions.

The discrepancy between the theory and practice of democratic governance is most visible wherever power is concentrated. This allegedly is a defining characteristic of a **military-industrial complex (MIC)**. This once popular concept was frequently used to explain the high levels of defense spending and other bellicose postures the United States assumed toward Soviet communism during the Cold War. President Dwight Eisenhower, a highly decorated World War II general who led the famous Normandy invasion in 1944, first brought national attention to the existence of a military-industrial complex when he warned in an often quoted passage from his farewell address given on January 17, 1961:

> This conjunction of an immense military establishment and a large arms industry is new in the American experience. The total influence—economic, political, even spiritual—is felt in every city, every state-house, every office of the federal government. We recognize the imperative need for this development. Yet we must not fail to comprehend its grave implications. Our toil, resources, and livelihood are all involved; so is the very structure of our society.
>
> In the councils of government we must guard against the acquisition of unwarranted influence, whether sought or unsought, by the military-industrial complex. The potential for the disastrous rise of misplaced power exists and will persist.

Eisenhower worried that the military-industrial complex was a threat because its vast power undermined the countervailing forces that would otherwise keep the abuse of power in check. "We must never let the weight of this combination endanger our liberties or democratic processes," he cautioned.

Eisenhower's warning came at about the same time as Harold D. Lasswell (1962) prophesied that a "garrison state" governed by "specialists in violence" would arise to dominate policy making and as C.

Wright Mills (1956) argued that a power elite promoted policies designed to serve its own, rather than the nation's, interests. Mills, using a somewhat different label than Eisenhower, described the military-industrial partnership this way:

> The "Washington military clique" is not composed merely of military men, and it does not prevail merely in Washington. Its members exist all over the country, and it is a coalition of generals in the roles of corporation executives, of politicians masquerading as admirals, of corporation executives acting like politicians, of civil servants who become majors, of vice-admirals who are also the assistants to a cabinet officer, who is himself, by the way, really a member of the managerial elite.

According to Mills, the partnership among these interests was more a natural coalition than a conspiracy. The interests might occasionally join forces to strive for the same self-serving ends, but not necessarily by design and infrequently through coordinated activities. "The power elite," wrote Mills, "is composed of political, economic, and military [personnel], but this institutionalized elite is frequently in some tension: it comes together only on certain coinciding points and only on certain occasions of 'crisis.'" Later theorists would describe the military-industrial complex as a partnership of "(1) the professional soldiers, (2) managers and . . . owners of industries heavily engaged in military supply, (3) top government officials whose careers and interests are tied to military expenditure, and (4) legislators whose districts benefit from defense procurement" (Rosen 1973).

It is not surprising that members of this elite lacked a unified voice on key issues. Nonetheless, its entrenched (if disorganized) power was believed to derive naturally from a capitalist economic system dependent on foreign involvement for economic benefit. In particular, the post–World War II arms race and the high level of U.S. military spending during the period were often attributed to the self-aggrandizing activities of the military and industrial sectors, which (so the reasoning goes) propagated

policies favorable to its interests. As a "peddler of crisis" (Sanders 1983) that benefited from trouble abroad, the complex justified its existence during the Cold War by provoking fear of the Soviet menace and the need for vigilance in order "to wage a war against cutbacks and not the Soviets" (Thompson 1990). External dangers were allegedly exaggerated to rationalize unnecessary weapons programs and ensure that the military budget would continue to grow "regardless of whether there is war or peace" (Parenti 1988). In so doing, it promoted policies beneficial to itself but arguably detrimental to the country as a whole.

Adherents to the thesis of a powerful military-industrial force in American society stressed that its combined components outweighed other, potentially countervailing domestic forces. Thus the complex was able to predominate over other societal groups (compare Friedberg 1992). "Each institutional component of the military-industrial complex [had] plausible reasons for continuing to exist and expand. Each [promoted] and [protected] its own interests and in doing so [reinforced] the interests of every other. That is what a 'complex' is—a set of integrated institutions that act to maximize their collective power" (Barnet 1969). As Eisenhower put it,

> The Congressman who seeks a new defense establishment in his district; the company in Los Angeles, Denver, or Baltimore that wants an order for more airplanes; the services which want them, the armies of scientists who want so terribly to test their newest views; put all of these together and you have a lobby.

In short, the military-industrial partnership became so influential after World War II because it permeated the whole of American society. Does it remain so?

The Military-Industrial Complex: Retrospect and Prospect

Shortly after 9/11, political journalist James Fallows (2002) wrote an essay about the MIC concept and concluded it retains cogency even today. But he argues that what Eisenhower, a fiscal conservative, was most concerned with were the budgetary implications of defense spending. Certainly he would have been startled at some of the ways his ideas were applied. Military spending and weapons procurement are nonetheless key elements of the MIC concept. In this section we examine some of the (often anecdotal) evidence on these elements.

The Evidence, Part I: The Cold War Years   The belief that the interests of the military-industrial complex were unfairly served to the possible detriment of the national interest is buttressed by circumstantial evidence. Some of it, drawn from the waning Cold War years, is described as follows:

- "In the mid-1980s, at the height of the Reagan administration's planned $2.3 trillion defense buildup, the Pentagon was spending an average of $28 million an hour. . . . By 1990 . . . the total defense-spending boom for the Cold War years [would] total $3.7 trillion in constant 1972 dollars—nearly enough 'to buy everything in the United States except the land: every house, factory, train, plane and refrigerator'" (Ignatius 1988).

- One of every sixteen American workers relied directly on the military-industrial complex for his or her paycheck, and millions more were indirectly dependent on them as customers (Thompson 1990). "More than thirty percent of mathematicians, twenty-five percent of physicists, forty-seven percent of aeronautical engineers, and eleven percent of computer programmers worked in the military-industrial complex" (Lipsitz and Speak 1989). "For every billion dollars that the Pentagon [cut] from its arms budget, almost 30,000 jobs [would] be lost by industry" (Reifenberg 1990).

- The list of top fifteen companies receiving prime contract awards from the Pentagon remained remarkably stable, especially among aerospace manufacturers. "Six of the eight aerospace production lines have had a continuous contracting relationship with one military service . . . in most cases back to World War II" (Kurth 1989).

- The prime aerospace contractors typically [receive] a new contract as a current production line [phased] out an existing award according to the *follow-on imperative,* which [held] that "a large and established aerospace production line is a national resource" (Kurth 1989).

- "The imperatives of the industrial structure [were] reinforced . . . by the imperatives of the political system. Four of the major production lines [were] located in states that loom large in the Electoral College: California (Rockwell and Lockheed-Missiles and Space), Texas (General Dynamics), and New York (Grumman). Three others [were] located in states that for many years had a senator who ranked high in the Senate Armed Services Committee or Appropriations Committee" (Kurth 1989).

- Fraud, waste, bribery, and corruption have been chronic in military contracting, as attested by procurement abuses in the 1980s that included "$748 . . . for a pair of $7.61 pliers, a $7,000 coffee pot, and $600 toilet seats" (Meier 1987). In the wake of such disclosures "the military . . . added 7,000 additional staffers to solve its spare parts problems" (Reich 1985). One study concluded that "virtually all large military contracts have cost overruns from 300 to 700 percent" (Parenti 1988).

- Support for Rand Corporation and other federally funded research and development centers (FFRDCs) that design and test weapon systems and devise war-fighting strategies increased by 30 percent between 1987 and 1991 (Pearlstein 1994). The centers receive Pentagon contracts without competitive bidding.

These anecdotes provide some support for the alleged existence of a complex of military-industrial interests—at least during the Cold War—but its influence on American foreign policy is easily overestimated. It may be true that pressures for increasing or continuing defense spending were (and are) brought to bear by some lobbyists and defense contractors, but it does not follow that the military-industrial partnership single-mindedly pursued this objective above all others. Thus the military-industrial complex undoubtedly colored much activity during the Cold War, particularly the structure of defense spending and the shape of the country's military capabilities. But where there is interest, there is not necessarily influence.

The Evidence, Part II: Beyond the Berlin Wall   The end of the Cold War portended important changes in the politics of defense spending as first the George H. W. Bush and then the Clinton administrations cut actual or projected defense spending and downsized the military. Critics of the military-industrial complex theory argue that these changes demonstrate it was "at best, inadequate and, at worst, inaccurate. The power of the military-industrial complex, if it was real, ought to have been sufficient to prevent severe budget decline, hardware cancellation, and base closings, the very events [that took place] in the 1990s" (Adams 1994; see also Anton and Thomas 1999).

Certainly there is merit in this critique, but it overstates the extensiveness of the changes that took place after the Berlin Wall fell and, in particular, the political dynamics that sustain defense procurement and production. "Pork-barrel politics" and a new "industrial policy" now shaped the domestic politics of defense spending and weapons procurement.

As the post–Cold War military build-down gained momentum during the first Bush administration, defense advocates offered several arguments designed to slow its pace. Protecting the nation's "defense industrial base" and maintaining "excess capacity" that could be brought into production in the event of a major war were critical arguments. At the same time, sales of U.S. military equipment to other states increased dramatically. Liberal Democrats in Congress, who previously opposed such arms transfers, now supported them, as concern about jobs back home and related presumed economic benefits took precedence (see

Renner 1994). National security and industrial policy became closely linked.

The sale of seventy-two advanced F-15 aircraft to Saudi Arabia in 1992 was particularly notable, as it enjoyed the support not only of congressional Democrats but also of presidential candidates George H. W. Bush and Bill Clinton. The Bush administration earlier had shelved the Saudi request, but Bush revived it during the campaign to keep production lines at McDonnell Douglas Corporation going and to preserve an estimated 7,000 jobs. Clinton went a step further, supporting two weapons systems the Bush administration wanted to ax: the Seawolf submarine and the V-22 Osprey tilt-rotor aircraft. Meanwhile, the Pentagon began to pick up costs military contractors had previously paid as they sought to sell U.S. military hardware in trade shows around the world.

The ill-fated effort of the George H. W. Bush administration to kill the V-22 Osprey—a vertical-takeoff transport plane ordered by the Marine Corps but opposed by top-level Pentagon officials (including Dick Cheney, then secretary of defense) as unnecessary and too expensive—illustrates how the ***iron triangles*** inside the defense policy process preserve weapons systems even in the face of stiff opposition. The concept refers to the bonds that link defense contractors and interest groups (the private sector), defense bureaucrats (the Defense Department), and members of Congress (the legislative branch) into a single entity that is exceedingly difficult to break. In the case of the Osprey, one side of the triangle was shaky—defense bureaucrats at the top. But they faced determined opposition from the two other sides of the triangle as well as opposition from within the Pentagon itself.

The interest group side was represented by the aerospace companies (led by Boeing) and unions (led by the United Auto Workers) that produced the plane. They mobilized a national network of workers and supplier companies with a toll-free hotline to Congress, and a national "Tilt Rotor Appreciation Day" capped off by a flight demonstration in Washington. Members of Congress whose districts would lose jobs and money were brought on board. Several members began weekly strategy sessions with lobbyists, and one representative hosted a cocktail party that drew 200 lobbyists and industry officials, checkbooks at the ready. Defense PACs (political action committees) vowed to step up contributions to members of key congressional committees, who had already received $2 million the year before. And the bureaucratic side of the triangle, working inside the Pentagon, was the Marine Corps, which wanted the program (Bennett 1994).

The Osprey survived—helped in part by the support it received in the presidential campaign. Thus, by the time Bill Clinton was sworn into office, the pattern was clear: "Politicians of all stripes [had become] preoccupied with keeping military spending high for economic and political reasons" (*The Defense Monitor,* 22 [2] 1993).

But tragedy lurked in the background: two Ospreys crashed after production began, killing twenty-three Marines. In a now highly politicized environment, the Osprey's future had to be faced again. Ironically, Vice President Dick Cheney would be among those responsible for a decision. Meanwhile, the commander of the Osprey squadron was fined after it was revealed he ordered subordinate officers to lie about the Osprey's maintenance records.

The Seawolf nuclear attack submarine was projected to cost $2.4 billion, making it among the most expensive weapons ever built. Its primary mission was to defeat the Soviet Union, which by 1992 had imploded. Moreover, construction of a newer, less costly submarine was projected to begin before the end of the decade. Political support for the nuclear submarine by the Pentagon, in Congress, and elsewhere was, however, vigorous. By the mid-1990s, the Submarine Industrial Base Preservation Council could report that the navy had granted construction subcontracts to firms in forty-five of the fifty states (Priest and Mintz 1995). Senator Bob Dole (R-Kansas), who earlier had voted against the Seawolf, came out in support of it as he positioned himself for a run at the presidency in 1996. Then House Speaker Newt Gingrich, other members of Congress, and many governors also supported the submarine out of obvious concern for protecting defense jobs in their constituencies.

Supporters of the submarine introduced "industrial policy" into the debate. They argued that if the Seawolf was not funded, General Dynamics' Electric Boat Division, which had long produced submarines at its Groton, Connecticut facility, would likely close shop. This would leave only one shipbuilder capable of producing nuclear ships or submarines, a situation perceived dangerous for national security (Priest and Mintz 1995). Navy Secretary John H. Dalton defended that viewpoint, saying "We live in an uncertain world. . . . Two shipyards capable of building nuclear submarines are important because 'we may need a surge capacity to build more than one submarine a year.'" Senator John McCain (R-Arizona), an influential member of the Senate Arms Services Committee and among the Seawolf critics, did not buy that argument: "This whole thing reminds me of 'Let's Make a Deal' and the taxpayer gets to pay. We've kept the shipyards in business well into the next century."

A combination of Cold War thinking, pork-barrel politics, and industrial policy also punctuated debate about two other expensive weapons systems: the air force's F-22 Raptor stealth fighter, now in advanced stages of development and near ready for production and the other the proposed Joint Strike Fighter plane, which is in early stages of production.

The F-22 was conceived in the early 1980s as a next-generation replacement for the F-15 fighter, long the mainstay of the U.S. fighter force and arguably still the most sophisticated plane of its kind. Development of the F-22 has taken more than two decades. Much has changed in that time. Not only did the Cold War end, but technical problems and cost overruns have pushed the estimated cost of each copy of the plane to $361 million according to the Government Accountability Office (GAO), which translates into more than $100 billion for the fleet of more than three hundred jets the air force wants. Critics also argue that the F-15 will continue to dominate the skies for many years into the future, and that other planes planned by the Pentagon obviate the need for the F-22. Supporters counter that the F-15 has been sold to many other countries, which levels the playing field between the United States and potential adversaries. The F-22 is therefore necessary if the United States is to maintain air superiority. Supporters also note that production of the plane would lead to 21,000 jobs throughout the United States

The Joint Strike Fighter is designed to replace aging air force, navy, and Marines fighters with a single, new, cost-effective plane that will fit each of the services' needs, something not done previously. The Pentagon initially made the decision to award the contract to only one company. Boeing and Lockheed Martin were the competitors and the stakes were enormous. The Pentagon anticipated that 5,000 copies of the plane would be built at a cost ranging from $28 million to $38 million each, making it the single most expensive weapons system ever (Wayne 1999). Lockheed Martin eventually won the contract and rolled out the first test version of the now X-35 in early 2006. As in the case of the Seawolf submarine, in Congress and elsewhere during the Joint Strike Fighter debate voices were raised about relying on a single defense contractor well into the future (Wayne 2000).

Fear that the widespread consolidation of the defense industry in the 1990s could have an adverse long-term impact on the ability of the United States to maintain its security again raises troublesome questions. In particular, has the downsizing of the defense industry reduced the ability of the United States to produce sophisticated weapons of war? Did the absence of a single, overarching security threat reduce the financial incentives of corporate America to produce the weapons necessary to combat twenty-first century security threats?

Eugene Gholz and Harvey Sapolsky (1999–2000), defense policy analysts at the Massachusetts Institute of Technology, have addressed issues directly related to these questions. Their findings are instructive.

First, their analysis supports the conclusion that the congressional-business-bureaucratic iron triangle remains highly effective. The politics of jobs and congressional districts that many analysts thought governed the Cold War have triumphed in its aftermath. As long as a decade after the collapse of the Soviet Union, not one Cold War weapon platform line had been closed in the United States. The same factories still produced the same aircraft, ships, and armored vehicles (or their incremental descents). (See Table 9.1.)

The drawdown after the Cold War was often portrayed as one of the harshest when compared to the defense cuts after other wars fought by the United States. It was actually the gentlest; more than a decade after the defense budget cuts started, government contracts still supported 2.1 million private defense-sector employees—400,000 more than at the budgetary low point of the Cold War (Gholz and Sapolsky 1999–2000).

Second, Gholz and Sapolsky dispute the argument advanced by MIC theorists that the defense industry enjoyed a cozy relationship with government during the Cold War that minimized their risks. Pointing to more than a dozen prime contractor production lines closed between the early 1950s and the early 1990s, the analysts suggest that in fact defense contracting was a high-risk venture during the Cold War resulting from the political and technological uncertainty the defense industry faced. They further argue that prime contractors' ability to please their customer, namely the Pentagon, is the reason why the same ones won awards year after year. "The way to please the customer was often to promise still more enhancements, which compounded technological uncertainty. . . . Responsiveness to the military customers rather than to Congress was a highly prized, contract-winning trait during the Cold War" (Gholz and Sapolsky 1999–2000).

Members of Congress, as we have seen, are sensitive to the impact of defense spending in their own states and districts. Intense lobbying by a highly effective industry lobby is also a potent force. In 1997, for example, an off-election year, Boeing made $424,000 in campaign contributions, and McDonnell Douglas (later acquired by Boeing) contributed $331,000 (Wayne 1998). The financial mergers of many of the large defense contractors in recent years has enhanced their already powerful voices. By the end of the 1990s, just three companies, Boeing, Lockheed Martin, and Raytheon,

TABLE 9.1 Active Post-Cold War Production Lines

	Current Product	Likely Follow-on
Aircraft		
Lockheed—Marietta, Ga.	C-130	C-130J, F-22
Lockheed—Fort Worth, Tex.	F-16	Joint Strike Fighter
Lockheed—Palmdale, Calif.	Aurora[a]	Another secret aircraft
Northrop—Palmdale, Calif.	B-2	B-X
Northrop—Lake Charles, La.	JSTARS	Small surveillance aircraft
Northrop—St. Augustine, Fla.	E-2C	New Navy support aircraft
Boeing—St. Louis, Mo.	F-15, F/A-18C/D, AV-8B, T-45	F/A-18 E/F
Boeing—Long Beach, Calif.	C-17	C-17
Helicopters		
United Technologies-Sikorsky—Stratford, Conn.	UH-60 Blackhawk	CH-60, UH-60 Upgrade, Comanche
Boeing-Vertol—Philadelphia, Pa.	V-22	V-22, Comanche
Textron-Bell—Fort Worth, Tex.	OH-58D Kiowa Warrior, V-22	V-22
Boeing-Hughes—Mesa, Ariz.	AH-64D Apache Longbow	AH-64D
Kaman—Bloomfield, Conn.	SH-2 Seasprite (export)	SH-2G Super Seasprite (export)
Shipyards		
Newport News Shipbuilding—Newport News, Va.	CVN-77	CVNX, NSSN
Litton Ingalls—Pascagoula, Miss.	DDG-51, LHD	DD-21, LHD
General Dynamics-Bath Ironworks—Bath, Me.	DDG-51	DD-21, LPD-17
General Dynamics—Electric Boat—Groton, Conn.	SSN 21 (Seawolf)	NSSN
Litton-Avondale—Avondale, La.	LMSR, LPD-17	LPD-17, T-ADC(X)
General Dynamics-NASSCO—San Diego, Calif.	LMSR	T-ADC(X), JCC
Armored Vehicles		
General Dynamics—Lima, Ohio	M1A2	M1A3
General Dynamics—Woodbridge, Va.	AAAV Design	AAAV
United Defense—York, Pa.	Hercules, Grizzly, M2 Bradley	Crusader
General Motors—London, Ontario	LAV	LAV

[a]Aurora is allegedly a secret reconnaissance airplane built in Lockheed's Skunk Works. It is not officially acknowledged by the U.S. Air Force or DoD, but there is reason to believe that Skunk Works has a substantial project.

SOURCE: Eugene Gholz and Harvey M. Sapolsky. "Restructuring the U.S. Defense Industry," *International Security* 24 (Winter 1999–2000): 13.

controlled 70 percent of U.S. defense business and a growing share of markets abroad (Wayne 1998). A consolidated defense industry likewise faces less competition, which reduces its risks. "The contractors no longer have to cut each other's throat to compete," observed the director of the Center for Defense Information. "Now they are giants who are beefing up their case for more spending" (cited in Wayne 1998). Moreover, since defense spending came to rely more on a climate of politics to sustain it than on the threat posed by Soviet Communism, its investment climate has become less risky (Gholz and Sapolsky 1999–2000).

After 9/11   The behavior discussed in the preceding paragraphs has not disappeared. Instead, it has intensified. The massive defense budgets of the post-9/11 era have afforded lawmakers, lobbyists, and military contractors more opportunities to secure lucrative funding for their pet projects. Jobs rather than strategic needs often become the driving factor in determining the weapons the Pentagon receives. As a result, one observer noted, "Five years after the September 11 attacks changed American military priorities, the U.S. defense machine is still churning out weapons made for old-style conventional conflicts, even as it needs new tools to battle terrorists and insurgents" (Karp 2006). As we discuss in Chapter 11, this reality impeded Secretary of Defense Rumsfeld's six-year quest to transform the military.

However, it is possible that special interests beyond the traditional military-industrial complex are motivated to influence the direction of American foreign policy. Twice in little more than a decade the United States attacked Iraq, a major supplier of oil consumed in Europe, the United States, and elsewhere. Officially the Persian Gulf War was explained by Iraq's aggression against Kuwait, and the Iraq war by its presumed possession of weapons of mass destruction and ties to Al Qaeda. Insuring access to Iraq's oil was never openly discussed. But "blood for oil" was often used by critics of the two Bushes' policies. The controversial Michael Moore movie *Fahrenheit 9/11,* for example, alleged that the Bush family itself had close personal ties to the ruler of Saudi Arabia, a major supplier of oil to the United States (see also Phillips 2004). So does a *"military-petrochemical-industrial complex"* now shape American foreign policy? The hypothesis is troublesome and perhaps impossible either to prove or disprove. But in a world of tight oil supplies, declining reserves, inadequate refining capabilities, and growing demand from the United States, China, India, and elsewhere in the Global South, it is not easily dismissed.

Do Special Interest Groups Control American Foreign Policy?

The power-elite thesis and the corollary military-industrial complex construct challenge the theoretical tenets of liberal democracy. If in practice an elite indeed rules, then "democratic" policy formation is a political myth. Foreign policy making under such conditions is little more than a reflection of the motives and interests of a privileged few.

Juxtaposed to this is an alternative view—that "average" Americans influence policy by organizing themselves into groups to petition the government on behalf of their shared interests and values. James Madison, one of the three contributors to *The Federalist Papers,* designed to win support for the Constitution, worried that a single interest (which he called a "faction") might tyrannize others. To counter that, Madison supported a constitution that would encourage multiple interests that would counter one another.

If Madison were alive today, he might at first blush applaud the description of the United States as an interest group society. These groups are the bedrock of American pluralism. From the pluralist perspective, interest groups serve the public interest by lubricating the system of checks and balances the nation's founders devised. Indeed, interest groups are a key element defining the United States as a society-dominated political system. Still, pluralism also raises perplexing questions about democracy in practice, as we will see. After looking a second time, Madison might himself be perplexed and troubled.

Types of Interest Groups   Today thousands of organizations purport to represent Americans' interests. The number of lobbyists along the famous K Street in Washington is often thought to have doubled to 34,000 since George W. Bush took office and the Republicans control of Congress. They lobby Congress on behalf of companies, labor unions, foreign countries, and others. In 2004, lobbyists spent an average of $4.1 million on every congressional member—a record total of $2.16 billion in federal lobbying alone that promises to grow even higher (Center for Responsive Politics, "Who Gives," at www.opensecrets.org, accessed 5/2/06).

The interest groups themselves range from those representing comparatively heterogeneous constituencies, such as AARP (formerly the American Association of Retired Persons), the largest interest group in the United States, to smaller, more homogeneous groups organized around rather specific issues, such as the Sierra Club.

Most are concerned primarily with economic issues and seek to promote policies that benefit the special interests of their members. The AFL-CIO is an example in the area of organized labor, as is the American Farm Bureau in agriculture.

Among the smaller proportion of non-economic groups, two types stand out: public interest groups and ideological/single-issue groups. **Public interest groups** differ from the economic interest groups in that they seek to represent the interests of society as a whole and to realize benefits that are often less tangible. Common Cause, the League of Women Voters, and Ralph Nader's Public Citizen are among the most visible public interest groups. **Ideological/single-issue groups** seek to influence policy in more narrowly defined arenas. Examples again include the Sierra Club, which concentrates on environmental protection issues, the National Rifle Association, which opposes restrictions on gun ownership, and the United Nations Association of America, which seeks to influence U.S. policy toward the UN. Various ethnic interest groups with special foreign policy concerns are also properly regarded as single-issue groups. Often, however, their activities are not distinguishable from groups that emphasize a particular philosophical viewpoint. Americans for Democratic Action and Empower America are clear examples of ideologically motivated groups.

They support liberal and conservative positions, respectively, in foreign and domestic policy. Some religious groups, notably the conservative Christian right, also combine a particular political viewpoint with their religious message as they seek to influence U.S. foreign policies (Martin 1999).

Three other types of actors should be regarded as interest groups, broadly defined. First, foreign governments hire lobbyists in an effort to influence the decisions of American policy makers on salient issues. Between 1977 and 1996, the number of countries with representation in Washington grew from 110 to 150, and the number of the firms or individuals who represent them from 220 to more than 1,100 (McCormick 1998). European and Asian countries in particular have stepped up their activities. Japan has been especially active in promoting its interests and protecting itself from attacks on its trade policies.

In addition to hiring lobbyists, it has supported various think-tanks and academic institutions (Judis 1990; see also Choate 1990). Several other Asian countries either directly or indirectly contributed vast sums to the Democratic Party in 1996, trying to influence the outcome of the presidential election. The contributions, some in contravention of U.S. law, provoked considerable controversy, congressional investigations, and grist for Senator John McCain's (R-Arizona) drive four years later to make campaign finance reform a centerpiece of his campaign for the Republican Party presidential nomination.

Second, departments and agencies of the U.S. government act much like interest groups. They have their own conceptions of appropriate policy and take steps to ensure their views are represented in decision-making circles. The Pentagon, for example, historically has employed (using taxpayers' dollars) hundreds of "congressional liaisons" whose purpose is to secure legislation favorable to itself. Iron triangles are not confined to defense issues but are widely evident in other policy areas as well. Often called *issue networks* rather than iron triangles, they comprise government officials, lobbyists, and policy specialists whose shared interest and expertise in a particular issue bring them together.

Third, both state and local governments conduct their own foreign economic policies. Their activities (often in competition with one another) in the solicitation of foreign direct investment resemble those of special interest groups generally.

Interest Groups and Foreign Policy   However reassuring to democratic theory the pluralist interpretation may be, in the foreign policy arena, where the questions at issue are often technical and remote from the daily lives of Americans, the presence of organized interests raises the specter of policy domination by narrow vested interests. Because interest group activities are not always visible or attended by the press, interest groups are often assumed to be working secretly behind the scenes to devise policies that serve their own interests, not those of the country. Indeed, many people firmly believe that foreign policy is determined by special interests. Their beliefs are reinforced by some persuasive evidence.

The *American Israel Public Affairs Committee (AIPAC)*—a key cog in the so-called "Jewish" or "pro-Israeli" lobby—is often thought to control America's Middle East policy (see Bard 1994; Mearsheimer and Walt 2006; Smith 2000; Tivnan 1987; Uslaner 1998). Certainly it is widely recognized as one of the most influential of all lobby groups pressuring Congress. Lending credence to this supposition: U.S. recognition of Israel only eleven minutes after it declared its independence; congressional passage of the Jackson-Vanik amendment denying the Soviet Union promised trade benefits unless it changed its policies governing the emigration of Soviet Jews; a parade of votes in the United Nations supporting controversial Israeli policies and actions; and the continuing flow of enormous sums of military and other aid to Israel. AIPAC is believed to be so powerful that its detractors claim it has made Israel "America's fifty-first state."

Some critics have gone so far as to allege that the war in Iraq was motivated not by the war on terrorism but instead by the perceived need to protect the security of Israel. John Mearsheimer and Stephen Walt (2006) advance that thesis in an exceptionally controversial and biting article titled "The Israel Lobby." Domestic forces both within and without the government, they argue, trumped the other reasons for the war.

> For the past several decades, and especially since the Six-Day War in 1967, the centrepiece of U.S. Middle Eastern policy has been its relationship with Israel. The combination of unwavering support for Israel and the related effort to spread "democracy" throughout the region has inflamed Arab and Islamic opinion and jeopardized not only U.S. security but that of much of the rest of the world. This situation has no equal in American political history. Why has the U.S. been willing to set aside its own security and that of many of its allies in order to advance the interests of another state? . . .
>
> The thrust of U.S. policy in the region derives almost entirely from domestic politics, and especially the activities of the "Israel Lobby." Other special-interest groups have managed to skew foreign policy, but no lobby has managed to divert it as far from what the national interest would suggest, while simultaneously convincing Americans that U.S. interests and those of the other country—in this case, Israel—are essentially identical.
>
> *(Mearsheimer and Walt 2006)*

With respect to the war on terrorism, they add that "saying that Israel and the U.S. are united by a shared terrorist threat has the causal relationship backwards: the U.S. has a terrorism problem in good part because it is so closely allied with Israel, not the other way around. Support for Israel is not the only source of anti-American terrorism, but it is an important one, and it makes winning the war on terror more difficult."

Ethnic interest groups—representing Americans of Arab, Armenian, Greek, Irish, and Jewish descent, and those with ancestry in the so-called Captive European Nations (the former communist states in Eastern Europe), among others—have long played an active role in seeking to shape American foreign policy (understandable in a nation of immigrants). African and Cuban Americans have also recently emerged as visible proponents of their special interests and perspectives (Smith 2000; Uslaner 1998). The African American lobby Trans-Africa played a visible role in the politics surrounding the decision to intervene militarily in Haiti during the Clinton administration. Earlier it contributed importantly to shaping the sanctions policies toward South Africa believed to have contributed to the demise of its apartheid regime (McCormick 1998).

In the case of Cuba, several organizations since Castro seized power in the early 1960s have pressured Washington to keep sanctions against Cuba in hopes of toppling Castro's leftist regime. The conservatively oriented Cuban American National Foundation (CANF) is the most visible among them and has been credited with largely dictating U.S.-Cuban policy since it was formed in the early 1980s (Haney and Vanderbush 1999; Brenner et al. 2004). It also has shaped the major political parties' approach to Cuban policies (McCormick 1998), particularly in Florida where conservatively oriented ethnic Cubans are concentrated. George W. Bush's narrow and controversial victory in the state in 2000, which sealed the election in his favor, may have been decided by the state's Cuban-American community.

The ubiquity and seeming influence of ethnic groups caused longtime Senator Charles McCurdy "Mac" Mathias to worry some years ago that the effects of their lobbying may be more harmful than beneficial:

> Ethnic politics . . . have generated both unnecessary animosities and illusions of common interest where little or none exists. There are also baneful domestic effects: fueled as they are by passion and strong feelings about justice and rectitude, debates relating to the interplay of the national interest with the specific policies favored by organized ethnic groups

generate fractious controversy and bitter recrimination.
>
> *(Mathias 1981, 997)*

Nearly two decades later, political scientist Samuel Huntington (1997) would echo Mathias's lament: "America remains involved in the world, but its involvement is now directed at commercial and ethnic interests rather than national interests. Economic and ethnic particularism define the current American role in the world. . . . Increasingly people are arguing that these are precisely the interests foreign policy should serve."[3]

As Huntington suggests, economic policy and particularly trade issues stimulate considerable interest group activity—because jobs and profits are at stake. Congress is the favored target of these organized efforts. Historically the Chamber of Commerce and the AFL-CIO have figured prominently in these efforts. A veritable cacophony of more narrowly focused interest groups also have often been vocal contestants.

Economic interest groups were especially visible in the fight over NAFTA during the early Clinton administration, when scores of groups contended on both sides of the issue and millions of dollars were spent to influence not simply the final outcome but also the details of the agreement (Avery 1998; Cohen, Paul, and Blecker 1996; Rothgeb 2001). Near the end of the Clinton administration, intense lobbying would again characterize the fight over granting normal trade relations (NTR) to China. The unexpectedly lopsided vote in favor of NTR may have been the product of "the new China lobby" (Bernstein and Munro 1999), which knits in close partnership business and consulting interests on both sides of the Pacific.

Interestingly, however, organized labor, once a champion of free trade, increasingly has sided with environmental and other groups opposed to trade liberalization and, more broadly, globalization. It opposed CAFTA-DR, for example, the free trade agreement between the United States, Central American governments, and the Dominican Republic approved (narrowly) by Congress in 2005.

Labor believes globalization encourages the export of jobs to low-wage countries at the expense of American workers while corporate executives profit. In the words of Robert Reich, secretary of labor in the Clinton administration, "Even though the business cycle in recent years has improved things for the country as a whole, labor does not feel that it has really shared in the expansion. It feels that manufacturing jobs are still vanishing—whether because of technology or globalization and free trade" (see Mazur 2000; Newland 1999). Loss of manufacturing jobs became a key issue in the 2004 presidential election, particularly in the industrial Midwest.

Despite the ubiquity of ethnic interest groups and those involved in trade policy, which often turns as much on domestic as foreign policy concerns, the interest groups involved in other foreign policy issues historically have not figured prominently in policy debates. (There are some notable exceptions, such as the "old" China lobby, which for two decades sought to prevent U.S. diplomatic recognition of communist China.) Recently defense policy questions have emerged as an important exception. U.S. policy toward Central America during the Reagan administration also did not fit the historical mold. In both cases, ideological/single-issue groups sought to influence policy using the tactics normally associated with domestic interest group activity, including writing letters to members of Congress, testifying at congressional hearings, meeting with members of the media, publicizing the voting records of candidates for office, working in electoral campaigns, engaging in protests and demonstrations, and the like.

On defense issues, for example, the Committee on the Present Danger, formed during the late 1970s to stall the process of détente, launched a major, nationwide campaign to reverse what it (and later President Reagan) claimed to be the unilateral disarmament of the United States begun with SALT I. Joined by other interest groups, the committee was an especially visible and vocal critic of the 1979 SALT II treaty. It doubtless played a critical role in creating a domestic political environment inhospitable to its ratification (see Caldwell 1991; Sanders 1983). Two decades later, as we have seen, Project

for the New American Century (PNAC) again emerged as a pro-defense advocate.

In Central America, the Reagan administration created and supported the counterrevolutionaries (*contras*) seeking to overthrow the leftist Sandinista government in Nicaragua. Despite concerted efforts to gain congressional support for increased funding, however, the president consistently failed. His administration confronted a broad array of organized opponents who enjoyed the upper hand. The countercoalition included prominent religious groups and other single-issue groups, which at one time numbered more than fifty (Arnson and Brenner 1993). Reagan complained six weeks prior to leaving the presidency that an "iron triangle" in a "Washington colony" comprising Congress, the news media, and special interest groups was "attempting to rule the nation according to its interests and desires more than the nation's." He lamented in his memoirs that "one of the greatest frustrations during those eight years was my inability to communicate to the American people and to Congress the seriousness of the threat we faced in Central America" (Reagan 1990).

Are Interest Groups Influential?   Asking whether interest groups are influential may seem curious, as we have already given several examples where the answer seems clear-cut. Still, as with the military-industrial complex, we must remind ourselves that where there is interest and activity, there is not necessarily influence. Research on the foreign policy influence of interest groups during the Cold War supports this conclusion. Briefly, those findings show the following.

- Interest groups exert a greater impact on domestic than on foreign policy issues, where the foreign policy elite are relatively immune from domestic pressures due to national security considerations.

- Interest group influence during crises is rare, as the president has enormous power to shape public opinion and receives little effective challenge from others.

- Interest groups exert their greatest influence on nonsecurity issues that entail economic considerations commanding attention over long periods.

- The impact of interest groups varies with the issue: the less important the issue, the greater the likelihood of interest group influence.

- Interest groups most effectively exercise power over policy through Congress.

- When congressional interest in a foreign policy issue mounts, interest group activity and influence increase.

- Interest group influences increase during election years, when candidates for office are most prone to open channels of access and communication.

- Interest groups are most influential when only a narrow segment of society is affected and the issue is not in the public spotlight, attended by the mass media. "A lobby is like a night flower," observed AIPAC's director of foreign policy issues. "It thrives in the dark and dies in the sun" (cited in Grove 1991).

- Influence between the government and interest groups is reciprocal. However, government officials are more likely to manipulate interest groups than the latter are to shape government policy.

- Single-interest groups have more influence than large, national, multipurpose organizations, but their influence is limited to their special policy interest.

- Interest groups often attempt to influence public opinion rather than policy itself, but mass attitudes are seldom amenable to manipulation by interest group efforts.

- Interest groups sometimes seek inaction and maintenance of the status quo; such efforts are generally more successful than efforts to bring about policy change. Thus interest groups act as "veto groups" that inhibit policy change.

This summary of findings shows that while interest groups seek to persuade, their mere presence, indeed, ubiquity, does not guarantee their penetration of the foreign policy-making process.

Interest groups may be effective on certain special issues. More often, foreign policy making is relatively immune to interest group influence. First, national security frequently requires secrecy. This reality leads to decision making behind closed doors rather than within the legislative process with its many access points. Second, within the policy-making arena, interest group influences often counterbalance one another. Groups line up on either side of an issue and politically cancel out one another.

Many of the above generalizations drawn from the Cold War era remain compelling, but the tremendous growth in interest group and lobbying activity witnessed recently raises important questions. James McCormick (1998), a preeminent scholar of Congress and foreign policy, suggests several factors that have had the effect of encouraging greater interest group influence. Among them are (1) congressional reforms that have encouraged greater interest group access; (2) the growth of partisan and ideological divisions among the American people, which have stimulated interest group interests and enhanced opportunities to exercise foreign policy influence; (3) the rise of new groups with foreign policy concerns—"foreign lobbies, some religious lobbies, think tanks, and scattered single-issue lobbies"; (4) the increased salience of trade and related issues compared with traditional national security issues; (5) a changing locus of decision making away from the small groups that make crisis decisions toward broader involvement by others interested in structural decisions (for example, goals and tactics of defense policy); and (6) procedural requirements imposed on the executive by Congress that have opened new points of access to others seeking to shape foreign policy preferences.

McCormick offers evidence to support each of these ideas, and his conclusions are compelling: "While involvement and access may arguably be necessary conditions for policy influence, they are not sufficient ones....Significant barriers still hamper interest groups from working their will on foreign policy making even as these groups are increasingly involved in the process.... The usual judgment that interest groups can be more effective in stopping action than in changing directions remains as accurate in the foreign policy arena as it does in the domestic arena."

The Politics of Policy Making: Elitism and Pluralism Revisited

The popularity of the pluralist model of policy making rests on the democratic belief that the public good is served when each group in a society of diverse interests seeks to maximize its own interests, much as Adam Smith hypothesized in his classic *The Wealth of Nations* that the invisible hand of the marketplace, driven by self-interest, would serve the public interest. In the marketplace of ideas and self-interest, the ability of any one group to exert disproportionate influence is offset by the tendency for ***countervailing powers*** to materialize. When an interest group seeks vigorously to push policy in one direction, another (or a coalition of others aroused by perceived threats to their interests) will be stimulated to push policy in the opposite direction. Indeed, today's losers often become tomorrow's winners.

The positive side of this picture is that no one interest dominates policy. That was the wish and intent of the nation's founders. The negative side is *gridlock,* a popular description of the Washington policy-making scene during the first Bush presidency as Democrats on Capitol Hill and Republicans in the White House repeatedly found themselves at loggerheads. When the pursuit of one group's interests are balanced by another's, can anything be accomplished?

Political economist Mancur Olson addressed this dilemma and its consequences in two classic works, *The Logic of Collective Action* (1965) and *The Rise and Decline of Nations* (1982). His arguments draw on the theory of collective goods and the "free rider" problem we discussed in Chapter 7. With respect to interest groups, Olson argues that small, private organizations (such as trade associations) often have an advantage over others as they seek to promote their interests, because larger groups (the

American consumer) are unorganized. Individuals also have an incentive to free ride on organized interest groups, because they benefit from their activities even if they fail to share in the costs (nonunion labor, for instance, often enjoys the benefits that unionized labor has won through collective bargaining).

Building on the logic of these arguments, writer/journalist Jonathan Rauch (1994) argues that "demosclerosis" is the result: democratic government can accomplish little that is meaningful, because each of the organized interests in American society seeks a share of the government's pie (taxes), even if this means redistributing wealth from one segment of society to another. "We have met the special interests and they are us," Rauch observes (see also Lowi 1979).

The pervasiveness of countervailing interests in American society contributes to demosclerosis. Money not only fuels group lobbying activities, it also funds elections. The 2004 presidential campaign cost more than any other in history—more than $1 billion according to the Federal Election Commission (FEC)—and the number promises to grow even higher. A variety of sources contribute money, including ***political action committees (PACs)*** representing interests of corporations and groups, wealthy individuals, and ***527 organizations,*** a new group of "political organizations" as defined by section 527 of the federal tax code. Like PACs, 527 organizations raise money to provide campaign funds for political parties or individual candidates for office. Unlike PACs, they fall within the purview of the Internal Revenue Service (IRS) rather than the FEC. Thus, they are not subject to FEC oversight and restrictions as are traditional PACs. 527 organizations were particularly active during the 2004 campaign. (The derogatory "Swift Boat" ads challenging Senator John Kerry's military record, for example, were financed by 527s.) With PACS, 527s are now a major source of campaign funds, with aerospace, defense, pro-Israeli, and "New Right" organizations near the top of the list of contributors.

There is little doubt that money has altered the character of contemporary campaign politics. Still, in some sense campaign finance patterns reinforce the veracity of pluralism as they reinforce the image of policy making as a taffy-pull among countervailing forces. Average Americans are able to contribute to the causes of the groups that represent their interests, pool their resources, and use them to influence electoral outcomes and, hence, policy choices. But few Americans are able to give the vast sums that the most wealthy contribute. So the taffy-pull becomes another arena of competition among the elite.

So which model of the politics of policy making is correct? The answer favors the elitist model, lending credence to Richard Barnet's (1972) observation that American foreign policy is "an elite preserve . . . made for the benefit of that elite." "The flaw in the pluralist heaven," writes E. E. Schattschneider in his classic study, *The Semisovereign People* (1960), "is that the heavenly chorus sings with a strong upper-class bias." In fact, the elitist and pluralist accounts both depict a process in which the ordinary citizen matters very little in any direct sense when it comes to foreign policy making.

THE ROLE OF THE MASS MEDIA IN THE OPINION-INTEREST-POLICY PROCESS

If anyone is in a position to challenge the power of the privileged in American society, arguably it is the mass media. The communications industry—print, radio, and television—plays two pivotal roles. First, public attitudes may be influenced (created, some would say) by the information the media disseminates. Second, the behavior of policy makers themselves may be affected by the news the media reports and by the images of the world it conveys. From either perspective, the media is an important link in the causal chain that transmits Americans' values, beliefs, and preferences into the foreign policy process. Figure 9.1 shows the pivotal role the media plays in what Robert Entman calls a *cascading activation model.* It portrays how thoughts

and feelings about foreign policy news *frames* are passed downward from the White House through the rest of the political system. We will return to his model and the critical role of news frames shortly.

Many Americans are apparently taken with the notion the media shapes public opinion either directly or by transmitting what government officials say is "true." Some might even say that the media *is* public opinion. Government officials likewise attribute vast powers to the media. They may be right, as the evidence suggests that policy makers are able to use the mass media to mold public preferences to support their policies. The presidential "bully pulpit" is particularly powerful.

Policy makers themselves, however, are typically less than sanguine about the media. Their views have ranged from awe and fear to downright hatred. Nearly every president has come to believe his administration is victimized by the media. Such views are captured in Oscar Wilde's famous remark that "the President reigns for four years, but Journalism reigns forever." Thus many consider the mass media as a fourth branch of the government, often called the *fourth estate.* It is no accident, therefore, that presidents actively court the media's favor and ascribe to it the power to make or break government policy.

Still, the notion that the media is somehow able to "determine" either foreign policy or even foreign policy attitudes is questionable. The relationship between media influences and other societal sources of foreign policy behavior is more complex than this simple view suggests. A preferable hypothesis is that the mass media performs a mediating role, helping to shape foreign policy attitudes and choices but determining neither. The hypothesis contrasts with the typical views of the media, which tend to embrace one of two alternatives: "The media either take foreign policy out of the hands of the elite and open the process to an ill-informed public or they are indentured servants of the foreign policy elite" (Kovach 1996). Neither of those polar extremes is without veracity, but neither is completely accurate either. We can learn why by examining, first, the relationship between the mass media and the public

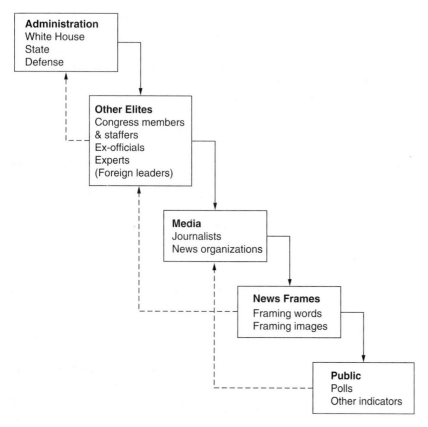

FIGURE 9.1 A Cascading Activation Model Linking the White House and Elites to the Public Through the Media and News Frames

SOURCE: Robert M. Entman. *Projections of Power: Framing News, Public Opinion, and U.S. Foreign Policy.* Chicago: University of Chicago Press, 2004, p. 10. Reprinted by permission.

and, second, the relationship between the mass media and policy makers.

The Mass Media and the Public

The proposition that the mass media shapes public attitudes is tempting if for no other reason than that it comprises the primary vehicle for the transmission of knowledge—and "knowledge is power." The institutions that provide Americans with political information are pervasive and sophisticated. Nearly all American households own at least one television set; well over half own two or more. There are roughly 1,400 daily newspapers in the United States, with total daily circulations exceeding 55 million. The three major

weekly news magazines also claim nearly 10 million readers. This extraordinary establishment has the ability to determine "what the news is," to define behaviors as important actions, and thereby to make them into events.

The *agenda-setting* role of the mass media is particularly important (McCombs and Shaw 1972; Weaver et al. 2004). Most people may be inattentive to foreign or other issues of public policy most of the time, but when they do show interest or are exposed to issues, the mass media tells them what to care about. Put succinctly, "the mass media may not be successful in telling people what to think, but [they] are stunningly successful in telling their audience what to think about" (Cohen 1963). By telling us what to think about, however, the media also provides cues as to what to think, precisely because of its capacity to determine what we think about (Entman 1989).

The media's ability to set the agenda and to influence thinking in other ways is greatest among those who are neither interested nor involved in politics and hence lack political sophistication. Because many who comprise the mass public have no prior information to draw on in forming attitudes about new developments, the media exert a potentially powerful impact on perceptions about events simply because the information it supplies is new—and is often presented in a sensational way in an effort to influence "appropriate" preferences. Noteworthy is that nearly 40 percent of Americans report that the media is their source of information about important international problems, compared with 25 percent who turn to it when it comes to domestic issues (Wittkopf and Hinckley 2000).

Furthermore, the attention the media gives to different issues may contribute to its symbolic significance. During 1987, for example, the United States became increasingly involved in the Gulf war between Iran and Iraq. However, news about its air attack on Iranian bases in the gulf region and the destruction of an Iranian domestic airliner by the USS Vincennes in October of that year was dwarfed by news of the dramatic Wall Street stock market crash, the steepest since the infamous crash of 1929. In "calmer times," Doris A. Graber (1993) observes, the Persian Gulf incidents "would have been the top stories."

Framing is widely used by political communication scholars to describe how the media shapes political discourse. During the continuing conflict in the Balkans during the 1990s, the media failed to report high levels of public support for U.S. involvement there. Instead, the media framed the issue in terms of opposition to involvement, which may have had the effect of misdirecting policy away from public preferences (Sobel 1998b). We can also surmise that this meant many Americans came to believe U.S. interests were not at stake in that troubled region.

In the foreign and national security policy domain, the president is the primary source of "news."

The key questions are how the news will be framed, by whom, and whether White House frames will dominate or counterframes win the contest in shaping foreign policy discussions. "The White House, its supporters, and its critics peddle their messages to the press in hopes of gaining political leverage," writes Robert Entman (2004). "The media's political influences arises from how they respond—from their ability to frame the news in ways that favor one side over another." Framing consists of "selecting and highlighting some facets of events or issues and making connections among them so as to promote a particular interpretation, evaluation, and/or solution." Framing, then, "refers to the process of selection and highlighting some aspects of a perceived reality, and enhancing the salience of an interpretation and evaluation of that reality." Figure 9.2 illustrates how a political event (surprise attack), actor (Al Qaeda,) and issue (destroy Al Qaeda) intersect with one another to form an idealized frame of the 9/11 terrorist attacks (see also Norris et al. 2003b.)

The media not only sets the agenda and frames the issues, it also functions as a *gatekeeper* by filtering the news and shaping how it is reported. The media's gatekeeping role is especially pronounced in foreign affairs, as the menu of foreign affairs coverage offered the American people comes from remarkably few major sources. Principal among them are three prestigious newspapers of record (the *New York Times, Washington Post,* and *Los Angeles Times*), two wire services (the Associated Press [AP] and United Press International [UPI]), national television broadcast networks (ABC, CBS, and NBC), and two prominent cable news networks (CNN [Cable News Network] and Fox News Channel [FNC]). The *New York Times* provides news to other newspapers, which typically follow its lead in the way they present news stories about foreign affairs to local audiences.

The *New York Times* motto promises "all the news that's fit to print," but in fact there is too much news even for it. Thus, in choosing what to print, the media gatekeepers also shape the values to which Americans are exposed. Over the long run, "the media tend to reinforce mainstream social values. They transmit 'normal' or legitimate issues and ideas

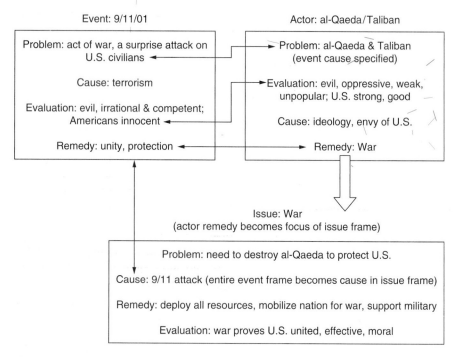

FIGURE 9.2   A Representative Frame of the 9/11 Event, Actor, and Issue

SOURCE: Robert M. Entman. *Projections of Power: Framing News, Public Opinion, and U.S. Foreign Policy.* Chicago: University of Chicago Press, 2004, p. 125. Reprinted by permission.

to the public and [filter] out new, radical, or threatening perspectives" (Bennett 1980). Similarly, *pack journalism*—a troublesome phenomenon in which reporters follow the lead of one or a few others in deciding what is (or is not) news and how it should be framed—often leads to remarkably similar news accounts, particularly among the national print and electronic media (Graber 1997).

Clearly, as the foregoing ideas suggest, the media plays a powerful role in American society. Why, then, is its impact on the public's foreign policy attitudes less direct and pervasive than might be expected?

Media Inattention to Foreign Affairs   The mass media's ability to shape foreign policy attitudes is undermined in part by its relative inattention to foreign affairs and its comparatively greater concern for domestic news. Few reporters are paid to cover foreign affairs, and television programming is overwhelmingly oriented toward local, not national or international news.

By some standards, coverage of foreign affairs is not inconsequential. Doris Graber (1993) reports that major Chicago newspapers devote about 6 percent of their space to international news and that national television networks give about 20 percent of their time to it. Still, foreign affairs certainly do not command overwhelming attention. In part this is due to the absence of a mass market for foreign policy news in the face of industry efforts to boost profits.[4] A survey of newspaper reading habits sponsored by the *Washington Post* led to the conclusion that "local news is the franchise for America's newspapers. . . . It is why people buy newspapers." Whereas nearly two-thirds of the respondents said they were very interested in local news, fewer than one in five said they were interested in foreign news—"a snore for most Americans," according to the *Post* (Morin 1996). Newspapers also suffer a competitive disadvantage compared with television. Seven of ten Americans responded in the *Post* that television is their primary source of all news (Morin 1996).

In the post–Cold War environment, however, even network television news turned decidedly inward. Garrick Utley, longtime foreign correspondent for several major TV news networks, reported that the "total foreign coverage of network nightly news programs . . . declined precipitously, from 3,733 minutes in 1989 to 1,838 minutes in 1996 at ABC, the leader, and from 3,351 minutes to 1,175 minutes at third-place NBC" (Utley 1997). The number of minutes devoted to foreign policy coverage in particular, always a smaller subset of foreign news, also declined. Similarly, Pippa Norris (1997) shows a dramatic decline in TV network coverage of international news during the transition to the post–Cold War world. Since 9/11 there has been a heightened interest in foreign policy news, however, especially in the war in Iraq, as we saw in Chapter 8.

An exception to the comparatively scant attention other media gives to foreign affairs is the coverage it receives in the national newspapers of record, sometimes called the *prestige press*. A study done some years ago showed that the *New York Times* allotted over 40 percent of its total national and international coverage to foreign news (Frank 1973). That proportion may have changed in recent years, but the *Times* remains an important source of international news. How many people consume that coverage remains problematic, however, as the circulation of the *Times* constitutes but a fraction of the nation's newspaper subscribers.

CNN, the twenty-four-hour Cable News Network, occupies a place providing world news that sets it apart from others. It maintains a global network of news-gathering offices, and its news broadcasts from around the world are seen by an international audience. Thus, courtesy of CNN, millions of Americans and others (including Saddam Hussein in Baghdad!) viewed at close range the dramatic aerial bombardment of Iraq at the onset of the 1991 Persian Gulf War (and, presumably, the Iraq war a decade later). Two years before the Persian Gulf War they witnessed the Chinese government's bloody suppression of pro-democracy forces on Tiananmen Square. Then–CNN anchor Bernard Shaw captured the drama unfolding in China this way: "Unbelievably, we all came here to cover a summit, and we walked into a revolution."

The CNN effect captures the presumed impact of CNN's news coverage. The phrase was especially popular in the early 1990s, when television coverage of developments in Somalia were credited by some as having "forced" the Bush administration to intervene there to stem widespread starvation and death. Journalist Warren Strobel (1999) described the **CNN effect** as "a loss of policy control on the part of policy makers because of the power of the media, a power they can do nothing about." Research has largely discredited the CNN effect as originally interpreted—the effects of the continuous CNN news reporting of dramatic events and home and abroad. Still, the phrase remains in the lexicon of communications research. The CNN effect, according to Stephen Hess and Marvin Kalb (2003), "included more than just CNN coverage–it meant that the world was wired, open to instantaneous coverage, and that the coverage affected everyone and everything, including world leaders and their tactics and strategies."

Since the early 1990s, CNN has itself been challenged. The birth and growing visibility of the Fox News Channel is the most obvious challenge. But changing preferences in favor of more commentary and "human interest" broadcasts championed by other cable companies pressured CNN to steer a new course in today's highly competitive media environment. The stream of 24-hour news coverage, long the mainstay of CNN, has given way to other programming formats as a result. Steven Livingston, who has written on the CNN effect, put it this way: "The contemporary version of CNN is that it's news as mini-series. . . . You have these periods of intense concentration on a story, and then somebody wakes up one morning and says, The war is over and we can go on to the next bang-bang, the next action. You're defining news as a dramatic event rather than as a process" (cited in Hess and Kalb 2003).

Finally, there is another way that cable television has impacted political news. Early in the last century, Theodore Roosevelt described the presidency as a **bully pulpit.** By that he meant the president could use the power of his office to cajole, to persuade, to get others inside and outside of government to support his policies and programs. The advent of television encouraged that process, as presidents could largely control their access to the media, whether through periodic press conferences or releasing "breaking news" that would break just in time for the evening news broadcasts. Today, however, the president can no longer count on media exposure. One *Washington Post* editorial board member put it rather caustically:

Technological advances now undermine the bully pulpit rather than amplify it. The rise of cable TV has changed television from a presidential megaphone into a presidential scourge. The three big networks—ABC, CBS, NBC—which once carried all presidential press conferences live, and which reported respectfully on initiatives emanating from the White House, have been displaced by new cable channels that compete for viewers by eschewing such deference. Rather than televise the president, these cable channels churn out irreverent talk shows. The bully pulpit has been drowned out by bullying pundits (Mallaby 2000).

Public Inattention to Foreign Affairs Most Americans are uninterested in and ill-informed about foreign affairs, as we learned in Chapter 8. In late 1990, for example, as the Cold War was winding down and the United States was in the midst of the crisis over Kuwait, only 36 percent of the American people said they were very interested in following news about other countries and barely more than half were very interested in news of U.S. relations with other countries (Rielly 1991). By the end of the decade, the proportions in all cases had dropped even further (Rielly 1999). An earlier study found that three-quarters of the public claimed they paid attention to government and public affairs, but only about a third had above-average knowledge on these matters. Over 40 percent were poorly informed. This finding led the authors to conclude that, "while seventy-six percent of the people say they pay attention to politics, they clearly aren't taking notes" (Ornstein, Kohut, and McCarthy 1988). Given a choice, Doris Graber (1997) observes, Americans "do not seek out foreign policy news."

The Imperviousness of Beliefs Research grounded in social psychology shows that most people do not easily change their beliefs. Popular myths notwithstanding, what they read in print and see and hear on television does not alter what they think.[5] Instead, as we saw in Chapter 8, they use information shortcuts that cause them to interpret new information in ways that reinforce, not restructure, prevailing attitudes. **_Selective perception_** is one reason. It is a pervasive human tendency: people search for "comfortable" information that fits with preexisting beliefs; they screen out or reject information with which they disagree. In short, we see what we want to see, we hear what we want to hear.

Selective perception is partially subconscious, stemming from the nearly universal need to maintain stable images when confronted with inconsistent and confusing information. In the parlance of psychology, everyone seeks to maintain **cognitive balance** (Festinger 1957). They either screen out information that runs counter to cherished beliefs or they suppress it if it challenges preexisting images. An individual who subscribes to the simplistic belief that all civil disturbances in the Middle East and North Africa are inspired by Islamic fundamentalists, for instance, is likely to reject or block out information that contradicts that view, such as reports that civil conflict in the Darfur region of Sudan stems from poverty and long-standing ethnic disputes.

Selective perception is also pervasive because people are prone to avoid information with which they disagree. Most people read magazines and listen to news programs that reinforce interpretations consistent with their preconceptions. Few seek out information that challenges them. Research shows, for example, that Republicans and conservatives prefer Fox News Channel as their television news source (Pew Research Center, "News Audiences Increasingly Politicized," http://people-press.org/reports/display.php3?ReportID=215, accessed 5/17/2006). On the other hand, liberals and moderates prefer CNN. Catch phrases like "Clinton News Network" to describe CNN and "White House Annex" to describe Fox News Channel capture the essence of selective perception.

Does the medium matter? Research by Steven Kull and his associates (Kull et al. 2003–2004) suggests it does. In three surveys taken between June and September 2003, they find that misperceptions of the *facts* of the war in Iraq were held by a larger proportion of Fox News viewers than other media. The surveys asked if weapons of mass destruction had been *found* in Iraq; whether clear evidence linking Saddam Hussein to Al Qaeda had been *found;* and whether world opinion *favored* the United States going to war. An average of 45 percent of the Fox News audience responded "yes" on all three questions—all factually wrong. For CNN, the number was 31 percent and for the broadcast networks, the answers ranged from 30 percent (ABC, NBC) to 36 percent (CBS). Those who relied on National Public Radio (NPR) and the Public Broadcasting System (PBS) were least prone to misperceptions, followed by consumers of (unspecified) print media. Interestingly, this tendency held for all Fox viewers, not just the Republicans and conservatives most likely to support President Bush's policies.

Individuals' lack of receptivity to wide-ranging ideas that challenge existing prejudices and stereotypes inhibits the mass media's ability to influence attitude change. Even among those who are relatively sophisticated politically, long-standing ideological predispositions toward conservative or liberal perspectives shape interpretations of events communicated by the media. Selective recall is a related tendency that reinforces attitude consistency.

Television's Inadvertent Audience   The pervasiveness of television in the homes and daily lives of millions of Americans requires that we add important caveats to the foregoing conclusions.

Television has provided Americans with an infusion of foreign affairs information that most neither like nor want. Instead, because most who watch television news see what does not interest them as well as what does—they don't "edit" the information television journalists supply by walking away from the set or turning it off—they have become an *inadvertent audience* (Ranney 1983). Even when the American people are attentive to foreign affairs, as clearly many were during the Persian Gulf War and the Iraq war that followed, the impact on their political knowledge of exposure to information remains slight (Bennett 1992).

What are the consequences of the intrusive force of television? First, television may explain the decline of confidence in the nation's institutional leadership witnessed during recent decades. As William Schneider (1982), a well-known political analyst, observes, "Negative news makes good video. Consequently, television presents much of the news as conflict, criticism, and controversy.... The public responds to this large volume of polarized information by becoming more cynical, more negative, and more critical of leadership and institutions."

Second, members of the inadvertent audience, being uninterested, are unlikely to have convictions as strong about issues as do those who regularly follow foreign policy concerns. "When people with weak opinions are exposed to new information, the impact of that information is very strong. They form new opinions, and if the information they receive is negative or critical, their opinions will develop in that direction" (Schneider 1982). As Kennedy adviser Theodore Sorensen (1994) observed, members of the inadvertent audience, who watch "the screen by the hour instead of by program,... often find their attention unintentionally engaged by the picture unfolding before them, their interest inadvertently aroused, their opinions almost involuntarily formed, and their actions as well as reactions as voters and citizens spontaneously motivated." Still, "there is no evidence that television changes the nature of the public's concerns in the area of foreign policy," observes Schneider (1984). "These concerns remain what they always have been: peace and strength. Television simply intensifies these concerns and creates more negative and unstable public moods."

Third, television has also affected the relationship between the mass public and policy makers in important ways. Members of Congress who wish to make names for themselves (read: all), for example, are induced to frame their foreign policy ideas in "one-liners" that will fit into the thirty-, sixty-, or ninety-second slots the evening news allocates to such issues. For the electorate, television has meant that "a presidential candidate without much prior international experience can come to office with a collection of half-minute clichés in his head masquerading as foreign policies" (Destler, Gelb, and Lake 1984). The compelling importance of television in shaping electoral outcomes magnifies the impact of these "sound bites."

The Internet   The remarkably rapid spread of the Internet in the past decade and its growing significance as a source of news inevitably challenges further our ideas about the role of the media in the opinion-policy process. Certainly it challenges the place of television as a source of political news. The Pew Research Center recently determined that 50 million Americans now get news online every day, a dramatic surge in just a few years fueled in part by the spread of broadband users (Horrigan 2006). Noteworthy, however, is that traditional media sources have established their own Web sites, including the newspapers of record, CNN, Fox, and other cable news outlets, and radio. All openly encourage readers and listeners to access them for additional information.

Certainly one of the medium's defining characteristics is the absence of gatekeepers. Virtually anyone can transmit information on the Internet (*blogs* have become an increasingly popular means of doing so). Without gatekeepers to filter the information and separate the wheat from the chaff, there are few ways to assess the accuracy or authoritativeness of the source. Nonetheless, Internet information often has important political content, and it may preempt more established news media. The *Drudge Report,* for example, was among the first sources of information about the events that led to President Clinton's impeachment trial.

Scholars are only now beginning to understand the impact of the Internet on political attitudes and foreign policy thinking. Because younger Americans are more prone than others to rely on the Internet as a source of political news, this promises to be an intriguing avenue of inquiry for many years. Meanwhile, we already know that the Internet, like television, challenges long-standing theories about how attitudes change.

How Do Attitudes Change?   Mass foreign policy attitudes are resistant to change, but they do change. How? Television, we have suggested, plays a role, especially among those with little knowledge about or interest in foreign policy. The relationship between elites and masses also has a bearing on attitudes in the general population. When those most attuned to foreign policy adjust their beliefs to accommodate new foreign policy realities, the changes can be expected to filter throughout society.

The classic explanation of the opinion-making and opinion-circulating process is known as the ***two-step flow theory of communications.*** As originally formulated, it says that "ideas often flow from radio and print to opinion leaders and from these to the less-active sections of the population" (Katz 1957). The dynamics of attitude change are best explained, the hypothesis holds, through the crucial channel of face-to-face contact. Members of the mass public do not actually sit down and exchange ideas with governing elites or those close to policy makers, of course. Instead, ideas become meaningful only after they have been transmitted to members of the mass public from opinion leaders such as teachers, members of the clergy, local political leaders, and others who have an above-average interest in public affairs and occupy positions allowing them to communicate frequently with others. Attitude change, according to this view, stems from changes in the thinking of the policy elite and those attentive to public affairs, with society at large following sometime later. Face-to-face contacts with opinion leaders are a crucial link in the diffusion process. Hence, the mass media is not the primary transmitters of ideas, nor is it the primary stimulus of mass attitude change. Instead, it is the conduit through which attitudes are first connected to the political system and then transmitted through interpersonal contact.

Television and the Internet complicate this view. There are few or no apparent face-to-face intermediaries between evening news anchors or blog writers and the consumers of their messages. The two-step flow theory is thus overly simple in today's world. Some analysts suggest that a multistep flow theory is preferable, as it provides a more accurate description of the opinion-making and opinion-circulating process in an age of mass electronic communication. The **multistep flow theory of communications** seeks to draw attention to the multiple channels through which ideas and opinions are circulated in America's complex society (Sandman, Rubin, and Sachsman 1982).

Clearly, though, even with a multistep flow of communications, the media plays a crucial role in the transmission of opinions within the political system. Hence it is pivotal in the process of opinion making and opinion diffusion. Syndicated columnist William Safire has drawn particular attention to the opinion-shaping role of the "Opinion Mafia"—those whom others might call "political pundits"—in his own retrospective comment on the original two-step flow theory. Arguing that in an environment where "political leaders tend to play it safe and consult polls before taking positions," more people turn to "those multimedia commentators who are ready to pound beliefs into shape while the iron of controversy and crisis is red hot" (Safire 1990).

The Mass Media and Policy Makers

Ordinary Americans may be impervious to the media's influence because they tune out its messages. On the other hand, those at the top of the public opinion pyramid—policy makers, policy influentials, and the attentive public—often rely heavily on the information the communications industry disseminates. Television has a leveling effect in that even those indifferent to foreign affairs get some information about it, while those making up the elite and attentive public take advantage of a broader array of information—virtually all of it from publicly available media sources, including the Internet. On the surface, then, it appears that the media may be most influential with those who have the most influence.

Policy Makers, Policy Influentials, and the Media To suggest that policy makers rely on the media—instead of the intelligence community, for instance—as a primary source of information may appear to be an exaggeration, but it is true. A study of roughly 100 officials in policy positions found that nearly two-thirds reported the media was generally their most rapid source of information in crisis situations, and over four-fifths indicated the media was an important source of policy-relevant information (O'Heffernan 1991).

This is the case partly because media reports about world developments are more timely and readable than official reports and are often perceived to be less biased than those of government agencies that gather data with a bureaucratic agenda in mind. Hodding Carter, a former State Department spokesperson, explained: "Most policy people, when they are not out there posturing and beating their chest in public about the effects of the media, would be happy to tell you how often they get information faster, quicker, and more accurately from the media than they get it from their official sources" (O'Heffernan 1991).

Policy influentials likewise depend on media reports. An often-cited example comes from conservative writer William F. Buckley (1970)—no admirer of the news establishment of which he is a part—who admitted that after hearing a radio bulletin of Egyptian President Gamal Abdel Nasser's death, "I slipped off to telephone the *New York Times* to see if the report was correct (one always telephones the *New York Times* in emergencies). The State Department called the *New York Times,* back in 1956, to ask if it was true that Russian tanks were pouring into Budapest." John Kenneth Galbraith (1969), a former American ambassador to India, has also testified to the accuracy of the nation's elite newspapers: "I've said many times that I never learned from a classified document anything I couldn't get earlier or later from the *New York*

Times." Bernard Cohen, a careful student of the subject, put the special role of the prestige press in a way that retains a timeless ring (as foreign policy professionals will readily admit):

> [The *New York Times*] is read by virtually everyone in the government who has an interest or responsibility in foreign affairs.... One frequently runs across the familiar story: "It is often said that Foreign Service Officers get to their desks early in the morning to read the *New York Times,* so they can brief their bosses on what is going on." This canard is easily buried: The "bosses" are there early, too, reading the *New York Times* for themselves.... The *Times* is uniformly regarded as the authoritative paper in the foreign policy field. In the words of a State Department official in the public affairs field, "You can't work in the State Department without the *New York Times.* You can get along without the overnight telegrams sooner."
>
> *(Cohen 1961)*

More recent evidence suggests that policy makers now also ascribe special importance to television news accounts (see Larson 1990). This is especially evident in insiders' and other accounts of the way they monitor the development of international crises in the White House Situation Room, where multiple television sets feed continuous electronic news coverage into the crisis nerve center. The long-popular television series *The West Wing* provided a glimpse into what others describe.

Media Vulnerability to Government Manipulation

To a considerable extent the media reflects, rather than balances, the attitudes of the government. During the 1979 Iranian hostage crisis, for example, the media rarely strayed from the government's line about what was happening (Larson 1990). Similarly, the media generally accepts the government's definition of America's friends and foes. When those

definitions change, the media reflects the changes. Even during the Vietnam War, the media continued to the very end to give the administration's account of the conflict considerable attention. (This is not to deny that the media contributed to the public's distaste for that unhappy and disconcerting venture.) After 9/11, the *war on terrorism* frame, quickly adopted by the Bush administration, became the benchmark used to identify friends and foes—the "axis of evil," for example. That frame also meant other important foreign policy problems, such as poverty reduction in the Global South and coping with the spread of AIDS, were made lower priorities by the administration—and given less media attention (Norris et al. 2003a).

By deferring to the government, the media encourages public acceptance of the government's view of the world; basically this means the viewpoints of the president and the executive branch, which remain the primary sources of foreign policy information. Therefore, it is able most of the time to "set the agenda of coverage and frame stories to reflect official perspectives" (Graber 1993; Entman 2004).

The 1990 crisis over Kuwait that led to the Persian Gulf War illustrates how the media and government together often shape opinion—and perhaps policy. Market research showed that the best way to frame the issue was to depict Saddam Hussein as an enemy of the American people and to use President George H. W. Bush to accomplish that end. Once the issue was cast and sold in this way, some policy options became more acceptable and others less so. In particular, "the Saddam framing...made it possible to dismiss the leading policy alternative of economic sanctions against Iraq long before there was any empirical basis for doing so (that is, long before it was reasonable to determine whether sanctions were working)" (Bennett 1994b). It is not surprising, then, that Bill Clinton would also invoke the Hitler image to describe Serbian President Slobodan Milošević as NATO war planes launched their air attack on Kosovo. What much of this suggests is that the media frequently operates as a conduit for the transmission of information from the governing elite to the American people rather than as a truly independent source of information about what the government is doing.

The seeming collusion between media and government, whether conscious or unconscious, stems from a variety of sources, including the media's dependence on government news releases, its inability to obtain classified information, media self-censure, the government's use of "privileged" and "on background" briefings, and the fact that self-restraint is often in the media's self-interest. Even the familiar news "leak," often used by incumbent administrations to float "trial balloons," by competing factions within the government to fight their bureaucratic battles publicly through the media, or by individuals to protect their political backsides, does not alter that conclusion. Indeed, it reinforces it. In addition to being required by their professional code of ethics to protect the confidentiality of high government sources,[6] reporters typically must offer such protection in order to be assured of receiving future news stories. It is clear that high-level officials (meaning White House staffers and members of the Cabinet) are often the source of government leaks.

The leak seems to have become an American political institution, a practice rooted in tradition and employed routinely by officials in every branch and at every level of government. Nonetheless, the highly secretive Bush was determined to stop the leaking. It brought charges against two staff members of American Israel Public Affairs Committee (AIPAC) for allegedly passing classified information from a Pentagon official to Israel, for example. Attorney General Alberto Gonzales also suggested that the government might have the legal authority to prosecute journalists for publishing classified information (*New York Times,* 5 May 2006, www.nytimes.com). The view, which involves First Amendment rights, may have been prompted by two prominent cases that for years after 9/11 had remained hidden from view: first, the *New York Times'* disclosure of eavesdropping by the National Security Agency (NSA) on thousands of phone calls between people in the United States and in foreign countries without obtaining prior court approval; second, *USA Today's* later disclosure of NSA's domestic "data mining" surveillance of billions of

phones calls in the United States designed to assess who called whom and for how long. Both were deemed tools in the war on terrorism and their secrecy protected in the name of national security. Both also led to a flurry of congressional activity, public commentary, and critical scrutiny—and potential legal challenges to the constitutionality of the actions.

Ironically, one of the most widely publicized leaks led to the White House and eventually to the president himself. Following the onset of war in Iraq, reporters unveiled the identity of an undercover CIA agent, Valerie Plame, whose husband was involved in the controversy over Iraq's alleged nuclear weapons program. A special prosecutor was appointed by the Justice Department to investigate who leaked the agent's name, a potential felony. Vice President Cheney's chief of staff and national security adviser, I. Lewis "Scooter" Libby, was eventually indicted for his participation in the leak. But the role of Bush's political adviser, Karl Rove, remained unresolved. The origin of the information was evidently a highly classified intelligence document, a National Intelligence Estimate (NIE), parts of which had been selectively declassified by the president.

Because of their interdependence, the media are vulnerable to government manipulation. News, in government parlance, is "manageable." Because what is reported often depends on what is leaked for public consumption rather than on what has actually occurred behind closed doors, public relations and the art of governance become closely intertwined. Public officials themselves not only engage in agenda setting and framing but also strive to place the correct "spin" on news stories that cast doubt on policy makers and their policies. The Clinton administration, in particular, elevated *spin control* to a near art form. Clinton's longtime press secretary Mike McCurry was admired by foes as well as friends for his deftness in deflecting media inquiries into the myriad scandals and sordid details that plagued Clinton's presidency. *Washington Post* media reporter Howard Kurtz (1998) even suggested that Clinton and his administration were so adept at spin control they were able to harness it for political advantage.

In the extreme, the government effectively censors the news. Censorship is anathema to democratic principles. It occurs nonetheless, especially during periods of crisis and peril, when the nation's vital interests or security are believed to be at stake. Thus the Reagan administration denied reporters permission to observe the Grenada assault force in 1983, an intervention later revealed to be fraught with mistakes. Journalists covering the 1989 invasion of Panama complained that the military deliberately kept them away from the action. The "pool" arrangement used during the Persian Gulf War had a similarly constraining impact. Only limited numbers of reporters were allowed to accompany military units. Their reports could only be passed on, even to journalists left behind, after having been "screened" by military authorities. Such scrutiny (censorship?) was defended as necessary to ensure that news reports would not jeopardize U.S. forces in the region. The control of information reflected the Pentagon's determination "never again to lose a public relations war." As political scientist W. Lance Bennett (1994b) explains, "Many policy officials in the Defense Department and the State Department became convinced that the U.S. military defeat and eventual withdrawal from Vietnam resulted, in part, from critical media coverage of battlefield activities and sympathetic coverage of domestic opposition to government policies back home."

A different approach was taken in the Iraq war. Reporters were "embedded" with military units in the field, including soldiers in combat zones. Though an attempt to answer some of the criticism growing out of earlier conflicts, now reporters often seemed to be champions of the war effort, reporting favorably on U.S. actions even as others saw a need for more introspective, critical reporting. *Al Jazeera,* a Qatar-based Arab satellite television station, in particular painted a quite different picture of the war than did the American media. Still, many of the courageous American reporters were injured or lost their lives trying to bring the story of the war to the American people.

The media and the government remain intertwined to a considerable extent in a process that invites collusion. The government's proven ability to manage the news, combined with the media's dependence on the government to get the news, perpetuates a symbiotic relationship between the two institutions (see Hess 1984). As one observer put it, "correspondents, editors, pundits, and publishers who work for major media outlets tend to see themselves as members of an opinion-making elite. They consider themselves on an intellectual and social par with high-level policy makers, an attribute that increases the prospect of their being co-opted by ambitious and determined policy makers" (Carpenter 1995).

The Foreign Policy Agenda and "Press Politics" Public officials' distaste for and fear of the media seems to reflect the view that the media, not policy makers, are often in control of what happens. They are particularly wary of television and the ability of highly visible and respected journalists, such as TV news anchors, to undermine their policies or influence. "A sixty-second verbal barrage on the evening news or a few embarrassing questions can destroy programs, politicians, and the reputations of major organizations. Political leaders fear this media power, because they often are unable to blunt it or repair the damage" (Graber 1993; see also Jordan and Page 1992).

During the 1990s, the media began to fragment, as more sources of news and ideologically based reporting became available. The George W. Bush administration was especially distrustful, even disdainful, of the "liberal" mainstream media. Stonewalling, or avoiding the press altogether, were commonplace. Few presidential news conferences were held until well into Bush's second term, for example. Then Bush's flagging presidential popularity caused him to turn to the media more frequently to get his message across. Noteworthy is that he appointed a new press secretary (Tony Snow, a well-known conservative commentator for Fox News) as part of a staff shakeup designed to shore up his administration's sagging fortunes.

We have already commented on the media's ability to set agendas and frame issues. Policy makers' reliance on media information further enhances its importance as an agent in the foreign policy process. Patrick O'Heffernan's (1991) survey of policy-making officials found that a majority rely most heavily on media information during the early stages of the policy cycle. This is a critical period, as the "definition of the situation" will dictate the response (see Chapter 13).

The increasingly rapid pace of electronic news and television's global coverage shorten the time frame for policy responses to new developments abroad—often called the *news cycle*. In 1961, when the Berlin Wall went up, President Kennedy took eight days to respond to the provocative action. In 1989, when the wall came down, President Bush was forced to respond overnight. Now, more than a decade later, the news cycle has been shortened from hours to minutes. Moreover, by publicizing foreign events or other international developments, the media draws attention to them. Journalist Marvin Kalb has used the term *press politics* to describe the growing "inseparability of foreign policy from its management in the news" (Bennett 1994b).

There are instances where journalists themselves or the media more generally have become agents in the diplomatic process. During the Cuban missile crisis, for example, an ABC news correspondent became a go-between for U.S. and Soviet officials. In 1977, CBS anchor Walter Cronkite was able to secure public pledges from Egyptian and Israeli leaders that paved the way for Anwar Sadat's historic visit to Jerusalem and the Camp David accord mediated by President Carter a year later. Similarly, there is little question that CNN provided an important communications node between the United States and Iraq during the Persian Gulf War.

In summary, the relationship between the media and policy makers is both subtle and complex, with no easy conclusions about who influences whom in what circumstances. Television has quickened the pace of news and inevitably shaped the way policy makers use the media and respond to events abroad, but it by no means determines American foreign policy. It is clear nonetheless that the fourth estate is a powerful institution that affects multiple facets of American political life. Theodore White, focusing once more on the

media's ability to set the agenda, usefully summarizes the media's importance:

> The power of the press in America is a primordial one. It sets the agenda of public discussion; and this sweeping political power is unrestrained by any law. It determines what people will talk and think about—an authority that in other nations is reserved for tyrants, priests, parties, and mandarins. No major act of the American Congress, no foreign adventure, no act of diplomacy, no great social reform can succeed in the United States unless the press prepares the public mind.
> *(White 1973, 327)*

THE IMPACT OF FOREIGN POLICY ATTITUDES AND ISSUES ON PRESIDENTIAL ELECTIONS

The press and public conventionally view elections as opportunities for policy change, if only for their potential to bring about new leadership. However, elections may also enable voters' preferences on foreign policy issues to be translated into policies that reflect those preferences. The important question, then, is whether voting is a viable means of expressing the public's policy preferences and thus translating them into policy.

It seems plausible that decision makers' fear of electoral punishment would lead them to propose policies designed to maintain their popularity and thus enhance their prospects for winning office. However, the "apparent immunity of the foreign policy establishment to electoral accountability" (Cohen 1973) is notable. Research on the two rival propositions has been extensive, and on the whole, the results have "not...been kind to democratic theory." They show "that policy voting is quite rare" and that, for a variety of reasons, citizens fail to vote for candidates on the basis of policy preferences. "In short, voters are incapable of policy rationality" (Page and Brody 1972).

The Electoral Impact of Foreign Policy Issues

Although controversial and not always consistent, evidence abounds to support the *issueless politics* hypothesis—that voter choice is determined neither by the nature of the issues nor candidates' positions on them (see Asher 1992). Foreign policy is no exception.

The role of the Vietnam War in 1968 is a classic case in point. The massive U.S. escalation of the war began in 1965. By 1968, as the war continued and its casualty lists grew, support declined. Campus unrest, mass demonstrations against the war, increasingly vocal minority opposition, including challenges from within the president's own party, were indicative of the changing climate of opinion. Johnson's decision not to run for a second full presidential term was widely interpreted as a direct result of this domestic opposition.

We would expect, therefore, that voters would have treated the election as a referendum on Vietnam, but they did not. Instead they (correctly) perceived little difference between the positions of the candidates (Vice President Hubert Humphrey and former Vice President Richard Nixon) on Vietnam policy. In short, from voters' perspective, the 1968 election, despite the centrality of Vietnam in American politics and society, was an issueless campaign (Page and Brody 1972).

Americans clearly do hold opinions about foreign policy matters, but they are not transmitted into the policy-formation system through the electoral process (compare Aldrich, Sullivan, and Borgida 1989). How do we account for such a failure?

One inviting explanation is that many Americans may regard foreign policy issues as among the most important facing the nation, but they fail to arouse the depth of personal concern raised by issues closer to their daily lives. In addition, foreign policy issues are not the ones that "divide the populace into contending groups. . . . In general foreign issues, involving as they do the United States versus others, tend to blur or reduce differences domestically" (Nie, Verba, and Petrocik 1976). The Iraq war, however, clearly challenges this long-standing conclusion. As we saw in Chapter 8, Republicans overwhelmingly supported the war; Democrats overwhelmingly opposed it.

Party outcomes can be unaffected by foreign policy issues during presidential elections. Public views of foreign policy were related to the partisan votes cast in each election between 1952 and 1988 (Asher 1992). Republicans benefited from those perceptions in eight of the ten elections. The 1964 election was the only one in which voter preferences on foreign policy issues clearly favored the Democrats. Although Democrats benefited from public fears of nuclear war in 1984, the Republicans benefited on the issue of war prevention.[7] By 1988, however, the Republicans could claim the high ground on both peace and prosperity. Michael Dukakis and the Democratic Party lost in a landslide—and the Republicans claimed the White House for the seventh time out of eleven Cold War presidential elections.

Four years later, George H. W. Bush found himself on the defensive. Peace was at hand—indeed, after a half-century of bitter conflict, the United States had "won" the Cold War with the Soviet Union and turned the tide against Iraq's aggression—but prosperity was not. The nation's economy was in recession, concern for debts and deficits punctuated campaign rhetoric, and Bill Clinton was determined to focus attention on domestic ills, not foreign policy challenges. The frequent use of the phrase "It's the economy, stupid!" reflected Democratic leaders' single-minded determination to stress domestic policy.

The end of the Cold War and the departure of virulent anticommunism from the domestic political agenda played to their strategy, while the partisan advantages Republicans once enjoyed on foreign policy mattered little this time (Weisberg and Kimball 1995). "Throughout the Cold War the Republican Party's reason for existence was anticommunism," observes Leon Sigal (1992–1993) in a retrospective look at what he calls "the last Cold War election" (see also Deudney and Ikenberry 1994). "Republicans could be counted on to shield America from the Red Menace, at home and abroad. . . . Now that the [Russian] bear has disappeared, what else does the GOP stand for?"

As we demonstrated in Chapter 8, the state of the economy is a powerful predictor of how Americans evaluate presidential performance. It is not surprising, therefore, that George H. W. Bush attracted their ire. Clinton, on the other hand, was quick to tie the state of the economy to the United States' continuing ability to play an active role in world affairs. "America must regain its economic strength to play a proper role as leader of the world," he declared. "And we must have a president who attends to prosperity at home if our people are to sustain their support for engagement abroad." Domestic policy was Clinton's strong suit, and he played to it repeatedly.

Admittedly weak on domestic policy issues, Bush also proved vulnerable on the very issues perceived to be his long suit. The "foreign policy president" largely confined himself to "tidying up the details of the old agenda.... He failed by and large to assist eastern Europe and the Soviet Union in their perilous transitions, to devise a foreign policy squaring national self-determination with state sovereignty and minority rights, to stanch bloodletting in Bosnia, and to prevent the proliferation of all arms, not just weapons of mass destruction." For most Americans these were not issues of burning significance (Miller and Shanks 1996). Even the brief euphoria sparked by victory in the Persian Gulf War soon gave way to "more pressing subjects" (Omestad 1992–1993). Indeed, Bush's decision to stop the war before Iraq's leader was driven from power eventually soured the views of many as they wondered whether the war had been worth the effort. A popular bumper sticker captured the irony of Bush's situation: "Saddam Hussein still has his job. What about you?"

By 1996, Bill Clinton, now the incumbent president, was in a surprisingly strong position on foreign policy. Although Republican standard-bearer Bob Dole attacked Clinton's policies toward Iraq, North Korea, Bosnia, and China, arguing that he (Dole) would provide more aggressive leadership, public opinion polls showed that a majority of Americans regarded Clinton as a strong leader in foreign policy (see also Ladd 1997). Indeed, for Clinton, foreign policy "became a surprisingly useful

forum for refuting...GOP charges that [he] was feckless and lacked backbone" (Omestad 1996–1997).

More important, perhaps, the U.S. economy was bubbling and Americans were enjoying the prosperity of sharply reduced inflation and unemployment compared with four years earlier. So we should expect that the state of the economy would have "made it difficult for any challenger to get political traction from criticizing Clinton's foreign policy." Furthermore, on foreign policy, 1996 seemed like a classic "issueless, me-too-ism" campaign, as "voters strained to see any major difference on foreign and security policy between two mainstream internationalists, Clinton and Dole" (Omestad 1996–1997; see also Dionne 1996).

Al Gore and George W. Bush were also internationalists. Using the belief-system framework described in Chapter 8, Gore's platform and campaign leaned toward the accommodationist side of the internationalist/isolationist divide, while Bush's tipped toward the hard-line. With regard to the use of U.S. military force abroad, Bush advocated selective engagement, whereas Gore was more supportive of nation-building. Gore was a champion of the Kyoto Protocol, designed to cope with global warming; Bush was more circumspect, although he did promise to seek to lower CO_2 emissions (a pledge broken shortly after he was elected). Gore endorsed the Clinton plan for a limited national ballistic defense system that would cover the territorial United States; Bush pledged a more ambitious system that would include U.S. allies in the anticipated defense umbrella. Gore supported the downsizing of the U.S. military that had taken place during the 1990s; Bush attacked the Clinton-Gore defense posture as inadequate for meeting the challenges of the new century and promised to build a new generation of high-tech weapons to meet them.

Analysts have yet to determine what impact, if any, these foreign and national security policy postures had on the final presidential vote in 2000. Usually it is difficult to determine the separate effects of particular foreign policy questions on citizens' voting behavior. Because most elections involve a variety of often overlapping issues, some of those who vote for the winning candidate do so because of the candidate's stance on particular issues; others do so in spite of it. Foreign policy issues thus become part of a mix of considerations. Typically they are a less important ingredient than domestic political issues or judgments of past performance (Abramson, Aldrich, and Rohde 1986, 1990; Fiorina 1981). As a result, voters' behavior is more likely an aggregate judgment about prior performance than a guide to future action. This is known as *retrospective voting.*

Foreign Policy and Retrospective Voting

Consider President Carter's electoral fate. The public generally gave Carter high marks on personal attributes but low marks on performance. Evaluations of his foreign policy performance were especially critical. Carter's popularity surged in late 1979 in the immediate aftermath of the seizure of American embassy personnel in Teheran, but his inability to secure their release fueled public dissatisfaction with his overall performance. His challenger, Ronald Reagan, criticized the policy of détente Carter and his predecessors had promoted, called for sharply increased defense spending, and hammered away at the theme of alleged American impotence in international affairs. In this context, "the continuing crisis in Iran came to be seen as a living symbol and constant reminder of all that Reagan had been saying" (Hess and Nelson 1985).

Four years later, Reagan's reputation for leadership proved a strong force motivating voters to choose the incumbent president over his challenger, Walter Mondale. Elements of Reagan's foreign policy record could easily be criticized, but four years of relative peace had put to rest fears about Reagan's recklessness. "No longer fearful that the President's policies might lead to war, the public had no compelling reason to abandon him" (Keeter 1985). In many respects the senior Bush's candidacy became a retrospective judgment on the Reagan years. Peace and prosperity thus redounded to Bush's benefit, as noted. Moreover, because Reagan had moved during his second term toward an accommodationist foreign policy posture and away from his "evil empire"

approach to the Soviet Union, the ideological differences on foreign policy issues that bore on the electoral outcomes in 1980 and 1984 tended to disappear in 1988. Still, to the extent that voters perceived differences between the candidates on foreign policy issues, particularly their willingness to "stand up for America" (Pomper 1989), they favored Bush.

We have already commented on Bush I and Clinton. Clinton swamped Bush on domestic policy, with foreign policy a distinctly secondary issue in spite of Bush's distinguished foreign policy record. Clinton again swamped Dole on domestic policy. The irony, perhaps, is that four years later Vice President Al Gore would not capitalize on the state of the economy during the Clinton-Gore years to put him in the White House (in part because of his determination to distance himself from other aspects of the Clinton presidency). In the absence of an overriding foreign policy issue in 2000, Gore could not capitalize on his slim margin of support among voters to carry the day.

Foreign policy was on the agenda in 2004. Indeed, not since Vietnam had foreign policy figured so prominently in a presidential election. Nineteen percent of the electorate saw terrorism as the most important issue in the election; 15 percent viewed Iraq as most important (Ceaser and Busch 2005, 138). George W. Bush's reelection in 2004 was nonetheless a clear instance of retrospective voting. As one group of scholars concluded, "Incumbent President George W. Bush survived Senator John F. Kerry's challenge mainly because he convinced a small majority of voters that he had done a good enough job and that the prospects for positive government performance were sufficiently good that he should be reelected" (Abramson et al. 2005). Bush scored better with voters than Senator John Kerry on terrorism, moral values, and taxes. Surprisingly, perhaps, Kerry scored better on Iraq, the economy and jobs, health care, and education. But compared with Kerry, Bush was also perceived to be a strong leader by a substantially greater margin of voters (Ceaser and Busch 2005, 138).

The conditions going into the election favored the incumbent, argues elections specialist James Campbell (2005). Among them were Bush's incumbency, an improving economy, and Bush's record in the war on terrorism. In the end, however, Campbell concludes ideology was an overriding factor: "More [voters] thought Senator Kerry was too liberal than thought President Bush was too conservative." The closeness of the vote (51.2 versus 48.8 percent) also reflects the deep partisan divisions in the country.

Despite the acknowledged importance of retrospective voting, the elitist model of policy making invites the conclusion that "elections are primarily a symbolic exercise that . . . offer the masses an opportunity to participate in the political system, but electoral participation does not enable them to determine public policy." "Parties do not offer clear policy alternatives," and a "candidate's election does not imply a policy choice by the electorate" (Dye and Zeigler 1990). Noteworthy is that Ralph Nader charged during the 2000 election that Republican and Democratic candidates Bush and Gore did not differ on the environmental issues central to Nader's presidential campaign. Nader's percent of the presidential vote barely registered on the national scale. Similarly, in 2004 Kerry made it clear he supported the war in Iraq, although he did effectively separate it from the war on terrorism.

Ironically, even when parties would seem to offer distinct alternatives, elections still do not set the course of foreign policy. That is nowhere more clear than in the 1964 presidential contest, when Vietnam became a major foreign policy issue. Republican challenger Barry Goldwater campaigned on the pledge to pursue "victory" against communism in all quarters of the globe, but especially in Vietnam "by any means necessary." The incumbent Lyndon Johnson campaigned on a theme of greater restraint in Vietnam, and his landslide victory was widely interpreted that way. Yet it was Johnson, armed with the Gulf of Tonkin Resolution passed by Congress, who would soon escalate the war in Southeast Asia. Why? Because, despite popular impressions of the foreign policy alternatives the electorate faced, the results of the election as they related to popular support for various Vietnam options were so ambiguous as to lead to the conclusion "that the 1964 vote . . . could have told [Johnson] anything he cared to believe" (Boyd 1972; see also Pomper 1968).

Despite evidence to the contrary, particularly in the foreign policy domain, policy makers nonetheless act as though voters make choices on the basis of their policy preferences. Hence, they pay attention to the anticipated responses of voters in shaping their policy choices. Miroslav Nincic offers an interesting example. He found that of fourteen U.S. military interventions since World War II, *only one* was initiated in the fourth year of an electoral cycle (Carter's disastrous attempt to rescue diplomats held by Iranian revolutionaries) (Nincic 2004, 125). He argues this shows that political leaders are risk-averse, particularly with Americans so sensitive to the casualties of war.

So elections do matter, particularly in terms of the character of the personnel a new president appoints to key positions in a new administration and the general shape, if not the specific direction, of the president's foreign policy.

LINKAGES BETWEEN SOCIETAL SOURCES AND AMERICAN FOREIGN POLICY

The question posed at the outset of this and the preceding chapter—"In what ways do societal factors influence American foreign policy?"—has invited a series of additional questions, and, inevitably, provoked a variety of answers. It is clear, however, that the view of the United States as a society-dominated political system provides insight into the potential impact of the political culture, public opinion, elites and masses, the media, and presidential elections.

The ability of citizens "to mobilize support for their demands and to organize themselves" is a characteristic feature of society-dominant systems (Risse-Kappen 1991). Similarly, elections and interest groups help to channel mass preferences and private interests into public policy in the United States, where, as we noted at the outset of this chapter, the power of both the state and societal groups is more decentralized than in many other industrial societies. Thus elites are unable to dictate completely what American foreign policy will be—which is the "top-down" view of policy making akin to the elitist model described earlier. Similarly, the mass of the American people do not determine American foreign policy from the "bottom up," a view that parallels the pluralist model. Instead, there is a constant interaction between policy makers and the public, elites and masses alike, much of it promoted through the media and the electoral system. American foreign policy emerges out of this continuing interaction. Policy makers and other elites enjoy a competitive advantage in shaping the agenda and are ultimately responsible for final decisions; important caveats and qualifications must be attached to the role that mass preferences and private interests play in shaping policy.

Societal factors explain more about the process of formulating American policies toward the external environment than about the objectives of those actions and the particular means chosen to achieve them. Moreover, it is difficult to isolate causal connections between particular societal variables and particular actions abroad. Thus societal factors rarely if ever "determine" foreign policy actions. Instead, they exert influence primarily as part of the context within which decisions are formulated. In particular, they operate more as forces constraining foreign policy than as forces stimulating radical departures from the past.

To pinpoint better the sources of American foreign policy decisions and initiatives, we need to turn from considering factors within American society to examining the political institutions from which most foreign policy initiatives spring. As we will discover in the next three chapters, these institutions—part of the domestic structures of the American political system—are comparatively decentralized into competing power centers, thus providing multiple access points to those in the society-dominated American political system who seek to shape American foreign policy.

KEY TERMS

527 organizations
agenda-setting
American Israel Public
    Affairs Committee
    (AIPAC)
bully pulpit
CNN-effect
cognitive balance
Council on Foreign
    Relations

countervailing powers
elitism
fourth estate
framing
gatekeeper
ideological/single-issue
    groups
inadvertent audience
iron triangles

military-industrial
    complex (MIC)
multistep theory of
    communications
pack journalism
pluralism
political action
    committees (PACs)

Project for the New
    American Century
    (PNAC)
public interest groups
retrospective voting
selective perception
think-tanks
two-step flow theory of
    communications

SUGGESTED READINGS

Carpenter, Ted Galen. *The Captive Press: Foreign Policy Crises and the First Amendment.* Washington, DC: Cato Institute, 1995.

Entman, Robert M. *Projections of Power: Framing News, Public Opinion, and U.S. Foreign Policy.* Chicago: University of Chicago Press, 2004.

Grose, Peter. *Continuing the Inquiry: The Council on Foreign Relations from 1921 to 1996.* New York: Council on Foreign Relations Press, 1996.

Hess, Stephen, and Marvin Kalb, eds. *The Media and the War on Terrorism.* Washington, DC: Brookings Institution, 2003.

Kotz, Nick. *Wild Blue Yonder: Money, Politics, and the B-1 Bomber.* Princeton, NJ: Princeton University Press, 1988.

Mann, James. *Rise of the Vulcans: The History of Bush's War Cabinet.* New York: Viking, 2004b.

Norris, Pippa, Montague Kern, and Marion Just, eds. *Framing Terrorism: The News Media, the Government, and the Public.* New York: Routledge, 2003.

O'Heffernan, Patrick. *Mass Media and American Foreign Policy: Insider Perspectives on Global Journalism and the Foreign Policy Process.* Norwood, NJ: Ablex, 1991.

Roberts, Priscilla. "All the Right People: The Historiography of the American Foreign Policy Establishment," *Journal of American Studies* 26 (December 1992): 409–454.

Smith, Tony. *Foreign Attachments: The Power of Ethnic Groups in the Making of American Foreign Policy.* Cambridge, MA: Harvard University Press, 2002.

Vernon, Raymond, Debora L. Spar, and Glenn Tobin. *Iron Triangles and Revolving Doors: Cases in U.S. Foreign Economic Policymaking.* New York: Praeger, 1991.

Wittkopf, Eugene R., and James M. McCormick, eds. *The Domestic Sources of American Foreign Policy: Insights and Evidence.* Lanham, MD: Rowman and Littlefield, 2004.

NOTES

1. Education, training, and experience do not prevent foolish policy decisions. Indeed, one of the main points of Halberstam's book is that intelligent people are capable of making stupid, even wicked decisions.

2. For more on PNAC and its members and philosophy, see www.newamericancentury.org.

3. Others have joined in this chorus. Morris P. Fiorina (2001), a prominent congressional scholar, argues that "The political class today allows national problems to fester because its members insist on having the entire loaf, not just a portion, because they would rather have an election issue than incremental progress, and because parties that have only shallow roots in the population at large are increasingly dependent on specific constituencies whose interests are not shared by the general population."

4. Market considerations may have other untoward effects. Commenting on media coverage of stock markets, economist Robert Shiller (2001) notes that because "the news media are in constant competition to capture the public's attention . . . the media often seem to disseminate and reinforce ideas that are not supported by real evidence. . . . Too often the media are swayed by competitive pressures to skew their presentations toward ideas best left alone."

5. Evidence and critiques of the "minimal-effects" thesis as it relates to television can be found in Dalton, Beck, and Huckfeldt (1998), Iyengar, Peters, and Kinder (1982), and Page, Shapiro, and Dempsey (1987).

6. In 2005 *New York Times* reporter Judith Miller spent more than 80 days in jail on contempt of court charges for refusing to cooperate with federal prosecutors seeking information in the Valerie Plame leak case.

7. In contrast with once popular political lore—that the Republican Party produced "peace with poverty" and the Democrat Party "war with wealth"—Gallup poll data from the mid-1970s through the early 1990s shows that the Democratic Party was more often perceived as the party of peace than the Republican Party. Since 1992, the Democrats also have more often been perceived as the party of "peace with wealth." (The Gallup Poll: www.galluppoll.com).

PART V

Governmental Sources
of American Foreign Policy

10

Presidential Preeminence in Foreign Policy Making

In the areas of defense and foreign affairs, the nation must speak with one
voice, and only the president is capable of providing that voice.
PRESIDENT RONALD REAGAN, 1984

I'm the decider, and I decide what is best.
PRESIDENT GEORGE W. BUSH, 2006

Observing President George W. Bush respond to the September 11 terrorist attacks on the United States, launch a global "war on terrorism," and initiate and sustain a military campaign in Iraq, it is easy to understand why the president of the United States is widely regarded at home and abroad as the most powerful individual in the world. The president is commander-in-chief of the world's most powerful military forces and the leader of the world's most prosperous and advanced economy. The increasing global popularity of the political ideas often associated with the United States provides the U.S. president with additional influence. Also, the advantages of the presidential form of government over other democratic systems such as the British parliamentary system allow the president to respond quickly and pragmatically to emergent challenges (Waltz 1967).

Furthermore, a half-century of Cold War competition with the Soviet Union and the ideological challenge of communism contributed measurably to presumption of presidential preeminence in foreign policy making. Indeed, prior to Vietnam it was commonplace to argue that "the United States has one president, but it has two presidencies," one for domestic policy, the other for foreign and defense policy. The two are distinguished by the president's greater influence in the latter domain compared with the former. As political scientist Aaron Wildavsky (1966) argued in a classic essay, "The president's normal problem with domestic policy is to get congressional support for the programs he prefers. In foreign affairs, in contrast, he can almost always get support for policies that he believes will protect the nation."

During and after the Vietnam War, however, the premise of *presidential preeminence* was questioned as Congress more vigorously asserted its foreign policy prerogatives. Of particular concern to lawmakers was the question of control over American commitments and presidential war powers. A series of legislative efforts to circumscribe the executive's authority resulted: the National Commitments Resolution (1969), the repeal of the Tonkin Gulf Resolution (1970), the Case Act (1972), and the War Powers Resolution (1973). They tried to make it more difficult for presidents to initiate war single-handedly and to otherwise circumscribe their foreign policy latitude.

With the demise of the Cold War and the associated changes in both the international and domestic policy environments, Congress continued its activism and other foreign policy actors now also challenged the premises of presidential preeminence. As one commentator wrote, "The end of the Cold War has changed the stature of the president—moving him off the imperial heights of the 'most powerful man in the world' to the mundane level of a political leader struggling over incremental domestic policy questions" (Lauter 1994). By the end of the twentieth century, presidential scholars wrote persuasively about the "weakening White House" and the "end of the imperial presidency" (Beschloss 2000; Neustadt 2001). Even Arthur M. Schlesinger, Jr., joined the chorus (Schlesinger 1998). It was Schlesinger (1973) who coined the term *imperial presidency* to describe the gradual but significant growth in executive power that began with Franklin D. Roosevelt and peaked with Richard M. Nixon. Schlesinger's view was that the American presidency by the Nixon era had become too powerful, secretive, and unaccountable.

Yet the death of the "imperial presidency" at the dawn of a new century was ephemeral. Observers, including Schlesinger, soon declared its return in the early years of the George W. Bush administration (see Fritz 2001; Gleckman 2002; Wolfensberger 2002; Schlesinger 2004a; Schlesinger 2004b; Rudalevige 2005). In fact, the imperial presidency not only reemerged, but it was taken to an unprecedented level by the forty-third president. According to presidential scholar Allan Lichtman, "The Bush White House has been extremely aggressive in expanding presidential power. Previous presidents have used presidential power, have used executive orders, but this president has really sent it into the stratosphere" (quoted in Hutcheson 2005). Certainly this dramatic expansion of executive power was a product of the crisis environment that emerged with September 11, 2001, terrorist attacks on the United States and the war on terrorism that followed. However, it is important to note the Bush administration came to office in January 2001 intent on reversing a three-decade decline in presidential power that began with Nixon's Watergate scandal (Hutcheson 2005; Silva 2006b). See Focus 10.1.

THE PRESIDENCY: THE CENTER OF THE FOREIGN AFFAIRS GOVERNMENT

In this chapter, we examine the forces giving rise to the power of the presidency, particularly in the last six decades, the efforts of presidents to enhance their control over the machinery of government responsible for making and executing the nation's foreign policy, and the factors that shape presidential preeminence, including the return of the imperial presidency. To guide our inquiry, we will draw on Roger Hilsman's (1967) conceptualization of the foreign policy-making process as a series of concentric circles (see Figure 10.1). In Hilsman's conceptualization, the innermost circle in the policy-making process consists of the president, his or her immediate advisers, and such important political appointees as the secretaries of state and defense, the director of national intelligence, and various under- and assistant secretaries who bear responsibility for carrying out policy decisions.

Outside this core, the second circle contains the various departments and agencies of the executive branch or, more specifically, the career professionals of those agencies who provide continuity in the implementation of policy from one administration to the next, regardless of who occupies the White House. Their primary task—in theory—is to

F O C U S 10.1   The Return of the Imperial Presidency

The reassertion and expansion of presidential power within and beyond foreign affairs has been considerable in recent years. Former Nixon administration aide John W. Dean has written, "George W. Bush and Richard B. Cheney have created the most secretive presidency of my lifetime. Their secrecy is far worse than during Watergate" (quoted in Schlesinger 2004a). Steven Aftergood, director of the Project on Government Secrecy at the Federation of American Scientists, commented in 2006, "...we are gradually shifting into another kind of government in which executive authority is supreme and significantly unchecked [by either Congress or the courts]" (quoted in Silva 2006b). Here is a sample of developments from the George W. Bush administration that lead observers to conclude the "imperial presidency" has returned and intensified.

- A White House with a strong penchant for secrecy, including remarkable internal discipline regarding *unauthorized* leaks of information

- Efforts to reestablish executive privilege by refusing lawmakers access to presidential and other executive branch documents

- Executive order granting the sitting president and his predecessors authority to block the release of presidential papers from previous administrations

- Dramatic rise in classification actions, making millions of documents, e-mail messages, and databases unavailable to the public

- Executive agencies resealing information already within the public domain

- Significant increase in the number of federal court cases with secret docket numbers and sealed records

- Aggressive use of a precedent known as the state secrets privilege to convince courts to dismiss cases that challenge the administration's counterterrorism practices rather than risk public exposure of national security secrets

- Use of "signing statements"[1] to bypass laws that circumscribe presidential authority, such as the McCain Amendment (discussed in Chapter 12)

- Appointment of judges who support broad executive authority and presidential prerogative, such as Supreme Court justices John Roberts and Samuel Alito

- Aversion to international treaties that enfranchise Congress by requiring Senate ratification

- Passage and subsequent extension of the USA Patriot Act, which affords the executive branch broad authority to surveil, search, detain, and deport terrorist suspects

- Indefinite detention of "unlawful enemy combatants"—terrorist suspects held in military prisons and subject to trial by military tribunals without due process of U.S. law or the full protection of international law, including the Third Geneva Convention

- Use of secret CIA flights to whisk foreign citizens suspected of terrorist ties to prisons in third countries

- Maintenance of a global network of secret prisons established by the CIA where detainees are subjected to harsh interrogation tactics

- Considerable congressional deference to the president on trade promotion authority, homeland security initiatives, counterterrorism, and war powers, including two broad authorizations for the use of military force and hundreds of billions of dollars in supplemental appropriations to finance undeclared wars in Iraq and Afghanistan

- Reliance on the 2001 congressional resolution authorizing the use of military force against those responsible for the September 11, 2001, terrorist attacks to justify expansions of executive authority to wage the war on terrorism

- Secret presidential approval for the National Security Agency (NSA) to monitor (without court warrants) telephone calls and e-mail messages between people in the United States and suspected terrorists overseas

- A doctrine of preventive war where the president decides unilaterally when, where, and why to go to war

- A 33 percent growth in the national budget (Baker and VandeHei 2006) and ever-expanding federal bureaucracy

SOURCE: Based on: Baker and VandeHei 2006; Chapman 2006; Gellman 2006; Gleckman 2002; Hensen 2001–2002; Priest 2005b; Shane 2005; Silva 2006b; Silva 2006c; Sniffen and Soloman 2006 and Zajac 2005.

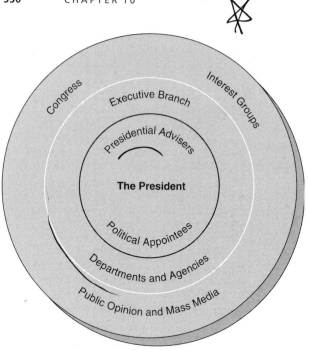

FIGURE 10.1 The Institutional Setting: The Concentric Circles of Policymaking

SOURCE: Adapted from Roger Hilsman, *To Move a Nation*. New York: Doubleday, 1967, 541–544.

provide top-level policy makers with the information necessary to make decisions and then to carry those decisions out. The outermost circle is what Hilsman called the "public one," consisting of Congress, interest groups, public opinion, and the mass media. According to Hilsman's image, the institutions, groups, and individuals at this level are least involved in the day-to-day foreign policy process. The clear implication is that important decisions involving the fate of the nation are made within the innermost circle; when it comes to policy leadership, the role and influence of various players involved in policy making declines with their distance from the center.

Using this conceptualization as a starting point, we will describe the foreign affairs government in three phases. First, in this chapter, as noted, we will examine the factors that affect presidential preeminence in the foreign policy domain. We direct particular attention to the rise of the National Security Council system and the role of the president's national security adviser as a more White House–centered policy process has evolved over the past sixty years. Second, in Chapter 11 we consider the foreign policy bureaucracy and its information-gathering and policy-implementation roles. The structural characteristics of the foreign affairs government, which define authority and divide the labor among those responsible for making and executing foreign policy, influence presidential decisions, policy implementation, and policy performance. The impact of this structure therefore requires examination. Finally, in Chapter 12 we examine the role of Congress in the policy-making process, investigating the tools available to Congress to influence foreign policy, the ways members exert that influence, and some of the patterns of congressional influence and legislative-executive relations that occur.[2]

THE SETTING OF PRESIDENTIAL PREEMINENCE

The U.S. Constitution shapes the president's role in foreign policy by empowering the president to lead, but it also creates constraints and challenges to that leadership. The Constitution does not assign "the foreign policy power" to any branch, but forces them to share responsibility by breaking foreign policy power into pieces and assigning various portions to the Congress and to the executive. Because the Constitution does not specify which branch is to lead, it provides the political branches an "*invitation to struggle*" (Corwin 1948).

Foreign Affairs and the Constitution

For the president, constitutional foreign policy power derives from Article II, which assigns the general executive power and the roles of *commander-in-chief, chief negotiator* ("He shall have the power, by and with the advice and consent of the Senate, to make treaties"), and *chief diplomat* (" . . . shall appoint ambassadors . . . and shall receive ambassadors and other public ministers") to the president.[3] Clearly, the specific grants of constitutional authority are limited. The president has important opportunities, but not unambiguous authority, to lead.

These limits are even more obvious when the Constitution's treatment of congressional foreign policy powers is considered. In Article I, Congress is entrusted with the general legislative power ("all legislative powers herein granted shall be vested in a Congress of the United States"), which empowers it to make laws and appropriate funds ("no money shall be drawn from the Treasury but in consequence of appropriations made by law"). Together, the general legislative power and "power of the purse" grant Congress nearly limitless authority to affect the flow and form of foreign relations.

The Constitution further forces the sharing of the war power by countering the president's power as commander-in-chief with the congressional injunction to provide for the common defense, to declare war, to raise and support armies, to provide and maintain a navy, to make rules for the government and regulation of the land and naval forces, and to organize, arm, discipline, and call forth the militia. The president's diplomatic powers are constrained by the Senate's constitutionally mandated role to "advise and consent" on treaties as well as the appointment of ambassadors and other executive branch personnel. Additionally, Congress is to regulate international commerce and immigration, to define and punish piracies, to grant letters of marque and reprisal, to make rules concerning capture on land and water, and to "make all laws necessary and proper for carrying into execution the foregoing powers."

It would seem then, far from concentrating foreign policy authority, that the Constitution disperses it and forces it to be shared. Were the Constitution itself the only basis for presidential leadership, Hilsman's conception of decision-making authority over foreign affairs shown in Figure 10.1 would be hard to sustain. As one observer noted, "It seems incredible that these few meager grants support the most powerful office in the world and the multi-varied, wide-flung webwork of foreign activity of the most powerful nation in the world" (Henkin 1972). However, other important factors help to develop the preeminent role of the president.

First, the Constitution's provisions have combined with practice to expand, over time, the central role of the president in the formulation as well as execution of American foreign policy. Presidents have undeniably taken advantage of their ability to act decisively and set the foreign policy bureaucracy in motion. By concluding treaties and other agreements with foreign states, by public declarations, by recognizing or not recognizing new governments, by attending international conferences, by deploying military power here or there, by encouraging or denouncing the actions of other states, and so forth, presidents have established the precedent of presidential preeminence. Moreover, Congress has acquiesced in such exercises of power and has even delegated further responsibilities to the president (including some specifically assigned to Congress by the Constitution), thereby increasing the force behind presidential preeminence. Examples of such delegation include the responsibility to propose budgets to Congress as required by the 1921 budget reforms (thus strengthening the president's ability to set the spending agenda) as well as the power to conclude trade agreements (often without congressional approval) established by the 1934 Reciprocal Trade Agreements Act. Additionally, the post–World War II growth of executive foreign policy institutions, most notably the Department of Defense, the Central Intelligence Agency, and the National Security Council established by the 1947 National

Security Act, gave the president even greater tools with which to take foreign policy action.

The U.S. role in a changing international environment further expanded the role of the president. The ability of the president to act assertively and decisively in the crisis-ridden atmosphere of the post–World War II period dramatically increased the foreign policy powers of the presidency. The widely shared consensus that the international environment demanded an active American world role contributed to the belief that strong presidential leadership was needed. Hence, because most members of Congress fundamentally agreed on the requirements of Cold War foreign policy, the president's policy decisions went largely unchallenged. The Vandenberg Resolution (1949), in which Congress supported a permanent American alliance with European countries (which later became NATO), and the Formosa Strait (1955), Middle East (1957), Cuban (1962), Berlin (1962), and Gulf of Tonkin (1964) resolutions, in which Congress gave the president broad power to deal with external conflict situations, fostered presidential preeminence by demonstrating a unity of purpose between the president and Congress. Together these factors eventually gave rise to the imperial presidency (discussed in the introduction to this chapter) and laid a foundation for the deference lawmakers continue to show the president in many matters of foreign policy.

The Courts

The judicial branch has been known to place important limits on presidential power. For example, in the 1952 case of *Youngstown Sheet and Tube Co. et al. v. Sawyer,* the Supreme Court determined that presidential authority was greatest when explicitly authorized by Congress and circumscribed when explicitly prohibited by Congress. In the "zones of twilight" between them, authority is less certain and possibly shared with Congress. Also, in two cases during the Nixon administration (*New York Times v. United States,* 1971, and *U.S. v. Nixon,* 1974), the Supreme Court limited the president's ability to control information on the grounds of national security or executive privilege. More recently, during the Clinton administration, the investigations into the Whitewater affair, the Paula Jones sexual harassment case, and the Monica Lewinsky episode, coupled with the subsequent impeachment and trial of the president, further weakened some presidential powers. In a number of decisions, the federal courts ruled: (1) sitting presidents may be sued while in office; (2) government lawyers may be compelled to testify regarding their counsel and advice to a president; (3) presidents' conversations with advisers may not be protected by executive privilege; and (4) presidential security forces may be required to testify about presidential behavior. Clinton also became the first president to testify before a grand jury while in office (see, for example, Holmes 1998). Despite these developments, the courts have done far more to enhance presidential power over time than to limit it, particularly in the realm of national security (Silverstein 1994). In fact, the courts generally have refrained from involvement in foreign policy issues. When the judiciary has addressed such issues, it has tended to support presidential claims of authority, which has solidified the president's foreign policy–making role. In a seminal case in 1936, for instance, the Supreme Court ruled in *United States v. Curtiss-Wright Export Corporation* that the president acts "as the sole organ of the federal government in the field of international relations." With few exceptions, the courts, in this and other cases, have repeatedly conferred on the president broad powers in foreign affairs.[4]

The courts have also furthered presidential preeminence when they have refrained from decisions. The Supreme Court has usually avoided refereeing contests between the executive and legislative branches because it considers the issues involved as political rather than legal. Frequently, the court does this by use of the ***doctrine of political questions,*** a judicial construct that enables the courts to sidestep politically contentious foreign policy issues. Three cases from the Cold War era illustrate the effects of this long-standing tradition. In 1981, several members of Congress brought suit against President Reagan, arguing that he had violated the Constitution and the War Powers Resolution by sending military advisers to El Salvador.[5] The court dismissed the suit with the ruling that a determination of whether U.S. forces in El Salvador were involved in actual or potential hostilities was a political, not a judicial, finding.

Six years later, as U.S. forces reflagged Kuwaiti ships with American flags to protect them in the Persian Gulf during the Iran-Iraq War, lawmakers again asked the court to enter the war powers fracas by declaring that the president should submit a report to Congress under the War Powers Resolution. Again the court concluded the issue was a political, not a justiciable question.[6]

The third case also involved the Persian Gulf. In late 1990, fifty-four Democratic members of Congress sought to derail further Bush administration military deployments and action in the Persian Gulf.[7] They argued that the Constitution required that Congress debate and authorize a declaration of war before the president could initiate hostilities. This time, the (U.S. district) court left open the door to a possible ruling against the president's war-making power without congressional involvement—but it also waffled: "It would be both premature and presumptuous for the court to render a decision on the issue of whether a declaration of war is required...when the Congress itself has provided no indication whether it deems such a declaration either necessary, on the one hand, or imprudent, on the other."

The tradition of the courts refraining from decisions affecting foreign policy has continued in the post-9/11 era. The Bush administration informed Russia in December 2001 that the United States was withdrawing from the 1972 Anti-Ballistic Missile (ABM) Treaty. Citing the need to defend against potential long-range terrorist threats to the American homeland, Bush stated that "as the events of September 11 made all too clear, the greatest threats to both our countries come not from each other, or from other big powers in the world, but from terrorists who strike without warning or rogue states who seek weapons of mass destruction" ("U.S. Quits ABM Treaty," www.cnn.com, 12/14/01). Though both Russia and China were less than thrilled about the ABM Treaty decision, lawmakers also challenged this new tilt in strategic policy. Moreover, shortly after the announcement, thirty-two members of Congress filed suit in federal court against the administration's decision (naming President Bush,

Secretary of State Colin Powell, and Secretary of Defense Rumsfeld directly). Ultimately, a federal district judge dismissed the case, stating that the "issues concerning treaties are largely political questions best left to the political branches of government, not the courts, for resolution" ("ABM Treaty Suit Dismissed," www. cnn.com, 12/31/02).

More recently, the Supreme Court has used *technical grounds* rather than the doctrine of political questions to enhance presidential power. In June 2004, the Supreme Court sidestepped an appeal by José Padilla, an enemy combatant held in military prison without formal indictment or the protection of traditional legal rights. Padilla, an American citizen arrested in Chicago in 2002 for his alleged ties to Al Qaeda and a plot to detonate a radiological "dirty bomb" in the United States, argued that his indefinite detention was a violation of his constitutional rights. In a 5–4 decision (*Rumsfeld v. Padilla, 03-1027*), the court rejected Padilla's appeal, maintaining the petition should have been filed in federal court in South Carolina (the location of the military prison where he was being held) rather than New York (Lane 2004). In April 2006, the Supreme Court dismissed a second appeal by Padilla. In a 6–3 judgment (*Padilla v. Hanft, 05-533*), the court ruled that his legal status changed with the Bush administration's decision to charge him in civilian court. Thus there were no grounds for his appeal (Vincini 2006). By avoiding a ruling on President Bush's authority to order the indefinite detention of suspected terrorists, the Supreme Court enhanced presidential war power by leaving that policy intact.

Overall, the general pattern of the courts contributing to the president's dominant role in U.S. foreign policy making over the last half-century lends strong support for placing the president at the core of Hilsman's conceptualization.

THE STRUCTURES OF PRESIDENTIAL PREEMINENCE

The president's greatest resource—at least in principle—in exercising policy leadership is the vast executive establishment. Most of the federal government's work force of three million civilians (2004) work in the executive branch, where collectively they bear responsibility for making and implementing the full range of America's domestic and foreign policies. The obvious challenge for a president is to harness the structures and personnel of the executive agencies to his or her foreign policy agenda. While their resources, expertise, and control over day-to-day policy provide the president with substantial assets, the numbers comprising the federal work force, diffusion, and their longevity also present challenges for leadership.

The Cabinet

The president is nominally "boss" of the employees who staff the executive departments and agencies of the foreign affairs government, but the president by no means *controls* them. That truism led Richard Neustadt (1980) to describe the president's power as the "*power to persuade*." The interests of executive branch organizations are not always synonymous with the interests of the president. The people who staff them commonly hold their positions long before and long after any given president's term in office. To them the president is often a "transient meddler in their business" (Destler 1974).

The tension between the White House and the executive agencies is a reason for the president's appointment of department and agency heads, who together form the *cabinet.* In principle, these appointed officials represent the president's authority over and need to harness the executive departments. Once George Washington established the principle of meeting with these department heads, for the next 140 years or so the cabinet served as the chief advisory body for the president in both foreign and domestic affairs. Strong cabinets were the norm in this period, as department heads enjoyed political capital and clout on Capitol Hill. For a variety of reasons, however, the cabinet declined in importance in the twentieth century. For example, the 1921 budget reforms placed greater power over department budgets in the hands of the White House, while the expansion of the bureaucracy enlarged the size of the cabinet, making it less useful as an advisory body. Other reforms gave rise to an expanded White House staff more closely aligned with the president.

As important, department chiefs often become captives of the interests of the departments they administer and of the positions advanced by career professionals within them. Because chiefs are necessarily advocates for the departments they head, they are often in conflict with one another and sometimes even with the president (discussed in Chapter 11). Indeed, "one of the strengths of cabinet members, namely their capacity to make a compelling case for their programs, has proved to be their chief liability with presidents" (Cronin 1973). Members of the cabinet thus quickly come to be viewed as the president's "natural enemies." Cabinet decision making is usually the casualty, and the cabinet itself is a "perennial loser" (Allison and Szanton 1976). Indeed, in spite of the occasional call for a return to "cabinet government," there has been a marked decrease in the influence of the cabinet since World War II, especially as it relates to foreign policy.

The erosion of cabinet policy making stems in part from "the cross-cutting nature of most presidential policy issues." These require "advice from a broader perspective than that of individual department heads" (Pfiffner 1990). It also grows from the disdain of bureaucrats and the permanent bureaucracy that most presidents nurture. *Adhocracy*—a system of decision making that "'minimizes reliance on regularized and systematic patterns of providing advice and instead relies heavily on the president to distribute assignments and select whom he listens to and when'" (Haass 1994a; see also Watson 1993)—is often the result. A common aspect of adhocracy is that "it neither trusts nor respects standing bureaucracies. They are viewed as slow, unimaginative, and disloyal" (Haass 1994a).

Such "government by inner circle" now commonly describes presidential policy making. Although cabinet members may sometimes be members of the circles, it is typically because of their individual ties with presidents, not their institutional roles. Prominent recent examples include Defense Secretary Dick Cheney and Secretary of State James Baker during the first Bush administration, Secretary of the Treasury Robert Rubin during the

Clinton administration, and Secretary of State Condoleezza Rice and Secretary of Defense Donald Rumsfeld in the second Bush administration.

The Presidential Subsystem

Despite what some see as its untoward effects, every American president since World War II has relied increasingly on his personal staff and the Executive Office of the President for advice and assistance in the development of policies and programs. A *presidential subsystem* within the executive branch is the result, which often leads to differences between the presidency, on the one hand, and the established bureaucracies comprising the second concentric circle of policy making, on the other.

The institutionalization of the presidency began with the Executive Reorganization Act of 1939, which authorized President Roosevelt to create the Executive Office, consisting of the White House Office and the Bureau of the Budget. The former unit was to house the president's personal assistants and their staffs. The latter, created in 1921 under the jurisdiction of the Treasury Department, was to ensure presidential control over budgetary matters and later over the president's entire legislative program.

Since 1939, the Executive Office of the President (EOP) has included a plethora of other offices and councils. The lists and labels change continually, reflecting both presidential preferences and policy priorities. Midway through the second term of George W. Bush, for example, the EOP included, among others, the Council of Economic Advisers, the Office of Management and Budget, the Office of National Drug Control Policy, the President's Foreign Intelligence Advisory Board, the United States Trade Representative, and the White House Office. The White House Office encompassed ten administrative components, including the Domestic Policy Council, the Homeland Security Council, and the National Economic Council.

With new offices and functions have come more people and demands for more money. During the George W. Bush administration, the EOP consisted of a staff of about 1,800 and a budget of over $330 million in fiscal year 2005. The institutionalized presidency is now "a powerful inner sanctum of government, isolated from traditional, constitutional checks and balances" (Cronin 1984). Moreover, an enlarged White House staff designed to increase presidential control of the executive branch becomes, in the eyes of critics, "a screen" between the executive and legislative branches that "[cuts] off the president from the government and the government from the president. The staff becomes a shock absorber around the president, shielding him from reality" (Arthur Schlesinger, in *The Wall Street Journal*, 7 January 1981).

The Chief of Staff   As the size of the presidential subsystem has increased, most presidents have eventually concluded they must rely on a *chief of staff* to ensure presidential leadership and to bring order to an otherwise potentially chaotic White House staff operation. This was one of the hallmarks of the Nixon administration, where H. R. Haldeman and John Ehrlichman played critical staff roles. Carter began his presidency with the pledge that he would never operate as Nixon had, but he, too, eventually found a strong chief of staff necessary for effective governance. Reagan and Bush I also began this way; eventually Clinton came to the same conclusion.

Clinton was renowned early in his presidency for others' easy yet time-consuming access to him, and especially for endless but inconclusive meetings ("schmooze-a-thons") involving large numbers of staff and cabinet members. Corrective action was taken when Leon Panetta replaced Thomas F. "Mack" McLarty, a lifelong friend of the president, as chief of staff in 1994. A former member of Congress and director of the Office of Management and Budget (OMB), Panetta sought a more orderly White House operation. To accomplish this, Panetta constructed a system that established himself as the sole gatekeeper for the president. All the various offices and departments in the White House reported to Panetta (or his deputies) and no one other than Panetta was given "walk-in" privileges to the president, not even the national security adviser or the president's personal advisers. Panetta also took control of the president's schedule and instituted weekly "long-term planning" meetings to encourage broader goals and strategies for the administration. Finally, and most important for foreign policy, while bringing National Security Adviser Anthony Lake into the president's daily 7:30 a.m. meeting to raise foreign policy issues to a more prominent level within the White House, Panetta also strengthened his influence on the National Security Council, adding himself to its top-level "Principals Committee" (Drew 1994). These moves greatly enhanced the centralization of the White House staff and substantially elevated the importance of the chief of staff in all policy matters.

When Panetta departed the administration at the end of Clinton's first term, he left a system that was substantially more centralized, but also significantly more personalized. His replacement, Erskine Bowles, sought to retain the organization and centralization, but also to revitalize the formal policy structures of the White House. Hence, structures such as the National Economic Council, the National Security Council, and the Domestic Policy Council were given more weight, and the tightly controlled access to the president was loosened somewhat (Solomon 1997). When Bowles left in 1999, he was replaced by his deputy, John Podesta, who retained Bowles's system.

Stressing a highly centralized and structured White House staff, George W. Bush chose Andrew Card for his first chief of staff. Card served in various roles during the Reagan and Bush I years, including deputy chief of staff in the latter administration. Card's central role in the Bush II administration stemmed from the president's MBA training and preference for a corporate model that delegated responsibility to subordinates (Berke 2001). With this authority, one observer noted, Card ran "the most button-down, leak proof, on-task, on-time, on-message White House in history" (Froomkin 2005). While Card worked incredibly long hours, kept the president's schedule, and embraced a hands-on daily management style, he was not the assertive gatekeeper that Panetta was. Card explained in October 2005, "I do not restrict access to the president. In fact, I have a rule, if anyone who is

on the White House staff or anyone who is in the cabinet needs to see the president, they should feel comfortable going to see the president." Condoleezza Rice added, "There have been chiefs of staff who want to control access all the time; that's just not Andy." Card's effectiveness, particularly in Bush's first term, came in his capacity to coordinate, but certainly not control, Vice President Dick Cheney, National Security Adviser Condoleezza Rice, and powerful senior White House officials Karl Rove and Joshua Bolten.

Although not a foreign policy expert, Card followed Panetta's practice of participating in National Security Council and Principals Committee meetings. He also chaired the White House Iraq Group (WHIG), charged with convincing Congress to adopt a resolution to use force against Saddam Hussein's regime, and "had regular private side conversations" with the president "about the progress of war planning" for the operation in Afghanistan (Woodward 2002; Woodward 2004). One journalist observed that for most of Card's tenure, "The most famous image of Mr. Card, whispering into the president's ear that the nation was under attack on September 11, 2001, [was] an apt one: when he [gave] his opinion to Mr. Bush, he [did] it so quietly that he [was] rarely assigned credit, or blame, for the decisions that followed" (Kornblut 2005).

By spring of 2006, however, Card was held responsible for the failed Supreme Court nomination of Harriet Miers and the slow pace of federal assistance to victims of Hurricane Katrina, both of which were coordinated by his office. These issues coupled with other White House missteps and the sharp decline in the president's public approval rating as midterm elections approached led the second longest serving White House chief of staff to resign in April 2006. Joshua Bolten, who had served as the administration's director of the Office of Management and Budget (OMB) and deputy chief of staff for policy, became the new chief of staff and oversaw a shakeup of the Bush White House. Moderate to strong chiefs of staff, such as Card and Panetta, have proven necessary to bring order to White House decision-making processes, but they also contribute to the view that the White House staff itself distances the president from the rest of the executive branch of government. This is especially true if, as in the Nixon administration, staff members like Henry Kissinger, H. R. Haldeman, and John Ehrlichman are more powerful than the secretaries of state or defense or the domestic department heads. In these situations, the staff serves not as channels of communication between the president and his "line" departments and agencies, but as an independent layer of decision-making authority between the president and the rest of the executive branch.

The Vice President For much of American history, the *vice president* was an exceedingly weak position within the federal government. John Adams, the nation's first vice president, said it was "the most insignificant office that ever the invention of man contrived or his imagination conceived." John Nance Garner, who served as the thirty-second vice president, quipped that the office was "not worth a pitcher of warm spit." Other than serving as the president of the U.S. Senate and occasionally being called upon to cast tie-breaking votes (the position's only constitutionally proscribed role), most vice presidents were more likely to attend a foreign dignitary's funeral than a meeting of the president's inner circle.

It was not until well into the twentieth century that the vice presidency began to grow gradually into a more significant position. President Warren G. Harding made a regular practice of inviting the vice president to cabinet meetings. The vice president became a statutory member of the newly created National Security Council (NSC) in the Truman administration. President Dwight D. Eisenhower allowed his assertive vice president, Richard M. Nixon, to chair cabinet meetings in his absence. During the Kennedy administration, Vice President Lyndon B. Johnson secured office space within the Old Executive Building, adjacent to the White House.

By the latter half of the twentieth century, the expanding role of the vice president was extended to foreign policy, with the five most active vice presidents being Richard Nixon, Walter Mondale, George H. W. Bush, Dan Quayle, and Al Gore (Kengor 2000b). Although each man's respective influence varied, they all participated in key foreign policy meetings, shaped significant substantive issues, and were at times given chief responsibility for a particular policy area, bilateral relationship, or region. According to Kengor (2000a), leading factors behind the vice president's growing involvement in foreign policy included but were not limited to "the prominence of foreign policy during the Cold War period and nuclear age; increases in the general size and scope of the U.S. government and demands on presidential time; changes in technology (television, air travel, etc.); the rise of the vice presidency as a springboard to the presidency; and desire of vice presidents for foreign policy exposure."

The trend toward an expanding role for the vice president continued in the George W. Bush administration but was elevated to an extraordinary level with Richard B. Cheney becoming "easily the most influential vice president in U.S. history" (Froomkin 2005). Upon entering office in 2001, Cheney was expected to play an important role in the administration. After all, the new president had limited experience in government and no public service in Washington, D.C. By contrast, Cheney was a seasoned Washington insider, who had served as defense secretary, White House chief of staff, and a member of Congress.

However, Cheney's broad authority and influence during President Bush's first term exceeded all expectations. In this regard, three developments are especially noteworthy. First, a central reason for Andrew Card's standing as a moderately powerful rather than a strong chief of staff (discussed in the previous section) is the fact that George W. Bush often seemed to rely on Cheney to perform roles played by such chiefs of staff as Panetta. For instance, Bush delegated chief of staff–like responsibilities on such issues as the budget and congressional relations to the vice president.

Second, Cheney established a "powerful parallel White House staff" to serve as an independent source of advice and assist him in shaping the president's agenda (Berke 2001). Moreover, no other vice president enjoyed a larger group of national security advisers and consultants, which at times ranged from 15 to 35 people, exceeding the size of President Kennedy's entire NSC staff (Rothkopf 2005a). This seasoned team of defense and foreign policy experts played an instrumental role the Bush administration's march toward war in Iraq. In addition, "Cheney . . . further expanded his own personal influence by putting loyalists in key positions throughout the White House" and drawing on an extensive network of associates across the federal government (Froomkin 2005; Rothkopf 2005a). His influence was also bolstered by his omnipresence. When they were both in Washington, Cheney would spend a good portion of his day with Bush. He attended the president's domestic, economic, and national security briefings, participated in the president's weekly session with his top foreign policy advisers, played a prominent role in Principals Committee meetings, and often stayed after meetings for one-on-one conversations with the president (Alvarez and Schmitt 2001; Bumiller 2004; and Rothkopf 2005b).

Third, Cheney took the lead in spearheading the administration's remarkable expansion of presidential powers (detailed earlier in this chapter) and in doing so protected and broadened his own authority. Cheney came to office intent on re-asserting and strengthening executive prerogative, which in his view, had been undermined in the post-Vietnam and post–Cold War eras and could not persist given the new post-9/11 security environment. He championed executive power, privilege, and secrecy at the expense of legislative oversight, judicial review, and public transparency. This was most apparent when interest groups and Congress's Government Accountability Office (GAO) demanded information about the inner workings of Cheney's energy taskforce, especially whom from the energy industry the vice president had consulted when he took the lead in shaping the administration's new national energy policy. It required a legal fight that reached as far as the Supreme Court, but Cheney prevailed and

successfully blocked the disclosure effort (see Montgomery 2005–2006).

However, Cheney's expansive view of executive power and considerable personal influence extended well beyond energy policy. It included key national security decisions related to a warrantless domestic eavesdropping program, the use of the classification "unlawful enemy combatant," and the approval of harsh CIA and military interrogation tactics, not to mention the president's decision to topple Saddam Hussein's regime in March 2003. In short, Cheney transformed the Office of the Vice President into a foreign policy powerhouse. According to one observer, "From 2001 to 2005, the vice president's influence over U.S. foreign policy may have been greater than that of any individual other than the president since Henry A. Kissinger held the positions of national security adviser and secretary of state during the Nixon years." However, the same analyst expressed doubt whether Cheney would enjoy the same level of foreign policy influence by the end of the second Bush term. Secretary of State Condoleezza Rice's power was on the rise, the National Security Council (a main vehicle for Cheney's exercise of power) was in decline under the quiet leadership of National Security Adviser Stephen Hadley, and I. Lewis "Scooter" Libby, Cheney's chief aide and national security adviser, had resigned following a perjury indictment (Rothkopf 2006).[8] Moreover, Cheney's strong political ally, Secretary of Defense Donald Rumsfeld, was forced to resign in November 2006. Yet even with the prospect of Cheney's influence ebbing in the final years of the Bush administration, two realities were firmly established. The institution of the vice presidency is now a central component of the presidential subsystem; and modern vice presidents have demonstrated they possess the willingness and the opportunity to play active and influential roles in foreign policy.

The National Security Adviser The *National Security Council (NSC)* is the institutional umbrella within the presidential subsystem bearing primary responsibility for foreign policy. This council—and especially its staff—has grown from its creation in

1947 to be the center of most foreign policy making in most administrations. For example, it was as head of the NSC and its staff that Kissinger acquired greater influence than the secretaries of state or defense. Ever since, the national security adviser's role and relationship with the president have been closely scrutinized.

Kissinger's formal title was Special Assistant for National Security Affairs. The word "special" has since been dropped, and the position is sometimes referred to loosely as simply *national security adviser* (NSA). Others had occupied the post in previous administrations—Robert Cutler and later Gordon Gray under Eisenhower; McGeorge Bundy under Kennedy; and Bundy and Walt W. Rostow under Lyndon Johnson. While the role of the NSA grew steadily through his tenure, none had achieved the same level of prominence and influence in the foreign affairs government as did Kissinger. Zbigniew Brzezinski, Kissinger's successor in the Carter administration, was somewhat less dominant, but he, too, emerged as his boss's key foreign policy adviser. Although President Reagan initially sought to downgrade the role of the national security adviser—six different men held the position in Reagan's eight-year presidency—the Iran-Contra affair demonstrated that the national security adviser and his staff had embarked on operational activities that expanded the role of the NSC system in new and uncharted directions. In his final two years, Reagan turned to Frank Carlucci and Colin Powell to restore the centrality of the national security adviser and the NSC system.

More recently, Brent Scowcroft, George H. W. Bush's national security adviser, eschewed operational activities and pursued a role more akin to his pre-Reagan predecessors but without the publicity. Thus he played an active managerial role in the administration. Anthony Lake, Clinton's first NSA, assumed a low-profile role and worked within the system to build support for Clinton's foreign policy and to brief reporters "on background" (not for attribution) about it. His deputy was Samuel (Sandy) Berger, who took over as NSA when Lake stepped down at the end of the first Clinton term, gradually assumed the central role in foreign policy making that was by then becoming the norm for the national security adviser (see Heilbrunn 1998; Perlez 1999). George W. Bush's first national security adviser was Condoleezza Rice, who seemed destined to adopt a low-key approach, but quickly became a visible spokesperson and close adviser to the president. However, she found it exceedingly difficult to coordinate a group of assertive and high-profile foreign policy advisers. With Rice's appointment as secretary of state in 2005, her deputy, Stephen Hadley, assumed the NSA post in Bush's second term and operated as a behind-the-scenes manager of the NSC system. Rather than vying for influence, Hadley seemed inclined to defer foreign policy leadership to his former boss and the State Department.

Presidential personality and preferences explain in part the variations in how different presidents draw on and interact with their in-house foreign policy advisers. Still, all recent presidents, regardless of their initial predilections, have found it necessary to exert political control over foreign policy making by institutionalizing it within the White House. According to Theodore Sorensen (1987–1988), a White House staff member during the Kennedy administration, "Since the days when Dean Acheson could serve as both secretary of state and Truman's personal adviser and coordinator, the overlap between national and international issues, the number and speed of thermonuclear missiles, and the foreign policy pressures from Congress, the press, and public, have all mounted to a point where no president can conscientiously delegate to anyone his constitutional responsibilities in foreign affairs."

We can gain an appreciation of how presidential style and external pressures encourage the centralization of foreign policy in the White House through a historical examination of the way different presidents have used the National Security Council and its staff. By reviewing roles, structures, and operations of each administration's NSC system, we will gain insight into the endemic differences between the institutionalized presidency comprising the innermost circle of foreign policy making and the career professionals comprising the second concentric circle.

Organizing for Foreign Policy: The National Security Council System

Created by the National Security Act of 1947,[10] the purpose of the National Security Council is to "advise the president with respect to the integration of domestic, foreign, and military policies relating to the national security." Statutory members of the council include the president (as chair), vice president, and secretaries of state and defense. The director of national intelligence and the chairman of the Joint Chiefs of Staff (JCS) are statutory advisers. Because presidents can include anyone they wish, others often participate, including the secretary of the treasury, the attorney general, the U.S. ambassador to the United Nations, the director of the Office of Management and Budget (OMB), heads of such organizations as the Agency for International Development (USAID), and various presidential advisers and assistants, depending on the issues and presidential predilections.

The president is free to use the NSC as much or as little as he or she desires, and its deliberations and decisions are purely advisory. Still, over time it has become the primary mechanism for tackling problems all presidents face: acquiring information, identifying issues, coping with crises, making decisions, coordinating actions, and ensuring agency compliance with presidential wishes. Through the development of formal *interagency processes,* it has become the principal formal mechanism for coordinating the vast federal structure on foreign policy.

Institutionalizing the NSC System, 1947–1961

The Truman Administration   Although it was created during his administration, President Truman did not use the NSC extensively, fearing it might encroach on his constitutional prerogatives by imposing a parliamentary-type cabinet system over foreign policy decision making. In fact, Truman did not even attend NSC meetings before the outbreak of the Korean War in 1950. As a result, the council's role was largely perfunctory. With the outbreak of the Korean War, however, Truman recognized the wisdom of better coordination of policy and action.

He therefore directed that major national security policy recommendations come to him via the council, and he also instituted weekly meetings. Nevertheless, the State Department remained at the core of foreign policy: the secretary of state was even named the ranking member of the NSC in Truman's absence. In fact, the famous NSC-68 memorandum was coordinated chiefly by the State Department and outside formal NSC channels (see Chapter 4). Nevertheless, by the end of his term Truman also had begun to use the NSC staff for interagency planning purposes.

The Eisenhower Administration   As an instrument of presidential leadership, the NSC system developed substantially under President Dwight D. Eisenhower. Coming from a professional background that emphasized the need for staff work and overall coordination, former General Eisenhower took the largely undeveloped NSC structure he had inherited from Truman and transformed it into a highly formalized system which he viewed as "the central vehicle for formulating and promulgating policy" and "the primary means of imparting presidential direction and overall coherence to the activities of the departments and agencies" (Clark and Legere 1969). An interagency planning board and operations coordinating board made up of midlevel officials from the relevant foreign policy bureaucracies, both eventually chaired by the special assistant for national security affairs (the now familiar position created by Eisenhower and filled initially by Robert Cutler), became part of Eisenhower's NSC system. They were charged, respectively, with generating policy recommendations for consideration by the full NSC and with overseeing the implementation of presidential decisions (Greenstein 2000). Eisenhower attended (and chaired) 326 of the NSC's 366 meetings during his two terms and made these meetings the largest item on his weekly agenda (U.S. Department of State 1997). Still, formal council meetings were often followed by more intimate "rump" sessions, or the president would convene meetings of a small group of advisers outside the formal NSC structure to deal with urgent matters.[11]

Personalizing the Staff, 1961–1969

The Kennedy and Johnson Administrations   By the time Eisenhower left office, the highly institutionalized National Security Council system was being criticized as an excessively bureaucratized system that stifled innovation and diluted policy decisions (Jackson 1965; Henderson 1988; Prados 1991). Reacting to criticisms of Eisenhower's "paper mill," President Kennedy moved initially to dismantle most of the machinery. Shortly after his election in 1960, he appointed McGeorge Bundy as his special assistant for national security affairs and announced that the purpose of Bundy's staff would be "to assist me in obtaining advice from, and coordinating operations of, the government agencies concerned with national security." He also announced his intention to strengthen the role of the secretary of state in the area of interagency coordination.

Insiders' accounts of the Kennedy administration indicate that Kennedy was quickly disappointed with the docile role assumed by Dean Rusk, Kennedy's choice as secretary of state, in an otherwise action-oriented administration. The State Department as an organization also proved too sluggish for White House officials. When this happened, the White House staff stepped into the perceived vacuum—not only Bundy's staff but also other members of Kennedy's personal team, most of whom were specifically recruited for his administration rather than drawn from careerists in established bureaucracies.

The National Security Council itself remained largely moribund, however. Preferring informality and personal control, Kennedy relied instead on ad hoc interagency task forces designed to serve presidential needs rather than the agencies they represented. The 1961 Bay of Pigs fiasco, from which Kennedy learned "never to rely on the experts," contributed much to his reliance on decision-making groups formulated without regard for the institutional affiliations of their members. The most celebrated of these ad hoc groups was the so-called *Ex Comm (Executive Committee of the NSC),* initially comprising some thirteen advisers on whom Kennedy relied heavily in devising a response to the surreptitious installation of Soviet offensive weapons in Cuba in October 1962. Similar but less well known ad hoc groups dealt with crises in Berlin and Laos, paramilitary experiments being tried in Vietnam, and covert intelligence operations directed against Cuba. Bundy served on most of the informal groups and his staff acted aggressively as a sort of "president's personal State Department."

Another key innovation was the establishment of the White House *Situation Room* next to Bundy's office in the basement. Linked to the communication channels of the foreign policy bureaucracy, the Situation Room allowed Bundy and the NSC staff to become increasingly central to foreign policy making. It was expanded in each subsequent administration. Hence, while the NSC itself proved far less important in ensuring presidential control than these less formal groups, the National Security Council staff assumed a more significant role, as did the NSA.

Kennedy's assassination in November 1963 brought to the presidency a man with little interest and less experience in foreign affairs. Johnson's approach to national security matters was even less formal than Kennedy's style. The NSC as a formal deliberative mechanism languished—a fact that, in the view of Johnson's critics, contributed to the Vietnam morass (see Hoopes 1973b). Informal meetings of the tight inner circle—the famed *Tuesday Lunch* gatherings—substituted for more formal meetings. At these meetings of the president, the secretaries of state and defense (Rusk and Robert McNamara), the national security adviser (first McGeorge Bundy, then Walt W. Rostow, who replaced Bundy in 1966), and eventually the director of the CIA, the chairman of the Joint Chiefs, and the president's press secretary, Vietnam was the principal luncheon topic. Indeed, Vietnam gradually consumed more and more of the administration's attention. While it preserved personal control and organizational flexibility, the cost of Johnson's highly personal and informal approach was the exclusion of subordinates on whom the president and his close circle of advisers depended for implementation of top-level decisions. While the NSA and NSC staff remained key foreign policy players, Johnson utilized them as his personal staff and not as coordinators of the policy process. The informality and lack of structure impaired the Johnson administration's ability to plan, prepare, assess, and implement policy in a coordinated fashion. Moreover, when Walt W. Rostow took over the position of National Security Adviser, he continued to manage the flow of information to the president, to communicate presidential wishes to the bureaucracy, and to provide policy analysis and advice. But he did much less to encourage the free flow of ideas and alternatives to the president than had his predecessor. The result was bureaucratic distrust of Rostow's ability to present departmental viewpoints to Johnson objectively, which further hampered effective policy making (Hoopes 1973b; Mulcahy 1995).

The White House Ascendant, 1969–1989

Noncoherence describes the policy-making legacy Nixon inherited from a divided and demoralized Johnson administration in January 1969. The outgoing administration's "policymaking institutions, formal and informal, had little that would recommend them to its successor" (Destler 1974). Hence, Nixon, and subsequently his successors, worked to construct more organized NSC systems, each of which ultimately resulted in a White House–centered structure and process.

The Nixon Administration   Nixon moved rapidly to restore coherence by rebuilding a more formal NSC system and placing it at the hub of foreign policy making. Eschewing the informality and sloppiness of the preceding administrations while preserving the personalization of the NSC staff, Nixon named Harvard political scientist Henry Kissinger as his special assistant for national security affairs and directed Kissinger to establish an "Eisenhower NSC system" but "without the concurrences" (Destler 1974). According to Morton Halperin, who helped devise the system, the goal was to ensure presidential control and conduct of foreign policy (National Security Council Project 1998).

The system that Nixon and Kissinger established located decision-making authority in the White House. Kissinger tripled the NSC staff and

organized a system around a number of top-level interagency committees whose jurisdictions covered the entire waterfront of American foreign policy, from arms control negotiations with the Soviet Union (the Verification Panel) to crisis management (the Washington Special Actions Group) to covert operations (the 40 Committee, named for the National Security Decision Memorandum that set it up). Their task was to develop alternatives for consideration by the president and the full NSC. Because Kissinger directed nearly all of these bodies (the Under Secretaries Committee chaired by the deputy secretary of state was the exception, and it was soon marginalized), his role in the NSC system was pivotal (see Figure 10.2). The working committees served the top-level "Review Group," also chaired by Kissinger, which screened all interagency papers prior to their consideration by the NSC (U.S. Department of State 1997).

The system fit Richard Nixon's preferred operating style. In contrast to Eisenhower's approach (which encouraged the NSC system to focus on compromises among departments and agencies), and in contrast to the Kennedy and Johnson styles (which saw NSC meetings as forums for its members to advocate views), Nixon wanted all policy options to be laid out for his subsequent consideration and, above all, to maintain his flexibility. Kissinger's influence in the system derived in part from Nixon's preference for solo decision making. The president's trust in Kissinger further enhanced his influence. Indeed, Kissinger himself has written that "in the final analysis the influence of a Presidential Assistant derives almost exclusively from the confidence of the President, not from administrative arrangements" (Kissinger 1979, 40).

Two additional developments characterized the operations of the Nixon system. First, President Nixon increasingly used Kissinger to implement foreign policy, thereby expanding the role of the national security adviser into operational responsibilities. Kissinger's activism produced some spectacular diplomatic successes in China, the Soviet Union, the Middle East, and elsewhere, and culminated in Kissinger's appointment as secretary of state, an assignment he held concurrently with his

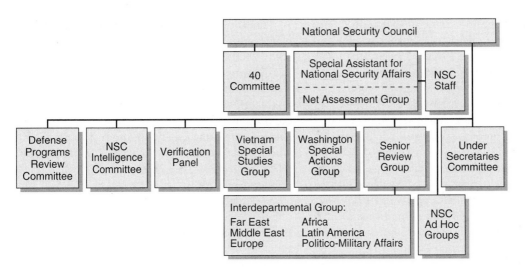

FIGURE 10.2 The Nixon Administration's National Security Council System

White House role. Second, even as Kissinger's personal influence rose, his elaborate NSC system atrophied. The decisions that led to the 1970 Cambodia incursion, for example, were a product of "catch-as-catch-can" gatherings between Nixon and his advisers outside the formal NSC framework (Destler 1974). Other major foreign policy initiatives involving China, the Middle East, and Vietnam also evolved outside the system. The "back channel" to the Soviet leadership that Kissinger established is perhaps his most celebrated bureaucratic end-run. It led to a breakthrough in the strategic arms negotiations with the Soviets even while formal negotiations between the two sides' delegations (the "front channel") continued (see Talbott 1979).

The Ford and Carter Administrations One of Gerald Ford's first moves on the eve of his inauguration as the first nonelected president was to ask Kissinger to remain as his secretary of state and national security adviser. In his dual capacity Kissinger continued to operate what some felt was a one-man foreign policy show, one all the more apparent because the president he served was a relative novice in international affairs. As public and congressional disapproval of the concentration of power in one adviser's hands grew, Kissinger's star and the popularity

of the policies he engineered gradually waned. In response, Ford appointed Brent Scowcroft to the NSA slot. Scowcroft restored a less elaborate version of the Nixon-Kissinger NSC system, but limited his own role to managing the process. Kissinger remained the primary foreign policy adviser with unlimited access to President Ford, while the NSC worked to present Ford with policy analysis and alternatives.

When Jimmy Carter took office after his defeat of Gerald Ford in 1976, he sought to construct an NSC system that would avoid concentrating foreign policy power into one individual's hands, while preserving the White House role in coordinating the foreign policy bureaucracy and ensuring that a broad spectrum of ideas and a vigorous debate over policy alternatives occurred. President Carter's designation of Zbigniew Brzezinski as assistant for national security affairs, which came before he named his secretary of state, reaffirmed the determination of the White House to exercise foreign policy control. The elaborate NSC system of the preceding years was replaced with one based on two committees: a Policy Review Committee (PRC) responsible chiefly for long-term projects, to be chaired by a cabinet member whose department had the greatest stake in a given issue; and a Special

Coordinating Committee (SCC) chiefly responsible for short-term projects (including covert intelligence operations and crisis management), to be chaired by the national security adviser.

The latter committee eventually emerged as the most influential body within the NSC structure. Brzezinski also emerged as the pivotal foreign policy adviser, and eventually expanded his role into operational activities as well. Initially one of a "collegium" of key advisers that included Secretary of State Cyrus Vance, Secretary of Defense Harold Brown, and UN Ambassador Andrew Young, Brzezinski transformed his role through his control over the SCC, his easy access to the president, and Carter's practice of avoiding NSC meetings in favor of more informal meetings of some of the key principals. The formal NSC met only ten times during the administration.

Fundamental conflict between the secretary of state and the president's national security adviser on foreign policy also emerged as a major problem. Although the principal members worked reasonably well together for the first half of the administration, by the second some serious fissures had developed. Brzezinski stressed a hard-line posture toward the Soviet Union and focused on the East–West conflict. Vance and Young stressed détente and appeared more sensitive to North–South relations and global-order issues. For a time, Carter seemed unable to reconcile the often conflicting thrusts of his principal advisers. However, Young resigned when his contacts with the Palestine Liberation Organization (in violation of established policy) were disclosed. Vance resigned in the spring of 1980 to protest the president's abortive military rescue of American hostages in Iran, the first time in sixty years a secretary of state resigned because of a policy dispute with the president. The White House–State Department rift did not end with Vance's departure, either. Carter named Senator Edmund S. Muskie as Vance's successor, but he was barely confirmed in office when Carter signed PD 59, which, as discussed in Chapter 4, moved U.S. strategic doctrine in the direction of an explicit counterforce posture—and without ever consulting the new secretary of state.

The rift between Brzezinski and Vance perpetuated what by 1980 had become a recurrent concern. Should the national security adviser be primarily a manager of the decision process or primarily a personal adviser and "resident intellectual" to the president? What is the proper relationship between the national security adviser and the secretary of state? Based on the experiences of the five presidents who occupied the Oval Office in the 1960s and 1970s, a degree of consensus emerged among practitioners and scholars about what the national security adviser should—and should not—be doing (Destler 1983b; "The National Security Adviser: Role and Accountability" 1980). Their activities fall along a continuum between an "inside management" role, where the adviser performs the role of facilitator, and a "leadership" role, which often places him in the potential position as a second secretary of state. The thrust of the consensus that emerged toward the end of the Carter administration is that the NSA should emphasize the inside role and eschew the outside. Exemplary tasks associated with each role are listed in Focus 10.2, which also suggests that some activities midway between the inside and outside orientations may be acceptable.

The Reagan Administration Ronald Reagan's efforts to address the lessons of previous administrations produced an NSC system that began as a cabinet-style approach and ended in a more White House–centered structure. Initially preferring to restore the cabinet and National Security Council per se, redress the balance between the White House and the State Department, and de-emphasize the role of the NSC staff and national security adviser, Reagan constructed a system whose problems eventually led him to replace it.

Reagan's initial system revolved around strong department heads and a weak national security adviser. Reagan's choice of Alexander Haig as secretary of state was spotlighted as an indication of the president's desire to relocate primary control over foreign policy making in the State Department. The former NATO commander had been schooled in the ways of the White House as an assistant to Henry Kissinger and later as chief of staff during the

---

F O C U S 10.2 The National Security Assistant: The Professionals' Job Description

YES ("Inside Management")	OKAY In Moderation	NO ("Outside Leadership")
Briefing the president, handling foreign policy in-box	Discreet advice/advocacy	Conducting particular diplomatic negotiations
Analyzing issues and choices:	Encouraging advocacy by NSC staff subordinates	Fixed operational assignments
a. Ordering information/ intelligence	Information and "background"	Public spokesperson
b. Managing interagency studies	Communicating with press, Congress, foreign officials	Strong, visible internal advocacy (except of already established presidential priorities)
Managing presidential decision processes		
Communicating presidential decisions and monitoring their implementation		Making policy decisions
General interagency brokering, circuit-connecting, crisis management		

SOURCE: I. M. Destler, "The Rise of the National Security Assistant," in Charles W. Kegley, Jr., and Eugene R. Wittkopf, eds., *Perspectives on American Foreign Policy: Selected Readings*. New York: St. Martin's, 1983, 262.

---

final, embattled days of the Nixon White House. Reagan also selected Caspar Weinberger, formerly the director of the Office of Management and Budget under Nixon, to serve as secretary of defense. Richard V. Allen was selected as the national security adviser. Reagan publicly stated that the secretary of state was going to be his "primary adviser ... [and] the chief formulator and spokesman for foreign policy for this administration."

Haig's initial attempts to act on this premise, including his proposal, submitted on inauguration day, to establish himself as the administration's "foreign policy vicar," were rebuffed. No clearly defined organizational structure for the management of foreign policy emerged during the administration's first year, as it gave priority to domestic rather than foreign policy. In February 1981, top officials did agree to establish Senior Interdepartmental Groups (SIGs) on foreign, defense, and intelligence issues (chaired by the heads of the relevant agencies) and a series of Interdepartmental Groups (IGs) at the assistant secretary level, each chaired by the agency most responsible for the issue. These groups would report to the NSC. Later that year, the National Security Planning Group (NSPG) was established to

strengthen planning and policy coordination. A smaller and less formal body, the NSPG included the original statutory members and advisers to the NSC designated in the 1947 National Security Act and held regular weekly meetings with the president.

This initial system soon broke down for at least two reasons. First, with a weak NSA, no mechanism existed for resolving disagreements among the leading executive agencies and departments. Second, as Robert C. McFarlane, who became Reagan's national security adviser late in 1983, would later testify before Congress, the system was characterized by the absence of an organizational framework within which to engage in a "thorough and concerted government-wide analysis" of critical foreign policy proposals (McFarlane 1994).

In early 1982, Reagan replaced Allen with William Clark (a former California Supreme Court Justice and then deputy secretary of state) and issued a presidential directive to establish a more organized NSC system. Although it preserved the secretary of state's responsibility for the "overall direction, coordination, and supervision of the interdepartmental activities incident to foreign policy formulation," it also made NSA Clark responsible for "developing, coordinating, and monitoring national security policy" (U.S. Department of State 1997). Shortly thereafter, Haig resigned as secretary of state, to be replaced with George Shultz. Unfortunately, these changes did little to solve the personality conflicts and internecine warfare that were occurring. The newly formalized system did not make a dramatic improvement because of its hybrid combination of White House–centered coordination and department-centered structures.

In fact, while Clark first sought to operate as an *honest broker* for others in the foreign affairs government, he eventually concluded, "Cabinet secretaries are all parochial, so you've got to decide yourself what to do." Thus he played an increasingly active role, enhancing the policy-making role of the NSC staff generally and increasing the number of professional staff serving the council to a level greater than at any time since Kissinger's tenure (Destler 1983a). Consequently, by the summer of 1983, Clark was widely regarded as having become the most influential foreign policy figure in the White House. As the most conservative of the president's inner circle of advisers, he also came into conflict with other, more pragmatic White House staffers, particularly Chief of Staff James Baker. The squabbling (especially on the issue of defense spending) may have contributed to Clark's sudden and unexpected departure for the Interior Department in October 1983. Clark's successors presided over three years of increasingly incoherent, fragmented, contentious, and uncoordinated foreign policy efforts complicated by the president's unwillingness to correct the underlying problems with the system that gave rise to these results. Clark's immediate successor was Robert C. "Bud" MacFarlane, a former NSC staffer under Kissinger and Scowcroft and a troubleshooter for Secretary of State Haig, who inherited an elaborate, but still incoherent NSC organizational structure and sought to use it to contend with the centrifugal forces of cabinet government and a relatively inattentive president.

MacFarlane enjoyed some successes as national security adviser, but he resigned in late 1985 after becoming "overwhelmed by 'Cabinet government'"

and his inability to resolve interminable squabbles among key administration officials (Cannon 1988). MacFarlane was replaced by his deputy, Rear Admiral John Poindexter, who lasted just over a year in the position before he was forced to retire over the Iran-Contra scandal in late 1986.

The Iran-Contra affair represented the failure of President Reagan's NSC system and illuminates many of the problems and deficiencies that system entailed. The "Iran initiative," as it was called by the special review board led by former Senator John Tower, former Secretary of State Ed Muskie, and former NSA Brent Scowcroft (the Tower Commission), included an attempted strategic opening to Iran, the sale of arms to Iran via Israel and by the United States itself in an effort to secure the release of hostages held in Lebanon, and, ultimately, the diversion of profits from the arms sales to the contras fighting the Sandinista regime in Nicaragua. Because the record indicates, for example, that Secretary of State Shultz and Secretary of Defense Weinberger vigorously opposed the transfer of arms to Iran, that key covert action findings that authorized the arms-for-hostages swap were approved by the president without their knowledge, and that John Poindexter authorized the transfer of arms profits to the contras without the president's knowledge, the Tower Board concluded that the proper use of existing structures might have averted the single most damaging foreign policy failure of the Reagan presidency. Such problems led Colin Powell to reaffirm the truism that an effective process is critical to a sound policy. "Issues come and go," observed Powell. "Process is always important." Perhaps recognition of Powell's observation finally led the Reagan White House to address the incoherence of its NSC system, because Poindexter's immediate successor—Frank Carlucci—quickly "set out to restore the credibility of the institution, to restore it to its proper role as an interagency body . . . That is its 'honest broker' role, and we set out to reestablish it. We took the NSC out of operations." Carlucci also established the national security adviser as a more central coordinator rather than another policy advocate. When he left the position in December 1987 to replace Weinberger as secretary of defense, his deputy, General Colin Powell, assumed the role. Under their leadership, the NSC played an important and positive role in preparing for the Washington and Moscow superpower summits, and the NSA once more emerged as an effective facilitator of the foreign affairs policy process (Cannon 1988; Kirschten 1987).

White House Centralization *The Bush I Administration* When George H. W. Bush moved from vice president to president through his 1988 election victory, he constructed an NSC system that reflected his experiences in the Reagan administration. His system had several characteristics. First, it was White House–centered; the NSA and NSC staff managed the process and coordinated policy, while the stakeholders from the foreign policy bureaucracy worked through an interagency process to formulate policy options. Also, while Bush placed great weight on the role of the Departments of State and Defense, the key interagency committees designed to serve the NSC were chaired by the NSA and deputy NSA, placing the White House in a position to control bureaucratic differences. Further, Bush selected his top-level advisers to create a collegial team that would work well together with the president, who would play an active and attentive role in making foreign policy decisions. Hence, Bush essentially sought to counter the key deficiencies of the early Reagan system: its decentralized cabinet government approach; its lack of White House coordination; its personal and bureaucratic divisions; and its lack of presidential attentiveness.

The structure of the Bush NSC system had three layers. At the top was the Principals Committee, consisting of the national security assistant (as chair), the secretaries of state and defense, the director of central intelligence, the chairman of the Joint Chiefs of Staff, and the president's chief of staff, with participation by the attorney general and treasury secretary when issues required. The Principals Committee was charged with reviewing, coordinating, and monitoring the development and implementation of national security policy. Serving the Principals Committee was the *Deputies*

Committee, chaired by the deputy national security adviser, with participants at the rank of under secretary. This committee coordinated and reviewed the work of the third layer and had the responsibility for preparing policy issues, papers, and recommendations for the Principals Committee. A series of *Policy Coordinating Committees* (PCCs), consisting of eight permanent regional and functional committees, and others on an ad hoc basis, were responsible for initially developing policy options and for overseeing policy implementation. These PCCs consisted of representatives from across the foreign policy bureaucracy at the assistant secretary level.

To knit the system together, Bush assembled an experienced team of advisers with collegial relationships. James Baker, a friend of Bush who ran his 1988 presidential campaign and also served as Reagan's chief of staff and secretary of the treasury, was named secretary of state. Dick Cheney, a congressman from Wyoming, became secretary of defense after former Senator John Tower failed to win Senate approval for the job. Earlier Cheney had served President Ford as chief of staff. Colin Powell returned to active military duty at the end of the Reagan administration and was named chairman of the Joint Chiefs of Staff. As his national security adviser, Bush selected Brent Scowcroft, who had occupied that role in the Ford administration and was, as noted, a member of the Tower Commission that investigated the Iran-Contra affair. Bush himself played a critical role, participating in virtually every high-level meeting of his administration (National Security Council Project 1999a).

As the NSA, Scowcroft tried, apparently successfully, to involve the secretaries of state and defense in the policy process and to himself maintain close contact with the president. Baker and Scowcroft agreed at the outset that "Baker would have the lead on foreign policy, Scowcroft and the NSC would have no operational role, and Scowcroft himself would be a low profile 'honest broker' within the administration." With this they hoped to avoid "niggling disagreements over public speeches, television interviews, ambassadorial visits, and the like" (Gergen 1989). As one observer explained late in the Bush presidency, Scowcroft "managed both to be a highly influential adviser to the president and to coordinate effectively the debate among the president's top foreign policy officials. Scowcroft was able to combine these two functions because he lacked the insatiable drive toward power and fame that has crippled previous National Security Council heads" (Judis 1992).

Paralleling this NSC system, however, was a less formal advisory structure on which Bush relied heavily. This informal advisory process, centered around the president himself, usually included Scowcroft, Cheney, Baker, Powell, and Chief of Staff John Sununu. Stressing teamwork and solidarity, this small group supplemented, and at times supplanted, the more formal NSC system. It reflected Bush's preference for a tight inner circle of confidants chosen on the basis of loyalty and friendship, not institutional ties. A similar informal system evolved at the deputies level as well, with key officials from different agencies working closely and collegially together (National Security Council Project 1999a).

There were, of course, a few problems. While military actions in Panama and the Persian Gulf were largely successful, they both involved far less systematic policy review than might have been expected. With regard to Panama, "so far as is . . . evident, there was . . . no NSC meeting in connection with Bush's most ambitious foreign policy move of his first year . . . " (Prados 1991). The decision process that led to the defense of Saudi Arabia in August 1990 and later to the war against Iraq also indicates that the decision making leading up to the Gulf War was less formal than it should have been, and that the decisions to end the war were taken with little formal review (Woodward 1991; Gordon and Trainor 1995). Finally, Bush's decision to dispatch U.S. troops to Somalia was curiously disconnected to careful NSC consideration. While his Deputies Committee prepared options and the NSC met to consider them on November 25, 1992, Bush's decision to pursue the most interventionist of the options did not reflect the analysis of the NSC or the preferences of the major stakeholders in the review process (Schraeder 1998).

Nonetheless, most observers believe the Bush I administration system to be a model in terms of structure and in terms of the role and behavior of the NSA (for example, National Security Council Project 1999a, 1999b). Indeed, subsequent administrations have essentially adopted the structures and procedures put in place by the first Bush administration. In most policy areas the formal and informal advisory systems complemented each other well. Former members of the NSC staff pointed to German unification, the end of the Cold War, most of the Gulf War policy making, the Middle East peace process, and a few others as good examples of the structure and process at work (National Security Council Project 1999a; Zelikow and Rice 1995).

The Clinton Administration According to James Steinberg, who later became the Deputy NSA, President Clinton's team concurred that the Bush NSC system had been highly successful and so sought to preserve it (National Security Council Project 2000). Hence the incoming administration retained much of the previous administration's system, adopting the same three-layered structure: a Principals Committee, a Deputies Committee, and a series of *Interagency Working Groups* (IWGs), the equivalent of the Bush administration's Policy Coordinating Committees, to "review and coordinate the implementation of presidential decisions in their respective policy areas" (U.S. Department of State 1997). The Clinton NSC system was also White House–centered, with the national security adviser and the deputy national security adviser chairing the Principals Committee and the Deputies Committee, respectively.

While retaining the fundamental structure, the administration made several important, if incremental, changes. To support the focus of the president's foreign policy agenda on economics and transnational issues, the membership of the Principals Committee was expanded. The secretary of the treasury, the ambassador to the UN, the assistant to the president for economic policy (head of the National Economic Council), and the director of the Office of Management and Budget were added.

Other officials, including the attorney general and the director of the Office of National Drug Control Policy, attended as necessary. Similarly, the composition and responsibilities of the Deputies Committee changed to include the deputy assistant for economic policy and the national security adviser to the vice president. In addition, this committee's responsibilities in assigning and overseeing the work of the IWGs were strengthened to the point where it became "the principal daily operating committee of the interagency process" (National Security Council Project 2000).

The Clinton administration's NSC staff mirrored the by-now familiar structure of regional and functional offices that parallel the structure of the State Department, although this bureaucracy of the NSC system was somewhat reorganized to reflect the realities of the post–Cold War world. Initially downsized from the Bush administration, the NSC staff was substantially expanded in the second Clinton term (see Figure 10.3).

Clinton selected Anthony Lake as his first national security adviser. Lake's experience included service on Kissinger's NSC staff and in Carter's State Department. Having witnessed Kissinger and Brzezinski firsthand, Lake was determined on becoming NSA himself to avoid the foreign policy flare-ups and pitfalls each of them experienced. He described his conception of the NSA's task shortly after his selection as making sure that Clinton "gets the wide array of alternatives, the concise information, and the broad range of advice [for decision making] that he requires."

For all its formal coherence, the evidence indicates that the Clinton NSC system did not function well for much of the president's first term. First, Clinton showed little interest in foreign policy issues and even less in formal NSC meetings. Instead, policy was discussed in less structured settings among the administration's foreign policy "principals"—Lake, Secretary of State Warren Christopher, UN Ambassador Madeleine Albright, Secretary of Defense Les Aspin, the director of the CIA, the chairman of the Joint Chiefs of Staff, and, later, the White House chief of staff. (For additional discussion, see Halberstam 2001). Second, Lake

failed to perform the NSA tasks effectively. Administration policies were not clearly articulated, State and Defense officials complained their views were not given a fair hearing with the president, and Lake and Christopher pursued different sets of foreign policy issues in the absence of effective White House coordination and leadership (Pine 1994; Harris 1997b; Helibrunn 1998). Third, the administration's propensity to "adhocracy" helped little. Indeed, the "lines of authority" in the Clinton White House were likened to "a plate of spaghetti: everyone seems to be in charge of everyone so that no one is held accountable, there is little hierarchy, and there are loops of influence and access that collide, coincide, or work in blissful ignorance of one another until some fiasco looms" (Devroy 1994). Last and perhaps most important, Lake did not develop a close, comfortable relationship with the one person with whom such a relationship was critical: Bill Clinton. Consequently, the relationship became strained as the president turned more and more to Sandy Berger, Lake's deputy, for advice (Halberstam 2001). By mid-1994, improvements began. Lake asserted himself more as a central coordinator for foreign policy. The new White House chief of staff, Leon Panetta, brought greater discipline to the process—and to the president himself—forcing regular foreign policy meetings. Deputy National Security Adviser Sandy Berger strengthened the role and activities of the Deputies Committee to instill greater direction to the administration's foreign policy efforts. Vice President Gore assumed an increasingly visible foreign policy role (Devroy and Barr 1995; Sciolino and Purdum 1995). These efforts paid off as President Clinton completed his first term with a series of foreign policy achievements (North Korea, Haiti, trade, the Dayton Accords) that contrasted well with the miscues of the first eighteen months.

With the onset of a second term, Christopher, Lake, and William Perry (Les Aspin's successor at the Pentagon) all departed, to be replaced by Madeleine Albright, the first female secretary of state, Berger, who moved up from Deputy NSA to NSA, and William Cohen, the former maverick Republican Senator from Maine, who took over

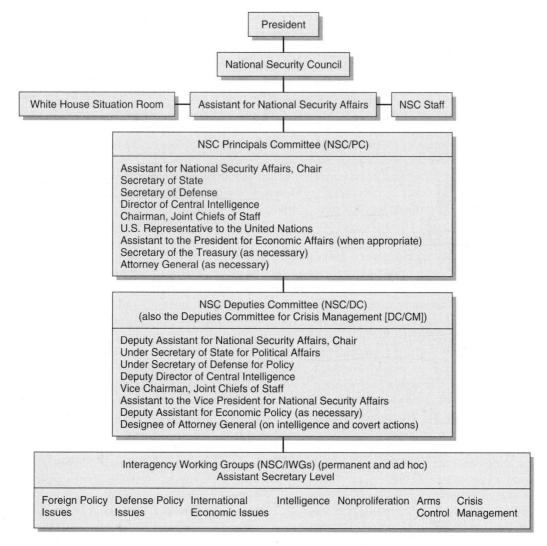

FIGURE 10.3 The Clinton Administration's National Security Council System

NOTES: The White House chief of staff later became a member of the NSC Principals Committee.

SOURCE: Adapted from Presidential Decision Directive (PDD) 2, January 20, 1993.

the defense secretary's position. This *"ABC" club* moved quickly to solidify a more effective NSC system.

While the essential structures remained constant, there were a number of positive changes that helped correct many of the problems of the first term. One major development was simply Clinton's improved discipline and engagement on foreign policy matters. Despite their disagreements on issues related to the use of U.S. military force, as in Bosnia and Kosovo, Albright and Cohen helped to strengthen the NSC system by forming an effective team (with Berger) and generally accepting Berger's strong role (Harris 1997b; Lancaster 2000). According to administration officials, behind the public profiles of Albright and Cohen, Berger soon became "the most influential policy maker on a day-to-day basis" (Harris 1999).

The most significant change, however, was the way in which Berger and his first deputy, James Steinberg, substantially improved the functioning and central coordination of the NSC system. Berger exerted control through his "involvement in virtually every important detail of foreign policy" and by ensuring that the Principals Committee, which he chaired, became a more central locus of decision making than before (Harris 1999; National Security Council Project 2000). At the same time, a strengthened Deputies Committee emerged as the "chief operating committee for American foreign policy" with Steinberg and later his successor, General Donald L. Kerrick, running daily meetings (National Security Council Project 2000). Related to this, the NSC staff itself expanded to over two hundred professionals and nineteen regional and functional offices in order to increase its capacity to coordinate and oversee policy (Patterson 2000).

The rise of Berger and his NSC staff as the locus of foreign policy was accompanied by waning policy influence from the foreign policy bureaucracy, especially the State Department. While Albright began the second term with the highest profile of the foreign policy team, her influence declined dramatically thereafter. Despite her continued visibility on foreign policy issues, her role in policy formulation was much more limited. This diminished role became especially apparent after the Kosovo operations in the spring of 1999 (Perlez 1999; Lancaster 2000). Consequently, another challenge for Berger was to maintain collegial and cooperative relationships with Albright and Cohen even as he asserted himself in foreign policy. Signs of tension, especially between Albright and Berger, were apparent, especially after Kosovo, as Albright was increasingly bypassed in policy making, appearances before the press, interaction with lawmakers, and, eventually, in policy implementation (for example, Harris 1999; Perlez 1999; Lancaster 2000). To control these tensions, Berger took several steps to nurture the "ABC" relationship. In addition to regular meetings of the Principals Committee, Albright, Berger, and Cohen met at least once a week

for lunch together, and held a breakfast meeting with other members of the Principals Committee every week as well. During significant events, they also held "near daily strategy sessions," always at the White House and always chaired by Berger (Harris 1997b; Harris 1999). In addition, the three devised a set of principles to guide their work together and in the public eye; these principles emphasized respect, public solidarity, and open, direct communication (Patterson 2000).

These efforts aided Berger immeasurably to control "the historic antagonism between national security advisers and secretaries of State and Defense" as he consolidated decision making in the White House and placed himself at the center of the NSC system (Harris 1999). The consequence was a smoother, more focused policy-making process based on Clinton's engagement and Berger's management skills and consensus building. To the extent that the President Clinton administration could point to a record of progress at the end of his administration on issues such as peace in the Middle East and Northern Ireland, conflict in the Balkans, engagement with China, revitalizing and enlarging NATO, and other areas, it was in large measure due to the greater competence of the NSC system in his second term.

Bush II Administration   At the start of 2001, the son of the forty-first president assumed the office of the presidency and leaned heavily on his father's foreign policy personnel, first selecting former Secretary of Defense Dick Cheney as his vice president. As his national security adviser, Bush named a member of his father's NSC staff, Condoleezza Rice. A foreign policy adviser to Bush during the 2000 campaign, Rice was reputed to be "a good manager and an honest broker of ideas" (Sciolino 2000). For his secretary of state, Bush selected Colin Powell, former NSA for Reagan and chair of the Joint Chiefs of Staff for Bush and the first year of the Clinton administration. As secretary of defense Bush named Donald Rumsfeld, who had served in that capacity under President Ford.

Unsurprisingly, in National Security Presidential Directive 1 (February 13, 2001), the new

Bush administration structured its foreign policy system along the lines of the first Bush administration. Like Clinton, along with the usual NSC members, Bush also included the secretary of the treasury, U.S. representative to the United Nations, the assistant to the president for economic policy, the chief of staff, and the counsel to the president. Serving this council was the now-traditional three-tiered interagency structure centralized in the White House: a Principals Committee, a Deputies Committee, and a series of eleven regional and functional policy coordinating committees. The president or vice president chairs the NSC meeting, the national security adviser (or his or her deputy) chairs the Principals and Deputies Committees, and different personnel at the assistant secretary rank chair the policy coordinating committees.

Initially, the overall size of the NSC staff was reduced by more than 30 percent (to seventy staffers) and the structure was initially simplified. The Clinton administration practice of having a legislative affairs and communications function in the NSC staff was ended, with both handled by the political staff of the White House (Daalder and Destler 2001). Counterterrorism was also downgraded. Over time, Rice found it necessary to undo all these changes given the demands of the job and a newfound focus on terrorism in the post-9/11 environment. By the end of her four-year tenure, the NSC staff had grown by 50 percent since 2001, a new NSC office for counterterrorism was established to better coordinate U.S. policy efforts, and several new deputy posts had been added, including the first deputy national security adviser for communications (Rothkopf 2005b).

As she assumed her duties, Condoleezza Rice appeared committed to managing the NSC system as a low-key coordinator or honest broker in much the same way her mentor Brent Scowcroft performed his NSA duties in the Bush I White House. Rice described her "insider" role as "working the seams, stitching the connections together tightly . . . providing the glue for many, many agencies and instruments the United States is now deploying around the world" (Daalder and Destler 2001). Increasingly, however, Rice took up a more visible and operational role, including a highly assertive presence in the public arena. Additionally, she played her position just down the hall from the Oval Office into a role that went beyond the "traffic cop" description she initially offered. As one observer noted early in Rice's tenure: "Bush wants his info whittled down to one-page memos, and she writes them; he likes one-person oral briefings, and she provides them. He doesn't want to hear a cacophony of competing voices; she ensures that disputes are resolved before they reach him" (McGeary 2001). Reflecting on her service as national security adviser, another analyst wrote of Rice: "In that vital role, she was closer to the president she served than any of her 16 predecessors. By her own account, she often spent as many as six or seven hours a day at the president's side. But she was also an unofficial member of the Bush family, with her own cabin at Camp David, coming as a regular guest to Sunday dinners, and relaxing with the president and his family on vacations" (Rothkopf 2005a).

However, there is consensus that Rice's standing as the president's most trusted and attentive aide had two serious implications for the Bush NSC system (Woodward 2004; Rothkopf 2005a; Rothkopf 2005b). First, she had less time to coordinate and control the seasoned heavyweights within the foreign policy advisory system. Although generally out of step with his more conservative colleagues in the administration, Powell's stature and bureaucratic acumen ensured him some influence, especially early on in the administration. Rumsfeld was a skilled Washington infighter with a reputation for toughness and a long-standing relationship with Cheney. In fact, the Cheney–Rumsfeld partnership afforded the defense secretary considerable influence given the closeness of their respective staffs and Cheney's integral role within the Bush NSC system. As discussed earlier in the chapter, Cheney maintained his own group of experienced foreign policy advisers, which was akin to a "mini-NSC staff." He also enjoyed greater access and authority on foreign policy than any previous vice president. With the president's blessing and unencumbered by Rice, Cheney became the equivalent of "an 800-pound gorilla" whose ideological views came to dominate meetings and shape a range of post-9/11 issues, most notably war in Iraq (Rothkopf 2005a, Rothkopf 2005b).

Moreover, each man—Powell, Rumsfeld, and Cheney—maintained a direct conduit to the president and showed little hesitation in pleading their case before Bush when they felt it necessary (Woodward 2004). Scowcroft observed, "The guys in the administration are old hands, experienced players, and you can't leave them to their own devices, or they will eat your lunch" (quoted in Rothkopf 2005a). Rice's preoccupation with serving as the president's personal adviser had the effect of bringing limited coordination and balance to the Bush NSC system, thereby enhancing the influence of the most powerful principals.

The other major implication of Rice's NSA leadership style was the emergence of serious tensions that impacted the functioning of the Bush NSC system. First, there was a philosophical rift between those in the administration and foreign policy bureaucracy who were "traditionalists" and favored a foreign policy based on pragmatism and multilateralism and those who were "transformationalists" and advocated a more aggressive, morally motivated foreign policy backed by unilateralism. Members of this latter group were often labeled the *neocons* or **_neoconservatives_** and dominated the staffs of both Cheney and Rumsfeld. Second, this concentration created a rift between bureaucracies given Powell's State Department staff was largely composed of more risk-averse traditionalists. This divide was exacerbated by the perennial tension between the Pentagon and Foggy Bottom over appropriate means for advancing the national interest, force or diplomacy. Not surprisingly, the administration's embrace of a military response after in the post-9/11 era significantly strengthened the position of the Defense Department in this regard. Tension at the staff level was also created by Rumsfeld's Office of the Secretary of Defense (OSD), which manifested blatant disregard for Rice's NSC staff through "repeated disinclination to play by the rules, arriving at meetings unprepared, refusing to discuss or advance issues, and working through back channels." According to

one NSC staffer, they were "just out of control, an endless nightmare" (Rothkopf 2005a).

The third and final rift was at the upper echelon of the administration with the secretaries of defense and state as the principal antagonists. From the onset of the administration, Rumsfeld, supported by Cheney and either backed or unobstructed by Rice, consistently pressed for firmer, often more unilateralist positions on a host of issues, from whether to sign on to various international treaties to North Korea to the Middle East peace process. While the September 11 attacks dampened the disputes, it did not eliminate them entirely and the march to war in Iraq in 2002 and 2003 only intensified the fissures. Disagreements surfaced over prewar intelligence, the war plan, strained relations with U.S. allies, whether to take the case for disarming Iraq to the United Nations, and, later, postwar reconstruction in Iraq. In most instances, Rumsfeld, allied with Cheney, prevailed over Powell in shaping the administration's foreign policy. One observer suggested early on that George W. Bush's NSC principals (supported by their deputies and staffers) resembled a hybrid of his father's and Ronald Reagan's: a collegial group (like the first Bush administration) divided into moderate and hard-line factions (like Reagan's) (Perlez 2001). By the end of Bush's first term, the hard-liners had prevailed, with Rice leaving her NSA position to become secretary of state following the resignation of a beleaguered Powell (discussed more in Chapter 11).

In sum, the challenges facing Rice as the NSA formally tasked with running the system were substantial. An assertive vice president, an experienced secretary of defense, and a high-profile secretary of state challenged her ability to control and coordinate foreign policy. Philosophical and bureaucratic rivalries between these advisers, their staffs, and institutions constituted formidable obstacles for an effective system. However, Richard Armitage, deputy secretary of state during Rice's tenure as NSA, blamed a "dysfunctional NSC system," in which there was too little policy debate and coordination, on Rice's inability "to be a good, knock-down-drag-out fighter . . . and enforce discipline"

(Woodward 2004). Certainly, Rice's strong emphasis on being a personal adviser to the president was a major contributing factor to her inability to act as an effective facilitator and mediator within the Bush foreign policy-making process. However, experienced observers of the NSC system also attribute Rice's problems to the fact that she was "the most publicly visible holder of [the] office since Henry Kissinger." Her public activity included frequent media appearances and overseas diplomatic missions as well as several speeches on behalf of the president's foreign policy during the 2004 campaign season. "Time spent preparing for and engaging in public activity is time not spent on the job only the national security adviser can do—managing the process by which effective foreign policy is made. This function is particularly critical when an administration is internally divided" (Daalder and Destler 2004).

Stephen J. Hadley became George W. Bush's second national security adviser as the president began his second term in 2005. A lawyer by training, Hadley brought considerable experience to the position. Before serving as a foreign policy adviser to the Bush 2000 campaign and Rice's deputy director, he served as a defense analyst in the Nixon administration, an NSC staffer in the Ford administration, and an assistant secretary of defense in the Bush I administration. He also assisted the Tower Commission (discussed earlier) during the Reagan administration. However, Hadley did not assume his NSA job with an unblemished record. With Rice consumed by her presidential advisory duties, most of the daily management of the problem-plagued NSC fell to him. In addition, Hadley and Rice were responsible for the fact that terrorism was not a focal point of Bush's NSC before the September 11, 2001, attacks (Clarke 2004; Rothkopf 2005b). In fact, the "[9/11] Commission report was critical of Hadley's handling of policy development in several areas. Hadley was also thrust into an uncomfortable spotlight when he accepted blame in 2003 for allowing faulty intelligence [regarding a supposed attempt by Iraq to obtain uranium in Africa] to appear in the president's State of the Union address" (Kessler 2004b).

Notwithstanding such issues, Hadley sustained his long-standing reputation for being very bright, a workaholic, and attentive to detail (Ignatius 2005). As he assumed his new post in January 2005, Hadley was "very much inclined to be a dependable, thoughtful, and mostly behind-the-scenes national security advisor in the mold of his former colleague Brent Scowcroft" (Rothkopf 2005b). Unlike Rice, who seemed to possess the same initial predilection but soon gravitated, Hadley followed through during his first year and a half on the job. He downplayed the role of personal adviser to the president, appeared infrequently before the media, and avoided overseas diplomatic activity. Instead his focus was concentrated on the "inside management" tasks (see Focus 10.2). As a result, he earned "high marks for improving interagency coordination" (Rothkopf 2006). In fairness to Rice, however, Hadley had the benefit of operating in a different environment with a more experienced and confident president, a less influential vice president and secretary of defense (post-Iraq invasion), and an excellent working relationship with the secretary of state. Based on his early service as NSA, some observers worried Hadley was perhaps too low profile and too inclined to defer foreign policy leadership to Rice. What was interesting, however, is some of this concern emanated from the State Department (see Rothkopf 2006), whose foreign policy influence has declined dramatically in the face of the National Security Council's six-decade ascendancy. Clearly, this is recognition that a strong, well-functioning NSC with an effective national security adviser is essential to the success of all actors within a modern, presidentially centered foreign policy process.

Summary: Presidential Leadership and the NSC System As the preceding review suggests, the evolving NSC system has become the central structure for presidential leadership in U.S. foreign policy making. In fact, Rothkopf (2005a) asserts it "is probably the most powerful committee in the history of the world, one with more resources, more power, more license to act, and more ability to project force further and swifter than any other convened by king, emperor, or president." Based on the preceding discussion, several noteworthy patterns stand out. First, the NSC system is very much a creature of presidential preference. Over time, it has been tailored and personalized to individual styles and needs, reflecting its central role as an extension of presidential authority over the foreign policy bureaucracy. As Colin Powell has explained, "At the end of the day, the duty of the National Security Council staff and the [NSA] is to mold themselves to the personality of the president. And that is why it has to remain a flexible organization with no statutory organization or devices in it. . . . The NSC has to mold itself to the will and desire and feelings of the president. . . . [I]f he's satisfied, that's all that counts" (National Security Council Project 1999b). At the same time, the development suggests that the system works best with an attentive president who is engaged in the process. As former NSA Brent Scowcroft observed, "The NSC system was really developed to serve an activist president in foreign policy. . . . I don't know that the system works all that well when you don't have the president there all the time, because by himself the national security adviser can't really do it" (National Security Council Project 1999b).

Additionally, the NSC system has grown substantially as a White House institution, especially through the evolution of the NSC staff into the president's personal foreign policy advisers and coordinators. From its early days as a little-used advisory board with a tiny staff to handle paperwork, an NSC bureaucracy has evolved to serve the needs of presidential decision making and policy coordination. Far from the collection of cabinet officials that originally comprised the NSC, the system that evolved instead relies on the national security adviser and a professional staff to manage a complex interagency process. Despite some inclinations to the contrary (for example, Reagan and Carter), this personal State Department has become the core of foreign policy making in every administration since Johnson. Indeed, two experienced observers recently suggested that "the NSC has become more like an agency than a presidential staff," to the detriment of both (Daalder and Destler 2000).

As the role of the NSA and NSC staff has grown with the development of the NSC system, a number of tensions have arisen that have required attention. Most notable of these are the persistent rivalries among key members, including those between the NSA and the secretary of state and between the NSC staff and the State Department. Although the NSC was established in part to manage the rivalries between departments and agencies, it has fueled these new tensions. Reflecting on the development of the NSC since the 1950s, Frank Carlucci asserted, "These tensions between the national security adviser and the secretary [of] state seem to run through every administration" (National Security Council Project 1999b).

Those tensions bring us back to the issue of the role of the NSA. As suggested earlier, a kind of consensus has developed over the preferred nature of that role (see Focus 10.2), but it is still hard to implement. A gathering of former national security advisers confirmed the consensus, stressing the need for a low-profile honest broker committed to the process first and to advising second, and out of the business of operational activities. According to Scowcroft, "My sense is that in order for the system to work, you first have to establish yourself in the confidence of your colleagues to convince them you are not going to pull fast ones on them. That means when you are in there with the president alone, which you are more than anybody else, that you will represent them fairly. . . . And after you have done that, then you are free to be an adviser" (National Security Council Project 1999b). A former NSC staff member from the first Bush administration put it this way: "The NSA has to have two hats. . . . [T]he first has to be the management hat, and everyone has to feel the process is legitimate. . . . His first responsibility has got to be the whole. But he can still have his own voice so long as everyone around there has confidence that he doesn't get so persuaded by his own voice that he's no longer a legitimate broker" (National Security Council Project 1999a). Easier said than done, if history is any guide.

The evolution of the NSC system suggests a kind of pendulum of reactions as succeeding administrations responded to the problems, strengths, and weaknesses of the systems utilized by their predecessors. Inexorably, it seems, these pendulum swings zeroed in on the need for a White House–centered approach to ensure presidential foreign policy leadership, the need for a strong but collegial national security adviser to manage the process and act as honest broker, and the need for presidential attention and engagement. The NSC itself today bears little resemblance to its ancestry. "Today most people asked about the NSC would think of the national security *adviser* and his small *staff* in the West Wing and Old Executive Office Building. In Ike's day the NSC was the president in council or, at a minimum, a reference to the NSC principals—the vice president and the secretaries of state and defense" (Prados 1991). What today is better conceived as the *National Security Council system* is nonetheless critically important. How to make both the council and the assistant for national security affairs most effective is now the issue, as neither the wisdom nor determination of presidents to exercise control over American foreign policy from the White House is any longer in question.

Other Executive Office Functions: Managing Economic Affairs

Before leaving the presidential subsystem, mention should be made of other units within the Executive Office which, along with the NSC, are at the immediate disposal of the president and thus contribute to presidential leadership in foreign policy making. Principal among them are the offices and personnel responsible for budgetary, economic, and homeland security decision making.

Managing the Budget   The largest, with more than 500 staff members (as of 2004), is the *Office of Management and Budget* (OMB). OMB has responsibility for reviewing budgetary and other legislative requests coming from departments and agencies and for examining legislation passed by Congress before it is signed into law by the president. It also assists in devising plans for the organization and management

of executive branch functions. Those tasks assign the OMB a potentially critical voice in ensuring that agencies' plans and programs are consistent with presidential priorities. Different presidents have employed different budgetary and management techniques to realize their objectives. In the early 1960s, after Robert McNamara introduced the Planning, Programming, and Budgeting System (PPBS) into the Defense Department, Lyndon Johnson ordered that PPBS be applied throughout the government as a procedure for making more-informed budgetary choices. President Nixon emphasized "management by objectives." The approach entailed assigning priorities to competing objectives and choosing some programs over others. As concern for restraining public spending mounted, Jimmy Carter implemented zero-based budgeting (ZBB), which required that each program be justified anew each year. It did not prove effective, however, in stemming the flow of public spending.

Fueled in part by the priority the Reagan administration gave to rebuilding the nation's defensive posture, budget deficits by the mid-1980s topped $200 billion annually. As the OMB attempted to cope with the deficit, it found that the largest item in the budget—national defense—involved other players with a stronger suit. Rather than challenge a steamroller, the politically wise strategy was to trim at the margins rather than launch a frontal attack. The result, however, is that the OMB was notably less effective in imposing a presidential imprimatur on the nation's foreign policy spending priorities during the 1980s than might have been expected.

As George H. W. Bush moved into the Oval Office, the government's flow of red ink was too great to ignore. Despite a "no new taxes" campaign pledge, Bush found it necessary to reach a politically contentious (and eventually costly) budget agreement with Congress. Designed to curb federal spending, it exposed defense as well as social programs to the budgetary ax. Bush's controversial OMB director, Richard G. Darman, often found himself in the unenviable position of the messenger people wanted to kill.

During the Clinton administration, the OMB was directed first by Leon E. Panetta, and then by Alice M. Rivlin, Panetta's deputy until 1994 when the former congressman became Clinton's chief of staff. Jacob J. Lew, Rivlin's deputy, succeeded her as director in May 1998. These directors became leading advocates of strict budgetary discipline in an administration that promised budget reductions but found them difficult (see Woodward 1994). Meanwhile, the "management" side of the OMB, already a low priority, was dealt twin blows as proposed reforms of the office promised to merge its dual functions into one and as Vice President Al Gore's "reinventing government" initiative promised dramatic reductions in the size of the federal bureaucracy. "Total Quality Management" (TQM) became the core concept in this latest effort to reform management practices in the federal government (see also Chapter 13).

Under George W. Bush, the OMB was led first by Mitchell Daniels, and then by Joshua Bolten. Former United States Trade Representative Robert Portman became OMB director when Bolten assumed the position of White House chief of staff in 2006. These directors presided over an OMB with a role in all budget, policy, legislative, regulatory, procurement, and management issues. However, they also faced a challenging fiscal environment. For instance, Bolten reduced discretionary spending in two consecutive budgets, but oversaw the three largest federal deficits in U.S. history, including a record $413 billion in 2004. The wars in Afghanistan and Iraq, new homeland security spending, an expensive Medicare prescription drug benefit, and the recovery from Hurricane Katrina contributed significantly to these annual shortfalls. Overall, the size of the federal budget coupled with the continuing demand for new expenditures and low taxes ensure that OMB will remain a critical player in the presidential subsystem in the years ahead.

Managing Economic Policy   Over time, economics has become a more central element of U.S. foreign policy. The White House has turned to several different components of the presidential subsystem to formulate and coordinate economic policy.

The Council of Economic Advisers   To assist in the economics of economic policy making, the president has relied on the Council of Economic Advisers (CEA). Together with officials from the OMB and the Treasury Department, the council makes economic forecasts on which the income and expenditures of the federal government are based. It has no operational responsibilities. Instead, it serves exclusively in an advisory capacity to the president (Porter 1983). The council itself comprises three presidential appointees, usually drawn from the ranks of the most respected academic economists. The council's chairperson becomes the administration's senior economist and is responsible for establishing the positions the council takes. One of two remaining members is typically assigned international responsibilities.

Created in 1946 with an eye toward short-run economic stabilization, today the CEA advises the president on the entire range of domestic and foreign economic policy issues; the value of the dollar and the U.S. trade balance are among them. The council also plays a role in managing the delicate relationship between the president and the Federal Reserve Board, an independent federal agency with broad powers over monetary policy (Feldstein 1992; Solomon 1994). As we saw in Chapter 7, monetary policy exerts a direct impact on the dollar and trade balance. Channels of influence available to the CEA include face-to-face meetings between the president and the chair of the council, interaction with the secretary of the treasury and other senior personnel, membership on the National Economic Council, involvement of the CEA members and its staff in interagency groups, testimony before Congress, and public commentary (Feldstein 1992). The CEA also prepares the influential *Economic Report of the President,* presented annually to Congress, which is widely used inside and outside of government.

The Office of the United States Trade Representative   For assistance in trade policy, presidents have relied on the Office of the United States Trade Representative. Headed by a presidential appointee who carries the rank of ambassador as well as membership in the cabinet, the **U.S. Trade Representative (USTR)** exercises primary responsibility for developing and coordinating the implementation of international trade policy and acting as the principal trade spokesperson for the U.S. government. The office directs American participation in trade negotiations with other states, including bilateral talks, such as the Structural Impediments Initiative with Japan, and multilateral ventures, such as the Uruguay Round of GATT negotiations concluded in 1993.

The trade representative originated in the Kennedy administration as the Special Trade Representative. The USTR achieved cabinet status during the Ford administration, when it wrested control over multilateral trade affairs from the State Department, and the office became a major player in multilateral negotiations during the Carter administration. A subsequent reorganization of the trade office in 1980 gave the USTR a greater voice among the many government agencies involved in determining overall American trade policy. President Reagan pledged that his trade representative would continue to play a dominant role in orchestrating the nation's trade policies. Growing trade deficits led to efforts to negotiate voluntary export restrictions (VERs) covering particular products with Japan and others in an effort to ameliorate the adverse effects of the strong dollar (see Chapter 7). Although Reagan had announced his trade representative would play the dominant role in orchestrating U.S. trade policy, in practice the USTR proved too weak to do anything more than negotiate market-sharing agreements with others. Instead, benign neglect characterized the administration's general approach to trade policy.

Congress became increasingly agitated with Reagan's unwillingness to take corrective action to deal with the nation's burgeoning trade deficit and passed the Omnibus Trade and Competitiveness Act of 1988. The new trade law contained no radical new departures from existing U.S. trade policy, despite many highly protectionist measures figuring prominently in the deliberations during its long gestation period. The *Super 301* provision was perhaps the exception. As noted in Chapter 7, Super 301 required the president to identify countries engaged in unfair trade practices and negotiate

remedies with them. The USTR was charged with that responsibility, effectively solidifying the office's role as the government's principal trade policy actor in a way not previously done.

Since the first Bush administration was uncomfortable with the confrontational, unilateralist thrust of Super 301 and did little to push it, Bush's USTR (Carla A. Hills) fared little better than Reagan's (Clayton Yeutter) in devising a government-wide response to the trade challenges the United States faced. However, "rather than leading trade policy, a bureaucratically weak and directionless USTR . . . often [became] a victim of the political pressures around it." That "reactive stance" often led to "bad trade policy" in which "U.S. interests . . . suffered" (Stokes 1992–1993).

Given President Clinton's emphasis on economic policy, both domestic and foreign, trade policy was destined to be an administration priority. Clinton named Mickey Kantor, a California attorney skilled in regulatory problems and chair of the Clinton-Gore 1992 campaign, as his trade representative. Kantor quickly assumed a high profile role in a series of contentious trade issues involving the European Union, NAFTA, the Uruguay Round, and Japan. His brusque personal style and aggressive policy postures offended some both within the United States and abroad, but he had a reputation for loyalty to the president and reflected the administration's preference for a posture of assertive unilateralism on trade issues. Kantor was replaced in 1996 with longtime USTR staff member Charlene Barshevsky. Under Barshevsky's leadership, the office of the USTR pursued a similar direction in bilateral trade relations with Japan, Europe, and others. Barshevsky was also a principal proponent of and decision maker in the efforts to extend U.S.-Chinese trade relations. She played a pivotal roles in engineering the Permanent Normal Trade Relations agreement with China in 1999, selling it to the U.S. Congress in 2000, and negotiating China's entry into the World Trade Organization.

George W. Bush turned to Robert Zoellick for the USTR position. Zoellick served in various positions within President Reagan's Treasury Department and as an under secretary of state and

White House deputy chief of staff. Reputed to be a "master strategist and policy analyst" (Blustein 2001), Zoellick devoted his early attention to securing **trade promotion authority (TPA)** (formerly known as "fast-track authority") from Congress. With the Trade Act of 2002, Congress granted President Bush the power to negotiate trade agreements, subject to consultation with Congress, after which lawmakers agree to vote accords up or down without amendments. With this new authority, Zoellick took the lead in concluding the 2005 Central America-Dominican Republic-United States Free Trade Agreement (CAFTA-DR) as well as several bilateral free trade agreements (FTAs). Reaching bilateral and regional FTAs became the Bush administration's central free trade strategy given developing states' opposition to the U.S. trade agenda within the World Trade Organization's Doha Round. When Zoellick became deputy secretary of state in 2005, Representative Robert Portman (R-Ohio) succeeded him. Portman was on the job little more than a year before he was asked to head the Office of Management and Budget. Deputy USTR Susan Schwab was named as his replacement.

The National Economic Council   Different presidents have devised different means to seek top level coordination of foreign economic policy making (see Cohen 1994). President Clinton's major innovation was the **National Economic Council (NEC),** created by executive order as the economic policy counterpart to the National Security Council. Creation of the council symbolized Clinton's determination to show that economic policy would be at least equal in importance to national security policy during his administration.

The NEC built on efforts by previous presidents. Twenty years earlier President Nixon had launched a Council on International Economic Policy in an unsuccessful effort to centralize control over foreign economic policy making. Ford created an Economic Policy Board, chaired by the secretary of the treasury, whose purpose was to oversee the entire range of foreign and domestic economic policy. Carter followed with a similarly structured

Economic Policy Group, but eventually relied on a special presidential representative to facilitate policy coordination. During the Reagan administration, the Cabinet Council on Economic Affairs was given responsibility over economic policy, and the administration's NSC apparatus eventually contained a Senior Interagency Group for International Economic Policy. The Bush I administration adopted similar practices. Clinton's National Economic Council was therefore simply the most ambitious mechanism for top-level coordination of foreign economic policy making. Like the National Security Council, the National Economic Council was intended to coordinate the cabinet departments and agencies with interests and responsibilities in economic policy, to advise the president on economic policy decisions, and to monitor their implementation. To accomplish these tasks, the NEC relied on a staff of about thirty to manage its responsibilities in both the domestic and foreign economic policy arenas. Moreover, since the assistant and deputy assistant had roles on the NSC's Principals Committee and Deputies Committee, the NEC and NSC staff cooperated. In fact, to facilitate that cooperation, Robert E. Rubin, national economic adviser and director of the NEC, and then–national security adviser Anthony Lake agreed to share staff for international economic matters, who would then report to both men (Destler 1996). Also, like Lake, Rubin viewed his role as an honest broker in representing the views of executive branch departments and agencies in White House decision making.

During Clinton's first term, the NEC was central to several foreign economic policy issues, including the North American Free Trade Agreement (NAFTA) in 1993 and the completion of the Uruguay Round in 1994. After initially taking a back seat to the State Department on China and its most-favored-nation (MFN) status in 1993, the NEC assumed a central role in 1994. It was also key in U.S.-Japan relations in this period.

When Rubin moved on to take up the position of secretary of the treasury in 1995, he was succeeded by Laura D'Andrea Tyson, former chair of the Council of Economic Advisers. Tyson, however, enjoyed far less success. A slow transition and several months of suspended meetings forced the NEC out if its modest role into the background. In the breach, other offices stepped forward to handle such crises as the Mexican peso collapse in late 1994. Moreover, Rubin continued to assert himself on international economic matters from his new position, making Tyson's role even more difficult. By most accounts, the NEC simply receded into the background until Tyson managed to carve out a role on trade issues in mid-1996 (Destler 1996).

When Tyson stepped down, Gene Sperling, her deputy, took over. Most observers expected the NEC role to again decline, but instead, Sperling helped solidify its place on matters of both domestic and international policy. For instance, Sperling and the NEC were the central coordinators for the U.S. response to the Asian financial crises of 1997–1998, working closely with Treasury Secretary Bob Rubin. Additionally, Sperling worked closely with USTR Charlene Barshevsky on the China–WTO Permanent Normal Trade Relations agreements in 1999–2000. Along with these contributions, Sperling's NEC was the locus of the administration's efforts on the budget and overall economic policy in the second term as well.

The prominence of Clinton's NEC was in part a function of Clinton's own preferences and priorities. For Clinton, "the interplay between trade, technology, educational training, economics and jobs [seemed to engage him] intellectually and animate him politically" (Friedman 1994b). Still, the rapid globalization of the world political economy, which Clinton's policies encouraged, has elevated the importance of economic issues and blurred the distinction between foreign and domestic economic policy. Today, more departments and agencies with important domestic roots and often powerful congressional allies have a greater stake in international economic policy. Clinton sought to give clear and consistent direction on economic issues from the White House, thus managing interagency politics that otherwise would dominate the process and the outcome.

George W. Bush found the same imperative when he assumed the office of the presidency. He retained the NEC and named Lawrence Lindsay, former member of Reagan's Council of Economic Advisers and George H. W. Bush's White House policy staff, as assistant to the president for economic policy. Additionally, he established a new deputy national security adviser for international economic policy to coordinate with the NEC. Under Lindsay, while keeping a low profile, the NEC for the Bush administration coordinated economic policy making on domestic and international issues and monitored economic policy implementation to ensure its consistency with the White House agenda. For example, after the September 11, 2001, attacks on the United States, Lindsay played the key role in monitoring the impact of the attacks on the U.S. economy and recommending responses to the problems faced by New York City and a number of industries. A year later, he was forced out in a shake-up of the president's economic team. Besides being held accountable for an underperforming economy, Lindsay lost favor within the administration for publicly stating a "war with Iraq and its aftermath could cost between $100 and $200 billion" (Raum 2005). Lindsay's successors, Stephen Friedman (2002–2005) and Allan Hubbard (2005–present) labored quietly behind the scenes, often dealing more with domestic economic issues than foreign economic policy. As an increasingly military-centric foreign policy took center stage, one observer noted that "by the beginning of the second term of the Bush administration, the once powerful NEC had become all but invisible (Rothkopf 2005b).

Managing Homeland Security

The newest component of the presidential subsystem emerged just weeks after the September 11, 2001, terrorist attacks on the United States. An executive order issued by President George W. Bush on October 8, 2001, established the Homeland Security Council (HSC). A subsequent presidential directive later that same month set forth its structure and operation. Just as the National Economic Council (NEC) in 1993 was a reflection of prevailing domestic and international realities and President Clinton's economic-centric agenda, the

HSC was a direct response to a new national security threat and a chief executive with post-9/11 priorities. Moreover, like the NEC, the HSC was also developed to mirror the National Security Council (NSC) and bring together the major agencies and other stakeholders to manage the development and implementation of homeland security policies. Specifically, the **Homeland Security Council** "is responsible for advising and assisting the President with respect to all aspects of homeland security." It is also the principal "mechanism for ensuring the coordination of homeland security-related activities of executive departments and agencies and effective development and implementation of homeland security policies" (Executive Order 13228, 2001). Similar to the NSC, HSC meetings are chaired by the president. The other permanent members of the council are the vice president, secretary of homeland security, secretary of defense, secretary of treasury, secretary of health and human services, secretary of transportation, the attorney general, the director of national intelligence, the director of the Federal Bureau of Investigation, and the assistant to the president for homeland security and counterterrorism. The national security adviser, chairman of the Joint Chiefs of Staff, the chiefs of staff to the president and vice president, White House counsel, and the director of the Office of Management Budget (OMB) are invited to attend any HSC session. Other officials may be invited to particular meetings given the particular matter under consideration.

Again, like the NSC, the HSC is supported by a staff, which in 2006 numbered about thirty-five. The assistant to the president for homeland security and counterterrorism supervises it with the help of a deputy and six special assistants. The assistants oversee specific policy areas, including border and transportation and security, chemical and biological defense, continuity of government, emergency preparedness and response, prevention strategy, and nuclear defense. There is also an interagency process structured around eleven HSC policy coordination committees (HSC/PCCs). Each committee, which is focused on one functional policy area related to homeland security (such as medical and public

health preparedness, to cite one example), brings together officials from different departments and agencies. These committees constitute the main conduit for daily coordination of homeland security policy. While antiterrorism is a central focus, the scope of HSC attention and activity is much broader. Recently, for example, it has included a review of emergency planning after Hurricane Katrina and influenza pandemic planning between states and the federal government.

PRESIDENTIAL PREEMINENCE IN THE TWENTY-FIRST CENTURY

The president and the presidency are central to U.S. foreign policy making. No other governmental source of foreign policy has the combination of stature, resources, authority, and opportunity. But will the presumption of presidential preeminence with which we began this chapter persist into the new century?

There are good reasons to expect continued foreign policy dominance by the president. As suggested at the outset of this chapter, the broad powers and opportunities granted to the chief executive will continue to allow the president to act on constitutional roles as chief executive, commander-in-chief, and chief diplomat, and the less formal, but still vital roles of chief communicator, chief legislator, and, perhaps, chief lobbyist. Together these will provide occasion for presidents' efforts to forge foreign policy. Furthermore, regardless of the occupant of the position, the president is likely to play a vital role in foreign policy agenda setting—the process of identifying problems, setting priorities, and the like. As our review of the NSC system indicates, ordering policy reviews, requiring the development of options on one issue and not another, and assigning responsibilities to certain executive branch structures and agencies rather than others give the president the capability to influence heavily the "list of subjects or problems to which government officials, and people outside of government closely associated with those officials, are paying some serious attention at any given time" (Kingdon 1995). Although other players can influence the agenda, if the president chooses to address an issue, others must as well. Just as clearly, presidential command of the foreign policy departments, agencies, and personnel, along with the continued importance of the United States in the international system, provide the White House with the ability to initiate action. Although this is closely related to the agenda-setting power possessed by the White House, this capability to take action enables the White House to force other players to respond, and constitutes another source of presidential preeminence not likely to disappear in the twenty-first century. George W. Bush's leadership in response to the September 11 attacks nicely illustrates this capacity.

Some would argue that the fundamental nature of the international system itself supports continued presidential preeminence in the twenty-first century. According to this view, the rise of presidential-centered foreign policy making occurred in response to demands, foreign and domestic, to which the other branches of government, notably Congress, could not respond adequately. That was most emphatically true in the foreign policy domain—and it remains so. The reasons inhere in the nature of the international system, the central element in the theory of political realism evident in American foreign policy thinking since its founding, but especially so since World War II, during which presidential government and the imperial presidency became the operative norms (and constitutional challenges). As one analyst argued:

> The role played by the executive in foreign affairs . . . is rooted in the requirements imposed on the nation-state by the potentially anarchic quality of the international system. . . . Policy takes precedence over politics because the international system both severely limits the sensible choices a country can make and shapes the processes by which these decisions are reached.
>
> *(Peterson 1994, 231–232)*

According to this logic, the very structure of the international system may alter the agenda of American politics and priorities, but it will not alter the responsibility of the president to respond to the challenges and opportunities posed by the external environment. Again the changed international context after September 11 supports this observation.

There are, however, other aspects of the policy-making environment that would seem to limit presidential preeminence, or at least generate challenges to it. Given the fundamentally fragmented nature of power in the American political system (that is, the governmental sources), one could also argue that the ability of the president to lead during the past years depended as much on policy agreement among the different actors as anything else. Hence, during the first two decades of the Cold War, the fundamental agreement embodied in the Cold War foreign policy consensus generated a much greater tendency toward executive branch (especially White House) foreign policy leadership in the making of U.S. foreign policy than previously had been the case. Similarly, the return of the imperial presidency in the post–9/11 era is largely a product of elite and mass consensus concerning a recognizable national security threat, which in turn has afforded the chief executive considerable latitude. However, is this consensus sustainable over the long term? What if the threat level within the global environment were to diminish? What will be the cumulative effect of a lame-duck president and a Democratic-controlled Congress during the final two years of the Bush administration? Will the same deference the president has enjoyed since 9/11 continue, particularly as the public becomes increasingly concerned over the situation in Iraq? Moreover, will a new chief executive, perhaps one who is less willing or capable of asserting executive prerogative than George W. Bush, carry on the imperial presidency? The Vietnam experience destroyed much of the Cold War consensus, and the ensuing policy disagreements largely ended the so-called "era of bipartisanship," making presidential leadership more difficult (see Melanson 2005). Such a pattern could easily emerge and pose significant challenges to presidential preeminence in the years ahead.

Finally, our discussion of the past sixty years or so of White House efforts to exercise foreign policy leadership suggests that other variables will condition the effectiveness of that leadership. Our review of the evolution of the NSC system drives the conclusion that part of the president's ability to lead depends first on establishing and using structures that allow leadership. Moreover, presidential leadership also depends on staffing those structures with the right people. Selection of appointees and staff, decision and advisory structures, management of time and information, and other aspects related to the management of the executive branch obviously matter. The record of the past six decades suggests that not every president succeeds in these areas; failure to do so inhibits leadership opportunities. Beyond structure and personnel, personality, style, attentiveness, interest, initiative, and other varying personal characteristics produce different results in the exercise of presidential leadership. (We address presidents' individual characteristics in greater detail in Chapter 14). Our review of the NSC systems indicates that presidents must be engaged, attentive, and informed to exercise leadership. Indeed, our review may even suggest that no system will work *unless* the president is involved.

Factors related to the policy context or situation will also impact presidential leadership. For example, crisis situations tend to activate presidential preeminence, while noncrisis situations tend to involve a broader set of policy actors. It is also widely agreed that intermestic issues are considerably less subject to presidential leadership, prompting instead the involvement of Congress, interest groups, and others. Moreover, variation in policy issue—from military force to aid to trade to intelligence to others—also prompts changing patterns of role and influence, while different policy instruments also generate similar shifts. Finally, as suggested by Chapter 8, and variation in public opinion, involvement of interest groups, and the media—all of which can stem from the international environment, policy context, and other sources—can also affect the president's ability to lead and dominate.

In sum, presidential preeminence in twenty-first century foreign policy is not a foregone conclusion. Certainly, continued and direct White House involvement in foreign policy is now a permanent feature of the governmental structures responsible for making and executing American foreign policy. Yet, just as the last century witnessed considerable shifts in foreign policy leadership, from decade to decade, administration to administration, and issue to issue, so too might we expect foreign policy to emerge in a similar fashion in the twenty-first century.

KEY TERMS

adhocracy
cabinet
chief of staff
doctrine of political questions
Homeland Security Council

honest broker
imperial presidency
interagency processes
national security adviser
National Economic Council (NEC)

National Security Council
neoconservatives
presidential preeminence
presidential subsystem

trade promotion authority
U.S. Trade Representative (USTR)
vice president

SUGGESTED READINGS

Bock, Joseph G. *The White House Staff and the National Security Assistant: Friendship and Friction at the Water's Edge.* New York: Greenwood, 1987.

Daalder, Ivo H., and James M. Lindsay. *America Unbound: The Bush Revolution in Foreign Policy.* Washington, DC: Brookings Institution Press, 2003.

Edwards, George C. III, and Stephen J. Wayne. *Presidential Leadership: Politics and Policymaking*, 7th ed. Belmont, CA: Wadsworth/Thomson Learning, 2005.

George, Alexander L. *Presidential Decisionmaking in Foreign Policy: The Effective Use of Information and Advice.* Boulder, CO: Westview, 1980.

Greenstein, Fred I. *The Presidential Difference: Leadership Style from FDR to George W. Bush*, 2nd ed. Princeton, NJ: Princeton University Press, 2004.

Gregg, Gary L., and Mark J. Rozell, eds. *Considering the Bush Presidency.* New York: Oxford University Press USA, 2003.

Hastedt, Glenn P., and Anthony J. Eksterowicz, eds. *The President and Foreign Policy: Chief Architect or General Contractor?* Hauppauge, NY: Nova Publishers, 2005.

Inderfurth, Karl F., and Loch K. Johnson, eds. *Fateful Decisions: Inside the National Security Council.* Oxford: Oxford University Press, 2004.

Koh, Harold H. *The National Security Constitution: Sharing Power after the Iran-Contra Affair.* New Haven, CT: Yale University Press, 1990.

Melanson, Richard A. *American Foreign Policy since the Vietnam War: The Search for Consensus from Richard Nixon to George W. Bush*, 4th ed. Armonk, NY: M. E. Sharpe, 2005.

Neustadt, Richard E. *Presidential Power and the Modern Presidents: The Politics of Leadership from Roosevelt to Reagan.* New York: Free Press, 1990.

Preston, Thomas. *The President and His Inner Circle: Leadership Style and the Advisory Process in Foreign Policy Making.* New York: Columbia University Press, 2001.

Rothkopf, David J. *Running the World: The Inside Story of the National Security Council and the Architects of American Power.* New York: PublicAffairs, 2005.

Schlesinger, Arthur M., Jr. *The Imperial Presidency.* New York: First Mariner Books/Houghton Mifflin, 2004.

Shoemaker, Christopher C. *The NSC Staff: Counseling the Council.* Boulder, CO: Westview, 1992.

Strong, Robert A. *Decisions and Dilemmas: Case Studies in Presidential Foreign Policy Making Since 1945*, 2nd ed. Armonk, NY: M. E. Sharpe, 2005.

Woodward, Bob. *Bush at War.* New York: Simon & Schuster, 2002.

———. *Plan of Attack.* New York: Simon & Schuster, 2004.

———. *State of Denial: Bush at War, Part III.* New York: Simon and Schuster, 2006.

NOTES

1. For further discussion, see Fisher (2006).

2. Because we discussed interest groups, the general public, and the mass media in Chapters 8 and 9, attention in Chapter 12 to Hilsman's outermost concentric circle will be confined to Congress.

3. Schlesinger (1989a) observes that the framers of the Constitution saw designation of the president as commander-in-chief "as conferring a merely ministerial function, not as creating an independent and additional source of executive authority." As we will see in Chapter 12, this presidential power has figured prominently in the executive-legislative dispute over war powers, especially since the Vietnam War.

4. On constitutional issues, see J. Smith (1989), Henkin (1990), Koh (1990), and Fisher (1991).

5. *Crockett v. Reagan,* 558 F. Supp. 893 (D.D.C. 1982).

6. *Lowry v. Reagan,* 676 F. Supp. 333 (D.D.C. 1987).

7. *Dellums v. Bush,* 752 F. Supp. 1141 (D.D.C. 1990).

8. Vice President Dick Cheney's chief of staff, I. Lewis "Scooter" Libby, was indicted in October 2005 on five counts of perjury. The charge was in connection to an investigation regarding his role in leaking the name of a CIA operative to journalists. The CIA agent was Valerie Plame, the wife of retired diplomat Joseph Wilson, who criticized the Bush administration's rationale for going to war with Iraq in 2003.

9. George (1980) identifies three key personality variables that affect a president's decision making and management style: cognitive style, personal

sense of efficacy and competence, and orientation toward political conflict. Generally, these factors lead presidents to select one of three approaches. In the competitive model, the president purposely seeks to promote conflict and competition among his advisers, thus forcing problems to be brought to the president's attention for resolution and decision. The formalistic model seeks to establish clear lines of authority to minimize the need for presidential involvement in the politicking among cabinet officials and key advisers. A chief of staff often provides a buffer between the president and cabinet heads. The collegial model emphasizes teamwork and group problem solving. The president operates like the hub of a wheel with spokes connecting to individual advisers and department heads, who often act as generalists rather than functional specialists concerned only with parts of particular problems.

10. As noted in earlier chapters, the Central Intelligence Agency, the Defense Department, and the Joint Chiefs of Staff were also created by the National Security Act.

11. These rump sessions may explain the apparent incongruity between Eisenhower's emphasis on the NSC system and the widespread belief that Secretary of State John Foster Dulles operated as the chief architect of American foreign policy during most of the Eisenhower years (in contrast, see Greenstein 1982, 1994). Dulles's biographer, Townsend Hoopes (1973a), also argues that the close working ties between Eisenhower and Dulles "compromised" Eisenhower's effort to use the NSC system to "orchestrate" the activities of the various foreign policy agencies into a coordinated foreign policy.

11

The Foreign Policy Bureaucracy and Foreign Policy Making

Our political system is too cumbersome to deal effectively with decisionmaking on the complex problems of the modern world.
ROBERT RUBIN, NATIONAL ECONOMIC ADVISER AND DIRECTOR OF THE NATIONAL ECONOMIC COUNCIL, 1993

It's very hard to give policy advice and not somehow become identified with the policy, or at least have an intellectual stake in wanting that policy to succeed.
R. JAMES WOOLSEY, DIRECTOR OF THE CENTRAL INTELLIGENCE AGENCY, 1994

Global activism is a pattern of American foreign policy. In response to international challenges such as the Cold War, the global economy, and, more recently, global terrorism, and in pursuit of U.S. political, economic, and military interests, the United States has constructed an elaborate complex of organizations and instruments through which to engage in the world. Recall from Chapters 4 and 5 the United States manifestations at the beginning of the twenty-first century: diplomatic relations with nearly every foreign government; participation in scores of international organizations; billions of dollars in economic and military assistance and sales; military deployments in many parts of the world; the capacity to strike virtually anywhere else; international cooperation critical to U.S. counterterrorism efforts; and trade and investment connections with other countries far beyond the nation's proportion of world population. Whose activities are reflected in such involvements? Whose responsibility is it to protect the interests they represent?

The executive departments of government, and the political appointees who head them, are at the core of the foreign policy-making process, particularly the Departments of State and Defense. The secretary of state, in principle at least, is the president's foremost foreign policy adviser and the State Department is the agency of government charged with coordinating U.S. activities overseas. The tense international political environment of the post–World War II period, which directed primary emphasis toward security considerations, also made the Defense Department and intelligence community particularly important. In recent decades, other executive agencies have also gained importance in the foreign policy process. Most notably, agencies with responsibilities in international economic affairs and homeland security have gained greater voices in many foreign policy debates.

In Chapter 10, we drew a distinction between executive branch agencies comprising the second concentric circle of policy making and the presidential subsystem, which makes up the innermost circle. In practice, the various secretaries of state, defense, and homeland security who serve the nation are simultaneously members of the inner circle as well as heads of the large, complex organizations found in the second concentric circle. These organizations are critically important to those in the innermost circle. The president and his closest advisers must depend on them and on their thousands of career professionals to manage America's day-to-day foreign relations and to implement the decisions of the president and presidential advisers. Hence, the scope and magnitude of the responsibilities of major organizations in the second concentric circle require scrutiny.

THE DEPARTMENT OF STATE

As the "first among equals" in the foreign affairs government, the Department of State is the principal agent of the executive branch of government responsible for managing U.S. foreign relations. In 2006, it operated a network of nearly 265 embassies, consulates, and diplomatic missions (namely delegations to international organizations) in 172

countries. At home and through these field missions, the State Department engages in a wide range of activities. Its responsibility to coordinate U.S. overseas activity would seem to give it the leadership role in foreign policy. Yet, the most obvious pattern for the Department of State since World War II has been its loss of influence in the formulation of foreign policy. As we will see, there are several factors that account for this state of affairs, but the department and its personnel continue to grapple with the foreign policy opportunities and challenges of the new century.

Structure and Mission

The State Department is organized in the hierarchical pattern typical of most large organizations, with the secretary of state perched on top of a series of more narrowly defined offices and bureaus that divide the labor within the department. As shown in Figure 11.1, that division reflects the department's orientation to the major geographic regions of the world through its *regional bureaus* under the direction of the under secretary of state for political affairs. Its *functional bureaus* show the necessity to cope with problems that transcend geographic boundaries, such as international security, nonproliferation, human rights, international narcotics, and the environment. The department is further staffed through a series of "support" offices to aid in analysis, planning, public affairs, and legislative affairs. The boxes in the figure reflect changes related to the post-9/11 era. For example, the newly established Bureau for International Security and Nonproliferation focuses on the nexus between terrorism and weapons of mass destruction, whereas the renaming of the under secretary for global affairs to the under secretary for democracy and global affairs reflects the Bush administration's desire to institutionalize democracy promotion.

Decision-making responsibility within the State Department itself follows the hierarchical pattern of its organization chart. Indeed, a common criticism of the State Department when it comes to decision making is its rigid hierarchy. Decisions of greatest importance are made by the secretary, the deputy

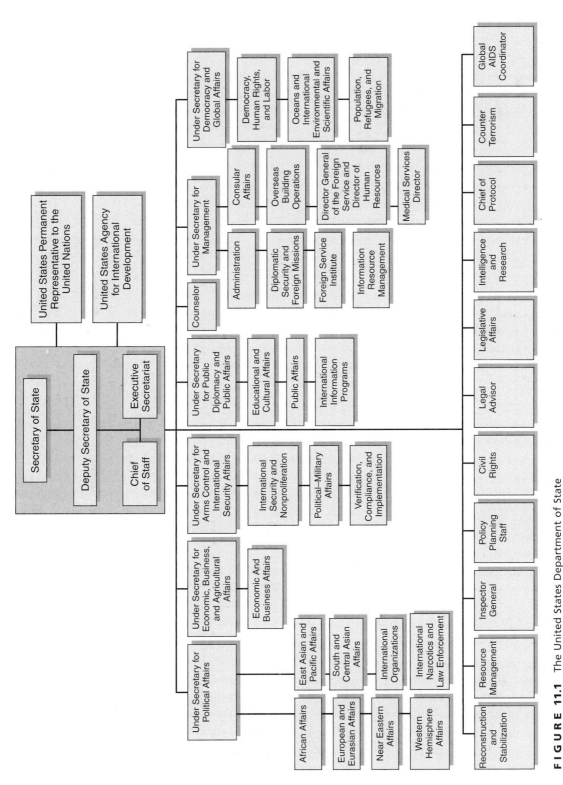

FIGURE 11.1 The United States Department of State

SOURCE: Based on information from www.state.gov/documents/organization/54806.pdf (U.S. Department of State 2006).

secretary, and the under secretaries who occupy the seventh floor of the State Department offices in the area of Washington, D.C., known as Foggy Bottom, and who frequently interact with the White House. Routine decisions, important more for policy implementation than development, are often made by the assistant and deputy assistant secretaries. Country directors and "desk officers" within each regional bureau arguably comprise the backbone of the State Department when it comes to coordinating U.S. policy toward particular countries abroad. In practice, however, the responsibilities of the regional bureaus have been greatly diluted by the involvement of several dozen other federal agencies in the management of foreign affairs, whose personnel also staff overseas embassies. Well over 60 percent of U.S. government personnel under the authority of ambassadors are not State Department employees, but come from other agencies, many traditionally associated with domestic policy (Talbott 1997; see also Warwick 1975 and Wiarda 2000).

Through this hierarchical structure, department personnel manage much of the day-to-day foreign relations of the United States. They *represent* the United States to other countries as well as convey the viewpoints and preferences of foreign governments and other international actors to the United States; they *negotiate* with foreign and international diplomats; and they analyze and *report* on events and information overseas. Department personnel also *recommend policy,* providing advice in the formulation and reformulation of initiatives through their participation in interagency groups. In short, the department manages, helps to shape, and implements many aspects of American foreign policy.

The Foreign Service and
Its Subculture

Within the State Department itself, the individuals who matter most are the *Foreign Service officers (FSOs),* who accounted (in 2005) for 11,000 of the 28,000 employees of the department (it also employs 8,000 civil servants at home and abroad and 9,000 foreign nationals at overseas posts). This elite corps of professional diplomats traditionally holds the most important positions within the State Department (outside of the high-level political and ambassadorial appointments made by the president). The popular image of the Foreign Service, based partly on legend as well as historical fact, is that of a remarkably homogeneous diplomatic corps comprising upper-class men from the Northeast with degrees from Ivy League colleges. However, the Foreign Service officer corps has sought to open itself to a broader geographical, educational, ethnic, and socioeconomic spectrum. Between 2001 and 2005, minority hires "increased from 14 percent of all Foreign Service generalists to 21 percent. Women now routinely comprise close to half [of all] entry-level hiring" (Pearson 2005). "Still, if the Foreign Service is no longer a smug men's club, it is more like one than any other part of the U.S. government" (Rubin 1985).

One of the distinctive elements of the Foreign Service is its relatively powerful *organizational subculture,* which is, according to James Q. Wilson (1989), "a persistent, patterned way of thinking about the central tasks of and human relationships within an organization." In fact, this powerful subculture is one of the reasons for the department's waning influence since World War II. It consists of several major characteristics. The first of these attributes stems in part from the Foreign Service's personnel system, separate from the Civil Service to which most federal employees belong. This unique system leads to *elitism.* As a longtime observer noted, "FSOs see themselves as members of an elite corps of talented, nonpartisan, close-knit, and unjustly beleaguered professionals" (Clarke 1989).

A second key element of the distinctive Foreign Service subculture is its *resistance to outside ideas.* As one officer put it, "'The Foreign Service officer believes that his is an arcane craft which people on the outside cannot hope to understand.' We listen carefully and politely but seldom change our views" (*Diplomacy for the 70s: A Program of Management Reform for the Department of State 1970*). According to another observer, "The stock in trade of the regular Foreign Service officers . . . is a large supply of cold water with which to dash ideas that emanate elsewhere or which challenge prevailing professional perspectives" (Rockman 1981). Thus it should come as no surprise that members of the State Department have been relatively less effective in the interagency working groups that have been so central to American foreign policy making.

A third characteristic of the Foreign Service subculture is the widely held belief that the only experience that is relevant to the activities of the Department of State is experience gained in the Foreign Service. This parochialism derives partly from the assignments of the typical Foreign Service officer. Viewed as a generalist rather than a specialist, a diplomat's career pattern usually involves two- or three-year tours of duty both in Washington and abroad in a variety of operating and functional positions (see Melbourne 1992). Its consequence, especially in combination with the elitism and resistance to outside ideas, is personnel who are overly dismissive and often disdaining of ideas, experiences, and expertise gained outside the service.

A fourth characteristic of the subculture is its emphasis on the essence or central mission of the department: negotiation, representation, and reporting. "It doesn't matter if it was a junior officer hoping for tenure, an FS-1 seeking to get into the Senior Foreign Service, or an ambassador or assistant secretary," observed one Foreign Service officer, "the qualities judged begin with reporting, analysis, and policy" (Bushnell 1989). Hence, Foreign Service personnel generally believe that overseas operations of the kind conducted by the U.S. Agency for International Development (USAID), Central Intelligence Agency (CIA), and Department of Defense are peripheral to the main foreign policy task (Scott 1969; see also Clarke 1989). For example, while the 1998 Foreign Affairs Restructuring Act integrated the USIA into the department to elevate the role and centrality of public diplomacy, this function is not part of the traditional mission and is resisted by the careerists throughout the agency.

The way the Foreign Service manages its personnel contributes to another characteristic of the subculture: its *cautiousness and risk-aversion*. The Foreign Service employs an *"up-or-out" promotion system,* under which a Foreign Service officer must advance beyond his or her present rank within a specified time or be "selected out." In addition to generating a highly competitive environment, that principle, together with the exceptional importance of the efficiency rating, tends, as one department self-study put it, "to stifle creativity, discourage risk-taking, and reward conformity" (*Diplomacy for the 70s: A Program of Management Reform for the Department of State 1970*). Whether one's star is allowed to shine in an assignment to political affairs in Paris rather than to budgetary affairs in Ouagadougou is heavily dependent on the outcome of one's evaluation by superiors. Foreign Service officers tend therefore to avoid rocking the boat and to eschew controversial views that may be viewed as challenges to the wisdom of one's superiors.

Over the years a number of developments both inside and outside the Foreign Service have disrupted the professional diplomatic corps, helping to reinforce this penchant for caution and traditionalism. Preeminent among them were the effects of *McCarthyism*. In the winter of 1950, Senator Joseph McCarthy claimed, "I have in my hand a list of 205 people that were known to the Secretary of State as being members of the Communist party and who, nevertheless, are still working and shaping the policy in the State Department." With those words, McCarthy launched an all-out attack against suspected "disloyalty" in the Foreign Service. The immediate thrust was directed against those charged with responsibility for the "loss" of China to communism in 1949. Eventually the entire corps of Foreign Service officers suffered the grueling humiliation of security investigations engendered by an atmosphere of hysterical anticommunism.

Among the serious consequences of McCarthyism for the State Department, two stand out. First, the devastating attacks promoted certain harmful values among its personnel: "The virtues inculcated were caution, conformity, discretion, and prudence" (Warwick 1975). Second, extraordinary security consciousness and an elaborate system of horizontal clearances resulted. The latter in particular has made State's operating procedures among the most complex of all federal agencies. The result is, according to many, a slowness and inefficiency in the department's processes, as well as "a most cautious way of doing business. It reflects an institutionalized desire to diffuse responsibility among many different offices and colleagues rather than to accept responsibility oneself" (Campbell 1971; see also U.S. Department of State 1992).

Other factors since World War II contributed to the decline of the State Department's influence in the wider foreign policy circles. Among them were increased presidential interest in and control over foreign policy, the security-centric issue agendas of the Cold War and post-9/11 eras (which elevate the importance of the military establishment and intelligence community), and the growing importance of economic and other "intermestic" issues to the foreign policy issue agenda (which fall beyond the department's traditional competencies).

The State Department in the Foreign Affairs Government

The combination of the subculture of the State Department and factors external to the organization are critical in explaining why a department that theoretically sits center-stage in the foreign affairs government is in fact ill-equipped to play a leadership role. Three additional factors circumscribe the State Department's ability to exercise leadership in the larger foreign affairs government: the tension between careerists and appointees, the fact that the department is a bureaucratic pygmy among giants, and the role and orientation of secretaries of state.

Careerists versus Political Appointees A tension in the role of the State Department (indeed, in any agency) that works against its ability to exercise effective leadership is the natural tension between career employees and the political appointees generally placed above them. Careerists frequently view political appointees as "in-and-outers," more concerned with political advantage and short-term

results than good policy. Appointees, on the other hand, frequently view careerists as overly cautious and unresponsive to the White House and department leadership. Often, a contest ensues.

A major manifestation of this tension involves the mid-level positions and ambassadorships to which FSO careerists aspire and into which political appointments from outside the Foreign Service are frequently made.[1] Not only does this reduce the opportunities available to career officers at the prime of their careers, when their potential to make a meaningful contribution is greatest, but it also generates resentment among the most senior members of the Foreign Service toward the appointees. In George W. Bush's first year, for example, 1,700 people sought jobs in American embassies, mostly in Europe and the Caribbean (the "plum" postings). Two hundred became finalists, and a fortunate forty-nine were named. Not surprisingly, in addition to former politicians being rewarded for service, the list was heavily laden with major contributors to the president's election campaign. Few such rewards go to "hardship" postings in Latin America, Africa, and Asia, which tend to be dominated by careerists (Lacey and Bonner 2001).

Presidents have long used ambassadorial appointments to reward their political supporters, but the propensity to make political appointments also reflects their profound distrust of careerists. Politicians often believe that careerists are not only disloyal to their policies but also actively seek to undermine them. Often, however, the demands political appointees make on those expected to serve them are contradictory. They want the career staff to be detached, but accuse it of being bland; they demand discipline, but can brand this as lack of imagination; they require experienced judgment, but may call this negativism. One FSO complains, "Presidents and their aides need scapegoats. They can't blame the administration so they blame the secretary of state, and if they can't blame the secretary of state they criticize the department's staff" (Rubin 1985).

Another manifestation of this tension can be seen in the presidential propensity to establish special envoys outside the department structure (using political appointees rather than career officials) to deal with major problems. The Clinton administration was particularly fond of such positions, appointing special envoys like former Senator George Mitchell for Ireland, and other similar, if lower profile "ambassadors at large " for NATO enlargement, war crimes, the Comprehensive Test Ban Treaty, religious freedom, counterterrorism, and newly independent states. In addition, U.S. generals and admirals who serve as regional commanders-in-chief (CINCs) around the globe have become independent foreign policy players in their own right. They wield enormous influence as emissaries of the world's largest military and often outflank career diplomats stationed in the same region (see Priest 2000). The use of such actors illustrates the "adhocracy" discussed in Chapter 10 (and will be revisited in Chapter 13). They constitute efforts to work around the established bureaus and offices and better "control" career employees.

Without Bureaucratic Muscle A second reason for the State Department's inability to exercise greater leadership is its relative lack of resources and bureaucratic muscle in Washington's intensely political environment. As one Foreign Service officer put it three decades ago, the secretary of state "is [the] most senior of cabinet members, and is charged (in theory) with responsibility for the coordination of all foreign policy activities, [but] he presides over a bureaucratic midget" (Pringle 1977–1978). Nothing has changed since. The State Department's budget for 2006 was about $9 billion compared with roughly $419 billion for the Defense Department. Remarkably, the figure for the Defense Department excluded tens of billions of dollars in supplemental appropriations used to fund ongoing military operations in Iraq and Afghanistan. The total international affairs budget (also referred to as Function 150 of the federal budget) represents little more than 1 percent of all federal expenditures. Meanwhile, the expenditures of every other department in the executive branch exceed those of the State Department—a pygmy among giants.

Centralization of foreign policy making in the White House grows naturally out of the State Department's lack of leadership but typically results in the "exclusion of the bureaucracy from most of the serious, presidential foreign policy business" (Destler, Gelb, and Lake 1984). Both circumstances reflect the State Department's inattentiveness to presidential needs: "Once a president comes to believe that Foggy Bottom is not attuned to politics, they are doomed to being ignored" (Gelb 1983). Specific presidential complaints are that the State Department produces bad staff work and is slow to respond, resistant to change, reluctant to follow orders, and incapable of putting its own house in order.

Part of the reason for the belief that the State Department is insensitive to a president's political needs is that the department necessarily represents in the councils of government the interests of other countries, who are its "clients." "From a White House perspective, efforts to accommodate the legitimate concerns of other countries are often viewed as coming at the expense of American interests, and the accommodationists are viewed as not being tough enough. Presidents usually do not have much patience with this kind of advice, find they cannot change State's penchant for it, and soon stop listening" (Gelb 1983; see also Clarke 1989). Within the interagency groups who play a key role in policy formulation, this *clientitis* is also damaging, causing other participants to discount the State Department representative.

Secretaries of State and the State Department

A third reason for the State Department's relative weakness is the secretary of state may or may not be influential in foreign policy, despite his or her assumed role as the president's leading foreign policy adviser. Since the 1950s, most secretaries have had to choose between two basic role orientations: to maximize their relationship with the president and distance themselves from the department itself, or to maximize their leadership and use of the department, only to see their influence with the president wane. Few manage both; some manage neither.

Let us consider secretaries over the past fifty years or so. John Foster Dulles (1953–1959) is widely regarded as one of the most influential secretaries of state in the twentieth century, but he did little to infuse the organization with a corresponding capacity to lead. Dulles reportedly told President Eisenhower he would accept the job only if he did not have to assume responsibility for managing the department and the Foreign Service. Dean Rusk (1961–1969) was a less dramatic secretary, and his personality and preoccupation with Vietnam prevented a more effective use of the department's expertise (*Diplomacy for the 70s: A Program of Management Reform for the Department of State 1970*).

Those who followed Dulles and Rusk— including Kissinger, Vance, Muskie, Haig, Shultz, Baker, Eagleburger, Christopher, and Albright— did no more to build bridges between top officials and careerists in order to involve the latter more actively in policy making. Kissinger (1973–1977) took many of his NSC staffers with him to Foggy Bottom when he left the White House, but largely ignored the department. Vance (1977–1980) was apparently more popular at the State Department "partly due to memories of his predecessor—tales of Kissinger mistreating FSOs and ashtray-throwing tantrums [were] legion" (Rubin 1985)—but eventually Vance became enmeshed in a bureaucratic duel with the White House, which he ultimately lost. Alexander Haig (1981–1982), Reagan's first secretary of state, also resigned when he found himself outside the charmed circle of White House advisers in an administration otherwise known for its friction with the career staff. If there was an exception, it was George Shultz (1982–1989), Haig's successor, whose survival through the end of the Reagan era suggests he was better able to satisfy the competing demands of organization person and presidential adviser. In contrast, James A. Baker (1989–1992) reopened the chasm separating the secretary of state from the department's career professionals and attempted to keep himself inside George H. W. Bush's inner circle. Whereas Shultz

"used the brightest stars of the career Foreign Service as the core of his policy-making team," Baker's style was to keep them at arm's length. "Many Foreign Service officers [complained] that Baker and his coterie of insiders ... turned the department's seventh-floor executive suite into an inaccessible redoubt where even the most senior professional diplomats [felt] unwelcome and ignored" (Goshko 1989).

President Clinton's secretaries of state did not fare much better than Baker. Although he sometimes acted as a leading spokesperson for Clinton's foreign policy, and he did administer structural and procedural changes at State, Warren Christopher (1993–1997) and his top aides were viewed by both administration officials and Foreign Service officers as "nice guys," but generally ineffective (see Goshko 1994). When Madeleine Albright (1997–2001) became the first woman to hold the position of secretary of state, she was hailed by most observers—including longtime State Department critic Jesse Helms, Republican chair of the Senate Foreign Relations Committee—as a major improvement over Christopher. Respected by the president and potentially able to add prestige to the department through her efforts, her highly visible role seemed to place her in a position to restore the secretary of state to an influential adviser role, as well as to elevate the department to a more prominent position. Notwithstanding a few successes (most notably, involving U.S. Balkans policy and the Kosovo conflict of 1999, dubbed "Madeleine's War"), Albright did not wield significant influence as an adviser. Instead her role in policy was more of an implementer, and her relationship to President Clinton was formal, not close (Isaacson 1999). Albright also failed within her department. Department officials allegedly viewed her as an "insecure, indifferent leader who [was] quick to anger and obsessed by her public image" (Lancaster 2000). One foreign policy specialist characterized her tenure as "largely unsuccessful in either getting control over her own building or her own policy generally" (quoted in Lancaster 2000).

George W. Bush's choice for secretary of state began with even more accolades than Albright. Colin Powell (2001–2005) was widely regarded as the star of the Bush foreign policy team during the transition period and early days of the administration. One political analyst asserted that Powell was "uniquely positioned to become the most influential voice in foreign affairs within the Bush administration" (Kitfield 2001a). Most observers, it seemed, expected Powell to use his star power and political clout to make the secretary of state the lead voice on foreign policy. Moreover, Powell's early statements to lawmakers and State Department employees suggested that he was determined to actually lead the department with the goal of restoring it to a more prominent position.

Powell did not live up to the conventional wisdom and emerge as President Bush's foreign policy vicar. Instead he was marginalized within the Bush foreign policy team, more often than not losing out to Vice President Dick Cheney, Secretary of Defense Donald Rumsfeld, and National Security Adviser Condoleezza Rice in the struggle to shape the administration's foreign policy. As early as 2001, *Time* (10 September, 24–32) ran a cover story entitled "Odd Man Out," commenting on the impression Powell was less influential than expected— even "invisible." After the September 11 attacks, Powell became an effective front man on the international stage for the Bush White House, but held little sway on the substance of policy. Once the focus shifted from Afghanistan to Iraq, he found himself virtually isolated in his support for renewed UN weapons inspections and the formation of a broad international coalition to deal with Iraq. Powell's deputy, Richard Armitage, likened his boss's predicament to being in the administration's "refrigerator" (Woodward 2004). One U.S. official recalls being told by French President Jacques Chirac: "When Powell agrees with us, we know it doesn't mean anything" (quoted in Steinberger 2004).

To be sure, Powell had his successes. As one observer suggested, "The White House lets him run free on Africa and AIDS" (McGeary 2001). He diffused the administration's first diplomatic crisis following the collision of a U.S. spy plane with a Chinese fighter jet. His many foreign visits played a key role in building an international coalition against terrorism and in support of U.S. military operations in Afghanistan. Before the Iraq war, it was Powell who insisted that the president go to the United Nations Security Council for a resolution of support. However, in terms of the issues most central to the Bush administration's foreign policy— Iraq, North Korea, Middle East peace talks, and U.S. opposition to various international treaties— Powell lost repeatedly and often in humiliating fashion. It was not uncommon for his preferences and public statements to be reversed or contradicted by Cheney, Rumsfeld, or the president, often publicly. Thus it came as little surprise when he announced that he would not serve a second term as secretary of state. *but not as effective policy maker*

In stark contrast to his performance as a foreign adviser, Powell earned high marks as the leader of the State Department's notoriously rigid and resistant bureaucracy. John Naland, former president of the American Foreign Service Association, labeled Powell, "easily the best leader and manager State has seen since George Schultz . . . As far as the Foreign Service is concerned, Powell has been an absolute standout" (quoted in *Government Executive*, 27 January 2003). The nonpartisan Foreign Affairs Council wrote of Powell's management in its November 2004 task force report: "In short, the achievements have been extraordinary—even historic . . . To use the vernacular, the Powell team has 'talked the talk' and 'walked the walk.' The Secretary has been an exemplary CEO of the State Department" (Foreign Affairs Council 2004). What accounts for these rave reviews?

When Powell walked into Foggy Bottom in January 2001, he encountered a critically underfunded bureaucracy with poor congressional relations, insecure and crumbling embassies, and antiquated information technology. The workforce was severely depleted, inadequately trained, and poorly managed. Not surprisingly these conditions created, in the words of former National Security Adviser Frank Carlucci, "a severe crisis in morale among employees" (Carlucci 2001). But by the third year of Powell's tenure, one of his under secretaries, Grant

---

F O C U S 11.1 **Secretary Powell's State Department: An Independent Assessment**

The Foreign Affairs Council, a nonpartisan umbrella group of 11 organizations concerned with effective diplomatic management, credited Colin Powell with several "extraordinary achievements" in its November 2004 task force report. The following developments were among the cited accomplishments.

- Employees at all levels, Foreign Service and Civil Service alike, feel empowered and respected. Morale is robust. "One Mission, One Team" has taken root as a value.

- Leadership and management training are now mandatory for all mid-level and senior officers. Career candidates for Ambassador or Deputy Chief of Mission (DCM) appointments have the inside track if they have demonstrated leadership qualities.

- Congress has given State virtually all the resources Secretary Powell requested. Congress understands that the increases for diplomatic readiness, information technology, overseas buildings and diplomatic security are permanent parts of the budget, not one-time catch-up costs.

- State has achieved most of its Diplomatic Readiness Initiative (DRI) staffing goals. With its new,

first-rate recruitment and marketing program, State has redressed in three years almost the entire personnel deficit of the 1990s (some 2,000 employees hired above attrition) and increased diversity and the quality of Foreign Service officers and specialists.

- All the hardware for modern IT is now installed and on a four-year replacement cycle. All desks are finally linked worldwide. Information security is greatly enhanced. A new, robust, state-of-the-art message and archiving system (SMART) is being tested to do away with yesteryear's tele-grams and their risky distribution and storage.

- The new Overseas Building Office (OBO) has completed 13 safe, secure, functional buildings in two years under budget. Twenty-six more are on the way. This contrasts with pre-2002 rate of about one building per year. Congress and OMB have praised OBO effusively. Security up-grades have thwarted terrorist attacks at several posts.

SOURCE: Excerpts from Foreign Affairs Council, *Task Force Report: Secretary Colin Powell's State Department: An Independent Assessment* (November 2004), www.diplomatsonline.org/taskreprot1104.pdf, iii–vi. Reprinted by permission of American Foreign Services Association.

Green, boasted, "Morale is sky-high" (Green 2003). The reason for this change was simple: Powell transformed State in real and meaningful ways. (See Focus 11.1.) There were tangible improvements, some fairly dramatic, in each of the areas that was an identified source of concern in January 2001. When Powell left the department four years later, he had laid the groundwork for making it, perhaps not a more influential bureaucracy, but certainly a more viable and effective one.

Several factors explain Powell's ability to succeed where so many other secretaries of state failed. For instance, Powell also brought with him a record of leadership and managerial experience, not to mention impressive interpersonal skills and a reservoir of political capital to tap. He also demonstrated a consistent willingness to be accessible to lawmakers and frequently testified before congressional committees to justify programs and appropriations

requests. In addition, Powell took a true "hands on" approach to State Department management, which was aided by his limited travel. According to the official historian of the State Department, he was the least-traveled secretary of state in thirty years, including a record of 45 percent fewer trips than Christopher, Albright, or Baker. Over the course of his tenure, Powell reduced the "average length of his trips from 4.6 days in 2001 to 2.9 days [in 2004]" (Kessler 2004a). When Powell did travel, he empowered State Department careerists. He limited the number of aides accompanying him from Washington, preferring instead to rely on the advice of ambassadors and their country teams. In the same direction, Powell eliminated nearly half (23 of 55) of the special envoy and ambassador-at-large positions that emerged during the Clinton years (Friel 2003; Diamond 2001; Peckenpaugh 2001). Most important, Powell's groundwork for success included a decision to set reasonable goals that a risk-averse organizational culture would accept. He avoided the controversy often associated with sweeping structural changes, such as merging State's regional and functional bureaus, and focused his attention on discrete problems—morale, embassy security and construction, information technology, public diplomacy, and diplomatic readiness (see Jones 2006a).

Working from a stronger organizational foundation, Powell's successor, Condoleezza Rice (2005–present), had something more dramatic in mind. In an effort to advance President Bush's call "to seek and support the growth of democratic movements and institutions in every nation and culture," Rice articulated a bold, new vision for U.S. diplomacy at the start of her second year as secretary of state. *"Transformational diplomacy,"* in her words, "not only reports about the world as it is, but seeks to change the world itself." The emerging Rice Doctrine, as one observer dubbed it (see Nolan 2006), called for large numbers of diplomats to be repositioned from Europe to pivotal states in the developing world. Mobile teams of diplomats would be established to respond to transnational and regional challenges. Diplomats would be expected to serve at hardship posts; and they would be required to have expertise in at least two regions and fluency in two languages to secure promotion to the senior ranks of the Foreign Service. Additionally, the plan called for the State Department's presence to be extended to the hinterlands of developing states through one-person posts and virtual diplomacy. Diplomats would be assigned to military commanders as political advisers; and the department's recently created Office of Reconstruction and Stabilization was to be strengthened and expanded to aid democratic transitions around the globe. Seeing foreign assistance as a major asset of transformational diplomacy, Rice also sought to strengthen USAID by granting its administrator a rank equivalent to a deputy secretary of state and pushing Congress to consider foreign aid as national security spending.

Whether Rice would be judged successful remained to be seen. However, she did possess a number of helpful assets: a more viable organization thanks to Powell's four-year revitalization effort, a seemingly supportive Foreign Service, and an experienced leadership team at the State Department. Most important, she enjoyed the trust and support of the president. Rice and Bush established a very close working relationship during the 2000 presidential campaign, which continued and intensified during her four years as national security adviser (see Chapter 10). Her personal standing with Bush boded well for her chance to remain an influential presidential adviser in her new role as secretary of state. It also positioned her to be a potentially successful leader at the State Department, especially if her policy and organizational initiatives complement the administration's overall foreign policy direction. Transformational diplomacy clearly met that criterion.

Of course, there was the issue whether of Rice could be both an effective organizational person and adviser as secretary of state. During her first two years, she traveled extensively (far more than Powell) and benefited from the trust of the president (perhaps her greatest asset), raising the question of whether she would be disciplined enough to devote steady attention to managing Foggy Bottom over the course of her tenure. While transformational diplomacy sought to carve out a niche for the State Department in implementing the Bush administration's foreign policy, it raised the prospect of taking the department in a new demanding direction without full appreciation of its continuing organizational challenges.

Twenty-First Century Challenges

As the State Department moves through the first decade of the twenty-first century, it faces several challenges. The same nonpartisan report, which praised Powell's accomplishments, stressed that "many are vulnerable in a budget crisis, and others require more work." In short, there remain several "vulnerabilities" that have not disappeared over the course of Rice's short tenure. According to the report, the State Department must maintain and actively promote good relations with Congress, continue its improvements in information technology, and remedy its "deficient" public diplomacy. The department also needs to engage the public on a sustained basis to build greater confidence in the institution. More personnel must be hired to make up for the positions shifted from diplomatic readiness to Iraq and Afghanistan and to satisfy the post-9/11 demands of overseas consular staffing. In addition, the report warns the department must continue to direct attention to competitive recruitment and adequate training, noting "sending [diplomats] abroad without the requisite training is like deploying soldiers without weapons." Meeting such objectives will be difficult, because "budget outlooks are grim" (Foreign Affairs Council 2004). Furthermore, the State Department remains saddled with the tradition deficiencies detailed in this chapter—its Foreign Service subculture, the perennial tension between political appointees and careerists, an absence of bureaucratic muscle, and secretaries of state pulled in two often competing directions.

Finally, the State Department will have to struggle with the impact of an issue agenda that seems to diminish its centrality. Just as in the Cold War military and security concerns reduced the dominance of the State Department while enhancing the roles of the defense and intelligence agencies, the leading foreign policy matters of the twenty-first century seem to diminish the centrality of State Department. The prevalence of transnational and economic issues coupled with the emphasis on counterterrorism and related security issues in the post-9/11 era invite influence by others, require coordination by the White House, and continue the long-standing pattern of there being serious challenges to the State Department's role.

THE DEPARTMENT OF DEFENSE

Given the international environment that has dominated much of the last sixty years, it is no surprise that the Department of Defense (DOD) has been an important voice in foreign policy making. The secretary of defense and the chairman of the Joint Chiefs of Staff bear the heaviest responsibility for advising the president on national security policy. Because the DOD is also thoroughly interwoven into the fabric of American social, political, and economic life, the defense secretary's recommendations greatly influence both the foreign and domestic environments.

Structure and Mission

As Figure 11.2 shows, the Defense Department is a complex agency. In truth, the Defense Department, popularly referred to simply as the *Pentagon* because of the shape of its headquarters in Arlington, Virginia, is far more complex than the figure is able to convey. The organizational chart shows the formal relationship between the secretary of defense, the military departments, each of which is headed by a civilian, the military services that comprise them, and the Joint Chiefs of Staff. It also indicates the importance of civilian control of the military, as the defense secretary and the service secretaries are all civilians, an issue to which we will return in more detail later. However, it fails to reveal fully the complicated chain of command that exists on national security policy and the increasing commitment to and adoption of *"jointness,"* by which the services are more integrated in their forces, doctrines, and commands. It is clear, however, that the department is a massive agency. As of 2002, it encompassed 1.4 million active duty personnel, 654,000 civilian employees, 1.2 million National Guard and Reserve forces, 2 million retirees or benefit-receiving family members, and 600,000 individual buildings located at more than 6,000 sites.

The complex organization portrayed in Figure 11.2 performs four important roles in American national security policy (see also Jordan, Taylor and Mazarr 1999). First, it has a *policy* role, providing advice and analysis to the White House on national security matters. This function is chiefly performed by the secretary and the Office of the Secretary of Defense (OSD) along with the Joint Chiefs of Staff (JCS) and their chair, who is the "principal military adviser" to the civilian leadership. Second, the DOD exercises *military command* over the nation's armed

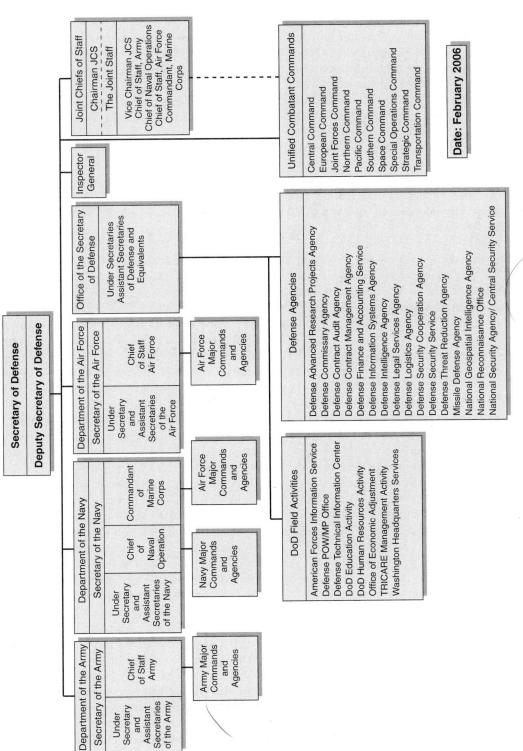

FIGURE 11.2   The United States Department of Defense

SOURCE: U.S. Department of Defense.

forces, under the overall authority of the president (who is commander-in-chief). This function is chiefly performed at the strategic level by the OSD, and at the tactical level by the services themselves, especially through their unified commands. The JCS is technically not in the operational chain of command, but also plays a role. Third, the DOD *administers* the military services, managing personnel and budgets, weapons and supplies, and training forces. This function is performed chiefly by the services themselves, with general oversight and supervision by the OSD. Finally, the DOD *collects intelligence* for use in devising and reviewing policy through intelligence units of the services and the Defense Intelligence Agency. Thus, implementing the role and mission of the department—providing policy advice and carrying out the security policy of the United States—is less easily coordinated and centralized than the organizational chart suggests.

The Secretary of Defense and the Office of the Secretary of Defense

The secretary of defense is the president's chief adviser on defense matters, including such issues as force size and structure and weapons procurement. The secretary is assisted in carrying out his or her responsibilities by the **Office of the Secretary of Defense (OSD),** comprising under secretaries, assistant secretaries, and other personnel responsible for more discrete issues, such as policy development, acquisitions and technology, personnel and readiness, and command, control, communications, and intelligence.

Managing the Military: Autonomy versus Centralization   Like all bureaucratic organizations, the military services within the Defense Department prize their autonomy in what historically has been the "services-dominated architecture" of the defense establishment. As one analyst noted wryly in commenting on the 1986 defense reorganization proposals, "In more than two hundred years [the Navy Department] had never met a centralization proposal that [it] liked" (Davis 1987). Hence, secretaries

of defense have their work cut out for them as they seek to lead the department in its foreign and national security functions.

Over time, different secretaries of defense have used different management strategies to coordinate the disparate military organizations. One strategy is *decentralization.* This is the preferred strategy of the military services, because it means delegating authority for both resources and strategy to them (Hammond 1994). Secretary of Defense Caspar Weinberger (1981–1987) pursued this management strategy, which is best suited to a time of growing defense spending, as during the 1980s. However, Bill Clinton's third defense secretary, former Republican Senator William Cohen (1997–2001), also falls into this category, much to the surprise of many observers who expected him to be more aggressive in managing the department (see Halberstam 2001).

A second strategy focuses on *"management of the acquisition process,"* including the development of new technologies and equipment. This strategy "permits the secretary of defense to have a major impact on the shape and functions of the armed services in the longer term by guiding their development and application of new technologies" (Hammond 1994). In this approach, the secretary of defense actively shapes key aspects of the resource planning and can shape overall strategy without imposing a blanket, top-down, managerial style in either resources or strategy. Harold Brown (1977–1981), defense secretary under President Carter and William Perry (1994–1997), Clinton's second defense secretary followed this route.

A third approach concentrates on developing overall strategy while delegating much of the resource management and planning. This *"top-down, directive planning guidance"* approach, which is promoted by the 1986 Defense Reorganization Act, prompts the military services to integrate their operations, and it encourages greater attention to "operational and contingency planning" and "long-range force...planning" (Hammond 1994). Not surprisingly, many of the post-1986 defense secretaries adopted this approach, including George H.

W. Bush's defense chief, Dick Cheney (1989–1993) and Bill Clinton's first secretary of defense, Les Aspin (1993–1994).

The final strategy is *"central resource management,"* which concentrates both budgetary and strategic planning in the OSD. In this approach, which is exemplified by Robert McNamara (1961–1968) during the Kennedy and Johnson administrations and Frank Carlucci (1987–1989) in the waning days of the Reagan administration, civilian control is most extensive. Under McNamara, for example, the Office of the Secretary of Defense was staffed with "acerbic, even arrogant, analytically brilliant men, most of whom had made their mark in business or academic life" (Nathan and Oliver 1994). McNamara and the OSD were "soon involved at virtually every level of national security management and military planning" (Nathan and Oliver 1994).

Although the 1986 defense reforms expanding the role of the JCS has made this last approach more difficult, George W. Bush's first secretary of defense, Donald Rumsfeld, embraced it, seeking to exercise strong leadership across both strategy and resource management. Equipped with a strong familiarity of the Pentagon from his days as President Ford's defense secretary and a reputation for political skill and toughness that led Kissinger to label him "the most ruthless man" he has ever met (quoted in Rothkopf 2005a), Rumsfeld set out to transform the DOD in 2001. Four years later, one scholar contended Rumsfeld had "earned a place in American bureaucratic history as one of the most ambitious organizational reformers" (Light 2005).

Examples of Rumsfeld's impact abound. He replaced an outdated civilian personnel system with a pay-for-performance system,[2] outsourced a number of administrative services, and reduced senior-level positions (career and political appointee) by 21 percent. He rebuilt OSD into an aggressive *policy shop* (see the following), pushed a new round of military base closures at home, and repositioned forces from large installations in Western Europe and East Asia to small bases in and around the Middle East and Central Asia (see Light 2005). Most significant, Rumsfeld sought to transform how the U.S. armed forces fight, leaving his imprint on the department's post-9/11 military strategy, force configuration, and weapons procurement.

By most accounts, however, Rumsfeld elevated the central resource management strategy to a new level, perhaps to a dangerous extreme. Thomas White, who was fired as secretary of the army in May 2003, characterized Rumsfeld as very smart, tough, and disciplined, but also someone who "micromanages, overcontrols, [and] can be intimidating, almost abusive. He tends to stifle communication, [and] overworks things that he ought to delegate" (White 2004).

Perhaps nothing epitomized the Rumsfeld style more than his deep involvement in nearly every dimension of the 2003 Iraq war. Rumsfeld was an early and ardent advocate of toppling Saddam Hussein, first expressing an interest to hit the Iraqi regime on the morning of September 11, 2001. He dominated prewar planning and dismissed the concerns of generals who believed the U.S. force needed more troops and heavy armor. Rumsfeld maintained there was no need to fight the war according to the tenets of the Powell Doctrine, which ensured the 1991 Gulf War victory. Consistent with his vision of military transformation, he insisted the war be waged with a smaller, lighter force that would overwhelm the enemy with its speed, precision strikes, and cutting-edge communications technology. In addition, Rumsfeld gave his approval to the plan to begin the war before all U.S. forces were in the area of operations and ready to go. Perhaps most famously, he rejected the advice of the army's chief of staff, General Eric K. Shinseki, who cautioned that hundreds of thousands of troops would be needed to hold territory and maintain order in postwar Iraq. Similarly, Rumsfeld ignored State Department recommendations regarding postwar reconstruction. In the midst of the war, he went so far as to raise the specter of expanding the conflict when he declared unilaterally that "hostile acts" by Iran and Syria would be met with severe consequences (see Purdum 2003; Woodward 2004). And at every turn, Rumsfeld was the Bush administration's chief public spokesperson on the war. However, instead of deftly handling controversies, such as the humiliation and torture of Iraqi prisoners at Abu Ghraib or the critical shortage of body armor for U.S. soldiers, he seemed to antagonize his audience with a dismissive attitude and often brusque remarks, such as "stuff happens" (in response to postwar looting and chaos in Iraq).

Given the foregoing discussion, scholar Lawrence Freedman made the case in early 2005 that the Rumsfeld legacy will be profoundly negative and forever connected to Iraq. In confronting his critics, Freedman wrote, "Rumsfeld cannot complain that he was the victim of poor advice, because the only advice he appears to trust is his own. This was evident from the moment he arrived at the Pentagon and is one reason why comparisons . . . with Robert McNamara, are apt and illuminating. And just as McNamara left behind the 'Vietnam syndrome,' when Rumsfeld departs his bequest may well be an 'Iraq syndrome' . . . that is even more burdensome" (Freedman 2005). The cases of McNamara and Rumsfeld, respectively and collectively, raise serious questions about the wisdom of future secretaries of defense adopting the central resource management model.

The Policy Shop: The Office of the Secretary of Defense   One of the major developments in the U.S. foreign policy bureaucracy was the rise of the Office of the Secretary of Defense as a source of policy ideas. With Robert McNamara's tenure as secretary of defense in the 1960s, the OSD emerged as an important bureaucratic player, often vying with bureaus in the State Department and offices in the NSC staff. The OSD is, technically, the staff of the secretary of defense. However, this sizable staff is organized into a wide variety of offices. Some are designed to facilitate management over the defense department itself (for example, the offices of the under secretary for personnel and readiness and for acquisition, technology, and logistics). However, within the OSD, the office of the under secretary for policy houses a series of units designed to formulate and analyze policy options. Although the names and assignments have varied since the

McNamara's era, historically these "policy shop" units have been among the most powerful in the department.

During the 1960s, for example, the *Office of International Security Affairs (ISA)* emerged as an influential Defense Department voice in the foreign affairs government. Called by many the "little State Department," its influence stemmed from McNamara's ability to establish control over the sprawling military complex and the fact that Vietnam was the principal foreign policy problem of the era. After the Johnson administration, however, the OSD declined in influence until the Reagan administration restored its significance. Under Reagan, the "policy shop," now divided into an International Security Affairs office, an International Security Policy (ISP) office, and a Special Operations and Low-Intensity Conflict (SO/LIC) office, exercised a powerful voice in OSD and in the interagency groups used to formulate policy ideas.

After declining in influence during the Bush I administration, OSD and its key policy offices regained some of their clout in the Clinton administration. Les Aspin, Clinton's first secretary of defense, sought an even greater role for policy, as he brought in a number of "defense intellectuals" whose tasks extended beyond traditional defense issues to encompass more novel threats to national security in the post–Cold War era. Aspin, whose tenure as secretary of defense was marked mostly by managerial failures, reorganized the OSD and the policy office to better reflect the emerging foreign policy and security environment. Indeed, by paralleling the State Department structure in many ways, and by adding such offices as environmental security and regional security, Aspin clearly set up the OSD to compete with the State Department. Aspin's successors, Perry and Cohen, further reorganized the OSD to reflect changing priorities, but Perry stripped away a number of Aspin's innovations by eliminating some of the newer offices.

George W. Bush's first defense secretary, Donald Rumsfeld, followed the pattern of his predecessors and set up offices within OSD to compete effectively in foreign and national security policy circles. For instance, the Office of Force Transformation was created to advance his goal of a smaller, lighter, and technologically sophisticated military. Yet the most prominent (and controversial) example of OSD behaving as an aggressive policy shop during Rumsfeld's tenure was the establishment of the Office of Special Plans (OSP) in 2002. Conceived by Deputy Secretary of Defense Paul Wolfowitz, overseen by Under Secretary of Defense for Policy Douglas Feith, and managed by William Luti and Abram Shulsky (all neoconservative political appointees), OSP was a small but influential intelligence unit charged with making the case for going to war with Iraq. Wolfowitz believed OSP was necessary to uncover facts overlooked by the broader intelligence community and to reexamine existing information from a different perspective. Critics charged OSP was nothing more than a vehicle for OSD officials to "politiciz[e] intelligence to fit their hawkish views [on Iraq]" (Purdum 2003). Ultimately, this is the key: the role and influence of the OSD, both within and outside the department, depends on the style and preferences of the secretary of defense.

The Joint Chiefs of Staff

The 1947 National Security Act created the ***Joint Chiefs of Staff (JCS)*** to provide military advice to the NSC. The ***Defense Reorganization Act of 1986*** further expanded the JCS to an even more prominent role in foreign and national security policy. This first major reorganization of the Defense Department since the 1950s, popularly known as the *Goldwater-Nichols Act* after its congressional architects, sought in particular to strengthen the role of the institutions associated with the Joint Chiefs of Staff and to ameliorate the interservice rivalry that has long plagued the defense establishment. Since its implementation, the JCS has played an increasingly central role in both policy formulation and implementation. This is especially true when the use of force is being considered but, ironically, less so once the decision to apply force is taken. The wars in Kosovo (1999)

and Afghanistan (2001) illustrate this well. In both situations, the chairman of the Joint Chiefs was central to the decisions to use force, but lost influence to the theater commanders and the civilian command authority once the campaigns began (see Halberstam 2001; Locher 2002).

The JCS consists of six officers—the senior military officer within each uniformed service and a chairman and vice chairman (a position added by Goldwater-Nichols) appointed by the president. The chairman of the JCS serves as the nation's chief military officer. Each service chief—the chief of staff of the army, the chief of staff of the air force, the chief of naval operations, and the commandant of the Marine Corps—is responsible for advising his civilian secretary on military matters and for maintaining the efficiency and operational readiness of the military forces under his command. Until the 1986 reorganization, the Joint Chiefs were assisted in that task by a ***Joint Staff*** comprising some 400 officers selected from each branch of the armed forces. Since 1986, however, the Joint Staff serves the chairman, operating solely under his direction, authority, and control.

Additionally, the Goldwater-Nichols Act made three other changes that have impacted policy formulation and implementation. First, it stimulated the creation of a new "joint specialty" designed to make service on the Joint Staff more rewarding professionally. Today one cannot rise to the rank of general or admiral without first serving as a "purple suiter" (the color that results from blending the traditional colors of the four armed services). Thus Joint Staff tours of duty have become coveted. Second, it centralized and expanded the staff, which now numbers roughly 1,600, while also permitting civilians to serve. Finally, the act explicitly named the chairman of the Joint Chiefs as the principal military adviser to the president, the secretary of defense, and the National Security Council (but not a member, as some had proposed). Before the Goldwater-Nichols Act, that task fell to the Joint Chiefs as a collective body. Now, in fact, the JCS chairman has "the right to give advice [to civilian policy makers] not only when asked, but also when not asked" (Perry 1989).

The law did not, however, make the chairman a commander with direct control over U.S. combat forces, a move many believed would have undermined the primacy of civilian control over the military. In fact, although the JCS system comprises the nation's senior military officers, they do not command combat forces in the field. Instead, they are essentially an administrative unit outside the operational chain of command. The actual command of combat forces in the field rests with ten commanders-in-chief (CINCs),[3] who receive their orders from the president as commander-in-chief through the secretary of defense. Thus, for example, in the 1999 Kosovo campaign, General Wesley Clark, commander-in-chief of the European theater (and supreme allied commander in Europe), was more influential in the application of force than the JCS. Indeed, Clark, who sought to use American military might more aggressively than the JCS wished to do, was able to circumvent their obstruction and appeal directly to the civilian chain of command (see Halberstam 2001; Clark 2001). A similar pattern occurred in the campaign against Afghanistan, where Chairman of the JCS General Hugh Shelton and his successor, Air Force General Richard Myers, were central to the initial planning only to see operational influence shift to Army General Tommy Franks, commander-in-chief of the Central Command. The Iraq war of 2003 also seems to fit this model, although it must be noted Franks was a central player in the war planning process and enjoyed unprecedented access to key decision makers and a close relationship with Rumsfeld (see, for example, Franks 2004; Woodward 2004).

Nevertheless, while the Goldwater-Nichols Act moved tentatively on this issue, it did give the JCS authority to transmit orders from the president or the secretary of defense to the CINCs. It also authorized, per the defense secretary's discretion, the chair of the JCS to oversee the CINCs. The CINCs of unified combatant commands in turn were given "operational command" but not complete command over forces assigned to them. Since the first Bush administration (1989–1993), the White House and the secretary of defense have, in practice, put the chair of the JCS into the command loop in this way.

Although the Defense Reorganization Act of 1986 did not accomplish all that its proponents had hoped,[4] it has had major effects on both the formulation and implementation of military policy. According to some, "the dominant norm for the JCS is no longer parochial protection of individual service interests, but a norm of jointness, in which service perspectives, forces, and doctrines are genuinely integrated" (Roman and Tarr 1998). Indeed, the JCS produced a *Joint Vision 2010* plan in 1996, and then developed the strategy even further in its 2001 plan entitled *Joint Vision 2020*. Operations in Kosovo (1999), Afghanistan (2001), and Iraq (2003) illustrate key aspects of the concept. General Franks, who oversaw the latter two campaigns, made it clear that as a CINC he was not an "army" soldier but a "joint" warrior, remarking, "I am absolutely purple" (quoted in Woodward 2004).

Second, Goldwater-Nichols has dramatically enhanced the role of the chairman of the JCS and the Joint Staff at his command to plan, organize, and coordinate the nation's military forces and operations. No longer required to submit corporate advice, the chair is empowered to provide independent recommendations. This development has encouraged the other chiefs to work more closely with the chair because they know he or she can advise as desired (Roman and Tarr 1998). For example, Colin Powell remembered that during his time as chairman he "did not have to take a vote among the chiefs before recommending anything. I did not even have to consult them, though it would have been foolish not to do so" (Powell 1995). Powell's successors—John Shalikashvili, Henry "Hugh" Shelton, Richard Myers, and Peter Pace— enjoyed the same advantage.

Third, Goldwater-Nichols changes have transformed the chair's role within interagency processes as well. Not only is representation on interagency working groups the responsibility of the staff of the JCS, the chair's (and vice chair's) participation in meetings of the deputies and principals committees is "indistinguishable from that of the cabinet officers and other politicians who are members of that body.

In this context, the chairman is a decision maker, not simply an adviser" (Roman and Tarr 1998). Consequently, "the participation of the military in public policy making has never . . . been more centralized, integrated, and effective than it is today" (Roman and Tarr 1998). David Halberstam's (2001) account of applications of force in the 1990s and Bob Woodward's (2002, 2004) examinations of the wars in Afghanistan and Iraq reveal this transformation.

The recent past supports this conclusion. The first chairman who truly took advantage of the reform was Colin Powell, schooled in the art of politics in part by his experience as national security adviser during the Reagan presidency. He became, in the words of defense specialist Richard Kohn (1994), "the most powerful military leader since George C. Marshall, the most popular since Dwight D. Eisenhower, and the most political since Douglas MacArthur." Further evidence can be found in Clinton's efforts to shape the JCS to better fit his administration's conception of the utility of force in "operations other than war." According to one observer, "Clinton's experience with Powell taught him that he would have to choose his next chairman carefully" (Worth 1998). He did so by going outside the current JCS to select his next two chairmen, believing Shalikashvili, CINC of Europe, and Shelton, CINC of U.S. Special Operations Command, would be supportive of nontraditional military missions, also known as *Operations Other Than War (OOTW)* and pronounced "ootwah" in military parlance.

While George W. Bush tapped two vice chairmen of the JCS to serve as his chairmen, he did so, like Clinton, with a sense of their policy preferences. Myers, the first air force general to hold the post, was known as a fan of technological sophistication and a supporter of antimissile systems. Pace, the first Marine Corps general to serve as chairman of the JCS, helped shaped the administration's global counterterrorism strategy. Both Myers and Pace were seen as men who could work with Rumsfeld, Bush's powerful secretary of defense. The fact that presidents take such factors into consideration when they nominate the chairman of

the JSC is a clear indicator of the occupant's important role and influence within the foreign policy-making process.

Twenty-First Century Challenges

As we look toward the end of the first decade of the new century, two questions about the Defense Department's foreign policy role must be addressed. The first concerns the overall force posture, doctrines, and strategies of the department in light of the dramatically changed global environment. As the new century began, the American military looked remarkably similar to its Cold War version in spite of the dramatically different strategic and security environment. The need for reform and restructuring was punctuated sharply when three airliners piloted by terrorists crashed into the towers of the World Trade Center and the Pentagon on September 11, 2001.

Critics had long been pressing for restructuring in light of the new threats and security concerns likely to face the country, stressing unconventional threats such as those revealed by the terrorist strikes. However, previous efforts to restructure forces and strategies in light of the altered environment produced few major changes. For example, although the 1997 *Quadrennial Defense Review* was initiated—with much fanfare—to plan for America's defense needs, its final report disappointed most defense analysts. Its proposals continued to envision a two-war strategy (which the United States would be prepared to fight concurrently two major regional wars) and a force structure built around Cold War era weapons systems. Few defense analysts were pleased. One group saw the strategy as appropriate, but contended there were inadequate funding and force levels to sustain it. Another group maintained it was seriously outdated and merely a justification for preserving a large force structure favored by the armed services and weapons contractors (see Wittkopf and Jones 1999).

A new strategic direction did not emerge until nine months into George W. Bush's presidency. It was first shaped by the administration's established commitment to defense transformation and then accelerated by the terrorist attacks of September 11, 2001. Secretary of Defense Rumsfeld issued the 2001 *Quadrennial Defense Review* on September 30. Even though much of the work on the report had been completed during the preceding summer, its substance corresponded well to the post-9/11 world. For one, homeland defense was explicitly identified as a key mission. Originally tied to the administration's support of national missile defense, this emphasis took on broader significance in the aftermath of multiple terrorist attacks on U.S. soil and led to the establishment of the Northern Combatant Command. In addition, there was a shift within the 2001 QDR from a "threat-based" force planning model, which focuses on *who* the adversary might be or *where* a war might occur, to a "capabilities-based model," which stresses *how* unknown enemies might attack the United States. Thus tools of war—terrorism, chemical and biological weapons, cyberattacks, and nuclear missile threats—rather than specific states, non-state actors, or regions became the focus of military planning and force structure decisions. Furthermore, the 2001 QDR abandoned the requirement to win two regional wars in decisive fashion at the same time, embracing essentially a "win–hold–win" strategy where combat operations might transpire in two theaters at the same time, but victories would be won consecutively rather than simultaneously.

At the center of the 2001 QDR was a strong commitment to revolutionary defense transformation. The report stated the new strategy "will require exploiting U.S. advantages in superior technological innovation; its unmatched space and intelligence capabilities; its sophisticated military training; and its ability to integrate highly distributed military forces in a synergistic combinations for highly complex joint military operations" (see *Quadrennial Defense Review Report*, September 30, 2001). The first sign of this transformation was Rumsfeld's move to scale back or eliminate weapons programs associated with the present-day military or "legacy force"—fighter jets, large ships, and heavy artillery—and redirect money to futuristic, unconventional systems that advanced his vision of a lighter, more agile, and technologically sophisticated

military. The best example was Rumsfeld's elimination of the Crusader mobile artillery system in 2002, which was a conventional weapons platform strongly supported by the army and its congressional supporters (see Jones 2005b).

However, the release of the 2006 *Quadrennial Defense Review* illustrated Rumsfeld was no longer prepared to wage political battles against the armed services' prized conventional programs as he did with the army's Crusader. Instead the report revealed concurrent commitments to the transformational force outlined in the 2001 QDR *and* the legacy force of the past (see *Quadrennial Defense Review Report,* February 6, 2006). What accounted for this shift? First, the presence of "iron triangles" (alliances of lawmakers, weapons contractors, and armed services that protect weapons procurement programs) made it difficult for Rumsfeld to cut conventional weapons systems that enjoyed wider and more politically powerful backing than the Crusader. Second, "[w]hen Rumsfeld suggested in his first QDR that the United States must choose between the status quo and the future force he did not reckon on an ocean of new money that would provide for both" (Von Drehle 2006). The Defense Department budget request for fiscal year 2007 was $439 billion, an amount when adjusted for inflation far exceeded "the annual average of $366 billion spent during the Cold War era when the United States faced the threat of nuclear annihilation or a Soviet invasion of Western Europe" (Rosenberg 2006). Third, the 2001 QDR envisioned a smaller, high-tech "transformational" force capable of waging quick, decisive wars against terrorists and tyrants. However, "postwar" Iraq proved that occupation and stabilization operations demand something different: ground troops and conventional weapons. Moreover, many defense experts believed the rise in spending for conventional, legacy force weapons systems was tied to an unspoken future threat, namely China, whose military expenditures have risen dramatically in recent years (see Rosenberg 2006).

As the second decade of the twenty-first century approached, the Pentagon found itself in control of a massive and unrivaled military machine deployed around the world, engaged in an unconventional war against global terrorism, mired in an unpopular occupation and counterinsurgency, and planning for future conventional conflicts. These realities coupled with the absence of tough decisions explain why annual and supplemental U.S. defense expenditures now surpass the military spending of the next 30 countries combined (Center for Arms Control and Non-Proliferation 2006). Of course, the question remains how long the United States can sustain this pattern given its ever-expanding federal budget deficit and national debt.

The second major concern involves *civil-military relations* in the new century. Civilian control of the military is a principle as old as the Republic itself and thoroughly interwoven into the nation's liberal political culture (Huntington 1957). As we have discussed, many believe that the uniformed military is more influential and capable in its policy role than ever before. Critics express concern that the balance between civilian and military control of the defense establishment now—to an alarming degree—tilts toward the military. In their view, augmenting the authority and independence of the chair of the Joint Chiefs under the Goldwater-Nichols Act has had the unintended consequence of so dramatically enhancing the power of the armed services that they now challenge the very principle of civilian control of the military (see Powell et al. 1994).

By the late 1990s, this potential crisis in civil-military relations was seen to have several facets. First, the military has become more politicized, steadily more open in its political views and affiliations, and increasingly willing to manipulate political leaders and processes to secure their own preferences (Cohen 1997). Second, there is an increasing gap between the military and broader society, as fewer citizens serve in the armed forces and as recruits are drawn from an increasingly narrow segment (mostly from military families). This may indicate "a growing gap between military and societal values" (Cohen 1997). Finally, the rise of the centralized staff and the power of the JCS and its chair, as noted, shifts the balance between

civilian and military officials (Cohen 1997; see also Holsti 1998–1999; Ricks 1997). These factors coupled with issues specific to the Clinton presidency, first the attempt to remove the ban on open homosexuals serving in the military, and then proceeding to several other issues ("sexual harassment concerns within the military, charges of military insubordination at the highest ranks, concerns about the moral authority of the commander-in-chief, [and] questions over who should shape the roles and missions of the post–Cold War force") seriously strained civil-military relations (Feaver 2003).

Although less overtly strained, civil-military relations continued to be a significant concern within the Bush administration. The difficulty, however, emanated from different sources than in the Clinton administration. For example, there was considerable animosity created by Rumsfeld's systematic campaign to reestablish civilian control over the military in the early months of the Bush administration. This development was followed by the armed services' concern over the effect Rumsfeld's defense transformation would have on the legacy force. While tensions subsided in the aftermath of the 9/11 attacks and the war in Afghanistan, the Iraq war and its continuing aftermath have significantly damaged civil-military relations. By some accounts, anger in the officer corps stemmed from a belief that the civilian leadership surrounded itself with "yes-men" (Myers and Franks who supported the Rumsfeld's approach) and then marched into Iraq without heeding the uniformed military's advice about adequate troop levels and the merits of the Powell Doctrine. As a result, the army and the National Guard and Reserves were stretched to a breaking point without sufficient recruitment to provide relief. News of extended tours of duty and a bloody, protracted conflict damaged new enlistments significantly. In addition, there was considerable resentment and concern within the army over its status as an occupying force. Moreover, without a plan to stabilize and rebuild Iraq, the belief was that civilian leaders had enmeshed the military in a bloody counterinsurgency that may not be winnable (see Owens 2003; Bassford 2004; Pant 2005). In fact, the long-term effect could be particularly demoralizing and damaging to an armed force that, in the words of President George H. W. Bush, had "kicked the Vietnam Syndrome once and for all" with its 1991 Gulf War victory. One scholar wrote: "[Rumsfeld] will leave behind an even more burdensome Iraq syndrome—the renewed, nagging, and sometime paralyzing belief that any large-scale U.S. military intervention abroad is doomed to practical failure and moral iniquity" (Freedman 2005). Rumsfeld's controversial tenure came to a close when Robert M. Gates, a former deputy national security adviser and director of central intelligence in the Bush I administration, was nominated in November 2006 to become George W. Bush's second secretary of defense.

THE INTELLIGENCE COMMUNITY

Like the military, the intelligence community has played a prominent role in American foreign policy for nearly half a century. Established to be "America's eyes and ears in a dangerous world" (Kober 1998), the intelligence community was, as a former chair of the House Permanent Select Committee on Intelligence suggested, "a spyglass focused on the Soviet Union, keeping track of Soviet military research and development and watching Soviet activities throughout the developing world" (McCurdy 1994). With the end of the Cold War, the intelligence community was increasingly challenged over its continuing relevance and its capabilities, with many critics calling for major overhauls of the community.

When members of the Al Qaeda terrorist network successfully hijacked four airliners and crashed three of them into the World Trade Center and the Pentagon on September 11, 2001, the intelligence community found its new mission for the twenty-first century. However, its failure to warn of the attacks, apprehend terrorist leader Osama bin Laden, or provide sound intelligence prior to the 2003 Iraq war ensure that questions and criticism will continue. How the intelligence community should serve American foreign policy and security interests remains a critical question. How it should be structured to do so is equally critical.

Since its inception, the intelligence community has engaged in five basic activities (some of which were discussed in Chapter 5): *research and analysis* (CIA and most members), *espionage* (mostly CIA), *technical surveillance* (mostly non-CIA members), *covert action* (mostly CIA), and *counterintelligence* (mostly CIA and FBI) (Hilsman 1995; Johnson 1996). In the post-9/11 era, with its new emphasis on non-state and transnational threats such as terrorism, these remain the central activities. The nature, extent, and objectives of these activities remain vital questions.

Structure and Mission

Foreign policy decision makers need *finished intelligence*—"data . . . which has been carefully collated and analyzed by substantive experts specifically to meet the needs of the national leadership" (Marchetti and Marks 1974)—to understand the varied military, economic, political, scientific, domestic, and foreign issues and events requisite to sound policy making. Such information comes from at least four sources. Much of what constitutes *raw intelligence* (the uncollated and unanalyzed data) must be sifted from *open sources*—reports of journalists and the publications of government agencies, private businesses, and scholars. Additional information is acquired through cloak-and-dagger escapades often called *human intelligence (HUMINT)* because it comes from human, not technical sources. *Imagery intelligence (IMINT)* (computer code that must be converted into images) from cryptanalysis and reconnaissance satellites and *signal intelligence (SIGINT)*—information gathered from interception and analysis of communications, electronic, and telemetry signals—are *technical sources* that provide a wealth of intelligence from around the world.

As Figure 11.3 indicates, gathering and analyzing these different forms of information occurs in and through a vast complex of sixteen actors that together make up the intelligence community. Five elements of the community—the Central

Independent Agency

1. Central Intelligence Agency

Department of Defense Elements

2. Air Force Intelligence, Surveillance, and Reconnaissance
3. Army Military Intelligence
4. Defense Intelligence Agency
5. Marine Corps Intelligence
6. National Geospatial-Intelligence Agency
7. National Reconnaissance Office
8. National Security Agency
9. Office of Naval Intelligence

Department Intelligence Elements (Other than Department of Defense)

10. Coast Guard Intelligence (Department of Homeland Security)
11. Department of Energy's Office of Intelligence
12. Department of Homeland Security's Information Analysis and Infrastructure Protection Directorate
13. Department of State's Bureau of Intelligence and Research
14. Department of the Treasury's Office of Intelligence and Analysis
15. Drug Enforcement Agency's Office of National Security Intelligence (Department of Justice)
16. Federal Bureau of Investigation's Directorate of Intelligence (Department of Justice)

FIGURE 11.3 The Members of the United States Intelligence Community (2006)

SOURCE: Based on www.intelligence.gov/1-members.shtml.

Intelligence Agency (CIA), Defense Intelligence Agency (DIA), National Security Agency (NSA), National Reconnaissance Office (NRO), and National Geospatial-Intelligence Agency (NGA)—are concerned solely with national intelligence. Thus each organization in its entirety is a member of the intelligence community. The other eleven actors are constituent units of larger bureaucracies with roles and responsibilities that lie outside intelligence work. In these cases, only the office or bureau of the organization with an intelligence responsibility is a member of the intelligence community. For example, the Department of the Treasury, as a whole, is not a member of the intelligence community, but its Office of Intelligence and Analysis is.

The word "community" may suggest "members" function in a cooperative manner. In practice, however, the character of the intelligence community is much more decentralized and disorderly. "Indeed, tribal and feudal metaphors often seem more appropriate in describing how the various collection, processing, and analytic organizations interact with one another and with policy makers" (Flanagan 1985; see also Lowenthal 1992). While this can spark creative tension and promote a diversity of outlook that can enhance the overall quality of national intelligence, it can also produce vertical *"stovepipes."* Lowenthal (2006) defines stovepipes as "agencies in similar or analogous lines of work (collection or analysis) that tend to compete with one another, sometimes to a wasteful and perhaps harmful extent." Such behavior, particularly the failure to share information between agencies, impeded the community's ability to thwart the 9/11 attacks and was a central reason behind the abolishment of the director of central intelligence (DCI).

Responsibility for managing the intelligence community from 1947 until 2004 rested with the DCI, who was also the director of the CIA. However, this dual-hatted role made it difficult to exercise effective leadership within the community. Heads of other intelligence agencies were inclined to view the DCI as a bureaucratic competitor rather than an honest broker and coordinator. Today the CIA chief is only responsible for managing the CIA bureaucracy and carries the new title, *director of the Central Intelligence Agency (DCIA).* Overall management of the intelligence community now rests with the *director of national intelligence (DNI),* the nation's new senior intelligence official. This position, which was recommended by the 9/11 Commission, was established by the *Intelligence Reform and Terrorism Prevention Act of 2004* and constitutes the most significant reorganization of U.S. intelligence since the National Security Act of 1947. Although the DNI is a cabinet-level official, the post is not affiliated with any of the organizations within the intelligence community. The responsibilities of the DNI are twofold. First, the DNI heads and coordinates the entire intelligence community through the Office of the Director of National Intelligence (ODNI) and with particular assistance from the principal deputy director of national intelligence (PDDNI) and a supporting staff of about fifty (see Figure 11.4). The DNI's coordinating responsibilities include but are not limited to the following tasks: establishing goals and priorities for the intelligence community, ensuring information is shared between organizations, providing guidance to agencies as they develop individual budgets, developing an annual budget for the intelligence community based on proposals from the sixteen members, monitoring budget implementation, ensuring differences in analytical judgment are fully considered and brought to the attention of decision makers, and coordinating interactions with foreign intelligence services.

To facilitate these responsibilities, the DNI is supported by and has authority over the National Counterterrorism Center, National Counterproliferation Center, National Intelligence Council, and National Counterintelligence Executive. In addition, the DNI is assisted by a number of coordinating committees—the Joint Intelligence Community Council, a deputy-level version of the Joint Intelligence Community Council, and the Intelligence Community Leadership Committee. The DNI also has access to all intelligence related to national security held by any organization of the intelligence community and possesses the authority to set community-wide standards and procedures related to the protection of intelligence sources and methods. Last, the DNI plays a role in the appointment process of most (but not all) of the directors of the sixteen agencies or offices that make up the intelligence community (discussed later).

The second main responsibility of the DNI is to serve as the statutory intelligence adviser to the president, the National Security Council, and the Homeland Security Council. He or she is responsible to the National Security Council and, through it, to the president. Thus the DNI has regular access to the president and responsibility for producing and, on most days, delivering the *President's Daily Brief (PDB).* With additional obligations to the Homeland Security Council, whose concern is domestic security and intelligence, the DNI has a broader purview than the former DCI, whose authority was limited to foreign intelligence matters. President George W. Bush named John Negroponte the first director of national intelligence in February 2005. Negroponte, a veteran career Foreign Service officer, served as U.S. ambassador to the United Nations and the first U.S. ambassador to Iraq following the toppling of Saddam Hussein's regime.

Both the executive and legislative branches conduct oversight of the intelligence community. In the executive branch, in addition to the National Security Council's Office of Intelligence Programs, the *President's Foreign Intelligence Advisory Board (PFIAB)* gives general counsel on the conduct of the intelligence community, including the collection and evaluation of intelligence and the execution of intelligence policy. In 1993, President Clinton's Executive Order 12863 established the *Intelligence Oversight Board* as a standing committee for the PFIAB to focus specifically on the legality of intelligence activities. In practice, however, the

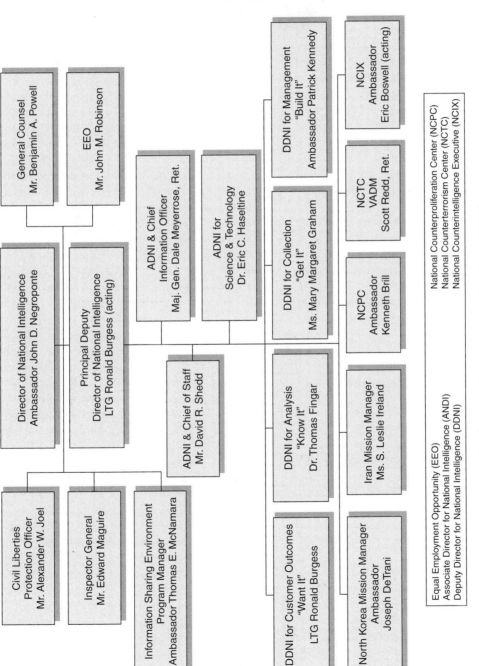

FIGURE 11.4 Office of the Director of National Intelligence Organizational Chart (2006)

SOURCE: www.odni.gov/aboutODNI/printer_friendly/organization_print.htm.

PFIAB has not been a central player in the intelligence community, as presidents have viewed its utility quite differently (Holt 1995; also see Lowenthal 2006).

Congress developed its current oversight mechanisms in the late 1970s following revelations of abuses committed over the previous quarter-century by intelligence agencies. It established the House and Senate *Select Committees on Intelligence* to authorize appropriations for the intelligence community, receive reports on intelligence analysis and production, and oversee the conduct of covert activities once the president has presented a "finding" on the need for such activities (discussed in Chapter 5). More broadly, the president is required by law to keep Congress "fully and currently informed" of all intelligence activities, and Congress as a whole appropriates all money for the intelligence community, including money for intelligence activities secretly tucked away in the Pentagon's budget. In highly sensitive matters, however, "[i]ntelligence officials may brief only the [congressional] leadership (known as the *Gang of 4*), or the leaders and chairmen and ranking members of the Intelligence Committees (known as the *Gang of 8*)" (Lowenthal 2006).

Intelligence and the Department of Defense

The exact size of the intelligence community, in money and personnel, remains uncertain owing to the secrecy in which the community and its activities are shrouded. However, it is widely believed that the top-line budget figure for the post-9/11 intelligence community is about $42 billion (Fessenden 2005). This is a significant increase from the budget estimates of the 1990s. In 1997 and 1998, George Tenet, the director of central intelligence at the time, revealed the aggregate budget levels for those years, which were $26.6 billion and $27.6 billion, respectively (Jehl 2004b). Figure 11.3 makes it clear that the Department of Defense (DOD) is the largest component of the intelligence community. Through the agencies

and elements shown in the figure, the Pentagon consumes 80 percent of the federal intelligence budget (Gates 2004) with the preponderance being absorbed by three DOD organizations—the National Reconnaissance Office (NRO), National Security Agency (NSA), and National Geospatial-Intelligence Agency (NGA).

The ***National Reconnaissance Office (NRO),*** which designs and operates the U.S. government's reconnaissance satellites, is the biggest spender and may alone account for nearly a quarter of the current national intelligence budget.[5] The NRO was created in 1960 to replace the U-2 spy-plane program. Its existence was not revealed until 1973, when its name was inadvertently included in a declassified congressional document, and it remained officially unacknowledged until 1992. "The magic phrase '*national technical means*' was invented so that the parties could talk to each other about reconnaissance satellites without using those words" (Holt 1995). Controlled jointly by the CIA and Defense Department, it operates under the "cover" of the air force, which reportedly pays the bills for the extremely costly photographic and electronic reconnaissance satellites and the rockets necessary to put them into orbit. The imaging (previously photographic) satellites for years provided enormous amounts of detailed information on military and related strategic developments in the Soviet Union and elsewhere. According to one anonymous source, the NRO imaging capability "could start with a satellite picture covering all of downtown Washington and get down so close you can almost read license plates on cars" (Pincus 1994).

The ***National Security Agency (NSA),*** which is responsible for signal intelligence (SIGINT), communications security, and cryptology, follows the NRO as the second most expensive DOD intelligence agency, spending about $7 billion per year. It is also the largest agency with collection sites scattered across the globe and an estimated 38,000 employees (Safire 2002). NSA's operations are extraordinarily technology-intensive, requiring massive supercomputers to discharge its responsibilities. "Its collection systems scoop up enough data every three hours to fill the Library of Congress" (Loeb 2001). Created by a classified presidential directive in 1952, NSA was not generally acknowledged as a government organization until 1957 and, much like the NRO, did not acknowledge its own existence until 1991. Indeed, its legendary silence led people to joke that its initials stood for "No Such Agency."

Scrutiny has heightened in recent years, however. Publicity over a Cold War era program known as *Echelon,* by which the NSA collected information from commercial communication satellites, led to concerns over an NSA role in stealing trade secrets from allies and invading the privacy of American citizens (Strobel 2000; Munro 2000). Early in 2000, its massive array of computers—nearly half the computing power in the entire world—crashed and remained shut down for three days. Although it is now believed that human error and computer glitches are responsible, the crash raised questions about the security of the NSA operations and the age and capability of its technology (Strobel 2000; Vistica 2000). In late 2005, the agency found itself, once again, on the front pages of the nation's newspapers when it was revealed that in an effort to uncover Al Qaeda-linked terrorist activity President Bush signed an executive order in 2002 authorizing the NSA to monitor the international telephone calls and e-mail messages of people with the United States without first obtaining court warrants. Critics of the program and of the Bush administration charged that the NSA's activities constituted illegal domestic spying, because the Foreign Intelligence Surveillance Act (FISA) prohibits electronic surveillance of individuals within the United States without the approval of the U.S. Foreign Intelligence Surveillance Court. The president maintained it was a "terrorist surveillance program" that lawmakers had implicitly approved with their resolution to use force in the wake of the 9/11 attacks.

With an estimated 14,000 employees and a likely operating budget of a few billion dollars,[6] *National Geospatial-Intelligence Agency (NGA)*

ranks as the third largest of the DOD-related intelligence agencies. As its name suggests, the mission of NGA is to prepare geospatial intelligence and imagery—national security information in a cartographic, photographic, digital, or computerized format. NGA data encompass topographical and hydrographical information and can involve natural or manmade objects. Until 2003 NGA was known as the National Imaging and Mapping Agency (NIMA), which was established in 1996 to manage all military and civilian surveillance and mapping operations. It combined the functions of the Defense Mapping Agency, the Central Imagery Office, the Defense Dissemination Program Office, and the CIA's National Photographic Interpretation Center, along with the imagery processing and dissemination functions of the Defense Intelligence Agency and the NRO. One recent development involving NGA has been the emergence of a strong working relationship with the NSA. "[A] previously undisclosed [joint] unit, code-named Geocell, has rushed real time tips and warnings to field operatives and White House officials. More than two dozen NSA-NGA teams were posted together in Iraq [during the 2003 war], with scores more in other military commands" (Drogin 2005).

Like NRO, NSA and NGA, the *Defense Intelligence Agency (DIA)* also operates under the authority of the secretary of defense, but it is the smallest of all DOD intelligence operations, with about 8,500 employees and a budget of approximately $600 million dollars (Pike 1996). Created by Robert McNamara in 1961, the DIA was to consolidate in one agency the various intelligence units of the armed services: Army Military Intelligence, Air Force Intelligence, Surveillance and Reconnaissance, the Office of Naval Intelligence, and Marine Corps Intelligence. These units are involved in the collection of "departmental" intelligence as opposed to "national" intelligence—that is, in collecting information germane to their tactical (battlefield) missions.

Designed to provide direct intelligence support to the secretary of defense and the Joint Chiefs of Staff (for whom the director of DIA is the principal intelligence adviser), the DIA's assignment is to improve coordination and management of Defense Department intelligence resources. For instance, the DIA represents the Defense Department on the National Foreign Intelligence Board (NFIB) and manages the defense attaché system (which places military representatives in U.S. field missions abroad). In 1995, the Defense HUMINT Service unit was formed, which collects the military's spies and clandestine operatives into single system (rather than one for each service) under the DIA (but, interestingly, overseen in the field by the CIA) to improve the coordination and analysis of military intelligence (Waller 1995). Without congressional authorization and drawing on "reprogrammed funds," Secretary of Defense Donald Rumsfeld secretly established the *Strategic Support Branch (SSB)* in 2001 as an arm of the Defense HUMINT Service to end, in the words of his order, "near total dependence on the CIA" for human intelligence. The branch consists of "small teams of case officers, linguists, interrogators and technical specialists" who have aided special operations forces in Afghanistan, Iraq, and several other undisclosed countries. The existence of the unit, which clearly encroaches on the traditional turf of the CIA, was not revealed publicly until early 2005 (Gellman 2005).[7]

Although the functions assigned the DIA appear to place it in a position superior to the army, navy, air force, and Marines, the DIA collects little information on its own, relying instead on the service intelligence agencies for its raw intelligence data. Moreover, the individual military departments send observers to the NFIB meetings, and military attachés themselves are drawn from the armed services (Holt 1995). Hence the DIA has chiefly analyzed information collected by the DIA, the Pentagon's satellites, and the embassy attachés, but has been less effective as a central coordinator (Waller 1995). These and other problems have led critics to question the need for DIA's continued existence, but as long as it enjoys the backing of the secretary of defense it will remain a formidable rival of other intelligence agencies.

Beyond the control of DIA, the Defense HUMINT Service, military attachés, and the new

Strategic Support Branch (not to mention the director of national intelligence), additional DOD intelligence units have emerged in recent years, providing further evidence of an ever-increasing trend in the militarization of U.S. intelligence. For example, *Special Operations Command* has placed small teams of its troops (referred to as military liaison elements) in dozens of U.S. embassies to collect operational intelligence and plan counterterrorism raids in Africa, Latin America, and Southeast Asia (Shanker and Shane 2006). In addition, the *Counterintelligence Field Activity* was established in 2002. With $1 billion in expenditures over three years, "[CIFA] has grown to become an analytic and operational organization with nine directorates and widening authority focused on protecting defense facilities and personnel from terrorist attacks" (Pincus 2006). In late 2005, CIFA sought congressional authority to conduct domestic surveillance activities related to counterterrorism, treason, and economic espionage.

Intelligence and the Department of State

The ***Bureau of Intelligence and Research (INR)*** is the State Department's representative in the intelligence community. The department's intelligence functions arise naturally out of its general foreign affairs responsibilities, and much of what the department routinely does in the way of analyzing and interpreting information might be regarded as intelligence work. INR is the unit through which the State Department makes its input into the various interagency committees that seek to guide intelligence operations (other than covert activities. The director of INR is also the secretary of state's senior in-house intelligence adviser.

In addition to representing the State Department within the intelligence community, INR's primary objective is to introduce a "diplomatic sensitivity to intelligence reports", and its own reports "are among the most highly regarded in the government—some say the best" (Johnson 1989). While far from flawless, the intelligence generated by

INR before the 2003 Iraq war was considered the best (or least wrong) of any member of the U.S. intelligence community (see Jehl 2004a). But INR does not independently collect intelligence except through normal cable traffic and reporting from overseas posts. Instead, it depends on input from other agencies, which its small staff of 300 (as of 2004) then turns into finished intelligence reports. Within the intelligence community, therefore, the State Department has been more a consumer than a producer of intelligence. This fact combined with INR's comparatively small size place the State Department in a relatively disadvantageous position within the highly competitive intelligence community.

Intelligence and Other Agencies

Other than the CIA (which will be discussed in the next section), there are five remaining officially designated members of the intelligence community—elements of the Treasury Department, the Energy Department, the Federal Bureau of Investigation (FBI), the Drug Enforcement Agency (DEA), and the Homeland Security Department (DHS). Each plays an important role in intelligence operations, although none is concerned primarily with the collection of foreign intelligence.

Department of the Treasury   The intelligence activities of the Department of the Treasury derive in part from the collection of foreign economic intelligence by its overseas attachés. The department also uses collection, analysis, counterintelligence, and enforcement tools (freezing of assets, for example)—to protect the U.S. banking and financial system; to undermine financial support networks for rogue states, terrorists, money launderers, drug traffickers, and other threats; and to assist policy makers with foreign economic and monetary issues. Two units within Treasury, both of which were established following the 9/11 attacks, are central to these responsibilities—the Office of Terrorism and Financial Intelligence (TFI) and the Office of Intelligence and Analysis (OIA). OIA is a member of the intelligence community.

Department of Energy   The Department of Energy maintains an Office of Intelligence (IN), which is responsible for the overt collection and analysis of intelligence on energy policies and developments, including energy security, nuclear weapons and nonproliferation, energy-related science and technology, and nuclear energy, waste, and safety. As the department responsible for conducting nuclear weapons research, development, and production, it maintains counterintelligence capabilities regarding those weapons. It also participates with other government agencies in monitoring nonproliferation issues. In providing policy makers with energy-related intelligence, IN draws on Energy's vast complex of bureaucratic resources, including the National Nuclear Security Administration (NNSA), which manages the nation's nuclear weapons and (as of 2005) had a staff of 35,000 and a budget of $6.6 billion (Deutch 2005).

Federal Bureau of Investigation   The Federal Bureau of Investigation (a Justice Department agency) is represented within the intelligence community through its Directorate of Intelligence, which was established in 2004. It is responsible for collecting and analyzing information to aid national security and law enforcement officials in thwarting terrorist attacks, foreign espionage, cyberterrorism, and national and transnational crime. Beyond furnishing intelligence, the FBI has a long-standing role in domestic counterintelligence, and makes an important contribution in counterterrorism, particularly since the 9/11 attacks. The FBI's Counterterrorism Division (with a large infusion of personnel and money in recent years) and Counterintelligence Division carry out these field activities. In fact, the work of these units has increasingly shifted the FBI's entire institutional focus. In 2003, for instance, the FBI filed more than 1,700 electronic surveillance warrants for espionage and counterterrorism cases compared with 1,442 warrants for criminal cases (Eggen and Schmidt 2004).

The FBI's mandate is strictly domestic; therefore, it must work with the CIA, which bears responsibility for counterintelligence and counterterrorism abroad. However, the relationship between the two agencies has long been marked by conflict (Riebling 1994), fed in part by their different perspectives and responsibilities. When the FBI catches spies, it thinks in terms of putting them in jail or, if they have diplomatic immunity, of expelling them from the country. When the CIA catches spies, it thinks in terms of turning them into double agents—that is, using them to spy on the government they have been working for (Holt 1995). However, fueled in part by the 1994 Aldrich Ames spy case (which was characterized by a lack of cooperation between the FBI and the CIA) as well as emergent security threats such as terrorism and drugs, the two agencies have begun to cooperate more closely.

Although they cannot collect foreign intelligence or conduct overseas counterintelligence investigations, the FBI's 59 legal attachés or *"legats"* (as of 2006) allow the agency to maintain a global presence. ("Legats" often have responsibilities in multiple countries.) Based at U.S. diplomatic posts around the world, these offices play a coordinating role with foreign law enforcement and security agencies. They facilitate FBI training for foreign police forces, share information and resources in combating crime and terrorism, pursue global leads related to U.S. domestic criminal investigations, and coordinate investigations of interest to both countries. When terrorist attacks occur against American targets overseas, as in the 1998 attacks against U.S. embassies in the Sudan and Tanzania, "legats" are typically first on the scene, demonstrating the FBI's increasing cooperation with foreign governments, the State Department, and the CIA (see Kampeas 2001).

Drug Enforcement Agency Recognizing the seriousness of global drug trafficking and the nexus between the production and sale of illicit narcotics and other security threats, such as terrorism, the Office of National Security Intelligence within the *Drug Enforcement Agency (DEA)* was named the newest member of the intelligence community in February 2006. Despite this recent action, the DEA has had a long-standing relationship with the intelligence community through the collection and

analysis of drug-related intelligence to support law enforcement activities and national policy making. Like the FBI, the DEA is a law enforcement agency housed within the Justice Department. However, its jurisdiction over foreign and domestic aspects of illicit narcotics can cause its activities to overlap with the CIA. Much like the FBI and CIA, the two agencies have quite different perspectives on their bureaucratic roles. Indeed, many accounts indicate that the DEA's efforts to combat the drug trade in the 1980s and early 1990s came into direct conflict with the CIA's activities in Central and South America, especially in Nicaragua. The DEA's global presence has expanded to 86 offices in 63 countries (as of 2006), stimulated in large part by the "war on drugs" waged by the Bush I, Clinton, and Bush II administrations.

Department of Homeland Security Two elements of the Department of Homeland Security (DHS) are also members of the intelligence community. First, the Coast Guard, which is part of the DHS and also one of the nation's military services, collects information germane to its maritime and homeland security duties. Coast Guard Intelligence (CGI) also shares information with other agencies concerning port and waterways security, drug and alien migrant interdiction, and maritime defense. Second, the Information Analysis and Infrastructure Protection (IAIP) Directorate analyzes and integrates law enforcement information and national intelligence related to terrorist threats to the U.S. homeland. However, like the State Department's Bureau of Intelligence and Research, IAIP does not collect intelligence. It is relies on finished intelligence reports from other sources, namely the CIA and FBI. Once it receives information from these actors, IAIP assesses it from a homeland security perspective to identify threats, issue warnings, assess vulnerabilities, and make policy recommendations. IAIP also works with the FBI to disseminate information from the broader intelligence community to assist local and state law enforcement in responding to terrorist threats.

The responsibilities of IAIP correspond to the Department of Homeland Security's organizational

Border and Transportation Security	**Former Department**
U.S. Customs Service	Treasury
The Immigration and Naturalization Service (part)	Justice
The Federal Protection Agency	General Services Administration
The Transportation Security Administration	Transportation
Federal Law Enforcement Training Center	Treasury
Animal and Plant Health Service (part)	Agriculture
Office for Domestic Preparedness	Justice

Emergency Preparedness and Response	**Former Department**
The Federal Emergency Management Agency	Independent Agency
Strategic National Stockpile	Health and Human Services
National Disaster Medical System	Health and Human Services
Nuclear Incident Response Team	Energy
Domestic Emergency Support Team	Justice
National Domestic Preparedness Office	Federal Bureau of Investigation

Science and Technology	**Former Department**
CBRN Countermeasures Programs	Energy
Environmental Measurements Laboratory	Energy
National BW Defense Analysis Center	Defense
Plum Island Animal Disease Center	Agriculture

Information Analysis and Infrastructure Protection	**Former Department**
Federal Computer Incident Response Center	General Services Administration
National Communications System	Defense
National Infrastructure Protection Center	Federal Bureau of Investigation
Energy Security and Assurance Program	Energy
Secret Service	Treasury
Coast Guard	Transportation

FIGURE 11.5 Agencies Transferred into the Department of Homeland Security

SOURCE: Department of Homeland Security, www.dhs.gov/xabout/history/editorial_0133.shtm.

mission to deter, prevent, and mitigate terrorist acts within the United States. The department was created little more than a year after the September 11 attacks when George W. Bush signed the Homeland Security Act of 2002 into law on November 24, 2002. President Bush named former Pennsylvania governor Tom Ridge the first secretary of homeland security on January 23, 2003, and *Department of Homeland Security* (DHS) was officially activated as the fifteenth cabinet-level department on January 24, 2003. The establishment of DHS is considered the most sweeping and significant reorganization of the federal government since the passage of the National Security Act of 1947, which created the Department of Defense. DHS was formed through a consolidation of 22 federal agencies with over 170,000 employees (see Figure 11.5). As of 2005, the department stood as a massive federal bureaucracy with approximately 183,000 employees and an annual budget of roughly $40 billion.

Despite its size, DHS emerged as a weak actor during the tenure of Tom Ridge, who resigned as secretary of homeland security in December 2004 and was succeeded by federal appeals court judge Michael Chertoff. Through the daily terrorist threat briefing, Ridge enjoyed daily access to the president and according to White House Chief of Staff Andrew Card, was "among the closest of the president's friends in the Cabinet and the political environment" (Mintz 2003). Nonetheless, Ridge lost battles on a number of levels.[8] Within the executive branch, the FBI and CIA won control of key analytic centers, depriving DHS of responsibilities it was promised under the Homeland Security Act and the means to promote better information sharing across the government (a central lesson of 9/11). On Capitol Hill, Ridge's failure to produce a national list of critical infrastructure targets and a strategy to protect such sites allowed pork-barrel politics to shape funding allocations, which resulted in rural regions garnering more per capita homeland security funding than high threat areas (Prieto 2004). In the realm of public affairs, Ridge saw the department's color-coded terrorist warning system and his advice to stock up on duct tape and plastic sheeting become subjects of ridicule. Most important, DHS officials and outside experts maintained that "personality conflicts, bureaucratic bottlenecks and an atmosphere of demoralization" prevailed inside the department. A former DHS inspector general commented in early 2005, "DHS is still a compilation of 22 agencies that aren't integrated as a cohesive whole." When asked to offer examples of ineffectiveness, the same official replied, "I don't know where to start . . . I've never seen anything like it before" (quoted in Mintz 2005). The statement seems prophetic in light of the department's inept response to Hurricane Katrina in late 2005.

Of course, we would be remiss if we did not mention that as DHS struggled with these problems, the U.S. homeland was kept free of terrorist attack. This is a significant point given the department's

central mission and the potential devastating consequences. Moreover, a bureaucratic experiment as extensive as the Department of Homeland Security cannot be judged after a few short years. It will take a decade or more before the wisdom of the 2002 reorganization and the true effectiveness of DHS can be fully assessed.

Central Intelligence Agency

We now turn our attention to the most prominent member of the intelligence community. Often referred to as the "Agency," "Langley" (for its location in Virginia), or the "Company" (by its employees), the ***Central Intelligence Agency (CIA)*** is the only independent agency within the community. It was established by the National Security Act of 1947, largely out of concern for the quality of intelligence analysis available to policy makers— stemming in part from the surprise attack by the Japanese at Pearl Harbor in 1941. The CIA was assigned responsibilities for (1) advising the National Security Council (NSC) on intelligence matters relating to national security; (2) making recommendations to the NSC for coordinating the intelligence activities of the various federal executive departments and agencies; (3) correlating and evaluating intelligence and providing for its dissemination; and (4) carrying out such additional services, functions, and duties relating to national security intelligence as the NSC might direct. Before long, covert psychological, political, paramilitary, and economic activities were added to the CIA's charge (see Chapter 5).

Although it may be the best known U.S. intelligence actor, the CIA is a relatively small agency with an estimated budget of $5 billion (as of 2003) and a staff about 20,000 (which is expected to expand significantly in coming years). Moreover, the CIA's stature within the intelligence community has diminished over the last decade or so. It is no longer maintains exclusive control of human intelligence; the Aldrich Ames spy scandal led the FBI to become more centrally responsible for counterintelligence; and imagery analysis capability was lost to a Pentagon agency (see Jones 2001). Most important, the agency's director does not head the post-9/11 intelligence community, serve as the nation's lead intelligence official, or stand as the president's primary intelligence adviser. As discussed, those duties now fall within the purview of the new director of national intelligence. Yet the CIA remains a seasoned, all-source intelligence agency; and the national security information it gathers, analyzes, and disseminates is vital to policy-makers who must make difficult decisions.

Two men have held the newly created post of director of the Central Intelligence Agency (DCIA): Porter J. Goss (2005–2006), a former chairman of the House Select Committee on Intelligence and a retired CIA case officer, and General Michael Hayden (2006–present), who served as the director of the National Security Agency and, later, as the first deputy director of national intelligence. Assisted by a deputy director, executive director, and a deputy executive director, the primary responsibility of the DCIA is to manage the CIA bureaucracy (see Figure 11.6). Although it clearly has many elements and support offices, the core of the CIA consists of four main divisions, two of which have had the greatest impact in shaping the identity, work, and reputation of the agency over time. The *Directorate of Intelligence* is the analysis division of the CIA. Its responsibilities are to sift through and analyze the vast quantity of data gathered from public and intelligence community sources and produce the CIA's intelligence assessments. Espionage (human intelligence collection), covert actions, and counterintelligence are the responsibility of the *National Clandestine Service*, formerly known as the Directorate of Operations (see, for example, Nye 1994; Andrew 1995; Berkowitz and Goodman 2000; Lowenthal 2006).

The Directorate of Operations was renamed in October 2005 in response to findings of the 9/11 Commission and a specific recommendation made by the 2004–2005 WMD Commission, formally known as the President's Commission on Intelligence Capabilities of the United States Regarding Weapons of Mass Destruction. The change also reflected the new standing of the DCIA as the National HUMINT Manager. The DCIA through

the director of the National Clandestine Service—whose identity is classified—coordinates human intelligence collection across the government. Such collection involves HUMINT units in the FBI and Pentagon, for example. However, it is important to note that this coordination does not afford the DCIA or CIA direction or control over these units. Moreover, the Office of the Director of National Intelligence (ODNI) oversees the work of the National Clandestine Service. A former senior intelligence official explained the logic of the decision to place the National Clandestine Service within the CIA in this way: "[If the coordinating] role had not remained in the CIA, it would have been bad for agency morale, which is already down. Despite the recent faults of the CIA, it is more disciplined and sophisticated on human intelligence than elsewhere [in the intelligence community]" (quoted in Pincus 2005a). Yet it remains to be seen whether the change will have any meaningful impact on the CIA's influence within the intelligence community or create a better coordinated, national human intelligence effort.

In the next few pages, we take a closer look at some of the CIA's most critical roles and responsibilities: intelligence gathering, intelligence analysis, and covert action (including within the latter area, the management and oversight of such action).

Intelligence Gathering   Recruiting and running spy networks in other countries is perhaps the signature effort of the CIA in the public's mind. However, the September 11 terrorist attacks revealed a serious problem: the lack of HUMINT caused by the over-reliance on technical means and the long-term decay of the CIA's human intelligence assets. The shocking success of the surprise attacks exposed the flip side of the HUMINT dilemma: such assets may be unsavory, but the lack of them can cause intelligence failures with devastating results. Addressing this problem, a former CIA counterterrorism expert argued, "We have a major gap here . . . There's been a lot of emphasis on technical collection at the expense of human resources" (Freedberg 2001). Both the long-term

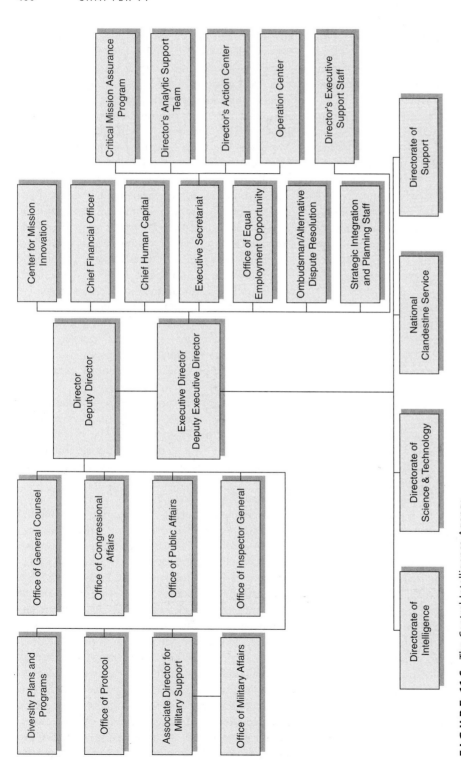

FIGURE 11.6 The Central Intelligence Agency

SOURCE: International Security Research and Intelligence Agency, www.isria.net/article.php?art=593, accessed 12/8/06.

emphasis on technical means and the more recent "human rights checks" on human assets have combined to create a deficient agency. To respond to such concerns, the CIA rescinded the 1995 guidelines requiring its operatives to secure high-level CIA approval before recruiting informers with criminal activity or human rights abuses in their backgrounds (Risen 2002). Moreover, agency funds were significantly increased and President Bush ordered a 50 percent expansion in the number of CIA clandestine officers (Pincus 2005c).

The difficulty, of course, is attracting the right personnel. Although the CIA enjoyed a dramatic increase in applications after the September 11 attacks, its needs are more difficult to meet. As a longtime analyst of intelligence affairs noted, "The ideal candidate is an Arab-American citizen, has knowledge about the culture and the Middle East, has language ability, and is willing to work for the CIA." An anonymous CIA officer added, "You [also] need to put people in place and let them sit there for ten years" (quoted in Freedberg 2001).

Traditionally, the CIA has had difficulty in minority recruitment (see Jones 2001). However, they have placed a major emphasis on such hiring in recent years and enjoyed some success. One troubling issue is whether there will be enough veteran operatives to train and mentor new employees. In his first year as head of the CIA, Porter Goss "lost [in the clandestine service] one director, two deputy directors, and at least a dozen department heads, station chiefs and division directors—many with the key language skills and experience . . . the agency needs" (Linzer 2005). The reasons for the departures have been varied, from low morale tied to post-9/11 inquiries and the agency's loss of standing in the intelligence community to anger over Goss's critique of CIA operatives before becoming CIA chief to dissatisfaction with aspects of his management style (see Linzer 2005). Whatever the cause, the agency can ill afford to lose such experience and expertise when the need for high quality human intelligence collection is critical in the ongoing war on terrorism.

Intelligence Analysis Analyzing intelligence—whether HUMINT, TECHINT, or open source—is similarly problematic. Clearly assessing situations and providing policy makers with information is a vital role and responsibility of the CIA and the broader intelligence community (Berkowitz and Goodman 2000). One of the key contributions the CIA's intelligence directorate plays in this effort is its dominant (although not exclusive) role in the production of the *President's Daily Brief*, which is now supervised and delivered by the director of national intelligence. It also prepares the *Senior Executive Intelligence Brief*, formally the National Intelligence Daily, which provides daily descriptions and analyses of events and developments around the world of potential importance to policy makers. Other, longer-term reports and papers are produced by the intelligence directorate, whose officers draw from open sources, HUMINT, and technical sources to anticipate trends and developments. As Joseph Nye (1994) has described their efforts, "Intelligence analysts sift through reams of information, trying to sort the accurate from the erroneous, and when not enough facts are available, estimating what the picture would look like if all facts were available."

George J. Tenet, who served as the CIA's director from 1997 to 2004, proclaimed publicly that analysis was his agency's core function. Consequently, he hired more analysts, instituted a new training program for recruits, established a CIA school for intelligence analysis, and created the Senior Analytic Service to keep and reward the most seasoned intelligence analysts (see Jones 2001). His successor has sought to fulfill President Bush's mandate to increase the number of analysts by 50 percent (Pincus 2005c). But how good has CIA analysis been?

Wide agreement exists on the high quality and usefulness of the daily intelligence documents, called by one intelligence officer the "most important product of the CIA." Many instances of timely, accurate papers and assessments exist and even critics acknowledge a body of excellent analyses (Goodman 1997). A recently released set of CIA estimates on Soviet spending and policy suggests a reasonably accurate set of documents (Berkowitz and Richelson 1995; Firth and Noren 1998; Fischer 1999; Haines and Leggett 2001).

However, others would argue that, on major questions, the CIA has repeatedly failed to provide good analysis. A listing would include its failure to anticipate North Korea's invasion of South Korea in 1950 and the Chinese intervention later that year; the Soviet Union's placement of missiles in Cuba in 1962; the Soviet intervention in Czechoslovakia in 1968; the 1973 attack on Israel by Egypt and its allies; and the fall of the Shah of Iran and the Soviet invasion of Afghanistan in 1979. Accusations of poor performance on the issue of Vietnam have been leveled as well (see Adams 1994). More recently, it would include its failure to anticipate Iraq's 1990 invasion of Kuwait, the precipitous decline of the Soviet Union, the 1998 test of nuclear weapons by India, and mistakenly selecting the Chinese embassy in Yugoslavia as a bombing target during the 1999 Kosovo war (see, for example, Goodman 1997; Pipes 1995; Jones 2001).

Some would argue that the intelligence community's failure to warn against, much less prevent, the September 11 strikes on New York and Washington constitute another catastrophic failure. This one highlighted an additional weakness: not only is the CIA lacking in adequate HUMINT, it does not have sufficient analysts to comb through and make sense of the intelligence data it does collect. The House Intelligence Committee noted, "At the National Security Agency and the Central Intelligence Agency, thousands of pieces of data were never analyzed, or were analyzed after the fact, because there are too few analysts; even fewer with the necessary language skills. . . . Written materials can sit for months, and sometime years, before a linguist with proper security clearances can begin a translation." According to Loch Johnson (2001), writing before the September strikes, "Between 1993 and 1997, fully 1,000 analysts retired from the CIA alone—a one-third reduction, back to 1977 levels. By the year 2005, CIA director George Tenet anticipates that up to 40 percent of the workforce at the agency will have served for five years or less. As a result, the secret agencies lack enough talented interpreters of information to make sense of the data that flood their offices."

Just a few years later, CIA-dominated analysis was blamed once again for a serious post-9/11 intelligence debacle. In a March 2005 letter transmitting their panel's final report to the president, the co-chairs of the WMD Commission (referenced earlier), Judge Laurence Silberman and former Senator Charles Robb, stated bluntly, " . . . the Intelligence Community was dead wrong in almost all of its pre-war judgments about Iraq's weapons of mass destruction. This was a major intelligence failure. Its principal causes [included] . . . serious errors in analyzing what information it could gather, and a failure to make clear just how much of its analysis was based on assumptions, rather than good evidence. On a matter of this importance, we simply cannot afford failures of this magnitude." The commission's conclusion was consistent with an earlier inquiry by the Senate Select Committee on Intelligence. The lawmakers wrote in their final report, "The failure . . . to accurately analyze and describe the intelligence in the [2002] National Intelligence Estimate was the result of a combination of systematic weaknesses, primarily in analytic trade craft, compounded by a lack of information sharing, poor management, and inadequate intelligence collection."

National Intelligence Estimates (NIEs), are routinely prepared on various parts of the world and take several months (if not longer) to prepare. ***Special National Intelligence Estimates (SNIEs)*** are prepared more quickly in response to specific requests by top-level policy makers who require information about urgent issues. These reports, signed by the DNI, are supposed to be the "best judgments" of the intelligence community on their respective subjects. Their value, however, is suspect. One senator described them as "overly cautious, caveated, and consensus-oriented" (Boren 1992). General Norman Schwarzkopf, who led U.S. forces during Operation Desert Storm in the 1991 Persian Gulf War, characterized the intelligence estimates as "unhelpful mush." In short, the many perspectives and voices that must be incorporated into estimates have a centrifugal effect, working to either water them down to common denominators or to weigh them down with exceptions, footnotes, alternate views, and the like, so that there is no true "estimate" involved but, rather, a series of agency-based positions.

However, the sources of the prewar Iraq intelligence failure extended well beyond the infamous 2002 NIE. One former CIA official has maintained that the Iraq intelligence failure was a result of more than inferior analysis. It was also the product of poor producer-consumer relations and the politicization of intelligence (see Pillar 2006). The *producer-consumer challenge*[9] refers to the difficulty in getting the information—accurate and objective—into key policy makers' hands in useful forms and at opportune moments. The publicly available evidence indicates intelligence analysts (producers) failed policy makers (consumers) on the issue of WMD. According to the CIA official, however, on the larger issues concerning the wisdom of going to war and the need to prepare for an unstable aftermath (if war was pursued) policy makers ignored intelligence analysts' valid warnings by failing to request or consult CIA reports.

Traditionally, the *politicization of intelligence* refers to a problem that occurs when those responsible for providing intelligence also become policy advocates. In such situations, top CIA officials or analysts may "slant" intelligence and reports to fit their own policy preferences. This was a common occurrence in the Reagan administration when William Casey and his deputy, Robert Gates, headed the agency (see Waller 1996). The inquiries conducted by both the WMD Commission and the Senate Select Committee found no evidence of such behavior in the Iraq case. According to Pillar (2006), however, more subtle types of politicization emerged. These included the questions that analysts were asked to pursue, the ease in which *some* reports reached policy makers (and others did not), and the highly visible use of the intelligence community to support the administration's march to war. On the last point, one clear example was George Tenet's conspicuous position behind Colin Powell as he delivered his February 2003 briefing to the United Nations Security Council. Finally, the most

troubling form of politicization from the perspective of Pillar (2006) was the Bush administration "aggressively using intelligence to win public support for its decision to go to war. This meant selectively adducing data—'cherry-picking'—rather than using the intelligence community's own analytic judgments."

Management and Oversight of Covert Actions Because the CIA's responsibilities also include covert operations (discussed in Chapter 5) and espionage in other countries, which by their nature require secrecy, how to exercise control over such intelligence operations has been a regular concern for both the president and Congress. The National Security Council (NSC) bears this responsibility in the presidential subsystem. Hence, the NSC apparatus has been ultimately responsible for approving covert actions and seeing that they meet applicable legal regulations (such as the prohibition against assassination of foreign political leaders).[10]

However, the concept of *plausible denial* complicates this relatively straightforward responsibility. Plausible denial means that the president is not appraised of current or pending covert actions in order to save him or her from the possible embarrassment of a "blown" operation. Hence, as the investigations of the 1970s showed, presidents can (and have) denied knowledge of covert operations undertaken on their behalf. As testimony during one of these investigations indicated, "One means of protecting the president from embarrassment was not to tell him about certain covert operations, at least formally" (*Final Report of the Select Committee to Study Governmental Operations with Respect to Intelligence Activities* 1976, I).

Partly as a result of such revelations in the 1970s, Congress has attempted to clarify the responsibility for the initiation and monitoring of covert operations. The Hughes-Ryan Amendment to the 1974 Foreign Assistance Act required that the president certify to Congress (that is, "find") that an executive-approved covert action is "important to the national interests of the United States." The law required that the CIA inform Congress of the *presidential finding* in a "timely manner," but also thereby required that the president be aware of and formally approve covert actions. In practice, the requirement meant informing roughly forty-five to two hundred members of Congress in the House and Senate committees on intelligence, armed services, appropriations, and foreign affairs and relations. The 1980 Intelligence Oversight Act, which superseded the Hughes-Ryan requirements, cut the number of committees to only two and, in some circumstances, allowed notification of merely the Gang of 8 (discussed earlier).

The evidence from the 1970s suggests other problems with top-level management of covert operations by the nation's elected officials. As one analyst observed in commenting on the Carter administration, "A tendency reportedly has grown within the CIA to forward only a few broad covert action categories to the president and make in-house decisions on all the supposedly routine ones... [which] permits the agency to bypass the White House and Congress" (Johnson 1980). Even when they are issued, the nature of the findings is also problematic. As some observers have indicated, they have often been too broad to be useful as instruments of control, management, and oversight (see Turner 1985; Holt 1995).

The Iran-Contra affair during the Reagan administration prompted another wave of concerns about managing covert actions. As many investigations and accounts indicate, in its efforts to maintain support for the rebels fighting against the leftist Sandinista regime in Nicaragua, as well as to secure the release of American hostages held by terrorists with ties to Iran, the Reagan administration concealed the operations from Congress, failed to issue written findings, circumvented congressional restrictions on aid to the contras, and provided false and misleading information about its activities.

The Iran-Contra revelations reinforced Congress's uneasiness about its oversight responsibilities with respect to covert actions and led to further changes. President Reagan issued an executive order in 1987 designed to address some of the problems. Among other things, it required all agencies to report on their activities; precluded the NSC staff

from involvement in covert operations; and required written findings prior to the initiation of the operation, and access by all members of the NSC to those findings. The administration and Congress agreed to establish an independent inspector general for the CIA to improve the agency's ability to monitor itself. Congress pressed the administration even further, seeking to require written notification of all covert actions within specified time periods, thus closing the loophole the Reagan administration had used to ignore Congress as it pursued its Iranian initiative and support of the contras (Holt 1995). The legislation failed to pass the House and was then dropped when George H. W. Bush assumed the presidency. However, in 1991, Congress succeeded in passing legislation (as part of the intelligence authorization bill) that defined covert actions, required written findings in all cases, and banned retroactive findings.

Nonetheless, new covert activities in the campaign against terrorism raise further concerns, especially since George W. Bush determined that assassinations of terrorists are permissible under existing executive orders, and because he has authorized the CIA to "take the gloves off" in its efforts. One manifestation of this broad latitude has been the CIA's rendition system. Suspected Al Qaeda terrorists are captured in one country, boarded on an unmarked plane, and secretly transferred to friendly but less than democratic "third countries" where CIA operatives or foreign intelligence personnel are free to use aggressive interrogation tactics (Priest 2005a). The CIA has also developed a global network of secret prisons, known as "black sites," where suspected terrorists have been detained indefinitely and are not privy to the protections associated with U.S. civil or military law (Priest 2005b).

On the one hand, national security officials, who are reluctant even to acknowledge these measures exist, see such actions as absolutely essential if the United States is to prevail in the war on terror. Lawmakers and human rights advocates, on the other hand, worry about the potential for torture and inhumane treatment of prisoners, particularly in light of such behavior at U.S. military prisons in Iraq and Guantanamo Bay where CIA personnel were present. Not surprisingly, they push for full disclosure and oversight of CIA practices. Thus an inherent tension exists between the principle of democratic governance, which depends on access to information so that citizens can make informed decisions, and on the secrecy that surrounds the collection of intelligence and covert intelligence operations. The question remains: Can a democratic society long absolve itself from responsibility for the conduct of its government officials without also running the risk of losing sight of who is serving whom, for what purpose, and in pursuit of what ideals? The question goes to the heart of a fundamental and persistent democratic dilemma.

Twenty-First Century Challenges

One major challenge that has always confronted the U.S. intelligence community is coordination. Mistrust, bureaucratic competition, and poor integration plagued the intelligence community of the Cold War and post–Cold War periods, and often adversely affected the quality of national intelligence. As previously discussed, significant structural adjustments were made in response to the 9/11 intelligence debacle. The question is whether the new director of national intelligence (DNI) can succeed where former directors of central intelligence too often failed.

On the positive side, the DNI enjoys a number of advantages his DCI predecessors lacked. The post is not affiliated with any institution within the intelligence community, and therefore the DNI is not likely to be seen as a bureaucratic competitor as was the DCI. For this reason, the DNI stands a better chance of being viewed across the community as an honest broker and coordinator. The DNI also possesses some budget authority and appointment power. For instance, he or she may recommend to the president a candidate for DCIA, has the right to concur in the appointments of eight other intelligence chiefs, and must be consulted in the appointments of the directors of the DIA and Coast Guard Intelligence. At the same time, the DNI, as previously noted, has the inherited powers of the former DCI. These include supervision of the community's key intelligence products, including NIEs, SNIEs and the *President's Daily Brief (PDB)*. Lastly, the DNI carries the standing and influence associated with being the statutory intelligence adviser to the president and the National Security Council.

Unfortunately, there are several reasons to believe the DNI may have considerable difficulty coordinating the intelligence community in the years ahead. For example, the DCIA retains significant power through the dominance of CIA analysis within the *President's Daily Brief* and his responsibility for managing day-to-day human intelligence activity across the government. Under the law, the DCIA must keep the DNI informed of covert action, but there are no reporting guidelines or mechanisms in place. While the DNI delivers the *PDB* as the principal national intelligence adviser, President Bush has "confused the situation once again" by also allowing the DCIA to attend morning briefings at the White House (Lowenthal 2006).

In addition, as of late 2005, "the office of the DNI was still negotiating with the FBI and Congress on just how robust [its] powers over the FBI's national security functions will be" (Fessenden 2006). More important, there is the matter of the Pentagon. Even with DNI budget and appointment authority (which is by no means comprehensive), roughly 80 percent of national intelligence resources are controlled on a day-to-day basis by the secretary of defense. These include new (previously discussed) elements that fall outside the parameters of the U.S. intelligence community's sixteen recognized members and the purview of the DNI. The secretary of defense's role and influence within intelligence matters is also well protected by the language of the intelligence reform act, which states the DNI will not "abrogate the statutory responsibilities" of department heads (see Section 1018 of the *Intelligence Reform and Terrorism Prevention Act of 2004*). Furthermore, if the DNI wishes to assert authority or promote timely, productive change within the intelligence community, such action may be stymied by the congressional appropriations process, which unlike intelligence authorization, is not centralized but rather is fragmented across a dizzying array of multiple accounts and committees (see Fessenden 2006).

Finally, the intelligence community remains cumbersome and dominated by entrenched bureaucratic interests, raising the prospect that the forces that plagued the DCI for nearly six decades will continue to impede the DNI.

ECONOMIC AGENTS IN A GLOBALIZING WORLD

As our discussion in Chapters 6 and 7 suggested, substantial changes in the international political and economic systems have raised new challenges for American foreign policy. One involves the role and impact of chiefly domestically oriented departments and agencies on foreign policy. They had foreign policy roles before, but they tended to be played at the margins of key foreign and national security policy issues. However, with the end of the Cold War and the acceleration of globalization, these other executive departments and agencies have seen their role in foreign policy expand. Moreover, their primary domestic constituencies—finance for the Treasury Department, business for the Commerce Department, farmers for the Agriculture Department, and workers for the Labor Department—have become increasingly interested and engaged in international economic issues. As the issues addressed by these executive branch departments—such as trade, international finance, and economics—have become more important, a greater leadership role for those agencies principally responsible for them has ensued. And while they are increasingly involved in the interagency groups and committees that comprise the executive branch's coordinating bodies, they have added complexity to the process of coordination.

Department of the Treasury

In the Eisenhower administration, Under Secretary of State Douglas Dillon played the key role in international economic policy, and throughout the 1960s the National Security Council had the principal coordinating role. The trend since that time has been toward the rise of the *"economic complex"*

(Destler 1994, 1998). No organization better reflects this than the Treasury Department, which today is the dominant voice on international economic policy.

Concern for the position of the U.S. dollar in the international monetary system gives the Treasury Department a keen interest in international affairs. Its responsibilities include tax policy, tariffs, the balance of trade and payments, exchange rate adjustments, and the public debt. Thus the Treasury is the principal department in which domestic and international financial and fiscal policy recommendations are formulated. Its ascendance in the area of international economic policy making may be "the outstanding organizational feature of U.S. international economic policy since the end of World War II" (Cohen 1994).

The importance of the Treasury Department has often brought the secretary of the treasury, who serves as the chief financial officer of the United States, into the most intimate circle of presidential advisers, where he has been able to influence foreign as well as domestic policy making. The roster of influentials would begin with Alexander Hamilton, the nation's first treasury secretary. In the past half century, it would include George M. Humphrey, Douglas Dillon, John Connally, William Simon, Michael Blumenthal, G. William Miller, James A. Baker, Nicholas F. Brady, Lloyd Bentsen, Robert Rubin, Paul O'Neill, John W. Snow, and Henry M. Paulson, Jr., among others.

Many recent department secretaries have participated in foreign policy making. In both the Clinton and Bush II administrations, the secretary formally became not only a *designated member* of the National Security Council, but also of the NSC's Principals Committee and the National Economic Council (see Chapter 10). Other key roles for the treasury secretary include the secretary's duties as the U.S. governor of the International Monetary Fund, the World Bank, and the Inter-American, Asian, and African development banks. Those assignments give the treasury secretary and Treasury Department a major voice in the often contentious decisions regarding United States participation in, and the level of contributions to, multilateral lending institutions, and in the complex issues involved in maintaining and operating the international monetary system.

Within the department, the office of the under secretary for international affairs and the assistant secretary for international affairs are the main units that carry out the department's international responsibilities. It is organized into subunits responsible for international monetary and financial policy; trade and investment policy; multilateral development institutions and policy; technical assistance; and two broad geographic areas (Eurasia and the Western Hemisphere; and Africa, the Middle East and Asia). Through these units the office assists the secretary of the treasury and the under secretary for international affairs in the formulation and execution of international financial, monetary, commercial, energy, and trade policies and programs. It is now rare that an NSC interagency working does not have a participant from this office.

Department of Commerce

The Commerce Department is especially concerned with foreign economic policy issues that relate to the expansion and protection of American commerce abroad. Unlike the secretary of the treasury, however, the secretary of commerce and the Commerce Department as a whole historically have not been principal actors in foreign economic policy making. Instead, as indicated in Chapter 10, the United States Trade Representative plays the lead role in the *development* of trade policy. Since 1980, however, when the government's trade-related responsibilities were reorganized, the Commerce Department has been the principal agency for *implementing* trade policy (other than agricultural trade). Thus, as former Commerce Secretary Malcolm Baldrige (1983) observed, "Trade is the only major cabinet function where policy is made in one department (the United States trade representative) and carried out in another (Department of Commerce)."

Specific trade responsibilities of the Commerce Department include all import-export programs: administration of countervailing duty and antidumping statutes,[11] foreign commercial representation and export promotion, trade policy analysis, and foreign compliance with trade agreements. Those duties are discharged by two subunits of the department: the International Trade Administration and the Bureau of Industry and Security (formerly known as the Bureau of Export Administration). The *International Trade Administration (ITA)* is headed by the under secretary for international trade, whose charge relates to issues of import administration, international policy and programs, and trade development. This office also supports the *Trade Promotion Coordinating Committee,* an interagency committee established in 1992 to promote exports. Also headed by an under secretary, the *Bureau of International Security (BIS)* has the primary mission of trade regulation—evaluating and processing export licenses for U.S. goods with a special focus on sensitive products and *dual use technology* (goods with civilian and military applications). According to the bureau, its activities also include "enforcing export control, antiboycott, and public safety laws; cooperating with and assisting other countries on export control and strategic trade issues; assisting U.S. industry to comply with international arms control agreements; monitoring the viability of the U.S. defense industrial base; and promoting federal initiatives and public-private partnerships across industry sectors to protect the nation's critical infrastructures."

Another aspect of Commerce's increasing role stems from the fact that since 1980 the Commerce Department, not the State Department, has been responsible for U.S. commercial representation abroad. The *U.S. and Foreign Commercial Service* seeks to enhance the competitiveness of American businesses abroad through an extensive network of 107 district offices throughout the United States and 145 posts located in U.S. embassies and consulates throughout the world (as of 2006). In conjunction with the domestic network of Export Assistance Centers created by the National Export Strategy and the expanded export centers in key markets overseas, Commerce personnel were well placed to encourage and support American firms to sell abroad.

Export markets of welfare of American farmers are critical

Department of Agriculture

The United States is one of the largest producers of agricultural products for the world marketplace, and agriculture is one of the few sectors of the American economy that consistently yields a trade surplus. Therefore, ensuring continued access to overseas markets is a priority goal of American negotiators in all their trade talks, ranging from multilateral efforts during the Uruguay Round of GATT trade talks to discussions today in the World Trade Organization (WTO) and in bilateral efforts with individual countries. Export markets are critical to the welfare of American farmers, so the Agriculture Department has a major stake in the administration of foreign economic policy.

Most of Agriculture's foreign economic responsibilities are conducted under the direction of the under secretary for farm and foreign agricultural services, out of the office bearing the same name. One key function is promoting U.S. agricultural commodities abroad. This includes the sale or distribution of surplus commodities owned by the government under the **Food for Peace Program.** Created by the Agricultural Trade Development and Assistance Act of 1954 (PL 480), the program sells agricultural commodities on credit and makes grants to provide emergency relief, promote economic development, and assist voluntary relief agencies. In short, the program is designed to meet immediate needs in the Global South and improve developing economies in the long run while at the same time enhancing market opportunities for American exporters. Other important overseas duties of the Agriculture Department include allocating import quotas for certain agricultural commodities, and participating in international negotiations related to world trade in agricultural products.

Principally, the **Foreign Agricultural Service (FAS)** conducts or supports the aforementioned services through its agricultural counselors and attachés, who are located in about 100 embassies worldwide (with responsibilities that extend to 130 countries), and a parallel group of international trade specialists in Washington. The FAS is also responsible for formulating, administering, and coordinating Agriculture

Department policies and programs as they relate to multilateral conventions and organizations, such as the WTO and the Food and Agriculture Organization (FAO) of the UN. Lastly, its overseas attachés act as a worldwide agricultural intelligence and reporting system on supply, demand, and commercial trade conditions relating to agricultural products.

Department of Labor

Gathering information, proffering advice, administering selected programs, and participating in international negotiations (especially in the International Labor Organization [ILO], the World Trade Organization, and the Organization for Economic Cooperation and Development [OECD]) are also the international affairs functions of the Labor Department. However, Labor performs these activities with a view toward their importance for the American wage earner rather than the agricultural, business, or financial communities. Specifically, they are carried out by the *Bureau of International Labor Affairs (BILA),* headed by the deputy under secretary for international affairs. The bureau carries out its functions through its offices of foreign relations, trade agreement implementation, international economic affairs, international child labor, and international organizations.

Among other things, the department's authority traditionally has carried with it a special concern for immigrant labor and immigration policy, and for assessing the impact of trade agreements, such as NAFTA, on American workers. As the U.S. economy has become increasingly dependent on foreign markets, for both imports and exports, these efforts on behalf of American workers have become increasingly significant. In addition, Labor has been involved with the State Department in the provision of labor attachés for assignment abroad and with the Agency for International Development in the execution of technical assistance activities overseas. The department also bears responsibility for the administration of the trade adjustment assistance programs for workers under the Trade Act of 1974, which provides restitution to those adversely affected by foreign trade competition.

THE FOREIGN POLICY BUREAUCRACY AND THE POLITICS OF POLICY MAKING

The executive departments and agencies that comprise the foreign affairs government are so numerous and multifaceted that no brief description could adequately capture either the breadth of their interests or the depth of their involvement in matters of foreign policy. As a way of explicating governmental sources of American policy, however, the description provided here demonstrates a distinguishing characteristic of American foreign policy making: decision making by and within a disparate set of exceedingly large and complex organizational structures. Effecting control over them and dealing with the consequences of their behavior are important presidential concerns for political, legal, and other reasons. Still, presidents depend on the organizations and agencies comprising the foreign affairs government, without which it would be impossible to accomplish their foreign policy agendas. The organizations comprising the second concentric circle of policy making also often have their own agendas, as we have seen in this chapter. And they have the capacity to derail presidential preferences, an idea we will explore in more detail in Chapter 13. Since more of them are increasingly engaged in foreign policy concerns, presidential leadership is a more difficult task. Moreover, as we have seen in this and previous chapters, because the Cold War imperatives had such an impact on their structures, resources, personnel, and missions, the changing agenda of the new century raises questions about the capacity of many of these departments, agencies, or units within them to master new challenges.

It is, of course, the case that foreign policy is not solely determined by the White House and executive branch agencies. Congress and its members—another concentric circle in the scheme we introduced in Chapter 10 to organize our discussion—often plays a role. How, when, and to what extent are the subjects of our next chapter.

KEY TERMS

Bureau of Intelligence and Research (INR)
Central Intelligence Agency (CIA)
Defense Intelligence Agency (DIA)
Defense Reorganization Act of 1986 (Goldwater-Nichols Act)
Department of Homeland Security
director of national intelligence (DNI)
director of the Central Intelligence Agency (DCIA)

finished intelligence
Food for Peace Program
Foreign Agricultural Service (FAS)
Foreign Service officers (FSOs)
human intelligence (HUMINT)
Imagery intelligence (IMINT)
Intelligence Reform and Terrorism Prevention Act of 2004
Joint Chiefs of Staff (JCS)

Joint Staff
National Geospatial-Intelligence Agency (NGA)
National Intelligence Estimates (NIEs)
National Reconnaissance Office (NRO)
National Security Agency (NSA)
Office of the Secretary of Defense (OSD)
organizational subculture
plausible denial
politicization of intelligence

presidential finding
producer-consumer challenge
signal intelligence (SIGINT)
Special National Intelligence Estimates (SNIEs)
stovepipes
U.S. and Foreign Commercial Service
Central Intelligence Agency (CIA)

SUGGESTED READINGS

Bamford, James. *Body of Secrets: Anatomy of the Ultra-Secret National Security Agency*. New York: Anchor Books (Random House), 2002.

Binnendijk, Hans, ed., *Transforming America's Military*. Washington, DC: National Defense University Press, 2002.

Clarke, Duncan L. *American Defense and Foreign Policy Institutions: Toward a Sound Foundation*. Lanham, MD: University Press of America, 1989.

Cohen, Stephen D. *The Making of United States International Economic Policy: Principles, Problems, and Proposals for Reform*, 4th ed. Westport, CT: Praeger, 1994.

Dizard, Wilson P. *Digital Diplomacy: U.S. Foreign Policy in the Information Age*. Westport, CT: Greenwood Publishers, 2001.

Feaver, Peter D. *Armed Servants: Agency, Oversight, and Civil-Military Relations*. Cambridge, MA: Harvard University Press, 2003.

Godson, Roy S. *Dirty Tricks or Trump Cards: U.S. Covert Action and Counterintelligence*. New Brunswick, NJ: Transaction Publishers, 2000.

Halberstam, David. *War in a Time of Peace: Bush, Clinton and the Generals*. New York: Scribner, 2001.

Herspring, Dale R. *The Pentagon and The Presidency: Civil-military Relations from FDR to George W. Bush*. Lawrence, KS: University of Kansas Press, 2005.

Johnson, Loch H. *Bombs, Bugs, Drugs, and Thugs: Intelligence and America's Quest for Security*. New York: New York University Press, 2000.

Lederman, Gordon Nathaniel. *Reorganizing the Joint Chiefs of Staff: The Goldwater-Nichols Act of 1986*. Westport, CT: Greenwood Press, 1999.

Locher, James R., III. *Victory on the Potomac: The Goldwater-Nichols Act Unifies the Pentagon*. College Station, TX: Texas A&M University Press, 2002.

Lowenthal, Mark M. *Intelligence: From Secrets to Policy*. Washington, DC: CQ Press, 2006.

Pillar, Paul R. *Terrorism and U.S. Foreign Policy*. Washington, DC: Brookings Institution, 2003.

Rubin, Barry. *Secrets of State: The State Department and the Struggle over U.S. Foreign Policy*. New York: Oxford University Press, 1985.

Woodward, Bob. *Plan of Attack*. New York: Simon & Schuster, 2004.

Zegart, Amy B. *Flawed by Design: The Evolution of the CIA, JCS, and NSC*. Stanford, CA: Stanford University Press, 1999.

NOTES

1. The 1980 Foreign Service Act specified that ambassadorial appointments will "normally" go to career officers, but the law has had little practical effect. Since the 1960s the number of political (noncareer) appointments has averaged about 30 percent.

2. As of February 2006, a federal court had blocked the implementation of much of Rumsfeld's new civilian personnel system. "In a 77-page decision, U.S. District Judge Emmet G. Sullivan ruled that the Pentagon's National Security Personnel System (NSPS) fails to ensure collective bargaining rights, does not provide an independent third-party review of labor relations decisions and would leave employees without a fair process for appealing disciplinary actions" (Lee 2006).

3. There are currently five geographically oriented unified commands, the Central, European, Pacific, Northern, and Southern, and five others organized by function, the Joint Forces, Space, Special Operations, Strategic, and Transportation commands.

4. For a discussion of concerns, see Bourne (1998), Locher (2001) and Locher (2002).

5. *Defense Week* (1 February 1999) reported the estimated annual budget of the National Reconnaissance Office (NRO) was $7 billion, which would constitute roughly 25 percent of the total national intelligence budget based on the 1998 top-line figure ($27.6 billion) provided by former DCI George Tenet in 1998 (Jehl 2004). There is no publicly available evidence to suggest that the NRO's budget as a percentage of national

intelligence spending has changed significantly in the post-9/11 era. Thus the NRO's current budget could be roughly $10.5 billion today, based on a $42 billion national intelligence budget.

6. Dorgin (2005) provides the estimate of 14,000 employees at the National Geospatial-Intelligence Agency (NGA). In a Congressional Research Service Report, Daggett (2004) states the budgets of the National Reconnaissance Office (NRO), National Security Agency (NSA), and National Geospatial-Intelligence Agency (NGA) and Defense Intelligence Agency (DIA), collectively, constitute "over $15–20 billion." Thus if the NRO budget is approximately $10.5 billion (see Note 5), the NSA budget is roughly $7 billion (see Safire 2002), and the DIA budget is about $650 million (Pike 1996), then one might estimate the NGA budget is in the area of $3 billion. Of course, these budget figures can only be considered best guesses given that the real amounts remained classified information.

7. "The Defense Department has decided that it will coordinate its human intelligence missions with the CIA but will not, as in the past, await consent. It also reserves the right to bypass the agency's Langley headquarters, consulting CIA officers in the field instead. The Pentagon will deem a mission 'coordinated' after giving 72 hours' notice to the CIA" (Gellman 2005).

8. The Department of Homeland Security did win at least one turf battle, receiving the final authority to determine who receives a U.S. visa. This new responsibility came at the expense of the perennially weak Department of State (see Shenon 2003).

9. For an interesting discussion of the relationship between intelligence producers and consumers, see Lowenthal (1999).

10. Reviews of covert operations and their oversight include Knott (1996), Godson (2000), Johnson (2000a), and Lowenthal (2006).

11. Countervailing duties are import taxes that offset subsidies provided by the exporting country. Antidumping regulations are designed to make up for the advantage gained by selling exports for prices below those in the exporter's own domestic market.

12

The Congress and Foreign
Policy Making

Congress . . . could, should, and will have
an influence on the fashioning of foreign policy.
HENRY HYDE,
HOUSE INTERNATIONAL RELATIONS COMMITTEE CHAIR 2001

The preferred stance is to let the president make the decisions and,
if it goes well, praise him, and if it doesn't, criticize him.
LEE HAMILTON, HOUSE FOREIGN AFFAIRS COMMITTEE CHAIR 1994

During the 1990s, President Bill Clinton saw his attempt to establish a new strategy for dealing with ethnic conflict in the Global South blocked, his effort to redesign foreign aid policy thwarted, his request for authority to negotiate expanded trade denied, his design for curbing global warming ignored, and his commitment to ending nuclear testing rejected. At the same time, he was forced to accept restructuring of the Department of State, restrictions on funding the International Monetary Fund, and substantially higher defense spending. All of these actions resisted by the president were driven by Congress. Similarly, in 2001, President George W. Bush faced opposition in Congress on several foreign policy issues, including defense strategy and spending and national missile defense.

In contrast, when terrorists attacked the United States, crashing airliners into the World Trade Center and the Pentagon on September 11, 2001, Congress rallied behind President Bush, not only by handing him broad authority to begin a campaign against terrorism, but also by working out and muting differences on a variety of other issues, both foreign and domestic, in a bipartisan fashion. Thirteen months later, substantial majorities in the House and the Senate approved a joint resolution authorizing the president to use force against Iraq. When serious questions emerged over the government's inability to head off the September 11 attacks and the intelligence underlying the president's rationale for war in Iraq, Congress responded with the establishment of the <u>Department of Homeland</u>

Security and a major reorganization of the U.S. intelligence community. As President Bush grew politically weaker during his second term, Congress became increasingly less deferential. The administration's antiterrorism law, the USA Patriot Act, was renewed but with limits. The 2006 defense-spending bill was blocked until the president reversed his position and accepted an amendment by Senator John McCain (R-Arizona), banning the inhumane treatment of suspected terrorists and other detainees in military custody. Strong congressional opposition compelled a United Arab Emirates–based company to drop its bid to manage several U.S. seaports, a deal favored by the Bush administration.

While few would argue that Congress makes foreign policy, these recent examples—and the contrast they reveal—suggest that Congress can have a real impact. The actions and the contrast raise important questions. How and when do members of Congress assert themselves on foreign policy issues? What impact, on what issues, and in what situations, do members have?

The traditional view of Congress's role relegates it to the outer circle of the concentric circles of policymaking we discussed in Chapter 10. Thus Congress's role is typically seen as primarily a negative one—to function as a public critic of the president and place constraints on presidential behavior. Examples of bipartisanship—in which most members of Congress support the president's foreign policy regardless of their party affiliation—and congressional deference—in which presidents have their way—are legion, especially in the early Cold War years. Even today, most observers would argue that Congress looks to the president for leadership.

As we have seen in previous chapters, presidents' ability to exert foreign policy leadership is uneven. Some of that variability can be traced to Congress. Congress cannot replace the president as the central actor in American foreign policy making, but it often influences, shapes, and occasionally even determines foreign policy.

In this chapter, we examine Congress's role in American foreign policy making. We begin with a look at the setting of congressional foreign policy

behavior, briefly reviewing the Constitution's stipulations and ambiguities and the key players in Congress who affect foreign policy. Second, we examine the instruments and avenues of influence Congress uses to shape foreign policy. Third, we discuss the obstacles to congressional influence and survey the record of executive–legislative foreign policy interactions since World War II and their implications.

THE SETTING OF CONGRESSIONAL FOREIGN POLICY MAKING

Understanding the role and influence of Congress requires that we understand the powers and responsibilities the Constitution assigns it and how Congress wields those powers and exercises those responsibilities.

The Constitution and Congress

As we saw in Chapter 10, the Constitution creates an uncertain playing field in its assignment of foreign policy powers.[1] In Article II, the president is made commander-in-chief and given the power to name ambassadors, receive foreign officials, and negotiate treaties. He is also afforded general executive power. By contrast, in Article I, Congress is granted more extensive responsibilities, including the general legislative power, the "power of the purse," the powers to declare war, to raise and support armies, to provide and maintain a navy, to make rules for the government and regulation of the land and naval forces, and to organize, arm, discipline, and call forth the militia. Congress is also to regulate international commerce and immigration, to define and punish piracies, to grant letters of marque and reprisal, and to make rules concerning capture on land and water. Moreover, the U.S. Senate is constitutionally empowered to "advise and consent" on treaties as well as the appointment of ambassadors and other executive branch personnel. Finally, the Constitution directs Congress to "make all laws necessary and proper for carrying into execution the foregoing powers."

Just a cursory glance at these assignments suggests that Congress has considerable power and authority in foreign policy making if it chooses to act. Furthermore, the overlapping of several areas (for example, the war, diplomatic, and appointment powers) is the basis for the "invitation to struggle" description of executive-legislative relations, as it establishes a system of *separate institutions sharing power.* Although these characteristics presage an environment of substantial congressional foreign policy activity, that has rarely been the case. Several factors explain this apparent paradox. We will discuss them in more detail later in this chapter, but we begin with a particularly important one: the congressional setting that permits many congressional actors to have a voice in foreign policy.

Congressional Foreign Policy Actors

When speaking of Congress and foreign policy it is important to recognize that many actors comprise the institution. Indeed, "Congress" need not act at all to affect American foreign policy; influence may flow from a variety of players without a formal action or output by the collective institution. Broadly speaking, Congress is:

- The *institution,* acting collectively through its procedures, when majorities can be mustered to take action on legislation and other activities

- One or the other of the two *political parties in the institution*

- Any of the many *committees or subcommittees* of either house, an increasing number of which are involved in some aspect of foreign policy

- *Congressional caucuses*—voluntary associations of legislators—many of which have foreign policy emphases (for example, the Senate Caucus on International Narcotics Control, the Congressional Black Caucus, the bipartisan House and Senate Caucuses on U.S./Israel Security Cooperation, the Congressional

Taiwan Caucus, and the Congressional Human Rights Caucus)

- *Congressional leaders* such as the House Speaker and minority leader, the Senate majority and leaders, committee and subcommittee chairs and ranking members, and others, most of whose actions have become increasingly partisan (Sinclair 1993; Smith 1994)

- Individual members of Congress who become *foreign policy activists* and *foreign policy entrepreneurs* (Carter and Scott 2004; Carter, Scott and Rowling 2004)

- Congressional staff and *"congressional bureaucracies"* composed of staff members and specialists (Carter 1998), such as the Congressional Research Service, the Government Accountability Office, and the Congressional Budget Office

Any one or any combination of these congressional foreign policy actors can exercise influence on a given issue. This is one reason why Congress has a difficult time asserting itself on foreign policy: different actors may advocate different policies, making it difficult for any to succeed. Any one may interact with the executive branch or seek to engage the public, interest groups, and the media. Occasionally, some may even engage other countries' representatives. Finally, each actor also has access to other levers of policy influence. Indeed, because there are so many avenues of foreign policy influence, these congressional actors have far more routes to policy influence than the Constitution's formal assignment of responsibilities suggests.

AVENUES OF CONGRESSIONAL FOREIGN POLICY INFLUENCE

Along with recognition of the constitutional setting and the array of congressional actors who may or may not play a role on a given foreign policy issue, we must understand two more factors: the avenues available for congressional foreign policy influence, and all the avenues that require interest, engagement, and activity on the part of the congressional

TABLE 12.1 Avenues of Congressional Influence

	Direct	Indirect
Legislative	Issue-Specific Legislation	Nonbinding Legislation
	Treaties (Senate)	Appointments (Senate)
	War Power	Procedural Legislation
	Appropriations	
	Foreign Commerce	
Nonlegislative	Informal Advice/Letters	Framing Opinion
	Consultations	Foreign Contacts
	Oversight/Hearings	
	Use of Courts	

SOURCE: Adapted from Scott (1997b).

players. The first indicates opportunity, the second that taking advantage of opportunity is, ultimately, a political issue. Lawmakers can act, but they must choose to act in order to have foreign policy influence of any kind. That they often do not is a reflection of their own political and policy interests, as well as some of the obstacles to the exercise of congressional influence that we will discuss later.

Categorizing the Avenues of Influence

There are many ways to categorize the avenues of influence available to members of Congress. One useful way is to distinguish between *legislative* and *nonlegislative* actions (Burgin 1997), and between *direct* and *indirect* efforts (Lindsay 1993). Legislative actions involve those related to the passage of specific laws or resolutions; nonlegislative actions are those that do not involve a legislative output. Direct actions are tied to specific issues and cases; indirect actions are aimed at influencing the broader political environment or climate of a debate. If these two dimensions are combined, then four categories of congressional influence avenues can be identified: direct-legislative, direct-nonlegislative, indirect-legislative, and indirect-nonlegislative (see Scott 1997b). These possibilities are summarized in Table 12.1 and highlighted through examples in the four subsections that follow. While each of the four

avenues will be discussed independently, it is important to note that, in practice, lawmakers combine and link efforts across these categories, thereby amplifying their effects.

Direct-Legislative Avenues The direct legislative foreign policy activities Congress may engage in are fairly impressive and are the most obvious and most scrutinized. They include the powers to declare war, to appropriate funds, and to regulate international commerce. The Senate also has the power to approve treaties. The key to this avenue of influence is ***substantive legislation*** developed through the institution's legislative procedures. Substantive legislation may involve treaty ratification, legislation regarding the use of force, trade and foreign aid legislation, budget appropriations, and any other issue-specific legislation passed by Congress that requires or prohibits specific policy actions.

Every year a long list of bills and amendments relating to foreign policy is considered in some fashion by one or both houses of Congress (Lindsay 1994b). While "major legislation" (for example, the *Omnibus Trade and Competitiveness Act* of 1988, the *Homeland Security Act of 2002* or the *Intelligence Reform and Terrorism Prevention Act of 2004*) is relatively infrequent (Hinckley 1994), "minor" legislative actions abound. Most notably, Congress relies on this avenue of influence when it attaches limits, restrictions, and conditions to foreign aid. One of the most prominent examples was the 1985 Pressler Amendment, named for former Senator Larry Lee Pressler (R-South Dakota), that tied American economic and military assistance to the president's annual certification that Pakistan did not possess a nuclear explosive device. Pakistan's standing as a key ally in the war on terrorism led to a repeal of the law in 2001. Similarly, the Leahy Law, named for Senator Patrick Leahy (D-Vermont), has prohibited military security assistance to foreign armed forces involved in gross violations of human rights since its passage in 1997. Many other restrictions on aid to various countries have existed or continue to exist for reasons related to drug trafficking, support for terrorism, and nuclear proliferation issues. Note, too, that besides limiting aid, members can earmark funds to go to specific projects they favor, which also constitutes substantive legislation, as we discuss later.

One last point should be made regarding substantive legislation. Members of Congress need not be successful in gaining passage of a particular piece of legislation for it to shape foreign policy. The mere *threat* of legislation may be used to trigger **anticipated reactions** whereby the president surveys the preferences of Congress on a policy issue and tailors his proposal to meet those preferences. An example occurred in 1986, when the Reagan administration's Congress enacted a series of partial sanctions against South Africa it had previously rejected. While Congress never actually passed legislation requiring sanctions, its proposals prompted the administration to preempt congressional policy making (Baker 1989). In 1994, the Clinton administration's "Presidential Decision Directive 25" bore the fingerprints of Congress as well. Although it was a presidential policy decision regarding the use of force under multilateral conditions, and although Congress did not pass legislation in either 1993 or 1994 on the matter, the administration substantially revised its initial proposals to accommodate congressional signals about its content (Daalder 1994).

Direct-Nonlegislative Avenues Through the direct-nonlegislative avenues, members of Congress rely on activities other than legislation to exercise influence. Such efforts could include consultations

and communications with the president and other administration officials, oversight activities like hearings and other investigations, fact-finding missions, and lawsuits against the president or administration. Such behavior may be linked to legislative and other actions as well.

Examples are numerous. In the 1960s, Senators Frank Church (D-Idaho) and William Fulbright (D-Arkansas) relied heavily on their ability to use oversight hearings to address foreign policy in the government operations and foreign relations committees, respectively (see Johnson 1998–1999; Woods 1998). Senator Church's select committee investigation and hearings on CIA abuses in the 1970s are another example. More recently, congressional intelligence committee hearings to explore the intelligence community's performance leading up to the September 11 terrorist attacks and the Iraq war in 2003 led to a restructuring of the intelligence community.

Many members rely on letters and other communications with the White House or departments to express their policy views. In early 1998, for instance, Senator Jesse Helms (R-North Carolina), chairman of the Foreign Relations Committee, sent a letter to President Clinton to indicate the Comprehensive Test Ban Treaty was "very low on the Committee's list of priorities." Similarly, Helms sent a letter in late 2000 to the secretary of state stating that a proposal for U.S. participation in the new International Criminal Court would be "dead on arrival" in the Senate. In October 2005, thirty-four Senate Democrats, led by Harry Reid (D-Nevada), sent a letter to President Bush raising concerns about Iraq, including continuing violence, the readiness of Iraqi security forces, postwar reconstruction, political strife, and limited international support for U.S. policy (see Reid 2005).

Use of the courts include efforts by Ron Dellums (D-California) in 1989 and Tom Campbell (R-California) a decade later to hold the president accountable for the requirements of the War Powers Resolution. More recently, Representative Jim McDermott (D-Washington) and five other members of Congress sought a court injunction in February 2003 to block military action by the Bush administration in Iraq.

Indirect–Legislative Avenues   Members of Congress can also use legislative approaches to have a more indirect influence on foreign policy. Here, lawmakers do not set out to determine a particular decision or issue, but rather, through their constitutional powers, select the players and processes that will determine future foreign policy. More specifically, the Senate has the ability to approve or not approve top administration personnel appointments, and both houses can introduce *procedural legislation* that alters processes, requires reports, or creates new agencies or institutions to shape the way policy is formulated and implemented (Burgin 1997; Lindsay 1994b).

The Senate's appointment powers enable members to play a role in shaping the president's foreign policy team. Generally the premise is that presidents should be entitled to their appointments, but the Senate has regularly intervened to block objectionable nominees. In 1989, for example, former Senator John Tower (R-Texas), President George H. W. Bush's first choice for secretary of defense, was rejected by a majority of senators, led by Georgia Democrat Sam Nunn. In 1997, conservative senators led by Richard Shelby (R-Alabama) blocked Anthony Lake, President Clinton's selection for the director of central intelligence. In 2005, Bush's nominee for U.S. ambassador to the United Nations, John Bolton, was blocked by Senate Democrats, who expressed concern over Bolton's "derogatory remarks about the United Nations . . . [his abrasive] temperament . . . [and] allegations [that he] manipulated intelligence to support his views as the top State Department official for arms control" (VandeHei and Lynch 2005). In an unusual move for such a high level position, Bush resorted to a *recess appointment* (naming an official when the Senate is in recess in order to circumvent Senate confirmation). This move in August 2005 allowed Bolton to serve until January 2007, the period remaining in the term of the sitting Congress. In addition, senators scrutinize lower level appointments, frequently blocking or holding hostage objectionable appointments. For instance, George W. Bush's nomination of Otto Reich as assistant secretary of state for the Western Hemisphere drew substantial opposition. Senators John Kerry (D-Massachusetts) and Christopher Dodd (D-Connecticut) blocked Reich, whose service in the Reagan administration involved him in the Iran-Contra affair.

Furthermore, key senators can use their ability to block appointments to exact concessions on other foreign policy matters. No one was more active in this regard than Jesse Helms (R-North Carolina). In 1989, Helms held up numerous presidential appointments to gain policy concessions across a range of issues. In 1995, as chair of the Foreign Relations Committee, he blocked several ambassadorial and other appointments to force Clinton administration support for his plan to reorganize the State Department and other foreign policy agencies (see Hook 1998). At times members will also use appointment approval power to link to their interests in non-foreign policy issues. In 1999, for example, Senator James Inhofe (R-Oklahoma) blocked the appointments of Lawrence Summers to be treasury secretary and Richard Holbrooke to be UN ambassador to protest the recess appointment of an openly gay man, James Hormel, as ambassador to Luxembourg (Shenon 1999).

Congress frequently resorts to procedural legislation to ensure a voice in policy. This may involve creating new agencies, requiring specific processes or agency involvement in policy decisions, or requiring reports (Lindsay 1994b). Again, many examples exist. The 1973 War Powers Resolution is essentially a procedural policy, as it specifies a decision process for using force abroad. The 1976 Arms Export Control Act not only required certain reporting to Congress, but also specified that certain agencies must participate in the decision. The 1980 Intelligence Oversight act established congressional oversight committees and reporting requirements to better control the executive's use of the intelligence community. The 1998 Foreign Affairs Restructuring Act revised the relationships between the State Department and the Agency for International Development (USAID) and eliminated the U.S. Information Agency (USIA) and the Arms Control and Disarmament Agency (ACDA), folding their operations into the State Department. More recently, Congress transferred coordination of the U.S. intelligence community from the director of central intelligence, who also served as CIA director, to the Office of the Director of National Intelligence (ODNI) headed by the director of national intelligence (see Chapter 11).

Through actions such as these, members of Congress seek to shape the way the executive branch formulates and implements policy, as well as to ensure that information on policy decisions is shared with Congress (Lindsay 1994c).

Indirect-Nonlegislative Avenues On the indirect-nonlegislative avenue of influence, lawmakers engage in the process of *framing*—trying to "change the climate of opinion surrounding the policy" (Lindsay 1994c). Increasing access to the media as well as increased opportunities for direct foreign contact make this venue a frequent means to exert congressional foreign policy activity and exercise influence. Through framing activities, members both signal the White House of their preferences and help shape public opinion.

Such efforts include participation in media talk shows and writing opinion pieces for newspapers. The participation and subsequent arrest of members of Congress in 1985 protests over South Africa's apartheid are another. In 1988, members sought to frame trade policy debates by appearing on the steps of the Capitol and smashing an electronic device made by Toshiba in protest of that company's sale of sophisticated electronics to the Soviet Union. Representative Pete Geren's (D-Texas) role in getting a prototype of the V-22 Osprey to land on the Capitol grounds in the early 1990s was also fundamentally a framing exercise.

The increasing prevalence of members of Congress meeting directly with foreign leaders offers another avenue for indirect-nonlegislative activities. For example, in 1997, Senator Jesse Helms met with UN Secretary General Kofi Annan to discuss U.S.–UN relations. Two years later, Helms delivered a speech before UN delegates. At about the same time then–House Speaker Newt Gingrich (R-Georgia) repeatedly attacked the Clinton administration for pressuring the Israeli government to make concessions

to the Palestinians in Middle East peace talks. The attacks followed numerous private meetings between Gingrich and then–Israeli Prime Minister Benjamin Netanyahu and a 1998 Gingrich speech before the Israeli Knesset. In 2002, a delegation of leading U.S. senators, including Senator John McCain (R-Arizona) and Senator Joseph Lieberman (D-Connecticut), visited the new interim leader of Afghanistan and then traveled to a number of other Central Asian capitals to thank leaders for their support in the war on terrorism. More recently, congressional delegations have visited Iraq, India, and Pakistan, and several other countries; and lawmakers have held meetings on Capitol Hill with a range of foreign leaders, from the Israeli prime minister to the Chinese vice president to the king of Jordan.

To summarize, these four avenues of influence in combination with the Constitution's grants of authority would seemingly make Congress a dominant power in the "invitation to struggle" with the president for a voice in foreign policy making. That is, these resources would appear to enable Congress to set overall policy much like a board of directors does in private enterprise. Remember, though, that the availability of these avenues does not necessarily mean they are used. That depends, as noted previously, on whether lawmakers, individually or collectively, have the *willingness* to act. Hence, while Congress has opportunities to influence foreign policy, it may or may not take advantage of them.

Avenues of Influence in Practice: Treaties, War, and Money

We now review three areas in which Congress has an obvious role to play because of the Constitution: treaties, war, and money. As we review these areas, we will assess whether the appearance of Congress as a foreign policy rival of the president matches the reality. We will use examples of how members of Congress use the avenues of influence just summarized to shape policy to fit their preferences.

Treaties Treaty-making powers rest in the Senate, whose advice *and* consent by a two-thirds vote is necessary before the president can consummate (with the exchange of instruments of ratification) a treaty with another country. (This effectively gives control to only 34 of the 535 members of Congress.) The Senate Foreign Relations Committee bears primary responsibility for conducting the hearings and investigations on which senatorial advice and consent are based. These and related foreign affairs responsibilities once made the Foreign Relations Committee the most prestigious of all Senate committees.

In recent years, however, ideological divisions have prevented the committee from speaking with a single voice. More important, service on the committee does not appear to advance senators' other interests. According to Nebraska Republican Chuck Hagel, "Foreign Relations has been kind of a wasteland" (cited in Lindsay 2000b). In 1995, following the Republican victory in the midterm elections, Senate Majority Leader Bob Dole had to cajole four senators into taking seats on the committee (Sciolino 1995). As one member of the committee once put it: "Well, you know, it is fun to hobnob with foreign leaders and discuss world affairs, but it doesn't get me anyplace with my Senate colleagues. . . . Foreign Relations doesn't have much legislative jurisdiction that's important to other senators—it's nothing like Finance or Appropriations" (cited in Smith and Deering 1990). The committee nonetheless remains a primary forum for the discharge of Congress's foreign policy responsibilities.

Despite the importance of the Constitution's treaty clause, the precise mechanism through which the Senate proffers advice and consent to the president is ambiguous. In barest form the process consists of the president, in the capacity of the nation's chief diplomat, negotiating through representatives a treaty with another state, and the Senate then merely voting up or down. More frequently, advice and guidance is offered in a variety of communications between the executive branch and the legislature, including letters and even resolutions.

In 1997, for example, the Senate communicated its preferences on the global warming treaty under negotiation at Kyoto, Japan, to President Clinton through the Byrd–Hagel resolution, named for West Virginia Democrat Robert Byrd and Nebraska Republican Chuck Hagel. The resolution, which passed 95-0, warned the administration that any global warming treaty that did not apply to developing states as well as the developed world would face substantial opposition in the Senate. Moreover, Senate opposition to the treaty, which would require a 5 percent reduction in 1990 greenhouse gas levels for all industrialized countries by 2012, continued even more strenuously after the Clinton administration signed the Kyoto Protocol on Global Climate Change in November 1998. The treaty languished without support on Capitol Hill until March 2001, when President Bush's Environmental Protection Agency (EPA) administrator, Christine Todd Whitman, stated Kyoto was "dead" (from an American standpoint), because the president had "no interest in implementing the treaty."

Another form of advice involves naming members of the Senate to the negotiating team. This practice has been widespread ever since the Senate rejected the Versailles Treaty ending World War I, which was negotiated without senatorial representation on the Peace Commission headed by Woodrow Wilson. By incorporating members of the Senate into the negotiation team, presidents have often been able to circumvent Senate opposition and develop internal advocates for treaties. In addition, senators have visited ongoing international negotiations or served as official observers, affording them opportunities to consult with, advise, and potentially influence U.S. negotiators. For instance, the Senate Arms Control Observer Group played an important role in the negotiations that resulted in the 1987 Intermediate-Range Nuclear Forces (INF) Treaty between the United States and the former Soviet Union.

Consent to treaties is established by a two-thirds vote, but the Senate can attach **reservations** to treaties. These may take the form of amendments that require the executive to renegotiate the terms of the treaty with other signatories—a potentially inhibiting obstacle, particularly with the increase in the number of multilateral treaties. Alternatively, reservations or conditions may simply incorporate the Senate's interpretation of the treaty without any binding effect on the parties to it. Other variants are reservations that apply only to the United States. The most celebrated example is the so-called *Connally Amendment* to the Statute of the International Court of Justice. According to this reservation, the United States reserves the right to determine whether matters falling under the court's compulsory jurisdiction clause are essentially within the domestic jurisdiction of the United States, and hence beyond the Court's purview.

Until recently, the Senate's treaty ratification record has been quite positive. The most famous treaty failure occurred in 1920, when the Versailles Treaty came up short of the two-thirds majority that would have opened the way for U.S. membership in the League of Nations. From then until the end of the Cold War, the Senate rejected only three treaties, while two others that failed to receive a two-thirds majority were subject to reconsideration (*Treaties and Other International Agreements: The Role of the United States Senate,* 1993).

Since 1993, however, the record has been considerably more mixed. In fact, the Clinton administration was able to gain ratification of just two of five major treaties during its two terms. As noted, the administration signed but failed to gain ratification of the Kyoto Protocol (see Balakrishnan 2002). It also negotiated a *Comprehensive Test Ban Treaty* that was rejected outright by the Senate in a highly partisan vote in October 1999 (see Jones 2005a). Finally, although the administration helped to design and supported a treaty for the establishment of an International Criminal Court, opposition by the Senate (and the Department of Defense) kept President Clinton from signing the treaty until December 31, 2000. When he did so, he declined to submit it to the Senate or even to recommend its ratification (see Jackson and Carter 2005).

Of the two successes, only one came relatively easily. On May 1, 1998, the Senate ratified the Clinton administration's decision to enlarge NATO, paving the way for the eastward movement of the alliance to include, a year later, Poland, Hungary, and the Czech Republic (Goldgeier 1998, 1999; Grayson 1999). Exhaustive meetings between members of the administration, Congress, and NATO

allies laid the groundwork for the expansion. According to Senator Dan Coats (R–Indiana), the agreement was "one of the least partisan issues I've been involved with since I came here" (Lippmann and Dewar 1999).

The other—the April 1997 ratification of the *Chemical Weapons Convention* (originally negotiated by the Reagan and Bush administrations)—occurred only after a difficult and highly charged political fight enabled the Clinton administration to win ratification with seventy-four votes in the Senate. However, it took complex maneuvering within the Senate to break loose the treaty from Foreign Relations Committee Chair Jesse Helms's hold inside the committee and then to assemble a coalition of supporters for the treaty on the Senate floor. Moreover, it took substantial bargaining between the White House and the Senate to gain passage. The White House had to agree to a long list of over two dozen conditions and to accede to demands for the restructuring of the foreign affairs agencies along lines advocated by Senator Helms. Ultimately, all forty-five Democratic senators voted in favor of the treaty, while members of the Republic Party split twenty-nine to twenty-six in favor of the accord originally negotiated by presidents of their own party (Krepon, Smithson, and Parachini 1997). Focus 12.1. sheds light on why some arms control treaties are able to secure Senate ratification and others are not.

Hence, while much of the Cold War period attests simultaneously to congressional deference to presidential initiatives and to general agreement between the president and Congress on many foreign policy issues, those areas of agreement as they related to recent treaty approvals have narrowed substantially. Increasing policy disagreement and partisanship appear to have persuaded members of the Senate to wield the treaty ratification power more forcefully than in previous years. Moreover, individual members of the Senate seem quite willing to use the ratification power to exact concessions on other foreign policy issues. There are signs of increased partisanship and politicization as well. The political battle surrounding CTBT offers countless examples (see Jones 2005a).

F O C U S 12.1   **What Factors Ensure Ratification of an Arms Control Treaty?**

Krepon and Caldwell (1991: 462–465) and their contributors identify five factors that were critical to winning Senate approval of arms control treaties during the 1919–1988 period:

- The perception that the treaty significantly enhances national security by offering substantive benefits
- The president enjoys popularity
- The perception that the president is a staunch protector of U.S. national security interests
- The perception that the president is an experienced and skilled practitioner of foreign policy
- The president's demonstrated skill in working with Congress

"Perception" refers largely to the views held by U.S. senators and to a lesser extent the views of the general public. The more a president lacks these five keys to success, the more dependent he or she will be on four additional variables to ensure ratification:

- Highly competent advisers
- Nonthreatening international environment
- Support of military leaders

- Support of Senate leaders and other pivotal lawmakers

Parachini (1997) identifies eight factors that were essential to the Senate's bipartisan approval of the Chemical Weapons Convention in April 1997:

- Treaty's clear entry-into-force date
- President's strong push for Senate approval
- Absence of election-year politics
- Framing ratification as a test of bipartisanship
- Political bargains struck by the president with Senate Republicans
- Backing of the U.S. military
- Support from key senators on the Foreign Relations Committee
- Endorsements from the Senate's leaders

Significantly, few of the factors identified by Krepon and Caldwell (1991) or Parachini (1997) were present in 1999 when the Senate failed to ratify the Comprehensive Test Ban Treaty (Jones 2003). For detailed accounts of the Senate's consideration of the CTBT, see Jones (2002a, 2005a); Deibel (2002; 2003); and Evans and Oleszek 2003).

Other than its approval in March 2003 to extend NATO membership to Bulgaria, Estonia, Latvia, Lithuania, Romania, Slovakia, and Slovenia, the Senate did not ratify a major treaty during the first six years of the George W. Bush administration. However, this fact was not the result of President Bush withholding treaties from the Senate that he knew would be rejected. Other chief executives have pursued this tactic, such as President Jimmy Carter with the Threshold Test Ban Treaty, the Peaceful Nuclear Explosives Treaty, and SALT II, or President Clinton with the Kyoto Protocol. Rather, the dearth of treaties before the Senate during the Bush years was tied to the president's strong opposition to specific international agreements coupled with his general wariness toward most multilateral frameworks, especially in the realm of security

affairs. As a result, the Bush administration did not seek Senate approval of the Comprehensive Test Ban Treaty, the Treaty Banning Antipersonnel Mines, a protocol to create a compliance regime for the Biological Weapons Convention, and the International Criminal Court's *Rome Statute* (to name just a few). President Bush also withdrew from treaties. Most notably, he unilaterally abandoned the 1972 Antiballistic Missile (ABM) Treaty with Russia in December 2001 in order to move forward with his National Missile Defense plan. While treaty termination can be controversial, as it was in 2001 or two decades earlier when Carter ended the mutual defense pact with Taiwan to establish diplomatic relations with the People's Republic of China, it is a clear advantage the president has over the Congress. The Constitution does not address the issue of treaty termination and more than two hundred years of precedent has favored the president, who heads the branch of government with the responsibility for the day-to-day management of U.S. foreign relations.

Executive agreements are another advantage of the president and the usual method presidents use to make international agreements in order to avoid the necessity of securing the advice and consent of the Senate. The Supreme Court has ruled that these government-to-government agreements have the same legal force as treaties, and thus become part of the "supreme law of the land," but they may be concluded without legislative scrutiny. Early examples include the agreements governing the Lend-Lease Act of 1941, which enabled the United States to provide war materials to its World War II allies, and President Truman's aid to Greece and Turkey in the late 1940s. Others include the Paris peace agreement on Ending the War and Restoring Peace in Vietnam (1973), the SALT I arms control accord (1972), and various bilateral agreements covering American military base rights in Bahrain, Diego Garcia, and Japan, to name just a few.

Of the nearly 8,000 international agreements concluded between 1946 and 1992, for example, 95 percent were executive agreements (*Treaties and Other International Agreements: The Role of the United States Senate,* 1993) and hence not subject to the formal approval procedures of the Senate. Many of these were based on statutory directives, and others were entered into pursuant to treaty provisions, both of which require legislative input. Still, the vast number affirms the president's wide latitude to negotiate international agreements unrestrained by constitutional checks and balances.

Evidence that executive agreements pose a potential challenge to congressional oversight is seen in Congress's periodic attempts to block such maneuvers. One effort occurred in 1953–1954, when Senator John Bricker's (R-Ohio) proposal for a constitutional amendment to restrict the president's treaty-making powers and ability to manage the day-to-day conduct of foreign affairs fell only one vote short of the two-thirds majority necessary for Senate approval. Two decades later,

concern over the breadth and depth of overseas commitments the executive branch had entered into without Congress's knowledge led to the 1972 ***Case Act*** (named after its sponsor, Republican Senator Clifford Case of New Jersey). The statute required the president to submit to Congress all international agreements within sixty days of their execution.

Although the Case Act augmented Congress's capacity to be informed of executive agreements, the president remained the initiator of agreements with other countries, determining which are to be treaties and which executive agreements. Moreover, the law protected the secrecy of executive agreements by providing that they need be forwarded only to the relevant Senate and House committees if the president determines that public disclosure would endanger national security. Thus the law may have complicated presidents' lives, but it has not substantially restricted their freedom.

War   The Constitution is less than clear on where war-making powers lie. It states in Article I, Section 8 that "the Congress shall have power . . . to declare war." Elsewhere, however (Article II, Section 2), the Constitution also specifies that "the President shall be Commander-in-Chief of the Army and Navy of the United States." Of the two provisions, the latter has proven the more important, as the president has used that provision to justify stationing troops all over the world. Presidents have also used it to justify American military intervention in Korea (1950–1953), Lebanon (1958), the Dominican Republic (1965–1966), Vietnam (1965–1973), Grenada (1983), Panama (1989), the Persian Gulf (1990–1991 and 1994), Somalia (1992–1994), Bosnia (1995–present), Kosovo (1999), Afghanistan (2001), and Iraq (2003). Yet in none of those cases was military action accompanied by a formal declaration of war. In Kosovo, for example, Congress refrained from any authorization. Shortly thereafter, in Afghanistan and Iraq, it authorized the use of force without actually declaring war.

Protracted American involvement in Vietnam prompted congressional efforts to redress the war-making balance. President Lyndon Johnson argued that his authority rested on the **Gulf of Tonkin Resolution,** passed by Congress in August 1964. The joint resolution gave the president approval "to take all necessary measures to repel any armed attack against the forces of the United States and to prevent further aggression." As the quagmire of Vietnam deepened, the meaning of the Gulf of Tonkin Resolution became the source of intense debate. The Johnson administration insisted that the resolution was the "functional equivalent" of a declaration of war, but Congress eventually repudiated that interpretation when it repealed the Gulf of Tonkin Resolution in 1970. It then took concrete steps to limit future presidential war-making prerogatives, embodying them in the **War Powers Resolution,** passed in 1973 over President Nixon's veto.

The War Powers Resolution: Key Provisions and Dilemmas Several provisions in the War Powers Resolution (or Act) try to ensure congressional consent in decisions to deploy American troops abroad. Three sections are particularly relevant. Section III of the resolution stipulates that "the president in every possible instance shall consult with Congress before introducing United States Armed Forces into hostilities or into situations where imminent involvement in hostilities is clearly indicated by the circumstances." This first provision triggers a second. When troops have been introduced into immediate or imminent hostilities, Section IV calls on the president to report to Congress within 48 hours regarding the circumstances necessitating U.S. forces, the authority under which the action was taken, and the "estimated scope and duration of the hostilities or involvement." The report is to be transmitted in writing. Section V prohibits troop commitments from extending beyond sixty days after the report is submitted or required unless Congress declares war, authorizes the use of force, or grants an extension. However, this period can be extended up to ninety days if the safety of American troops is at stake. It is important to note that any time American forces become engaged in hostilities without a declaration of war or a specific congressional authorization, the law enables Congress to direct the president to disengage such troops by a concurrent resolution of the two houses of Congress. Because such a measure would not require the president's signature to take effect, it constitutes a **legislative veto** and may no longer be constitutional under the Supreme Court's *INS v. Chadha* ruling in 1983. The sixty-day limit and consulting and reporting requirements, however, remain intact.

President Richard Nixon argued that the sixty-day limit and the concurrent resolution provisions "purport to take away, by a mere legislative act, authorities which the president has properly exercised under the Constitution for almost two hundred years." They are unconstitutional, he asserted, because "the only way in which the constitutional powers of a branch of government can be altered is by amending the Constitution—and any attempt to make such alterations by legislation alone is clearly without force." He also claimed the resolution would "seriously undermine the nation's ability to act decisively and convincingly in times of international crisis" and that it would "give every future Congress the ability to handcuff every future president." Although the Senate rejected Nixon's argument and overrode the veto to make the War Powers Resolution law, virtually every president since Nixon has also questioned the constitutionality of the act. The courts' typical resort to the *doctrine of political questions* (discussed in Chapter 10) makes it unlikely that the constitutionality of the War Powers Resolution will ever be judicially tested. However, several other dilemmas regarding the provisions of that law also exist.

First, what are *consultations?* The War Powers Resolution seeks to ensure greater congressional participation in decisions authorizing the use of force by requiring consultation between the executive and legislative branches "in every possible instance" prior to committing U.S. forces to hostilities or to situations likely to result in such. However, there are no specific guidelines regarding what entails consultation, which lawmakers in Congress should be consulted, or to what lengths presidents should in their efforts to consult. Despite this ambiguity, presidents generally claim to have met the consultation requirement. However, rarely has serious and meaningful debate between the two branches occurred before a presidential decision on the use of force. Indeed, most presidents have resorted to *notifying* congressional leaders shortly before the use of force but have not consulted with them on specific courses of action (Collier 1994b; Fisher 1998; Fisher and Adler 1998; Hendrickson 2002). Such presidential practice would seem to violate the spirit, if not the letter, of the War Powers Resolution.

In short, there is no agreed-on mechanism to ensure that the president will weigh congressional views before making a decision to use force. The consultations issue is critical to the effectiveness of the War Powers Resolution, because once the decision to use force is implemented, Congress's power is severely circumscribed. Two examples make the point. President George H. W. Bush informed members of Congress of his intention to invade Panama at 6:00 P.M. on December 19, 1989. The actual invasion began seven hours later, at 1:00 A.M., December 20. In 1999, President Clinton began meeting with members of Congress only six days in advance of the initiation of the Kosovo bombing campaign, seeking their support for the decision he had already made. While this "consultation" left members with time to initiate opposition to the action had they so desired, there is little to suggest that the president did much more than notify members of his plans and ask for their support. With the decisions made in both cases prior to the notification—and with additional pressure from NATO in the second instance—there would seem to be little that Congress could have done.

Second, what are *imminent hostilities?* Many U.S. force deployments since the passage of the War Powers Resolution have involved situations short of outright combat, leaving open the opportunity for presidents to define them as outside the arena of "imminent hostilities." This reality has greatly complicated the application of the act's provisions and, occasionally, triggered substantial political debates.

For example, in the Reagan administration's deployment of American forces in Lebanon (1983) and the Persian Gulf (1987), the question of whether American troops were placed in danger of "imminent hostilities" as envisaged by the War Powers Resolution figured prominently in the congressional-executive contest. U.S. Marines were first sent to Lebanon in 1982 as part of a multinational force with the expectation that their presence there would be brief. In August 1983 the Marines suffered two fatalities and several casualties, prompting Reagan to seek congressional authorization for the deployment. Negotiations between Congress and the president resulted in a compromise resolution passed by both houses involving the War Powers Resolution but authorizing the Marines to stay in Lebanon for eighteen months. When he signed the resolution, however, the president stated, "I do not and cannot cede any of the authority vested in me under the Constitution as president and as commander-in-chief of the United States armed forces. Nor should my signing be viewed as any acknowledgment that the president's constitutional authority can be impermissibly infringed by statute." In the end, the October truck bombing of Marine headquarters in Beirut, which killed 241 Marines, persuaded the administration to withdraw the troops. In February 1984, the Marines were stationed on ships offshore and shortly thereafter, a complete evacuation from Lebanon was ordered.

The definition of "imminent hostilities" also played a role in the debate over the war power and the dispatch of American troops to Somalia in 1992–1993. Billed as a humanitarian mission in December 1992 by the outgoing George H. W. Bush administration, the continued deployment and expanding activities of the American troops later evoked substantial congressional debate and discussion, especially as the American forces became increasingly involved in military operations. Calls for the application of the War Powers Resolution, for President Clinton to seek congressional authorization for continued deployment, and for immediate withdrawal of the troops came from both sides of the aisle on Capitol Hill. Ultimately, when ninety-six American soldiers were killed or wounded in early October 1993, the criticism from Congress and elsewhere reached a crescendo and generated sufficient pressure for the administration to announce it would withdraw troops from the troubled country by the end of March 1994. Notably, the War Powers Resolution, while mentioned and threatened, was not formally invoked.

In contrast, there was little question about the nature of hostilities in the Afghanistan (2001) and Iraq (2003) cases. A strong military response was inevitable after Osama bin Laden's Al Qaeda network, with safe havens and training facilities in Afghanistan, attacked the United States in September 2001. Similarly, there was a clear understanding before the Iraq war that a military option to enforce UN resolutions or topple the Saddam Hussein regime would require combat operations. In both instances, Congress passed resolutions before forces were deployed that provided a broad grant of war-making authority to the Bush administration, affording the president the capacity to "use all necessary and appropriate force." These authorizations also specifically referenced the War Powers Resolution. While congressional influence can be seen in each instance, the unevenness with which the War Powers Resolution has been applied, as illustrated by the preceding examples, raises the question of the effectiveness of the Act.

The War Powers Resolution: Impact and Effectiveness   The United States has engaged in significant and sizable uses of its armed forces abroad nearly two dozen times since the War Powers Resolution was passed, and it has deployed forces in relatively minor actions in nearly eighty other instances. While presidents have often submitted reports to Congress under the resolution (more than fifty times through the end of the Clinton administration), the law has never been fully implemented. In particular, Section 4(a)(1), which would set the sixty-day clock in motion, has almost never been cited, nor has reference been made to actual or imminent hostilities. For its part, Congress has invoked the provisions of the act only once, in 1983, when in connection with the deployment of U.S. Marines to Lebanon, it declared that Section 4(a)(1) had become operative—but it went on to authorize the Marines to stay in Lebanon for eighteen months.

In the case of the 1991 Persian Gulf War, Congress stated that its authorization to use force against Iraq "constituted specific statutory authorization within the meaning of the War Powers Resolution" (Collier 1994a), and its authorization for the 2001 campaign in Afghanistan and 2003 invasion of Iraq contained similar language.

So has the War Powers Resolution had an effect on presidents and the use of U.S. force abroad? A brief review of some recent uses of force highlights the dilemmas that impinge upon the effectiveness of the law and assessments, pro and con, that have emerged among policymakers and scholars. First, although the act has been vigorously discussed in Congress and its application threatened, it has never been formally applied. Second, the political will of Congress to invoke the provisions of War Powers Resolution in conflict situations is questionable, because that would pose profound confrontation between Congress and the president. Third, the War Powers Resolution is poorly designed for dealing with uses of force short of large deployments of combat troops on the ground (that is, peacekeeping forces, air strikes, covert operations, and other more limited applications), which are far more commonplace than overt uses of military force. On the other hand, Congress appears to have drawn on the power of the War Powers Resolution to shape presidential behavior in some conflict situations, even though it did not seek to apply the act formally. Consider the following examples.

When President George H. W. Bush ordered military forces into Panama in December 1989, he submitted a report about the intervention to Congress "consistent with the War Powers Resolution" but neither cited the provision of the act that would limit the duration of force deployments nor recognized the legitimacy of the act itself. "I have an obligation as president to conduct the foreign policy of this country as I see fit," he exclaimed. He also announced, however, that U.S. troops were expected to be home in less than two months—within the sixty-day framework of the War Powers Resolution.

Bush adopted a similar posture during the crisis over Kuwait leading to the Persian Gulf War. A week after Iraq's August 1990 invasion of Kuwait he submitted a report "consistent with the War Powers Resolution" indicating that he had deployed U.S. forces to the region to deter further Iraqi aggression. He did not cite section 4(a)(1) of the resolution, which would have started the sixty-day clock, and specifically stated, "I do not believe involvement in hostilities is imminent." He reaffirmed that posture in November 1990 following the dispatch of another 150,000 troops to the region, claiming only that "The deployment will ensure that the coalition has an adequate offensive military option should that be necessary."

On November 29, 1990, the UN Security Council authorized the use of "all necessary means" to evict Saddam Hussein from Kuwait if he did not comply with UN mandates by January 15 1991. The Bush administration maintained that "the president did not need any additional congressional authorization for this purpose" (Collier 1994b; see also Moore 1994). Representative Ronald Dellums (D-California) and more than fifty of his colleagues, fearing that the administration would press forward without congressional authorization, took the administration to court.[2] While the case was dismissed, the U.S. district court left open the door to a possible ruling against the president's war-making power without congressional involvement. In the end, of course, the Bush administration did seek congressional authorization, but the president insisted to the very end that he had a legal right to make war against Iraq "regardless of any action that Congress might or might not take" (Moore 1994). Nevertheless, it could be argued that congressional concerns, the suit brought by Dellums, and the threat of the War Powers Resolution combined to force the president to bring the decision to Congress before acting.

The Persian Gulf War and, later, interventions in the Clinton administration added new elements to the War Powers debate, as they invited questions about Congress's role in authorizing U.S. participation in United Nations military or peacekeeping operations. The issue was left unresolved at the United Nations' creation in 1945, when it was anticipated that member states would conclude agreements placing military forces at the disposal of the organization. The *UN Participation Act,* the implementing legislation for U.S. participation in the United Nations, makes it clear that congressional approval is required for any agreement designating U.S. military forces for United Nations use, but that further congressional approval would not be necessary before they could be made available to the UN Security Council for enforcement action.

Like his predecessor, President Bill Clinton looked increasingly to the United Nations Security Council for his authority to use force, not to Congress or the Constitution. As he honed the military option to unseat Haiti's military regime in 1994, for example, he said he "welcomed" congressional support for the contemplated action, but added, "Like my predecessors of both parties, I have not agreed that I was constitutionally mandated to get it." Shortly after that, "he told the American public that he was prepared to use military force to invade Haiti, referring to a UN Security Council [resolution] as authority and his willingness to lead a multilateral force 'to carry out the will of the United Nations'"(Fisher 1994–1995).

The climate for congressional acquiescence to presidential deployments seemed to shift significantly in 1995. The Republican Congress, which came into power in January, determined to rein in U.S. participation in UN operations. The *National Security Revitalization Act* passed by the House sought to increase congressional control over peacekeeping deployments. It also proposed to bar the president from placing U.S. forces under foreign command as part of a UN peacekeeping operation—a move opposed by Clinton officials as an affront to the president's powers—and to reduce U.S. contributions to UN operations by the amount the Defense Department spent supporting past peacekeeping activities. Presidential contender Senator Robert Dole (R-Kansas) also introduced the *Peace Powers Act.* While repealing much of the War Powers Resolution, it would have strengthened its consultation provisions and the congressional oversight of UN-sponsored peacekeeping missions (similar legislation was introduced and later defeated in the House). "It makes sense to untie the president's hands in the use of force to defend U.S. interests," Dole told the Senate Foreign Relations Committee, "but we need to rein in the blank check for UN peacekeeping."

Nevertheless, in the fall of 1995 President Clinton committed 20,000 American troops to Bosnia-Herzegovina as part of the Dayton peace accords (Hendrickson 1998). Clinton's action followed his decisions to commit American forces to NATO enforcement of a UN-authorized "no-fly" zone over Bosnia and to dispatch roughly 350 U.S. troops to Macedonia to join a mission authorized by the UN Security Council intended to prevent a widening of the Balkan conflict. Clinton's decision took place in the climate of heightened congressional concern over force deployments generally and the president's authorization of NATO air strikes against the Bosnian Serbs in August. In the months that followed the Dayton peace accords, Clinton pledged to consult with Congress before committing American troops to the peace enforcement mission. Instead, he basically presented Congress with his decisions and then asked Congress to support him. Despite some grumbling and opposition and complaints, both houses of Congress would pass resolutions supporting Clinton's actions. Congressman Henry Hyde (R-Illinois) lamented that "the die is cast, now we have to fall in line."

Four years later, in early 1999, Clinton committed additional American forces to another operation in the former Yugoslavia, this time engaging in a massive bombing campaign against Serbia in reaction to its actions in Kosovo, a autonomous Serbian province heavily populated by ethnic Albanians (see Moskowitz and Lantis 2002). Secretary of Defense William Cohen and Secretary of State Madeleine Albright had asserted earlier that NATO had the authority to use force without either UN or congressional approval. That view was later challenged, leading to heated debates in the House of Representatives. But, in spite of the obvious opposition to Clinton's initiative, no substantive actions were taken to derail it.

Clinton did initiate discussions with Congress a few days before the start of the campaign, hoping to win members' support for the action. Under the leadership of several prominent Republican Senators, the Senate in March 1993 passed a resolution supporting the president's initiative. The House, however, was considerably more divided on the issue and failed to pass a similar resolution (Dionne 1999; Pianin 1999; Gugliotta 1999).

Then, three weeks into the Kosovo campaign, resolutions were introduced in the House calling for the withdrawal of American troops from the conflict and for a declaration of war. Intense debates over war powers followed. Secretary of State Albright informed members of the House International Relations Committee that "we do not believe in a war powers resolution . . . there is a conflict going on . . . The President has, we believe, the constitutional authority to do what he is doing." When the issue went to the House, a series of resolutions that would have constrained Clinton's authority failed.

Not to be denied, Representative Thomas Campbell (R-California) filed a suit in court against President Clinton for violation of the War Powers Act. This case was dismissed for lack of standing, as well as court use of the political questions doctrine (see Chapter 10) (Fisher 2000b). So, did Congress exercise influence, or was it denied? On the surface it appears that Congress again failed to rein in the president, but it should be remembered that Clinton also seems to have responded to the congressional climate by publicly ruling out the use of American ground troops in the Balkans conflict.

In sharp contrast to the controversy surrounding U.S. applications of force in Somalia, Haiti, Bosnia, and Kosovo, substantial consensus characterized the climate around the use of force against the Al Qaeda network and the Taliban regime in Afghanistan. In response to the attacks on the United States, Congress moved swiftly to authorize the Bush administration to use force against the perpetrators of the attack. The resolution, which passed the House 420–1 and the Senate 98–0 just three days after the attacks, authorized the president to use "all necessary and appropriate force . . . against nations, organizations, or persons . . . [who] planned, authorized, committed, or aided" the attacks. Nevertheless, the resolution fell short of the authority requested by George W. Bush, who sought the power to respond to the September 11 attacks and any future attacks. Cognizant of mistakes like the Gulf of Tonkin Resolution of 1964, some lawmakers tried to avoid "blank check" grants of war-making authority. According to Democratic Senator John Kerry (D-Massachusetts), not only did the resolution require Bush to provide regular updates to Congress, it also stipulated that Congress had to vote on funding military actions.

Moreover, as Democratic Chair of the Foreign Relations Committee Joseph Biden (D-Delaware) argued, the resolution "was narrowly drawn to apply only to responses to [September 11] terrorist actions" and invoked the War Powers Resolution by requiring the president to return to Congress for a formal declaration of war if he desired to expand the U.S. action (Povich 2001). Other observers acknowledged the careful language and the fact that Congress had not provided Bush with a "blank check," but cautioned that the resolution probably did not substantially limit the president. For example, national security law scholar Harold Koh of the Yale Law School stated, "I think it is extremely broad because no nations are named, the nations are to be determined by the president and the president could theoretically name lots of nations. . . . There is also no time limit" (Lewis 2001).

Koh's assessment was correct. As the Bush administration began its march toward war with Iraq, the president maintained that he already held the authority to topple Saddam Hussein's regime. This assertion in 2002 was based on the president's constitutional authority as commander-in-chief, congressional authorization of the 1991 Persian Gulf War and Iraq's ongoing violation of UN Security Council Resolutions tied to that conflict, *and* the 2001 congressional authorization. As discussed, the 2001 authorization granted the president the capacity to use force against states that aided the September 11 attacks. Lawmakers on both sides of the aisle strongly opposed the president's position. Some insisted he was legally required to seek congressional approval for any military action against Iraq. Others believed the president possessed the authority to act, but underscored the political wisdom of seeking a congressional resolution explicitly

focused on Iraq. Bush was persuaded by the latter logic and launched a concerted public relations campaign in the fall of 2002 to win support for going to war. His efforts included a major address before the UN General Assembly, several other speeches and public statements, and a televised address in which he specifically requested congressional authorization. These actions, which linked the Iraqi regime to Al Qaeda and weapons of mass destruction, coupled with lawmakers' desire to appear strong on national security as the midterm election approached, led the House (299–133) and the Senate (77–23) to pass a resolution authorizing the use of force (see Schonberg 2004; Lantis and Moskowitz 2005).

The action was a clear victory for President Bush and executive war powers. Congress did ensure the resolution explicitly referenced the War Powers Resolution and the president's reporting obligations. It was also successful in shifting language that tied U.S. national security interests to "international peace and security in the [entire] Persian Gulf region" from the substantive portions of the bill to the preamble (see *Joint Resolution to Authorize the Use of United States Armed Forces Against Iraq,* October 2, 2002). However, most observers agree the document granted President Bush exceedingly broad authority. One scholar observes that no time or geographical limits were placed on the president's authority and every attempt to create such constraints or link the use of force to a UN Security Council vote or the exhaustion of diplomatic means was overwhelming rejected (Schonberg 2004). Senator Robert Byrd (D-West Virginia) complained the resolution allowed "the president to use the military forces of this nation wherever, whenever and however he determines . . . and for as long as he determines, if he feels he can somehow make a connection to Iraq."

So does the War Powers Resolution matter? In many respects, the historical record suggests that the 1973 law has failed in its intention to redress the balance between Congress and the president. Quite simply, the president has not conceded its provisions bind him, and Congress cannot ensure enforcement. Many observers have endorsed this view

(Fisher and Adler 1998; Lowi 1985b; Hendrickson 2002). Even congressional luminaries, including Bob Dole, a co-sponsor of the War Powers Resolution, and Henry Hyde, have proposed its repeal.

Senator Jacob K. Javits (R–New York), architect of the War Powers Resolution, wrote shortly before his death that the resolution "did not, and does not, guarantee the end of presidential war, but it does present Congress with the means by which it can stop presidential war if it has the will to act" (Javits 1985). In most instances it appears that Congress lacks the will—in part because short, decisive military actions by the president (like the interventions in Grenada, Panama, and the Persian Gulf) tend to be politically popular at home. Conflicts that become protracted and unpopular may embolden Congress to act. However, there is no guarantee. Lawmakers are often reluctant to cut funding for ongoing military operations for fear they will be perceived as abandoning U.S. soldiers in the field.

Yet, other observers conclude that the act has, indeed, constrained presidential uses of force (see Gartzke 1996; Auerswald and Cowhey 1997). A recent analysis of uses of force before and after the War Powers Resolution concludes, for instance, that "The use of force after the Act is significantly different than it was before the Act, despite seeming congressional passivity" (Auerswald and Cowhey 1997). According to this analysis, presidents have, even while denouncing the act, engaged in more selective and careful applications of force. Moreover, Congress has, even while failing to invoke the law, generated anticipated reactions from presidents because of its provisions. Still, the president continues to enjoy considerable latitude in using military force to respond to international threats and there are no immediate signs that presidential dominance within this area will wane as long as the United States remains engaged in a global war on terrorism.

Money   What about the *power of the purse?* Since Congress has the exclusive power to appropriate funds for foreign as well as domestic programs, we should expect that here, more than in any other area, Congress would assert its authority over foreign affairs, and in many respects it does. Examples include the Boland amendments of the 1980s barring or restricting aid to the Nicaraguan contras, the 1995 vote to cut off funds to enforce the arms embargo against Bosnia, and a 1999 amendment to withhold half of U.S. aid to Russia until that country ended its nuclear and ballistic missile cooperation with Iran. In addition, throughout the last half of the 1990s, Congress repeatedly held American contributions to the United Nations hostage to a variety demands, including UN reforms, reduced American dues, and even abortion policy.

It is also noteworthy that lawmakers are able to link the power of the purse to other avenues of influence. Indeed, the mere threat of a linking issue enables members of the House and Senate to have an impact on policy. For example, the power of the purse enables them to conduct regular oversight hearings in conjunction with budgetary decisions. These hearings address military, diplomatic, trade, and intelligence issues, among others. Because budgeting is about voting, the process enables members to bargain for influence on one issue or another, frequently by tying apparently unrelated policy questions together. As members of Congress utilize this potentially powerful tool, they are guided by both policy and electoral concerns. The politics of defense and foreign aid budgeting highlight the dynamics.

Managing Foreign Aid Expenditures   Because it depends directly on Congress's appropriation of money, the perennially unpopular foreign aid program enables Congress to scrutinize the executive branch's conduct of foreign policy.[3] "Here is where the specter of '535 secretaries of state' is inevitably raised by critics of an aggressive congressional role" (Warburg 1989). Congress frequently exercises its power of the purse by adjusting presidential requests and adding its own. For instance, in 1995, House Speaker Newt Gingrich added $18 million to the budget for efforts to overthrow Saddam Hussein. Additionally, Congress often uses statutory requirements or **earmarks** to fund foreign aid for particular countries. Israel and Egypt have been the largest recipients over the last three decades; and in the post-9/11 era, substantial amounts of assistance have been earmarked for Iraq, Afghanistan, and Pakistan. Lawmakers also tie earmarks to particular programs, such as the Middle East Partnership Initiative (MEPI) or International Military Education and Training (IMET), to cite just two examples.

In addition, *conditionality* has become a centerpiece of congressional-presidential struggles over foreign aid funding (see Turner 1988). Bans on aid to countries taking certain actions—such as human rights violations, seizing U.S. fishing vessels, granting sanctuary to terrorists, and the like—are commonplace. In the case of the Freedom Support Act of 1992, which authorized U.S. assistance for the republics of the former Soviet Union, Congress linked the flow of aid to the removal of Russian troops from the Baltic States. Aid also has been made conditional on recipients meeting certain standards, such as cooperating with the United States in the interdiction of drug trafficking, holding free elections, or supporting the United States on UN resolutions. In fact, Congress reportedly directs where half of all development loan funds and over 90 percent of all U.S. security assistance are to go (Kondracke 1990).

Congress also resorts to *reporting requirements* to ensure executive compliance with legislative restrictions. The pervasiveness of reporting is indicated by the explosion in the reporting requirements, from 200 in 1973 to more than 800 in 1988 (Collier 1989, 37). In recent decades the number has continued to grow. For example, the Department of Homeland Security faces 256 reporting requirements every year, with the Transportation Security Administration alone obligated to deliver 62 annual reports to Capitol Hill (Miller 2005). From Congress's point of view, reporting requirements provide lawmakers with information, promote consultation, focus attention on a problem, provide a means of control, and oversee implementation (Collier 1988).

Although reporting requirements are useful to Congress, their number is now so great that "Congress has difficulty keeping track of them" (Collier 1988). Moreover, the required reports and certifications may generate **micromanagement**—detailed legislative involvement in the conduct of America's foreign relations often regarded by presidents as excessive interference in executive responsibilities. In the late 1980s, USAID employees in Global South countries complained "that they spend so much time filling out reports to Congress that they have only an afternoon a week to help the poor" (Kondracke 1990). Republicans and Democrats are equally guilty. As Democratic Senator Joseph R. Biden caustically observed, "When the Republicans were in the White House, they kept on saying, 'Don't micromanage foreign policy.' But they have turned out to be the biggest micromanaging, tinkering fools around."

Presidents can often avoid such situations by taking advantage of loopholes. Congress typically provides loopholes to permit the president flexibility to ignore restrictions that he believes compromise the United States' security interests. For instance, it is commonplace for penalties against major drug producing and transit countries to be waived, because presidents deem the continuation of U.S. foreign assistance to these states as vital to American national interests. Very few drug producing and transit countries are actually punished. Another example involves U.S. policy toward Cuba. After the passage of the Helms-Burton Act in 1996—which requires secondary sanctions against foreign companies and individuals doing business with Cuba, as well as allowing legal action by Americans against such companies—President Clinton took advantage of the law's waiver provision and suspended key requirements every six months until the end of his second term.

Recent presidential administrations have sought unsuccessfully to overhaul the foreign aid program by sweeping away congressional restrictions. In 1994, the Clinton administration proposed to appropriate aid not for specific countries or programs but in pursuit of broad foreign policy goals. Earmarks and distinctions between military and economic assistance would be eliminated. It quickly became clear that Congress was reluctant to relinquish its ability to influence aid allocations. "We will not give to an unelected bureaucracy . . . authority to spend dollars any way they want, so long as they call it 'pursuit of democracy' or 'expanding economic development,'" asserted Democratic Congressman David R. Obey of Wisconsin, a member of the House Appropriations Subcommittee on Foreign Operations. Republicans were even less interested. When they assumed the reins of congressional leadership following the 1994 elections, earmarks across all areas of federal spending expanded from 1,349 in 1995 to 13,997 in 2005 (Murray 2006, A21). Foreign aid was no exception.

In 2004, the Bush administration established the **Millennium Challenge Account (MCA)** in an effort to circumvent the congressional earmarks associated with traditional U.S. foreign assistance. This bilateral development assistance account is administered by a new government agency, the Millennium Challenge Corporation (MCC), rather than USAID. Aid is awarded on a competitive basis to a select group of "qualified" developing countries based on clearly specified criteria designed to reward good governance and economic and political reform. President Bush expressed a commitment to use the MCA to increase foreign aid permanently by five billion dollars a year. At the same time, he proposed major cuts in USAID funding. During the first five years of the Bush administration, however, Congress was unwilling to fund the MCA to the levels requested by the president or expand the more rigorous, goal-oriented MCA model to the more than one hundred countries and $14 billion worth of accounts overseen by USAID (Fisher 2006). This reality raised serious doubts that Secretary of State Condoleezza Rice would be able to win support on Capitol Hill for her plan to overhaul the U.S. foreign aid system and bring the work of USAID more in line with Bush administration policy goals, such as democracy promotion.

Managing Military Expenditures   Military spending is another budgetary area in which Congress can and does play a major role. During the 1950s and 1960s, Congress often voiced its views on the defense budget by appropriating *more* for defense than was asked for by the president. After that, Congress began cutting administration requests substantially, much as it did with foreign aid. Moreover, its

micromanagement of the Pentagon increased steadily. A White Paper from the Bush I administration complained that "some thirty committees and seventy-seven subcommittees claim some degree of oversight . . . and more than 1,500 congressional staffers devote nearly all of their time to defense issues" (*Wall Street Journal,* 18 December 1989, A10). The administration also complained that "the Pentagon alone spent $50 million and 500 'man-years' in fiscal 1989 writing reports to satisfy Congress" (cited in Burgin 1993). Meanwhile, Congress made an increasing number of changes in the president's defense budget requests. In 1970, Congress made 830 program changes during the annual budgetary cycle; by the end of the Cold War the number had grown to nearly 2,800 (Blechman 1990).

The motivation to micromanage is tied directly to the factors that differentiate the perspective of members of Congress on foreign and national security policy issues from that of the president. Political grandstanding for electoral purposes is a powerful incentive. For example, Congress publicly debated (and voted on) virtually all of the important strategic and many conventional weapons systems requiring production decisions during the Reagan administration's military buildup in the 1980s, when the incentives to micromanage were especially strong. The decisions Congress faced included the MX missile, the Strategic Defense Initiative (SDI), the Stealth bomber program, antisatellite systems, chemical weapons, the Trident II submarine, the B-1 bomber, cruise missiles, nuclear-powered aircraft carriers, and antiaircraft guns and tactical aircraft. Before Reagan, decisions on them typically would have been made in congressional committees. As Democratic Senator Gaylord Nelson of Wisconsin noted wryly, "The floor is being used as an instrument of political campaigning far more than it ever was before." Electoral incentives in the form of financial contributions and constituency support also multiplied as the guns-instead-of-butter spending priorities of the Reagan administration helped to politicize defense policy (Lindsay 1987).[4]

The same parochialism that motivates members of Congress to serve on committees fuels Congress's micromanagement of the defense budget, as members are alert to the impact of defense spending on their constituencies, as we saw in Chapter 9. As one defense expert observed caustically, "Politicians of both parties see the [defense] budget as a jobs program. No longer does the defense debate take place between hawks and doves, but between those who have defense facilities and those who don't" (Korb 1995a). Hence, immediate constituency interests promise to figure prominently in the calculations. A persistent question, then, is how to get Congress to focus on policy rather than micromanaging individual programs.

Defense "intellectuals" in Congress, notably Sam Nunn, chair of the Senate Armed Services Committee, and Les Aspin, chair of the House Armed Services Committee, did strike out in new strategic directions in the early post–Cold War years, believing, as Aspin put it, that "there are new realities in the world, but no new thinking at home to match them" (Stockton 1993). The two drafted their own defense budgets, setting out markedly different priorities from the Bush administration's budget requests.

Nunn's and Aspin's response to broad policy issues as the Cold War waned is not easily explained by the imperative of reelection or the demands of constituent service. A sense of "duty" and a belief that addressing policy issues is "part of their job" are perhaps better explanations (Stockton 1993). But Nunn and Aspin would soon leave Congress, and Congress throughout the Clinton years would continue micromanaging the defense budget. According to one accounting:

> Congress cut Bush [I]'s requests for HARM missiles (52 percent), high-speed cargo ships (49 percent), U.S. troops stationed in Europe after FY 1996 (33 percent), C-17 cargo planes (28 percent), Strategic Defense Initiative (SDI) funding (25 percent), FA-18 Aircraft (25 percent), and the development of a new Centurion-class nuclear submarine (14 percent). Bush was also forced to accept a total fleet of twenty B-2 Stealth bombers, rather than

the seventy-five he had requested. . . . Congress increased funding for modernization of M-1 tanks (492 percent), Bradley fighting vehicles (120 percent), JSTARS radar aircraft (65 percent), and a helicopter-borne laser for use as a minesweeper (50 percent). Members also added $1.2 billion for an unrequested helicopter carrier, continued to fund the V-22 Osprey air transport, and refused to stop the Seawolf submarine program after building only one such submarine. . . . Facing a Republican Congress . . . [President Clinton's] budget battles intensified. Congress tried to increase antimissile defense funding and gain more control over peacekeeping activities, but was unable to override Clinton's veto. Clinton also vetoed the Foreign Operations appropriations bill, as it cut his requests for Arms Control and Disarmament Agency (53 percent), UN peacekeeping costs (49 percent), U.S. Information Agency (16 percent), and the Department of State (13 percent). Congress was more successful in cutting multilateral aid requests by 48 percent, bilateral aid requests by 15 percent, and export assistance requests by 10 percent.
> *(Carter 1998, 112–113)*

Indeed, in each of the last four years of his term, Congress increased the defense budget beyond Clinton's request. Moreover, Congress was clearly the driving force behind the reincarnation of the Strategic Defense Initiative in its current form: National Missile Defense (NMD). It was Congress that sought additional funds for an expanded program beginning in 1995, Congress that voted to go forward with the program in 1999, and Congress that pressured Clinton to endorse NMD in 2000. In this context, the Bush II administration's commitment to NMD is merely the continuation of congressional policy.

Congress continued to use its power of the purse over military expenditures during George W. Bush's administration, although the nature of that use shifted in the wake of the September 2001 terrorist attacks on the United States. Prior to the attacks, Bush's budget faced congressional micromanagement similar to those of his predecessors. The overall amount, the specific programs, and, especially, the commitment to spending over $8 billion on national missile defense drew substantial congressional activism, especially after the Democrats assumed the majority in the Senate after Vermont Senator James Jeffords switched parties. For example, Carl Levin (D-Michigan), the chair of the Senate Armed Services Committee, indicated his intention to oppose missile defense spending. Senator Joseph Biden (D-Delaware) appeared before the National Press Club the day before the terrorist strikes to announce in strong terms his opposition to missile defense.

In the wake of the attacks, the climate changed substantially. First, many of those most likely to oppose the President Bush's budget proposals backed away from their opposition. Levin, for instance, decided to suspend plans to block missile defense spending in the interest of bipartisanship and unity (Hartung 2001). The global war on terrorism, force modernization associated with Secretary of Defense Donald Rumsfeld's military transformation initiative (discussed in Chapter 11), wars in Afghanistan (2001) and Iraq (2003), and continued postwar fighting in these theaters led Congress to approve major annual increases in defense spending throughout the Bush administration. While the defense budget hovered around $300 billion a year by the end of the Clinton administration, the Defense Department request for fiscal year (FY) 2007 stood at $439.3 billion, nearly a 5 percent increase over FY 2006. Moreover, the $400 billion-plus annual defense budgets of the Bush years did not include hundreds of billions of dollars in supplemental congressional appropriations to finance ongoing military operations in Afghanistan and Iraq. For instance, lawmakers approved $120 billion in supplemental military funding in *both* 2005 and 2006 and a similar level was anticipated in 2007 (Silva 2006a).

The supplemental defense spending bills of the Bush era provided great opportunities for lawmakers to add on money for programs unrelated to the war on terrorism or the campaigns in Iraq and Afghanistan, but which financed pet projects in their districts and states. One watchdog group, the Taxpayers for Common Sense, "identified more than $12 billion in add-ons [in 2004] and expected the number to be higher [in 2005]." The same group observed, "Parochially and politically motivated [defense] earmarks totaled 2,671 [in 2004], compared to just 62 in 1980" (quoted in Bender 2005). These pork-barrel appropriations included billions of dollars for a range of weapons systems the armed services did not request as well as millions of dollars for nonmilitary items, such as a wastewater treatment plant in Mississippi, a medical center in Texas, and a fire sciences academy in Nevada (Bender 2005).

Still, in some ways the end of the Cold War has added incentives to strategize as well as to micromanage. For example, the Defense Reorganization Act of 1986 (the Goldwater-Nichols Act) required that each annual budget request to Congress be accompanied by a comprehensive report on overall national security strategy, enabling Congress to consider strategic concerns as well as budget lines. In addition, the National Defense Authorization Act of 1996 required *Quadrennial Defense Reviews*. These four-year reviews, which have now been conducted in 1997, 2001, and 2006, were to include: " . . . a comprehensive examination of the defense strategy, force structure, force modernization plans, infrastructure, budget plan, and other elements of the defense program and policies with a view toward determining and expressing the defense strategy of the United States. . . ." To be sure, both of these requirements place the executive branch in the position of conducting the studies, but they ensure that Congress has opportunities to review more than annual budgets.

Constraints on the Power of the Purse Congressional actions on the foreign aid and defense budgets demonstrate Congress's willingness to exercise its power of the purse, although its instruments for doing so are not finely honed and its motives sometimes suspect. Indeed, there are limits to

Congress's ability use its fiscal powers. Briefly, they include:

- *Problems associated with political will and political costs.* On some issues, members of Congress are reluctant to challenge a president because of the potential costs involved. It is difficult to get even a majority of the 535 members of Congress organized into two competing political parties to agree on a particular policy priority, especially if it challenges the president. Nowhere is this more evident than in controlling the use of force. Members are reluctant to use the power of the purse to control uses of force for fear that they will be vulnerable to the criticism that they left American forces exposed. For example, in spite of the outcry over the 1970 American incursion into Cambodia order by the Nixon administration, Congress cut off Cambodian war funds only after (then known) U.S. military activity had ceased. Congress never failed to appropriate the funds for the war that the Johnson and Nixon administrations sought. Three decades later, lawmakers (as of early 2006) avoided any call for a reduction in spending for the military campaign in Iraq even though there was mounting concern over the strength of insurgency, the potential for full-fledged civil war, and the continuing loss of American lives.

- *Problems associated with the instrument itself.* It is often noted that "policy is what gets funded." However, while the power of the purse is central to some foreign policy initiatives, its link to others is not. The extent to which money can be used to affect the nation's foreign policy is limited. Simply put, it is difficult to legislate foreign policy or to equate lawmaking with foreign policy making. Programs, but not necessarily policies, require appropriations. Hence, some of the most important aspects of America's foreign relations do not require specific and direct appropriations of money

- *Problems associated with the budget process.* The budget process itself is long, drawn-out, complex, and fragmented, which makes difficult the prospect of coordinating the process and policy. This problem is especially acute because, within each house of Congress, the substantive committees having jurisdiction over particular programs authorize expenditures, but another committee makes the actual appropriations. Moreover, opportunities for individuals to pursue their own agendas and pressures for logrolling (vote trading) and compromises tend to blunt the sharp edge of the power of the purse

- *Problems associated with presidential discretion.* The president has important budgetary powers that also limit the ability of Congress to turn its power of the purse into direct policy results. For one, the 1921 budget reform act gave the president the agenda-setting power of presenting a budget to Congress, which places lawmakers on the defensive and compels them to react to presidential proposals. For example, each year from 1989 through 1992, the Bush I administration removed funding for the development of the Marine Corps' V-22 Osprey. And each year, the plane's supporters on Capitol Hill challenged executive branch opposition and restored funding. More significantly, presidents have opportunities for **impoundment** or refusals to spend money appropriated by Congress, which the Office of the Secretary of Defense attempted during the four-year battle over the V-22 (see Jones 2002b). Presidents also have **discretionary funds**—monies provided by Congress the president to deal with situations unforeseen at the time of the annual budget process—on which they can draw to evade congressional restrictions. For example, President Johnson used $1.5 billion in contingency funds embedded in the Pentagon budget to finance military operations in Southeast Asia during 1965 and 1966 (Nathan and Oliver 1976). Similarly, President Reagan used $10 million in CIA discretionary funds to finance the Nicaraguan contras during its first term (Copson 1988). The Clinton administration used discretionary funds to aid Mexico in 1995 during that country's financial crisis after Congress rejected its request for emergency assistance. George W. Bush used discretionary funds to support the CIA's expanded counterterrorist intelligence and covert activities

- *Reprogramming* permits funds within an appropriation category to be moved from one purpose to another (for example, from shipbuilding to submarine construction). Although the 1974 Budget and Impoundment Control Act sought to constrain such executive flexibility, it still specified that the president could order *deferrals* (temporary spending delays, which can extend up to twelve months) and *rescissions* (permanent efforts to cancel budget authority), subject to congressional review.[5]

In summary, our review of the congressional power of the purse suggests that members of Congress use multiple instruments and opportunities to shape American foreign policy. These avenues range from substantive legislation to less direct means, all of which may be linked together to shape policy. Moreover, our review suggests that members may have influence even when the institution does not produce legislation, as presidents respond to congressional preferences, often through "anticipated reactions," and adjust policies accordingly. However, the president retains important advantages in foreign policy leadership, including control over the implementation of policy. Other presidential advantages stem from obstacles that obstruct congressional foreign policy making, to which we now turn.

OBSTACLES TO CONGRESSIONAL FOREIGN POLICY MAKING

Because of its access to powerful avenues of influence such as those discussed previously, Congress can, at times, play an assertive foreign policy role. However, as an institution, Congress suffers from some key disadvantages when it comes to

competing effectively with the president over the direction of the nation's foreign relations. Three interrelated factors—parochialism, organizational weaknesses, and lack of expertise—help to explain this disadvantage and shed light on the reasons that members of Congress frequently fail to utilize its apparently powerful and numerous avenues of foreign policy influence.

Parochialism

Congress is more oriented toward domestic than foreign affairs. All 435 members of the House are up for reelection every two years, as is a third of the Senate. Continual preoccupation with reelection creates pressure to attend more to domestic than to international concerns. The pressure is especially acute on the House side, and perhaps explains why the ten provisions of the House Republicans' *Contract with America* during the 1994 election included only one foreign policy item. The president has a national constituency. In contrast, all 535 members of Congress have much more narrowly construed electoral bases and correspondingly restricted constituency interests. Thus, in the words of former Under Secretary of State William D. Rogers (1979), "With the fate of the entire House and a third of the Senate in the hands of the voters every 730 days, Congress is beholden to every short-term swing of popular opinion. The temptation to pander to prejudice and emotion is overwhelming."

The twenty-first century environment arguably exacerbates these tendencies. For one thing, globalization and the concomitant rise of intermestic issues dramatically increase the range of constituency interests in issues formerly thought to be either purely domestic or purely international. Increased ethnic diversity may also heighten the concerns and interests of constituents (Shain 1994–1995). These developments present often powerful incentives for Congress to address specialized issues that relate to foreign policy. Moreover, the international threat environment plays a critical role in such calculations. Without pressing threats, constraints on foreign policy activism erode, as the costs related to narrow, often single-issue-driven policy concerns are diminished. The combination of more concerns and lowered political risks may simply encourage more members to act on their parochial interests. Conversely, when clear threats appear, as after September 11, 2001, members are more likely to control parochial urges.

Because senators and representatives depend for their survival on satisfying their constituents' parochial interests, "being national-minded can be a positive hazard to a legislative career" (Sundquist 1976). Thus a foreign policy problem may be viewed from a representative's Polish, Israeli, or Irish constituent viewpoint. Similarly, military needs may be weighed by the benefits of industries located within a senator's state or representative's district. "Asked one day whether it was true that the navy yard in his district was too small to accommodate the latest battleships," Henry Stimson (chair of the House Naval Affairs Committee early in the twentieth century) replied, 'That is true, and that is the reason I have always been in favor of small ships' (cited in Sundquist 1976).

The president's perspective is much different. Having a nationwide constituency, the president's outlook on foreign policy problems is broader. The president can usually afford to alienate some local or narrow interests (by refusing to support a protective trade restriction, for example) without fear of electoral retribution; and while the president is rewarded for thinking in long-run terms rather than for the moment, a senator or representative is not. "With their excessively parochial orientation," former Senator J. William Fulbright explains, lawmakers "are acutely sensitive to the influence of private pressure and to the excesses and inadequacies of a public opinion that is all too often ignorant of the needs, the dangers, and the opportunities in our foreign relations." (Fulbright and two of his successors as chairs of the Senate Foreign Relations Committee, Frank Church of Idaho and Charles Percy of Illinois, lost reelection bids in part because they assumed leadership roles in foreign rather than domestic affairs.)

Interest in and attention to foreign policy issues by members of Congress is typically short-lived and strongly influenced by their newsworthiness (Crabb

and Holt 1992). According to Republican Senator Daniel J. Evans of Washington, the legislative process has degenerated into "reading yesterday's headlines so that we can write today's amendments so that we can garner tomorrow's headlines." Often amendments are passed with little expectation of becoming law. As one Senate aide observed, "It has come to be an accepted part of the game that amendments are passed and press releases claiming credit are issued, with the understanding that most of these items will be tossed in the wastebasket when the bill goes to conference with the House." The *"hundred barons phenomenon"*—all senators want to be seen as directing the nation's foreign policy—explains the seemingly pointless behavior (Oberdorfer and Dewar 1987).

The congressional committee system, where the institution's real work is done, reinforces parochialism. Lawmakers serve on committees to enhance their prospects for reelection, expand their influence within chambers, devise good public policy, and position themselves for new careers (Fenno 1973; see also Burgin 1993; Smith and Deering 1990). Although distinguished performance in congressional committees may further each of those goals, reelection depends primarily on *constituent service.* Such concerns deflect congressional attention from substantive policy issues. Gaining a committee assignment germane to the interests of people back home is therefore critical to the effective performance of constituent service. Congressional committees reflect these preferences, which in turn help to shape the legislative process.

> Farm state members want to deal with agriculture while city people do not, so the agriculture committees are rural and proagriculture in their composition. The military affairs committees are dominated by partisans of the military, urban affairs committees by members from the cities, interior committees by proreclamation westerners, and so on. By custom, the judiciary committees are made up exclusively of lawyers. Within each committee, there is further specialization of

subcommittees and of individual members.... And through logrolling, the advocates of various local interests form coalitions of mutual support.

(Sundquist 1976, 600)

Given these incentives and the behaviors they encourage, congressional attention to foreign affairs is often fleeting and shallow. Indeed, "sacrificing overall consistency and coherence of national policy for narrow interests and short term objectives ... is the natural consequence of the political calculus that inevitably dominates congressional decision making" (Blechman 1990).

Organizational Weaknesses

Foreign policy influence by members of Congress is also hindered by the fragmentation of power and responsibility within Congress. President Truman's famous quip, "The buck stops here!" has no counterpart in Congress. Over half of the standing committees in both the House and Senate have broadly defined jurisdictions that give them some foreign affairs responsibility (see Table 12.2). Unlike the executive branch, where policy debates take place in private with a single individual, the president often making the final choice, congressional debates are perforce public, with final choices made by counting yeas and nays, and with decision making diffuse. Under these conditions, policy consistency and coordination are most unlikely.

During the 1970s, Congress undertook several procedural reforms that decentralized power from the committee to the subcommittee level, encouraged challenges to the seniority system, and reduced the importance of leadership positions.[6] As a consequence it became more difficult than ever to locate power and authority in Congress. "There are 165 different people in the House and Senate who can answer to the proud title 'Mr. Chairman,' having been given committees or subcommittees of their own" (Broder 1986). Accordingly, the congressional leadership cannot speak for the institution as a whole, and Congress rarely speaks with a single voice. Newt Gingrich reversed the trend toward

fragmented leadership when he became speaker of the House by gathering and concentrating some powers and authority to the leadership. Overall, his success was marginal in an institution as decentralized and sprawling as the House of Representatives. In fact, the Republican decision to limit the tenure of any committee chair probably exacerbates the problem by reducing the impact of expertise (Gugliotta 1998).

The rise of *single-issue politics*—which subjects members of Congress to evaluation not on the basis of their entire record but only their performance on particular issues—magnifies the problems associated with the diffusion of power. Noting that the 385 committees and subcommittees of Congress are scouted by hundreds of registered lobbyists, one former official lamented that instead of a two-party system Capitol Hill resembles "a 385-party system" (cited in Crabb and Holt 1992). As the foreign-domestic policy divide has become increasingly porous, this effect has increasingly had foreign policy consequences. Business groups, ideological groups, ethnic groups, labor groups, environmental groups, and virtually every other special interest group seems to be able to find something "international" on which to focus their efforts.

The fragmentation of power and responsibility in Congress also frustrates executive–legislative consultation and coordination and makes Congress appear irresponsible. When facing a skeptical electorate, for example, these conditions enable individual senators and representatives to deflect criticism with the defense, "I didn't do it; it was everyone else."

Individual accountability is reduced further by the congressional penchant for dealing with issues in procedural terms rather than confronting them directly. A striking illustration occurred with the Senate's consideration of two controversial treaties to cede American control of the Panama Canal to Panama. Senators took record votes on more than fifty amendments, nearly twenty reservations, a dozen understandings, and several conditions—nearly ninety proposals for change of one kind or another. Many of the proposed changes were billed as "improvements," which made it easier to vote for

T A B L E 12.2 **Foreign Affairs Responsibilities of Committees in the House and Senate, 109th Congress (Number of Foreign Policy-Related Subcommittees in Parentheses)**

Senate Committee	Foreign Affairs Responsibility	House Committee
Agriculture, Nutrition, and Forestry (4)	Foreign agricultural policy and assistance	Agriculture (5)
Appropriations (12)	Appropriation of revenues, rescission of appropriations	Appropriations (10)
Armed Services (6)	Defense, national security, national security aspects of nuclear energy, defense production,	Armed Services (7)
Banking, Housing, and Urban Affairs (5)	International economic policy, export and foreign trade promotion	Financial Services (5); Energy and Commerce (4); International Relations (6)
Budget	Budgetary matters, concurrent budget resolution	Budget
Commerce, Science, and Transportation (10)	Merchant marine, marine fisheries, oceans, coastal zone management, nonmilitary space sciences and aeronautics	Energy and Commerce (6); Resources (3); Science (3)
Energy and Natural Resources (4)	Energy policy, nonmilitary development of nuclear energy	Energy and Commerce (4); Science (4); Resources (5)
Environment and Public Works (4)	Environmental policy, regulation of nuclear energy, ocean dumping, environmental aspects of outer continental shelf lands	Science (3)
Finance (5)	Revenue measures, customs, foreign trade agreements, tariffs, import quotas	Ways and Means (6)
Foreign Relations (7)	Relations with foreign nations, treaties, executive agreements, international organizations, foreign assistance, international economic policy, trade and export promotion, intervention abroad, declarations of war, terrorism, international environmental and scientific affairs	International Relations (7)
Homeland Security and Governmental Affairs (3)	Organization and reorganization of the executive branch, organization and management of nuclear export policy, homeland security, studying relations with intergovernmental organizations, relations with oil producing and consuming countries	Government Reform (7); Homeland Security (6)
Intelligence (1)	Intelligence activities, covert operations	Intelligence (4)
Judiciary (8)	Immigration and refugees, terrorism, espionage	Judiciary (6)
Health, Education, Labor, and Pensions (4)	Regulation of foreign labor	Education and the Workforce (5)

NOTE: Descriptions of the foreign affairs responsibilities are derived from the jurisdictions of the Senate committees in the 109th Congress, with the corresponding jurisdictions of House committees matched to those as closely as possible. All are standing committees of the respective houses of Congress except the Intelligence committees, which are select committees.

SOURCE: Congress Merge Online, www.congressmerge.com.

a politically unpopular document. (In the case of the Panama Canal, however, it is noteworthy that over half of the thirty-eight senators who supported the treaties lost in their next campaign for reelection.) Procedure therefore becomes a useful tool for coping with single-issue politics, allowing lawmakers to conceal their true positions, thereby avoiding direct confrontation with the president and deflecting potential electoral criticism.

> If done directly, a Congressional decision—for example, to disapprove money for a new aircraft carrier—would require that more than half of all Congressmen conclude that the Navy can do with fewer carriers. . . . This would involve a stark confrontation with expertise that would be very uncomfortable for a Congressman. If a showdown is reached on the carrier issue, the vote is almost certain to be cloaked in procedures (motions to table, and so on) that would allow the Congressman to justify his vote, if he needed to, on a procedural question rather than on the merits of the case.
>
> *(Aspin 1976, 165)*

A different sort of Congress's seeming irresponsibility arises out of the very sluggishness of the legislative process. As freshman Senator Barak Obama (D-Illinois) observed in 2006, "Things move extraordinarily slowly." Slow, deliberative procedures may be inherent in a body charged with reconciling disparate views, but delays are prolonged by the dispersion of power and responsibility between two houses, their further fragmentation within a complex structure of committees and subcommittees (which slows the legislative process on major issues to "near paralysis" [Burgin 1993]), and the near absence of party discipline. The Senate's cloture rule, requiring an extraordinary majority for terminating debate, is another restraint on initiative. "The result is that any piece of legislation must surmount an obstacle course of unparalleled difficulty. . . . Few things happen quickly. Policies eventually adopted are often approved too late . . . .

And in the process of overcoming the countless legislative hurdles, policies may be compromised to the point of ineffectiveness" (Sundquist 1976). Contrast that picture with the president's proven ability to act quickly and decisively, as rapidly moving international developments frequently require. "Presidents can procrastinate too," James L. Sundquist (1976) observes, "but unlike Congress they are not compelled to by any institutional structure."

A final form of irresponsibility is found in the frequent tendency of members of Congress to "leak" information. A glaring example of the recurrent problem took place in 1987, when the Senate Intelligence Committee voted not to make public a report on its closed-door hearings on the Iran-Contra affair, only to have NBC News acquire the first half of it three days later. Within two weeks, the other half appeared in the *New York Times.* Senator Patrick J. Leahy (D-Vermont) later resigned as vice chair of the committee when it was learned he had leaked the unclassified committee report—and at precisely the time the committee was trying to demonstrate that Reagan administration officials, not lawmakers, were most often responsible for leaking classified government information.

Recent violations occurred in 1995 and 2001. In 1995, when Representative Robert C. Torricelli, a Democrat from New Jersey, revealed classified information allegedly implicating the CIA in a pair of murders in Guatemala—despite his oath "not [to] disclose any classified information received in the course of my service with the House of Representatives."[7] Such leaks arise from the independence that senators and representatives prize and from the benefits they can realize by placing issues in the mass media's spotlight. (Torricelli cited "moral obligation" in defending his behavior.) Unfortunately, one of the consequences is that the president often uses "executive privilege" to conceal information—particularly classified information—thus preventing congressional involvement in policy making. In 2001, George W. Bush restricted briefings of Congress on military actions around Afghanistan because of his frustration with congressional leaks of previous briefings.

Lack of Expertise

The third weakness limiting Congress's ability to exercise foreign policy leadership derives from the White House's comparatively greater command of technical expertise and from its ability to control the flow of information. We have already observed this in our discussion of the departments and agencies comprising the foreign policy bureaucracy, all of which are executive branch organizations. Although they sometimes resist presidential orders, as we will see in Chapter 13, these organizations contribute enormously to presidential leadership. Congress must often depend on the executive branch for the information critical to sound policy recommendations (see West and Cooper 1990).

Congress has tried to overcome its lack of expertise in several ways. First, Congress dramatically increased the size of the professional staff serving congressional committees and individual members of Congress. Growth exploded during the 1970s and continued throughout the 1980s, bringing the total number of personal and committee staff employees to more than 15,000 by 1991 (Mann and Ornstein 1993). In the mid-1990s, with the Republicans in the majority, the total number of congressional staff was trimmed by about 25 percent, with committee and support agency staff sustaining much larger reductions than personal staff. However, after 1996, personal and committee staff numbers began to increase. By 2000, there were roughly 24,000 congressional staffers on Capitol Hill (C-SPAN 2000).

Staff resources give Congress a greater capacity to assert an independent congressional position and the means to become involved in policy questions where congressional interest and expertise previously may have been lacking (Crabb and Holt 1992). Furthermore, in an atmosphere where knowledge is power, congressional staffs exercise greater influence over the direction of policy. The technical experts filling staff roles, and the networks of communications and coalitions that have developed among them, enable them to steer policy, operating as an "invisible force in American lawmaking" (Fox and Hammond 1977).

Second, Congress has, as noted previously, increased the reporting requirements on practically every bureaucratic agency, and has strengthened oversight since the mid-1970s as well. This trend has improved the ability of members to extract relevant information from the executive branch in a timely fashion.

Third, Congress has developed "congressional bureaucracies" to assist it in assembling information and analysis. For example, it has periodically expanded the overseer role of the Government Accountability Office (formerly the General Accounting Office). In 1972, Congress created the Office of Technology Assessment to evaluate scientific and technical proposals, and in 1974, it added the Congressional Budget Office to assist in analyzing budget options and preparing the annual budget resolution. In 1995, the Republican majority attempted to reverse the growth of legislative staff and support agencies. Not only did it reduce staff (mostly those serving committees), it also eliminated the Office of Technology Assessment (parceling outs its responsibilities to the GAO and to the newly established House Science Committee).

Individual members of Congress often develop considerable policy expertise. The committee system and the penchant to allocate positions of authority according to the rules of seniority mean that some senators and representatives often spend their entire legislative careers specializing in their committees' areas of jurisdiction. For example, Senator Richard Lugar (R-Indiana) has served three decades on the Senate Foreign Relations Committee, including two terms as the committee's chair, and is widely recognized as a foreign and national security policy expert. Given the electoral advantage that incumbents enjoy, it is not uncommon to find many congressional careers that span a quarter-century or more—much longer than the president is allowed by the Constitution to remain in office.

Historically, specialization by entrenched members of Congress has been especially prominent in the Senate and House Armed Services committees (the latter now called the Committee on National Security), where southern Democrats in particular have claimed considerable expertise on national security issues. Members of these committees now also receive large amounts of intelligence from the CIA, contributing to their ability to arrive at policy judgments independent of the president. Congress's committee and seniority systems also facilitate the patron-client relationships between Congress and the foreign policy bureaucracy described in the previous chapter. Such relationships sometimes subvert presidential interests, but they also provide Congress power vis-à-vis the executive branch.

Still, all members of Congress cannot be experts on all matters of policy. Moreover, members of Congress are especially ill-equipped to acquire the kinds of information that would enable them to better monitor, and hence influence, decision making in times of crisis. Following the Ford administration's use of Marines to rescue the ship *Mayaguez* from its Cambodian captors in May 1975, for example, a survey revealed that the press was the principal source of information for many members of Congress. This was even true for a majority of those serving on congressional committees directly concerned with foreign and national security policy. Little wonder that one (anonymous) member of Congress cynically observed, "The actions of the United States are not secret to other nations, only to Congress and the American people" (*Congressional Quarterly Weekly Report,* 13 November 1976).

CONGRESS AND THE PRESIDENT

Having reviewed the setting, avenues of influence, and obstacles facing members of Congress on foreign policy issues, how do we assess broad patterns of congressional-executive interactions in the foreign policy domain? How do we make sense of the shifts between acquiescence and assertiveness? As we have noted, Congress has been active and deferential at different times. It also seems clear that congressional deference is not primarily a matter of lack of opportunity or instrument of influence. What, then, has been the post–World War II pattern of legislative-executive relations?

A key pattern that helps to explain the mixed accounts in our previous discussion concerns the willingness of members of Congress to follow the president's lead. As that discussion hinted, members of Congress seem to have been much more assertive in foreign policy since the Vietnam War. The percentage of congressional foreign policy behavior that is compliant with presidential leadership has dropped by nearly 50 percent from its Cold War level (Scott and Carter 2002). During the Cold War, the president got all of what he wanted in foreign policy almost half the time. Since then, members were likely to give the president what he wanted less than a quarter of the time. Conversely, members of Congress are now almost twice as likely to resist the president and tend to engage in their own independent attempts to make foreign policy. Indeed, in the decade and a half since the fall of the Berlin Wall, congressional members were more likely to push their own foreign policy preferences than to follow those of the president. Moreover, as we discuss later, a number of studies indicate that partisanship also increased across each period as well. (McCormick, Wittkopf, and Danna 1997; Wittkopf and McCormick 1998; Carter and Scott 2004).

The increasing assertiveness and partisanship are significant for our analysis for two reasons. First, they substantiate our argument that presidential leadership of Congress became more difficult after the Vietnam War. Second, they suggest continued challenges for the president in the new century. These two results help us bring into sharper relief the broad patterns characterizing the relationship between Congress and the President since World War II. Activism and deference both have been characteristic at different times and on different issues. To highlight these shifts, we now turn to a review of the phases in legislative-executive relations, and then examine the role of partisanship and bipartisanship, especially as it illuminates the climate of the new century.

Phases in the Relationship between Congress and the President

As we have suggested, the role and influence of Congress has varied over the post–World War II years. Broadly speaking, legislative-executive relations generally divides into three phases: the Cold War (1945–1968), post–Vietnam (1969–1989), and post–Cold War (1989–present). Each era has had some distinctive characteristics with respect to congressional foreign policy involvement and influence.[8]

The Cold War Phase   The primary pattern of this phase was congressional deference to presidential leadership. This era, the so-called era of bipartisanship, was fundamentally characterized by foreign policy consensus over the goals and purposes and over the means of U.S. foreign policy. A key element of this period was the relative clarity—and therefore agreement about—the nature of the threats to U.S. interests (see, for example, Holsti and Rosenau 1984; Melanson 1996). Congress therefore generally deferred to presidential leadership, in part because of the general policy agreement that existed.

Within this period, several different patterns developed. From World War II to roughly 1951, *accommodation* describes the pattern of relations between Congress and the president. The nation's goals of globalism, anticommunism, and containment of perceived Soviet expansionism were forged during that time through a variety of specific foreign policy initiatives and programs in which Congress willingly participated. Bipartisanship captures the essence of the accommodative atmosphere of the period.

Accommodation was followed by a brief period of *antagonism*, a phase that lasted from 1951 to 1955. McCarthyism fell within this period. So, too, did congressional recriminations over who "lost" China; disenchantment with "limited" war in Korea and the firing of General Douglas MacArthur, who independently sought to expand that war; and growing concern over the cost of foreign aid and Truman's commitment of troops to Europe. Efforts by the Senate to curb presidential treaty-making powers symbolized the antagonisms of the period. A period of congressional foreign policy *acquiescence* followed during the decade ending in 1965. It was then that Congress passed the "area resolutions" granting presidents broad authority to deal with

conflict in the Middle East, Berlin, Cuba, the China straits, and Vietnam as they alone saw fit. A bipartisan spirit was again dominant as Congress agreed with most of the specific foreign policy decisions made by the three presidents who held office during the period. Any lingering doubts Congress may have had about some of them were "simply swallowed," as Congress preferred "not to share the responsibility of decision with the president" (Bax 1977). By backing presidential decisions in a manner that legitimated them to the public, Congress helped to build a broad-based, anticommunist foreign policy consensus.

Presidents, for their part, encouraged the acquiescent congressional mood, since a passive role made consultation with or deference to "mere legislators" unnecessary. Following the massive Vietnam buildup in 1965, however, congressional docility began to dissipate. Highly publicized Senate Foreign Relations Committee hearings, chaired by J. William Fulbright, fed the growing perception that the war in Vietnam was a major mistake. Still, Congress refused to exercise the constitutional prerogatives at its disposal to constrain presidential behavior. Congress was in a state of *ambiguity*.

Post–Vietnam Phase   In contrast to the relative deference of the Cold War phase, the post–Vietnam phase was generally characterized by congressional *activism* and assertiveness. With the Cold War consensus shattered by the Vietnam War, members of Congress began to reassert congressional prerogatives and seek greater roles on shaping American foreign policy. Without common agreement on policy or common perspectives on the nature of the problems facing the United States, presidential leadership became more difficult, and members of Congress sought to rein in the excesses of the "imperial presidency" many observers argued had developed through the deference of Congress. As one observer suggested, "In no previous era of congressional ascendancy has the United States borne the burdens of world leadership. And in no previous era of presidential counterreformation has the White House confronted such a formidable array of procedural weapons at the legislature's disposal" (Warburg 1989). The following summaries of congressional action are characteristic of the post–Vietnam era:

- In 1970, Congress "repealed" the Gulf of Tonkin Resolution that gave President Johnson, as he interpreted it, a "blank check" for prosecuting undeclared war in Southeast Asia.

- In 1973, Congress overrode President Nixon's veto to write the War Powers Resolution into law, thus requiring the president to consult Congress before dispatching troops abroad.

- In 1974, Congress embargoed arms sales to Turkey in retaliation for its invasion of Cyprus, despite the objectives of the Ford administration.

- In 1974, Congress refused to permit the president to extend most-favored-nation (MFN) trade treatment to the Soviet Union by linking MFN to the emigration of Soviet Jews.

- In 1975, Congress ensured American withdrawal from Vietnam by denying the president authority to provide the South Vietnamese government emergency military aid to forestall its imminent collapse in the face of communist forces.

- In 1976, Congress prohibited continued CIA expenditures to bolster anti-Marxist forces fighting in Angola.

- In 1978, the Senate adopted a reservation to the Panama Canal neutrality treaty permitting the United States to use military force to reopen the canal if it were closed for any reason.

- In 1980, Congress passed legislation asserting its right to receive prior executive branch notice of impending covert intelligence activities.

- In 1982, Congress denied the Defense Department and the CIA funds for the purpose of overthrowing Nicaragua's government.

- In 1983, Congress invoked provisions of the War Powers Resolution to limit the time military forces could remain in Lebanon.

- In 1985, Congress cut from two hundred to fifty the number of land-based MX missiles to be deployed in fixed silos.

- In 1986, Congress overrode a presidential veto to place economic sanctions on South Africa.

These examples of congressional activism in response to the so-called "imperial presidency" of the Vietnam era reflect Congress's effort to ensure itself a greater voice in foreign policy making. By writing certain conditions into legislation and otherwise placing a distinctively legislative stamp on American foreign policy, a sometimes submissive Congress raised its voice in shaping the nation's foreign affairs, often at the expense of the president. As Under Secretary of State William D. Rogers lamented in 1979, "Foreign policy has become almost synonymous with lawmaking. The result is to place a straitjacket of legislation around the manifold complexity of our relations with other nations." President Reagan echoed that sentiment in 1985, exclaiming, "We have got to get to the point where we can run a foreign policy without a committee of 535 telling us what we can do." Indeed, in the latter half of this phase, critics charged that Congress, not the president, was acting in an "imperial" fashion (Jones and Marini 1988; see also Califano 1994).

The impact of Vietnam and subsequent events in moving Congress from acquiescence toward assertiveness deserves emphasis. Acquiescence is possible only when a broad national consensus exists on the general purposes of policy and when the specific means the president chooses to pursue them are generally successful (Bax 1977). It seems most likely in an environment characterized by relatively clear—and significant—threats to U.S. interests. Those conditions crumbled in the wake of Vietnam. The experience born of that war thus affirms an earlier historical pattern: An assertive congressional mood typically has coincided with and followed each major American war. The post–Civil War Reconstruction era, the post–World War I "return to normalcy" period, and the years following the Korean War provide striking parallels. Concerted congressional efforts to preempt presidential foreign policy prerogatives followed each of them.

Like the Cold War phase, the post–Vietnam period involved several different patterns as well. Richard Nixon's decision to expand the Vietnam War into Cambodia in the spring of 1970 transformed ambiguity into *acrimony*. During the next three years, the Senate passed a variety of measures to curtail the president's ability to keep or use American troops in Indochina, but the House typically refused to support them. However, in 1971 both chambers adopted language that proscribed the use of funds authorized or appropriated by Congress "to finance the introduction of United States ground combat troops into Cambodia, or to provide United States advisors to or for Cambodian military forces in Cambodia." Significantly, the bill was passed only *after* the spring offensive of 1970 had been completed. Other efforts to restrict expenditures were also largely symbolic. Nevertheless, Congress had begun to participate in the termination of America's role in the tragic Indochina conflict.

The high point of congressional acrimony occurred in 1973, when Congress passed the War Powers Resolution over President Nixon's veto. As noted earlier, for at least a decade after this, congressional *assertiveness*—though subject to ebbs and flows—best describes how Congress sought to be heard and treated as a coequal in foreign policy-making. While the Reagan administration challenged a broad array of reforms put into place by the "imperial Congress" to assert its own foreign policy prerogatives (Warburg 1989), Congress remained aggressive in its efforts to shape foreign policy. The trend continued until the end of the Cold War.

Between the fall of the Berlin Wall in 1989 and the Persian Gulf War in 1991, the first Bush administration contended with members of Congress in trying to adapt to the changing landscape. In some ways, Congress remained assertive and active: pushing for defense policy changes; pressing the administration for more proactive responses to the dissolution first of the Warsaw Pact and then of the Soviet Union itself; championing the promotion of democracy. However, George H. W. Bush adopted an almost defiant posture toward Congress's foreign policy role. He "wielded the threat of a veto

effectively, and even when signing important foreign policy legislation, made claims of executive power which implied that Congress did not have the same legislative authority in foreign policy as in other fields and that seemed to ignore the role of Congress in foreign policy granted by the Constitution" (*Congress and Foreign Policy 1991*, 1992).

The Post–Cold War Phase   The post–Cold War phase takes us into the first decade of the twenty-first century. It mirrors in many ways the patterns that developed toward the end of the post–Vietnam phase: struggle between the president and the Congress over foreign policy. However, with all vestiges of the Cold War's guideposts swept away, the dissensus characterizing American foreign policy makers opened the door for even greater contests. The hallmark of this latest phase of congressional-executive relation is its *partisanship,* as politics and party interests have increasingly trumped policy and national interests.

Curiously, perhaps, in some regards the latest phase also invited greater participation by Congress in shaping an American foreign policy, at least initially. "As perceptions of external threat have receded," political scientist James M. Lindsay (1994a) observed, "the American public is now more likely to tolerate legislative dissent on foreign affairs. Faced with fewer electoral costs in opposing the president, members of Congress are more likely to deal the president public rebuffs." For example, the Democratic-led Congress passed legislation broadening the agenda for negotiation of a North American Free Trade Agreement (NAFTA) to include such matters as environmental protection. It adopted conditions for continuing China's most-favored-nation (MFN) trade status (twice vetoed by George H. W. Bush). It held hearings on U.S. policy toward Iraq prior to the Persian Gulf War that seemed to vindicate Congress's position that sanctions should have been imposed on Iraq long before Bush applied them. It proposed to initiate sanctions against those states would assist Iran or Iraq in developing weapons of mass destruction or advanced conventional weapons. Later the Republican-led Congress took steps to curtail the new interventionism on behalf of humanitarian values, notably in Somalia. It terminated funding for the enforcement of a United Nations embargo on the sale of arms to Bosnia and later demanded that the arms embargo be lifted. It launched a determined effort to hamstring American participation in future UN peacekeeping operations, to slash foreign affairs spending while increasing defense spending, and to defeat multilateral agreements on global warming, nuclear testing, and efforts to control genocide and other war crimes. To these examples, others could be added. In general, though, while both Bush and Clinton had some success on big issues—the Gulf War for George H. W. Bush, and Russian aid and NATO expansion for Clinton—the overall pattern was sharply partisan and antagonistic.

At least initially, the pattern in George W. Bush's administration seemed destined to be consistent with that of his predecessors. The persistence of divided government (with Democrats taking control of the Senate after Senator Jeffords of Vermont switched parties in the late spring of 2001), disagreements over the general course of the United States in its relations with friends and rivals (for example, over unilateralism and multilateralism, and between internationalism and selective engagement), and dissensus over policy goals in a variety of areas indicated continued partisanship and political strife consistent with the post–Vietnam trend. Much of that discord fell away after the September 11 attacks on the United States and the onset of the Iraq war.

In the changed environment, bipartisanship was reasserted in many ways, driven in the short term by the recognition of the clear threat facing the United States. Thus, as we have discussed, the Bush administration and Congress moved toward more cooperation and accommodation on a number of issues. At first blush, it appeared that presidential leadership and congressional deference had returned.

Certainly the partisan environment was muted considerably. However, a closer look indicates that substantial congressional activism and assertiveness remained. Even while being more supportive of the president, Congress compelled the administration to accept compromises related to the creation of a Department of Homeland Security and antiterrorism legislation, took actions on global warming and energy policy that diverged from presidential preferences, and continued to resist objectionable administration foreign policy appointments. Hence, even with a more urgent threat to security driving greater cooperation, different interests and perspectives continued to motivate lawmakers to resist presidential preferences. Congressional activism and assertiveness, sometimes driven by partisanship, are likely to persist as part of the pattern of legislative-executive relations in the present era. In this light, we now turn to a consideration of the patterns and shifts between bipartisanship and partisanship since World War II.

Bipartisanship and Partisanship

The proposition that "politics stops at the water's edge," long a part of the nation's cherished political mythology, was a sure victim of the changed and changing nature of executive-legislative relations in the post–Vietnam War era. Increasing partisanship—"foreign policy as a continuation of politics"—has been the dominant pattern ever since. Even the bipartisanship triggered by the 2001 terrorist attacks on the United States is not likely to eliminate it.

Bipartisanship is the practical application of the "water's edge" consensual ideal. As noted, it is often used to describe the cordial and cooperative relationship between Congress and the executive branch during much of the Roosevelt, Truman, and Eisenhower presidencies—the period when the United States rejected isolationism, embraced internationalism, and developed the postwar strategy for containment of the Soviet Union. Congress and the president often acted as partners in these efforts, especially on matters involving Europe. The famous conversion of Arthur Vandenberg, Republican senator from Michigan who coined the "water's edge" aphorism, symbolized the emergent bipartisan spirit. Once a staunch isolationist, Vandenberg used his position as chair of the powerful Senate

Foreign Relations Committee after World War II to engineer congressional support for NATO and the Marshall Plan.

To be sure, partisan and ideological differences between the president and Congress and within the latter were never absent during the heyday of bipartisanship. Republican Senator Robert A. Taft of Ohio, for example, personified many of the elements of congressional antagonism between 1951 and 1955. He opposed NATO, criticized Truman for failing to declare war in Korea and concentrating too much power in the White House, and worried that containment would result in continuing U.S. involvement in world affairs, which he opposed. His neoisolationist sentiment and its associated criticisms were a minority voice, however—one that the anticommunist consensus muted as Congress moved from a posture of antagonism toward the president in the early 1950s to acquiescence in the latter half of the decade. Not until the Vietnam War challenged the premises of the anticommunist consensus were the premises of bipartisanship itself also questioned. Now foreign policy increasingly became the object of factional and partisan dispute. No longer did politics stop at the water's edge.

Presidents invariably appeal to bipartisanship to win political support for their programs. Often they use bipartisan commissions as a vehicle to that end. The commissions President Reagan appointed to seek alternative policies for Central America, strategic defense, and military base closings, are prominent examples. More recently, President George W. Bush signed congressional legislation establishing the well-known 9/11 Commission and a 2004 executive order creating a WMD commission to probe the root causes of intelligence failures related to the September 11, 2001, terrorist attacks and the absence of weapons of mass destruction in Iraq. Beset by particularly intense partisanship during his two terms, President Clinton sought to reduce it with respect to foreign policy, first by appointing William Cohen, a former Republican senator from Maine, as secretary of defense for his second term. Late in his second term, Clinton sought to restore some bipartisanship by creating the Commission on National Security for the Twenty-First Century,

headed by former Democratic Senator Gary Hart of Colorado and former Republican Senator Warren Rudman of New Hampshire. The panel worked throughout 1999 and 2000 to outline a blueprint for the new century that would rebuild a consensus.

The urge to restore bipartisanship to foreign policy making stems from a desire to restore the halcyon mood of the early post–World War II era. Beyond this, advocates of bipartisanship see it as a vehicle for promoting the policy coherence and consistency necessary to an effective foreign policy (Kissinger and Vance 1988; Winik 1989). Such a view assumes a broad-based agreement within American society about the appropriate American role in world affairs, similar to that once provided by deeply held anticommunist values. It also seems to require a relatively clear and urgent threat environment.

Critics, on the other hand, argue that bipartisanship is a tool used to stifle the expression of divergent viewpoints, which is the heart of democratic governance (Falk 1983; Nathan and Oliver 1994). Too often, they say, its appeal is motivated by the goal of blurring the separation of powers, which assigns different foreign policy roles and responsibilities to Congress and the president. As one member of Congress put it, "Calls for bipartisanship usually seek to have Congress follow the president, never the opposite" (Hamilton 1988). Yet, as Justice Louis Brandeis wrote (in *Myers v. United States,* 1926), the purpose of the separation-of-powers doctrine is "not to avoid friction but . . . to save the people from autocracy."

Because the bipartisan concept itself is often used for partisan purposes, its precise meaning is unclear.[9] One simple yet useful measure is how often a majority of Republicans and Democrats agree with the president's position on foreign policy issues that come before Congress. Figure 12.1 uses this measure to trace bipartisan behavior in each house of Congress from President Truman to President Clinton. It shows a gradual decline in bipartisanship following the Eisenhower administration and an especially sharp decline in the House beginning with President Ford. Clearly bipartisanship is in retreat, especially since Vietnam.

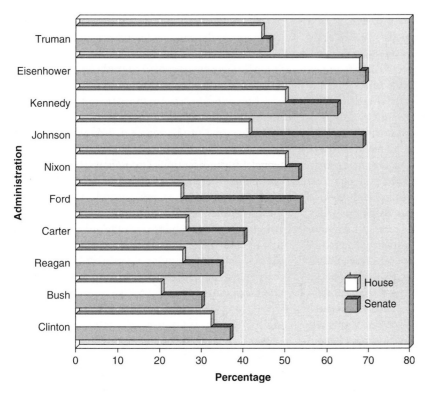

FIGURE 12.1 Congressional Support of Presidential Policy from Truman to Clinton

NOTE: Each bar represents the percentage of foreign policy votes on which a majority of both parties supported the president's position. Data for Clinton are for the 103rd Congress (1993–1994) only.

SOURCE: Data through 1988 from James M. McCormick and Eugene R. Wittkopf, "Bipartisanship, Partisanship, and Ideology in Congressional-Executive Foreign Policy Relations, 1947–1988," *Journal of Politics* 52 (November 1990): 1085; data for the Bush and Clinton administrations compiled by McCormick and Wittkopf from various issues of the *Congressional Quarterly Weekly Report*.

Shifts in the partisan and ideological support accorded different presidents underlie these changes. During the Cold War, Democratic presidents consistently enjoyed their greatest foreign policy support not only from their own partisans but also from liberals, regardless of party. Eisenhower, a Republican president, also enjoyed support from liberal Democrats as well as members of his own party. This pattern underlies the *two presidencies thesis,* which posits the legislative and judicial branches allow broad executive discretion and unilateral action in foreign policy, while they exercise checks and balances to a greater degree in domestic policy (Wildavsky 1966).

Since Eisenhower, however, Republican presidents have received their greatest support from conservatives and comparatively little from liberals. The changing patterns of foreign policy voting in Congress suggest that partisan attachments and ideological predispositions now reinforce one another. Before Vietnam, partisanship and ideology crosscut one another, muting differences between Congress and the president. After Vietnam, they magnified them. Republicans have become the party of conservative internationalism and Democrats the party of liberal internationalism, thus bringing both parties into alignment with their postures on domestic policy.

In such a situation, as might be expected, the "two presidencies" thesis finds little support, as analyses of the post–Vietnam and post–Cold War eras indicate (for example, Fleisher, Bond, and Krutz 2000).

The end of the Cold War might have been expected to moderate the partisan and ideological disputes characteristic of congressional-executive relations since Vietnam, as many of them played out in differing perceptions about how best to deal with the perceived Soviet threat. As perceptions of external threat receded, however, members of Congress also found incentives to distance themselves from presidential initiatives (Lindsay 1994a; see also McCormick and Wittkopf 1990b). Indeed, rather than receding, partisanship increased in just about every way imaginable. Party leaders have shown "increasingly partisan patterns in their support for presidential positions (Smith 1994). Congressional voting behavior on foreign and defense policy has also shown increasing partisanship (Carter 1998; McCormick, Wittkopf and Danna 1997; Rohde 1994; Sinclair 1993; Wittkopf and McCormick 1998). Those individual members of Congress who choose to make foreign policy a focus of their attention—foreign policy entrepreneurs—have also become increasingly partisan over the three phases discussed previously (Carter and Scott 2004). As we have suggested, the more obvious threat environment after September 11, 2001, reduced but did not eliminate the general pattern. Moreover, the prospect for increased partisanship intensified in George W. Bush's second term as fighting in Iraq dragged on, the president became politically weaker, and Congress, now controlled by the Democrats, exhibited less deference.

CONGRESS AND TWENTY-FIRST CENTURY FOREIGN POLICY

How foreign policy will fare in the contest between Congress and the president in the years ahead remains uncertain—a conclusion made all the more stark by an uncertain security environment at home and abroad, the rise of intermestic issues and the forces of globalization, and the closely balanced divisions between Democrats and Republicans in American society that Congress mirrors. The unity of purpose generated by the nation's response to the terrorist attacks of September 2001 provided some cause for optimism, but other indications of dissensus discussed in this chapter limit such views. The potential for dissensus will intensify in the absence of immediate threats or with the return of divided government.

Two intriguing questions remain. First, how active will members of Congress be on foreign policy as the new century continues to unfold? The dramatic changes just noted would seem to presage considerable activity. Second, how assertive will members of Congress be? Will they attempt to forge their own foreign policies and resist presidential leadership? The patterns of the past sixty years give us ambiguous guidance. The increasing levels of assertiveness seem to suggest that the current president will have his hands full. Much of the historical record suggests that it is policy consensus that smoothes relations between the two branches. But is broad, sustained consensus possible in today's complex, globalized environment?

In all likelihood, the pattern is likely to be mixed. Foreign and defense policy issues are sometime described as falling into three categories: crisis policy, structural policy, and strategic policy (Ripley and Franklin 1991).[10] Congress has virtually no role in crisis decision making, but it is a central component of the exceedingly complex institutional labyrinth in which less salient (structural and strategic) policy is made. We should expect more presidential leadership on some policy issues but less on others. The president may well remain the leading partner—if not always the senior partner—in devising responses to the challenges and opportunities the nation now faces. Still, as one analysis concluded, "Post–Cold War presidents should fasten their seat belts securely; foreign and defense policy making is likely to be an increasingly bumpy ride" (Carter 1998).

KEY TERMS

anticipated reactions
bipartisanship
Case Act
deferrals
discretionary funds
earmarks

executive agreements
framing
Gulf of Tonkin
    Resolution
impoundment
legislative veto

micromanagement
Millennium Challenge
    Account (MCA)
partisanship
procedural legislation
reprogramming

rescissions
reservations
single-issue politics
substantive legislation
two presidencies thesis
War Powers Resolution

SUGGESTED READINGS

Bacchus, William I. *The Price of Foreign Policy: Congress, the Executive and Foreign Affairs Funding*. College Park, PA: Pennsylvania State University Press, 1997.

Blechman, Barry M. *The Politics of National Security: Congress and U.S. Defense* Policy. New York: Oxford University Press, 1990.

Campbell, Colton C., Nicol C. Rae, and John F. Stack, Jr., eds., *Congress and the Politics of Foreign Policy*. Upper Saddle River, NJ: Prentice Hall, 2003.

Crabb, Cecil V., Glenn Antizzo, and Leila S. Sariedinne. *Congress and the Foreign Policy Process: Modes of Legislative Behavior*. Baton Rouge, LA: Louisiana State University Press, 2000.

Deibel, Terry L., and Karen M. Rohan, eds., *Clinton and Congress: The Politics of Foreign Policy*. New York: Foreign Policy Association, 2000.

Fisher, Louis. *Presidential War Power*. Lawrence, KS: University of Kansas Press, 1995.

Franck, Thomas M., and Edward Weisband. *Foreign Policy by Congress*. New York: Oxford University Press, 1979.

Hendrickson, Ryan C. *The Clinton Wars: The Constitution, Congress, and War Powers*. Nashville, TN: Vanderbilt University Press, 2002.

Hersman, Rebecca K. C. *Friends and Foes: How Congress and the President Really Make Foreign Policy*. Washington, DC: Brookings Institution Press, 2000.

Hess, Gary R. "Presidents and the Congressional Resolutions of 1991 and 2002." *Political Science Quarterly* 121 (Spring 2006): 93–118.

Hinkley, Barbara. *Less than Meets the Eye: Foreign Policy Making and the Myth of the Assertive Congress*. Chicago, IL: University of Chicago Press, 1994.

Lindsay, James M. *Congress and the Politics of U.S. Foreign Policy*. Baltimore: Johns Hopkins University Press, 1994.

Ripley, Randall B., and Grace A. Franklin. *Congress, the Bureaucracy, and Public Policy*. Pacific Grove, CA: Brooks/Cole, 1991.

Ripley, Randall B., and James M. Lindsay, eds., *Congress Resurgent: Foreign and Defense Policy on Capitol Hill*. Ann Arbor, MI: University of Michigan Press, 1993.

Warburg, Gerald Felix. *Conflict and Consensus: The Struggle between Congress and the President over Foreign Policymaking*. New York: Harper and Row, 1989.

Weissman, Stephen R. *A Culture of Deference: Congress's Failure of Leadership in Foreign Policy*. New York: Basic Books, 1995.

NOTES

1. On constitutional issues, see J. Smith (1989), Henkin (1990), Koh (1990), Fisher (1995, 1997), and Silverstein (1996).

2. *Dellums v. Bush*, 752 F. Supp.1141 (D.D.C. 1990).

3. See Bacchus (1997) for an analysis of the tug of war between Congress and the president over foreign aid and international affairs spending.

4. Defense procurement is typically regarded as a pork-barrel issue, which members of Congress use

to cultivate constituency support. During the debate on the B-1 bomber, for example, the Air Force and its industrial allies lobbied Congress with the argument that they would profit from the project with increased jobs and dollars in their states and congressional districts (Kotz 1988; Ornstein and Elder 1978). Interestingly, however, congressional votes on strategic weapons issues are best explained not by constituency interests (as the military-industrial complex thesis would argue) but instead on the basis of Congress members' political ideology (Lindsay 1990). Although foreign and national security policy often are thought to be above politics, evidence abounds to show that they are as frequently characterized by partisan and ideological disputes as are domestic issues. See Bernstein (1989), Bernstein and Anthony (1974), Fleisher (1985), McCormick (1985), McCormick and Black (1983), McCormick and Wittkopf (1990a, 1990b), Moyer (1973), Taylor and Rourke (1995), and Wayman (1985).

5. Court rulings in the aftermath of the Chadha decision on the legislative veto restricted the comprehensiveness of Congress's role in these matters compared with the intent of the 1974 budget law (Fisher 1991; Fisher 1993). Also, the Iran-Contra affair suggests another area: "problems associated with 'creative policy funding.'" Presidents may be able to pursue policies with monies from third parties. For example, between $3 and $4 million in profits from the sale of arms to Iran in early 1986 and as much as $50 million from private contributors and foreign governments was supplied to the contras at precisely the time the Boland amendment banned U.S. government support for the guerrillas. Lieutenant Colonel Oliver North and Admiral John Poindexter, North's boss at the NSC, both testified before Congress that they believed the withholding of appropriations by Congress did not prevent the president from pursuing his foreign policy objectives using private or foreign-donated funds. Congress debated, but ultimately defeated, a 1990 bill that would have explicitly legislated against such activities.

6. See Cavanagh (1982–1983), Pfiffner (1992), and Smith and Deering (1990) for examinations of changes in Congress since the 1960s, and Drischler

(1985) and Lindsay (1987, 1988) for insight into their importance for the enactment of foreign affairs legislation.

7. The Torricelli incident is more complicated than it appears, as the information "leaked" by the representative actually came from a State Department employee, Richard Nuccio (*Washington Post*, 12 September, 1997, A24; *New York Times*, 11 September, 1997, A30; Marks 1997). Whether one considers Nuccio a "whistleblower" or a "leaker," the example illustrates what many observers have been arguing for decades: the most prolific "leakers" in Washington are not members of Congress, but members of the executive branch.

8. In addition to the three-phase breakdown utilized here, this section also extends the chronology suggested by Bax (1977) into six comparatively distinct phases of executive-legislative relations during the past half-century.

9. One definition associates bipartisanship with "unity in foreign affairs" as reflected in "policy supported by majorities within each political party"; another depicts it as a set of "practices and procedures designed to bring about the desired unity" (Crabb 1957). For a review of the idea and practice of bipartisanship, see Collier (1989).

10. The difference between structural and strategic policy is not clear-cut. Ripley and Franklin (1991) suggest that "structural policies and programs aim primarily at procuring, deploying, and organizing military personnel and materiel, presumably within the confines of previously determined strategic decisions." What they call "subgovernments"— typically "composed of members of the House and Senate, members of congressional staffs, bureaucrats, and representatives of [interested] private groups and organizations"—are principal actors in the structural policy arena. Strategic policies, on the other hand, "assert and implement the basic military and foreign policy stance of the United States toward other nations. Policy planning and proposals resulting from that planning stem primarily from executive branch activities . . . Although congressional influence can be important, that influence is often used to respond supportively to executive branch agencies."

Role Sources of American Foreign Policy

13

The Process of Decision Making:

Roles, Rationality, and the Impact of Bureaucratic Organizations

As modern bureaucracy has grown, the understanding of change and the formulation of new purposes have become more difficult. Like men, governments find old ways hard to change and new paths difficult to discover.
PRESIDENT RICHARD M. NIXON, 1970

[The foreign policy apparatus] was often a witch's brew of intrigue, elbows, egos, and separate agendas.
FORMER SECRETARY OF STATE JAMES A. BAKER, 1995

In 1992, Bill Clinton made a more assertive American response to ethnic conflict and aggression in places such as the former Yugoslavia part of his campaign for the presidency. After his victory, he signed a Presidential Review Directive to initiate just such a policy change, calling for a policy shift to *assertive multilateralism*. It would expand U.S. cooperation with UN peace operations and devote more American military resources and personnel to multilateral efforts. Clinton even called for a standing UN force with American participation, and for American troops to serve under foreign

commanders. Over a year later, the administration released Presidential Decision Directive 25 announcing the administration's policy on peace operations. Far from the policy shift initially advocated, PDD-25 rejected expanded American participation in and cooperation with UN operations, announcing instead a list of conditions that had to be met before the United States would agree to, much less support materially, such operations.[1] Clinton also announced that American troops would not serve under foreign officers. How did the bold, aggressive policy of the first few months of the

Clinton administration evolve into the cautious, unimaginative policy announced in April 1994?

Understanding this policy decision, like understanding so many others, requires that we consider the many different people, widely dispersed throughout the agencies and institutions of the American government, who make American foreign policy. It also requires that we examine the decision-making process through which they interact to make such policy choices. Our inquiry in previous chapters gives a glimpse of what we can expect to find.

First, the very size of the government—the incredibly complex organizational structures into which the millions of federal employees fit and the maze of channels through which innovative ideas must pass before they become new policies—is likely to work against policy change and the formulation of new purposes. Apart from cabinet-level departments, the federal roster includes more than sixty different departments and agencies and countless advisory boards and commissions. Add Congress—which, as we have seen, often acts more like 535 separate interests than one unified body—and we can begin to appreciate how the very size of government inhibits policy change in response to new realities.

Second, the politics of policy making within this maze of multiple and often overlapping institutions is more conducive to the status quo than to change. Money and personnel mean political power. Once acquired, institutions protect them. They oppose changes that threaten to erode their sources of influence. Incremental changes at the edge are acceptable, but fundamental reorientations that would require massive budgetary and personnel cuts must be resisted.

President Clinton's choice to abandon the ambitious ideas of "assertive multilateralism" as a post–Cold War foreign policy strategy was the consequence of a complex environment with multiple voices and stakeholders. It may have been rationally calculated to cope with the emerging international (and domestic) environment. Perhaps, and more likely, it was a consequence of confrontation, bargaining, and compromise among competing individuals and agencies over the proper use of American military force. Surely it was conditioned by a variety of players, each of whom was influenced by the roles they occupy and the patterns of demands and expectations that define those roles.

In this chapter, we reflect on the impact of roles and two interpretations of American decision-making procedures that embrace rival images of role-induced behavior—the rational decision-making model and the bureaucratic politics model. As we will see, the two offer sometimes competing, sometimes complementary views of roles as sources of American foreign policy.

ROLES AS A SOURCE OF FOREIGN POLICY

Role theory posits that the positions decision makers occupy, rather than their individual characteristics, influence their behavior and choices in making and executing the nation's foreign policy. As colorfully summarized in ***Miles's Law,*** role theory suggests that "where you stand (on a policy issue) depends on where you sit (in the government)."[2] Each role (or position) carries with it social and psychological demands and expectations that shape perceptions of how it should be performed. These pressures, which include personal and peer pressures as well as those of "the boss," affect both attitudes and actions. They influence *anyone* filling a particular role, regardless of personal preferences. Thus every individual behaves similarly to others who have occupied the same role. Furthermore, changes in policy presumably result from changes in *role conceptions* rather than from changes in the individuals who occupy the roles. Individuals are not unimportant, from this perspective, but the institutional roles that individuals occupy mold their behavior and constrain their decision-making latitude.

Policy makers are not immune to this phenomenon. Each policy-making role carries with it certain expectations, obligations, and images of appropriate behavior—pressures that push the new occupant of an office to think and act like his or her predecessor. The newcomer's style and mannerisms may be markedly different from his or her predecessor's, but orientations toward crucial issues will be similar. "It's an old story in Washington that where you stand depends on where you sit. That's a practical acknowledgment of the fact that people's views change as they change responsibilities," political journalist David Broder observed.

There are limits to role theory's ability to explain policy-making behavior, of course. A forceful personality may actually redefine the role to extend the boundaries of permissible behavior, as Franklin Roosevelt did when he expanded the scope and authority of the presidency. Ronald Reagan's habit of taking many naps and frequent vacations—a propensity that reflected his relaxed style in an office that heretofore demanded sleepless attention to the duties of governance— also transcended customary role requirements, although in another direction. George W. Bush's penchant for retiring early at night fits that same pattern.

Particular roles may also permit more than one interpretation, and some have boundaries so wide and elastic that the behavior of individuals within them is almost unpredictable. Moreover, individuals, especially at higher levels of government, often have multiple roles whose conflicting pressures may pull him or her in multiple directions. Resolving such role conflicts may involve a number of factors, but surely indicates that, in some cases at least, "role by itself cannot explain positions taken by individual decision makers" (Vertzberger 1990).[3] The individual source category (discussed in Chapter 14) is a key place to look for additional explanation. Indeed, as Downs (1967) has argued, there are different types of decision makers (climbers, conservers, zealots, advocates, and statesmen) with different values and goals (power, personal security, advancement of a few core goals, loyalty to the organization, desire for the best possible policy) who will react to and manipulate roles in different ways.[4]

Nevertheless, this line of reasoning has substantial implications for American foreign policy. Role theory's premise—that people's conduct conforms to their roles—means that if we are to understand the nature of American foreign policy we must examine the behavior most often associated with foreign policy-making roles in addition to examining individuals themselves. That focus also enables us to understand a potentially potent source of foreign policy change. Because roles shape goals, policy innovations may derive from changes in major policy-making roles or individuals' conceptions of them. If the decision-making system with its existing roles and their prevailing interpretations changes, then policy redirections may follow.

FOREIGN POLICY MAKING AS A RATIONAL PROCESS

In December 1998, President Clinton sat resolutely in the Oval Office before a bank of television cameras preparing to announce to his "fellow Americans" that he was about to launch Operation Desert Fox, an extensive bombing campaign in which American and British forces would punish Saddam Hussein for forcing UN weapons inspectors to leave Iraq. Saddam's move was in violation of the ceasefire agreed to by the United States and Iraq in 1991 and of later Security Council resolutions. Five years later, in March 2003, the same scene was played out again. This time President Bush prepared to tell the nation that Operation Iraqi Freedom was about to begin, whose purpose, among others, was to remove Saddam Hussein from power.

Sitting behind the desk in the Oval Office, dressed in coat and tie, and flanked by the American and the presidential flags, both Clinton and Bush sought to project a similar image: a resolute commander-in-chief at the helm, armed with the best evidence and judgment of his most trusted advisers, someone with the experience, dedication, energy, and diligence to make the right choices for the nation.

The image reinforced a popular view of the policy-making process at the nation's nerve center on Pennsylvania Avenue: that fateful decisions are made by rational actors engaged in orderly, contemplative processes. In this **rational decision-making model,** American foreign policy results from a deliberate intellectual process in which the central figures carefully choose what is best for the country and select tactics appropriately designed to promote its national interests.

Thus the question, "Is foreign policy making rational?" is a curious one. We tend, almost instinctively, to think, "How could it be otherwise?" Indeed, where the stakes are the lives of thousands of people and, if WMD may be involved, perhaps the survival of the nation itself, it is disconcerting to imagine something as important as foreign policy choice being governed by incoherence, emotions, or irrational impulses. The notion of rational policy making is much more comforting. Political leaders also try to cultivate public images of themselves as decisive, unfettered by subconscious psychological drives, able to manage the stress and burden of their positions, endowed with boundless energy, and prepared to guide the country safely through crises while pursuing the nation's best interests. Their efforts are frequently successful because we prefer to think of our leaders' decisions as the product of rational deliberations.

What constitutes rationality as it applies to foreign policy decision making? Although "rationality" is loosely used in a variety of ways, it generally refers to "actions chosen by the nation . . . that will maximize strategic goals and objectives" (Allison 1971). This implies purposeful, goal-directed behavior that occurs when "the individual responding to an international event . . . uses the best information available and chooses from the universe of possible responses that alternative most likely to maximize his goals" (Verba 1969; see also Levi 1990; Moser 1990).

The Rational Actor Model

The *rational actor model* treats the nation-state as a **unitary actor,** a single, homogeneous entity, and presumes that all policy makers go through the same rational thought processes to make *value-maximizing choices* to define national interests and identify options. In this vein, scholars who study decision making and advise policy makers on ways to improve their policy-formulation skills describe the perfect rationality role model as a sequence of decision-making activities involving the following intellectual steps:

1. *Problem recognition and definition.* The necessity for choice begins when policy makers perceive an external problem and attempt to define objectively its distinguishing characteristics. Objectivity requires full information about the actions, motivations, and capabilities of other actors as well as the state of the international environment and trends within it. The search for information must be exhaustive, and all the facts relevant to the problem must be gathered.

2. *Goal selection.* Next, those responsible for making foreign policy choices must decide what they want to accomplish. This disarmingly simple requirement is often difficult. It requires the identification and ranking of *all* values (such as security, democracy, freedom, and economic well-being) in a hierarchy from most- to least-preferred.

3. *Identification of alternatives.* Rationality also requires the compilation of an exhaustive list of *all* available policy options and an estimation of the costs associated with each alternative course of action as it relates to the goals and values decision makers hope to realize.

4. *Choice.* Finally, rationality requires selecting from competing options the single alternative with the best chance of achieving the desired goal(s). For this purpose, policy makers must conduct a rigorous means–ends, cost–benefit analysis, one guided by an accurate prediction of the probable success of each option.

Clearly, the requirements of comprehensive or perfect rationality are stringent. Nonetheless, elements of this idealized version of decision making have been approximated in some instances. The 1962 Cuban missile crisis—described by Secretary of State Dean Rusk as "the most dangerous crisis the world has ever seen"—illustrates several ways the deliberations of the key American policy makers conformed to a rational process.[5] Once Washington discovered the presence of Soviet missiles in Cuba, President Kennedy charged the crisis decision-making group he formed to "set aside all other tasks to make a prompt and intensive survey of the dangers and all possible courses of action." Six options were ultimately identified: Do nothing; exert diplomatic pressure; make a secret approach to Cuban leader Fidel Castro; invade Cuba; launch a surgical air strike against the missiles; and blockade Cuba. Goals had to be prioritized before a choice could be made among these six. Was removing the Soviet missiles, retaliating against Castro, or maintaining the balance of power the objective? Or did the missiles pose little threat to vital U.S. interests? "Do nothing" could not be eliminated as an option until the missiles were determined to pose a serious threat to national security.

The first Bush administration's decisions to apply force in the Persian Gulf crisis with Iraq in 1991 (Smith 1992; Gordon and Trainor 1995; Bush and Scowcroft 1999) and to send ground troops to Somalia late the following year also illustrate the approximation of rationality often used to describe decision-making processes. Rational decision making does not reflect the whole story of those decision processes, of course, but we do have a sense that they were punctuated by value priorities, efforts to relate means to ends, and preferred courses of action to cope with the situations—all central canons of rational choice.

Rationality and Reality: The Limits to Rational Choice

Despite the apparent application of rationality in these (and other) cases, the rational actor model is more an idealized standard used to evaluate behavior than an actual description of real-world behavior. One participant in the Cuban missile deliberations, Theodore Sorensen, suggested why rational procedures are difficult to follow:

Each step cannot be taken in order. The facts may be in doubt or dispute. Several policies, all good, may conflict. Several means, all bad, may be all that are open. Value judgments may differ. Stated goals may be imprecise. There may be many interpretations of what is right, what is possible, and what is in the national interest.

(Sorensen 1963, 19–20)

Despite the virtues promised by rational choice, then, there are impediments. Some are human. They derive from deficiencies in the intelligence, capability, and psychological needs and aspirations of those who make foreign policy decisions under conditions of uncertainty. Others are organizational. Individuals meeting in groups make most policy decisions. As a result, most decisions require group agreement about the national interest and the wisest course of action to pursue. Reaching agreement is not easy, however. Reasonable people with different human characteristics and values understandably disagree about goals, preferences, and the probable results of alternative options. Thus the impediments to sound (rational) policy making are substantial. Let us examine them in greater detail.

Tardy Problem Recognition Decision makers often neglect evidence of an impending problem until it confronts them directly or reaches crisis proportions. People seldom foresee improbable events. Most are prone psychologically to deny the existence of troublesome problems (even when they might be partially responsible for them), and often avoid facing information suggesting the necessity for difficult choices.

Inadequate Information Henry Kissinger once observed that "when the scope for action is greatest, the knowledge on which to base such action . . . is at a minimum." The information required to define a problem is often incomplete, outdated, or unavailable, and critical variables such as others' intentions are not open to scrutiny. In addition, *information overload*—the availability of too much information—may also undermine rationality. Discrepant and contradictory information makes distinguishing the significant from the irrelevant difficult.

Inaccurate Information The information on which decision makers' choices are based is screened, sorted, and rearranged by their advisers. Distortion is compounded by the tendency of advisers to tell their superiors what they want to hear rather than supplying them with the cold, hard facts, and by policy makers' all-too-human tendency to reject unfamiliar or disturbing information. "Cherry-picking" from intelligence reports allegedly caused the second Bush administration to base its decision for war against Iraq on erroneous information.

Deficient Information Gathering Policy makers rarely search for *all* pertinent information. Instead, they base decisions on partial information.[6] Rationality is compromised, because if an exhaustive search had generated additional information, conceivably a different set of policy choices would have been considered. Moreover, rather than admit error, leaders are prone to cling to bad decisions and to search energetically for new information that justifies their previous mistaken choices.

Ambiguous National Interests When facing a policy problem, it is not sufficient to insist that the national interest be served. That merely begs the question. The more difficult intellectual task requires *prioritizing* all possible goals according to their ability to promote the nation's welfare. Rationally identifying what is best is difficult because every goal has associated costs as well as possible unanticipated long-run consequences. "Rational" goal selection, therefore, frequently means choosing the lesser of two evils. For instance, if a leader's goals include promoting democracy in the Middle East and maintaining access to Saudi Arabian oil, one may be achieved only at the expense of the other. Or consider support for the principle of national self-determination and a promise to stem the spread of ethnopolitical conflict. The latter may undermine the former by rationalizing suppression of minority ethnic groups.

The Constraint of Time Pressure Since policy makers work constantly with overloaded agendas

and short deadlines, time is rarely available for careful identification of possible courses of action and for a cool-headed assessment of their consequences. "There is little time for leaders to reflect. They are locked in an endless battle in which the urgent constantly gains on the important. The public life of every political figure is a continual struggle to rescue an element of choice from the pressure of circumstance" (Kissinger 1979).

Options that are not identified cannot be considered. As economist Thomas Schelling asks, "How do you make a list of things you would never have thought of?" (cited in Bloomfield 1974). Did anyone seriously consider that air passenger airliners laden with jet fuel could purposely be crashed into a building with the hope of killing thousands?

Instead of identifying options on their own, presidents usually are presented with an abbreviated list of "feasible" options by their advisers and by bureaucratic agencies. Whether defensively or offensively, the pressure to shorten the search for options is intense, which limits the range of alternatives considered to the first ones that come to mind (usually those derived from prior analogous situations).

Satisficing Rational decision making is compromised most by the way foreign policy choices are actually reached. Policy makers do not choose the option or set of options that has the maximum chance of realizing desired goals (Lindblom 1959; March and Simon 1958). Instead, they typically terminate their evaluation as soon as an alternative surfaces that appears superior to those already considered. Management guru Herbert Simon (1957) describes this as ***satisficing*** behavior. Rather than seeking optimal alternatives, decision makers are routinely content to select the choice that meets minimally acceptable standards.

The difficulties of correctly ascertaining the payoffs attached to available options reduce the prospects for rational choice (and promote satisficing instead). Even in the best of circumstances—even if policy makers could obtain full information and were able to identify all the options available to realize the preferred goal—"guesstimates" about the relative utility and efficacy of each alternative still often guide the choice. Because determining the best (rational) choice is difficult, *muddling through* better describes how choices perceived to be feasible and pragmatic often win out. "A wise policy maker," Charles Lindblom (1959) surmises, "expects that his policies will achieve only part of what he hopes and at the same time will produce unanticipated consequences he would have preferred to avoid. If he proceeds through a succession of incremental changes, he avoids serious lasting mistakes." Some past leaders have been known to advocate this less-than-comprehensive, trial-and-error method for making difficult decisions. "It is common sense," noted President Franklin D. Roosevelt, "to take a method and try it; if it fails, admit it frankly and try another."

Psychological Restraints   Foreign policy is made not by states but by human beings acting on behalf of states. Hence, decision-making processes cannot be separated from psychodynamics (Simon 1985). Decisions therefore may be rooted less in logic than in the subconscious needs and drives of decision makers. The need to be liked, the desire to be popular, and the temptation to look decisive, even heroic, may interfere with rational judgment and ultimately sacrifice the nation's welfare. Decision makers also tend to be overconfident about their judgments and analytical skills and to overestimate their abilities and wisdom so as to maintain their *illusion of control* (Langer 1975).

Personal emotional needs and passions also may lead decision makers to confuse their own goals with those of the state. If they come to see themselves as indispensable to national welfare, they may equate what is good for them with what is good for the country. When this happens, policy may be driven by a leader's perceived need to maintain or strengthen his or her power and popularity, possibly at the expense of the national interest. There is reason to believe this is what drove Lyndon Johnson during the Vietnam War.

The confusion of national and personal needs is sometimes used to show how irrefutably irrational many foreign policy choices have been. The classic example is Adolf Hitler, whose determination to seek military conquest of the entire European continent proved disastrous for Germany. More recent examples include Saddam Hussein's determination twice to fight the technologically superior United States and its coalition of allies, facing sure defeat both times, rather than to withdraw from Kuwait or to submit to United Nations disarmament demands. Slobodan Milošević's decision to use force against Kosovo and defy NATO, which proved devastating for both Serbia and Milošević's own political career, is another example. In all of these instances we can explain the apparent discrepancy between what is good for the state and what is good for its leaders by distinguishing between *procedural rationality* and *instrumental rationality* (Zagare 1990).

Procedural rationality is what we have described to this point, a conceptualization of rationality based on perfect information and careful weighing of all possible courses of action. It is the kind of rationality that relates to the decision-making dynamics of small groups and large-scale bureaucratic organizations. It is the definition of rationality that underlies the theory of political realism, which sees all states as acting in fundamentally similar ways. Like the rational actor model we have described, realism, too, sees states as single, unitary actors whose (rational) decision processes result in choices that seek to maximize benefits to national interests and minimize costs.

Instrumental rationality, on the other hand, is a more limited view of rationality. It says simply that individuals have preferences, and that when faced with two (or more) alternatives, they will choose the one that yields the preferred outcome—and this is rational behavior. Although we might dispute some individuals' preferences, we cannot dismiss them as "crazy" or their choices as "irrational" simply because they result in negative consequences for the state as a whole or for the individuals themselves.

Our review of how policy makers actually make decisions warrants the conclusion that the ideal requirements of rational problem solving are seldom met in real life (see Focus 13.1). Preconceived notions pass for facts. Decisions are made to

---

F O C U S 13.1   Foreign Policy Decision Making in Theory and Practice

The Ideal Process	Actual Performance
Accurate, comprehensive information	Distorted, incomplete information
Clear definition of national goals	National goals biased by personal motivations and organizational interests
Exhaustive analysis of all options	Limited number of options considered, none thoroughly analyzed
Selection of optimal course of action most capable of producing desired results	Selection of course of action by political bargaining and compromise
Effective statement of decision and its rationale to mobilize domestic support	Confusing and contradictory statements of decision, designed primarily for media
Instantaneous evaluation of consequences followed by correction of errors	Superficial policy evaluation, uncertain responsibility, poor follow-through, and delayed correction

---

satisfy immediate, not long-term, needs. Decision makers avoid the task of formulating a coherent strategy. They have a natural reluctance to reach decisions and a strong temptation to pass the buck. They usually weigh only a few alternatives and ponder only a small number of consequences. Decision makers rarely achieve full knowledge, even though the volume of information may be staggering. Instead, they scan only what they regard as most relevant to the decision. Often they reach a decision first and find reasons (information) to support it only later. The result is not rationality, with each step leading logically to a value-maximizing choice, but something quite different—a haphazard, trial-and-error, seat-of-the-pants process conducted in a rush based on "gut-it-out," best-guess calculations strongly influenced by social pressures (Anderson 1987). Thus the process looks decidedly indecisive and improvisational, and the degree of rationality in foreign policy decision making typically "bears little relationship to the world in which officials conduct their deliberations" (Rosenau 1980).

What are the implications of such a conclusion? If the nation's behavior is not the product of public officials laden with exceptional skills and cognitive powers, untiringly collecting accurate information and logically deriving conclusions to maximize the country's national interests, is the rational actor model completely irrelevant to the "real world"?

In some respects, the model is little more than a caricature, a straw man easily destroyed by even superficial knowledge about how people and organizations make choices on a daily basis, as they must. Still, even if we know that rationality is more ideal than real, the rational actor model is useful in understanding how decision making occurs, all the more so because policy makers aspire to rational decision-making behavior, and on occasion may even approximate it. As one political scientist put it, "Officials have some notion, conscious or unconscious, of a priority of values; . . . they possess some conceptions, elegant or crude, of the means available and their potential effectiveness; . . . they engage in some effort, extensive or brief, to relate means to ends; and . . . therefore, at some point they select some alternative, clear-cut or confused, as the course of action that seems most likely to cope with the immediate situation" (Rosenau 1980).

Administrative Theory and Foreign Policy Rationality

The practical relevance of the rational model finds expression in *administrative theory,* which seeks to explain how bureaucratic organizations should be designed to serve the best interests of the state and its citizens. The theory is relevant in any modern organization, public or private, and nowhere more so than in American foreign policy making. Sufficient time or resources to manage foreign relations are not available without the support of large organizations, which facilitate rational decision making in ways that would otherwise be impossible. Before we reject the rational actor model completely, then, we must first consider a subsidiary hypothesis: that the U.S. foreign policy-making machinery enhances the prospects for rational decision making, even if the ideal is not always realized.

The idea that modern bureaucracy—by virtue of the roles it creates—enhances the prospects for rational decision making stems from the German scholar Max Weber's (1864–1920) seminal theories. Large-scale bureaucracies contribute to efficient administration and rationality, Weber reasoned, by how they are organized and operate:

- Structured on the principle of division of labor, bureaucracies make each person in the machinery of government a specialist, even an expert, at her or his job; functional divisions among agencies as well as within them (as, for example, in the separation of diplomatic and defense responsibilities between the State and Defense departments) achieves *specialization* by assigning different tasks to different people qualified in different ways.

- Dividing authority among competing organizations enhances the probability that all policy options will be considered before decisions are reached. *Multiple advocacy* (George 1972) results from interagency bargaining, because the process requires defending positions and negotiation prevents any one agent from unilaterally making a critical policy decision.

- Authority is distributed hierarchically, and a clear *chain of command* delineates who is responsible for what and to whom. It is easier to get things done when everyone has a clear idea of who is subordinate to whom, who has authority over what, and what role each cog in

the machinery should perform. Precious time does not have to be devoted to deciding who has the power to decide.

- Rules specify how each major function or task is to be performed and prescribe *standard operating procedures* for each task. Hence, rather than deliberating about the best method for handling a problem, the professional bureaucrat can concentrate on mastering those methods.

- Bureaucracies rely on a system of records, written documents systematically gathered and stored to facilitate retrieval. These provide a data bank of past decisions, and increase the information available for making future decisions.

- In principle, bureaucracies recruit "the best and brightest" personnel on the basis of achievement and aptitude rather than on the basis of ascriptive criteria such as ethnicity, gender, wealth, or family background.

- Similarly, personnel are compensated and promoted on the basis of their achievements, thus placing decision-making responsibility in the hands of those deemed most competent. Merit determines who is "selected up" and who is "selected out," rather than criteria such as seniority, personal characteristics, ingratiation, or favors to superiors.

- Administrative norms allow some specialists the luxury of engaging in "forward planning." Unlike the president, whose role requires that attention be focused on the crisis (foreign or domestic) of the moment, bureaucracies can consider long-term needs.

This brief overview of administrative theory portrays a bureaucratic policy process that contributes to rational decision making. There is considerable merit in that viewpoint. Still, before we jump to the conclusion that bureaucratic decision making is a modern panacea, these theoretical propositions, as with the rational actor model, tell us how bureaucratic decision making *should* occur but not necessarily how it *does* occur. The reality of bureaucratic practice suggests that bureaucracies cause problems as well as solve them.

THE CASE AGAINST BUREAUCRATIC FOREIGN POLICY MAKING

In principle, bureaucracies are expected to help the president carry out presidential policies. In practice, the president depends on the bureaucracies comprising the foreign affairs government to get things done. Thus, as Henry Kissinger advised, "To understand what the government is likely to do, one has to understand the bureaucratics of the problems."

What are some of the consequences of presidential dependency on bureaucracies? Does it enhance or constrain the president's power over American foreign policy? Are bureaucracies "ruling servants," in control of policy by virtue of their power to impede? Indeed, does the bureaucracy rule while the president merely reigns? Those troublesome questions have been raised by past presidents' recurrent complaints that they were unable to persuade, even coerce, their own bureaucracy to support their policies. Subordinates have often appeared insubordinate; rather than helping to get things done, they have opposed presidential directives. "You know," Ronald Reagan once said, "one of the hardest things in a government this size is to know that down there, underneath, is that permanent structure that's resisting everything you're doing." Political scientist and former presidential adviser Richard E. Neustadt observed that, "to a degree, the needs of bureaucrats and president are incompatible. The better one is served, the worse will be the other."

Although it is an exaggeration to speak of the *bureaucratic captivity* of presidents, they are heavily dependent on the bureaucracy for information, for identifying problems, for advocating solutions and, most importantly, for implementing presidential orders. Correspondingly, presidents' leeway is markedly constrained by the government they are elected to run. The very enormity of the federal bureaucracy is a constraint. The federal civilian workforce (excluding postal workers) totaled 1.9 million in 2002. Just over a million more were on active military duty. Federal employees are ensconced in roughly 2,000 separate but overlapping government agencies. Presidents come and go, but these millions of bureaucrats remain, providing continuity from one administration to the next. Something over 7,000 are "policy makers" as described in the "Plum Book," which lists the jobs available for individuals appointed by and able to be fired by the president. The rest are career civil servants, whose independence and job security are protected by an elaborate system of rules and regulations. As a result, foreign policy decisions necessarily are made by many individuals within a massive but fragmented governmental structure, most of whom are beyond the immediate reach of elected public officials. As Woodrow Wilson put it in a timeless description, "Nobody stands responsible for the policy of government...a dozen men originate it; a dozen compromises twist and alter it; a dozen offices put it into execution."

Bureaucratic Behavior: Interorganizational Attributes

How do large bureaucratic organizations relate to one another? How do individuals behave within complex organizational settings? At least five *interorganizational* (how the organizations relate to each other) characteristics of administrative decision making are important to an understanding of bureaucratic behavior and its impact on foreign policy. Four other *intraorganizational* features (how the organizations shape the roles of the people within them), discussed later, combine to summarize the **bureaucratic politics model** of foreign policy decision making. In short, this is a perspective that stresses the policy making effects of interaction and competition among bureaucratic organizations and the competing roles of people within them.[7]

Parochialism Bureaucracies are driven to protect their jurisdictions. As Drezner (2000) notes, organizations "resist or subvert new tasks that are assigned to them, for fear they will lose their cohesion and ability to function." In short, they define issues and take stands on them to promote their self-interests. As James M. Fallows, President Carter's chief speechwriter, observed, "The chief force motivating most top bureaucrats, cabinet secretaries, and even some White House aides is job security—you can predict a bureaucrat's reaction to almost any issue by the way it will affect their job or fiefdom. That's what comes first."

Parochialism is a characteristic of many organizational subcultures in which views, experiences, and values of the agency are considered paramount, often leading to elitism, resistance to outside ideas, and narrow definition of interests. It can manifest itself in several ways. Consider the bureaucratic hurdles the Clinton administration both created and faced as it sought to move counterterrorism higher on its agenda of priorities. They began with the administration's treatment of acts of terrorism as crimes, not acts of war.

In the mid-1990s, the U.S. government developed the capabilities to strike Al Qaeda training camps, cells, and individual terrorists. Yet planned missions were never executed.... "Mutually reinforcing, self-imposed constraints...kept the special units sidelined."

Terrorism as Crime: The designation of terrorism as criminal activity (rather than acts of war) placed the Justice Department, not the Pentagon, at the center of U.S. counterterrorism efforts. As a result, legal instruments like extradition became the weapon of "choice" employed against terrorists and precluded the Defense Department from coordinating a military response.

Not a Clear and Present Danger for War: Both the Pentagon and the CIA were resistant to classifying actions that were not conducted by "armies of other nations" as acts of war. The Pentagon believed that attacks on targets like the USS Cole [in Yemen] and the Khobar Towers facility in Dhahran [Saudi Arabia] were a "force protection issue." Terrorism was understood as an ongoing threat that required vigilance, but it was not grounds for war....

No Legal Authority: In the 1990s, lawyers at the Pentagon and in the intelligence community argued that the Department of Defense did not have the legal authority to execute the clandestine missions of the SOF [Special Operations Forces] and related counterterrorism units.... But ultimately "the Pentagon did not want the authority to strike terrorists secretly or to employ Special Forces against states that aided and sheltered them."

(Tulis 2004, based on Shultz 2004)

Or consider the V-22 Osprey, a tilt-rotor aircraft capable of taking off and landing like a helicopter, but flying like an airplane. The Pentagon has worked diligently for over a decade to acquire the Osprey. The Marines greatly desired the Osprey to ensure their ability to transport units swiftly and efficiently into faraway places. Thus, the Marine Corps and its supporters worked against the first Bush administration's repeated efforts (led by then–Defense Secretary Dick Cheney) to cancel the program for broader strategic and budgetary reasons. From the perspective of advocates of the Osprey, its contribution to Marine Corps interests and capabilities was paramount (Jones 2002b; Jones 2004). The success of the Marine Corps and its advocates during the first Bush administration—plans to purchase more than 900 of the aircraft continued in spite of the White House decision to cancel the program—led to additional efforts later in 2001 when, in the face of rising costs, troubling maintenance and safety records, and several well publicized crashes killing Marines, high-ranking officers went so far as to falsify maintenance records to protect the program (Flaherty 2001; Marquis 2001).

A third example: After the 9/11 terrorist attacks, it was revealed that the classified report of the *National Commission on Terrorism: Countering the Changing Threat of International Terrorism* established by President Clinton in 2000 had recommended a series of changes in the security, intelligence, and law enforcement communities to deal with a threat for

---

F O C U S 13.2   Bureaucracy and the Terrorist Threat

Prior to September 11, a major reason why a succession of government commissions and legislators called for organizational changes in the homeland security areas was to draw attention to the problem of terrorism and the need to respond. Advocates of change argued that terrorism constituted a very real threat to U.S. security—yet this threat did not receive the priority attention of the U.S. government that they believed it deserved. Consolidating homeland security functions would give it that priority—by creating what the General Accounting Office called a "focal point." Most proposed placing the new organization within the Executive Office of the President in an effort to make homeland security a White House priority.

Clearly, before terrorists turned commercial jetliners into conventional weapons of mass destruction and killed more than 5,000 people on U.S. soil, homeland security was not a top priority for the U.S. government. To be sure, successive presidents had talked about the threat of terrorism. Clinton frequently worried, often publicly, about a germ weapons attack by terrorists on U.S. soil. Bush mentioned the threat of terrorism during his campaign, and continued to talk about the threat as president (although often as an argument for developing missile defenses). Spending on counterterrorism activities also increased dramatically—from $6 billion in 1998 to well over $10 billion in 2001. And with the appointment of a national coordinator for security, infrastructure protection, and counterterrorism in 1998, there was an attempt to improve coordination among the myriad of agencies and interests involved in preparing for, preventing, and responding to terrorist attacks.

But even with heightened presidential interest, increased funding, and improved coordination, the terrorist threat had not moved to the top— or even near the top—of the daily agenda of the president and his senior national security advisers. The national coordinator was a special assistant to the president and senior director on the NSC staff, reporting to the national security adviser—not the president. And while the issue of terrorism was rising in importance in every agency with a role to play in guarding against the threat, terrorism remained just one among their many concerns. For the Pentagon, preparing to fight two major theater wars remained the priority—and in the distance loomed the rise of China and the acquisition of long-range missiles by nuclear-armed rogue states. The customs agents searched luggage and shipments coming across borders—to sniff out illegal drug shipments more than germ weapons. Foreign service officers working their first tour of duty in consular sections in U.S. embassies abroad, and Immigration and Naturalization Services personnel at U.S. ports of entry worried more about preventing entry of people who wished to stay for good than keeping out people who wished to do the United States. harm. The FBI tracked federal criminals at home and sought to garner evidence that could stand up in U.S. courts against terrorists abroad, but did not take the initiative to track people who might terrorize our nation. And the list goes on. In each and every case other critical agency functions were, for very understandable reasons, given priority over countering the terrorism threat.

SOURCE: Prepared statement of W. H. Daalder and I. M. Destler before the Committee on Governmental Affairs, U.S. Senate, October 12, 2001 (www.puaf.umd.edu/faculty/destler/Organizing%20for%20Homeland %20Security.pdf. accessed 12/1/06).

---

which the commission found a dreadful lack of preparation (see Focus 13.2). Nearly every proposal was embraced by the White House and Congress after the 2001 attacks. Had the Commission's recommendations been followed early, might 9/11 have been averted? Why weren't they? Virtually every agency head, including FBI director Louis Freeh, CIA director George Tenet, Secretary of State Madeleine Albright, and Attorney General Janet Reno, opposed parts of the report because they challenged their bureaucratic purview or turf. Thus,

organizational interests were elevated above the national security interests.

Competitiveness   The departments and agencies comprising the foreign affairs government frequently compete with one another for influence. Rarely are they impartial participants in the policy process that obediently carry out presidential orders. As a staff member of the Clinton administration's National Security Council once noted, organizations take stands on issues that advance their interests and maneuver to protect them against other organizations and senior officials, including the president (Halperin 1971). Although not intentionally malicious, many agency heads nonetheless confuse their organization's welfare with the country's. The V-22 case just discussed is a good example of the observation that national security managers have a personal investment in the health and aggrandizement of their own bureaucratic organizations. They equate the national interest and their organization's interest as a matter of course. As Drezner (2000) argues, "Agencies that prefer the status quo or fear losing power will resist the introduction of new ideas [or new players] into the policy mix and use any means at their disposal to avoid unpalatable ideas."

Heads of bureaucratic organizations are not insensitive to the nation's interests, but they struggle over defining what is best for the country. For several years prior to the Persian Gulf War, for example, the United States authorized the sale of advanced-technology goods to Iraq (which, ironically, may have enhanced Iraq's ability to wage war against the United States). The Commerce Department, following its mandate to promote international trade, became a vigorous proponent of technology sales to Iraq. Commerce usually prevailed in the interorganizational policy process because it was able to build a "'winning' coalition in favor of liberal export controls" with the State Department, whose arguments extended beyond economics to an array of diplomatic concerns. Together the Commerce and State Departments blocked the Defense Department's objections. Thus, "each agency's separate organizational mission led it to embrace a different conception of national security and, therefore, different reasons for supporting either trade promotion or trade control" (Jones 1999).

The incidence with which agency officials propose and pursue policies that blatantly benefit their own organizations attests to the parochial outlook and the arguably selfish concerns that typically dominate bureaucratic thinking. Consider the following example. After the collapse of the Soviet Union, the CIA's clandestine services,

officially known as the Directorate of Operations, shut down its operations there, believing that Russia no longer posed much of a threat. Less than two years later, the decision was reversed by the CIA official responsible for operations in the former Soviet Union and Eastern Europe. Why? Because "a decision to stop targeting Russia would cost the agency 500 overseas jobs for case officers [those whose job is to recruit and oversee individuals who conduct espionage and provide information to the agency]" (*U.S. News and World Report,* 4 July 1994).

Another example comes from the weeks following the report of the Clinton administration's National Commission on Terrorism, headed by former national security adviser Brent Scowcroft. The Commission recommended that several Defense Department intelligence agencies be transferred to the CIA for better intelligence coordination and analysis. The CIA predictably favored the restructuring, but the Defense Department and Defense Secretary Donald Rumsfeld—also predictably—were opposed to it (Pincus 2001).

Does a similar fate await the newly created cabinet-level director of national intelligence with broad powers over the sixteen agencies comprising the intelligence community (most of which are in the Defense Department) and its estimated $40 billion annual intelligence budget? Instructively, in testimony before the *9/11 Commission* in March 2004, Defense Secretary Rumsfeld declared that an intelligence czar would do the nation "a great disservice" by creating reliance on a single, centralized source of information. Where you stand depends on where you sit?

The reasons for competitive intergovernmental politics are numerous. Former Secretary of State Henry Kissinger (1969) suggests one: "The decision maker will always be aware of the morale of his staff. . . . [He] cannot overrule it too frequently without impairing its efficiency. . . . Placating the staff then becomes a major preoccupation of the executive." Another reason is that most agency heads are not only tied *to* their own organization but also *by* it: "A secretary of a federal department almost invariably becomes more the agent of the permanent bureaucracy under his command than a free agent, mainly because he must rely upon the permanent officials for expert information and analysis" (MacMahon 1951). Thus, caught in the middle between higher-level elected officials and their advisers on one side, and the career professionals in an organization on the other, the typical agency head must try to satisfy both. The pressures encourage competition with other organizations for scarce resources and power. Policy success in such an atmosphere tends to be defined more in terms of organizational interests than of the national interest.

Risk Aversion   Risk aversion also impeded the Clinton administration's efforts to pursue a more vigorous counterterrorism policy. As we saw in Chapter 11, risk averse behavior is pervasive among individuals in bureaucratic settings, often understandably so. Those who rock the boat are more likely to be promoted out than up.

> Organizations are not immune from risk aversion. Consider the following:
> Not only were SOF [Special Operations Forces] missions considered too dangerous and unpredictable in general, but the political and military leadership demanded "fail-safe operations." Opportunities to strike at Al Qaeda were lost because of fear of potential casualties. . . .
> As originally conceived, an SOF counterterrorism unit would be "small, flexible, adaptive, and stealthy"; each of its operations would leave a "footprint" that was very small, even invisible. However, when SOF missions against Al Qaeda were proposed, senior military officials would demand that the plans be revised to include conventional forces—hundreds of men, gunships, planes, a quick-reaction force ready to assist—that would mitigate "risk" but leave a huge "footprint."
> *(Tulis 2004; based on Shultz 2004)*

The military's risk aversion is rooted in Vietnam. Stung by high casualties that fell disproportionally across racial and other groups and a loss of

support at home, the "Vietnam syndrome" embodied the caution with which the officers' corps viewed civilian policy makers' penchant to draw the sword in response to post-Vietnam diplomatic and military challenges. Richard A. Clarke, counterterrorism director under both Clinton and George W. Bush, issued a recommendation less than a week before the 9/11 attacks that proposed a strategy for responding to the threat posed by Al Qaeda. Stimulated by Clarke's controversial book *Against All Enemies: Inside America's War on Terrorism*, *Newsweek* describes the context and response to the proposal (see Focus 13.3). Less than favorable puts it succinctly.

Imperialistic Task Expansion   Driven to protect their own interests and promote their own influence, bureaucratic agencies invariably seek to enlarge their budgets and staffs, both absolutely and in relation to other agencies. Bureaucratic agencies also typically seek to increase their prerogatives and functional powers. Thus the Defense Department (among others) sought aggressively to capture part of the CIA's $3 billion share of the intelligence budget at a time when the agency searched for a new post–Cold War mission in the face of intense scrutiny by Congress and others. At the same time, the CIA sought to defend its roles and budgets and to find new missions in the changing threat environment of the new century. Later, in 2001, the roles reversed as the CIA supported a proposal to give it three DOD intelligence agencies, while the DOD resisted.

Another example is Madeleine Albright's support in 1998 for the restructuring of the foreign affairs agencies that gave the State Department greater control over the Agency for International Development and absorbed the US. Information Agency into the department. The reasons are clear. Size is a sign of security, expansion an indicator of importance, and, to some extent, prestige and influence can be conferred only by growth. Other things being equal, larger bureaucracies have greater access, greater credibility, greater resources, greater durability—and greater influence. (Such organizations usually have more enemies as well.) Thus,

---

F O C U S 13.3   Risk Aversion, Then and Now

Everyone agrees that the [Clarke] plan would have taken three to five years to accomplish. The squabbling over plans and progress masks a much deeper problem in the "risk-averse" attitude of the national-security bureaucracy of the past two decades. It is a mind-set rooted in history—in the scandals over assassination plots and spying on American citizens that engulfed the CIA and FBI after Watergate. . . .

The culture of risk aversion has been just as pronounced in the post-Vietnam military. Asked to stage a commando raid to kill a terrorist, the Joint Chiefs typically respond by piling on the logistical requirements. The generals understand that the politicians, confronted with re-enacting Operation Overlord [the 1944 invasion of Normandy during World War II], will back off. President Clinton wanted to put Special Forces troops into Afghanistan to chase Al Qaeda in the late '90s. The chairman of the Joint Chiefs, General Hugh Shelton, set up a planning exercise with requirements so elaborate that the whole operation collapsed of its own weight. . . .

It takes a determined president to overcome such inertia, and Clinton, plagued by his own scandals, was not that man. Nor was Bush, at least at first. It is not clear he understood the seriousness of the threat. "Before 9/11, I didn't feel that sense of urgency . . . I was not on point," Bush told *Washington Post* reporter Bob Woodward in December 2001. As a "war president," Bush is more likely to press. Do Bush and his aides discuss the problem of risk aversion?, *Newsweek* asked [former National Security Adviser Condoleezza] Rice. "All the time," she replied. "All the time."

SOURCE: Evan Thomas, Michael Isikoff, and Tamara Lipper, "The Insider: Special Report," *Newsweek*, 5 April 2004, 25. Reprinted by permission.

---

most organizations strive to maintain and enhance their budgets and grow their personnel.

The raison d'être of administrative organization is efficiency through the performance of discrete tasks by independent units; a division of labor that clearly differentiates functions permits experts to specialize. This rationale led in 1947 to creation of a separate Central Intelligence Agency, whose ostensible purpose was to coordinate the gathering of foreign intelligence, and in 1961 to creation of the U.S. Agency for International Development (USAID) to specialize in the administration of foreign aid and technical assistance.

Practice, however, frequently fails to conform to theory. Imperialistic bureaucracies seek to perform the tasks for which other agencies have been assigned responsibility. That inclination explains why the Council on International Economic Policy created by President Nixon did not become an effective coordinator of economic policy making: it became merely another competitor jockeying for a piece of the policy action among those preexisting units needing coordination. The Clinton administration's National Economic Council fared better, but still struggled with many of the same "turf wars,"

especially after Robert Rubin moved from the White House to the Treasury Department. George W. Bush experienced similar tension early in his administration between his Treasury Department, headed by Paul O'Neill, and his NEC, headed by Lawrence Lindsay. O'Neill was Bush's first cabinet-level official to resign his post.

Bureaucratic imperialism also explains why so many different agencies are independently involved in gathering roughly the same intelligence information (for example, the State Department, the Defense Department, and the CIA, among others), and why the three military services have found it "absolutely essential" that each develop its own capabilities in areas where the other services specialize (as evidenced by the fact that the army at one time had more support aircraft than the air force). The result: instead of a bureaucratic division of labor, functions are often duplicated.

The bureaucratic imperatives of the uniformed military services, which include not only imperialism but also competitiveness and endurance, are well illustrated by the activities and strategies advocated by the different branches in the run-up to the 1991 Persian Gulf War (Gordon and Trainor 1995;

F O C U S 13.4   Bureaucratic Competitiveness and Task Expansion: Military Rivalry in the Aftermath of Victory in the Persian Gulf

As the Defense Department begins its most dramatic restructuring of the armed forces in decades, the services are in tough competition for declining dollars. Although such budget rivalries are hardly new, the Persian Gulf War is being used to reshape the debates on the future roles and missions of the military. . . . Senior U.S. military officials say they were most concerned during the initial days of the Gulf crisis about the vulnerability of Saudi Arabia. . . . The only ground-based American forces aligned against Iraqi troops in late August were an airborne infantry division and marine units illequipped to battle heavy armor, plus an air force fighter wing with no more weapons than it could carry under its wings.

This experience has spurred the air force to create two special combat wings that, for the first time, would include a mix of fighter, bomber and attack planes that could be dispatched in crises. Until now, air force tactical wings have been composed of a single type of aircraft.

The army, with its thousands of tons of heavy armor and hundreds of thousands of combat troops, was hit hardest by the military's limited sealift and airlift capacity. Once content to let the navy and air force worry about such capacity, army officials now say they will press the other services to increase resources for sealift and airlift operations.

The army wants the navy, for instance, to be able to transport at least two divisions simultaneously within thirty days of call-up—not just one division, as the navy had planned. Navy officials readily agree that more of the Pentagon budget needs to be invested in transport ships. . . . The Marine Corps, which has spent billions of dollars on amphibious landing operations, conducted no amphibious assaults against Iraq, but argues that this kind of war-fighting capability should not be abandoned because the fear of an amphibious attack kept several Iraqi divisions diverted toward the sea during the war.

All the services have appeared equally eager to use the Gulf War in sales pitches for more purchases of the kinds of weapons that proved most successful. The air force and navy, for instance, are using memories of the pinpoint strikes by "stealth" F-117A fighter-bombers to push for continuation of the stealth B-2 bomber and development of a stealth carrier-based plane for the navy.

At the same time, the services are pointing to the deficiencies that were evident in the war in arguing for improved and expanded new systems. The navy, for example, which dropped primarily "dumb bombs" and had only a limited number of high-technology, precision-guided missiles, is now using the success of the air force's "smart" weapons in lobbying to expand its own arsenal. . . . The navy, annoyed that it received so little credit for its aerial bombing attacks, discovered what officials believe is one of the reasons. "We didn't realize," says one naval official, "how lousy the video recorders were on our aircraft until we saw them side by side with the air force's. We had junk. The air force guys had nice clean pictures." Better recorders are sure to be on the navy's new shopping list.

SOURCE: Molly Moore, "The Armed Services and the Nibbling Rivalries," *Washington Post National Weekly Edition,* 17–23 June 1991, 31. Reprinted by permission of The Washington Post.

Holland 1999). They are also seen in the meaning that each branch attached to the Persian Gulf War as each positioned itself for the oncoming debate about the military's role in the post–Cold War world. Focus 13.4 provides a glimpse of how the war stimulated "new thinking" in the Pentagon and among its congressional and interest-group supporters shortly after its victorious conclusion.

Endurance   Bureaucracies are survival oriented. Both the number and size of administrative units responsible for promoting and protecting America's activist foreign policy interests have increased enormously. More new units have been created or expanded than phased out or cut back. Same with taxes. The federal excise tax on long-distance phone calls was instituted at the turn of the twentieth century as a temporary tax designed to pay for the Spanish-American War. Check your latest phone bill.

Bureaucratic growth is arguably a response to new challenges and changing circumstances. With the end of the Cold War, for example, the State Department opened fourteen new embassies in the former Soviet Union and expected to increase its number of diplomats there by nearly half. The Commerce Department also quadrupled the number of trade promotion officials assigned to the region, the Treasury Department increased its economic analysts from three to eleven, and USAID, traditionally oriented exclusively toward the Global South, created a twenty-five person team to speed delivery of technical and humanitarian assistance to the former Soviet Union (Priest 1992, 33).

Historically, however, organizational "reforms" designed to streamline government have often created *new* organizations to coordinate and regulate the activities of existing ones. The new Department of Homeland Security (DHS), discussed in Chapter 11, is a recent example. It draws approximately 180,000 people from twenty-two different organizations throughout the government, seeking to rally all of them behind a single responsibility: to make America more secure. The agencies range from the U.S. Secret Service and the Federal Emergency Management Agency (FEMA) to the National Domestic Preparedness Office, and from the National Infrastructure Protection Center and the Federal Computer Incident Response Center to the U.S. Coast Guard and four existing border protection agencies, including Immigration and Customs Enforcement.

Each organization and its people bring with them certain skills, but they also are encumbered by a distinctive organizational subculture and set of standard operating procedures. Perhaps the department will be an exception to the normal bureaucratic rule, but too often the result is not enhanced efficiency but, instead, the addition of new bureaucratic layers to an already burgeoning bureaucracy. As Ronald Reagan's Secretary of the Navy John Lehman once complained, "It would be impossible for me or anyone to accurately describe to you the system with which, and within which, we must operate. There are thousands upon thousands of offices and entities and bureaus that have been created over the years to deal episodically with aspects of defense."

Bureaucratic Behavior: Intraorganizational Attributes

The interorganizational side of bureaucratic behavior just described is easily summarized: all bureaucratic organizations pursue their own purposes, promote their own power, enhance their own position in the governmental hierarchy, and strive to endure. Successful pursuit of those objectives flows in part from and in turn reinforces internal **standard operating procedures** (SOPs), rules and routines for dealing with recurring tasks and situations, as well as the way bureaucratic organizations mold the behavior of their role occupants.

Secrecy and Exclusiveness   Bureaucratic agencies seek to minimize interference in and regulation of their operations. To the extent possible, they keep their proceedings secret from potential enemies—including the president—who might use such knowledge to attack their operations publicly, and they conceal activities that can injure their public image. Efforts by the Marines to falsify maintenance records for the V-22 Osprey are simply a more egregious form of this behavior. "There are no secrets in Washington," President Kennedy once observed, "except the things I need to know." Conversely, bureaucratic secrets are "leaked" selectively for propaganda purposes when their release is politically advantageous.

Attitudinal Conformity   Every bureaucracy eventually develops a shared "mind set" or dominant way of looking at reality, which few challenge. The process of recruitment and self-selection brings together individuals who already share many basic attitudes. The Foreign Service, for instance, has sought "young people they consider most like the successful officers already in the system" (Harr 1969). Free thinkers or people who might "rock the boat" or "make waves" are not welcomed; instead, those subscribing to the agency's dominant values are preferred.[8] Moreover, the State Department's *organizational subculture*—a common set of goals and norms shared by members of the organization—spreads quickly among its personnel, creating patterned ways of thinking and acting (Wilson 1989; Scott 1969).

Attitudinal conformity is reinforced in small group decision-making situations, where social pressures that reinforce group norms sometimes produce *groupthink,* a cohesiveness and solidarity of outlook that may lead to dysfunctional policy choices as the group's search for unanimity overrides the realistic appraisal of alternative policy choices (Janis 1982).[9] Indeed, several recent studies indicate that groupthink has been associated with poor outcomes in numerous foreign policy decisions (for example, Herek, Janis, and Huth 1987; Schafer and Crichlow 1996). President Johnson's habit of addressing Bill Moyers, his resident "dove" on Vietnam, as "Mr. Stop-the-Bombing" illustrates the pressures toward conformity small decision-making groups often generate.

The Kennedy administration's disastrous Bay of Pigs decision in 1961 contained numerous elements of groupthink (Janis 1982). So did the Reagan administration's policy revisions regarding Iran and the Lebanese hostage crisis in 1985–1986 that led to the Iran-Contra affair ('t Hart 1990). Even decision processes that lead to success, as those that brought about victory in the Gulf War, are susceptible to concurrence-seeking behavior and pressures toward attitudinal conformity. Even some in the "inner circle" of decision making, such as Secretary of State James A. Baker and JCS Chairman Colin Powell, were unwilling to challenge the dominant views articulated by President Bush and his national security adviser, Brent Scowcroft. To do so "would have meant undermining one's own political standing at the White House" (Hybel 1993). In 1998, when President Clinton and his advisers decided to retaliate with force against Osama bin Laden and Al Qaeda for the bombing of U.S. embassies in Africa, similar concurrence-seeking behavior occurred (see Hendrickson 2002).

Once an individual joins a bureaucratic organization, socialization to its "mission" and its "essence" (Allison and Halperin 1972) reinforces conformity to the organization's central norms. Recruits are quickly educated into their role and the acceptable attitudes that go with it. Nonconformity

can result in loss of influence or, in the extreme, one's job. On the other hand, those who conform to peer-group attitudes, who are perceived as team players, are rewarded. "Promotions are awards given to bureaucrats for accepting organizational myths" cynically describes this phenomenon.

Shared convictions about an organization's role and mission are important in maintaining organizational morale, but the line is not always clear between a healthy commitment to an organization's welfare and what is detrimental to larger purposes. Institutional mind sets discourage creativity, dissent, and independent thinking, undermining rational policy making. The Department of State, for instance, has found in numerous self-studies that pressures producing uniformity of thought and stifling creativity have been persistent problems.

Groupthink is usually applied to small group decision making. Still, it is instructive that the Senate Intelligence Committee report on intelligence failures in the run-up to the Iraq war concluded that "'Groupthink' caused the [intelligence] community to interpret ambiguous evidence . . . as conclusive."

Deference to Tradition Because decision making in complex organizations is conducted according to rules, bureaucrats are prone to defer to tradition rather than invent a new way to deal with a new problem. "A man comes to an assignment," Charles Frankel (1969) observed, "and he is told what the policy is. He must find a way to navigate through the storms, to resist the pressures of people and events, and to turn over the policy to his successor in the same condition in which it was when he received it from his predecessor." A former staff member of the National Security Council dubbed this respect for ritual and precedent the *curator mentality* (Thomson 2004).

Reliance on Historical Analogies The Clinton administration's cautious approach to Al Qaeda and bin Laden was shaped in part by an historical event and corresponding analogy dubbed the *Somalia Syndrome.* The administration was "haunted by the image of Somalis dragging the body of a U.S. solder through the streets of Mogadishu following the 1993 special operations forces mission to capture Mohammed Aidid. The Somalia catastrophe also reinforced 'wariness' of the [special operations forces] within the senior ranks of the military" (Tulis 2004).

The Somalia Syndrome illustrates the tendency of policy makers to search history impressionistically for parallels that suggest options for dealing with (or avoiding) emergent policy problems. That tendency—which often results in a misreading of historical lessons (Neustadt and May 1986; Khong 1992)—helps account for continuity in American foreign policy. The "Munich" analogy, for example, was drawn on by a generation of policy makers as evidence that it is impossible to appease aggressors. As described in Chapter 3, the analogy refers to the 1938 British and French agreement that permitted Nazi Germany to annex a large part of Czechoslovakia in return for what British Prime Minister Neville Chamberlain called "peace in our time." Instead, war broke out in Europe a year later, with the apparent lesson that an aggressor cannot be stopped short of fighting it.[10]

Bill Clinton invoked the Hitler analogy to describe Serbian President Slobodan Milošević as NATO warplanes launched an extensive air attack in Kosovo in 1999. George H. W. Bush drew on the Munich analogy directly as he prepared the nation for war against Saddam Hussein, whom he also described as a modern-day Hitler. Indeed, so strong was his commitment to the analogy that, according to one scholar, it "acted as a barrier to the search for information that could have jeopardized its validity" (Hybel 1993). Heavy reliance on analogical thinking before and after Iraq's invasion of Kuwait in August 1990 limited the Bush administration's ability to follow the canons of *procedural rationality,* thus calling into question the *instrumental rationality* of its decisions, particularly the choice of war over containment through the sustained application of sanctions. By no means does this detract from the administration's success in bringing Iraq to its knees, but it does show that "success does not prove rationality" (Hybel 1993).

The war in Iraq inevitably invites comparisons with the unpopular Vietnam War. Consider the rhetoric of Presidents Bush and Johnson:

"Our military is confronting terrorists in Iraq and Afghanistan and in other places so our people will not have to confront terrorist violence in New York or St. Louis or Los Angeles."
George W. Bush, 2003

"If we don't stop the Reds in South Vietnam, tomorrow they will be in Hawaii, and next week they will be in San Francisco."
Lyndon B. Johnson, 1966

Washington Post reporter Robert C. Kaiser, who covered the Vietnam War in 1969 and 1970, wrote in early 2004 about the similarities and dissimilarities between Iraq and Vietnam. Here, in Focus 13.5, we emphasize what Kaiser regards as similarities between the two conflicts as seen through the prism of achieving political rather than strictly military objectives.

Other attributes of bureaucratic behavior as it relates to foreign policy making could be added to this discussion, but they would not change the conclusion drawn from it: that the decision-making system profoundly influences the behavior of those who occupy institutionally defined decision-making roles. Given this, we now shift attention to some of the major policy consequences of those attributes.

POLICY CONSEQUENCES OF ORGANIZATIONAL DECISION MAKING

Because American foreign policy is a product of organizational decision-making processes, it is useful to consider how bureaucratic behavior shapes both policy and policy making. Some conspicuous repercussions of bureaucratic processes follow.

Bureaucratic Resistance to Change

In the realm of broad foreign policy conceptions and goals, the president and the executive

---

F O C U S 13.5 Iraq and Vietnam: Rhyme and Reason

The first President Bush and his national security adviser, Brent Scowcroft, wrote a book together in 1998 that defended their decision not to take Baghdad at the end of the 1991 Persian Gulf War. In a section written by the elder Bush, it said: "Trying to eliminate Saddam, extending the ground war into an occupation of Iraq . . . would have incurred incalculable human and political costs. . . . The United States could conceivably still be an occupying power in a bitterly hostile land."

Today the United States is an occupying power in a divided Iraq whose rivalrous Shia, Sunni, and Kurdish communities eye us nervously. Though we are rushing to establish a government that will allow us to withdraw, so far there is no plan describing the path to that end that is broadly accepted in Iraq. What started as a pristinely military undertaking now has a primarily political objective. But there is no obvious way to achieve that objective. This is just what happened in Vietnam. . . .

If we see that a neat military victory is difficult to reach, then Iraq and Vietnam begin to have more in common. Sometimes the rhymes ring like chimes. . . .

- **Official optimism.** Johnson told the country again and again how well things were going in Vietnam. So did key members of his administration and commanders in the field. The happy endings they repeatedly promised never materialized. Cheney's "welcomed as liberators" prediction is one example of the official optimism about Iraq that proved overly optimistic. Another was the projection made by Pentagon planners last May [2003] that the United States would need only about 30,000 troops in Iraq by the end of summer. Today [early 2004] we have 132,000 men and women in the country, and another 30,000 next door in Kuwait.

- **American isolation on the ground.** In Iraq, as they were in Vietnam, most U.S. installations are surrounded by armed guards, concertina wire, or high walls. In Vietnam, few Americans spoke Vietnamese. In Iraq, only a handful speak Arabic, and contacts between Iraqis and Americans are surprisingly rare and often strained. When the war in Vietnam was launched, Americans knew little of Vietnam's history, most critical the centuries of rivalry between Vietnam and China. The complexities of Shia and Sunni history, compounded by Kurdish issues that transcend the borders of Iraq (because large numbers of Kurds live in Turkey and Iran) have similarly eluded many Americans on the ground in Iraq who are prosecuting the current war.

- **American isolation in the world.** Robert S. McNamara, Kennedy's and Johnson's secretary of defense, said in a recent interview that if the United States had listened to its allies in the 1960s, when all of them cautioned us not to go to war in Vietnam, we could have avoided that disaster. In 2003 Britain joined the war against Iraq, but all our other traditional allies refused. Vietnam became an unpopular war in many parts of the world; Iraq appears even more so. . . .

Vietnam undermined the U.S. economy, nearly destroyed the U.S. army and contributed to a generation or more of public cynicism and distrust of government. There are no grounds today for predicting consequences as grave from the war in Iraq. Indeed, a successful outcome, including a new democratic Iraq, remains possible. But the rhymes should give us pause.

SOURCE: Robert G. Kaiser, "Iraq and Vietnam, Rhyme and Reason," The *Washington Post National Weekly Edition*, 5–11 January 2004, 22.

---

bureaucracies may be natural enemies. Because many upper-echelon career officials have retained their positions for years, sometimes even decades, their long-held assumptions about American foreign policy may be as deeply entrenched as the bureaucracies for which they work. Fundamental assumptions—about Soviet motives during the Cold War and Russian and Chinese intentions since, about the continuing wisdom of globalism and the utility of force, and about other themes that have defined American foreign policy for more than five decades—have become conventional bureaucratic wisdom, unworthy of further reexamination. Presidents intermittently come to power with fresh ideas about foreign policy essentials, eager to implement new approaches, only to find that old ways of thinking are firmly entrenched in agencies that are resistant to change.

With communism and the Soviet challenge as the guideposts of American foreign policy for decades, it is not surprising that attempts at fundamental policy changes were rare. Even as the end of the Cold War demanded a fresh appraisal of old ways of thinking, however, many bureaucratic agencies continued to view the future through the prism of the past. "The ghost in the Pentagon" (Iklé 1990) is the way a former under secretary of defense described the "enduring mind-set" of military planners as they contemplated the first evidence that the Cold War was indeed passing. A decade later—and after terrorist bombings of the World Trade Center in 1993, the American embassies in Kenya and Tanzania in 1998, and the USS Cole in Yemen in 2000—bureaucratic resistance to new counter-terrorism approaches was evident, as we saw earlier (see Focus 13.2).

Arguably the Bush administration's invasions of Afghanistan and Iraq also mimicked the Cold War military approach to threats from abroad. As two conservative critics of neoconservative logic argue, "An ideology that highlights conventional state-against-state conflict as its one-size-fits-all policy option has been adapted for an era when threats are unconventional, transnational, and non-state-specific. Little wonder," they continue critically, "that no one feels safer" (Halper and Clarke 2004). In this instance, however, the reasons are likely to be as much shared visions among key policy makers as bureaucratic resistance to new ideas. Among them are people described by writer James Mann (2004b; see also Buchanan 2004) as the *vulcans*. All gained their national security credentials in previous Republican administrations during the 1970s into the early 1990s, including Vice President Dick Cheney, Secretaries of Defense and State Donald Rumsfeld and Colin Powell, Deputy Secretaries of Defense and State Paul Wolfowitz and William Armitage, and National Security Adviser Condoleezza Rice. Among their shared world views is an emphasis on the "high politics" of national security rather than the "low politics" of political economy and social welfare issues (Mann 2004b).

Even if new realities are recognized, reorienting existing procedures and reallocating resources to new problems is not easy. (See Focus 13.6 for an example from the CIA.) Nowhere is that more apparent than in the Pentagon, where decisions on weapons systems and their intended purposes often take decades to come to fruition (as illustrated by the fight over the V-22 Osprey). Not surprisingly, then, when Clinton's first secretary of defense, Les Aspin, undertook a "bottom-up" review of the U.S. military, he confronted a simple yet enduring fact: "The military machine cannot turn around on a dime" (Sweetman 1994).

The new Bush administration concluded the need for change was even more apparent than earlier, but it ran into a similar problem. Throughout 2001, the president and Secretary of Defense Rumsfeld signaled their desire for a more fundamental change of strategy and planning to meet the challenges and imperatives of the new century. However, Rumsfeld's much anticipated Quadrennial Defense Review Report, released in September 2001 just days after the September 11 terrorist strikes, was far less sweeping than expected. Moreover, even with the jarring reality of the terrorist attacks fresh in everyone's minds, initial proposals for the reorganization of the Pentagon's regional command structure to better promote cooperation and coordination against the terrorist threat were resisted. High-level officials, including Rumsfeld, concluded that "the current structure is too balkanized to execute a global campaign against terrorism," and that "transnational concerns, such as terrorism and weapons proliferation, have not received adequate attention from senior commanders" (Ricks 2001b). Nevertheless, plans for restructuring encountered fierce opposition from the services, especially the regional commanders-in-chief (CINCs), whose independence and influence in the current structure is substantial (Ricks 2001b).

Eventually Rumsfeld was successful in creating a new Northern Command, whose mission included homeland security.[11] Not unexpectedly, the new command immediately faced the unenviable bureaucratic challenges of integrating its tasks with those of the Department of Homeland Security and overcoming the technical and cultural problems of sharing communications internally and

---

F O C U S   13.6   Bound by Tradition?

The CIA had been created to wage the Cold War. Its steady focus on one or two primary adversaries, decade after decade, had at least one positive effect: it created an environment in which managers and analysts could safely invest time and resources in basic research, detailed and reflective. Payoffs might not be immediate. But when they wrote the estimates, even in brief papers, they could draw on a deep base of knowledge.

When the Cold War ended, those investments could not easily be reallocated to new enemies. The cultural effects ran even deeper. In a more fluid international environment with uncertain, changing goals and interests, intelligence managers no longer felt they could afford such a patient, strategic approach to long-term accumulation of intellectual capital. A university culture with its versions of books and articles was giving way to the culture of the newsroom.

During the 1990s, the rise of round-the-clock news shows and the Internet forced pressure on

analysts to pass along fresh reports to policymakers at an ever-faster pace, trying to add context or supplement what their customers were receiving from the media. Weaknesses in all-source and strategic analysis were highlighted by a panel, chaired by Admiral David Jeremiah, that criticized the intelligence community's failure to foresee the nuclear weapons tests by India and Pakistan in 1998, as well as by a 1999 panel, chaired by Donald Rumsfeld, that discussed the community's limited ability to assess the ballistic missile threat to the United States. Both reports called attention to the dispersal of effort on security rules that prevented adequate sharing of information. Another Cold War craft had been an elaborate set of methods for warning against surprise attack, but that too failed in analyzing new dangers like terrorism.

SOURCE: The 9/11 Commission Report. New York: Norton, 2004, pp. 90–91.

---

with other government agencies that plagued the run-up to 9/11.

Bureaucratic Competition and Foreign Policy Inertia

Bureaucratic competition encourages its own inertia as well as policy inertia. The overwhelming complexity of the foreign affairs machinery, with its entrenched and competing bureaucracies, limits what leaders can do and casts doubt on Washington's capacity to act expeditiously. Reaching consensus and taking decisive action is inhibited because policy is formulated and implemented by many individuals situated in a complex institutional arrangement. Bureaucrats in charge of the different agencies usually disagree: they want different policies and define situations differently because of their differing vantage points. The result is policy formulation that often comes down to a tug-of-war among competing agencies, a high-stakes political game in which differences are settled at the lowest common denominator.

Consider the tug-of-war evident in two recent examples. Bureaucratic disagreement and competition—notably between the State and Defense Departments—over the proper course of U.S. policy in the former Yugoslavia contributed heavily to the Clinton administration's failure to forge an effective approach to the problem until 1995. Progress did not come until the State Department used internal policy reviews to enlist the support of Deputy National Security Adviser Sandy Berger to propose a more aggressive approach. With the help of National Security Adviser Tony Lake, who used his position as process manager to force the issue, this more aggressive approach prevailed when President Clinton opted for a more assertive U.S. effort despite continued Defense Department opposition (Daalder 2000).

A few years later, George W. Bush's team experienced a policy logjam because of a fundamental dispute about how to deal with Iraq. Prior to 9/11, the administration was locked in a serious competition between the State and Defense Departments over sanctions against Iraq. Colin Powell and his staff, including Richard Haass, director of the Policy and Planning staff, preferred a revision of U.S. policy to reduce the sanctions, while Donald Rumsfeld and his staff, including deputy secretary Paul Wolfowitz, preferred an even more aggressive effort to topple Saddam Hussein's regime. Both sides blocked the other, with the result that policy was locked in place (McGeary 2001; Perlez 2001c). After the 9/11 strikes, the two sides squared off over Iraq again, with Wolfowitz advocating a widening of U.S. military action against Afghanistan to include attacks on Iraq with the ultimate purpose of eliminating Hussein's regime. Powell and his team, concerned about the need to build and preserve a broad coalition against Al Qaeda and the Taliban regime in Afghanistan, argued against widening the war. Bush's decision to identify Iraq as part of an "axis of evil" (with Iran and North Korea) in his 2002 State of the Union address hinted at the direction of the U.S. antiterror campaign after Afghanistan. The internal wrangling now turned to the question of when to move militarily against Iraq. Powell continued to be a voice for diplomacy and multilateralism. This stance put him directly at odds with the "hawks," particularly Vice President Cheney, who, according to journalist Bob Woodward (2004), Powell felt "was beyond hell-bent for action against Saddam."

Inertia as well as competition characterizes organizational behavior. Bureaucracies typically administer programs created by prior decisions. Most career professionals therefore see themselves as loyal, even unquestioning implementers of past policies rather than the creators of their own. The greater the loyalty to specific administrative tasks, the greater the commitment to existing policy. "To try and believe in what one is doing, . . . to see broader problems in narrow terms derived from one's own specific activities," is a natural part of a bureaucrat's role. The result, however, is that "the information and judgments bureaucrats provide for use in the making of policies tend to be strongly biased in favor of the continuation, rather than the modification, much less the reversal, of existing policies. . . . Thus a bureaucracy inevitably comes down heavily on the side of established policies and strongly resists change" (Reischauer 1968).

Bureaucratic Sabotage of Presidential Foreign Policy Initiatives

The popular impression that American foreign policy is little more than what the president says it is can be misleading. The president alone does not make foreign policy. Policy must not only be pronounced but also carried out, and for that task the chief executive must rely on the bureaucracies comprising the foreign affairs government. Hence, what the government's departments and agencies choose to implement becomes American foreign policy: Policy is what is done, not just what is said.

Given that bureaucracies are by nature exclusive, parochial, and interested primarily in protecting their own power and authority, we should not be surprised that few agencies cheerfully carry out presidential directives they perceive as harmful to their organizations. When threatened, bureaucrats are inclined to put themselves first and to defend their own welfare. The often intractable foreign affairs machinery is therefore capable of disloyalty to the president it ostensibly serves. And since change, or the prospect of change, usually threatens someone (because policy change almost invariably entails some redistribution of influence in the foreign affairs hierarchy), bureaucratic agencies frequently resist top-level policy proposals. "The only decision that's final is the one you agree with" is a favorite Washington cliché.

Nearly every president has complained at one time or another that the federal bureaucracy ostensibly designed to serve him undercuts his policy by refusing to carry out orders expeditiously. Witness President Truman's prediction prior to General Eisenhower's succession to the White House: "He'll sit here and he'll say, 'Do this! Do that!' *And nothing will happen.* Poor Ike—it won't be a bit like the army. He'll find it very frustrating." Another example is President Kennedy's observation that giving the State Department an instruction was like dropping it in the dead-letter box. As Dick Cheney put it when he was President Ford's chief of staff, "There is a tendency before you get to the White House or when you're just observing it from the outside to say, 'Gee, that's a powerful position that person has.' The fact of the matter is that while you're here trying to do things, you are far more aware of the constraints than you are of the power. You spend most of your time trying to overcome obstacles to getting what the president wants done."

Bureaucratic inaction and lack of responsiveness often manifest themselves as lethargy. The government machinery grinds slowly. (To quote the tongue-in-cheek characterization by James H. Boren, founder of the International Association of Professional Bureaucrats, "One must always remember that freedom from action and freedom from purpose constitute the philosophical basis of creative bureaucracy.") Procrastination appears endemic and is easily interpreted as intentional when in fact it is often inadvertent. It takes time to move people, paper, and processes along, and completing even the simplest requests routinely involves delay. An impatient president can easily mistake the crawling pace for insubordination, even sedition, because the effect—braking or abrogating policy decisions—is the same.

We must be careful not to equate everyday bureaucratic inaction with intentional foot dragging and disobedient noncompliance. Still, willful bureaucratic sabotage is not a mere figment of leaders' imaginations. It can take several forms. Bureaucracies can withhold or slant vital information. They can provide advice showing reasons why recommended policy changes will not work. They can leak information to Congress or discreetly contact interest groups capable of mobilizing opposition to a directive bureaucrats find intolerable. They can delay policy implementation by demanding time to study the problem thoroughly (to death, that is)—a tactic known as *paralysis by analysis*—or by complexifying it into incomprehensibility (violating the KISS principle: "Keep It Simple, Stupid!"). And bureaucracies can buck a presidential directive by interpreting it in such a way that it is administered differently than proposed or with a change in emphasis. The result, of course, is no result. It has been said in this context that bureaucracies never change the course of the ship of state, they just adjust the compass.

A widely cited example of "adjusting the compass" occurred in the months leading up to the dangerous Cuban missile crisis of October 1962, in which ballistic missiles already pointed at the Soviet Union became an important bargaining issue. President Kennedy had concluded in March 1961 that Jupiter missiles in Turkey should be removed. He felt they were obsolete and exacerbated Soviet fears of encirclement and possible American attack from just beyond the Soviet border. The president therefore instructed the State Department to negotiate withdrawal of the American missiles. Turkish officials disapproved, however, so the State Department reasoned that the diplomatic thing to do was to comply with the Turkish request that the missiles stay until American Polaris submarines armed with nuclear missiles took their place. However, according to the president's brother Robert Kennedy (1969), "The president believed he was president and that, his wishes having been made clear, they would be followed and the missiles removed." Kennedy was surprised later to discover that the missiles had not been removed.[12]

President Clinton experienced a form of indirect bureaucratic sabotage of his policies toward Haiti and the former Yugoslavia. At the same time that he sought to return Jean-Bertrand Aristide to power, replacing Haiti's military regime with the country's last popularly elected president, the CIA repeatedly told Congress that, according to its psychological profile of Aristide, he was mentally unfit to rule. As the Clinton administration considered options for deposing Haiti's military leader, it shunned covert action, as officials in both the White House and State Department did not trust the CIA to carry out its mission. They believed the agency was anti-Aristide, partly because of his leftist political platform (Devroy and Smith 1993).

The conflict between the administration and the CIA was particularly embarrassing to the president, whose policies toward Haiti were already widely under attack from various quarters, but it was a classic illustration of the different purposes and perspectives policy makers and intelligence analysts bring to policy problems. Indeed, intelligence consumers and producers rarely speak the same language. Instead, they characteristically appear like "two closely related tribes that believe, mistakenly, that they speak the same language and work in the same manner for agreed outcomes. . . . Indeed, one is often reminded of George Bernard Shaw's quip about Britons and Americans being divided by a common tongue" (Lowenthal 1992).

The White House and the Pentagon are also often at cross-purposes. In the former Yugoslavia, after the Dayton peace accords in 1995, the U.S. military deployed to enforce the peace took advantage of ambiguity in the language of the agreement ("authority" rather than "responsibility") to avoid aggressive efforts to enforce the terms of the agreement. In particular, the military assiduously avoided efforts to apprehend suspected war criminals (Daalder 2000; Holbrooke 1998). Later, during the Kosovo campaign in 1999, the military—especially the Joint Chiefs of Staff—limited the air war in ways that frustrated the Clinton administration, while at the same time, the theater commander, Wesley Clark, used his control over the campaign to press for wider action than the administration preferred (Halberstam 2001; Clark 2001).

Managing Bureaucratic Intransigence

The *bureaucratic captivity* of American foreign policy is easily exaggerated. Although bureaucracies have a grip on presidential policies, presidents are not powerless to respond. There are ways to handle recalcitrant agencies and obstructionist officials. Consider Franklin D. Roosevelt, the "master" of managing federal bureaucracies. An astute politician, Roosevelt overcame policy-implementation obstacles through a divide-and-rule strategy. "Planned disorganization and confusion" aptly describes it.

> [He] deliberately organized—or disorganized—his system of command to insure that important decisions were passed on to the top. His favorite technique was to keep grants of authority incomplete, jurisdictions uncertain, charters overlapping. The result of this competitive theory of administration was often confusion and exasperation on the operating level; but no other method could so reliably insure that in a large bureaucracy, filled with ambitious

> men eager for power, the decisions, and the power to make them, would remain with the president. . . . Franklin allowed no one to discover the governing principle.
>
> *(Schlesinger 1958, 527; see also George 1980)*

In short, Roosevelt sought to control policy by denying control to those around him.

The "Kissinger solution" is an interesting, rather blunt, but highly effective strategy: punish the disobedient agency by excluding it from future decision making or circumvent it by creating a smaller, substitute unit. Removing a bureaucracy from influence—especially on issues that vitally concern it—can have considerable therapeutic value, making a hostile agency less intent on opposing presidential policy every time its own parochial interests are at stake.

The Bush administration's Defense Department used this tactic deliberately and with apparent effect. After the terrorist attacks of 9/11, Defense Secretary Rumsfeld and his deputy, Paul Wolfowitz, were determined to show a connection between Saddam Hussein and Al Qaeda—and hence to the suicide attacks on the Pentagon and WTC. The Office of Special Plans (OSP) was created within the Pentagon after 9/11 with this specific purpose in mind (and reportedly with the patronage of Vice President Cheney [Borger 2003]). By the fall of 2002, "The operation rivaled both the CIA and the Pentagon's own Defense Intelligence Agency, the DIA, as the president's main source of intelligence regarding Iraq's possible possession of weapons of mass destruction and connection with Al Qaeda" (Hersh 2003).

The "Iraqi intelligence cell" was especially aggressive. An adjunct of the OSP created in 2002 and headed by Douglas Feith, the number three man in the Defense Department, the cell was populated by people on contract to the government and hence were beyond congressional oversight. Few if any had intelligence experience (Borger 2003). Nonetheless, they were able to challenge conclusions drawn by the CIA and others that questioned what higher-level policy makers wanted to hear. Three members of the Senate Intelligence Committee commented on the cell's reaction to a CIA report titled *Iraq and Al-Qaeda: A Murky Relationship:*

> Even though the CIA's June 2002 report was "purposefully aggressive" in seeking to draw connections between Iraq and Al Qaeda, the intelligence analysis did not find the relationship sought by Pentagon policy officials. One of the individuals working for the self-named "Iraqi intelligence cell" at the Pentagon stated the June report " . . . should be read for content only—and the CIA's interpretation ought to be ignored." This criticism of the CIA's analysis was sent by Under Secretary for Policy Feith to Deputy Secretary Paul Wolfowitz and Secretary Rumsfeld.
>
> *("Additional Views of Vice Chairman John D. Rockefeller IV, Senator Carl Levin, and Senator Richard Durbin,"* Report of the U.S. Intelligence Community's Prewar Intelligence Assessment on Iraq, *July 7, 2004, p. 457)*

In another instance, the OSP briefed the president directly without the knowledge of the director of central intelligence, George Tenet.

These and other findings led the same three members of the Senate Intelligence Committee's inquiry into pre-Iraqi intelligence to conclude that the intelligence community had in fact been cowed to support the administration's line, not to challenge it. "By the time American troops had been deployed overseas and were poised to attack Iraq, the administration had skillfully manipulated and cowed the intelligence community into approving public statements that conveyed a level of conviction and certainty that was not supported by an objective reading of the underlying reporting."

The Bush administration also used a third strategy to cope with bureaucratic intransigence, a kind of variant of the Kissinger solution: *ignore* the bureaucracy. George W. Bush went to Washington determined that the Kyoto Protocol to the United Nations Framework Convention on Global Climate Change undermined American interests by threatening the U.S. economy. He and his advisers also questioned the science underlying the proposition that human activity was responsible for the upward trend in global temperatures. Bush quickly moved to reject the protocol. At the same time, however, the Environmental Protection Agency and others continued their research and reports on global climate change. When they issued a report in June 2002 to the United Nations under an existing climate change treaty that agreed with the prevailing science, namely that human activity was responsible for global climate change, the president responded simply: the report was something "put out by the bureaucracy" (Revkin 2004).

President Kennedy employed a fourth tactic: causing disturbance *within* a recalcitrant agency by skipping the normal chain of command and dealing directly with lower-echelon officials. By upsetting standard operating procedures and going through unusual channels of communication, Kennedy obtained needed information and avoided bureaucratic bottlenecks. A related Kennedy tactic was to encourage a recalcitrant official's voluntary resignation by hinting that he or she was no longer in favor. Kennedy "would plant newspaper reports that the official was planning to resign. After reading a sufficient number of these reports, the official would grasp what was happening and turn in his resignation" (Berkley 1978).

Richard Nixon practiced yet a fifth strategy, described best by his words to George Shultz when the latter was director of the Office of Management and Budget (OMB):

> You've got to get us some discipline, George. You've got to get it, and the only way you get it, is when a bureaucrat thumbs his nose, we're going to get him.
> . . . They've got to know that if they do it, something's going to happen to them, where anything can happen. I know the Civil Service pressure. But you can do a lot there. There are many unpleasant places where Civil Service people can be sent.

This punitive approach requires a stomach for vindictiveness, because dismissals, forced resignations, and demotions risk adverse publicity and are time consuming. These obstacles may explain why the common approach is to remove an obstructionist employee by giving him or her a promotion or special assignment to a prestigious sounding but meaningless position. To "squeeze" an intransigent bureaucrat from a position, the victim is "layered over" by assigning others to perform his or her duties.

President Carter practiced a sixth method by attacking causes instead of symptoms: he proposed to regain control of government by reorganizing it. "We must give top priority to a drastic and thorough revision and reorganizing of the federal bureaucracy." Reorganization attempts have been frequent and were implemented not only by Carter but also Truman, Johnson, Nixon, Reagan, Clinton, and George W. Bush. Symptomatic of the magnitude of the problem—and indicative of why solutions are so intractable—is the fact that reorganization seldom demolishes existing organizations. As noted earlier, most entrenched bureaucracies have perfected survival tactics: In the words of former Secretary of State James F. Byrnes, the "nearest thing to immortality on Earth is a government bureau."

Carter was able to revise regulations governing civil servants' employment with the Civil Service Reform Act, which put some 7,000 top bureaucrats into a Senior Executive Service, entitling them to earn bonuses for outstanding job performance but separating them from job tenure (a virtual guarantee of permanent employment). The reform permitted the chief executive and cabinet officers to reassign upper-middle management personnel and, where deemed necessary, to replace them. Similar reforms followed in the Foreign Service with the creation of Senior Foreign Service. These innovations augmented the president's managerial capabilities, but they did not guarantee agency responsiveness to presidential orders.

Like his predecessors, Ronald Reagan sought to exercise greater control over the federal bureaucracy. Reagan declared in his first inaugural speech that "Government is not the solution, it is the problem." Since then, running against Washington has become a favorite campaign theme. To achieve his objectives, Reagan sought to control the bureaucracy by infiltrating it with political operatives. To gain a

top government post, candidates were required to pass an "ideological censorship" test (Barber 1985). The number of political appointees increased by a third, from roughly 2,200 to more than 3,300 (Struck 1985). The goal was driven by the perceived need, in the words of Navy Secretary John Lehman, "to roll back the accretion of layers of centralized bureaucracy and restore a crisper accountability."

Vice President Al Gore, point man of the Clinton administration's "reinventing government" initiative launched in 1993, echoed some of Reagan's earlier sentiments. "Our problems don't come from bad workers," he noted. "Rather, we have good people trapped in bad systems." The Clinton administration thus proposed energizing the government by cutting red tape, making it more consumer oriented, eliminating unnecessary programs and consolidating others, and making government workers more productive. The administration's goal, as described by Gore (1993), was to focus "on how well [the government] performs." *Total Quality Management (TQM)* became the buzzword. Drawing on the ideas of management consultant W. Edwards Deming, the core idea was to make the government operate more like a business.[13]

The Clinton plan won high praise for its objectives but many, particularly in Congress, were skeptical of the administration's ability to achieve its lofty goals. Reagan's failure to live up to his promises may have colored their assessments. During Reagan's presidency big government got bigger, as federal spending went up, not down, and budget outlays as a percentage of the GNP rose to peacetime records. Moreover, while reductions in some agencies' personnel were implemented, overall the number of federal civilian and military employees grew.

Thus the goal of making the federal bureaucracy responsive to presidential priorities and political preferences remains as elusive as ever. Indeed, whether the federal bureaucracy can be made measurably more tractable is questionable. A key problem is that most presidents serve for only four years, a few for eight at most. It is impossible to reform a complex and recalcitrant bureaucracy so quickly. Whether the foreign affairs government's responsiveness and willingness to take direction can be increased thus also remains doubtful.

Compartmentalized Policy Making and Foreign Policy Inconsistency

Because each foreign affairs department and agency has its own definition of proper goals, the U.S. government sometimes pursues incompatible foreign policies. A former official gives a disturbing recollection of policy inconsistency that bureaucratic competition produced:

> The Agency [CIA] supported Indonesian rebels against Sukarno while State was trying to work with Sukarno. It supplied and emboldened the anticommunist Chinese guerrillas in Burma over the protests of the Burmese government and the repeated protestations of the State Department in Washington and our ambassador in Burma that we were doing no such thing. . . . [The CIA] meddled elsewhere, to the consternation of the State Department and friendly governments. In the mid-1950s, its agents intruded awkwardly in Costa Rica, the most stable and democratic country in Latin America. While the agency was trying to oust José Figueres, the moderate socialist who became the Costa Rican president in a fair election in 1953, the State Department was working with him and our ambassador was urging President Eisenhower to invite him to the United States to enhance his prestige. So it went the world around.
>
> *(Simpson 1967, 103)*

Another example is an incident that occurred during the Shah's final days in Iran, which set the stage for the taking of the American embassy and American diplomatic personnel. The American response to the unfolding drama was clouded by a quarrel between the National Security Council staff in Washington and the State Department's representatives in both Teheran and Washington. The

divergent views, and the bickering and struggle that followed, led to a tragic outcome. William Sullivan, the U.S. Ambassador to Iran, concluded that the difference in views held by the competing bureaucracies in Washington extended to the "instructions that were sent to the embassy or, more often, to the absence of any instructions whatsoever. . . . By November 1978 [National Security Adviser] Brzezinski began to make his own policy and established his own 'embassy' in Iran." According to Sullivan (1980), the White House ignored his recommendation that, upon the Shah's fall from power, the United States should not cast its fate with the successor (Bakhtiar) government because, in his view, it "was a chimera the Shah had created to permit a dignified departure, that Bakhtiar himself was quixotic and would be swept aside by the arrival of Khomeini and his supporters in Teheran." As history records, the ambassador's dire predictions proved correct even while Brzezinski's policy prevailed. Iran fell into revolution, and American diplomats became its victims.

A third example comes from the first Bush administration, when differences about what to do with, for, and about Mikhail Gorbachev generated turf battles and the pursuit of incompatible objectives. While President Bush and Secretary of State Baker spent their time attempting to convince the Soviets (and the American public) that they truly wished Gorbachev's domestic reforms and foreign policy redirection to succeed, Secretary of Defense Cheney and Vice President Quayle publicly proclaimed their reservations about Gorbachev's prospects and peaceful intentions. Meanwhile, a secret team was established in the White House to discredit Gorbachev's credibility. Because the professed goal of "ending the Cold War" was not endorsed by all of the administration's factions, initiatives to end that conflict appeared timid, tardy, and inconsistent (see Beschloss and Talbott 1993).

Recent American policy toward Mexico also illustrates the problem. With an immense range of different agencies involved in various aspects of policy (more than forty on drug policy alone), some in several different strands, struggle and inconsistency are virtually unavoidable. As Wiarda (2000) argues, "We do not have a single U.S. foreign policy in

Bureaucratic Consensus-Seeking (groupthink at the extreme)		Bureaucratic Confrontation (warfare at the extreme)
	Indicators	
Limited	Number of Actors	High
Aligned	Positioning of Interests	Opposed
Closed Arena	Contingent Power Structure	Open Network
Collegial	Interaction by "pulling and hauling"	Competitive
Quick	Compromise Formation	Slow
Low	Implementation Slippage	High

F I G U R E 13.1 The Continuum of Bureaucratic Politics

SOURCE: Adapted from Thomas Preston and Paul 't Hart, "Understanding and Evaluating Bureaucratic Politics: The Nexus Between Political Leaders and Advisory Systems." *Political Psychology,* 20 (Spring 1999): 49–98.

Mexico; instead we have approximately sixty-seven policies—one or several policies for each of the U.S. agencies operating there.... [T]he bureaucratic politics of U.S.-Mexican relations has now become so complex, so multilayered, so conflicting, that it hamstrings, frustrates, and often paralyzes policy and makes it virtually impossible for the United States to carry out a successful foreign policy there."

Bureaucratic Pluralism and Foreign Policy Conflict and Compromise

Bureaucratic pressures diminish presidents' ability to assert control and lead. Rather than selecting policies from alternative recommendations and turning to the bureaucracy to implement them, presidents often choose among agreed-on bureaucratic solutions and then seek to mobilize their action on the decisions reached.

That image does not conform to the popular view of presidents determining policy goals through rational processes. However, most if not all presidential decisions are affected by the options that bureaucracies offer. Hence, policy determination is more realistically pictured as a product of bargaining through an accommodative and sometimes conflictual political process. Policy results from competition, compromise, and even conflict, not necessarily the president's priorities. Presidents, rather than deciding, act as "power brokers" who resolve their competing agencies' conflicting demands.

Seen in this way, the nation's chief executive is an arbitrator of interagency disputes, and policy making entails settling jurisdictional struggles. In many ways, the captive president's role is primarily to govern by managing his own bureaucracy. "The president is beset with too many often conflicting opinions," James Baker observed in 1987 while serving as Reagan's chief of staff. "He spends an inordinate time resolving differences among his advisers who are there because their existence has been legislated." More recently, George W. Bush found it necessary to manage disputes during his first term between Colin Powell, on the one hand, and Dick Cheney and Donald Rumsfeld, on the other. Thus, how to get bureau chiefs, assistant secretaries, and agency heads to do what is needed and prevent their rebellion dominates presidents' attention. "Somehow a president must try to make a ministry out of what is at best a coalition" (Lowi 1967).

As portrayed in Figure 13.1, the result of this organizational setting is a continuum of policy-making possibilities that ranges from the *consensus-seeking* characteristics of smaller groups, which sometimes exhibit groupthink, to the *bureaucratic confrontation* characteristic of the bureaucratic rivalries we have highlighted. As the figure suggests, movement along the continuum may be conditioned by any of several factors, including the number of actors involved, the positioning of interests, the contingent power structure, the nature of the "pulling and hauling" that occurs, and others.

Presidents must grapple with the forces that pull in either of these directions to avoid the extreme versions of groupthink and turf wars at either end of the continuum.

When viewed from the perspective of the role any president must play, the reasons for compromise, incrementalism, and caution in policy making become apparent. The president is surrounded on a daily basis by advisers, including members of the cabinet, who so interpret their jobs as to make maximum claims on their agencies' behalf. Having heard from one supplicant the extreme of one side of a policy dispute, and then the other extreme from another, the president must forge the terms of settlement.

Permitting foes to save face is also an important part of this game. Because policy making involves constant struggle, with much give and take, "the profusion of so many centers of power makes building the kind of consensus necessary for positive action a formidable task" (Hilsman 1990). Ironically, then, American foreign policy's resistance to adaptive change may flow not from the concentration of power but from its diffusion. The jumble of policy-making centers and increases in their number decrease presidents' capacity to take visionary initiatives. Because policy directions are set through long-established intra- and interagency bargains that reflect an established distribution of influence, policy disruptions are unlikely unless the distribution of influence itself is changed. Perhaps it was this kind of environment that stimulated Dean Acheson's memorable remark that a secretary of state's most essential quality is "the killer instinct."

It is important, however, to remember that the president is not simply another actor in the process (Krasner 1972). When presidents assert themselves, they can prevail. Indeed, the evidence suggests that attentive and engaged presidents are capable of overcoming the most damaging aspects of bureaucratic politics. As Goldgeier (1999) has argued, "If the question is whether policy outcomes inside the executive branch reflect presidential dominance over the foreign policy apparatus or the pulling and hauling of bureaucratic interests, the answer is: when the president gets involved he wins (unless the bureaucracy can get outside actors, for example Congress, to constrain him)."

Other Effects of Bureaucratic Decision Making

The preceding discussion has identified some of the basic characteristics and consequences of bureaucratic policy-making behavior, but still others are discernible and deserve note.

Ad Hoc Decision Making   Preoccupied with each day's immediate crisis, leaders rarely think long-term. Often, they confront only issues that have reached crisis proportions. Rather than choices being made in light of carefully considered national goals and long-term planning, trial-and-error responses to policy problems as they surface seem more characteristic.

Decision Avoidance   Presidents are expected to be decisive—an image they willingly cultivate. Harry Truman (1966) put it this way: "The greatest part of the president's job is to make decisions—big ones and small ones. . . . The president—whoever he is—has to decide. He can't pass the buck to anybody. No one else can do the deciding for him. That's his job." Unfortunately, few presidents adhere to Truman's advice. Many, quite proficient at passing the buck, manage not to decide. "Presidents are, in the eyes of bureaucrats, notorious for putting off decisions or changing their minds. They have enough decisions to make without looking for additional ones. In many cases, all the options look bad and they prefer to wait" (Gelb and Halperin 1973).

Risky-Shift Phenomenon   People deciding in groups are reluctant to appear overly cautious or, worse, fearful. Hence they act differently together than they would alone. For psychological reasons, they reach shift-to-risk decisions under peer group pressure. Thus, it has been argued, groups are usually dominated by their most reckless (and neurotic) member. People will sacrifice themselves for and take chances on behalf of others that they would not normally take when acting for themselves alone.

When decision responsibilities are shared, risky alternatives are more likely because no member of the group making the risky decision can be held personally responsible for proposing a policy that produces failure. "Madness," Friedrich Nietzsche argued, "is the exception in individuals but the rule in groups."

Unmanaged Policy Initiatives If policy making is determined at the implementation stage and not at the declaratory stage (when the president or his staff proclaims the policy), then what bureaucrats actually do defines the real policy. In a sense, every bureaucrat has the opportunity to be a policy maker. "In the intricate sticky webs of paperwork, the principle of accountability flutters and expires. Responsibility gets diffused; finally it disappears. Everyone is responsible; therefore no one is responsible. It is 'the system'" (Kilpatrick 1985).

An interesting example occurred during the run-up to war in the Pacific between the United States and Japan. The United States used an oil embargo against Japan, a resource on which Japan was critically dependent, to curtail its territorial and imperial ambitions in China and elsewhere. As tensions mounted following the Tripartite Pact linking Japan with the fascist states in Europe (Germany and Italy), the United States froze Japanese assets in the United States. The new economic policy required Japan to get export licenses on a case-by-case basis before it could buy more oil, effectively further tightening the embargo noose but not completely eliminating further sales. Assistant Secretary of State Dean Acheson was put in charge of the program. Apparently on his own initiative, Acheson used the new economic policy to stop the flow of oil to Japan altogether.

> Japan received no oil after its assets were frozen in late July. FDR [President Roosevelt] did not realize this until early September. The Japanese of course did, and this set in the panic that Japan had a very limited time before the navy would run out of oil, thereby putting it in the position of either negotiating [with the United States] or attacking [it]. A hard-line

> American bureaucrat in the right place at the right time was able to force the issue.
> *(Vasquez and Gibler 2001, 33)*

A more recent illustration comes from the covert actions of Lt. Colonel Oliver North in the infamous Iran-Contra affair. A gung-ho underling with a desire to pursue Cold War confrontation by any means necessary, North "seized upon the 'neat idea'" of making clandestine arms sales to what Secretary of State George Shultz had termed a terrorist regime (the anti-American government of Iran) and using the profits to support the contras, opponents of the leftist Sandinista government in Nicaragua. Moving under cover, North set up an illegal plan to divert secret funds from the arms sales in order to provide the contras with clandestine military support. In essence, his operation established a secret government or government within a government to conduct a secret war. This "junta" believed it had been forced to manipulate the real U.S. government to get what it wanted because it could not secure public approval or congressional authorization for its action (Draper 1990).

In the end, the carefully crafted plan backfired at the same time that it jeopardized basic democratic principles. Convicted of lying to Congress (even though he claimed to have received the tacit approval of President Reagan), North was given a light sentence by presiding judge Gerhard A. Gesell, who, in pronouncing the sentence "reiterated the jurors' view that North was not a leader but a 'low-ranking subordinate' who presumably was not entirely responsible for what he did" (Fitzgerald 1989). North's conviction was later set aside by a U.S. Appeals Court.

ROLES AND THE PROCESS OF DECISION MAKING: CREDITS AND DEBITS

The impact of role-induced bureaucratic behavior on foreign policy making is seriously at odds with the rational actor model. Although the texts we are likely to read in a high school civics course make historical policy decisions sound reasonable, the memoirs of past participants in the decision-making process—including presidents—and an objective treatment of the diplomatic record leave quite a different impression. To contemporary eyewitnesses and to others who have later probed the record of events, those happenings often did not look orderly or rational. At times they appear more like scenes from the theater of the absurd. To some, the American foreign policy-making process contributes to its recurrent failures (Etheredge 1985); to others, it makes the United States its "own worst enemy" (Destler, Gelb, and Lake 1984).

Still, we must be careful not to overstate or misrepresent the impact of large-scale organizations on American foreign policy making. "Bureaucrat" need not be a dirty word. (If a bureaucrat is anyone who works for a publicly funded organization at the federal, state, or local level, their numbers are very large indeed!) The negative side of the ledger must be balanced by the clear advantages of modern bureaucracy. In fact, the conduct of American foreign policy would not be possible without a modern bureaucracy and the kind of organizational support capable career professionals alone can provide. Though deficient in many respects, bureaucratic government is nonetheless indispensable to a great power's practices.

It is not the enormous size of the government alone that makes officials appear to be continually tripping over each other (although that is part of the problem); nor is the propensity for the policy-making system to stumble and blunder due merely to self-serving people (although they contribute to the problem as well). The formidable challenges posed by today's complex, globalizing world make bureaucratic government necessary even as they make it look unresponsive to a changing environment. "Inveighing against big government," observes syndicated columnist George Will, "ignores the fact that government, though big, is often too weak." The solution, therefore, is not to do away with bureaucratic government, but to run it efficiently and shape its power to national purposes. For that, vigorous leadership is required.

In the final analysis, then, bringing out the best that the foreign affairs government has to offer—and preventing the worst that it can produce—rests with the president and his principal advisers. But can they make a difference? Or was the eminent sociologist Max Weber correct when he argued, "In a modern state the actual ruler is necessarily and unavoidably the bureaucracy"? To address that question, we must examine the fifth and final source of American foreign policy: individual leaders.

KEY TERMS

ad hoc decision making	instrumental rationality	rational decision-	standard operating
administrative theory	Miles's Law	making model	procedures
bureaucratic politics	organizational	risky-shift	unitary actor
model	subculture	phenomenon	unmanaged policy
decision avoidance	parochialism	role theory	initiatives
groupthink	procedural rationality	satisficing	

SUGGESTED READINGS

Allison, Graham T., and Philip Zelikow. *Essence of Decision: Explaining the Cuban Missile Crisis.* Boston: Little, Brown, 1999.

Clarke, Richard A. *Against All Enemies: Inside America's War on Terror.* New York: Free Press, 2004.

Daadler, Ivo H. *Getting to Dayton: The Making of America's Bosnia Policy.* Washington, DC: Brookings Institution, 2000.

Garrison, Jean. *Games Advisors Play: Foreign Policy in the Nixon and Carter Administrations.* College Station, TX: Texas A&M University Press, 1999.

Janis, Irving L. *Groupthink: Psychological Studies of Policy Decisions and Fiascoes.* Boston: Houghton Mifflin, 1982.

Khong, Yuen Foong. *Analogies at War: Korea, Munich, Dien Bien Phu, and the Vietnam Decisions of 1965.* Princeton, NJ: Princeton University Press, 1992.

Preston, Thomas. *The President and His Inner Circle: Leadership Style and the Advisory Process in Foreign Policy Making.* New York: Columbia University Press, 2001.

't Hart, Paul, Eric Stern, and Bengt Sundelius, eds. *Beyond Groupthink: Political Group Dynamics and Foreign Policy-Making.* Ann Arbor, MI: University of Michigan Press, 1997.

Woodward, Bob. *Plan of Attack.* New York: Simon & Schuster, 2004.

NOTES

1. For discussion and analysis of the decision-making on *assertive multilateralism* and the former Yugoslavia, see Sterling-Folker (1998) and Daalder (1994).

2. On *Miles's Law,* see Neustadt and May (1986) and Allison and Zelikow (1999).

3. An interesting exchange on the relative importance of roles, role conflicts, ideas, and interests focused on the preferences and policy behavior of the chief of naval operations may be found in Rhodes (1994) and Mitchell (1999).

4. We are indebted to Scott Crichlow for these points.

5. For studies of the Cuban Missile Crisis, see Allison and Zelikow (1999); Blight (1990); Blight, Nye, and Welch (1987); Blight and Welch (1989); Brugioni (1993); Hilsman (1996); May and Zelikow (1997); and Nathan (1993).

6. This may not be entirely illogical. Anthony Downs (1957) suggests that the rational voter cannot afford to gather all the information available about all candidates prior to deciding for whom to vote: The costs involved are too high for the resultant payoff. Instead, voters base decisions on partial information such as the candidate's party label. Similar logic about the costs of acquiring information apply to a wide array of decision situations.

7. The literature on the bureaucratic political model is extensive. For a useful overview, see Stern and Verbeek (1998). For classic treatments, see Allison (1971); Allison and Halperin (1972); and Allison

and Zelikow (1999). For critiques, see Art (1973); Bendor and Hammond (1992); Caldwell (1977); Krasner (1972); Rhodes (1994); and Welch (1992).

8. Some organization theorists note that *new* units within administrative agencies (for example, the State Department's Bureau of Human Rights in the Carter administration) recruit ideologues and risk takers, whereas old ones recruit cautious, security-conscious personnel who are more likely to protect their stakes in the status quo than to express their policy preferences and push reforms. See also Drezner (2000) on the clash between newer, ideas-based agencies and older, entrenched bureaucracies.

9. More recent formulations of the *groupthink* model include 't Hart (1990), 't Hart, Stern and Sundelius (1997), and Preston and 't Hart (1999).

10. The lessons of the 1930s also led policy makers to conclusions about the appropriateness of interventionist and noninterventionist trade policy regarding manufactured and agricultural goods (Goldstein 1989). The result, as we noted in Chapter 7, is that international trade in the industrial and agricultural sectors developed quite differently.

11. Rumsfeld was also successful in canceling the army's program for a new cannon, called the Crusader mobile artillery system. See Jones (Jones 2005b) for an analysis of the reasons for Rumsfeld's success compared with then-Defense Secretary Cheney's inability during the first Bush

administration to eliminate the controversial V-22 Osprey weapon system.

12. The Turkish missiles have long figured prominently in the Cuban missile story. Kennedy was believed to have been intransigent on the issue of trading U.S. missiles in Turkey for Soviet missiles in Cuba, but a transcript of a crucial meeting of the ExComm declassified twenty-five years after the event reveals that Kennedy was more willing to compromise on the U.S. missiles issue than previously thought. He apparently worried about how he could justify going to nuclear war over missiles his own advisers considered obsolete (Bundy and Blight 1987–1988; see also May and Zelikow 1997).

13. Deming's is "the philosophy of nonhierarchical management style, employee 'empowerment,' and customer satisfaction. . . . The problem with this 'entrepreneurial' model of government, its critics say, is that government is not and should not function like a business. Businesses respond to the bottom line; government is supposed to respond to laws written in the public interest" (Carney 1994). The effort to make government behave more like the private sector actually began during the first Bush administration. Richard G. Darman, Bush's director of OMB, was a primary catalyst behind the 1990 Chief Financial Officers Act, designed to improve government agencies' financial management. For a critical review of TQM as applied to government, see Wieseltier (1993).

PART VII

Individuals as Sources
of American Foreign Policy

14

Leader Characteristics and Foreign Policy Performance

*If I have learned anything in a lifetime in politics and government,
it is the truth of the famous phrase, "History is biography"—that
decisions are made by people, and they make them based on what they
know of the world and how they understand it.*
VICE PRESIDENT GEORGE H. W. BUSH, 1987

*One of the most unsettling things for foreigners is the impression
that our foreign policy can be changed by any new president
on the basis of the president's personal preference.*
HENRY KISSINGER, FORMER SECRETARY OF STATE 1979

Picture a president sitting alone in the Oval Office, wrestling with a crisis that threatens the lives of thousands of Americans and non–Americans. Assume that this particular president is impulsively competitive, is prone to take risks to attract attention and to exploit opportunities, views the world as a jungle in which one must perpetually claw and scratch for power, is contemptuous of his adversaries, and has a quick temper. Assume also that the president is driven by a fear of failure stemming from low self-esteem, a fear overcome in the past by dramatic and successful actions that restored his self-confidence. How is such a president likely to respond to the crisis he faces? Will he calculate rationally, considering only the interests of the United States? Or will his response be driven by his background, his beliefs, and his personality traits?

Properly speaking, states are incapable of acting or thinking. In reality, foreign policy decisions are made by remarkably few people acting on behalf of states, most conspicuously the president and the president's inner circle of advisers. "The management of foreign affairs," Thomas Jefferson maintained, is "executive altogether." Harry Truman concurred, exclaiming, "I make American foreign policy." For these reasons, the personal characteristics of those empowered to make decisions on behalf of the state are crucial.

In this chapter, we examine individuals as a source of American foreign policy. We look at the people who occupy the decision-making roles at the highest echelons of government, particularly presidents, and explore whether and how their personal aspirations, anxieties, convictions, memories, and experiences influence American foreign policy.

INDIVIDUALS AS A SOURCE OF FOREIGN POLICY

Because of the president's power and preeminence, it is tempting to think of foreign policy as determined exclusively by presidential preferences and to personalize government by identifying a policy with its proponents. Ralph Waldo Emerson's aphorism, "There is properly no history, only biography," dramatizes the popular impression that individual leaders are the makers and movers of history. This *hero-in-history model*[1] of foreign policy making finds expression in the practice of routinely attributing foreign affairs successes and failures to the administration in which they occurred, not to mention attaching the names of presidents to the policies they promulgate (for example, the Bush Doctrine, the Kennedy Round). The conviction that the individual who holds office makes a difference is also one of the major premises underlying the democratic electoral system, as new administrations seek to distinguish themselves from their predecessors and those reelected to affirm their "mandates." Hence leadership and policy are portrayed as synonymous, and changes in policy and policy direction are often perceived as results of the predispositions of the leadership.

A consideration of the idiosyncratic characteristics of individuals draws attention to the psychological foundations of human conduct. Perceptions, personal needs, and drives are all important determinants of the way people act. Correspondingly, decision makers' inner traits influence how they respond to various situations. The cognitions and responses of decision makers are determined not by "the 'objective' facts of the situation...but [by]

their 'image' of the situation;" that is, they "act according to the way the world appears...not necessarily according to the way it 'is'" (Boulding 1959). That principle correctly suggests that images shape foreign policy behavior.

Perceptions are not simple reflections of what is passively observed. Instead, they are influenced by the memories, values, needs, and beliefs the observer brings to the situation (see Falkowski 1979; Jonsson 1982; Vertzberger 1990). Everyone's perceptions are biased by personality predispositions and inner drives, as well as by prior experiences and future expectations. What occurs in decision makers' heads (their cognitions) is therefore important.

As we shift attention from the way issues are debated to the debaters themselves, we must ask if contrasts among decision makers make a difference in policy—in content as well as in style. Do the particular personal qualities of the people holding policy positions determine the course a state charts for itself in foreign affairs? Or would others holding those positions during the same period have acted similarly? Do changes in leadership stimulate changes in foreign policy? If so, in what ways, and under what conditions? We now turn to these intriguing questions.

INDIVIDUALS AND FOREIGN POLICY PERFORMANCE

No two individuals are identical; each person differs in some way from every other. This personal diversity is exhibited by the major figures in post–World War II American foreign policy. Compare "give 'em hell" Harry Truman, charismatic Jack Kennedy, "Tricky Dick" Nixon, Hollywood "Dutch" Reagan, and "Slick Willie" Clinton. Apparent differences in policy elites' personalities may nevertheless mask important similarities. The relevant question, therefore, is not how different are the individuals, but, instead, what impact do leaders' peculiar traits have on their decision-making behavior.

Although it is difficult to generalize, it is easy to demonstrate that policy makers' personal characteristics influence their behavior, as in-depth case studies of particular decision-makers abound.[2] Many probe the life history of policy makers to describe their psychological makeup and world view. These *psychobiographies* invariably assume that leaders' personalities are determined by their early childhood experiences, their relationships with parents and peers, their self-concept, and the like. These background factors are presumed to mold the leaders' personalities and beliefs and their later decision-making styles and policy-making behavior. The following brief synopses of Presidents Wilson and Kennedy and Secretary of State Henry Kissinger are illustrative.

Psychobiography: Personal Characteristics and Foreign Policy Behavior

Woodrow Wilson   Wilson grew up in a stern and often punitive childhood environment. The psychological effects proved consequential. Unable to please his rigid father as a child, this created an all-consuming need in later life to attain self-esteem. As president, Wilson compulsively strove to perform great deeds to compensate for his fear of rejection. Most notable was his intense battle to create the League of Nations, a passion explained by Wilson's overriding need to attain a puritanical "state of grace" (George and George 1964). Ironically, then, Wilson's unmet psychological needs, which also contributed to his "active-negative" presidential character (see below), led to the failure of what he wanted most—acceptance of his idealistic foreign policy initiatives.

John F. Kennedy   The possible relationship between a leader's psychological profile and his or her policy behavior is suggested by the ways President Kennedy's personality may have been instrumental in the decisions he made during the Cold War crises he faced. According to one (controversial) interpretation (Mongar 1974), Kennedy suffered most of his life from a neurotic conflict between an

overpowering fear of failure, on one hand, and an overwhelming need for assistance, on the other. The first stemmed from his inability to compete successfully with his older brother. Joe Kennedy, Jr., was introduced by his father to friends as a future president of the United States, and his mother held him up as a model for the other children, especially Jack, giving him a free hand in disciplining them. In that atmosphere, it became impossible for Jack to gain recognition and affection from his parents, which undermined the younger Kennedy's self-assurance. A succession of childhood illnesses permitted him to avoid fruitless competition, and he resorted to "the manipulation of fantasy to protect his [preferred self-] image of greatness." Thus self-deception served as a defense mechanism to protect him from his fears of weakness.

Maturity helped young Jack Kennedy strengthen his self-image. As his personality took shape, Kennedy still needed to prove his personal worth. His search for adventure, and his restlessness, intellectualism, and acceptance of difficult tasks reflected this abiding compulsion. To protect his preferred self-image, he habitually disarmed criticism "by modestly calling attention to minor shortcomings. This witty self-derision, which reflected a merciless introspection, undermined criticism early and simultaneously elicited reassurance and support from other people." Political problems, even foreign policy crises, became "games," opportunities to recover self-esteem. Kennedy's major decisions, Mongar argues, were shaped by his personal motives.

Is Kennedy's situation unique, or do emotional and personality needs strongly influence other policy makers' responses to foreign policy situations? Consider the case of Henry Kissinger, a decision maker whose extraordinary childhood deviated markedly from the typical route to power.

Henry A. Kissinger   Henry Kissinger's path to influence over U.S. foreign affairs (including stints as national security adviser for Nixon and secretary of state for Presidents Nixon and Ford) was both a difficult and distinct one that helped mold Kissinger into one of the more interesting and noteworthy figures in the recent history of U.S. foreign policy.

Born in 1923 into a Jewish family in Germany, Kissinger encountered the true face of hatred and fear growing up as a teenager in a developing Nazi Germany. Kissinger and his family escaped from Nazi persecution in 1938 and began living in New York City. Life was not easy for the young Jewish immigrant, as Kissinger worked all day while studying at night in high school, giving an early indication of the work ethic that would help propel and distinguish Kissinger's career.

In 1943, while attending City College in New York, Kissinger was drafted into the army, where he became a German interpreter. Following his military service, Kissinger attended college at Harvard, where he excelled in his studies (and where he wrote an undergraduate thesis that was over 300 pages in length!), receiving his B.A., M.A., and Ph.D., before becoming a Harvard professor in 1954. After being chosen by Nixon, Kissinger became the first Jewish secretary of state. Kissinger arguably relied on ideas developed during his difficult early experiences to deal with analogous personal and national problems later in life (Isaak 1975). Personally insecure, yet egocentric, Kissinger felt that uncertainty was the very essence of international politics. As a policy maker, he consistently acted on two basic beliefs: first, that people are limited in what they can do, and second, that because of the complexity of life, many imponderables make history move. Ironically, the principle of uncertainty that supported his pessimistic world view may also have been the source of his successes, for Kissinger's achievements may be attributed in part to his ability to use ambiguity, negotiate compromise, and secrecy—as well as public relations strategies ingeniously devised to enhance his image in his conduct of diplomacy (Walker 1997; Caldwell 1983). Kissinger's embrace of political realism as a theory of international politics also was shaped by his unusual past. *Realpolitik* stresses the expectation of conflict between states, not collaboration, the need to increase power relative to one's adversaries, the inadequacy of moral precepts as a guide to foreign affairs, and distrust of others' motives. Each of these finds a counterpart in the "lessons" Kissinger derived from his personal experiences during

the crucial formative period of his political awakening in Germany. It seems, then, that Kissinger's disdain of moralism and his corresponding preference to ask not "What is right, and what is wrong?" but "Who is strong, and who is weak?" was rooted in his uncertain, insecure youth.

These brief synopses of Wilson, Kennedy, and Kissinger illustrate the varied personalities of those who have risen to positions of power in the American foreign policy establishment and the impact of their needs, background, and prior experiences on their later outlook and policy-making behavior. We can explore these ideas further by looking specifically at the relationship between presidential character and presidential performance. Here James David Barber's analysis of presidents' personal traits and leadership styles is particularly informative.[3]

Presidential Character:
Types and Consequences

According to Barber, presidents can be understood best by observing their *style* (habitual ways of performing political roles), *world view* (politically relevant beliefs), and especially *character*—"the way the President orients himself toward life—not for the moment, but enduringly" (Barber 1992). "Character," others argue, "reflects a person's basic and habitual ways of relating to circumstances."

> Individuals with substantial levels of ambition and the [necessary] talent, along with the focused persistence to reach the top, are more likely to be successful. And, having achieved success *because* of their past behavior, they are more likely to persist in patterns they have developed.
> *(Renshon 2003, 128, 129; see also Renshon 2004)*

In Barber's formulation, two dimensions of **presidential character** are critical: the energy presidents put into the job (active or passive) and their personal satisfaction with their presidential duties (negative or positive). The first captures presidents' images of their job description. Active presidents are movers and shakers, energetically engaged in the challenge of leading, eagerly attentive to the responsibilities of office, and willing to accept the task of policy formulation and management. Conversely, passive presidents prefer to steer an even course, maintaining existing arrangements and avoiding the conflict that invariably accompanies changes in policy.

The second dimension reflects presidents' levels of contentment with their job. This varies because some presidents have not enjoyed the position they achieved and have looked with disfavor on the burden of awesome responsibility. Such negative types, Barber notes, tend to have had childhood experiences that make them dutifully accept but not enjoy the demands that go with holding power.

These two dimensions of presidential character create four categories: passive-negative, passive-positive, active-negative, and active-positive. Barber distinguishes among the four this way: "*Active-positive* presidents want most to achieve results. *Active-negatives* aim to get and keep power. *Passive-positives* are after love. *Passive-negatives* emphasize their civic virtue. The relation of activity to enjoyment in a president thus tends to outline a cluster of characteristics, to set apart the adapted from the compulsive, compliant, and withdrawn types."

Not surprisingly, Barber contends that presidents with active-positive characters are best equipped to direct the nation's foreign policy and to meet its challenges and crises. Active-positives are self-respecting and happy, open to new ideas, and able to learn from their mistakes. Their energies are no longer consumed with conquering the developmental traumas associated with youth but instead are directed outward toward achievement. As policy makers, therefore, active-positives have a greater capacity for growth and flexibility. Figure 14.1 identifies active-positive presidents as well as the other types comprising Barber's typology.

Barber's research shows that the behavior of leaders with similar skills and values can be quite different, depending on their character. A leader's inner self, and especially his or her degree of self-confidence and self-esteem, critically affect

performance and influence decision makers' careers and conduct.

Let us consider some vignettes from Barber's work[4] and then, emulating his methodology, extrapolate from it to assess the character of the nation's forty-second and forty-third presidents, William Jefferson Clinton and George Walker Bush. We will find that those with sufficient ambition and skill to make it to the top do not always succeed, that childhood and developmental experiences, including habitual ways of relating to the environment, can result in failure as well as success.

Woodrow Wilson   As we noted earlier, Woodrow Wilson was an active-negative president who proved incapable of compromising with Senate irreconcilables and others disposed against the League of Nations. "'Accept or reject'—that was the way Wilson posed the question." In the end his "narrow insistence on a failing course of action" cost him what he cherished so deeply.

Warren G. Harding   A passive-positive, Harding longed to be America's "best loved" president, but history remembers him as perhaps "'the worst President,' the zero point for all scales of 'presidential greatness.'" He came to power at the end of the first

PERSONAL SATISFACTION

Energy	Personal Satisfaction	
	Positive	Negative
Active	Franklin Roosevelt Harry Truman John Kennedy Gerald Ford Jimmy Carter George H.W. Bush Bill Clinton George W. Bush	Woodrow Wilson Herbert Hoover Lyndon Johnson Richard Nixon
Passive	William Taft Warren Harding Ronald Reagan	Calvin Coolidge Dwight Eisenhower

F I G U R E 14.1 Barber's Classification of Twentieth Century Presidents by Their Character Type epic struggle of the twentieth century and set aside the national debate on the League of Nations in favor of a "return to normalcy" (read, "isolationism") and then initiated the Washington Conference on Naval Disarmament and related agreements designed to secure peace in the Pacific. But "his early success was based on illusions—illusions that helped to produce the debacle of the 1930s" (Wolfowitz 1994).

Harry S. Truman   An active-positive president, Harry Truman took "massive initiatives at a time when such initiatives seemed unlikely, given the circumstances of his accession to office, his own qualifications, and the condition of the country." Why? Many of Truman's bold foreign policy actions—the Truman Doctrine, the Marshall Plan, NATO, and the Korean intervention—arguably stemmed from Truman's decisive personality.

Dwight D. Eisenhower   Although Barber submits that Eisenhower is difficult to categorize, he concludes Ike was a passive-negative. Eisenhower "did not feel a duty to save the world or become a great hero, but simply to contribute what he could the best he was able." This was the passive side of his character. The negative side, observes Barber, was reflected in his feelings that he was imposed on by an unnecessarily heavy schedule. Indeed, Eisenhower claimed his heart attack in September 1955 was triggered "when he was repeatedly interrupted on the golf links by unnecessary phone calls from the State Department."

Lyndon B. Johnson   Barber concludes that Johnson was, like Wilson, an active-negative president. The "fantastic pace of action in his presidency," motivated by humanitarian concerns and a commitment to the pursuit of happiness and creating a better world, revealed the activism in Johnson's character. The "tough, hard, militaristic" posture he assumed toward his enemies evinced his negativism. A 1952 statement while a member of the Senate, in which he declared that he was "prepared to reduce Moscow to rubble to stop communist aggression anywhere," revealed that side of his character.

Richard M. Nixon   Another active-negative president, Richard Nixon is a revealing contrast with Truman and Kennedy. According to Barber, Nixon's decision to widen the Vietnam War by invading Cambodia in the spring of 1970 was symptomatic of this character: "To see in President Nixon the character of Richard Nixon—the character formed and set early in his life—one need only read over his speech on the Cambodian invasion, with its themes of power and control, its declaration of independence, its self-concern, its damning of doubters, and its coupling of humiliation with defeat" (Barber 1977). Nixon reached this critical decision without urging from his advisers, and the manner in which the president announced his decision "flabbergasted" his defense secretary, Melvin Laird. Extreme personal isolation ultimately destroyed the Nixon presidency.

Gerald R. Ford   Entering office in the wake of the Watergate scandal and Nixon's resignation, Barber notes that Ford exceeded the low expectations many held for his presidency and showed a capacity to grow and learn. Although "a step-by-step thinker," Ford approached the task of policy making with the positive attitude and activism characteristic of active-positives: "Just as all the props were collapsing in Vietnam, he unrealistically called for hundreds of millions more in military aid. He turned foreign policy over to a wizard of dramatic negotiation [Henry Kissinger] whose ad hoc successes obscured deepening world chaos, and he stood as firm and fast as he could against all sorts of 'wild' schemes to spend the country out of recession, countering them with some tame schemes of his own."

Jimmy Carter   Noting that Carter came to Washington full of high expectations at a time of low hopes, Barber predicted that the energetic, "up and at 'em" active-positive Carter would enjoy life in the Oval Office and would find that it could be fun. Barber also warned, however, that Carter's troubles would spring "from an excess of an active-positive virtue: the thirst for results." His prediction proved accurate. Carter's character eventually led him impatiently to pursue too many goals simultaneously—a penchant that lent credibility to the frequent charges that he was inconsistent and indecisive, that he lacked a clear sense of priorities, and that he abandoned policy objectives almost as soon as they were announced in favor of still newer objectives, which then also were shelved.

Ronald Reagan   Reagan's personality and ideology reveal inconsistent traits, but his "take it easy" style and optimism made Reagan a passive-positive: "the receptive, compliant, other-directed character whose life is a search for affection as a reward for being agreeable and cooperative rather than personally assertive." Several facets of his passive-positive orientation stand out. First, Reagan's aides described him even during crisis situations "as 'uninvolved in the planning process,' 'secluded,' and 'disconcertedly disengaged'" (McElvaine 1984). As one scholar of the presidency recently observed, Reagan "was more dependent than any other modern president on others to accomplish his aims. As a result, the policies of Reagan's presidency were to a large extent a function of the shifting cast of aides who served him" (Greenstein 2000). Moreover, Reagan adhered to a simple "black and white" outlook and was uninterested in facts and unaffected by them (see Dallek 1984; Glad 1983). Finally, Reagan's thirty years of show business, following scripts written and directed by others, instilled a theatrical style in his performance. As he once revealingly commented, "Politics is just like show business. You have a hell of an opening, coast for a while, and then have a hell of a close."

George H. W. Bush   Coming to office with a wealth of experience as a public servant—member of Congress, chair of the Republican National Committee, director of the CIA, envoy to China, ambassador to the United Nations, and vice president—George Herbert Walker Bush was an active-positive president. Noting that "Mr. Bush wants a mission...[and] sees himself as enlivened and inspired," Barber also worried, however, that "The basic question about Bush...is not character, but world view. What is his vision?" Many others asked the same question.

Bush himself disparaged "the vision thing," but it dogged his entire presidency. His preference for prudence and pragmatism seemed often to lead to a cautious—indeed, timid—response to the dramatic developments in Europe and the Soviet Union leading to the end of the Cold War.[5] However, Bush's active, hands-on style and character—neatly summed up in his own claim to have the responsibility "to conduct the foreign policy of this country in the way I see fit"—was illustrated in his leadership and style during the Persian Gulf War. Drawing on his extensive contacts with and courtship of world leaders, Bush personally engineered the coalition that fought the 1991 war against Iraq, reflecting a long-standing preference for personal politics (Mullins and Wildavsky 1992). At home, his preference for a small, inner circle of advisers chosen on the basis of personal ties and loyalty rather than expertise or independent thinking promoted secrecy that helped to conceal the president's thinking from Congress and the public. This style not only preserved the administration's flexibility, but also enhanced Bush's decision-making freedom.[6]

Bill Clinton   On Bill Clinton's first inauguration, Barber wrote that "William Jefferson Clinton is politically active-positive, has strong political skills, and keeps working for what he believes is best" (*The News and Observer,* [Raleigh, NC] 17 January 1993, 10). Educated at Georgetown, Oxford, and Yale Universities, Clinton returned to Arkansas, where he lost a bid for Congress in 1974 but won the attorney general's office two years later. Five terms as governor followed, during which he garnered a reputation for active efforts in political leadership.

As president, in many ways Clinton was an ideal illustration of the active-positive character. His interest in politics and policy was unique among modern presidents, and his energy, enthusiasm, intelligence, and confidence dominated his public career.[7] A self-described "policy wonk," Clinton thoroughly relished a hands-on role in the political and policy process (see, for example, Drew 1994). Furthermore, his philosophy of government stressed activism, if by moderate means. His goal, as he told one of his chief speechwriters in 1998, was "to save government from its own excesses so it can again be a progressive force" (quoted in Weisberg 1999; see also Purdum 1996). Additionally, Clinton had a genuine enthusiasm for the political aspects of the presidency, thriving on the campaigning style adopted by his White House and relishing opportunities for personal contact with advisers, other policy makers, and the public. Intellectually, Clinton also seemed to savor debate and discussion of the ideas underlying policy and democratic governance, as exemplified by his penchant for "seminaring" on policy issues (Drew 1994; Daalder 1994) and his persistent engagement with academic and policy specialists throughout his presidency.

These characteristics and others certainly indicate the active-positive nature of Bill Clinton's character. However, other, frequently less flattering characteristics temper that assessment. There was, for example, Clinton's lack of discipline and tendency toward exaggeration and dishonesty (see Drew 1994; Purdum 1996; Maraniss 1995; Maraniss 1998a). An aspect of this trait found expression in Clinton's well-publicized ability to make everyone believe he had agreed with them without actually doing so. Even during his time as governor of Arkansas, "Clinton began to garner a reputation . . . for slipperiness and waffling in excess of even the norm of politics" (Kelly 1994). Leaving aside the personal implications, in political terms these characteristics complicated his efforts to exercise policy leadership on such issues as Bosnia, Somalia, Haiti, China, and elsewhere. Frequently, promises were made and pledges taken, only to be revised, reversed, or remain unfulfilled. It soon became "the conventional diplomatic wisdom" that "the pledges of the president of the United States are to be regarded more as well-meaning sentiments than actual commitments" (Kelly 1994).

In the wake of the Monica Lewinsky affair and the impeachment and trial of President Clinton in 1998–1999, these and other aspects of Clinton's character became even more salient.[8] As one of his biographers summed up, the characteristics included:

> His tendency to block things out, to compartmentalize different aspects of his life, to deny reality at times, to keep going no matter what obstacles face him, and to feel a constant hunger for affirmation. Other traits are more familiar to historians and psychiatrists as the generic characteristics of many powerful and ambitious men. These include an enormous appetite for life, a powerful sex drive . . . a lack of normal standards of self-control, an addiction to the privileges of public office and a reliance on aides to shield him from public scrutiny of private behavior.
>
> *(Maraniss 1998b, 6)*

Indeed, according to one specialist on addictive behaviors, this "Clinton Syndrome" rested on insecurity, low self-esteem, and a need for affirmation and reassurance (Levin 1998). None is a trait generally associated with active-positive presidents.

George W. Bush   When he began his presidency, the forty-third president—and only the sixteenth to be reelected to a second term—George W. Bush could not easily be classified according to Barber's scheme. By the time of his second inauguration, however, there was little doubt the president was an active-positive.

Bush's positive attitude toward the presidency, its duties, and toward public service generally was clear from the start. It reflected his sunny self-confidence and a substantial degree of satisfaction from his pursuits in the political arena. Less clear was his orientation toward the job in terms of his energy and involvement. He delegated responsibility and relied on aides and advisers to an unusual degree. He once proudly announced that he did not read newspapers—that he got all the news he needed from his advisers. Furthermore, he was notoriously uninterested in the details of policy or process. In contrast, at the onset of his second term, *Newsweek* (24 January 2005) would describe Bush as an "ambitious," "hands-on," "detail-oriented" president who "hates 'yes' men." The events of 9/11 seem to have been the catalyst to change, as Bush now proclaimed himself a wartime president.

James David Barber argues that the roots of presidential character are in the past. For George

W. Bush, that past includes a family with an extensive public service record, the challenge of living up to the standard of his father, whose name (mostly) he shares, the learning experiences offered by a failed business and run for Congress, and a stint as governor of one of the largest states in the country.

In spite of successfully portraying himself as a Washington outsider, not to mention an average citizen, George W. Bush hails from a political family with more than a little status. On his mother's side, he is a direct descendant of President Franklin Pierce. On his father's side, his grandfather, Prescott Bush, was a U.S. senator, and his father, George H. W. Bush, had a thirty year political career that culminated as vice president and then president. A sense of civic duty (perhaps even opportunity) thus runs deep in the Bush family. One observer suggests the Bush family trusts deeply in its own competence and management abilities, appearing to believe that "if someone has to run things it should be a Bush" (Bennet 2001).

The younger Bush's career marched closely in lock-step with his father's. Like him, George W. was educated at Andover and then Yale University, where he also followed his father by being inducted into the elite Skull and Bones secret society. Like his father, he entered military service (the Air National Guard during the Vietnam War), where he became a jet pilot. After earning a master's degree from the Harvard Business School, George W. moved to Midland, Texas, to begin an oil company (which failed), just as his father had done twenty-seven years earlier. A year later, he ran unsuccessfully for a Texas seat in the United States House of Representatives; his father had successfully captured a seat in 1966 but failed in a bid for the Senate in 1970. Just as the elder Bush ran successfully for president in 1988, George the younger ran and won in 2000. These parallel tracks have led many to speculate that George W. Bush's efforts are explained by his motivation to fill his father's shoes or compete with his father's aspirations. It should be noted, however, that until his successful presidential run, the younger Bush had failed to match his father in each of these steps: the elder Bush did better in school, flew in combat, ran a successful oil company, and won a seat in the House of Representatives. But George W. did

the one thing his father could not—win reelection to a second presidential term.

The comparison of father and son perhaps explains some of the other characteristics of George W.'s first forty years. By most accounts, the younger Bush showed little interest in public affairs or a political career until his unsuccessful run for the House seat. A Yale classmate, for example, remarked, "If I had to go through my class, and pick five people who were going to run for president, it would never have occurred to me he would ever run" (Romano and Lardner 1999a). Indeed, George W. largely ignored the convulsions surrounding the Vietnam War, the leading political issue of his time. Instead he developed a reputation in college and after as "a rabble-rouser of sorts" (Kristof 2000a), an undisciplined "Bombastic Bushkin" devoted to good times and parties (Romano and Lardner 1999a). If not an alcoholic, he was at least a frequent heavy drinker. Late in the 2004 presidential campaign it was revealed that he had been arrested in Maine in the 1970s for DUI (driving under the influence). Living up to the high standards and achievements of his father was difficult, generating a relationship some have characterized as "a shadow, a competition, [and] an opportunity" all at once (Romano and Lardner 1999a). Only at his fortieth birthday in 1986 did he break this pattern: George W. stopped drinking.

That date also marks the beginning of his second effort at his own political career. He served as an informal adviser and guardian of his father's presidency, acting as the elder Bush's "pit bull" to enforce loyalty. It was George W., for example, who confronted his father's chief of staff, John Sununu, with the news that he would have to resign after the imperious Sununu had overstepped his authority one too many times (Verhovek 1998). After advising his father during the painful 1992 electoral loss to Bill Clinton, the younger Bush defeated incumbent Texas Governor Ann Richards in 1994, and then won reelection in 1998 with 69 percent of the vote, catapulting himself into the hunt for the Republican presidential nomination. After locking up the party's nomination in the summer of 2000, George W. successfully defeated then–Vice President Al Gore (in the electoral college) to become the forty-third president of the United States.

This quick review of George W. Bush's past suggests that he has grown from an undisciplined, disinterested citizen to a more disciplined, focused leader. In each of his campaigns from 1994 to 2004, along with his time in office in both Texas and Washington, D.C., Bush revealed himself as an enthusiastic, "methodical, disciplined candidate and officeholder" (Bennet 2001). His presidential character supports his placement in the active-positive quadrant of Barber's typology.

As we noted earlier, active-positives tend to be happy and self-respecting, open to new ideas, and able to learn from their mistakes. For Bush, there is, first, his energy, enthusiasm, and charisma, which he has used to great effect. Second, there is his deep reservoir of self-confidence—even arrogance, some say—that supports him in all his efforts. "He is a cheery guy whose success has arisen not from self-doubt but from self-confidence," writes one journalist (Kristof 2000c), "and when setbacks have arisen he has normally shrugged and moved on." Not only did this trait enable Bush to accept compromise, and even defeat, but it also made him comfortable in surrounding himself with high-quality, formidable advisers without fear that they would outshine him (Kristof 2000d).

These characteristics aided Bush as he led the U.S. response to the September 2001 terrorist attacks. Once detached from foreign policy matters, Bush's "emotional intelligence," "self-assurance," and "calm determination" (Greenstein 2004) worked to his advantage as he coached the country through the crisis. Furthermore, his deep sense of patriotism and love of country led to "great personal anguish" as he contemplated the tragedy. "But it [9/11] also had the effect of providing strong emotional fuel to an already high level of resolve, framed by an intense focus on bringing those responsible, and their allies, to justice" (Renshon 2002).

In his public career since 1994, George W. Bush was focused and agenda-driven, holding fast to a set of values[9] and priorities and managing his time and staff to see them realized. In his campaign for governor in Texas in 1994, for example, Bush ran on a four-part agenda unified by an emphasis on economic opportunity and development. As president, he initially adopted a similar approach, emphasizing education reform and a faith-based initiative toward helping less fortunate Americans. After September 11, he shifted his attention to the new war on terrorism and the threat of weapons of mass destruction (WMD), which rationalized the invasion of Iraq in March 2003. Where Bush once insisted on a disciplined, organized structure and process that kept his staff tightly focused on his themes and preferences, he now relied on a more "improvisational administration" (Milbank and Graham 2001) that called for close interaction with his war cabinet, known as the *vulcans* (Mann 2004b). As we note again later, early in his administration Bush embraced the views of the liberal multilateralists in his war cabinet; after 9/11 his preferences turned sharply toward the "hawks" and "neocons" (Robison 2006).

A believer in spending his political capital wisely, Bush began his second term emphasizing an "ownership society" that called for major reform of the nation's largest entitlement program, Social Security (Moens 2004). Homeland security and the war on terrorism were also top priorities for the second term. Interestingly, the phrase "outposts of tyranny" (successor to the "axis of evil"?) referenced by Secretary of State Rice in her confirmation hearings was not mentioned in Bush's second inaugural address or in his State of the Union message. Although his new secretary of state often talked about "transformational diplomacy"—the task of spreading democracy to the Middle East and elsewhere, much as the United States promoted democracy in Japan and Germany following World War II—foreign policy generally seemed to have been moved to a lower rung on his foreign policy agenda.

James David Barber argues that a willingness to learn from mistakes is characteristic of active-positive presidents. At times Bush displayed this quality, but not, say critics, in his policies toward Iraq. Critics argued that his administration did not prepare adequately for the post-invasion reconstruction phase in Iraq and that the president did not put enough "boots on the ground" to quell the bloody insurgency that erupted after the end of major fighting was declared. Bush responded to critics, repeatedly saying more troops would be sent if the generals asked for them and maintained that no such request had been forthcoming (a position challenged in some published accounts). He also proclaimed during the 2004 presidential campaign that "you may not agree with me, but you know where I stand." Indeed, much like Ronald Reagan, Bush maintained a Manichean, black-and-white view of the world that extended not only to adversaries abroad but also to critics at home. Extreme sensitivity to secrecy and loyalty complemented that world view.

Despite campaign controversy over Iraq, the American people continued to give Bush high marks for his conduct of the war on terrorism. That applause contributed markedly to his successful reelection bid (Abramson et al. 2005; Campbell 2005).

Leadership and the Impact of Leadership Styles

Leaders' personalities impact foreign policy performance in many ways, ranging from grand designs to their choice of advisers and way they organize their advisory systems. Alexander George (1988) describes three different approaches presidents have evolved for managing the tasks they all face of mobilizing available information, expertise, and analytical resources for effective policy making: the formalistic, competitive, and collegial models. In a **formalistic model,** clear lines of authority minimize the need for presidential involvement in the inevitable politicking among cabinet officers and presidential advisers. In the **competitive model,** the president purposely seeks to promote conflict and competition among presidential advisers. And in the **collegial model,** teamwork and group problem solving are sought, with the president acting like the hub of a wheel with spokes connecting to individual advisers and agency heads. Bush's **corporate or "CEO" model** might be described as a variant on the formalistic. Bush acted as a CEO, delegating substantial authority and control over details to members of his cabinet and others in his administration, while he concentrated on "the big

picture." In practice the administration was also characterized by a high degree of secrecy and loyalty. Few members of the cabinet left during the first term, and some, even the highly controversial Secretary of Defense Donald Rumsfeld, were kept on into the second term.

Thomas Preston and Margaret G. Hermann (2004) argue that presidents structure and use their advisory systems depending on three leadership characteristics: "(1) [their] need for control and involvement in the policy process; (2) [their] . . . need for information and sensitivity to the political context; and (3) [their] prior policy experience or expertise in a particular policy domain." *Control and involvement* reflect presidents' determination "to have their preferences prevail" and to act as "the ultimate authority." *Information and sensitivity* to context affects the kinds of information a president will seek. And *prior experience or expertise* shapes how likely presidents are to become personally involved in the foreign policy process.

The interactions among these three concepts reveal an eight-fold typology of possible foreign policy advisory systems. The typology illustrates how different leadership styles are likely to shape the relationship between a president and his foreign policy advisers. It is shown in Figure 14.2, with brief descriptive labels assigned to nine post–World War II presidents depending on their placement in the eight categories. The placements are based on systematic psychological "at a distance" measurements of their leadership characteristics (see Hermann 1987b; Hermann 1987c). The "high" and "low" refer to the scores each president received compared with the others on the involvement, sensitivity, and experience dimensions. The labels in each cell "describe the role that a president with each set of characteristics is likely to play in the policymaking process and, in turn, the kinds of advisers such a president will choose and how they will be organized" (Preston and Hermann 2004).

Figure 14.3 in turn summarizes the presidential advisory systems associated with the leadership characteristics depicted in Figure 14.2. It suggests several interesting variations. Presidents' advisory systems are more hierarchical and formal the higher

			Prior Experience or Expertise in Policy Domain	
			High	Low
High Need to Control Or Be Involved Low	Sensitivity to Context	High	**Director-Navigator** (Eisenhower and Kennedy foreign policy style)	**Magistrate-Observer** (Carter foreign policy style)
		Low	**Director-Sentinel** (Johnson domestic policy style)	**Magistrate-Maverick** (Truman and Johnson foreign policy style)
	Sensitivity to Context	High	**Administrator-Navigator** (Clinton domestic policy style and George Bush Sr. foreign policy style)	**Delegator-Observer** (Clinton foreign policy style and George Bush Sr. domestic policy style)
		Low	**Administrator-Sentinel** (Ronald Reagan domestic policy style)	**Delegator-Maverick** (George W. Bush and Ronald Reagan foreign policy style)

FIGURE 14.2 Typology of Possible Presidential Advisory Systems Based on the Presidents' Leadership Styles

SOURCE: Thomas Preston and Margaret G. Hermann. "Presidential Leadership Style and the Foreign Policy Advisory Process," in *The Domestic Sources of American Foreign Policy: Insights and Evidence*, Eugene R. Wittkopf and James M. McCormick, eds. Lanham, MD: Rowman and Littlefield, 2004, p. 369. Reprinted by permission of Rowman & Littlefield.

the president's need for control and involvement. There is more centralization of authority in the president. Advisers' input to problem definition, option generation, and planning is more valued the more sensitive the president is to the political context, while there is more emphasis on advisers who share the concerns, vision, and ideology of presidents who are less sensitive to the political context. The advisory systems are more open to outside influences the more sensitive and responsive the president is to contextual information. As the prior policy experience or substantive expertise increases, so does a president's willingness to be actively engaged in the process, to trust [his] own policy judgment, and to perceive accurately the nature and characteristics of constraints in the policy environment. (Hermann and Preston 2004, 371, 373).

Presidents Clinton and the senior Bush illustrate aspects of the ideas summarized in Figures 14.2 and and 14.3 (Hermann and Preston 1999). Bush, for

example, came to the White House with extensive foreign policy experience. He largely ignored domestic policy (to his detriment, as we saw in Chapter 8), choosing instead to concentrate on foreign policy issues. Bush generally preferred a collegial style relationship with his staff, Indeed, as we saw in Chapter 10, loyalty was highly prized during his administration. Hermann and Preston also note that Bush became less sensitive to the political context and less inclusive of his advisers when he was under pressure and "the more he perceived a threat not only to the policies of his administration but to policies important to his political well-being and place in history." We also know that Bush could personalize issues, as during the crisis leading to the Gulf War in 1991. When backed into a corner, he personalized the situation, "tending to see the world in black and white terms. . . . Bush became a man with a mission wanting advisers who also shared his perspective on the problem. . . . Only

			Prior Experience or Expertise in Policy Domain	
			High	Low
High Need to Control Or Be Involved Low	Sensitivity to Context	High	Interested in planning and anticipating problems. Advisers used as sounding board. Time spent considering options and consequences. Coherence in policy is valued. Advisers represent important constituencies.	Seek doable solution that will sell politically. Advisers seen as part of team. Advisers propose and delineate problems and options. Compromise is valued. Seek experts as advisers. Policy by discussion.
		Low	Interested in framing policy agenda. Interested in focusing on important decisions. Loyalty is important. Procedures well-defined and highly structured. Disagreements allowed on means but not ends.	Interested in evaluating not generating options. Select advisers with similar policy concerns. Decision shaped by shared vision. Advisers viewed as implementers and advocates of policy.
	Sensitivity to Context	High	Interested in noncontroversial policy. Advisers' input is valued. Sharing of accountability. Seek advisers whom they know. Interested in reactions inside and outside advisory system. Consensus valued.	Advisers have leeway to decide policy. Seek advisers with skills that match position. Seek advisers who are interested in acting independently.
		Low	Interested in shaping option. Seek advisers with similar vision. Discussion focuses on how to coordinate policy. Groupthink is possible. Advisers provide psychological support.	Interested in overseeing policy. Seek advisers who can act on own within particular framework. One or two advisers play gatekeeper role for information and access.

FIGURE 14.3 The Proposed Influence of Presidential Leadership Style on the Selection and Organization of Advisers

SOURCE: Thomas Preston and Margaret G. Hermann. "Presidential Leadership Style and the Foreign Policy Advisory Process," in *The Domestic Sources of American Foreign Policy: Insights and Evidence*, Eugene R. Wittkopf and James M. McCormick, eds. Lanham, MD: Rowman and Littlefield, 2004, p. 372. Reprinted by permission of Rowman & Littlefield.

advisers who had his vision concerning what was happening were included in the inner circle."

In contrast to Bush, Clinton chose to focus on domestic, not foreign policy. This led him to appoint people to staff positions and cabinet posts with foreign policy expertise, but also none who would eclipse his own power and authority. Clinton was notorious for deciding not to decide. As we saw in Chapter 10, "talkathons" were commonplace, especially during his first term. (Interestingly, Clinton later spoke admiringly of his successor's ability to run a tight ship and to keep everything on schedule—the CEO model.) Clinton was also the consummate politician. This meant that while he chose advisers with expertise, he also preferred those politically attuned to the issue at hand. Clearly Clinton was a successful politician. He was the first Democratic president to win reelection since Franklin Roosevelt. And he weathered his impeachment trial and assorted other charges lodged against him and other members of his administration.

George W. Bush's style changed during his presidency. Initially he preferred a more detached, structured approach consistent with a corporate model and CEO style. For example, his early (and relatively rare) NSC meetings tended to be structured around short summaries of adviser positions and presentations of a few previously agreed upon options for Bush to consider. After the September 11 attacks on the United States, Bush adopted a less formal style and structure, a more engaged and active role for himself, and a more free-wheeling discussion and debate. On foreign policy, at least, Bush's initial style gave way to a more informal approach (Allen and Sipress 2001). Bush consistently stressed delegation, however, preferring to concentrate on the bigger picture. As observers have noted, Bush continued his preferred management style: "Once the strategy [in the war on terror] was ordained, the execution of the war [was] left, to a remarkable extent, in the hands of the military" (Engel 2001)

Why are some leaders successful and others not? Presidential scholar Fred Greenstein (2000) argues that successful modern presidencies have rested on a president's communication skills, effective organization, political skills, vision, cognitive style, and emotional intelligence. David Gergen (2001), who has worked for and observed presidents since Nixon, argues that the "must-have list" includes personal integrity, a sense of mission, the ability to persuade, the ability to work with other politicians, skilled advisers, the ability to inspire, and a successful "honeymoon period" after inauguration.

Historian Garry Wills (1994a; 1994b; see also Hermann 1986) argues that followers are essential to leaders (their "first and all-encompassing need") and suggests that leaders and followers must share a common goal. "Followers do not submit to the person of the leader. They join him [or her] in pursuit of the goal" (Wills 1994b). The effective leader, then, "is one who mobilizes others toward a goal shared by leader and followers." In part, then, successful presidential leadership is determined by how presidents respond to the demands and expectations of presidential advisers, the departments and agencies that make up the foreign affairs government, Congress, other world leaders, and, of course, the electorate. In a democracy, Wills argues, this often means an effective leader must defer to the demands of public opinion and abandon principle for the sake of compromise—actions typically held in low regard but perhaps necessary to sustain followership, without which leaders cannot exist and leadership be sustained.

Others, however, are seemingly uncomfortable with this viewpoint, particularly when it comes to foreign policy and interactions with other states, friend and foe. Henry Kissinger (1994a), a distinguished political historian as well as former policy maker, urges in his book *Diplomacy* that power, principle, and analytical thinking are the bedrock of successful foreign policy leadership throughout history. He specifically disparages contemporary political leaders "who measure their success by the reaction of the television evening news," which makes them prisoners of "the purely tactical, focusing on short-term objectives and immediate results."

Charisma is a concept often associated with successful leadership. We used the concept to describe why George W. Bush should be regarded as an active-positive president. But what is charisma? And how does it relate to foreign policy performance?

Long associated with early Christendom, the concept derives from the Greek word for "gift." Christ, Muhammad, and other early religious leaders were described as "charismatic" because of their exceptional leadership qualities. That notion was eventually secularized and used to describe political and business leaders (Halverson et al., 2004). Today, charisma is generally regarded as an attribute of leadership often accorded them by others, not something that inheres in their personal, psychological makeup. "Whereas an emphasis on the fantastic and mystical was appropriate for the church, the shift to secular charismatic leadership revolutionized the perception of authority figures." Now, "the mark of a good politician became his or her unwillingness to accept the status quo, and promises to change the system" (Halverson et al., 2004).

Years ago, the German political sociologist Max Weber argued that crises provide the circumstances in which charismatic leadership may emerge. Although not a necessary condition, "the existence of a crisis situation is antecedent to the emergence of charisma: A crisis situation leads to distress, which in the presence of a leader and a doctrine may lead to charismatic attributions. In other words, people become increasingly susceptible to the leader and his or her vision in the wake of a crisis" (Bligh et al. 2004). Thus the intersection of crisis situations and exceptional leadership are easily linked to the hero-in-history model we discussed briefly at the beginning of this chapter.

The 9/11 terrorist attacks provoked a crisis of epic proportions. More people were killed in New York and Washington, D.C., than at Pearl Harbor on December 7, 1941; the notion that America was invincible was shattered; and the president himself believed the United States was under attack by unknown assailants. How did Bush respond?

Before 9/11, critics worried that the new president did not have the skills essential to effectively lead the country. Michael Moore's controversial movie *Fahrenheit 9/11* also depicted Bush as ill-equipped to handle the volatile situation following the terrorist attacks, virtually "paralyzed" much like a deer looking into the headlights of an oncoming car in the dark of night. Instead, Bush eventually rose to the occasion wrapped in the cloak of charisma. His "rhetorical language [as revealed in his public speeches] became more charismatic after the crisis of 9/11. In addition, the media's portrayal of Bush reflected a similar increase in charismatic rhetoric, suggesting an increased receptivity to a more charismatically based leadership relationship after the crisis" (Bligh et al. 2004). Approval of Bush's presidential performance soared in the aftermath of the crisis, as we saw in Chapter 8. Nationalistic "rally round the flag" sentiments certainly stimulated the extraordinary change in the public's evaluation of Bush's job performance, but Bush's own (charismatic) leadership style contributed to an environment conducive to the policy changes at home and abroad deemed necessary to prosecute the war on terrorism.

THE IMPACT OF INDIVIDUALS' PERSONALITY AND COGNITIVE CHARACTERISTICS[10]

Another way to assess the impact of individuals' personal characteristics on their foreign policy behavior is to investigate which behaviors and preferences are associated with particular personality traits and related beliefs. Individuals can be described as embracing a variety of personal characteristics. The following eight concepts are among those that have been linked to the foreign policy attitudes, beliefs, and behavior of foreign policy elites.

- **Nationalism:** A state of mind that gives primary loyalty to one state to the exclusion of other possible objects of affection (such as other countries, family, or transnational entities like the European Union or a religion). Nationalists glorify their own state and exaggerate its virtues while denigrating others. Because nationalists develop an ego involvement with their own state, they tend to defend its acclaimed right to superiority (Stagner 1971).

- **Need for power:** An individual's need to have influence or prestige when interacting with others. This basically connotes the level of one's need for control over others. Political leaders with a high need for power typically hold strong nationalist sentiments (Hermann 1980; Hermann 1984). They also are more likely than others to engage in aggressive behavior. Thus different presidents' need for power has been found to predict to whether or not the United States engaged in war during their administrations (Winter 1987).

- **Need for affiliation:** An individual's level of concern with maintaining friendly relationships with others. The felt need for interpersonal warmth may affect foreign policy decision making in several ways. Leaders with a need for affiliation rely more than others on the opinions of friends than on those of experts (Winter and Carlson 1988). Additionally, individuals concerned with maintaining friendly relationships prefer to engage in cooperative relations with other states rather than pursue tougher policy options. A concern with cooperation and friendship, however, may also a cause leader to respond aggressively if he or she feels betrayed by a friend (Winter 1993).

- **Need for achievement:** An individual's level of concern with attaining excellence in whatever the person does. Political leaders with a high need for achievement are often motivated by a desire to make a favorable impact on history. This heightened concern affects foreign policy decision making by making leaders who experience it more likely to rely on the advice of experts when making policy decisions (Winter and Stewart 1977). It also increases their willingness to take risks if they see opportunities to leave a positive imprint on world events (McClelland 1961).

- **Distrust of others:** A personality characteristic that reflects an individual's suspicion of the motivations and actions of others. Individuals distrustful of others are reluctant to make commitments. Thus they are wary of the risks involved in engaging in cooperative international behavior and skeptical of its potential benefits. Distrustful leaders also typically embrace nationalist sentiments and tend to have an exaggerated need for power (Hermann 1980).

- **Conceptual complexity:** How leaders structure their views of the world. Those who see a great deal of ambiguity in their surroundings and believe that multiple factors explain particular events are more "conceptually complex" than leaders who see the world around them in terms of a few clearly defined characteristics. Those high in complexity generally see many possibilities and believe they can be flexible in their reactions to events, while those low in complexity usually prefer either/or choices (Hermann 1987). Less conceptually complex leaders see themselves as having comparatively few policy options and thus are more likely than more conceptually complex leaders to adopt conflictual policies (Hermann 1980; Hermann 1984; Hermann and Hermann 1989). They also are generally more likely than conceptually complex leaders to take risks and to test accepted norms of international behavior (Hermann and Kegley 1995). Furthermore, variation in conceptual complexity leads to different advisory systems and structures (Preston 1997; Preston 2001), a matter to which we return later.

- *Historical analogies:* Political leaders frequently structure their understanding of the world by relying on their interpretations of the lessons of the past (Neustadt and May 1986). They typically see current situations as analogous to previous events, essentially equating them with previous circumstances they perceive common to both. They then take the "lessons" they learned from the outcome of an earlier situation and use them as guides when making decisions dealing with the new, seemingly similar event. But which past events are deemed relevant to the new situation and the lessons an individual associates with those events depends critically on that person's perceptual lens. So determining which analogy someone chooses can provide important insight into his or her behavior (Jervis 1976; Khong 1992). As we have seen in previous chapters, "Munich" and "Vietnam" are popular analogies, and they can lead to quite different foreign policy choices.

- **Operational codes:** A construct that includes several different personal characteristics relating to individuals' views about fundamental factors affecting the course of world affairs. Taken together in the form of an *operational code,* these provide insight into a person's basic beliefs about how the world operates (George 1969). Operational codes include a policy maker's beliefs about the basic nature of his or her political environment. Does he or she see the world as basically cooperative or conflictual? Can individuals make an impact on history? Or is the course of world events beyond any one person's control? Those beliefs also include the individual's preferred foreign policy strategies and tactics. Does the policy maker believe that engaging in cooperative acts is the most effective way to attain one's goals? Or does he or she prefer reliance on threats?

Analyses of political leaders' operational codes show that they have an important influence on their own behavior (Holsti 1970; Johnson 1977; Starr 1984), and, in some cases, on their country's foreign policy behavior as well. One study of U.S. policy during the Vietnam War found that changes in American tactics closely mirrored predictions based on Henry Kissinger's operational code (Walker 1977). Another found that changes in the Carter administration's foreign policies reflected changes in the president's operational code (Walker, Schafer, and Young 1998).

George W. Bush changed his operational code quite markedly following 9/11, as we noted earlier. Using their public speeches, Robison (2006) systematically analyzes Bush's operational code and that of four members of his war cabinet both before and after 9/11. He determined that before 9/11 Bush leaned toward the views of the liberal multilateralists in the State Department (Secretary Powell and Deputy Secretary Richard Armitage); after 9/11 his preferences shifted sharply toward the neoconservative unilateralists in the Defense Department (Secretary Rumsfeld and Deputy Secretary Paul Wolfowitz). (Focus 14.1. illustrates these competing viewpoints or as seen through the operational code beliefs of Secretaries Powell and Rumsfeld.) Bush's decision to abandon diplomacy and invade Iraq without broad international support reflects the change in his operational code from one of optimism to pessimism.

The foregoing eight concepts illustrate how individuals' personality traits and cognitive characteristics may influence foreign policy behavior. The list is not exhaustive, and some of these factors can work in tandem with others to affect leaders' behavior. But knowledge of these characteristics is important as they provide insight into leaders' policy choices when faced with particular international events. To illustrate how a leader's personal characteristics may influence his or her policy preferences, we turn to a well-known example.

John Foster Dulles and the Soviet Union

According to an authoritative interpretation of Eisenhower's Secretary of State John Foster Dulles (Holsti 1962), Dulles's behavior toward the Soviet Union was driven by his prior beliefs rather than by Soviet conduct. "Built on the trinity of atheism, totalitarianism, and communism, capped by a deep belief that no enduring social order could be erected upon such foundations," his belief system was predicated on three strong convictions: (1) the Russian people were basically good, but Soviet leaders were irredeemably bad; (2) Soviet national interest, which sought to preserve the state, was good, in contrast

---

F O C U S 14.1   Inside Bush's War Cabinet: Operational Codes of Colin Powell and Donald Rumsfeld

Colin Powell

In many ways, former U.S. Secretary of State Colin Powell is the template of a "dovish" operational code. Powell saw the world outside the United States as a generally friendly place, and this feeling held even after 9/11, demonstrating that he was relatively unfazed by the vicious terrorist attacks perpetrated that day. He continued to believe others would treat the United States in a cooperative rather than hostile fashion. Further, within this perceived friendly environment, Powell was fairly optimistic regarding realization of his political values, including his role in promoting peace and restraint in the world. Even though 9/11 shook Powell's confidence in his ability (and that of the United States) to control international events, he never felt that others had more control than he did. Furthermore, Powell preferred cooperation over conflict in dealing with others, a preference that continued beyond 9/11. Thus, Powell seemed to view the terrorist attacks as isolated incidents carried out by a small band of malcontents; they did not fundamentally alter his generally cooperative and optimistic view of the world or the United States' international role. Powell's beliefs may originate, in part, from his (negative) experiences during the Vietnam War, the effects of which are reflected in the "Powell Doctrine," which advocates the use of publicly supported, overwhelming force with clear political and military objectives. This doctrine is a testament to Powell's cautious, generally diplomatic operational code.

President Bush's beliefs matched Powell's fairly well prior to 9/11. Both saw the environment as friendly, were optimistic toward realizing their values, and seemed to prefer cooperation over conflict as a foreign policy strategy. However, while Powell's operational code remained fairly steady over time, Bush's post-9/11 operational code shifted away from Powell toward the more "hawkish" posture of his Defense Department advisers, eventually choosing force over diplomacy to deal with Saddam Hussein. The post-9/11 differences between the secretary of state and the president may have led to Powell's apparent frustration with and relative lack of influence regarding post-9/11 U.S. policy, culminating in his resignation early in Bush's second term.

Donald Rumsfeld

Donald Rumsfeld consistently viewed the world in a conflict-oriented "hawkish" manner. To him the world was an extremely hostile place, where even apparently friendly actions by others were seen as attempts to exploit the United States and hence were treated with suspicion. Even before 9/11, Rumsfeld held a

---

with the implacably bad, atheistic international communism; and (3) the Soviet state was good, but the Communist Party was bad.

What were the sources of Dulles's beliefs? His perceptions were shaped in part by his childhood experiences, his relationship with his parents and his peer groups, and his psychological needs and personal predispositions—his basic personality. Dulles came from a celebrated, well-connected elite background that boasted two previous secretaries of state. He presumably inherited his moralistic, evangelic attitude toward most issues from his father, a stern Presbyterian minister. John Foster Dulles was perhaps the most unabashed moralist ever to sit in the office of the secretary of state (Barnet 1972); for him the purpose of policy was the pursuit of morality. He believed that the Cold War was essentially a

moral rather than a political conflict. In his mind, the "insincere," "immoral," and "brutal" Soviet leadership was hateful because its creed was "godless." Two universal faiths competed, one good and the other evil.

Other aspects of Dulles's background also may have affected his later outlook. For instance, his early training and practice in business law may have inculcated an aggressive "can do" attitude, "an inspired ability to calculate risks and gamble on them," and a habit of mind that "carried over into his diplomacy, where countries 'were all instinctively rivals and opponents of his own client, America'" (Barnet 1972). Moreover, Dulles "was never in touch with people who knew hunger, poverty, or personal failure. Believing in addition that everyone must make the most of themselves in life and that "might makes right" attitude, preferring the use of force and conflict over cooperative gestures and diplomatic maneuvers. Further, Rumsfeld was pessimistic about realizing his own political values, including his role of promoting the nation's security and maximizing its military power. Rumsfeld saw himself and the United States as having a fairly low level of control over international outcomes compared to others in the world, indicating that he was not satisfied with what he perceived to be the United States' insufficient preexisting levels of military power and its seeming unwillingness to use that power to control political outcomes. The 9/11 attacks had little effect on Rumsfeld's beliefs; on the contrary, they reinforced his belief that the international system is an arena of conflict in which force must be met with force. He feared that overestimating the utility of cooperation may be dangerous to American national security.

The origins of Rumsfeld's beliefs may be attributed in part to considerable "institutional indoctrination." Rumsfeld had a long history of public service and experience, particularly with the military, before joining the Bush administration, including a previous stint as defense secretary during the Ford administration. His operational code during the Bush administration thus fit well with his prior experience and the expectations attached to the role of secretary of defense, whose primary tasks are war-making and protecting the nation's security. Though George W. Bush's pre-9/11 operational code was similar to Colin Powell's, and may even be called "dovish," his post-9/11 beliefs more closely followed Rumsfeld's more hostile, conflict orientation, indicating that 9/11 had a significant impact on the president's operational code. The similarities in beliefs between Bush and Rumsfeld following 9/11 may thus have contributed to the "hawkish" movement of U.S. foreign policy following 9/11. (Rumsfeld and like-minded advisers such as Dick Cheney and Paul Wolfowitz had already advocated the overthrow of Saddam Hussein prior to Bush's election in 2000.) These similarities may also have contributed to Bush's apparent affinity for Rumsfeld, as Bush steadfastly defended his defense adviser and refused to accept his resignation on multiple occasions. Despite several missteps on Iraq over the course of three and a half years, it was not until November 2006 that President Bush finally decided to replace Rumsfeld.

SOURCE: Adapted by the author and with the permission of the editors, from: Sam Robison, "George W. Bush and the Vulcans: Leader-Advisor Relations and America's Response to the 9/11 Attacks," in *Beliefs and Leadership in World Politics: Methods and Applications of Operational Code Analysis*, Mark Schafer and Stephen G. Walker, eds. New York: Palgrave, 2006. Reprinted by permission of Palgrave Macmillan Ltd.

those who do not have something wrong with them, he never seriously tried to understand the people whose misfortune it is to get left on the bottom rungs of the ladder" (cited in Barnet 1972).

As secretary of state, Dulles's rigid, doctrinaire beliefs and personality traits predetermined his reactions to the Soviets and led him to distort information so as to reduce any discrepancies between his knowledge and his perceptions (Holsti 1962). Dulles's psychological need for image maintenance led him to reject all information that conflicted with his preexisting belief that the Soviet Union could not be trusted. Friendly Soviet initiatives were seen as deception rather than true efforts to reduce tension. For example, Soviet military demobilizations were attributed to necessity (particularly economic weakness) and bad faith (the released men would be put to work on lethal weapons). Similarly, the Austrian State Treaty—a Soviet initiative for the withdrawal of Soviet and American occupation forces from Austria in return for the promise that the Austrians would maintain a policy of neutrality in the East–West dispute—was explained as Soviet frustration (the failure of its European policy) and weakness (their system was "on the point of collapse") (Holsti 1962). Thus, in Dulles's image, the Soviets could do only harm and no good. If they acted cooperatively, it was either because they were dealing from a position of weakness or because they were trying to deceive the United States into a position of unpreparedness. When they did anything bad, it supported Dulles's prior image that the Soviets were incapable of virtuous behavior. The Cold War policies of John Foster Dulles, we may reasonably conclude, were derived from his entrenched negative beliefs—what Henry Kissinger

(1962) termed an *"inherent bad faith"* model of the Soviet leadership.

Dulles's inflexible image and unwillingness to accept any uncomfortable information was reinforced by his extreme faith in his own judgment and lack of respect for that of others, whom he regarded as his inferiors. Dulles felt "he was uniquely qualified to assess the meaning of Soviet policy. This sense of indispensability carried over into the day-to-day operations of policy formulation, and during his tenure as secretary of state he showed a marked lack of receptivity to advice" (Holsti 1962).

The Dulles example makes a convincing case for the influence of individual variables on policy behavior, as Dulles's foreign policy behavior clearly seems to have been firmly rooted in his belief system and its antecedent personality traits.

The Impact of the Individual on Foreign Policy: Additional Examples

Madeleine Albright, the first woman secretary of state, is another interesting example of a powerful person whose personality and socialization experiences colored her foreign policy approach. Born in Czechoslovakia, Albright's experience as a young refugee from the dictates of Stalinist Russia and Nazi Germany appears to have profoundly shaped her career choices and especially her beliefs about how the United States should respond to the Balkans' crises when they were beset by civil conflict and ethnic cleansing during her tenure as U.S. ambassador to the United Nations and, later, secretary of state. While others in the Clinton administration were wary of U.S. involvement in the genocidal conflict, including then–Chairman of the Joint Chiefs of Staff Colin Powell, Albright was a firm advocate of the use of force. One journalist described Albright as "a tough-talking, semimuscular interventionist [who] believes in using force—including limited force such as calibrated air power, if nothing heartier is possible, to back up a mix of strategic and moral objectives" (Isaacson 1999). Once NATO launched its air campaign against Serbia, it was sometimes called "Madeleine's War."

Similarly, LBJ's intense need to be loved and feel in control of his fate fed his penchant during the Vietnam War to surround himself with advisers who provided him with information he wanted to hear (Kearns 1976). Johnson's immense ego involvement with affairs of state also led him to "personify" his policies, as illustrated by his statements regarding his Vietnam policies: "By 1965, Johnson was speaking of 'my Security Council,' 'my State Department,' 'my troops.' It was *his* war, *his* struggle; when the Vietcong attacked, they attacked *him*. On one occasion, a young soldier, escorting him to an army helicopter, said: 'This is your helicopter, sir.' 'They are *all* my helicopters, son,' Johnson replied" (Stoessinger 1985). "The White House machinery became the president's psyche writ large" (Kearns 1976).

Consider Harry Truman, for example, a president who "was prone to back up his subordinates to an extent that was indiscriminate" (DeRivera 1968). A decisive person, Truman expected loyalty and was intolerant of disrespect. Hence when he was confronted with blatant insubordination from General Douglas MacArthur (an authoritarian who wanted to call the shots and expand the war with the communists in Asia), the president dealt with the situation decisively: "You're fired!" Able to give loyalty himself, Truman expected it from others.

President Eisenhower, on the other hand, illustrates the difficulties of evaluating the psychological bases of diplomatic conduct. His low-key approach produced results that were not at the time recognized as a part of his design. Historians have since reevaluated his presidency. Where previously they perceived inattention and indifference to the duties of office they now see strength and command (see Ambrose 1990). Eisenhower's personality contributed to his "hidden hand" managerial approach and its quiet effectiveness (Greenstein 1982).

Richard Nixon and Bill Clinton also present perplexing cases. Some of Nixon's conduct, both in and out of office, appears explicable only in light of his private conflicts and emotional problems. Consider the portrayals of Nixon's character and personality offered by Summers and Summers (2000) and Abrahamsen (1977). These scholars diagnose

Nixon as a disturbed personality, at war with himself since the traumatic events and parental disputes of his unhappy childhood. Those conflicts were never resolved, making Nixon unstable, indecisive, and, above all, self-consciously unsure of himself. They account for Nixon's obvious discomfort in the White House, his inability to maintain warm personal relationships, his paranoid distrust of those around him, his self-absorption, and his competitive, adversarial approach toward his political opponents. They almost certainly led him to conquer and destroy, to become the "victor," and they may have subconsciously attracted Nixon to failure, because inwardly he felt inadequate and suspected that he did not deserve success. Decisions motivated by such personal factors may have contributed to the tragedies of Vietnam and Watergate.

Similarly, what one careful observer characterized as "the Clinton enigma" (Maraniss 1998a) can be traced to individual characteristics. As David Maraniss (1995; 1998a) and Stanley Renshon (1998) have suggested, many aspects of Clinton's behavior, including his tendency to avoid decisions, his evasiveness, his license with the truth, and his lack of self-control, can be attributed to his personal ambition, his experiences in a troubled home, and the environment in which he learned his political behavior. According to Maraniss (1998a), for instance, "It was not difficult to find the darker corners of Clinton's life. He could be deceptive, and he came from a family in which lying and philandering were routine, two traits that he apparently had not overcome. As he grew older, the more tension he felt between idealism and ambition, the more he gave in to his ambition, sometimes at the expense of friends and causes that he had once believed in." Persistently troubling throughout his political career, these characteristics led to the Monica Lewinsky episode and, ultimately, Clinton's loss of effectiveness for much of his second term as he faced impeachment.

Our sketch of George W. Bush earlier in this chapter suggests additional examples of such linkages. They show that the content and conduct of American foreign policy may in some instances be profoundly influenced by policy makers' personal characteristics. Still, both the occasions for the exercise of that influence and its extent are likely to be constrained by a variety of factors, to which we now turn.

LIMITS ON THE EXPLANATORY POWER OF INDIVIDUAL FACTORS

Can continuities and change in American foreign policy be traced to leaders' personal attributes? As intuitively inviting as that interpretation might be, it ignores the fact that individuals are only one of several sources of American foreign policy, any of which can limit severely the impact that leaders exert on the direction of foreign policy. The question, then, is under what conditions are leaders' individual characteristics likely to be influential?

When Are Individual Factors Influential?

In general, the influence of personal characteristics on policy-making conduct *increases* in response to the following factors:

- The individual's level of advancement in the decision-making structure. The higher one climbs in the hierarchy of the foreign affairs government, the more the occupant's personality will affect policy.

- The ambiguity and complexity of the decision-making situation. Because people respond to bewildering and uncertain situations emotionally rather than rationally and calmly, perceptions of circumstances are important. At least four types of such foreign policy situations bring psychological (nonlogical) drives into play: (1) new situations, where the individual has had little previous experience and few familiar cues to assist in the definition of the situation; (2) complex situations, involving a large number of different factors; (3) contradictory situations, which encompass many inconsistencies and incompatibilities; and (4) situations devoid of social sanctions, which permit freedom of choice because societal definitions of appropriate options are unclear (DiRenzo 1974).

- The level of self-confidence and ego in the individual. Decision makers' subjective faith in their own ability to control events—their self-esteem, self-confidence, and belief in themselves—strongly determines the extent to which they will dare to allow their own preferences to set policy directions (DeRivera 1968). Conversely, in the absence of such assurance (or narcissistic ego inflation), self-doubt will inhibit risk taking and leadership.

- The level of the individual's personal involvement in the situation. When people believe their own interests and welfare are at stake, their response is governed primarily by their private psychological needs. They cease to appear cool and rational and begin to act emotionally. Compare student behavior when mechanically taking class notes during a lecture with behavior when called upon to recite or when negotiating with a professor over an exam grade. Likewise, when policy makers assume personal responsibility for policy management (and become ego-involved in outcomes, as Johnson did during the Vietnam war), their reactions frequently display heightened emotion and their personalities are revealed.

- A scarcity of available information. When facing a decision in which pertinent information is unavailable, gut likes or dislikes tend to dictate policy choices. Conversely, "the more information an individual has about international affairs, the less likely is it that his [or her] behavior will be based upon non-logical influences" (Verba 1969). Other things being equal, ample information reduces the probability that decisions will be based on psychological drives and personal needs.

- Power having been assumed recently or under dramatic circumstances. When an individual first enters office, the formal requirements of the role are least likely to circumscribe what he or she can do. That holds true especially for newly elected presidents, who often enjoy

a "honeymoon" period during which they are relatively free of criticism and extraordinary pressure. So, too, cabinet members and other top-level officials usually experience a brief period during which their personal freedom is great and their decisions encounter little resistance. Moreover, when a leader comes to office following a dramatic event (a landslide election or the assassination of a predecessor), "the new high-level political leader can institute his [or her] policies almost with a free hand. Constituency criticism is held in abeyance during this time" (Hermann 1976).

- Crisis conditions—although they capture only a fraction of the countless decisions made by members of the foreign affairs government—often bring together circumstances that enhance individuals' potential impact on the policy process. Because crises upset "business as usual," they typically upset the influences that otherwise affect how foreign policy is made, thus permitting individual factors to play a larger-than-usual role in affecting foreign policy decisions. It is not coincidental that the great (charismatic) leaders of history have customarily arisen during periods of extreme challenge. The moment may make the person rather than the person the moment, in the sense that crisis can liberate a gifted leader from the constraints that normally would inhibit his or her capacity to engineer change.

- A *foreign policy crisis* is "a situation that (1) threatens high-priority goals of the decision-making unit: [for example, foreign policy makers]; (2) restricts the amount of time available for response before the decision is transformed; and (3) surprises the members of the decision-making unit by its occurrence" (Hermann 1972). When such a situation arises, several things typically happen (Hermann 1969):

  - The highest level of government officials will make the decision(s) (because of the perceived threat to national goals or interests).

- Bureaucratic procedures usually involved in foreign policy making will be side-stepped (because high-ranking officials can commit the government to action without the normal deference to bureaucracies).

- Information about the situation is at a premium (because time limits decision makers' ability to acquire new information).

- Selection among options is often based on something other than information about the immediate situation (for example, because of the short time, analogies with prior situations may be inaccessible).

- Personal antagonisms and disagreements among policy makers will remain subdued (because of the urgent need for consensus).

- Extreme responses are encouraged (because of limited information and the enhanced importance of the policy makers' personalities).

Especially noteworthy for our purposes is that crises encourage formation of ad hoc decision-making groups that are given broad authority (Hermann and Hermann 1989). In crises, then, decision-making elites truly govern. Bureaucratic procedures are short-circuited and decision responsibility is redistributed from the usual centers of government power. Hence, one of the greatest role-induced constraints on individual decision makers is circumvented.

Finally, evidence from case studies indicates that the domestic political implications of policy options are not given their usual intense consideration in crisis situations (Paige 1972; compare Hampson 1988). This helps liberate individuals from their typical constraints, thus encouraging the expression of individual values and increasing the likelihood that decision makers' personal characteristics will imprint policy. Indeed, the individual leader's personality may now be determinative, as the usual institutional and societal barriers to decisive action are suspended. In a situation that simultaneously challenges a nation's will and the president's self-esteem, governmental decision processes can easily become fused with the chief executive's psychodynamic processes. Furthermore, the resolution of a policy crisis under such circumstances could depend ultimately on the outcome of a personal, emotional crisis (DiRenzo 1974). It is instructive to note in this context that the influence of personality on the decisions of American foreign policy makers has been especially strong when the use of force has been involved (Etheredge 1978)—and force is often the option chosen in crisis situations.

There may be other situations that elevate the potency of leaders' personal characteristics as policy determinants. One is when a decision centers on broad, abstract conceptions of the nation's basic policy goals. Unlike occasions when policy makers are asked to find a pragmatic solution to a specific problem, in this case attention focuses on doctrinal and ideological issues, thus making leaders' value preferences, fundamental beliefs, and inner needs especially influential. The divergent "strategies of containment" (Gaddis 1982) adopted by different presidents, reveal how different persons and personalities shaped the broad outlines of how the "war" against communism should be conducted. With respect to the five-decade struggle over Indochina and Vietnam, for example, a former policy planner (Kattenburg 1980) describes presidential behavior thus:

> Truman was obdurate, tough, and determined to demonstrate these traits in his policies.... [H]e felt challenged by the rise of communism in Southeast Asia and became determined to arrest it. Eisenhower, far more at ease in the office, accustomed to high command, and not in need of establishing his credentials as a tough leader.... He alone among the five presidents involved was able to absorb a defeat to communism in Indochina [that of the French] and to provide such a defeat with a domestic appearance of success by way of gradually increasing U.S. responsibility in Southeast Asia.... Kennedy was sophisticated, eager, and daring to the point of adventurousness. He accordingly did not

shy away from undertaking new commitments. . . . Johnson suffered from the combination of an enormous inferiority complex in regard to handling affairs of state, and an enormous feeling of superiority, experience, and self-confidence in handling and manipulating the movers, shakers, and sleepers in American politics. His inferiority complex. . . . put him in wholly unwarranted awe of the national security and foreign affairs expert advisers he inherited from Kennedy [and] the intellectuals who surrounded him. . . . Accordingly, Johnson accepted the ill-conceived scenarios of the graduated escalation school of thought in regard to Vietnam. . . . Finally, Nixon's negative manipulative traits of a highly insecure (proto-paranoid) but extremely ambitious power-seeker . . . led him to deceive the public into believing he was withdrawing from Vietnam when in fact he was not only continuing but intensifying the war. . . . [H]e managed also to convince the public that he was turning defeat in Vietnam into standoff . . . by changing the most fundamental premise of American foreign policy, namely, the co-equation in the U.S. public's mind of American security with the defeat of communism everywhere.

(Kattenburg 1980, 227)

Knowing that different presidents responded differently to similar situations, another intriguing question follows: How different are the personalities of those comprising the decision-making elite?

Do Policy-Making Elites and Politicians Have Similar Personality Profiles?

In terms of background and experience, a remarkably homogeneous collection of people have made up America's postwar foreign policy establishment. Recall from Chapter 9 the similarities of those who have managed American foreign policy

in the past. When we carefully examine America's foreign policy makers, we discover that—in spite of their varied personality predispositions and beliefs—they share a distinctive set of personal characteristics that set them apart from the average person. Those attracted to political careers conventionally are thought to possess an instinct for power. As power seekers, they pursue power "as a means of compensation against deprivation. *Power is expected to overcome low estimates of the self,* by either changing the traits of the self or of the environment in which it functions" (Lasswell 1974). Accordingly, politicians seek positions of power that confer attention and command deference, respect, and status to overcome their personal sense of inadequacy. Erich Fromm has argued in a similar vein that "the lust for power is rooted in weakness and not in strength, and that fundamentally this motive is a desperate attempt to gain secondary strength where genuine strength is lacking" (cited in DiRenzo 1974).

The disturbing suggestion here is that policy makers are power-hungry. Though they may claim they enter politics to do good and serve the public, in fact they subconsciously seek leadership to compensate for their personal insecurities and to bolster their own self-esteem by holding power over others. As Bruce Buchanan (1978) has argued, "those who make the final presidential sweepstakes are [persons] of near fanatical personal ambition who show themselves willing to sacrifice health, family, peace of mind, and principle in order to win the prize."

This image of leaders' psychological motives can easily be exaggerated, as clear differences in motivation and belief are also evident. Generalizations about the *response* of people to the acquisition of power are less risky, perhaps. Those with power, whether conferred by election or appointment to high office, become personally absorbed in the roles they play, let their egos and identity become involved with it, and become intoxicated with the sense of power, purpose, and importance they derive from the experience. After all, they find themselves making history, attended by press and public.

Even the most self-assured individuals can easily confuse personal identity with the role played and mistake the power conferred by the position for personal power. The next step is to inflate one's own importance in the overall scheme of things: to think that one has made things happen when in fact things have happened only because of the power one controls, or to assume that, being powerful, one is indispensable. People become elite only because they occupy elite positions and not because, as they sometimes assume, they are inherently special. Individuals playing roles often become, in their own minds, the masks they wear. In this respect the impact of the office on the officeholder makes those in the foreign policy elite more alike than different.

Do Individuals Make a Difference? Psychological Limits on Policy Change

In a sense, I had known that "power" might feel like this, just as I had known, before I ever had a drink, that whiskey goes to the head. The taste of power, or whatever it was that I tasted that first day, went to my head too, but not quite as I had been warned it would. I had come into the office with projects and plans. And I was caught in an irresistible movement of paper, meetings, ceremonies, crises, trivialities. There were uncleared paragraphs and cleared ones, and people waiting for me to tell them what my plans were, and people doing things that had nothing to do with my plans. I had moved into the middle of a flow of business that I hadn't started and wouldn't be able to stop. There were people in place to handle this flow, and established machinery in operation to help me deal with it. The entire system was at my disposal. In a word, I had power. And power had me.

(Frankel 1969, 5–6)

This recollection by a new policy maker of his first day in office illuminates the connection between policy maker and policy position. The policy-making system influences the behavior of those who work within it. Although we cannot speak precisely about what makes a politician a politician, our discussion in the previous chapter documented the similarity of outlook among those who occupy roles within the foreign affairs government—regardless, by implication, of the idiosyncratic variations among the individuals themselves and their projects and plans. As individuals enter new groups, they experience enormous pressure to conform to the prevailing and preexisting views of that group. They find that they must "go along to get along." Rewarded for accepting the views of their superiors and predecessors, and punished or ostracized for questioning them, few resist. Authority and tradition are seldom challenged.

The psychological tendency to accept the views of those with whom we interact frequently is sobering. It suggests that certain types of situations elicit certain uniform behaviors regardless of the different personalities involved. Because people behave differently when in different groups and when engaged in different activities, it is uncommon for all but those with unusually strong personalities to resist group pressures and role demands. All people are inclined to adapt to their roles or positions (see Lieberman 1965), each of which has certain expected ways of behaving and attitudes associated with it. Often these are governed by preexisting decision norms embedded in and reinforced by social processes within an institutional structure. All role occupants tend to conform to the rituals, vocabulary, and beliefs defined by these preexisting norms. One review of research on this phenomenon concludes:

> If there has been one important lesson coming from all the research in social and personality psychology . . . it is that situations control behavior to an unprecedented degree. It is no longer meaningful, as it once was, to talk in terms of personality "types," of persons "low in ego strength," or of "authoritarians"—at least it is not meaningful if we wish to account for

any substantial portion of an individual's behavior. . . . Rather, we must look to the situation in which the behavior was elicited and is maintained if we hope ever to find satisfactory explanations for it. The causes of behavior we have learned are more likely to reside in the nature of the environment than inside the person. And although the operation of situational forces can be subtle and complex in the control of behavior, it can also be extremely powerful. . . . Research . . . seems to indicate that . . . [in] "real life" we are often faced with a situation or role which demands behavior of a certain kind and, over a period of time, our beliefs are likely to change in a way consistent with this situation or role behavior.

(Haney and Zimbardo 1973, 40–42; for a contrasting view, see Gallagher 1994)

This conclusion applies to the presidency as well, where the formal and informal norms of the office—the demands of the job, its constitutional obligations, and its public pressures—arguably permit less freedom of individual expression than many others. As political scientist James Rosenau (1980) concluded, "Even the president must function within narrowly prescribed limits, so much so that it would be easier to predict the behavior of any president from prior knowledge of the prevailing state of that role than from data pertaining to his past accomplishments, orientations, and experiences."

That insight helps us understand why, following World War II and even earlier, durable policy prescriptions were advanced for decades, despite changing international circumstances. The names of the actors may have changed as the script was played out, but the script itself remained largely intact. Changing it now may be imperative, as the external world of the early twenty-first century is radically different with the passing of the Cold War and the events of 9/11. But many of the individuals remain the same and, as we have seen, people are slow to adjust their thinking to new realities. Even those associated with a new political generation, such as

Bill Clinton and George W. Bush, remain prisoners not only of their own political ambitions but also of the domestic and international forces that continue to mold the behavior of individuals once they rise to positions of prominence. As President Clinton once noted: "At least on the international front, I would say the problems are more difficult than I imagined them to be [as a candidate]."

When we add these psychological and circumstantial restraints on policy initiatives to the many domestic and external factors discussed in the preceding chapters, we can appreciate why policy change, when it occurs, "does so in acts of renewing, repairing, or improving existing relationships or commencing new ones that correspond to familiar patterns [and why] diplomacy . . . normally resembles more the act of gardening than of bulldozing" (Seabury 1973).

QUESTIONABLE UTILITY OF THE "HERO-IN-HISTORY" THESIS

The interpretation at the beginning of this chapter articulated a potentially powerful source of change in American foreign policy. Since so much authority is concentrated in the hands of so few, it is logical to assume that the decision-making elite in charge of foreign policy can, with relative ease, choose to revise—indeed, revolutionize—America's foreign policy. Change the people in charge, it is assumed, and the policy itself will often change. In short, change the leadership, and then look for a change in American foreign policy.

The theory and evidence summarized in this chapter force us to question the utility of this "hero-in-history" model of American foreign policy making. At the very least, the thesis is much too simple. By attributing policy variation to a single source, it tries to explain everything and succeeds in explaining little.

Why? To recapitulate, we find that the people who make American foreign policy are not that different from one another after all. Only certain types of people seek positions of power, and top leaders are recruited from similar backgrounds and rise to the top in similar ways. Consequently, they share many attitudes and personality characteristics. Moreover, once in office, their behaviors are shaped by the positions they occupy; they typically see their options differently from within the system than they did outside it. Often they conform their beliefs to the beliefs of their peers and predecessors. The pressures imposed by the office and decision- making setting elicit similar policy responses from diverse personalities. The result: Different individuals often pursue their predecessors' policies and respond to international events consistently. American policy makers thus routinely display a propensity for incremental change, perpetuation of established routines of thought and action, and preservation of established policies.

This reasoning invites the conclusion that, even though the president and his or her immediate circle of advisers constitute one of the most powerful institutions in the world, and even though, in principle, they have the resources to bring about prompt and immediate change by the decisions they make, those powers are in fact seldom exercised. In today's complex world, it is difficult for great leaders to "emerge," and momentous decisions are rare. Personal characteristics influence the style with which decisions are reached, but the overall thrust of American foreign policy remains highly patterned and informed by the past. As Ole Holsti (1973) puts it, "Names and faces may change, interests and policies do not."

KEY TERMS

collegial model
competitive model

corporate or "CEO"
   model
foreign policy crisis

formalistic model
hero-in-history model
historical analogies

operational code
presidential character

SUGGESTED READINGS

Ambrose, Stephen E. *Eisenhower: Soldier and President.* New York: Simon & Schuster, 1990.

Etheredge, Lloyd S. *A World of Men: The Private Sources of American Foreign Policy.* Cambridge, MA: MIT Press, 1978.

George, Alexander L., and Juliette L. George. *Presidential Personality and Performance.* Boulder, CO: Westview, 1998.

Gergen, David R. *Eyewitness to Power: The Essence of Leadership from Nixon to Clinton.* New York: Macmillan, 2001.

Greenstein, Fred I. *The Presidential Difference: Leadership Style from FDR to Clinton.* New York: Free Press, 2000.

Hatfield, J. H. *Fortunate Son: George W. Bush and the Making of an American President.* New York: Soft Skull Press, 2001.

Jones, Charles O. *The Trusteeship Presidency: Jimmy Carter and the United States Congress.* Baton Rouge, LA: Louisiana State University Press, 1988.

Maraniss, David. *The Clinton Enigma: A Four-and-a-Half-Minute Speech Reveals This President's Entire Life.* New York: Simon & Schuster, 1998.

Post, Jerrold M., ed. *The Psychological Assessment of Political Leaders.* Ann Arbor, MI: University of Michigan Press, 2003.

Preston, Thomas. *The President and His Inner Circle: Leadership Style and the Advisory Process in Foreign Policy Making.* New York: Columbia University Press, 2001.

Renshon, Stanley A. *In His Father's Shadow: The Transformations of George W. Bush.* New York: Palgrave Macmillan, 2004.

Wills, Garry. *Certain Trumpets: The Call of Leaders.* New York: Simon & Schuster, 1994.

Wilson, Robert A., ed. *Power and the Presidency.* New York: PublicAffairs, 1999.

NOTES

1. The terminology is borrowed from the timeless "great man" versus "Zeitgeist" debate. At the core of the controversy is the perhaps unanswerable question of whether the times must be conducive to the emergence of great leaders, or whether, instead, great people would have become famous leaders regardless of when and where they lived. For a discussion, see Greenstein (1969).

2. Studies by Barber (1992), Donovan (1985), and Stoessinger (1985) provide insights to the personalities and beliefs of the postwar presidents that are particularly relevant to foreign policy formulation.

3. Recent examinations of presidential style and character include Gergen (2001), Greenstein (2000, 2004), Landy and Milkis (2000), Renshon (2004), Schlesinger (1997), and Wilson and Beschloss (2000).

4. Unless otherwise noted, all quotations from Barber in this section are from the fourth (1992) edition of his book.

5. See also Beschloss and Talbott (1993). However, Zelikow and Rice (1995) argue that Bush's management of the dramatic changes in Europe, including the reunification of Germany, was both effective and proactive.

6. See also Hermann (1989), Mullins and Wildavsky (1992), and Schneider (1990).

7. During Clinton's first term, observers frequently concluded that he had "the dreaded Carter disease—no focus, no continuity, confusing motion with accomplishment," in the words of one frustrated Democratic member of Congress (see also Greenstein 1993–1994). After the staffing changes late in his first term (discussed in Chapter 10), this criticism was less common, although others quickly took its place.

8. On the Lewinsky scandal and the investigation of the president by independent counsel Kenneth Starr, see Peter Baker (2000) and Richard A. Posner (2000).

9. Alexander Moens describes Bush's values this way: Compassionate conservatism is not a political ploy or campaign spin but contains the key principles he sought in Texas and pursues in the White House. The term includes values of personal responsibility and traditional family, faith-based communities helping the needy, and the quest to rebuild an American society and culture that respects faith and favors life. He is unwavering in these, but also unhurried.
(Moens 2004, 2)
   Secretly taped conversations between then-governor Bush and Doug Wead, a close friend, also reveal Bush's religious faith and how it would "play" as he considered a run for the presidency. In one conversation he said, "I am going to say that I've accepted Christ into my life. And that's a true statement" (Kirkpatrick 2005).

10. Scott Crichlow contributed to the revision of this section.

Pattern and Process
in American Foreign Policy

15

Beyond Bush: The Future of American Foreign Policy

I claim not to have controlled events,
but confess plainly that events have controlled me.
PRESIDENT ABRAHAM LINCOLN, 1864

We choose leadership over isolationism,
and the pursuit of free and fair trade and open markets over
protectionism.... We seek to...influence events for the better instead
of being at their mercy.... The path we have chosen is consistent with
the great tradition of American foreign policy. Like the policies of Harry
Truman and Ronald Reagan, our approach is idealistic about our
national goals, and realistic about the means to achieve them.
PRESIDENT GEORGE W. BUSH, 2006

The months and years since terrorists attacked the World Trade Center and the Pentagon in September 2001 have been tumultuous ones for the United States and its foreign policy strategy. The legacy of George W. Bush will forever be the linked with those fateful events. The outcome of the war in Iraq which followed on the heels of 9/11 and which Bush consistently defended as part of the war on terrorism promises to be a centerpiece of history's judgment of the Bush presidency. Of the two, Iraq seems to be dominant.[1]

With the end of the Bush years now in view, we briefly inquire in our concluding chapter about the elements of his **grand strategy** (see Chapter 1)

that are likely to affect future judgments of his legacy and his role in shaping American foreign policy future. We also examine how external and domestic forces interact to shape America's foreign policy in the post-9/11 era.

THE BUSH DOCTRINE: RETROSPECT AND PROSPECT

The **Bush Doctrine** outlines a foreign policy grand strategy that has often been described as

521

"revolutionary" or "transformational." Recall from Chapter 1 its principal tenets:

- Pursuing terrorists and the states that harbor them

- Halting the proliferation of nuclear and other weapons of mass destruction

- Promoting the spread of liberty and democracy throughout the world

These ideas were codified in the 2002 *National Security Strategy* (NSS) statement. That statement also identified Iraq as a major threat to international order and stability. ***Preemptive war, unilateralism,*** and ***hegemony*** are intimately related to the Bush vision as it was first articulated. Products of that vision included the war in Iraq and, as part of Bush's self-declared war on terrorism, the earlier invasion of Afghanistan that toppled the Taliban regime that harbored Osama bin Laden and his Al Qaeda training camps.

Writing toward the end of Bush's first term, as we saw in Chapter 1, Gary Hart, a former senator and co-chair with former Senator Warren Rudman of *The United States Commission on National Security/21st century,* worried that the terrorist threat provided a thin thread with which to weave a tapestry for the future: "Few would argue that this war *by itself* represents an American grand strategy—the application of its powers to large national purposes—worthy of a great nation. Rather, terrorism and the responses it requires might best be seen as a metaphor for an emerging new revolutionary age to which a national grand strategy must respond" (Hart 2004).

Then, shortly after Bush's reelection in 2004, historian John Lewis Gaddis (2005) offered a critical assessment of the strengths and shortcomings of what he saw as the administration's grand strategy during its first term. His assessment included the following:

The president and his advisers [seemed] to have concluded that the shock the United States suffered on September 11 required that shocks be administered in return, not just to the part of the world from which the attack came, but to the international system as a whole. Old ways of doing things no longer worked. The status quo everywhere needed shaking up. Once that happened, the pieces would realign themselves in patterns favorable to U.S. interests. . . . The breaking up of an old international order would encourage a new one to emerge, more or less spontaneously, based on a universal desire for security, prosperity, and liberty. . . .

. . . The assumption that things would fall neatly into place after the shock was administered was the single greatest misjudgment of the first [George W.] Bush administration. It explains the failure to anticipate multilateral resistance to preemption. It accounts for the absence of planning for the occupation of Iraq. It . . . produced an overstretched military for which no "revolution in military affairs" [could] compensate. . . . And it . . . allowed an inexcusable laxity about legal procedures—at Guantanamo, Abu Ghraib, and elsewhere—to squander the moral advantage the United States possessed after September 11 and should have retained.

(Gaddis 2005, 14–15)

In March 2006, the administration released its second *National Security Strategy (NSS)*. It repeated many of the principles of the first, but the second NSS placed greater emphasis on ***multilateralism*** or working with other states than did the first. It also included for the first time a chapter on globalization. And Iran, because of its nuclear (weapons?) program, replaced Iraq as a major security threat. Iran and Iraq along with North Korea were identified early in the Bush administration as comprising an "axis of evil." That phrase was largely absent from the administration's rhetoric in the years that followed, but all three states along with Syria remained primary national security concerns.

Democracy promotion also remained a central focus in the 2006 NSS. "Ending tyranny throughout the world," a theme first given prominence in the president's second inaugural address in January 2005, was emphasized as an element of the administration's democracy promotion strategy. Ending tyranny is not a realistic goal, however. Indeed, some of America's closest allies in the war on terrorism, such as Saudi Arabia and Pakistan, are paragons of authoritarianism. Nor is it clear that democracy is an unmitigated blessing. Venezuela's leftist president Hugo Chavez was democratically elected in 1998. He allied himself with Castro's Cuba and later sought close ties with the democratically elected socialist president of Bolivia, Evo Morales. Chavez, who presides over vast oil resources on which the United States has depended in the past, is virulently anti-American. He views Washington as harboring "imperialist designs" (Shifter 2006). The autocratic direction in which democratically elected president Vladimir Putin has continued to take Russia is also troubling (Goldman 2004).

We saw in Chapter 8 that neither opinion leaders nor the mass public attaches priority to promoting democracy. The findings were reinforced in a 2005 survey by the Pew Research Center (2006a). It found that of thirteen issues regarded as top foreign policy priorities, "promoting democracy in other nations" ranked dead last. Despite these facts, political scientist Joseph Nye reports that senior administration officials believe that Bush's aggressive democratization [in Iraq and elsewhere] will prove successful and that the next president will be bound to follow the broad lines of Bush's new strategy. Vice President Dick Cheney expressed the administration's confidence in January [2006], predicting that in a decade observers will "look back on this period of time and see that liberating 50 million people in Afghanistan and Iraq really did represent a major shift, obviously, in U.S. policy in terms of how we dealt with the emerging terrorist threat—and that we've fundamentally changed circumstances in that part of the world." (Nye 2006, 140). Cheney's prediction may be correct. Others observers are less sanguine. "Machiavelli famously asked whether it is better to be feared or to be loved. The problem for the United States is that it is likely to be neither," writes political scientist Robert Jervis (2005b). "Bush's unilateralism and perceived bellicosity have weakened ties to allies, dissipated much of the sympathy that the United States had garnered after September 11, and convinced many people that America was seeking an empire with little room for their interests or values. It will be very hard for any future administration to regain the territory that has been lost" (see also Fuller 2006).

At home, the Iraq war became a highly partisan issue, as we have seen in previous chapters, contributing to the sharp divisions between Republicans and Democrats across a range of foreign and domestic policy disputes.[2] The divisions on Iraq were especially apparent in the summer of 2006, when Congress debated whether and how to set a course for ending U.S. involvement in the war. Bush had earlier said that not he, but his successor, would decide when to bring the troops home. He pledged to "stay the course." Generally that seemed to mean the United States would stay in Iraq until its own military and other security forces could by themselves provide security for the Iraqi people. Republicans in Congress for the most part supported Bush's stand. Democrats wanted to set a deadline for either withdrawal of U.S. forces or their redeployment. A few months later, the issue figured prominently in the 2006 midterm congressional elections. Voter discontent over the direction of Iraq policy was the primary reason Democrats successfully regained control of both the House and Senate for the first time in twelve years.

The War on Terrorism[3]

George W. Bush and members of his administration, particularly Vice President Dick Cheney, continually defended the war in Iraq as a part of the war on terrorism. Democrats effectively divorced the two issues during the 2004 presidential campaign, with John Kerry, Democratic senator from

Massachusetts, enjoying greater support on the Iraq issue than President Bush, but with Bush carrying the day on terrorism. The inability of the United States to find weapons of mass destruction in Iraq or to prove a link between Saddam Hussein and Al Qaeda contributed to the Democrats' successful separation of the issues. But Bush not only used the terrorist theme effectively in his own 2004 re-election bid but also in the earlier 2002 midterm elections. By building on the terrorist fear factor, Republicans actually increased their number of seats in Congress, historically an unusual feat when the White House incumbent is of the same party.

Iraq was supposed to be a quick and tidy "liberation" of the Iraqi people from the tentacles of Saddam Hussein's tyrannical regime. It was anything but. Bush could eventually claim victories in Iraq, including the capture of Saddam, national elections, a new constitution, and a new government embracing Shia, Sunnis, and Kurds. But the insurgency raged on—even after the head of Al Qaeda in Iraq, Abu Mussab al-Zarqawi, was killed in a June 2006 U.S. bombing raid. The war in Afghanistan also raged on. The Taliban reasserted themselves, insurgent tactics against American and NATO forces similar to those in Iraq increased, and Osama bin Laden remained at large. Against this background, as before, critics asked, Who is the enemy?

Former Assistant Secretary of Defense Lawrence Korb and his colleague, Caroline Wadhams of the Center for American Progress, wrote a critical appraisal of the 2006 *National Security Strategy* (Korb and Wadhams 2006). They concluded that the document "fails to offer a realistic plan with achievable goals to safeguard American interests, contradicts the actual policies and actions of the administration and reveals an absence of introspection and lessons learned from the mistakes of the first term." They argue with respect to the terrorist threat in particular that "Perhaps the greatest weakness of the new strategy is the failure once again to define the enemy, place it in the proper context, and offer a coherent, realistic strategy to defeat it." Their argument is spelled out in some detail in Focus 15.1. Note in particular they reject the views that terrorists despise Americans' values

and way of governance and that the term "terrorist" fits all stripes and colors.

Three years after the war in Iraq started, a solid majority of Americans opposed it. They believed U.S. involvement was a mistake and, in retrospect, not worth the costs. On the other hand, a cross section of public opinion polls taken between January and June 2006 showed that 56 percent of the public thought the United States was winning the war on terror ("The Terrorism Index" 2006, 52). Evidently most Americans agreed with the Bush's administrations argument that it was better to fight terrorists abroad than at home, and that success had been made in the war on terror. Furthermore, the war remained a high priority among the public.

Foreign policy elites, on the other hand, embraced a strikingly different posture. *Foreign Policy* magazine in 2006 teamed with the Center for American Progress to survey about a hundred members of "the highest echelons of the America's foreign-policy establishment" to determine their views on the global war on terrorism.[4] Stunningly, on a bipartisan basis 84 percent of the respondents said the United States was *not* winning the war on terror (71 percent conservative, 90 percent moderate, and 89 percent liberal). Eighty-seven percent expressed the view that the war in Iraq was having a *negative* impact on the ability of the United States to protect the American people from global terrorist networks; and 86 percent said the world had become *more* or *somewhat more dangerous* for the United States and the American people ("The Terrorism Index" 2006, 50, 54). Leslie Gelb, former president of the Council on Foreign Relations and a participant in the elite survey, surmised that "foreign-policy experts have never been in so much agreement about an administration's performance abroad. The reason is that it's clear to nearly all that Bush and his team have had a totally unrealistic view of what they can accomplish with military force and threats of force."

The view from abroad among mass publics is generally in line with American elites. Surveys in 2006 by the Pew Research Center (2006b) of more than 15,000 people in fourteen foreign countries reveal that most people hold unfavorable views of

---

F O C U S 15.1   A Critique of the 2006 National Security Strategy (NSS): Not Defining the Threat

The NSS opens by informing us once again that America is at war. But nowhere does it tell us exactly with whom we are at war and why, and what we must do about it in specific terms. According to the [2006] NSS, the American people are threatened by the rise of terrorism fueled by an aggressive ideology. But terrorism cannot be an enemy. It is a tactic, not a state or even a political movement. The document then proceeds to state that the United States must keep on the offensive against terrorist networks, but without telling us which terrorist networks threaten us.

In the Pentagon's Quadrennial Defense Review, released approximately a month prior to the NSS, Secretary of Defense Rumsfeld spoke about the "long war." In order for the United States to eliminate all terrorist networks and terrorism itself, it will indeed be a long war. The vagueness of this terminology and timeline confuse the American people and the world. The NSS exemplifies this confusion by conflating the attacks on the streets of Fallujah, Iraq, with the bombings in London. These are two different threats, unrelated to international terrorist networks, with separate causes, requiring different responses. The attacks in Fallujah were carried out by native Iraqis against those civilians cooperating with the American occupiers. Their gruesome attacks against American contractors seemed to be an expression of opposition to the occupation. On the other hand, the perpetrators of the London bombings, according to an official British government report, were British citizens largely motivated by their opposition to the invasion of Iraq and the British government's foreign policy, with no apparent connection to Al Qaeda.

The NSS also exaggerates the threat from these violent extremists, telling us that we are in the early years of a long struggle against a new, totalitarian ideology, similar to what our country faced in the early

days of the Cold War. But comparing Osama bin Laden and his scattered followers to the Red Army is quite a stretch. . . . Whereas the United States was threatened in the Cold War by a global superpower, it is threatened now by largely disconnected extremists who seek to capitalize on local grievances. In other words, comparison of the current terrorist threat to the emerging Soviet behemoth in the 1950s is spurious and misleading.

Furthermore, the NSS misreads the motivations of the violent extremists. The president tells us that their resort to terrorism is not simply a result of hostility to our occupation of Iraq, Israeli-Palestinian issues, or our response to Al Qaeda. Rather, the terrorists' ideology is based on "enslavement," and that terrorists see individuals as objects to be exploited and then to be ruled and oppressed. The implication from the NSS is clear: the terrorists hate our freedoms. The truth is that these violent extremists hate our policies, feel threatened by our influence and power, and are galvanized by extremist religious beliefs. . . . In their view, our direct and indirect support keeps what they view as heretical, oppressive, and corrupt regimes in places like Saudi Arabia and Egypt in power. . . .

Osama bin Laden and his followers do not care if we separate church and state, protect minority rights, give women an equal vote, or conduct free and open elections. They want the United States and its influence out of the Arab world. A misreading of what terrorists want and stand for undermines U.S. efforts to battle them.

SOURCE: Lawrence Korb and Caroline Wadhams, "A Critique of the Bush Administration's National Security Strategy," *The Stanley Foundation Policy Analysis Brief*, June 2006, pp. 3–4. The Stanley Foundation encourages use of this report for educational purposes. Any part of the material may be duplicated with proper acknowledgment.

---

the United States, their support for the war on terrorism has waned, they believe the removal of Saddam Hussein has made the world a more dangerous place, and they are pessimistic about bringing democracy to Iraq.

Preemptive War/Preventive War

The 2002 *National Security Strategy* articulates a case for preventive war. It states that the United States

will act preemptively to exercise its inherent right of self-defense. The 2006 version of the NSS reasserts that right:

> It is an enduring . . . principle that [that the government has an obligation to protect the American people and the nation's interests]. . . . This duty obligates the government to anticipate and counter threats . . . before the threats can do grave

---

F O C U S 15.2   Preemption or Prevention?

The decision to use military force can be made in a variety of different situations, and in response to numerous different triggers or actions taken by an enemy or adversary. A preemptive strike is a military action taken to forestall an imminent military attack or other type of threat. This type of activity is different from a *preventive action*, which is undertaken to counter a more distant threat. In this respect, a preemptive strike deals with a current threat, while preventive action deals with a potential, or future, threat.

Preemptive strikes are generally motivated by the fear of an impending attack or invasion. In this scenario, the leadership of a state believes its adversary is preparing for an attack or invasion. Instead of waiting for the attack to actually occur, the leadership decides to take action first—launch a preemptive strike against the adversary.

The Israeli decision to strike against Egyptian forces on June 5, 1967, is an example of a preemptive strike. The Israelis believed that the Egyptians were poised for their own attack and that Israel could ill afford to absorb such an attack. As a result, the Israelis decided to launch a preemptive strike to forestall the imminent Egyptian attack.

A preventive action, on the other hand, would be undertaken to deal with a threat that could develop sometime in the future. With preventive action, the "threat" posed by the target is distant in nature, and in some cases a mere potentiality. The Israeli strike against the Iraqi nuclear reactor at Osiraq in June 1981

is an example of a preventive action. Israel struck the Iraqi facility in order to forestall the further development of the Iraqi nuclear program, which the Israelis viewed as a threat. This action was not really "preemptive" in nature, however, in that Iraq did not pose an imminent threat to Israel.

The distinctions between preemptive and preventive actions are important, but often confused. The 2002 *National Security Strategy of the United States of America* (NSS) describes a strategy identified as "preemptive," but in actuality is closer to being preventive in nature. The NSS . . . states, in the context of the threat from weapons of mass destruction, that "The greater the threat, the greater is the risk of inaction— and the more compelling the case for taking anticipatory action to defend ourselves, even if uncertainty remains as to the time and place of the enemy's attack." The fact that the NSS stresses that the "time and place" of the attack are unknown makes the policy preventive. However, the NSS . . . goes on to state, "To forestall or prevent such hostile acts by our adversaries, the United States will, if necessary, act preemptively." While the NSS does use the word "prevent," it describes the policy as "preemptive." Regardless of the terminology used to describe the policy, it fits squarely with the criteria of preventive actions.

SOURCE: Rachel Bzostek, "Preemptive Strikes," in *International Encyclopedia of the Social Sciences*, 2nd ed., William A. Darity, ed. Farmington Hills, MI Macmillan:, 2007. Reprinted with permission of Thomson, a division of Thomson Learning: www.thomsonrights.com. Fax 800 730-2215.

---

damage. . . . There are few greater threats than a terrorist attack with WMD. . . .

To forestall or prevent such hostile acts by our adversaries, the United States will, if necessary, act preemptively in exercising our inherent right of self-defense.

Under law and practice, every state has the right to act preemptively to protect its own security. Preventive war is another matter. The key issue has to do with the timeline of the threat. **Preemption** is a response to an *imminent threat*. **Prevention** is a response to a more *distant threat*. From this perspective, despite the rhetoric surrounding the war in Iraq, it was a preventive war, not a preemptive war, as

Bzostek explains in Focus 15.2. Might the continued application of sanctions, weapons inspections by United Nations and American experts, and concerted diplomacy have averted the war altogether? An imminent threat, particularly the threat of an imminent use of weapons of mass destruction against the United States or others, would have called for an immediate attack against Saddam Hussein. Preventive war in response to a more distant threat would have allowed time to pursue these alternatives to war.

Whether purposely or inadvertently, the Bush administration conflated the two concepts, with potentially dangerous long-term consequences. Since Bush presented the ideas in the 2002 NSS somewhat earlier at West Point, if not before, critics have argued that the logic of U.S. policy may encourage other states to act similarly. "If it is legitimate or lawful for the United States to attack Iraq because in its view the country posed a potential or latent longer-term danger, what is to prevent India from claiming it would be legitimate to use military force to remove the regime of General Musharraf in Pakistan? Or Russia, to attack Georgia? Or China, Taiwan" (Korb and Wadhams 2006).

Unilateralism

The United States has a long history of acting unilaterally, going back as far as George Washington and Thomas Jefferson. The tradition held throughout the nineteenth century and well into the twentieth. The policy of nonentanglement, the Monroe Doctrine, the Open Door toward China, and repeated military interventions in Central American and the Caribbean are examples. More recent ones include the Bush administration's opposition to the global Comprehensive Test Ban Treaty (CTBT), its refusal to sign onto the multilateral Kyoto Protocol on global warming, its shunning of the widely approved International Criminal Court agreement, and its abrogation of the bilateral Anti-Ballistic Missile treaty with Russia.

In 2006, Bush traveled to India, where he made a bilateral agreement with India regarding its nuclear program, which includes weapons of mass destruction. Some, but not all, of India's nuclear facilities would be placed under international inspection. Those excluded are used to build weapons. According to the Nuclear Non-Proliferation Treaty (NPT)—to which India is *not* a party—*all* nuclear facilities are to be subject to international inspection with punishments for those who use nuclear facilities to produce bombs. The agreement came at precisely the time the United States was seeking to persuade North Korea to drop its active nuclear weapons program and Iran not to move forward with its plan to produce highly enriched uranium, which could be used for weapons production. (Both North Korea and Iran are NPT signatories.)

Claiming India to be an ally, the apparent strategic purpose of the agreement was to enable India to balance China in the Asian theater. But critics claim the Indian agreement "[damaged] one of our country's most strategic, effective and 'realistic' agreements: the Nuclear Non-Proliferation Treaty (NPT) .... The instant we announced our willingness to disregard the NPT, we forever undermined its coercive power" (Korb and Ogden 2005). And that, say Korb and Ogden, is a more effective strategic weapon against China than the bilateral agreement with India.

This view is not universally shared. Fareed Zakaria, writer and editor of *Newsweek* international, calls the agreement a more "realistic" approach to the Indian nuclear program than the "fantasy" of hoping India would renounce its nuclear weapons program (see Focus 15.3, written shortly before Bush's visit to India). He notes that India has withstood U.S. pressure for thirty-two years, and that it was prepared to do the same for another thirty-two.

While the Indian agreement in particular reinforced the notion that unilateralism continued to characterize Bush's approach during his second term, and while the rhetoric may have appeared as strident as before, in practice the neoconservative, ultra-nationalist ideological edge of the first term was more muted following Bush's reelection in 2004. So changed was his posture that foreign policy analyst Philip Gordon (2006) declared "the end of the Bush revolution."[5] Accommodation and conciliation now became more evident, unilateralism more muted. Judging by the 2006 NSS statement, the administration's "revolutionary" posture remained intact. So "the question is not whether the president and most of his team still hold to the basic tenets of the Bush doctrine—they do—but whether they can sustain it," wrote Gordon midway through Bush's second term. He added: "They cannot."

> By overreaching in Iraq, alienating important allies, and allowing the war on terrorism to overshadow all other national priorities, Bush has gotten the United States bogged down in an unsuccessful war, overstretched the military, and broken the domestic bank. Washington now lacks the reservoir of international legitimacy,

F O C U S 15.3 A Nuclear Reality Check: The U.S.-Indian Proliferation Pact

Many of the Bush administration's critics argue, with some merit, that it has often pursued a foreign policy based on ideology and fantasy, not the realities of the world. But now the critics are lost in their own reveries. They fantasize that the United States and India will sign a nuclear agreement in which the latter renounces its nuclear weapons. They criticize the Bush administration's proposed deal with India because it does no such thing. (Instead, India commits to placing 14 of its 22 reactors under permanent inspections, and retains eight for its weapons program.) But this is a dream, not a deal. India has spent 32 years under American sanctions without budging—even when it was a much poorer country than it is today—and it would happily spend 32 more before it signed such a deal. The choice we face is the proposed deal with India or no deal at all.

The nuclear nonproliferation regime has always tempered idealism with a healthy dose of realism. After all, the United States goes around the world telling countries that a few more nuclear warheads are dangerous and immoral—while it has 12,000 nukes of its own. The nonproliferation treaty arbitrarily determined that countries that had nuclear weapons in 1968 were legitimate nuclear-weapons states, and that all latecomers were outlaws. (It was the mother of all grandfather clauses.) India is the most important country, and only potential global power, that lies outside the nonproliferation system. Bringing it in is crucial to the system's survival. That's why Mohamed El Baradei, the man charged with protecting and enforcing global nonproliferation, has been a staunch supporter of the agreement.

This deal, shorn of all the jargon, comes down to something quite simple: should we treat India like China, or like North Korea? If the former, then we have to accept the reality that it is a nuclear power and help make its program as safe and secure as possible. If the latter, then we'll never stop trying to reverse India's weapons program.

Actually, even if this deal goes through, India will have second-class status compared with China, Russia, and the other major nuclear powers. In all those countries, not one reactor is under any inspection regime whatsoever, yet India would place at least two thirds of its program under the eye of the International Atomic Energy Agency.

The inequity with China is particularly galling to New Delhi. China has a long history of abetting nuclear proliferation, most clearly through Pakistan. Yet the United States has an arrangement to share civilian nuclear technology with Beijing. India, meanwhile, is a democratic, transparent country with a perfect record of nonproliferation. Yet it has been denied such cooperation for the past 32 years.

There are some who are willing, grudgingly, to give up their full-blown fantasy and settle for a minor one—a deal in which India would agree to cap its production of fissile material. . . . But look at a map. India is bordered by China and Pakistan, both nuclear-weapons states, neither of which has agreed to a mandatory cap. (China appears to have stopped producing plutonium, as have the other major powers, but this is a voluntary decision, made largely because it's awash in fissile material.) For India to accept a mandatory cap is to adopt a one-sided nuclear freeze. Would the United States do that? India has declared a commitment to support such a cap when it is accepted by all nuclear states, which is what we should push for.

There is a broader strategic issue for the United States. It has been American policy for decades to oppose the rise of a single hegemonic power in either Europe or Asia. If India were forced to halt its plutonium production, the result would be that China would become the dominant nuclear power in Asia. Why is this in American interests? Should we not prefer a circumstance where there is some balance between the major powers on that vast continent?

The agreement is also a crucial step forward in tackling the problem of global energy. If India and China keep guzzling gas as they grow, any and all Western efforts at energy conservation are pointless. We have to find a way that these two rising giants can satisfy their energy needs, while also reducing their dependence on fossil fuels. Civilian nuclear power can help fill the gap. . . .

A more workable nonproliferation regime, a more stable strategic balance in Asia—and it's even good for the environment. This is a reality that's better than most fantasies.

SOURCE: Fareed Zakaria, "A Nuclear Reality Check," *Newsweek*, 17 April 2006, 35. Reprinted by permission of Newsweek.

resources, and domestic support necessary to pursue other key national interests. *(Gordon 2006, 75–76)*

In what is perhaps the most remarkable sign of Bush's second-term conciliatory turn, the administration joined with the European Union, Russia, and China, under whose leadership the radical Iranian regime was presented a package of incentives designed to curb its determination to produce highly enriched uranium that could be used to produce nuclear weapons. The United States (with Israel) had long been suspected of developing military options to "take out" Iran's existing nuclear infrastructure (Hersh 2005, 2006a). It also sought to impose sanctions against the Iranian regime for breaking its obligations under the NPT. By joining forces with other states (who also opposed sanctions) the military option—while still "on the table"—seemed to become less urgent. Similarly, the administration continued to hold out hope of dealing diplomatically with North Korea's nuclear challenge, even after the reclusive state tested several short-range missiles and a longer-range one thought (before its failed test) to be able to reach the United States. (Bush quipped during a 2006 news conference: "You know, the problem with diplomacy: it takes a long time to get something done. If you're acting alone, you can move more quickly.")

Hegemony

The United States will likely remain the preponderant power in world politics well into the future, thus laying claim to this as the "second American Century." China's rise to power as a regional and perhaps global power is widely anticipated, but its ability to challenge the United States militarily or economically is likely to be circumscribed for decades. India, too, is moving rapidly forward as a formidable technological power. And even though it is a nuclear power, it is unlikely to pose a serious, broad-based challenge for decades to come. Meanwhile, the Bush administration has made clear its determination that the United States will remain a hegemonic power.

Leadership is a key component of hegemony. Every American president from Harry Truman to George W. Bush has urged the United States to accept the leadership mantle to ensure creation and maintenance of a world compatible with its interests in an otherwise disorderly and unstable international environment. During the Cold War, the United States became leader of the "free world." With that conflict's end, Presidents Clinton, Bush senior, and George W. Bush worried that isolationist sentiments would again capture the country's imagination, as they had following World War I, so they argued that creating a world safe for American security, interests, values, and, indeed, global justice, depended on American leadership.

What does "leadership" in international politics mean? Historian Garry Wills, author of *Certain Trumpets: The Nature of Leadership* (1995), addresses that question and reaches disquieting conclusions. Noting that the United States became "leader of the free world" after World War II as the defender of freedom anywhere, Wills also recites how the arrogance of power led the United States to engage in often unsavory interventionist practices that led to the removal of "inauthentic leaders—the enemies of freedom—even when the people had chosen them." Indeed, as we saw in Chapters 4 and and 5, the United States often engaged in overt and covert practices that debased its own cherished ideals.

This kind of leadership is best described in the contemporary context as **coercive hegemony**. The concept fits the pattern of much of the recent past, at least as seen from the perspective of other countries. Coercive hegemony tracks political realists' conception of international politics, which applauds the stabilizing influence of a dominant power and the role of *hard power* in international politics. It also fits with more radical views of hegemony (known as Gramscian after the radical thinker and Italian Communist Party leader Antonio Gramsci), which see hegemony as the source of dominant social and cultural values in the international system.[6] Many worry that coercive hegemony already drives America's war against terrorism.

Benevolent hegemony is leadership of a different sort. It conforms to the farsighted leadership Charles

Kindleberger talked about in his analysis of the causes of the Great Depression (see Chapter 7). Whereas coercive hegemony often involves "taxing" patrons to the benefit of the hegemon's interests, benevolent hegemons are more altruistic, providing public goods that create order, stability, and prosperity from which all can benefit (see also Snidal 1985).

Wills prefers benevolent to coercive hegemony. Leaders require followers—at home as well as abroad. Followership implies persuasion, not coercion. It implies openness, not secrecy; consultation, not confrontation (see also Haass 2000). Too often, Wills argues, American elites have failed to lead the American people, resorting instead in the name of "national security" to the notion that they "know better." (The numerous secret and often court-warrantless surveillance programs initiated by the Bush administration to thwart terrorism are good examples.[7]) And too often they have chosen to dictate to other states rather than consult with them. "A framework of mutually enriching exchanges protects far better than nuclear weapons in space," Wills agues. Although America's unilateralist approach to world affairs enjoys a long heritage, as we have noted, Wills argues that "until America's leaders address the American people and other nations with . . . respect, attention, and persuasion, we shall lack foreign policy leadership of any sort."

Others share that sentiment. Ardent political realist Henry Kissinger (2001b), for example, challenges twenty-first century American foreign policy to embrace a posture that will "recognize its own preeminence but [will] conduct its policy as if it were still living in a world of many centers of power. In such a world, the United States will find partners not only for sharing the psychological burdens of leadership but also for shaping an international order consistent with freedom and democracy."

Neoconservative and former State Department official Robert Kagan cautions critics of American foreign policy arrogance. Describing the United States as "the benign empire," Kagan (1998) says "the truth is that the benevolent hegemony exercised by the United States is good for a vast portion of the world's population. It is certainly a better international arrangement than all realistic alternatives." And he quotes from political scientist Samuel Huntington (1993b) (before Huntington "joined the plethora of scholars disturbed by the 'arrogance' of American hegemony"): "'A world without U.S. primacy will be a world with more violence and disorder and less democracy and economic growth than a world where the United States continues to have more influence than any other country shaping world affairs.'" Kagan adds that the truth is no other state wants to assume even an equal share of responsibility for managing global crises or making the kinds of sacrifices hegemonic powers must make (see also Mandelbaum 2006).

Noteworthy, in Kagan's view, is the continuing penchant of American policy makers to define the "national security" in terms that extend well beyond Fortress America. "Americans seem to have internalized and made second nature a conviction held only since World War II: Namely, that their own well-being depends fundamentally on the well-being of others; that American prosperity cannot occur in the absence of global prosperity; that American freedom depends on the survival and spread of freedom elsewhere; that aggression anywhere threatens the danger of aggression everywhere; and that American national security is impossible without a broad measure of international security."

Cementing America's benevolent leadership role implies a form of multilateralism similar to that described by Richard Haass (1999), president of the Council on Foreign Relations: "The proper goal for American foreign policy . . . is to encourage a multipolarity characterized by cooperation and concert rather than competition and conflict. In such a world, order would not be limited to peace based on a balance of power or a fear of escalation, but would be founded in a broader agreement on global purposes and problems." The international institutions the United States fostered during the post–World War II era contributed to those objectives in the latter half of the twentieth century. Perpetuating that vision into the twenty-first century may continue to serve the interests of all, not just Americans (Ikenberry 1989, 1999, 2001; see also Tucker 1999; but compare Maynes 1998).

Meanwhile, the United States remains the world's preponderant power. "The United States is probably as benign a hegemon as the world has ever seen," writes Robert Jervis (2005a). "Its large domestic market, relatively tolerant values, domestic diversity, and geographic isolation all are helpful. But a hegemon it remains, and by that very fact it must make others uneasy." Furthermore, although America's *soft power,* its ideas and values, has suffered a setback, it remains a global force that cannot be ignored.

WHAT TO DO WITH AMERICAN PRIMACY?

Well into its second term, the Bush administration could rightly claim that during its watch nothing approaching the catastrophic events of 9/11 had been repeated on American soil. Simultaneously, the president would claim that it was preferable to fight terrorists abroad than at home. What he could not say with any certainty is that the same Al Qaeda that masterminded the horrific tragedy of that memorable day still had the capability to do something similar in the near future (see Fallows 2006). Nor could he champion the Bush Doctrine and the war on terrorism as a new foreign policy paradigm around which a bipartisan majority of Americans could rally as they looked toward the second American Century. Indeed, as the events of 9/11 faded into memory, the push/pull of history, not a new vision of the future, seemed increasingly to drive the country. The vicious urban warfare in Iraq remained paramount as the president looked increasingly toward his place in history. The sudden and unexpected outbreak of war between Israel and the militant Islamic group Hezbollah in mid-2006 further complicated future judgments of Bush's foreign policy record, as it threatened to undermine the president's goal of bringing stability and democracy to the Middle East.

The rhetorical push/pull of history is evident in the epigraph to this chapter. It comes from Bush's letter to Congress transmitting the 2006 *National Security Strategy of the United States of America.* "Like the policies of Harry Truman and Ronald Reagan," Bush writes, "our approach is idealistic about our national goals, and realistic about the means to achieve them." The Truman administration and the Truman Doctrine set in motion the long, arduous containment of Soviet communism that would infuse American foreign policy with purpose and deep domestic support for decades. Truman would also preside over the development of a set of multilateral institutions—the United Nations, the International Monetary Fund, the World Bank, and the GATT framework—that enmeshed the United States in a webwork of global connections designed to avert a repetition of the catastrophe of the 1930s. Ronald Reagan in turn governed not at the onset of containment and the Cold War but at their sunset. During the 1980s, he and Soviet President Mikhail Gorbachev turned from confrontation to conciliation, as they solved first one and then others of the multiple issues that had long fueled Soviet-American conflict, especially the division of Europe between East and West. The decades-long Cold War ended. Ronald Reagan is given substantial credit in American political history for his role in the conflict's (unexpectedly peaceful) demise, which occurred early in the senior Bush presidency.

George W. Bush seemingly sought to link his own legacy to the historic policies engineered by these two great presidents, not to create a revolutionary heritage of his own that deviates markedly from past practices, which have created a long-term consistency in American foreign policy. Notable is that Bush increasingly stressed the virtues of internationalism, which characterized the Cold War era, fearing a reversion to the introversion of the 1920s and 1930s that set the stage for World War II and its aftermath. The intense isolationism of that period is unlikely to recur, but it is interesting to recall Frank Klingberg's thesis of cycles of introversion and extroversion in American diplomatic history (see Focus 8.1). By his logic, the second decade of the twenty-first century will witness an inward turn in American foreign policy. John Mueller (2005) also argues that the war in Iraq will give rise to an "Iraq syndrome" not unlike the Vietnam Syndrome that constrained policy makers' foreign policy initiatives from the mid-1970s into the 1990s.

The menu of choices that will likely engage policy discussions after Bush remains essentially the same as that outlined in Chapter 1 by Robert Art. We reiterate his brief summary below:

Dominion aims to transform the world into what America thinks it should look like. This strategy would use American military power in an imperial fashion to effect the transformation. *Isolationism* aims to maintain a free hand for the United States, and its prime aim is to keep the United States out of most wars. *Offshore balancing* generally seeks the same goals as isolationism, but would go one step further and cut down an emerging hegemon in Eurasia so as to maintain a favorable balance of power there. *Containment* aims to hold the line against a specific aggressor that either threatens American interests in a given region or that strives for world hegemony, through both deterrent and defensive uses of military power. *Collective security* aims to keep the peace by preventing war by any aggressor. *Global collective security* and *cooperative security* aim to keep the peace everywhere; *regional collective security* to keep peace within specified areas. All three variants of collective security do so by tying the United States to multilateral arrangements that guarantee military defeat for any aggressor that breaches the peace. Finally, *selective engagement* aims to do a defined number of things well (Art 2003, 83). To a considerable extent, the Bush administration's hard-line-unilateralist-selective-engagement posture coupled with the Bush Doctrine outlines a grand strategy of *dominion*. This is particularly evident with the addition of ridding the world of tyranny to the goal of promoting democracy abroad. Both objectives imply an interventionist posture consistent with the policies of Presidents McKinley, Roosevelt, Wilson, Harding, and Hoover at the turn of the last century. Despite these historical precedents, our previous discussion of the Bush Doctrine and its related concepts raises questions about its durability. Still, the attraction of remaking the world in America's image and exercising U.S. military might to that end will continue to enjoy support after Bush among neo-conservatives, conservative ultra-nationalists, and their political compatriots.

Political realists will continue to be drawn to a strategy of offshore balancing (Walt 2005), believing that America's immediate foreign policy interests are best served in, say, the Middle East, by reducing its immediate physical presence while "standing by offshore" in the event U.S. interests are directly affected. Containment is a related strategy tried by the Clinton administration to deal with Iraq and Iran (see Lake 1994). Selective engagers and collectivists are likely to draw continuing support from liberal internationalists.

Who will dominate the long-running debate about the nation's appropriate grand strategy? There is no easy answer. Today, as before, contention will focus on the priorities perceived to enhance and protect American national security and other interests. The outcome of the debate will doubtless be shaped by the complex interaction among the domestic and external sources of American foreign policy, to which we now turn.

THE SOURCES OF AMERICAN FOREIGN POLICY REVISITED

The intrusion of domestic politics into foreign policy making in democratic polities is a disadvantage that—at least in the eyes of some—undermines their ability to deal effectively with foreign policy crises and other external challenges. French political sociologist Alexis de Tocqueville ([1835] 1969) argued more than a century ago that democracies are "decidedly inferior" to centralized governments in the management of foreign affairs because they are prone to "impulse rather than prudence." Democracies, according to this reasoning, are slow to respond to external dangers but, once aroused, they overreact to them. George Kennan, intellectual father of the Cold War foreign policy strategy of containment and a strong proponent of realist thinking, reflected on democratic foreign policy performance this way:

I sometimes wonder whether a democracy is not uncomfortably similar to one of those prehistoric monsters with a body as long as this room and a brain the size of a pin: he lies there in his comfortable primeval mud and pays little attention to his environment; he is slow to wrath—in fact, you practically have to whack his tail off to make him aware that his interests are being disturbed; but, once he grasps this, he lays about him with such blind determination that he not only destroys his adversary but largely wrecks his native habitat. You wonder whether it would not have been wiser for him to have taken a little more interest in what was going on at an earlier date and to have seen whether he could not have prevented some of these situations from arising instead of proceeding from an undiscriminating indifference to a holy wrath equally undiscriminating.

(Kennan 1951, 59)

Arguably the U.S. response to the terrorist attacks on its assets in New York and Washington, D.C., reflected its "blind determination" to have its own way on the global response to terrorism—of which the war in Iraq was continually asserted to be a part.

Many scholars and policy makers have joined the long-standing chorus lamenting the role that domestic politics play in the American foreign policy process. Before 9/11 nearly all began with the premise that domestic politics now figure more prominently due to the absence of a dominant external challenge and a corresponding foreign policy paradigm around which American elites and followers could unite (see, for example, Huntington 1997; Kissinger 2001a). The response to 9/11 and the Bush Doctrine changed the ground rules. But the intensely partisan and ideological character of the responses to that doctrine and the actions that flowed from it highlighted a classic **democratic dilemma:** how to balance the requirements of national security with the requisites of democracy. Democracy demands openness and easy access to

information on which to make sound policy judgments. National security requires closedness. Security information is typically classified and hence not accessible in a way that might aid and abet an adversary. Open, closed. We will return to this sensitive issue when we discuss governmental sources of American foreign policy. First, however, we turn our attention to individual and then role sources of foreign policy, reversing the order in which they were discussed in previous chapters.

Individuals as Sources of American Foreign Policy

Any administration's foreign policy reflects the character of the person sitting in the innermost sanctum of power, the Oval Office. A president's individual or idiosyncratic qualities influence policy style, but many restraints reduce the impact of individuals on policy itself. All recent presidents have found it necessary to bend strong convictions to the force of competing political pressures, because successful presidential performance requires a willingness to satisfy political constituents at home and abroad on whom their popularity and power depend. George W. Bush certainly experienced those pressures. In part his second-term embrace of diplomacy reflected growing sensitivity toward other countries who largely stepped away from either support for or involvement in the war in Iraq.

Following James David Barber's typology, we classified George W. Bush in Chapter 14 as an *active-positive* president. His May 2006 assertion during a controversy about then–Secretary of Defense Donald Rumsfeld, and whether Rumsfeld should resign, affirmed that characterization. "I'm the decider," declared Bush, and "I decide what's best." (Six months later, the president did decide to replace Rumsfeld with Robert Gates, George H. W. Bush's deputy national security adviser and director of central intelligence.)

Early in the Bush administration, Thomas Preston and Margaret Hermann (2004) drew a picture of what they thought Bush's leadership characteristics would look like. "One would expect a very rapid, decisive decisionmaking style," they wrote, "[one] driven by black-and-white reasoning, rigid adherence to existing ideological beliefs, extensive use of simple stereotypes and analogies, and advice from people who share his general idiosyncratic views of the world." Interestingly, those predictions proved to be remarkably accurate. They also revealed similarities to the leadership style of Woodrow Wilson, another president who pursued a transformational foreign policy.

Wilson sought to transform the game of world politics following World War I. Multilateralism, the League of Nations, was central to his vision of the future. That vision finally carried the day after World War II (although it was then laced with a heavy dose of *realpolitik*), but it failed in Wilson's lifetime and the conflict-ridden years of the 1920s and 1930s. Political scientist Joseph Nye draws a parallel between Wilson's and Bush's characters and their political strategies that may ultimately bear on Bush's attempted transformation of world politics as well as his legacy:

> Overall, the similarities between Bush and Wilson are uncanny. Both highly religious and moralistic men, they were both elected president initially without a majority of the popular vote. Bush portrays the world in black and white rather than shades of gray; so did Wilson. Bush was successful in Congress at first with his transformational domestic agenda and paid little heed to foreign policy until a crisis struck; same with Wilson. Bush... proposed the promotion of democracy and freedom abroad as the central feature of his foreign policy vision, as did Wilson. In fact, many of Bush's speeches [sounded] as though they could have been delivered by Wilson.... Bush defined a vision that failed to balance ideals with national capabilities; Wilson made the same miscalculation....
>
> Persistence can be admirable, but it is dangerous when it slows the process of making corrections. Like Wilson, Bush is

not very receptive to new information once his mind is made up. Former Secretary of State Colin Powell has said of Bush that "he knows kind of what he wants to do and what he wants to hear is how to get it done."
> *(Nye 2006, 147–148)*

What Nye calls "persistence" others might describe as "inflexibility." Bush's persona is more that of a crusader than a pragmatist (Stoessinger 1985). *Newsweek* reporter Richard Wolffe accompanied the president on Air Force One to Moscow for the G-8 summit, when the war broke out in Lebanon between Israel and Hezbollah. Wolffe had the opportunity to view the president close at hand and to have personal conversations with him. He offered this assessment of Bush:

> Over the next several days [of the summit], Bush huddles with presidents and prime ministers, showing how far he has traveled since 9/11—and also how little he has changed. Bush thinks the new war vindicates his early vision of the region's struggle: of good versus evil, civilization versus terrorism, freedom versus Islamic fascism. He still believes that when it comes to war and terror, leaders need to decide whose side they are on.
> *(Richard Wolffe, "Backstage at the Summit," Newsweek, 1 July 2006, 32)*

Bush promised at the time of his first inauguration to be a uniter, not divider. But his persona and his policies came to defy that description. Under the tutelage of political adviser Karl Rove, Bush mastered a domestic political strategy that continually built on the unity and strength of his conservative base. The approach served him well at home for most of his presidency.

Abroad the story was different. The Bush administration was repeatedly criticized for its aggressive, unilateral foreign policy. Although Bush embraced diplomacy and multilateralism more often during his second term, his approach toward the Lebanese conflict between Hezbollah and Israel led to widespread criticism. As most of the world called for an immediate ceasefire, Bush was determined to let the conflict rage until Israel had inflicted crippling damage on Hezbollah's terrorist capabilities. As the outside kingpin in Middle East conflict, the position of the United States on the war was critical. The Bush administration did eventually play a lead role in bringing about a respite in the fighting, but not before again stirring much anti-Americanism in the Muslim world and in the "Old Europe," which earlier shunned U.S. policies in Iraq. As Zbigniew Brzezinski, President Carter's national security adviser, put it caustically as the fighting continued, "[President] Bush and [Secretary of State Condoleezza] Rice are pursuing a remarkably successful policy of self-ostracism."

As discussed earlier, voters used the opportunity of the 2006 mid-term elections to voice their growing discontent with Bush's leadership on foreign policy, particularly the deteriorating situation in Iraq. Interestingly, voters turned their backs on Wilson and his internationalist policies in the 1920 presidential election. Most historians also judge Wilson's political skills harshly. But "Wilsonianism," like few other ideas, has profoundly colored American diplomatic history for more than a century. Will history conclude that Bush's seemingly intransigent posture toward terrorism, liberty, democracy, and tyranny has had a similarly enduring impact?

Roles as Sources of American Foreign Policy

A president is not the personification of the state. George W. Bush, like all of his predecessors, discovered that his ability to move in new directions was restricted by the interests and preferences of U.S. friends and allies, his predecessors' prior commitments and policies, and the actions and preferences of the individuals already in position to implement their vision of the *role* of president they expected him to fulfill.

Roles define patterns of expectations, and the constraints of the past are powerful. Presidents are free from neither. Presidents almost never end up meeting their own expectations and role

conceptions. Foreign policy typically figures prominently in the changes they experience both personally and in the larger environment. As Simon Serfaty (2002) writes, President Truman had few post–World War II goals in mind, but the Korean War changed that, setting the stage for global activism that continues to describe American foreign policy. John Kennedy began his presidency as a "Cold Warrior" but ended as a champion of detente. Ronald Reagan began and ended his presidency in much the same way, first dismissing negotiations with "the evil empire" and then ending up engaged in them. Every president becomes what he did not want to be.

George W. Bush could not have anticipated the profound havoc Bin Laden and Al Qaeda would wreak on his presidency. Indeed, no one could have predicted the unprecedented attacks the terrorists visited on America's territorial virginity and how profoundly they would affect the nation. Moreover, George W. Bush became an unlikely war president. After all, he went to Washington determined to avoid the lapses in his father's domestic policy agenda; suddenly he was pressed into a foreign policy role for which he arguably was ill prepared. Circumstances often dictate priorities and the roles needed to address them. Thus, Bush found himself pursuing "a fight to save the civilized world and values common to the West, to Asia, [and] to Islam." "Freedom from fear" was now the overriding goal (Serfaty 2002). It is consistent with American interests and values since the beginning of the Republic more than two centuries ago. Almost from the beginning of the war on terrorism, however, contention arose about the extension of the Bush Doctrine to include an invasion of Iraq, which quickly set in motion constraints on the budget, the ability of the military to meet and execute multiple roles, the willingness of other states to join actively in the war on terrorism, and the domestic support the president enjoyed. The president's eagerness to play repeatedly on fear of future terrorist attacks also proved troublesome, sharpening the wedge between Republicans and Democrats that came to characterize the Bush presidency across multiples issues (See Table 15.1).

TABLE 15.1 Bush's Issue Approval by Partisan Groups, July 21–23, 2006

	Republicans	Independents	Democrats
	%	%	%
Terrorism	82	39	25
Foreign affairs	77	28	15
The situation in Iraq	77	27	8
The economy	75	33	13
The situation in the Middle East	75	29	14
Overall Job Performance	82	27	9

NOTE: Based on percentage who approve of Bush on each issue.

SOURCE: "Bush Job approval of 37%," *The Gallup poll*, July 25, 2006, 4–5.

The backgrounds of those appointed to fill foreign policy-making roles invariably shape the decisions that are made. It is noteworthy that many of George W. Bush's appointees were veterans of the Republican administrations of Presidents Ford, Reagan, and his own father. Inevitably they brought well-worn conceptual baggage with them. These foreign policy managers were insiders, which helps explain why Cold War precepts and related experiences often shaped their perspectives. At the same time, many of those with prior Republican experience also brought with them a renewed sense of the role that American power could—and should—play in today's world. The neoconservatives, exemplified by Paul Wolfowitz and Douglas Feith, the second and third ranking civilians in the Defense Department, were articulate champions of regime change in Iraq. They envisioned a democratic Iraq as a step toward a broader transformation of the Middle East designed to bring peace, stability, and freedom to a region wracked by decades, even centuries of violent conflict and authoritarian rule. For neoconservatives, the vigorous exercise of American power could be used to do good. Publications of the Project for the New American Century (PNAC) contained the blueprint of much of their thinking and program of action, as we saw earlier.

Neoconservatives were less visible in Bush's second term foreign policy team than in his first. Condoleezza Rice was appointed secretary of state, and midway through Bush's second term Robert Gates was nominated to replace Donald Rumsfeld as secretary of defense. Rice and Gates were realists who were more inclined to embrace a foreign policy marked by moderation and multilateralism. Nonetheless, "neocons" remained and continued to exercise an impact on policy. In terms of foreign policy officials, UN Ambassador John Bolton was perhaps the most politically visible of the "neocons." (Bolton's appointment as UN ambassador was a controversial recess appointment, described in Chapter 12.) Moreover, the influence of Vice President Cheney, while weaker in the second term, could not be discounted given how forcefully and effectively he championed the neoconservative foreign policy agenda. Furthermore, the role and influence of Stephen Hadley could not be ignored. Hadley, whom Cheney and the "neocons" worked through repeatedly during Bush's first term, was elevated from deputy national security adviser to national security adviser in January 2005.

Wolfowitz, Feith, and Bolton were among the several thousand policy makers comprising part of the foreign affairs government. They were political appointees who served at the president's pleasure and helped to give his administration a distinctive presidential imprint. At the next echelon of the executive branch are career service personnel charged with the day-to-day management and implementation of the nation's public policy, domestic as well as foreign. For the most part they are beyond the immediate reach of the president, the White House, and the secretaries of the departments comprising the Cabinet. Try as presidents have, most found they can do little to transform the face of bureaucracy. This was especially apparent in the Bush administration's attempt to revamp the national intelligence community and to create a streamlined Department of Homeland Security. In both cases, long-established bureaucratic subcultures worked against substantial changes in the way the government protects the nation's homeland security and how it gathers and organizes foreign intelligence for policy-making purposes. Even before Bush became president, U.S. intelligence agencies knew they had to change to meet the challenges of the post–Cold War world. But a combination of factors worked against adaptation, including the nature of the bureaucratic organizations themselves (Zegart 2005).

Here in the "permanent government," the role requirements that constrain individual latitude are particularly acute. "Bureaucratic politics" is the phrase we used to explain the how and why of individuals' behavior in the multitude of large-scale organizations that comprise the foreign affairs government. "Bureaucrat" is often used pejoratively by Americans to disparage the careerists and what they do and how they do it. Nonetheless, the fundamental premise is that the position and its corresponding subculture shape an individual's perspectives and policy preferences. Because both the personnel and their perspectives are more enduring than elected officials, they often act as a brake on policy innovation. Their role conceptions may also condition the options that high-level officials consider, ultimately making political appointees, including cabinet secretaries, more responsive to the career bureaucracy's agenda rather than careerists conforming to the priorities of the administration.

Governmental Sources of American Foreign Policy

Despite the power of the "permanent government," presidents enjoy enormous advantages as they seek to exercise their leadership roles. Indeed, as we saw in Chapter 10, their power in the foreign policy arena is preeminent. The advantages they enjoy include constitutional and legal prerogatives, precedents set by previous presidents, and the power to persuade, which flows in part from presidents' roles as chief executive and head of the White House–based presidential subsystem. George W. Bush nonetheless went to Washington determined to change things. A hallmark of his White House years will be his determined effort to strengthen the power of the president and the presidency. History will remember the intense secrecy that surrounded

his administration. Likely to be of more enduring impact were his persistent, concerted efforts to extend the power of the president into previously uncharted waters. Congress, the courts, and the American public all felt the currents of Bush's expansive interpretation of executive powers.

Vice President Dick Cheney was a champion of expanded executive powers. His experiences during the Watergate affair that led to Richard Nixon's resignation (1974) and the later Iran-Contra affair during the Reagan administration (1986) led Cheney to the conclusion that the post-Vietnam years severely circumscribed presidential prerogatives. He was determined to reverse course and encouraged every effort by President Bush to accomplish that goal.

The 9/11 terrorist attacks and the congressional resolution supporting the president's pursuit of terrorists opened the door to broad interpretations of presidential power. Many of them were claimed under the guise of the president's constitutional role as commander-in-chief.

> Known as the New Paradigm [the administration's] strategy [rested] on a reading of the Constitution that [said] . . . the President, as Commander-in-Chief, has the authority to disregard virtually all previously known legal boundaries, if national security demands it. Under this framework, statutes prohibiting torture, secret detention, and warrantless surveillance have been set aside.
>
> *(Mayer 2006, 44)*

The Bush administration engaged in all of these activities—shrouding them in secrecy and often beyond congressional approval or oversight—in the name of national security. Even some of Bush's own top-level officials, including many lawyers, were left outside the loop when the activities were vetted and approved (Mayer 2006). The National Security Agency's (NSA) surveillance without court order of Americans' international phone calls (and perhaps Internet activities) was one of the most widely publicized of Bush's controversial programs. When the press leaked information about it (and other surreptitious activities), the president defended his actions as necessary instruments in the war on terror. The administration also threatened to take legal action against reporters or their publishers who leaked the information, arguably in violation of their First Amendment rights protecting freedom of speech and the press. Thus in the balance between secrecy and openness posed by the democratic dilemma, the Bush administration tilted sharply toward secrecy.

Survey research shows many Americans are willing to trade some of their liberties to fight the war on terror. But some of the government's activities provoked serious questions about the legality, even constitutionality, of how the Bush administration pursed the war on terror. Bush's position that the president as commander-in-chief has virtually unlimited power during wartime was dealt a blow by the Supreme Court in an important case (*Hamdan v. Rumsfeld*) decided in early summer 2006. The Court ruled that the administration could not use military commissions to try detainees captured during the war on terror because the commissions afforded only limited legal protections for the rights of the accused. Further, it ruled that the government's treatment of prisoners violated Geneva Conventions on the treatment of prisoners of war. Earlier the Court had decided against Bush's contention that prisoners held at Guantanamo Bay—"illegal enemy combatants"—were beyond the U.S. court system and could not challenge their detention.[8] Of the hundreds of enemy combatants held at the military base in Cuba (some of them going back to the early days of the campaign against the Taliban in Afghanistan), none had been charged legally with an offense.

Following the *Hamdan v. Rumsfeld* case, *Washington Post* writers commented that "the decision-echoed not simply as a matter of law but as a rebuke of a governing philosophy of a leader who at repeated turns...operated on the principle that it is better to act than to ask permission. This ethos is why many supporters [found] Bush an inspiring leader, and why many critics in the country and abroad [reacted] so viscerally against him" (Baker and Abramowitz 2006).

Signing statements, referenced in Chapter 10 , are another means Bush used to enhance his presidential prerogatives. These statements, attached to laws passed by Congress, give a president's interpretation of how he views the law and whether it contains provisions he cannot support or enforce. All modern presidents have used this instrument, a prerogative that they have guarded jealously. But Bush made far more liberal use of them than any of his predecessors, issuing more than 750 of them (Mayer 2006, 55).[9] Some effectively challenged the basic purpose of the legislation. Among them was a law sponsored by Republican Senator John McCain, which sought to outlaw torture in the treatment of prisoners held by the United States. (The move was stimulated by the Abu Ghraib prison scandal in Iraq.) Bush's signing statement reserved "the right to construe the legislation only as it was consistent with the Constitution" (Mayer 2006). The president also issued a statement in connection with an effort by Democratic Representative John Murtha to forbid "the use of federal funds for any intelligence-gathering that violates the Fourth Amendment, which protects the privacy of American citizens." (The background in this case was the NSA's warrantless surveillance of Americans.) The White House took exception; Bush said "that the executive branch would 'construe' the spending limit only 'in a manner consistent with the President's constitutional authority as Commander-in-Chief, including for the conduct of intelligence operations.'" (Mayer 2006)

The Constitution and *The Federalist Papers* make clear that the founders intended that executive opposition to congressional legislation be registered with a veto. Bush cast only one veto in the first six years of his presidency—on stem cell research. The ultimate effect of signing statements on law-in-practice may well become a controversial Bush legacy.

The revival of presidential preeminence during the Bush years contrasts sharply with the direction of events in the 1990s. Then the Clinton administration charged Congress with usurping presidential power. Clinton himself "[accused] members of Congress of launching 'nothing less than a frontal assault on the authority of the president to conduct the foreign policy of the United States'" (Lindsay 2004). Under Bush, members of Congress themselves worried that they may have abdicated Congress's foreign policy role: "When President Bush asked Congress to give him authority to wage war on Iraq, Congress quibbled with some of the language of the draft resolution. Nonetheless, the revised bill, which the House and Senate passed overwhelmingly, amounted to a blank check that the president could cash as he saw fit" (Lindsay 2004). As we have seen throughout previous chapters, that legislation and laws and resolutions passed soon after 9/11, including the resolution that authorized the pursuit of terrorists and the renewed USA Patriot Act, turned out to have had very consequential effects.

The ebb and flow of Congress's assertions of its foreign policy powers closely follows the seemingly cyclical patterns of war and peace. Lindsay (2004) nicely summarizes "the rule": "Times of peace favor congressional activism. Times of war favor congressional deference." He adds that "both modes of congressional behavior have advantages—as well as create dangers."

The Clinton administration and the interlude between the fall of the Berlin Wall and 9/11 was a period of relative calm. To be sure, the United States intervened in Somalia, Haiti, and the Balkans, but globalization was the dominant order of the day. It encouraged the presence and deepened the salience of intermestic issues, ones that sit at the rather amorphous line separating foreign and domestic policy issues. International trade, a key component of the globalizing process, is an example. Members of Congress are more likely to be interested and involved in such issues than in matters of national security, where the president is usually recognized as the dominant player. Absent an obvious and pressing strategic threat at the time reduced the costs to members of Congress of challenging Clinton, thereby reducing the political risk to those who asserted their individual preferences. The American people's comparative indifference to foreign policy issues encouraged this tendency. "General public disinterest in foreign policy gives many members

[of Congress] a lot of latitude to pursue particular foreign policy interests without fear of political backlash, even if their views do not correspond with mainstream America or even with their own constituents" (Hersman 2000).

Although neither helpless nor without influence, Clinton watched as (since 1994) the Republican-controlled House of Representatives and the closely divided Senate scuttled his efforts to address the problem of global climate change, eliminate nuclear weapons testing, expand free trade arrangements, strengthen American involvement in multilateral peace operations, and reorient foreign economic aid policy. Clinton also found it necessary to accept congressional preferences on a host of issues not to his liking, including defense spending and national missile defense.

During roughly half of the twentieth century, bipartisanship, born of a broad foreign policy consensus supporting America's rise to global leadership, muted the Constitution's invitation for struggle between Congress and the president. Recent trends have been toward greater partisanship, particularly since the fractious Vietnam War. The highly partisan "culture wars" of recent years have also fueled the intensely partisan character of executive-legislative relations. There is no reason to expect these divisions will not persist beyond Bush. Without an overarching consensus about the U.S. world role and broad support of a dominant grand strategy, words like "usurp" and "abrogate" will likely characterize the invitation to struggle well into the future.

The structure of the American system of government, which divides authority between the executive and legislative branches, can act as a brake on presidential leadership and policy innovation. So can the executive bureaucracy, as we suggested earlier. National security issues dominated the foreign policy agenda under George W. Bush. However, the influence of career professionals comprising the foreign affairs government on the formulation and implementation of policy was also apparent on the evolving agenda of global challenges and opportunities evident for some years. Issues ranging from trade to the environment, from immigration to the continuing war on drugs, were among them. The range of issues now engages more elements of the foreign affairs government than ever before, thereby raising more interests, voices, and perspectives. They in turn complicate the challenge of coordinating the increasingly sprawling and disparate stakeholders on any given issue. As the country faces a complex environment fraught with dangers and opportunities that blur the distinction between foreign and domestic policy, the State Department and other traditional foreign policy agencies typically find themselves joined by Homeland Security, the Treasury, Commerce, Justice, and Agriculture Departments and agencies like the Drug Enforcement Agency and the Environmental Protection Agency in their search for appropriate responses to unfolding problems.

Ironically, the changing nature of contemporary world politics calls into question the relevance of the missions and capabilities of at least some of the foreign affairs organizations created and shaped during America's twentieth-century rise to globalism. Virtually all of them were designed to address Cold War threats. Today, many struggle to adapt to the new context. Presidents and their appointees must in turn grapple with how to reorient entrenched bureaucracies toward new goals and purposes. Again, Bush's efforts to reorganize America's foreign intelligence collection and homeland security exposed many entrenched interests and inappropriate structures.

The challenge is formidable; few presidents have succeeded in the past. In many ways a "new wine in old bottles" problem, the challenge is to move stubborn bureaucratic structures (and the traditions, born in another era, that sustain them) in a direction suitable for addressing twenty-first century problems while also jettisoning old mind-sets. Organizations, like individuals, are prone to cling to the past and the assumptions with which they are comfortable. Illustrative are the obstacles George W. Bush and his first Secretary of Defense Donald Rumsfeld faced as they sought to implement the president's bold campaign promise to discard Cold War premises and assumptions and transform the Pentagon to meet twenty-first century challenges in new and innovative ways. Ironically, with ample

budget resources at hand, Rumsfeld still chose to keep on line some major weapons systems first conceived as long ago as the Reagan administration rather than scuttle them in favor of the fast, highly mobile military machine he often touted.

The overlapping organizations that comprise the foreign affairs government, while nominally at the president's command, are not easily directed or led, as the role requirements of career professionals reward caution, not innovation. Furthermore, new presidents—often viewed as "transient meddlers" in the business of the people who staff the foreign affairs government—frequently find that their preferences are not top priorities in an environment that equates organizational survival with individual survival. Substantial bureaucratic resistance to White House direction complicates and confounds the exercise of *presidential leadership,* making it more difficult for the chief executive to direct the policy agenda, shape policy choices, and manage the activities of the many players, agencies, departments, and institutions of government. As political scientist Theodore Lowi aptly put it more than two decades ago:

> Presidents operate on the brink of failure and in ignorance of when, where, and how failure will come. They do not and cannot possibly know about even a small proportion of government activity that bears on their failure. They can only put out fires and smile above the ashes. They don't know what's going on—yet they are responsible for it. And they feed that responsibility every time they take credit for good news not of their own making.
> *(Lowi 1985b, 190)*

Societal Sources of American Foreign Policy

Because the United States is a society-dominant political system, the ability of the president to work his will in Congress is ultimately influenced by the support he and his policies enjoy among the American people. Judging by President Bush's approval ratings, which skyrocketed immediately after 9/11, his policies at the time appropriately enjoyed considerable support in Congress. Midway through his second term, however, Bush's approval ratings were among the lowest of all post–World War II presidents, including Truman, Nixon, Carter, and Bush I. The war in Iraq was clearly the cause. Bitter partisanship also characterized the relations among members of Congress and their approach to other policy issues. The data in Table 15.1 suggest that Congress and the American public were on the same page. We cannot say who is influencing whom, but the mirror images are unmistakable. Note in particular that the issues approval of Bush generally follows the same patterns as his overall approval.

During times of peace and prosperity and no imminent external threat, the American people's definition of national priorities understandably is driven by domestic concerns. Although it has been commonplace during the past decade to argue that the American people are turning inward, there is little evidence to suggest this is an isolationist plunge reminiscent of the period between the twentieth century World Wars. Americans want their leaders to prioritize issues and to be selective. The conflicts in Iraq and elsewhere in the Middle East remain unresolved, and terrorism, as Americans have been repeatedly warned, poses a long war. Surprisingly, however, Americans' recovery from the shock of 9/11 was remarkably quick. "This changes everything" was a popular cliché used to describe the impact of the terrorist attacks. Instead, "politics as usual" soon returned as the norm.

> A Gallup poll in December 2001 found that 71 percent of Americans said that religion as a whole was increasing its influence on American life, a sharp turnabout from findings of almost 20 years of polling. By March 2002, according to a Pew Research poll, the 9/11 effect had worn off and the public's view had reverted to pre-attack levels, with 37 percent saying religion's influence on American life was increasing.

> Fear of attack also spiked, but then quickly began to recede.... Fear of flying increased, then began to decline within weeks of the attack. The attacks understandably scrambled the nation's issue agenda. Combating terrorism rose to the top of the country's priorities, while concern over other issues dropped. But by the end of 2001, concern about jobs and the economy once again were as high as terrorism and security.
>
> (Broder and Balz 2006, 7)

In short, as one opinion analyst reported, "It didn't take America five years to recover [from 9/11]. It was like a year" (cited in Broder and Balz 2006).

Putting aside the war in Iraq, if the American people seem to evince misinformation about and a lack of interest in American foreign policy, the reasons are understandable. Doubtless this is worrisome from the perspective of democratic theory, which says that an informed citizenry will shape American leaders' policy choices. It also casts doubt on policy makers' claims when they profess they know what "the American people" want. Iraq aside again, the reality is that the preeminence of the United States in twenty-first century world politics leads most Americans to attach comparatively little salience to what happens beyond Fortress America. Terrorist threats against the United States may be a worry; whether attacks in London, Madrid, and Bali are of equal concern is questionable. This disjuncture also means presidents cannot ignore—without inviting political peril—the priorities that the American people attach to the home front.

The opinions of policy influentials and the mass public often differ, as we saw in Chapter 8. The mass public typically attributes greater importance to foreign policy issues with a distinctly domestic tinge, for example. The meaning for democratic theory of the gap between influentials and the public is not entirely clear, however. Public ignorance and misunderstanding is the obvious elitist interpretation of this persistent empirical finding.

But the counterweight to that interpretation is the failure of some pursuits that American leaders favored despite public dissension that turned out to be fundamentally flawed. Vietnam heads the list, but it is not alone.

In a careful study of the gap between leaders and the general public, Benjamin Page and Jason Barabas conclude:

> Taken as a whole, the gaps . . . between the foreign policy preferences of citizens and those of leaders do not appear . . . to result from a contrast between leaders' wisdom and expertise and the public's ignorance, misunderstanding, selfishness, or short-sightedness. In many cases public opinion may be reasonably well informed and deliberative, and the gaps may reflect differences between leaders and citizens with respect to values, goals, and interests. In such cases democratic theory would seem to recommend responsiveness to what the citizens favor.
>
> *(Page and Barabas 2000, 362)*

Still, others worry that the nature of contemporary American politics militates against the development of a coherent foreign policy framework to guide the United States in the twenty-first century. Charles Maynes, editor emeritus of the influential magazine *Foreign Policy,* is among them:

> At the beginning of the last century, Americans interested in foreign policy had an advantage that those similarly interested today do not: Leading the debate over foreign policy choices were two exceptionally eloquent national figures— Theodore Roosevelt and Woodrow Wilson.
>
> By contrast, today's politics produce— perhaps require—political figures of narrow electoral calculation rather than lofty policy conviction. Since Reagan in the 1980s, no recent president or presidential candidate has been willing to make his vision of America's role in the world a major thrust of his message to the country. All have suffered from the lack of the "vision thing," and perhaps all agree in private that displaying it might prove politically lethal.
>
> *(Maynes 2001, 57)*

Even as the American people look outward as well as inward in these tumultuous times, pressures from powerful interests in the United States continue to dictate large expenditures on national defense outside the special appropriations for the wars in Afghanistan and Iraq. Defense spending declined each year in the decade ending in 1995, but since then, with the support of both Republicans and Democrats, it has been on an upward spiral. Today, as during the Cold War, defense spending consumes a lion's share of discretionary federal spending. A concern for jobs and an urge to keep the defense industrial base "warm" are potent domestic sources behind the urge to spend on the military. Meanwhile, expenditures on other foreign affairs activities remain minuscule, even as the federal budget accumulated massive surpluses during a time of unparalleled economic prosperity in the 1990s. Since then, of course, large tax deductions combined with an upward spiral in federal spending have led to budget deficits in excess of $300 billion.

Interest groups and political action committees continue to press their special causes, leading policy makers to navigate a middle course among the shoals of America's political pluralism. The changing face of America, documented in the 2000 census, promises to encourage even greater interest group activity. President Clinton once remarked that "you can't be president anymore unless you understand the concerns of at least fifty different groups." For those fifty groups, the best way to have their concerns expressed is through organized political activity. Foreign governments also are taking advantage of channels of access and influence made possible by America's open political system. With the United States the world's preeminent power, others want to be sure their voices are heard. "Today Washington is . . . inundated by foreign diplomats and revolving-door lobbyists working to ensure that the interests of America's partners are not over-looked" (Ikenberry 2001; see also Huntington 1997).

The electronic media also play an increasingly prominent role in shaping political agendas and causing policy makers to pander to public preferences. In particular, the Internet and Internet blogs have been among the most recent devices used in the chorus of voices seeking to influence policy makers. The traditional print media have themselves found the Internet a useful outlet. Although less assertive than during the heyday of investigative journalism prominent during the Watergate era, they continue to perform the watchdog function expected of a free press in a democratic society. When the *New York Times* published high profile leaks of classified information about the Bush administration's warrantless surveillance programs, the *Washington Post (National Weekly Edition*, 10–16 July 2006, 26) defended the *Times'* controversial actions:

> All administrations jealously guard secrets. But this [Bush] administration, more than any since the one that prosecuted the Pentagon Papers case, has resisted disclosure and effective oversight, whether by Congress or the press. This across-the-board aversion to scrutiny makes it all the more difficult for responsible media organizations to separate the legitimate claims of national security from the overblown.
>
> Those who complain about disclosures assert that the war on terrorism has changed the calculus of risk. They would prefer a media meekly obeying official demands for secrecy. But in the end, as Justice Stewart understood, the nation stands to benefit far more than it could lose from a press that is "alert, aware, and free."

The allusion to Supreme Court Justice Potter Stewart is from his concurring opinion in the Pentagon Papers case from the early 1970s. The *New York Times* at that time published a classified Pentagon self-study of the Vietnam War that had been leaked by Daniel Ellsberg. Stewart wrote:

> In the absence of the governmental checks and balances present in other areas of our national life, the only effective restraint upon executive policy and power in the areas of national defense and international affairs may lie in an enlightened citizenry—in an informed and critical public opinion which alone can here protect the values of democratic government. . . . For this reason, it is perhaps here that a press that is alert, aware, and free most vitally serves the basic purpose of the First Amendment. For without an informed and free press, there cannot be an enlightened people.

Our earlier discussion of public opinion (Chapter 8) raises serious questions about how enlightened the people are. Nonetheless, their opinions cannot easily be discounted. The **perpetual election**—constant polling to determine presidents' standing with the American people—arguably forces presidents to choose the path of convenience, not conscience, when faced with tough choices. Foreign policy challenges and crises often boost presidents' popularity at home, as witnessed by the dramatic surge in George W. Bush's popularity following the 9/11 terrorist attacks. But the state of the economy typically exerts a more enduring impact. Even here, however, the challenges facing the United States in a rapidly changing world political economy have caused skittishness in the public mood, as witnessed not only by protests against globalization but also by sharp divisions in Congress and the public about how to deal with the influx of largely Hispanic, often illegal, immigrants. Indeed, Bush's attempt to devise a comprehensive immigration policy that would deal not only with incoming illegal immigrants but also amnesty or some other venue for those already in the United States proved to be one of the most divisive issues in the summer preceding the 2006 midterm congressional elections.

Fear that immigrants threaten Americans' jobs motivates one side of the immigration argument; concern that as low wage workers they perform jobs essential for the economy that Americans do not want, and that immigrants often make positive contributions to the nation's culture as well as economy, is an opposing viewpoint. Still, as we saw in Chapter 8, multiculturalism—an expression of new immigrant groups' rejection of the "melting pot" metaphor long used to describe the process that assimilated new Americans into the established social system—promises to be a source of continuing debate about issues ranging from affirmative action to the use of Spanish in classrooms. The only certainty is that the urge to migrate to "the land of the free" and plenty will continue as population growth, environmental degradation, and religious and ethnic conflicts push millions from their homelands. A more diverse American society will manifest significant domestic political differences, making it more difficult for the nation to reach consensus on an appropriate world role for today and tomorrow.

The Cold War stimulated the cohesiveness that bound the American nation together for decades. What historian John Lewis Gaddis called "the long war" against communism strengthened Americans' national identity, providing a "unifying dynamic [that] helped overcome ethnic and sectional differences and the ideological heritage of individualism" (Deudney and Ikenberry 1994). In contrast, the narrowness of the 2000 and 2004 presidential elections and the slender majorities in Congress in recent years are mirror images of contemporary American politics and society. Division, not unity, now characterizes the American polity. The widespread popularity of the electoral map of "red states" and "blue states" shows clearly the country's sectional (and typically corresponding partisan) divisions.

The closely divided elections were unusual in some respects, but not atypical. The electoral process rarely clarifies the range of public support for specific policies. Instead, voter preferences are a breeding ground for policy evolution, not revolution. Mapping a new foreign policy strategy for the twenty-first century in such an environment is nearly impossible. Critical elections for Americans lie in the years ahead. But, as we have seen, in a society-dominant political system, elections are only one element in a complex process that determines policy outcomes.

External Sources of American Foreign Policy

As George W. Bush approached the midpoint of his second term, crises seemed to loom on every horizon: the unexpected outbreak of war between Israel and the militant Hezbollah in Lebanon; violent insurgency in Iraq that threatened to degrade into a full-fledged civil war; growing violence in Afghanistan just as NATO forces took on an expanded peacekeeping role; persistent challenges from a nuclear-armed North Korea; intransigence from a near-nuclear radical regime in Iran; and the revelation of an unsuccessful terrorist plot in which airliners were to be blown up over the Atlantic by suicide bombers after takeoff from London's Heathrow airport.

The war between Israel and Hezbollah along the border separating Israel and Lebanon revealed how quickly events abroad can threaten American interests. A non-state actor, Hezbollah has long been deeply entrenched in Southern Lebanon, where it operates as both a guerrilla organization and a social service agency. Although Hezbollah is predominantly Shia, it nonetheless developed links with the Sunni-oriented Hamas, the militant Palestinian movement that won election to the Palestinian parliament in early 2006. Syria and Iran have long supported Hezbollah and are believed to be its major arms suppliers.

Out of this crucible of conflict, which included the sectarian insurgency in Iraq, the threat of a wider war loomed large. As we said earlier, that would undo virtually the centerpiece of Bush's grand strategy—namely, bringing stability and democracy to the Middle East. Many Arabs blamed the United States for the fighting because of its close ties with Israel, including its roles as major supporter, consultant, and supplier of arms to the Jewish state.[10] Still, other states, because of the Unites States' close ties to Israel, looked to it for leadership in bringing the conflict to an end. But the exercise of leadership was made more difficult by the tense, almost nonexistent relations between the United States and Syria, and by the U.S. refusal to recognize either Iran or the Hamas Palestinian government—both consistent with the Bush

Doctrine, which calls for going after terrorists and the states that support them.

The United States has long had a hand in the conflict in Lebanon between Hezbollah and Israel. In 1983, for example, 241 American Marines and navy personnel, all part of a multilateral peace-keeping force, were killed in a terrorist bombing at the Beirut international airport. Although many thought the United States could stop the fighting in the summer of 2006 at will, the crisis seemed to illustrate once more the limits of America's hard power. The United States and Israel maintained the military upper hand. But neither by themselves nor together could they impose a solution to the long-standing political and religious divisions rending the region.

Here and in the larger picture of Middle East conflict, some saw as essential the need for the United States to recapture the moral high ground. As an (unidentified) senior army officer of an allied state fighting along side the United States in Iraq put it:

> The United States is so powerful militarily that by its very nature it represents a threat to every other [state] on earth. The only country that could theoretically destroy every single other country is the United States. The only way we can say that the U.S. is *not* a threat is by looking at intent, and that depends on moral authority. If you're not sure that United States is going to do the right thing, you can't trust it with that power, so you begin thinking, How can I balance it off and find other alliances to protect myself?
>
> *(Cited in Fallows 2006, 70; see also Ferguson 2003b)*

The unipolar distribution of power in the international system, which finds the United States the preponderant power, has encouraged its unilateralist policies and its doctrine of preemptive war. Both have been primary irritants among other states. This is particularly true since the United States has already proclaimed its determination to remain a hegemonic power in a series of official documents, going back as early as the first Bush presidency. As former Secretary of State Henry Kissinger (2001b) warned: "No matter how selfless America perceives its aims, an explicit insistence on predominance would gradually unite the world against the United States and force it into impositions that would eventually leave it isolated and drained."

Although not yet in a multipolar world, we would still expect other states to form alliances or pool their power and resources in other ways designed to *balance* the hegemon. They have. The very fact of its preponderance, however, makes balancing the United States difficult. Still, "other countries have deployed a multiplicity of strategies and tactics designed to weaken, divert, alter, complicate, limit, delay or block the Bush agenda through a death by a thousand cuts." Although their motives are diverse and often reflect narrowly defined parochial interests, "their unifying theme—usually unspoken—is resistance to nearly anything that serves to buttress a unipolar world." Much the same is true among Europeans, where the unstated "goal has been to lessen the superpower's freedom of action and to work towards a more multipolar world. This global trend will stamp the character of global politics for a decade or more." Among the other major powers, Russia, China, and India "have acted subtly, or even not so subtly, to complicate or block many of Washington's major initiatives" (Fuller 2006).

Surprisingly, the emphasis on ***democratization*** (the move from authoritarian or semi-authoritarian rule to a democratic political system) within American foreign policy is a project that has become an irritant to other states. The United States claims both to be values universally shared. But they are not. Certainly the Muslim world has not embraced democracy as a "universal norm," and several Latin American states have also backed away from it. The absence of a universal (and equal) promotion of democracy is one reason. As Graham Fuller writes,

> We may perceive democracy as a universal good—and in principle it may well be. But the ideal now becomes transformed into an instrument of U.S. policies. And as a policy tool, the call for democratization in fact has become an instrument to intimidate,

pressure or even overthrow regimes that resist the global American project. . . . Democratization just might gain some international credence if truly applied across the board as the central principle of U.S. policy. But to date, democratization has largely been a punishment visited upon our enemies, never a gift bestowed upon our friends. . . . In the eyes of others it merely becomes another superpower tool opportunistically employed for its own transient ends.

(Fuller 2006, 40)

Another irritant is ***globalization,*** the rapid intensification and integration of states' economies, not only in terms of markets but also ideas, information, and technology, which is having a profound impact on political, social, and cultural relations across borders. Like democratization, the United States often touts globalization as a universal process from which all can benefit. Yet others have not always seen it that way. Hegemonic powers, as we saw in Chapter 7, benefit from an open world political economy. They control markets, capital, production, and valued goods, like technology. Others do not share equally in the benefits of an open system. Hence, "for better or worse, globalization is now increasingly perceived as a particular American agenda designed to serve American interests. It is therefore held in suspicion by many" (Fuller 2006).

It is noteworthy that the Bush administration professed to be a champion of multilateralism in its approach to the world political economy, particularly in the Western Hemisphere. However, of the more than twenty free trade agreements (FTAs) currently in force or pending, most were negotiated during the Bush presidency and were either bilateral or regionally based. As we observed in Chapter 7, the norms being established by these agreements may undermine the Liberal International Economic Order promoted by the United States after World War II, and also the principles and rules of the World Trade Organization (WTO), which monitors the global free trade system. Furthermore, the Doha Round of multilateral trade negotiations launched in 2001 under the auspices of the WTO with U.S. support, is at a standstill and may never be revived.

For some neoconservatives and neoisolationists, slowing the momentum of globalization, particularly the enhancement of the role of multilateral institutions in international governance, is a good thing, as it thwarts challenges to America's sovereign prerogatives. Others disagree. Indeed, President Clinton, a liberal internationalist, argued that "the train of globalization cannot be reversed." But, he added, "it has more than one possible destination. If we want America to stay on the right track, if we want other people to be on that track and have the chance to enjoy peace and prosperity, we have no choice but to try to lead the train."

Free markets and democracies often go hand in hand. This was part of the logic of the Clinton administration's focus on democratic enlargement: democracies do not fight one another. The post–Cold War experiment in globalization has a counterpart early in the twentieth century. Norman Angell's (1914) acclaimed book *The Great Illusion,* published on the eve of World War I, is part of the legacy that argues globalization (intensified interdependence) reduces the probability of war. That experiment was interrupted by two world wars and the economically, socially, and politically disruptive experiments in fascism and communism. Will the widening expanse and sophistication of terrorism today disrupt the current experiment in globalization, perhaps postponing it again for nearly a century?

There is no easy answer to the question of terrorism's effect on globalization and the dilemma it poses for policy makers.[11] It should not be surprising that terrorists can easily take advantage of the open society that is America, and with which Americans themselves so closely identify. Liberty ultimately means freedom of choice unencumbered by the dictates of government. So we should not be surprised that many around the world who harbor a deep-seated hatred for the United States simultaneously take advantage of its freedoms to attack the very liberal foundations on which it was built and continues to prosper.

Historian Niall Ferguson (2005) reminds us that today's world looks suspiciously like the world that led to the collapse of the early twentieth century experiment with globalization. "The present political situation," he writes, "has the same five flaws as the pre-1914 international order: imperial overstretch, great-power rivalry, an unstable alliance system, rogue regimes sponsoring terror, and the rise of a revolutionary terrorist organization hostile to capitalism." And the world "is no better prepared for calamity now" than it was then.

Despite what may be an impending calamity, globalization proceeds apace (see A. T. Kearney, Inc. and the Carnegie Endowment for International Peace 2006). Its effects stretch beyond culture and economics to national security issues. China comes readily to mind. It is now one of the most important trade partners of the United States. The U.S. trade deficit with China is at or in excess of $2 billion annually, and U.S. multinational corporations invest heavily in China. Increasingly, China also invests in the United States (as well as in Latin America and Europe).

Most strategic analysts view China, the most populous of the emerging industrial economies, as the most likely competitor and rival of the United States in this century. The flashpoint in their relations is Taiwan. How China's rise to power and how the contentious Taiwan issue are handled will likely shape the entire panoply of security and nonsecurity issues in the Far East, including relations with Japan, the two Koreas, and perhaps others. And the repercussions will extend beyond Asia, helping to shape the contours of a new multipolar distribution of power widely believed to be on the distant horizon of the twenty-first century.

The first Bush administration pursued a policy of engagement toward China rather than confrontation. Bill Clinton criticized that strategy during the 1992 presidential campaign but would later adopt it as his own under the guise of *comprehensive engagement*. His administration first de-linked trade from human rights issues, and then ultimately became the champion of granting China Permanent Normal Trade Relations (PNTR). This paved the way for its entry into the World Trade Organization. Clinton believed this was the best way to integrate China into the mainstream world political economy, thus opening the Chinese economy and

society to external influences and the possibility that these might encourage the spread of democratizing forces in the communist country.

The George W. Bush administration at first did not follow the path of either of its predecessors. Instead, it viewed China not as a strategic partner but as a *strategic competitor*. In the eyes of China's leaders, its hostile intent was affirmed when early in his presidency Bush submitted a bill to Congress calling for the sale of advanced weapons to Taiwan, which China vigorously opposed. The president also articulated more clearly than had his predecessors the determination of the United States to defend Taiwan against an armed attack. Previously what the United States would do in such an eventuality was purposely shrouded in ambiguity. China viewed the administration's determination to build a missile defense system as an offensive threat, encouraging it to engage in a military buildup of its own. It is perhaps notable that the administration devoted attention to the concerns expressed by both Europe and Russia on this issue, but virtually none expressed by China.

The terrorist attacks in 2001 changed American rhetoric from strategic competition to partnership. The Bush administration now sought to enlist China in the war on terrorism. To a large extent it was successful. Then–Secretary of Defense Donald Rumsfeld visited China in 2005. He said at the time that China's record of military spending was potentially ominous. But he also said that while China posed a security threat to much of Asia, it did not pose a threat to the United States.

On the other side, China engaged in "balancing" diplomacy in the United Nations Security Council and in other venues. For the most part, however, it supported the Bush administration on terrorist matters. The consequence was a distinctly more cordial relationship with the United States across both security and nonsecurity matters. How this will affect the long-term relations between the two states remains to be seen.

If China is the next superpower, India may not be far behind. The United States' agreement with India on its nuclear program is an implicit recognition of India as an increasingly major player in international politics. India also plays an increasingly important role in the globalization process. Computer users who call their software providers for technical help often find that help comes from someone in India. This is a microcosm of the rapid advances India has made in recent years in developing sophisticated technological skills. With that, India has developed, particularly around its technology centers, a growing middle class. As elsewhere, a dynamic middle class is widely deemed to be critical in sustaining long-term economic growth. Still, India remains a very poor country with a population of more than a billion, most of whom live a life of poverty.[12]

We should also put Japan into this equation. As Kenneth Waltz (1993) argues, it would be an anomaly if Japan were not to build nuclear weapons. Because the United States provides a nuclear umbrella that promises to protect Japan, the possibility that Japan, already constrained by its own constitution, would build nuclear weapons has been slight. Now, however, North Korea's aggressive nuclear weapons and missile programs increasingly pose a direct threat to Japan. If in response Japan were to discard its post–World War II phobia against nuclear weapons, this would have a profound effect on U.S.-Japanese relations and the entire balance of power in Asia.

Beyond the strategic challenges China, India, and Japan face, the whole of Asia confronts economic challenges that inevitably involve the United States, the world's unchallenged economic hegemon. Japan's economy has largely stalled during much of the past decade or more. Elsewhere, particularly in Southeast Asia, growing religious conflicts and the hangover from the economic meltdown of the late 1990s have imperiled the stellar economic progress the emerging economies of the region once displayed (Hartcher 2001).

If the United States chooses to lead the globalization train, that will require its attention to those globalization has left behind, causing widening disparities between the rich of the Global North and those less fortunate in the Global South, as we saw in Chapter 6. Harvard economist Jeffrey Sachs observes that poor economic performance among poor countries goes "beyond direct economic returns." "As a general proposition, economic failure abroad raises the risk of state failure as well. When foreign states malfunction, in the sense that they fail to provide basic public goods for their populations, their societies are likely to experience steeply escalating problems that spill over to the rest of the world. . . . Failed states are seedbeds of violence, terrorism, international criminality, mass migration and refugee movements, drug trafficking, and disease" (Sachs 2001). Sachs adds a clear policy prescription: "If the United States wants to spend less time responding to failed states, . . . it will have to spend more time helping them achieve economic success to avoid state failure."

THE SECOND AMERICAN CENTURY: A CHALLENGING FUTURE

Former Secretary of State Dean Acheson once said that "there are fashions in everything, even in horrors . . . and just as there are fashions in fears, there are fashions in remedies." Today the remedies are very much American fashions. Whether committed to liberal internationalism or to neoconservatism, America's leadership will be essential to meet the challenges ahead. As President Clinton put it in his December 2000 speech on "A Foreign Policy for the Global Age":

> We must not squander the best moment in our history on small-mindedness. We don't have to be fearful. We've got the strongest military in the world, and in history. . . .
> We don't have to be cheap. Our economy is the envy of the world. We don't have to swim against the currents of the world. The momentum of history is on our side, on the side of freedom and openness and competition. And we don't have the excuse of ignorance, because we've got a 24-hour global news cycle. So we know what's going on out there.

Whether the fashions of today will persist will depend in part on the capacity of the American democracy to recruit into office farsighted, courageous leaders able to offer a positive vision of the future and a program to reach it. Emergent twenty-first century developments will be influenced by the assumptions policy makers make about global realities and by their capacity to act decisively and wisely in responding to the challenges of today and tomorrow.

The person empowered to make the fundamental choices, the president, is only one element in the equation that will define the outcome. Other factors will join presidential influence to collectively drive the policy process, ultimately shaping the policy patterns that eventually emerge. Indeed, the process—more than the individuals involved in it—will parent the policy, for the policy-making process and the conditions that influence it will not only stimulate efforts to cope with external challenges but also constrain a president's ability to implement the design chosen.

Nearly two centuries ago, Secretary of State John Quincy Adams declared, "I know of no change in policy, only of circumstance." Over a century later, Emmet John Hughes (1972), an adviser to President Eisenhower, wrote that "All of [the nation's past presidents], from the most venturesome to the most reticent, have shared one disconcerting experience: the discovery of the limits and restraints—decreed by law, by history, and by circumstances—that sometimes can blur their clearest designs or dull their sharpest purposes." Most of the assumptions made by American policy makers in the immediate circumstances following World War II proved to be remarkably resilient for more than six decades. Arguably they served the nation well. Now, however, the structure of the international system on which those assumptions were based no longer exists. Old solutions may no longer fit new realities. Although past policy has the awesome force of momentum behind it, today the question is whether American leaders have the will to chart new foreign policy directions and the means to realize them. George W. Bush assuredly sought to do so. History will be the ultimate judge of his success.

When Henry Luce in 1941 predicted the twentieth century would be the American Century, he based his conviction not only on the potential military might of the United States but also on its ability to maintain "a vital international economy" and "an international moral order." If the twenty-first century is to be a second American Century, the United States must rise to the challenge.

KEY TERMS

benevolent hegemony
Bush Doctrine
coercive hegemony
democratic dilemma
democratization

globalization
grand strategy
hegemony
multilateralism
perpetual election

preemption/preemptive war
presidential leadership
prevention/preventive war

signing statements
unilateralism

SUGGESTED READINGS

Brokaw, Tom. *The Greatest Generation.* New York: Random House, 1998.

Fromkin, David. *In the Time of the Americans: FDR, Truman, Eisenhower, Marshall, MacArthur—The* Generation That Changed America's Role in the World. New York: Knopf, 1995.

Haass, Richard N. *The Opportunity: America's Moment to Alter History's Course.* New York: PublicAffairs, 2005.

Hodge, Carl Cavanagh. *Atlanticism for a New Century: The Rise, Triumph, and Decline of NATO.* Upper Saddle River, NJ: Pearson/Prentice Hall, 2005.

Jervis, Robert. *American Foreign Policy in a New Era.* New York: Routledge, 2005a.

Kissinger, Henry A. *Does America Need a Foreign Policy? Toward a Diplomacy for the 21st Century.* New York: Simon &Schuster, 2001.

Mann, Thomas E., and Norman J. Ornstein. *The Broken Branch: How Congress Is Failing America and How to Get It Back on Track.* New York: Oxford University Press, 2006.

Nye, Joseph, Jr. *The Paradox of American Power: Why the World's Only Superpower Can't Go It Alone.* New York: Oxford University Press, 2002.

Rudalevige, Andrew. *The New Imperial Presidency: Renewing Presidential Power after Watergate.* Ann Arbor, MI: University of Michigan Press, 2006.

Trubowitz, Peter. *Defining the National Interest: Conflict and Change in American Foreign Policy.* Chicago: University of Chicago Press, 1998.

Tucker, Robert W., and David C. Hendrickson. "The Sources of American Legitimacy," *Foreign Affairs* 83 (November/December), 2004: 18–32.

NOTES

1. A June 2006 survey sponsored by the *Washington Post* and ABC News asked Americans whether Bush would be remembered most for Iraq or for his efforts to combat terrorism: 79 percent picked Iraq, only 15 percent picked terrorism (*Washington Post National Weekly Edition,* July 24–30, 8).

2. Surprisingly, a June 2005 poll by the nonprofit organization Public Agenda found that divisions on the war on terrorism and the reconstruction of Iraq followed religious as well as partisan lines. "The more often Americans attend religious services, the more likely they are to be content with current U.S. foreign policy" (Yankelovich 2005).

3. James Fallows (2006) offers a positive assessment of the success of the United States and its allies in the war on terror. He writes, "The United States is succeeding in its struggle against terrorism. The time has come to declare the war on terror over, so that an even more effective military and diplomatic campaign can begin."

4. *Foreign Policy* describes the respondents this way: Participants include people who have served as secretary of state, national security advisor, retired top commanders from the U.S. military, seasoned members of the intelligence community, and distinguished academics and journalists. Nearly 80 percent of the . . . participants have worked in the U.S. government—of these more than half were in the executive branch, one third in the military, and 17 percent in the intelligence community ("The Terrorism Index" 2006).

5. See Leffler (2004) for a contrary view that sees Bush's foreign policy as no more "revolutionary" that his predecessors, going all the way back to Thomas Jefferson.

6. Writing in the 1920s and 1930s, Gramsci used the concept of hegemony in trying to understand why, when faced with the rise of fascism, the European working class did not rise up in revolution as Karl Marx had predicted. He concluded that "Dominant groups in society, including fundamentally but not exclusively the ruling class, maintain their dominance by securing the 'spontaneous consent' of subordinate groups, including the working class, through the negotiated construction of a political and ideological consensus which incorporates both dominant and dominated groups" (Strinati 1995).

7. "Their policy is 'Trust us,' and that may not be good enough anymore." *Newsweek* (July 3/July 10, p. 33) reported that comment by Steven Aftergood, director of the Project on Government Secrecy of the Federation of American Scientists after the *New York Times* revealed the Bush administration was operating a secret program designed to track bank transactions without court approval.

8. In contrast, during his first term Bush enjoyed several court victories or non-decisions bearing on his controversial actions.

9. David S. Addington, Vice President Cheney's chief of staff and longtime legal adviser, was reportedly the author of many of these statements. Addington

was a principal architect of the administration's legal approach to the war on terror and an advocate of the "New Paradigm" governing a president's power as commander-in-chief (Mayer 2006).

10. According to an article by Seymour M. Hersh in the August 2006 issue of *The New Yorker*, the United States was closely involved with Israel in the planning of its attack on Hezbollah even before the capture of two Israeli soldiers by Hezbollah on July 12, 2006 (Hersh 2006b).

11. See Naim (2003) for a provocative view of the way globalization affects other "wars," including illegal trade in drugs, arms, intellectual property, people, and money.

12. A series of articles in *Foreign Affairs* deals extensively with issues pertinent to relations between the United States and China (September/October 2005) and between the United States and India (July/August 2006).

Glossary

527 organizations A new group of political organizations as defined by Section 527 of the federal tax code. Like political action committees (PACs), these entities raise money to provide campaign funds for political parties or individual candidates. Unlike PACs, they fall within the purview of the Internal Revenue Service and are not subject to the oversight and restrictions of the Federal Elections Commission.

absolute poverty A condition of life in which one lacks the resources to meet the basic needs for healthy living, such as access to safe water, adequate nutrition, sanitation, and medical care.

accommodationists Those who, in the wake of the Vietnam War, emphasized cooperative ties with other states, particularly détente with the Soviet Union, and rejected the view that the United States could assume a unilateralist posture in the world; proponents of multilateralism in the post–Cold War world.

ad hoc decision making A behavior in which decisions are made in reaction to others' decisions or issues as they arise, focusing on each day's immediate crisis and avoiding long-term planning.

adhocracy A system of decision making that allows the president flexibility to devise advisory committees and make assignments to address a specific situation or need without relying on the usual, established patterns of providing advice through cabinet officials or bureaucratic organizations.

administrative theory A theory tied to the work of German sociologist Max Weber (1864–1920) that seeks to explain how bureaucratic organizations should be designed to promote efficient administration and rationality to better serve the state and its citizens.

agenda–setting The role that the mass media play in telling the public which issues to think and care about.

Al Qaeda A transnational terrorist organization responsible for the September 11, 2001, attacks on the United States.

American Century A prolonged period in which American interests shape the world.

American Israel Public Affairs Committee (AIPAC) A key cog in the so-called pro-Israeli lobby within the United States. It is widely recognized as one of the most influential of all lobby groups on Capitol Hill.

anticipated reactions A process whereby the president surveys the preferences of Congress on a policy issue and tailors his proposal to meet those preferences.

assured destruction The capacity to survive an aggressor's worst possible attack with sufficient firepower to inflict unacceptable damage on the attacker in retaliation; a key feature of the Kennedy and Johnson administrations' doctrine of strategic deterrence.

asymmetrical warfare As defined by the U.S. military, a form of warfare that attempts to circumvent or undermine an opponent's strengths while exploiting his weaknesses using methods that differ significantly from the opponent's usual mode of operations.

attentive public People who are attentive to and knowledgeable about foreign affairs but who do not necessarily have access to decision makers.

ballistic missile defense (BMD) A means of defending against attacks from intercontinental ballistic missiles.

beggar-thy-neighbor policies Efforts to enhance domestic welfare by means of currency devaluations, tariffs, quotas, export subsidies, and other strategies that promote trade surpluses at other states' expense.

belief system Conceptual lens through which individuals receive and process information that orients them to their physical and social environment, helping them to establish goals, order preferences, and relate ideas systematically to one another.

benevolent hegemony The use of preponderant power to provide leadership and public goods such as order, stability, and prosperity for the benefit of all members of the international system.

biodiversity The natural abundance of plant and animal species, humankind's genetic heritage, which is threatened by rapidly increasing extinctions due to deforestation and other environmental damage.

bipartisanship The practical application of the proposition that "politics stops at the water's edge"; used to describe the cordial and cooperative relationship between Congress and the executive branch during much of the Roosevelt, Truman, and Eisenhower presidencies.

bipolar/bipolarity A global structure in which power is concentrated in two countries or centers (poles).

bipolycentrism A global power structure somewhat looser and more fluid than a bipolar one, in which the alliance partners of the primary powers form relationships among themselves while continuing to rely on their great power patrons for security.

Brezhnev Doctrine A Soviet doctrine, named after Premier Leonid Brezhnev, intended to justify the 1968 invasion of Czechoslovakia and to put other communist states on warning about the dangers of defection from the socialist fold and the Soviet sphere of influence.

brinkmanship A willingness during the Eisenhower administration to go to the brink of nuclear war as a means of bargaining with the Soviet Union.

bully pulpit The president's use of his office and considerable access to the media to cajole and persuade others inside and outside of government to support his polices and programs.

Bureau of Intelligence and Research The State Department's representative in the intelligence community, which is charged with introducing a diplomatic sensitivity to intelligence reports.

bureaucratic politics model A perspective that stresses the policy-making effects of interaction and competition among bureaucratic organizations and the competing roles of people within them.

Bush Doctrine George W. Bush's foreign policy grand strategy as outlined in the National Security Strategy of 2002. Its chief objectives were to pursue terrorists and the states that harbor them, halt the proliferation of weapons of mass destruction, and promote the spread of democracy throughout the world. Preemptive war, hegemony, and unilateralism were identified as critical for realizing these goals.

cabinet The advisory body to the president made up of the department secretaries and agency heads.

Carter Doctrine President Jimmy Carter's declaration that the United States was willing to use military force to protect its security interests in the Persian Gulf.

Case Act Named after its sponsor, Republican Senator Clifford Case of New Jersey, this 1972 statute required the president to submit to Congress all international agreements within sixty days of their execution.

casualty hypothesis A theory supported by empirical evidence that maintains Americans' tolerance for war is limited by the number of casualties suffered by its soldiers.

Central Intelligence Agency (CIA) Established by the National Security Act of 1947, the most prominent member of the U.S. intelligence community and the only member with the status of an independent agency. It has collection, analysis, counterintelligence, and covert action responsibilities.

Chemical Weapons Convention (CWC) An international agreement concluded in 1995 that bans the development, production, acquisition, transfer, stockpiling, and use of chemical weapons. The United States ratified the CWC in 1997.

chief of staff A member of the presidential staff selected by presidential appointment to manage and coordinate the activities and agendas of the White House staff. Chiefs of staff may be strong or weak and, in addition to bringing order to White House operations, may be key advisers if presidents so desire.

civil religion The appeal to or use of the American people's religious values and religiosity in public life and foreign policy.

Clinton Doctrine President Bill Clinton's vision of the world following the 1999 NATO intervention in Kosovo, in which international values would reign supreme.

He stated, "If somebody comes after innocent civilians and tries to kill them en masse because of their race, their ethnic background, or their religion, and it's within our power to stop it, we will stop it."

CNN effect The supposed loss of policy control by decision makers because of the power of the media.

code of conduct on arms transfers Congressional effort to develop requirements for the sale of U.S. weapons to other states; stimulated by concern over the role of the military in fomenting regional conflict, instability, civil wars, and repressive regimes, and in spreading widely advanced military technology that may be dangerous to U.S. national security.

coercive hegemony The use of preponderant power to secure national interests, often by "taxing" other members of the international system to benefit the hegemon.

cognitive balance When individuals seek to maintain a balance in their cognitions either by screening out information that runs counter to cherished beliefs or by suppressing information that challenges preexisting images.

collective goods (public goods) Benefits shared by everyone, from which no one can be excluded on a selective basis (e.g., national security).

collective security A system embodied within international organizations, such as the United Nations, in which member states pledge to join together to oppose aggression by any state whenever and wherever it occurs.

collegial model An executive decision-making approach that emphasizes teamwork and group problem solving, in which the president is likened to the hub of a wheel, with spokes connecting to individual advisers and agency heads.

compellence The view of nuclear weapons as the means by which one state can coerce other states to conform to its will.

competitive model An approach to executive decision making in which the president purposely seeks to promote conflict and competition among presidential advisers.

Comprehensive Test Ban Treaty (CTBT) A treaty that seeks to stall further nuclear proliferation by banning all explosive nuclear weapons tests. The agreement enters into force when it is ratified by the forty-four countries in the world that possess nuclear power and research reactors. The treaty was rejected by the U.S. Senate in 1999.

containment A foreign policy strategy, initiated by President Truman and carried out by subsequent Cold War presidents, designed to inhibit the expansion of the Soviet Union's power and influence in world affairs.

cooperative internationalism Support for active involvement in world affairs that stresses the United States' willingness to cooperate with other states to solve global as well as national problems.

corporate (CEO) model A variant of the formalistic model in which the president acting as a CEO (chief executive officer) delegates substantial authority and control over the details of policy to members of his cabinet and others in the administration while he concentrates on the "big picture."

Council on Foreign Relations (CFR) A highly influential policy-planning group that publishes the journal *Foreign Affairs* and whose limited membership occupies prominent governmental and nongovernmental positions with the American foreign policy community.

counterfactual reasoning A reasoning strategy that poses a series of questions that effectively drop a key variable from the equation and then speculates about what might have been.

counterforce A nuclear weapons strategy that seeks deterrence by targeting an adversary's weapons and military forces.

counterintelligence Operations directed specifically against the espionage efforts of foreign intelligence services, including efforts to penetrate them.

counterproliferation A concept that implies the United States itself will act as the sole global arbiter and destroyer of weapons of mass destruction.

countervailing powers A description of interest group activity in which disproportionate political influence possessed by one group will cause one or more opposing groups to balance it by pushing policy in the opposite direction.

countervailing (war-fighting) strategy A plan, embodied in President Carter's Presidential Directive (PD) 59, to enhance deterrence by targeting not only the Soviet Union's population and industrial centers but also its military forces and weapons.

countervalue A nuclear weapons strategy that seeks deterrence by threatening destruction of the things an adversary is believed to value most—its population and military-industrial centers.

covert action Clandestine activity typically undertaken against foreign governments to influence political, economic, or military conditions abroad, where it is intended that the role of the U.S. government will not be apparent or acknowledged.

Cuban missile crisis Soviet-American confrontation in 1962 resulting from the surreptitious placement of Soviet offensive missiles in Cuba; high point of the cold war.

decision avoidance Bureaucratic behavior in which policy makers delay decision making or delegate it by "passing the buck."

Defense Intelligence Agency (DIA) The Defense Department agency responsible for collecting national (rather than tactical) intelligence; the principal intelligence adviser to the secretary of defense and the Joint Chiefs of Staff.

Defense Reorganization Act of 1986 (Goldwater-Nichols Act) A law that sought to shift power from the separate branches of the armed services to the institutions associated with the Joint Chiefs of Staff in an effort to ameliorate interservice rivalry.

deferrals Temporary spending delays by which the president, subject to congressional review, can impound funds for up to twelve months.

democratization The move from authoritarian or semi-authoritarian rule to a democratic political system.

democratic capitalism A set of beliefs that blends the premises of classical democratic theory and capitalism that are embedded in American culture and foreign policy.

democratic dilemma The classic challenge in American foreign policy of how to balance the requirements of national security with the requirements of democracy.

Department of Homeland Security Established by the Homeland Security Act of 2002 and activated in January 2003, this cabinet-level department is responsible for U.S. homeland security. It was created through a consolidation of twenty-two federal agencies with more than 170,000 employees, constituting the most sweeping reorganization of federal government since the National Security Act of 1947.

dependency theory A conceptual lens in international politics, which argued that the relationship between rich and poor states (the core and periphery) explained the persistent underdevelopment of developing states.

dependent variable That which an investigator seeks to explain; in the foreign policy context, a state's foreign policy behavior is the dependent variable.

desertification A sustained decline in land productivity resulting from long-term environmental stress, often caused by population growth.

détente A strategy of containment initiated in 1969 that emphasized the need for superpower cooperation and restraint and sought to create a movement away from competition and toward cooperation.

deterrence A strategy intended to dissuade an adversary from using force by convincing it that the costs of such action outweighs the potential gains.

development assistance Grants and loans to specific countries for specific social and economic development projects related to health, education, agriculture, rural development, or disaster relief.

digital divide The gap between people with regular access to information and communications technology (ICT) and those without such access.

Director of the Central Intelligence Agency (DCIA) A title created in 2004 for the organizational leader of the Central Intelligence Agency (CIA). Unlike his predecessors who carried the title of director of central intelligence, this official does not oversee the U.S. intelligence community or serve as the president's chief intelligence adviser.

Director of National Intelligence (DNI) As of 2004, the nation's new senior (cabinet-level) intelligence official, who heads and coordinates the U.S. intelligence community as well as serves the statutory intelligence adviser to the president, National Security Council, and Homeland Security Council.

discretionary funds Monies the Congress provides the president to deal with situations unforeseen at the time of the annual budget process.

doctrine of political questions A judicial construct that enables the courts to sidestep contentious foreign policy issues separating Congress and the president, such as war powers, by holding that the issues are political rather than legal.

dollar convertibility A U.S. government commitment during the Bretton Woods regime to exchange gold for dollars at any time on demand. Convertibility is an arrangement in which a government permits its currency to be freely exchanged for the currencies of other states.

dollar diplomacy U.S. policy from 1900 to 1913, intended to protect rapidly growing business interests in the Caribbean and Central America and characterized by President Taft as "substituting dollars for bullets."

domino theory A popular metaphor in the 1960s which asserted that one country's fall to communism would stimulate the fall of those adjacent to it.

earmarks Statutory requirements that a minimum amount of government funding or foreign aid be provided to a specific program or country.

economic liberalism The existence or development of market economies.

economic nationalists (mercantilists) Those who assign the state an aggressive role in fostering national economic welfare, stressing their own national interests in international economic transactions rather than the mutual benefit of all trading partners.

elitism A perspective that emphasizes the influence of a few within the policy process.

environmental refugees People forced to abandon lands no longer fit for human habitation due to environmental degradation.

espionage The illegal collection of intelligence; spying to obtain secret government information.

exceptional American experience The absence of pronounced class and religious strife at the time of America's founding complemented by its geographic isolation from European political turmoil.

executive agreements International agreements that do not require the advice and consent of the Senate. These agreements have the same legal force as treaties, which require Senate approval.

extended deterrence A strategy that seeks to dissuade an adversary from attacking one's allies.

external source category The attributes of the international system and the characteristics and behaviors of the state and non-state actors comprising it; includes the global environment and any actions occurring abroad that influence a state's foreign policy decisions.

failed states States that can no longer perform basic functions such as security or governance, usually due to fractious violence or extreme poverty.

fair trade A precept stating that state's exporters should be given the same access to foreign markets as foreign producers enjoy in that state.

finished intelligence Data obtained from all sources—secret as well as public—that have been expertly assembled and analyzed specifically to meet the nation's foreign policy needs.

fixed exchange rate system A monetary system in which a government sets the value of its currency at a fixed rate in relation to the currencies of other states.

flexible response A U.S. and NATO defense posture that implied the United States and its allies were willing and able to respond to a hostile attack at whatever level was appropriate, ranging from conventional to nuclear weapons.

Food for Peace program A program created by the Agricultural Trade Development and Assistance Act of 1954 (PL 480) that sells agricultural commodities on credit and makes grants to provide emergency relief, promote economic development, and assist voluntary relief agencies.

force-short-of-war Displays of conventional military power short of war intended to persuade an adversary to change its political calculations.

Foreign Agricultural Service (FAS) The principal subdivision of the Agriculture Department concerned with international affairs, which is designed to promote sales of American agricultural commodities overseas.

foreign economic aid Low interest loans and grants to other countries, often tied to purchases of goods and services in the United States.

Foreign Military Financing (FMF) The largest of the three accounts associated with foreign military assistance that allows countries to receive military equipment from the U.S. government or to access equipment directly through U.S. commercial programs.

foreign policy The goals that a state's officials seek to attain abroad, the values that give rise to those objectives, and the means or instruments used to pursue them.

foreign policy crisis A situation that threatens the core values of decision makers, imposes time constraints for a response, and surprises decision makers by its occurrence.

Foreign Service officers (FSOs) Members of an elite corps of professional diplomats traditionally holding the most important positions within the State Department (outside of the high-level political and ambassadorial appointments made by the president).

formalistic model An approach to executive decision making in which clear lines of authority minimize the need for presidential involvement in the inevitable politicking among cabinet officers and presidential advisers.

fourth estate The mass media, regarded by some as so powerful as to be considered a fourth branch of the U.S. government.

framing The process of lawmakers using access to the media and other means to try to change the climate of opinion surrounding a policy; also a term widely used by political communications scholars to describe how the media shapes political discourse.

free-floating exchange rates Currency values that are determined by market forces rather than government intervention.

free riders Those who enjoy the benefits of collective (public) goods but pay little or nothing for them.

gatekeeper The function of the mass media in filtering the news and shaping how it is reported, particularly noticeable in foreign affairs.

General Agreement on Tariffs and Trade (GATT) An international agreement created after World War II to promote and protect the most-favored-nation (MFN) principle as the basis for free international trade. *See* most-favored-nation principle and World Trade Organization.

Global North A term used in the post–Cold War system to denote the states formerly thought of as the First World. Defining characteristics are democracy, sophisticated technology, wealth, and near zero population growth.

Global South A term used in the post–Cold War system to denote the countries previously comprising the Third World. Global South states may possess some but not all of the defining characteristics of the Global North (democracy, sophisticated technology, wealth, and steady-state populations). A significant proportion of the population in this part of the world lives in poverty and without hope.

global warming A change in the earth's temperature that occurs when carbon dioxide and other gas molecules trap heat that would otherwise be remitted from earth back into the atmosphere.

globalization The process of rapid intensification and integration of states' economies, not only in terms of markets but also ideas, information, and technology, with an accompanying profound impact on political, social, and cultural relations across national borders.

governmental source category Those aspects of a government's structure that limit or enhance decision makers' foreign policy choices. Examples in the United States include the constitutional separation of powers and the bureaucratization of policy making in the executive branch.

grand strategy A statement of national goals and the means to realize those goals, with an emphasis on the use of military instruments to achieve foreign policy objectives.

Group of 8 (G-8) The world's seven largest industrialized democracies (Canada, France, Germany, Italy, Japan, the United Kingdom, and the United States) plus Russia.

Group of 77 (G-77) A loose coalition at the United Nations of the world's poor states (Global South) allied to press for concessions from the world's rich states (the Global North). Formed in 1964, the G77 now comprises more than 130 developing states.

groupthink Social pressures that reinforce group norms in small decision-making groups; a cohesiveness and solidarity of outlook that may lead to dysfunctional policy choices.

Gulf of Tonkin Resolution A joint resolution passed by Congress in 1964 that gave the president approval "to take all necessary means to repel any armed attack against the forces of the United States and to prevent further aggression." The Johnson administration insisted that the resolution was the "functional equivalent" of a declaration of war in the Vietnam conflict.

hardliners Those who, in the wake of Vietnam, viewed communism as a threat to the United States, opposed détente with the Soviet Union, and embraced an interventionist position; proponents of unilateralism in the post–Cold War world.

hegemon/hegemony (primacy) A single country that dominates the global political, military, and economic arenas. This preponderant power is beyond the challenge of any other state or combination of states.

hegemonic stability theory A perspective that focuses on the role of the preponderant power in stabilizing the international economic system; defines the special roles and responsibilities of the major economic power (hegemon) in a commercial order based on market forces.

hero-in-history model The view that individual leaders are the makers and movers of history; in foreign policy making, it finds expression in the practice of attaching presidents' names to the policies they promulgate.

historical analogies The use of interpretations of the lessons of the past to structure one's understanding of the contemporary world.

Homeland Security Council Established by executive order in 2001, this top-level interagency body within the presidential subsystem advises and assists the president on all aspects of homeland security and serves as a mechanism for coordinating homeland security policy.

honest broker The role fulfilled by the national security adviser when he or she faithfully presents all the views and recommendations of members of the National Security Council. Although he or she can share his or her thoughts with the president, this role is concerned more with coordination of the policy process rather than the national security adviser behaving as an independent player or advocate.

human intelligence (HUMINT) The fruits of espionage that come from human, not technical, sources of intelligence.

idealism A body of thought that believes fundamental reforms of the system of international relations are possible. The idealist agenda includes open diplomacy, freedom of the seas, removal of trade barriers, self-determination, general disarmament, and collective security.

ideological/single issue groups Interest-group organizations that seek to influence policy in narrowly defined areas. Often times, their activities are not distinguishable from groups that emphasize a particular philosophical viewpoint.

imagery intelligence (IMINT) Information gathered from cryptanalysis satellites in computer code, which must be converted into images.

IMF conditionality Loans tied to the adoption of particular policies designed to resolve a country's balance of payments difficulties and promote long-term economic growth.

imperial overstretch A state of affairs when a hegemon's global interests and commitments exceed its domestic resources and international capabilities.

imperial presidency A term coined by Arthur M. Schlesinger, Jr., to describe the gradual but significant growth in executive power that began with Franklin D. Roosevelt and peaked with Richard M. Nixon. Many observers agree the imperial presidency returned and was taken to an unprecedented level during the George W. Bush administration.

impoundment A presidential refusal to spend money appropriated by Congress.

inadvertent audience People who are exposed to foreign affairs information transmitted by television that most neither like nor want.

independent variables Factors that exert a causal impact on a dependent variable. In the foreign policy context, a state's foreign policy behavior is the dependent variable and the source categories and factors contained within them are the independent variables, or inputs.

individual source category A decision maker's personal traits—including values, talents, and prior experiences—that influence his or her foreign policy choices and thus potentially impact a state's foreign policy.

instrumental rationality A conceptualization of rationality that stresses individual preferences; it predicts that decision makers, when faced with multiple alternatives, will choose the one believed to yield their preferred outcome.

Intelligence Reform and Terrorism Prevention Act of 2004 A law providing for the most significant reorganization of U.S. intelligence since the National Security Act of 1947. The act established the position of Director of National Intelligence (DNI) and the National Counterterrorism Center (NCTC). It also introduced significant changes related to the Federal Bureau of Investigation, homeland security, transportation and border security, and terrorism prevention.

interagency processes The principal mechanism for coordinating the vast federal structure in foreign policy. Interagency processes bring together different decision makers, organizations, interests, and information in an effort to coordinate and integrate national policy.

intergovernmental organizations (IGOs) International organizations whose members are governments (e.g., the United Nations).

International Monetary Fund (IMF) An intergovernmental organization established to assist states in dealing with such matters as maintaining stability in their financial inflows and outflows (balance of payments) and exchange rates (the rate used by one state to exchange its currency with another's).

international regimes Coalitions of state and non-state actors observing common principles, norms, rules, and decision-making procedures to facilitate cooperative efforts in a given area of international activity.

internationalism A policy of active engagement in world affairs.

internationalists Supporters of active American involvement in international affairs, favoring a combination of conciliatory and conflictual strategies to solve global and national problems.

intervening variable A factor that links an independent variable to a dependent variable. In the foreign policy context, the foreign policy–making process is the intervening variable that links inputs (the source categories) to outputs (foreign policy behavior).

iron triangles A powerful and highly durable coalition of defense contractors and interest groups (the private sector), defense bureaucrats (the executive branch), and lawmakers (the legislative branch) that work together to preserve weapons programs.

isolationism A policy of aloofness or political detachment from international affairs; Thomas Jefferson advocated isolationism as the best way to preserve and develop the United States as a free people.

isolationists Those who oppose the United States actively involving itself in international affairs, whether by conciliatory or conflictual means.

Joint Chiefs of Staff (JCS) A six-member advisory body consisting of the senior military officer within each uniformed service, a vice chairman, and a chairman. The chairman is appointed by the president and serves as the nation's chief military officer.

Joint Staff A staff of about 1,600 composed primarily of military officers from each branch of the armed forces who serve the chairman of the Joint Chiefs of Staff and operate solely under his direction, authority, and control.

Kellogg-Briand Pact A 1928 agreement, also known as the Pact of Paris, that renounced war as an instrument of national policy.

Kyoto Protocol to the United Nations Framework Convention on Climate Change An international agreement designed to stabilize and then reduce the concentration of greenhouse gases in the atmosphere; an addendum to the Framework Convention negotiated at the 1992 Earth Summit in Rio de Janeiro.

laager mentality A heightened sense of nationalism in response to economic coercion; related to the Afrikaner phrase, "circle the ox wagons to face oncoming enemies."

law of anticipated reactions A potential constraint of political culture that posits that decision makers screen out certain alternatives because they foresee they will be adversely received by the American people.

legislative veto The ability of Congress to express disapproval of a presidential initiative, such as a major arms sale, by a concurrent or joint resolution of both houses. It may no longer be constitutional under the Supreme Court's *INS vs. Chadha* ruling in 1983.

Lend-Lease Act A law enacted in 1941 that permitted the United States to assist other states deemed vital to U.S. security, thus committing the United States to the Allied cause against the Axis powers.

Liberal International Economic Order (LIEO) A system of rules and institutions that have governed post–World War II economic relations, in which barriers to the free flow of trade and capital have been progressively reduced. Limited government intervention in economic affairs is a key principle of the system.

liberal internationalism A political tradition based on global activism and a belief that liberal democracies must lead in creating a peaceful world order through multilateral cooperation and effective international organizations.

liberalism A tradition based on the political philosophy of John Locke and codified by Thomas Jefferson in the Declaration of Independence; it is based on the advocacy of liberty and the belief that legitimate political power arises only from the consent of the governed, whose participation in decisions affecting public policy and the quality of life is guaranteed.

liberty Individual freedom.

linkage theory A strategy of containment fashioned by Richard Nixon and Henry Kissinger that stressed economic, political, and strategic ties designed to bind the United States and the Soviet Union in a common fate that would lessen the incentives for war. It made the entire range of superpower relations interdependent where cooperation in one policy area was contingent on acceptable conduct in other areas.

long peace A term coined by historian John Lewis Gaddis to capture the reality that while the Cold War was marked by endemic threats and recurring crises, major war between the great powers did not occur.

managed trade A system in which a government intervenes to steer trade relations in a direction that the government itself has predetermined.

manifest destiny The belief, widespread in the nineteenth century, that Americans were a chosen people who were destined to expand across the North American continent and eventually embody it.

Marshall Plan A program that used American capital to rebuild Western Europe's economic, social, and political infrastructures after World War II in order to ensure a market for U.S. products and to enhance Europe's ability to resist communist subversion.

mass public The large proportion of Americans who are neither policy influentials nor members of the attentive public. *See* **policy influentials** and **attentive public.**

massive retaliation A doctrine proclaimed by the Eisenhower administration designed to deter attack and accomplish foreign policy goals by threatening mass destruction of Soviet population and military-industrial centers.

micromanagement Detailed legislative involvement in the conduct of America's foreign relations, often regarded by presidents as excessive interference in executive responsibilities.

Miles's Law A long-standing tenet of role theory that suggests "where you stand (on a policy issue) depends on where you sit (in the government)."

militant internationalism Support for active involvement in world affairs, stressing the United States' willingness to protect its self-defined national interests with the use of force if necessary.

military-industrial complex (MIC) A partnership of military professionals, leaders of industries dependent on military contracts, high government officials whose political interests are linked to military expenditure, and legislators whose constituents benefit from defense spending.

Millennium Challenge Account (MCA) A new bilateral assistance account established by the Bush administration in 2004 and administered by a new government agency in an effort to circumvent the congressional earmarks associated with traditional American foreign assistance. *See* **earmarks.**

Missile Technology Control Regime (MCTR) An informal voluntary arrangement established in 1987 to slow the development of missiles capable of delivering weapons of mass destruction.

Monroe Doctrine A policy articulated by President James Monroe stating that the New World would not be subject to the same forces of colonization that the Europeans had perpetrated on others.

most-favored-nation (MFN) principle The cornerstone of free trade, which states that the tariff preferences granted to one state must be granted to all other states exporting the same product, thus ensuring equality in a state's treatment of its trade partners. *See* **normal trade relations (NTR).**

multiculturalism An emphasis on the importance of ethnicity in shaping individuals' identities and interests, thus promoting communal rights over individual rights and universal opportunity.

multilateralism A means to foreign policy ends that coordinates relations among three or more states on the basis of generalized principles of conduct (e.g., collective security).

multilevel interdependence A global power structure illustrated by the metaphor of a layer cake. The top layer, military might, is unipolar; the middle layer, economics, is tripolar; and the bottom layer, transnational interdependence, shows a diffusion of power.

multinational corporations (MNCs) Business enterprises organized in one society with activities abroad growing out of direct investment, as opposed to portfolio investment through share holding.

multipolar/multipolarity A global structure in which power is distributed among four or more major powers.

multistep theory of communications A theoretical perspective that seeks to draw attention to the multiple channels through which ideas and opinions are circulated in America's complex society.

Munich Conference A 1938 meeting among Britain, France, and Germany leading to a failed agreement that ceded much of Czechoslovakia to Nazi Germany in exchange for what the British prime minister called "peace in our time." Source of the widespread conviction that aggressors cannot be appeased.

mutual assured destruction (MAD) A "balance of terror" in which combatants' essentially equal capability to cause widespread death and destruction in a nuclear exchange encourages stability and the avoidance of war; a description of U.S. and Soviet nuclear strategy during much of the Cold War.

mutual security The belief that a diminution of the national security of one's adversary reduces one's own security.

National Economic Council (NEC) Established by executive order in 1993, this top-level interagency body within the presidential subsystem serves as a counterpart to the National Security Council and advises and assists the president on the integration and coordination of national economic policy.

National Geospatial-Intelligence Agency (NGIA)
Formerly known as the National Imaging and Mapping Agency (NIMA), this Defense Department agency is responsible for preparing geospatial intelligence and imagery—national security information in cartographic, photographic, digital, or computerized format.

National Intelligence Estimates (NIEs) Reports prepared on various parts of the world, intended to be the "best judgments" of the intelligence community on their respective subjects.

national missile defense Missile defense that seeks to protect the United States.

National Reconnaissance Office (NRO) The agency responsible for managing the nation's satellite reconnaissance programs; controlled jointly by the Central Intelligence Agency and Defense Department and operated under the "cover" of the Air Force.

national security adviser (NSA) The head of the National Security Council staff and the president's principal foreign policy adviser within the presidential subsystem.

National Security Agency (NSA) The Defense Department agency responsible for signal intelligence (SIGINT), communications security, and cryptology.

National Security Council (NSC) A top-level interagency body within the presidential subsystem created by the National Security Act of 1947 to "advise the president with respect to the integration of domestic, foreign, and military policies relating to the national security."

national security policy The weapons and strategies on which the United States relies to ensure security and survival in an uncertain, dangerous, and often hostile global environment.

nationalism A state of mind that gives primary loyalty to one's own country and the promotion of its culture and interests as opposed to those of other countries.

neoconservatives Originally liberal internationalists who soured with the strategy and outcome of the Vietnam War, this group embraced the view that American power should be exercised not with restraint but proactively to promote American values and ideals. Military strength and moral clarity were cornerstones of their convictions.

neo-isolationism An international strategy of avoiding foreign entanglements. Today this approach would include distancing the United States from the United Nations and other international organizations when they seek to make or enforce peace in roiling conflicts.

neomercantilism State intervention in economic affairs designed to strengthen national economic fortunes by maintaining a balance-of-trade surplus by stimulating domestic production, reducing imports, and promoting exports.

New Independent States (NIS) The former republics of the Union of Soviet Socialist Republics (USSR).

New International Economic Order (NIEO) A movement in the 1970s among Third World states seeking to gain a greater role in shaping their own economic futures and determining who would govern the distribution of world wealth and how they would make their choices.

new interventionism A term associated with the Clinton years, representing a willingness to intervene in foreign conflicts based on humanitarian and international values.

new world order George H. W. Bush's vision of the world following the Persian Gulf war in which "the principles of justice and fair play protect the weak against the strong. . . . A world in which freedom and respect for human rights find a home among all nations."

Newly Industrializing Economies (NIEs) Among the more advanced of the developing states, a small group of fast-growing exporters of manufactured goods. Principal among them are the "Asian Tigers": Hong Kong, Singapore, South Korea, and Taiwan.

Nixon Doctrine President Richard Nixon's pledge in 1970 that the United States would provide military and economic assistance to its friends and allies but would hold those states responsible for protecting their own security.

nonalignment Newly emerging states in the Third World determined to strike a neutral course in the Cold War.

nongovernmental organizations (NGOs) International organizations whose members are individuals or societal groups (e.g., the International Federation of Red Cross and Red Crescent Societies).

nontariff barriers (NTBs) Government regulations that reduce or distort international trade (e.g., health and safety regulations and restrictions on the quality of goods that may be imported).

normal trade relations (NTR) A term replacing the most-favored-nation principle, which states that the tariff preferences granted to one state must be granted to all other states exporting the same product, thus ensuring equality in a state's treatment of its trade partners.

NSC-68 A top-secret memorandum issued by the National Security Council in 1950, which called for increased military spending and a nonmilitary counter-offensive against the Soviet Union that included covert economic, political, and psychological warfare designed to foment unrest and revolt in Soviet bloc countries.

Nuclear Non-Proliferation Treaty (NPT) Policed by the International Atomic Energy Agency (IAEA), the treaty declares that nuclear states will transfer to non-nuclear states nuclear know-how for peaceful purposes in return for the promise that such knowledge will not be used to make nuclear weapons.

Office of the Secretary of Defense (OSD) The civilian leadership of the Department of Defense; the under secretaries, assistant secretaries, and other person-nel responsible for supporting the secretary of defense as he manages the Pentagon and carries out his duties as the president's chief adviser on defense matters.

Open Door policy The U.S. policy toward China initiated by Secretary of State John Hay in 1899, which supported free competition for trade with China and opposed dividing China into spheres of influence.

operational codes Elements of the basic beliefs about the nature of an individual's political environment, factors affecting world affairs, and the individual's role and orientation toward both. These codes shape per-ceptions and preferred strategies and tactics.

organizational subculture A common set of goals and norms shared by members of an agency that shapes their perceptions, actions, and policy preferences, while also affecting agency processes and procedures.

pack journalism A troublesome phenomenon in which reporters follow the lead of one or a few others in deciding what is (or is not) news and how it should be framed. This behavior often leads to remarkably similar news accounts, particularly among the national print and electronic media.

parochialism A characteristic of many organizational subcultures in which the views, experiences, and values of the agency are considered paramount, often leading to elitism, resistance to outside ideas, and narrow definitions of interests.

partisanship A state of affairs where politics and party interests trump policy and national interests.

peace enforcement The use of an outside military force (e.g., UN, NATO, etc.) to impose a settlement on the parties in a political or military conflict.

peacekeeping The use of an outside military force (UN, NATO, etc.) to keep contending parties apart to prevent fighting.

perpetual election Constant polling to determine presidents' standing with the American people.

plausible denial A tenet by which the president is not apprised of current or pending covert actions in order to save him or her from the possible embarrassment of a "blown" operation.

pluralism A perspective that emphasizes the influence of a broader array of actors and preferences within the policy process; also a model of public policy making in which individual citizens organize themselves into groups to petition the government on behalf of their shared interests and values, and whose competition explains political decisions.

policy influentials People who are knowledgeable about foreign affairs and who have access to decision makers.

political action committees (PACs) Branches of business and interest groups that raise money to provide campaign funds for political parties or individual candi-dates for office.

political culture The political values, ideas, and ideals about a state's society and politics that the people hold in common.

political realism A school of thought in international relations that holds that the structure of the international system, defined by the distribution of power among states, is the primary determinant of states' foreign policy behavior. Political realism views conflict as a natural state of affairs and urges states to seek power to protect their national interests.

political realists Analysts who argue that the distribu-tion of power in the international system, more than anything else, influences how its member states act.

politicization of intelligence A problem that occurs when those responsible for providing intelligence also become policy advocates. In such situations, intelligence analysts may distort, filter, or select intelligence to serve his or her policy preferences. Another form involves decision makers selectively adducing intelligence data to support their policy preferences rather than using the intelligence community's own analytic judgments.

politics of prestige The logic that the more popular a president is, the more likely he is to accomplish his political agenda.

Powell Doctrine A set of guidelines that stress the United States should go to war with clear political and military objectives (including an exit strategy), strong public backing, a commitment to operational flexibility, and a willingness to use overwhelming force to ensure a quick, decisive victory.

preemption/preemptive war A defense strategy of striking militarily an adversary who poses an imminent threat before the adversary can strike first.

presidential character The way a president orients himself or herself to life, especially the level of energy that goes into the job and the level of satisfaction derived from presidential duties.

presidential finding The president's certification to Congress that an executive approved covert action is "important to the national interests of the United States." Presidential findings are to specify the need, purposes, and (general) means of the operation.

presidential leadership The president's varying ability to direct the policy agenda, shape policy choices, and manage the activities of the many players, agencies, departments, and institutions of the government.

presidential preeminence The perspective that the president dominates the American foreign policy–making process.

presidential subsystem A division within the executive branch that has arisen as presidents rely increasingly on their personal staffs and on the Executive Office of the President for advice and assistance in developing policies and programs, often leading to differences between the presidency and the established bureaucracy.

procedural legislation Legislation passed by Congress that alters processes, requires reports, or creates new agencies or institutions to shape the way policy is formulated and implemented.

procedural rationality A conceptualization of rationality that is based on perfect information and a careful weighing of all possible courses of action; it underlies the theory of political realism, which views all states as acting in fundamentally similar ways as they make value-maximizing choices to enhance their national security.

"producer-consumer" challenge The difficulty in getting accurate and objective information into key policy makers' hands in useful forms and at opportune moments.

Project for the New American Century (PNAC) A think-tank dominated by neoconservatives that provided the new George W. Bush administration with both foreign policy ideas and key personnel.

public diplomacy The methodical spreading of information to influence public opinion; a polite term for propaganda.

public interest groups Organizations that seek to represent the interests of society as a whole and to realize benefits that may be intangible (e.g., Ralph Nader's Public Citizen).

public opinion Citizens' foreign policy attitudes and preferences.

"rally round the flag" phenomenon A condition whereby dramatic foreign policy events boost a president's short-term popularity and offers strong public support for the use of executive power in the name of national security.

rational decision-making model A perspective that hypothesizes that foreign policy results from a deliberate intellectual process in which the central figures carefully choose what is best for the country and select tactics appropriately designed to promote the national interest.

Reagan Doctrine President Ronald Reagan's pledge of American support for anticommunist insurgents who sought to overturn Soviet-supported Marxist regimes.

reprogramming A nonstatutory control mechanism devised by Congress and the executive to deal with unanticipated contingencies by permitting funds within an appropriation category to be moved from one purpose to another.

rescissions A mechanism by which the president, subject to congressional review, can impound funds by permanently canceling budget authority.

reservations Amendments or conditions the Senate may attach to an international treaty.

retrospective voting When voters cast their votes for a candidate based on judgments of past performance.

revolution in military affairs (RMA) A rapid and radical increase in the effectiveness of military units that changes the nature of warfare and alters the strategic environment.

risky-shift phenomenon A potential effect of bureaucratic decision making in which members of decision-making groups, reluctant to appear fearful, act more recklessly together than they would individually.

role source category This category includes the socially prescribed behaviors and legally sanctioned norms attached to policy-making positions; it takes into account the impact of an office on the behavior of the officeholder.

role theory A perspective that posits that the positions decision makers occupy, rather than their individual characteristics, influence their behavior and choices in making and executing foreign policy.

rollback A strategy that called for the liberation of communist-dominated areas during the Cold War.

Roosevelt Corollary President Theodore Roosevelt's extension of the Monroe Doctrine that justified the use of American power, including military force, to oppose Latin American revolutions and to bring hemispheric economic affairs under U.S. control.

sanctions Governmental actions designed to inflict economic deprivation on a target state or society by limiting or cutting off customary economic relations; often used as alternatives to military force.

satisficing The behavior by which decision makers are content to select an alternative that meets minimally acceptable standards rather than continuing to seek an optimal solution.

second-strike nuclear capability The ability of offensive strategic forces to withstand an aggressor's initial strike and retain the capacity to respond with a devastating second blow.

security assistance A program of foreign military grants and sales plus economic support funds intended to serve a wide range of U.S. policy objectives.

security dilemmas Vicious-circle situations in which the defensive weapons a country acquires are perceived by its adversary to be offensive, thus causing it, too, to build up its "defensive" arsenal.

selective engagement A grand strategy that maintains the United States should remain militarily strong and engaged overseas through alliances and forward bases to advance its vital national security interests. It seeks to avoid the more aggressive postures associated with unilateralism or a world's policeman role.

selective perception A pervasive human tendency to search for "comfortable" information that fits with one's preexisting beliefs and to screen out or reject information with which one disagrees.

signal intelligence (SIGINT) Information gathered from the interception and analysis of communications, electronic, and telemetry signals.

signing statements Statements attached to laws passed by Congress in which the president provides an interpretation of how he views the law and whether it contains provisions he cannot support or enforce.

Single Integrated Operational Plan (SIOP) A top-secret master plan for waging nuclear war that operationalizes strategic doctrine by selecting the military and nonmilitary targets to be attacked in the event of war.

single-issue politics A condition in which members of Congress are evaluated not on the basis of their entire record but only on their performance on particular issues.

smart sanctions Sanctions designed to target crucial economic sectors or individuals within a target country rather than punish the general population.

societal source category Those nongovernmental characteristics of a state's society that influence its relations with other states; examples include major value orientations, degree of national unity, and extent of industrialization.

society-dominated system A political system characterized by strong domestic influences on foreign policy behavior (e.g., the United States). Such a system focuses policy makers' attention on societal sources of foreign policy.

soft power The ability to get another country to do something it otherwise would not do without the use of military or economic power. Soft power includes cultural attractiveness, values, political beliefs, and the ability to establish rules and institutions.

source categories Five forces that influence a state's foreign policy: (1) the external (global) environment; (2) the societal environment; (3) the governmental setting in which policy is made; (4) the roles policy makers occupy; and (5) policy makers' individual characteristics.

sovereignty A cardinal principle in international law and politics, sovereignty affirms that no authority is above the states; it protects the territorial inviolability of the state, its freedom from interference by others, and its authority to rule its own population.

Special National Intelligence Estimates (SNIEs) Prepared more quickly than standard national intelligence estimates, these special reports by the intelligence community are in response to requests from high-level policy makers. These estimates are intended to be the "best judgments" of the intelligence community on a given issue.

standard operating procedures (SOPs) Rules and routines for dealing with recurring tasks and situations, as well as the way bureaucratic organizations mold the behavior of their role occupants.

stovepipes Intelligence agencies involved in similar work, such as analysis or collection, that compete and may fail to share information with one another, which can create waste and have a negative effect on the overall quality of national intelligence.

Strategic Arms Limitation Talks (SALT) Negotiations initiated in 1969 that sought to restrain the Soviet-American arms race by limiting offensive strategic weapons. They produced two sets of agreements: the 1972 SALT I agreement limiting strategic offensive weapons and the Antiballistic Missile (ABM) treaty, and the 1979 SALT II treaty.

Strategic Arms Reduction Talks (START) Negotiations aimed at reducing the strategic forces of the United States and the Soviet Union and its successors. Agreements reached in 1991 and 1993 commit the nuclear powers (including the nuclear heirs of the former Soviet Union) to eliminate or reduce significantly the number of strategic weapons in their arsenals.

Strategic Defense Initiative (SDI) A futuristic, "defense dominant" ballistic missile defense strategy initiated during the Reagan administration. Also known as "Star Wars," SDI sought to use space-based technology to interdict offensive weapons launched toward the United States.

Strategic Offensive Reductions Treaty (SORT) An agreement reached between the United States and Russia in 2002 limiting each country's total number of operationally deployed strategic nuclear weapons to 1,700 to 2,200. The projected targets are to be met by 2012, when the treaty will either expire or be extended by a follow-on agreement.

strategic trade A form of industrial policy that seeks to create comparative advantages in international trade by targeting government subsidies toward particular industries.

strategic weapons Nuclear and other weapons of mass destruction capable of annihilating an adversary.

structural realism A theory that holds that the distribution of power defines the structure of the international system, which in turn defines states' behavior. States protect their interests against external threats by balancing power with power.

substantive legislation Issue-specific legislation passed by Congress that requires or prohibits specific policy actions.

Super 301 A provision of the 1988 Omnibus Trade and Competitiveness Act that required the president to identify countries engaged in unfair trade practices, with a view toward negotiation to seek remedies or face U.S. retaliation.

sustainable development A concept encapsulating the belief that the world must work toward a model of economic development that also protects the delicate environmental systems on which humanity depends for its existence.

tactical nuclear weapons Nuclear weapons designed for the direct support of combat operations.

terrorism An instrument of the weak against the strong. There is no universally accepted definition. The U.S. Department of State defines terrorism as a "premeditated, politically motivated violence perpetrated against noncombatant (civilian) targets by subnational groups or clandestine agents, usually intended to influence an audience."

theater missile defense Missile defense that seeks to protect American allies in their local settings.

theater nuclear forces Nuclear forces directed toward regional rather than global threats.

think-tanks Privately run public policy research organizations that seek to exercise influence across the broad spectrum of American foreign policy.

Third World A term used during the Cold War era to designate states that had failed to grow economically or otherwise advance toward the degree and type of economic development experienced in Western Europe and North America; included most countries in Asia, Africa, and Latin America.

trade promotion authority Congressional authorization to the president to negotiate trade arrangements, in consultation with Congress, which will then be voted up or down by Congress without any amendments; formerly known as fast track authority.

triad of strategic weapons A force consisting of manned bombers and land- and sea-based intercontinental ballistic missiles that the United States maintains as a means of strategic deterrence.

trip wire A situation where policy makers are militarily obligated to respond.

Truman Doctrine President Harry S. Truman's dictum that "it must be the policy of the United States to support free peoples who are resisting attempted subjugation by armed minorities or by outside pressures." The doctrine led to a containment strategy based on substantial quantities of U.S. political, economic, and military aid.

twin pillars strategy A Cold War plan designed to protect American interests in the Middle East by building up the political and military stature of Iran and Saudi Arabia.

two presidencies thesis A thesis from the work of Aaron Wildavsky that posits the legislative and judicial branches allow broad executive discretion and unilateral action in foreign policy, while they exercise "checks and balances" to a greater degree in domestic policy.

two-step flow theory of communications A hypothesis staring that ideas do not flow directly from the mass media to the general population; rather they are transmitted first to opinion leaders and through them to the less interested, less knowledgeable members of society.

two-war strategy A strategy in which U.S. forces have the capacity to fight two major regional conflicts (MRCs) on the scale of the 1991 Persian Gulf War nearly simultaneously.

unilateralism Conducting foreign affairs individually rather than acting in concert with others.

uni-multipolar system A global structure characterized by one superpower and several major powers. The superpower is capable of vetoing actions by others but is also dependent on others to cope with key international issues.

unipolar/unipolarity A global power structure in which one state enjoys unparalleled supremacy, possessing the military and economic might to defend unilaterally its security and sovereignty (e.g., the United States' status as the "sole remaining superpower" in the post–Cold War world).

unipolar moment The concentration of power in the hands of a single state, such as the United States in the immediate aftermath of World War II and the Persian Gulf War.

unitary actor The state viewed as a single, homogeneous decision-making entity; the concept presumes that all policy makers go through the same rational processes to make value-maximizing choices defining national interests and choices.

unmanaged policy initiatives A potential effect of decision making in complex organizations, in which policy is effectively determined at the implementation stage, thereby empowering bureaucrats.

U.S. Agency for International Development (USAID) The government organization that since 1961 has been responsible for administering most U.S. foreign economic assistance programs.

U.S. and Foreign Commercial Service A branch of the Commerce Department that seeks to enhance the competitiveness of American businesses abroad by bringing together those who encourage U.S. firms to export and those who deal with potential buyers of American products.

U.S. Trade Representative (USTR) A presidential appointee who carries the rank of ambassador, holds membership in the cabinet, and exercises primary responsibility for developing and coordinating the implementation of international trade policy. The USTR acts as the principal trade spokesperson for the U.S. government.

vice president The officer in the U.S. government next in rank to the president and one who has become increasingly active and influential in foreign policy in recent decades.

War Powers Resolution Legislation passed in 1973 to limit presidential war-making prerogatives.

Washington Consensus A common outlook shared by the U.S. government, the International Monetary Fund, and the World Bank that encourages privatization of industries and other institutions, financial deregulation, and reductions of barriers to trade as the path to economic development.

Weinberger Doctrine A set of six principles to govern the use of force abroad: vital national interests, sufficient resources, clear objectives, operational flexibility, congressional and public support, and the use of force as a last resort.

Wilsonianism liberalism A strategy that sees the United States as the world's leader and emphasizes the soft power of American ideals and values rather than the hard power of its military strength.

win-hold-win strategy A strategy in which U.S. military forces will be prepared to fight and win decisively a single major conflict in one theater while conducting a defensive holding operation against another opponent in a second theater. Once the first opponent is defeated, U.S. military will shift its attention and resources to win decisively in the second theater.

World Bank An intergovernmental organization charged with assisting postwar reconstruction and development following World War II by facilitating the transnational flow of investment capital. Today, it is the principal means to channel multilateral development assistance to the Global South in an effort to reduce global poverty and improve living standards.

World Trade Organization (WTO) An international organization created by the Uruguay Round to replace GATT and which formally came into existence in January 1995. The WTO seeks to extend GATT's coverage of products, sectors, and conditions of trade and will have broader authority over trade disputes. *See* General Agreement on Tariffs and Trade (GATT).

zero-sum A situation in which, when one side wins, the other necessarily loses.

References

THE 9/11 COMMISSION REPORT. (2004) New York: W. W. Norton.

ABRAHAMSEN, DAVID. (1977) *Nixon vs. Nixon: An Emotional Tragedy.* New York: Farrar, Straus, and Giroux.

ABRAMSON, PAUL R., JOHN H. ALDRICH, AND DAVID W. ROHDE. (1986) *Change and Continuity in the 1984 Elections.* Washington, DC: CQ Press.

———. (1990) *Change and Continuity in the 1988 Elections.* Washington, DC: CQ Press.

———. (1994) *Change and Continuity in the 1992 Elections.* Washington, DC: CQ Press.

———. (2005) "The 2004 Presidential Election: The Emergence of a Permanent Majority?" *Political Science Quarterly,* 120 (Spring): 33–57.

ADAMS, GORDON. (1994) "The New Politics of the Defense Budget," in *The Domestic Sources of American Foreign Policy: Insights and Evidence,* Eugene R. Wittkopf, ed. New York: St. Martin's, pp. 106–119.

ADELMAN, KENNETH L. (1981) "Speaking of America: Public Diplomacy in Our Time," *Foreign Affairs* 59 (Spring): 913–936.

AIZENMAN, NURITH C. (1999) "Intelligence Test," *New Republic* 220 (22 March): 22–27.

ALDRICH, JOHN H., JOHN L. SULLIVAN, AND EUGENE BORGIDA. (1989) "Foreign Affairs and Issue Voting: Do Presidential Candidates 'Waltz Before a Blind Audience?'" *American Political Science Review* 83 (March): 123–141.

ALLEN, MIKE, AND ALAN SIPRESS. (2001) "Attacks Refocus White House on How to Fight Terrorism. *Washington Post,* 26 September (www.washingtonpost.com, accessed 9/26/01).

ALLISON, GRAHAM T. (1971) *Essence of Decision: Explaining the Cuban Missile Crisis.* Boston: Little, Brown.

———. (2004a) "How to Stop Nuclear Terror," *Foreign Affairs,* 83 (1): 64–75.

———. (2004b) *Nuclear Terrorism: The Ultimate Preventable Catastrophe.* New York: Times Books/Henry Holt.

ALLISON, GRAHAM T., AND MORTON H. HALPERIN. (1972) "Bureaucratic Politics: A Paradigm and Some Policy Implications," *World Politics* 24 (Spring Supplement): 40–80.

ALLISON, GRAHAM T., AND PETER SZANTON. (1976) "Organizing for the Decade Ahead," in *Setting National Priorities: The Next Ten Years,* Henry Owen and Charles L. Schultze, eds. Washington, DC: Brookings Institution, pp. 227–270.

ALLISON, GRAHAM, AND PHILIP ZELIKOW. (1999) *The Essence of Decision: Explaining the Cuban Missile Crisis.* New York: Addison Wesley.

ALMOND, GABRIEL A. (1960) *The American People and Foreign Policy.* New York: Praeger.

ALPEROVITZ, GAR. (1985) *Atomic Diplomacy: Hiroshima and Potsdam,* rev. ed. New York: Penguin.

———. (1989) "Do Nuclear Weapons Matter?" *New York Review of Books* 36 (April): 57–58.

ALPEROVITZ, GAR, AND KAI BIRD. (1994) "The Centrality of the Bomb," *Foreign Policy* 94 (Spring): 3–20.

ALSOP, JOSEPH, AND DAVID JORAVSKY. (1980) "Was the Hiroshima Bomb Necessary? An Exchange," *New York Review of Books,* 23 October: 37–42.

ALTER, JONATHAN. (1999) "Playing Politics with the Bomb," *Newsweek,* 134 (18 October): 41.

ALTMAN, ROGER C. (1994) "Why Pressure Tokyo?" *Foreign Affairs* 73 (May/June): 2–6.

ALVAREZ, LIZETTE, AND ERIC SCHMITT. (2001) "Cheney Ever More Powerful as Crucial Link to Congress," *New York Times,* 13 May (www.nytimes.com, accessed 5/13/01).

AMBROSE, STEPHEN E. (1990) *Eisenhower: Soldier and President.* New York: Simon & Schuster.

———. (1993) *Rise to Globalism: American Foreign Policy Since 1938,* 7th ed. New York: Penguin.

AMUZEGAR, JAHANGIR. (1987) "Dealing with Debt," *Foreign Policy* 68 (Fall): 140–158.

———. (1997) "Adjusting to Sanctions," *Foreign Affairs* 76 (May/June): 31–41.

ANDERSON, PAUL A. (1987) "What Do Decision Makers Do When They Make a Foreign Policy Decision?" in *New Directions in the Study of Foreign Policy,* Charles F. Hermann, Charles W. Kegley, Jr., and James N. Rosenau, eds. Boston: Allen and Unwin, pp. 285–308.

ANDREAS, PETER. (1996) "U.S.-Mexico: Open Markets, Closed Border," *Foreign Policy* 103 (Summer): 51–69.

ANDREW, CHRISTOPHER. (1995) *For the President's Eyes Only: Secret Intelligence and the American Presidency from Washington to Bush.* New York: HarperCollins.

ANDREWS, EDMUND L. (2001) "Bush Angers Europe by Eroding a Pact on Warming," *New York Times,* 1 April, p. 3.

ANGELL, NORMAN. (1914) *The Great Illusion.* London: Heinemann.

ANJARIA, S. J. (1986) "A New Round of Global Trade Negotiations," *Finance & Development* 23 (June): 2–6.

ANTON, GENEVIEVE, AND JEFF THOMAS. (1999) "The Politics of Military Base Closures," in *The Domestic Sources of American Foreign Policy: Insights and Evidence,* Eugene R. Wittkopf and James M. McCormick, eds. Lanham, MD: Rowman and Littlefield, pp. 61–70.

APPLE, R. W., JR. (1997) "Clinton's NATO Vision: Crisp on Expansion, Murky on What Comes After," *New York Times,* 17 July, p. 4.

ARAT, ZEHRA. (1988) "Democracy and Economic Development: Modernization Theory Revisited," *Comparative Politics* 21 (October): 21–36.

ARNSON, CYNTHIA J., AND PHILIP BRENNER. (1993) "The Limits of Lobbying: Interest Groups, Congress, and Aid to the Contras," in *Public Opinion in U.S. Foreign Policy: The Controversy over Contra Aid,* Richard Sobel, ed. Lanham, MD: Rowman and Littlefield, pp. 191–219.

ARORA, VIVEK B., AND TAMIM A. BAYOUMI. (1994) "Reductions in World Military Expenditure: Who Stands to Gain?" *Finance & Development* 31 (March): 24–27.

ART, ROBERT J. (1973) "Bureaucratic Politics and American Foreign Policy: A Critique," *Policy Sciences* 4 (December): 467–490.

———. (1991) "A Defensible Defense: America's Grand Strategy After the Cold War," *International Security* 15 (Spring): 5–53.

———. (1998–1999) "Geopolitics Updated: The Strategy of Selective Engagement," *International Security* 23 (Winter): 5–53.

———. (2003) *A Grand Strategy for America.* Ithaca, NY: Cornell University Press.

ART, ROBERT J., AND PATRICK M. CRONIN. (2003) *The United States and Coercive Diplomacy.* Washington, DC: United States Institute of Peace Press.

ASHER, HERBERT B. (1992) *Presidential Elections and American Politics,* 5th ed. Pacific Grove, CA: Brooks/Cole.

ASPIN, LES. (1976) "The Defense Budget and Foreign Policy: The Role of Congress," in *Arms, Defense Policy, and Arms Control,* Franklin A. Long and George W. Rathjens, eds. New York: Norton, pp. 115–174.

———. (1992) "Three Propositions for a New Era Nuclear Policy," commencement speech delivered at the Massachusetts Institute of Technology, Cambridge, MA, 3 June (http://web.mit.edu/newsoffice/1992/propositions-0603.html).

A. T. KEARNEY, INC. AND THE CARNEGIE ENDOWMENT FOR INTERNATIONAL PEACE. (2005) "Measuring Globalization," *Foreign Policy* 148 (May/June): 52–60.

A. T. KEARNEY, INC. AND THE CARNEGIE ENDOWMENT FOR INTERNATIONAL PEACE. (2006) "The Globalization Index," *Foreign Policy* 157 (November/December): 74–81.

ATKINSON, RICK, AND FRED HIATT. (1985) "Oh, That Golden Safety Net: The Pentagon Never Met a Defense Contractor It Wouldn't Bail Out," *Washington Post National Weekly Edition,* 22 April, pp. 6–8.

ATLAS, JAMES. (1995) "The Counterculture," *New York Times Magazine,* 12 February, pp. 32–38ff.

AUER, MATTHEW R. (1998) "Agency Reform as Decision Process: The Reengineering of the Agency for International Development," *Policy Sciences* 31 (June): 81–105.

AUERBACH, STUART. (1993) "How the U.S. Built Japan Inc.," *Washington Post National Weekly Edition,* 26 July–1 August, p. 21.

AUERSWALD, DAVID P., AND PETER F. COWHEY. (1997) "Ballotbox Diplomacy: The War Powers Resolution and the Use of Force," *International Studies Quarterly* 41 (September): 505–528.

AUSTER, BRUCE B. (1998) "Enviro-Intelligence: The CIA Goes Green," *U.S. News & World Report* 124 (16 March): 34.

AVERY, WILLIAM P. (1998) "Domestic Interests in NAFTA Bargaining," *Political Science Quarterly* 113 (Summer): 281–305.

BACCHUS, WILLIAM I. (1997) *The Price of American Foreign Policy: Congress, the Executive and Foreign Affairs Funding.* College Park, PA: Pennsylvania State University Press.

BACEVICH, ANDREW J. (1999) "Policing Utopia: The Military Imperatives of Globalization," *National Interest* 56 (Summer): 5–13.

———. (2002) *American Empire: The Realities and Consequences of U.S. Diplomacy.* Cambridge: Harvard University Press.

BAILEY, KATHLEEN. (1995) "Why We Have to Keep the Bomb," *Bulletin of the Atomic Scientists* 51 (January/February): 30–37.

BAKER, PAULINE H. (1989) *The United States and South Africa: The Reagan Years.* New York: Ford Foundation/Foreign Policy Association.

BAKER, PETER. (2000) *The Breach: Inside the Impeachment and Trial of William Jefferson Clinton.* New York: Scribner.

BAKER, PETER, AND MICHAEL ABRAMOWITZ. (2006) "A Governing Philosophy Rebuffed," *Washington Post,* 30 June.

BAKER, PETER, AND JIM VANDEHEI. (2005–2006) "Commander of All: With Cheney's Help, Bush Pushes for Broader Executive Power," *Washington Post National Weekly Edition,* 26 December–8 January, p. 13.

BALAKRISHNAN, UMA. (2002) "The Kyoto Protocol on Climate Change: A Balance of Interests," in *Contemporary Cases in U.S. Foreign Policy: From Terrorism to Trade,* 1st ed., Ralph G. Carter, ed. Washington, DC: CQ Press, pp. 317–338.

BALDRIGE, MALCOLM. (1983) "At Last, Hope for Coherent Policy," *New York Times,* 19 June, p. F2.

BALL, DESMOND. (1989) "Can Nuclear War Be Controlled?" in *The Nuclear Reader: Strategy, Weapons, War,* Charles W. Kegley, Jr., and Eugene R. Wittkopf, eds. New York: St. Martin's, pp. 284–290.

BALL, DESMOND, AND ROBERT C. TOTH. (1990) "Revising the SIOP: Taking War-Fighting to Dangerous Extremes," *International Security* 14 (Spring): 65–92.

BALL, GEORGE. (1984) "White House Roulette," *New York Review of Books* 31 (8 November) p. 5–11.

BALZ, DAN. (2001) "U.S., Britain Launch Airstrikes Against Targets in Afghanistan." *Washington Post,* 8 October, p. A1.

BAMFORD, JAMES. (1983) *The Puzzle Palace.* New York: Penguin.

BANDOW, DOUG. (1992–1993) "Avoiding War," *Foreign Policy* 89 (Winter): 156–174.

———. (1996) "Shaping a New Foreign Aid Policy," *USA Today* 124 (May): 16–17.

BARBER, BENJAMIN R. (1992) "Jihad vs. McWorld," *Atlantic Monthly* 269 (March): 53–63.

———. (2001) *The Truth of Power: Intellectual Affairs in the Clinton White House.* New York: W.W. Norton.

BARBER, JAMES DAVID. (1977) *The Presidential Character,* 2nd ed. Englewood Cliffs, NJ: Prentice Hall.

———. (1985) *The Presidential Character,* 3rd ed. Englewood Cliffs, NJ: Prentice Hall.

———. (1989) "George Bush: In Search of a Mission," *New York Times,* 19 January, p. A31.

———. (1992) *The Presidential Character: Predicting Performance in the White House,* 4th ed. Englewood Cliffs, NJ: Prentice Hall.

BARD, MITCHELL. (1994) "The Influence of Ethnic Interest Groups on American Middle East Policy," in *The Domestic Sources of American Foreign Policy: Insights and Evidence,* Eugene R. Wittkopf, ed. New York: St. Martin's, pp. 79–94.

BARDES, BARBARA A., AND ROBERT W. OLDENDICK. (2003) *Public Opinion: Measuring the American Mind.* Belmont, CA: Thomson/Wadsworth.

BARITZ, LOREN. (1985) *Backfire: A History of How American Culture Led Us into Vietnam and Made Us Fight the Way We Did.* New York: Morrow.

BARNES, FRED. (1994) "Saudi Doody," *New Republic,* 14 March, pp. 10–11.

BARNET, RICHARD J. (1969) *The Economy of Death.* New York: Atheneum.

———. (1972) *Roots of War: The Men and Institutions Behind U.S. Foreign Policy.* Baltimore: Penguin.

———. (1990) "U.S. Intervention: Low-Intensity Thinking," *Bulletin of the Atomic Scientists* 46 (May): 34–37.

———. (1993) "Still Putting Arms First," *Harper's* 286 (February): 59–65.

BARNET, RICHARD J., AND JOHN CAVANAGH. (1994) *Global Dreams: Imperial Corporations and the New World Order.* New York: Simon & Schuster.

BARNET, RICHARD J., AND RONALD E. MÜLLER. (1974) *Global Reach: The Power of the Multinational Corporations.* New York: Simon & Schuster.

BARNETT, ROGER W. (2003) *Asymmetrical Warfare.* Washington, DC: Brassey.

BASSFORD, CHRISTOPHER. (2004) "Bushies Vex U.S. Military—But It's War," *Newsday,* 3 February (www.clausewitz.com/VITA/CivMilRel.htm, accessed 11/3/06).

BAX, FRANS R. (1977) "The Legislative-Executive Relationship in Foreign Policy: New Partnership or New Competition?" *Orbis* 20 (Winter): 881–904.

BELLAH, ROBERT N. (1980) *Civil Religion in America.* San Francisco: Harper and Row.

———. (1992) *The Broken Covenant: American Civil Religion in Time of Trial.* Chicago: University of Chicago Press.

BELLAH, ROBERT, AND PHILLIP HAMMOND. (1988) "Civil Religion in America," *Daedalus* 117 (Summer): 97–119.

BENDER, BRYAN. (2005) "Congress Said to Steer Military Funds to Pet Projects," *Boston Globe,* 17 June (www.boston.com, accessed 4/15/06).

BENDOR, JONATHAN, AND THOMAS H. HAMMOND. (1992) "Rethinking Allison's Models," *American Political Science Review* 86 (June): 301–322.

BENDYNA, MARY E., AND CELINDA C. LAKE. (1995) "Gender and Voting in the 1992 Presidential Election," in *American Government: Readings and Cases,* Karen O'Connor, ed. Boston: Allyn and Bacon, pp. 372–382.

Benjamin, Matthew. (2003) "Greenback Game: Will the Bush Administration's Cheaper-Dollar Talk Backfire?" *U.S. News & World Report,* 13 October (www.usnews.com/usnews/biztech/articles/03101-3/13dollar.htm, accessed 5/3/2006).

BENNET, JAMES. (2001) "C.E.O., U.S.A," *New York Times Magazine,* 14 January (www.nytimes.com/library/magazine/home/20010114mag-bennet.html).

BENNETT, STEPHEN EARL. (1992) "The Persian Gulf War's Impact on Americans' Political Information," revised version of a paper presented at the American National Election Studies' Conference on "The Political Consequences of War," Washington, DC , 28 February.

BENNETT, W. LANCE. (1980) *Public Opinion in American Politics.* New York: Harcourt Brace Jovanovich.

———. (1994a) *Inside the System: Culture, Institutions, and Power in American Politics.* New York: Harcourt Brace Jovanovich.

———. (1994b) "The Media and the Foreign Policy Process," in *The New Politics of American Foreign Policy,* David A. Deese, ed. New York: St. Martin's, pp. 168–188.

BERGEN, PETER L. (2001) *Holy War Inc.: Inside the Secret World of Osama bin Laden.* New York: Free Press.

BERGER, SAMUEL R. (2000) "A Foreign Policy for the Global Age," *Foreign Affairs* 79 (November–December): 22–39.

BERGSTEN, C. FRED. (1988) *America in the World Economy: A Strategy for the 1990s.* Washington, DC: Institute for International Economics.

———. (1994) "APEC and World Trader," *Foreign Affairs* 73 (May/June): 20–26.

———. (2001) "America's Two-Front Economic Conflict," *Foreign Affairs* 80 (March/April): 16–27.

BERGSTEN, C. FRED, AND MARCUS NOLAND. (1993) *Reconcilable Differences? United States-Japan Economic Conflict.* Washington, DC: Institute for International Economics.

BERKE, RICHARD. (2001) "Bush Is Providing Corporate Model for White House," *New York Times,* 11 March (www.nytimes.com/2001/03/11/politics/11GOVE.html).

BERKLEY, GEORGE E. (1978) *The Craft of Public Administration.* Boston: Allyn and Bacon.

BERKOWITZ, BRUCE D., AND ALLAN E. GOODMAN. (1998) "The Logic of Covert Action," *National Interest* 5 (Spring): 38–46.

———. (2000) *Best Truth: Intelligence in the Information Age.* New Haven, CT: Yale University Press.

BERKOWITZ, BRUCE D., AND JEFFREY T. RICHELSON. (1995) "The CIA Vindicated: The Soviet Collapse Was Predicted," *National Interest* 41 (Fall): 36–47.

BERNSTEIN, BARTON J. (1995) "The Atomic Bombings Reconsidered," *Foreign Affairs* 74 (January/February): 135–152.

BERNSTEIN, RICHARD. (2003) "Foreign Views of U.S. Darken since September 11," *New York Times,* 11 September (www.nytimes.com, accessed 6/12/06).

BERNSTEIN, RICHARD, AND ROSS H. MUNRO. (1999) "The New China Lobby," in *The Domestic Sources of American Foreign Policy: Insights and Evidence,* Eugene R. Wittkopf and James M. McCormick, eds. Lanham, MD: Rowman and Littlefield, pp. 71–83.

BERNSTEIN, ROBERT A. (1989) *Elections, Representation, and Congressional Voting Behavior: The Myth of Constituency Control.* Englewood Cliffs, NJ: Prentice Hall.

BERNSTEIN, ROBERT A., AND WILLIAM ANTHONY. (1974) "The ABM Issue in the Senate, 1968–1970: The Importance of Ideology," *American Political Science Review* 68 (September): 1198–1206.

BERRIGAN, FRIDA, AND WILLIAM D. HARTUNG WITH LESLIE HEFFEL. (2005) *Special Report – Weapons at War 2005: Promoting Freedom or Fueling Conflict? U.S. Military Aid and Arms Transfers since September 11.* New York: World Policy Institute.

BESCHLOSS, MICHAEL. (2000) "The End of the Imperial Presidency," *New York Times,* 18 December (www.nytimes.com, accessed 5/15/06).

BESCHLOSS, MICHAEL R., AND STROBE TALBOTT. (1993) *At the Highest Levels: The Inside Story of the End of the Cold War.* Boston: Little, Brown.

BETTS, RICHARD K. (1994) "The Delusion of Impartial Intervention," *Foreign Affairs* 73 (November/December): 20–33.

———. (1996) "The Downside of the Cutting Edge," *National Interest* 45 (Fall 1996): 80–83.

———. (1998) "The New Threat of Mass Destruction," *Foreign Affairs* 45 (January/February): 26–41.

BHAGWATI, JAGDISH. (1993) "The Case for Free Trade," *Scientific American* 269 (November): 41–49.

———. (2001) *The Wind of a Hundred Days: How Washington Mismanaged Globalization.* Cambridge, MA: MIT Press.

BIENEFELD, MANFRED. (1994) "The New World Order: Echoes of a New Imperialism," *Third World Quarterly* 15 (March): 31–48.

BINNENDIJK, HANS. (1997) "Tin Cup Diplomacy," *National Interest* 49 (Fall): 88–91.

BIRDSALL, NANCY. (1998) "Life Is Unfair: Inequality in the World," *Foreign Policy* 101 (Spring): 76–91.

BISSELL, RICHARD E. (1990) "Who Killed the Third World?" *Washington Quarterly* 13 (Autumn): 23–32.

BITZINGER, RICHARD A. (1994) "The Globalization of the Arms Industry: The Next Proliferation Challenge," *International Security* 19 (Fall): 170–198.

BLACHMAN, MORRIS J., AND DONALD J. PUCHALA. (1991) "When Empires Meet: The 'Long Peace' in Long-Term Perspective," in *The Long Postwar Peace,* Charles W. Kegley, Jr., ed. New York: HarperCollins, pp. 177–201.

BLACKBURN, PAUL P. (1992) "The Post–Cold War Public Diplomacy of the United States," *Washington Quarterly* 15 (Winter): 75–86.

BLECHMAN, BARRY M. (1990) *The Politics of National Security: Congress and U.S. Defense Policy.* New York: Oxford University Press.

BLECHMAN, BARRY M., AND TAMARA COFMAN WITTES. (1999) "Defining Moment: The Threat and Use of Force in American Foreign Policy," *Political Science Quarterly* 114 (Spring): 1–30.

BLECKER, ROBERT A. (2004) "U.S. Steel Import Tariffs: The Politics of Global Markets," in *Contemporary Cases in U.S. Foreign Policy,* Ralph G. Carter, ed. Washington, DC: CQ Press, pp. 249–279.

BLIGH, MICHELLE, JEFFREY C. KOHLES, AND JAMES MEINDL. (2004) "Charisma Under Crisis: Presidential Leadership, Rhetoric, and Media Responses Before and After the September 11 Terrorist Attacks," *Leadership Quarterly* 15 (2): 211–239.

BLIGHT, JAMES G. (1990) *The Shattered Crystal Ball: Fear and Learning in the Cuban Missile Crisis.* Lanham, MD: Rowman and Littlefield.

BLIGHT, JAMES G., JOSEPH S. NYE JR., AND DAVID A. WELCH. (1987) "The Cuban Missile Crisis Revisited," *Foreign Affairs* 66 (Fall): 170–188.

BLIGHT, JAMES G., AND DAVID A. WELCH. (1989) *On the Brink: Americans and Soviets Reexamine the Cuban Missile Crisis.* New York: Hill and Wang.

BLOCK, FRED L. (1977) *The Origins of International Economic Disorder.* Berkeley and Los Angeles: University of California Press.

BLOOMFIELD, LINCOLN P. (1974) *The Foreign Policy Process: Making Theory Relevant.* Beverly Hills: Sage.

BLUMENTHAL, SIDNEY. (1988) *The Rise of the Counter Establishment.* New York: Harper and Row.

BLUSTEIN, PAUL. (1993) "East Asia's Economic Lesson for America," *Washington Post National Weekly Edition,* 15–21 March, p. 20.

———. (2001) "Getting Out in Front on Trade," *Washington Post,* 13 March, p. E1

BOBROW, DAVIS B., AND MARK A. BOYER. (2005) *Defensive Internationalism: Providing Public Goods in an Uncertain World.* Ann Arbor, MI: University of Michigan Press.

BOFFEY, PHILIP M. (1983) "'Rational' Decisions Prove Not To Be," *New York Times,* 6 December, pp. C1, C7.

BOLLEN, KENNETH A. (1979) "Political Democracy and the Timing of Development," *American Sociological Review* 44 (August): 572–587.

BOLTON, M. KENT. (2005) *U.S. Foreign Policy and International Politics: George W. Bush, 9/11, and the Global-Terrorist Hydra.* Upper Saddle River, NJ: Pearson/Prentice Hall.

BOOT, MAX. (2004) "Neocons," *Foreign Policy* 140 (January/February): 20–28.

BOREN, DAVID L. (1992) "The Intelligence Community: How Crucial?" *Foreign Affairs* 71 (Summer): 52–62.

BORGER, JULIAN. (2003) "The Spies Who Pushed for War," *The Guardian,* 17 July (www.guardian.co.uk, accessed 12/01/06).

BORRUS, MICHAEL, STEVE WEBER, JOHN ZYSMAN, AND JOSEPH WILLIHNGANZ. (1992) "Mercantilism and Global Security," *National Interest* 29 (Fall): 21–29.

BOSTDORFF, DENISE M., AND STEVEN R. GOLDZWIG. (1994) "Idealism and Pragmatism in American Foreign Policy Rhetoric: The Case of John F. Kennedy and Vietnam," *Presidential Studies Quarterly* 24 (Summer): 515–530.

BOULDING, KENNETH E. (1959) "National Images and International Systems," *Journal of Conflict Resolution* 3 (June): 120–131.

BOURNE, CHRISTOPHER M. (1998) "Unintended Consequences of the Goldwater-Nichols Act," *Joint Force Quarterly* 18 (Spring): 99–108.

BOUTON, MARSHALL M. (2004) *Global Views 2004: American Public Opinion and Foreign Policy.* Chicago: Chicago Council on Foreign Relations.

———. (2002) *Worldviews 2002: American Public Opinion and Foreign Policy.* Chicago: Chicago Council on Foreign Relations.

BOUTROS-GHALI, BOUTROS. (1992) *An Agenda for Peace: Preventive Diplomacy, Peacemaking, and Peacekeeping.* New York: United Nations.

———. (1992–1993) "Empowering the United Nations," *Foreign Affairs* 72 (Winter): 89–102.

BOVARD, JAMES. (1991) "Fair Trade Is Unfair," *Newsweek,* 9 December, p. 13.

BOYD, RICHARD W. (1972) "Popular Control of Public Policy: A Normal Vote Analysis of the 1968 Election," *American Political Science Review* 66 (June): 429–449.

BOYER, MARK A., AND TARA M. LAVALLEE. (2002) "Slovenia and NATO Enlargement: Understanding American Perspectives and the Prospects for Round 2 Enlargement," in *Small States in the Post–Cold War World: Slovenia and NATO Enlargement,* Zlatko Sabic, ed. Westport, CT: Praeger Publishers.

BRACE, PAUL, AND BARBARA HINCKLEY. (1992) *Follow the Leader: Opinion Polls and the Modern Presidents.* New York: Basic Books.

———. (1993) "George Bush and the Costs of High Popularity: A General Model with a Current Application," *PS: Political Science and Politics* 26 (September): 501–506.

BRANDS, H. W. (2000) *The Use of Force After the Cold War.* College Station, TX: Texas A&M University Press.

BRENNER, PHILIP, PATRICK J. HANEY, AND WALTER VANDERBUSH. (2004) "Intermestic Issues and U.S. Policy Toward Cuba," in *The Domestic Sources of Foreign Policy: Insights and Evidence,* Eugene R. Wittkopf and James M. McCormick, eds. Lanham, MD: Rowman and Littlefield, pp. 67–83.

BRESLAU, KAREN. (2000) "Snooping Around the Valley: The CIA Sets Up a High-Tech Investment Fund," *Newsweek,* 10 April, p. 45.

BREWER, GARRY D., AND PAUL BRACKEN. (1984) "Who's Thinking About National Security?" *Worldview* 27 (February): 21–13.

BRILMAYER, LEA. (1994) *American Hegemony: Political Morality in a One-Superpower World.* New Haven, CT: Yale University Press.

BRINKLEY, DOUGLAS. (1997) "Democratic Enlargement: The Clinton Doctrine," *Foreign Policy* 106 (Spring): 110–127.

BROAD, ROBIN, AND JOHN CAVANAGH. (1988) "No More NICs," *Foreign Policy* 72 (Fall): 81–103.

BRODER, DAVID S. (1986) "Who Took the Fun Out of Congress?" *Washington Post National Weekly Edition,* 17 February, pp. 9–10.

BRODER, DAVID S., AND DAN BALZ. (2006) "How Common Ground of 9/11 Gave Way to Partisan Split," *Washington Post,* 16 July (www.washingtonpost.com, accessed 12/2/06).

BRODER, DAVID S., AND RICHARD MORIN. (1998) "Two Different Bill Clintons," *Washington Post National Weekly Edition,* 31 August, pp. 6–7.

———. (1999) "A Question of Values," *Washington Post National Weekly Edition,* 11 January, pp. 6–7.

BRODER, JOHN M. (1997) "In Washington, It's Never Farewell to Arms," *New York Times,* 11 May, p. E16.

BROOKS, LINTON F., AND ARNOLD KANTER. (1994) "Introduction" in *U.S. Intervention Policy for the Post–Cold War World: New Challenges and New Responses.* New York: Norton.

BROOKS, STEPHEN G., AND WILLIAM C. WOHLFORTH. (2005) "Hard Times for Soft Balancing," *International Security* 30 (Summer): 72–108.

BROWER, RALPH S, AND MITCHEL Y. ABOLAFIA. (1997) "Bureaucratic Politics: The View from Below," *Journal of Public Administration Research and Theory* 7(a): 305–331.

BROWN, HAROLD. (2000) "Is Arms Control Dead?" *Washington Quarterly* 23 (Spring).

BROWN, JANET WELSH. (1998) "Population, Consumption, and the Path to Sustainability," in *The Global Agenda: Issues and Perspectives,* 5th ed., Charles W. Kegley, Jr., and Eugene R. Wittkopf, eds. Boston: McGraw-Hill, pp. 407–414.

BROWN, LESTER R. (2001) "Eradicating Hunger: A Growing Challenge," in *State of the World 2001,* Lester R. Brown, Christopher Flavin, Hilary French, et al., eds. New York: Norton, pp. 43–62.

BROWNSTEIN, RONALD, AND NINA EASTON. (1983) *Reagan's Ruling Class.* New York: Pantheon.

BRUGIONI, DINO A. (1993) *Eyeball to Eyeball: The Inside Story of the Cuban Missile Crisis.* New York: Random House.

BRUNE, LESTER. (1999) *The United States and Post–Cold War Interventions: Bush and Clinton in Somalia, Haiti, and Bosnia, 1992–1998.* Claremont, CA: Regina Publishers.

BRZEZINSKI, ZBIGNIEW K. (1998) *The Grand Chessboard: American Primacy and Its Geostrategic Imperatives.* New York: HarperCollins.

BUCHANAN, BRUCE. (1978) *The Presidential Experience: What the Office Does to the Man.* Englewood Cliffs, NJ: Prentice Hall.

BUCHANAN, PATRICK J. (1990) "America First-and Second, and Third," *National Interest* 19 (Spring): 77–82.

———. (1993) "America First—NAFTA Never," *Washington Post National Weekly Edition,* 15–21 November, p. 25.

———. (2004) *Where the Right Went Wrong.* New York: Thomas Dunne Books/St. Martin's Press.

BUCKLEY, WILLIAM F. (1970) "On the Right," *National Review,* 24 October, pp. 1124–1125.

BUMILLER, ELISABETH. (2004) "A Partner in Shaping an Assertive Foreign Policy," *New York Times,* 7 January (www.nytimes.com, accessed 1/7/04).

BUNDY, MCGEORGE. (1988) *Danger and Survival.* New York: Random House.

BUNDY, MCGEORGE, AND JAMES G. BLIGHT. (1987–1988) "October 27, 1962: Transcripts of the Meetings of the ExCom," *International Security* 12 (Winter): 30–92.

BURCH, PHILIP H., JR. (1980) *Elites in American History: The New Deal to the Carter Administration.* New York: Holmes and Meier.

BURGIN, EILEEN. (1993) "Congress and Foreign Policy: The Misperceptions," in *Congress Reconsidered,* 5th ed., Lawrence C. Dodd and Bruce I. Oppenheimer, eds. Washington, DC: CQ Press, pp. 333–363.

———. (1997) "Assessing Congress' Role in the Making of Foreign Policy," in *Congress Reconsidered,* 6th ed., Lawrence Dodd and Bruce Oppenheimer, eds. Washington, DC: Congressional Quarterly, pp. 293–324.

BURK, JAMES. (1999) "Public Support for Peacekeeping in Lebanon and Somalia: Assessing the Casualties Hypothesis," *Political Science Quarterly* 114 (Spring): 53–78.

BURKHART, ROSS E., AND MICHAEL S. LEWIS-BECK. (1994) "Comparative Democracy: The Economic Development Thesis," *American Political Science Review* 88 (December): 903–910.

BURKI, SHAHID JAVED. (1983) "UNCTAD VI: For Better or for Worse?" *Finance & Development* 20 (December): 16–19.

BURR, WILLIAM. (2005) "The Nixon Administration, the 'Horror Strategy,' and the Search for Limited Nuclear Options, 1969–1972: Prelude to the Schlesinger Doctrine," *Journal of Cold War Studies,* 7 (Summer): 34–78.

BUSH, GEORGE H. W., AND BRENT SCOWCROFT. (1999) *A World Transformed.* New York: Knopf.

BUSH, GEORGE W. (2001) *A Charge to Keep.* New York: Harper Trade.

BUSHNELL, PRUDENCE. (1989) "Leadership at State: The Neglected Dimension," *Foreign Service Journal* 66 (September): 30–31.

BYMAN, DANIEL, KENNETH POLLACK, AND GIDEON ROSE. (1999) "The Rollback Fantasy," *Foreign Affairs* 78 (January/February): 24–41.

BYRNES, MARK S. (1999) "'Overruled and Worn Down': Truman Sends an Ambassador to Spain," *Presidential Studies Quarterly* 29 (June): 263–279.

CALDER, KENT E. (2006) "China and Japan's Simmering Rivalry," *Foreign Affairs* 85 (March/April): 129–139.

CALDWELL, DAN. (1977) "Bureaucratic Foreign Policy Making," *American Behavioral Scientist* 21 (September–October): 87–110.

———. (1978) "A Research Note on the Quarantine of Cuba October 1962," *International Studies Quarterly* 22 (December): 625–633.

———, ed. (1983) *Henry Kissinger: His Personality and Policies.* Durham, NC: Duke University Press.

———. (1991) *The Dynamics of Domestic Politics and Arms Control: The SALT II Treaty Ratification Debate.* Columbia, SC: University of South Carolina Press.

CALIFANO, JOSEPH A., JR. (1994) "Imperial Congress," *New York Times Magazine,* 23 January, pp. 40–41.

CALLAHAN, PATRICK. (2004) *Logics of American Foreign Policy: Theories of America's World Role.* New York: Pearson/Longman.

CALLEO, DAVID P. (2003) "Power Wealth, and Wisdom: The United States and Europe After Iraq," *National Interest* 72 (Summer): 5–15.

CAMBONE, STEPHEN. (2000) "An Inherent Lesson in Arms Control," *Washington Quarterly* 23 (Spring), 207–218.

CAMPBELL, ANGUS, PHILIP E. CONVERSE, WARREN E. MILLER, AND DONALD E. STOKES. (1960) *The American Voter.* New York: Wiley.

CAMPBELL, JAMES E. (2005) "Why Bush Won the Presidential Election of 2004: Incumbency, Ideology, Terrorism, and Turnout." *Political Science Quarterly,* 120 (Summer): 219–241.

CAMPBELL, JOEL, AND LEILA CAIN. (1965) "Public Opinion and the Outbreak of War," *Journal of Conflict Resolution* 9 (September): 318–329.

CAMPBELL, JOHN FRANKLIN. (1971) *The Foreign Affairs Fudge Factory.* New York: Basic Books.

CAMPBELL, KURT M. (2002) "Globalization's First War?" *Washington Quarterly* 25 (Winter): 7–14.

CANNON, LOU. (1988) "An 'Honest Broker' at the NSC," *Washington Post National Weekly Edition,* 22–28 August, pp. 6–8.

CANTLUPE, JOE. (2000) "Mexico Might Have U.S. to Thank if Big Drug Arrests Are Made," *San Diego Union-Tribune,* 5 November, p. 11.

CAPACCIO, TONY. (2000) "Foreign Military Sales Show Sustained Growth," *Defense Week,* 6 November, p. 5.

CAPORASO, JAMES A., ed. (1978) *International Organization* 32 (Winter): 1–300.

CAPRIOLI, MARY. (1999) "Gendered Conflict," *Journal of Peace Research,* 37 (1): 51–68.

CAPRIOLI, MARY, AND BOYER, MARK A. (2001) "Gender, Violence and International Crisis," *Journal of Conflict Resolution,* 45 (4): 503–518.

CARLUCCI, FRANK. (2001) "What State Needs: Resources for Reform," *Foreign Service Journal* 78 (May) (www.afsa.org/fsj/may01/carluccimay01.cfm, accessed 10/29/06).

CARNEY, ELIZA NEWLIN. (1994) "Still Trying to Reinvent Government," *National Journal,* 18 June, pp. 1442–1443.

CAROTHERS, THOMAS. (1994a) "The Democracy Nostrum," *World Policy Journal* 11 (Fall): 47–53.

———. (1994b) "The NED at 10," *Foreign Policy* 95 (Summer): 123–138.

———. (1995) "Democracy Promotion Under Clinton," *Washington Quarterly* 18 (Autumn): 13–25.

———. (1997) "Democracy Without Illusions," *Foreign Affairs* 76 (January/February): 85–99.

———. (1999) *Aiding Democracy Abroad: The Learning Curve.* Washington, DC: Carnegie Endowment for International Peace.

CARPENTER, TED GALEN. (1995) *The Captive Press: Foreign Policy Crises and the First Amendment.* Washington, DC: Cato Institute.

———. (1998) "Roiling Asia: U.S. Coziness with China Upsets the Neighbors," *Foreign Affairs* 77 (November/December): 2–6.

CARR, CALEB. (1994) "Aldrich Ames and the Conduct of American Intelligence," *World Policy Journal* 11 (Fall): 19–28.

CARR, E. H. (1939) *The Twenty-Years' Crisis 1919–1939: An Introduction to the Study of International Relations.* London: Macmillan.

CARTER, ASHTON, JOHN DEUTCH, AND PHILIP ZELIKOW. (1998) "Catastrophic Terrorism," *Foreign Affairs* 77 (November/December): 80–94.

CARTER, HODDING, III. (1981) "Life Inside the Carter State Department," *Playboy* 28 (February): 96ff.

CARTER, RALPH G. (1998) "Congress and Post–Cold War U.S. Foreign Policy," in *After the End: Making U.S. Foreign Policy in the Post–Cold War World,* James M. Scott, ed. Durham, NC: Duke University Press, pp. 108–137.

———, ed. (2002) *Contemporary Cases in U.S. Foreign Policy: From Terrorism to Trade.* Washington, DC: Congressional Quarterly.

CARTER, RALPH G., AND JAMES M. SCOTT. (2000a) "Patterns of Leadership: Congressional Foreign Policy Entrepreneurs and U.S. Foreign Policy," *International Studies Association/Midwest.* St. Louis, MO , October: 27–28.

———. (2000b) "Senator Chuck Hagel as a Foreign Policy Entrepreneur," *Annual Convention of the International Studies Association.* Los Angeles, CA , March: 14–18.

———. (2001) "Taking the Lead: Congressional Foreign Policy Entrepreneurs in U.S. Foreign Policy," *Annual Convention of the International Studies Association.* Chicago, IL , February: 20–24.

———. (2004) "Taking the Lead: Congressional Foreign Policy Entrepreneurs in U.S. Foreign Policy," *Politics & Policy* 32 (March): 34–70.

CARTER, RALPH G., JAMES M. SCOTT, AND CHARLES M. ROWLING. (2004) "Setting a

Course: Congressional Foreign Policy Entrepreneurs in Post–World War II U.S. Foreign Policy," *International Studies Perspectives* 5 (August): 278–299.

CASPARY, WILLIAM R. (1970) "The 'Mood Theory': A Study of Public Opinion," *American Political Science Review* 64 (June): 536–547.

CAVANAGH, THOMAS E. (1982–1983) "The Dispersion of Authority in the House of Representatives," *Political Science Quarterly* 97 (Winter): 623–637.

CEASER, JAMES W., AND ANDREW E. BUSCH. (2005) *Red Over Blue: The 2004 Elections and American Politics*. Lanham, MD: Rowman and Littlefield.

CENTER FOR ARMS CONTROL AND NON-PROLIFERATION. (2006) "U.S. Military Spending vs. the World," 6 February (www. armscontrolcenter.org/archives/002244.php, accessed 12/3/06).

CHACE, JAMES. (1996) "Sharing the Atom Bomb," *Foreign Affairs* 75 (January/February): 129–144.

CHAN, STEVE. (1997) "In Search of Democratic Peace: Problems and Promise," *Mershon International Studies Review* 41 (May): 59–91.

CHAN, STEVE, AND ALEX MINTZ, eds. (1992) *Defense, Welfare, and Growth*. London: Routledge.

CHAPMAN, STEVE. (2006) "Government Secrecy Is Not Always a Good Thing," *Chicago Tribune*, 30 April, sec. 1, p. 7.

CHASE, ROBERT S., EMILY B. HILL, AND PAUL KENNEDY. (1996) "Pivotal States and U.S. Grand Strategy," *Foreign Affairs* 75 (January/February): 33–51.

CHILDS, HAROLD L. (1965) *Public Opinion: Nature, Formation, and Role*. Princeton, NJ: Van Nostrand.

CHOATE, PAT. (1990) *Agents of Influence*. New York: Knopf.

CHRISTIANSEN, DREW, AND GERARD F. POWERS. (1993) "Unintended Consequences," *Bulletin of the Atomic Scientists* 49 (November): 41–45.

CHRISTOPHER, ROBERT C. (1989) *Crashing the Gates: The De-WASPing of America's Power Elite*. New York: Simon & Schuster.

CHUBIN, SHAHRAM. (1993) "The South and the New World Order," *Washington Quarterly* 16 (Autumn): 87–107.

CIRINCIONE, JOSEPH. (1997) "Why the Right Lost the Missile Defense Debate," *Foreign Policy* 106 (Spring): 39–55.

———. (2005) "The Declining Ballistic Missile Threat, 2005," in *Policy Outlook* (February):1–16.

CITRIN, JACK, ERNST B. HAAS, CHRISTOPHER MUSTE, AND BETH REINGOLD. (1994) "Is American Nationalism Changing?: Implications for Foreign Policy," *International Studies Quarterly* 38 (March): 1–31.

CLARK, KEITH C., AND LAURENCE J. LEGERE, eds. (1969) *The President and the Management of National Security: A Report by the Institute for Defense Analyses*. New York: Praeger.

CLARK, WESLEY. (2001) *Waging Modern War*. New York: Public Affairs Press.

CLARKE, DUNCAN L. (1989) *American Defense and Foreign Policy Institutions: Toward a Sound Foundation*. New York: Harper and Row.

———. (1997) *Send Guns and Money: Security Assistance and U.S. Foreign Policy*. Westport, CT: Praeger.

CLARKE, RICHARD A. (2004) *Against All Enemies: Inside America's War on Terror*. New York: Free Press.

CLARKE, WALTER, AND JEFFREY HERBST. (1997) *Learning from Somalia: The Lessons of Armed Humanitarian Intervention*. Boulder, CO: Westview Press.

CLAUDE, INIS L., JR. (1971) *Swords into Plowshares*, 4th ed. New York: Random House.

COHEN, BERNARD C. (1961) "Foreign Policy Makers and the Press," in *International Politics and Foreign Policy*, James N. Rosenau, ed. New York: Free Press, pp. 220–228.

———. (1963) *The Press and Foreign Policy*. Princeton, NJ: Princeton University Press.

———. (1973) *The Public's Impact on Foreign Policy*. Boston: Little, Brown.

COHEN, EDWARD S. (2001) *The Politics of Globalization in the United States*. Washington, DC: Georgetown University Press.

COHEN, ELIOT A. (1996) "A Revolution in Warfare," *Foreign Affairs* 75 (March/April): 37–54.

———. (1997) "Are U.S. Forces Overstretched? Civil-Military Relations," *Orbis* 41 (Spring): 177–186.

COHEN, STEPHEN D. (1994) *The Making of United States International Economic Policy: Principles,*

Problems, and Proposals for Reform, 4th ed. New York: Praeger.

COHEN, STEPHEN D., JOEL R. PAUL, AND ROBERT A. BLECKER. (1996) *Fundamentals of U.S. Foreign Trade Policy: Economics, Politics, Laws, and Issues.* Boulder, CO: Westview Press.

COHEN-TANUGI, LAURENT. (2005) "The End of Europe?" *Foreign Affairs* 84 (November/December): 55–67.

COLLIER, ELLEN C. (1988) "Foreign Policy by Reporting Requirement," *Washington Quarterly* 11 (Winter): 75–84.

———. (1989) "Bipartisan Foreign Policy and Policy-making Since World War II" in *CRS Report for Congress,* 9 November. Washington, DC: Congressional Research Service.

———. (1994a) "War Powers Resolution: Presidential Compliance" in *CRS Issue Brief 81050,* 15 February. Washington, DC: Congressional Research Service.

———. (1994b) "The War Powers Resolution: Twenty Years of Experience" in *CRS Report for Congress,* 11 January. Washington, DC: Congressional Research Service.

COLLIER, PAUL, AND DAVID DOLLAR. (1999) *Aid Allocation and Poverty Reduction.* Washington, DC: World Bank.

COMMAGER, HENRY STEELE. (1965) "A Historian Looks at Our Political Morality," *Saturday Review,* 10 July, p. 16–18.

———. (1983) "Misconceptions Governing American Foreign Policy," in *Perspectives on American Foreign Policy,* Charles W. Kegley, Jr., and Eugene R. Wittkopf, eds. New York: St. Martin's, pp. 510–517.

CONGRESS AND FOREIGN POLICY 1991, U.S. HOUSE OF REPRESENTATIVES, 102ND CONGRESS. (1992) Washington, DC: Government Printing Office.

CONGRESSIONAL RESEARCH SERVICE. (1989) "Soviet-U.S. Relations: A Briefing Book" in *CRS Report for Congress.* Washington, DC: Congressional Research Service.

CONOVER, PAMELA J., AND STANLEY FELDMAN. (1984) "How People Organize the Political World: A Schematic Model," *American Journal of Political Science* 28 (February): 95–126.

CONSTABLE, PAMELA. (1998) "The Holdup on the Nuclear Test Ban Treaty," *Washington Post National Weekly Edition,* 19 October, p. 17.

CONVERSE, PHILIP E. (1964) "The Nature of Belief Systems in Mass Publics," in *Ideology and Discontent,* David E. Apter, ed. New York: Free Press, pp. 206–261.

CONWAY, M. MARGARET. (2000) *Political Participation in the United States,* 3rd ed. Washington, DC: CQ Press.

COOK, CHARLES E., JR. (2001a) "How Does 2000 Stack Up?" *Washington Quarterly* 23 (Spring): 213–220.

———. (2001b) "The Silver-Bullet Presidency," *Washington Quarterly* 23 (Summer): 229–234.

COOLEY, ALEXANDER. (2005) "Base Politics," *Foreign Affairs,* 84 (6): 72–92.

COOPER, RICHARD N. (1988) "International Economic Cooperation: Is It Desirable? Is It Likely?" *Washington Quarterly* 11 (Spring): 89–101.

———. (1998) "Toward a Real Global Warming Treaty," *Foreign Affairs* 77 (March/April): 66–79.

COPSON, RAYMOND W. (1988) "The Reagan Doctrine: U.S. Assistance to Anti-Marxist Guerrillas" in *CRS Issue Brief,* 11 March. Washington, DC: Congressional Research Service.

COREN, MICHAEL. (2005) "Experts: Cyber-crime Bigger Threat than Cyber-terror," 24 January (www.cnn.com, accessed 6/25/06).

CORTRIGHT, DAVID, AND GEORGE A. LOPEZ, eds. (2000) *The Sanctions Decade: Assessing UN Strategies in the 1990s.* Boulder, CO: Lynne Rienner.

———. (2002) *Smart Sanctions: Targeting Economic Statecraft.* New York: Rowman and Littlefield.

CORWIN, EDWARD S. (1948) *The President: Office and Powers.* New York: New York University Press.

COX, ARTHUR MACY. (1976) *The Dynamics of Détente.* New York: Norton.

CRABB, CECIL V., JR. (1957) *Bipartisan Foreign Policy: Myth or Reality.* Evanston, IL: Row, Peterson, and Company.

CRABB, CECIL V., JR., AND PAT M. HOLT. (1992) *Invitation to Struggle,* 4th ed. Washington, DC: CQ Press.

CRAIG, GORDON A., AND ALEXANDER L. GEORGE. (1990) *Force and Statecraft: Diplomatic Problem of Our Time.* New York: Oxford University Press.

CRAIG, STEPHEN C. (1993) *The Malevolent Leaders: Popular Discontent in America.* Boulder, CO: Westview Press.

CRISTENSEN, THOMAS J. (1999) "China, the U.S.-Japan Alliance, and the Security Dilemma in East Asia," *International Security* 23 (Spring): 49–80.

CROCK, STAN. (1998) "Gore's Foreign Policy Guru," *New Republic,* 7 December, p. 18.

CROCKER, CHESTER. (1995) "The Lessons of Somalia," *Foreign Affairs* 74 (May/June): 2–8.

———. (2003) "Engaging Failed States," *Foreign Affairs* 82 (September/October): 32–44.

CRONIN, THOMAS E. (1973) "The Swelling of the Presidency," *Saturday Review of the Society* 1 (February): 30–36.

———. (1984) "The Swelling of the Presidency: Can Anyone Reverse the Tide?" in *American Government: Readings and Cases,* Peter Woll, ed. Boston: Little, Brown, pp. 345–359.

CROPSEY, SETH. (1994) "The Only Credible Deterrent," *Foreign Affairs* 73 (March/April): 14–20.

C-SPAN. (2000) "Capitol Questions with Ilona Nickels, C-SPAN Resident Congressional Scholar" (www.c-span.org/questions/weekly35.htm, accessed 11/3/06).

CUKIER, KENNETH NEIL. (2005) "Who Will Control the Internet?" *Foreign Affairs* 84 (November/December): 7–13.

CUPITT, RICHARD T. (2000) *Reluctant Champions: U.S. Presidential Policy and Strategic Export Controls, Truman, Bush Eisenhower, and Clinton.* New York: Routledge.

DAALDER, IVO. (1994) *The Clinton Administration and Multilateral Peace Operations, Case 462.* Washington, DC: Institute for the Study of Diplomacy.

———. (1999) "Emerging Answers: Kosovo, NATO, and the Use of Force," *Brookings Review* 17 (Summer): 22–25.

———. (2000) *Getting to Dayton: The Making of America's Bosnia Policy.* Washington, DC: Brookings Institution.

DAALDER, IVO H., AND I. M. DESTLER. (2000) "A New NSC for a New Administration." *Brookings Institution Policy Brief #68.* Washington, DC: Brookings Institution.

———. (2001) "How Operational and Visible an NSC?" The Brookings Institution Opinion Piece (website publication only), 23 February (www.brookings.edu/views/op-ed/daalder/20010223.htm, accessed 11/11/01).

———. (2004) "More than a Few Campaign Stops: How Rice Has Changed the Role of National Security Adviser," *Center for American Progress,* 22 October (www.americanprogress.org, accessed 5/28/06).

DAALDER, IVO, AND MICHAEL E. O'HANLON. (2000) "The United States in the Balkans: There to Stay," *Washington Quarterly* 23 (Autumn): 157–170.

DAGGETT, STEPHEN. (2004) *CRS Report for Congress: The U.S. Intelligence Budget: A Basic Overview,* September 24. Washington, DC: Congressional Research Service.

DAHL, ROBERT. (1989) *Democracy and Its Critics.* New Haven, CT: Yale University Press.

DALLEK, ROBERT. (1983) *The American Style of Foreign Policy: Cultural Politics and Foreign Affairs.* New York: Knopf.

———. (1984) *Ronald Reagan: The Politics of Symbolism.* Cambridge, MA: Harvard University Press.

DALTON, RUSSELL J., PAUL A. BECK, AND ROBERT HUCKFELDT. (1998) "Partisan Cues and the Media: Information Flows in the 1992 Presidential Election," *American Political Science Review* 92 (March): 111–126.

DALY, HERMAN E. (1993) "The Perils of Free Trade," *Scientific American* 269 (November): 50–57.

DANZIGER, SHELDON, AND DEBORAH REED. (1999) "Winners and Losers: The Era of Inequality Continues," *Brookings Review* 17 (Fall): 14–17.

DAS, DILIP K. (2001) *Global Trading System at Crossroads: A Post-Seattle Perspective.* New York: Routledge.

DAVIS, JENNIFER. (1993) "Squeezing Apartheid," *Bulletin of the Atomic Scientists* 49 (November): 16–19.

DAVIS, VINCENT. (1987) "Organization and Management," in *American Defense Annual, 1987–1988,*

Joseph Kruzel, ed. Lexington, MA: Lexington Books, pp. 171–199.

DE BORCHGRAVE, ARNAUD. (1996) "Globalization-The Bigger Picture: An Interview with Dr. Ismail Serageldin, World Bank Vice President for Environmentally Sustainable Development," *Washington Quarterly* 19 (Summer): 159–178.

DE LA GARZA, RODOLFO O., AND HARRY PACHON, eds. (2000) *Latinos and U.S. Foreign Policy: Representing the Homeland?* Lanham, MD: Rowman and Littlefield.

DE TOCQUEVILLE, ALEXIS. ([1835] 1969) *Democracy in America.* New York: Doubleday.

DE YOUNG, KAREN. (2001) "Allies Are Cautious on 'Bush Doctrine'," *Washington Post,* 16 October, p. A1.

DE YOUNG, KAREN, AND DANA MILBANK. "Military Plans Informed by Polls," *Washington Post,* 19 October, p. A19.

DE YOUNG, KAREN, AND ALAN SIPRESS. (2001) "Dual Strategy of Assault, Reward," *Washington Post,* 8 October, p. A1.

DECONDE, ALEXANDER. (1992) *Ethnicity, Race, and American Foreign Policy.* Boston: Northeastern University Press.

DEFENSE SECURITY ASSISTANCE AGENCY. (2004) *Facts Book.* Washington, DC: Administration and Management Business Operations, DSCA (www.dsca.mil, accessed 6/15/06).

DEFENSE SECURITY COOPERATION AGENCY. (2002) *Strategic Plan, 2003–2008* (www.dsca.mil, accessed 5/20/05).

DEIBEL, TERRY L. (1992) "Strategies Before Containment: Patterns for the Future," *International Security* 16 (Spring): 79–108.

———. (2002) "The Death of a Treaty," *Foreign Affairs* 81 (September/October): 142–161.

———. (2003) "Inside the Water's Edge: The Senate Votes on the Comprehensive Test Ban Treaty," *Pew Cases Studies in International Affairs,* Case 263, 1–32.

DERIVERA, JOSEPH H. (1968) *The Psychological Dimension of Foreign Policy.* Columbus, OH: Merrill.

DESTLER, I. M. (1974) *Presidents, Bureaucrats, and Foreign Policy: The Politics of Organizational Reform.* Princeton, NJ: Princeton University Press.

———. (1983a) "The Evolution of Reagan Foreign Policy," in *The Reagan Presidency,* Fred I. Greenstein, ed. Baltimore, MD: Johns Hopkins University Press, pp. 117–158.

———. (1983b) "The Rise of the National Security Assistant," in *Perspectives on American Foreign Policy* Charles W. Kegley, Jr., and Eugene R. Wittkopf, eds. New York: St. Martin's, pp. 260–281.

———. (1994) "A Government Divided: The Security Complex and the Economic Complex," in *The New Politics of American Foreign Policy,* David A. Deese, ed. New York: St. Martin's, pp. 132–147.

———. (1996) *The National Economic Council: A Work in Progress.* Washington, DC: Institute for International Economics.

———. (1998) "Foreign Economic Policymaking Under Bill Clinton," in *After the End: Making U.S. Foreign Policy in the Post–Cold War World,* James M. Scott, ed. Durham, NC: Duke University Press, pp. 89–107.

———. (1999) "Trade Policy at a Crossroads," *The Brookings Review* 17 (Winter): 26–30.

DESTLER, I. M., AND PETER J. BALINT. (1999) *The New Politics of American Trade: Trade, Labor, and the Environment.* Washington, DC: Institute for International Economics.

DESTLER, I. M., LESLIE H. GELB, AND ANTHONY LAKE. (1984) *Our Own Worst Enemy: The Unmaking of American Foreign Policy.* New York: Simon & Schuster.

DEUDNEY, DANIEL, AND G. JOHN IKENBERRY. (1994) "After the Long War," *Foreign Policy* 94 (Spring): 21–35.

DEUTCH, JOHN. (2005) "Nuclear Posture for Today," *Foreign Affairs,* 84 (1): 49–60.

DEUTCH, JOHN, HAROLD BROWN, AND JOHN WHITE. (2000) "National Missile Defense: Is There Another Way?" *Foreign Policy* 119 (July/August): 91–100.

DEUTSCH, KARL W., AND RICHARD L. MERRITT. (1965) "Effects of Events on National and International Images," in *International Behavior,* Herbert C. Kelman, ed. New York: Holt, Rinehart, and Winston, pp. 132–187.

DEVROY, ANN. (1994) "The Shakedown Cruise: Year Two," *Washington Post National Weekly Edition,* 11–17 April, p. 11.

DEVROY, ANN, AND STEPHEN BARR. (1995) "Reinventing the Vice Presidency," *Washington Post National Weekly Edition,* 27 February–5 March, pp. 6–7.

DEVROY, ANN, AND R. JEFFREY SMITH. (1993) "Oceans Apart Over Intervention," *Washington Post National Weekly Edition,* 3–9 October, pp. 8–9.

DIAMOND, JOHN. (2001) "Powell's Aim: Remove 'Rust'," *Chicago Tribune,* 29 January (www.nci.org/p/powell-ct12901.htm, accessed 11/3/06).

DIAMOND, LARRY. (1999) *Developing Democracy: Toward Consolidation.* Baltimore, MD: Johns Hopkins University Press.

DICKEY, CHRISTOPHER, MARK DENNIS, GREGORY VISTICA, AND RUSSELL WATSON. (1998) "How to Get Rid of Him," *Newsweek,* 9 March, p. 31.

DIONNE, E. J., JR. (1996) "Why Foreign Policy Is No Big Issue," *Washington Post Weekly Edition,* 28 October–3 November, p. 26.

———. (1999) "War as an Opening for Partisan Payback," *Washington Post Weekly Edition,* 10 May, p. 26.

DIPLOMACY FOR THE 70'S: A PROGRAM OF MANAGEMENT REFORM FOR THE DEPARTMENT OF STATE. (1970) Washington, DC: Department of State.

DIRENZO, GORDON J., ed. (1974) *Personality and Politics.* Garden City, NY: Doubleday/Anchor.

DIXON, WILLIAM J., AND STEPHEN M. GAARDER. (1992) "Presidential Succession and the Cold War: An Analysis of Soviet-American Relations, 1948–1988," *Journal of Politics* 54 (February): 156–175.

DOBBS, MICHAEL. (1999) "Post-Mortem on NATO's Bombing Campaign," *Washington Post National Weekly Edition,* 19–26 July, p. 23.

———. (2001) "Aid Abroad Is Business Back Home," *Washington Post,* p. A1.

DOMBROWSKI, PETER, AND RODGER A. PAYNE. (2003) "Global Debate and the Limits of the Bush Doctrine," *International Security,* 4 (November): 395–408.

DOMHOFF, G. WILLIAM. (1984) *Who Rules America Now?* Englewood Cliffs, NJ: Prentice Hall.

DONOVAN, HEDLEY. (1985) *Roosevelt to Reagan.* New York: Harper and Row.

DONOVAN, JOHN C. (1974) *The Cold Warriors: A Policy-Making Elite.* Lexington, MA: Heath.

DORAN, MICHAEL SCOTT. (2001) "Somebody Else's Civil War: Ideology, Rage, and the Assault on America." in *How Did This Happen: Terrorism and the New War,* James F. Hoge, Jr. and Gideon Rose, eds. New York: Public Affairs Press, pp. 31–52.

DORRIEN, GARY. (2003) "Axis of One," *Christian Century* 120 (8 March): 30–35.

DOWNS, ANTHONY. (1957) *An Economic Theory of Democracy.* New York: Harper and Row.

———. (1967) *Inside Bureaucracy.* Boston: Little, Brown.

DOXEY, MARGARET. (1990) "International Sanctions," in *World Politics: Power, Interdependence, and Dependence,* David G. Haglund and Michael K. Hawes, eds. Toronto: Harcourt Brace Jovanovich, pp. 242–261.

DOYLE, MICHAEL W. (1986) "Liberalism and World Politics," *American Political Science Review* 80 (December): 1151–1169.

———. (1995) "Liberalism and World Politics Revisited," in *Controversies in International Relations Theory: Realism and the Neoliberal Challenge,* Charles W. Kegley, Jr., ed. New York: St. Martin's, pp. 83–106.

DRAPER, THEODORE. (1968) *The Dominican Revolt.* New York: Commentary.

———. (1990) *A Present of Things Past.* New York: Hill and Wang.

———. (1991) *A Very Thin Line: The Iran-Contra Affair.* New York: Hill and Wang.

DREW, ELIZABETH. (1994) *On the Edge: The Clinton Presidency.* New York: Simon & Schuster.

DREYFUS, ROBERT. (1998) "Risky Business," *New Republic* 218 (5 January): 18–20.

DREZNER, DANIEL W. (2000) "Ideas, Bureaucratic Politics, and the Crafting of Foreign Policy," *American Journal of Political Science* 44 (October): 733–749.

———. (2003) "How Smart Are Smart Sanctions?" *International Studies Review* 5 (Spring): 107–110.

———. (2004) "The Outsourcing Bogeyman," *Foreign Affairs,* 83 (3): 22–34.

DRISCHLER, ALVIN PAUL. (1985) "Foreign Policy Making on the Hill," *Washington Quarterly* 8 (Summer): 165–175.

DROGIN, BOB. (2005) "U.S. Trains its 'Eyes and Ears' against Nation's Enemies," *San Francisco Chronicle,* 9 January (www.sfgate.com, accessed 2/4/06).

DROZDIAK, WILLIAM. (1997) "Down with Yankee Dominance," *Washington Post National Weekly Edition,* 24 November, p. 15.

DRURY, A. COOPER. (2000) "U.S. Presidents and the Use of Economic Sanctions," *Presidential Studies Quarterly* 30 (4) (December): 623–642.

DULLES, JOHN FOSTER. (1952) "A Policy of Liberation," *Life,* 19 May, p. 19 ff.

DUNN, MICHAEL SCOTT. (2001) "Somebody Else's Civil War: Ideology, Rage, and the Assault on America," in *How Did This Happen? Terrorism and the New War,* James F. Hoge, Jr. and Gideon Rose, eds. New York: Public Affairs, pp. 31–52.

DUNN, ROBERT M., JR. (2001) "Has the U.S. Economy REALLY Been Globalized?" *Washington Quarterly,* (Winter): 53–64.

DWYER, JIM. (2003) "A Gulf War Commander Sees a Longer Road," *New York Times,* 28 March.

DYE, THOMAS R. (1990) *Who's Running America?: The Bush Era,* 5th ed. Englewood Cliffs, NJ: Prentice Hall.

———. (1995) *Who's Running America?: The Clinton Years,* 6th ed. Englewood Cliffs, NJ: Prentice Hall.

DYE, THOMAS R., AND HARMON ZEIGLER. (1990) *The Irony of Democracy,* 8th ed. Pacific Grove, CA: Brooks/Cole.

———. (2000) *The Irony of Democracy: An Uncommon Introduction to American Politics,* Millennial ed. Fort Worth, TX: Harcourt Brace College Publishers.

EAGLEBURGER, LAWRENCE, AND ROBERT BARRY. (1996) "Dollars and Sense Diplomacy," *Foreign Affairs* 75 (4) (July/August): 2–8.

EBERSTADT, NICHOLAS. (1991) "Population Change and National Security," *Foreign Affairs* 70 (Summer): 115–131.

———. (2001) "The Population Implosion," *Foreign Policy* 123 (March/April): 42–53.

ECKHOLM, ERIK. (2001) "Experts Try to Make Missile Shield Plan Palatable to China," *New York Times,* 28 January, p. 1.

ECONOMIST INTELLIGENCE UNIT. (2006) "The World's Largest Economies," *Economist* (1 April): 84.

EDSALL, THOMAS B. (2001) *Washington Post National Weekly Edition,* 23–29 April, p. 14.

EDWARDS, GEORGE C., III, WILLIAM MITCHELL, AND REED WELCH. (1995) "Explaining Presidential Approval: The Significant of Issue Salience," *American Journal of Political Science* 39 (February): 108–134.

EGGEN, DAN, AND SUSAN SCHMIDT. (2004) "It's a Whole New Spy Game," *Washington Post National Weekly Edition,* 10–16 May, p. 29.

EHRLICH, PAUL R., AND ANNE H. EHRLICH. (1990) *The Population Explosion.* New York: Simon & Schuster.

EICHENBERG, RICHARD C. (2003) "Gender Differences in Public Attitudes Toward the Use of Force by the United States, 1990–2003." *International Security* 28 (Summer): 110–141.

EICHENGREEN, BARRY. (1999) *Toward a New International Financial Structure.* Washington, DC: Institute for International Peace.

———. (1998) *Globalizing Capital: A History of the International Monetary System.* Princeton, NJ: Princeton University Press.

EINHORN, JESSICA. (2006) "Reforming the World Bank," *Foreign Affairs* 85 (January/February): 17–22.

EIZENSTADT, STUART. (1998) "Stick with Kyoto: A Sound Start on Global Warming," *Foreign Affairs* 77 (May/June): 119–121.

ELAND, IVAN. (1993) "Think Small," *Bulletin of the Atomic Scientists* 49 (November): 36–40.

ELAZAR, DANIEL J. (1970) *Cities of the Prairie.* New York: Basic Books.

———. (1994) *The American Mosaic: The Impact of Space, Time, and Culture on American Politics.* Boulder, CO: Westview Press.

ELLIOTT, KIM ANDREW. (1989–1990) "Too Many Voices of America," *Foreign Policy* 77 (Winter): 113–131.

ELLIOTT, KIMBERLY ANN. (1993) "A Look At the Record," *Bulletin of the Atomic Scientists* 49 (November): 32–35.

———. (1998) "The Sanctions Glass: Half Full or Completely Empty," *International Security* 23 (Summer): 50–65.

ELLIS, JOHN. (1993) *The World War II Databook.* London: Aurum Press.

EMMOTT, BILL. (1994) *Japanophobia: The Myth of the Invincible Japanese.* New York: Times Books.

ENGEL, MATTHEW. (2001) "The Good-News President Risks a Higher Profile," *Guardian Unlimited,* 7 November (www.guardian.co.uk, accessed 12/03/06).

ENTMAN, ROBERT M. (1989) "How the Media Affect What People Think: An Information Processing Approach," *Journal of Politics* 51 (May): 347–370.

———. (2004) *Projections of Power: Framing News, Public Opinion, and U.S. Foreign Policy.* Chicago: University of Chicago Press.

ESTY, DANIEL. (1994) *Greening the GATT: Trade, Environment, and the Future.* Washington, DC: Institute for International Economics.

ETHEREDGE, LLOYD S. (1978) *A World of Men: The Private Sources of American Foreign Policy.* Cambridge, MA: MIT Press.

———. (1985) *Can Governments Learn? American Foreign Policy and Central American Revolutions.* New York: Pergamon.

EVAN, THOMAS. (2000) *Robert Kennedy: His Life.* New York: Simon & Schuster.

EVANS, C. LAWRENCE, AND WALTER J. OLESZEK. (2003) "A Tale of Two Treaties: The Practical Politics of Treaty Ratification in the U.S. Senate," in *Congress and the Politics of Foreign Policy,* Colton C. Campbell, Nicol C. Rae, and John F. Stack, Jr., eds. Upper Saddle River, NJ: Prentice Hall, pp. 90–111.

FAGEN, RICHARD R. (1960) "Some Assessments and Uses of Public Opinion in Diplomacy," *Public Opinion Quarterly* 24 (Fall): 448–457.

FALK, RICHARD. (1983) "Lifting the Curse of Bipartisanship," *World Policy Journal* 1 (Fall): 127–157.

FALKOWSKI, LAWRENCE S., ed. (1979) *Psychological Models in International Politics.* Boulder, CO: Westview Press.

FALLOWS, JAMES. (1994) *Looking at the Sun.* New York: Pantheon.

———. (2002) "The Military Industrial Complex." *Foreign Policy,* 133 (November/December): 46–48.

———. (2006) "Declaring Victory," *Atlantic Monthly* 298 (September): 60–73.

FARAH, BARBARA G., AND ETHEL KLEIN. (1989) "Public Opinion Trends," in *The Elections of 1988:* *Reports and Interpretations,* Gerald M. Pomper, Ross K. Baker and Walter. Dean Burnham, Marjorie Randon Farah, and Ethel Klein McWilliams, eds. Chatham, NJ: Chatham House, pp. 103–128.

FEAVER, PETER D. (2003) *Armed Servants: Agency, Oversight, and Civil-Military Relations.* Cambridge, MA: Harvard University Press.

FEAVER, PETER D., AND CHRISTOPHER GELPI. (1999) "Shattering a Foreign Policy Myth," *Washington Post National Weekly Edition,* 15 November, pp. 22–23.

———. (2004) *Choosing Your Battles: American Civil-Military Relations and the Use of Force.* Princeton, NJ: Princeton University Press.

FELDSTEIN, MARTIN. (1992) "The Council of Economic Advisers and Economic Advising in the United States," *Economic Journal* 102 (September): 1223–1234.

FENNO, RICHARD F., JR. (1973) *Congressmen in Committees.* Boston: Little, Brown.

FERGUSON, NIALL. (2003a) "An Empire in Denial: The Limits of U.S. Imperialism," *Harvard International Review* 25 (Fall): 64–69.

———. (2003b) "Power," *Foreign Policy* 134 (January/February): 18–24.

———. (2004) "A World Without Power," *Foreign Policy* 143 (July/August): 32–39.

———. (2005) "Sinking Globalization," *Foreign Affairs* 84 (March/April): 64–77.

FERRELL, ROBERT H. (1988) *American Diplomacy: The Twentieth Century.* New York: Norton.

FESSENDEN, HELEN. (2005) "The Limits of Intelligence Reform," *Foreign Affairs* 84 (6) (November/December): 106–120.

FESTINGER, LEON. (1957) *A Theory of Cognitive Dissonance.* Evanston, IL: Row, Peterson.

FIORINA, MORRIS P. (1981) *Retrospective Voting in American National Elections.* New Haven, CT: Yale University Press.

———. (2001) "Keystone Reconsidered," in *Congress Reconsidered,* 7th ed., Lawrence C. Dodd and Bruce I. Oppenheimer, eds. Washington, DC: CQ Press, pp. 141–162.

FIRTH, NOEL E., AND JAMES H. NOREN. (1998) *Soviet Defense Spending: A History of CIA Estimates,*

1950–1990. College Station, TX: Texas A&M University Press.

FISCHER, BENJAMIN B., ed. (1999) *At Cold War's End: U.S. Intelligence on the Soviet Union and Eastern Europe, 1989–1991.* Washington, DC: Government Printing Office.

FISHER, LOUIS. (1991) *Constitutional Conflicts Between Congress and the President.* Lawrence, KS: University of Kansas Press.

———. (1993) *The Politics of Shared Power: Congress and the Executive,* 3rd ed. Washington, DC: CQ Press.

———. (1994–1995) "Congressional Checks on Military Initiatives," *Political Science Quarterly* 109 (Winter): 739–762.

———. (1995) *Presidential War Power.* Lawrence, KS: University of Kansas Press.

———. (1997) *Constitutional Conflicts Between Congress and the President.* Lawrence, KS: University of Kansas Press.

———. (1998) "Military Action Against Iraq," *Presidential Studies Quarterly* 28 (Fall): 793–798.

———. (2000a) *Congressional Abdication on War and Spending.* College Station, TX: Texas A&M University Press.

———. (2000b) "Litigating the War Power with Campbell v. Clinton," *Presidential Studies Quarterly* 30 (September): 564–574.

———. (2006) "Signing Statements: What to Do?" *The Forum,* 4 (2): Article 7. (www.bepress.com/forum/vol4/iss2/art7/, accessed 12/7/06).

FISHER, LOUIS, AND DAVID GRAY ADLER. (1998) "The War Powers Resolution: Time to Say Goodbye," *Political Science Quarterly* 113 (Spring): 1–20.

FISHER, WILLIAM. (2006) "The End of U.S. Aid?" *Common Dreams News Center,* 30 January (www.commondreams.org, assessed 4/15/06).

FITE, DAVID, MARC GENEST, AND CLYDE WILCOX. (1990) "Gender Differences in Foreign Policy Attitudes: A Longitudinal Analysis," *American Politics Quarterly* 18 (October): 492–512.

FITZGERALD, FRANCES. (2000) *Way Out There in the Blue: Reagan, Star Wars, and the End of the Cold War.* New York: Simon & Schuster.

FITZGERALD, FRANCIS. (1989) "Annals of Justice: Iran-Contra," *New Yorker,* 16 October, pp. 51–84.

FIXDAL, MONA, AND DAN SMITH. (1998) "Humanitarian Intervention and Just War," *Mershon International Studies Review* 42 (November): 283–312.

FLAHERTY, MARY PAT, AND THOMAS E. RICKS. (2001) "Osprey Probe Reaches Pentagon's Top Ranks," *Washington Post,* 2 March (www.washingtonpost.com, accessed 3/2/01).

FLANAGAN, STEPHEN J. (1985) "Managing the Intelligence Community," *International Security* 10 (Summer): 58–95.

FLANAGAN, STEPHEN J., ELLEN L. FROST, AND RICHARD L. KUGLER. (2001) *Challenges of the Global Century: Report of the Project on Globalization and National Security.* Washington, DC: National Defense University.

FLAVIN, CHRISTOPHER. (2001) "Rich Planet, Poor Planet," in *State of the World 2001,* Lester R. Brown, Christopher Flavin, Hilary French, et al., eds. New York: Norton, pp. 3–20.

FLEISHER, RICHARD. (1985) "Economic Benefit, Ideology, and Senate Voting on the B-1 Bomber," *American Politics Quarterly* 13 (April): 200–211.

FLEISHER, RICHARD, JON R. BOND, AND GLEN S. KRUTZ. (2000) "The Demise of the Two Presidencies." *American Politics Quarterly.* 28 (1) (Spring): 3–25.

FLETCHER, MARTIN. (1990) "CIA Ordered by Bush to Plot Fall of Saddam," *Times* (London), 7 August, p. 1.

FLICKNER, CHARLES. (1994–1995) "The Russian Aid Mess," *National Interest* 38 (Winter): 13–18.

FLORINI, ANN M. (1999) "Does the Invisible Hand Need a Transparent Glove? The Politics of Transparency," paper prepared for the Annual World Bank Conference on Development Economics, Washington, DC, April 28–30 (www.worldbank.org/wbi/governance/pdf/florini.pdf, accessed 11/19/06).

FLYNN, STEPHEN E. (2004a) *America the Vulnerable.* New York: HarperCollins.

———. (2004b) "The Neglected Home Front," *Foreign Affairs,* 83 (5): 20–33.

FOLEY, TIMOTHY D. (1994) "The Role of the CIA in Economic and Technological Intelligence," *Fletcher Forum on World Affairs* 18 (Winter/Spring): 135–145.

FORD, GERALD R. (1979) *A Time to Heal.* New York: Harper and Row.

FOREIGN AFFAIRS COUNCIL. (2004) *Secretary Colin Powell's State Department: An Independent Assessment* (Task Force Report) (www.diplomatsonline.org/taskreprot1104.pdf, accessed 11/3/06).

FOSTER, GREGORY D. (1989) "Global Demographic Trends to the Year 2010: Implications for U.S. Security," *Washington Quarterly* 12 (Spring): 5–24.

FOX, HARRISON W., JR., AND SUSAN WEBB HAMMOND. (1977) *Congressional Staffs: The Invisible Force in American Lawmaking.* New York: Free Press.

FRANCK, THOMAS M. (1999) "Sidelined in Kosovo? The United Nations Decline Has Been Exaggerated," *Foreign Affairs* 78 (July/August): 116–118.

FRANK, CHARLES R., JR., AND MARY BAIRD. (1975) "Foreign Aid: Its Speckled Past and Future Prospects," *International Organization* 29 (Winter): 133–167.

FRANK, ROBERT S. (1973) *Message Dimensions of Television News.* Lexington, MA: Lexington Books.

FRANKEL, CHARLES. (1969) *High on Foggy Bottom.* New York: Harper and Row.

FRANKOVIC, KATHLEEN A. (1982) "Sex and Politics-New Alignments, Old Issues," *PS* 15 (Summer): 439–448.

————. (1998) "Public Opinion and Polling," in *The Politics of News: The News of Politics,* Doris Graber, Denis McQuail, and Pippa Norris, eds. Washington, DC: CQ Press, pp. 150–170.

FRANKS, TOMMY, WITH MALCOLM MCCONNELL. (2004) *American Soldier.* New York: HarperCollins.

FREEDBERG, SYDNEY J. (2001) "Where Are the Humans?" *National Journal,* 15 September, pp. 2834–2836.

FREEDMAN, LAWRENCE. (2005) "Rumsfeld's Legacy: The Iraq Syndrome?" *Washington Post,* 9 January, p. B4.

FREEMAN, J. LEIPER. (1965) "The Bureaucracy in Pressure Politics," in *Bureaucratic Power in National Politics,* Francis E. Ranke, ed. Boston: Little, Brown, pp. 23–35.

FRENCH, HILARY F. (1993) "The GATT: Menace or Ally," *World Watch* 6 (September–October): 12–19.

FRENCH, HILARY, AND LISA MASTNY. (2001) "Controlling International Environmental Crime," in *State of the World 2001,* Lester R. Brown, Christopher Flavin, Hilary French, et al., eds. New York: Norton, pp. 166–188.

FRIEDBERG, AARON L. (1989) "The Strategic Implications of Relative Economic Decline," *Political Science Quarterly* 104 (Fall): 401–431.

————. (1992) "Why Didn't the United States Become a Garrison State?" *International Security* 16 (Spring): 109–142.

FRIEDMAN, THOMAS L. (1994a) "Never Mind Yen. Greenbacks Are the New Gold Standard," *New York Times,* 3 July, p. E5.

————. (1994b) "Trade War Isn't So Swell Either," *New York Times,* 6 March, p. E4.

————. (1999) *The Lexus and the Olive Tree: Understanding Globalization.* New York: Farrar, Straus, Giroux.

FRIEL, BRIAN. (2001) "The Powell Leadership Doctrine," *Government Executive,* 1 June (www.govexec.com/features/0601/0601s1.htm, accessed 11/3/06).

FRITZ, SARA. (2001) "Unchecked Power Can Be Dangerous," *St. Petersburg Times,* 26 November (www.sptimes.com, accessed 5/19/06).

FROOMKIN, DAN. (2005) "Who's Who in the White House," *Washington Post,* 22 June (www.washingtonpost.com, accessed 5/25/06).

FRUM, DAVID, AND RICHARD PEARLE. (2003) *An End to Evil: Strategies for Victory in the War on Terror.* New York: Random House.

————. (2004) *An End to Evil: Strategies for Victory in the War on Terror.* New York: Random House.

FRYE, ALTON. (1996) "Banning Ballistic Missiles," *Foreign Affairs* 75 (November/December): 99–112.

————, ed. (2000) *Humanitarian Intervention: Crafting a Workable Doctrine.* New York: Council on Foreign Relations.

FUKUYAMA, FRANCIS. (2004a) "Nation–Building 101," *Atlantic Monthly,* 293 (1) (January–February): 159–162.

————. (2004b) "The Neoconservative Moment," *National Interest* 76 (Summer): 57–68.

FULLER, GRAHAM. (1995) "The Next Ideology," *Foreign Policy* 98 (Spring): 145–158.

———. (2006) "Strategic Fatigue," *National Interest* 84 (Summer): 37–42.

THE FUND FOR PEACE AND THE CARNEGIE ENDOWMENT FOR INTERNATIONAL PEACE. (2005) "Failed States Index," *Foreign Policy* 149 (July/August): 56–65.

GABEL, JOSIANE. (2004–2005) "The Role of U.S. Nuclear Weapons after September 11," *Washington Quarterly,* 28 (1): 181–195.

GABELNICK, TAMAR. (1999) "Problems with Current U.S. Policy," *Foreign Policy in Focus* 21 (May): 2.

GABELNICK, TAMAR, AND ANNA RICH. (2000) "Globalized Weaponry," *Foreign Policy in Focus* 5 (June): 1–4.

GADDIS, JOHN LEWIS. (1972) *The United States and the Origins of the Cold War.* New York: Columbia University Press.

———. (1982) *Strategies of Containment: A Critical Appraisal of Postwar American National Security Policy.* New York: Oxford University Press.

———. (1983) "Containment: Its Past and Future," in *Perspectives on American Foreign Policy,* Charles W. Kegley, Jr., and Eugene R. Wittkopf, eds. New York: St. Martin's, pp. 16–31.

———. (1986) "The Long Peace: Elements of Stability in the Postwar International System," *International Security* 10 (Spring): 99–142.

———. (1987–1988) "Containment and the Logic of Strategy," *National Interest* 10 (Winter): 27–38.

———. (1992) *The United States and the End of the Cold War: Implications, Reconsiderations, Provocations.* New York: Oxford University Press.

———. (1997) *We Now Know: Rethinking Cold War History.* New York: Clarendon.

———. (2002) "A Grand Strategy of Transformation," *Foreign Policy* 133 (November/December): 50–57.

———. (2004) *Surprise, Security, and the American Experience.* Cambridge, MA: Harvard University Press.

———. (2005) "Grand Strategy in the Second Term," *Foreign Affairs* 84 (January/February): 2–15.

GALBRAITH, JOHN KENNETH. (1969) "The Power of the Pentagon," *The Progressive* 33 (June): 29.

GALLAGHER, WINIFRED. (1994) "How We Become What We Are," *Atlantic Monthly* 274 (September): 38–55.

GALLUP POLL NEWS SERVICE. (2006) "Americans More Negative than Positive About Economy," 7 February, Washington, DC: The Gallup Poll.

GARDNER, RICHARD N. (1990) "The Comeback of Liberal Internationalism," *Washington Quarterly* 13 (Summer): 23–39.

GARFINKLE, ADAM. (1998) "Anatomy of a Farce," *National Interest* 52 (Summer): 123–126.

GARRETT, LAURIE. (2001) "Encroaching Plagues: The Return of Infectious Disease," in *The Global Agenda: Issues and Perspectives,* 6th ed., Charles W. Kegley, Jr., and Eugene R. Wittkopf, eds. Boston: McGraw-Hill, pp. 425–433.

———. (2005a) "The Lessons of HIV/AIDS," *Foreign Affairs* 84 (July/August): 51–64.

———. (2005b) "The Next Pandemic?" *Foreign Affairs* 84 (July/August): 3–23.

GARTEN, JEFFREY E. (1998) *The Big Ten: The Big Emerging Markets and How They Will Change Our Lives.* New York: Basic Books.

———. (2005) "The Global Economic Challenge," *Foreign Affairs* 84 (January/February): 37–38.

GARTHOFF, RAYMOND L. (1994) "Looking Back: The Cold War in Retrospect," *Brookings Review* 12 (Summer): 10–13.

GARTZKE, ERIC. (1996) "Congress and Back Seat Driving: An Information Theory of the War Powers Resolution," *Policy Studies Journal* 24 (Summer): 259–286.

GASIOROWSKI, MARK J. (1987) "The 1953 Coup D'Etat in Iran," *International Journal of Middle East Studies* 19 (August): 261–286.

GATES, ROBERT M. (2004) "Racing to Run the C.I.A.," *New York Times,* 8 June, p. 25.

GAUSE, F. GREGORY III. (1994) "The Illogic of Dual Containment," *Foreign Affairs* 73 (March/April): 56–66.

———. (1999) "Getting It Backward on Iraq," *Foreign Affairs* 78 (May/June): 54–65.

GELB, LESLIE H. (1983) "Why Not the State Department?" in *Perspectives on American Foreign Policy,* Charles W. Kegley, Jr., and Eugene R. Wittkopf, eds. New York: St. Martin's, pp. 282–298.

————. (1994) "Quelling the Teacup Wars: The New World's Constant Challenge," *Foreign Affairs* 73 (November/December): 2–6.

GELB, LESLIE H., AND MORTON H. HALPERIN. (1973) "The Ten Commandments of the Foreign Affairs Bureaucracy," in *At Issue: Politics in the World Arena,* Steven L. Spiegel, ed. New York: St. Martin's Press, pp. 250–259.

GELLMAN, BARTON. (1992a) "On Second Thought, We Don't Want to Rule the World," *Washington Post National Weekly Edition,* 1–7 June, p. 31.

————. (1992b) "The U.S. Aims to Remain First Among Nonequals," *Washington Post National Weekly Edition,* 16–22 March, p. 19.

————. (1993) "Pin Stripes Clash with Stars and Bars," *Washington Post National Weekly Edition,* 28–June–3 July, pp. 31–32.

————. (1999) "Learning from Kosovo," *Washington Post National Weekly Edition,* 14 June, pp. 6–9.

————. (2005) "Secret Unit Expands Rumsfeld's Domain," *Washington Post,* 23 January (www.washingtonpost.com, accessed 3/4/06).

————. (2006) "Administration Revives Dispute over Eavesdropping Authority," *Washington Post,* 4 March (www.washingtonpost.com, accessed 3/4/06).

GENTRY, JOHN A. (1998) "Military Force in an Age of National Cowardice," *Washington Quarterly* 21 (Autumn): 179–191.

GEORGE, ALEXANDER L. (1969) "The 'Operational Code': A Neglected Approach to the Study of Political Leaders and Decision-Making," *International Studies Quarterly* 13 (June): 190–222.

————. (1972) "The Case for Multiple Advocacy in Making Foreign Policy," *American Political Science Review* 66 (September): 751–785.

————. (1980) *Presidential Decisionmaking in Foreign Policy: The Effective Use of Information and Advice.* Boulder, CO: Westview Press.

————. (1988) "Presidential Management Styles and Models," in *The Domestic Sources of American Foreign Policy: Insights and Evidence,* Charles W. Kegley, Jr., and Eugene R. Wittkopf, eds. New York: St. Martin's, pp. 107–126.

————. (1992) *Forceful Persuasion: Coercive Diplomacy as an Alternative to War.* Washington, DC: United States Institute of Peace Press.

GEORGE, ALEXANDER L., AND JULIETTE L. GEORGE. (1964) *Woodrow Wilson and Colonel House: A Personality Study.* New York: Dover.

GERGEN, DAVID. (1989) "The Bush Administration's Three Musketeers," *Washington Post National Weekly Edition,* 17–23 April, pp. 23–24.

————. (2001) *Eyewitness to Power: The Essence of Leadership from Nixon to Clinton.* New York: MacMillan.

GHOLZ, EUGENE, DARYL G. PRESS, AND HARVEY M. SAPOLSKY. (1997) "Come Home, America: The Strategy of Restraint in the Face of Temptation," *International Security* 21 (Spring): 5–48.

GHOLZ, EUGENE, AND HARVEY M. SAPOLSKY. (1999–2000) "Restructuring the U.S. Defense Industry," *International Security* 24 (Winter): 5–51.

GILBERT, FELIX. (1961) *The Beginnings of American Foreign Policy: To the Farewell Address.* New York: Harper Torchbooks.

GILBOA, EYTAN. (1987) *American Public Opinion toward Israel and the Arab-Israeli Conflict.* Lexington, MA: Lexington Books.

GILL, STEPHEN, AND DAVID LAW. (1988) *The Global Political Economy: Perspectives, Problems, and Policies.* Baltimore, MO: Johns Hopkins University Press.

GILPIN, ROBERT. (1981) *War and Change in World Politics.* New York: Cambridge University Press.

————. (1987) *The Political Economy of International Relations.* Princeton, NJ: Princeton University Press.

————. (2000) *The Challenge of Global Capitalism: The World Economy in the 21st Century.* Princeton, NJ: Princeton University Press.

GILPIN, TODD. (1995) "After the Failed Faiths: Beyond Individualism, Marxism, and Multiculturalism," *World Policy Journal* 12 (Spring): 61–68.

GINGRICH, NEWT. (2003) "A Grand Strategy," *Foreign Policy* 137 (July/August): 42–48.

GLAD, BETTY. (1983) "Black-and-White Thinking: Ronald Reagan's Approach to Foreign Policy," *Political Psychology* 4 (March): 33–76.

GLASER, CHARLES L. (1992) "Nuclear Policy Without an Adversary: U.S. Planning for the Post-Soviet Era," *International Security* 16 (Spring): 34–78.

GLASER, CHARLES L., AND STEVE FETTER. (2001) "National Missile Defense and the Future of

U.S. Nuclear Weapons Policy," *International Security* 26 (1): 40–92.

GLECKMAN, HOWARD. (2002) "Return of the Imperial Presidency," *Business Week Online,* 6 August (www.businessweek.com, accessed 5/19/06).

GLENNON, MICHAEL J. (1999) "The New Interventionism: The Search for a Just International Law," *Foreign Affairs* 78 (May/June): 2–7.

GODSON, ROY S. (2000) *Dirty Tricks or Trump Cards: U.S. Covert Action and Counterintelligence.* New Brunswick, NJ: Transaction Publishers.

GODSON, ROY S., AND ERNEST MAY. (1995) *U.S. Intelligence at the Crossroads: Agendas for Reform.* Herndon, VA: Brassey's, Inc.

GOLDGEIER, JAMES M. (1998) "NATO Expansion: Anatomy of a Decision," *Washington Quarterly* 21 (Winter): 88–102.

———. (1999) *Not Whether but When: The U.S. Decision to Enlarge NATO.* Washington, DC: Brookings Institution Press.

GOLDMAN, MARSHALL I. (2004) "Putin and the Oligarchs," *Foreign Affairs* 83 (November/December): 33–44.

GOLDSBOROUGH, JAMES O. (1993) "California's Foreign Policy," *Foreign Affairs* 72 (Spring): 88–96.

GOLDSTEIN, JOSHUA S. (1988) *Long Cycles: Prosperity and War in the Modern Age.* New Haven, CT: Yale University Press.

GOLDSTEIN, JUDITH. (1989) "The Impact of Ideas on Trade Policy: The Origins of U.S. Agricultural and Manufacturing Policies," *International Organization* 43 (Winter): 31–71.

GOODMAN, ALLAN E. (1975) "The Causes and Consequences of Détente, 1949–1973," paper presented at the National Security Education Seminar, Colorado Springs, CO, July.

GOODMAN, MELVIN A. (1997) "Ending the CIA's Cold War Legacy," *Foreign Policy* 106 (Spring): 128–143.

———. (2000) "The Politics of Getting It Wrong," *Harper's* 301 (November): 74–80.

GOODPASTER, ANDREW J. (1995) *An Evolving U.S. Nuclear Posture.* Washington, DC: The Henry L. Stimson Center.

———. (1997) *An American Legacy: Building a Nuclear-Weapon-Free World.* Washington, DC: The Henry L. Stimson Center.

GOODSELL, CHARLES T. (1985) *The Case for Bureaucracy,* 2nd ed. Chatham, NJ: Chatham House.

GOOZNER, MERRILL. (1997) "U.S. Arms Makers Strike Hard," *Toronto Star, p.* A1.

GORDON, MICHAEL, AND BERNARD TRAINOR. (1995) *The General's War: The Inside Story of the Conflict in the Gulf.* Boston: Little, Brown.

GORDON, PHILIP H. (2006) "The End of the Bush Revolution," *Foreign Affairs* 85 (July/August): 75–86.

GORE, AL. (1993) "This Time We Mean Business," *Washington Post National Weekly Edition,* 20–26 September, p. 25.

GOSHKO, JOHN M. (1989) "Foreign Policy in Turmoil—or Transition?" *Washington Post National Weekly Edition,* 13–19 March, p. 7.

———. (1994) "Undiplomatic Doubts at Foggy Bottom," *Washington Post National Weekly Edition,* 27 June–3 July, p. 31.

GOWA, JOANNE. (1999) *Ballots and Bullets: The Elusive Democratic Peace.* Princeton, NJ: Princeton University Press.

GOWING, NIK. (1994) "Discounting the 'CNN Factor'," *Washington Post National Weekly Edition,* 8–14 August, p. 23.

GRABER, DORIS A. (1993) *Mass Media and American Politics,* 4th ed. Washington, DC: CQ Press.

———. (1997) *Mass Media and American Politics,* 5th ed. Washington, DC: CQ Press.

GRAHAM, BRADLEY, AND THOMAS RICKS. (2001) "Rangers Hit Taliban in Ground Combat." *Washington Post,* 20 October, p. A1.

GRAHAM, THOMAS W. (1986) "Public Attitudes Towards Active Defense: ABM and Star Wars, 1945–1985." Cambridge, MA: Center for International Studies, Massachusetts Institute of Technology.

GRAYSON, GEORGE W. (1999) *Strange Bedfellows: NATO Marches East.* Lanham, MD: University Press of America.

GREEN, GRANT. (2003) "Transforming the State Department 'Quietly and Effectively'," *Washington Times,* 6 July. Distributed by the Bureau of International Information Programs, U.S. Department of State (http://usinfo.org/wf-archive/2003/030707/epf110.htm, accessed 11/3/06).

GREENSTEIN, FRED I. (1969) *Personality and Politics.* Princeton, NJ: Princeton University Press.

———. (1982) *The Hidden Hand Presidency: Eisenhower as Leader.* New York: Basic Books.

———. (1993–1994) "The Presidential Leadership Style of Bill Clinton: An Early Appraisal," *Political Science Quarterly* 108 (Winter): 589–601.

———. (1994) "The Hidden-Hand Presidency: Eisenhower as Leader: A 1994 Perspective," *Presidential Studies Quarterly* 24 (Spring): 233–241.

———. (2000) *The Presidential Difference: Leadership Style from FDR to Clinton.* New York: Free Press.

———. (2004) "The Changing Leadership of George W. Bush: A Pre- and Post-9/11 Comparison," in *The Domestic Sources of American Foreign Policy: Insights and Evidence,* Eugene R. Wittkopf and James M. McCormick, eds. Lanham, MD: Rowman and Littlefield, pp. 353–362.

GREENSTEIN, FRED I., AND RICHARD H. IMMERMAN. (2000) "Effective National Security Advising: Recovering the Eisenhower Legacy," *Political Science Quarterly* 115 (Fall): 335–345.

GRIEVE, MALCOLM J. (1993) "Debt and Imperialism: Perspectives on the Debt Crisis," in *The Politics of Global Debt,* Stephen P. Riley, ed. New York: St. Martin's, pp. 51–68.

GRIMMETT, RICHARD F. (1995) "The War Powers Resolution: Fifteen Years of Experience" in *CRS Report for Congress.* Washington, DC: Congressional Research Service.

———. (1999) "Conventional Arms Transfers to the Developing Nations, 1991–1998" in *CRS Report for Congress.* Washington, DC: Congressional Research Service.

———. (2001) *Conventional Arms Transfers to Developing Nations, 1993–2000.* Washington, DC: Congressional Research Service.

———. (2004) *Conventional Arms Transfers to Developing Nations, 1996–2003.* Washington, DC: Congressional Research Service.

GROELING, TIM, AND SAMUEL KERNELL. (1998) "Is Network Coverage of the President Biased?" *Journal of Politics* 60 (November): 1063–1086.

GRONLUND, LISBETH, AND DAVID WRIGHT. (1997) "Missile Defense: The Sequel," *Technology Review* 100 (May/June): 28–36.

GROVE, LLOYD. (1991) "Israel's Force in Washington," *Washington Post National Weekly Edition,* 24–30 June, pp. 8–9.

GUGLIOTTA, GUY. (1998) "Playing Musical Chairs in the House," *Washington Post National Weekly Edition,* 30 March, p. 12.

———. (1999) "A Balkanized Congress," *Washington Post Weekly Edition,* 17 May, p. 14.

GURR, TED ROBERT. (1991) "America as a Model for the World? A Skeptical View," *PS: Political Science and Politics* 24 (December): 664–667.

HAASS, RICHARD N. (1994a) "Bill Clinton's Adhocracy," *New York Times Magazine,* 29 May, pp. 40–41.

———. (1994b) *Intervention: The Use of American Military Force in the Post–Cold War World.* Washington, DC: Carnegie Endowment.

———. (1995) "Paradigm Lost," *Foreign Affairs* 74 (January/February): 43–58.

———. (1997) "Sanctioning Madness," *Foreign Affairs* 76 (November/December): 74–85.

———, ed. (1998) *Economic Sanctions and American Diplomacy,* 2nd ed. New York: Council on Foreign Relations.

———. (1999) "What to Do with American Primacy," *Foreign Affairs* 78 (September/October): 37–49.

———. (2000) "Five Not-So-Easy Pieces: The Debates on American Foreign Policy," *Brookings Review* 18 (Spring): 38–40.

HAINES, GERALD K., AND ROBERT S. LEGGETT, eds. (2001) *CIA's Analysis of the Soviet Union, 1947–1991.* Washington, DC: Center for the Study of Intelligence.

HAKIM, PETER. (2006) "Is Washington Losing Latin America?" *Foreign Affairs* 85 (January/February): 39–53.

HALBERSTAM, DAVID. (1972) *The Best and the Brightest.* New York: Random House.

———. (2001) *War in a Time of Peace: Bush, Clinton, and The Generals.* New York: Scribner.

HALL, BRIAN. (1998) "Overkill Is Not Dead," *New York Times Magazine,* 15 March, pp. 42–49ff.

HALLIDAY, DENIS J. (1999) "Iraq and the UN's Weapon of Mass Destruction," *Current History* 98 (February): 65–68.

HALPER, STEFAN, AND JONATHAN CLARKE. (2004) *America Alone: The Neo-Conservatives and the Global Order.* New York: Cambridge University Press.

HALPERIN, MORTON H. (1971) "Why Bureaucrats Play Games," *Foreign Policy* 2 (Spring): 70–90.

HALVERSON, STEFANIE K., SUSAN ELAINE MURPHY, AND RONALD E. RIGIO. (2004) "Charismatic Leadership in Crisis Situations: A Laboratory Investigation of Stress and Crisis," *Small Group Research,* 35 (October): 495–514.

HAMILTON, LEE H. (1988) "Congress and The Presidency in American Foreign Policy," *Presidential Studies Quarterly* 18 (Summer): 507–511.

HAMMOND, PAUL Y. (1994) "Central Organization in the Transition from Bush to Clinton," in *American Defense Annual, 1994,* Charles F. Hermann, ed. New York: Lexington Books, pp. 163–181.

HAMPSON, FEN OSLER. (1988) "The Divided Decision-Maker," in *The Domestic Sources of American Foreign Policy,* Charles W. Kegley, Jr., and Eugene R. Wittkopf, eds. New York: St. Martin's, pp. 227–247.

HAN, ALBERT. (1992–1993) "No Defense for Strategic Defense," *Harvard International Review* 156 (Winter): 54–57.

HANCOCK, JAY. (2000) "Military Expected to Be Used Sparingly; 'Powell Doctrine' Calls for Measured Troop Use," *Baltimore Sun,* 17 December, p. 1A.

HANDELMAN, STEPHEN. (1994) "The Russian 'Mafiya'," *Foreign Affairs* 73 (March/April): 83–96.

HANEY, CRAIG, AND PHILIP ZIMBARDO. (1973) "Social Roles, Role-Playing, and Education," *Behavioral and Social Science Teacher* 1 (1): 24–45.

HANEY, PATRICK J., AND WALT VANDERBUSH. (1999) "The Role of Ethnic Interest Groups in U.S. Foreign Policy: The Case of the Cuban American National Foundation," *International Studies Quarterly* 43 (June): 341–361.

HANSEN, ROGER D. (1980) "North-South Policy—What's the Problem?" *Foreign Affairs* 58 (Summer): 1104–1128.

HARKAVY, ROBERT E. (1997) "Images of the Coming International System," *Orbis* 41 (Fall): 569–590.

HARPER, JOHN L. (1997) "The Dream of Democratic Peace," *Foreign Affairs* 76 (May/June): 117–121.

HARR, JOHN ENSOR. (1969) *The Professional Diplomat.* Princeton, NJ: Princeton University Press.

HARRIS, JOHN F. (1997a) "The Man Who Squared the Oval Office," *Washington Post Weekly Edition,* 13 January, p. 11.

———. (1997b) "Mixing Stagecraft with Statecraft," *Washington Post Weekly Edition,* 14 July, pp. 12–13.

———. (1999) "A Man of Caution," *Washington Post National Weekly Edition,* 24 May, pp. 6–7.

———. (2001) "On the World Stage Bush Shuns the Spotlight," *Washington Post National Weekly Edition,* 23–29 April, p. 11.

HARRIS, SHANE. (2003) "Powell's Army," *Government Executive,* 4 November (www.govexec.com, accessed 6/12/06).

HART, GARY. (2004) *The Fourth Power: A Grand Strategy for the United States in the Twenty-First Century.* New York: Oxford University Press.

HARTCHER, PETER. (2001) "From Miracle to Malaise," *The National Interest* 62 (Spring): 76–85.

HARTUNG, WILLIAM D. (1993) "Welcome to the U.S. Arms Superstore," *Bulletin of the Atomic Scientists* 49 (September): 20–26.

———. (1994b) "The Phantom Profits of the War Trade," *New York Times,* 6 March, p. 13.

———. (1995) "Nixon's Children: Bill Clinton and the Permanent Arms Bazaar," *World Policy Journal* 12 (Summer): 25–35.

———. (1998) "Reagan Redux: The Enduring Myth of Star Wars," *World Policy Journal* 15 (Fall): 17–24.

———. (2001) "New War, Old Weapons." *The Nation,* 29 October, p. 4.

HARTZ, LOUIS. (1955) *The Liberal Tradition in America.* New York: Harcourt Brace and World.

HASLAM, JONATHAN. (1997) "Russian Archival Revelations and Our Understanding of the Cold War," *Diplomatic History* 21 (Spring): 217–228.

HATFIELD, J. H. (1999) *Fortunate Son: The Making of an American President.* New York: St. Martin's.

HAUSMANN, RICARDO. (1999) "Should There Be Five Currencies or One Hundred and Five?" *Foreign Policy* 116 (Fall): 65–79.

HEILBRUNN, JACOB. (1997) "The Great Equivocator," *New Republic,* 24 March, pp. 23–27.

———. (1998) "Mr. Nice Guy," *New Republic,* 13 April, pp. 19–25.

HELMS, JESSE. (1999) "What Sanctions Epidemic?" *Foreign Affairs* 78 (January/February): 2–8.

———. (2000–2001) "American Sovereignty and the UN," *National Interest* 62 (Winter): 31–45.

HENDERSON, PHILLIP G. (1988) *Managing the Presidency: The Eisenhower Legacy from Kennedy to Reagan.* Boulder, CO: Westview Press.

HENDRICKSON, DAVID C. (1994) "The Recovery of Internationalism," *Foreign Affairs* 73 (September/October): 26–43.

———. (1994–1995) "The Democratist Crusade: Intervention, Economic Sanctions, and Engagement," *World Policy Journal* 11 (Winter): 26–43.

HENDRICKSON, RYAN. (1998) "War Powers, Bosnia, and the 104th Congress," *Political Science Quarterly* 113 (Summer): 241–258.

———. (2002) *The Clinton Wars: The Constitution, Congress, and War Powers.* Nashville, TN: Vanderbilt University Press.

HENKIN, LOUIS. (1972) *Foreign Affairs and the Constitution.* Mineola, NY: Foundation Press.

———. (1990) *Constitutionalism, Democracy, and Foreign Affairs.* New York: Columbia University Press.

HENRIKSEN, THOMAS. (2000) "Covert Operations, Now More than Ever," *Orbis* 44 (Winter): 145–156.

HENSEN, STEVEN L. (2001–2002) "All the President's Papers," *Washington Post National Weekly Edition,* 24 December–6 January, p. 27.

HEREK, GREGORY M., IRVING JANIS, AND PAUL HUTH. (1987) "Decision Making During International Crisis: Is Quality of Process Related to Outcome?" *Journal of Conflict Resolution* 31 (June): 203–226.

HERMANN, CHARLES F. (1969) "International Crisis as a Situational Variable," in *International Politics and Foreign Policy,* James N. Rosenau, ed. New York: Free Press, pp. 409–421.

———. (1972) "Some Issues in the Study of International Crisis," in *International Crises: Insights from Behavioral Research,* Charles F. Hermann, ed. New York: Free Press, pp. 3–17.

HERMANN, MARGARET G. (1976) "When Leader Personality Will Affect Foreign Policy: Some Propositions," in *In Search of Global Patterns,* James N. Rosenau, ed. New York: Free Press, pp. 326–333.

———. (1980) "Explaining Foreign Policy Behavior Using Personal Characteristics of Political Leaders," *International Studies Quarterly* 24 (March): 7–46.

———. (1984) "Personality and Foreign Policy Decision Making: A Study of 53 Heads of Government," in *Foreign Policy Decision-Making: Perceptions, Cognition, and Artificial Intelligence,* Donald A. Sylvan and Steve Chan, eds. New York: Praeger, pp. 53–80.

———. (1986) "Ingredients of Leadership," in *Political Psychology,* Margaret G. Hermann, ed. San Francisco: Jossey-Bass, pp. 167–192.

———. (1987) "Foreign Policy Role Orientations and the Quality of Foreign Policy Decisions," in *Role Theory and Foreign Policy Analysis,* Stephen G. Walker, ed. Durham, NC: Duke University Press, pp. 123–140.

———. (1987b) "Handbook for Assessing Personal Characteristics and Foreign Policy Orientations of Political Leaders," *Mershon Occasional Papers* (Spring): n.p.

———. (1987c) "Workbook for Developing Personality Profiles of Political Leaders from Content Analysis Data," *Mershon Occasional Papers* (Summer): n.p.

———. (1989) "Defining the Bush Presidential Style," *Mershon Memo* (Spring): 1.

———. (2001) "Stereotypes Build Solidarity but Limit Our Understanding," *Maxwell Perspective* 12 (Fall): 10–11.

HERMANN, MARGARET G., AND CHARLES F. HERMANN. (1989) "Who Makes Foreign Policy Choices and How: An Empirical Inquiry," *International Studies Quarterly* 33 (December): 361–387.

HERMANN, MARGARET G., AND CHARLES W. KEGLEY, JR. (1995) "Rethinking Democracy and International Peace: Perspectives from Political Psychology," *International Studies Quarterly* 39 (September): 511–533.

———. (2001) "Stereotypes Build Solidarity, but Limit Our Understanding," *Maxwell Perspective* 12 (Fall): 10–11.

HERMANN, MARGARET G., AND THOMAS PRESTON. (1999) "Presidents, Leadership Style, and the Advisory Process," in *The Domestic Sources of American Foreign Policy: Insights and Evidence,* 3rd ed., Eugene R. Wittkopf and James M. McCormick, eds. Lanham, MD: Rowman and Littlefield, pp. 351–368.

HERRMANN, RICHARD K. (1986) "The Power of Perceptions in Foreign-Policy Decision Making: Do Views of the Soviet Union Determine the Policy Choices of American Leaders?" *American Journal of Political Science* 30 (November): 841–875.

HERSH, SEYMOUR. (1983) *The Price of Power: Kissinger in the Nixon White House.* New York: Summit Books.

———. (1994) "Missile Wars," *New Yorker,* 26 September, pp. 86–99.

———. (2003) "Selective Intelligence," *New Yorker,* 12 May (www.newyorker.com, accessed 12/1/06).

———. (2005) "The Coming Wars," *New Yorker,* 24 June, pp. 40–47.

———. (2006a) "Last Stand," *New Yorker,* 10 July, pp. 42–49.

———. (2006b) "Watching Lebanon," *New Yorker,* 21 August, pp. 28–33.

HERSMAN, REBECCA K. C. (2000) *Friends and Foes: How Congress and the President Really Make Foreign Policy.* Washington, DC: Brookings Institution.

HESS, GARY R. (2006) "Presidents and the Congressional War Resolutions of 1991 and 2002," *Political Science Quarterly,* 121 (Spring): 93–118.

HESS, STEPHEN. (1984) *The Government/Press Connection.* Washington, DC: Brookings Institution.

HESS, STEPHEN, AND MICHAEL NELSON. (1985) "Foreign Policy: Dominance and Decisiveness in Presidential Elections," in *The Elections of 1984,* Michael Nelson, ed. Washington, DC: CQ Press, pp. 129–154.

HILLEN, JOHN. (1999) "Defense's Death Spiral," *Foreign Affairs* 78 (July/August): 2–7.

HILSMAN, ROGER. (1967) *To Move a Nation.* New York: Doubleday.

———. (1990) *The Politics of Policy Making in Defense and Foreign Affairs,* 2nd ed. Englewood Cliffs, NJ: Prentice Hall.

———. (1995) "Does the CIA Still Have a Role?" *Foreign Affairs* 74 (September–October): 104–116.

———. (1996) *The Cuban Missile Crisis: The Struggle Over Policy.* Westport, CT: Preager.

HINCKLEY, BARBARA. (1994) *Less than Meets the Eye: Foreign Policy Making and the Myth of the Assertive Congress.* Chicago: University of Chicago Press.

HINCKLEY, RONALD H. (1993) "Neo/Isolationism: A Threat or a Myth?" *Wirthlin Report* 3 (January): 1–3.

HIRSHBERG, MATTHEW S. (1993) *Perpetuating Patriotic Perceptions: The Cognitive Function of the Cold War.* Westport, CT: Praeger.

HOBSBAWM, ERIC J. (2004) "Spreading Democracy: The World's Most Dangerous Ideas," *Foreign Policy,* 144 (September/October): 40–41.

HOCKIN, THOMAS A. (2001) *The American Nightmare: Trade Politics After Seattle.* Lanham, MD: Lexington Books.

HODGE, CARL CAVANAGH. (2005) *Atlanticism for a New Century: The Rise, Triumph, and Decline of NATO.* Upper Saddle River, NJ: Pearson/Prentice Hall.

HOFFMAN, DAVID. (1999) "A Weakened Bear: An Impoverished Russian Military Envies NATO," *Washington Post National Weekly Edition,* 21 June, p. 18.

HOFFMANN, STANLEY. (1978) *Primacy or World Order: American Foreign Policy Since the Cold War.* New York: McGraw-Hill.

———. (1979–1980) "Muscle and Brains," *Foreign Policy* 37 (Winter): 3–27.

———. (1992) "Bush Abroad," *New York Review of Books* 39 November: 54–59.

———. (1995) "The Crisis of Liberal Internationalism," *Foreign Policy* 98 (Spring): 159–177.

———. (2003) "The High and the Mighty: Bush's National Security Strategy and the New American Hubris," *American Prospect* 13: 28ff.

HOGE, JAMES F., JR. (1994) "Media Pervasiveness," *Foreign Affairs* 73 (July/August): 136–144.

———. (2004) "A Global Power Shift in the Making," *Foreign Affairs* 83 (July/August) 2–7.

HOLBROOKE, RICHARD. (1998) *To End a War.* New York: Random House.

HOLLAND, LAUREN. (1999) "The U.S. Decision to Launch Operation Desert Storm: A Bureaucratic

Politics Analysis," *Armed Forces and Society: An Interdisciplinary Journal* 25(Winter): 219–242.

HOLLOWAY, DAVID. (1994) *Stalin and the Bomb: The Soviet Union and Atomic Energy 1939–1956.* New Haven, CT: Yale University Press.

HOLMES, GENTA HAWKINS. (1994) "Diversity in the Department of State and the Foreign Service," *State Magazine* 375 (March): 18–25.

HOLMES, JENNIFER S. (2005) "Terrorism Drugs, and Congressional Politics: The Colombian Connection," in Ralph G. Carter, ed. *Contemporary Cases in U.S. Foreign Policy.* Washington, DC: CQ Press, pp. 33–64.

HOLMES, STEVEN A. (1998) "Losers in Clinton-Starr Bouts May Be Future U.S. Presidents," *New York Times,* 23 August, p. A1.

HOLSTI, K. J. (1998) "International Relations Theory and Domestic War in the Third World: The Limits of Relevance," in *International Relations Theory and the Third World,* Stephanie G. Neuman, ed. New York: St. Martin's, pp. 103–132.

HOLSTI, OLE R. (1962) "The Belief System and National Images: A Case Study," *Journal of Conflict Resolution* 6 (September): 244–252.

———. (1970) "The 'Operational Code' Approach to the Study of Political Leaders: John Foster Dulles' Philosophical and Instrumental Beliefs," *Canadian Journal of Political Science* 3 (March): 123–157.

———. (1973) "Foreign Policy Decision-Makers Viewed Psychologically," paper presented at the Conference on the Successes and Failures of Scientific International Relations Research, Ojai, CA, June 25–28.

———. (1976) "Foreign Policy Formation Viewed Cognitively," in *Structure of Decision: The Cognitive Maps of Political Elites,* Robert Axelrod, ed. Princeton, NJ: Princeton University Press, pp. 18–54.

———. (1987) "Public Opinion and Containment," in *Containing the Soviet Union,* Terry L. Deibel and John Lewis Gaddis, eds. Washington, DC: Pergamon-Brassey's, pp. 20–58.

———. (1992) "Public Opinion and Foreign Policy: Challenges to the Almond-Lippmann Consensus," *International Studies Quarterly* 36 (December): 439–466.

———. (1994) "Public Opinion and Foreign Policy: Attitude Structures of Opinion Leaders After the Cold War," in *The Domestic Sources of American Foreign Policy,* 2nd ed., Eugene R. Wittkopf, ed. New York: St. Martin's, pp. 36–56.

———. (1995) "Theories of International Policies and Foreign Policy: Realism and Its Challengers," in *Controversies in International Relations Theory: Realism and the Neoliberal Challenge,* Charles W. Kegley, Jr., ed. New York: St. Martin's, pp. 35–65.

———. (1996) *Public Opinion and American Foreign Policy.* Ann Arbor, MI: University of Michigan Press.

———. (1998–1999) "A Widening Gap Between the U.S. Military and Civilian Society? Some Evidence, 1976–96," *International Security* 23 (Winter): 5–42.

———. (2004) *Public Opinion and American Foreign Policy,* Revised Edition. Ann Arbor: University of Michigan Press.

HOLSTI, OLE R., AND JAMES N. ROSENAU. (1980) "Does Where You Stand Depend on When You Were Born? The Impact of Generation on Post-Vietnam Foreign Policy Beliefs," *Public Opinion Quarterly* 44 (Spring): 1–22.

———. (1984) *American Leadership in World Affairs.* Boston: Allen and Unwin.

———. (1990) "The Structure of Foreign Policy Attitudes: American Leaders, 1976–1984," *Journal of Politics* 52 (February): 94–125.

———. (1994) "The Foreign Policy Beliefs of American Leaders After the Cold War: Persistence or Abatement of Partisan Cleavages?" in *The Future of American Foreign Policy,* 2nd ed., Eugene R. Wittkopf, ed. New York: St. Martin's, pp. 127–147.

———. (1999a) "Internationalism: Intact or in Trouble?" in *The Future of American Foreign Policy,* 3rd ed., Eugene R. Wittkopf and Christopher M. Jones, eds. New York: St. Martin's, pp. 125–139.

———. (1999b) "The Political Foundations of Elites' Domestic and Foreign-Policy Beliefs," in *The Domestic Sources of American Foreign Policy: Insights and Evidence,* 3rd ed., Eugene R. Wittkopf and James M. McCormick, eds. Landham, MD: Rowman and Littlefield, pp. 33–50.

HOLT, PAT M. (1995) *Secret Intelligence and Public Policy: A Dilemma of Democracy.* Washington, DC: CQ Press.

HOMER-DIXON, THOMAS. (1999) *Environment, Scarcity, and Violence.* Princeton, NJ: Princeton University Press.

HONEY, MARTHA. (1997) "Guns 'R' Us: The Clinton Administration Is Helping U.S. Arms Dealers Corner the Global Market," *Baltimore Chronicle,* 5 November (http://baltimorechronicle.com, accessed 6/24/06).

HOOK, STEVEN W. (1998) "The White House, Congress, and the Paralysis of the U.S. State Department," in *After the End: Making U.S. Foreign Policy in the Post–Cold War World,* James M. Scott, ed. Durham, NC: Duke University Press, pp. 305–329.

———. (2004) "Sino American Trade Relations: Privatizing Foreign Policy," in *Contemporary Cases in U.S. Foreign Policy,* Ralph G. Carter, ed. Washington, DC: CQ Press, pp. 303–329.

HOOPES, TOWNSEND. (1973a) *The Devil and John Foster Dulles: The Diplomacy of the Eisenhower Era.* Boston: Little, Brown.

———. (1973b) *The Limits of Intervention.* New York: McKay.

HORRIGAN, JOHN B. (2006) "For Many Home Broadband Users, the Internet Is a Primary News Source," 22 March (www.pewinternet.org/pdfs/PIP_News.and.Broadband.pdf, accessed 11/4/2006).

HOWELL, LLEWELLYN D. (2000) "Isolationism or Unilateralism?" *USA Today* 128 (January): 13.

HOY, PAULA. (1998) *Players and Issues in International Aid.* West Hartford, CT: Kumarian Press.

HUFBAUER, GARY. (1998) "Foreign Policy on the Cheap," *Washington Post National Weekly Edition,* 20–27 July, pp. 22–23.

HUFBAUER, GARY CLYDE, JEFFREY J. SCHOTT, AND KIMBERLY ANN ELLIOTT. (1990) *Economic Sanctions Reconsidered: History and Current Policy,* 2nd ed. Washington, DC: Institute for International Economics.

HUGHES, EMMET JOHN. (1972) *The Living Presidency.* New York: Coward, McCann, and Geoghegan.

HUGHES, NEIL C. (2005) "A Trade War with China?" *Foreign Affairs* 84 (July/August): 94–106.

HUMAN DEVELOPMENT REPORT 1993. (1993) New York: Oxford University Press.

HUNT, MICHAEL H. (1987) *Ideology and U.S. Foreign Policy.* New Haven, CT: Yale University Press.

HUNTINGTON, SAMUEL P. (1957) *The Soldier and the State: The Theory and Politics of Civil/Military Relations.* Cambridge, MA: Belknap.

———. (1988–1989) "The U.S.–Decline or Renewal," *Foreign Affairs* 67 (Winter): 76–96.

———. (1991) *The Third Wave: Democratization in the Late Twentieth Century.* Norman OK: University of Oklahoma Press.

———. (1993a) "The Clash of Civilizations?" *Foreign Affairs* 72 (Summer): 22–49.

———. (1993b) "Why International Primacy Matters," *International Security* 17 (Spring): 68–83.

———. (1997) "The Erosion of American National Interests," *Foreign Affairs* 76 (September/October): 28–49.

———. (1999) "The Lonely Superpower," *Foreign Affairs* 78 (March/April): 35–49.

———. (2004a) *Who Are We: The Challenges to America's National Identity.* New York: Simon & Schuster.

———. (2004b) "The Hispanic Challenge," *Foreign Policy* 141 (March/April): 30–45.

HURWITZ, JON, AND MARK PEFFLEY. (1987) "How Are Foreign Policy Attitudes Structured? A Hierarchical Model," *American Political Science Review* 81 (December): 1099–1120.

———. (1990) "Public Images of the Soviet Union: The Impact of Foreign Policy Attitudes," *Journal of Politics* 52 (February): 3–28.

———. (1992) "International Events and Foreign Policy Beliefs: Public Response to Changing Soviet-U.S. Relations," *American Journal of Political Science* 36: 431–461.

HUTCHESON, RON. (2005) "Bush Pushing Power," *Advocate,* 22 May, p. 2D.

HYBEL, ALEX ROBERTO. (1993) *Power Over Rationality: The Bush Administration and the Gulf Crisis.* Albany, NY: State University of New York Press.

IGNATIUS, DAVID. (1988) "Is This Any Way for a Country to Buy Weapons?" *Washington Post National Weekly Edition,* 4–10 July, p. 23.

———. (1994) "Reinvent the CIA," *Washington Monthly* 26 (April): 38–42.

———. (1995) "Is the CIA's New Mission Impossible?" *Washington Post National Weekly Edition,* 13–19 March, pp. 23–24.

————. (2005) "The New Player in Foreign Policy," *San Diego Union-Tribune,* 11 February (http://signonsandiego.com, accessed 5/29/06).

IKENBERRY, G. JOHN. (1989) "Rethinking the Origins of American Hegemony," *Political Science Quarterly* 104 (Fall): 375–400.

————. (1993) "Salvaging the G-7," *Foreign Affairs* 72 (Spring): 132–139.

————. (1999) "America's Liberal Hegemony," *Current History* 98 (January): 23–28.

————. (2001) "Getting Hegemony Right," *National Interest* 63 (Spring): 17–24.

IKLÉ, FRED CHARLES. (1990) "The Ghost in the Pentagon," *National Interest* 19 (Spring): 13–20.

IMMERMAN, RICHARD H. (1982) *The CIA in Guatemala: The Foreign Policy of Intervention.* Austin, TX: University of Texas Press.

THE INDEPENDENT GROUP ON THE FUTURE OF US DEVELOPMENT COOPERATION. (1992) *Reinventing Foreign Aid: White Paper on US Development Cooperation in a New Democratic Era.* Washington, DC: Overseas Development Council.

ISAACS, JOHN. (1996) "Right Wing Targets Treaty," *The Bulletin of the Atomic Scientists* 52 (November–December): 13.

————. (1997) "Treaty Tactics," *Bulletin of the Atomic Scientists* 53 (July–August): 13.

ISAACSON, WALTER. (1993) *Kissinger: A Biography.* New York: Simon & Schuster.

————. (1999) "Madeleine's War," *Time,* 17 May, pp. 26–27ff.

ISAAK, ROBERT A. (1975) *Individuals and World Politics.* North Scituate, MA: Duxbury Press.

————. (1977) *American Democracy and World Power.* New York: St. Martin's.

————. (1995) *International Political Economy: Managing World Economic Change,* 2nd ed. Englewood Cliffs, NJ: Prentice Hall.

IVANOV, IGOR. (2000) "The Missile Defense Mistake/Undermining Strategic Stability and the ABM Treaty," *Foreign Affairs* 79 (September/October): 15–20.

IYENGAR, SHANTO, MARK D. PETERS, AND DONALD R. KINDER. (1982) "Experimental Demonstrations of the 'Not-So-Minimal' Consequences of Television News Programs," *American Political Science Review* 76 (December): 848–858.

JACKMAN, ROBERT W. (1973) "On the Relationship of Economic Development to Political Performance," *American Journal of Political Science* 17 (August): 611–621.

JACKSON, DONALD W., AND RALPH G. CARTER. (2005) "The International Criminal Court: Present at the Creation," in *Contemporary Cases in U.S. Foreign Policy: From Terrorism to Trade,* 2nd ed., Ralph G. Carter, ed. Washington, DC: CQ Press, pp. 363–388.

JACKSON, HENRY M. (1965) *The National Security Council: Jackson Subcommittee Papers on Policy-Making at the Presidential Level.* New York: Praeger.

JACOBS, LAWRENCE R., AND ROBERT Y. SHAPIRO. (2000) *Politicians Don't Pander: Political Manipulation and the Loss of Democratic Responsiveness.* Chicago: University of Chicago Press.

JACOBS, MARK. (2003) "Brain and Brawn: Putting Money and Muscle into Public Diplomacy Training," *State Magazine* 472 (October): 34–35.

JACOBSON, GARY C. (2007) *A Divider, Not a Uniter: George W. Bush and the American People, the 2006 Election and Beyond.* New York: Pearson/Longman.

JACOBSON, HAROLD K. (1984) *Networks of Interdependence: International Organizations and the Global Political System.* New York: Knopf.

JACOBSON, JODI. (1989) "Abandoning Homelands," in *State of the World 1989,* Lester R. Brown et al., eds. New York: Norton, pp. 59–76.

JACOBY, HENRY, RONALD PRINN, AND RICHARD SCHMALENSEE. (1998) "Kyoto's Unfinished Business," *Foreign Affairs* 77 (July/August): 54–66.

JACOBY, TAMAR. (2004) "Commentary on 'The Hispanic Challenge'," *Foreign Policy* 142 (May/June): 10, 12.

JAMES, PATRICK, AND JOHN R. ONEAL. (1991) "The Influence of Domestic and International Politics on the President's Use of Force," *Journal of Conflict Resolution* 35 (June): 307–332.

JANIS, IRVING. (1982) *Groupthink: Psychological Studies of Policy Decisions and Fiascoes,* 2nd ed. Boston: Houghton Mifflin.

————. (1989) *Crucial Decisions: Leadership in Policymaking and Crisis Management.* New York: Free Press.

JAVITS, JACOB K. (1985) "War Powers Reconsidered," *Foreign Affairs* 64 (Fall): 130–140.

JEHL, DOUGLAS. (2004a) "Tiny Agency's Iraq Analysis Is Better than Big Rival," *New York Times,* 19 July (www.nytimes.com, accessed 7/19/04).

————. (2004b) "White House Considers Disclosing Intelligence Budgets," *New York Times,* 29 July (www.nytimes.com, accessed 3/29/04).

JENKINS, MICHAEL. (2000–2001) "Columbia: Crossing a Dangerous Threshold," *National Interest* 62 (Winter): 47–55.

JENTLESON, BRUCE W. (1992) "The Pretty Prudent Public: Post-Vietnam American Opinion on the Use of Military Force," *International Studies Quarterly* 36 (March): 49–74.

————. (1998) "Still Pretty Prudent: Post–Cold War American Public Opinion on the Use of Force," *Journal of Conflict Resolution* 42 (August): 395–417.

JERVIS, ROBERT. (1976) *Perception and Misperception in International Politics.* Princeton, NJ: Princeton University Press.

————. (1991) "Will the New World Be Better?" in *Soviet-American Relations After the Cold War,* Robert Jervis and Seweryn Bialer, eds. Durham, NC: Duke University Press, pp. 7–19.

————. (1991–1992) "The Future of World Politics: Will It Resemble the Past?" *International Security* 16 (Winter): 39–73.

————. (1993) "International Primacy: Is the Game Worth the Candle?" *International Security* 17 (Spring): 52–67.

————. (2002) "Mutual Assured Destruction," *Foreign Policy* 144 (November/December): 40–42.

————. (2003) "Understanding the Bush Doctrine," *Political Science Quarterly* 118 (Fall): 365–388.

————. (2005a) *American Foreign Policy in a New Era.* New York: Routledge.

————. (2005b) "Why the Bush Doctrine Cannot Be Sustained," *Political Science Quarterly* 120 (Fall): 351–377.

————. (2006) "The Remaking of a Unipolar World," *Washington Quarterly* 29 (Summer): 7–19.

JOFFE, JOSEF. (1997) "America the Inescapable," *New York Times Magazine,* 8 June, pp. 38–43.

JOHNSON, CHALMERS, AND E. B. KEEHN. (1995) "The Pentagon's Ossified Strategy," *Foreign Affairs* 74 (July/August): 103–114.

JOHNSON, DOUGLAS, AND STEVEN METZ. (1995) "Civil-Military Relations in the United States: The State of the Debate," *Washington Quarterly* 18 (Winter): 197–213.

JOHNSON, LOCH. (1977) "Operational Codes and the Prediction of Leadership Behavior: Senator Frank Church at Midcareer," in *A Psychological Examination of Political Leaders,* Margaret G. Hermann, ed. New York: Free Press, pp. 80–119.

————. (1980) "Controlling the Quiet Option," *Foreign Policy* 39 (Summer): 143–153.

————. (1989) *America's Secret Power: The CIA in a Democratic Society.* New York: Cambridge University Press.

————. (1996) *Secret Agencies: U.S. Intelligence in a Hostile World.* New Haven, CT: Yale University Press.

————. (2000a) *Bombs, Bugs, Drugs, and Thugs: Intelligence and America's Quest for Security.* New York: New York University Press.

————. (2000b) "Spies," *Foreign Policy* 120 (September–October): 18–26.

————. (2001) "The CIA's Weakest Link," *Washington Monthly,* 33 (July): 9–11.

JOHNSON, ROBERT D. (1998–1999) "The Government Operations Committee and Foreign Policy During the Cold War," *Political Science Quarterly* 113 (Winter): 645–671.

JONAS, MANFRED. (1966) *Isolationism in America 1935–1941.* Ithaca, NY: Cornell University Press.

JONES, CHRISTOPHER M. (1994) "American Prewar Technology Sales to Iraq: A Bureaucratic Politics Explanation," in *The Domestic Sources of American Foreign Policy: Insights and Evidence,* Eugene R. Wittkopf, ed. New York: St. Martin's, pp. 279–296.

————. (1998) "The Foreign Policy Bureaucracy in a New Era," in *After the End: Making U.S. Foreign Policy in the Post–Cold War World,* James M. Scott, ed. Durham, NC: Duke University Press, pp. 57–88.

————. (1999) "Trading with Saddam: Bureaucratic Roles and Competing Conceptions of National Security," in *The Domestic Sources of American Foreign Policy: Insights and Evidence,* Eugene R. Wittkopf and James M. McCormick, eds. Lanham, MD: Rowman and Littlefield, pp. 267–285.

———. (2001) "The CIA under Clinton: Continuity and Change," *International Journal of Intelligence and Counterintelligence,* 14 (4) (Winter): 503–528.

———. (2002a) "Rejection of the Comprehensive Test Ban Treaty: The Politics of Ratification?" in *Contemporary Cases in U.S. Foreign Policy: From Terrorism to Trade,* 1st ed., Ralph G. Carter, ed. Washington, DC: CQ Press, pp. 160–195.

———. (2002b) "The V-22 Osprey: Pure Pork or Cutting -Edge Technology?" in *Contemporary Cases in U.S. Foreign Policy: From Terrorism to Trade,* 1st ed., Ralph G. Carter, ed. Washington, DC: CQ Press, pp. 217–247.

———. (2003) "Rejection of the Comprehensive Test Ban Treaty: A Political Fait Accompli," *Annual Convention of the International Studies Association.* Portland, OR , February 26–March 1.

———. (2004) "Roles, Politics, and the Survival V-22 Osprey," in *The Domestic Sources of American Foreign Policy: Insights and Evidence,* Eugene R. Wittkopf and James M. McCormick, eds. Lanham, MD: Rowman and Littlefield, pp. 183–195.

———. (2005a) "Rejection of the Comprehensive Test Ban Treaty: The Politics of Ratification," in *Contemporary Cases in U.S. Foreign Policy: From Terrorism to Trade,* 2nd ed., Ralph G. Carter, ed. Washington, DC: CQ Press, pp. 181–216.

———. (2005b) "The Crusader Mobile Artillery System: Who Determines the Army's Needs," in *Contemporary Cases in U.S. Foreign Policy: From Terrorism to Trade,* 2nd ed., Ralph G. Carter, ed. Washington, DC: CQ Press, pp. 217–247.

———. (2006a) "The Other Side of Powell's Record." *American Diplomacy* (www.unc.edu/depts/diplomat/item/2006/0103/jone/jonesc_powell.html, accessed 11/3/06).

———. (2006b) "NATO's Transformation," in *Old Europe, New Security: Evolution for a Complex World,* Janet Adamski and Mary. Troy Johnson, and Christina M. Schweiss, eds. Aldershot, United Kingdom: Ashgate Publishing Limited, pp. 71–84.

JONES, GORDON S., AND JOHN A. MARINI, eds. (1988) *The Imperial Congress: Crisis in the Separation of Powers.* New York: Pharos Books.

JONSSON, CHRISTER. (1982) *Cognitive Dynamics and International Politics.* New York: St. Martin's.

———. (1982) *Cognitive Dynamics and International Politics.* New York: St. Martin's.

JORDAN, AMOS A., WILLIAM J. TAYLOR, JR., AND MICHAEL MAZARR. (1999) *American National Security.* Baltimore, MD: Johns Hopkins University Press.

JORDAN, DONALD L., AND BENJAMIN I. PAGE. (1992) "Shaping Foreign Policy News: The Role of TV News," *Journal of Conflict Resolution* 36 (June): 227–241.

JOYNER, CHRISTOPHER C. (1992) *Intervention into the 1990s: U.S. Foreign Policy in the Third World,* 2nd ed. Peter J. Schraeder, ed. Boulder, CO: Lynne Rienner.

——— (1993) "When Human Suffering Warrants Military Action," *Chronicle of Higher Education,* 27 January, p. A52.

———. (2005) *International Law in the 21st Century: Rules for Global Governance.* Lanham, MD: Rowman and Littlefield.

JUDIS, JOHN B. (1990) "The Japanese Megaphone," *New Republic,* 22 January, pp. 20–25.

———. (1992) "Statecraft and Scowcroft," *New Republic,* 24 February, pp. 18–21.

KAEMPFER, WILLIAM H., AND ANTON D. LOWENBER. (1999) "Unilateral versus Multilateral International Sanctions: A Public Choice Perspective," *International Studies Quarterly* 43 (March): 37–58.

KAGAN, DONALD. (1997) "Are U.S. Forces Overstretched? Roles and Missions," *Orbis* 41 (Spring 1997): 187–198.

KAGAN, ROBERT. (1998) "The Benevolent Empire," *Foreign Policy* 111 (Summer): 24–34.

———. (2003) *Of Paradise and Power: America and Europe in the New World Order.* New York: Knopf.

KAGAN, ROBERT, AND IRVING KRISTOL, eds. (2000) *Present Dangers: Crisis and Opportunity in American Foreign and Defense Policies.* San Francisco: Encounter Books.

KAHLER, MILES. (1995) "A World of Blocs: Facts and Factoids," *World Policy Journal* 12 (Spring): 19–27.

KAHN, DAVID. (1984) "The United States Views Germany and Japan in 1941," in *Knowing One's*

Enemies: Intelligence Assessment Before the Two World Wars, Ernest R. May, ed. Princeton, NJ: Princeton University Press, pp. 476–501.

KALB, MARVIN L., AND STEPHEN HESS, eds. (2003) *The Media and the War on Terrorism.* Washington, DC: Brookings Institution.

KAMP, KARL-HEINZ. (1999) "A Global Role for NATO?" *Washington Quarterly* 22 (Winter): 7–11.

KAMPEAS, RON. (2001) "FBI Expands Global Reach, Earning Success and Friends," *Advocate,* 6 August, p. 7A.

KANBUR, RAVI, AND TODD SANDLER, WITH KEVIN MORRISON. (1999) *The Future of Development Assistance: Common Pools and International Public Goods.* Washington, DC: Overseas Development Council.

KANTER, ARNOLD, AND LINTON F. BROOKS, eds. (1994) *U.S. Intervention Policy for the Post–Cold War World: New Challenges and New Responses.* New York: Norton.

KAPLAN, LAWRENCE F. (2001a) "Containment," *New Republic,* 5 February, pp. 17–20.

———. (2001b) "Drill Sergeant: The Oil Industry's Man at the State Department," *New Republic,* 26 March, pp. 17–20.

KAPLAN, MORTON A. (1957) *System and Process in International Politics.* New York: Wiley.

KAPLAN, ROBERT D. (2000) *The Coming Anarchy: Shattering the Dreams of the Post–Cold War World.* New York: Random House.

KAPSTEIN, ETHAN B. (1994) "America's Arms-Trade Monopoly," *Foreign Affairs* 73 (May/June): 13–19.

———. (1996) "Workers and the World Economy," *Foreign Affairs* 75 (May/June): 16–37.

———. (1999) "Global Rules for Global Finance," *Current History* 98 (November): 355–360.

KAPUR, DEVESH. (1998) "The IMF: A Cure or a Curse?" *Foreign Policy* 111 (Summer): 114–128.

KARP, JONATHAN. (2006) "Pet Projects Prevail in U.S. Military-Spending Boom," *Wall Street Journal,* 16 June (http://online.wsj.com/public/us/, accessed 11/21/06).

KATE, KERRY TEN, AND SARAH A. LAIRD. (1999) *The Commercial Use of Biodiversity: Access to Genetic Resources and Benefit-Sharing.* London: Earthscan.

KATTENBURG, PAUL. (1980) *The Vietnam Trauma in America Foreign Policy, 1945–75.* New Brunswick, NJ: Transaction Books.

KATZ, ELIHU. (1957) "The Two-Step Flow of Communications," *Public Opinion Quarterly* 21 (Spring): 61–78.

KATZENSTEIN, PETER J. (1977) "Introduction: Domestic and International Forces of Foreign Economic Policy," *International Organization* 31 (Spring): 587–606.

KAUFMAN, HERBERT. (1976) *Are Government Organizations Immortal?* Washington, DC: Brookings Institution.

KAUL, INGE, AND ISABELLE GRUNBERG. (1999) *Global Public Goods: International Cooperation in the 21st Century.* New York: Oxford University Press.

KAY, DAVID A. (1998) "Iraq Beyond Crisis Du Jour," *Washington Quarterly* 21 (Summer): 10–14.

KEARNS, DORIS. (1976) *Lyndon Johnson and the American Dream.* New York: Harper and Row.

KEETER, SCOTT. (1985) "Public Opinion in 1984," in *The Election of 1984: Reports and Interpretations,* Gerald M. Pomper et al., eds. Chatham, NJ: Chatham House, pp. 91–111.

KEFALAS, A. G. (1992) "The Global Corporation: Its Role in the New World Order," *National Forum* 72 (Fall): 26–30.

KEGLEY, CHARLES W., JR. (1994) "How Did the Cold War Die? Principles for an Autopsy," *Mershon International Studies Review* 38 (April): 11–41.

———, ed. (1995) *Controversies in International Relations Theory: Realism and the Neoliberal Challenge.* New York: St. Martin's.

KEGLEY, CHARLES W., JR., AND SHANNON L. BLANTON. (1994) "America's Policy Conundrum: The Promotion of Democratic Nation Building and U.S. Arms Exports," *Brown Journal of World Affairs* 2 (Winter): 65–75.

KEGLEY, CHARLES W., JR., AND STEVEN W. HOOK. (1991) "U.S. Foreign Aid and UN Voting: Did Reagan's Linkage Strategy Buy Deference or Defiance?" *International Studies Quarterly* 35 (September): 295–312.

KEGLEY, CHARLES W., JR., AND GREGORY A. RAYMOND. (1998) "Great-Power Relations in the 21st Century: A New Cold War, or Concert-Based Peace?" in *The Global Agenda: Issues and*

Perspectives, 5th ed., Charles W. Kegley, Jr., and Eugene R. Wittkopf, eds. Boston: McGraw-Hill, pp. 170–183.

KEGLEY, CHARLES W., JR., AND EUGENE R. WITTKOPF. (2001) *World Politics: Trend and Transformation,* 8th ed. Boston: Bedford/St. Martin's.

KELLER, PAUL. (2000) "Backlash in Peru to CIA's Flawed Battle Against Drugs," *Financial Times,* London, 15 November, p. 1.

KELLY, MICHAEL. (1994) "The President's Past," *New York Times Magazine,* 31 July, pp. 20–29ff.

KENGOR, PAUL. (2000a) "The Vice President, Secretary of State, and Foreign Policy," *Political Science Quarterly* 115 (Summer): 175–199.

———. (2000b) *Wreath Layer or Policy Player? The Vice President's Role in Foreign Policy.* Lanham, MD: Lexington Books.

KENNAN, GEORGE F. ("X"). (1947) "The Sources of Soviet Conduct," *Foreign Affairs* 25 (July): 566–582.

———. (1951) *American Diplomacy, 1900–1950.* New York: New American Library.

———. (1954) *Realities of American Foreign Policy.* Princeton, NJ: Princeton University Press.

———. (1967) *Memoirs.* Boston: Little, Brown.

———. (1976) "The United States and the Soviet Union, 1917–1976," *Foreign Affairs* 54 (July): 670–690.

———. (1995) "On American Principles," *Foreign Affairs* 74 (March/April): 116–126.

KENNEDY, DAVID M. (2005) "What 'W' Owes to 'WW'," *Atlantic Monthly* 295 (March): 36–40.

KENNEDY, PAUL. (1987) *The Rise and Fall of the Great Powers.* New York: Random House.

———. (1992) "A Declining Empire Goes to War," in *The Future of American Foreign Policy,* Charles W. Kegley, Jr., and Eugene R. Wittkopf, eds. New York: St. Martin's, pp. 344–346.

———. (1994) "Overpopulation Tilts the Planet," *New Perspectives Quarterly* 11 (Fall): 4–6.

KENNEDY, ROBERT F. (1969) *Thirteen Days.* New York: Norton.

KEOHANE, ROBERT O. (1984) *After Hegemony: Cooperation and Discord in the World Political Economy.* Princeton, NJ: Princeton University Press.

———. (1986a) "Realism Neorealism, and the Study of World Politics," in *Neorealism and Its Critics,* Robert

O. Keohane, ed. New York: Columbia University Press, pp. 1–26.

———, ed. (1986b) *Neorealism and Its Critics.* New York: Columbia University Press.

KEOHANE, ROBERT O., AND JOSEPH S. NYE JR. (1975) "International Interdependence and Integration," in *International Politics. Handbook of Political Science,* vol. 8, Fred I. Greenstein and Nelson W. Polsby, eds. Reading, MA: Addison-Wesley, pp. 363–414.

———. (2000) "Globalization: What's New? What's Not? (And So What?)," 118 *Foreign Policy,* Spring 104–118.

———. (2001) *Power and Interdependence.* New York: Longman.

KERNELL, SAMUEL. (1999) "The Challenge Ahead for Explaining President Clinton's Public Support," *PRG Report* 21 (3): 1–3.

KESSLER, GLENN. (2001) "More than Meets the Eye," *Washington Post National Weekly Edition.* 15–21 October, p. 18.

———. (2004a) "Powell Flies in the Face of Tradition: The Secretary of State Is the Least Traveled in 30 Years," *Washington Post,* 14 July (www.washingtonpost.com/wp-dyn/articles/A48010-2004Jul13.html, accessed 11/3/06).

———. (2004b) "For New National Security Adviser, a Mixed Record," *Washington Post,* 17 November (www.washingtonpost.com, accessed 11/19/2004).

———. (2006) "Karen Hughes: Changing Public Diplomacy's Face," *Pittsburgh Post-Gazette,* 23 April (www.post-gazette.com, accessed 6/13/06).

KETTLE, MARTIN. (2001) "Powell Losing Policy Battle to Hardliners," *The Guardian,* 12 March, p. 13.

KEY, V. O. (1961) *Public Opinion and American Democracy.* New York: Knopf.

KHONG, YUEN FOONG. (1992) *Analogies at War.* Princeton, NJ: Princeton University Press.

KIBBE, JENNIFER D. (2004) "The Rise of the Shadow Warriors," *Foreign Affairs* 83 (2) (March/April): 102–115.

KILPATRICK, JAMES J. (1985) "An Overstuffed Bureaucracy," *The State,* 23 April, p. 8A.

KINDLEBERGER, CHARLES P. (1973) *The World in Depression, 1929–1939.* Berkeley: University of California Press.

————. (1988) *Manias, Panics, and Crashes: A History of Financial Crises.* New York: Basic Books.

KINGDON, JOHN W. (1995) *Agendas, Alternatives, and Public Policies.* New York: HarperCollins.

————. (1999) *America the Unusual.* New York: St. Martin's/Worth.

KINSELLA, DAVID. (1994) "Conflict in Context: Arms Transfers and Third World Rivalries During the Cold War," *American Journal of Political Science* 38 (August): 557–581.

KINZER, STEPHEN. (2003) "Regime Change: The Legacy," *The American Prospect,* 14 (10): 40–42.

KIRKPATRICK, DAVID D. (2005) "In Secretly Taped Conversations, Glimpses of the Future President," *New York Times,* 20 February (www.nytimes.com, accessed 2/20/05).

KIRSCHTEN, DICK. (1987) "Competent Manager," *National Journal,* 28 February, pp. 468–469 passim.

KISSINGER, HENRY. (1962) *The Necessity of Choice.* Garden City, NY: Doubleday.

————. (1969) "Domestic Structure and Foreign Policy," in *International Politics and Foreign Policy,* James N. Rosenau, ed. New York: Free Press, pp. 261–275.

————. (1979) *White House Years.* Boston: Little, Brown.

————. (1994a) *Diplomacy.* New York: Simon & Schuster.

————. (1994b) "Reflections on Containment," *Foreign Affairs* 73 (May/June): 113–130.

————. (2001a) "America at the Apex: Empire or Leader?" *National Interest* 64 (Summer): 9–17.

————. (2001b) *Does America Need a Foreign Policy? Toward a Diplomacy for the 21st Century.* New York: Simon & Schuster.

KISSINGER, HENRY, AND CYRUS VANCE. (1988) "Bipartisan Objectives for American Foreign Policy," *Foreign Affairs* 66 (Summer): 899–921.

KITFIELD, JAMES. (2000) "Covert Counterattack," *National Journal* 32, 16 September, pp. 2858–2865.

————. (2001a) "A Diplomat Handy with a Bayonet," *National Journal* 33, 27 January, pp. 250–251.

————. (2001b) "A Small Study Carries a Heavy Burden," *National Journal* 33, 3 March, pp. 644–646.

KLARE, MICHAEL. (1984) *American Arms Supermarket.* Austin, TX: University of Texas Press.

————. (1994–1995) "Awash in Armaments: Implications of the Trade in Light Weapons," *Harvard International Review* 17 (Winter): 24–26, 75–76.

KLARE, MICHAEL T., AND DANIEL C. THOMAS, eds. (1998) *World Security: Challenges for a New Century,* 3rd ed. Boston: Bedford.

KLINE, JOHN. (1983) *State Government Influence in U.S. International Economic Policy.* Lexington, MA: Lexington Books.

KLINGBERG, FRANK L. (1983) *Cyclical Trends in American Foreign Policy Moods: The Unfolding of America's World Role.* Lanham, MD: University Press of America.

————. (1990) "Cyclical Trends in Foreign Policy Revisited in 1990," *International Studies Notes* 15 (Spring): 54–58.

————. (1996) *Positive Expectations of America's World Role: Historical Cycles of Realistic Idealism.* Lanham, MD: University Press of America.

KNOTT, STEPHAN F. (1996) *Secret and Sanctioned Covert Operations and the American Presidency.* New York: Oxford University Press.

KOBER, STANLEY. (1998) "Why Spy? The Uses and Misuses of Intelligence," *USA Today* 126 (March): 10–14.

KOH, HAROLD H. (1990) *The National Security Constitution: Sharing Power after the Iran-Contra Affair.* New Haven, CT: Yale University Press.

KOHN, RICHARD H. (1994) "Out of Control: The Crisis in Civil-Military Relations," *National Interest* 35 (Spring): 3–17.

KOHUT, ANDREW. (2003) "Anti-Americanism: Causes and Characteristics," *Pew Research Center for the People and the Press,* 10 December (http://people-press.org, accessed 6/12/06).

KOHUT, ANDREW, AND ROBERT C. TOTH. (1994) "Arms and the People," *Foreign Affairs* 73 (November/December): 47–61.

————. (1998) "A World of Difference: The Public and Opinion Leaders Are Poles Apart on the U.S. Role in Global Affairs," *Washington Post National Weekly Edition,* 5 January, p. 22.

KOLKO, GABRIEL. (1968) *The Politics of War.* New York: Random House.

————. (1969) *The Roots of American Foreign Policy.* Boston: Beacon Press.

KONDRACKE, MORTON. (1990) "How to Aid A.I.D," *New Republic,* 26 February, pp. 20–23.

KOPPEL, ANDREA, ELISE LABOTT, AND PAM BENSON. (2005) "Terror Threat to U.S. Called 'Significant,'" *CNN.com* (www.cnn.com/2005/US/04/27/terror.report/index.html, accessed 11/4/06).

KORANY, BAHGAT. (1994) "End of History, or Its Continuation? The Global South and the 'New Transformation' Literature," *Third World Quarterly* 15 (March): 7–15.

KORB, LAWRENCE J. (1995a) "The Indefensible Defense Budget," *Washington Post National Weekly Edition,* 17–23 July, p. 19.

———. (1995b) "The Readiness Gap. What Gap?" *New York Times Magazine,* 26 February, pp. 40–41.

KORB, LAWRENCE, AND PETER OGDEN. (2005) "A Bad Deal with India," *Defense Monitor* 34 (July/August): 2–3.

KORB, LAWRENCE, AND CAROLINE WADHAMS. (2006) *Policy Analysis Brief: "A Critique of the Bush Administration's National Security Strategy."* Muscatine, IA: Stanley Foundation, 6 June (http://reports.stanleyfoundation.org).

KORNBLUH, PETER. (1998) *Bay of Pigs Declassified: The Secret CIA Report on the Invasion of Cuba.* New York: The New Press.

KORNBLUT, ANNE E. (2005) "Crises Raise Criticisms of Bush's Chief of Staff," *New York Times,* 18 October (www.nytimes.com, accessed 5/25/06).

KOTZ, NICK. (1988) *Wild Blue Yonder: Money, Politics, and the B-1 Bomber.* Princeton, NJ: Princeton University Press.

KOVACH, BILL. (1996) "Do the News Media Make Foreign Policy," *Foreign Policy* 102 (Spring): 169–179.

KRAMER, DAVID J. (2000) "No Bang for the Buck: Public Diplomacy Should Remain a Priority," *Washington Times,* 23 October (www.state.gov/r/adcompd/kramer.html).

KRASNER, STEPHEN D. (1972) "Are Bureaucracies Important? (Or Allison Wonderland)," *Foreign Policy* 7 (Summer): 159–179.

———. (1982) "Structural Causes and Regime Consequences," *International Organization* 36 (Spring): 185–206.

———. (1985) *Structural Conflict: The Third World Against Global Liberalism.* Berkeley: University of California Press.

KRAUTHAMMER, CHARLES. (1991) "The Unipolar Moment," *Foreign Affairs* 70 (Winter): 23–33.

———. (1999) "The Clinton Doctrine," *Time,* 5 April, p. 88.

———. (2004) "Democratic Realism," American Enterprise Institute for Public Policy Research, 12 February (www.aei.org, accessed 7/23/04).

KRENN, MICHAEL L., ed. (1999) *The Impact of Race on U.S. Foreign Policy: A Reader.* New York: Garland Publishing.

KREPON, MICHAEL, AND DAN CALDWELL. (1991) *The Politics of Arms Control Ratification.* New York: St. Martin's Press and Henry L. Stimson Center.

KREPON, MICHAEL, AMY E. SMITHSON, AND JOHN PARACHINI. (1997) *The Battle to Obtain U.S. Ratification of the Chemical Weapons Convention.* Washington, DC: Henry L. Stimson Center.

KRISTOF, NICHOLAS. (2000a) "Ally of an Older Generation Amid the Tumult of the 1960s," *New York Times,* 19 June, p. 1.

———. (2000b) "Learning How to Run: A West Texas Stumble," *New York Times,* 27 July, p. 1.

———. (2000c) "How Bush Came to Tame His Inner Self," *New York Times,* 29 July, p. 1.

———. (2000d) "The Republicans: Man in the News; Confident Son of Politics Rises," *New York Times,* 3 August, p. 1.

———. (2000e) "The 2000 Campaign: Running Texas; A Master of Bipartisanship with No Taste for Details," *New York Times,* 16 October, p. 1.

KRUGMAN, PAUL. (1990) *The Age of Diminished Expectations: U.S. Economic Policy in the 1990s.* Cambridge, MA: MIT Press.

———. (1994a) "Competitiveness: A Dangerous Obsession," *Foreign Affairs* 73 (March/April): 28–44.

———. (1994b) *Peddling Prosperity: Economic Sense and Nonsense in the Age of Diminished Expectations.* New York: Norton.

KRUGMAN, PAUL R., AND ROBERT Z. LAWRENCE. (1994) "Trade, Jobs, and Wages," *Scientific American* 270 (April): 44–49.

KULL, STEVEN, AND I. M. DESTLER. (1999) *Misreading the Public: The Myth of the New Isolationism.* Washington, DC: Brookings Institution.

KULL, STEVEN, I. M. DESTLER, AND CLAY RAMSAY. (1997) *The Foreign Policy Gap: How Policymakers Misread the Public.* College Park, MD: The Center for International and Security Studies at Maryland (CISSM).

KULL, STEVEN, CLAY RAMSAY, AND EVAN LEWIS. (2003–2004) "Misperceptions, the Media, and the Iraq War," *Political Science Quarterly,* 118 (4): 569–598.

KUNZ, DIANE B. (1997) *Butter and Guns: America's Cold War Economic Diplomacy.* New York: Free Press.

KUPCHAN, CHARLES A. (1998) "After Pax Americana: Benign Power, Regional Integration, and the Sources of Stable Multipolarity," *International Security* 23 (Fall): 40–79.

KUPERMAN, ALAN J. (1999) "The Stinger Missile and U.S. Intervention in Afghanistan," *Political Science* Quarterly 114 (2): 219–263.

KURKJIAN, STEPHEN. (1991) "CIA Wages Quiet War on Iraq," *Boston Globe,* 11 February, p. 1.

KURTH, JAMES R. (1989) "The Military-Industrial Complex Revisited," in *American Defense Annual 1989–1990,* Joseph Kruzel, ed. Lexington, MA: Lexington Books, pp. 196–215.

KURTZ, HOWARD. (1993) "How Sources and Reporters Play the Game of Leaks," *Washington Post National Weekly Edition,* 15–21 March, p. 12.

———. (1996) *Hot Air: All Talk, All the Time.* New York: New York Times Books.

———. (1998) *Spin Cycle: Inside the Clinton Propaganda Machine.* New York: Free Press.

KUSNITZ, LEONARD A. (1984) *Public Opinion and Foreign Policy: America's China Policy, 1949–1979.* Westport, CT: Greenwood.

LABOTT, ELISE. (2003) "U.S. Launches Arab Gen-X Mag," 14 August (www.cnn.com, accessed 11/18/04).

LACEY, MARC, AND RAYMOND BONNER. (2001) "A Mad Scramble by Donors for Plum Ambassadorships." *New York Times,* 19 March, p. A1.

LADD, EVERETT CARL. (1997) "1996: The 'No Majority' Realignment Continues," *Political Science Quarterly* 112 (Winter): 1–28.

LAFEBER WALTER. (1976) *America, Russia, and the Cold War 1945–1975.* New York: Wiley.

———. (1994) *The American Age: United States Foreign Policy at Home and Abroad,* 2nd ed. New York: Norton.

LAI, BRIAN. (2003) "Examining the Goals of U.S. Foreign Assistance in the Post–Cold War Period, 1991–96," *Journal of Peace Research* 40 (January): 103–128.

LAIRD, MELVIN R. (2005) "Iraq: Learning the Lessons of Vietnam," *Foreign Affairs,* 85 (6): 22–43.

LAIS, SAMI. (1997) "Groups Clash Over Mapping Agency's Role," *Government Computer News* 16, 14 July, p. 1.

LAKE, ANTHONY. (1994) "Confronting Backlash States," *Foreign Affairs* 73 (March/April): 45–55.

LANCASTER, CAROL. (2000a) *Transforming Foreign Aid: United States Assistance in the 21st Century.* Washington, DC: Institute for International Economics.

———. (2000b) "Redesigning Foreign Aid," *Foreign Affairs* 79 (September/October): 74–88.

LANCASTER, JOHN. (1993) "Ammunition Against Budget Cuts," *Washington Post National Weekly Edition,* 22–28 November, p. 32.

———. (2000) "No Clout Where It Counts," *Washington Post National Weekly Edition,* 17 April.

LANDY, MARC, AND SIDNEY M. MILKIS. (2000) *Presidential Greatness.* Lawrence, KS: University of Kansas Press.

LANE, CHARLES. (2000) "'Superman' Meets Shining Path: Story of a CIA Success," *Washington Post,* 7 December, p. A1.

———. (2004) "Justices Back Detainee Access to U.S. Courts," *Washington Post,* 29 June (www. washingtonpost.com, accessed 5/11/06).

LANG, TIM. (2001) "Dietary Implications of the Globalization of the Food Trade," in *The Global Agenda: Issues and Perspectives,* 6th ed., Charles W. Kegley, Jr., and Eugene R. Wittkopf, eds. Boston: McGraw-Hill, pp. 420–424.

LANGER, E. J. (1975) "The Illusion of Control," *Journal of Personality and Social Psychology* 32 (6): 311–328.

LANTIS, JEFFREY S., AND ERIC MOSKOWITZ. (2005) "The Return of the Imperial Presidency? The Bush Doctrine and U.S. Intervention in Iraq," in *Contemporary Cases in U.S. Foreign Policy: From Terrorism to Trade,* 2nd ed., Ralph G. Carter, ed. Washington, DC: CQ Press, pp. 89–121.

LAQUEUR, WALTER. (1994) "Save Public Diplomacy," *Foreign Affairs* 73 (September/October): 19–24.

———. (1998) "The New Face of Terrorism," *Washington Quarterly* 21 (Autumn): 169–178.

LARSON, DEBORAH WELCH. (1985) *Origins of Containment: A Psychological Explanation.* Princeton, NJ: Princeton University Press.

LARSON, ERIC V. (1996) *Casualties and Consensus: The Historical Role of Casualties in Domestic Support for U.S. Military Operations.* Santa Monica, CA: RAND Corporation.

LARSON, ERIC V., AND BOGDAN SAVYCH. (2005) *American Public Support for U.S. Military Operations from Mogadishu to Baghdad.* Santa Monica, CA: RAND Corporation.

LARSON, JAMES F. (1990) "Television and U.S. Foreign Policy: The Case of the Iran Hostage Crisis," in *Media Power in Politics,* 2nd ed., Doris A. Graber, ed. Washington, DC: CQ Press, pp. 301–312.

LASKI, HAROLD J. (1947) "America-1947," *The Nation* 165 (December): 641–644.

LASSWELL, HAROLD D. (1962) "The Garrison State Hypothesis Today," in *Changing Patterns of Military Politics,* Samuel P. Huntington, ed. New York: Free Press, pp. 51–70.

———. (1974) "The Political Personality," in *Personality and Politics,* Gordon J. DiRenzo, ed. Garden City, NY: Doubleday-Anchor, pp. 38–54.

LAUTER, DAVID. (1994) "Anti-Politician Hate Becoming Institutional Phenomenon," *Sunday Advocate,* 10 July, p. 4E.

LAVALLEE, TARA. (2003) "Globalizing the Iron Triangle: Policy-Making Within the US Defense Industrial Sector," *Defense and Security Analysis,* 19 (2) (June): 149–164.

———. (2005) *Globalizing the Iron Triangle? The Changing Face of the United States Defense Industry.* Ph.D. dissertation, University of Connecticut.

LAYNE, CHRISTOPHER. (1993) "The Unipolar Illusion: Why New Great Powers Will Rise," *International Security* 17 (Spring): 5–51.

———. (1998) "Rethinking American Grand Strategy: Hegemony or Balance of Power in the Twenty-First Century?" *World Policy Journal* 15 (Summer): 8–28.

———. (2002) A New Grand Strategy, *Atlantic Monthly* 289 (January): 36–42.

LEE, CHRISTOPHER. (2006) "Court Blocks DOD's New Rules for Workers," *Washington Post,* 28 February (www.washingtonpost.com, accessed 2/28/06).

LEFFLER, MELVYN P. (1996) "Inside Enemy Archives: The Cold War Reopened," *Foreign Affairs* 75 (July/August): 120–135.

———. (2004) "Bush's Foreign Policy," *Foreign Policy* 144 (September/October): 22–28.

LEGRO, JEFFREY W., AND ANDREW MORAVCSIK. (2001) "Faux Realism," *Foreign Policy* 125 (July/August): 80–82.

LEIGH, MICHAEL. (1976) *Mobilizing Consent: Public Opinion and American Foreign Policy, 1937–1947.* Westport, CT: Greenwood.

LEVERING, RALPH B. (1976) *American Opinion and the Russian Alliance, 1939–1945.* Chapel Hill, NC: University of North Carolina Press.

———. (2005) "Overstretch Myth-Can the Indispensable Nation Be a Debtor Nation?" *Foreign Affairs* 84 (2): 2–7.

LEVI, ISAAC. (1990) *Hard Choices: Decision Making Under Unresolved Conflict.* New York: Cambridge University Press.

LEVIN, JEROME D. (1998) *The Clinton Syndrome: The President and the Self-Destructive Nature of Sexual Addiction.* New York: Random House.

LEWIS, MICHAEL. (1998) "The World's Biggest Going-Out-of-Business Sale," *New York Times Magazine,* 31 May, pp. 35–41ff.

LEWIS, NEIL A. (2001) "A Nation Challenged: The Resolution." *New York Times,* 18 September, p. B7.

LEWY, GUENTER. (1978) *America in Vietnam.* New York: Oxford University Press.

LEYTON-BROWN, DAVID. (1987) "Introduction," in *The Utility of International Economic Sanctions,* David Leyton-Brown, ed. New York: St. Martin's, pp. 1–4.

LI, YITAN, AND A COOPER DRURY. (2004) "Threatening Sanctions When Engagement Would Be More Effective," *International Studies Perspectives,* 5 (4) (November): 378–394.

LIAN, BRADLEY, AND JOHN R. ONEAL. (1993) "Presidents, the Use of Military Force, and Public

Opinion," *Journal of Conflict Resolution* 37 (June): 277–300.

LICHTER, S. ROBERT, AND STANLEY ROTHMAN. (1981) "Media and Business Elites," *Public Opinion* 4 (October/November): 42–46, 59–60.

LIEBER, KEIR A., AND GERARD ALEXANDER. (2005) "Waiting for Balancing: Why the World Is Not Pushing Back," *International Security* 30 (Summer): 109–139.

LIEBER, KEIR A., AND DARYL G. PRESS. (2006) "The Rise of U.S. Nuclear Primacy," *Foreign Affairs* 85 (March/April): 42–54.

LIEBERMAN, SEYMOUR. (1965) "The Effects of Changes in Roles on the Attitudes of Role Occupants," in *Human Behavior and International Politics,* J. David Singer, ed. Chicago: Rand McNally, pp. 155–168.

LIGHT, PAUL C. (1991) *The President's Agenda: Domestic Policy Choice from Kennedy to Reagan.* Baltimore, MD: Johns Hopkins University Press.

———. (2005) "Rumsfeld's Revolution at Defense," *The Brookings Institution Policy Brief* 142 (July): 1–8.

LIM, LINDA Y. C. (2001) "Whose 'Model' Failed? Implications of the Asian Financial Crisis," in *The Global Agenda: Issues and Perspectives,* Charles W. Kegley, Jr., and Eugene R. Wittkopf, eds. Boston: McGraw-Hill, pp. 285–296.

LINDBLOM, CHARLES E. (1959) "The Science of Muddling Through," *Public Administration Review* 19 (Spring): 79–88.

LINDSAY, JAMES M. (1986) "Trade Sanctions As Policy Instruments: A Re-examination," *International Studies Quarterly* 30 (June): 153–173.

———. (1987) "Congress and Defense Policy: 1961 to 1986," *Armed Forces and Society* 13 (Spring): 371–401.

———. (1988) "Congress and the Defense Budget," *Washington Quarterly* 11 (Winter): 57–74.

———. (1990) "Parochialism, Policy, and Constituency Constraints: Congressional Voting on Strategic Weapons Systems," *American Journal of Political Science* 34 (November): 936–960.

———. (1993) "Congress and Foreign Policy: Why the Hill Matters," *Political Science Quarterly* 107 (Winter): 607–628.

———. (1994a) "Congress and Foreign Policy: Avenues of Influence," in *The Domestic Sources of American*

Foreign Policy: Insights and Evidence, Eugene R. Wittkopf, ed. New York: St. Martin's, pp. 191–207.

———. (1994b) *Congress and the Politics of U.S. Foreign Policy.* Baltimore, MD: Johns Hopkins University Press.

———. (1994c) "Congress, Foreign Policy, and the New Institutionalism," *International Studies Quarterly* 38 (June): 281–304.

———. (2000a) "Looking for Leadership: Domestic Politics and Foreign Policy," *Brookings Review* 18 (Winter): 40–43.

———. (2000b) "The New Apathy: How an Uninterested Public Is Shaping Foreign Policy," *Foreign Affairs* 79 (September/October): 2–8.

———. (2004) "From Deference to Activism and Back Again: Congress and the Politics of American Foreign Policy," in *The Domestic Sources of American Foreign Policy: Insights and Evidence,* Eugene R. Wittkopf and James M. McCormick, eds. Lanham, MD: Rowman and Littlefield, pp. 183–195.

LINDSAY, JAMES M., AND MICHAEL E. O'HANLON. (2002a) "Missile Defense After the ABM Treaty," *Washington Quarterly* 25: 163–176.

———. (2002b) "Limited National and Allied Missile Defense," *International Security* 26 (4): 190–201.

LINK, MICHAEL W., AND CHARLES W. KEGLEY, JR. (1993) "Is Access Influence? Measuring Adviser-Presidential Interactions in Light of the Iranian Hostage Crisis," *International Interactions* 18 (4): 343–364.

LINZER, DAFNA. (2005) "A Year Later, Goss's CIA Is Still in Turmoil," *Washington Post,* 19 October (www.washingtonpost.com, accessed 10/19/05).

LIPPMAN, THOMAS. (1996) "The Decline of U.S. Diplomacy," *Washington Post National Weekly Edition,* 22–28 July, pp. 6–7.

LIPPMANN, THOMAS W., AND HELEN DEWAR. (1999) "Who Says Bipartisanship Is Dead?" *Washington Post National Weekly Edition,* 16 March, p. 16.

LIPPMANN, WALTER. (1943) *U.S. Foreign Policy: Shield of the Republic.* Boston: Little, Brown.

———. (1947) *The Cold War: A Study in U.S. Foreign Policy.* New York: Harper.

LIPSET, SEYMOUR M. (1959) "Some Social Requisites of Democracy," *American Political Science Review* 53 (March): 69–105.

————. (1996) *American Exceptionalism: A Double-Edged Sword.* New York: Norton.

LIPSET, SEYMOUR MARTIN, AND WILLIAM SCHNEIDER. (1987) "The Confidence Gap During the Reagan Years, 1981–1987," *Political Science Quarterly* 102 (Spring): 1–23.

LIPSITZ, LEWIS, AND DAVID M. SPEAK. (1989) *American Democracy.* New York: St. Martin's.

LISKA, GEORGE. (1978) *Career of Empire: America and Imperial Expansion over Land and Sea.* Baltimore: Johns Hopkins University Press.

LLOYD, JOHN. (1999) "The Russian Devolution," *New York Times Magazine,* 15 August, pp. 34–41ff.

LOCHER, JAMES R., III. (2001) "Has It Worked? The Goldwater-Nichols Reorganization Act," *Naval War College Review* 54 (4) (August): 95–115.

————. (2002) *Victory on the Potomac: The Goldwater-Nichols Act Unifies the Pentagon.* College Station, TX: Texas A&M University Press.

LOEB, VERNON. (1998) "Where the CIA Wages Its New World War," *Washington Post National Weekly Edition,* 14 September, p. 18.

————. (1999) "Bin Laden Still Seen as Threat," *Washington Post, p. A1.*

————. (2001) "Test of Strength," *Washington Post,* 31 July (www.washingtonpost.com, accessed 7/31/01).

LORD, CARNES. (1988) *The Presidency and the Management of National Security.* New York: Free Press.

LOVEN, JENNIFER. (2005) "Bush, Blair Work on Plan for African Aid," *San Francisco Chronicle,* 7 June (www.sfgate.com, accessed 6/14/06).

LOW, PATRICK. (1993) *Trading Free: The GATT and U.S. Trade Policy.* New York: Twentieth Century Fund Press.

LOWENTHAL, MARK M. (1992) "Tribal Tongues: Intelligence Consumers, Intelligence Producers," *Washington Quarterly* 15 (Winter): 157–168.

————. (1999) "Tribal Tongues: Intelligence Consumers, Intelligence Producers," in *The Domestic Sources of American Foreign Policy: Insights and Evidence,* Eugene R. Wittkopf and James M. McCormick, eds. Lanham, MD: Rowman and Littlefield, pp. 253–266.

————. (2006) *Intelligence: From Secrets to Policy.* Washington, DC: CQ Press.

LOWI, THEODORE J. (1967) "Making Democracy Safe for the World," in *Domestic Sources of Foreign Policy,* James N. Rosenau, ed. New York: Free Press, pp. 295–331.

————. (1979) *The End of Liberalism.* New York: Norton.

————. (1985a) *The Personal President.* Ithaca, NY: Cornell University Press.

————. (1985b) "Presidential Power: Restoring the Balance," *Political Science Quarterly* 100 (Summer): 185–213.

LOWI, THEODORE J., AND BENJAMIN GINS-BERG. (1990) *American Government.* New York: W. W. Norton.

LOWRY, RICHARD. (1999) "Test-Ban: How the Treaty Went Down," *National Review,* 8 November, p. 20.

————. (2004) "Never Again?" *National Review,* 25 June.

LUND, MICHAEL S. (1995) "Underrating 'Preventive Diplomacy'," *Foreign Affairs* 74 (July/August): 160–163.

LUNDESTAD, GEIR. (1990) *The American Empire.* London: Oxford University Press.

LUTTWAK, EDWARD N. (1993) *The Endangered American Dream: How to Stop the United States from Becoming a Third World Country and How to Win the Geo-Economic Struggle for Economic Supremacy.* New York: Simon & Schuster.

————. (1994) "Where Are the Great Powers?" *Foreign Affairs* 73 (July/August): 23–28.

MACKINNON, MICHAEL. (1999) *The Evolution of U.S. Peacekeeping Policy Under Clinton.* London: Frank Cass Publishers.

MACMAHON, ARTHUR W. (1951) "The Administration of Foreign Affairs," *American Political Science Review* 45 (September): 836–866.

MAGDOFF, HARRY. (1969) *The Age of Imperialism.* New York: Monthly Review Press.

MAHARIDGE, DALE. (1996) *The Coming White Minority: California, Multiculturalism, and America's Future.* New York: Vintage.

MALLABY, SEBASTIAN. (2000) "The Bullied Pulpit," *Foreign Affairs* 79 (January/February): 2–8.

MANDELBAUM, MICHAEL. (1994) "A Struggle Between Two Pasts," *World Policy Journal* 11 (Fall): 95–103.

————. (1996) "Foreign Policy as Social Work," *Foreign Affairs* 75 (January/February): 16–32.

————. (1999) "A Perfect Failure: NATO's War Against Yugoslavia," *Foreign Affairs* 78 (September/October): 2–8.

————. (2006) "David's Friend Goliath," *Foreign Policy* 152 (September/October): 50–56.

MANGOLD, TOM. (1991) *Cold Warrior: James Jesus Angleton, the CIA's Master Spy Hunter.* New York: Simon & Schuster.

MANKIW, N. GREGORY, AND SWAGEL PHIL L., (2005) "Antidumping: The Third Rail of Trade Policy." *Foreign Affairs* 84 (July/August): 107–119.

MANN, JAMES. (1993) "Post–Cold War CIA Fighting for Its Life," *Los Angeles Times,* p. A1.

————. (1999) "America Is World's Arms Superstore," *Baltimore Sun,* p. A.

————. (2004a) "The Armageddon Plan," *Atlantic Monthly* 293 (2) March (www.theatlantic.com/doc/prem/200403/mann).

————. (2004b) *Rise of the Vulcans: The History of Bush's War Cabinet.* New York: Viking.

MANN, THOMAS E., AND NORMAN J. ORN-STEIN. (1993) *Renewing Congress: A Second Report.* Washington, DC: American Enterprise Institute for Public Policy and the Brookings Institution.

MANNING, ROBERT A. (1999) "Futureshock or Renewed Partnership? The U.S.-Japan Alliance Facing the Millennium," in *The Future of American Foreign Policy,* 3rd ed., Eugene R. Wittkopf and Christopher M. Jones, eds. New York: St. Martin's/Woth, pp. 192–203.

MANSBACH, RICHARD W., AND JOHN A. VAS-QUEZ. (1981) *In Search of Theory: A New Paradigm for Global Politics.* New York: Columbia University Press.

MANSFIELD, EDWARD D., AND HELEN V. MILNER, eds. (1997) *The Political Economy of Regionalism.* New York: Columbia University Press.

MARANISS, DAVID. (1995) *First in His Class: The Biography of Bill Clinton.* New York: Simon & Schuster.

————. (1998a) *The Clinton Enigma: A Four-and-a-Half Minute Speech Reveals this President's Entire Life.* New York: Simon & Schuster.

————. (1998b) "Clinton's Personality Patterns," *Washington Post National Weekly Edition,* 2 February, pp. 6–8.

MARCH, JAMES G., AND HERBERT M. SIMON. (1958) *Organizations.* New York: Wiley.

MARCHETTI, VICTOR, AND JOHN D. MARKS. (1974) *The CIA and the Cult of Intelligence.* New York: Knopf.

MARCUS, JONATHAN. (2000) "Kosovo and After: American Primacy in the Twenty-First Century," *Washington Quarterly* 23 (Winter): 79–94.

MAREN, MICHAEL. (1997) *The Road to Hell: The Ravaging Effects of Foreign Aid and International Charity.* New York: Free Press.

MARKS, ALEXANDRA. (1997) "Do Whistleblowers Threaten Security When Telling Congress of Spies' Lies," *Christian Science Monitor,* 15 July, p. 1.

MARKUSEN, ANN. (1999) "The Rise of World Weapons," *Foreign Policy* 114 (Spring): 40–51.

MARQUIS, CHRISTOPHER. (2001) "Eight Marine Officers Are Charged in Osprey False-Records Case," *New York Times,* 18 August (www.nytimes.com, accessed 8/19/01).

————. (2003) "Study Finds Europeans Distrustful of U.S. Global Leadership," *New York Times,* 4 September (www.nytimes.com, accessed 6/12/06).

MARTIN, ANDREW, AND ROSS GEORGE. (1999) "Europe's Monetary Union: Creating a Democratic Deficit?" *Current History* 98 (April): 171–175.

MARTIN, WILLIAM. (1999) "The Christian Right and American Foreign Policy," *Foreign Policy* 114 (Spring).

MASTANDUNO, MICHAEL. (1991) "Do Relative Gains Matter? America's Response to Japanese Industrial Policy," *International Security* 16 (Summer): 73–113.

————. (1997) "Preserving the Unipolar Moment: Realist Theories and U.S. Grand Strategy After the Cold War," *International Security* 21 (Spring): 49–88.

MATHIAS, CHARLES MCC., JR. (1981) "Ethnic Groups and Foreign Policy," *Foreign Affairs* 59 (Summer): 975–998.

MAY, ERNEST R. (1992) "Intelligence: Backing into the Future," *Foreign Affairs* 71 (Summer): 63–72.

MAY, ERNEST R., AND PHILIP D. ZELIKOW, eds. (1997) *The Kennedy Tapes: Inside the White House During the Cuban Missile Crisis.* Cambridge, MA: Harvard University Press.

MAYER, JANE. (2005) "Outsourcing Torture," *New Yorker,* 14 February (www.newyorker.com, accessed 6/25/06).

———. (2006) "The Hidden Power: The Legal Mind behind the White House's War on Terror," *New Yorker,* Letter from Washington, 26 June (www.newyorker.com/fact/content/articles/060703fa_fact1, accessed 11/28/06).

MAYNES, CHARLES WILLIAM. (1993–1994) "A Workable Clinton Doctrine," *Foreign Policy* 93 (Winter): 3–20.

———. (1995) "Relearning Intervention," *Foreign Policy* 98 (Spring): 96–113.

———. (1998) "The Perils of (and for) an Imperial America," *Foreign Policy* 111 (Summer): 36–47.

———. (2001) "Contending Schools," *National Interest* 63 (Spring): 49–58.

MAZUR, JASON. (2000) "Labor's New Internationalism," *Foreign Affairs* 79 (January/February): 79–93.

MAZZAR, MICHAEL J. (1990) "Beyond Counterforce," *Comparative Strategy* 9 (2): 147–162.

———. (2002) "Saved from Ourselves," *Washington Quarterly* 25 (Spring): 221–232.

MCCALLISTER J. F. O. (2001) "Why the Spooks Screwed Up. *Time,* 24 September, p. 44.

MCCLARAN, JOHN M. (2000) "U.S. Arms Sales to Taiwan," *Asian Survey* 40 (July): 622–640.

MCCLELLAND, DAVID C. (1961) *The Achieving Society.* Princeton, NJ: Van Nostrand.

MCCLOSKY, HERBERT, AND JOHN ZALLER. (1984) *The American Ethos: Public Attitudes Toward Capitalism and Democracy.* Cambridge, MA: Harvard University Press.

MCCOMBS, MAXWELL E., AND DONALD L. SHAW. (1972) "The Agenda-Setting Function of Mass Media," *Public Opinion Quarterly* 36 (Summer): 176–185.

MCCORMICK, JAMES M. (1985) "Congressional Voting on the Nuclear Freeze Resolutions," *American Politics Quarterly* 13 (January): 122–136.

———. (1992) *American Foreign Policy and Process.* Itasca, IL: F. E. Peacock.

———. (1993) "Decision Making in the Foreign Affairs and Foreign Relations Committees," in *Congress Resurgent: Foreign and Defense Policy on Capitol Hill,* Randall B. Ripley and James M. Lindsay, eds. Ann Arbor, MI: University of Michigan Press, pp. 115–153.

———. (1998) *American Foreign Policy and Process.* Itasca, IL: F. E. Peacock.

MCCORMICK, JAMES M., AND MICHAEL BLACK. (1983) "Ideology and Voting on the Panama Canal Treaties," *Legislative Studies Quarterly* 8 (February): 45–63.

MCCORMICK, JAMES M., AND EUGENE R. WITTKOPF. (1990a) "Bipartisanship, Partisanship, and Ideology in Congressional-Executive Foreign Policy Relations, 1947–1988," *Journal of Politics* 52 (November): 1077–1100.

———. (1990b) "Bush and Bipartisanship: The Past as Prologue?" *Washington Quarterly* 13 (Winter): 5–16.

MCCORMICK, JAMES M., EUGENE R. WITTKOPF, AND DAVID DANNA. (1997) "Politics and Bipartisanship at the Water's Edge: A Note on Bush and Clinton," *Polity* 30 (Fall): 133–150.

MCCURDY, DAVE. (1994) "Glasnost for the CIA," *Foreign Affairs* 73 (January–February): 125–140.

MCELVAINE, ROBERT S. (1984) "Do We Really Want an 'Active President?'" *Washington Post National Weekly Edition,* 2 July, p. 28.

MCFARLANE, ROBERT C. (1994) *Special Trust.* New York: Cadell and Davies.

MCFAUL, MICHAEL. (2002) "The Liberty Doctrine: Reclaiming the Purpose of American Power," *Policy Review,* April/May, pp. 3–21.

MCGEARY, JOHANNA. (2001) "Odd Man Out," *Time,* 10 September, pp. 24–32

MCGLEN, NANCY E., AND MEREDITH REID SARKEES. (1993) *Women in Foreign Policy: The Insiders.* New York: Routledge.

MCNAMARA, ROBERT S. (1983) "The Military Role of Nuclear Weapons: Perceptions and Misperceptions," *Foreign Affairs* 62 (Fall): 59–80.

———. (1995) *The Tragedy and Lessons of Vietnam.* New York: Times Books.

MEAD, WALTER RUSSELL. (1988–1989) "The United States and the World Economy," *World Policy Journal* 6 (Winter): 1–45.

———. (1989) "American Economic Policy in the Antemillennial Era," *World Policy Journal* 6 (Summer): 385–468.

MEARSHEIMER, JOHN J. (1990a) "Back to the Future: Instability in Europe After the Cold War," *International Security* 14 (Summer): 5–56.

———. (1990b) "Why We Will Soon Miss the Cold War," *Atlantic Monthly* 266 (August): 35–50.

MEARSHEIMER, JOHN, AND STEPHEN WALT. (2003) "An Unnecessary War," *Foreign Affairs,* 84 (January/February): 50–59.

———. (2006) "The Israeli Lobby," *London Review of Books* 28 (26 March) (www.lrb.co.uk, accessed 4/2/06).

MEERNIK, JAMES. (1994) "Presidential Decision Making and the Political Use of Military Force," *International Studies Quarterly* 38 (March): 121–138.

MEERNIK, JAMES, AND STEVEN C. POE. (1996) "U.S. Foreign Aid in the Domestic and International Environments," *International Interactions* 22 (July): 21–40.

MEIER, KENNETH J. (1987) *Politics and the Bureaucracy,* 2nd ed. Monterey, CA: Brooks/Cole.

MELANSON, RICHARD A. (1983) *Writing History and Making Policy: The Cold War, Vietnam, and Revisionism.* Lanham, MD: University Press of America.

———. (1996) *American Foreign Policy Since the Vietnam War: The Search for Consensus from Nixon to Clinton.* Armonk, NY: M. E. Sharpe.

———. (2005) *American Foreign Policy since the Vietnam War: The Search for Consensus from Richard Nixon to George W. Bush,* 4th ed. Armonk, NY: M. E. Sharpe.

MELBOURNE, ROY M. (1992) *Conflict and Crisis: A Foreign Service Story.* Lanham, MD: University Press of America.

MELMAN, SEYMOUR. (1974) *The Permanent War Economy.* New York: Simon & Schuster.

MENDELSOHN, JACK. (1997) "Arms Control: The Unfinished Agenda," *Current History* 96 (April): 145–150.

MERELMAN, RICHARD M. (1984) *Making Something of Ourselves: On Culture and Politics in the United States.* Berkeley: University of California Press.

METZ, STEVEN. (1997) "Racing Toward the Future: The Revolution in Military Affairs," *Current History* 96 (April): 184–188.

MICHALAK, STANLEY. (1995) "Bill Clinton's Adventures in the Jungle of Foreign Policy," *USA Today* 123 (March): 10–14.

MILBANK, DANA, AND BRADLEY GRAHAM. (2001) "No Time for 'Strategy'," *Washington Post National Weekly Edition,* 15–21 October, p. 13.

MILES, RUFUS E., JR. (1985) "Hiroshima: The Strange Myth of Half a Million American Lives Saved," *International Security* 19 (Fall): 121–140.

MILLER, LESLIE. (2005) "Security Deadlines Ignored," *Advocate,* 31 October, p. 2A.

MILLER, WARREN E., AND J. MERRILL SHANKS. (1996) *The New American Voter.* Cambridge, MA: Harvard University Press.

MILLS, C. WRIGHT. (1956) *The Power Elite.* New York: Oxford University Press.

MINTER, WILLIAM. (1986–1987) "South Africa: Straight Talk on Sanctions" *Foreign Policy* 65 (Winter): 43–63.

MINTZ, JOHN. (2003) "Ridge's Rise to Homeland Security," *Washington Post Weekly Edition,* 10–16 March, p. 29.

———. (2005) "Infighting Cited at Homeland Security," *Washington Post,* 2 February (www.washingtonpost.com, accessed 3/7/06).

MINUTAGLIO, BILL. (1999) *First Son: George W. Bush and the Bush Family Dynasty.* New York: Random House.

MITCHELL, JENNIFER D. (2001) "The Next Doubling: Understanding Global Population Growth," in *The Global Agenda: Issues and Perspectives,* 6th ed., Charles W. Kegley, Jr., and Eugene R. Wittkopf, eds. Boston: McGraw-Hill, pp. 446–456.

MITCHELL, PAUL T. (1999) "Ideas, Interests, and Strategy: Bureaucratic Politics and the United States Navy," *Armed Forces and Society: and Interdisciplinary Journal* 25 (2): 243–266.

MOEN, MATTHEW C., AND GARY W. COPELAND. (1999) *The Contemporary Congress: A Bicameral Approach.* Belmont, CA: West/Wadsworth.

MOENS, ALEXANDER. (2004) *The Foreign Policy of George W. Bush: Values, Strategy, and Loyalty.* Hants, England: Ashgate.

MOFFETT, GEORGE D. (1994) "Global Population Growth: 21st Century Challenges," *Headline Series* 302 (Spring). New York: Foreign Policy Association.

MOHAN, GILES. (2000) *Structural Adjustment: Theory, Practice, and Impacts*. New York: Routledge.

MONGAR, THOMAS M. (1974) "Personality and Decision-Making: John F. Kennedy in Four Crisis Decisions," in *Personality and Politics,* Gordon J. DiRenzo, ed. Garden City, NY: Doubleday-Anchor, pp. 334–372.

MONROE, ALAN D. (1979) "Consistency Between Public Preferences and National Policy Decisions," *American Politics Quarterly* 7 (January): 3–19.

———. (1998) "Public Opinion and Public Policy 1980–1993," *Public Opinion Quarterly* 62 (Spring): 6–28.

MONTGOMERY, BRUCE P. (2005–2006) "Congressional Oversight: Vice President Richard B. Cheney's Executive Branch Triumph," *Political Science Quarterly* 120 (Winter): 581–617.

MOORE, MOLLY. (1994) "The CIA Gets Stung by Afghan Rebels' Stingers," *Washington Post National Weekly Edition,* 14–20 March, p. 18.

MORGAN, DAN. (2001) "House Panel Allocates $1.67 Billion for Pentagon Counterterrorism Bid," *Washington Post,* 9 November, p. A12.

MORGAN, EDMUND S. (1988) *Inventing the People: The Rise of Popular Sovereignty in England and America*. New York: Norton.

MORGENTHAU, HANS J. (1969) "Historical Justice and the Cold War," *New York Review of Books,* 10 July, pp. 10–17.

———. (1985) *Politics Among Nations,* revised by Kenneth W. Thompson. New York: Knopf.

MORICI, PETER. (1997) "The United States, World Trade, and the Helms-Burton Act," *Current History* 96 (February): 87–88.

MORIN, RICHARD. (1996) "City Editors for a Day," *Washington Post National Weekly Edition,* 6–12 May, p. 35.

———. (1998) "Keeping the Faith," *Washington Post National Weekly Edition,* 12 January, p. 37.

MORRISON, PHILIP, KOSTA TSIPIS, AND JEROME WIESNER. (1994) "The Future of American Defense," *Scientific American* 270 (February): 38–45.

MOSER, PAUL K., ed. (1990) *Rationality in Action: Contemporary Approaches*. New York: Cambridge University Press.

MOSKOWITZ, ERIC, AND JEFFREY S. LANTIS. (2002) "The War in Kosovo: Coercive Diplomacy," in *Contemporary Cases in U.S. Foreign Policy: From Terrorism to Trade,* 1st ed., Ralph G. Carter, ed. Washington, DC: CQ Press, pp. 59–87.

MOYER, WAYNE. (1973) "House Voting on Defense: An Ideological Explanation," in *Military Force and American Society,* Bruce Russett and Alfred Stepan, eds. New York: Harper and Row, pp. 106–142.

MUELLER, JOHN. (1971) "Trends in Popular Support for the Wars in Korea and Vietnam," *American Political Science Review* 65 (June): 358–375.

———. (1973) *War, Presidents, and Public Opinion*. New York: Wiley.

———. (1994) *Policy and Opinion in the Gulf War*. Chicago: University of Chicago Press.

———. (2004–2005) What Was the Cold War About? Evidence from Its Ending," *Political Science Quarterly,* 119 (Winter 2004–2005): 609–631.

———. (2005) "The Iraq Syndrome," *Foreign Affairs* 84 (November/December): 44–54.

MUELLER, JOHN, AND KARL MUELLER. (1999) "Sanctions of Mass Destruction," *Foreign Affairs* 78 (May/June): 43–53.

MUFSON, STEVEN. (1992) "Superpower or Sri Lanka?" *Washington Post National Weekly Edition,* 7–13 September, pp. 6–7.

MULCAHY, KEVIN V. (1995) "Rethinking Groupthink: Walt Rostow and the National Security Advisory Process in the Johnson Administration," *Presidential Studies Quarterly* 25 (Spring): 237–250.

MÜLLER, HARALD, AND MITCHELL REISS. (1995) "Counterproliferation: Putting New Wine in Old Bottles," *Washington Quarterly* 18 (Spring): 143–154.

MULLINS, KERRY, AND AARON WILDAVSKY. (1992) "The Procedural Presidency of George Bush," *Political Science Quarterly* 107 (Spring): 31–62.

MUNRO, NEIL. (2000) "Undercover Agency Sheds Its Security Blanket," *National Journal* 32 (7 October): 3176.

MURRAY, ALAN. (1992–1993) "The Global Economy Bungled," *Foreign Affairs* 72 (1): 158–166.

MURRAY, SHAILAGH. (2006) "Capital's New Four-Letter Word," *Washington Post,* 27 January, p. A21.

MURRAY, SHOON KATHLEEN. (1994) "Change and Continuity in American Elites' Foreign Policy Beliefs: A 1988–1992 Panel Study," paper presented at the annual meeting of the International Studies Association, Washington, DC, March 29–April 1.

MURRAY, SHOON KATHLEEN, AND CHRISTOPHER SPINOSA. (2004) "The Post 9/11 Shift in Public Opinion: How Long Will It Last?" in *The Domestic Sources of American Foreign Policy: Insights and Evidence,* Eugene R. Wittkopf and James M. McCormick, eds. Lanham, MD: Rowman and Littlefield, pp. 97–115.

MYERS, ROBERT J. (1999) *U.S. Foreign Policy in the Twenty-First Century: The Relevance of Realism.* Baton Rouge, LA: Louisiana State University Press.

MYERS, STEVEN LEE. (1997) "Why Washington Likes Land Mines," *New York Times,* 24 August, p. 5.

MYRDAL, GUNNAR. (1944) *An American Dilemma: The Negro Problem in Modern Democracy.* New York: Harper.

NACHT, ALEXANDER. (1995) "U.S. Foreign Policy Strategies," *Washington Quarterly* 18 (Summer): 195–210.

NAFTALI, TIMOTHY. (2005) *Blind Spot: The Secret History of American Counterterrorism.* New York: Basic Books.

NAIM, MOISES. (2000) "Washington Consensus or Washington Confusion?" *Foreign Policy* 118 (Spring): 87–102.

———. (2002) "The New Diaspora," *Foreign Policy* 131 (July/August): 95–96.

———. (2003) "The Five Wars of Globalization," *Foreign Policy* 134 (January/February): 29–36.

NAIMARK, NORMAN M. (2004) "Sudan: Bosnia Repeated?" *National Review,* 2 August.

NATHAN, JAMES A., ed. (1993) *The Cuban Missile Crisis Revisited.* New York: St. Martin's.

NATHAN, JAMES A., AND JAMES K. OLIVER. (1976) *United States Foreign Policy and World Order.* Boston: Little, Brown.

———. (1994) *Foreign Policy Making and the American Political System,* 3rd ed. Baltimore, MD: Johns Hopkins University Press.

NATIONAL INTELLIGENCE COUNCIL. (2004) *Mapping the Global Future* (www.dni.gov/nic/NIC_globaltrend2020.html, accessed 12/5/06).

NATIONAL SECURITY COUNCIL PROJECT. (1998) *The Nixon Administration National Security Council.* Center for International and Security Studies at Maryland and the Brookings Institution, 1998.

———. (1999a) *The Bush Administration National Security Council.* Center for International and Security Studies at Maryland and the Brookings Institution.

———. (1999b) *The Role of the National Security Adviser.* Center for International and Security Studies at Maryland and the Brookings Institution.

———. (2000) *The Clinton Administration National Security Council.* Center for International and Security Studies at Maryland and the Brookings Institution.

NELSON, TREVOR. (1995) "My Enemy's Friends: In Guatemala, the DEA Fights the CIA," *New Republic* 212, 5 June, pp. 18–20.

NEUMAN, W. RUSSELL. (1986) *The Paradox of Mass Politics: Knowledge and Opinion in the American Electorate.* Cambridge, MA: Harvard University Press.

NEUSTADT, RICHARD E. (1980) *Presidential Power.* New York: Wiley.

———. (2001) "The Weakening White House," *British Journal of Political Science* 31 (January): 1–11.

NEUSTADT, RICHARD E., AND ERNEST R. MAY. (1986) *Thinking in Time: The Uses of History for Decision Makers.* New York: Free Press.

NEWLAND, KATHLEEN. (1999) "Workers of the World, Now What?" *Foreign Policy* 114 (Spring): 52–64.

NEWMAN, RICHARD J. (1998) "America Fights Back: Clinton Raises the Stakes in the War Against Terrorism," *U.S. News and World Report* 125, 31 August, pp. 38–43.

NEWMAN, RICHARD J., AND ALAN COOPERMAN. (1997) "Getting Ready for the Wrong War," *U.S. News and World Report* 122, 12 May, pp. 30–32.

NIE, NORMAN H., SIDNEY VERBA, AND JOHN R. PETROCIK. (1976) *The Changing American Voter.* Cambridge, MA: Harvard University Press.

NIEBUHR, REINHOLD. (1947) *Moral Man and Immoral Society.* New York: Scribner's.

NIJMAN, JAN. (1998) "United States Foreign Aid: Crisis? What Crisis?" in *The Global Crisis in Foreign Aid,* Richard and Jan Nijman Grant, eds. Syracuse, NY: Syracuse University Press, pp. 29–43.

NINCIC, MIROSLAV. (2004) "Elections and U.S. Foreign Policy," in *The Domestic Sources of Foreign Policy: Insights and Evidence,* Eugene R. Wittkopf and James M. McCormick, eds. Lanham, MD: Rowman and Littlefield, pp. 117–127.

NOLAN, JANNE E., ed. (1994) *Global Engagement: Cooperation and Security in the 21st Century.* Washington, DC: The Brookings Institution.

NOLAN, ROBERT. (2006) "The Rice Doctrine: A Look at Transformational Diplomacy," *Foreign Policy Association Newsletter,* 26 January (www.fpa.org/newsletter_info2583/newsletter_info.htm, accessed 11/3/06).

NORRIS, PIPPA. (1997) "News of the World," in *Politics and the Press: The News Media and Their Influences,* Pippa Norris, ed. Boulder, CO: Lynne Reinner, pp. 275–290.

NORRIS, PIPPA, MONTAGUE KERN, AND MARION JUST. (2003a) "Framing Terrorism," in *Framing Terrorism: The News Media, the Government, and the Public,* Pippa Norris, Montague Kern, and Marion Just, eds. New York: Routledge.

———, eds. (2003b) *Framing Terrorism: The News Media, the Government, and the Public.* New York: Routledge.

NOWZAD, BAHRAM. (1990) "Lessons of the Debt Decade," *Finance & Development* 27 (March): 9–13.

NUNN, SAM. (1987) "The ABM Reinterpretation Issue," *Washington Quarterly* 10 (Autumn): 45–57.

NUNN, SAM, AND PETE DOMENICI. (1992) *The CSIS Strengthening of America Commission.* Washington, DC: Center for Strategic and International Studies.

NUNN, SAM, AND JAMES R. SCHLESINGER. (2000) *The Geopolitics of Energy into the 21st Century. Vol. 1: An Overview and Policy Considerations.* Washington, DC: Center for Strategic and International Studies.

NYE, JOSEPH S., JR. (1990) *Bound to Lead: The Changing Nature of American Power.* New York: Basic Books.

———. (1992) "What New World Order?" *Foreign Affairs* 71 (Spring): 83–96.

———. (1994) "Peering into the Future," *Foreign Affairs* 73 (July/August): 82–93.

———. (1996) "Conflicts After the Cold War," *Washington Quarterly* 19 (Winter): 5–24.

———. (1999) "Redefining the National Interest," *Foreign Affairs* 78 (July/August): 22–35.

———. (2001/02) "Seven Tests: Between Concert and Unilateralism," *The National Interest* 66 (Winter): 5–13.

———. (2002a) "The Dependent Colossus," *Foreign Policy* (March/April): 74–75.

———. (2002b) *The Paradox of American Power: Why the World's Only Superpower Can't Go It Alone.* New York: Oxford University Press.

———. (2004) "The Decline of America's Soft Power," *Foreign Affairs* 83 (May/June): 16–20.

———. (2006) "Transformational Leadership and U.S. Grand Strategy," *Foreign Affairs* 85 (July/August): 139–148.

NYE, JOSEPH S., JR., AND WILLIAM A. OWENS. (1996) "America's Information Edge," *Foreign Affairs* 75 (March/April): 20–36.

NYE, JOSEPH S., JR., PHILIP D. ZELIKOW, AND DAVID C. KING, eds. (1997) *Why People Don't Trust Government.* Cambridge, MA: Harvard University Press.

O'HALLORAN, MICHAEL A. (2005) "NSC-68 and the Global War on Terrorism," *USAWC Strategy Research Project.* Carlisle Barracks, PA: U.S. Army War College (www.strategicstudiesinstitute.army.mil/pdffiles/ksil207.pdf, accessed 11/18/06).

O'HANLON, MICHAEL. (1998–1999) "Can High Technology Bring U.S. Troops Home?" *Foreign Policy* 113 (Winter): 72–85.

———. (1999) "Defense and Foreign Policy: The Budget Cuts Are Going Too Far," *Brookings Review* 17 (Winter): 22–25.

———. (2000) "Doing It Right," *Brookings Review* 18 (Fall): 34–37.

O'HANLON, MICHAEL, AND CAROL GRAHAM. (1997) *A Half Penny on the Federal Dollar: The Future of Development Aid.* Washington, DC: Brookings Institution Press.

O'HANLON, MICHAEL, AND NINA KAMP. (2005) "Afghanistan Index: Tracking Variables of Reconstruction and Security in Post-Taliban Afghanistan," the Brookings Institution, 15 September (www.didgah.de/English/Afghanistan/afghanistanindex.pdf).

———. (2006) "Iraq Index: Tracking Variables of Reconstruction and Security in Post-Saddam Iraq," the Brookings Institution, 16 November (www.brookings.edu/fp/saban/iraq/index.pdf).

O'HEFFERNAN, PATRICK. (1991) *Mass Media and American Foreign Policy: Insider Perspectives on Global Journalism and the Foreign Policy Process.* Norwood, NJ: Ablex.

OBERDORFER, DON. (1993) "U.S. Had Covert Plan to Oust Iraq's Saddam," *Washington Post,* 20 January, p. A4.

OBERDORFER, DON, AND HELEN DEWAR. (1987) "The Capitol Hill Broth Is Being Seasoned by a Lot of Cooks," *Washington Post National Weekly Edition,* 26 October, p. 12.

OLSON, MANCUR. (1965) *The Logic of Collective Action.* Cambridge, MA: Harvard University Press.

———. (1982) *The Rise and Decline of Nations.* New Haven, CT: Yale University Press.

OMESTAD, THOMAS. (1992–1993) "Why Bush Lost," *Foreign Policy* 89 (Winter): 70–81.

———. (1996–1997) "Foreign Policy and Campaign '96," *Foreign Policy* 105 (Winter): 37–54.

ORGANSKI, A. F. K., AND JACEK KUGLER. (1980) *The War Ledger.* Chicago: University of Chicago Press.

ORME, JOHN. (1997–1998) "The Utility of Force in a World of Scarcity," *International Security* 22 (Winter): 138–167.

ORNSTEIN, NORMAN J., AND SHIRLEY ELDER. (1978) *Interest Groups, Lobbying, and Policymaking.* Washington, DC: CQ Press.

ORNSTEIN, NORMAN J., ANDREW KOHUT, AND LARRY MCCARTHY. (1988) *The People, the Press, and Politics.* Reading, MA: Addison-Wesley.

OSGOOD, ROBERT E. (1953) *Ideals and Self-Interest in America's Foreign Relations.* Chicago: University of Chicago Press.

OSTROM, CHARLES W., JR., AND BRIAN L. JOB. (1986) "The President and the Political Use of Force," *American Political Science Review* 80 (June): 541–566.

OSTROM, CHARLES W., JR., AND DENNIS M. SIMON. (1985) "Promise and Performance: A Dynamic Model of Presidential Popularity," *American Political Science Review* 79 (June): 334–358.

———. (1989) "The Man in the Teflon Suit: The Environmental Connection, Political Drama, and Popular Support in the Reagan Presidency," *Public Opinion Quarterly* 53 (Fall): 353–387.

OTTAWAY, DAVID B., AND STEVE COLL. (1995) "Streamlining the Nuclear Order," *Washington Post National Weekly Edition,* 24–30 April, pp. 10–11.

OTTAWAY, MARINA, AND THOMAS CAROTHERS. (2004) "The Greater Middle East Initiative: Off to a False Start," *Carnegie Policy Brief,* 29: 1–8.

OWEN, JOHN M. (1994) "How Liberalism Produces the Democratic Peace," *International Security* 19 (Fall): 87–125.

OWENS, MACKUBIN THOMAS. (2003) "Civilian Rumsfeld: Overseeing the Military," *National Review Online,* 17 July (www.nationalreview.com, accessed 3/1/06).

PAARLBERG, ROBERT. (2000) "The Global Food Fight," *Foreign Affairs* 79 (May/June): 24–38.

PAGE, BENJAMIN I. (1994) "Democratic Responsiveness? Untangling the Links Between Public Opinion and Policy," *PS: Political Science and Politics* 27 (March): 25–29.

PAGE, BENJAMIN I., AND JASON BARABAS. (2000) "Foreign Policy Gaps Between Citizens and Leaders," *International Studies Quarterly* 44 (September): 339–364.

PAGE, BENJAMIN I., AND RICHARD A. BRODY. (1972) "Policy Voting and the Electoral Process: The Vietnam War Issue," *American Political Science Review* 66 (September): 979–995.

PAGE, BENJAMIN I, AND ROBERT Y. SHAPIRO. (1992) *The Rational Public.* Chicago: University of Chicago Press.

PAGE, BENJAMIN I., ROBERT SHAPIRO, AND GLENN R. DEMPSEY. (1987) "What Moves Public Opinion?" *American Political Science Review* 81 (March): 23–43.

PAIGE, GLENN D. (1972) "Comparative Case Analysis of Crises Decisions: Korea and Cuba," in *International Crises: Insights from Behavioral Research,* Charles F. Hermann, ed. New York: Free Press, pp. 41–55.

PANT, HARSH V. (2005) "Donald Rumsfeld: A New Phase in Civil-Military Relations in U.S," Observer Research Foundation (www.observerindia.com/analysis/A195.htm, accessed 11/3/06).

PAPE, ROBERT A. (1997) "Why Economic Sanctions Do Not Work," *International Security* 22 (Fall): 90–136.

———. (1998) "Why Economic Sanctions Still Do Not Work," *International Security* 23 (Summer): 66–77.

———. (2005) "Soft Balancing Against the United States," *International Security* 30 (Summer): 7–45.

PARACHINI, JOHN V. (1997) "U.S. Senate Ratification of the CWC: Lessons for the CTBT," *Nonproliferation Review* 5 (Fall): 62–72.

PARENTI, MICHAEL. (1969) *The Anti-Communist Impulse*. New York: Random House.

———. (1981) "We Hold These Myths to Be Self-Evident," *The Nation* 232 (April): 425–429.

———. (1986) *Inventing Reality*. New York: St. Martin's.

———. (1988) *Democracy for the Few*, 5th ed. New York: St. Martin's.

PARRY, ROBERT, AND PETER KORNBLUH. (1988) "Iran-Contra's Untold Story," *Foreign Policy* 72 (Fall): 3–30.

PASTOR, ROBERT A., ed. (1999) *A Century's Journey: How the Great Powers Shape the World*. New York: Basic Books.

———. (1999) "The Great Powers in the Twentieth Century: From Dawn to Dusk," in *A Century's Journey: How the Great Powers Shape the World*, Robert A. Pastor, ed. New York: Basic Books, pp. 1–31.

———. (2004) "North America's Second Decade," *Foreign Affairs*, 83 (1): 124–135.

PATERSON, THOMAS G. (1979) *On Every Front: The Making of the Cold War*. New York: Norton.

PATTERSON, BRADLEY. (2000) *The White House Staff: Inside the West Wing and Beyond*. Washington, DC: Brookings Institution Press.

PAUL, T. V. (2005) "Soft Balancing in the Age of U.S. Primacy," *International Security* 30 (Summer): 46–71.

PAYASLIAN, SIMON. (1996) *U.S. Foreign Economic and Military Aid: The Reagan and Bush Administrations*. Lanham, MD: University Press of America.

PAYNE, RICHARD J. (1996) *The Clash with Distant Cultures: Values, Interests, and Force in American Foreign Policy*. Albany, NY: State University of New York Press.

PEARLSTEIN, STEVEN. (1994) "The Hill Shines a Light on the Shadow Pentagon," *Washington Post National Weekly Edition,* 5–11 August, p. 31.

PEARSON, W. ROBERT. (2005) "Our Diverse Department of State," *State Magazine* 49 (June): 2.

PECKENPAUGH, JASON. (2001) "State Department Will Not Privatize Foreign Buildings Office," *Government Executive,* 23 March (www.govexec.com/dailyfed/0301/032301p1.htm, accessed 11/3/06).

THE PENTAGON PAPERS as published by the *New York Times*. (1971) Toronto: Bantam Books.

PERLEZ, JANE. (1999) "With Berger in Catbird Seat, Albright's Star Dims," *New York Times,* 14 December, p. A1.

———. (2001) "Washington Memo: Divergent Voices Heard in Bush Foreign Policy," *New York Times,* 12 March, p. A1.

PERLMUTTER, DAVID D. (1998) *Photojournalism and Foreign Policy: Icons of Outrage in International Crises*. Boulder, CO: Praeger.

PERRY, JAMES M. (1989) "Reagan's Last Scene: Blaming the 'Iron Triangle' for U.S. Budget Deficit Draws Mixed Reviews," *Wall Street Journal,* 5 January, p. A12.

PETERSON, PAUL E. (1994) "The President's Dominance in Foreign Policy Making," *Political Science Quarterly* 109 (Summer): 215–234.

PETERSON, PETER G. (1999) "Gray Dawn: The Global Aging Crisis," *Foreign Affairs* 78 (January/February): 42–55.

PEW RESEARCH CENTER FOR THE PEOPLE AND THE PRESS. (1997) *America's Place in the World II*. Washington, DC: Pew Research Center.

———. (2000) *Campaign 2000 Typology Survey*. Washington, DC: Pew Research Center.

———. (2004) *Foreign Policy Attitudes Now Driven by 9/11 and Iraq*. Washington, DC: Pew Research Center.

———. (2006a) *Commentary: Bush's Concern Over Isolationism Reflects More than Just Rhetoric*. Washington, DC: Pew Research Center.

———. (2006b) *Pew Global Attitudes Project*. Washington, DC: Pew Research Center.

PFIFFNER, JAMES P. (1990) "Establishing the Bush Presidency," *Public Administration Review* 50 (January/February): 64–73.

———. (1992) "The President and the Postreform Congress," in *The Postreform Congress,* Roger H. Davidson, ed. New York: St. Martin's, pp. 211–232.

PHILLIPS, KEVIN. (2004) *American Dynasty: Aristocracy, Fortune, and the Politics of Deceit in the House of Bush.* New York: Viking.

PIANIN, ERIC. (1999) "How Much Longer Can This Last," *Washington Post Weekly Edition,* 31 May, p. 11.

PIERRE, ANDREW, AND SAHR CONWAY-LANZ. (1994–1995) "Desperate Measures: Arms Producers in a Buyer's Market," *Harvard International Review* 17 (Winter): 12–15, 70–72.

PIKE, JOHN. (1996) "Intelligence Agency Budgets: Commission Recommends No Release but Releases Them Anyway," FAS Intelligence Resource Program, March 14 (www.fas.org/irp/commission/budget.htm, accessed 12/3/06).

PILAT, JOSEPH F., AND WALTER F. KIRCHNER. (1995) "The Technological Promise of Counterproliferation," *Washington Quarterly* 18 (Winter): 153–166.

PILLAR, PAUL R. (2006) "Intelligence, Policy, and the War in Iraq," *Foreign Affairs* 85, 2 (March/April): 15–27.

PINCUS, WALTER. (1985) "The Military's New, Improved 'Revolving Door,'" *Washington Post National Weekly Edition,* 18 March, p. 33.

———. (1994) "A Highflier, but Still Mired in the Cold War," *Washington Post National Weekly Edition,* 15–21 August.

———. (2001) "Intelligence Shakeup Would Boost CIA." *Washington Post,* 8 November, p. A1.

———. (2005a) "CIA to Remain Coordinator of Overseas Spying," *Washington Post,* 13 October (www.washingtonpost.com, accessed 3/8/06).

———. (2005b) "Counterterrorism Center Awaits Presidential Action," *Washington Post,* 3 June (www.washingtonpost.com, accessed 6/25/06).

———. (2005c) "CIA Spies Get a New Home Base," *Washington Post,* 14 October (www.washingtonpost.com, accessed 3/8/06).

———. (2006) "Pentagon Agency's Contracts Reviewed," *Washington Post,* 3 March (www.washingtonpost.com, accessed 3/3/06).

PINCUS, WALTER, AND DAN EGGEN. (2006) "325,000 Names on Terrorism List," *Washington Post,* 15 February (www.washingtonpost.com, accessed 6/25/06).

PINE, ART. (1994) "Perry's Steady Hand Stands Out on Foreign Policy Team," *Los Angeles Times,* 29 May.

PIPES, RICHARD. (1995) "What to Do About the CIA," *Commentary* 99 (March): 36–43.

POMPER, GERALD M. (1968) *Elections in America: Control and Influence in Democratic Politics.* New York: Dodd, Mead.

———. (1989) "The Presidential Election," in *The Election of 1988: Reports and Interpretations,* Gerald M. Pomper et al., eds. Chatham, NJ: Chatham House, pp. 129–152.

PORTER, BRUCE D. (1992) "A Country Instead of a Cause: Russian Foreign Policy in the Post-Soviet Era," *Washington Quarterly* 15 (Summer): 41–56.

PORTER, ROGER B. (1983) "Economic Advice to the President: From Eisenhower to Reagan," *Political Science Quarterly* 98 (Fall): 403–426.

POSEN, BARRY R. (2001/02) "The Struggle against Terrorism: Grand Strategy, Strategy, and Tactics." *International Security* 26 (Winter): 39–55.

POSEN, BARRY R., AND ANDREW L. ROSS. (1996–1997) "Competing Visions for U.S. Grand Strategy," *International Security* 21 (Winter): 5–53.

———. (1997) "Competing U.S. Grand Strategies," in *Eagle Adrift: American Foreign Policy at the End of the Century,* Robert J. Lieber, ed. New York: Longman, pp. 100–134.

POSNER, RICHARD A. (2000) *An Affair of State: The Investigation, Impeachment, and Trial of President Clinton.* Cambridge, MA: Harvard University Press.

POSTOL, THEODORE A. (1991–1992) "Lessons of the Gulf Experience with Patriot," *International Security* 16 (Winter): 119–171.

POVICH, ELAINE S. (2001) "Terrorist Attacks: Quick Vote on Use of Force." *Newsday,* 15 September, p. W10.

POWELL, COLIN L. (1992–1993) "U.S. Forces: Challenges Ahead," *Foreign Affairs* 71 (Winter): 32–45.

———. (1995) *My American Journey: An Autobiography.* New York: Random House.

POWELL, COLIN, JOHN LEHMAN, WILLIAM ODOM, SAMUEL HUNTINGTON, AND RICHARD KOHN. (1994) "An Exchange on

Civil-Military Relations," *National Interest* 36 (Summer): 23–31.

POWLICK, PHILIP J. (1991) "The Attitudinal Bases for Responsiveness to Public Opinion Among American Foreign Policy Officials," *Journal of Conflict Resolution* 35 (December): 611–641.

PRADOS, JOHN. (1991) *Keepers of the Keys: A History of the National Security Council from Truman to Bush.* New York: William Morrow.

———. (1996) "No Reform Here," *Bulletin of the Atomic Scientists* 52 (September–October): 55–59.

PRESTON, THOMAS. (1997) "Following the Leader: The Impact of U.S. Presidential Style Upon Advisory Group Dynamics, Structure, and Decision," in *Beyond Groupthink: Political Group Dynamics and Foreign Policymaking,* Paul 't Hart, Eric Stern, and Bengt Sundelius, eds. Ann Arbor, MI: University of Michigan Press, pp. 191–248.

———. (2001) *The President and His Inner Circle: Leadership Style and the Advisory Process in Foreign Policy Making.* Columbia, NY: Columbia University Press.

PRESTON, THOMAS, AND MARGARET G. HERMANN. (2004) "Presidential Leadership Style and the Foreign Policy Advisory Process," in *The Domestic Sources of American Foreign Policy: Insights and Evidence,* Eugene R. Wittkopf and James M. McCormick, eds. Lanham, MD: Rowman and Littlefield, pp. 363–380.

PRESTON, THOMAS, AND PAUL 'T HART. (1999) "Understanding and Evaluating Bureaucratic Politics: The Nexus Between Political Leaders and Advisory Systems," *Political Psychology* 20 (March): 49–98.

PRESTOWITZ, CLYDE V., JR. (1992) "Beyond Laissez Faire," *Foreign Policy* 87 (Summer): 67–87.

———. (2003) *Rogue Nation: American Unilateralism and the Failure of Good Intentions.* New York: Basic Books.

PRIEST, DANA. (1992) "Showing Up Where You'd Least Expect," *Washington Post National Weekly Edition,* 27 April–3 May, p. 33.

———. (2000) "A Four-Star Foreign Policy? U.S. Commanders Wield Rising Clout, Autonomy," *Washington Post,* 28 September (www.washingtonpost.com, accessed 1/2/06).

———. (2005a) "An Open Secret," *Washington Post National Weekly Edition,* 3–9 January, p. 30.

———. (2005b) "The CIA's Secret Prisons," *Washington Post National Weekly Edition,* 7–13 November, p. 10.

PRIEST, DANA, AND JOHN MINTZ. (1995) "The Unsinkable Seawolf," *Washington Post National Weekly Edition,* 23–29 October, p. 33.

PRIETO, DANIEL B. (2004) "Ridge's Mixed Legacy on Homeland Security," *Chicago Tribune,* 5 December, sec. 2, 9.

PRINGLE, ROBERT. (1977–1978) "Creeping Irrelevance at Foggy Bottom," *Foreign Policy* 29 (Winter): 128–139.

PROGRAM ON INTERNATIONAL POLICY ATTITUDES. (2001) "Americans on Foreign Aid and World Hunger: A Study of U.S. Public Attitudes," *Executive Summary,* 2 February (www.worldpublicopinion.org/pipa/, accessed 10/29/06).

PRUGH, THOMAS, AND ERIK ASSADOURIAN. (2003) "What Is Sustainability, Anyway?" *World Watch* 16 (September/October): 10–21.

PURDUM, TODD S. (1996) "Facets of Clinton," *New York Times Magazine,* 19 May, pp. 35–41ff.

———. (2003) *A Time of Our Choosing: America's War in Iraq.* New York: Times Books.

PURDUM, TODD S., AND ALLISON MITCHELL. (2001) "Bioterror Drills Warned of Gaps in Preparedness," *New York Times,* 20 October (www.nytimes.com, accessed 10/21/01).

PUTNAM, ROBERT D. (1988) "Diplomacy and Domestic Politics: The Logic of Two-Level Games," *International Organization* 42 (Summer): 427–460.

———. (2000) *Bowling Alone: The Collapse and Revival of American Community.* New York: Simon & Schuster.

QUADRENNIAL DEFENSE REVIEW REPORT. (2001) 30 September.

RABKIN, JEREMY. (1994) "Trading in Our Sovereignty?" *National Review,* 13 June, pp. 34–36, 73.

RADELET, STEVE. (2003) "Bush and Foreign Aid," *Foreign Affairs* 82 (5) (September/October): 104–117.

RANELAGH, JOHN. (1987) *The Agency: The Rise and Decline of the CIA.* New York: Simon & Schuster.

RANGER, ROBIN. (1993) "Theater Missile Defenses: Lessons from British Experiences with Air and Missile Defenses," *Comparative Strategy* 12 (4): 399–413.

RANNEY, AUSTIN. (1983) *Channels of Power.* New York: Basic Books.

RANSOM, HARRY HOWE. (1970) *The Intelligence Establishment.* Cambridge, MA: Harvard University Press.

RAUCH, JONATHAN. (1994) *Demosclerosis: The Silent Killer of American Government.* New York: Times Books.

RAUM, TOM. (2005) "White House Basks in Recent Economic Data," *ABC News,* 22 December (www.abcnews.go.com, accessed 5/26/05).

RAY, JAMES LEE. (1995) *Democracy and International Conflict: An Evaluation of the Democratic Peace Proposition.* Columbia, SC: University of South Carolina Press.

REAGAN, RONALD. (1990) *An American Life.* New York: Simon & Schuster.

REICH, ROBERT B. (1985) "How Much Is Enough?" *New Republic,* 12 and 19 August, pp. 33–37.

REID, HARRY. (2005) "Democrats Raise Key Questions for President Bush on Iraq," *Letter to President George Bush,* 5 October (http://democrats.senate.gov/~dpc/press/05/2005A06425.html, accessed 12/10/06).

REIFENBERG, JAN. (1990) "Economies Built on Arms," *World Press Review* 37 (January): 22–23.

REISCHAUER, EDWIN O. (1968) "Redefining the National Interest: The Vietnam Case," paper presented at the annual meeting of the American Political Science Association, Washington, DC, September 2–7.

RENNER, MICHAEL. (1994) "Monitoring Arms Trade," *World Watch* 7 (May–June): 21–26.

RENSHON, STANLEY A. (1998) *High Hopes: The Clinton Presidency and the Politics of Ambition.* New York: Routledge.

———. (2002) "The World According to George W. Bush: Good Judgment or Cowboy Politics?" in *Good Judgment in Foreign Policy,* Stanley A. Renshon and Deborah Welch Larson, eds. Lanham, MD: Rowman and Littlefield, pp. 271–308.

———. (2003) "Psychoanalytic Assessments of Character and Performance in Presidents and Candidates," in *The Psychological Assessment of Political Leaders,* Jerrold M. Post, ed. Ann Arbor, MI: University of Michigan Press, pp. 105–133.

———. (2004) *In His Father's Shadow: The Transformations of George W. Bush.* New York: Palgrave Macmillan.

REVKIN, ANDREW C. (2004) "U.S. Report Turns Focus to Greenhouse Gases," *New York Times* on the Web, 26 August (www.nytimes.com, accessed 8/26/04).

REYNOLDS, DAVID, ed. (1994) *The Origins of the Cold War in Europe: International Perspectives.* New Haven, CT: Yale University Press.

RHODES, EDWARD. (1994) "Do Bureaucratic Politics Matter: Some Disconfirming Findings from the Case of the U.S. Navy," *World Politics* 47 (October): 1–41.

RICE, CONDOLEEZZA. (2000) "Promoting the National Interest," *Foreign Affairs* 79 (January/February): 45–62.

RICKS, THOMAS E. (1997) "The Widening Gap Between the Military and Society," *Atlantic Monthly* 280 (July): 66–78.

———. (2001a) "Time for a Military Shake-Up." *Washington Post National Weekly Edition,* 15–21 October, p. 29.

———. (2001b) "U.S. Arms Unmanned Aircraft," *Washington Post,* 18 October, p. A1.

———. (2001c) "Bull's Eye War: Pinpoint Bombing Shifts Role of GI Joe," *Washington Post,* 2 December, p. A1.

RICKS, THOMAS, AND VERNON LOEB. (2001) "Special Open Ground Campaign." *Washington Post,* 19 October, p. A1.

RICKS, THOMAS AND ALAN SIPRESS. (2001) "Attacks Restrained by Political Goals." *Washington Post,* 23 October, p. A1.

RIEBLING, MARK. (1994) *Wedge: The Secret War Between the FBI and CIA.* New York: Knopf.

RIEFF, DAVID. (1999) "A New Age of Liberal Imperialism?" *World Policy Journal* 16 (Summer): 1–10.

RIELLY, JOHN E., ed. (1991) *American Public Opinion and U.S. Foreign Policy 1991.* Chicago: Chicago Council on Foreign Relations.

———, ed. (1995) *American Public Opinion and U.S. Foreign Policy 1995.* Chicago: Chicago Council on Foreign Relations.

———, ed. (1999) *American Public Opinion and U.S. Foreign Policy 1999.* Chicago: Chicago Council on Foreign Relations.

RILEY, STEPHEN P. (1993) "Conclusions," in *The Politics of Global Debt,* Stephen P. Riley, ed. New York: St. Martin's, pp. 189–196.

RIPLEY, RANDALL B., AND GRACE A. FRANKLIN. (1991) *Congress, the Bureaucracy, and Public Policy.* Pacific Grove, CA: Brooks/Cole.

RISEN, JAMES. (2000) "The Clinton Administration's See-No-Evil CIA," *New York Times,* 10 September, p. 5.

———. (2001a) "Clinton Creates Post to Protect Nation's Secrets," *New York Times,* 5 January, p. 1.

———. (2001b) "Gaps in CIA's Ames Case May Be Filled by FBI's Own Spy Case," *New York Times,* 20 February, p. 16.

———. (2001c) "Moles Often Burrow Deeper than Spy Hunters Can Dig," *New York Times,* 25 February, p. 12.

———. (2002) "After Criticism, CIA Eases Policy on Recruiting Informers," *New York Times,* 19 July, p. A13.

RISSE-KAPPEN, THOMAS. (1991) "Public Opinion, Domestic Structure, and Foreign Policy in Liberal Democracies," *World Politics* 43 (July): 479–512.

ROBB, CHARLES S. (1997) "Challenging the Assumptions of U.S. Military Strategy," *Washington Quarterly* 20 (Spring): 115–131.

———. (1999) "Star Wars II," *Washington Quarterly* 22 (Winter): 81–86.

ROBINSON, JAMES A. (1972) "Crisis: An Appraisal of Concepts and Theories," in *International Crises: Insights from Behavioral Research,* Charles F. Hermann, ed. New York: Free Press, pp. 20–35.

ROBISON, SAMUEL. (2006) "George W. Bush and the Vulcans: Leader Advisor Relations and America's Response to the 9/11 Attacks," in *Beliefs and Leadership in World Politics: Methods and Applications of Operational Code Analysis,* Mark Schafer and Stephen G. Walker, eds. New York: Palgrave Macmillan.

ROCA, SERGIO. (1987) "Economic Sanctions Against Cuba," in *The Utility of International Economic Sanctions,* David Leyton-Brown, ed. New York: St. Martin's, pp. 87–104.

ROCKMAN, BERT A. (1981) "America's Departments of State: Irregular and Regular Syndromes of Policymaking," *American Political Science Review* 75 (December): 911–927.

RODMAN, PETER W. (1999) "His Own Fault," *National Review,* 22 November, pp. 18ff.

RODRIK, DANI. (1997) *Has Globalization Gone Too Far?* Washington, DC: Institute for International Economics.

ROGERS, WILLIAM D. (1979) "Who's in Charge of Foreign Policy?" *New York Times Magazine,* 9 September, pp. 44–50.

ROGOW, ARNOLD A. (1963) *James Forrestal: A Study in Personality, Politics, and Policy.* New York: Macmillan.

ROHDE, DAVID. (1994) "Partisan Leadership and Congressional Assertiveness in Foreign and Defense Policy," in *The New Politics of American Foreign Policy,* David Deese, ed. New York: St. Martin's, pp. 76–101.

ROMAN, PETER J., AND DAVID W. TARR. (1998) "The Joint Chiefs of Staff: From Service Parochialism to Jointness," *Political Science Quarterly* 113 (Spring): 91–111.

ROMANO, LOIS, AND GEORGE LARDNER, JR. (1999a) "The Unlikely Candidate," *Washington Post National Weekly Edition,* 9 August, pp. 6–8.

———. (1999b) "A Son Follows in a Famous Father's Footsteps," *Washington Post National Weekly Edition,* 9 August, pp. 9–11.

ROOSEVELT, ANN. (2001) "Combating Terrorism, Other Threats: Lawmakers Boost Anti-Terror Funds for '02 Defense Budget." *White House Weekly,* 11 September, p. 1.

ROSATI, JEREL A. (1993) "Jimmy Carter, a Man Before His Time? The Emergence and Collapse of the First Post–Cold War Presidency," *Presidential Studies Quarterly* 23 (Summer): 459–476.

———. (1981) "Developing a Systematic Decision-Making Framework," *World Politics* 33 (January): 234–252.

ROSE, GIDEON. (2000–2001) "Democracy Promotion and American Foreign Policy," *International Security* 25 (Winter): 186–203.

ROSECRANCE, RICHARD. (1990) *America's Economic Resurgence: A Bold New Strategy.* New York: Harper and Row.

ROSEN, STEVEN J., ed. (1973) *Testing the Theory of the Military-Industrial Complex.* Lexington, MA: Heath.

ROSENAU, JAMES N. (1966) "Pre-Theories and Theories of Foreign Policy," in *Approaches to*

Comparative and International Politics, R. Barry Farrell, ed. Evanston, IL: Northwestern University Press, pp. 27–92.

———. (1980) *The Scientific Study of Foreign Policy.* New York: Nichols.

ROSENBERG, ERIC. (2006) "Bush Pushes to Increase Defense Spending; Jump of 7% Would Top Rest of World's Military Budgets," *San Francisco Chronicle,* 12 February (www.sfgate.com, accessed 2/28/06).

ROSENBERG, MILTON J. (1965) "Images in Relation to the Policy Process: American Public Opinion on Cold War Issues," in *International Behavior,* Herbert C. Kelman, ed. New York: Holt, Rinehart, and Winston, pp. 277–336.

ROSENTHAL, URIEL, PAUL 'T HART, AND ALEXANDER LOUZMIN. (1991) "The Bureaupolitics of Crisis Management," *Public Administration* 69: 211–233.

ROSTOW, EUGENE V. (1993) *Toward Managed Peace: The National Security Interests of the United States, 1759 to the Present.* New Haven, CT: Yale University Press.

ROTHGEB, JOHN M. (2001) *U.S. Trade Policy: Balancing Economic Dreams and Political Realities.* Washington, DC: CQ Press.

ROTHKOPF, DAVID J. (2005a) "Inside the Committee that Runs the World," *Foreign Policy* 147 (March/April): 30–40.

———. (2005b) *Running the World.* New York: PublicAffairs.

———. (2006) "End of the Cheney Era," *Washington Post National Weekly Edition,* 20–26 March, pp. 22–23.

ROWE, EDWARD T. (1974) "Aid and Coups d'Etat: Aspects of the Impact of American Military Assistance Programs in the Less Developed Countries," *International Studies Quarterly* 18 (June): 239–255.

RUBIN, BARRY. (1985) *Secrets of State: The State Department and the Struggle Over U.S. Foreign Policy.* New York: Oxford University Press.

RUDALEVIGE, ANDREW. (2005) *The New Imperial Presidency: Renewing Presidential Power after Watergate.* Ann Arbor, MI: University of Michigan Press.

RUGGIE, JOHN GERARD. (1992) "Multilateralism: The Anatomy of an Institution," *International Organization* 46 (Summer): 561–598.

RUSSETT, BRUCE. (1998) "A Community of Peace: Democracy, Interdependence, and International Organization," in *The Global Agenda: Issues and Perspectives,* 5th ed., Charles W. Kegley, Jr., and Eugene R. Wittkopf, eds. New York: McGraw-Hill, pp. 241–251.

RUSSETT, BRUCE, AND THOMAS W. GRAHAM. (1988) "Public Opinion and National Security Policy Relationships and Impact," in *Handbook of War Studies,* Manus Midlarsky, ed. London: Allen and Unwin, pp. 239–257.

RUSSETT, BRUCE, THOMAS HARTLEY, AND SHOON MURRAY. (1994) "The End of the Cold War, Attitude Change, and the Politics of Defense Spending," *PS: Political Science and Politics* 27 (March): 17–21.

RUSSETT, BRUCE, AND JOHN ONEAL. (2000) *Triangulating Peace: Democracy, Interdependence, and International Organization.* New York: Norton.

RUTTAN, VERNON W. (1996) *United States Development Assistance Policy: The Domestic Politics of Foreign Economic Aid.* Baltimore, MD: Johns Hopkins University Press.

SACHS, JEFFREY. (1989) "Making the Brady Plan Work," *Foreign Affairs* 68 (Summer): 87–104.

———. (2001) "The Strategic Significance of Global Inequality," *Washington Quarterly* 24 (Summer): 187–198.

———. (2005) "The Development Challenge," *Foreign Affairs* 84 (March/April): 78–90.

SACHS, JEFFREY, AND FELIPE LARRAIN. (1999) "Why Dollarization Is More Straitjacket than Salvation," *Foreign Policy* 116 (Fall): 80–91.

SACHS, SUSAN. (2004) "Poll Finds Hostility Hardening toward U.S. Policies," *New York Times,* 17 March (www.nytimes.com, accessed 6/12/06).

SAFIRE, WILLIAM. (1990) "Forming Public Opinion," *New York Times,* 10 December, p. A15.

———. (2002) "The 'Big Ear' Gone Deaf," *New York Times,* 13 June, p. A35.

SAGOFF, MARK. (2001) "Do We Consume Too Much?" in *The Global Agenda: Issues and Perspectives,* 6th ed., Charles W. Kegley, Jr., and Eugene R. Wittkopf, eds. Boston: McGraw-Hill, pp. 404–419.

SAHN, DAVID E., PAUL A. DOROSH, AND STEPHEN D. YOUNGER. (1999) *Structural Adjustment*

Reconsidered: Economic Policy and Poverty in Africa. London: Cambridge University Press.

SANDERS, JERRY W. (1983) *Peddlers of Crisis: The Committee on the Present Danger and the Politics of Containment.* Boston: South End Press.

SANDMAN, PETER M., DAVID M. RUBIN, AND DAVID B. SACHSMAN. (1982) *Media,* 3rd ed. Englewood Cliffs, NJ: Prentice Hall.

SANGER, DAVID E. (1994) "Who Won in the Korean Deal," *New York Times,* 23 October, p. E3.

———. (1999) "America Finds It Lonely at the Top," *New York Times,* 18 July, pp. 1, 4.

SANGER, DAVID E., AND FRANK BRUNI. (2001) "In His First Days, Bush Plans Review of Clinton's Acts," *New York Times,* 14 January, p. A1.

SCHAFER, MARK, AND SCOTT CRICHLOW. (1996) "Antecedents of Groupthink: A Quantitative Study," *Journal of Conflict Resolution* 40: 415–435.

SCHATTSCHNEIDER, E. E. (1960) *The Semisovereign People.* New York: Holt, Rinehart, and Winston.

SCHELL, JONATHAN. (1982) *The Fate of the Earth.* New York: Avon Books.

———. (1984) *The Abolition.* New York: Knopf.

———. (1999) "The Unthinkable," *The Nation* 269 (8 November): 7ff.

SCHELLING, THOMAS C. (1966) *Arms and Influence.* New Haven, CT: Yale University Press.

SCHERLEN, RENEE G. (1998) "NAFTA and Beyond: The Politics of Trade in the Post–Cold War Period," in *After the End: Making U.S. Foreign Policy in the Post–Cold War World,* James M. Scott, ed. Durham, NC: Duke University Press, pp. 358–385.

SCHLESINGER, ARTHUR, JR. (1958) *The Coming of the New Deal.* Boston: Houghton Mifflin.

———. (1967) "Origins of the Cold War," *Foreign Affairs* 46 (October): 22–52.

———. (1973) *The Imperial Presidency.* Boston: Houghton Mifflin.

———. (1977) "America: Experiment or Destiny?" *American Historical Review* 82 (June): 505–522.

———. (1986) *The Cycles of American History.* Boston: Houghton Mifflin.

———. (1989) "The Legislative-Executive Balance in International Affairs: The Intentions of the Framers," *Washington Quarterly* 12 (Winter): 99–107.

———. (1992) *The Disuniting of America: Reflections on a Multicultural Society.* New York: Norton.

———. (1997) "Rating the Presidents: Washington to Clinton." *Political Science Quarterly* 122 (Summer): 179–190.

———. (1998) "So Much for the Imperial Presidency," *New York Times,* 3 August (www.nytimes.com, accessed 5/15/06).

———. (2004a) *The Imperial Presidency.* New York: First Mariner Books/Houghton Mifflin.

———. (2004b) "The Imperial Presidency Redux," in *War and the American Presidency.* New York: W. W. Norton, pp. 45–67.

SCHMITT, ERIC. (1999) "Bombs Are Smart. People Are Smarter," *Washington Post National Weekly Edition* 4 July, p. 6.

———. (2001a) "Helms Urges Foreign Aid Be Handled by Charities," *New York Times,* 12 January.

———. (2001b) "Cheney Draws on Seasoned Veterans to Support His New Role," *New York Times,* 3 February, p. A1.

SCHNEIDER, BARRY R. (1989) "Invitation to a Nuclear Beheading," in *The Nuclear Reader,* 2nd ed., Charles W. Kegley, Jr., and Eugene R. Wittkopf, eds. New York: St. Martin's, pp. 291–301.

SCHNEIDER, WILLIAM. (1982) "Bang-Bang Television: The New Superpower," *Public Opinion* 5 (April/May): 13–15.

———. (1984) "Public Opinion," in *The Making of America's Soviet Policy,* Joseph S. Nye, Jr., ed. New Haven, CT: Yale University Press, pp. 11–35.

———. (1990) "The In-Box President," *Atlantic Monthly* 265 (January): 34–43.

SCHNEIDER, WILLIAM, AND L. A. LEWIS. (1985) "Views on the News," *Public Opinion* 8 (August/September): 6–11, 58–59.

SCHONBERG, KARL K. (2004) "Global Security and Legal Restraint: Reconsidering War Powers after September 11," *Political Science Quarterly* 119 (Spring 2004): 115–142.

SCHRAEDER, PETER J., ed. (1992) *Intervention into the 1990s: U.S. Foreign Policy in the Third World.* Boulder, CO: Rienner.

———. (1998) "From Ally to Orphan: Understanding U.S. Policy Toward Somalia After the Cold War," in *After the End: Making U.S. Foreign Policy in the*

Post–Cold War World, James M. Scott, ed. Durham, NC: Duke University Press, pp. 330–357.

SCHWARTZ, HERMAN M. (1994) *States Versus Markets: History, Geography, and the Development of the International Political Economy.* New York: St. Martin's.

SCHWARTZ, STEPHEN. (2000) "Outmaneuvered, Outgunned, and Out of View," *Bulletin of the Atomic Scientists* 56 (January/February): 24–31.

SCHWARZ, BENJAMIN. (1998) "The Enduring Myth of a Liberal America," *World Policy Journal* 15 (Fall): 69–77.

SCHWARZ, BENJAMIN, AND CHRISTOPHER LAYNE. (2002) "A Grand New Strategy," *Atlantic Monthly* 289 (January): 38–42.

SCHWEIZER, PETER. (1993) *Friendly Spies: How America's Allies Are Using Economic Espionage to Steal Our Secrets.* New York: Atlantic Monthly Press.

SCHYDLOWSKY, DANIEL. (1995) *Structural Adjustment: Retrospect and Prospect.* Westport, CT: Greenwood.

SCIOLINO, ELAINE. (1995) "Global Concerns? Not in Congress," *New York Times,* 15 January, p. 1.

———. (2000) "Woman in the News: Condoleezza Rice," *New York Times,* 18 December, p. A1.

SCIOLINO, ELAINE, AND TODD S. PURDUM. (1995) "Gore Is No Typical Vice President in the Shadows," *New York Times,* 19 February, pp. 1, 16.

SCOTT, ANDREW M. (1969) "The Department of State: Formal Organization and Informal Culture," *International Studies Quarterly* 13 (March): 1–18.

SCOTT, JAMES M. (1996) *Deciding to Intervene: The Reagan Doctrine and American Foreign Policy.* Durham, NC: Duke University Press.

———. (1997a) "Trade and Tradeoffs: The Clinton Administration and the 'Big Emerging Markets' Strategy," *Futures Research Quarterly* 13 (Summer): 37–66.

———. (1997b) "In the Loop: Congressional Influence in American Foreign Policy," *Journal of Political and Military Sociology* 25 (Summer): 47–76.

———. (1998a) "Competing for Markets: The Dilemmas of the 'Big Emerging Markets' Strategy," *International Studies Association/Midwest Annual Conference.* Chicago, Illinois.

———, ed. (1998b) *After the End: Making U.S. Foreign Policy in the Post–Cold War World.* Durham, NC: Duke University Press.

SCOTT, JAMES M., AND RALPH G. CARTER. (1999) "Acting on the Hill: Congressional Assertiveness in U.S. Foreign Policy," *International Studies Association Annual Convention.* Washington, DC, February 16–20.

———. (2002) "Acting on the Hill: Congressional Assertiveness in U.S. Foreign Policy," *Congress and the Presidency* 29 (Autumn): 151–170.

SCOTT, PETER DALE. (1998) *Cocaine Politics: Drugs, Armies, and the CIA in Central America.* Berkeley: University of California Press.

SEABURY, PAUL. (1973) *The United States in World Affairs.* New York: McGraw-Hill.

SEMMEL, ANDREW K. (1983) "Evolving Patterns of U.S. Security Assistance 1950–1980," in *Perspectives on American Foreign Policy,* Charles W. Kegley, Jr., and Eugene R. Wittkopf, eds. New York: St. Martin's, pp. 79–95.

SEN, AMARTYA. (1999) *Development as Freedom.* New York: Knopf.

SERABIAN, JOHN A., JR. (2000) "Statement for the Record before the Joint Economic Committee on Cyber Threats and the U.S. Economy," 23 February (www.odci.gov/cia/public_affairs/speeches/2000/cyberthreats_022300.html, accessed 10/29/06).

SERFATY, SIMON. (1972) *The Elusive Enemy: American Foreign Policy Since World War II.* Boston: Little, Brown.

———. (1978) "Brzezinski: Play It Again, Zbig," *Foreign Policy* 32 (Fall): 3–21.

———. (2002) "The New Normalcy," *Washington Quarterly* 25 (Spring): 209–219.

SHAIN, YOSSI. (1994–1995) "Ethnic Diasporas and U.S. Foreign Policy," *Political Science Quarterly* 109 (Winter): 811–841.

SHALOM, STEPHEN ROSSKAMM, ed. (1993) *Imperial Alibis: Rationalizing U.S. Intervention After the Cold War.* Boston: South End Press.

SHANE, SCOTT. (2005) "Behind Power, One Principle as Bush Pushes Prerogatives," *New York Times,* 17 December (www.nytimes.com, accessed 12/17/05).

SHANKER, THOM, AND SCOTT SHANE. (2006) "Elite Troops Get Expanded Role on Intelligence,"

New York Times, 8 March (www.nytimes.com, accessed 3/8/06).

SHANNON, ELAINE. (1995) "Skirts and Daggers," *Time,* 12 June, p. 46–47.

SHANNON, THOMAS RICHARD. (1989) *An Introduction to the World-System Perspective.* Boulder, CO: Westview Press.

SHAPIRO, ROBERT Y., AND HARPREET MAHAJAN. (1986) "Gender Differences in Policy Preferences: A Summary of Trends from the 1960s to the 1980s," *Public Opinion Quarterly* 50 (Spring): 42–61.

SHAPIRO, ROBERT Y., AND BENJAMIN I. PAGE. (1988) "Foreign Policy and the Rational Public," *Journal of Conflict Resolution* 32 (June): 211–247.

SHEEHAN, JIM. (1998) "The Case Against Kyoto," *SIAS Review* 18 (Summer/Fall): 121–133.

SHENON, PHILIP. (1999) "In Protest of Clinton Action, Senator Blocks Nominations," *New York Times,* 9 June, p. 20.

———. (2003) "Homeland Security Dept. Planning 7 Offices Overseas to Screen Visas," *New York Times,* 7 October, p. A19.

SHIFTER, MICHAEL. (2006) "In Search of Hugo Chavez," *Foreign Affairs* 85 (May/June): 45–59.

SHILLER, ROBERT J. (2001) "Exuberant Reporting," *Harvard International Review* 23 (Spring): 60–65.

SHIRLEY, EDWARD G. (1998) "Can't Anybody Here Play this Game?" *Atlantic Monthly* 281 (February): 45–55.

SHULSKY, ABRAM N., AND GARY J. SCHMITT. (1994–1995) "The Future of Intelligence," *National Interest* 38 (Winter): 63–72.

SHULTZ, RICHARD H., JR. (2004) "Showstoppers: The Incompetent Clinton Administration's Perspective in Terrorism," *Weekly Standard,* 26 January (www.freerepublic.com/focus/f-news/1065193/posts, accessed 12/1/06).

SICHERMAN, HARVEY. (1997) "The Strange Death of Dual Containment," *Orbis* 41 (Spring): 223–240.

SICK, GARY. (1999) "Iran Has Changed, Why Can't We?" *Washington Post National Weekly Edition,* 5 August, p. 23.

SIGAL, LEON V. (1992–1993) "The Last Cold War Election," *Foreign Affairs* 71 (Winter): 1–15.

SILVA, MARK. (2006a) "$70 Billion Sought for War Costs," *Chicago Tribune,* 3 February, sec. 1, pp. 1, 18.

———. (2006b) "Bush Team Imposes Thick Veil of Secrecy," *Chicago Tribune,* 30 April, sec. 1, pp. 1, 11.

———. (2006c) "Selective Secrecy by Bush Debated," *Chicago Tribune,* 1 May, sec. 1, pp. 1, 16.

SILVERSTEIN, GORDON. (1994) "Judicial Enhancement of Executive Power," in *The President, the Congress, and the Making of Foreign Policy,* Paul E. Peterson, ed. Norman, OK: University of Oklahoma Press, pp. 23–45.

———. (1996) *Imbalance of Powers: Constitutional Interpretation and the Making of American Foreign Policy.* New York: Oxford University Press.

SIMES, DIMITRI K. (2003) "America's Imperial Dilemma," *Foreign Affairs* 82 (November/December): 91–102.

———. (2003/2004) "Realism: It's High Minded… and It Works," *National Interest* 74 (Winter): 168–172.

SIMON, DENNIS M., AND CHARLES W. OSTROM, JR. (1988) "The Politics of Prestige: Popular Support and the Modern Presidency," *Presidential Studies Quarterly* 18 (Fall): 741–758.

SIMON, HERBERT A. (1957) *Administrative Behavior.* New York: Macmillan.

———. (1985) "Human Nature in Politics: The Dialogue of Psychology with Political Science," *American Political Science Review* 79 (June): 293–304.

SIMPSON, SMITH. (1967) *Anatomy of the State Department.* Boston: Houghton Mifflin.

SINCLAIR, BARBARA. (1993) "Congressional Party Leaders in the Foreign and Defense Policy Arena," in *Congress Resurgent: Foreign and Defense Policy on Capitol Hill,* Randall B. Ripley and James M. Lindsay, eds. Ann Arbor, MI: University of Michigan Press, pp. 207–231.

SINGER, J. DAVID. (1991) "Peace in the Global System: Displacement, Interregnum, or Transformation?" in *The Long Postwar Peace,* Charles W. Kegley, Jr., ed. New York: HarperCollins, pp. 56–84.

SINGER, MAX, AND AARON WILDAVSKY. (1993) *The Real World Order: Zones of Peace/Zones of Turmoil.* Chatham, NJ: Chatham House.

SINGH, JASWANT. (1999) "Against Nuclear Apartheid," *Foreign Affairs* 77 (September/October): 41–52.

SIPRESS, ALAN, AND VERNON LOEB. (2001) "The CIA's Stealth War: U.S. Covert Efforts Include Winning the Loyalty of Taliban Defectors," *Washington Post National Weekly Edition,* 15–21 October, p. 6.

SITARZ, DANIEL, ed. (1993) *Agenda 21: The Earth Summit Strategy to Save Our Planet.* Boulder, CO: Earthpress.

SKIDMORE, DAVID. (1993–1994) "Carter and the Failure of Foreign Policy Reform," *Political Science Quarterly* 108 (Winter): 699–729.

SKLAIR, LESLIE. (1991) *Sociology of the Global System.* Baltimore, MD: Johns Hopkins University Press.

SLOSS, LEON. (1999) *Ballistic Missile Defense Revisited.* Washington, DC: The Atlantic Council.

SMITH, JEAN E. (1989) *The Constitution and American Foreign Policy.* New York: West Publishers.

———. (1992) *George Bush's War.* New York: Henry Holt.

SMITH, MICHAEL JOSEPH. (1987) *Realist Thought from Weber to Kissinger.* Baton Rouge, LA: Louisiana State University Press.

SMITH, R. JEFFREY. (1994a) "The CIA's Ill-Advised Dumping Ground," *Washington Post National Weekly Edition,* 1–7 August, p. 32.

———. (1994b) "Clinton Goes For the Bush Nuclear Plan," *Washington Post National Weekly Edition,* 26 September–2 October, pp. 16–17.

———. (1997) "A Believer No More," *Washington Post National Weekly Edition,* 22–29 December, pp. 6–10.

SMITH, STEVEN. (1994) "Congressional Party Leaders," in *The President, The Congress, and the Making of Foreign Policy,* Paul E. Peterson, ed. Norman, OK: University of Oklahoma Press, pp. 129–157.

SMITH, STEVEN S., AND CHRISTOPHER J. DEERING. (1990) *Committees in Congress,* 2nd ed. Washington, DC: CQ Press.

SMITH, TOM W. (1984) "The Polls: Gender and Attitudes Toward Violence," *Public Opinion Quarterly* 48 (Spring): 384–396.

SMITH, TONY. (1994a) *America's Mission: The United States and the Worldwide Struggle for Democracy in the Twentieth Century.* Princeton, NJ: Princeton University Press.

———. (1994b) "In Defense of Intervention," *Foreign Affairs* 73 (November/December): 34–46.

———. (1994c) "Winning the Peace: Postwar Thinking and the Defeated Confederacy," *World Policy Journal* 11 (Summer): 92–102.

———. (2000) *Foreign Attachments: The Power of Ethnic Groups in the Making of American Foreign Policy.* Cambridge, MA: Harvard University Press.

SMITHSON, AMY E. (1995) "Dateline Washington: Clinton Fumbles the CWC," *Foreign Policy* 99 (Summer): 168–182.

SMYSER, W. R. (1993) "Goodbye, G-7," *Washington Quarterly* 16 (Winter): 15–28.

SNIDAL, DUNCAN. (1985) "The Limits of Hegemonic Stability Theory," *International Organization* 39 (Autumn): 579–615.

———. (1991) "Relative Gains and the Pattern of International Cooperation," *American Political Science Review* 85 (September): 701–726.

SNIFFEN, MICHAEL J., AND JOHN SOLOMAN. (2006) "Secret Court Cases Increase under Bush Administration," *Chicago Tribune,* 5 March, sec. 1, p. 7.

SNOW, DONALD M. (1998) *National Security: Defense Policy for a Changed International Order,* 4th ed. New York: St. Martin's.

SNYDER, JACK. (1991) *Myths of Empire: Domestic Politics and International Ambition.* Ithaca, NY: Cornell University Press.

———. (2003) "Imperial Temptations," *National Interest* 71 (Spring): 29–39.

SOBEL, ANDREW C. (2005) *Political Economy and Global Affairs.* Washington, DC: CQ Press.

SOBEL, RICHARD. (1998a) "The Polls-Trends: United States Intervention in Bosnia," *Public Opinion Quarterly,* (Summer): 250–278.

———. (1998b) "Portraying American Public Opinion Toward the Bosnia Crisis," *Harvard Journal of Press/ Politics* 3 (2): 16–33.

———. (2001) *The Impact of Public Opinion on U.S. Foreign Policy Since Vietnam: Constraining the Colossus.* New York: Oxford University Press.

SOFAER, ABRAHAM D. (1987) "The ABM Treaty: Legal Analysis in the Political Cauldron," *Washington Quarterly* 10 (Autumn): 59–75.

SOLOMON, BURT. (1994) "Though Clinton's Got the Willies … the Fed May Be Doing Him a Favor," *National Journal,* 7 May, pp. 1086–1087.

———. (1997) "Advisers Used to Clinton Time Now Set Their Watches by Bowles," *National Journal,* 18 January, p. 128.

SOPKO, JOHN F. (1996–97) "The Changing Proliferation Threat," *Foreign Policy* 105 (Winter): 3–20.

SORENSEN, THEODORE C. (1963) *Decision Making in the White House: The Olive Branch or the Arrows.* New York: Columbia University Press.

———. (1987–1988) "The President and the Secretary of State," *Foreign Affairs* 66 (Winter): 231–248.

———. (1994) "Foreign Policy in a Presidential Democracy," *Political Science Quarterly* 109 (Summer): 515–528.

SPANIER, JOHN. (1988) *American Foreign Policy Since World War II,* 11th ed. Washington, DC: CQ Press.

———. (1990) *Games Nations Play,* 7th ed. Washington, DC: Congressional Quarterly Press.

SPEAR, JOANNA. (1994–1995) "Beyond the Cold War: Changes in the International Arms Trade," *Harvard International Review* 17 (Winter): 8–11, 70.

SPERO, JOAN EDELMAN. (1990) *The Politics of International Economic Relations,* 4th. ed. New York: St. Martin's.

SPERO, JOAN EDELMAN, AND JEFFREY A. HART. (1997) *The Politics of International Economic Relations,* 5th. ed. New York: St. Martin's.

SPIRO, DAVID E. (1994) "The Insignificance of the Liberal Peace," *International Security* 19 (Fall): 50–86.

———. (1999) *The Hidden Hand of American Hegemony: Petrodollar Recycling and International Markets.* Ithaca, NY: Cornell University Press.

STAGNER, ROSS. (1971) "Personality Dynamics and Social Conflict," in *Conflict Resolution: Contributions of the Behavioral Sciences,* Clagett G. Smith, ed. Notre Dame, IN: University of Notre Dame Press, pp. 98–109.

STARKEY, BRIGID, MARK A. BOYER, AND JONATHAN WILKENFELD. (2005) *Negotiating a Complex World,* 2nd ed. Boulder, CO: Rowman and Littlefield.

STARR, HARVEY. (1984) *Henry Kissinger: Perceptions of International Politics.* Lexington, KY: University Press of Kentucky.

STEDMAN, STEPHEN JOHN. (1992–1993) "The New Interventionists," *Foreign Affairs* 72 (Winter): 1–16.

———. (1995) "Alchemy for a New World Order," *Foreign Affairs* 74 (May/June): 14–20.

STEEL, RONALD. (1994) "The Lure of Detachment," *World Policy Journal* 11 (Fall): 61–69.

STEINBERGER, MICHAEL. (2004) "Misoverestimated," *American Prospect* 15 (4), 1 April (www.prospect.org/print/V15/4/steinberger-m.html, accessed 11/3/06).

STEINBRUNER, JOHN D. (1995) "Reluctant Strategic Alignment: The Need for a New View of National Security," *Brookings Review* 13 (Winter): 5–9.

STERLING-FOLKER, JENNIFER. (1998) "Between a Rock and a Hard Place: Assertive Multilateralism and Post–Cold War U.S. Foreign Policy Making," in *After the End: Making U.S. Foreign Policy in the Post–Cold War World,* James M. Scott, ed. Durham, NC: Duke University Press, pp. 277–304.

STERN, ERIC, AND BERTJAN VERBEEK. (1998) "Whither the Study of Governmental Politics in Foreign Policymaking? A Symposium," *Mershon International Studies Review* 42 (November): 205–210.

STEVENSON, ADLAI E., AND ALTON FRYE. (1989) "Trading with the Communists," *Foreign Affairs* 68 (Spring): 53–71.

STEVENSON, JONATHAN. (1995) *Losing Mogadishu: Testing U.S. Policy in Somalia.* Washington, DC: Naval Institute Press.

STIGLITZ, JOSEPH E. (2003) *The Roaring Nineties: A New History of the World's Most Prosperous Decade.* New York: Norton.

STIMSON, HENRY L., AND MCGEORGE BUNDY. (1947) *On Active Service in Peace and War.* New York: Harper and Row.

STIMSON, JAMES A., MICHAEL B. MACKUEN, AND ROBERT S. ERIKSON. (1994) "Opinion and Policy: A Global View," *PS: Political Science and Politics* 27 (March): 29–35.

STOCKTON, PAUL N. (1993) "Congress and Defense Policy-Making in the Post–Cold War Era," in *Congress Resurgent: Foreign and Defense Policy on Capitol Hill,* Randall B. Ripley and James M. Lindsay, eds. Ann Arbor, MI: University of Michigan Press, pp. 235–259.

————. (1995) "Beyond Micromanagement: Congressional Budgeting for a Post–Cold War Military," *Political Science Quarterly* 110 (Summer): 233–259.

STOESSINGER, JOHN G. (1985) *Crusaders and Pragmatists: Movers of Modern American Foreign Policy.* New York: Norton.

STOKES, BRUCE. (1992–1993) "Organizing to Trade," *Foreign Policy* 89 (Winter): 36–52.

————. (1994) "The American Marketplace Has Gone Global," *National Journal,* 18 June, pp. 1426–1430.

————. (1999–2000) "The New Protectionist Myth," *Foreign Policy* 117 (Winter): 88–102.

————. (2001) "Free Trade-Offs," *Foreign Policy* 124 (May/June): 62–63.

STOKES, BRUCE, AND PAT CHOATE. (2004) "Trade Policy Making: The Changing Context," in *The Domestic Sources of American Foreign Policy: Insights and Evidence,* 4th ed., Eugene R. Wittkopf and James M. McCormick, eds. Lanham, MD: Rowman and Littlefield, pp. 237–246.

STRANGE, SUSAN. (1987) "The Persistent Myth of Lost Hegemony," *International Organization* 41 (Autumn): 551–574.

————. (1998) *Mad Money: When Markets Outgrow Governments.* Ann Arbor, MI: University of Michigan Press.

STREMLAU, JOHN. (1994–1995) "Clinton's Dollar Diplomacy," *Foreign Policy* 97 (Winter): 18–35.

STRINATI, DOMINIC. (1995) *An Introduction to Theories of Popular Culture.* London: Routledge.

STROBEL, WARREN P. (1999) "The CNN Effect: Myth or Reality?" in *The Domestic Sources of American Foreign Policy: Insights and Evidence,* 3rd ed., Eugene R. Wittkopf and James M. McCormick, eds. Landham, MD: Rowman and Littlefield, pp. 85–93.

————. (2000) "The Sound of Silence," *U.S. News and World Report,* 14 February, p. 24.

STRUCK, MYRON. (1985) "A Bumper Crop of Plums: Political Appointments Are Proliferators," *Washington Post National Weekly Edition,* 20 May, p. 31.

SUEDFELD, PETER, RAYMOND S. CORTEEN, AND CARROLL MCCORMICK. (1986) "The Role of Integrative Complexity in Military Leadership: Robert E. Lee and His Opponents," *Journal of Applied Social Psychology* 16 (6): 498–507.

SULLIVAN, WILLIAM H. (1980) "Dateline Iran: The Road Not Taken," *Foreign Policy* 40 (Fall): 175–186.

SUMMERS, ANTHONY, AND ROBIN SWAN SUMMERS. (2000) *The Arrogance of Power: The Secret World of Richard Nixon.* New York: Viking Penguin.

SUMMERS, HARRY G., JR. (1997) "Are U.S. Forces Overstretched? Operations, Procurement, and Industrial Base," *Orbis* 41 (Spring): 199–207.

SUNDQUIST, JAMES L. (1976) "Congress and the President: Enemies or Partners?" in *Setting National Priorities: The Next Ten Years,* Henry Owen and Charles L. Schultze, eds. Washington, DC: Brookings Institution, pp. 583–618.

SUSSMAN, BARRY. (1988) *What Americans Really Think: And Why Our Politicians Pay No Attention.* New York: Pantheon.

SWEETMAN, BILL. (1994) "Aspin's Review Didn't Go Deep Enough," *Washington Post National Weekly Edition,* 27 December–2 January, pp. 8–9.

TALBOTT, STROBE. (1979) *Endgame.* New York: Harper and Row.

————. (1984) *Deadly Gambits.* New York: Knopf.

————. (1989) "Why Bush Should Sweat," *Time,* 6 November, p. 59.

————. (1990) "Rethinking the Red Menace," *Time,* 1 January, pp. 66–72.

————. (1996) "Democracy and the National Interest," *Foreign Affairs* 75 (November/December): 47–63.

————. (1997) "Globalization and Diplomacy: A Practitioner's Perspective," *Foreign Policy* 108 (Fall): 69–83.

————. (1999) "Dealing with the Bomb in South Asia," *Foreign Affairs* 78 (March/April): 110–122.

TARNOFF, CURT, AND LARRY NOWELS. (2005) *Foreign Aid: An Introductory Overview of U.S. Programs.* Washington, DC: Congressional Research Service/The Library of Congress.

TAYLER, JEFFREY. (2001) "Russia Is Finished," *Atlantic Monthly* 287 (May): 35–52.

TAYLOR, ANDREW J., AND JOHN T. ROURKE. (1995) "Historical Analogies in the Congressional Foreign Policy Process," *Journal of Politics* 57 (May): 460–468.

TAYLOR, PAUL. (1988) "The GOP Has a Woman Problem," *Washington Post National Weekly Edition,* 4–10 July, p. 9.

TAYLOR, TERRENCE. (2004) "The End of Imminence," *Washington Quarterly* 27 (Autumn): 57–72.

'T HART, PAUL. (1990) *Groupthink in Government: A Study of Small Groups and Policy Failure.* Baltimore, MD: Johns Hopkins University Press.

'T HART, PAUL, ERIC STERN, AND BENGT SUNDELIUS. (1997) *Beyond Groupthink: Political Group Dynamics and Foreign Policy-making.* Ann Arbor, MI: University of Michigan Press.

THOMAS, EVAN, AND CHRISTOPHER DICKEY. (1998) "Bay of Pigs Redux," *Newsweek,* 23 March, pp. 36–41.

THOMAS, JO. (2000) "After Yale, Bush Ambled Amiably into His Future," *New York Times,* p. A1.

THOMAS, KEITH. (1988) "Just Say Yes," *New York Review of Books* 35, 24 November, pp. 43–45.

THOMPSON, KENNETH W. (1960) *Political Realism and the Crisis of World Politics.* Princeton, NJ: Princeton University Press.

THOMPSON, RANDAL JOY. (1990) "Mandates for AID Reform," *Foreign Service Journal* 67 (January): 34–36.

THOMSON, ALLISON. (1998) "Defense-Related Employment and Spending, 1996–2006," *Monthly Labor Review* 121 (July): 14–33.

THOMSON, JAMES C., JR. (1972) "On the Making of U.S. China Policy, 1961–69: A Study in Bureaucratic Politics," *China Quarterly* 50 (April/June): 220–243.

———. (1994) "How Could Vietnam Happen? An Autopsy," in *The Domestic Sources of Foreign Policy: Insights and Evidence,* Eugene R. Wittkopf, ed. New York: St. Martin's, pp. 255–264.

———. (2004) "How Could Vietnam Happen? An Autopsy," in *The Domestic Sources of Foreign Policy: Insights and Evidence,* Eugene R. Wittkopf and James M. McCormick, eds. Lanham, MD: Rowman and Littlefield, pp. 259–270.

THUROW, LESTER. (1992) *Head to Head: Coming Economic Battles Among Japan, Europe, and America.* New York: William Morrow.

TILLEMA, HERBERT K. (1973) *Appeal to Force: American Military Intervention in the Era of Containment.* New York: Crowell.

———. (1989) "Foreign Overt Military Intervention in the Nuclear Age," *Journal of Peace Research* 26 (May): 179–195.

TIMMERMAN, KENNETH. (2001) "State's Saddamists," *Insight on the News,* 19 March, pp. 14–16.

TISCH, SARAH J., AND MICHAEL B. WALLACE. (1994) *Dilemmas of Development Assistance: The What, Why, and Who of Foreign Aid.* Boulder, CO: Westview Press.

TIVNAN, EDWARD. (1987) *The Lobby: Jewish Political Power and American Foreign Policy.* New York: Simon & Schuster.

TOLCHIN, MARTIN, AND SUSAN TOLCHIN. (1988) *Buying into America: How Foreign Money Is Changing the Face of Our Nation.* New York: Times Books.

TOTH, ROBERT C. (1989) "U.S. Shifts Nuclear Response Strategy," *Los Angeles Times,* 23 July, p. A1.

TOWNSEND, JOYCE CAROL. (1982) *Bureaucratic Politics in American Decision Making.* Washington, DC: University Press of America.

TRADE BLOCS. (2000) New York: Oxford University Press.

TRAVERS, RUSSELL E. (1997) "A New Millennium and a Strategic Breathing Space," *Washington Quarterly* 20 (Spring): 97–114.

TRAVIS, RICK. (1998) "The Promotion of Democracy at the End of the Twentieth Century: A New Polestar for American Foreign Policy," in *After the End: Making U.S. Foreign Policy in the Post–Cold War World,* James M. Scott, ed. Durham, NC: Duke University Press, pp. 251–276.

TREATIES AND OTHER INTERNATIONAL AGREEMENTS: THE ROLE OF THE UNITED STATES SENATE, COMMITTEE ON FOREIGN RELATIONS, United States Senate. (1993) Washington, DC: Government Printing Office.

TREVERTON, GREGORY F. (1987) *Covert Action: The Limits of Intervention in the Postwar World.* New York: Basic Books.

TRIFFIN, ROBERT. (1978–1979) "The International Role and Fate of the Dollar," *Foreign Affairs* 57 (Winter): 269–286.

TRUBOWITZ, PETER. (1992) "Sectionalism and American Foreign Policy: The Political Geography of Consensus and Conflict," *International Studies Quarterly* 36 (March): 173–190.

TRUMAN, DAVID B. (1951) *The Governmental Process.* New York: Knopf.

TRUMAN, HARRY S. (1966) *Public Papers of the 'Presidents of the United States, Harry S. Truman, 1952–1953.* Washington, DC: Government Printing Office.

TUCKER, ROBERT W. (1990) "1989 and All That," *Foreign Affairs* 69 (Fall): 93–114.

———. (1999) "Alone or With Others: The Temptations of Post–Cold War Power," *Foreign Affairs* 78 (November/December): 1520.

TUCKER, ROBERT W., AND DAVID C. HENDRICKSON. (2004) "The Sources of American Legitimacy," *Foreign Affairs,* 83 (6): 18–32.

TUGWELL, REXFORD GUY. (1971) *Off Course: From Truman to Nixon.* New York: Praeger.

TULIS, ELIZABETH. (2004) "Counterterrorism and the Clinton Administration," Project for the New American Century, 20 January (www.newamericancentury.org/defense-20040120.htm, accessed 12/1/06).

TURNER, ROBERT F. (1988) "The Power of the Purse: Controlling National Security by Conditional Appropriations," *Atlantic Community Quarterly* 26 (Spring): 79–96.

TURNER, STANSFIELD. (1985) *Secrecy and Democracy: The CIA in Transition.* Boston: Houghton Mifflin.

TUSSIE, DIANA. (1993) "Holding the Balance: The Cairns Groups in the Uruguay Round," in *The Developing Countries in World Trade: Policies and Bargaining Strategies,* Diana Tussie and David Glover, eds. Boulder, CO: Lynne Rienner, pp. 181–203.

TUSSIE, DIANA, AND DAVID GLOVER, eds. (1993) *The Developing Countries in World Trade: Policies and Bargaining Strategies.* Boulder, CO: Lynne Rienner.

TYSON, LAURA D'ANDREA. (1992) *Who's Bashing Whom? Trade Conflict in High-Technology Industries.* Washington, DC: Institute for International Economics.

U.S. ARMS CONTROL AND DISARMAMENT AGENCY. (2000) *World Military Expenditures and Arms Transfers 1998.* Washington, DC: Government Printing Office.

U.S. DEPARTMENT OF STATE. (1992) *State 2000: A New Model for Managing Foreign Affairs.* Washington, DC: Department of State.

———. (1999) *History of the National Security Council, 1947–1997.* Washington, DC: Bureau of Public Affairs, Department of State.

ULAM, ADAM B. (1985) "Forty Years of Troubled Coexistence," *Foreign Affairs* 64 (Fall): 12–32.

ULLMAN, HARLAN. (2006) "Slogan or Strategy?" *National Interest* 84 (Summer): 43–49.

UNITED NATIONS PROGRAMME ON TRANS-NATIONAL CORPORATIONS. (1993) "World Investment Report 1993," *Transnational Corporations* 2 (August): 99–123.

UNITED STATES AGENCY FOR INTERNATIONAL DEVELOPMENT. (2005) "World Wide Anti-Terrorism Certification," *Fact Sheet,* 4 March (www.usaid.gov, accessed 6/15/05).

UNITED STATES DEPARTMENT OF STATE. (2005) *International Narcotics Control Strategy Report.* Washington, DC: Bureau for International Narcotics and Law Enforcement Affairs.

UNITED STATES DEPARTMENT OF STATE AND UNITED STATES AGENCY FOR INTERNATIONAL DEVELOPMENT. (2003) *Strategic Plan–Fiscal Years 2004–2009: Aligning Diplomacy and Development Assistance.* Washington, DC: Department of State/USAID Publication 11084.

———. (2005) *U.S. Foreign Assistance Reference Guide.* Washington, DC: Department of State Publication 11202.

USLANER, ERIC M. (1998) "All in the Family? Interest Groups and Foreign Policy," in *Interest Group Politics,* 5th ed., Allan J. Cigler and Burdett A. Loomis, eds. Washington, DC: CQ Press, pp. 365–386.

UTLEY, GARRICK. (1997) "The Shrinking of Foreign News," *Foreign Affairs* 76 (March/April): 2–10.

VAN EVERA, STEPHEN. (1990a) "Why Europe Matters, Why the Third World Doesn't: American Grand Strategy After the Cold War," *Journal of Strategic Studies* 13 (June): 1–51.

———. (1990b) "The Case Against Intervention," *Atlantic Monthly* 266 (July): 72–80.

VANDEHEI, JIM, AND COLUM LYNCH. (2005) "Bush Names Bolton U.N. Ambassador in Recess Appointment," *Washington Post,* 2 August (www.washingtonpost.com, accessed 8/2/05).

VASQUEZ, JOHN A. (1983) *The Power of Power Politics.* New Brunswick, NJ: Rutgers University Press.

VASQUEZ, JOHN A., AND DOUGLAS GIBLER. (2001) "The Steps to War in Asia, 1931–1941," *Security Studies* 10 (Spring):1–45.

VERBA, SIDNEY. (1969) "Assumptions of Rationality and Non-rationality in Models of the International System," in *International Politics and Foreign Policy,* James N. Rosenau, ed. New York: Free Press, pp. 217–231.

VERHOVEK, SAM HOWE. (1998) "Is There Room on a Republican Ticket for Another Bush," *New York Times Magazine,* 13 September, pp. 52–59ff.

VERTZBERGER, YAACOV. (1990) *The World in Their Minds: Information Processing, Cognition, and Perception in Foreign Policy Decisionmaking.* Stanford, CA: Stanford University Press.

VICTOR, DAVID G. (2006) "Recovering Sustainable Development," *Foreign Affairs* 85 (January/February): 91–103.

VINCINI, JAMES. (2006) "Supreme Court Rejects Padilla Appeal," *Boston Globe,* 3 April (www.boston.com, accessed 5/11/06).

VISTICA, GREGORY. (1999) "The Plot to Get Slobo," *Newsweek,* 12 April, p. 36.

———. (2000) "Inside the Secret Cyberwar: Facing Unseen Enemies, the Feds Try to Stay a Step Ahead," *Newsweek,* 21 February, p. 48.

VON DREHLE, DAVID. (2006) "Rumsfeld's Transformation," *Washington Post,* 11 February (www.washingtonpost.com, accessed 2/22/06).

VON HIPPEL, FRANK. (1997) "Paring Down the Arsenal," *Bulletin of the Atomic Scientists* 53 (May/June) pp. 33–40.

WAGNER, R. HARRISON. (1993) "What Is Bipolarity?" *International Organization* 47 (Winter): 77–106.

WALKER, STEPHEN G. (1977) "The Interface Between Beliefs and Behavior: Henry Kissinger's Operational Code and the Vietnam War," *Journal of Conflict Resolution* 21 (March): 129–168.

WALKER, STEPHEN G., MARK SCHAFER, AND MICHAEL D. YOUNG. (1998) "Systematic Procedures for Operational Code Analysis: Measuring and Modeling Jimmy Carter's Operational Code," *International Studies Quarterly* 42 (March): 175–190.

WALLER, DOUGLAS. (1995) "Soldier Spies," *Time,* 29 May, p. 24.

———. (1996) "Master of the Game," *Time,* 6 May, pp. 40–43.

———. (1998) "Inside the Hunt for Osama," *Time,* 21 December, pp. 32–34.

WALSH, KENNETH T. (2001) "A Right-Stuff Kind of Guy," *U.S. News and World Report,* 9 April, p. 24.

WALSH, LAWRENCE E. (1997) *Firewall: The Iran-Contra Conspiracy and Cover-Up.* New York: W. W. Norton.

WALT, STEPHEN M. (1990) *The Origins of Alliances.* Ithaca, NY: Cornell University Press.

———. (2000) "Two Cheers for Clinton's Foreign Policy," *Foreign Affairs* 79 (March–April): 63–79.

———. (2005) *Taming American Power: The Global Response to U.S. Primacy.* New York: Norton.

WALTERS, ROBERT S., AND DAVID H. BLAKE. (1992) *The Politics of Global Economic Relations,* 4th ed. Englewood Cliffs, NJ: Prentice Hall.

WALTZ, KENNETH N. (1964) "The Stability of a Bipolar World," *Daedalus* 93 (Summer): 881–909.

———. (1967) *Foreign Policy and Democratic Politics.* Boston: Little, Brown.

———. (1971) "Opinions and Crisis in American Foreign Policy," in *The Politics of U.S. Foreign Policy Making,* Douglas M. Fox, ed. Pacific Palisades, CA: Goodyear, pp. 47–55.

———. (1979) *Theory of International Politics.* Reading, MA: Addison-Wesley.

———. (1993) "The Emerging Structure of International Politics," *International Security* 18 (Fall): 44–79.

———. (1997) "Evaluating Theories," *American Political Science Review* 91 (December): 915–916.

———. (2000a) "Structural Realism After the Cold War," *International Security* 25 (Summer): 5–41.

———. (2000b) "Globalization and American Power," *National Interest* 59 (Spring): 46–56.

WARBURG, GERALD FELIX. (1989) *Conflict and Consensus: The Struggle Between Congress and the President over Foreign Policymaking.* New York: Harper and Row.

WARNER, GEOFFREY. (1989) "The Anglo-American Special Relationship," *Diplomatic History* 13 (Fall): 479–499.

WARWICK, DONALD P. (1975) *A Theory of Public Bureaucracy: Politics, Personality, and Organization in the State Department.* Cambridge, MA: Harvard University Press.

WASTELL, DAVID. (2001) "President's Men Vie for Control of Foreign Policy," *Sunday Telegraph,* 11 March, p. 31.

WATSON, JACK H., JR. (1993) "The Clinton White House," *Presidential Studies Quarterly* 23 (Summer): 429–435.

WATTENBERG, BEN J. (1989) *The Birth Dearth.* New York: Pharos Books.

———. (2004) *Fewer: How the New Demography of Depopulation Will Shape Our Future.* Chicago: Ivan R. Dee Publisher.

WAYMAN, FRANK WHELON. (1985) "Arms Control and Strategic Arms Voting in the U.S. Senate," *Journal of Conflict Resolution* 29 (June): 225–251.

WAYNE, LESLIE. (1998) "800–Pound Guests at the Pentagon," *New York Times,* 15 March, pp. WK, 5.

———. (1999) "Dogfight Over a Must-Win Contract," *New York Times,* 15 August, pp. 3, 9–10.

———. (2000) "Winner May Not Take All in Pentagon Jet Deal," *New York Times,* 14 May, p. BU 4.

WEAVER, DAVID, MAXWELL MCCOMBS, AND DONALD L. SHAW. (2004) "Agenda Setting Research: Issues, Attributes, and Influence," in *Handbook of Political Communication Research,* Lynda Lee Kaid, ed. Mahwah, NJ: Lawrence Erlbaum Associates, pp. 257–282.

WEBER, STEVEN. (1997) "The End of the Business Cycle," *Foreign Affairs* 76 (July/August): 65–82.

WEINBERG, GERHARD L. (1994) *A World at Arms: A Global History of World War II.* New York: Cambridge University Press.

WEINER, TIM. (1994) "The Men in the Gray Federal Bureaucracy," *New York Times,* 10 April, p. E4.

WEISBAND, EDWARD. (1973) *The Ideology of American Foreign Policy: A Paradigm of Lockian Liberalism.* Beverly Hills, CA: Sage.

WEISBERG, HERBERT F., AND DAVID C. KIMBALL. (1995) "Attitudinal Correlates of the 1992 Presidential Vote: Party Identification and Beyond," in *Democracy's Feast: Elections in America,* Herbert F. Weisberg, ed. Chatham, NJ: Chatham House, pp. 72–111.

WEISBERG, JACOB. (1999) "The Governor/President: Bill Clinton," *New York Times Magazine,* 17 January, pp. 30–35ff.

WELCH, DAVID A. (1992) "The Organizational Process and Bureaucratic Politics Paradigms: Retrospect and Prospect," *International Security* 17 (Fall): 112–146.

WEST, WILLIAM F., AND JOSEPH COOPER. (1990) "Legislative Influence v. Presidential Dominance: Competing Models of Bureaucratic Control," *Political Science Quarterly* 104 (Winter): 581–606.

WHITE, JULIE. (2000) "U.N. Hosts Historic Millennium Summit," *The InterDependent* 26 (Fall): 5–7.

WHITE, RALPH K. (1984) *Fearful Warriors: A Psychological Profile of U.S.-Soviet Relations.* New York: Free Press.

WHITE, THEODORE H. (1973) *The Making of the President, 1972.* New York: Atheneum.

WHITE, THOMAS. (2004) "Rumsfeld's War: Interviews," *PBS Frontline* (www.pbs.org/wgbh/pages/frontline/shows/pentagon/interviews/white.html, accessed 11/3/06).

WIARDA, HOWARD J. (1996) *American Foreign Policy: Actors and Processes.* New York: HarperCollins.

———. (1997) "Back to Basics: Reassessing U.S. Policy in Latin America," *Harvard International Review* 19 (Fall): 16–19, 57.

———. (2000) "Beyond the Pale: The Bureaucratic Politics of United States Policy in Mexico," *World Affairs* 162 (Spring): 174–190.

WIESELTIER, LEON. (1993) "Total Quality Meaning," *New Republic,* 19 and 26 July, pp. 16–18ff.

WILCOX, CLYDE, JOSEPH FERRARA, AND DEE ALLSOP. (1993) "Group Differences in Early Support for Military Action in the Gulf: The Effects of Gender, Generation, and Ethnicity," *American Politics Quarterly* 21 (July): 343–359.

WILDAVSKY, AARON. (1966) "The Two Presidencies," *Trans-Action* 4 (December): 7–14.

WILLIAMS, CINDY. (2006) "Beyond Preemption and Preventive War: Increasing U.S. Budget Emphasis on Conflict Prevention," *Policy Analysis Brief.* Muscatine, IA: Stanley Foundation.

WILLIAMS, WILLIAM APPLEMAN. (1972) *The Tragedy of American Diplomacy,* 2nd ed. New York: Delta.

———. (1980) *Empire as a Way of Life.* New York: Oxford University Press.

WILLS, GARRY. (1994a) *Certain Trumpets: The Call of Leaders.* New York: Simon & Schuster.

———. (1994b) "What Makes a Good Leader?" *Atlantic Monthly* 273 (April): 63–80.

———. (1995) *Certain Trumpets: The Nature of Leadership.* New York: Touchstone.

WILSON, ERNEST J. III. (2002) *Closing the Digital Divide.* Washington, DC: Internet Policy Institute.

WILSON, GEORGE C. (2001a) "Guns Aplenty, Butter Be Damned," *National Journal* 33, 27 January, pp. 252–253.

———. (2001b) "CEO Rumsfeld and His Pentagon Inc," *National Journal* 33, 17 March, p. 812.

WILSON, JAMES Q. (1989) *Bureaucracy: What Government Organizations Do and Why They Do It.* New York: Basic Books.

WILSON, ROBERT A., AND MICHAEL R. BESCHLOSS, eds. (2000) *Power and the Presidency.* New York: MacMillan.

WINIK, JAY. (1989) "Restoring Bipartisanship," *Washington Quarterly* 12 (Winter): 109–122.

WINTER, DAVID G. (1987) "Leader Appeal, Leader Performance, and the Motives Profiles of Leaders and Followers: A Study of American President and Elections," *Journal of Personality and Social Psychology* 52 (1): 196–202.

———. (1993) "Personality and Leadership in the Gulf War," in *The Political Psychology of the Gulf War,* Stanley A. Renshon, ed. Pittsburgh: University of Pittsburg Press, pp. 107–117.

WINTER, DAVID G., AND LESLIE A. CARLSON. (1988) "Using Motive Scores in the Psychobiographical Study of an Individual: The Case of Richard Nixon," *Journal of Personality* 56 (March): 75–103.

WINTER, DAVID G., AND ABIGAIL J. STEWART. (1977) "Content Analysis as a Method of Studying Political Leaders," in *A Psychological Examination of Political Leaders,* Margaret G. Hermann, ed. New York: Free Press, pp. 27–61.

WISE, DAVID. (1995) *Nightmover: How Aldrich Ames Sold the CIA to the KGB for $4.6 million.* New York: HarperCollins.

WITKOW, BRANDON J. (2000) "A New 'Spook Immunity': How the CIA and American Business Are Shielded from Liability for the Misappropriation of Trade Secrets," *Emory International Law Review* 14 (Spring) 451–489.

WITTKOPF, EUGENE R. (1990) *Faces of Internationalism: Public Opinion and American Foreign Policy.* Durham, NC: Duke University Press.

———. (1994) "Faces of Internationalism in a Transitional Environment," *Journal of Conflict Resolution* 38 (September): 376–401.

———. (1996) "What Americans Really Think About Foreign Policy," *Washington Quarterly* 19 (Summer): 91–106.

———. (2000) "U.S. Foreign Policy Formulation: Internal Processes and External Impact," *Malaysian Association of American Studies,* Kuala Lumpur, September 12–13, 2000.

WITTKOPF, EUGENE R., AND RONALD H. HINCKLEY. (2000) "Internationalism at Bay? A Contextual Analysis of Americans' Post–Cold War Foreign Policy Attitudes" in *Decision-Making in a Glass House: Mass Media, Public Opinion, and American and European Foreign Policy in the 21st Century,* Brigitte Nacos, Robert Y. Shapiro, and Pierangelo Isernia, eds. Lanham, MD: Rowman and Littlefield, pp. 133–153.

WITTKOPF, EUGENE R., AND CHRISTOPHER M. JONES. (1999) *The Future of American Foreign Policy,* 3rd ed. New York: St. Martin's/Worth.

WITTKOPF, EUGENE R., AND JAMES M. MC-CORMICK. (1993) "The Domestic Politics of Contra Aid: Public Opinion, Congress, and the President," in *Public Opinion in U.S. Foreign Policy: The Controversy over Contra Aid,* Richard Sobel, ed. Lanham, MD: Rowman and Littlefield, pp. 73–103.

———. (1998) "Congress, the President, and the End of the Cold War," *Journal of Conflict Resolution* 42 (August): 440–467.

WOHLFORTH, WILLIAM C. (1999) "The Stability of a Unipolar World," *International Security* 24 (Summer): 5–41.

WOLFE, FRANK. (2001) "Modernizing NSA Technology Likely to Be Priority of Senate Intel Committee," *Defense Daily* 209, 31 January.

WOLFENSBERGER, DONALD R. (2002) "The Return of the Imperial Presidency?" *Wilson Quarterly* 26 (Spring): 36–41.

WOLFERS, ARNOLD. (1962) *Discord and Collaboration.* Baltimore, MD: Johns Hopkins University Press.

WOLFOWITZ, PAUL D. (1994) "Clinton's First Year," *Foreign Affairs* 73 (January/February): 28–43.

WOODS, RANDALL B. (1998) *J. William Fulbright, Vietnam, and the Search for a Cold War Foreign Policy.* Cambridge, MA: Cambridge University Press.

WOODWARD, BOB. (1987) *Veil: The Secret Wars of the CIA 1981–1987.* New York: Simon & Schuster.

———. (1991) *The Commanders.* New York: Simon & Schuster.

———. (1994) *The Agenda: Inside the Clinton White House.* New York: Simon & Schuster.

———. (2000) *Maestro: Greenspan's Fed and the American Boom.* New York: Simon & Schuster.

———. (2001) "CIA Told to Do 'Whatever Necessary' to Kill Bin Laden," *Washington Post,* 21 October (www.washingtonpost.com, accessed 10/21/01).

———. (2002) *Bush at War.* New York: Simon & Schuster.

———. (2004) *Plan of Attack.* New York: Simon & Schuster.

WOODWARD, BOB, AND CARL BERNSTEIN. (1979) *The Final Days.* New York: Simon & Schuster.

WOODWARD, SUSAN L. (1993) "Yugoslavia: Divide and Fall," *Bulletin of the Atomic Scientists* 49 (November): 24–27.

WORLD BANK. (1998) *Assessing Aid: What Works, What Doesn't, and Why.* New York: Oxford University Press.

WORLD DEVELOPMENT REPORT 1988. (1988) New York: Oxford University Press.

WORLD DEVELOPMENT REPORT 2000/2001. (2001) New York: Oxford University Press.

WORLD RESOURCES 1994–95. (1994) New York: Oxford University Press.

WORLD RESOURCES 1998–99. (1998) New York: Oxford University Press.

WORLD RESOURCES 2000–2001. (2000) Washington, DC: World Resources Institute.

WORTH, ROBERT. (1998) "Clinton's Warriors: The Interventionists," *World Policy Journal* 15 (Spring): 43–48.

WREN, CHRISTOPHER S. (2001) "The U.N. Offers 87 Remedies to Help Poor Nations Develop," *New York Times,* 4 February, p. 1.

WRIGHT, ROBIN. (1997) "Democracy: Challenges and Innovations in the 1990s," *Washington Quarterly* 20 (Summer): 23–36.

———. (2004) "Transforming the Islamic World 101," *Washington Post National Weekly Edition,* 30 August–5 September, p. 17.

WRIGHT, ROBIN, AND SHAUL BAKHAS. (1997) "The U.S. and Iran: An Offer They Can't Refuse?" *Foreign Policy* 108 (Fall): 124–136.

YANKELOVICH, DANIEL. (2005) "What Americans Really Think About Foreign Policy." *Foreign Affairs* 84 (September/October): 2–16.

YANKELOVICH, DANIEL, AND SIDNEY HARMAN. (1988) *Starting with the People.* Boston: Houghton Mifflin.

YARMOLINSKY, ADAM. (1970–1971) "The Military Establishment (Or How Political Problems Become Military Problems)," *Foreign Policy* 1 (Winter): 78–97.

———. (1971) *The Military Establishment: Its Impact on American Society.* New York: Harper and Row.

YERGIN, DANIEL. (1978) *Shattered Peace: The Origins of the Cold War and the National Security State.* Boston: Houghton Mifflin.

———. (2006) "Ensuring Energy Security," *Foreign Affairs* 85 (March/April): 69–82.

YOST, DAVID S. (1998) *NATO Transformed: The Alliance's New Roles in International Security.* Washington, DC: United States Institute of Peace Press.

ZAGARE, FRANK C. (1990) "Rationality and Deterrence," *World Politics* 42 (January): 238–260.

ZAJAC, ANDREW. (2005) "Bush Wielding Secrecy Privilege to End Suits," *Chicago Tribune,* 3 March.

ZALLER, JOHN R. (1992) *The Nature and Origins of Mass Opinion.* New York: Cambridge University Press.

ZEGART, AMY B. (2005) "September 11 and the Adaptation Failure of U.S. Intelligence Agencies," *International Security* 29 (Spring): 78–111.

ZELIKOW, PHILLIP. (2001) *American Military Strategy: Memos to a President* (Aspen Policy Series). New York: W. W. Norton and Company.

ZELIKOW, PHILIP, AND CONDOLEEZZA RICE. (1995) *Germany Unified and Europe Transformed: A Study in Statecraft.* Cambridge, MA: Harvard University Press.

ZENGERLE, JASON. (1998) "Hegelianism," *New Republic* 218, 9 February, p. 10ff.

ZIMMERMAN, ROBERT F. (1993) *Dollars, Diplomacy, and Dependence: Dilemmas of U.S. Economic Aid.* Boulder, CO: Lynne Rienner.

ZOELLICK, ROBERT B. (2000) "A Republican Foreign Policy," *Foreign Affairs* 79 (January/February): 63–78.

ZUELI, KIMBERLY A., AND VERNON W. RUTTAN. (1996) "U.S. Assistance to the Former Soviet Empire: Toward a Rationale for Foreign Aid," *Journal of Developing Areas* 30 (July): 493–524.

Index